Handbook of Clinical
Psychophysiology

Wiley Psychophysiology Handbooks

Series Editor: Anthony Gale
University of Southampton

Handbook of Social Psychophysiology
Edited by Hugh Wagner and Antony Manstead

Handbook of Clinical Psychophysiology
Edited by Graham Turpin

Handbook of Psychophysiology of Human Eating
Edited by Richard Shepherd

Further titles in preparation

Handbook of Clinical Psychophysiology

Edited by
Graham Turpin

Plymouth Polytechnic, Plymouth, UK

WILEY

Chichester · New York · Brisbane · Toronto · Singapore

Library of Congress Cataloging in Publication Data:

Handbook of clinical psychophysiology.

   (Wiley psychophysiology handbooks)
   Includes bibliographies and indexes.
   1. Mental illness—Physiological aspects.
2. Psychophysiology. I. Turpin, Graham. II. Series.
[DNLM: 1. Psychophysiology WL 103 H2355]
RC455.4.B5H356 1989   152   88–33829

ISBN 0 471 91159 3

British Library Cataloguing in Publication Data:

Handbook of clinical psychophysiology.
   1. Medicine. Psychophysiology
   I. Turpin, Graham
   612'.8

ISBN 0 471 91159 3

Phototypeset by Input Typesetting Ltd, London
Printed and bound in Great Britain by
Courier International Ltd, Tiptree, Essex

Handbook of Clinical Psychophysiology

Contents

List of Contributors   ix
Preface by Series Editor   xi
Preface   xv

SECTION 1—GENERAL APPLICATIONS: 1
METHODOLOGICAL AND THEORETICAL
ISSUES

Chapter 1.   *An overview of clinical psychophysiological techniques: tools or*   3
theories?
Graham Turpin

Chapter 2.   *Research strategies employing psychophysiological measures:*   45
identifying and using psychophysiological markers
William G. Iacono and John W. Ficken

Chapter 3.   *Psychophysiological assessment: conceptual, psychometric, and*   71
statistical issues
Gerhard Stemmler and Jochen Fahrenberg

Chapter 4.   *Imagery, memory and emotion: a psychophysiological analysis of*   105
             clinical anxiety
             Bruce N. Cuthbert and Peter J. Lang

Chapter 5.   *Lateralization and central mechanisms in clinical psychophysiology*   135
             John H. Gruzelier

Chapter 6.   *Psychophysiological assessment in behaviour therapy*   175
             Stephen N. Haynes, Shelley Falkin and Kathy Sexton-
             Radek

Chapter 7.   *Psychophysiological interventions in behavioural medicine*   215
             Andrew Steptoe

Chapter 8.   *Psychophysiological and biochemical indices in 'stress' research:*   241
             applications to psychopathology and pathophysiology
             Mats Fredrikson

             SECTION 2—APPLICATIONS TO SPECIFIC   281
             DISORDERS

Chapter 9.   *Simple phobias*   283
             Kenneth Hugdahl

Chapter 10. *Panic disorder, agoraphobia, and social phobia*   309
             Lars-Göran Öst

Chapter 11. *Obsessional–compulsive disorder*   329
             Gudrun Sartory

Chapter 12. *Affective disorders*   357
             Jeffrey B. Henriques and Richard J. Davidson

Chapter 13. *Schizophrenic disorders*   393
             Michael E. Dawson, Keith H. Nuechterlein and
             Robert M. Adams

Chapter 14. *Sexual disorders*   419
             James H. Geer and Cathy Orman Castille

Chapter 15. *Hypertension*   441
             Iris B. Goldstein

Contents   vii

Chapter 16. *Raynaud's disease*   469
             Robert R. Freedman

Chapter 17. *Gastrointestinal disorders*   495
             Rupert Hölzl

Chapter 18. *Respiratory disorders: asthma and hyperventilation syndrome*   519
             Paul Grossman and Cornelis J. E. Wientjes

Chapter 19. *Motor disorders*   555
             Marjan Jahanshahi and C. David Marsden

Author index   585

Subject index   623

Handbook of Clinical Psychophysiology

List of Contributors

Robert M. Adams, *Department of Psychology, University of Southern California, USA*

Bruce N. Cuthbert, *Department of Clinical and Health Psychology, University of Florida, Gainesville, USA*

Richard J. Davidson, *Department of Psychology, University of Wisconsin-Madison, USA*

Michael E. Dawson, *Department of Psychiatry and Biobehavioral Sciences, University of Southern California, USA*

Jochen Fahrenberg, *Forschungsgruppe Psychophysiologie, University of Freiburg, Freiburg, FRG*

Shelley Falkin, *Department of Psychology, Illinois Institute of Technology, Chicago, USA*

John W. Ficken, *Department of Psychology, University of Minnesota, Minnesota, USA*

Mats Fredrikson, *Department of Medical Psychology, Karolinska Institute, Stockholm, Sweden*

Robert R. Freedman, *Behavioral Medicine Laboratory, Departments of Psychiatry and Psychology, Wayne State University, USA*

James H. Geer, *Department of Psychology, Louisiana State University, USA*

Iris B. Goldstein, *Department of Psychiatry, University of California, Los Angeles, USA*

Paul Grossman, _Forschungsgruppe Psychophysiologie, University of Freiburg, Freiburg, FRG_

John H. Gruzelier, _Department of Psychiatry, Charing Cross and Westminster Medical School, London, UK_

Stephen N. Haynes, _Department of Psychology, University of Hawaii at Manoa, Honolulu, USA_

Jeffrey B. Henriques, _Department of Psychology, University of Wisconsin-Madison, USA_

Rupert Hölzl, _Psychophysiological Research Unit, Max Planck Institute of Psychiatry, Munich, FRG_

Kenneth Hugdahl, _Department of Somatic Psychology, University of Bergen, Norway_

William G. Iacono, _Department of Psychology, University of Minnesota, Minnesota, USA_

Marjan Jahanshahi, _Department of Clinical Neurology, Institute of Neurology, The National Hospital, London, UK_

Peter J. Lang, _Center for Research in Psychophysiology, University of Florida, Gainesville, USA_

C. David Marsden, _Department of Clinical Neurology, Institute of Neurology, The National Hospital, London, UK_

Keith H. Nuechterlein, _Department of Psychology, University of California, Los Angeles, USA_

Cathy Orman Castille, _Department of Psychology, Louisiana State University, USA_

Lars-Göran Öst, _Psychiatric Research Center, University of Uppsala, Sweden_

Gudrun Sartory, _Department of Psychology, University of Wuppertal, FRG_

Kathy Sexton-Radek, _Department of Psychology, Elmhurst College, Elmhurst, USA_

Gerhard Stemmler, _Forschungsgruppe Psychophysiologie, University of Freiburg, Freiburg, FRG_

Andrew Steptoe, _Department of Psychology, St Georges Hospital Medical School, London, UK_

Graham Turpin, _Department of Psychology, Plymouth Polytechnic, Plymouth, UK_

Cornelis J.E. Wientjes, _TNO Institute for Perception, Soesterberg, The Netherlands_

Preface by Series Editor

Psychophysiology is still an emerging discipline even though its key journal *Psychophysiology*, published by the Society for Psychophysiological Research, is now in its 25th year. The very complexity of the subject matter of psychophysiology makes theory building particularly hazardous. Even where a theory has sound formal properties, the move to empirical data is rarely straightforward. The inclusion of variables which are easy to justify from a theoretical point of view in no way guarantees that the outcome of an experiment will be easy to interpret, will relate to previous data, or will settle theoretical issues once and for all. Typically, some of the data tell one story, while the remainder offer a puzzle. Psychophysiology, still in its intellectual infancy, suffers from the imperative of being too ambitious and the move from laboratory findings to clinical applications offers an even greater challenge.

Psychophysiology seeks to integrate data along a bio-social continuum. It therefore has to tackle several major issues, drawing upon a number of separate, even disparate, approaches or sub-disciplines. Genetic predisposition is recognized as a source of variance both for general characteristics and for individual variations. Inherent biological characteristics are expressed in terms of the biochemistry of the nervous system and its functional organization. Yet these too are seen to be open to the influence of ontogeny and learning.

The measurement of biological variables has been a major concern in psychophysiology and the development of the minicomputer and then the micro computer has revolutionized the acquisition and analysis of data. In this sphere, that of measurement, several psychophysiologists have made their mark.

While the burden of experimentation and measurement has fallen on the assessment of central and autonomic nervous system variables, psychophysiologists recognize the need to integrate such data with data describing behaviour, performance and subjective state. Without reference to observable behaviour and subjective experience psychophysiology remains a physiological and not a psychological discipline. It is the measurement of both behaviour and experiential state as well as non-invasive assessment of physiological change, which marks off psychophysiology from its parent discipline, physiological psychology. Yet measurement in these non-physiological domains creates major problems for a systematic scientist to tackle, even when they are taken separately. The notion that the psychophysiologist seeks to *integrate* data derived from such disparate domains of description distinguishes psychophysiology from most other disciplines of psychology. It imposes a tremendous intellectual burden on the researcher and of course, upon the theorist and practitioner.

Given that psychophysiologists employ human subjects as their experimental material, the issues of consciousness, self-regulation and self-control must also be handled. As Porges, Ackles and Truax (1983) point out, there are multiple logical relations between the domains of physiology, behaviour, experience and subjective report, and each logical relation, in its turn, creates special difficulties for experimental design, measurement, and the interpretation of data.

Clinical psychology offers a perfect example of the appropriateness of the psychophysiological approach. Explanations of mental illness extend from biological to socio-cultural causation. The patient presents unusual patterns of response in our three key domains. For example, it is likely that schizophrenia has biological anomolies in its causation, and powerful chemical medication seems to change the behaviour of the patient. Research studies of electrophysiological variables reveal unusual patterns of responding. The schizophrenic person's world of subjective experience can seem bizarre and incomprehensible to others. He or she may suffer from disorders of perception and attention, can perform poorly in cognitive tests, may behave strangely in social situations, and can be clearly affected by characteristics of family life and institutional living. A similar story can be told about anxiety and depression and their physiological, behavioural, subjective, and inter-personal components.

Graham Turpin, in his masterly introduction to the *Handbook of Clinical Psychophysiology* defines clinical psychophysiology as '. . . the application of psychophysiological techniques, concepts and theories to the explanation of psychological factors which influence health behaviours and risks. Health in this context, is taken to mean a state of both physical and psychological well-being'. This definition indicates how far clinical psychophysiology has travelled from its early preoccupations with psychosomatic disorders and its attempt to offer support for psychiatric accounts of pathology by identifying physiological markers of mental illness (Lader, 1975). There has also been a clear shift away from concern with individual response parameters to an appreciation of the interactional nature of psychophysiological systems. Clinical psychophysiology has emerged as a powerful theoretical and practical tool in the broad fields of behavioural medicine and health.

The *Handbook* is divided into two sections. The first considers the conceptual and methodological problems associated with clinical psychophysiology and explores the fundamental science which it presupposes. The second section is devoted to applications of fundamental research findings in relation to specific psychopathological conditions. The *Handbook of Clinical Psychophysiology* therefore has an appeal for both basic psychological scientists and practitioners, demonstrating the symbiotic relationship between theory and practice.

Other volumes in the Series address overlapping concerns in different spheres of theory and application. Volume 1, edited by Hugh Wagner and Antony Manstead, focuses on the fast growing field of social psychophysiology and, in particular, on biological and social-psychological aspects of emotion and its expression. Volume 3, edited by Richard Shepherd, explores the psychophysiology of human eating and nutritional behaviour and will introduce psychophysiologists to new concerns, for the field of human eating has yet to attract the research interest which it clearly deserves. Volume 4, edited by myself and Michael Eysenck, reviews the long-established field of the psychophysiological study of individual differences in personality and intelligence. Finally, Volume 5, edited by Richard Jennings and Michael G. H. Coles, explores central and autonomic nervous system correlates of cognitive processes in a radical fashion, by focusing on processes rather than response systems.

In inviting world authorities in their fields to contribute to the *Wiley Psychophysiology Handbooks* Series we have encouraged them to offer state-of-the-art reviews. We hope that these well-referenced and timely papers will stand as essential sources for students, advanced researchers, and practitioners. We have focused on depth of approach rather than breadth; thus even within a Series it has been impossible to address all the key issues in each area of concern and the reader should treat the Series as an essential complement to other major volumes (for example Coles, Donchin and Porges, 1986).

It is clear that psychophysiology raises more questions than answers, but would science be fun if everything were clear-cut? One advantage of uncertainty is that new discoveries are that much sweeter.

ANTHONY GALE
University of Southampton, October 1988

REFERENCES

Coles, M. G. H., Donchin, E. and Porges, S. W. (1986) *Psychophysiology: Systems, Processes, and Applications*, New York: Guilford.

Lader, M. (1975) *The Psychophysiology of Mental Illness*, London: Routledge and Kegan Paul.

Porges, S. W., Ackles, P. A. and Truax, S. R. (1983). Psychophysiological measurement: methodological constraints. In A. Gale and J. A. Edwards (eds) *Physiological Correlates of Human Behaviour. Volume 1. Basic Issues*, London: Academic Press.

Preface

A prerequisite of any text on psychophysiology is usually an introductory statement to define the essential nature of this relatively new discipline. Clinical psychophysiology, the topic of this current handbook, is no exception (see Chapter 1). The use of the term 'clinical', however, necessitates further efforts at clarification and definition. Although it originally described 'bedside practice', clinical disciplines generally refer to medical and psychiatric applications of a particular science. The purpose of this present handbook is to maintain both these definitions. It is intended to provide a comprehensive review of the scientific background subsuming the application of psychophysiology to clinical problems. This has largely been the brief of Section 1. However, it was also planned that the handbook would provide a reference source for practitioners wishing to apply psychophysiological techniques to particular clinical problems and disorders. It is for this reason that Section 2 provides overviews of psychophysiological research for a number of common medical and psychiatric disorders. An attempt has been made to provide comprehensive coverage of common clinical problems, but, due to the usual vagaries of editing arrangements, some notable clinical areas, such as headache and sleep disorder, have had to be dropped from the final handbook. Nevertheless, it is hoped that Section 2 provides examples of how psychophysiological techniques can usefully be applied to clinical problems. Another area which has received only relatively brief attention is that of central measures. There are two reasons for this apparent bias. First, clinical electroencephalographic techniques are commonly employed to investigate pathophysiological and not psychophysiological mechanisms. Since the former application has been dealt with in many recent neurological handbooks, it has been omitted from the current text, which focuses specifically on psychophysiological processes. Second, in keeping with a 'bedside' definition of clinical psychophysiology, an attempt has been made to emphasize the role of simpler and more easily applicable psychophysiological paradigms and measures which can be easily adopted for clinical research.

The present status of clinical psychophysiology as an area of study is a reflection of many diverse scientific disciplines, which have included experimental psychology, psychosomatic medicine, physical medicine, psychiatry, physiology and the neurosciences. Recent additions to this list might include psychotherapy, behaviour therapy, behavioural medicine and health psychology. A further aim of this text is that it should be accessible to all these disciplines. Authors have been requested, therefore, to orientate their chapters both to the fundamental researcher, providing relevant clinical background information, and to the clinician, by explaining basic psychophysiological principles.

The range of clinical disciplines which have employed psychophysiological techniques is clearly extensive, and raises the question as to whether any single unifying theme can be identified. Moreover, psychophysiological research has a tendency to be empirically based, and to reflect the mere application of particular recording techniques. The final aim of this handbook has been, therefore, to try to promote the role of psychophysiological concepts, principles and theories in attempting to understand clinical phenomena. Significant advances in clinical psychophysiology will be achieved only by the application of appropriate theories.

I would like to thank Tony Gale, the Series Editor, and Michael Coombs of Wiley for encouraging me to undertake this project. I owe an incalculable debt to Marilyn Darch for secretarial support and an infinite resource of patience when encountering impossible deadlines, and Wendy Hudlass from John Wiley & Sons for her persistent but always pleasant prompting. Finally, I should like to thank my wife, Trish, for her enduring support and enviable understanding of the idiosyncrasies of English language.

GRAHAM TURPIN

Plymouth Polytechnic, May 1988

SECTION 1

GENERAL APPLICATIONS: METHODOLOGICAL AND THEORETICAL ISSUES

Chapter 1

An Overview of Clinical Psychophysiological Techniques: Tools or Theories?

Graham Turpin

Department of Psychology,
Plymouth Polytechnic,
Drake Circus,
Plymouth PL4 8AA

ABSTRACT

An overview of clinical psychophysiology is provided. Issues of definition and the historical development of psychophysiological approaches to psychopathology are discussed. Three main rationales underlying the adoption of clinical psychophysiology are reviewed. These are: discrimination and diagnosis, elaboration of psychological theories of psychopathology, and clinical assessment and treatment. Finally, the application of psychophysiological techniques and measures to clinical practice is critically reviewed.

Handbook of Clinical Psychophysiology Edited by G. Turpin
© 1989 John Wiley & Sons Ltd

INTRODUCTION

The title of this introductory chapter seeks to emphasize the choice between conceptualizing clinical psychophysiology as a diverse collection of applied techniques or as an integrated body of knowledge and theory. The question to be addressed, therefore, is whether clinical psychophysiology may be considered as an area of study in its own right or as a mere collection of empirical findings and techniques associated with various health-related disciplines such as clinical psychology, psychiatry, medicine, etc. It is hoped that an answer to this question can be achieved by examining the conceptual foundations and rationales underlying the application of clinical psychophysiology and its utility as an area of study. In addition, the present chapter will also seek to provide a basis for the understanding of psychophysiological techniques and concepts. This will include discussion of physiological substrates and measures, instrumentation and recording techniques, and concepts and theoretical positions.

DEFINITIONS

Psychophysiology

Essentially, psychophysiology is concerned with the application of physiological measurement to the understanding of psychological processes underlying behaviour. Previous definitions have emphasized the physiological nature of the dependent variables under study (Stern, 1964) and the tendency to employ human experimental subjects (Sternbach, 1966). It differs from physiological psychology since its major aim is the elucidation of psychological processes, as opposed to the identification of physiological substrates that may subserve behaviour. Accordingly, physiological psychology primarily examines the effects of physiological manipulations (i.e. brain lesions, stimulation, etc.) upon behaviour, whereas psychophysiology is concerned with the effects of psychological or behavioural manipulations upon physiological activity. Traditional areas of psychophysiologal study, therefore, have included the physiological identification of such different behavioural states as sleep, anger and sexual arousal, and the study of physiological correlates of psychological processes said to underlie conditioning, emotional behaviour, arousal, attention, etc.

  Although much psychophysiological research has tended to be of a correlational nature, seeking to identify parallels between inferred psychological processes and observed physiological events, recent theoretical accounts have emphasized the interactional nature of psychophysiologal processes. Hence, the distinction between physiological correlate and psychological process becomes blurred since behavioural outcomes are seen as a product of *psychophysiological* processes. For example, it has been established that specific patterns of heart rate change are associated with different environmental events (cf. Coles, Jennings and Stern, 1984). In particular, it has been claimed that heart rate slowing or cardiac deceleration is a possible correlate of attention and may reflect the degree and location of attention directed towards environmental stimuli. This relationship between cardiac deceleration and attention has been viewed in several different ways. First, deceleration can be seen as a physiological correlate reflecting the operation of orienting, a psychological process said to subserve attention (Graham, 1979). This account does not specifically address either the functional relationship or the physiological mechanism which relates heart rate slowing to enhanced information processing in the form of the orienting response. A complementary account suggests that heart rate slowing accompanies the 'intention to note and detect external stimuli' (Lacey and Lacey, 1978, p. 99) and that the physiological response may itself enhance processing via a biological baroreceptor feedback mechanism. Hence, heart rate slowing is both a component of the process, and also a product and correlate of the attentional mechanism. Although the Laceys' notion of afferent feedback is a controversial one (Carroll and Anastasiades, 1978), it does serve to illustrate how the relationship between physiological response and psychological process may be integrated within a psychophysiological mechanism. Finally, an alternative perspective has been advanced by Obrist (1981) which relies on the premise that much of cardiac activity is regulated in accord with metabolic demand and consequently motor activity. Cardiac deceleration, therefore, is seen as a physiological concomitant of a behavioural response (i.e. general body quietening) which accompanies changes in attention. Hence, the relationship between cardiac activity and environmental intake is accounted for both at a behavioural ad physiological level. Indeed, Obrist (1981) has strongly argued that adequate psychophysiological explanations must take into account physiological substrates and mechanisms. This he has termed a 'psychobiological' approach.

Clinical Psychophysiology

It would seem, therefore, that psychophysiological measures can be considered as psychological correlates, psychophysiological processes or psychobiological mechanisms. The distinction between psychophysiological correlates and processes reflects an uneasy separatism between mind and body. Indeed, the problem of dualistic distinctions between psychological and physiological processes is particularly relevant when considering a definition of clinical psychophysiology. Historically, clinical psychophysiology has been associated with so-called 'functional psychiatric' and 'psychosomatic' disorders. Both these areas have suffered from the adoption of dualist principles either in relation to psychoanalytic explanations of psychosomatic disorder (Wittkower, 1977) or the interdisciplinary divisions between psychiatry and medicine (Engel, 1986;

Leigh, 1982). There would appear to be two major alternatives to the dualist approach: monist and interactionalist positions. The former attempts to account for both physical and psychological disorder in terms of single elementary processes, whether they be based upon operant conditioning (e.g. Engel, 1986) or some undisclosed pathological process, as is the case with the medical model (Guze, 1977; but see Tarrier, 1979). The latter approach adopts an interactionalist perspective which is either based upon systems theory (Schwartz, 1983) or upon interdisciplinary models which seek to account for physical and psychological wellbeing and/or disorder at several levels of explanation including the sociological, psychological and physiological domains of discourse (Engel, 1977; Ohman, 1981a; Weiner, 1977). Given the current trend towards interactionalist accounts of psychophysiology which seek to identify both relationships and interactions at a process level between environment and physiology, it would appear that this discipline should be well placed to provide a basis with which to examine 'biobehavioural' models of health and disease.

We are still left with the need for a definition of clinical psychophysiology which will reflect the diversity of disciplines that have previously employed psychophysiological techniques. Traditionally, clinical psychophysiology has been approached from several distinct directions. Perhaps the most established application concerns the extension of laboratory-based psychophysiological paradigms to the study of psychopathological groups in psychiatry. Previous texts which have adopted this approach have included those by Fowles (1975), Lader (1975) and Van Praag, Lader, Rafaelsen and Sachar (1980). A recent overview of the application of psychophysiology to psychopathology in general is to be found in Zahn's (1986) excellent review. A second area from which clinical psychophysiology has originated involves its application as a collection of clinical assessment instruments in psychotherapy research (Crits-Christoph and Schwartz, 1983; Lacey, 1959; Lang, 1971; Schwartz, 1978; Stern and Plapp, 1969) and behaviour therapy, in particular (Haynes and Wilson, 1979; Kallman and Feuerstein, 1986; Ray and Raczyuski, 1981; Sturgis and Arena, 1984; Sturgis and Gramling, 1988). A third but related source of influence stems from the psychophysiological foundations of biofeedback and self-regulation (Blanchard and Epstein, 1978; Carroll, 1984; Gatchel and Price, 1979; Olton and Noonberg, 1980). Finally, the advent of both behavioural medicine and the related disciplines of medical and health psychology has also seen a rapid expansion of the use of psychophysiological techniques for the assessment and treatment of a vast range of physical or non-psychiatric conditions (Doleys, Meredith and Ciminero, 1982; Feuerstein, Labbe and Kuczmierczyk, 1986; Gentry, 1984; Haynes and Gannon, 1981; Surwit, Williams, Steptoe and Biersner, 1982).

A definition of clinical psychophysiology ought, therefore, to represent the above diverse interests. Accordingly, it should be interdisciplinary in nature, linking both biological and social sciences, and should be applied to both psychiatry and medicine. It is proposed, therefore, that clinical psychophysiology is the application of psychophysiological techniques, concepts and theories to the explanation of psychological factors which influence health behaviours and risks. Health, in this context, is taken to mean a state of both physical and psychological wellbeing.

PSYCHOPHYSIOLOGICAL APPROACHES TO PSYCHOPATHOLOGY

A general distinction can be made between psychophysiological techniques which have been adopted merely as pathological correlates of some physiological or psychological process and applications based upon psychophysiological theories which emphasize the interaction between psychological and physiological processes. The former approach is exemplified by two general rationales. First is the use of typical psychophysiological measures as pathophysiological indices. Shagass (1976) has distinguished between psychophysiological and pathophysiological indices on the basis that the latter reflect directly biological dysfunction (i.e. neural substrates of abnormal behaviour) without recourse to psychological states. Examples of this approach would include the use of brain evoked potentials to localize anatomical or neurophysiological dysfunction (e.g. Harding, Boylan and Clement, 1985). Essentially, psychophysiological measures used in this manner do not differ from any other physiological index of brain function. This is not to say that psychophysiologists are not interested in neural substrates, only that identification of brain dysfunction *per se* in isolation of behaviour is of limited interest. Therefore this handbook has omitted coverage of the use of physiological measures (e.g. evoked potentials) which have been employed exclusively for diagnostic testing of neurological function. This topic has been comprehensively dealt with elsewhere (Aminoff, 1986; Halliday, 1982; Halliday, Butler and Paul, 1987 Harmony, 1984).

The second example of the isolated use of psychophysiological techniques is the converse of the pathophysiological approach. Here psychophysiological measures are used as physiological correlates of psychological states but without recourse to any functional relationship or psychophysiological context. Examples of this approach would include the use of autonomic measures as *sole* indices of psychological constructs such as anxiety, arousal, emotional discharge, attention, etc. Usually, specific measures are adopted with minimal explanation and may be frequently interchanged with other psychophysiological or behavioural indices. The major problem which arises from this approach concerns the interpretation of the psychophysiological measures obtained. It is likely that for most psychophysiological measures, the variance accounted for by specific psychological processes may be relatively small. Accordingly, if measures are to be reliably employed, this variance needs to be identified, together with sources of variation (see Turpin, 1983a, pp. 56–57) arising from other physiological and psychological influences unrelated to the psychological correlate in question.

The logical extension of the above critiques would be the clinical application of psychophysiological techniques firmly based upon a body of psychophysiological theory. Unfortunately, until recently, psychophysiology has tended to be a rather empirical and, hence, descriptive discipline. However, several areas of recent psychophysiological endeavour have direct relevance to psychopathology. The following section provides a brief overview of some common psychophysiological constructs which may help to illustrate how these models can be applied to questions of psychopathology.

PSYCHOPATHOLOGY AND PSYCHOPHYSIOLOGICAL THEORIES

Perhaps the earliest illustration of the application of psychophysiologically based theories to psychopathology concerns biological substrates of personality and abnormal personality function. In particular, Russian researchers (cf. Nebylitsyn and Gray, 1972) have employed psychophysiological measures in order to extend Pavlov's (1957) early formulations of personality. Pavlov suggested that both individual differences and abnormal reactions such as neuroses could be accounted for in terms of a stable personality dimension, the strength of the nervous system, which determined conditioning and subsequent personality development. This individual difference dimension relied upon an underlying physiological substrate which gave rise to the possibility of psychophysiological investigation. Research into the strength of the nervous system has been reviewed elsewhere (Gray, 1964; Nebylitsyn and Gray, 1972). Indeed, these ideas have influenced European theories of personality such as those of Eysenck (1967) and Claridge (1967, 1985). The later reformulation has important implications for psychophysiological models of psychosis. Recent reviews of psychophysiological approaches to personality include those by Gale and Edwards (1986) and O'Gorman (1983).

Much of the above theorizing concerning biological substrates of personality has been founded upon the notion of arousal (Claridge, 1967; Gray, 1964). Indeed, the concept of arousal has had an important influence on the development of psychophysiological theories and, in particular, on their applications to psychopathology (Lader, 1975). Ironically, arousal and psychophysiology have grown apart, resulting in a decline in the use of arousal as an intervening variable in psychophysiological research (Fowles, 1984a; Venables, 1984). Several reasons for the demise of arousal or activation theory, as originally advocated by Duffy (1962), can be identified. First, despite its use as a general concept, a variety of different definitions of arousal exist. These range from behavioural definitions concerning the intensity of behaviour to various physiological definitions which emphasize different measures and neural substrates (Andrew, 1974; Claridge, 1981). In addition, complementary terms and concepts such as 'arousability' (Claridge, 1967, 1981) and 'activation and effort' (Priabram and McGuinness, 1975) have also been evolved. Second, correlational studies which have attempted to examine both the construct and concurrent validity of these definitions have failed to demonstrate convincing results (Venables, 1984). Indeed, the demise of arousal theory is associated with Lacey's (1967) classic paper which stressed situational stereotypy in determining the behaviour of different autonomic response systems. Hence, the individual patterning of autonomic measures is considered to be governed more by specific stimulus and response characteristics than by some general construct such as arousal. More recent advocates of arousal theory have also stressed the complex nature of stimulus–response relationships (Fahrenberg and Foerster, 1982) and the different arousal systems which may reflect different control systems (Claridge, 1981; Venables, 1984), motivational systems (Fowles, 1980, 1982), and neurophysiological (Routtenberg, 1968) or neurochemical (Vanderwolf and Robinson, 1981) substrates.

The apparent disrepute of arousal theory poses a problem for clinical psychophysiology since, as Lader (1975) has emphasized, 'arousal' is a potentially useful explanatory concept for psychopathology. Lader stresses that the paucity of correlational data may reflect more the inexact nature of our understanding of psychophysiological measurement than the non-existence of an underlying physiological arousal substrate. A similar argument concerning the limitations of different measurement techniques has also been suggested by Cone (1979) and Cone and Hawkins (1977) for the failure to observe synchrony between different 'modes' of anxiety responding (see later).

In summary, arousal may still provide an economic explanation of psychobiological relationships under certain specified conditions. Nevertheless, researchers should be aware that more specific explanations concerning stimulus–response characteristics may prove to be of greater worth in the longer term (Steptoe, 1980).

Some of the issues raised in relation to arousal may also be levelled at the concept of 'stress'. Limitations on space prevent an adequate discussion of the relationship between psychophysiology and stress research. Fortunately, this topic has been covered both in recent reviews (Cox, 1978; Engel, 1985; Steptoe, 1980; Turpin and Lader, 1986) and also in Chapter 8 of this volume.

Another traditional area of psychophysiological pursuit has been the identification and differentiation of emotion. In particular, physiological and hormonal measures have been frequently employed in order to assess biological substrates associated with different emotions such as fear and anger (e.g. Ax, 1953). More recent theories of emotion have stressed the interaction of cognitive and physiological processes (Schachter and Singer, 1962) and the ascendancy of cognitive evaluative theories of emotional states (Lazarus, 1966). Recently, Zajonc (1980) has challenged the primary role of cognition in determining affective states and has reintroduced the notion of preconscious early affective processing prior to cognitive appraisal. This controversial reformulation (Lazarus, 1984; Zajonc, 1984) is said to have important implications for behaviour therapy (Greenberg and Safran, 1984; Rachman, 1981, 1984). Readers interested in contemporary psychophysiological approaches to emotional behaviour should also consult the reviews by Fridlund, Gibson and Newman (1984) and Schwartz (1986).

Another important area of psychophysiological research concerns human classical conditioning (Davey, 1987; Dawson and Schell, 1985; Öhman, 1983). These paradigms have been used by Ohman and his colleagues (see Chapter 9) to examine the equipotentiality premise concerning the acquisition of phobias. This states that phobic responses should be acquired equally across a range of neutral stimuli. The converse is that some so-called 'prepared stimuli' (i.e. common phobic objects) are more easily conditioned and demonstrate greater resistance to extinction. Seligman (1971) has claimed that for phobias, the latter premise holds and may be explained in terms of selection and evolutionary advantage. This research has culminated in the 'evolutionary- -cognitive' approach to emotion (Öhman, 1986) and draws heavily upon earlier information-processing models proposed by Öhman (1979, 1983, 1986) to account for autonomic classical conditioning.

A further application which is also related to psychophysiological models of fear concerns Lang's model of emotional imagery (Lang, 1979). This is based upon numerous observations that people respond similarly to imagined fearful situations as they do to real-life encounters with fearful objects. Psychophysiological activation will also occur in response to subjects reading affectively descriptive text. Lang accounts for these patterns of activation by suggesting that in each situation an emotional action set is accessed from memory which when processed gives rise to efferent output in the form of somatic and autonomic events. Further discussion of this model is provided by Cuthbert and Lang in Chapter 4.

Perhaps one of the most important areas of contemporary psychophysiology concerns information processing. Physiological measures have commonly been employed as indices of attention, especially with respect to the orienting paradigm (Siddle, 1983). Indeed, the concepts of 'orienting and defence responses' (cf. Turpin, 1986) are commonly used to account for differences in fearful behaviour in different psychopathological groups (cf. Sartory, 1983). More recently, cortical measures especially have become incorporated into cognitive psychology paradigms (Donchin, Karis, Bashore, Coles and Gratton, 1986). These paradigms have been frequently applied to psychopathological states such as anxiety, obsessional–compulsive disorder, depression and, in particular, schizophrenia (Sartory, 1985; Zahn, 1986). With respect to schizophrenia, early applications had sought to reveal deficits in psychophysiological responding which could be related to psychological dysfunctions associated with orienting (Bernstein, 1970) or selective filtering (Venables, 1973). Although, incontrovertible evidence of a substantial processing deficit(s) has yet to be obtained (see Nuechterlein and Dawson, 1984a; Zahn, 1986), psychophysiological data have contributed generally to innovative models of psychosis (Gruzelier, 1979; and see Chapter 5) and schizophrenic relapse (Nuechterlein and Dawson 1984b; Turpin, Tarrier and Sturgeon, 1988; and see Chapter 13).

Finally, psychophysiological models have begun to be applied to areas of behavioural medicine concerned with conditions such as coronary heart disease and hypertension (Obrist, 1981; Steptoe, 1981; and see Chapters 8 and 15), peripheral vascular disorders (see Chapter 16), headache (Andrasik, Blanchard, Arena, Saunders and Barron, 1982), etc. Since many of these applications are dealt with separately by chapters in Section 2 of this handbook, they will not be discussed further here. Similarly, the impact of psychophysiologically based interventions such as biofeedback, etc. are reviewed in both Sections 1 and 2 of this handbook (see Chapters 7, 16 and 19, in particular).

Although it has been argued that a general distinction can be made between 'tools and theories' regarding rationales underlying clinical psychophysiology, it is probably more useful to the unfamiliar reader to review each specific approach individually. The next part of this chapter will examine several frequently adopted rationales for employing psychophysiological methods in clinical research and practice.

PRINCIPLES AND RATIONALES UNDERLYING CLINICAL PSYCHOPHYSIOLOGY

The successful adoption of psychophysiological techniques requires an appropriate rationale for their application, together with adequate measurement and quantification methods. The purpose of this section is to explore rationales which have previously been proposed for clinical psychophysiological research and to critically evaluate current applications. As has already been stated, clinical psychophysiology has evolved from several disparate sources, each with its own rationales and paradigms of study. It is important, therefore, that these are individually recognized and applied appropriately as foundations for future research.

DISCRIMINATION AND DIAGNOSIS

Many early psychophysiological studies in psychopathology were motivated by the promise of identifying objective diagnostic criteria with which to distinguish individuals experiencing different disorders. The identification and subsequent classification of psychiatric syndromes have generally been confined to the elicitation and clarification of abnormal phenomenological states, together with the careful observation of behaviour (Wing, Cooper and Sartorius, 1974).

Psychiatric diagnosis has been fraught with numerous methodological difficulties such as poorly operationalized criteria and assessment techniques, poor
inter-observer reliability, and limited construct and predictive validity (Morey,
Skinner and Blashfield, 1986). Recognition of these problems has resulted both
in attempts to refine the diagnostic process, and in the search for so-called
'objective indices' of psychopathological states (Usdin and Hanin, 1982).
Psychophysiological measures have been advocated as potential diagnostic
markers either as correlates of some underlying biological dysfunction or as
objective indicators of psychological dysfunction. The former approach is exemplified by research on possible arousal dysfunctions in anxiety disorders (Lader,
1975). A more recent example is Ward and Doerr's (1986) adoption of electrodermal measures as possible markers of cholinergic dysfunction in affective
states. These applications tend towards the use of psychophysiological measures
as pathophysiological markers and may be seen as synonymous with other
biological markers associated with biological psychiatry. However, one
important characteristic of psychophysiological techniques is that they are
generally non-invasive.

Psychophysiological measures may also be employed as indices of psychological dysfunction associated with the disorder in question. An obvious
example is the use of autonomic measures in conjunction with self-report and
behavioural ratings in order to assess anxiety (Lang, 1968; Rachman and
Hodgson, 1974). Similarly, psychophysiological measures have been frequently
employed as correlates of attentional dysfunction in schizophrenia (Zahn, 1986;
and see Chapter 13). The latter use is consistent with Neale and Oltmann's
(1980) attempt to operationalize the term 'schizophrenia' and employ it
as an open, hypothetical, scientific construct as opposed to a diagnostic
entity.

Before examining the use of psychophysiological measures as discriminative
markers, a distinction should be made between the sensitivity and specificity
of a marker. Sensitivity refers to the likelihood that the marker will identify
specific disorders (i.e. the 'hit' rate), whereas specificity concerns the ratio of
specific cases identified versus non-related cases (i.e. the false alarm rate).
Hence, elevated autonomic activity may be reliably associated with a specific
disorder but also evident in numerous other conditions. This would be an
example of high sensitivity but low specificity. In terms of diagnostic discrimination, psychophysiological markers should be both highly sensitive and specific. Low specificity may indicate the presence of some common and hence
non-specific antecedent or consequence of psychopathological dysfunction, such
as psychosocial stressors, non-specific affective changes or psychological
discomfort. The interpretation of psychophysiological differences with respect
to different clinical populations, within the same population and in relation to
the natural history of the disorder will be discussed next.

Comparing Psychophysiological Measures Across Clinical Populations

Traditional applications of psychophysiological measures for diagnostic purposes have sought to discriminate particular clinical populations from either other clinical groups or so-called 'normal' populations. A detailed review of this enterprise is outside the scope of the present overview and the reader is referred to recent reviews (Lader, 1975; Zahn, 1986) and to Section 2 of this handbook.

The basis underlying many of these investigations concerned the premise that clinical populations would differ from 'normals' in terms of arousal. An early example of this approach was Lader's attempt to discriminate individuals experiencing anxiety and affective disorders from controls who had not formerly displayed any psychiatric history (Lader, 1967; Lader and Wing, 1966; Noble and Lader, 1971, 1972). This was based originally on the assumption that people with anxiety disorders were generally over-aroused whereas depressives would be under-aroused. Lader employed several different psychophysiological indices but relied principally upon the rate of habituation of electrodermal responses to auditory stimuli and the frequency of spontaneously occurring electrodermal responses in the absence of specific stimulation. The findings from these studies indicated that relative to normal subjects, people with anxiety disorders demonstrated slower response habituation and greater spontaneous response frequencies. People with affective disorders, however, tended to display depressed skin conductance levels and fewer spontaneous responses, especially if the depression was of a retarded or endogenous type and in the absence of anxiety. These data demonstrate a limited utility for the differentiation of anxiety and affective states using relatively simple psychophysiological procedures.

The adoption of an approach similar to the one described above to schizophrenia has proved less successful. Numerous reviews of the application of psychophysiological measures to the assessment of arousal in schizophrenia have been published (e.g. Bernstein, 1967; Depue and Fowles, 1973; Gruzelier and Venables, 1975; Gruzelier, Lykken and Venables, 1972; Ohman, 1981b; Rubens and Lapidus, 1978). It is evident from these reviews that different, and sometimes contradictory, conclusions regarding hypo- or hyperarousal in schizophrenia can be drawn depending upon the nature of the measures employed, the clinical characteristics of the schizophrenic group studied, and whether the subjects were medicated, etc.

The current failure of psychophysiological measures as diagnostic markers in schizophrenia reinforces the limitations of this approach. In order to yield adequate specificity and sensitivity, the markers have to be reliable and insensitive to potentially confounding factors which are associated with the study of pathological populations, such as medication, institutionalization, laboratory stress, diet, etc (see Chapter 2). It must also be assumed that the target clinical populations in these studies have also been adequately and reliably defined. The lack of consistent and operationally defined diagnostic criteria, particularly amongst early psychophysiological studies, may have also resulted in contradictory findings. Finally, it must be assumed that the psychophysiological measure is a specific index of either some physiological or psychological dysfunction which is directly associated with the dimension of psychopathology in question.

In summary, the use of psychophysiological indices as diagnostic markers which would have clinical as opposed to theoretical implications is a promise which has remained unfulfilled. Since psychophysiological measures are influenced by a variety of physiological and psychological processes, it is unlikely that a single measure will have sufficient specificity to discriminate between individual psychopathological states. The major exception to this rule is where the psychophysiological measure itself is intricately related with a major dysfunction or process associated with the major psychopathology. Hence, the use of such measures in the assessment of sexual (see Chapter 14) or sleep dysfunctions (cf. Hartmann, 1981) may result in valid and useful data which may help to discriminate abnormal populations. In these cases, the measures are being adopted as part of an assessment of the target dysfunction *per se* and not just as potential diagnostic markers.

Comparing Psychophysiological Measures Within Clinical Populations

More recent psychophysiological studies of clinical populations have tended to focus upon single psychophysiological groups as opposed to seeking to discriminate between different clinical populations or non-psychiatric controls. Essentially, three main purposes underlying these investigations may be identified: subgroup classification, determination of prognosis and prediction of response to treatment.

The first concerns the subgroup problem. Given that many classes of psychiatric disorder are often quite globally and polythetically defined (Blashfield, 1986), and that a single diagnostic label may be associated with numerous different types and combinations of symptoms, psychophysiological measures have been frequently employed in order to study patterns of similarity and dissimilarity amongst various subgroups. For example, Nobel and Lader (1972) attempted to discriminate between 'endogenous' and 'reactive' depression using physiological measures. Similarly, numerous studies have examined possible subgroup differences in schizophrenia including pre-morbid adjustment (Crider, Greenspoon and Maher, 1965), clinical status (Bernstein, 1967; Gruzelier, 1976), chronicity (Venables and Wing, 1962), and presence or absence of paranoia (Horvath and Meares, 1979).

An alternative approach has been to identify clinical subgroups on the basis of psychophysiological reactivity and to subsequently identify clinical features associated with these physiological differences. Once again, schizophrenia provides examples of this strategy. In particular, the orienting response paradigm has been employed to categorize subtypes of schizophrenia. At least two categories of response type have been identified. For example, the failure to elicit electrodermal orienting responses (i.e. non-responding) is more frequently observed in schizophrenia (0–75%) than in normal controls (0–40%) (Zahn, 1986). It would appear that non-responding is associated with ratings of confusion, conceptual disorganization, emotional withdrawal, and depressive symptoms (Venables and Bernstein, 1983). Other categories of electrodermal responding observed in schizophrenia include fast and slow habituators (Ohman, 1981b; Zahn, 1986). Over-responding has been said to be associated with clinical ratings of anxiety, agitation and behavioural disturbance (Gruzelier, 1976).

The identification of clinical subtypes, whether based upon behavioural or physiological criteria, may be of both aetiological and prognostic significance. Indeed, it has been suggested that psychophysiological measures may be important prognostic indicators. With respect to schizophrenia, Zahn (1986) has reviewed several studies where a relationship between psychophysiological reactivity and clinical outcome has been established. In particular, slow clinical improvement has been associated with slow electrodermal habituation (Frith, Stevens, Johnstone and Crow, 1979; Zahn, Carpenter and McGlashan, 1981) and poorer social outcome with electrodermal non-responding (Öhlund *et al.*, 1987). Similarly, higher rates of non-specific skin conductance responding in acutely ill patients may predict future episodes of relapse (Sturgeon, Turpin, Kuipers, Berkowitz and Leff, 1984). Straube, Wagner, Foerster, Boven and Schmid (1987) have also reported a relationship between autonomic activity and schizophrenic outcome. Accordingly, psychophysiologically defined subgroups have also contributed to high-risk research. (cf. Watt, Anthony, Wynne and Rolf, 1984). Electrodermal hyporeactivity has also been associated with suicidal behaviour in depressives (Thorell, 1987). Finally, cardiovascular hyper-reactivity has also been said to be a possible future indicator of relapse with respect to behavioural treatments of phobias (Grey, Rachman and Sartory, 1981).

Psychophysiological measures might also identify differential treatment response and clinical subtypes. This topic will not be discussed further since it has been covered within Zahn's (1986) comprehensive review, and will also be dealt with in later sections on assessment and treatment evaluation.

Psychophysiological Vulnerability Markers

The use of psychophysiological measures as diagnostic markers is implicitly associated with a biomedical disease model, the assumption being that comparisons across different groups will reveal psychophysiological differences indicative of some underlying pathological process. However, recent aetological approaches, termed vulnerability models (see later), have stressed the interaction between long-term causal factors associated with increased population risk for developing a specific psychiatric disorder, and short-term precipitating factors which lead to the expression of dormant risk within the population, in the form of individuals exhibiting particular psychiatric symptoms and patterns of psychopathological functioning (cf. Turpin and Lader, 1986). An example of a recent vulnerability model is provided by Nuechterlein and Dawson (1984b, see also Chapter 13) and essentially consists of four components: enduring vulnerability characteristics, external environmental stimuli (e.g. psychosocial stressors), transient intermediate states (e.g. arousal and information-processing deficits) and outcome behaviours (e.g. schizophrenic symptoms and impaired social functioning). It should be stressed that these models attempt to deal with the *episodic* nature of psychiatric disorders and, hence, emphasize the natural history of the development of episodes of dysfunctioning within a population over time. A consequence of this temporal perspective is that several different categories of marker can be identified (see also Chapter 2). Vulnerability markers, therefore, are associated with increased risk for the development of the disorder. They may be potentially identified in the population at large, even for people who have not experienced symptom breakdown, and are traditionally associated with personality or behavioural traits which are associated with the development of the disorder. In relation to schizophrenia, psychophysiological markers have been used as vulnerability indicators both with respect to high-risk research (Venables, 1978; Watt *et al.*, 1984) and also in association with pre-morbid personality traits in the population at large. The latter approach is exemplified by Buchsbaum's research on input dysfunction and monoamine oxidase inhibitors (Haier, Buchsbaum and Murphy, 1979) and the concept of schizophrenia proneness (e.g. Miller, 1986; Simons, 1981). Vulnerability markers might also be identified by comparing people who have experienced a psychopathological episode, but who are not currently demonstrating symptoms and are therefore said to be in remission. The study of remitted patients has been commonly adopted both in schizophrenia (Iacono, 1982) and depression (Iacono, Peloquin, Lumry, Valentine and Tuason, 1982). It is also possible that psychophysiological vulnerability measures may act as genetic markers for certain psychiatric disorders (see Chapter 2).

Finally, markers can be identified during the actual episode itself. These constitute traditional diagnostic differences between symptomatic and non-symptomatic groups. However, these differences may also reflect the onset of some psychopathological process, the presence of a precipitating environmental event, a mere correlate of symptomatic behaviour, the psychological response to illness onset, an indicator of breakdown in coping resources or an interaction between stressor and vulnerability. The last category has been termed 'a mediating vulnerability' factor (Nuechterlein and Dawson, 1984b) and may be identified both during the episodic stage and earlier during any evident prodromal phase.

The adoption of vulnerability models, in conjunction with the longitudinal study of the natural history of episodic psychological disorder, provides a relatively complex framework in which to evaluate potential diagnostic psychophysiological differences. It is, therefore, not too surprising that the conclusions drawn from cross-sectional studies of diagnostic groups have generally resulted in markers of limited specificity and sensitivity.

PSYCHOLOGICAL THEORIES OF PSYCHOPATHOLOGY

A major rationale underlying the application of clinical psychophysiology, as has already been discussed, is the use of physiological measures as correlates or process measures of psychological dysfunction. Hence, it is insufficient to adopt a solely comparative approach. Instead, psychophysiological differences ought to facilitate the interpretation and explanation of psychopathology in terms of psychological theory. Accordingly, recent applications of these measures have been guided by the promise of identifying specific areas of psychological dysfunction. Since specific psychophysiological concepts and theories relevant to psychopathology have been dealt with in the previous section of this chapter, only a brief overview of these rationales will be provided.

The use of psychophysiological paradigms to study conditioning and learning has resulted in a diverse range of studies which have applied this approach to psychopathology. Stern and Janes (1973) have reviewed the application of electrodermal conditioning paradigms to the study of various psychopathological states, including schizophrenia, depression and mental retardation. More recently, conditioning paradigms have been applied to examine the equipotentiality premise in relation to the acquisition of phobias (Ohman, 1986) and also in the development of hypertension (Engel, 1986).

Psychophysiological measures are frequently adopted within cognitive paradigms as measures of attention, expectancy, memory function, response preparation and selection, etc (Coles, Donchin and Porges, 1986). Accordingly, such measures have commonly been employed to study information-processing deficits which may be associated with psychopathology. In particular, the use of central measures such as evoked potentials and the contingent negative variation have been adopted to explore cognitive dysfunction (cf. Zahn, 1986) in both psychiatric and brain-damaged populations. Autonomic information-processing indices such as the orienting response (Siddle, 1983) have also been frequently employed.

The psychophysiological differentiation of different subjective and behavioural states has obvious implications for psychopathology. In particular, electroencephalographic (EEG) studies of sleep have been frequently conducted in psychiatric groups (Hartmann, 1981). In relation to waking states, psychophysiological measures are often employed in studies of emotional behaviour (Schwartz, 1986). Commonly, autonomic (Ekman, Levenson and Friesen, 1984) and electromyographic (EMG; Fridlund and Izard, 1983) measures have been used to distinguish different types of emotional experience. This research has particular relevance to negative affective states and the development of depression (see Chapter 12). A related area concerns the use of psychophysiological measures to investigate social interaction (Cacioppo and Petty, 1983). The social psychophysiological paradigm has been recently applied to psychopathology in relation to marital functioning (Levenson and Gottman, 1983) and the effects of expressed emotion upon relapse in schizophrenia (Turpin *et al.*, 1988).

Finally, the emergence of psychobiological theories of disease (Engel, 1977; Van Praag, 1981) has provided a further impetus for the use of psychophysiological measures. The traditional biomedical model with its emphasis upon endogenous biological pathogens has been critically dismissed as an adequate explanation of both physical and mental health problems (Engel, 1977; Öhman, 1981a; Tarrier, 1979; Zubin and Spring, 1977). Similarly, psychodynamic explanations of so-called 'psychosomatic' disorders have also been described as insufficient, since they fail to adequately predict those individuals at risk for disorder, the temporal onset of the disorder and, most importantly, the mediational processes involved (Weiner, 1977). Accordingly, a variety of multidisciplinary-based biopsychosocial models of psychopathology have evolved which emphasize the interaction of biological, psychological and social processes (Turpin and Lader, 1986; Turpin *et al.*, 1988). Typically, these models adopt a 'diathesis–stress' (Rosenthal, 1970) approach whereby the expression of a disorder results from an environment–vulnerability interaction. It has been argued that psychophysiological measures may provide both noninvasive techniques and a theoretical basis with which these models can be evaluated (Turpin *et al.*, 1988). Moreover, these models help to argue against a simplistic equation that 'biology' is equivalent to 'disease' (cf. Fowles, 1984b).

The notion that behavioural processes may be important in the development of specific vulnerabilities and the onset of pathophysiology in physical disorders has been central to the development of behavioural medicine as a discipline (see Chapter 8). Accordingly, the 'stress-coping' model, which is concerned with the effects of psychological stresses and coping processes upon physiological reactivity, has become an influential paradigm in behavioural medicine (but see Steptoe, 1980).

CLINICAL ASSESSMENT AND TREATMENT

The previous sections have dealt with the clinical application of psychophysiological largely in terms of research. A major rationale for employing psychophysiological measures is their potential contribution to assessment and treatment in clinical practice. Some of the earliest examples of clinical psychophysiology were in relation to the study of psychotherapeutic processes. Indeed, both Jung (see Walrath and Stern, 1981) and Reich (1982) employed psychogalvanic responses to study psychotherapeutic processes. Excellent reviews of early psychotherapeutic applications are available (Lacey, 1959; Lang, 1971). Similarly, psychophysiological measures were frequently employed in large-scale psychometric assessments both during and immediately following the Second World War. This approach is best exemplified by Wenger's (1941) studies of autonomic balance. Essentially, autonomic balance referred to the relative activities of the parasympathetic and sympathetic branches of the autonomic nervous system. Wenger (1941) sought evidence of this construct by measuring within a large number of US servicemen a variety of physiological indices said to reflect sympathetic and parasympathetic activity.

More recent applications have been derived mainly from behaviourally orientated approaches to the assessment and treatment of health problems. The purpose of this section is to describe the rationales underlying the use of psychophysiological measures in clinical practice. Four areas of interest will be identified: assessment, treatment outcome evaluation, treatment process evaluation and psychophysiologically based interventions. It should be noted that some of these issues are also covered elsewhere in this handbook (see particularly Chapters 6 and 7).

Assessment

Several different rationales may be identified for adopting psychophysiological assessment procedures. Originally, these measures were employed as objective indices of arousal or emotional states (i.e. 'affect or arousal meter'; see Lacey, 1959, p. 160). Relative to self-report questionnaires, psychophysiological indices might be considered to provide continuous, objective and sensitive measures (Levenson, 1983). Hence, measures of autonomic reactivity (e.g. skin conductance, heart rate) have commonly been used to assess anxiety (Lader, 1975). Unfortunately, dissociations are frequently observed between different modes of assessment such that the correlations between questionnaire, physiological and behavioural data have typically been low (Martin, 1961). Moreover, these relationships will also be affected by the context of the clinical interview. These points were clearly illustrated by Lacey (1959), who stated that 'autonomic responses . . . need to be *interpreted* in terms of the total behaviour of the organism' and that the implications of this 'are rather serious – even devastating – for those who wish to evaluate the effectiveness of psychotherapy in terms of the course of somatic arousal'. This substitutive use of psychophysiological measures, to use Lacey's term, *in vacuo* as objective measures of psychological states such as anxiety has limited usefulness.

Contemporary psychophysiological assessments are typically multimodal, involving physiological, behavioural and cognitive (subjective self-report) categories of responding. The use of these 'three systems' has largely been influenced by attempts to measure anxiety and fear behaviours during the course of behavioural treatments. Indeed, Lang (1968, 1971) advocated the adoption of the 'three-systems' approach in order to overcome the previously discussed problem of dissociation between measures (Lacey, 1967; Martin, 1961).

The multimodal approach has also been suggested on the basis of some assessment models advocated for behaviour therapy. Whereas original applications of operant conditioning relied upon the functional analysis of the effects of environmental events upon observed behaviours, more recent behavioural interventions, especially in relation to adult mental health, have stressed the importance of so-called organismic variables, together with a broader definition of behaviour which encompasses physiological, cognitive and overt modes of responding (cf. Nelson and Hayes, 1986). The stimulus–organism–response––consequences model of assessment (Goldfried and Sprafkin, 1976) provides two rationales for psychophysiological indices. First, in relation to organismic variables which may represent some underlying physiological substrate or disturbance (e.g. brain tumour, drug abuse, hunger, fatigue, etc). Second, as a component of measuring behavioural constructs associated with psychological states such as anxiety.

However, the adoption of a three-systems approach has given rise to several interpretative problems (cf. Hollandsworth, 1986). First, dissociations between avoidance behaviours and subjective and autonomic correlates of fear frequently occur. Rachman and Hodgson (1974) have termed poor correlations across different measures 'discordance' and dissociations across measures in time 'desynchrony'. Moreover, these authors (Hodgson and Rachman, 1974) argue that patterns of desynchrony may be strong determinants of therapeutic outcomes in behavioural treatments. Nevertheless, this emphasis upon three-systems measurement and its ensuing desynchronies has been criticized, since desynchrony may arise due to measurement artifact and differences in situational demands (Cone, 1979; Kaloupek and Levis, 1983). In addition, given that the three systems are correlates of a hypothetical construct labelled 'anxiety', these measures should not therefore be highly correlated (Hugdahl, 1981; Kaloupek and Levis, 1980). The reliance on three different modes of measurement also gives rise to problems of selectivity when interpretations of multimodal assessments are made. Peterson (1984) warns against the arbitrary use of one mode of responding as representative of the necessarily loosely defined construct under investigation. Similarly, Evans (1986) suggests that it is interactions between these different modes of responding which may be of value rather than viewing them as passive reflections of a behavioural construct using different modes of measurement. A similar argument has also been advanced by Schwartz (1978). Finally, it should be recognized that some behaviours (e.g. speech) are notoriously difficult to delineate in terms of the three-systems approach (Hollandsworth, 1986).

Although the implicit assumption of the three-systems approach is an equal weighting of the individual response modes, there are several cases when the physiological mode may take precedence over other measures. The first concerns situations when the target response is essentially of a physiological nature. Hence, in behavioural medicine, the measurement of blood pressure in hypertension or blood glucose levels in diabetes may assume some additional weighting with respect to other assessment measures. However, care should be exercised to ensure that the physiological index monitored is truly germane to the aetiology of the syndrome being studied. Recent research on headache using psychophysiological measures of muscle tension and peripheral blood flow have demonstrated that the aetiological distinctions made between 'tension' and 'migraine' headaches may be unfounded (Philips, 1980). Consequently, the sole reliance on psychophysiological indices of headache for problem assessment and treatment evaluation may be based upon a false premise.

Another area where physiological assessment has been suggested by some to be of greater importance than either behavioural or subjective measures concerns forensic and legal liability applications. For example, it has been assumed that physiological measures of sexual preference may be more reliable and valid than measures of self-report, since they are said to be less amenable to voluntary control and hence, possibly, deception (for a discussion of these issues see Chapters 6 and 14). A similar assessment situation which is presently receiving much attention is the physiological detection of post-traumatic stress disorder (Blanchard, Kolb, Gerardi, Ryan and Pallmeyer, 1986; Pitman, Scott, Forgue de Jong and Claiborn, 1987). However, given the severe consequences of these types of clinical decisions, the situation becomes analogous to the 'lie detection' paradigm. Accordingly, clinicians should be aware of the problems of interpretation and the consequences of both false alarms and miss rates associated with these types of paradigms (Furedy, 1986).

Treatment Outcome Measures

A logical extension of the use of psychophysiological measures for clinical assessment is their application to the evaluation of treatment outcome. Since this topic is covered elsewhere (see Chapters 6 and 7 and individual chapters in Section 2), only a brief overview will be provided. The major issue concerns desynchrony between measures during the course of treatment (Rachman and Hodgson, 1974). In particular, the interpretation of multimodal assessments when physiological measures fail to parallel behavioural and cognitive changes poses a difficult problem. Indeed, some researchers have questioned whether physiological measures should be considered as behavioural outcome measures at all (Wolff and Merrens, 1974). Similarly, the contribution of physiological measures such as heart rate have been questioned in relation to outcome evaluation in particular disorders such as agoraphobia (e.g. Holden and Barlow, 1986). Other investigators have employed psychophysiological measures essentially as interim process measures since they have been excluded from final outcome criterion measures (Michelson, Mavissakalian and Marchione, 1985). Despite these reservations, physiological assessments have shown promise in predicting individual differences in treatment outcome (Hollandsworth, 1986 and see Chapter 10). For example, Jerremalm, Jansson and Ost (1986) attempted to distinguish between 'behaviourally orientated' and 'physiologically orientated' social-phobic patients in relation to the differential effects of relaxation and self-instructional training.

Treatment Process Measures

Psychophysiological measures in outcome evaluation have principally been applied as process measures. It is argued that patterns of desynchrony between these measures are both prognostically and theoretically relevant to treatment outcome (Hodgson and Rachman, 1974). For example, different behaviourally based fear-reduction treatments are associated with different patterns of desynchrony over time. These have been interpreted as representing differences in theoretical processes such as habituation (Grey *et al.*, 1981) and self-efficacy (Bandura, Adams, Hardy and Howells, 1980).

A traditional aim of process evaluation is to assess the specificity of a given treatment. Hence, when interventions are employed in order to bring about a specific physiological change, as in the case of some fear reduction, relaxation and biofeedback treatments, physiological measures provide important indices of the specificity of the intervention adopted relative to the desired outcome behaviours. A distinction may be made between process measures that bear a direct relationship to the clinical outcome measures employed, and indirect measures that index some mediational process which reflects a hypothetical relationship to the outcome variables studied. Examples of direct process measures are the use of psychophysiological measures for behavioural treatments of fear and anxiety reduction (e.g. Bernstein, Borkovec and Coles, 1986) and the assessment of biofeedback control of specific physiological target responses (e.g. Blanchard and Epstein, 1978).

Indirect psychophysiological process measures are commonly employed to assess the effects of treatments upon relatively non-specific constructs such as somatic arousal or tension which are said to be important determinants of specific target problem behaviours. Examples of the latter approach include the physiological evaluation of relaxation treatments (Borkovec, Johnson and Bloch, 1984) in relation to clinical problems such as insomnia (Nicassio and Buchanan, 1981) and asthma (Erskine-Milliss and Schonell, 1981), and the use of arousal–relapse models for schizophrenic symptoms (Slade, 1973; Turpin, 1983b; Turpin *et al.*, 1988).

Psychophysiologically Based Treatments

From the above discussion of psychophysiological process measures, it is apparent that their use is not just related to assessment. Several specific treatment approaches are dependent upon psychophysiological measurement. Perhaps the most obvious examples are biofeedback therapies based upon the proposition of learnt control over the autonomic system (cf. Miller, 1977). Within the context of this overview, there is insufficient space to adequately deal with this topic. Instead, the interested reader is referred to the following reviews and texts: Andrasik and Blanchard (1983), Blanchard and Epstein (1978), Carroll (1984), Gatchel and Price (1979), Hatch, Fisher and Rugh (1987), Olton and Noonberg (1980), and Reed, Katkin and Goldband (1986). In addition, within this handbook, biofeedback is also reviewed generally in relation to behavioural medicine (Chapter 7) and also in relation to specific disorders (see Section 2).

Other psychophysiologically based interventions exist. Some proponents of relaxation training emphasize its physiological basis as a major determinant of therapeutic outcome (e.g. Benson, 1975). Recently, cue-controlled relaxation, which is based upon the notion of a conditioned autonomic relaxation response, has received some attention but unfortunately little favourable direct evidence to support its proposed mechanisms (Grimm, 1980). Finally, controlled breathing interventions have been advocated in order to control symptoms associated with 'hyperventilation syndrome' and some panic disorders (see Chapter 18).

TECHNIQUES

The successful application of psychophysiology to clinical assessment requires both knowledge and experience of psychophysiological techniques and paradigms. The purpose of this section is to provide an overview of the techniques available and to critically assess the adoption of these methods in clinical research and practice. Since there already exists a comprehensive literature on psychophysiological methodology (Coles *et al.*, 1986; Greenfield and Sternbach, 1972; Martin and Venables, 1980), details of instrumentation and procedures will not be discussed in any great depth. Readers unfamiliar with psychophysiological methods might want to approach either general introductory psychophysiology texts (e.g. Andreassi, 1980; Grings and Dawson, 1978; Stern, Ray and Davis, 1980) or texts and review articles written specifically for applications of psychophysiology to clinical practice (Cacioppo, Petty and Marshall-

Goodell, 1985; Feuerstein and Schwartz, 1977; Feuerstein *et al.*, 1986; Haynes and Wilson, 1979; Hollandsworth, 1986; Kallman and Feuerstein, 1986; Lader, 1975; Lang, 1971; Ray and Raczyuski, 1981; Sturgis and Arena, 1984; Sturgis and Gramling, 1988; Van Praag *et al.*, 1980; Williamson, Waters and Hawkins, 1986) and biofeedback (Andrasik and Blanchard, 1983; Blanchard and Epstein, 1978; Reed *et al.*, 1986). In addition, further details of specific psychophysiological techniques are to be found in Section 2 of the current volume. General aspects of electronic instrumentation and electrical safety have also been covered elsewhere (Pope, 1978; Rugh, Gable and Lemke, 1986).

SELECTION OF MEASURES

Perhaps the most daunting task facing the novice investigator is the choice of a psychophysiological measure or measures. This will be governed by several factors. Initial selection will depend upon the kind of rationale underlying the decision to adopt a psychophysiological approach. The choice of measure will result either directly, from the observation of some clinically relevant physiological behaviour (e.g. blood pressure in hypertension), or indirectly, via a psychophysiological index of some psychological construct, such as anxiety or attention. This latter case is accompanied by problems of both construct and concurrent validity as regards individual psychophysiological indices and the choice of an appropriate experimental paradigm.

A second factor concerns the physiological context in which the measurement is to be made. It has already been emphasized that the variance attributed to psychophysiological as opposed to physiological influences may be relatively small. Hence, the choice of measure may depend upon identifying other sources of physiological influence that may well determine the activity of the chosen index. For example, cardiovascular measures have frequently been developed as correlates of fear and anxiety during behavioural avoidance tasks (Sartory, 1981). However, it has also been argued that cardiovascular functioning is largely determined by the metabolic demand arising from both anticipated and actual physical movements (Obrist, 1981). In situations where motor activity itself is expected to vary and, hence, cannot be experimentally controlled, cardiovascular measures should also be accompanied by measures of either somatic activity or metabolic rate (see Turpin, 1985a) in order to separate out both physiological and psychophysiological influences. The need to examine psychophysiological indices within a physiological context should not be over-simplified or understated (Schwartz, 1978).

Practical or clinical considerations may also dictate the adoption of a particular measure. This will largely depend upon the instrumentation and transducer required for its measurement, together with the nature of the paradigm to be studied. For example, heart rate may be derived either from the electrocardiogram or from a pulse signal measured using a photoplethysmograph (Siddle and Turpin, 1980). Although for some purposes the former is said to be more accurate (Jennings, Westervelt and Ackles, 1987), the latter is the more easily obtained measure since it requires a single transducer attached to the ear-lobe rather than the attachment of a number of electrocardiogram electrodes either to the chest or limbs. Similarly, although electrodermal measures are the most frequently adopted indices of sweating, other more simple techniques such as sweat-gland imprints are also available (Clements and Turpin, 1987; Sutarman and Thomson, 1952). The susceptibility of different measures to movement artifacts will also help determine the choice of measure.

Finally, the scale and time-course of the psychophysiological index to be assessed require careful consideration. It is common for several different measures to be derived from a single channel of physiological activity. For example, skin conductance activity upon analysis may yield measures of response amplitude, response frequency, non-specific response frequency and level (Martin and Venables, 1980). These derived measures may all have different functional relationships with the psychological constructs being assessed. Similarly, response derivation is also determined by the time-course of events. Heart rate measures can either be obtained as short-term event-locked phasic changes or long-term time-locked tonic changes (Turpin, 1985b). In addition, tonic activity may be represented as changes in the mean and variance of the cardiac data. These different forms of derived measure should not be used interchangeably since they are said to reflect different psychophysiological processes. Similarly, long-term psychobiological changes may be better represented using biochemical as opposed to electrophysiological indices (see Chapter 8).

TYPES OF MEASURES

There is a wide range of measures which can be described as constituting a psychophysiological database and may be classified in a number of ways. First, they may be grouped according to the mode of measurement employed. This would result in invasive and non-invasive electrophysiological measures, biochemical measures, motoric measures (including observed overt behaviours) and self-report measures. Second, measures might be classified according to physiological dimensions underlying either the function or target organ presumed to be under investigation. For example, cardiovascular status might be considered both in terms of cardiac output from the heart and the peripheral resistance encountered within the circulation (Siddle and Turpin, 1980). These physiological variables can in turn be related to a variety of indices including heart rate, left ventricular performance, measures of cardiac impedance, peripheral blood flow, pulse volume, etc. (see Chapter 8). In addition to functional physiological distinctions, measures may also be classified according to assumed anatomical differences. Hence, psychophysiological measures are frequently subdivided according to central or electrocortical measures on the one hand, and autonomic or peripheral measures on the other. The latter are often further subcategorized into sympathetic and parasympathetic measures. However, it should be noted that many peripheral end-organs are dually innervated (e.g. heart and pupil) and hence, individual psychophysiological indices may have to be further differentiated with respect to sympathetic and parasympathetic effects. The functional integrity of the parasympathetic and sympathetic divisions of the autonomic nervous systems may also be an over-simplification (Turpin, 1983a, p. 46) due to specialization of particular branches of either the parasympathetic or sympathetic systems. Furthermore, the specific nature of the neurotransmitter systems subserving these branches of the autonomic nervous system should also be taken into consideration.

Finally, psychophysiological indices may be classified with respect to the nature of their presumed psychological significance. For example, psychophysiological indices of attention might include various cortical measures, together with peripheral autonomic measures (see Coles *et al.*, 1986). These latter measures are frequently said to be components of an orienting reflex (Turpin, 1983a). However, although several different measures are said to be associated with attentional processes, examination of the psychophysiological literature strongly suggests that different measures should not be employed interchangeably. For example, orienting is said to be indexed by a number of peripheral autonomic changes including heart rate deceleration, increased skin conductance, peripheral vasoconstriction, etc. However, even within a simple habituation paradigm consisting of the repetition of an auditory stimulus, different measures will display different response habituation rates (Turpin, 1983a). The use of only a single measure, particularly in the absence of other behavioural data, may lead to erroneous conclusions concerning the psychophysiological process being studied (Turpin, 1986).

DESIGNS AND PARADIGMS

Psychophysiological research has tended to be rooted firmly in the traditions of group designs and accompanying analysis of variance or multivariate statistical procedures. Although this approach has been fruitful for traditional psychophysiological studies, clinical applications necessitate a greater degree of flexibility as regards type of design. In particular, single-case designs (Barlow and Hersen, 1984; Kratochwill, 1978) are probably under-represented in clinical psychophysiological research. It is likely that the traditional preoccupation with group comparison designs, together with an overcautious expectation of inter- and intra-measure variability, has contributed to the neglect of these potentially useful procedures. Indeed, several authors have reiterated the potential advantages of single-case methodology in relation to biofeedback (Bandeira, Bouchard and Granger, 1982; Barlow, Blanchard, Hayes and Epstein, 1977).

These include the ability to examine individual versus group mean data, the examination of clinical versus statistical significance, the detailed examination of individual variability and the ethical advantages of single-case innovative procedures. In addition, single-case studies have facilitated the use of psychophysiological procedures to study relatively rare clinical phenomena such as Tourette syndrome (Surwillo, Shafii and Barrett, 1978; Turpin and Powell, 1984). Indeed, the continuous nature of psychophysiological measurement makes it an ideal candidate for the adoption of single-case methodology. In selecting designs for psychophysiological research, the merits of single-case designs should, therefore, also be borne in mind, together with the traditional advantages of group comparison protocols (cf. Kazdin, 1980). Fortunately, there exists a growing literature which has employed single-case methodology in relation to blood–injury phobia (e.g. Kozak and Miller, 1985), schizophrenic relapse and expressed emotion (Tarrier and Barrowclough, 1984), mania (Hemsley and Philips, 1975) and depression (Blackburn and Bonham, 1980). In addition to the traditional limitations of group designs, psychophysiological research has tended to be strongly paradigm-bound. The purpose of this section is to review types of psychophysiological paradigm and their application to clinical research.

Given that most psychophysiological research is paradigm-bound, it is important to assess how these designs may be adapted for clinical research. The majority of studies have examined differences between clinical populations using existing paradigms such as classical conditioning, orienting and habituation, reaction time, vigilance and signal detection, and recently more complex cognitive tasks such as sentence completion and dichotic listening procedures, etc. Essentially, the tasks are relatively simple and require little active or overt participation by the subject so as to allow artifact-free collection of psychophysiological data. Although these paradigms may be of theoretical importance, their divergence from the behavioural assessment of clinical problems should be recognized. Indeed, in the context of individual differences, Gale and Edwards (1986, p. 497) have described many traditional psychophysiological paradigms as 'nontasks (i.e. sitting doing nothing); we believe that human subjects in a laboratory do not do or think about nothing, and that experimenters who believe the opposite are misleading themselves'. It is likely that the issue of stimulus control is even more apposite when subjects may be acutely psychologically disturbed and preoccupied with obsessional ruminations, hallucinations, delusions, etc. The apparently simple nature of the paradigms employed may also lead to the assumption of stimulus equivalence across subjects and conditions as regards task difficulty and requirements. Again this would appear to be an oversimplification. Even the nature of the instructions to 'sit and listen/attend' given within a simple habituation task may significantly affect the experimental outcome (Iacono and Lykken, 1979). As with all psychophysiological research, clinical applications require close scrutiny of the experimenter's assumptions and the frequent use of appropriate manipulation checks.

Studies which attempt to examine clinical phenomena *per se* confront two major problems. The first concerns the restricted nature of the psychophysiological laboratory and the range of activities which can be measured within a space-limited environment and relatively free of movement artifacts. The second problem concerns the availability of clinical populations and access to psychophysiological laboratories. Many laboratories are located away from hospitals and clinics, and present difficulties of enabling clinically distressed subjects to travel to and participate in psychophysiological studies. It is not surprising, therefore, that much clinical psychophysiological research has been essentially of an analogue nature. Either analogue subjects, in the form of so-called 'anxious, depressed or phobic' undergraduates, or analogue situations, such as role play or behavioural avoidance tests (cf. Haynes and Wilson, 1979), or sometimes both, have been employed. Although analogue research may overcome problems due to access to client populations and the need for a limited and restricted psychophysiological environment, problems of validity ensue. Researchers interested in analogue studies should be mindful of the various critiques and recommendations published concerning the validity of this approach (Borkovec and Rachman, 1979; Haynes and Wilson, 1979; Nay, 1986). Nevertheless, analogue studies have enabled the potential extension of psychophysiological hypotheses (e.g. Kartsounis and Turpin, 1987; Ohman, 1981a) to encompass clinical phenomena not easily assessed within the laboratory. Accordingly, they have an important role in clinical psychophysiological research, so long as their findings are treated cautiously and the generalizability to true clinical situations and populations tested.

A final category of paradigm concerns the combined collection of behavioural and psychophysiological data within an appropriate clinic or home environment. This approach requires the use of either portable or ambulatory psychophysiological equipment. As regards clinic settings, the use of psychophysiological assessments under 'resting' or non-dysfunctional conditions are probably of limited value (cf. Philips, 1980). Indeed, the use of specific, stressful conditions in order to assess psychophysiological reactivity has been particularly emphasized with respect to behavioural medicine (Steptoe, 1980). If the dysfunctional behaviour is infrequent or inappropriate within the clinic setting, situational analogues will need to be considered. The alternative is the collection of psychophysiological data in naturalistic settings during ongoing behaviour and social interaction, and without the strict 'stimulus control' of the psychophysiological laboratory. Although this approach is almost antithetical to the usually well-controlled psychophysiological study, social interactional studies are producing pertinent clinical data. For example, Levenson and Gottman (1983) have reported interesting associations between heart rate measures and self-reported affect between couples during marital interactions.

Similarly, electrodermal measures obtained from people with schizophrenia in the presence of a high expressed emotion relative have given rise to a psychobiological model of schizophrenic relapse (Tarrier, Vaughn, Lader and Leff, 1978; Turpin *et al.*, 1988). Social interaction *per se* would also appear to produce pronounced psychophysiological activation (e.g. Lynch, Thomas, Paskewitz, Malinow and Long, 1982) which would suggest that the new discipline of social psychophysiology (Cacioppo and Petty, 1983) may make important contributions to future research.

SITUATIONAL FACTORS

It is often naively assumed that psychophysiological measures provide objective and unconfounded measures of physiological activity which are in some respect 'purer' than other forms of behavioural assessment. Indeed, Sturgis and Arena (1984) have likened contemporary psychology's infatuation with scientific instrumentation to Dorothy's reliance on the wizard in the children's story 'The Wizard of Oz'. Indeed, as with all good fairy-tales, all that glitters is not gold! Psychophysiological measures are subject to a variety of confounding factors which either require careful experimental control or need to be considered when the data are interpreted. Perhaps one of the most important methodological considerations concerns the reactivity of measurement. As has previously been discussed, the traditional psychophysiological laboratory places constraints upon the range of activities and behaviours which can be appropriately studied. It is likely, therefore, that these constraints limit both the range of clinical problems and clients which may be studied. Moreover, the novel and often socially obtrusive nature of psychophysiological procedures may sometimes arouse feelings of apprehension and anxiety in both normal and abnormal populations. With acutely disturbed clients, the strict experimental demands of the laboratory may result either in normalizing behaviour or the selective rejection of clients whose clinical state prevents them from complying with experimental procedures, and hence leads to their exclusion from the study.

The potentially reactive effects of psychophysiological laboratory studies have provided an important impetus for the use of naturalistic psychophysiological studies (Turpin, 1983b) and the adoption of ambulatory monitoring (Turpin, 1985a). Ambulatory monitoring enables psychophysiological data to be recorded from a freely moving subject, in an unrestrained environment during the course of his/her daily activities. This is achieved either by the use of radiotelemetry or the wearing of portable data-loggers such as miniature cassette recorders or digital memory devices. Unfortunately, restrictions on space preclude a detailed discussion of clinical applications of ambulatory monitoring. However, the interested reader should consult the following articles: Holden and Barlow (1986); Margraf, Taylor, Ehlers, Roth and Agras

(1987); Mavissakalian and Michelson (1982); and review (Turpin, 1985a). Ambulatory monitoring also provides an opportunity to examine the generalizability of laboratory-based assessments (cf. McKinney, *et al.*, 1985; Turpin, 1985a).

Several other aspects of the experimental situation need to be considered. First, the personal characteristics of the experimenter (Cacioppo *et al.*, 1985; Gale and Baker, 1981) and therapist (Sturgis and Arena, 1984) may influence psychophysiological responding. Second, important subject variables such as age, sex, race, drug abuse (tobacco, alcohol, caffeine, etc), menstrual cycle, physical fitness and prior activity all have profound effects (Martin and Venables, 1980; Sturgis and Arena, 1984) on physiological baselines and reactivity. Finally, ambient environmental conditions (temperature and humidity) and also seasonal fluctuations (Sturgis and Arena, 1984) will affect psychophysiological measurements.

Even if the influences of these variables are recognized and controlled, it should not be assumed that they remain constant throughout a study. Psychophysiological measures frequently demonstrate changes over time in the absence of observed environmental changes. This has necessitated the use of adaptation periods or initial baselines in order to provide a standardized comparison datum with which other experimental data can be compared. Unfortunately, the choice of such a resting or adaptation period has not been standardized and lacks consensus (Hastrup, 1986; Linden and McEachern, 1985; Robinson, Whitsett and Kaplan, 1987).

Within-session changes in physiological baselines will also necessitate the use of 'counterbalancing' to reduce the systematic effects of different experimental conditions, if manipulated on a within-subject basis. Changes due to fatigue, or physiological and psychological adaptation pose a serious problem to the evaluation of treatments manipulated on a within-sessions basis (e.g. biofeedback) and will necessitate the adoption of 'placebo' controls (Borkovec *et al.*, 1984). Similarly, psychological measures frequently display large 'first-time testing' or between-session effects (Whitsett, Robinson and Kaplan, 1987). These may unduly influence the conclusions which can be drawn from both single- and multiple-session studies. For example, Tarrier *et al.* (1978) have claimed that electrodermal reactivity in schizophrenia is only sensitive to expressed emotion if studied in the home. Unfortunately, Tarrier *et al.*'s (1978) design confounded order of testing between home and laboratory with first-time testing effects (cf. Turpin, 1983b).

DATA MANIPULATION AND ANALYSIS

The collection of psychophysiological data is generally only a starting point for further quantification and analysis. Typically, these data are subjected to several stages of artifact rejection, time sampling and transformation in order to derive measures prior to statistical analysis. The principles underlying these procedures have been discussed elsewhere (cf. Coles *et al.*, 1986; Martin and Venables, 1980; and see Chapter 3). Analytical techniques usually require parametric statistical procedures and the advantages and limitations of these methods have been discussed in a number of recent reviews (Coles *et al.*, 1986; Levey, 1980; Ray and Kimmel, 1979). In particular, the problem of serial dependency across repeated measures poses serious problems for analysis of variance models, and requires careful consideration (Jennings and Wood, 1976; Vasey and Thayer, 1987).

INTERPRETATION AND RELIABILITY

The interpretation of psychophysiological data will clearly be guided by the rationale underlying its application. Indeed, in previous sections the import-ance of the physiological context surrounding a particular measure and the need to include additional behavioural and self-report measures has already been stressed when interpreting psychophysiological changes. Another major issue which has recently received particular attention concerns the reliability of psychophysiological changes. Most applications assume that psychophysiol-ogical measures are stable with respect to situational and temporal factors. Changes in these measures are thus thought to represent significant and relevant changes due to psychopathological processes or treatments. However, if psychophysiological measures are unstable, the significance of individual changes or the sensitivity of those measures to treatment effects within groups of subjects might be much reduced. Several recent studies have been conducted to assess the test–retest reliability of commonly employed clinical psychophysi-ological measures and procedures (Arena, Blanchard, Andrasik, Cotch and Myers, 1983; Faulstich, Williamson, McKenzie, Duchmann, Hutchinson and Blouin, 1986; Waters, Williamson, Bernard, Blouin and Faulstich, 1987). Arena *et al.* (1983) obtained only few and modest test–retest correlations from a sample of 15 college students, which led them to be cautious concerning the reliability of psychophysiological measures and hence their usefulness as applied clinical techniques. Using a larger sample of 48 students, Faulstich *et al.* (1986) reported adequate reliability for skin temperature, skin resistance vasomotor response, heart rate and diastolic/systolic blood pressure recorded during baseline and test (both physical and mental stressors) conditions. Differ-ence scores, together with the majority of EMG measures, were found to be unstable. A more recent study by this research group (Waters *et al.*, 1987) also reported significant and moderately stable coefficients for respiration rate, skin conductance responding, skin temperature and heart rate during baseline and test conditions, systolic blood pressure and skin conductance level only being stable during some baseline assessments.

In addition to the assessment of temporal stability, the above studies have also examined situational and individual response specificity (Engel, 1960). Situational, or stimulus, specificity refers to the ability of psychophysiological measures to discriminate between different conditions and, hence, may provide an index of treatment sensitivity. Individual response specificity concerns the stability of individual differences in psychophysiological response profiles. Both Waters *et al.* (1987) and Robinson *et al.* (1987) argue that the presence of individual response specificity requires the use of multivariate reliability methods which assess individual test–retest coefficients and also the analysis of the temporal consistency of response profiles. These issues are discussed further in Chapter 3.

SUMMARY

The extent of prior knowledge required by a naive investigator embarking on the application of psychophysiological techniques will obviously depend upon the level of sophistication of the methods to be employed. Ideally, researchers unfamiliar with those procedures should seek out help and collaboration from experienced psychophysiological researches. If help is not at hand, the inexperienced researcher should either consult the relevant handbooks (Coles *et al.*, 1986; Greenfield and Sternbach, 1972; Martin and Venables, 1980) or scan recent reports in the following journals: *Psychophysiology, Biological Psychology, International Journal of Psychophysiology* and the *Journal of Psychophysiology*. In particular, *Psychophysiology* has commissioned a series of articles concerning publication guidelines for the following measures: heart rate (Jennings, Berg, Hutcheson, Obrist and Turpin, 1981), electrodermal activity (Fowles, Christie, Edelberg, Grings, Lykken and Veriables, 1981) and electromyography. Similar guidelines have also been published for evoked potentials (Donchin *et al.*, 1977). Finally, naive investigators may also like to consult the 'seven deadly sins of psychophysiological research in individual differences', published by Gale and Edwards (1986) as a source of inspiration, and hopefully not exasperation, for designing future studies.

CONCLUSION

An underlying theme of this chapter has been to evaluate the diverse uses to which psychophysiological has been applied. Too frequently, introductory chapters concerning clinical psychophysiology have yielded rather unoriginal, albeit useful, accounts of psychophysiological techniques. The main purpose of the present overview has been to focus upon the different rationales which have been adopted for the use of psychophysiological measures. By emphasizing the *choice* of a *particular* rationale, it is hoped to modify the perception of clinical psychophysiological as a mere collection of assessment techniques which are arbitrarily and interchangeably applied. Instead, it is argued that the adoption of these techniques should be based upon a set of principles. To achieve this aim will necessitate the development of psychophysiological theories. Although psychophysiology has been an essentially empirically based discipline, theoretical advances relevant to psychopathology have recently begun to emerge. Hopefully, the following chapters in this handbook will help to reinforce the application of theory to clinical psychophysiology practice.

In addition to theoretical developments, future research must also address the assumptions underlying currently adopted rationales. The increasing availability of innovations in both equipment (e.g. Kazrin and Durac, 1983) and training (Feuerstein and Schwartz, 1977), together with the expanding application of psychophysiological techniques to clinical research in behaviour therapy and behavioural medicine, herald a potential renascence for the discipline of clinical psychophysiology. However, this expansion should not continue without a clear understanding of the psychophysiological processes underlying the application of these frequently complex and expensive methods of assessment.

REFERENCES

Aminoff, M. J. (1986). *Electrodiagnosis in Clinical Neurology*. London: Churchill Livingstone.

Andrasik, F., and Blanchard, E. B. (1983). Applications of biofeedback to therapy. In: C. E. Walker (Ed.) *Handbook of Clinical Psychology: Theory, Research and Practice*. Homewood: Dow-Jones.

Andrasik, F., Blanchard, E. B., Arena, J. G., Saunders, N. L. and Barron, K. D. (1982). Psychophysiology of recurrent headache: methodological issues and new empirical findings. *Behavior Therapy* **13**, 407–429.

Andreassi, J. L. (1980). *Psychophysiology*. London: Oxford University Press.

Andrew, R. J. (1974). Arousal and the causation of behaviour. *Behaviour* **51**, 135–165.

Arena, J. G., Blanchard, E. B., Andrasik, F., Cotch, P. A. and Myers, P. E. (1983). Reliability of psychophysiological assessment. *Behaviour Research and Therapy* **21**, 447–460.

Ax, A. F. (1953). The physiological differentiation between fear and anger in humans. *Psychosomatic Medicine* **15**, 433–442.

Bandeira, M., Bouchard, M. A. and Granger, L. (1982). Voluntary control of autonomic responses: a case for a dialogue between individual and group experimental methodologies. *Biofeedback and Self-Regulation* **7**, 317–330.

Bandura, A., Adams, N. E., Hardy, A. B. and Howells, G. N. (1980). Tests of the generality of self-efficacy theory. *Cognitive Therapy and Research* **4**, 39–66.

Barlow, D. H. and Hersen, M. (1984). *Single-Case Experimental Designs: Strategies for Studying Behavior Change*, 2nd edn. New York: Pergamon.

Barlow, D. H., Blanchard, E. B., Hayes, S. C. and Epstein, L. H. (1977). Single-case experimental designs and clinical biofeedback experimentation. *Biofeedback and Self-Regulation* **2**, 221–239.

Benson, H. (1975). *The Relaxation Response*. New York: Morrow.

Bernstein, A. S. (1967). Electrodermal base level, tonic arousal, and adaptation in chronic schizophrenics. *Journal of Abnormal Psychology* **72**, 221–232.

Bernstein, A. S. (1970). Phasic electrodermal orienting response in chronic schizophrenics. *Journal of Abnormal Psychology* **75**, 146–156.

Bernstein, D. A., Borkovec, T. D. and Coles, M. G. H. (1986). Assessment of anxiety. In: A. R. Ciminero, K. S. Calhoun and H. A. Adams (Eds) *Handbook of Behavioral Assessment*, 2nd edn. New York: Wiley.

Blackburn, I. M. and Bonham, K. G. (1980). Experimental effects of a cognitive therapy technique in depressed patients. *British Journal of Social and Clinical Psychology* **19**, 353–363.

Blanchard, E. B. and Epstein, L. H. (1978). *A Biofeedback Primer*. Reading, Mass: Addison-Wesley.

Blanchard, E. B., Kolb, L. C., Gerardi, R. J., Ryan, P. and Pallmeyer, T. P. (1986). Cardiac responses to relevant stimuli as an adjunctive tool for diagnosing post-traumatic stress disorder in Vietnam veterans. *Behavior Therapy* **17**, 592–606.

Blashfield, R. K. (1986). Structural approaches to classification. In: T. Millon and G. L. Klerman (Eds) *Contemporary Directions in Psychopathology: Towards DSMIV*. New York: Guildford.

Borkovec, T. D. and Rachman, S. (1979). The utility of analogue research. *Behaviour Research and Therapy* **17**, 253–261.

Borkovec, T. D., Johnson, M. C. and Bloch, D. L. (1984). Evaluating experimental designs in relaxation research. In: R. L. Woolfolk and P. M. Lehrev (Eds) *Principles and Practice of Stress Management*. New York: Guilford.

Cacioppo, J. T. and Petty, R. E. (1983). *Social Psychophysiology: A Sourcebook*. New York: Guilford.

Cacioppo, J. T., Petty, R. E. and Marshall-Goodell, B. (1985). Physical, social and inferential elements of psychophysiological measurement. In: P. Karoly (Ed.) *Measurement Strategies in Health Psychology*. New York: Wiley.

Carroll, D. (1984). *Biofeedback in Practice*. London: Longman.

Carroll, D. and Anastasiades, P. (1978). The behavioural significance of heart rate: the Laceys' hypothesis. *Biological Psychology* **1**, 249–275.

Claridge, G. S. (1967). *Personality and Arousal*. Oxford: Pergamon.

Claridge, G. S. (1981). Arousal. In: G. Underwood and R. Stevens (Eds) *Aspects of Consciousness*, Vol. 2: *Structural Issues*. London: Academic Press.

Claridge, G. (1985). *Origins of Mental Illness*. Oxford: Blackwell.

Clements, K. and Turpin, G. (1987). The validity of the Palmar Sweat Index: effects of feedback-induced anxiety and level of task difficulty on measures of palmar sweating. *Psychophysiology* **24**, 583–584 (Abs.).

Coles, M. G. H., Donchin, E. and Porges, S. W. (1986). *Psychophysiology: Systems, Processes and Applications*. New York: Guilford.

Coles, M. G. H., Jennings, J. R. and Stern, J. A. (1984). *Psychophysiological Perspectives: Festschrift for Beatrice and John Lacey*. New York: Van Nostrand Reinhold.

Cone, J. D. (1979). Confounded comparisons in triple response mode assessment research. *Behavioral Assessment* **1**, 85–95.

Cone, J. D. and Hawkins, R. P. (1977). Current status and future directions in behavioral assessment. In: J. D. Cone and R. P. Hawkins (Eds) *Behavioral Assessment: New Directions in Clinical Psychology*. New York: Brunner/Mazel.

Cox, T. (1978). *Stress*. London: Macmillan.

Crider, A. B., Greenspoon, L. and Maher, B. A. (1965). Autonomic and psychomotor correlates of pre-morbid adjustment in schizophrenia. *Psychosomatic Medicine* **27**, 201–206.

Crits-Christoph, P. and Schwartz, G. E. (1983). Psychophysiological contributions to psychotherapy research: a systems perspective. In: A. Gale and J. Edwards (Eds) *Physiological Correlates of Human Behaviour*, Vol. 3: *Individual Differences and Psychopathology*. London: Academic Press.

Davey, G. (1987). *Cognitive Processes and Pavlovian Conditioning in Humans*. Chichester: Wiley.

Dawson, M. E. and Schell, A. M. (1985). Information processing and human autonomic classical conditioning. In: P. K. Ackles, J. R. Jennings and M. G. H. Coles (Eds) *Advances in Psychophysiology*, Vol. 1, pp. 89–165. Greenwich, Conn. JAI Press.

Depue, R. A. and Fowles, D. C. (1973). Electrodermal activity as an index of arousal in schizophrenics. *Psychological Bulletin* **79**, 233–238.

Doleys, D. M., Meredith, R. L. and Ciminero, A. R. (1982). *Behavioral Medicine: Assessment and Treatment Strategies*. New York: Plenum.

Donchin, E., Callaway, E., Cooper, R., Desmedt, J. E., Goff, W. R., Hillyard, S. A. and Sutton, S. (1977). Publication criteria for studies of evoked potentials (EP) in man. *Progress in Clinical Neurophysiology* **1**, 1–11.

Donchin, E. Karis, D., Bashore, T. R., Coles, M. G. H. and Gratton, G. (1986). Cognitive psychophysiology and human information processing. In: M. G. H. Coles, E. Donchin and S. W. Porges (Eds) *Psychophysiology: Systems, Processes and Applications*. New York: Guilford.

Duffy, E. (1962). *Activation and Behavior*. New York: Wiley.

Ekman, P., Levenson, R. and Friesen, W. V. (1984). Autonomic nervous system activity distinguishes among emotions. *Science* **221**, 1208–1210.

Engel, B. T. (1960). Stimulus-response and individual response specificity. *Archives of General Psychiatry*, **2**, 305–313.

Engel, B. T. (1985). Stress is a noun! No, a verb! No, an adjective! In: T. M. Field, P. M. McCabe and N. Schneiderman (Eds) *Stress and Coping*. Hillsdale, NJ: Erlbaum.

Engel, B. T. (1986). Psychosomatic medicine, behavioral medicine, just plain medicine. *Psychosomatic Medicine* **48**, 466–479.

Engel, G. L. (1977). The need for a new medical model: a challenge for biomedicine. *Science* **196**, 129–136.

Erskine-Milliss, J. and Schonell, M. (1981). Relaxation therapy in asthma: a critical review. *Psychosomatic Medicine* **43**, 365–372.

Evans, I. M. (1986). Response structure and the triple-response mode concept. In: R. O. Nelson and S. C. Hayes (Eds) *Conceptual Foundations of Behavioral Assessment*. New York: Guilford.

Eysenck, H. J. (1967). *The Biological Basis of Personality*. Springfield, Ill.: C. C. Thomas.

Fahrenberg, J. and Foerster, F. (1982). Covariation and consistency of activation parameters. *Biological Psychology* **15**, 151–169.

Faulstich, M. E., Williamson, D. A., McKenzie, S. J., Duchmann, E. G., Hutchinson, K. M. and Blouin, D. C. (1986). Temporal stability of psychophysiological responding: a comparative analysis of mental and physical stressors. *International Journal of Neuroscience* **30**, 65–72.

Feuerstein, M., and Schwartz, G. E. (1977). Training in clinical psychophysiology: present trends and future goals. *American Psychologist* **32**, 560–568.

Feuerstein, M., Labbe, E. E. and Kuczmierczyk, A. R. (1986). *Health Psychology: A Psychobiological Perspective*. New York: Plenum.

Fowles, D. C. (1975). *Clinical Applications of Psychophysiology*. New York: Columbia University Press.

Fowles, D. C. (1980). The three systems arousal model: implications of Gray's two factor learning theory for heart rate, electrodermal activity and psychopathy. *Psychophysiology* **17**, 87–104.

Fowles, D. C. (1982). Heart rate as an index of anxiety: failure of a hypothesis. In: J. T. Cacioppo and R. E. Petty (Eds) *Perspectives in Cardiovascular Psychophysiology*. New York: Guilford.

Fowles, D. C. (1984a). Arousal: implications of behavioral theories of motivation. In: M. G. H. Coles, J. R. Jennings and J. A. Stern (Eds) *Psychophysiological Perspectives: Festschrift for Beatrice and John Lacey*. New York: Van Nostrand Reinhold.

Fowles, D. C. (1984b). Biological variables in psychopathology: a psychobiological perspective. In: H. E. Adams and P. B. Sutker (Eds) *Comprehensive Handbook of Psychopathology*. New York: Plenum.

Fowles, D. C., Christie, M. J., Edelberg, R., Grings, W. W., Lykken, D. T. and Venables, P. H. (1981). Publication recommendations for electrodermal measurement. *Psychophysiology* **18**, 232–239.

Fridlund, A. J., and Izard, C. E. (1983). Electromyographic studies of facial expressions of emotions. In: J. T. Cacioppo and R. E. Petty (Eds) *Social Psychophysiology*. New York: Guilford.

Fridlund, A. J., Gibson, E. L. and Newman, J. B. (1984). Putting emotion in behavioral medicine. Discrete-emotion psychophysiology and its relevance for research and therapy. In: L. Temoshok, C. Van Dyke and L. S. Zegous (Eds) *Emotions in Health and Illness: Applications to Clinical Practice*. New York: Grune-Stratton.

Frith, C. D., Stevens, M., Johnstone, E. C. and Crow, T. J. (1979). Skin conductance responsivity during acute episodes of schizophrenia as a predictor of symptomatic improvement. *Psychological Medicine* **9**, 101–106.

Furedy, J. J. (1986). Lie detection as psychophysiological differentiation: some fine lines. In: M. G. H. Coles, E. Donchin and S. W. Porges (Eds) *Psychophysiology: Systems, Processes and Applications*. New York: Guilford.

Gale, A., and Baker, S. (1981). *In vivo* or *in vitro*?: some effects of laboratory environments with particular reference to the psychophysiology experiment. In: M. J. Christie and P. Mellett (Eds) *Foundations of Psychosomatics*. Chichester: Wiley.

Gale, A., and Edwards, J. A. (1986). Individual differences. In: M. G. H. Coles, E. Donchin and S. W. Porges (Eds) *Psychophysiology: Systems, Processes and Applications*. New York: Guilford.

Gatchel, R. J. and Price, K. P. (1979). *Clinical Applications of Biofeedback: Appraisal and Status*. New York: Pergamon Press.

Gentry, W. D. (1984). *Handbook of Behavioral Medicine*. New York: Guilford.

Goldfried, M. R. and Sprafkin, J. N. (1976). Behavioral personality assessment. In: J. T. Spence, R. C. Carson and J. W. Thibout (Eds) *Behavioral Approaches to Therapy*. Morristown, NJ: General Learning Press.

Graham, F. K. (1979). Distinguishing among orienting, defense and startle reflexes. In: H. D. Kimmel, E. H. Van Olst and J. F. Orlebeke (Eds) *The Orienting Reflex in Humans*. Hillsdale, NJ: Erlbaum.

Gray, J. A. (1964). *Pavlov's Typology*. Oxford: Pergamon Press.

Greenberg, L. S. and Safran, J. D. (1984). Integrating affect and cognition: a perspective on the process of therapeutic change. *Cognitive Therapy and Research* **8**, 559–578.

Greenfield, N. S. and Sternbach, R. A. (1972). *Handbook of Psychophysiology*. New York: Holt.

Grey, S. J., Rachman, S. and Sartory, G. (1981). Return of fear: the role of inhibition. *Behaviour Research and Therapy* **19**, 135–143.

Grimm, L. G. (1980). The evidence for cue-controlled relaxation. *Behavior Therapy* **11**, 283–293.

Grings, W. W. and Dawson, M. E. (1978). *Emotions and Bodily Responses: A Psychophysiological Approach.* New York: Academic Press.

Gruzelier, J. H. (1976). Clinical attributes of schizophrenic skin conductance responders and non-responders. *Psychological Medicine* **6**, 245–249.

Gruzelier, J. H. (1979). Lateral asymmetries in electrodermal activity and psychosis. In: J. Gruzelier and P. Flor-Henry (Eds) *Hemispheric Asymmetries of Function in Psychopathology.* Amsterdam: Elsevier.

Gruzelier, J. H., and Venables, P. H. (1975). Evidence of high and low levels of physiological arousal in schizophrenia. *Psychophysiology* **12**, 66–73.

Gruzelier, J. H., Lykken, D. T. and Venables, P. H. (1972). Schizophrenia and arousal revisited. *Archives of General Psychiatry* **26**, 427–432

Guze, S. B. (1977). The future of psychiatry: medicine or social sciences. *Journal of Nervous and Mental Disease* **165**, 225–230.

Haier, R. J., Buchsbaum, M. S. and Murphy, D. L. (1979). Screening young adults for psychiatric vulnerability: a preliminary comparison of biological and clinical measures. *Psychopharmacology Bulletin* **25**, 7–9.

Halliday, A. M. (1982). Evoked potentials in clinical testing. In: *Clinical Neurology and Neurosurgery Monographs*, Vol. 3. Edinburgh: Churchill Livingstone.

Halliday, A. M., Butler, S. R., and Paul, R. (1987). *A Textbook of Clinical Neurophysiology.* Chichester: Wiley.

Harding, G. F. A., Boylan, C. and Clement, R. A. (1985). The visual evoked cortical potential and visually evoked sub-cortical potential, in ocular and oculocutaneous albinos. In: D. Papakostopoulos, S. Butler and I. Martin (Eds) *Clinical and Experimental Neuropsychophysiology.* London: Croom Helm.

Harmony, T. (1984). Neurometric assessment of brain dysfunction in neurological patients. *Functional Neuroscience*, Vol. 3. Hillsdale, NJ: Erlbaum.

Hartmann, E. (1981). Sleep and sleep disorders. In: H. M. Van Praag, M. H. Lader, O. J. Rafaelsen and E. J. Sachar (Eds) *Handbook of Biological Psychiatry*, Part II: *Brain mechanisms and Abnormal Behaviour – Psychophysiology.* New York: Marcel Dekker.

Hastrup, J. L. (1986). Duration of initial heart rate assessment in psychophysiology **23**, 15–18.

Hatch, J. P., Fisher, J. G., and Rugh, J. D. (1987). *Biofeedback: Studies in Clinical Efficacy.* New York: Plenum.

Haynes, S. N., and Gannon, L. (1981). *Psychosomatic Disorders: A Psychophysiological Approach to Etiology and Treatment.* New York: Praeger.

Haynes, S. N. and Wilson, C. C. (1979). *Behavioural Assessment.* San Francisco: Jossey-Bass.

Hemsley, D. R. and Philips, C. H. (1975). Models of mania: an individual case study. *British Journal of Psychiatry* **127**, 78–85.

Hodgson, R. and Rachman, S. (1974). Desynchrony in measures of fear. *Behaviour Research and Therapy* **12**, 319–326.

Holden, A. E. and Barlow, D. H. (1986). Heart rate and heart rate variability recorded *in vivo* in agoraphobics and nonphobics. *Behavior Therapy* **17**, 26–42.

Hollandsworth, J. G. (1986). *Physiology and Behavior Therapy: Conceptual Guidelines for the Clinician.* New York: Plenum.

Horvath, T. and Meares, R. (1979). The sensory filter in schizophrenia: a study of habituation, arousal and the dopamine hypothesis. *British Journal of Psychiatry* **134**, 39–45.

Hugdahl, K. (1981). The three systems model of fear and emotion – a critical examination. *Behaviour Research and Therapy* **19**, 75–86.

Iacono, W. G. (1982). Bilateral electrodermal habituation-dishabituation and resting EEG in remitted schizophrenics. *Journal of Nervous and Mental Disease* **170**, 91–101.

Iacono, W. G., and Lykken, D. T. (1979). The orienting response: importance of instructions. *Schizophrenia Bulletin* **5**, 11–14.

Iacono, W. G., Peloquin, L. J., Lumry, A. E., Valentine, R. H., and Tuason, V. B. (1982). Eye tracking in patients with unipolar and bipolar affective disorders in remission. *Journal of Abnormal Psychology* **91**, 35–44.

Jennings, J. R., Berg, W. K., Hutcheson, J. S., Obrist, P. A., and Turpin, G. (1981). Publication guidelines for heart rate studies in man. *Psychophysiology* **18**, 226–231.

Jennings, J. R., Westervelt, W. W. and Ackles, P. A. (1987). On plethysmographic measures of beat by beat heart rate. In: P. Ackles, J. R. Jennings and M. Coles (Eds) *Advances in Psychophysiology*, Vol 2. Greenwich, Conn.: JAI.

Jennings, R. J., and Wood, C. C. (1976). The epsilon-adjustment procedures for repeated-measures analyses of variance. *Psychophysiology* **13**, 277–278.

Jerremalm, A., Jansson, L., and Öst, L. G., (1986). Cognitive and physiological reactivity and the effects of different behavioural methods in the treatment of social phobia. *Behaviour Research and Therapy* **24**, 171–180.

Kallman, W., and Feuerstein, M. J. (1986). Psychophysiological procedures. In: A. R. Ciminero, K. S. Calhoun and H. E. Adams (Eds) *Handbook of Behavioral Assessment*. New York: Wiley.

Kaloupek, D. G., and Levis, D. J. (1980). The relationship between stimulus specificity and self-report indices in assessing fear of heterosexual social interaction: a test of the unitary response hypothesis. *Behavioral Assessment* **2**, 267–281.

Kaloupek, D. G., and Levis, D. J. (1983). Issues in the assessment of fear: response concordance and prediction of avoidance behavior. *Journal of Behavioral Assessment* **5**, 239–260.

Kartsounis, L. D., and Turpin, G. (1987). Effects of induced hyperventilation on electrodermal response habituation to agoraphobia-relevant stimuli. *Journal of Psychosomatic Research* **31**, 401–412.

Kazdin, A. E. (1980). *Research Design in Clinical Psychology*. New York: Harper Row.

Kazrin, A., and Durac, J. (1983). Group penile plethysmography: an apparatus for clinical research. *Behavior Therapy* **14**, 714–717.

Kozak, M. J., and Miller, G. A. (1985). The psychophysiological process of therapy in a case of injury-scene-elicited fainting. *Journal of Behavior Therapy and Experimental Psychiatry* **16**, 139–145.

Kratochwill, T. R. (1978). *Single Subject Research: Strategies for Evaluating Change*. New York: Academic Press.

Lacey, B. C., and Lacey, J. I. (1978). Two-way communication between the heart and the brain. *American Psychologist* **33**, 99–113.

Lacey, J. I. (1959). Psychophysiological approaches to the evaluation of psychotherapeutic process and outcome. In: E. I. Rubenstein and M. B. Parloff (Eds) *Research in Psychotherapy*. Washington, DC: American Psychological Association.

Lacey, J. I. (1967). Somatic response patterning and stress: some revisions of activation theory. In: M. H. Appley and R. Trumbull (Eds) *Psychological Stress*. New York: Appleton-Century-Crofts.

Lader, M. H. (1967). Palmar skin conductance measures anxiety and phobic states. *Journal of Psychosomatic Research* **11**, 271–281.

Lader, M. H. (1975). *The Psychophysiology of Mental Illness*. London: Routledge and Kegan Paul.

Lader, M. H. and Wing, L. (1966). *Physiological Measures, Sedative Drugs and Morbid Anxiety*. London: Oxford University Press.

Lang, P. J. (1968). Fear reduction and fear behavior: problems in treating a construct. In: J. M. Shlien (Ed.) *Research in Psychotherapy*. Washington, DC: American Psychological Association.

Lang, P. J. (1971). The application of psychophysiological methods to the study of psychotherapy and behavior modification. In: A. E. Bergin and S. L. Garfield (Eds) *Handbook of Psychotherapy and Behavior Change: An Empirical Analysis*. New York: Wiley.

Lang, P. J. (1979). A bio-informational theory of emotional imagery. *Psychophysiology* **16**, 495–512.

Lazarus, R. S. (1966). *Psychological Stress and the Coping Process*. New York: McGraw-Hill.

Lazarus, R. S. (1984). On the primacy of cognition. *American Psychologist* **39**, 124–129.

Leigh, H. (1982). Comment: the role of psychiatry in medicine. *American Journal of Psychiatry* **139**, 1581–1587.

Levenson, R. W. (1983). Personality research and psychophysiology: general considerations. *Journal of Research in Personality* **17**, 1–21.

Levenson, R. W. and Gottman, J. M. (1983). Marital interaction: physiological linkage and affective exchange. *Journal of Personal and Social Psychology* **45**, 587–597.

Levey, A. B. (1980). Measurement units in psychophysiology. In: I. Martin and P. H. Venables (Eds) *Techniques in Psychophysiology*. Chichester: Wiley.

Linden, W., and McEachern, H. M. (1985). A review of physiological prestress adaptation: effects of duaration and context. *International Journal of Psychophysiology* **2**, 239–245.

Lynch, J. P., Thomas, S. A., Paskewitz, D. A., Malinow, K. L., and Long, J. M. (1982). Inter-personal aspects of blood pressure control. *Journal of Nervous and Mental Disease* **170**, 143–153.

Margraf, J., Taylor, C. B., Ehlers, A., Roth, W. T., and Agras, W. S. (1987). Panic attacks in the natural environment. *Journal of Nervous and Mental Disease*, **175**, 558–565.

Martin, B. (1961). The assessment of anxiety by physiological and behavioral measures. *Psychological Bulletin* **58**, 234–255.

Martin, I., and Venables, P. H. (1980). *Techniques in Psychophysiology*. Chichester: Wiley.

Mavissakalian, M., and Michelson, L. (1982). Patterns of psychophysiological change in the treatment of agoraphobia. *Behaviour Research and Therapy* **20**, 347–356.

McKinney, M. E., Miner, M. H., Ruddel, H., McIlvain, H. E., Witte, H., Buell, J. C., Eliot, R. S., and Grant, L. B. (1985). The standardized mental stress test protocol: test–retest reliability and comparisons with ambulatory blood pressure monitoring. *Psychophysiology* **22**, 453–463.

Michelson, L., Mavissakalian, M., and Marchione, K. (1985). Cognitive and behavioral treatments of agoraphobia: clinical, behavioral and psychophysiological outcomes. *Journal of Consulting and Clinical Psychology* **53**, 913–925.

Miller, G. A. (1986). Information processing deficits in anhedonia and perceptual aberration: a psychophysiological analysis. *Biological Psychiatry* **21**, 100–115.

Miller, N. E. (1977). Biofeedback and visceral learning. *Annual Review of Psychology* **29**, 373–404.

Morey, L. C., Skinner, H. A., and Blashfield, R. K. (1986). Trends in the classification of abnormal behavior. In: A. R. Ciminero, K. S. Calhoun and H. E. Adams (Eds) *Handbook of Behavioral Assessment*, 2nd edn. New York: Wiley.

Nay, W. R. (1986). Analogue measures. In: A. R. Ciminero, K. S. Calhoun and H. E. Adams (Eds) *Handbook of Behavioral Assessment*, 2nd edn. New York: Wiley.

Neale, J. M., and Oltmanns, T. F. (1980). *Schizophrenia*. Chichester: Wiley.

Nebylitsyn, V. D., and Gray, J. A. (1972). *Biological Bases of Individual Behavior*. New York: Academic Press.

Nelson, R. O., and Hayes, S. C. (1986). *Conceptual Foundations of Behavioral Assessment*. New York: Guilford.

Nicassio, P. M., and Buchanan, D. C. (1981). Clinical application of behavior therapy for insomnia. *Comprehensive Psychiatry* **22**, 512–521.

Noble, P. J., and Lader, M. H. (1971). The symptomatic correlates of skin conductance changes in depression. *Journal of Psychiatric Research* **9**, 61–69.

Noble, P. J., and Lader, M. H. (1972). A physiological comparison of 'endogenous' and 'reactive' depression. *British Journal of Psychiatry* **120**, 541–542.

Nuetcherlein, K. H., and Dawson, M. E. (1984a). Information processing and attentional functioning in the developmental course of schizophrenic disorders. *Schizophrenia Bulletin* **10**, 160–203.

Nuetcherlein, K. H., and Dawson, M. (1984b). A heuristic vulnerability/stress model of schizophrenic episodes. *Schizophrenia Bulletin* **10**, 300–312.

Obrist, P. A. (1981). *Cardiovascular Psychophysiology: A Perspective*. New York: Plenum.

O'Gorman, J. G. (1983). Individual differences in the orienting response. In: D. Siddle (Ed.) *Orienting and Habituation: Perspectives in Human Research*. Chichester: Wiley.

Öhlund, L., Alm, T., Lindstrom, L., Wieselgren, I., Ost, L., and Ohman, A. (1987). Electrodermal nonresponding in schizophrenics: relationship to social outcome. *Psychophysiology*, **24**, 603 (Abstract).

Öhman, A. (1979). The orienting response, attention and learning: an information processing perspective. In: H. D. Kimmel, E. H. van Olst and J. F. Orlebeke (Eds) *The Orienting Reflex in Humans*. Hillsdale, NJ: Erlbaum.

Öhman, A. (1981a). The role of experimental psychology in the scientific analysis of psychopathology. *International Journal of Psychology* **16**, 229–321.

Öhman, A. (1981b). Electrodermal activity and vulnerability to schizophrenia: a review. *Biological Psychology* **12**, 87–145.

Öhman, A. (1983). The orienting response during Pavlovian conditioning. In: D. Siddle (Ed.) *Orienting and Habituation: Perspectives in Human Research*. Chichester: Wiley.

Öhman, A. (1986). Face the beast and fear the face: animal and social fears as prototypes for evolutionary analyses of emotion. *Psychophysiology* **23**, 123–145.

Olton, D. S., and Noonberg, A. R. (1980). *Biofeedback: Clinical Applications in Behavioral Medicine*. Englewood Cliffs, NJ: Prentice-Hall.

Pavlov, I. P. (1957). *Experimental Psychology and Other Essays*. New York: Philosophical Library.

Peterson, L. (1984). A brief methodological comment on possible inaccuracies induced by multimodal measurement analysis and reporting. *Journal of Behavioral Medicine* **7**, 307–313.

Philips, C. (1980). Recent developments in tension headache research: implications for understanding and management of the disorder. In: S. Rachman (Ed.) *Contributions to Medical Psychology*, Vol. 2. Oxford: Pergamon.

Pitman, R. K., Scott, P. O., Forgue, D. F., de Jong, J. B., and Claiborn, J. M. (1987). Psychophysiological assessment of post-traumatic stress disorder imagery in Vietnam combat veterans. *Archives of General Psychiatry* **44**, 970–975.

Pope, A. T. (1978). Electrical safety in the use of biofeedback instruments. *Behavior Research Methods and Instrumentation* **10**, 627–631.

Priabram, K. H., and McGuinness, D. (1975). Arousal, activation and effort in the control of attention. *Psychological Review* **82**, 116–149.

Rachman, S. (1981). The primacy of affect: some theoretical implications. *Behaviour Research and Therapy* **19**, 279–290.

Rachman, S. (1984). A reassessment of the 'Primacy of Affect'. *Cognitive Therapy and Research* **8**, 579–584.

Rachman, S. and Hodgson, R. (1974). Synchrony and desynchrony in fear and avoidance. *Behaviour Research and Therapy* **12**, 311–318.

Ray, R. L., and Kimmel, H. D. (1979). Utilization of psychophysiological indices in behavioral assessment: some methodological issues. *Journal of Behavioral Assessment* **2**, 107–122.

Ray, W. J., and Raczyuski, J. M. (1981). Psychophysiological assessment. In: M. Hersen and A. S. Bellack (Eds) *Behavioral Assessment: A Practical Handbook, 2nd edn.* Oxford: Pergamon.

Reed, S. D., Katkin, E. S., and Goldband, S. (1986). Biofeedback and behavioral medicine. In: F. H. Kanfer and A. P. Goldstein (Eds) *Helping People Change: A Textbook of Methods*, 3rd edn. New York: Pergamon.

Reich, W. (1982). *The Bioelectrical Investigation of Sexuality and Anxiety*. New York: Farrar, Straus and Giroux.

Robinson, J. W., Whitsett, S. F., and Kaplan, B. J. (1987). The stability of physiological reactivity over multiple sessions. *Biological Psychology* **24**, 129–139.

Rosenthal, D. (1970). *Genetic Theory and Abnormal Behavior*. New York: McGraw-Hill.

Routtenberg, A. (1968). The two-arousal hypothesis: reticular formation and limbic systems. *Psychological Review* **75**, 51–80.

Rubens, R. L., and Lapidus, L. B. (1978). Schizophrenic patterns of arousal and stimulus barrier functioning. *Journal of Abnormal Psychology* **87**, 199–211.

Rugh, J. D., Gable, R. S., and Lemke, R. R. (1986). Instrumentation for behavioral assessment. In: A. R. Ciminero, K. S. Calhoun and H. E. Adams (Eds) *Handbook of Behavioral Assessment*, 2nd edn. New York: Wiley.

Sartory, G. (1981). Some psychophysiological issues in behavioural psychotherapy. *Behavioral Psychotherapy* **9**, 215–230.

Sartory, G. (1983). The orienting response and psychopathology: anxiety and phobias. In: D. Siddle (Ed.) *Orienting and Habituation: Perspectives in Human Research*. Chichester: Wiley.

Sartory, G. (1985). The contingent negative variation (CNV) in psychiatric states. In: D. Papakostopoulos, S. Butler and I. Martin (Eds) *Clinical and Experimental Neuropsychophysiology*. London: Croom Helm.

Schachter, S., and Singer, S. (1962). Cognitive, social and physiological determinants of emotional states. *Psychological Review* **69**, 379–399.

Schwartz, G. E. (1978). Psychobiological foundations of psychotherapy and behaviour change. In: S. L. Garfield and A. E. Bergin (Eds) *Handbook of Psychotherapy and Behavior Change*, 2nd edn. New York: Wiley.

Schwartz, G. E. (1983). Social psychophysiology and behavioral medicine: a systems perspective. In: J. T. Cacioppo and R. E. Petty (Eds) *Social Psychophysiology*. New York: Guilford.

Schwartz, G. E. (1986). Emotion and psychophysiological organization: a systems approach. In: M. G. H. Coles, E. Donchin and S. W. Porges (Eds) *Psychophysiology: Systems, Processes and Applications*. New York: Guilford.

Seligman, M. E. P. (1971). Phobias and preparedness. *Behavior Therapy* **2**, 307–320.

Shagass, C. (1976). An electrophysiological view of schizophrenia. *Biological Psychiatry* **11**, 3–30.

Siddle, D. (1983). *Orienting and Habituation: Perspectives in Human Research*. Chichester: Wiley.

Siddle, D. A. T., and Turpin, G. (1980). Measurement, quantification and analysis of cardiac activity. In: I. Martin and P. H. Venables (Eds) *Techniques in Psychophysiology*. Chichester: Wiley.

Simons, R. F. (1981). Electrodermal and cardiac orienting in psychometrically defined high-risk subjects. *Psychiatry Research* **4**, 347–356.

Slade, P. (1973). The psychological investigation and treatment of auditory hallucinations. *British Journal of Medical Psychology* **46**, 293–296.

Steptoe, A. (1980). Stress and medical disorders. In: S. J. Rachman (Ed.) *Contributions to Medical Psychology*, Vol. II. Oxford: Pergamon.

Steptoe, A. (1981). *Psychological Factors in Cardiovascular Disease*. London: Academic Press.

Stern, J. A. (1964). Toward a definition of psychophysiology. *Psychophysiology* **1**, 90–91.

Stern, J. A. and Janes, C. L. (1973). Personality and psychopathology. In: W. F. Prokasy and D. C. Raskin (Eds) *Electrodermal Activity in Psychological Research*. New York: Academic Press.

Stern, J. A. and Plapp, J. M. (1969). Psychophysiology and clinical psychology. In: C. D. Spielberger (Ed.) *Current Topics in Clinical and Community Psychology*, Vol. I. New York: Academic Press.

Stern, R. M., Ray, W. J., and Davis, C. M. (1980). *Psychophysiological Recording*. New York: Oxford University Press.

Sternbach, R. A. (1966). *Principles of Psychophysiology*. New York: Academic Press.

Straube, E., Wagner, W., Foerster, K., Boven, K. H., and Schmid, H. (1987). Does ANS activity predict short- and long-term outcome in schizophrenia? *Psychophysiology* **24**, 615 (Abstract).

Sturgeon, D., Turpin, G., Kuipers, L., Berkowitz, R. and Leff, J. (1984). Psychophysiological responses of schizophrenic patients to high and low expressed emotion relatives: a follow up study. *British Journal of Psychiatry* **145**, 62–69.

Sturgis, E. T., and Arena, J. G. (1984). Psychophysiological assessment. *Progress in Behavior Modification*, Vol. 17. New York: Academic Press.

Sturgis, E. G., and Gramling, S. (1988). Psychophysiological assessment. In: A. S. Bellack and M. Hersen (Eds) *Behavioral Assessment: A Practical Handbook*, 3rd edn. New York: Pergamon.

Surwillo, W. W., Shafii, M., and Barrett, C. L. (1978). Gilles de la Tourette syndrome: a 20-month study of the effects of stressful life events and haloperidol on symptom frequency. *Journal of Nervous and Mental Disease* **169**, 812–816.

Surwit, R. S., Williams, R. B., Steptoe, A. and Biersner, R. (1982). *Behavioural Treatment of Disease*. New York: Plenum.

Sutarman, M., and Thomson, M. L. (1952). A new technique for enumerating active sweat glands in man. *Journal of Physiology* **117**, 51P–52P.

Tarrier, N. (1979). The future of the medical model: a reply to Guze. *Journal of Nervous and Mental Disease* **167**, 71–37.

Tarrier, N., and Barrowclough, C. (1984). Psychophysiological assessment of expressed emotion in schizophrenia: a case example. *British Journal of Psychiatry* **145**, 197–203.

Tarrier, N., Vaughn, C. E., Lader, M. H., and Leff, J. P. (1978). Bodily reactions to people and events in schizophrenia. *Archives of General Psychiatry* **36**, 311–315.

Thorell, L. H. (1987). Electrodermal activity in suicidal and nonsuicidal depressive patients and in matched healthy subjects. *Acta Psychiatrica Scandinavica* **76**, 420–430.

Turpin, G. (1983a). Unconditioned reflexes and autonomic nervous system. In: D. Siddle (Ed.) *Orienting and Habituation: Perspectives in Human Research*. Chichester: Wiley.

Turpin, G. (1983b). Psychophysiology, psychopathology and the social environment. In: A. Gale and J. Edwards (Eds) *Physiological Correlates of Human Behaviour*, Vol. 3: *Individual Differences and Psychopathology*. London: Academic Press.

Turpin, G. (1985a). Ambulatory psychophysiological monitoring: techniques and applications. In: D. Papakostopoulos, S. Butler and I. Martin (Eds) *Clinical and Experimental Neuropsychophysiology*. London: Croom Helm.

Turpin, G. (1985b). Quantification, analysis and interpretation of phasic cardiac responses. In: D. Papakostopoulos, S. Butler and I. Martin (Eds) *Clinical and Experimental Neuropsychophysiology*. London: Croom Helm.

Turpin, G. (1986). Effects of stimulus intensity on autonomic responding: the problem of differentiating orienting and defense reflexes. *Psychophysiology* **23**, 1–14.

Turpin, G., and Lader, M. (1986). Life events and mental disorder: biological theories of their mode of action. In: H. Katschnig (Ed.) *Life Events and Psychiatric Disorders: Controversial Issues*. Cambridge: Cambridge University Press.

Turpin, G. and Powell, G. E. (1984). The effects of massed practice and cue-controlled relaxation on tic frequency in Gilles de la Tourette's syndrome. *Behaviour Research and Therapy* **22**, 165–178.

Turpin, G., Tarrier, N., and Sturgeon, D. (1988). Social psychophysiology and the study of biopsychosocial models of schizophrenia. In: H. L. Wagner (Ed.) *Social Psychophysiology: Theory and Clinical Applications*. Chichester: Wiley.

Usdin, E., and Hanin, I. (1982). *Biological Markers in Psychiatry and Neurology*. Oxford: Pergamon.

Van Praag, H. M. (1981). Socibiological psychiatry. *Comprehensive Psychiatry* **22**, 441–449.

Van Praag, H. M., Lader, M. H., Rafaelsen, O. J., and Sachar, E. J. (1980). *Handbook of Biological Psychiatry*, Part II: *Brain Mechanisms and Abnormal Behavior – Psychophysiology*. New York: Marcel-Dekker.

Vanderwolf, C. H., and Robinson, T. E. (1981). Reticulo-cortical activity and behavior: a critique of arousal theory and a new synthesis. *Behavioral and Brain Sciences* **3**, 459–476.

Vasey, M. W., and Thayer, J. F. (1987). The continuing problem of false positives in repeated measures ANOVA in psychophysiology: a multivariate solution. *Psychophysiology* **24**, 479–486.

Venables, P. H. (1973). Input regulation and psychopathology. In: M. Hammer, K. Salzinger and S. Sutton (Eds) *Psychopathology*. New York: Wiley.

Venables, P. H. (1978). Psychophysiology and psychometrics. *Psychophysiology* **15**, 302–315.

Venables, P. H. (1984). Arousal: an examination of its status as a concept. In: M. G. H. Coles, J. R. Jennings and J. A. Stern (Eds) *Psychophysiological Perspectives: Festschrift for Beatrice and John Lacey*. New York: Van Nostrand Reinhold.

Venables, P. H., and Bernstein, A. S. (1983). The orienting response and psychopathology: schizophrenia. In: D. Siddle (Ed.) *Orienting and Habituation: Perspectives in Human Research*. Chichester: Wiley.

Venables, P. H., and Wing, J. K. (1962). Level of arousal and the subclassification of schizophrenia. *Archives of General Psychiatry* **7**, 114–119.

Walrath, L. C., and Stern, J. A. (1981). General considerations. In: H. M. Van Praag, M. H. Lader, O. J. Rafaelsen and E. J. Sachar (Eds) *Handbook of Biological Psychiatry*, Part II: Brain Mechanisms and Abnormal Behaviour – Psychophysiology. New York: Marcel-Dekker.

Ward, N. G., and Doerr, H. O. (1986). Skin conductance: a potentially sensitive and specific marker for depression. *Journal of Nervous and Mental Disease* **174**, 553–559.

Waters, W. F., Williamson, D. A., Bernard, B. A., Blouin, D. C., and Faulstich, M. E. (1987). Test–retest reliability of psychophysiological assessment. *Behaviour Research and Therapy* **25**, 213–223.

Watt, N. F., Anthony, E. J., Wynne, L. C., and Rolf, J. E. (1984). *Children at Risk for Schizophrenia: A Longitudinal Perspective*. Cambridge: Cambridge University Press.

Weiner, H. (1977). *Psychobiology and Human Disease*. New York: Elsevier.

Wenger, M. A. (1941). The measurement of individual differences in autonomic balance. *Psychosomatic Medicine* **3**, 427–434.

Whitsett, S. F., Robinson, J. W., and Kaplan, B. J. (1987). A comparison of three approaches for the determination of baseline levels of physiological activity. *International Journal of Psychophysiology* **5**, 53–61.

Williamson, D. A., Waters, W. F., and Hawkins, M. F. (1986). Physiologic variables. In: R. O. Nelson and S. C. Hayes (Eds) *Conceptual Foundations of Behavioral Assessment*. New York: Guilford.

Wing, J. K., Cooper, J. E., and Sartorious, N. (1974). *The Measurement and Classification of Psychiatric Symptoms*. Cambridge: Cambridge University Press.

Wittkower, E. D. (1977). Historical perspective of contemporary psychosomatic medicine. In: S. J. Lipowski, D. R. Lipsitt and P. C. Whybrow (Eds) *Psychosomatic Medicine: Current Trends and Clinical Applications*. New York: Oxford University Press.

Wolff, W. T., and Merrens, M. R. (1974). Behavioral assessment: a review of clinical methods. *Journal of Personality Assessment* **38**, 3–16.

Zahn, T. P. (1986). Psychophysiological approaches to psychopathology. In: M. G. H. Coles, E. Donchin and S. W. Porges (Eds) *Psychophysiology: Systems, Processes and Applications*. New York: Guilford.

Zahn, T. P., Carpenter, W. T., and McGlashan, T. H. (1981). Autonomic nervous system activity in acute schizophrenia: II. Relationships to short term prognosis and clinical state. *Archives of General Psychiatry* **38**, 260–266.

Zajonc, R. B. (1980). Feeling and thinking: preferences need no inferences. *American Psychologist* **35**, 151–175.

Zajonc, R. B. (1984). On the primacy of affect. *American Psychologist* **39**, 117–123.

Zubin, J., and Spring, B. (1977). Vulnerability: a new view of schizophrenia. *Journal of Abnormal Psychology* **86**, 103–126.

Chapter 2

Research Strategies Employing Psychophysiological Measures: Identifying and Using Psychophysiological Markers

William G. Iacono and John W. Ficken

University of Minnesota,
Department of Psychology,
N438 Elliott Hall,
75 E. River Road,
Minnesota, MN 55455, USA

ABSTRACT

A research strategy to identify and validate psychophysiological measures as potential markers of clinical disorders is outlined. The focus is on markers that have the potential to identify the genotype that predisposes an individual to a given disorder. The utility of this strategy for addressing different research questions is also discussed.

Handbook of Clinical Psychophysiology Edited by G. Turpin
© 1989 John Wiley & Sons Ltd

INTRODUCTION

The traditional approach to studying clinical populations with psychophysiological techniques has been to compare the affected group to normal individuals or other types of patients. These cross-sectional studies typically have one of two goals. One of these involves an effort to identify psychophysiological correlates of the disorder, in which case a search is launched to identify the parameters of the psychophysiological measures that differentiate the groups. Factors that are unique to the pathological group are presumed to provide clues to the underlying pathophysiology of the disorder. The second major goal involves the use of psychophysiological indices to provide insight into underlying psychological processes. For example, if children with conduct disorders commit more than the normal number of errors on a vigilance task and also appear underaroused on various indices of sympathetic nervous system activation, their poor performance might be explained by their less than optimal level of arousal during the task.

Although the pursuit of both of these objectives has yielded an informative array of data about the psychophysiological and psychology of behaviour disorders (Zahn, 1986), this traditional approach to research is not without its limitations. The use of psychophysiological techniques to understand psychological processes may be complicated by the fact that the psychophysiological mechanisms are themselves dysfunctional. For example, choosing an electrodermal measure to examine habituation of the orienting response in depression will be of little value if, as may be the case (Iacono, Lykken, Haroian, Peloquin, Valentine and Tuason, 1984), the physiology of the electrodermal system is disturbed in depressed people. The use of a psychophysiological measure that is made abnormal by the patient's condition will present a misleading picture of the psychological processes the measure is presumed to tap.

Likewise, attempts to identify psychophysiological correlates of a disorder also have associated difficulties. Often the clinical and comparison groups do not differ only by the fact that one group is lacking the affliction of the other. A host of factors, including drugs, diet, institutionalization, activity level, and the cumulative effects of prior treatments, are likely to differ across groups. The effects of such variables on the psychophysiological measures may account for much of the between-group variance as well as failures to replicate across settings. Inconsistent research findings may also stem from the aetiological heterogeneity that is increasingly believed to be present in many disorders. Failures to replicate psychophysiological findings could be due to the selection of samples that differ in the psychophysiology of their subjects because they also differ with respect to the relative proportions in which their subjects are drawn from different aetiological categories. Because of these problems of confounding variables and possible aetiological heterogeneity, our understanding of the psychophysiology of behaviour disorders has been both frustrated and slow to progress.

Another shortcoming of the traditional approach is that many interesting questions cannot be answered. Primary among them is whether a psychophysiological finding reflects a cause or effect of a disorder. In addition, many medical and most psychopathological conditions are conceptualized in terms of a diathesis–stress model (e.g. Gottesman and Shields, 1982). According to this formulation, every individual falls along a hypothetical dimension of liability. A person's initial position on this continuum is determined by the genetic diathesis, the constitutional predisposition to develop a given disorder. Environmental agents and experience interact with the genetic diathesis to regulate the degree of liability at any point in time. When the combined sources of genetic and environmental liability exceed a threshold value, the disorder is manifest. From this perspective, what is needed is a research strategy for the identification of the diathesis and the degree of liability present at a given time. Knowledge of these factors would make it possible to separate susceptible from non-susceptible individuals, provide clues to the nature of the genetic transmission, and facilitate the determination of the psychosocial and biological agents that interact with the diathesis to potentiate the development of the disorder (see also Chapter 1).

The limitations of the traditional approach to the study of behaviour disorders has led to the development of alternative strategies which have as their goal the identification and validation of various types of 'markers' for a disorder. The term *marker* has increasingly found its way into clinical vocabulary during the last decade, often modified by adjectives such as 'biological', 'vulnerability', or 'genetic', but no consensus has been reached on the meaning of these terms which are sometimes used interchangeably. In this chapter, we will define various types of markers and outline the research strategies used to uncover and validate them. When specific marker candidates are discussed, we will focus on psychophysiological measures. In our view, any psychophysiological variable that has utility as a marker is a psychophysiological (and, more generally, biological) marker, but within this large domain of markers, several distinct subtypes can be delineated.

TYPES OF MARKERS

A psychophysiological marker is a deviation in a psychophysiological variable that is reliably associated with a particular disorder. It may reflect a variation in structure, function, or performance that is present before, during, and/or after an episode of illness. The majority of marker traits that have been proposed are continuously distributed characteristics and only persons manifesting an extreme value of the characteristic are said to express the marker. However, variables that are truly dichotomous, that is either present or absent, may also function as markers.

Three types of markers may be distinguished: episode, vulnerability, and genetic. The defining property of *episode markers* is that they are manifest only during an episode of a disorder and therefore cannot be used to identify at-risk individuals. Episode markers are useful for delimiting the onset and termination of an episode (Zubin and Steinhauer, 1981), and may potentially suggest when treatment is required and when it may be withdrawn. Such a marker may also have utility for identifying subgroups of patients with a certain aetiology, prognosis, or treatment response.

An example of a putative episode marker is shortened rapid eye movement (REM) sleep latency. The first period of REM sleep usually appears 70–80 min after falling asleep. Persons with endogenous depression enter REM much earlier during their sleep cycle (Kupfer, 1982). Following clinical remission, however, REM latencies return to normal levels (Avery, Wildschiodtz and Rafaelsen, 1982; Hauri, Chernik, Hawkins and Mendels, 1974). Individuals with other disorders, such as narcolepsy (Zarcone, 1973) and schizophrenia (Zarcone, Benson and Bergen, 1987), also have abnormal REM latencies when acutely ill. In contrast to episode markers, *vulnerability markers* are stable traits present before, during, and after an acute episode. These characteristics identify individuals who are more likely than others in the general population to develop a disorder. Vulnerability markers may not be under genetic control and, like episode markers, need not be associated with disorders for which there is a genetic diathesis. Victims of mild anoxia at birth, who are therefore prone to develop pathology as adults, may possess a characteristic electroencephalographic (EEG) irregularity throughout their life that could serve as a vulnerability marker. If a vulnerability marker is genetically determined, it differs from a genetic marker in that it is expressed in family members whether or not they are genetically predisposed to develop the disorder. This could occur if a trait that has no pathophysiological significance is expressed in a family or group that is prone to the disorder. An example is black skin colour; it isolates a group at high risk for sickle-cell anaemia, but the genes that code for the sickling trait and skin colour are physiologically unrelated. Black skin colour selects persons at risk for sickle-cell anaemia in the general population, but does not indicate which family members carry the genes for illness.

Genetic markers are heritable traits that indicate the presence of a pathogene or set of genes. Genetic markers are similar to vulnerability markers in that both may indicate persons likely to develop illness in the general population and both are present before, during, and after illness onset. The distinguishing feature of genetic markers is that they indicate the presence of a genotype (hence, the choice of the term *genetic marker*).

It should be recognized that genetic marker traits may be expressed fully, partially, or not at all (this is also true of genetically based illnesses). An assumption we are making about the genetic markers described here is that they are highly penetrant (i.e. fully expressed in a large proportion of individuals carrying the pathogene or genes) and are manifest well before illness onset. A marker that appeared at the same time as the disease would be little more than an objective sign of illness onset. Another consideration is that genetically based characteristics, especially psychophysiological ones, are not necessarily immutable traits. Their expression can be altered by numerous medications, diets, smoking habits, and so on. The clinical state of the individual may also exert a powerful effect on the appearance of a genetic marker. This could be useful if the expression of a genetic marker is discernably different during an episode of illness because the genetic marker would also have utility as an episode marker.

There are several possible bases for the association between a psychophysiological genetic marker and the underlying pathological genotype. The marker may represent a direct manifestation of the genetic diathesis in that the gene or genes predisposing the individual to a disorder also control or influence the presence of the marker. It may be an antecedent factor that is aetiologically related to the development of the disorder or, as is more likely with psychophysiological variables, it may reflect a by-product of the pathogenic gene that is not part of the causal chain. In either case, the genetic marker indicates an underlying genetic predisposition to the disorder. Gottesman and Shields (1972) have applied the term *endophenotype* (implying the existence of an internal characteristic that is observable only with aid to the naked eye) to this type of genetic indicator.

Another way in which a trait could associate with a pathogene is via chromosomal linkage. In this case the gene that codes for the marker is actually located on the same chromosome in close proximity to the putative pathogene. This type of marker is linked to the pathogene because the genes controlling these two characteristics are unlikely to be separated during the exchange of chromosomal material that takes place during meiosis. As a result, both the marker and the gene are passed together from one generation to the next and the marker identifies the specific chromosome and where on that chromosome the illness gene lies. A large number of classical marker genes have been located on the 22 autosomal chromosomes (McKusick and Ruddle, 1977) and the X chromosome (Drayna and White, 1985); many of these represent biochemical factors detectable in human blood. When one of these factors is consistently coupled to the appearance of a disorder within a family from one generation to another, it identifies individuals who possess the illness genotype. An example of this type of marker was provided by Baron *et al.* (1987). These investigators found that colour blindness and the lack of glucose-6-phosphate dehydrogenase (an enzyme, the absence of which causes a form of haemolytic anaemia) tended to be inherited together with manic-depressive disorder in some families. Because these genetic markers are located on the distal arm of the X chromosome, it is possible to conclude that a gene predisposing to bipolar affective illness exists in this same region of the X chromosome. Recent advances in molecular genetic techniques have greatly increased the utility of linkage studies because it is now possible to identify and use as a marker a fragment of genomic DNA that has unknown function but that can be traced to a particular location on a chromosome (Housman and Gusella, 1981). This type of linkage marker has sometimes been referred to as a 'DNA marker' to distinguish it from the classical linkage markers. Using DNA markers, the gene for Huntington's disease has been located (Gusella *et al.*, 1983), as has a gene for a variant of Alzheimer's disease (St George-Hyslop *et al.*, 1987) and manic depression (Egeland *et al.*, 1987).

Historically, the use of the term *genetic marker* has been restricted to linkage markers. Our definition of genetic marker, which is consistent with the way many use the term in psychiatric genetics, subsumes classical and DNA linkage markers and expands the category of genetic markers to include characteristics that are manifestations of the deviant gene itself. However, for a variety of reasons, linkage markers are likely to be of limited utility to psychophysiologists. This is primarily because there are no psychophysiological characteristics with well-defined genetic properties, and certainly none with an identified chromosomal locus. There are other limitations in the use of this type of marker. The use of linkage markers requires assumptions about the mode of inheritance of the pathogene, and this type of marker cannot identify persons at risk outside of a given family where both the linkage marker and the disorder are present. Another factor limiting the application of linkage markers is that the size of the gene pool is vast, so the likelihood of easily locating a marker that happens to be proximal to a gene for a disorder is small. In the absence of leads suggesting where and on which chromosome to look, the use of the linkage approach requires both patience and luck. For these reasons, we will not deal with linkage markers further in this chapter.

A variety of psychophysiological measures have been advanced as putative vulnerability or genetic markers of different forms of psychopathology. Table 2.1 provides an overview of these measures. The particular psychophysiological deviations listed in the table have all been found to exist in the unaffected first-degree relatives of those with the disorder and/or in the patients themselves during symptom remission.

IDENTIFICATION AND VALIDATION

The types of variables that are examined as potential markers depend on whether a theoretical or an empirical approach is adopted. In the former case, the field of variables to be considered is constrained by the theoretical conception of the disorder. On the other hand, the empirical strategy is largely

Table 2.1
Some psychophysiological deviations that have potential as vulnerability or genetic markers.

Putative marker	Disorder	Reference
Reduced P300 amplitude in the ERP	alcoholism	Begleiter *et al.* (1984)
An excess of fast EEG activity	alcoholism	Gabrielli *et al.* (1982)
Abnormal visual evoked potential amplitudes	major affective disorder	Buchsbaum *et al.* (1982), Gershon and Buchsbaum (1977)
Electrodermal non-responding	major affective disorder	Iacono *et al.* (1984)
Abnormal smooth-pursuit eye tracking	schizophrenia	Holzman *et al.* (1974), Iacono (1987)
Electrodermal non-responding	schizophrenia	Iacono (1982), Venables *et al.* (1978)
Rapid electrodermal response recovery	schizophrenia	Mednick and Schulsinger (1968)
Decreased EEG alpha/increased EEG delta	schizophrenia	Iacono (1982), Itil (1977)
Failure to inhibit P50 amplitude in the ERP	schizophrenia	Siegal *et al.* (1984)
Attenuated P300 amplitude in the ERP	schizophrenia	Saitoh *et al.* (1984)

ERP = event-related potential, EEG = electroencephalogram.

exploratory, and virtually any variable might be considered. An empirical strategy would be appropriate for disorders in which the nature of the disorder is poorly understood, in cases where the theoretical approach has failed, or simply as a means of expanding the repertoire of markers. To the extent that a marker illuminates facets of the pathogenesis, empirical derivation may also suggest previously unforeseen pathogenic pathways.

The identification and validation of all types of markers involves a sequence of studies that typically begins with comparisons of ill and healthy subjects. Variables that distinguish these groups may have potential to serve as episode markers. However, as noted previously, the afflicted and comparison groups may differ on several characteristics in addition to the presence of the disorder. If these characteristics alter the expression of a variable, it might fortuitously be considered a marker of the disorder when it is actually an artifact. Consideration of possible confounding factors is particularly important in the identification of psychophysiological markers because their expression can be altered by many nuisance variables. Table 2.2 lists some of the variables that must be

Table 2.2
Some factors that may influence psychophysiological recordings.

Measure	Possible confound	Reference
EDA	Race does not affect SCR, blacks show lower SCL than whites	Johnson and Corah (1963)
	EDA decreases with age (may be true of males, not females)	Morimoto (1978)
	Males higher EDA than females	Morimoto (1978)
	Neuroleptics reduce SCL	Ohman (1981), Zahn (1986)
	Smoking decreases SCRs	Woodson et al. (1986)
HR	Tricyclic antidepressants raise HR	Iacono et al. (1983), Glassman and Bigger (1981)
	Neuroleptics elevate HR	Spohn et al. (1977)
	Smoking increases HR	Hastrup and Light (1984), Woodson et al. (1986)
	Higher HR responsiveness during luteal phase of menstrual cycle	Little and Zahn (1974)
	HR responsiveness declines with age	Gintner et al. (1986)
BP	Imipramine raises systolic and diastolic BP in children	Greenberg and Yellin (1975)
	Caffeine increases systolic and diastolic BP	Lane and Williams (1985)
	Higher systolic BP in males than females	Hastrup and Light (1984)
EEG	Smoking deprivation slows EEG	Knott and Venables (1977), Ulett and Itil (1969)
CNV	Amphetamines may increase or reduce CNV amplitude	Teece and Cole (1974)
	Chlorpromazine reduces CNV amplitudes	Teece et al. (1975)
ERP	P50 wave inhibition less developed in young people	Freedman et al. (1987)
	Decreased VEP during smoking deprivation	Hall et al. (1973)
	Chlorpromazine increases latencies of all SEP components and reduces amplitudes of late components	Saletu et al. (1972)

Measure	Possible confound	Reference
EOG measures of smooth-pursuit eye movements	Lithium reduces tracking ability	Iacono *et al.* (1982), Levy *et al.* (1985)
	Poorer tracking ability with age	Sharpe and Sylvester (1978)
Blinking	Neuroleptics reduce spontaneous blink rate in schizophrenics	Stevens (1978), Karson (1983)
	Blink rate increases with age	Karson *et al.* (1986)

SCR = skin conductance response, SCL = skin conductance level,
EDA = electrodermal activity, HR = heart rate, BP = blood pressure,
EEG = electroencephalogram, CNV = contingent negative variation,
VEP = visual evoked potential, SEP = somatosensory evoked potential,
EOG = electro-oculogram.

considered when comparing ill and healthy groups. This list is by no means comprehensive, but is intended to convey the range of characteristics that could confound psychophysiological studies. The specific effect of any of these characteristics will depend on several factors and may vary from study to study (see Andreassi, 1980). If drugs colour the expression of the variable, which is a strong possibility with psychophysiological measures, unmedicated patients should be employed, allowing due time for withdrawal symptoms to abate. Age and sex effects can be reduced by equating the groups as closely as possible on these attributes. Sex effects can also be eliminated by including only males or only females in the study.

The ocular artifacts that arise when recording brain potentials merit special comment. Although eye movements and blinking (Stern, Walrath and Goldstein, 1984) may serve as important dependent measures in psychophysiological experiments, the electro-oculographic (EOG) signals they generate have long been recognized to contaminate EEG recording. The most common method for removing EOG artifacts is to delete trials or epochs that contain ocular potentials. However, deviant groups such as psychotic patients may blink and move their eyes more often than normal (e.g. Karson, Goldberg and Leleszi, 1986). Deleting contaminated segments, either with or without replacing them by lengthening the experimental session and including more trials, may lead to data from patient groups that is unrepresentative. Hence, other methods for dealing with ocular artifacts that involve subtracting a proportion of the EOG from resting or evoked brain potentials must be considered (Gasser, Sroka and Mocks, 1986; Gratton, Coles and Donchin, 1983; O'Toole and Iacono, 1987; Semlitsch, Anderer, Schuster and Presslich, 1986).

After controlling for artifacts, many of the characteristics that differentiate patients and controls will be state-dependent and thus may serve only as episode markers. To separate episode from potential vulnerability and genetic markers, the traits that remain following symptom remission must be identified. When studying remitted patients, it is advisable to wait some time after the illness ends to ensure that all systems have recuperated fully.

Having demonstrated the presence of a deviation when patients are well, several other steps must be taken to confirm that the deviation qualifies as a vulnerability or genetic marker. Evaluation of several of these requirements can be accomplished by employing normal subjects as they are more accessible than patients. This strategy rests on the assumption that the marker trait is continuously distributed, so it is expressed to some degree in everyone. If not, studies of normal volunteers must be carried out on those selected for the presence of the marker. An additional assumption is that the same factors influence the marker trait in normals and patients. If this is not true, it may be inappropriate to generalize the findings from normals to patients. For example, a psychophysiological variable could be under strong environmental control in the general population. The genes regulating a particular illness may produce extreme values of the trait, so that it would be highly heritable in patients. Thus, although the marker trait would appear not to be heritable in normals, it would still qualify as a genetic marker of the disorder. This possibility dictates that the marker characteristics observed in healthy subjects be verified in patient groups whenever possible.

In the search for a genetic marker, studies of normal subjects should demonstrate that the putative marker (a) is expressed infrequently in the population at large, (b) is stable, (c) is heritable, and (d) identifies persons at risk to illness. Studies with patients should show that the putative marker (a) is specific, (b) is sensitive, (c) is present in remission, (d) is more common in patients with a family history of disorders than in those without such a history, (e) is prevalent in families of affected individuals, and (f) identifies family members who are at risk for illness. The search for vulnerability markers will require many of these same criteria to be met. However, a vulnerability marker that is not under genetic control will not be heritable, and vulnerability markers in general will not be able to separate family members at risk for a disorder from those who are not at risk.

Whether the strategy used to identify and evaluate a marker involves work with normal or patient subjects, it is essential that genetically related individuals be studied. Although psychophysiological experiments seldom include related subjects, any psychophysiological investigation with a focus on individual differences is made more interesting through the inclusion of such subjects. Boomsa and Gabrielli (1985) have illustrated univariate and multivariate classical and biometrical genetic techniques for the analysis of psychophysiological data. They stressed that when using these methods to estimate genetic contributions, investigators do not forfeit their ability to test their non-genetic hypotheses on the unrelated subjects included in the study.

Because the criteria listed above have been discussed in detail elsewhere

(Iacono, 1983, 1985), we will briefly summarize a few of the more salient methodoligical and conceptual issues entailed in their assessment. In doing so, the focus of discussion will be on genetic markers.

RESEARCH WITH NORMAL SUBJECTS

The putative marker should be present in only a small proportion of the general population. Several factors determine how large this fraction could be before the trait would lose its utility as a marker. Because not everyone who possesses the genetic diathesis will manifest the disorder, the marker will appear in some healthy persons. If the genetic diathesis is relatively weak, far more individuals can be expected to have the marker than actually succumb to the disorder. Even a marker with a relatively high prevalence may be used with some other indicator (e.g. sex, age, another marker) to define adequately a high-risk group. The base rate of a marker can be evaluated differently depending on whether it is used to estimate risk in the population at large or within a family (Shields, Heston and Gottesman, 1975). A commonly occurring trait may still be used to advantage in a family where the marker trait is associated with the occurrence of a disorder. Although occasional false-positive cases will arise, the marker would identify susceptible persons at above chance levels.

The stability of a marker trait is typically equated with the correlation between measures taken on two or more occasions, and is related inversely to the amount of time elapsing between occasions. The within-pair correlations of monozygotic twins on marker variables represent another index of stability (Lykken, 1975). These individuals possess identical genetic constitutions and are exposed to similar environments, and so should appear quite alike on stable characteristics.

Because genetic markers arise from the actions of genes, it is necessary to ascertain that the putative marker is heritable. Family studies are usually the first step in estimating heritability. The first-degree relatives of someone who possesses the marker should express the marker more frequently than do members of the general population. Another popular method of estimating heritability is to examine the degree of similarity in pairs of twins. Measures are assumed to have a heritable component if the concordance rate for monozygotic twins, who share all their genes, exceeds that of dizygotic twins, who share on average only half of their genes.

Perhaps the ultimate step in the validation of a genetic marker requires the longitudinal follow-up of unaffected individuals who possess the marker. The proportion of such a group who succumb to the disorder should be substantially larger than that of a comparison group of subjects who are without the marker. In addition to their increased level of susceptibility, unaffected members of such a high-risk group can be expected to display subsyndromal signs and symptoms and have a positive family history of the disorder (e.g. see Buchsbaum, Coursey and Murphy, 1976). Finally, normal individuals with the marker may generate values on other measures (e.g. personality tests) that overlap with those of affected persons.

RESEARCH WITH PATIENTS

A genetic marker will be most useful if it has relatively high specificity (i.e. it is found infrequently in persons with other disorders). One factor affecting specificity is diagnostic accuracy, which depends on the reliability with which clinical decisions are made and ultimately on the validity of the diagnostic system. Many diagnostic schemes, such as those proposed for mental disorders (e.g. see the *Diagnostic and Statistical Manual*, 3rd edn, American Psychiatric Association, 1980, or *International Classification of Diseases – 9 (ICD-9)*, contain vague and/or arbitrary criteria which could result in patients with the same diathesis, and therefore with the same marker, being placed in different categories. Specificity will also be reduced if two or more disorders share a genetic basis, or if multiple pathways lead to the expression of the marker.

Low specificity may be overcome by combining the marker with other indicators of illness. Enhanced specificity should result because it is improbable that two disorders would both deviate on several of the same variables. As evidenced in several recent studies (e.g. Akiskal, Walker, Puzantin, King, Rosenthal and Dranon, 1983; Feinberg and Carroll, 1984; Hanson, Gottesman and Heston, 1976), this strategy can substantially boost specificity. For example, Feinberg and Carroll (1984) examined the utility of an EEG measure of REM sleep abnormality and the dexamethasone suppression test for classifying endogenous depression. The specificity of either procedure alone was about 0.85. However, when both tests were required to be abnormal, the diagnostic specificity was raised to 0.99.

Genetic markers are also expected to be sensitive (i.e. a large proportion of those with the disorder should express the marker). Diagnostic imprecision may also lower estimates of sensitivity, but the principal challenge to sensitivity is probably aetiological heterogeneity: only a subset of the affected population may be expected to share a diathesis and therefore possess the marker. In this case, validation of a marker against current classifications may not permit a true assessment of the marker's efficacy. A more meaningful test may entail a reversal of the typical research design, basing marker sensitivity on the proportion of persons with the marker who are ill, instead of the converse (Buchsbaum and Haier, 1983).

A genetic marker must be present during remission, when patients are neither acutely nor chronically symptomatic. The presence of this feature clearly establishes the trait as more than an episode marker. Another interesting strategy to document this point is to examine identical twins discordant for the disorder. If the marker indicates presence of the genetic predisposition, it should be present in both the proband and the healthy co-twin. Expression of the marker only in the ill twin suggests that the marker is not solely a result of the pathogenes and may arise as a consequence of the illness.

Because genetic markers are associated with the underlying genetic diathesis, patients with a positive family history of disorder may be more apt to possess the marker than patients whose families lack such a history. The emergence of such a data pattern requires the assumption that the aetiology of the disorder is in some way different in the two types of family.

The final test of a potential genetic marker requires examining the families of probands who express the marker. The prevalence of the marker in the first-degree relatives of the proband should exceed the rate of expression in the general population. This is because many of these relatives, whether ill or not, presumably carry the pathogenes. In the case of identical twins discordant for a disorder, all of the unaffected twins should have the marker when it is present in their co-twin. Finally, to distinguish it from a vulnerability marker, a genetic marker must be shown to segregate with the illness in families (although see the discussion of the paper by Matthysse, Holzman and Lange (1986) later in this chapter). This means that, compared to family members who lack the marker, relatives who express the marker (a) are more likely to manifest subclinical and clinical symptoms of the illness, (b) are at higher risk for becoming ill, and (c) are expected to have an increased number of affected offspring. In addition, all family members with obvious manifestations of the illness should display the marker (Rieder and Gershon, 1978). Because of this latter requirement, multiplex families (i.e. those with more than one affected member) are especially well suited to the evaluation of a putative genetic marker.

DEFINING THE MARKER CRITERION

Ideally, the distribution of the marker trait would be bimodal: all persons carrying the pathogenes would display values of the trait different from all non-predisposed persons. Typically, however, the marker values displayed by predisposed and non-predisposed subjects will overlap. The question, then, is what criterion should be used for delimiting the presence of the marker?

The cut-off value one selects will depend on the base rate of the pathogenes in the general population and on the way in which the marker trait is distributed (e.g. whether positively skewed, quasi-bimodal, or normal). Another factor influencing the choice of cut-off values is the context in which the marker is to be applied. More extreme cut-offs generally increase specificity at the price of reduced sensitivity. Such thresholds are often necessary for research purposes where homogeneous samples are essential. In clinical contexts, however, the goal may be to identify all potentially treatable cases, even if some non-cases are treated, and a less extreme cut-off may be preferable. Finally, to achieve some objectives, such as testing genetic models, it is desirable to select a group composed of as many 'hits' (i.e. true positives and true negatives) as possible. Meehl (Meehl, 1972; Meehl and Golden, 1982) has outlined an algorithm for choosing a marker cut-off to meet this need. This technique requires identification of three or more putative genetic markers. Comparisons of the intercorrelations among these markers are used to derive the cut-off value on each marker that selects a maximum number of true positives and true negatives.

STANDARDIZATION

It should be clear that the extent to which a psychophysiological marker can be identified and validated as such will depend on numerous factors, including the threshold used to define the presence of both the disorder and the marker, the procedures and tasks employed for measuring the marker trait, and the parameters of the marker variable that are investigated. Procedural and measurement issues are especially critical to psychophysiological measures, which are readily influenced by subtle variations along these dimensions. In order to maximize the likelihood of replication within and across laboratories, it is desirable to develop a standard protocol for measuring the marker. This process can be effected empirically by subjecting a host of procedures and marker parameters to the above criteria. The use of normal populations to develop a protocol that minimizes error variance may be particularly worthwhile. The best procedures should be those with the highest retest reliability. Twin studies may also serve as a valuable aid at this stage; techniques that maximize the within-pair correlations in monozygotic twins are probably the best (Lykken, 1975).

PSYCHOPHYSIOLOGICAL VARIABLES AS MARKERS

Why search for markers using psychophysiological measures? Since virtually any biological or psychological variable might be considered as a marker, the first impulse might be to focus on biochemical abnormalities because they are the most basic components of an illness and are closest to the actions of genes. However, attempts at tapping the inextricable complexities of the human body with single biochemical parameters may be misleading. Notwithstanding the methodological difficulties associated with biochemical investigation and the lack of interesting leads, choosing the correct biochemical measure may be no simpler a task than finding the proverbial needle in the haystack. Our knowledge of human physiology and anatomy is quite limited and our understanding of how neurotransmitters, hormones, organs, and cell groups interact is very incomplete. Investigations based on a single biochemical cannot begin to tap these intricacies. Psychophysiological measures, on the other hand, are more likely to assess general aspects of bodily functioning and depend on the overall integrity of various anatomical units and physiological systems. If any one function is impaired, the dysfunction may be detected using psychophysiological techniques. However, because of their coarse nature, it will be difficult to use such global measures to identify the precise nature of any underlying deficiency.

Interest in these variables is also generated by their capacity to serve as indices of cognitive processing, attention, and arousal, all psychological processes that are hypothesized to be disturbed in many behavioural and physical disorders. Additional recommendations for their application include their unobtrusiveness, ease of measurement, and inherent interest to research subjects.

APPLICATIONS OF MARKERS

Several of the methodological refinements derivable from the applications of markers are discussed in this section.

REFINING DIAGNOSES

Contemporary diagnosis is based heavily on clinical presentation despite growing recognition that specific biological dysfunctions, many partly under genetic control, underlie a wide variety of disorders (Akiskal, 1983; Feighner, Robins, Guze, Woodruff, Winokur and Munoz, 1972). A consequence of reliance on symptom-based classification is that subgroups that are distinct on dimensions of aetiology and pathophysiology may be grouped together. The current practice of aggregating across diverse groups can dilute potentially meaningful results and breeds inconsistency between studies. Clinically, the price of pathogenic heterogeneity is imprecision in effecting prophylaxis, prognosis, and treatment.

Episode markers may be useful for delimiting subgroups sharing some aspect of pathophysiology. Genetic markers are more likely to define aetiologically homogeneous populations, and, because they permit the identification of high-risk subjects, may also allow clinical intervention earlier than is currently possible.

Another possibility worth considering is that the groupings suggested by markers may be at odds with those derived from symptom presentation. Since biological abnormalities may underlie many diseases, it may prove more profitable to suspend existing groupings, and to compare the biological correlates, family history, course, and treatment responses between groups derived on the basis of markers (Buchsbaum and Haier, 1983).

DELIMITING HIGH-RISK GROUPS

At present, our attempts to understand the development of pathology concentrate heavily on the clinical phase of illness while the pre-clinical stages of illness are relatively neglected. Yet, the nature of the illness may be such that the majority of interesting physiological deviations develop during the pre-clinical stages, and illness onset may be little more than a quantitative exacerbation of these deviations. If this is true, the clinical phase design will overlook a major portion of the pathogenesis. A second weakness of the clinical phase approach is that the events that precipitate illness must be established via retrospective reports that are readily subject to biases and distortions. For example, when the initiating agents act over a prolonged period, only those closest to onset appear salient, while earlier but equally important agents may go unnoticed. A related concern is the difficulty inherent in disentangling early manifestations of illness from precipitating events. For example, if depression is commonly observed in alcoholics, one cannot discern whether the depression incited excessive drinking, or the psychological and physiological trauma of extensive alcohol-abuse induced depression. Cross-sectional studies reconcile these weaknesses to a degree, but they cannot capture the dynamic interplay of the pathogenic variables (Gottesman and Shields, 1982).

An alternative to the clinical phase research design is the longitudinal prospective approach. This strategy using high-risk subjects permits the study of the disease as it unfolds, and so circumvents the aforementioned pitfalls of the conventional approach. An additional advantage of studying high-risk subjects is that various measures can be taken untainted by such episode-related artifacts as medication, hospitalization, diet, and inactivity. Finally, the study of persons at high risk who do not succumb to illness may uncover factors that indicate a reduced vulnerability or resistance to disorder.

The challenge, then, is to develop a method of detecting persons who are likely to succumb to illness. The earliest attempts at identifying a predisposed population examined the children of schizophrenic mothers (Mednick and Schulsinger, 1968), taking advantage of the modest increment in risk in first-degree relatives of psychotic individuals. Though this tack continues to be applied (e.g. Schulsinger, Knop, Goodwin, Teasdale and Mikkelsen, 1986), it is inefficient for studying the course of most disorders because only a small proportion of offspring ever develop the disease. Furthermore, because a large proportion of patients do not have an affected parent, the representativeness of this pool to the population at risk is dubious (Depue, Slater, Wolfstetter-Kausch, Klein, Goperlund and Farr, 1981).

Genetic markers may be useful adjuncts to the affected parent approach. By identifying those offspring who possess the genetic diathesis, the size of the risk group is greatly reduced since only those showing the marker need to be followed. Alternatively, a large-scale programme screening for the marker could be instituted to select a representative sample of predisposed subjects from the general population. Such a study was begun on the island of Mauritius in 1972 by Venables and his colleagues (Venables, 1978; Venables *et al.*, 1978). Eighteen hundred 3-year-old children underwent a psychophysiological examination in which various electrodermal measures served as the major dependent variables. Based on the results of prior research, different patterns of electrodermal activity were used to define subjects at high risk for schizophrenia and criminal psychopathic behaviour.

Few investigations have examined psychophysiological markers in preadolescent children; those that have have focused on the amplitude of the P300 wave in the event-related potential and have obtained results that can at best be described as inconclusive (Friedman, Cornblatt, Vaughan and Erlenmeyer-Kimling, 1986; Friedman, Erlenmeyer-Kimling and Vaughan, 1985; Friedman, Vaughan and Erlenmeyer-Kimling, 1982; Herman, Mirsky, Ricks and Gallant, 1977). At present, it is not known in what ways the psychophysiological reactivity and functioning of children can be expected to be like that of adults. Hence, great caution must be exercised when generalizing findings obtained in adults to a younger population. For some putative psychophysiological markers, it may be premature to define young children as at high risk because they possess the same psychophysiological deviation that has been identified in adults.

That a psychophysiological marker can be used successfully to identify adults at psychiatric risk has been demonstrated by Siever and associates (Siever, Coursey, Alterman, Buchsbaum and Murphy, 1982a, 1984; Siever *et al.*, 1982b). These investigators screened 284 undergraduate students for their ability to perform a smooth-pursuit eye-tracking task. Abnormal pursuit tracking has been associated with psychosis, especially schizophrenia (for a review, see Iacono, 1987). Contrasting the best and worst performers, they found, following a structured clinical interview, that deviant-pursuit trackers were more likely than normal trackers to have a schizotypal personality disorder and schizotypal features. The proportion of individuals with a history of either hypomania or mania was also elevated in the poor eye-tracking group. In another study, Siever *et al.* (1982b) reported that college students displaying tracking impairment were more likely than good-tracking subjects to have significant elevations on Minnesota Multiphasic Personality Inventory clinical scales.

Simons, Losito, Rose and MacMillan (1983) have adopted a similar approach for the identification of an adult high-risk group. They monitored electrodermal activity (EDA) in 250 college students and identified a small group who were non-responsive to non-signal auditory stimuli. Hypothesizing that reduced EDA may be associated with risk for schizophrenia, Simons *et al.* (1983) expected EDA non-responders to score higher than a comparison group of EDA responders on several self-report measures of proneness to schizophrenia. However, they found the questionnaire scores for these two groups to be very similar.

This finding is surprising given that Simons (1981) showed that college students who scored high on one of these measures, the Physical Anhedonia Scale (Chapman, Chapman and Raulin, 1976), were electrodermally hyporesponsive. One possible explanation for this discrepancy is that deficits in EDA may not be specific to risk for schizophrenia. For example, persons who are depressed or in remission from depression also evidence low EDA (e.g. Iacono, Lykken, Peloquin, Lumry, Valentine and Tuason, 1983). This possibility could be addressed in a future study by assessing both psychosis-proneness and depressive characteristics of electrodermal non-responders.

PREDICTING OUTCOME

Psychophysiological markers have potential to provide useful information in addition to identifying acutely ill and illness-prone individuals. Because they may appear in only some of those with a disorder or in varying degrees in affected and susceptible persons, vulnerability and genetic markers, and to a lesser extent episode markers, may have prognostic significance. Susceptible individuals in whom the marker is expressed most strongly may have the highest risk for developing the disorder, succumb at an earlier age, have the most severe episodes, and have the worst long-term prognosis. The strong expression of the marker may signify a strong genetic diathesis and a disorder whose development and maintenance is less affected by environmental events, including those that may have ameliorative qualities.

For example, abnormal smooth-pursuit eye tracking, a putative psychophysiological marker that appears in about 50% of schizophrenic patients, has been found to be an indicator of poor prognosis (Iacono, 1987). Compared to normal trackers, patients with this characteristic at the time of their first lifetime episode of psychosis have more symptoms and lower levels of social and occupational functioning 18 months later. Another example would be high blood pressure as an indicator of risk for heart disease, stroke, and multi-infarct dementia.

IDENTIFYING MODE OF INHERITANCE

If a disorder is found to have a genetic basis, discovering the mode in which the diathesis is inherited guides future research programmes and may also elucidate the nature of the disease (Gottesman and Shields, 1982). Support for the various genetic models is usually tested by examining the prevalence of diagnosable illness in pedigrees and in mono- and dizygotic twins. The principal pitfall of analysing only clinically diagnosable cases is that predisposed persons who are healthy or who show subclinical or variant forms of the illness will be excluded, while persons with non-genetic forms of the illness will be included. Consequently, the results of analyses based on illness prevalence may be at odds with the mode in which the diathesis is actually transmitted.

Genetic markers represent an appealing alternative to the customary approach because they select persons possessing the genetic diathesis independently of clinical presentation. Consequently, individuals who develop a variant of the illness are included in transmission analyses, while persons with non-genetic forms of the disorder are not, and this should provide a more accurate basis for testing the various genetic models. Furthermore, one must be aware that the demonstration of a genetic diathesis does not guarantee that a single genetic mechanism is responsible (Gottesman and Shields, 1982). Aggregating across aetiologically diverse families might fortuitously lend support to a model that is untenable. To the extent that genetic markers identify genetically distinct subgroups, they circumvent this problem and allow the most unequivocal test of the mode of inheritance (Gershon, 1978).

The study of multiple markers may reveal important information about the genetic heterogeneity of a disorder. If a number of putative genetic markers have been associated with a single disorder, it is important to determine the extent to which they are correlated in patients and their families. If the markers are highly interrelated, a single genetic aetiology with multiple manifestations is suggested. If a set of markers appear together in only a subcluster of patients and their relatives, a homogeneous subgroup that shares a common aetiology may exist. If the marker traits appear relatively independently of one another, different genetic mechanisms and causal paths are suggested and what may have been viewed as a single disorder may better be viewed as a heterogeneous class of disorders.

Unfortunately, there have been very few studies in which more than one putative genetic marker has been examined. While this is true about markers in general, it has been particularly true about psychophysiological markers such as those listed in Table 2.1. Hence, little is known about the interrelationship of these various traits.

ILLUMINATING THE NATURE OF PATHOGENESIS

The foregoing sections have discussed some of the methodological refinements afforded by genetic markers. Another potential application of markers involves illuminating the nature of the disease process itself.

Any attempt to evaluate the aetiological significance of a marker must proceed with extreme caution. It is hoped, and often gratuitously assumed, that markers invariably are linked directly to a causal component of pathogenesis. The association between a variable and a disease may arise via several other pathways, however. Episode markers may originate as a consequence of some environmental concomitant of the disorder, such as medical intervention,

dietary changes, or increased exposure to stressful events. The marker could
be a by-product far removed from the pathogenesis; minor biochemical deviations, for instance, may produce reverbations at several levels throughout the
nervous system.

Another possibility mentioned earlier is that the pathogene or genes induce
the disease and deviation in the marker variable via entirely independent
pathways (e.g. genetic pleiotropy). An example of such a possibility arises from
recent studies of smooth-pursuit eye tracking, a putative genetic marker of
schizophrenia. Matthysse *et al.* (1986) noted that examination of the transmission of schizophrenia and deviant-pursuit eye tracking in families leads to
the conclusion that neither characteristic segregates in a clear Mendelian
pattern. However, when the two traits are considered together, their pattern
of transmission is consistent with the notion that they are independent plei-
otropic effects of a single major gene. The gene may be expressed in an
individual as schizophrenia, bad eye tracking, or both schizophrenia and
tracking dysfunction. The model of Matthysse *et al.* (1986), besides suggesting
that schizophrenia is inherited as a Mendelian trait, can also account for the
seemingly anomalous observation that some schizophrenics with normal eye
tracking have relatives with impaired pursuit and also predicts that some
affected relatives of schizophrenics with deviant eye tracking will have normal
pursuit.

With so many potential derivations, interpretation of the pathogenic significance of a marker should be delayed until the specific pathway of origin is
ascertained. These considerations are especially applicable to psychophysiological markers, which are affected by complex and poorly understood interactions
of psychological and physiological forces (Edelberg, 1972). Furthermore, as
psychophysiological theories of psychopathology and other disorders are
lacking, one is forced to draw on hypotheses generated by studies of normal
populations. These interpretations may not generalize to those who are ill if
the processes underlying the marker characteristic are *qualitatively* different in
normal individuals and ill patients. For example, there is some evidence
suggesting that reduced EDA might serve as a genetic marker of the affective
disorders (Iacono *et al.*, 1984). In normals, low EDA might suggest low arousal,
leading to the conjecture that depressed patients produce less EDA because
they are less aroused. If replicated in high-risk subjects, it might be tempting
to develop a model of underarousal as a precursor for depression. An opposing
hypothesis that has received empirical support (Iacono *et al.*, 1984) is that the
diminished EDA accompanying depression stems from a *physiological*, not a
psychological basis, and so is entirely independent of arousability. One means
of evaluating these competing hypotheses is to compare the correlates of
diseases that share a marker. If reduced EDA is characteristic of a disorder
with which normal arousal levels are associated, a simple underarousal
interpretation of lower EDA is challenged. A dissociation between EDA and

other indices of arousal (e.g. heart rate, finger pulse amplitude) within ill subjects also would mitigate the viability of the arousal interpretation.

Another potentially profitable area of investigation is identifying markers of genes that are assets (Gottesman and Shields, 1982) and actually reduce the chances of a disorder developing. Identification of such variables would have substantial theoretical and practical value. For instance, such markers would give a more complete picture of the factors mediating the development of illness, and they may help explain the range of outcomes that has been observed in persons who possess the pathogenes. An example of a possible psychophysiological marker of invulnerability also derives from the study of EDA in affective disorders (Iacono *et al.*, 1983, 1984). The reduced EDA observed in remitted affective disorder patients was also observed in about half of a normal comparison group. However, almost none of those with affective disorder evidenced high levels of EDA. Such a pattern is consistent with the interpretation that high levels of EDA are a sign of reduced susceptibility or resistance to affective disorder.

CONCLUSION

Traditionally, psychophysiological studies of pathology have concentrated on comparisons of ill and healthy subjects. Broadly stated, the goal of these comparisons has been to provide clues to the aetiology of a disorder and to the psychobiological dysfunction present. While this approach has contributed much to our understanding of many disorders, it is not without its limitations. These include reliance on symptom-based diagnoses that are of unknown validity, the inability to distinguish factors that are related to cause from those that are effects, the difficulty in understanding the development of the disorder because preclinical phases can be studied only retrospectively, and the inability to identify meaningful subtypes of disorder.

The primary objective of this chapter was to call attention to an alternative way in which psychophysiological measures can be used to study illness. Each of the three types of psychophysiological markers we described provides interesting data as well as a means for circumventing many of the shortcomings of the traditional clinical phase design. All three types of markers can be used to help refine diagnosis and have potential to provide insight into the biological underpinnings and heterogeneity of a disorder. In addition, episode markers can be used as adjuncts to evaluate treatment efficacy. Vulnerability and genetic markers derive their usefulness from the fact that they identify healthy persons at risk for illness. Genetic markers allow us to pursue hitherto unanswerable questions, such as how a disorder is transmitted and what determines whether those with the genetic diathesis do or do not develop an illness.

REFERENCES

Akiskal, H. S. (1983). Diagnosis and classification of affective disorders: new insights from clinical and laboratory approaches. *Psychiatric Developments* **1**, 123–160.

Akiskal, H. S., Walker, P., Puzantin, V. R., King, D., Rosenthal, T. and Dranon, M. (1983). Bipolar outcome in the course of depressive illness: phenomenologic, familial and pharmacological predictors. *Journal of Affective Disorder* **5**, 115–128.

American Psychiatric Association (1980) *Diagnostic and Statistical Manual*, 3rd edn. Washington, DC: APA.

Andreassi, J. L. (1980). *Psychophysiology: Human Behavior and Physiological Response*. New York: Oxford University Press.

Avery, D., Wildschiodtz, G., and Rafaelsen, O. (1982). REM latency and temperature in affective disorder before and after treatment. *Biological Psychiatry* **17**, 463–470.

Baron, M., Risch, N., Hamburger, R., Mandel, B., Kushner, S., Newman, M., Drumer, D., and Belmaker, R. H. (1987). Genetic linkage between X-chromosome markers and bipolar affective illness. *Nature* **326**, 289–292.

Begleiter, H., Porjesz, B., Bihari, B., and Kissin, B. (1984). Event-related brain potentials in boys at risk for alcoholism. *Science* **225**, 1493–1496.

Boomsa, D. I., and Gabrielli, W. F. (1985). Behavioral genetic approaches to psychophysiological data. *Psychophysiology* **22**, 249–260.

Buchsbaum, M. S., and Haier, R. J. (1983). Psychopathology: biological perspectives. *Annual Review of Psychology* **34**, 401–430.

Buchsbaum, M. S., Coursey, R. D., and Murphy, D. L. (1976). The biochemical high risk paradigm: behavioral and familial correlates of low platelet monoamine oxidase activity. *Science* **194**, 339–341.

Buchsbaum, M. S., Haier, R. J., and Johnson, J. (1982). Augmenting and reducing: individual differences in evoked potentials. In: A. Gale and J. Edwards (Eds) *Psychophysiological Correlates of Human Behavior*. London: Academic Press.

Chapman, L. J., Chapman, J. P., and Raulin, M. L. (1976). Scales for physical and social anhedonia. *Journal of Abnormal Psychology* **85**, 374–382.

Depue, R. A., Slater, J. F., Wolfstetter-Kausch, H., Klein, D., Goperlund, E., and Farr, D. (1981). A behavioral paradigm for identifying persons at risk for bipolar depressive disorder: a conceptual framework and five validation studies. *Journal of Abnormal Psychology* **90**, 381–437.

Drayna, D., and White, R. (1985). The genetic linkage map of the human X chromosome. *Science* **230**, 753–758.

Edelberg, R. (1972). The electrodermal system. In: N. S. Greenfield and R. A. Sternbach (Eds) *Handbook of Psychophysiology*, pp. 367–418. New York: Holt, Rinehart and Winston.

Egeland, J. A., Gerhard, D. S., Pauls, D. L., Sussex, J. N., Kidd, K. K., Allen, C. R., Hostetter, A. M. and Housman, D. E. (1987). Bipolar affective disorders linked to DNA markers on chromosome 11. *Nature* **325**, 783–787.

Feighner, J. P., Robins, E., Guze, S. B., Woodruff, R. A., Winokur, G., and Munoz, R. (1972). Diagnostic criteria for use in psychiatric research. *Archives of General Psychiatry* **26**, 57–63.

Feinberg, M., and Carroll, B. J. (1984). Biological markers for endogenous depression in series and parallel. *Biological Psychiatry* **19**, 3–12.

Freedman, R., Adler, L. E., and Waldo, M. (1987). Gating of the auditory evoked potential in children and adults. *Psychophysiology* **24**, 223–227.

Friedman, D., Cornblatt, B., Vaughan, H., and Erlenmeyer-Kimling, L. (1986). Event-related potentials in children at risk for schizophrenia during two versions of the continuous performance test. *Psychiatry Research* **18**, 161–177.

Friedman, D., Erlenmeyer-Kimling, L., and Vaughan, H. (1985). Auditory event-related potentials in children at risk for schizophrenia revisited: re-diagnosis of the patient parents and inclusion of the psychiatric control group. *Psychophysiology* **22**, 590.

Friedman, D., Vaughan, H., and Erlenmeyer-Kimling, L. (1982). Cognitive brain potentials in children at risk for schizophrenia: preliminary findings. *Schizophrenia Bulletin* **8**, 514–531.

Gabrielli, W. F., Jr, Mednick, S. A., Volavka, J., Pollock, V. E., Schulsinger, F., and Itil, T. M. (1982). Electroencephalograms in children of alcoholic fathers. *Psychophysiology* **19**, 404–407.

Gasser, T., Sroka, L., and Mocks, J. (1986). The correction of EOG artifacts by frequency dependent and frequency independent methods. *Psychophysiology* **23**, 704–712.

Gershon, E. S. (1978). The search for genetic markers in the affective disorders. In: M. A. Lipton, A. DiMascio and K. F. Killiam (Eds) *Psychopharmacology: A Generation of Progress*, pp. 1197–1212. New York: Raven Press.

Gershon, E. S., and Buchsbaum, M. S. (1977). A genetic study of AER augmenting/reducing in affective disorder. In: C. Shagass, S. Gerson and A. J. Friedhoff (Eds) *Psychopathology and Brain Dysfunction* pp. 279–290. New York: Raven Press.

Gintner, G. G., Hollandsworth, J. G., and Intrieri, R. C. (1986). Age differences in cardiovascular reactivity under active coping conditions. *Psychophysiology* **23**, 113–120.

Glassman, A. H., and Bigger, J. T. (1981). Cardiovascular effects of therapeutic doses of tricyclic antidepressants: a review. *Archives of General Psychiatry* **38**, 815–820.

Gottesman, I. I., and Shields, J. (1972). *Schizophrenia and Genetics*. New York: Academic Press.

Gottesman, I. I., and Shields, J. (1982). *Schizophrenia: The Epigenetic Puzzle*. New York: Cambridge University Press.

Gratton, G., Coles, M. G. H., and Donchin, E. (1983). A new method for off-line removal of ocular artifact. *Electroencephalography and Clinical Neurophysiology* **55**, 468–484.

Greenberg, L. M., and Yellin, A. M. (1975). Blood pressure and pulse changes in hyperactive children treated with imipramine and methylphenidate. *American Journal of Psychiatry* **132**, 1325–1326.

Gusella, J. F., Wexler, N. S., Conally, P. M., Naylor, S. L., Anderson, M. A., Tanzi, R. E., Watkins, D. C., Ottina, K., Wallace, M. R., Sakaguchi, A. Y., Young, A. B., Shoulson, I., Bonilla, E., and Martin, J. B. (1983). A polymorphic DNA marker genetically linked to Huntington's disease. *Nature* **306**, 234–238.

Hall, R. A., Rappaport, M., Hopkins, H. K., and Griffin, R. (1973). Tobacco and evoked potential. *Science* **180**, 212–214.

Hanson, D. R., Gottesman, I. I., and Heston, L. L. (1976). Some possible childhood indicators of adult schizophrenia inferred from children of schizophrenics. *British Journal of Schizophrenia* **129**, 142–154.

Hastrup, J. L., and Light, K. C. (1984). Sex differences in stress responses: modulation as a function of menstrual cycle phases. *Journal of Psychosomatic Research* **28**, 475–483.

Hauri, P., Chernik, D., Hawkins, D., and Mendels, J. (1974). Sleep of depressed patients in remission. *Archives of General Psychiatry* **31**, 386–391.

Herman, J., Mirsky, A., Ricks, N., and Gallant, D. (1977). Behavioral and electrographic measures of attention in children at risk for schizophrenia. *Journal of Abnormal Psychology* **86**, 27–33.

Holzman, P. S., Proctor, L. R., Yasillo, N. J., Meltzer, H. Y. and Hurt, S. W. (1974). Eye-tracking dysfunctions in schizophrenic patients and their relatives. *Archives of General Psychiatry* **31**, 143–151.

Housman, D., and Gusella, J. (1981). Use of recombinant DNA techniques for linkage studies in genetically based neurological disorders. In: E. S. Gershon, S. Matthysse, X. O. Breakefield and R. D. Ciaranello (Eds) *Genetic Research Strategies for Psychobiology and Psychiatry*, pp. 17–24. Pacific Grove, Cal. Boxwood Press.

Iacono, W. G. (1982). Bilateral electrodermal habituation–dishabituation and resting EEG in remitted schizophrenics. *Journal of Nervous and Mental Disease* **170**, 91–101.

Iacono, W. G. (1983). Psychophysiology and genetics: a key to psychopathology research. *Psychophysiology* **20**, 371–383.

Iacono, W. G. (1985). Psychophysiological markers of psychopathology: a review. *Canadian Psychology* **26**, 96–112.

Iacono, W. G. (1987). Eye movement abnormalities in schizophrenic and affective disorders. In: C. W. Johnston and F. J. Pirozzolo (Eds) *Neuropsychology of Eye Movements*. Hillsdale, NJ: Erlbaum.

Iacono, W. G., Lykken, D. T., Haroian, K. P., Peloquin, L. J., Valentine, R. H. and Tuason, V. B. (1984). Electrodermal activity in euthymic patients with affective disorders: one-year retest stability and the effects of stimulus and intensity significance. *Journal of Abnormal Psychology* **93**, 304–311.

Iacono, W. G., Lykken, D. T., Peloquin, L. J., Lumry, A. E., Valentine, R. H., and Tuason, V. B. (1983). Electrodermal activity in euthymic unipolar and bipolar affective disorders: a possible marker for depression. *Archives of General Psychiatry* **40**, 557–565.

Iacono, W. G., Peloquin, L. J., Lumry, A. E., Valentine, R. H., and Tuason, V. B. (1982). Eye tracking in patients with unipolar and bipolar affective disorders in remission. *Journal of Abnormal Psychology* **91**, 35–44.

Itil, T. M. (1977). Qualitative and quantitative EEG findings in schizophrenics. *Schizophrenic Bulletin* **3**, 61–79.

Johnson, L., and Corah, N. (1963). Racial differences in skin resistance. *Science* **139**, 766–767.

Karson, C. N. (1983). Spontaneous eye-blink rates and dopaminergic systems. *Brain* **106**, 643–653.

Karson, C. N., Goldberg, T. E., and Leleszi, J. P. (1986). Increased blink rate in adolescent patients with psychosis. *Psychiatry Research* **17**, 195–198.

Knott, V. J., and Venables, P. H. (1977). EEG alpha correlates of non-smokers, smokers, smoking and smoking deprivation. *Psychophysiology* **14**, 150–156.

Kupfer, D. J. (1982). EEG sleep as biological markers in depression. In: E. Usdin and I. Hanin (Eds) *Biological Markers in Psychiatry and Neurology*, pp. 387–396. Oxford: Pergamon.

Lane, J. D., and Williams, R. B. (1985). Caffeine affects cardiovascular responses to stress. *Psychophysiology* **22**, 648–655.

Levy, D. L., Dorus, E., Shaughnessy, R., Yasillo, N. J., Ghanshym, N. P., Janicak, P. G., Gibbons, R. D., Gavira, M., and Davis, J. M. (1985). Pharmacologic evidence for specificity of pursuit dysfunction to schizophrenia. *Archives of General Psychiatry* **42**, 335–341.

Little, B. C., and Zahn, T. P. (1974). Changes in mood and autonomic functioning during menstrual cycle. *Psychophysiology* **11**, 579–590.

Lykken, D. T. (1975). The role of individual differences in psychophysiological research. In: P. H. Venables and M. J. Christie (Eds) *Research in Psychopathology*, pp. 3–15. London: Wiley.

Matthysse, S., Holzman, P. S., and Lange, K. (1986). The genetic transmission of schizophrenia: application of Mendelian latent structure analysis to eye tracking dysfunctions in schizophrenia and affective disorder. *Journal of Psychiatric Research* **20**, 57–76.

McKusick, U. A., and Ruddle, F. H. (1977). The status of the gene map of the human chromosomes. *Science* **196**, 390–405.

Mednick, S. A., and Schulsinger, F. (1968). Some premorbid characteristics related to breakdown in children with schizophrenic mothers. In: D. Rosenthal and S. S. Kety (Eds) *Transmission of Schizophrenia*, pp. 267–292. New York: Pergamon.

Meehl, P. E. (1972). *Psychodiagnosis: Selected Papers*. New York: Norton.

Meehl, P. E., and Golden, R. R. (1982). Taxometric methods. In: P. C. Kendall and J. N. Butcher (Eds) *Handbook of Research Methods in Clinical Psychology*, pp. 127–181. New York: Wiley.

Morimoto, T. (1978). Variations in sweating activity due to sex, age and race. In: A. Jarrett (Ed.) *The Physiology and Pathophysiology of the Skin*, Vol. 5: *The Sweat Glands, Skin Permeation, Lymphatics and the Nails*. New York: Academic Press.

Ohman, A. (1981). Electrodermal activity and vulnerability to schizophrenia: a review. *Biological Psychology* **12**, 87–143.

O'Toole, D. M., and Iacono, W. G. (1987). An evaluation of different techniques for removing eye blink artifact from visual evoked response recordings. *Psychophysiology* **24**, 487–497.

Rieder, R. O., and Gershon, E. S. (1978). Genetic strategies in biological psychiatry. *Archives of General Psychiatry* **35**, 866–873.

Saitoh, O., Niwa, S., Hiramatsu, K., Kameyama, T., Rymar, K., and Itoh, K. (1984). Abnormalities in late positive components of event-related potentials may reflect a genetic predisposition to schizophrenia. *Biological Psychiatry* **19**, 293–303.

Saletu, B., Saletu, M., and Itil, T. (1972). Effect of minor and major tranquillizers on somatosensory evoked potentials. *Psychopharmacologia* **24**, 347–358.

Schulsinger, F., Knop, J., Goodwin, D. W., Teasdale, T. W., and Mikkelsen, U. (1986). A prospective study of young men at high risk for alcoholism. *Archives of General Psychiatry* **43**, 755–763.

Semlitsch, H. V., Anderer, P., Schuster, P., and Presslich, O. (1986). A solution for reliable and valid reduction of ocular artifacts, applied to the P300 ERP. *Psychophysiology* **23**, 695–703.

Sharpe, J. A., and Sylvester, T. O. (1978). Effects of aging on horizontal smooth-pursuit. *Investigate Ophthalmology and Visual Science* **17**, 465–470.

Shields, J., Heston, L. L., and Gottesman, I. I. (1975). Schizophrenia and the schizoid: the problem of genetic analysis. In: R. R. Fieve, D. Rosenthal and H. Brill (Eds) *Genetic Research in Psychiatry*, pp. 167–198. Baltimore: Johns Hopkins University Press.

Siegal, C., Waldo, M., Mizner, G., Adler, L. E., and Freedman, R. (1984). Deficits in sensory gating in schizophrenic patients and their relatives: evidence obtained with auditory evoked responses. *Archives of General Psychiatry* **41**, 607–612.

Siever, L. J., Coursey, R. D., Alterman, I. S., Buchsbaum, M. S., and Murphy, D. L. (1982a). Psychological and physiological correlates of variation in smooth pursuit eye movements. In: E. Usdin and I. Hanin (Eds) *Biological Markers in Psychiatry and Neurology*, pp. 359–370. Elmsford, NY: Pergamon.

Siever, L. J., Coursey, R. D., Alterman, I. S., Buchsbaum, M. S., and Murphy, D. L. (1984). Impaired smooth pursuit eye movement: vulnerability marker for schizotypal personality disorder in a normal volunteer population. *American Journal of Psychiatry* **141**, 1560–1566.

Siever, L. J., Haier, R. J., Coursey, R. D., Sostek, A. J., Murphy, D. L., Holzman, P.

S., and Buchsbaum, M. S. (1982b). Smooth pursuit eye tracking impairment: relation to other 'markers' of schizophrenia and psychological correlates. *Archives of General Psychiatry* **39**, 1001–1005.

Simons, R. F. (1981). Electrodermal and cardiac orienting in psychometrically defined high-risk subjects. *Psychiatry Research* **4**, 347–356.

Simons, R. F., Losito, B. D., Rose, S. C., and MacMillan, F. W. (1983). Electrodermal nonresponding among college undergraduates: temporal stability, situational specificity, and relationship to heart rate change. *Psychophysiology* **20**, 498–506.

Spohn, H. E., Lacoursieve, R. B., Thompson, K., and Coyne, L. (1977). Phenothiazine effects on psychological and psychophysiological dysfunction in chronic schizophrenics. *Archives of General Psychiatry* **34**, 633–644.

St George-Hyslop, P. H., Tanzi, R. E., Polinsky, R. J., Haines, J. L., Nee, L., Watkins, P. C., Myers, R. H., Feldman, R. G., Pollen, D., Drachman, D., Growden, J., Bruni, A., Foncin, J.-F., Salmon, D., Frommelt, P., Amaducci, L., Sorbi, S., Piacentini, S., Stewart, G. D., Hobbs, W. J., Conneally, D. M., and Gusella, J. F. (1987). The genetic defect causing familial Alzheimer's disease maps on chromosome 21. *Science* **235**, 885–890.

Stern, J. A., Walrath, L. C., and Goldstein, R. (1984). The endogenous eye blink. *Psychophysiology* **21**, 22–33.

Stevens, J. R. (1978). Eye blink and schizophrenia: psychosis or tardive dyskinesia? *American Journal of Psychiatry* **135**, 223–226.

Teece, J. J., and Cole, J. O. (1974). Amphetamine effects in man: paradoxical drowsiness and lowered electrical brain activity (CNV). *Science* **185**, 451–453.

Teece, J. J., Cole, J. O., and Savignano-Bowman, J. (1975). Chlorpromazine effects on brain activity (contingent negative variation) and reaction time in normal women. *Psychopharmacologia* **43**, 293–295.

Ulett, J. A., and Itil, T. M. (1969). Quantitative electroencephalogram in smoking and smoking deprivation. *Science* **164**, 969–970.

Venables, P. (1978). Psychophysiology and psychometrics. *Psychophysiology* **15**, 302–315.

Venables, P. H., Mednick, S. A., Schulsinger, F., Raman, A. C., Bell, B., Dalais, J. C., and Fletcher, R. P. (1978). Screening for risk of mental illness. In: G. Serban (Ed.) *Cognitive Defects in the Development of Mental Illness*, pp. 273–303. New York: Brunner/Mazel.

Woodson, P. P., Buzzi, R., Nil, R., and Battig, K. (1986). Effects of smoking on vegetative reactivity to noise in women. *Psychophysiology* **23**, 272–282.

Zahn, T. P. (1986). Psychophysical approaches to psychopathology. In: M. G. H. Coles, E. Donchin and S. W. Porges (Eds) *Psychophysiology*, pp. 508–610. New York: Guilford.

Zarcone, V. (1973). Narcolepsy: a review of the syndrome. *New England Journal of Medicine* **288**, 1156–1166.

Zarcone, V. P., Benson, K. L., and Bergen, P. A. (1987). Abnormal rapid eye movement latencies in schizophrenics. *Archives of General Psychiatry* **44**, 45–48.

Zubin, J., and Steinhauer, S. (1981). How to break the logjam in schizophrenia: a look beyond genetics. *Journal of Nervous and Mental Disease* **169**, 477–492.

Chapter 3

Psychophysiological Assessment: Conceptual, Psychometric, and Statistical Issues

Gerhard Stemmler and Jochen Fahrenberg

Forschungsgruppe Psychophysiologie,
University of Freiburg,
Belfortstrasse 20,
D-7800 Freiburg,
Federal Republic of Germany

ABSTRACT

Psychophysiological assessment is discussed from the perspective of various conceptual and practical research aspects. Specific topics include: research questions, validity aspects, psychometric properties of difference scores, the Law of Initial Values, implicit measurement models, trends and baselines, artifacts, outliers and missing data, stability, generalizability, partitioning of variance and covariance, multivariate analysis of variance, and profile analysis.

Handbook of Clinical Psychophysiology Edited by G. Turpin
© 1989 John Wiley & Sons Ltd

INTRODUCTION

Psychophysiological assessment is not just the recording of a physiological measure and its analysis. Assessment can only be devised properly with reference to the research question, the particular theoretical constructs and their operationalization, the experimental design, and the statistical hypotheses. On the other hand, assessment methods often implicate a particular statistical treatment of the data and set the stage for subsequent interpretation. Assessment must, therefore, be placed within the context of conceptual and statistical issues.

CONCEPTUAL ISSUES

PSYCHOLOGICAL PERSPECTIVE ON PHYSIOLOGICAL DATA

A broad variety of physiological and biochemical data is used in the psychophysiological research literature. Compared to many fields of psychology, data acquisition in the laboratory does not seem to present a problem. Physiological functions can be measured in physical units with respect to amplitude and frequency components, and the objectivity and reproducibility of such measurements are obvious.

However, psychophysiologists are not usually interested in particular physiological or biochemical data *per se* but in these measures as indices of theoretical constructs such as arousal, anxiety, and stress. This leads to basic questions of construct validity that are specific to the psychophysiological approach and demand a psychophysiological theory of physiological data. Admittedly, not all psychophysiologists are concerned with the psychological–behavioural surplus meaning of physiological data but prefer to study distinct neurobiological mechanisms or specific symptoms. Different orientations and implicit assumptions have to be acknowledged.

A particular physiological parameter, e.g. heart rate, may have a variety of meanings:

(1) a direct measure of sinus rhythm
(2) an index of beta-adrenergic activity
(3) an index of actual haemodynamic regulation within the 'accentuated antagonism' of sympathetic and vagal control of the heart
(4) an index of the theoretical construct of a rather global activation state/ activation reaction (emotion, stress, etc.)
(5) an index of the cardiovascular component of a multicomponent model of activation
(6) an aspect of the organism's metabolic, muscular performance and thermoregulatory functioning

(7) an index of physical fitness
(8) an index of theoretical constructs like habitual autonomic reactivity (emotionality or anxiety as traits)
(9) a symptom of tachycardia as a psychophysiological disorder
(10) an aspect of a hyperkinetic cardiac regulatory pattern
(11) a symptom of physical disturbance or illness which is caused, for example, by endocrine dysfunction, fever, or intoxication
(12) a hypothetical or an empirically validated predictor for criteria of practical relevance, for example occupational strain or outcome of behaviour therapy in agoraphobia.

More items could easily be added to this list. The apparent multiplicity of meaning may consequently lead to much confusion.

The mere acquisition of physiological measures in a clinical psychological context does not yet constitute a sound psychophysiological approach. The researcher should also provide his or her basic assumptions. Which psychological/physiological state, process, trait, diagnostic category, criteria, etc. are purportedly indexed by a particular physiological measure? What are the specific operation–construct units and which evidence can be given for convergent and discriminant validity of particular measures? What is the psychological (behavioural) or the integrative psychophysiological hypothesis that can be tested more convincingly and validly with rather than without physiological data? What is their explanatory value?

The use of psychophysiological assessments in clinical as opposed to general psychology raises even more substantial issues. First, individual differences in activation state and reactivity have to be particularly noted because an individual's data are fundamental to clinical diagnosis and as indications for and evaluations of treatment. The clinical approach typically employs longitudinal studies (e.g. investigations on risk and development of disease), single-subject designs, and follow-up studies. With respect to practical applications, therefore, the assessment and prediction of inter- and intra-individual differences are crucial. Specifically, it remains an intriguing question whether individual differences in activation state and reactivity can be predicted reliably from particular physiological measures or from psychological variables (e.g. personality traits). Issues of such practical importance like these, as well as the development of standardized assessment procedures, have been very rarely raised.

Second, the degree of generalizability across various situations is much more pertinent in clinical than in experimental psychophysiology. Diagnostic and therapeutic decisions must assume that recordings taken in the clinical setting are fairly representative of the patient's normal life. Thus it is important to consider the external validity (i.e. is the physiological measurement predictive for disease- or treatment-related factors external to the laboratory?), incremental validity (i.e. does the externally valid physiological measurement carry relevant information in addition to psychological and clinical data?), and finally practical utility (i.e. does the incrementally valid physiological measurement lead to clinical decisions that would otherwise not have been reached?) of physiological data in clinical psychological decisions.

A more detailed discussion of these aspects of validity cannot be pursued further here (for more general aspects of the validity issue, cf. Averill and Opton, 1968; Fahrenberg, 1983; Gale and Edwards, 1983; Porges, Ackles and Truax, 1983; Ray, Cole and Raczynski, 1983; Rösler, 1983, 1984; see also the other chapters in Section 1 of this handbook). However, it must be acknowledtted that the development of a consistent conceptual framework incorporating these various aspects of validity still lies ahead.

Generally, a treatise on methodological issues in clinical psychophysiology would reveal many questions that correspond to principles and strategies of personality assessment. Within a broader conceptual framework of assessment theory (cf. Wiggins, 1973), several distinct assessment strategies have been identified. Psychophysiological methodology, especially in the clinical and applied field, could profit considerably from these and further developments in psychometrics and personality assessment theory.

THE QUEST FOR A MULTICOMPONENT MODEL OF ACTIVATION

A wide variety of theoretical orientations prevails in the literature, each of which provides a unique frame of reference for the interpretation of physiological data. A different and indeed more unifying approach would be the development of a general theory of activation integrating the common elements of these theories. We would like to give a short presentation of some of the empirical results which might serve as a starting point for a theory of activation.

Broad evidence has accumulated for response fractionation as a basic phenomenon in psychophysiology (Lacey, 1962). This has led to a growing criticism of unidimensional activation theory and the proposal of multicomponent models (Lacey, 1967). Arguments for this position are supported by the following observations (see Fahrenberg, 1986 and 1988, for an extended discussion):

(1) Physiology has accumulated a large body of evidence about the independence of various effector systems, partially acting synergistically and antagonistically.
(2) Activation processes for different stress–strain sequences are patterned rather than proportional to one another.
(3) The patterning of activation processes to some extent reflects situational characteristics or demands as postulated by the principle of situation-specific responses (SSR).

(4) The patterning of activation processes is idiosyncratic to a considerable extent, as postulated by the principle of individual-specific responses (ISR).

(5) There remains a consistent patterning of activation processes in particular subject–situation combinations, as, for example, within highly individualized phobic situations, as postulated by the principle of individual–situation-specific responses (ISSR).

What are the consequences of a multicomponent model for psychophysiological assessment? First, a single physiological variable can seldom claim to represent activation. Second, a single variable can seldom even safely represent a certain component of activation, because complex and often not well understood processes govern the variable's activity. A corollary to this is that a psychological construct can hardly be operationalized with one physiological variable, as the risk of false conclusions is too large. Third, the interrelationship between physiological variables should be taken into account by adopting multivariate statistical methods as well as the analysis of system dynamics. Fourth, frequently used terms in psychophysiology that explicitly refer to an ensemble of variables, as, for example, the *pattern* of activation processes (as distinguished from their intensity), should be statistically defined. Fifth, physiological data cannot replace psychological data, for example the self-report of affect, motivation, or cognitive evaluations.

In summary, it is our position that psychophysiological assessment is intricately related to the problem of validity. Common assumptions as to the external and incremental validity, or to the practical utility of physiological measures still have to be substantiated. An improved assessment methodology on the basis of a multicomponent activation theory would be a promising start.

OVERVIEW AND CONCLUSION

Thus far, we have emphasized the relationship of assessment, on the one hand, to theoretical and research design issues and on the other, to issues concerning the validation and interpretation of psychophysiological measures. Despite the importance of these issues, we have chosen to devote the major part of this chapter to the discussion of key biometric notions that provide the basic methodology for psychophysiological assessment. In accordance with our interest in the development of a multicomponent activation theory, we shall introduce a limited number of multivariate statistical analysis strategies which we have previously found useful. Other methods not mentioned here might be similarly applied and may include time-series analysis in the frequency or time domain, or differential equations for a systems analytic approach. However, lack of space precludes the discussion of only a few topics.

From the viewpoint of a researcher coming from another field and asking whether psychophysiological methods could help answer his or her questions, some issues in psychophysiological methodology may appear to be rather sophisticated. Accordingly, the authors will try to offer preliminary conclusions and recommendations wherever possible. But the reader is reminded that the intricate relationships between research questions, validity assumptions, assessment strategies, and statistical analyses stand against general methodological recommendations.

RESPONSE SCALING

In psychophysiological assessment, response scaling is the intermediate step between data acquisition and statistical analysis. Two of the problems often encountered during this step concern the measurement of change and the choice of a response measure.

The measurement of change, especially with only two measurement occasions arising from pre- and post-stimulus/treatment (x and y, respectively), has created many problems in the psychophysiological and statistical literature. The intuitively most appealing measure, the algebraical difference d between y and x, $d = y - x$, has been challenged for a number of reasons. First, difference scores are often more unreliable than either x or y; second, they are influenced by regression to the mean effects; third, they are subject to the influence of the so-called Law of Initial Values (LIV); fourth, the latent variable (the indicand) purportedly indexed by the measured variable (the indicator) might not be the same at the two measurement occasions (cf. Plewis, 1985).

While we shall ignore the last argument against the use of d, the first three shall be discussed subsequently, because d none the less is an unbiased estimate of true individual change if a linear growth model can be assumed (Rogosa, Brandt and Zimowski, 1982), i.e. if the change of the indicator is proportional to that of the indicand.

PSYCHOMETRIC PROPERTIES OF THE DIFFERENCE SCORE

Reliability

The reliability of the difference score (r_{dd}) is the accuracy with which individual differences in true change are gauged by the observed change. Two factors influence r_{dd}. First, unreliability of x (r_{xx}) and y (r_{yy}), or lack of measurement precision, reduces r_{dd}. Because of positively correlated errors in x and y, however, narrowly spaced retest measurements might lead to an overestimation of r_{dd}. Second, low inter-individual variance in true change reduces r_{dd}. This means that if subjects respond quite similarly to a stimulus, r_{dd} will be near zero, even if measurement precision was high! Thus it follows that r_{dd} depends not only on r_{xx} and r_{yy}, but also on the sample of subjects and stimuli used: unreliability of difference scores does not necessarily mean low measurement precision. Note that large inter-individual true-change variance (large r_{dd}) is desirable when exploring correlates of individual differences, while the opposite (low r_{dd}) holds when evaluating group differences in change (Overall and Woodward, 1975).

Pre-Post Correlation

The pre-post correlation (r_{xy}) and r_{dd} are often inversely related: given a high measurement precision and low true-change variance (low r_{dd}), r_{xy} is large; however, with large true-change variance (large r_{dd}), r_{xy} is low. (If the correlation between true pre-stimulus scores and true change is high positive, both r_{dd} and r_{xy} may attain large coefficients.) Thus, a physiological variable might be a good predictor of individual differences (e.g. in laboratory-field comparisons), yet have low r_{dd} and no correlates of change.

Stability

An important variant of the pre-post correlation issue arises when no stimulus intervenes between two measurements x and x'. Then $r_{xx'}$ is called a stability coefficient and estimates the reliability of x. The magnitude of $r_{xx'}$ depends largely on measurement precision, if both inter-individual true-change variance and true first-occasion with true-change correlation are low. Thus, a low $r_{xx'}$ does not necessarily indicate low measurement precision, because it is also reduced by systematic variations occurring between the measurements (see later in this chapter 'Psychometric issues: generalizability' for practical considerations).

Regression Towards the Mean

This effect means that scores x above (below) the common population mean tend to be followed by decreased (increased) x' scores. Formally, the slope of the linear regression of x' on x is less than one (Nesselroade, Stigler and Baltes, 1980). If x and x' have equal variances, the regression slope equals $r_{xx'}$, the stability coefficient, which in turn equals the reliability r_{xx} if no true-change variance is present (Goldstein, 1979).

Next, we shall consider two typical research situations, where regression towards the mean constitutes a potential source of artifacts. First, difference scores d are formed to evaluate individual treatment effects. Here, d is usually composed of treatment and regression effects. This may pose severe problems if individual treatment effects are the basis for interpretations or practical decisions (e.g. treatment allocation, modification, or evaluation), or if correlates of individual treatment effects are sought. One way to avoid this is to calculate an 'improved difference score' (Cronbach and Furby, 1970; Messick, 1981; Rogosa et al., 1982), mostly on the basis of at least one additional measurement. If, however, overall instead of individual treatment effects are sought (i.e. for a group of subjects), this problem does not arise.

In the second situation, subjects are assigned to groups by way of their pre-stimulus scores. It might be asked whether the groups differ in their reactivity to a stressful stimulus. If the pre-test measurements are not completely reliable, regression effects lead to false assignments and hence to a weak test of the experimental hypothesis. The statistical literature emphasizes the need to know the underlying measurement model (e.g. uncorrelated- or autocorrelated-error models, cf. Nesselroade et al., 1980; Weisberg, 1979) for handling this problem adequately.

We are not aware of recommendations concerning the appropriate measurement models for psychophysiological variables. Therefore our suggestion is to carefully plan multiple measurement occasions in order to obtain reliability estimates, to separate selection and experimental treatment, or to identify the underlying measurement model. If the uncorrelated-error model actually holds, a pre-pre measurement for selection and the ensuing pre-stimulus/post-stimulus measurements would be sufficient to cope with regression effects in this situation ('True-Score ANCOVA'; Huitema, 1980).

Digression: Kendall and Stuart's Proposals to Counteract Regression Effects

Attempts to equate for regression towards the mean effects focus on ways of how to obtain estimates of the slope of the linear regression of true post-stimulus scores (t_y) on true pre-stimulus scores (t_x). Kendall and Stuart (1967) proposed four estimates of the unknown regression slope $\alpha_{t_y t_x}$ of t_y on t_x, two of which ('Case 1' and 'Case 3') have been used more than the others. These proposals assume the uncorrelated-error measurement model of classical test theory to hold.

'Case 1': The reliability of x is known. Then (see also Goldstein, 1979; Messick, 1981) the regression slope of t_y on t_x may be estimated by dividing the covariance between x and y by the variance of x weighted by r_{xx}. The same solution is provided by True-Score ANCOVA, which starts with an estimate of a measure of change free from regression towards the mean effects (Huitema, 1980, p. 312).

'Case 3': The ratio of the error variances of y and x is assumed to adopt a certain value λ. Then the regression slope of true scores may be estimated using the covariance between x and y, and the variances of x and y. Letting

$\lambda = 1$, Myrtek and Foerster (1986a) called this estimate 'AHA' (see also Cleary, 1986; Myrtek and Foerster, 1986b).

Correlation Between Pre-stimulus Score and Change

The correlation r_{xd} between the pre-stimulus score x and change d is often termed 'spurious', because it systematically underestimates the correlation $\rho_{t_x\beta}$ between true pre-stimulus scores t_x and true change, $\beta = t_y - t_x$. Thus, even if $\rho_{t_x\beta} = 0$, r_{xd} will often be negative. Assuming uncorrelated errors, this bias is a function of the unreliability of x. An unbiased estimate of $\rho_{t_x\beta}$ can be obtained similarly as noted previously with Kendall and Stuart's (1967) 'Case 3' (cf. Goldstein, 1979, p. 136). Taken together, r_{xd} is an uninteresting artifact of measurement error. The correlation of pre-stimulus scores with change is meaningful only if unbiased estimates of $\rho_{t_x\beta}$ can be obtained. This conclusion has considerable impact on the following discussion of the LIV.

THE LAW OF INITIAL VALUES

Wilder (1931) stated the LIV as a general biological law demonstrable within individuals. It says that 'the higher the initial value, the smaller the response to function-raising, the larger the response to function-depressing stimuli' (Wilder, 1967, p. viii). With respect to the LIV, three questions have continually been asked: How should the LIV be statistically defined, and tested where it applies? What are the consequences, if the LIV is operating? How can LIV effects, if present and adverse for interpretation, be corrected for?

Definition and Test of the LIV

In the 1960s, there was an extended and controversial discussion on how to statistically define the LIV (cf. Campbell, 1981). Under the LIV we would expect a negative r_{xd} and α_{dx}, and a positive α_{yx} of less than one. But as shown above, these statistics are negatively biased: results expected under the LIV will also come about in its absence. Thus, these statistics should be avoided for defining or testing the LIV. A better choice instead is to use an unbiased estimator as discussed above.

Except for the work summarized by Myrtek and Foerster (1986a), we know of no published data that has examined the LIV with unbiased statistics. From between-subjects correlations, these authors concluded that in their data the LIV was a rare exception. A similar conclusion was drawn by Scher, Furedy and Heslegrave (1985), who used the biased r_{xd}. Furthermore, both studies reported evidence indicating an 'anti-LIV', i.e. a positive relationship between initial value and response. However, within-subjects correlations more often were consistent with LIV predictions (Scher *et al.*, 1985).

The discrepancy between Wilder's (1931) claim that the LIV is a general biological law and the empirical status of the LIV is bewildering. However, a closer look at LIV studies reveals that pre-stimulus scores are often obtained during rest periods only. This is a remarkably weak condition for the LIV to operate: individual activation differences during rest are probably small. The LIV, however, predicts differential changes for (clearly) different pre-stimulus activation states. It might be more rewarding to conceive of the LIV as a 'growth model', which posits a certain relationship between a latent, hypothetical variable (the indicand, e.g. 'activation') and an observed variable (the indicator, e.g. heart rate). Other growth models include the linear and the anti-LIV or fan-spread models (cf. Messick, 1981), discussions of which deserve much more attention in psychophysiological research than hitherto.

Consequences of LIV and Anti-LIV

The interpretation of individual difference scores depends on the pre-stimulus score and the variable's growth model (unless it is linear). If neither or only one of these is known, the magnitude of a hypothesized activation change may be difficult to infer. For example, the LIV predicts a small observed positive change only if pre-stimulus scores are high, whereas the anti-LIV predicts the same activation change only if pre-stimulus scores are low. Other interpretational problems arise where subjects have not been randomly assigned to groups. Then the groups are likely to differ in their mean pre-stimulus scores, and treatment effects are confounded with LIV or anti-LIV effects. The problem here is twofold: a correct analysis deserves specification of the growth model and of the selection model (how subjects were assigned to groups; Huitema, 1980, provides a highly recommended guide).

Correction of the LIV

Various methods have been proposed to 'undo' the LIV. The most prominent among them is the use of the Autonomic Lability Score (ALS) suggested by Lacey (1956). Apart from its particular scaling, it is the difference between obtained and predicted post-stimulus scores, where the prediction is based on the linear regression of y on x. Thus, the ALS is a conditional difference uncorrelated with observed pre-stimulus scores. Other approaches include the use of standardized difference scores ('ZDZ'; Heath and Oken, 1965), orthogonal polynomials (Weyer and Blythe, 1983), AHA scores (Myrtek and Foerster, 1986a), and multivariate regression (Thayer, Tanaka and Cohen, 1984).

Although these and other methods fit one or the other statistical criterion, practically none of them can claim to be the psychophysiologically optimal method. Reasons for this are to be found not so much in the methods *per se*, but in our limited knowledge of the growth models underlying physiological variables. Given these blind spots in our knowledge and remembering that methods 'to undo the LIV' merely correct for some undesirable statistical consequences of it, we propose to ask these questions:

(1) *Could the LIV have adverse effects on the results?*

This is likely to happen if the *amount* of individual change is important for practical or research decisions or if *correlates* of change are sought. When comparing groups, adverse LIV effects can be suspected with non-randomized assignments of subjects to groups and even more so if groups receive different treatments.

(2) *Is the LIV actually operating?*

An unbiased estimate of $\alpha_{t_y t_x}$ should be obtained (see above) and tested for deviation from one (consult Myrtek and Foerster, 1986a, for details).

(3) *Are the substantive results invariant over different alternative methods of LIV correction?*

If not, accept the more conservative conclusion to guard against false positives, unless the divergent results had been predicted. This proposition acknowledges that practically all correction methods are open to criticism. (With respect to the ALS, refer, e.g., to Corder-Bolz, 1978; Lykken, 1968; Zimmerman and Williams, 1982.)

(4) *How adverse are the actual LIV effects for the substantive results?*

A comparative analysis with simple difference scores can provide an answer. With identical conclusions, results using difference scores should be preferred, because they make fewer assumptions, are sample independent, and are the best estimators of true individual change under a linear growth model.

In conclusion, LIV effects, their correction, and the measurement of change in general (Bock, 1976; Rogosa and Willett, 1985) crucially depend on knowledge of growth models – for variables and for individuals. For the time being, comparative analyses and proper documentation of results seem warranted.

MEASUREMENT MODELS IMPLIED BY RESPONSE MEASURES

The importance of a knowledge of growth models has already been stressed. If we could specify them, response measures could be perfectly devised. For example, if one variable possessed logarithmic and another straight-line growth, their raw scores would be incompatible: with respect to the indicand (e.g. activation) they would have a different metric. Scale linearization (antilog transformation of the first variable) would provide a common metric. (Levey, 1980, reviews and classifies transformation proposals.) Thus, use of a particular transformation assumes knowledge of a variable's growth model.

Response measures also imply certain growth models. These can be inferred from the equation defining the raw score as a function of the response measure. A plot of this function, the 'transfer function', is a display of the assumed growth model. Depending on the particular response measure, these transfer functions can be identical over subjects or not (allowing for psychophysiological individuality) and invariant over variables or not (implying different growth models among variables). In summary, response measures imply particular measurement models. Differences among some of them will be reviewed shortly (see the detailed discussion by Stemmler, 1987a).

Response Measures and Indicand–Indicator Relationships

Indicands may reside at different levels of psychophysiological organization. An example relating to heart rate has been given earlier in this chapter (see 'Conceptual issues'): indicands ranged from effector activity over that of peripheral and central systems up to the level of psychological constructs. Probably, the 'farther apart' the indicand from the indicator, the more complex their relationship. Additionally, different indicators could follow quite different growth models. Therefore, response measures should allow for non-linear and variable-specific transfer functions. This should be emphasized for more 'distal' indicands. Transfer functions of raw scores, difference scores, range-corrected scores (Lykken, 1968), and, for a given base-value, ALS and percentage scores are linear. Those of square-root, logarithmic, or normalizing (McCall) transformations are non-linear, as are those of percentage scores for varying base-values.

Estimates of Growth Models

For more proximal indicands, some growth models have been determined by physiological experimentation (e.g. see Lidberg and Wallin, 1981, for skin resistance responses and sudomotor nerve impulses as indicand). This is far more difficult, if not impossible, for distal indicands (e.g. 'activation'). In the context of a suggestion by Lader (1975), Fahrenberg, Walschburger, Foerster, Myrtek and Müller (1979) and, with another methodology, Foerster, Schneider and Walschburger (1983a) and Stemmler (1984) have estimated growth models. Although still preliminary, these attempts confirmed the notion of clearly different growth models among variables.

Response Measures and Individual Differences

Research questions may be categorized as exploring either nomothetic laws or individual differences (general vs differential psychophysiology). Individual differences seem harder to evaluate than general laws, and the more distal an indicand, the larger this discrepancy. Reasons for this proposition are twofold. First, individuals differ in organismic structure and function. Some of the individual differences (those existing in the indicand) are of substantial interest. Others, however, are unrelated to the research question and lower the 'signal-to-noise' ratio. Nomothetic laws are more easily found, because individual differences are largely cancelled when averaging over individuals. Second, the more distal an indicand, the greater the likelihood of irrelevant individual differences intervening between indicand and indicator. In summary, response measures should preferably allow for person-specific transfer functions. Those which do include difference scores, range-corrected scores, and normalized difference scores. Raw scores, between-subjects ALS, percentage scores, and normalized scores, however, do not.

Response Measures and Experimental Design

Several response measures need reference values, for example a base-value (difference scores and ALS) or extreme values (range-corrected scores). It is not irrelevant how reference values are obtained (Ben-Shakhar, 1985; Obrist, 1985; see 'Artifacts and outliers' later in this chapter). Transfer functions of percentage scores depend crucially on the measurement scale's origin (which is often deliberately chosen): if it is below the range of observed data, an anti-LIV growth model is implied and partly corrected for, if above, it is the LIV model (cf. Stemmler, 1987a)!

Response Measures and Sample Dependencies

Some response measures depend on the sample of subjects (ALS, normalized and normalized difference scores; cf. Foerster, Schneider and Walschburger, 1983b), most depend on the sample of experimental conditions (difference, normalized difference, ALS, range-corrected, and normalized scores), others are completely nomothetic (raw and percentage scores). These sample dependencies may limit the generalizability of results to a varying extent.

Choice Among Response Measures

The objective of the preceding paragraphs was to offer a theoretical framework for an evaluation of response measures, complementing the usual psychometric and empirical *ad-hoc* comparisons. The lack of knowledge about the actual growth models of variables and individuals precludes any but the gross recommendations given above for choosing among response measures. Also, some of their features (e.g. generalizability of results) might outweigh other advantages (e.g. allowance for individual differences; cf. Stemmler, 1987b).

It has been stated that response measures implicitly assume certain measurement models, according to which the variance of raw scores is partitioned into 'valid' (and hence retained) and 'irrelevant' (and hence excluded) parts. Whether these parts are correctly identified most often remains unknown. An easily performed check would be an analysis of both the response measure and the excluded part of the raw score. The latter may be simply obtained by calculating the difference between raw scores and response measures.

PSYCHOMETRIC ISSUES

The internal validity of psychophysiological experiments is threatened by the many factors that were outlined by Campbell and Stanley (1963). In this regard a multitude of specific technical, physiological, and situational sources of artifacts and irrelevant variance components deserve attention (see Chapter 1). Usually, substantive interest is directed at task-specific arousal. The other variance components should then be reduced to a minimum by experimental and statistical controls. Gale and Baker (1981) suggest some appropriate research tactics. Generally, a thorough standardization of collative situational variables is needed. Reliability and generalizability estimates of psychophysiological measures depend on additional factors of data acquisition and analysis, especially the experimental and/or statistical control for trends within and between experimental sessions, the selection of appropriate baselines often needed for response scaling, the identification of outliers, and strategies for the treatment of missing data.

TRENDS AND THE DEFINITION OF BASELINES

Intra-experimental trends may result from recurrent circadian regulations (time of day), regular daily events (e.g. food intake), adaptation to the laboratory setting, increasing fatigue, boredom, or impatience, but also from the particular task sequence. The problems posed by trends and sequence effects are widely recognized but seldom thoroughly investigated (Erdmann, Janke, Kallus, Nutz and Schlömer, 1984; Fahrenberg, Foerster, Schneider, Müller and Myrtek, 1984; Foerster *et al.*, 1983a; Lichstein, Sallis, Hill and Young, 1981; Myrtek, 1985; Neus and von Eiff, 1985; Wieland and Mefferd, 1970). There are various experimental strategies to deal with these problems.

Steady States

It is generally recommended that the subject's response level should reach a steady state before the next task commences. However, in practice such stationary organismic phases hardly exist. The investigator may observe independently a rather steady heart rate, steady respiration, or a rather stable period of dominant electroencephalogram (EEG) alpha activity but as soon as multichannel recordings are taken, non-stationarities in other physiological functions often become evident. The term 'relative steady state', then, implies a stable condition without marked trends during the observation interval in particular variables.

Permutation of Tasks

Experimental psychologists usually plan a permutated sequence of tasks to deal with trend and sequence effects. In the analysis of variance, the main effect for tasks would then remain unconfounded with them. However, variance attributable to these effects inflates the error variance and reduces the power of the statistical test. In contrast, clinical psychophysiologists and other researchers interested primarily in individual differences tend to use a fixed sequence of tasks as is the case with test batteries. This allows for the comparison of individuals.

Referencing the Initial Rest Period

Assuming a relative steady state, some investigators use the initial rest period to obtain a reference for the response scaling of all subsequent experimental conditions. But this initial rest period is a potentially stressful condition and the magnitude of this effect could be confounded with subject characteristics, for example irritability, anxiety, and familiarity with laboratory, diagnostic, or treatment procedures. Serious concerns about such a 'psychophysiology of initial effects' are justified, especially when researchers do not insist on replicating their findings within and between laboratories. Obrist (1985), for example, abandoned the use of this reference period and instead used a second testing occasion when subjects were exclusively monitored in order to obtain a valid baseline measurement.

If, for whatever reasons, an initial (and perhaps a final) rest period provides the only available baseline, a duration of 5–10 min for baseline recordings will suffice in most cases, provided that (1) the subject was able to adapt to the laboratory setting in a 'dry-run' session on a previous day and (2) the time used for preparing the recordings allows further adaptation immediately before the experiment.

Referencing Multiple Baselines

The most simple control for trends is obtained if each task is preceded by a separate rest period. Task-specific responses are then determined with reference to the associated baseline or reference to the linear or higher order trend between the preceding and the following baseline. Note that in all cases of trend analysis, the experiment's real-time and not the sequence number of experimental conditions must enter into the calculation!

ARTIFACTS AND OUTLIERS

Sternbach, Alexander, Rice and Greenfield (1969) pointed to the lack of conventions that would indicate how to deal with artifacts and missing data. This observation still appears to hold. Despite some specific suggestions, for example concerning electro-oculogram artifacts in the EEG (e.g. Gasser, Sroka and Möck, 1986), these issues have not been settled satisfactorily; Society for Psycho-physiological Research (SPR) publication guidelines for heart rate (Jennings, Berg, Hutcheson, Obrist, Porges and Turpin, 1981), electrodermal activity (Fowles, Christie, Edelberg, Grings, Lykken and Venables, 1981), and electromyographic (Fridlund and Cacioppo, 1986) research still do not recommend specific strategies. Because of this fact, it is left to one's discretion which segments of a recording to eliminate because of 'technical failures', movement artifacts, etc. One of the great problems of elimination is that artifacts seldom occur randomly. Instead, they often covary with the degree of task challenge and the magnitude of the response level. Recordings from ambulatory monitoring provide illustrative examples for such phenomena (see Chapter 1). Note that with multichannel recordings and ambulatory monitoring the number of artifacts will increase.

Outlier Detection

Even one or two outliers can definitely distort statistical inference with conventional statistics, for example a coefficient of correlation. The jack-knife and the more refined bootstrap technique (Efron and Gong, 1983) were developed to handle such outlier problems in statistical testing.

Outlier detection has become an important issue in applied statistics. Approaches to this problem include:

(1) on-line data rejection (e.g. Gevins, Yeager, Zeitlin, Ancoli and Dedon, 1977)
(2) outlier detection utilizing techniques of exploratory data analysis (Tukey, 1977)
(3) reduction of outlier effects by employing comparatively robust sample statistics, for example the median instead of the mean (Wainer, 1982)

(4) bivariate outlier detection that takes into account differential covariate information (Clark *et al.*, 1987)

Missing Data

Various strategies for missing data 'correction' have been proposed and in some instances specifically investigated by simulation studies (for a review see Anderson, Basilevsky and Hum, 1983). An investigator may choose to eliminate cases with missing data, to accept incomplete data sets, or to find 'adequate' substitutions. If not too small, a reduced sample size may be acceptable with some statistical techniques (e.g. analysis of variance, correlation analysis) but not with others (e.g. spectral analysis may require substitutions). There is no generally accepted procedure for dealing with these difficulties.

Missing data substitutions may be performed at different stages of data processing and analysis. It is generally advisable to choose the earliest possible stage, although the time and effort required may be substantial. For example, some major problems such as beat-to-beat heart rate or time-series analyses demand extensive processing. In the order of analysis phases, missing data substitutions include the following procedures:

(1) Signal conditioning. Signals may be edited before or during parameterization.
(2) Parameter editing. The time-course of physiological parameters (e.g. inter-beat intervals) may be graphically displayed and edited in the case of 'unusual' values (Cheung, 1981).
(3) Time-series modelling. The time-series model underlying an individual's successive scores can be determined and used for prediction of the missing value (Gottman, 1981).
(4) Group data estimates. If the statistical parameter (e.g. the mean of an experimental condition) entering into an analysis of variance is missing, a substitution optimally tailored for the statistical design in question may be found (Kirk, 1982).

Authors should provide explicit information about the overall and variable-specific percentage of missing data (after the editing stages) and eventually about how substitutions were performed.

STABILITY OF PHYSIOLOGICAL MEASURES

Stability coefficients are the appropriate indices for assessing the reliability of physiological measures provided that no true change occurred between the two measurements (cf. 'Psychometric properties of the difference score' earlier in this chapter). The reproducibility of measurements in a strict sense would include the removal and reapplication of electrodes and transducers. Performed in a single session, this procedure would probably alter the assumed steady state and could introduce a bias due to repeated skin preparation and due to local interactions at the recording site. Thus, different approaches to the estimation of stability coefficients should complement each other.

Retest Intervals

With most physiological variables, short-term stabilities (electrodes and transducers not removed) at intervals of one or a few minutes are likely to approximate 0.90 (Epstein and Webster, 1975). Longer intervals (20–30 min) from extended rest periods or from equivalent experimental conditions would be more interesting. Short-term stabilities with electrodes and transducers removed have not been reported.

Many studies report stability coefficients based on intervals of days up to weeks (e.g. Arena, Blanchard, Andrasik, Cotch and Myers, 1983; Foerster *et al.*, 1983b; Freixa i Baqué 1982; Myrtek, 1984, 1985; Seraganian *et al.*, 1985). Long-term stability coefficients based on intervals of several months or even years are scarce (e.g. Fahrenberg, Schneider and Safian, 1987; Gasser, Bächer and Steinberg, 1985; Iacono and Lykken, 1981; Manuck and Garland, 1980; Wenger and Cullen, 1972). Very few investigations have tested the long-term stability of response patterns (Foerster, 1985; Lacey and Lacey, 1962; Robinson, Whitsett and Kaplan, 1987).

Magnitude of Stability Coefficients

Stability coefficients from different investigations are not easily compared since essential methodological differences frequently exist. These include parameter definitions, response scalings, experimental conditions, subject samples, length of sampling intervals, and the retest interval. In addition to these details, means and variances should be reported.

Within our laboratory, a comparison of stability coefficients for a broad spectrum of physiological measures was obtained within (Fahrenberg *et al.*, 1979) and over replications of an experiment at intervals of 3 weeks, 3 months, and 1 year (Fahrenberg, Foerster, Schneider, Müller and Myrtek, 1986; Fahrenberg *et al.*, 1987). The results indicated that:

(1) The linear trend component accounted for less than 10% of the total variance in a two-factorial analysis of variance (subjects × replications).
(2) Short-term stability coefficients (electrodes not removed) between roughly equivalent experimental conditions exceeded 0.70 for most physiological measures.
(3) Heart rate, pulse wave velocity, and respiration rate attained higher stab-

ilities than blood pressure, parameters from impedance cardiography, eye blinks, and electrodermal activity.
(4) Raw scores yielded relatively higher stability coefficients than change scores.
(5) Comparing 3-week and 1-year retest intervals, from a total of 30 stability coefficients (of different physiological measures and experimental conditions) the numerical values of 22 coefficients declined (8 increased), but 19 coefficients remained significant.

Obvious differences in the stability of physiological measures might serve to identify comparatively imprecise and/or unstable measures that should be further refined, for example, by reducing sources of measurement error, or by increasing the sampling interval (test lengthening).

GENERALIZABILITY

The degree of generalizability across various situations is relevant for the prediction of individual differences. Is it possible to reliably predict an individual's responses outside the laboratory from assessments during an experimental task (Dimsdale, 1984; Manuck, Krantz and Polefrone, 1985)? Research on inter-task consistency must gradually extend to include laboratory–field comparisons. Recent developments in techniques of ambulatory monitoring of physiological functions have encouraged such investigations, especially with the electrocardiogram, blood pressure recordings, and the EEG (cf. Stefan and Burr, 1982; Stott, Raftery, Clement and Wright, 1982; Weber and Drayer, 1984).

A generalizability (G) study, according to Cronbach, Gleser, Nanda and Rajaratnam (1972), is designed to identify important influences on the dependability or generality of scores. One of the studies mentioned above (Fahrenberg *et al.*, 1986) tested the generalizability of some commonly used physiological measures with respect to inter-task as well as laboratory-field consistency. The coefficients of generalizability were rather low, indicating a small percentage of common variance. Since there are no standards of reference for this first G-study with psychophysiological data, an evaluation of the findings is restricted to internal comparisons: generalizability coefficients for heart rate, respiration rate, pulse wave velocity, and ventricular ejection time exceeded those for electrodermal and eyeblink activity, blood pressure, and other variables. However, these coefficients have to be considered within the restrictions imposed by imperfect stability. These findings indicate that only few assessments from a typical psychophysiological study truly depict relatively enduring individual differences.

MULTIVARIATE STATISTICAL ANALYSIS STRATEGIES

A restriction to univariate statistical analyses of psychophysiological data has several shortcomings. On a technical level, the univariate approach does not account for the interrelation among variables, and a variable-wise testing of experimental effects may pose problems for the control of the overall alpha-error. On a conceptual level, the univariate statistical approach does not correspond to a multicomponent model of activation and hence does not account for the consequences drawn from such a conceptualization for psychophysiological assessments (see 'The quest for a multicomponent model of activation' earlier in this chapter).

It is the purpose of the following sections to discuss some of the multivariate techniques that might be profitably applied in psychophysiology. This discussion will emphasize conceptual rather than statistical issues (as to the latter, cf. Harris, 1985; Morrison, 1976; Timm, 1975; expositions of multivariate techniques within psychophysiology may be found in McHugo and Lanzetta, 1983; Ray and Kimmel, 1979; Van Egeren, 1974; Vasey and Thayer, 1987). The train of thought running through these sections concerns the psychophysiological interpretation of different variance and covariance components. After discussing some general principles of variance and covariance partitioning, multivariate analysis of variance (MANOVA) and profile analysis from this conceptual point of view will shortly be commented upon.

PARTITIONING OF VARIANCE AND COVARIANCE

Partitioning of variance and covariance is a consequence of the notion that a particular research question usually refers to certain sources of variation in the dependent variables. Examples for this are the decomposition of 'total variation' into specific sources of variation in the analysis of variance (ANOVA), or the distinction of 'relevant' and 'irrelevant' variance components made above in the context of response scaling.

Cronbach *et al.* (1972) based their generalizability theory on the same reasoning when they wrote, 'to ask which universe is relevant is to ask how the investigator proposes to interpret the measure' (p. 19), as did Wittmann (1988) with his multivariate reliability theory. Grice (1966) gave a highly readable and non-technical account on some aspects of variance and covariance partitioning. Gollob (1968a,b) proposed a factor analytic decomposition of the ANOVA subjects × conditions (S × C) interaction term if 'individual differences in patterns of performance' (Gollob, 1968b, p. 357) are the subject of research. Cleary (1974) advocated the analysis of the between-subjects plus S × C variance in order to describe inter-individual differences in psychophysiological reactivity. Fahrenberg and Foerster (1982) investigated various aspects of activation processes with the aid of covariance partitioning (for other psycho-physiological applications, see Andresen, 1987; Foerster *et al.*, 1983a; Stemmler, 1984). Yet, the advantages of this approach have not been fully explored.

Definitions

For a brief formal exposition, consider the breakdown of the total sums of squares (*SS*) for an ANOVA design with repeated measurements on one factor (Kirk, 1982).

$$SS(\text{T}) = SS(\text{BS}) + SS(\text{BC}) + SS(\text{R}), \tag{3.1}$$

where T = total, BS = between subjects, BC = between conditions, and R = residual (composed of the S $\times$ C interaction and error, separable only if replications are obtained). By definition,

$$SS(\text{WS}) = SS(\text{BC}) + SS(\text{R})$$
$$SS(\text{WC}) = SS(\text{BS}) + SS(\text{R}),$$

where WS = within subjects and WC = within conditions. Then Equation 3.1 can be rewritten in one of two forms:

$$SS(\text{T}) = SS(\text{BS}) + SS(\text{WS}) \tag{3.2}$$
$$SS(\text{T}) = SS(\text{BC}) + SS(\text{WC}). \tag{3.3}$$

The same relationships hold if, instead of the *SS* of a single variable, the sums of squares and cross-products matrix **S** of several variables is analysed,

$$\mathbf{S}_T = \mathbf{S}_{BS} + \mathbf{S}_{BC} + \mathbf{S}_R \tag{3.4}$$
$$= \mathbf{S}_{BS} + \mathbf{S}_{WS} \tag{3.5}$$
$$= \mathbf{S}_{BC} + \mathbf{S}_{WC}. \tag{3.6}$$

Given the sums of squares and cross-products matrices, variance–covariance and correlation matrices can be easily derived (cf. Morrison, 1976). In the following sections, the psychophysiological meaning of correlation coefficients determined from the various sources of variance is discussed. Table 3.1 gives a summary.

Between-Subjects Correlations (r_{BS})

These correlations indicate the degree of correspondence between two variables across subject means. One such mean is the average over the repeated measures (e.g. experimental conditions) of one subject. If an r_{BS} is large in absolute value, individual differences in mean physiological activity in one variable will be substantially predictable by another variable.

Obviously, the precise interpretation of between-subjects correlations depends on the sample of conditions during which scores are obtained. If this

Table 3.1
Evaluation of relationships between activation variables by partitioning of covariance
(subjects × conditions design).

Source of Covariation	Coefficient	Comments
Between Subjects (BS)	r_{BS}	Correlation over subject means. Correspondence of variables in predicting individual differences in average physiological reactivity. Average defined over sample of experimental conditions used.
Between Conditions (BC)	r_{BC}	Correlation over condition means, i.e. degree of synchronous increases/decreases over the course of conditions. Corrrespondence of variables in situation-specific physiological activity due to coupling of response systems but also due to physiological redundancy and technical/algebraical dependencies.
Residual (R)	r_R	Correlation over all data with subject and condition means removed. Subject × condition component (separable from error only with replications): correspondence of variables in predicting individual differences in individual–situation-specific activation processes. Error component: remaining systematic and unsystematic sources of covariance.
Within Subjects (WS)	r_{WS}	Correlation over all data with subject means removed. Correspondence of variables in the time domain. Uses situation-specific and individual–situation-specific plus error covariance. Contains complete information dealt with in General Psychophysiology.
Within Conditions (WC)	r_{WC}	Correlation over all data with condition means removed. Correspondence of variables in predicting all individual differences in activation processes. Uses covariance from average physiological reactivity and individual–situation-specific activation processes plus error. Contains complete information dealt with in Differential Psychophysiology.

sample is large and in a specifiable way representative of subjects' responsiveness, individual differences in 'habitual' physiological reactivity are depicted.
If this sample is small, individual differences consist of habitual and individual–situation-specific components of physiological reactivity.

Between-Conditions Correlations (r_{BC})

These correlations indicate the degree of correspondence between two variables across condition means. One such mean is the average over all subject scores in one experimental condition. If an r_{BC} is large in absolute value, the situation-specific physiological activity in two variables is essentially similar.

More specifically, an r_{BC} is a measure of shape similarity of two variables' condition-profiles (conditions are the elements of these profiles). Note that profile elevations and scatters (average responsiveness across all conditions and general response magnitude in excess of the average responsiveness, respectively; see 'Profile analysis' later in this chapter) of condition-profiles are irrelevant for the magnitude of an r_{BC}.

Under the assumption that the condition-profile of the 'average subject' is a valid representation of that of each single subject (this assumption is violated in the case of marked individual–situation-specific responses), the r_{BC}s indicate a systemic relationship of variables over conditions. Several factors may lead to systemic relationships. First, variables may be physiologically or physically closely related. Therefore, they covary irrespective of the type of condition and also within conditions, for example finger pulse volume amplitude and finger temperature. Psychophysiological research has repeatedly tried to identify such 'redundant' variables to find substitutes for those difficult to measure.

Second, variables may be part of a temporarily coordinated, functional mechanism to serve organismic requirements, behavioural goals, situational demands, etc. Variables of quite distinct physiological systems may then be more or less tightly coupled, as, for example, heart rate and muscular activity during certain tasks (passive coping tasks, after Obrist, 1976). Third, variables may be related over conditions because of technical confounds or algebraical dependencies. Obviously, if the substantive question relates to the first or second of these factors (i.e. identification of redundant variables or of functional integrative mechanisms), the remaining factors have to be ruled out as possible rival explanations.

Residual Correlations (r_R)

Since in a design without replications the $S \times C$ and error variances are confounded, residual variance is a mixture of distinct sources. First, the $S \times C$ correlation indicates the degree of correspondence between two variables across individual–situation-specific activation processes (see the ISSR principle, earlier). These activation processes are defined as the deviation of an individual from the 'average subject' condition-profile, centred around the subject's mean. The $S \times C$ correlation subsumes individual differences of considerable interest for clinical psychophysiology, because differential physiological reactivity to particular conditions may be clinically more relevant than the general level of over- or underactivation. If two variables are physiologically or physically closely related (near redundant, see above), or technically or algebraically dependent, these correlations necessarily will be high. Second, the error correlation is composed of covariance not accounted for by the previously described sources. The uncorrelated-error model of classical test theory assumes these correlations to vanish.

Within-Subjects Correlations (r_{WS})

These correlations are established from covariance complementing the between-subjects covariance, as shown in Equation (3.2). Thus, they give a summary account of the correspondence of two variables in the time domain, jointly for all subjects. They are based on the information inherent in all individual condition-profiles, stemming from the effects of experimental conditions, from individual–situation-specific reactivities, and from systemic or other relationships independent of conditions.

For an intercorrelation of physiological variables, r_{WS} should only be a first approach in establishing time domain correspondences. An investigation of r_{BC} and r_R would allow for more specific interpretations. However, for an intercorrelation of physiological variables with other time-domain data (e.g. self-report or behavioural data), r_{WS} should be chosen, because the more specific correlation coefficients usually would not have an interpretative advantage.

Within-Conditions Correlations (r_{WC})

These correlations are produced by covariance complementing the between-conditions covariance, as shown by Equation 3.3. They comprise all the available information on individual differences in activation processes. These are the coefficients of choice when studying, for example, the predictability of individual physiological differences both from other physiological variables and from data of other measurement domains.

Example

For illustrative purposes, an example with data from the laboratory–field generalizability study (Fahrenberg *et al.*, 1986) will be presented. Subjects ($N = 58$) were observed during ten experimental conditions (mental arithmetic, reaction time, speech, cold pressor, and various rest, relaxation, and anticipation periods). The analysis was performed with raw scores in order to completely describe the effects of covariance partitioning (response measures already exclude variance, see above). Table 3.2 (a) shows the correlations between heart rate and other physiological variables.

To evaluate the significance of the correlation coefficients, the conservative

Table 3.2
Illustrative example for covariance partitioning.

(a) *Correlations of Heart Rate with Selected Physiological Variables*

Physiological variable	Source of Covariation					
	Total	BS	WS	BC	WC	R
Stroke Volume Index	−0.13	−0.24	0.01	0.12	−0.21*	0.07
Heather Index	0.45*	0.35*	0.52*	0.81*	0.32*	0.40*
Pulse Volume Amplitude	−0.04	−0.09	0.03	−0.19	−0.04	0.07
Pulse Wave Velocity	0.64*	0.52*	0.83*	0.96*	0.53*	0.60*
Number of Eyeblinks	−0.11	−0.12	−0.10	−0.27	−0.09	−0.04
Skin Conductance Level	0.10	0.06	0.19	0.34	0.06	0.01
Number of Skin Conductance Reactions	0.37*	0.19	0.46*	0.86*	0.13	0.08
Respiratory Frequency	0.25*	0.22	0.29*	0.63*	0.13	−0.02
Horizontal Eye Movements	0.23*	0.19	0.27*	0.43	0.18	0.16
Systolic Blood Pressure	0.34*	0.13	0.46*	0.75*	0.12	−0.03
Diastolic Blood Pressure	0.28*	0.04	0.42*	0.62	0.02	0.01

(b) *Degrees of Freedom for Significance Tests*

Procedure	Source of Covariation					
	Total	BS	WS	BC	WC	R
Conventional ANOVA (repeated measures)	$NK-1$	$N-1$	$N(K-1)$	$K-1$	$K(N-1)$	$(N-1)(K-1)$
Conservative Greenhouse–Geisser	$2N-1$	$N-1$	N	1	$2(N-1)$	$N-1$

BS = between subjects, WS = within subjects, BC = between conditions, WC = within conditions, R = residual, N = no. of subjects, K = no. of variables. Data from Fahrenberg, Foerster, Schneider, Müller and Myrtek (1986), $N = 58$, $K = 10$. Significance tests according to conservative Greenhouse–Geisser degrees of freedom, except for BC, for which conventional ANOVA degrees of freedom were used.
* $P < 0.05$ (two-tailed).

estimate for degrees of freedom after Greenhouse and Geisser (Table 3.2 (b); cf. Kirk, 1982) was adopted except for the between-conditions correlations (with only one degree of freedom, these tests obviously would be too conservative).

Table 3.2 demonstrates that there are roughly four sets of variables each exhibiting a different correlation structure with heart rate. First, pulse wave velocity and Heather index (an estimate of left ventricular contractility derived from impedance cardiography) are significantly correlated with heart rate within all sources of covariance. Clearly, these three variables are systemically closely related. Second, pulse volume amplitude, number of eyeblinks, and skin conductance level are independent of heart rate under all aspects. Third, number of skin conductance reactions, respiratory frequency, systolic blood pressure, horizontal eye movements, and diastolic blood pressure have a significant overall time-domain relationship with heart rate. Except for the last two variables, this includes a similar shape of the condition-profiles. Fourth, the stroke volume index (again from impedance cardiography) is significantly negatively correlated with heart rate within conditions: both variables describe individual differences slightly similarly, differentiating between subjects with high heart rate and low stroke volume, and vice versa. These individual differences might reflect different states of 'cardiac fitness'. These substantial differences among variable sets would obviously not have been discerned without covariance partitioning.

MULTIVARIATE ANALYSIS OF VARIANCE

In this section we would like to point out briefly that a proper selection of methods and the interpretation of results might well profit from the considerations of the preceding section. We shall confine ourselves to a discussion of some MANOVA applications.

The basic idea of MANOVA is to find a linear combination of variables (called discriminant function, DF) for which the F ratio of hypothesis to error variance is maximal. Then a new DF is sought which is independent of the first and which again has a maximal F ratio, and so forth. Consider again the unifactorial repeated measurements design. The subjects main effect is constructed from the matrix product $S_{BS}S_R^{-1}$, the conditions main effect from $S_{BC}S_R^{-1}$. The DFs of the subjects main effect depict components of individual differences in average multivariate physiological activity; these are dimensions obviously related to the ISR postulate. The DFs of the conditions main effect depict components of situation-specific multivariate physiological activity; these are dimensions related to the SSR postulate.

Similar lines of reasoning may lead to the derivation of unconventional uses of MANOVA that might be more appropriate for the research question than conventional uses. Take, for example, a groups × conditions design, which is very common in clinical psychophysiology and in behavioural medicine. It is expected that group differences occur as a group main effect and as a groups × conditions (GR × C) interaction. The decomposition of the total sums of squares and cross-products matrix in this design reads

$$S_T = S_{GR} + S_{SWG} + S_{BC} + S_{GR \times C} + S_R, \tag{3.7}$$

where GR = groups and SWG = subjects within groups. While conventionally the group main effect and the GR × C interaction effect are tested separately (by $S_{GR}S_{SWG}^{-1}$ and $S_{GR \times C}S_R^{-1}$, respectively), their combined consideration by $(S_{GR} + S_{GR \times C})(S_{SWG} + S_R)^{-1}$ leads to DFs that include both group mean and group–situation-specific differences in physiological activation processes.

PROFILE ANALYSIS

In this section we will be concerned with variable-profiles (variables are the profile elements). It is assumed that variables are scaled in commensurable units of measurement, for example standard scores. The physiological variable-profile of a subject contains the complete information about the momentary state of measured activation. Mean variable-profiles for subjects (averaged over conditions) and for conditions (averaged over subjects) are the multivariate extensions of the respective univariate means. In the following, we shall introduce the notion of variance and covariance partitioning with respect to profile similarity. This might lead to an operationalization of two concepts that are of considerable and continued interest: intensity and pattern of activation (Cacioppo and Petty, 1983; Davidson, 1978; Duffy, 1972; Lacey, 1967; Schwartz, 1983).

Partitioning of Profile Similarity Covariance

Methods available for the analysis of profiles have been used only rarely in psychophysiology. Recently, discriminant analysis has been proposed to disentangle intensity and pattern aspects of activation processes 'Fridlund, Schwartz and Fowler, 1984). However, discriminant analysis *per se* does not automatically disentangle intensity and pattern effects (Stemmler 1988).

Cronbach and Gleser (1953) studied the squared Euclidian distance between profiles as a measure of profile dissimilarity and showed that it is composed of the profile parameters elevation, scatter, and shape. Thus, the total covariation among variable-profiles can be partitioned into these three sources. Usually, profile dissimilarity is analysed with respect to all three sources, or the last two, or shape alone. These distinctions are the basis for various analytical procedures: (1) identification of similar profiles (e.g. Q-factor analysis, Nunnally and Kotsch, 1983; linear typal analysis, Overall and Klett, 1972; modal profile analysis, Skinner, 1978), (2) standard tests for profile analysis (cf. Harris, 1975; Morrison, 1976; Timm, 1975), and (3) discrimination of group profiles (multistage discriminant analysis, Stemmler 1988).

Operationalization of Intensity and Pattern

The profile parameters elevation, scatter, and shape are obvious candidates for an operationalization of the concepts 'intensity' and 'pattern' of physiological activation processes. There will probably be no serious debate that 'intensity' be operationalized with profile elevation and 'pattern' with profile shape. Profile Scatter is more difficult to allocate to one of these concepts. Together with profile shape, it can be conceived of as a measure of 'pattern', because it is sensitive to the 'distinctiveness' of a profile. However, together with profile elevation, it can be conceived of as a measure of 'intensity', because it reflects 'amplification' (e.g. when comparing profiles of the same shape but different scatters).

Stemmler (1988) has discussed the effects of profile elevation, scatter, and shape on the geometrical representation of profiles in variable and in discriminant space. Given these developments, basic dimensions of activation patterns can be identified and interpreted separately from the intensity dimension. This might provide a useful frame of reference for the study of physiological activation processes.

LOOKING BACK

If we look back over the pages of this chapter, it may appear that psychophysiological assessment involves too many and, in part, too sophisticated issues for a researcher to be concerned with. Issues have ranged from research strategies, tactics, and designs, over psychometrics and statistics to experimental and data-processing considerations (not necessarily in that order), all coordinated by the substantive research question. This is a long list of topics and each is backed with a large literature. This is not meant to discourage the reader as yet unfamiliar with psychophysiological assessment. Our intention, instead, was to show that these topics are 'semantically' closely related even if quite apart in their specific 'syntax'.

If we look back over the contributions to psychophysiological assessment in the last 20 years, we see some encouraging lines of development. One of them is the increasing body of empirical work that substantiates specific procedures of psychophysiological assessment. Another is the growing awareness of and experience with developments from outside our discipline – philosophy of science, physiology, psychometrics, and statistics. A third is the steps in the direction of a multicomponent theory of activation. These developments should help to clear the path for further theoretical and empirically based progress in psychophysiological assessment.

REFERENCES

Anderson, A. B., Basilevsky, A., and Hum, D. J. (1983). Missing data: a review of the literature. In: P. H. Rossi, J. D. Wright and A. B. Anderson (Eds) *Handbook of Survey Research*, pp. 415–493. Orlando: Academic Press.

Andresen, B. (1987). *Differentielle Psychophysiologie valenzkonträrer Aktivierungsdimensionen.* Frankfurt: Lang.

Arena, J. G., Blanchard, E. B., Andrasik, F., Cotch, P. A., and Myers, P. E. (1983). Reliability of psychophysiological assessment. *Behaviour Research and Therapy* **21**, 447–460.

Averill, J. R., and Opton, E. M. (1968). Psychophysiological assessment: rationale and problems. In: P. McReynolds (Ed.) *Advances in Psychological Assessment*, pp. 265–288. Palo Alto: Science and Behavior Books.

Ben-Shakhar, G. (1985). Standardization within individuals: a simple method to neutralize individual differences in skin conductance. *Psychophysiology* **22**, 292–299.

Bock, R. D. (1976). Basic issues in the measurement of change. In: D. N. M. DeGruijter and L. J. T. van der Kamp (Eds) *Advances in Psychological and Educational Measurement*, pp. 76–96. New York: Wiley.

Cacioppo, J. T., and Petty, R. E. (1983). Foundations of social psychophysiology. In: J. T. Cacioppo and R. E. Petty (Eds) *Social Psychophysiology*, pp. 3–36. New York: Guilford.

Campbell, D. T., and Stanley, J. C. (1963). Experimental and quasi-experimental designs for research on teaching. In: N. L. Gage (Ed.) *Handbook of Research on Teaching*, pp. 171–246. Chicago: Rand McNally.

Campbell, M. E. (1981). Statistical procedures with the Law of Initial Values. *Journal of Psychology* **108**, 85–101.

Cheung, M. N. (1981). Detection of and recovery from errors in cardiac interbeat intervals. *Psychophysiology* **18**, 341–346.

Clark, L. A., Denby, L., Pregibon, D., Harshfield, G. A., Pickering, T. G., Blank, S., and Laragh, J. H. (1987). A data-based method for bivariate outlier detection: application to automatic blood pressure recording devices. *Psychophysiology* **24**, 119–125.

Cleary, P. J. (1974). Description of individual differences in autonomic reactions. *Psychological Bulletin* **81**, 934–944.

Cleary, P. J. (1986). L.I.V. R.I.P.? Comments on Myrtek and Foerster's 'The Law of Initial Value: a rare exception'. *Biological Psychology* **22**, 279–284.

Corder-Bolz, C. R. (1978). The evaluation of change: new evidence. *Educational and Psychological Measurement* **38**, 959–976.

Cronbach, L. J., and Furby, L. (1970). How we should measure 'change': or should we? *Psychological Bulletin* **74**, 68–80.

Cronbach, L. J., and Gleser, G. C. (1953). Assessing similarity between profiles. *Psychological Bulletin* **50**, 456–473.

Cronbach, L. J., Gleser, G. C., Nanda, H., and Rajaratnam, N. (1972). *The Dependability of Behavioral Measurements: Theory of Generalizability for Scores and Profiles*. New York: Wiley.

Davidson, R. J. (1978). Specificity and patterning in biobehavioral systems. *American Psychologist* **33**, 430–436.

Dimsdale, J. E. (1984). Generalizing from laboratory studies to field studies of human stress physiology. *Psychosomatic Medicine* **46**, 463–469.

Duffy, E. (1972). Activation. In: N. S. Greenfield and R. A. Sternbach (Eds) *Handbook of Psychophysiology*, pp. 577–622. New York: Holt, Rinehart and Winston.

Efron, B., and Gong, G. (1983). A leisurely look at the bootstrap, the jackknife and cross-validation. *American Statistician* **37**, 36–48.

Epstein, L. H., and Webster, J. S. (1975). Reliability of various estimates of electromyogram activity: within and between subject analyses. *Psychophysiology* **12**, 468–470.

Erdmann, G., Janke, W., Kallus, W., Nutz, B., and Schlömer, P. (1984). Untersuchungen zur Modifikation der psychophysiologischen Reaktionen in einer Belastungssituation durch Erfahrung. *Archiv für Psychologie* **136**, 301–315.

Fahrenberg, J. (1983). Psychophysiologische Methodik. In: K.-J. Groffmann and L. Michel (Eds) *Enzyklopädie der Psychologie, Verhaltensdiagnostik, Psychologische Diagnostik*, Vol. 4, pp. 1–192. Göttingen: Hogrefe.

Fahrenberg, J. (1986). Psychophysiological individuality: a pattern analytic approach to personality research and psychosomatic medicine. *Advances in Behaviour Research and Therapy* **8**, 43–100.

Fahrenberg, J. (1988). Psychophysiological processes. In: J. R. Nesselroade and R. B. Cattell (Eds) *Handbook of Multivariate Experimental Psychology*, 2nd edn. New York: Plenum.

Fahrenberg, J., and Foerster, F. (1982). Covariation and consistency of activation parameters. *Biological Psychology* **15**, 151–169.

Fahrenberg, J., Foerster, F., Schneider, H. J., Müller, W., and Myrtek, M. (1984). *Aktivierungsforschung im Labor–Feld-Vergleich.* München: Minerva.

Fahrenberg, J., Foerster, F., Schneider, H. J., Müller, W., and Myrtek, M. (1986). Predictability of individual differences in activation processes in a field setting based on laboratory measures. *Psychophysiology* **23**, 323–333.

Fahrenberg, J., Schneider, H. J., and Safian, P. (1987). Psychophysiological assessments in a repeated-measurement design extending over a one-year interval: trends and stability. *Biological Psychology* **24**, 49–66.

Fahrenberg, J., Walschburger, P., Foerster, F., Myrtek, M., and Müller, W. (1979). *Psychophysiologische Aktivierungsforschung.* München: Minerva.

Foerster, F. (1985). Psychophysiological response specificities: a replication over a 12-month period. *Biological Psychology* **21**, 169–182.

Foerster, F., Schneider, H. J., and Walschburger, P. (1983a). *Psychophysiologische Reaktionsmuster.* München: Minerva.

Foerster, F., Schneider, H. J., and Walschburger, P. (1983b). The differentiation of individual-specific, stimulus-specific, and motivation-specific response patterns in activation processes: an inquiry investigating their stability and possible importance in psychophysiology. *Biological Psychology* **17**, 1–26.

Fowles, D. C., Christie, M. J., Edelberg, R., Grings, W. W., Lykken, D. T., and Venables, P. H. (1981). Publication recommendations for electrodermal measurements. *Psychophysiology* **18**, 232–239.

Freixa i Baqué, E. (1982). Reliability of electrodermal measures: a compilation. *Biological Psychology* **14**, 219–229.

Fridlund, A. J., and Cacioppo, J. T. (1986). Guidelines for human electromyographic research. *Psychophysiology* **23**, 567–589.

Fridlund, A. J., Schwartz, G. E., and Fowler, S. C. (1984). Pattern recognition of self-reported emotional state from multiple-site facial EMG activity during affective imagery. *Psychophysiology* **21**, 622–637.

Gale, A., and Baker, S. (1981). *In vivo* or *in vitro?* Some effects of laboratory environments, with particular reference to the psychophysiology experiment. In: M. J. Christie and P. Mellett (Eds) *Foundations of Psychosomatics*, pp. 363–384. Chichester: Wiley.

Gale, A., and Edwards, J. A. (1983). A short critique of the psychophysiology of individual differences. *Personality and Individual Differences* **4**, 429–435.

Gasser, T., Bächer, P., and Steinberg, H. (1985). Test–retest reliability of spectral parameters of the EEG. *Electroencephalography and Clinical Neurophysiology* **60**, 312–319.

Gasser, T., Sroka, L., and Möck, J. (1986). The correction of EOG artifacts by frequency dependent and frequency independent methods. *Psychophysiology* **23**, 704–712.

Gevins, A. S., Yeager, C. L., Zeitlin, G. M., Ancoli, S., and Dedon, M. F. (1977). On-line computer rejection of EEG artifact. *Electroencephalography and Clinical Neurophysiology* **42**, 267–274.

Goldstein, H. (1979). *The Design and Analysis of Longitudinal Studies.* London: Academic Press.

Gollob, H. F. (1968a). Confounding of sources of variation in factor-analytic techniques. *Psychological Bulletin* **70**, 330–344.

Gollob, H. F. (1968b). Rejoinder to Tucker's 'Comments on confounding of sources of variation in factor-analytic techniques'. *Psychological Bulletin* **70**, 355–360.

Gottman, J. M. (1981). *Time-Series Analysis*. Cambridge: Cambridge University Press.

Grice, G. R. (1966). Dependence of empirical laws upon the source of experimental variation. *Psychological Bulletin* **66**, 488–498.

Harris, R. J. (1985). *A Primer of Multivariate Statistics*, 2nd edn. New York: Academic Press.

Heath, H. A., and Oken, D. (1965). The quantification of 'Response' to experimental stimuli. *Psychosomatic Medicine* **27**, 457–471.

Huitema, B. E. (1980). *The Analysis of Covariance and Alternatives*. New York: Wiley.

Iacono, W. G., and Lykken, D. T. (1981). Two-year retest stability of eye tracking performance and a comparison of electro-oculographic and infrared recording techniques: evidence of EEG in the electro-oculogram. *Psychophysiology* **18**, 49–55.

Jennings, J. R., Berg, W. K., Hutcheson, J. S., Obrist, P., Porges, S., and Turpin, G. (1981). Publication guidelines for heart rate studies in men. *Psychophysiology* **18**, 226–231.

Kendall, M. G., and Stuart, A. (1967). *The Advanced Theory of Statistics*, Vol. 2, 2nd edn. London: Griffin.

Kirk, R. E. (1982). *Experimental Design: Procedures for the Behavioral Sciences*, 2nd edn. Belmont, NY: Brooks/Cole.

Lacey, J. I. (1956). The evaluation of autonomic responses: toward a general solution. *Annals of the New York Academy of Sciences* **67**, 123–164.

Lacey, J. I. (1962). Psychophysiological approaches to the evaluation of psychotherapeutic process and outcome. In: E. A. Rubinstein and M. B. Parloff (Eds) *Research in Psychotherapy*, pp. 161–208. Washington: American Psychological Association.

Lacey, J. I. (1967). Somatic response patterning and stress: some revisions of activation theory. In: M. H. Appley and R. Trumbull (Eds) *Psychological Stress*, pp. 14–37. New York: Appleton-Century-Crofts.

Lacey, J. I., and Lacey, B. C. (1962). The Law of Initial Value in the longitudinal study of autonomic constitution: reproducibility of autonomic responses and response-patterns over a four-year interval. *Annals of the New York Academy of Sciences* **98**, 1257–1290.

Lader, M. (1975). Psychophysiological parameters and methods. In: L. Levi (Ed.) *Emotions – Their Parameters and Measurement*, pp. 341–367. New York: Raven.

Levey, A. B. (1980). Measurement units in psychophysiology. In: I. Martin and P. H. Venables (Eds) *Techniques in Psychophysiology*, pp. 597–628. New York: Wiley.

Lichstein, K. L., Sallis, J. F., Hill, D., and Young, M. C. (1981). Psychophysiological adaptation: an investigation of multiple parameters. *Journal of Behavioral Assessment* **3**, 111–121.

Lidberg, L., and Wallin, B. G. (1981). Sympathetic skin nerve discharges in relation to amplitude of skin resistance responses. *Psychophysiology* **18**, 268–270.

Lykken, D. T. (1968). Neuropsychology and psychophysiology in personality research. In: E. F. Borgatta and W. W. Lambert (Eds) *Handbook of Personality Theory and Research*, pp. 413–509. Chicago: Rand McNally.

Manuck, S. B., and Garland, F. N. (1980). Stability in individual differences in cardiovascular reactivity: a thirteen-month follow-up. *Physiology and Behavior* **21**, 621–624.

Manuck, S. B., Krantz, D., and Polefrone, J. (1985). Task influences on behaviourally-elicited cardiovascular reactions. In: A. Steptoe, H. Rüddel, and H. Neus (Eds)

Clinical and Methodological Issues in Cardiovascular Psychophysiology, pp. 16–29. Berlin: Springer.

McHugo, G. J., and Lanzetta, J. T. (1983). Methodological decisions in social psychophysiology. In: J. T. Cacioppo and R. E. Petty (Eds) *Social Psychophysiology*, pp. 630–665. New York: Guilford.

Messick, S. (1981). Denoting the base-free measure of change. *Psychometrika* **46**, 215–217.

Morrison, D. F. (1976). *Multivariate Statistical Methods*, 2nd edn. New York: McGraw-Hill.

Myrtek, M. (1984). *Constitutional Psychophysiology*. New York: Academic Press.

Myrtek, M. (1985). Adaptation effects and the stability of physiological responses to repeated testing. In: A. Steptoe, H. Rüddel and H. Neus (Eds) *Clinical and Methodological Issues in Cardiovascular Psychophysiology*, pp. 93–106. Berlin: Springer.

Myrtek, M., and Foerster, F. (1986a). The Law of Initial Value: a rare exception. *Biological Psychology* **22**, 227–237.

Myrtek, M., and Foerster, F. (1986b). Rejoinder to Cleary's 'Comments on Myrtek and Foerster's "The Law of Initial Value: a rare exception" '. *Biological Psychology* **22**, 285–287.

Nesselroade, J. R., Stigler, S. M., and Baltes, P. B. (1980). Regression towards the mean and the study of change. *Psychological Bulletin* **88**, 622–637.

Neus, H., and von Eiff, A. W. (1985). Selected topics in the methodology of stress testing: time course, gender and adaptation. In: A. Steptoe, H. Rüddel, and H. Neus (Eds) *Clinical and Methodological Issues in Cardiovascular Psychophysiology*, pp. 78–92. Berlin: Springer.

Nunnally, J., and Kotsch, W. E. (1983). A reciprocity principle that permits profile-factoring with very large numbers of people. *Educational and Psychological Measurement* **43**, 693–703.

Obrist, P. A. (1976). The cardiovascular–behavioral interaction – as it appears today. *Psychophysiology* **13**, 96–107.

Obrist, P. A. (1985). Beta-adrenergic hyperresponsivity to behavioural challenges: a possible hypertensive risk factor. In: J. F. Orlebeke, G. Mulder and L. J. P. van Doornen (Eds) *Psychophysiology of Cardiovascular Control*, pp. 667–682. New York: Plenum.

Overall, J. E., and Klett, C. J. (1972). *Applied Multivariate Analysis*. New York: McGraw-Hill.

Overall, J. E., and Woodward, J. A. (1975). Unreliability of difference scores: a paradox for measurement of change. *Psychological Bulletin* **82**, 85–86.

Plewis, I. (1985). *Analysing Change*. New York: Wiley.

Porges, S. W., Ackles, P. A., and Truax, S. R. (1983). Psychophysiological measurement: methodological constraints. In: A. Gale and J. A. Edwards (Eds) *Physiological Correlates of Human Behaviour*, Vol. I: *Basic Issues*, pp. 219–240. London: Academic Press.

Ray, R. L., and Kimmel, H. D. (1979). Utilization of psychophysiological indices in behavioral assessment: some methodological issues. *Journal of Behavioral Assessment* **1**, 107–122.

Ray, W. J., Cole, H. W., and Raczynski, J. M. (1983). Psychophysiological assessment. In: M. Hersen, A. E. Kazdin, and A. S. Bellack (Eds) *The Clinical Psychology Handbook*, pp. 427–453. New York: Pergamon.

Robinson, J. W., Whitsett, S. F., and Kaplan, B. J. (1987). The stability of physiological reactivity over multiple sessions. *Biological Psychology* **24**, 129–139.

Rösler, F. (1983). Physiologisch orientierte Forschungsstrategien in der Differentiellen und Diagnostischen Psychologie. I. Zur Konzeption des psychophysiologischen

Untersuchungsansatzes. *Zeitschrift für Differentielle und Diagnostische Psychologie* **4**, 283–299.

Rösler, F. (1984). Physiologisch orientierte Forschungsstrategien in der Differentiellen und Diagnostischen Psychologie: II. Zur Systematisierung psychophysiologischer Untersuchungen. *Zeitschrift für Differentielle und Diagnostische Psychologie* **5**, 7–36.

Rogosa, D. R., Brandt, D., and Zimowski, M. (1982). A growth curve approach to the measurement of change. *Psychological Bulletin* **92**, 726–748.

Rogosa, D. R., and Willett, J. B. (1985). Understanding correlates of change by modeling individual differences in growth. *Psychometrika* **50**, 203–228.

Scher, H., Furedy, J. J., and Heslegrave, R. J. (1985). Individual differences in phasic cardiac reactivity to psychological stress and the Law of Initial Value. *Psychophysiology* **22**, 345–348.

Schwartz, G. E. (1983). Social psychophysiology and behavioral medicine: a systems perspective. In: J. T. Cacioppo and R. E. Petty (Eds) *Social Psychophysiology*, pp. 592–608. New York: Guilford.

Seraganian, P., Hanley, J. A., Hollander, B. J., Roskies, E., Smilga, C., Martin, N. D., Collu, R., and Oseasohn, R. (1985). Exaggerated psychophysiological reactivity: issues in quantification and reliability. *Journal of Psychosomatic Research* **29**, 393–405.

Skinner, H. A. (1978). Differentiating the contribution of elevation, scatter and shape in profile similarity. *Educational and Psychological Measurement* **38**, 297–308.

Stefan, H., and Burr, W. (Eds) (1982). *Mobile Long-Term EEG Monitoring*. Proceedings of the MLE Symposium, Bonn, May 1982. Stuttgart: Fischer.

Stemmler, G. (1984). *Psychophysiologische Emotionsmuster*. Frankfurt: Lang.

Stemmler, G. (1987a). Implicit measurement models in methods for scoring physiological reactivity. *Journal of Psychophysiology* **1**, 113–125.

Stemmler, G. (1987b). Standardization within subjects: a critique of Ben-Shakhar's conclusions. *Psychophysiology* **24**, 243–246.

Stemmler, G. (1988). Effects of profile elevation, scatter, and shape on discriminant analysis results. *Educational and Psychological Measurement*.

Sternbach, R. A., Alexander, A. A., Rice, D. G., and Greenfield, N. S. (1969). Technical note: some views on the treatment of 'artifacts' in psychophysiological recordings. *Psychophysiology* **6**, 1–5.

Stott, F. D., Raftery, E. B., Clement, D. L., and Wright, S. L. (Eds) (1982). *ISAM-GENT-1981*. London: Academic Press.

Thayer, J. F., Tanaka, J. S., and Cohen, B. H. (1984). Removal of basal differences from patterned psychophysiological data. *Psychophysiology* **21**, 601.

Timm, N. H. (1985). *Multivariate Analysis*. Monterey, Cal.: Brooks/Cole.

Tukey, J. W. (1977). *Exploratory Data Analysis*. Reading, Mass.: Addison-Wesley.

Van Egeren, L. F. (1974). Multivariate statistical analysis. *Psychophysiology* **10**, 517–534.

Vasey, M. W., and Thayer, J. F. (1987). The continuing problem of false positives in repeated measures ANOVA in psychophysiology: a multivariate solution. *Psychophysiology* **24**, 479–486.

Wainer, H. (1982). Robust statistics: a survey and some perspectives. In: G. Keren (Ed.) *Statistical and Methodological Issues in Psychology and Social Sciences Research*. Hillsdale, NJ: Erlbaum.

Weber, M. A., and Drayer, J. I. M. (1984). *Ambulatory Blood Pressure Monitoring*. New York: Springer.

Weisberg, H. I. (1979). Statistical adjustments and uncontrolled studies. *Psychological Bulletin* **86**, 1149–1164.

Wenger, M. A., and Cullen, T. D. (1972). Studies of autonomic balance in children and adults. In: N. S. Greenfield and R. A. Sternbach (Eds) *Handbook of Psychophysiology*, pp. 535–576. New York: Holt, Rinehart and Winston.

Weyer, G., and Blythe, S. T. (1983). Zur Behandlung des Ausgangswertproblems durch die Datentransformation mit orthogonalen Polynomen. *Zeitschrift für Experimentelle und Angewandte Psychologie* **30**, 500–521.

Wieland, B. A., and Mefferd, R. B. (1970). Systematic changes in levels of physiological activity during a four-month period. *Psychophysiology* **6**, 669–689.

Wiggins, J. S. (1973). *Personality and Prediction: Principles of Personality Assessment*. Reading, Mass.: Addison-Wesley.

Wilder, J. (1931). Das 'Ausgangswert-Gesetz', ein unbeachtetes biologisches Gesetz und seine Bedeutung für Forschung und Praxis. *Zeitschrift für Neurologie* **137**, 317–338.

Wilder, J. (1967). *Stimulus and Response: The Law of Initial Value*. Bristol: Wright.

Wittmann, W. W. (1988). Multivariate reliability theory: principles of symmetry and successful validation strategies. In: R. B. Cattell and J. R. Nesselroade (Eds) *Handbook of Multivariate Experimental Psychology*, 2nd edn. New York: Plenum.

Zimmerman, D. W., and Williams, R. H. (1982). The relative error magnitude in three measures of change. *Psychometrika* **47**, 141–147.

Chapter 4

Imagery, Memory, and Emotion: a Psychophysiological Analysis of Clinical Anxiety

Bruce N. Cuthbert and Peter J. Lang

Department of Clinical and Health Psychology and
Center for Research in Psychophysiology,
University of Florida,
Box J-165 JHMHC,
Gainesville, FL 32610, USA

ABSTRACT

Anxiety disorders are considered from an information-processing perspective. In this view, emotions are held to be action dispositions. Their memorial representations are associative networks in the brain, which include information about the affective stimulus context, response pattern, and their semantic meaning. Psychophysiological analysis provides a real-time index to the processing of these networks. Research based on this approach has contributed significantly to the evaluation and treatment of anxiety disorders, and is offered as a model for the general study of affect in psychopathology.

Handbook of Clinical Psychophysiology Edited by G. Turpin
© 1989 John Wiley & Sons Ltd

INTRODUCTION

It is the thesis of this chapter that psychophysiological methods are essential to the study of cognitive processes and emotional reactivity, and thus, are integral to any analysis of psychopathology. In this paper, a theoretical rationale for this viewpoint is presented, and distinguished from other current views of emotion and psychopathology. A variety of illustrative experiments are discussed, drawn largely from a programme of research on the anxiety disorders; however, the concepts involved are seen as general to all areas of psychopathology. It is suggested that employment of such techniques does not have to await 'further research', but can be usefully implemented now for a variety of clinical problems. In brief, this chapter is intended as an illustration, with examples, of the potential of psychophysiology for expanding our knowledge and guiding treatment of emotional disorders.

PHENOMENA AND PHENOMENOLOGY

The Experience of Emotion

The approach to psychopathology presented here is based upon a view of affective processes somewhat different in its orientation from many traditional theories of emotion. Accordingly, some introduction is in order to provide a background for subsequent discussion. Much research and theorizing in the psychopathology literature are deeply rooted in assumptions about the nature and causes of emotion. Centuries of Western culture have bequeathed to us the view that human behaviour and thought are based upon the phenomenological experience of the sentient human. The primacy of one's own thought processes was seen as an irreducible axiom, defining to a large extent the uniqueness of man. We have referred elsewhere to this position as the 'homunculoid' view of human experience (Lang, 1984): i.e. one must posit some internal intelligence which is actually running the brain machinery itself, and which can be interrogated for information regarding the state of the system. In this view, emotions are simply a subset of phenomenological states, those that involve 'feelings' and 'moods' and are marked by the intensity of the internal experience: '. . . emotion is a fact upon which all introspection agrees. Anxiety, depression, elation, indifference, anger, fear, pleasurable anticipation and dread, for example, are undeniable because they are states which we have experienced personally' (Gellhorn and Loofbourrow, 1963, p. 41). In this approach the initial step in studying emotion is the simple compilation of distinct experiential states; many authors over several hundred years have attempted this task, but with considerable disagreement beyond three or four major emotions (e.g. see Panksepp, 1982).

The historical dominance of this view may be inferred by noting the immeasurable impact of Freud's realization that the system does not, in fact, always work that way: feeling and behaviour seem to occur in some circumstances, particularly those marked by affective intensity, even though the individual is unable to relate the underlying thoughts involved. Freud was able to synthesize these observations into his theory of personality, but only at the cost of adding yet another homunculus to the system (Skinner, 1953). That is, in addition to the public operator directing the mind operations normally available, there had to be a second, private operator generally hidden from the first, but who could gain access to the same final output systems. (See Lang, 1984, for a detailed discussion of the ramifications of this conception.)

In contrast, the view to be presented here, elaborated at greater length elsewhere (e.g. Lang, 1984, 1985), holds that an acceptable scientific definition of affect must replace phenomenological primacy, and include instead only those responses which are accessible for measurement by the scientific community. This is not to deny the place of subjective experience, but only to point out the distinct standards attendant upon the scientific enterprise. Neither does it say that systematic accounting cannot be made of subjective reports; however, for reasons discussed below, a reliance upon such reports as the primary criteria of emotion, or as alone reflecting its basic organization, is not likely to be successful.

Three Response Systems

A model of affect has been developed in the light of these concerns, which has proved fruitful in the experimental study and treatment of phobias (e.g. Cook, Melamed, Cuthbert, McNeil and Lang, 1988; Lang, 1985). The theory as currently elaborated has evolved in the context of the 'three-systems' model of emotion (Lang, 1968, 1978). Briefly, the latter is based upon the presumption that proper assessment of emotions must encompass activity which can appear in any of three measurement systems. These systems include (1) overt behavioural acts, such as escape, avoidance, etc.; (2) physiological activity in visceral and skeletomuscular systems; and (3) verbal report of affect, which can include specific emotions such as fear or anger, and also reports along dimensions such as pleasure or arousal. Such verbalizations are construed simply as one of the three measurement systems, and not as an insight into the 'real' emotion or as a unique window into the 'cognitive' processing of emotion (see Kozak and Miller, 1982, and Lang, 1978, for a detailed discussion of this point).

This construct has served well as an organizing principle and stimulus to research. Experience in our laboratory and others has shown that these are loosely coupled systems, which often are not concordant within a subject for many situations. Exploration of observed differences has yielded fruitful and systematic results. For example, in exposure therapies for fears and phobias, the behavioural component typically changes before the subject or patient reports any decrement of experienced fear in the situation (Rachman, 1978); knowledge of this fact helps in treating patients with anxiety disorders. As another example, it has been found that the ability to generate palpable physiological arousal during the visualization of fear-arousing images is positively correlated with successful therapy outcome (Lang, Melamed and Hart, 1970; Levin, Cook and Lang, 1982).

THE BIO-INFORMATIONAL APPROACH TO EMOTION

A working model, sometimes referred to as 'bio-informational theory' (Lang, 1977, 1979), has grown out of attempts to order findings arising from studies of emotional imagery and other related paradigms. In brief, we conceptualize emotion to be an *action set* – an active disposition to respond to a stimulus or situation. The latter typically involve contexts of marked personal and/ or phylogenetic significance, e.g. fighting, eating, reproduction; in turn, the behaviour occurring in such situations is frequently marked by its intensity. Note that this definition, in contrast to experientially-oriented theories, places an inherent emphasis upon *response* in emotional situations, and upon the *functional* nature of emotions. The reliance upon psychophysiological recording follows naturally from this view.

This action set is comprised of an information structure stored in the brain, and may be conceived as analogous to a computer program which directs the machinery of behaviour. The declarative information for the program is considered to be organized into associative networks, similar to those first proposed by Quillian (1966) for semantic analyses and later extended by other workers for different types of information (e.g. Anderson and Bower, 1974). The probability of accessing this network, and thus a specific emotional disposition, is a function of the extent to which inputs of various types match information in the network. When a sufficient number of the units in the network are activated, the entire network is brought into play, and run off, with both somatic and visceral consequences. Certain elements may be particularly high in associative strength, so that activation of only a few key concepts in the network may be sufficient to access the entire program. For example, a wriggling movement is frequently the only cue necessary to elicit a strong response in a snake phobic.

IMAGERY AND AFFECT

The original statements of bio-informational theory were developed in the early and middle 1970s, and were influenced by Pylyshyn's (1973) discussion of the nature of mental imagery. Accordingly, the information represented in memory was discussed in terms of a propositional structure (e.g. Lang, 1977). Propositions are elemental statements expressing the relationship between units of information. For instance, the phrase 'boy hits ball' might be regarded as a proposition in which 'boy' and 'ball' are connected by the predicate 'hit'. Such propositions were not necessarily seen as identical with linguistic systems but rather were held to be coded into the language of the brain, which is presumed to underlie any given native tongue (Chomsky, 1980; Pylyshyn, 1973).

The theoretical model, as originally posited, presumed two broad categories of information to be represented in memory for emotional images (Lang, 1977). Stimulus information describes the objective properties of a stimulus and/or situation. This category comprises the elements typically conceived in discussions of mental imagery. Response information refers to the entire spectrum of efferent activity, somatic and visceral, which might occur on a given occasion, and will be discussed further below. A third category was subsequently added to account for verbal information which may not be objectively present, but which is associatively connected, and elaborates upon the significance of the stimulus and response information (Lang, 1984); such a 'meaning' unit, for example, might involve the knowledge that a healthy-looking individual in fact has an incurable disease.

The theory emphasizes the representation in emotion networks of response information, which is seen as being doubly coded in memory. In the first instance, response information may be organized semantically as a part of the overall verbal description of an emotional situation. In this sense, response elements are coded like any other components of the network. In the second place, however, activation and processing of the response elements' deep structure (the behavioural program) result in palpable outflow to relevant somato-visceral structures. This effect, which has been referred to as 'efferent leakage' (Lang, 1984), occurs even when overt acts are inhibited (as in imagery), and can be measured by appropriate psychophysiological recording techniques. This has been demonstrated in a variety of emotional and non-affective situations. For example, in a classic study, Shaw (1940) had subjects lift a variety of weights, and after each trial asked them to imagine lifting the previous weight. The amplitude of the electromyogram (EMG) response during imagery varied linearly with the mass of the weight just lifted; furthermore, amplitudes were larger for trials where images were reported as vivid. A number of other studies, employing a wide range of paradigms, have found results supporting this position (recently reviewed by Cuthbert, Vrana and Bradley, in press). In summary, a central tenet of the theory holds that information about postural and somatic adjustments is part of the memory coding which takes place at the time of an experience, and the same information is recalled and processed along with the other elements of the memory structure when the experience is regenerated.

Since the initial presentations of this theory, many arguments have arisen regarding the ways in which mental images are represented in memory. On the one side have been the propositionalists such as Pylyshyn, advocating the view that our experience of an image is an epiphenomenon resulting from the processing of an information network (e.g. Pylyshyn, 1973, 1980). On the other hand, a number of investigators have developed theory and data suggesting that images are strongly linked to visual perception, and are stored as pictures in the mind's eye (e.g. Kosslyn, Pinker, Smith and Shwartz, 1979; Shepard and Cooper, 1982). The outcome of this debate is as yet unclear; at least one theorist regards the controversy as potentially unresolvable, due to the impossibility of differentiating at a sufficiently molecular level between the opposing points of view (Anderson, 1979). While such issues appear potentially relevant to the current discussion at first glance, the chief emphasis of bio-informational theory actually lies somewhat orthogonal to this controversy. As stated above, in contrast to most views of imagery, which conceive of imagery as a quasi-perceptual process, the current theory regards imagery – and, by extension, emotion – as primarily about responding. While this position has received substantial empirical support, it is also based upon theoretical considerations.

THE BIOLOGICAL COMPUTER

The metaphor of cognitive operations as similar to that of a digital computer has dominated modern cognitive psychology and research in artificial intelligence. There is no question that this approach has been heuristic and enormously productive in generating research and theory. However, the computer analogy is not perfect. For example, there is now increasing evidence that the brain operates with multiple processes in parallel (e.g. McClelland and Rumelhart, 1986), as opposed to the single-step operation of the traditional von Neumann architecture; fifth-generation computing machines making effective use of parallel processing are still in the very early stages of development. However, perhaps an even more enduring distinction regards the relative strong points of brain versus computer. The computer was specifically developed for the purpose of internal information transfers, and is unmatched at the tasks of extremely rapidly and accurately retrieving and processing information stored in memory. On the other hand, the most powerful super-computer struggles mightily with tasks that are simple for a toddler – those requiring immediate and effective response to and interaction with the environment.

It is somewhat curious that people often remark upon the deficiencies of the human brain compared to computers for high-speed processing, but yet take relatively for granted the superb adaptive response capabilities of the nervous system. The latter reflects the fact that, in an evolutionary sense, the function of our 'biological computer' is precisely the ability to enable the organism to respond appropriately to changes in the environment. In this sense, the 'information processing' of the human brain may be seen as that which has evolved to produce appropriate patterns of response to given circumstances. In other words, the brain's information processing is not primarily configured to contemplate or compute, but rather to organize responding (Sperry, 1952). Thus, it seems most appropriate, if we are to study information processing in humans, to study responses – not simply the reaction-time measures of so many cognitive paradigms, which are often employed to make inferences about internal computations – but rather the various patterns of efferent activity which people emit. This seems particularly true for the clinical domain, where we are primarily concerned with responses and situations defined as 'emotional'. Emotional reactions, by definition, are those that involve marked responses in a variety of measurement systems.

Thus, this orientation towards response information is seen as much more central for the present purposes than the actual nature of the representation (i.e. the propositional/non-propositional debate), or even its structural organization (a network of nodes and links or of 'connectionist' vectors). In the present view, the emphasis is not so much on how the information is stored, but on what kind of information – specifically, that information about responding is represented in memory and comprises an important part of the total network of associations, particularly for emotional material.

FIRMWARE: THE NEUROPHYSIOLOGICAL CONNECTION

As can be seen, the current approach emphasizes the brain's software. It should be noted, however, that this model is by no means incompatible with neurophysiological conceptions of how efferent information is stored and transmitted. For example, in a now classic paper on imagery, Hebb (1968) proposed that imagery could be construed in terms of the activity of cell assemblies at various levels of the cortex. As in scanning some original object (e.g. a squirrel), visual images were considered as dependent upon the activity of eye movements driven by simple cell assemblies in the visual system: '. . . the motor process may have an organizing function in the percept itself and in imagery . . . the motor accompaniments of imagery are not adventitious but essential' (p. 470). More complex images are dependent upon higher order cell assemblies, which abstract information and operate at successively more conceptual levels, up to the point of being completely 'non-representational'. Cell assemblies, particularly at the higher levels, are seen as dynamic and fluid in nature; any given neurone can participate in multiple organizations, thus permitting a very large number of possible images.

In an elegant updating and elaboration of this hypothesis, Freeman and associates (Freeman, 1983; Freeman and Schneider, 1982) employed arrays of electrodes to study electroencephalogram (EEG) patterns in the olfactory bulb of rabbits during conditioning, with various scents as unconditional stimuli. Although the results were complex, the main finding concerning the present context was that the conditioned response (CS) appeared as a topographical pattern across the surface of the entire bulb, rather than as a single localized event. This response reflected the learning that had occurred during conditioning, as the patterns were not apparent at the first presentation of an odour stimulus; rather, they were manifested after conditioning when the rabbit was in the experimental chamber and 'expecting' further trials. Changes in the odour CS led to the appearance of new EEG patterns over trials. Freeman (1983) interpreted these results as a neurophysiological demonstration of mental images, as the EEG responses after conditioning occurred in the absence of any actual stimulus. Furthermore, the efferent role of the EEG response was emphasized, as 'it shapes the output of the bulb ... By extrapolating the interactive properties of the bulb and cortex to other parts of the limbic system, such as the amygdalostriatum and hippocampus that have similar structures and dynamics, we can conceive of the activation or creation of images of expectant motor activity' (p. 1122).

Such results provide an intriguing model and analogue of the imagery process, and provide further support for an efferent-oriented view of imagery and emotion. While these neurophysiological approaches are not practicable for research and clinical practice with humans, they nevertheless encourage continued development and study of the 'software' of the brain.

EFFERENT MEDIATION IN LEARNING AND MEMORY

Once response information is considered as integral to brain associative networks, some interesting ramifications follow. A primary topic concerns the role of efferent activity in modulating learning and memory. If efferents are part of an information structure, they presumably possess attributes similar to those of more traditionally conceived elements. For instance, various aspects of verbally presented information have been extensively investigated in regard to their associative properties. Perhaps the simplest example is paired associate learning, where such factors as the extent of the imagery relating two words in a pair have been shown to enhance recall (Paivio, 1971). More recently, the structure of larger, sentence- or paragraph-sized networks has been explored, by utilizing the reaction time to a given target word when it is preceded closely in time by a priming word varying in its physical and/or logical proximity to the target (McKoon and Ratcliff, 1980).

Such functional effects should also accrue to efferent information, and particularly with respect to the salient efferent activity involved in affective states. Research with state-dependent learning has indicated that this is indeed the case. For instance, some years ago Gordon Bower (1981) demonstrated that memory for word lists was better when mood at recall (as instigated by hypnotic induction) matched that at learning, as opposed to other conditions when learning and recall moods were different. From the current perspective, however, a problem with Bower's work is that the putative moods were determined only by mood-induction procedures, and were not validated by actual measurements of any sort to confirm the extent of the states achieved. Thus, evidence confirming that the effects were actually due to differential efferent activity was only indirect, at best.

In a more overt manipulation of physiological states, Clark, Milberg and Ross (1983) conducted a state-dependent learning study in which subjects initially learned two word lists, one under a state of relaxation and the other while participating in a step test (continuously stepping up and down on a cinder block). Later, subjects recalled the lists after viewing one of two randomly determined films, either a relaxing nature film or a sexually arousing film. As predicted, subjects who had viewed the sexually arousing film recalled more of the words presented in the step test, while subjects who had viewed the nature film recalled more of the words learned in the initial relaxation condition. While no physiological measurements were recorded, the nature of the manipulations suggests that different physiological states were, in fact, achieved; in terms of the associative facilitation of recall by the states induced, it is noteworthy and intriguing that the higher activation state at recall (i.e. sexual arousal) was markedly different from that at learning (the step test). Results such as these are important in considering the nature of the mediation processes that are occurring.

PROCESSING ANXIETY INFORMATION

The idea that information about efferents is represented in memory, and significantly influences learning and memory, has important practical implications for the anxiety disorders. Physiological responses are a traditional, salient component of the syndrome. We speculated elsewhere (Lang, 1985) that the degree of integration of stimulus–response information in phobia seems to follow a gradient across diagnostic groups. That is, simple phobics show a physiology that, while marked, is specific to confrontation with the phobic object and to directly associated language. Social phobics tend to show a somewhat less-focused physiological response (e.g. Lang *et al.*, 1970). While the panic attack is seen as a core feature for most agoraphobics, it is also true that such attacks are somewhat capricious, in that they do not reliably occur in any given situation; rather, panics are only probabilistically related to prototypical agoraphobic contexts such as supermarkets, shopping malls, etc. Finally, in pure panic disorder, the bursts of overwhelming distress seem to come about almost totally at random, and sometimes strike while the patient is in what would usually be considered a 'safe place' for the agoraphobic, such as at home.

One way of considering these disorders, then, involves the extent to which the physiology is coupled to specific contexts, i.e. from the present perspective, the organization of stimulus and response information in associative memory. In simple phobia, physiological response is part of a strong, highly interrelated associative network; the avoidance-related patterns are not seen in other contexts, but are limited to actual phobic situations. In agoraphobia, in contrast, the information structure seems more diffuse. Episodes of extreme fear can occur in a variety of situations, not seemingly related to the original circumstances of panic; on the other hand, confrontation with even a highly threatening situation does not invariably result in panic (which engenders great frustration for both patient and therapist in trying to determine progress). If the elements that give rise to such attacks could be specified with greater precision, these occurrences might not seem so baffling.

An answer to such problems depends on a better understanding of how the activation of response information alters and maintains emotional behaviour. For instance, what are the aspects of physiology which generate associations across various information structures, and how does this modulation take place? Differential emotions theorists, as mentioned above, have argued that there are discrete emotional states. One of the difficulties of this position is that there may be multiple physiological responses associated with one culturally labelled emotion; for example, both freezing and avoidance may be considered as fear behaviour, but obviously involve markedly different patterns of response. Another possibility is that general dimensions of response predisposition are stored, such as arousal or affective valence. In addition to state-dependent experiments such as those mentioned above, evidence for this view has come from factor analytic studies of affective reports (e.g. Osgood, Suci and Tannen-baum, 1957), as well as a variety of other paradigms (reviewed in Lang, 1985). Finally, it is possible that specific response patterns within organ systems might modulate associations. For example, Obrist (1981) has demonstrated markedly different patterns of cardiovascular response between 'active coping' tasks which demand marked effort, and 'passive coping' tasks which involve a more inhibitory behavioural adjustment. Such modes are independent of affective valence, in the sense that active coping might be equally invoked by an appetitive or aversively motivated task, and also seem to represent possibly different states of arousal. Further differentiation among these various possibilities presents an exciting challenge for psychophysiological research; at present, the database in this area is clearly insufficient to support more than the vaguest adumbration as to how such associative mediation in emotion and psychopathology could take place.

Thus, intriguing questions remain to be answered, and will unquestionably clarify enormously our understanding of the ways in which efferent activity is represented in the brain and affects a wide variety of cognitive and behavioural activities. However, the state-dependent paradigms are by no means the only way to approach this area. Many studies have been carried out to investigate emotional response in a variety of imagery and behavioural paradigms, and one such programme of research is considered in the next section.

The direction taken here has proved highly useful in terms of ordering and suggesting new approaches to a variety of experimental data. One such example concerns the treatment of phobias. Imagery-based therapies such as systematic desensitization (e.g. Lang and Lazovik, 1963) and imaginal flooding (Rachman, 1969) have been widely employed for several years. However, some inconsistencies have appeared in the imagery literature. Some studies have shown that imagery therapies are not equally effective for treating fears, with flooding sometimes reported as superior to desensitization (e.g. Boulougouris, Marks and Marset, 1971). In addition, over the last decade reports have accumulated suggesting a superiority of real-life exposure compared to imagery techniques (reviewed in Foa and Kozak, 1985). The role of physiological activity in emotional imagery has also been studied extensively. While there is general agreement that physiological response is enhanced in imagery (see review by Cuthbert, Vrana and Bradley, in press), the precise role of such activity in the maintenance and reduction of fear has been debated (e.g. Foa and Kozak, 1986; Watts, 1979).

BASIC RESEARCH ON EMOTIONAL IMAGERY

In view of the conflicting reports and difficulty with theoretical integration in the literature on emotional imagery, an experimental series was initiated some years ago to explore the area in terms of the bio-informational model. The paradigm that was developed involved presenting subjects with tape-recorded imagery scripts, and requesting them first to listen to, and then imagine the scenes depicted by the scripts while psychophysiological measurements were taken. Each trial included a 30-s Rest period, a 50-s Read period, a 30-s Image period, and a 30-s Recovery period. Physiological responses were monitored continuously during Rest, Image, and Recovery periods, and during the final 30-s of the Read period. Subjects were instructed to imagine each scene as it was presented (Read period), and to continue to imagine the scene after the description was completed (Image period). A brief tone at the end of the Image period signalled subjects to stop imagining the scene and focus on relaxing their muscles. Following the Recovery period, the tone sounded again to indicate that the subject should open his or her eyes and report on the vividness and quality of the emotional experience. Post-image pleasure, arousal, and dominance ratings were obtained in random order over trials; vividness was always assessed last. When the ratings were completed, subjects were instructed to close their eyes, relax, and await the beginning of the next script.

To test aspects of the theory, the presence of stimulus and response propositions was manipulated systematically in the scripts read to the subjects. In addition, to ensure that the response material was being processed at the level of the motor outputs and not merely in a superficial semantic way, we developed training procedures for the various propositional elements. Subjects were given practice trials in which they reported the content of their imagery immediately following the trial, and received systematic feedback from the experimenter. Subjects given 'stimulus training' were shaped to include ever-richer details of the stimulus described in the script, e.g. colour, sizes, shapes, etc. 'Response-trained' subjects, in contrast, were encouraged to report details of their bodily activity in the scene – heart pounding, muscles tensing, sweat dripping from the brow, etc. By the end of training, groups of subjects were created whose verbal report differed markedly for a scene of identical overt content, but whose vividness reports were quite similar.

In the first studies, it was found that only subjects given the combination of both response training and response scripts exhibited a palpable physiological response to arousal or fear scenes; subjects with only one, or neither, of the response-oriented manipulations produced very little response (Lang, Kozak, Miller, Levin and McLean, 1980). This demonstrated the importance of training subjects to process propositions at the motor output level, and also the need to cue subjects properly for them to be able to include such response factors in the image.

Another experiment demonstrated the specificity of the information structure, while replicating and extending the first study (Lang, Levin, Miller and Kozak, 1983). Separate groups of snake phobics and speech-anxious subjects were selected from undergraduate classes by appropriate questionnaires. Subjects were initially given two behaviour tests, one pertaining to each of the two phobic situations. The results for the snake behaviour test were in accord with the prediction: subjects selected for snake fear exhibited increasing heart rate over the steps of the snake test, while socially anxious subjects were non-reactive in this context. However, both groups showed elevated heart rate and skin conductance in the speech behaviour test. The latter result was somewhat unexpected, and seemed to reflect the metabolic demand of giving a speech. Thus, as has been shown in a variety of paradigms (e.g. see Obrist, 1981), autonomic activation reflects to a large degree the metabolic demands of the task, and is not necessarily an automatic index of a putative 'fear' state.

Subsequently, the subjects imagined scenes pertaining both to their own and to the other group's fear content. The results were in the same direction as the exposure conditions, in that snake phobics displayed elevated heart rate responses only to imagery of the snake test; however, in spite of the immediately recent experience with actual situations, the differences which emerged were not significant.

Accordingly, another sample of snake- and speech-fearful subjects was drawn from the same population. This time, rather than the behaviour test given initially in the first sample, subjects were given either stimulus- or response-oriented imagery training as described above. Following such drill, response-trained subjects exhibited a pattern very much like the actual behaviour test given in the earlier procedure. Heart rates were elevated for both groups during the speech test; verbal report of arousal, however, was highly significant in separating the speech-anxious from the phobic subjects on the speech scenes. For the snake imagery scene, however, the snake-phobic subjects exhibited a heart rate response clearly and significantly higher than that for subjects in the social-fear group, appearing to reflect the response disposition of flight in the situation. Thus, the response training procedures do not induce a non-specific arousal to any script material, but cue response information in memory which is directly associated with the specific phobic context.

INDIVIDUAL DIFFERENCES: IMAGERY AS A COGNITIVE TRAIT

Another potential factor influencing the response to emotional imagery is the subject's ability to create a highly vivid image. A concern with imagery vividness reaches back to the pre-behaviourist, introspectionist time of psychology, with one of the earliest related questionnaires published by Betts (1909). Such inventories, of course, are based upon the assumption that images are primarily visual and perceptual in nature. An obvious possibility in studies of phobic imagery is that differences in response can be attributed to subjects' differential capacity to generate vivid images. In a recent experiment (Miller, Levin, Kozak, Cook, McLean and Lang, 1987), subjects were divided into two extreme groups based on their scores on a revised version of Betts' Questionnaire on Mental Imagery (QMI; Sheehan, 1967), in which subjects rate the vividness of their images in five sensory modalities as well as some interoceptive sensations. Heart rate and other physiological measures were recorded while the subjects listened to tape-recorded scenes, as in the Lang *et al.* (1980, 1983) studies. In addition to standard scripts involving fear, anger, and pleasure, 'personalized' scripts of negative and positive affect were included in the tape-recorded scene set given to each subject; these were obtained by a brief questionnaire given during an screening initial session. In a subsequent session, all subjects were given response-oriented imagery training as described above. Finally, the imagery session was repeated once more exactly as it had been given the first time.

Prior to the response-directed imagery training, the two groups did not differ on their response to any of the scripted materials, although the self-reported 'good' imagers tended to show greater physiological responsivity. However, after training, good imagers were significantly higher in heart rate response for the fear scenes given to all subjects. Thus, the value of the training procedure was reaffirmed, and led to a predicted difference between the two groups.

Interestingly, however, this was the case only for the 'standard' scenes given to the entire sample. For the personalized affective scenes, the heart rate response of 'poor' imagers was enhanced to a degree not significantly different from that of the good-imager group.

These results suggest that the deficit seen in poor imagers is not global to all possible imagery tasks. Images based on the recall of an actual, previous experience seem to be accessible for loading into the work space and processing at a level sufficiently deep to reach efferent pathways. It is in the construction of new images from an amalgam of previously unrelated material in memory that these subjects appear to be deficient. Similar findings have been reported in other studies (Bardach and Weerts, 1980; Weerts and Roberts, 1976). Good imagers, by contrast, are able to synthesize disparate memorial elements in response to the script and generate an affective physiology 'on line' in real time.

Research by Levin (1982) with volunteer snake phobics provides further insight into these issues. In the experiment, subjects imaged a specific, prior presentation of a live snake (rather than being prompted only by descriptive text). Under these conditions, palpable physiological responses were observed without prior training. Furthermore, significantly greater visceral activity was again observed for good than for poor imagers. This result has been confirmed by McLean (1981), who presented stimulus materials as in a theatrical play, instructing subjects to 'imagine' that the scene was real. Such effects are clearly consistent with theory, i.e. (1) imagery of a recently presented stimulus (or coincident stimuli, in McLean's (1981) study) will more likely match the relevant stimulus information in memory, than will the vagaries of a general text; furthermore, (2) as in the Levin (1982) experiment, the use of phobic subjects assures that the relevant emotional network is indeed there to be activated.

Overall, these findings suggest why the earlier literature may contain such mixed results. Variations in the imagery prompt (instructions, script composition, and wording), the behavioural demand, the presence or absence of psychopathology, the characteristics of the subject sample, or previous experience in the image target situation could easily result in the irregular pattern of previous experimental findings regarding fear imagery. In contrast, the studies just reviewed, driven by a coherent theoretical model, suggest that systematic, replicable findings can be achieved in this area. While all of the studies reported above used normal college student or volunteer phobic populations, the consistency of the data encourages the view that the approach could be applied to a clinical population as well. This seems particularly so in the light of the previous finding that the magnitude of response to clinical imagery is related to success at outcome (Lang et al., 1970; Levin et al., 1982).

IMAGERY AND THE ANXIETY DISORDERS: A CLINICAL STUDY

Building on the foundation laid by this programme of basic experimentation, a clinical research project was initiated as a test bed in which to explore a variety of hypotheses regarding the effects of diagnosis, imagery vividness, script type, and level of fear. With respect to diagnosis, a variety of clinical and research reports have suggested that patients' responses to fear imagery differ systematically among the phobic disorders. In several studies (Bardach and Weerts, 1980; Lang *et al.*, 1970; Weerts and Lang, 1978) small-animal phobics reported fear imagery to be more vivid, and/or reported a level of experienced arousal that is more consistent with physiological activation, than was observed for socially anxious subjects (i.e. speech phobics). Subjects frightened of small animals also showed distinct, large amplitude visceral responses when imagining the relevant fear objects – significantly greater than those shown by non-phobic subjects. Furthermore, for simple phobics, physiological patterns observed during imagery are concordant with those seen when phobics anticipate a confrontation with the fear object or are actually exposed to it.

The psychophysiological responses of socially anxious subjects, on the other hand, are less readily differentiated from those of their non-anxious peers when both groups imagine a speaking performance (or indeed, when they actually perform in one! – see Knight and Borden, 1979). They also show less consistent physiological patterns across related contexts of fear arousal (Lang *et al.*, 1983).

Finally, a preliminary investigation of anxiety patients (Levin *et al.*, 1982) suggested that agoraphobics might be even less responsive than social phobics to their own imaginal productions. Indeed, despite other evidence that they are highly reactive to external stimulation (Lader, Gelder and Marks, 1967), agoraphobics showed little sympathetic activation to personally selected fear imagery. A deficient imagery response might account for the results of earlier treatment-outcome studies in which agoraphobics responded less favourably to imagery therapies than did those with other phobic disorders (Gelder and Marks, 1968; Marks, 1969).

Based on such considerations, the initial study carried out with a clinical sample was intended to explore differences as a function of diagnostic grouping and imagery ability. (See Cook *et al.*, 1988, for a more detailed report.) In accord with the findings reviewed above, simple phobics were expected to show higher amplitude visceral responses during imaging of their own fear content than social phobics or agoraphobics. As all three diagnostic groups report intense fear of the phobic context, it is presumed that the physiological effect is independent of patients' appraisal of their own affect during imagery. That is to say, the physiological response differences among diagnoses would occur even if the three groups reported their fear images to be similar in subjective affective intensity.

A second hypothesis concerned imagery vividness. The research reviewed above has shown that efferent activity during imagery varies positively with imagery ability, as measured by questionnaire assessment (Miller *et al.*, 1987). Thus, observed differences among diagnostic groups in visceral response during emotional imagery could represent differences among groups in imagery processing, rather than differences in the fear memory content or organization. Imagery ability was assessed for all subjects prior to the experiment, and the overall effect of this variable on physiological response and affective appraisal, and its interaction with diagnosis, were evaluated.

Finally, to the extent that a patient's memory representation is a coherent network of stimulus, response, and meaning (semantic) concepts, concordance among response measures is expected during imagery of phobic scenes (Lang, 1979). Again, consistent with the hypothesis of diagnostic differences in phobic memory organization, it was anticipated that correlations between physiological response amplitude and judged affective intensity of the image would be highest for simple phobics and least for agoraphobics.

AN IMAGERY ASSESSMENT BATTERY

To test these hypotheses, an assessment battery was adapted from the procedure described above for use in research with a normal population by Lang *et al.* (1980). Subjects were instructed to imagine that they were active participants in a series of phobic, generally stressful, and affectively neutral situations, each prompted by a verbal script that described both context and response.

The subjects were patients seen in an anxiety disorders clinic at a university health centre. All patients were interviewed and administered a battery of paper-and-pencil questionnaires. Each patient was initially diagnosed according to the criteria of the *Diagnostic and Statistical Manual* (3rd edn; American Psychiatric Association, 1980) by two doctoral-level clinical psychologists, one of whom participated in the intake interview and testing, and a second who later reviewed a videotape of the intake interview as well as questionnaire materials. Disagreements between the two primary diagnosticians were resolved by consensus among a committee of the investigators. The sample included patients diagnosed in the three categories of agoraphobia with panic attacks ($N = 11$), social phobia ($N = 14$), or simple phobia ($N = 13$).

The study was part of an extensive treatment protocol which included the interview session, imagery and behavioural assessments, and three sessions of an imaginal flooding procedure as a standardized programme for all patients. Following these sessions, patients received further therapy as indicated, of a type and duration determined by the nature and severity of the problem. The imagery and behaviour test procedures were repeated at the time of termination, and again at 6–12 months post-therapy.

Following an intake interview (adapted from the *Anxiety Disorders Interview Schedule*, Di Nardo, O'Brien, Barlow, Waddell and Blanchard, 1983), each patient was administered a battery of paper-and-pencil questionnaires, including the QMI (Sheehan, 1967) and a variety of other general and specific fear questionnaires selected for their relevance to an individual patient's fears.

The actual imagery procedure was held at the next meeting one week later. The session consisted of 11 trials, each with a different imagery script, following the same general format as earlier studies. Personal scripts were developed from a Scene Construction Questionnaire given at the initial interview. Patients were asked to describe in their own words various personal, affective situations, and to check off physiological responses that had been experienced in each context. Two of the situations pertained to the patient's own phobia, while the remainder involved a setting of physical danger, an actively pleasant experience, and a relaxing, affectively neutral context. The other six scenes comprised standard imagery scripts that were the same for all subjects, and included two common fear situations (giving a speech, receiving dental treatment), active exercise situations (riding a bicycle, flying a kite), and two neutral situations (relaxing at home, sitting on a lawn chair). The latter scene was always given as a practice/warm-up trial, and not analysed.

Patients were instructed to imagine vividly each script, as if they were active participants in the described situation. Before script presentation, all patients received brief relaxation instructions. Following the unanalysed warm-up trial, the ten personal and standard scripts described above were presented in two randomized blocks of five trials; each block included one of the two personal fear, standard fear, and standard action scripts, as well as either the standard neutral or personal neutral script, and either the personal pleasure or personal danger script. Heart rate and skin conductance were recorded throughout the session, and expressed as change scores by deviating the averaged measurements for the Read/Image periods from that for the 30-s base-period before each trial.

The mean heart rate and skin conductance responses for each scene in the assessment battery are presented in Figure 4.1. The figure also shows the patients' judged experience of arousal during scene imagery. It is clear that the scenes varied widely both in the visceral reaction they evoked and in reported affective experience, and regardless of the physiological or affective appraisal measure tested (i.e. including dominance and pleasure ratings), overall scene differences were highly significant ($P < 0.00002$). Furthermore, there was a strong positive relationship across scenes between average amplitude of visceral response and arousal report. Scene images that patients found to be emotionally exciting (particularly those with negative valence) prompted a more active physiology, while imagery of a restful setting produced the greatest quiescence.

Overall, the results indicated that the imagery battery was a sensitive instru-

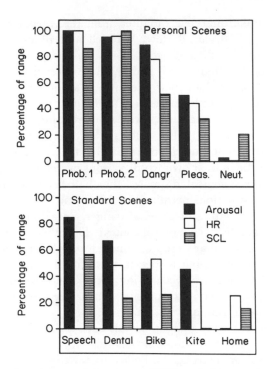

Figure 4.1. Arousal ratings, and heart rate (HR) and skin conductance level (SCL) responses for all scenes (see text) in an imagery assessment battery given to anxiety-disorder patients (N = 38). To facilitate comparison, all scores were range-corrected in terms of the largest and smallest mean across scenes for each measure. (Cook *et al.* © 1988 by the American Psychological Association. Reprinted by permission of the publisher.)

ment for use with anxiety patients. Visceral responses to phobic scenes were significantly greater than to neutral scenes, and in general, visceral activation during imagery covaried positively with intensity of reported affect. Furthermore, as predicted, patients generally showed significantly larger visceral reactions to their own emotional memories than to images based on scripts defined *a priori* as emotional.

PSYCHOPHYSIOLOGICAL DIFFERENCES AMONG ANXIETY DISORDERS

The primary hypothesis – that simple phobics would show a greater visceral reaction to phobic images than would other anxious patients – was supported for both heart rate change and skin conductance response (Figure 4.2). This result is consistent with Lang's (1985) hypothesis that the anxiety disorders differ in the organization of their relevant phobic memories. In this view, the

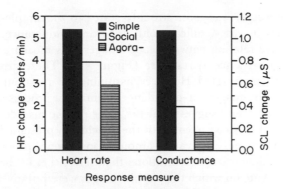

Figure 4.2. Average changes in heart rate (HR) and skin conductance level (SCL) responses to two phobic scenes for each of three groups of anxiety-disorder patients: simple phobics, social phobics and agoraphobics. (Cook *et al.* © 1988 by the American Psychological Association. Reprinted by permission of the publisher.)

memorial database for phobic expression (including imagery) is presumed to be a network of concepts – stimulus and response representations, and semantic elaborations of their meaning. The phobic response, including its somato-visceral components, is accessed when input concepts (in the present case, script and instructions) match concepts in the network. The probability of access is enhanced if the network is high in coherence (i.e. concepts are richly interconnected and these connections have high association probabilities). Agoraphobic fear networks are held to have the lowest coherence of the disorders studied here.

An alternative explanation of this result is that the phobic scripts for agoraphobics somehow failed to capture the essence of their prototypical fear situations, or did not include the propositions which prime physiological reactivity. One way of addressing this issue is to examine group differences in the phobic scene construction questionnaires. At initial interview, all subjects were asked to endorse those items, from a list of 52 response descriptors, which most closely represented their behavioural and physiological response during the selected, focal phobic scenes. An analysis of the total number of such items for each patient indicated that agoraphobics actually endorsed *more* responses than patients in the other groups. This argues strongly against the hypothesis that agoraphobics' clinical scenes had lower potential for physiological reactivity as compared to the other groups.

The three diagnostic groups did not differ in self-report of imagery vividness as measured by questionnaire prior to the experiment, nor in post-scene reports of vividness of the images presented in the battery. However, the groups did differ in the extent to which the psychometric measure (QMI) predicted visceral reactivity to phobic material. The expected relationship between good imagery and high sympathetic activation to fear scenes (heart rate and skin conductance increases) was most strongly stated in the simple-phobic group; for social phobics it was significant only for skin conductance; agoraphobics showed no positive relation between good imagery (as measured by the questionnaire) and either visceral response (Figure 4.3). These group differences might be variously interpreted. However, assuming the questionnaire measured capacity to generate images, or prevalence of imagery processing, the similar QMI group means would suggest that the three phobic disorders are equal in these capacities. This is consistent with the conclusion presented at the outset, that differences in imagery activation among disorders are prompted by group differences in the memory representations themselves, i.e. in the nature of the information aggregate on which the phobic images were putatively based. This view receives further support from the analysis of standard fear scripts.

The dental scene was selected as representative of normal fear and because it is widely distributed throughout the population. As there is a reasonably

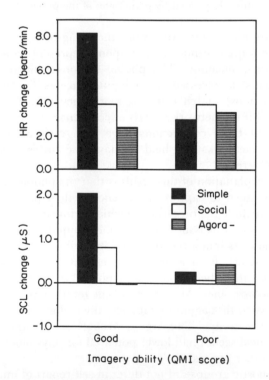

Figure 4.3. Average changes in heart rate (HR) and skin conductance level (SCL) responses to two phobic scenes for each of three groups of anxiety-disorder patients: simple phobics, social phobics and agoraphobics. Patients were classified as 'good' or 'poor' imagers using the Questionnaire on Mental Imagery (QMI) and the results are shown separately. (Cook *et al.* © 1988 by the American Psychological Association. Reprinted by permission of the publisher.)

high objective probability of pain in this context, the primary behavioural feature is simple escape and avoidance. Avoidance behaviour requires cardio-vascular mobilization, and thus, heart rate acceleration was anticipated in dental fear imagery.

Consistent with prediction, patients tended to show heart rate increase during dental imagery. However, unlike the pattern of response to their phobic scenes, agoraphobics were *not* differentiated from other phobics on the dental script. Furthermore, this time the good-imager agoraphobics responded in the same way as other good imagers (social and simple phobics), giving larger heart rate responses to the dental script than poor imagers. This uniformity of dental scene response is consistent with the conclusion that the effects of diagnosis found for the primary phobia scripts are mediated by differences in these fear memories, rather than in processing ability.

While few people approach public speaking with equanimity, a speech performance is more likely to be avoided by social phobics than other patients. As expected, heart rate increases during speech imagery were significantly larger for social phobics. Furthermore, social phobics with better imagery questionnaire scores also showed significantly larger skin conductance responses to the speech scene. It is noteworthy that social phobics' visceral responses to this standard material were just as large as those observed to specific phobic memories. This could be taken as evidence of the generality of their anxiety, and the reduced specificity in the activating fear cue.

Post-image reports of experienced emotion were moderately correlated with sympathetic reactivity during phobic imagery. This reflects the finding that all patients reported the expected differences between phobic and neutral images (that during fearful scenes they felt more aroused and unpleasant, and less dominant), while scene differences in physiological reactivity were less consistent over subjects. Only within the simple-phobic group was a strong relationship observed between affective judgments and physiology, i.e. simple phobics reporting intense affective feelings to phobic scenes reliably showed larger visceral responses (for example, the relationship between heart rate and arousal report accounted for nearly 60% of the variance). The relative absence of concordance among social phobics and agoraphobics is consistent with the hypothesis that their imagery is based on a less coherent phobic memory network.

MEMORY ORGANIZATION AND ANXIETY

Simple phobics showed both the most visceral reactivity to phobic imagery, and the least anxiety and depression on psychometric measures, such as the Fenz–Epstein anxiety scale (Fenz and Epstein, 1965) and the Beck Depression Inventory (Beck, Ward, Mendelsohn, Mock and Erbaugh, 1961). Accordingly, it might be concluded that attenuation of visceral responses in imagery is caused by group differences in a pathology-determined general deficit for all tasks (i.e. in the sense that a general deficit may be the basis of any specific performance difference between normal subjects and, for example, schizophrenic patients). However, it has already been noted that the groups did not differ in mean imagery ability, as measured by questionnaire (the QMI), nor in their visceral responses to a non-phobia-related fear scene. Furthermore, the actual correlations across the entire sample between psychopathology and visceral response to phobic scenes did not suggest any *general* relationship between these variables, i.e. they varied little from zero for any pair of measures.

As for the entire sample, correlations between psychopathology and visceral response were generally non-significant when separately assessed within the social-phobic and agoraphobic groups. It was only among simple phobics that greater visceral reactivity to phobic scenes was correlated with generalized anxiety and depression, and, in this case, a larger imagery response was associated with *more* anxiety and depression. This relationship is consistent with the view that the presenting fear is, itself, the main focus of distress in simple phobia, which is directly related to (perhaps, determinant of) other domains of pathological behaviour. The same logic argues that, for social phobics and agoraphobics, the presenting phobic material is not necessarily the pathological focus, i.e. that context-specific mobilization for avoidance (which would include, for example, cardiac rate increase) is not *the* primary feature of these disorders. These results also raise questions about the integrity of the group of phobic disorders as a nosological class, particularly in consideration of the significant differences in the extent of general psychopathology among these phobic categories.

The data are consistent with the hypothesis that the generative fear memory in simple phobia is a highly coherent, context-specific avoidance program. The results show that for simple phobics, a close association exists between the actual visceral responses in avoidance (i.e. sympathetic activation and cardiovascular mobilization) and semantic representations of fear in memory (i.e. of context and response concepts). This association is indicated on the input side by the strong visceral reactivity of simple-phobic patients to the linguistic medium of a phobic script, and on the output side by the orderly relationship (among simple phobics) between the amplitude of visceral response during phobic imagery and their subsequent appraisal (meaning analysis) of this affective experience.

The imagery questionnaire results lend further support to this view. It has been argued (Hebb, 1968; Lang, 1977, 1979; Sarbin, 1972) that imagery is the cognitive process through which patterns of efference are regenerated, duplicating the response array of perceptual–motor and action memories. Thus, assuming the phobic memory to be an action set, the degree to which the memory is accessed (and the associated efference manifested) varies systematically with a subject's basic capacity or disposition to process images, i.e. the questionnaire score. This relationship was most clearly seen in the simple-phobic group.

In contrast, Lang *et al.* (1983, pp. 291–292) previously noted a tendency for skin-conductance change to be a dominant sympathetic response in speech phobics. Considering the relationship between phasic skin conductance and 'orienting', they suggested that the fear program of socially anxious subjects might be different from that of simple phobics, having more to do with a state of vigilance (e.g. for social criticism) than cue-specific avoidance or escape. Öhman (1986) has made a similar suggestion, reasoning from an evolutionary perspective. In this view, socially anxious individuals are not really social avoiders; they are, in fact, highly affiliative. However, they are also hypersensitive to interpersonal rewards and punishments, and continually struggling for position in the human version of mammalian dominance hierarchies. Unlike simple phobics, who may have had only a single contact with the phobic object (or none!), the social phobic is continually forming new fear memories and conceivably moderating old ones, as he/she copes with the daily social milieu. From this perspective, the cues that elicit apprehension, the type of response, and their semantic representations form a less stable memorial structure than in simple phobia, with a consequent degradation in both the reliability of an overt action in any specific social context and the quality of a linguistically evoked image.

Finally, a similar set of factors could be implicated in the 'poor' phobic imagery of agoraphobics, with the additional consideration that distress is not restricted to a unique stimulus (as for simple phobics), or even limited to a class of stimuli (i.e. social cues). While it has been variously argued that agoraphobics are frightened of open spaces, distance from a 'safe' person, 'fear itself', 'going crazy', natural catastrophe and catastrophic illness, or their own uncontrolled physiology, there is no clear evidence that any of these cues is an invariable focus of avoidance. Furthermore, recent research suggests that overt avoidance (the prototypical phobic response) may be no better a predictor of panic (Craske, Sanderson and Barlow, 1987) or agoraphobic distress than imagery of the avoidance context proved to be here. Mavissakalian and Hamann (1986) administered both standard and personalized behavioural avoidance tests to a large sample of agoraphobics. 'Subgroups of avoiders and non-avoiders, classified simultaneously on both tests, did not differ significantly in their clinical characteristics or response to treatment' (p. 317). Assuming the phobic image to be a regeneration of a context-specific avoidance response from memory, these data raise the possibility that we found no visceral mobilization associated with imagery in agoraphobics precisely because they do not have such focused, associated avoidance-response concepts in memory. The further investigation of this hypothesis depends on direct comparison of image and *in-vivo* psychophysiology in these anxiety disorders.

The results support the conclusions of Turner, McCann, Beidel and Mezzich

(1986) concerning the reclassification of anxiety and phobic disorders. These researchers found no differences between agoraphobia and generalized anxiety states on a broad range of questionnaire measures of anxiety and depression; moreover, agoraphobia, like these generalized anxiety states, was associated with significantly more pathology than simple and social phobia. Within the phobic disorders, simple phobics showed less general distress than social phobics. Based on these data, Turner *et al* (1986) proposed that a distinction be made between phobic states and anxiety states, and that agoraphobia be included among the anxiety states. They noted further that 'an intriguing question' is raised: 'whether disorders characterized by circumscribed fear might have a totally different psychopathological basis than those characterized by more pervasive disturbance'. The data presented here answer the question positively: simple phobia is characterized by an explicit image of fear, with a coherent base-structure of stimulus, response, and semantic elements in memory. For patients with this disorder, the intensity of their fear image is directly related to the generality of behaviour pathology (e.g. generalized anxiety and depression). Social phobics are responsive to fear imagery, but there is much less context specificity, and individual images are not apparently the key to their broader pathology. While further data are clearly needed, the present findings suggest that agoraphobia might not be based on any organized fear imagery (or cluster of such images). Agoraphobics may be more like generalized anxiety disorder patients than phobics, in that there is no reliable focal fear in memory, or specific external stimulus, around which the distress response is organized.

CONCLUSIONS AND FUTURE DIRECTIONS

The purpose of presenting the above clinical study was twofold: first, to describe new data in the area of the anxiety disorders, and secondly, of at least equal importance, to illustrate how the theoretical orientation presented at the outset can be applied to an actual clinical problem and how a response-oriented view of emotion can shape a fruitful programme of clinical research. This model has also guided experiments by Pitman, Orr, Forgue, de Jong and Claiborn (1987), who used the same imagery procedure described in this chapter to successfully discriminate Vietnam veterans with chronic post-traumatic stress syndrome from other neurotics, and from non-disturbed veterans with similar combat experience. Similarly, Steinberg (1986) and Dekker and Everaerd (1988) investigated genital arousal in imagery to sexually provocative text, and both studies found clear support for the response information hypothesis. Indeed, imagery paradigms have been useful in psychophysiological analysis with a great variety of measures, and in studies of widely differing pathologies. Thus, Schwartz and colleagues (e.g. Schwartz, Fair, Salt, Mandel and Klerman, 1976) studied facial EMGs in normal subjects and depressed patients: the corrugator EMG (controlling the muscle over the eye involved in frowning) was significantly elevated for the depressed during imagery of clinical material. Graham (1972) proposed that 'psychosomatic medicine is psychophysiology in a clinical context' (p. 839), and used imagery procedures to analyse the psychological organization of different disease entities. In a now classic series of studies, Graham's group (see Graham, Kabler and Graham, 1962) demonstrated that response patterns specific to a given psychosomatic disorder could be evoked by the suggestion of attitudes previously found to be related to that disease. For example, suggestions of hypervigilance against threat were associated with rises in blood pressure (hypertension), while suggestions of being powerless in the face of unfair punishment led to increases in skin temperature (urticaria).

The paradigms discussed in this chapter are useful not only in assessment, but also to measure progress in treatment. Standardized presentation of relevant imagery materials and coincident physiological recording provide an invaluable guide to change in the distress response, which may be much more significant than the information gained from verbal report. Starting from the bio-information processing approach, Foa and Kozak (1986) have raised several important therapy issues, e.g. within- and between-session habituation, the significance of 'corrective information', and the role of meaning in the network structure, which depend on psychophysiological analysis for their explication and practical application.

In recent years, a variety of paradigms from experimental cognitive psychology have been adapted to clinical use. For example, Watts, McKenna, Sharrock and Trezise (1986) asked subjects to perform a Stroop-type test, in which spider-related words could potentially interfere with performance. Consistent with their hypothesis, phobics were significantly slower to name the colours of words referring to spiders, as compared to a variety of control words. This apparent interference effect was significantly reduced following therapy for the spider phobia. Mathews and MacLeod (1985) reported similar findings for a Stroop task with general-anxiety patients. In this case, the extent to which distress words interfered with performance was related to the anxiety level of the patient at the time of the testing.

In another study designed to investigate differences in the processing of emotionally relevant material in patients, Mathews and MacLeod (1986) used a dichotic listening task, in which subjects shadowed a neutral passage presented to one ear while threat or non-threat words were presented to the other ear. As compared to control subjects, anxiety-disorder patients were slower in responding to a superimposed reaction-time task when threat words were presented in the unattended channel. As all subjects were unable to report or recognize the content of the unattended words, it was concluded that threat cues are processed differently by anxiety-disorder patients and normals, and that a pre-attentive mechanism contributes to such differences.

These techniques, and others based on the information-processing approach (e.g. MacLeod, Mathews and Tata, 1986), offer great promise for investigating memory organization in psychopathology. Furthermore, considering the specificity of content-interference and the clear, post-treatment changes observed by Watts *et al.* (1986), these procedures could become important tools in diagnosing and assessing change in emotional disorders. However, understanding their mechanism may depend importantly on adding measurement of the physiological system to the experimental paradigm. For example, the slowed reaction times noted by Watts *et al.* (1986) may be described more precisely than as a reallocation of attention (e.g. from the colour-naming task to the spider words). From the bio-informational perspective, we would presume that the phobic words evoked in the Stroop test activate the phobic prototype, with its somatovisceral response structure. Slower colour-naming times are specifically predicted, determined by response interference between the reaction-time task and the demands of a phobic avoidance response. Because psychophysiological measurement can be accomplished coincident with the hypothesized cognitive processes, this methodology can be used to test precise predictions about mechanism.

The fact that the bio-informational model maps so well onto current notions about neural networks (illustrated earlier by the animal research of Freeman, 1983, and Freeman and Schneider, 1982) argues that it may prove equally productive in neurological studies. For example, Bauer (1982) recently reported the case of a man injured in a motorcycle accident, who complained subsequently of an inability to become emotionally aroused by, or to become involved in, any pleasurable visual material, such as art objects, natural scenery, or sexual stimuli. This visual stimulus deficit persisted, despite the fact that emotional arousal was prompted normally by other sensory information (e.g. a woman's 'sexy' voice). As lesions had been sustained on the inferior aspect of the posterior temporal lobes in the right hemisphere, in the region of the occipitotemporal gyrus, Bauer (1982) hypothesized that the patient's sensory-specific hypo-emotionality was due to a disconnection between peristriate cortex and limbic structures. To verify this more systematically, skin-conductance responses were recorded while various emotional and neutral stimuli were presented in visual and auditory modalities. The results confirmed the supposition, in that marked electrodermal activity occurred in response to auditory emotional stimuli, but was virtually nil for visually presented material. This case study provides strong evidence for the involvement of a specific brain area modulating one type of emotion network, altering connections between sensory and response information. It also suggests how studies of brain-injured patients could be used to define the firmware for cognitive programs which support emotional behaviour.

In conclusion, converging evidence encourages the use of psychophysiological analysis, not only in the anxiety disorders, but in the broad study of psychopathology. Furthermore, these developments have direct bearing on clinical practice, as well as research. Using physiological recording, the clinician can assess affective behaviour in the 'real-time' of cognition, without waiting for a retrospective report. Furthermore, its use avoids reliance solely upon a single response system (e.g. verbal report) when the evidence shows system intercorrelations are so often low (Lang, 1978). Indeed, clinical information is maximum when verbal report, physiological measures, and behavioural assessment can be multiplexed in the same or imaginally similar situations. Finally, systematic use of psychophysiology and other concomitant behavioural observations can bring the art of therapy much closer to the control-ideal of laboratory research. Each case can be an '*N* of 1' study, for which comparable, previous findings exist to guide diagnosis and treatment. Given the presence of organizing theory and a good, beginning database, the increased availability of recording instrumentation, and the ever-increasing population of scientifically trained consultants, the use of psychophysiological methods in the study of psychopathology holds great promise for both science and clinical practice.

ACKNOWLEDGEMENTS

This work was supported in part by NIMH grants 37757 and 41950.

REFERENCES

American Psychiatric Association (1980). *Diagnostic and Statistical Manual*, 3rd edn. Washington, DC: APA.

Anderson, J. R. (1979). Further arguments concerning representations for mental imagery: a response to Hayes-Roth and Pylyshyn. *Psychological Review* **86**, 395–406.

Anderson, J. R. and Bower, G. H. (1974). A propositional theory of recognition memory. *Memory and Cognition* **2**, 406–412.

Bardach, E., and Weerts, T. C. (1980). Assessment of controllability and vividness of visual imagery in two types of phobia. Unpublished manuscript.

Bauer, R. M. (1982). Visual hypoemotionality as a symptom of visual–limbic disconnection in man. *Archives of Neurology* **39**, 702–708.

Beck, A. T., Ward, C. H., Mendelsohn, M., Mock, J., and Erbaugh, J. (1961). An inventory for measuring depression. *Archives of General Psychiatry* **4**, 561–571.

Betts, G. H. (1909). *The Distribution and Functions of Mental Imagery*. Columbia University Teachers College, Contribution to Education Series, No. 26. New York: CUTC.

Boulougouris, J. C., Marks, I. M., and Marset, P. (1971). Superiority of flooding (implosion) to desensitization for reducing pathological fear. *Behavior and Research Therapy* **9**, 7–16.

Bower, G. H. (1981). Mood and memory. *American Psychologist* **36**, 129–148.

Chomsky, N. (1980). Rules and representations. *Behavioral and Brain Sciences* **3**, 1–61.

Clark, M. S., Milberg, S., and Ross, J. (1983). Arousal cues arousal-related material in memory: implications for understanding effects of mood on memory. *Journal of Verbal Learning and Verbal Behavior* **22**, 633–649.

Cook, E. W., III, Melamed, B. G., Cuthbert, B. N., McNeil, D. W., and Lang, P. J. (1988). Emotional imagery and the differential diagnosis of anxiety. *Journal of Consulting and Clinical Psychology* **56**, 734–740.

Craske, M., Sanderson, W. C., and Barlow, D. H. (1987). The relationships among panic, fear, and avoidance. *Journal of Anxiety Disorders* **1**, 153–160.

Cuthbert, B. N., Vrana, S. R., and Bradley, M. M. (in press). Imagery: function and physiology. In: P. K. Ackles, J. R. Jennings and M. G. H. Coles (Eds) *Advances in Psychophysiology*, Vol. IV. Greenwich, Conn.: JAI Press.

Dekker, J., and Everaerd, W. (1988). Attentional effects on sexual arousal. *Psychophysiology* **25**, 45–54.

Di Nardo, P. A., O'Brien, G. T., Barlow, D. H., Waddell, M. T., and Blanchard, E. B. (1983). Reliability of DSM-III anxiety disorder categories using a new structured interview. *Archives of General Psychiatry* **40**, 1070–1075.

Fenz, W. D., and Epstein, S. (1965). Manifest anxiety: unifactorial or multifactorial composition? *Perceptual and Motor Skills* **20**, 773–780.

Foa, E. B., and Kozak, M. J. (1985). Treatment of anxiety disorders: implications for psychopathology. In: A. H. Tuma and J. D. Maser (Eds) *Anxiety and the Anxiety Disorders*. Hillsdale, NJ: Erlbaum.

Foa, E. B., and Kozak, M. J. (1986). Emotional processing of fear: exposure to corrective information. *Psychological Bulletin* **99**, 20–35.

Freeman, W. J. (1983). The physiological basis of mental images. *Biological Psychiatry* **18**, 1107–1125.

Freeman, W. J., and Schneider, W. (1982). Changes in spatial patterns of rabbit olfactory EEG with conditioning to odors. *Psycophysiology* **19**, 44–56.

Gelder, M. G., and Marks, I. M. (1968). Desensitization and phobia: a crossover study. *British Journal of Psychiatry* **114**, 323–328.

Gellhorn, E., and Loofbourrow, G. N. (1963). *Emotions and Emotional Disorders: A Neurophysiological Study*. New York: Harper and Row.

Graham, D. T. (1972). Psychosomatic medicine. In: N. S. Greenfield and R. A. Sternbach (Eds) *Handbook of Psychophysiology*. New York: Holt, Rinehart and Winston.

Graham, D. T., Kabler, J. D., and Graham, F. K. (1962). Physiological response to the suggestion of attitudes specific for hives and hypertension. *Psychosomatic Medicine* **24**, 159–169.

Hebb, D. O. (1968). Concerning imagery. *Psychological Review* **75**, 466–477.

Knight, M. L., and Borden, R. J. (1979). Autonomic and affective reactions of high and low socially-anxious individuals awaiting public performance. *Psychophysiology* **16**, 209–213.

Kosslyn, S. M., Pinker, S., Smith, G. E., and Shwartz, S. P. (1979). On the demystification of mental imagery. *Behavioral and Brain Sciences* **2**, 535–581.

Kozak, M. J., and Miller, G. (1982). Hypothetical constructs vs. intervening variables: a re-appraisal of the three-systems concept of anxiety. *Behavioural Assessment* **4** 347–358.

Lader, M. H., Gelder, M. G., and Marks, I. M. (1967). Palmar skin conductance measures as predictors of response to densensitization. *Journal of Psychosomatic Research* **11**, 283–290.

Lang, P. J. (1968). Fear reduction and fear behavior: problems in treating a construct. In: J. M. Schlien (Ed.) *Research in Psychotherapy*, Vol. 3. Washington, DC: American Psychological Association.

Lang, P. J. (1977). Imagery in therapy: an information processing analysis of fear. *Behavior Therapy* **8**, 862–886.

Lang, P. J. (1978). Anxiety: toward a psychophysiological definition. In: H. S. Akiskal and W. L. Webb (Eds) *Psychiatric Diagnosis: Exploration of Biological Predictors.* New York: Spectrum.

Lang, P. J. (1979). A bio-informational theory of emotional imagery. *Psychophysiology* **16**, 495–512.

Lang, P. J. (1984). Cognition in emotion: concept and action. In: C. Izard, J. Kagan and R. Zajonc (Eds) *Emotion, Cognition, and Behavior.* New York: Cambridge University Press.

Lang, P. J. (1985). The cognitive psychophysiology of emotion: fear and anxiety. In: A. H. Tuma and J. D. Maser (Eds) *Anxiety and the Anxiety Disorders.* Hillsdale, NJ: Erlbaum.

Lang, P. J., and Lazovik, A. D. (1963). Experimental desensitization of a phobia. *Journal of Abnormal and Social Psychology* **66**, 519–525.

Lang, P. J., Kozak, M. J., Miller, G. A., Levin, D. N., and McLean, A., Jr (1980). Emotional imagery: conceptual structure and pattern of somato-visceral response. *Psychophysiology,* **17**, 179–192.

Lang, P. J., Levin, D. N., Miller, G. A., and Kozak, M. J. (1983). Fear behavior, fear imagery, and the psychophysiology of emotion: the problem of affective response integration. *Journal of Abnormal Psychology* **92**, 276–306.

Lang, P. J., Melamed, B. G., and Hart, J. D. (1970). A psychophysiological analysis of fear modification using an automated desensitization procedure. *Journal of Abnormal Psychology* **31**, 220–234.

Levin, D. N. (1982). The psychophysiology of fear reduction: role of response activation during emotional imagery. Unpublished doctoral dissertation, University of Wisconsin, Madison.

Levin, D. N., Cook, E. W., and Lang, P. J. (1982). Fear imagery and fear behavior: psychophysiological analysis of clients receiving treatment for anxiety disorders. *Psychophysiology* **19**, 571–572 (abstract).

MacLeod, C., Mathews, A., and Tata, P. (1986). Attentional bias in emotional disorders. *Journal of Abnormal Psychology* **95**, 15–20.

Marks, I. M. (1969). *Fears and Phobias.* New York: Academic Press.

Mathews, A., and MacLeod, C. (1985). Selective processing of threat cues in anxiety states. *Behavior Research and Therapy* **23**, 563–569.

Mathews, A., and MacLeod, C. (1986). Discrimination of threat cues without awareness in anxiety states. *Journal of Abnormal Psychology* **95**, 131–138.

Mavissakalian, M., and Hamann, M. S. (1986). Assessment and significance of behavioural avoidance in agoraphobia. *Journal of Psychopathology and Behavioral Assessment* **8**, 317–327.

McClelland, J. L., and Rumelhart, D. E. (Eds) (1986). *Parallel Distributed Processing: Explorations in the Microstructure of Cognition,* Vol. 2: *Psychological and Biological Models.* Cambridge, Mass.: MIT Press.

McKoon, G., and Ratcliff, R. (1980). Priming in item recognition: the organization of propositions in memory for text. *Journal of Verbal Learning and Verbal Behavior* **19**, 369–386.

McLean, A. (1981). Emotional imagery: stimulus information, imagery ability and patterns of physiological response. Unpublished doctoral dissertation, University of Wisconsin, Madison.

Miller, G. A., Levin, D. N., Kozak, M. J., Cook, E. W., III, McLean, A., and Lang, P. J. (1987). Individual differences in emotional imagery. *Cognition and Emotion* **1**, 367–390.

Obrist, P. A. (1981). *Cardiovascular Psychophysiology: A Perspective.* New York: Plenum.

Osgood, C., Suci, G., and Tannenbaum, P. (1957). *The Measurement of Meaning.* Urbana, Ill.: University of Illinois.

Öhman, A. (1986). Face the beast and fear the face: animal and social fears as prototypes for evolutionary analyses of emotion. *Psychophysiology* **23**, 123–145.

Paivio, A. (1971). *Imagery and Verbal Processes.* New York: Holt, Rinehart and Winston.

Panksepp, J. (1982). Toward a general psychobiological theory of emotions. *Behavioral and Brain Sciences* **5**, 407–422.

Pitman, R. K., Orr, S. P., Forgue, D. F., de Jong, J., and Claiborn, J. M. (1987). *Psychophysiological assessment of post-traumatic stress, disorder imagery in Vietnam veterans. Archives of General Psychiatry* **44**, 970–975.

Pylyshyn, Z. W. (1973). What the mind's eye tells the mind's brain: a critique of mental imagery. *Psychological Bulletin* **80**, 1–24.

Pylyshyn, Z. W. (1980). Computation and cognition: issues in the foundation of cognitive science. *Behavioral and Brain Sciences* **3**, 111–169.

Quillian, M. R. (1966). Semantic memory. In: M. L. Minsky (Ed.) *Semantic Information Processing.* Cambridge, Mass.: MIT Press.

Rachman, S. (1969). Treatment by prolonged exposure to high intensity stimulation. *Behavior Research and Therapy* **7**, 295–302.

Rachman, S. (1978). The return of fear. *Behaviour Research and Therapy* **17**, 164–166.

Sarbin, T. R. (1972). Imagining as muted role-taking: a historical–linguistic analysis. In: P. W. Sheehan (Ed.) *The Function and Nature of Imagery.* New York: Academic Press.

Schwartz, G. E., Fair, P. L., Salt, P., Mandel, M. R., and Klerman, G. L. (1976). Facial expression and imagery in depression: an electromyographic study. *Psychosomatic Medicine* **38**, 337–347.

Shaw, W. A. (1940). The relation of muscular action potentials to imaginal weight lifting. *Archives of Psychology* **247**, 1–50.

Sheehan, P. W. (1967). A shortened form of Betts' questionnaire upon mental imagery. *Journal of Clinical Psychology* **23**, 386–389.

Shepard, R. N., and Cooper, L. A. (1982). *Mental Images and their Transformations.* Cambridge, Mass.: MIT Press.

Skinner, B. F. (1953). *Science and Human Behavior.* New York: Macmillan.

Sperry, R. (1952). Neurology and the mind–brain problem. *American Scientist* **40**, 291–312.

Steinberg, J. L. (1986). The psychophysiology of sexual arousal: an information processing analysis. Unpublished doctoral dissertation, State University of New York, Stony Brook, NY.

Turner, S. M., McCann, B. S., Beidel, D. C., and Mezzich, J. E. (1986). DSM-III classification of the anxiety disorders: a psychometric study. *Journal of Abnormal Psychology* **95**, 168–172.

Watts, F. N. (1979). Habituation model of systematic desensitization. *Psychological Bulletin* **86**, 627–637.

Watts, F. N., McKenna, F. P., Sharrock, R., and Trezise, L. (1986). Colour naming of phobia-related words. *British Journal of Psychology* **77**, 97–108.

Weerts, T. C., and Lang, P. J. (1978). Psychophysiology of fear imagery: differences between focal phobia and social performance anxiety. *Journal of Consulting and Clinical Psychology* **46**, 1157–1159.

Weerts, T. C., and Roberts, R. (1976). The physiological effects of imagining anger-provoking and fear-provoking scenes. *Psychophysiology* **13**, 174.

Chapter 5

Lateralization and Central Mechanisms in Clinical Psychophysiology

John H. Gruzelier

Department of Psychiatry,
Charing Cross and Westminster Medical School,
St Dunstan's Road,
London W6 8RP

ABSTRACT

Localization of function – structural versus functional impairment; bilateral electro-dermal activity – multiple central determinants, hemispheric influences and individual differences in habituation, laterality of pain in migraine, and syndromes in schizo-phrenia; cortical–subcortical and limbic system dysfunction in schizophrenia – P300, brain-stem and middle latency evoked potentials, callosal transmission; smooth-pursuit eye movements; cerebral laterality – normal and pathological anxiety, pain, hyperventil-ation, psychoneuroimmunology; therapeutic intervention – hypnosis; brain electrical activity mapping.

Handbook of Clinical Psychophysiology Edited by G. Turpin
© 1989 John Wiley & Sons Ltd

INTRODUCTION

It is a basic premise of psychophysiology that through the measurement of electrocortical and autonomic activity insights will be gained about psychological functions. The use of physiological parameters as dependent variables theoretically gives psychophysiology close affinities with the disciplines of physiological psychology and neuropsychology which presume that functions have a basis in cerebral activity, often of a localized nature, unlike disciplines such as behavioural analysis or cognitive psychology which have often denied the importance of the brain altogether, adopt a 'black box' approach, or assume an equipotentiality of cerebral function.

In practice, psychophysiology has distanced itself from its theoretical neighbours with the result that central mechanisms in psychophysiology are a much neglected issue. Neglected, that is, in Western psychophysiology; Soviet science has always seen the theoretical kinship of neuropsychology, psychophysiology and physiological psychology (Meccaci, 1977), such that the neuropsychologist Luria was at home with the procedures of both neuropsychology and psychophysiology, and contemporary Soviet psychophysiology has been resourceful in developing invasive procedures with animals to elucidate central determinants of electrocortical and autonomic responses in man (Bechtereva, 1987). The more exclusive path followed by psychophysiology in the West has meant that investigations of neurological patients by psychophysiologists have been negligible outside of electroencephalography, which developed as a clinical speciality quite independently of psychophysiology.

Changes are afoot. An exchange and integration of the disparate activities of psychophysiology, neuropsychology and electroencephalography is emerging, and it is from the clinical field that this reapproachment is heralded. Increased communication with contemporary Soviet psychophysiology is also taking place, which should provide impetus to research on basic cerebral mechanisms in psychophysiology (Bechtereva, 1983).

Research on cerebral mechanisms has historically seen the influence of two contrasting schools of thought (Boring, 1957). One school, with its roots in phrenology, reflex physiology, associationist psychology and clinicopathological correlation, advocated a strict localization of cortical functions. Holistic theory opposed phrenology in showing that recovery of function after ablation was commonplace, irrespective of the cortical site of ablation. In the work of Lashley this led to the view that impairment of function depended on the size rather than the locus of the cortical lesion. The Pavlovian roots of psychophysiology owed much to reflex physiology and assocationist psychology, and accordingly have led to an often unstated alignment with the localizationalist school.

Recent developments in contemporary cognitive neuropsychology have drawn an important distinction between processes based on fixed structure, such as may give rise to the left hemisphere's advantages in linguistic functions and the right hemisphere's advantages in spatial-perceptual functions, and dynamic processes such as activation and attention that may reflect or determine the functional state of hemispheric activity (Cohen, 1982; Kinsbourne, 1975; Moscovitch, 1979). Psychophysiological measures would appear ideally suited to provide indices of brain functional activity (Gruzelier, 1984), an issue which is becoming of widespread interest in psychopathology through the advent of brain imaging procedures which are disclosing abnormalities of function through measures of cerebral blood flow, metabolism and topographical electroencephalography (EEG) (Maurer, 1988; Pfurtscheller and Lopes da Silva, 1988). Clarification of the distinction between brain structure and function, and understanding the remarkable ability of the brain to reconstitute its functions after damage, are likely to be crucial to advancement in the understanding of the cerebral mechanisms underpinning psychophysiological parameters, not to mention their clinical utility.

Considerations of space have necessitated both a selective treatment of what is potentially a vast topic and, in places, provision of references of review articles only or of individual papers where supplementary references may be obtained. The selection of topics to a large extent reflects the author's personal interests.

CEREBRAL LATERALITY AND PSYCHOPATHOLOGY

The most active area of research on localization of function in psychology has been concerned with lateralization, a dimension which has held considerable appeal for research on psychopathology, notably schizophrenia, affective psychoses, psychosomatic disorders and disorders related to anxiety. Therapeutic procedures such as relaxation and hypnosis have also been couched in neuropsychological terms with laterality playing a pivotal role. The degree of interest in the topic of lateralization and psychopathology is shown by the fact that three international conferences have been devoted to the issue (see Flor-Henry and Gruzelier, 1983; Gruzelier and Flor-Henry, 1979; Takahashi, Flor-Henry, Gruzelier and Niwa, 1987). The proceedings of these meetings indicate that schizophrenia has received the lion's share of attention.

It is perhaps salutary to note that last century there was lively interest in the possibility that schizophrenia arose from a disorder of inter-hemispheric functions, with the origins of the idea going back even further (see Harrington, 1985). One exponent was Wigan, who around the middle of last century wrote a book on the topic, emphasizing disturbed functional integration of the hemispheres across the corpus callosum. By the end of the century, enthusiasm for this line of thinking waned, one reason for which was the discovery of callosal agenesis and the fact that acallosals were not psychotic.

Interest in cerebral laterality and schizophrenia was revived through Flor-

Henry's (1969) survey of the laterality of EEG foci in a series of Maudsley patients with temporal lobe epilepsy and psychotic-like behaviour. He claimed a relationship between schizophrenia and left-sided or bilateral foci, and between affective psychosis and right-sided foci. This relationship was subsequently vindicated in studies of similar types of schizophrenic patients with temporal lobe epilepsy, though the evidence for a right-sided association with affective psychoses and epilepsy has been controversial (Trimble and Robertson, 1987).

Flor-Henry's (1969) survey struck a responsive chord in schizophrenia research at the end of the 1960s. The 1960s had seen widespread interest in hemisphere asymmetries of function revealed by the ingenious experiments on patients undergoing callosectomy (Sperry, 1964) and the evidence of dissociations between psychic functions in neurological patients with focal lesions, termed 'disconnection syndromes' (Geschwind, 1965). The focus in research on the psychopathology of schizophrenia at the time emphasized disordered linguistic functions, termed 'formal thought disorder'. These factors all contributed to the appeal of an association between left hemispheric disturbance and schizophrenia. The splitting of psychic functions in schizophrenia could conceivably stem from dissociations between the functions of the two brain hemispheres (Dimond, 1979; Galin, 1974). A double-bind situation could arise independently of parent–child relationships, through the failure to integrate perceptual and emotional non-verbal cues with verbal awareness (Gruzelier and Hammond, 1976). References for this and the preceding paragraphs may be found in Gruzelier (in press).

Every conceivable investigative technique has now been applied to the problem of cerebral laterality and schizophrenia. Heuristically, this has been a unique enterprise, because otherwise research in psychopathology has tended to be paradigm driven with little integration between techniques (Gruzelier, 1985), whether they involve measures of orienting responses, smooth-pursuit eye movements, exogenous or endogenous evoked potentials, or EEG rhythms, to mention only procedures from psychophysiology. The diversity of research on laterality in schizophrenia goes far beyond the scope of this handbook and readers may consult many recent reviews (Flor-Henry, 1983; Gruzelier, 1987a, in press; Walker and McGuire, 1982). Here the relevance of psychophysiological techniques will be outlined, together with a consideration of central mechanisms underpinning the polygraphic measure, before going on to consider other contemporary issues in the cerebral basis of clinical psychophysiology.

BILATERAL ELECTRODERMAL RECORDING

Investigation of lateralized dysfunction in schizophrenic patients was first reported with skin conductance orienting responses and tonic levels of reactivity (Gruzelier, 1973; Gruzelier and Venables, 1973, 1974). Studies with neurological patients, while methodologically somewhat sketchy, have nevertheless shown consistent results as to hemispheric influences on bilateral electrodermal activity. Sourek (1965) obtained recordings from lobectomy cases before and after surgery for the removal of tumours or relief of epilepsy. No matter how profound were the neurological impairments, only resections of the medial temporal lobe, rhinencephalon and frontal lobe produced consistent changes in skin potential responses; neither resection of other brain lobes nor unilateral coagulation of thalamic nuclei in Parkinsonian patients altered electrodermal reactivity. Post-operative lateral asymmetries were always in the direction of smaller responses on the limb homolateral to the lesion, as was shown by Luria and Homskaya (1963). Whether this is due to reduced excitation mediated ipsilaterally or increased inhibition mediated contralaterally is unknown, but in the debate that has surrounded this issue the fact that these interpretations are not mutually exclusive is often overlooked.

The hierarchical nature and multiplicity of central influences on electro-dermal activity must also be taken into account in interpreting hemispheric influences on skin potential. Destruction of the triggering mechanisms for autonomic responses in the brain stem (Davison and Koss, 1974) will have irreparable consequences for the influence of higher centres on responses. In contrast, the destruction of higher centres will not destroy the capacity for responses but may alter the interplay and hierarchical nature of cortical–sub-cortical influences, including hemispheric control. After damage to higher centres, but not to the brain stem, the brain has scope for functional recovery, as seen in the loss of post-operative response asymmetries in some frontal leucotomy cases in follow-up recordings 3 months or later (Elithorn, Piercy and Crosskey, 1954). Limitations in the evidence collected many years post-lobectomy have not always been observed (e.g. Toone, Cooke and Lader, 1979).

Awareness of the importance of hemispheric control has arisen from a study of unilateral lesion cases who showed opposite extremes of electrodermal responsivity according to the side of the lesion. Heilman, Schwartz and Watson (1978) examined seven right-sided, and six left-sided neurological cases who were compared with non-organic controls. Electrodermal activity was recorded from the hand ipsilateral to the lesion to brief electrical pulses delivered to the forearm. Levels of electrodermal activity were significantly reduced in the right-sided group and five out of seven patients were non-responders. In contrast, the magnitude of responses of the left-sided group was approximately four times that of the controls. A similar study was conducted by Morrow, Vrtunski, Kim and Boller (1981), where the right-sided group again produced smaller amplitude responses and showed no differentiation between stimuli consisting of emotional and neutral slides.

To complicate matters further, Sourek (1965) found that when unilateral surgical lesions produced response asymmetries, these were always independent of asymmetries in background levels of activity, indicating that central influences on levels and responses could be differentiated. It is often the case in normal subjects that lateral asymmetries in levels of activity do not correlate with asymmetries in responses (e.g. Gruzelier, Eves and Connolly, 1981b). This is also illustrated by differential drug influences on asymmetries in orienting responses, non-specific responses and levels (Gruzelier and Connolly, 1980). However, the popular notion of the predominance of contralateral inhibitory influences on bilateral electrodermal responses (Lacroix and Comper, 1979) has not acknowledged these distinctions and has, in fact, proceeded on the basis of evidence of the effects of cerebral lesions on electrodermal levels (Holloway and Parsons, 1969). Holloway and Parsons (1969) found that what distinguished patients with unilateral damage to frontal, temporal and parietal regions from controls was higher levels of skin conductance contralateral to the lesion; this they attributed to a contralateral release of the reticular activating system from cortical inhibition.

The study of Holloway and Parsons (1969) also provides a useful example in human subjects of the multiplicity of cerebral influences on electrodermal activity which were comprehensively charted by Wang (1964) in the cat. They examined levels of activity during passive sensory stimulation that was typical of the conventional orienting paradigm with a perceptual task and a motor-readiness task. The contralateral enhancement was only found during passive stimulation and at rest. It had earlier been shown (e.g. Schwartz, 1937) that premotor cortex had excitatory influences on electrodermal activity. Conceivably, this would counteract inhibitory factors and would come into play with active task deemands. Recent paradigms which fractionate the various stimulus and response processes have provided undeniable evidence of contralateral excitatory processes evinced by asymmetrical increases in response amplitude to those stimuli which signified a preparation for action on the hand which was subsequently to perform the action (Gruzelier, Sergeant and Eves, 1988).

The majority of studies on cerebral laterality in normal subjects with bilateral electrodermal measurement have not observed the distinctions disclosed by neuropathological studies between differential hemispheric influences on phasic and tonic reactivity, nor the predominance of contralateral inhibition in passive states and the involvement of contralateral excitation in sensory–motor tasks. It is therefore not surprising that a confusing picture has emerged, with some experiments showing a predominance of contralateral inhibitory influences, others contralateral excitation, and the majority no uniform asymmetry (Hugdahl, 1984).

Furthermore, the emphasis on reductions in skin conductance response amplitude as an accompaniment of active processing, which a unitary contralateral inhibition hypothesis requires, is of course paradoxical and runs counter to psychophysiological theory, which posits positive relationships between processing and response amplitude. Thus when consideration is given to neurophysiological evidence, unitary theories of electrodermal responses become a doubtful enterprise or lead to generalized notions such as 'a need for processing'; attention is also drawn away from Sokolovian concerns about enhancement of perceptual processing towards effector functions (Gruzelier, 1988).

Thus the neuropsychophysiological evidence to date requires in the planning of experiments that distinctions be observed between conditions of passive sensory stimulation and active task demands. In the former, when the brain is in an idling state, a less complex state of affairs will obtain and therefore the likelihood will be increased of revealing trait or state factors associated with hemisphericity in activational processes. When active tasks are imposed, central determinants will increase. Accordingly, a fractionation of stimulus and response functions is advocated, and here bilateral measurement will assist in unravelling the involvement of output functions. Consideration should also be given to the fact that lateral asymmetries in response may not coincide with asymmetries in tonic levels of skin conductance. Evidence also suggests that with adaptation and repeat testing, asymmetries in levels of activity will be affected (Gruzelier and Venables, 1974; Obrist, 1963).

Aside from the lateral dimension, the vertical cortical–subcortical dimension is likely to become increasingly important in understanding psychopathological conditions. Anterior cortex appears to have inhibitory influences over subcortex and these inhibitory functions appear to be contralaterally mediated (Holloway and Parsons, 1969). Given the increase in frontal blood flow, or hyperfrontality, known to obtain in the normal resting brain (Ingvar, 1976), it follows that, under conditions of rest or passive sensory stimulation, the relative balance in frontal influences is likely to be an important determinant of the electrodermal response asymmetry.

Notwithstanding the fact that the reader may find neuropsychophysiological considerations unfamiliar and daunting, it has also to be acknowledged that what is presently understood will prove to be grossly simplistic. Before abandoning a neuropsychophysiological perspective in despair, the reader may wish to consider evidence from clinicopathological correlation, a tradition following in the footsteps of Broca and Wernicke, which has shown striking, replicable associations between clinical syndromes and electrodermal asymmetries. In the work of the author and colleagues, associations have been uncovered with the laterality of pain in migraine and with syndromes in schizophrenia. Before outlining this evidence, the existence of individual differences in electrodermal lateral asymmetries will be briefly reviewed.

Individual Differences in Electrodermal Lateral Asymmetries

Research on cerebral lateralization has since its origins been aware that individual differences exist, notably with respect to handedness and more recently sex differences (Harris, 1978; Herron, 1980). These factors may be joined by a third one.

Serendipitously we discovered, in three experiments with a total of 109 subjects, that rates of habituation of the electrodermal response vary with lateral asymmetry in both the orienting response and the non-specific responses that occur during the orienting paradigm, a relationship that was independent of asymmetries in tonic levels of skin conductance (Gruzelier *et al.*, 1981b). This and subsequent work (Gruzelier, 1987a; Kopp and Gruzelier, in press) has led to a schema which posits reciprocal hemispheric influences on electrodermal response habituation. In the majority of individuals, fast habituation and a low incidence of non-specific responses are associated with higher response amplitudes on the left hand. As responsivity increases, this asymmetry at first reduces and then reverses. On the assumption that when the brain is in the idling state it is a passive recipient of intermittent stimulation, then as outlined above contralateral influences will predominate. Accordingly, it is the left hemisphere which is dominant for low levels of reactivity and fast habituation, and the right hemisphere for higher levels of reactivity. These relationships are shown in Figure 5.1.

Anxiety may interfere with these relationships. In one study, students' scores on the IPAT scale of anxiety (Krug, Scheier and Cattell, 1976) were found to

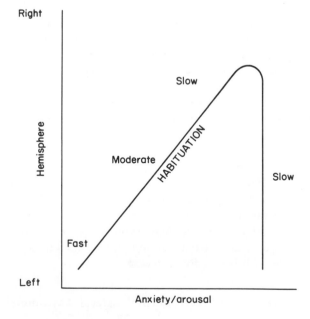

Figure 5.1. Habituation and electrodermal reactivity as a function of hemispheric activation and anxiety/arousal.

be higher in slow habituators than fast habituators; however, whereas moderate levels of anxiety were associated with larger right hand responses, higher levels of anxiety were associated with larger left hand responses. In other words, with higher states of anxiety, the left hemispheric influences predominate. A coupling of slow habituation with anxiety is consistent with other reports in students (Gruzelier and Phelan, in press; Maltzman, Smith and Cantor, 1971) and Mandell, 1971 and with studies of anxiety disorders (Lader and Wing, 1966). The relationships proposed in the schema have been partially supported by a study (Kopp and Gruzelier, in press) in which bilateral absolute auditory thresholds were examined in anxious patients and controls who were classified as low, medium or high in electrodermal reactivity measured unilaterally. The low and moderate groups showed no asymmetry in thresholds or left ear advantages, while the highly reactive group showed right ear advantages compatible with higher left hemispheric activation in temporal regions. The importance of lateralization for anxiety disorders will be returned to in a later section of the chapter.

Thus, while there are well-recognized important individual differences in electrodermal responsiveness (O'Gorman, 1977), in the light of the above evidence these must be extended to include lateral asymmetries in electrodermal responsivity. The central determinants of such effects are beginning to be charted and cerebral laterality and dynamic process factors, such as anxiety, are shown to be important.

Habituation and the Laterality of Pain in Migraine

Migraine, according to the Greek derivation of the word, means a one-sided headache. Pain is often felt unilaterally and some individuals characteristically experience the pain on the same side from one attack to another. Sensory discomfort is often a forerunner of an attack, and photophobia and phonophobia may accompany the migraine. We hypothesized that impairments in habituation may underlie such sensory sensitivity and studied patients whose pain was consistently lateralized. Groups with left- and right-sided pain were contrasted on measures of electrodermal response habituation to flashes in one experiment and tones in another (Gruzelier, Nikolau, Connolly, Peatfield, Davies and Clifford-Rose, 1987a). Patients were all severe cases of migraine, and were examined between headaches. In both experiments, we found that there was no overlap in rates of habituation between the groups. Left-sided migraineurs were fast habituators or non-responders, and right-sided migraineurs were slow habituators – in most cases with extremely slow habituation. In the second experiment which involved drug-free patients, extremes of habituation were found to have parallels in the number of non-specific responses and the degree of tonic electrodermal responsiveness. Thus, in migraineurs whose pain was consistently lateralized, extremes of responsiveness were found, the direction of which was predictive of the laterality of pain.

A review of the organic literature on neurological symptoms of mirgraine, which include hemianopia, hemiparesis and dysphasia, revealed that damage to thalamic nuclei can give rise to all such symptoms (Gruzelier, 1986b). When this evidence is taken in conjunction with the importance of thalamocortical mechanisms in the mediation of the autonomic orienting response (Lynn, 1966; Sokolov, 1963), it is tempting to conclude that in migraine there is a failure in the regulation of focal brain activation which involves thalamocortical mechanisms and which may be laterally imbalanced. Disturbance to a regulatory mechanism may have significance for the finding from a biofeedback study involving headache cases that stabilizing of frontalis muscle tension at a high level was as effective as lowering muscle tension (Cram, 1980).

Lateral Imbalance and Syndromes in Schizophrenia

The original finding of lateral asymmetries in schizophrenic patients in a passive orienting paradigm indicated larger right than left hand responses and a few instances of unilateral non-responding on the left hand (Gruzelier, 1973; Gruzelier and Hammond, 1976; Gruzelier and Venables, 1974). These were statistical relationships; not all schizophrenic patients showed the same right-greater-than-left asymmetry. These initial results in group tendency were nevertheless consistent with evidence of left hemispheric lesions in neurological patients and with Flor-Henry's (1969) survey showing an association of schizophrenic-like psychoses and EEG epileptic foci in the left temporal lobe. Examination of a group of endogenous depressives revealed the opposite response asymmetry and represented the first evidence from non-organic psychotic patients in support of Flor-Henry's schema relating schizophrenia to the left hemisphere and affective psychoses to the right hemisphere.

Some subsequent investigators comparing psychopathological groups with normals have concluded that there is no evidence of lateral asymmetry in electrodermal responses. What these authors really mean is that no directionally consistent asymmetries have differentiated the groups, not that subjects were symmetrical in their responses. In fact, individual differences in the direction of symmetry have proved to be the salient feature in more recent studies of schizophrenia. Work with remitting forms of schizophrenia diagnosed with the standardized diagnostic procedure, the Present State Examination (Wing, Cooper and Sartorius, 1974), showed almost as many schizophrenic patients with larger left as larger right hand responses. Using the direction of lateral asymmetry as a classifying procedure and symptoms as the dependent variable, two disparate syndromes in schizophrenia were disclosed (Gruzelier, 1984; Gruzelier and Manchanda, 1982). Patients with losses of left hemispheric function, i.e. with larger responses on the right hand, were characterized by negative symptoms such as poverty of speech, social and emotional withdrawal, and blunted affect. The symptoms of patients with losses of right hemispheric function, i.e. with larger responses on the left hand, included positive symptoms such as delusions, cognitive acceleration, positive affect and overactivity. The syndromes were termed 'Withdrawn' and 'Active', respectively, and were consistent with neuropsychological functional asymmetries. In the Withdrawn syndrome, the symptom of poverty of speech was in keeping with a reduction in left hemispheric functions, while withdrawal and negative affect have been associated with right hemispheric activation. In the Active syndrome, cognitive acceleration was consistent with left hemispheric activation, as was positive affect. Schneiderian symptoms of first rank did not distinguish the groups, because these symptoms, consisting predominantly of auditory hallucinations in the third person and passivity experiences such as being under the control of external forces, are cardinal to the diagnosis of schizophrenia and therefore were common to the majority of patients.

The neuropsychological basis of the Active and Withdrawn syndromes is posited to stem from imbalances in hemispheric activation: in other words, they represent the dynamic functional state of the brain and are not fixed in a structural sense. This allows for shifts from one syndrome to another within an episode or as the illness progresses. It also allows for shifts in hemispheric activational dominance with medication, as has been shown for the action of neuroleptics. In a chlorpromazine withdrawal study with institutionalized patients, auditory discriminations, which were superior in the right ear when patients were on the drug, reversed progressively as the drug was withdrawn, and switched back progressively as the drug was reinstated (Hammond and Gruzelier, 1978). In remitting patients, the administration of antipsychotic drugs which was followed by clinical improvement also coincided with shifts in lateral asymmetries in electrodermal orienting responses (Gruzelier *et al.*, 1981a). Evidence of a dynamic state of hemispheric imbalance also raises the possibility of therapeutic intervention in schizophrenia by non-pharmacological means aimed at influencing hemispheric balance.

Other psychological measures apart from skin conductance responses have produced evidence in support of opposite states of hemispheric imbalance in the two schizophrenic syndromes (Gruzelier, 1983, 1986, 1986a, 1987bc). These include measures of EEG power, the contingent negative variation, the recovery curve of the Hoffman reflex to somatosensory stimulation and lateral eye movements. Associations with skin conductance activity have been independently replicated and extended (Rabavilas, Liappas and Stefanis, 1986; White, Svali and Charles, 1987). Support also stems from other laterality procedures which reflect the dynamic functional state of brain activity. Dichotic listening procedures have indicated exaggerated right ear advantages in paranoid as distinct from non-paranoid schizophrenic patients. Corroboration has also followed from invasive imaging procedures of brain metabolism and blood flow (see Gruzelier, 1987b, for review).

In measures depicting structural process asymmetries, such as neuropsychological test procedures, a more complex situation obtains. Here, dynamic processes may interact with or mask asymmetries in hemispheric cognitive specialization based on structural processes, especially where a process may be performed by either hemisphere, even though one hemisphere is characteristically dominant (Levy, Heller, Banich and Burton, 1983; Sackheim, Weiman and Grega, 1984). This may be illustrated by a neuropsychophysiological study of examination anxiety in students (Gruzelier and Phelan, in press). Aside from the ecological validity of using examination stress as a means of manipulating anxiety, its effects were validated with a questionnaire of anxiety (IPAT) and with measures of electrodermal response habituation and non-specific reactivity. Students were used as their own control and were examined twice, one day before an examination and 4 weeks before or after, with order counterbalanced. The index of a structurally based hemispheric process was a lexical task involving divided visual-field presentation, which was known to produce right visual-field/left hemisphere advantages in normal subjects (Connolly, Gruzelier and Manchanda, 1983). Under the stress of an impending exam, frustration–tension scores on the anxiety questionnaire increased as did the number of specific and non-specific electrodermal responses. In confirmation of previous experiments, the lexical task showed a left hemispheric advantage in the non-anxious condition, but before the exam this was reversed. A left hemispheric advantage was shown by 23 out of 31 subjects in the non-anxious condition, whereas a right hemispheric advantage was shown by 21 out of 31 subjects under anxiety ($P < 0.001$).

In studies of schizophrenia there has been a striking example of a cognitive task which has revealed different cognitive strategies in schizophrenic patients belonging to Active and Withdrawn syndromes. Gaebel, Ulrich and Frick (1986) compared 20 schizophrenic outpatients with 20 normal controls on (1) lateral deviations in visual fixation of a stationary spot of light, (2) eye movements and reaction time during a letter matrix search task, and (3) ratings of symptoms on the Brief Psychiatric Rating Scale (Overall and Gorham, 1962). Consistent with the hemisphere-imbalance syndromes, 'emotional excitement' and a factor score termed 'activation' were associated with rightward eye movements, while 'withdrawal' was associated with leftward eye movements: lateral deviations in eye movements are controlled by the frontal eye fields, such that deviations are contralateral to the more activated hemisphere (Kinsbourne, 1975). Remarkably, the Withdrawn patients, who typically perform more poorly on cognitive tasks, were on a par with controls in their search time, and the search route shown by eye movements was compatible with a right hemispheric, parallel processing, perceptual style. In contrast, the Active patients had a significantly longer search time, and the search route indicated left hemispheric serial processing, as if reading a passage of text. These effects are shown in Fgure 5.2.

The administration of experimental neuropsychological tests of learning and memory to Active and Withdrawn patients with remitting forms of schizophrenia has shown that unilateral losses of function tend to correspond with the less activated hemisphere (Gruzelier, Seymour, Wilson, Jolley and Hirsch, 1988). Tests were selected which on the basis of studies with neurological patients distinguished left- from right-sided temporohippocampal and frontohippocampal functions (Milner, 1982). Patients with the Active syndromes showed impairments on the right hemispheric tests, while patients with the Withdrawn syndrome showed either impairments on the left hemispheric tests or bilateral impairments. The fact that 90% of remitting cases showed evidence of focal losses of function gives lie to the belief that schizophrenic patients show only generalized cognitive impairments. In fact, the learning, memory and verbal fluency of some of the Active syndrome patients was in the superior category. Evidence such as this releases the study of neuropsychological deficits

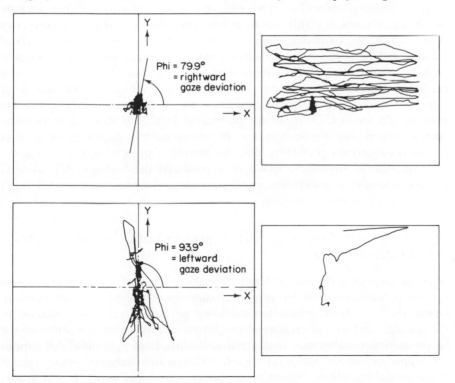

Figure 5.2. Traces for a patient characterized by 'activation' (top) show a rightward gaze deviation and a serial search strategy. Traces for a patient characterized by 'withdrawal' (bottom) show a leftward gaze deviation and a parallel search strategy.

in schizophrenia from the constraints of artifactual interpretations based on inattention, lack of motivation and generalized cognitive impairment. This does not, however, release the investigator from the necessity to provide evidence of double dissociations of function (Teuber, 1959).

The neuropsychological evidence of focal cerebral involvement in schizophrenia serves to introduce evidence from other sources that has not always considered cerebral laterality. This evidence will be reviewed before leaving the topic of schizophrenia and resuming discussion of the relevance of laterality to other types of psychopathology.

CENTRAL NERVOUS SYSTEM SIGNS IN SCHIZOPHRENIA

Brain damage of a widespread nature can occur in schizophrenia. Structural imaging procedures such as computed tomography (CT) have, since the 1970s, revealed bilateral cortical atrophy and ventricular enlargement in a varying percentage of cases. It is still not altogether clear what are the clinical correlates of the CT signs (Gruzelier, 1985). In view of the non-specificity of cortical atrophy and ventricular enlargement for schizophrenia, given their association with a range of neurological disorders, they are unlikely to underpin the cardinal features of schizophrenia. This is not to suggest that focal neurological signs may not be responsible for cardinal symptoms, but these have not as yet been sought for in CT investigations, though high-resolution scanners make such a strategy feasible. Nevertheless, neuropsychophysiological investigations cannot disregard the possibility that the sample of patients will include some with widespread pathology, which may confound the findings. Accordingly, CT scans should be undertaken on all patients and those with gross CT signs regarded as a separate subgroup.

CORTICAL–SUBCORTICAL AND LIMBIC SYSTEM DYSFUNCTION IN SCHIZOPHRENIA

Neuropsychological evidence of hippocampal involvement in schizophrenia (see earlier) is consistent with recent neuropathological evidence (summarized by Gruzelier *et al.*, 1988) which has disclosed pyramidal cell disorientation in the anterior and medial regions of the hippocampus; reduced volume of the hippocampus, parahippocampal gyrus and amygdala; pyramidal cell loss in the hippocampus and temporal cortex; and cytoarchitechtonic abnormalities of the rostral entorhinal regions of the parahippocampal gyrus. In one study, lateral asymmetries were examined and were found on the left side in ten patients and on the right side in three patients (Jakob and Beckmann, 1986).

Hippocampal involvement is also consistent with early psychophysiological evidence which, in fact, preceded the neuropathological studies (Gruzelier, Lykken and Venables, 1972; Mednick, 1970). After the discovery of a collection of nuclei in the brain stem and functional considerations that gave rise to the concept of the brain-stem activating system (Moruzzi and Magoun, 1949), Jaspers speculated that in psychosis there was a disruption of cortical–subcortical regulation. Darrow, Pathman and Kronenberg (1946), by recording simultaneously electrocortical and autonomic activity, offered a means of examining cortical–subcortical relationships. This led to a series of studies with schizophrenic patients, often using the two-flash threshold as a measure of cortical arousal and electrodermal activity as an autonomic parameter. In many studies, positive correlations were found between the two sets of measures and were interpreted as evidence of an abnormal state of simultaneous activation of cortical and subcortical systems (Gruzelier, Lykken and Venables, 1972; Lykken and Maley, 1968).

During the 1960s, there were discoveries of the modulatory influences of the limbic system over cortical–reticular interactions which took the form of a negative feedback loop (Douglas, 1967; Gray, 1967; Kimble, 1968; Redding, 1967). The electrodermal orienting response and its rate of habituation were found in animal studies to be disrupted by lesions to some limbic structures such as the amygdala and hippocampus, and by interconnected frontal regions. Much of this evidence has been reviewed by Pribram and McGuinness (1975). Lesions to the hippocampus produced a failure of habituation to auditory stimuli, whereas lesions to the amygdala produced in the majority non-responding and in the remainder hyper-responding. As reviewed in these studies, the findings were consistent with ablation experiments and evidence from electrical stimulation.

Mednick (1970), in a longitudinal study of children with severely schizophrenic mothers, found that in comparison with control children, those children with psychiatric breakdowns in early adulthood showed in puberty shorter electrodermal response latencies in an orienting and conditioning paradigm, a failure of response latencies to habituate, a resistance of response to extinction, and short response half-recovery times. Many of these features were subsequently found to characterize the hippocampectomized monkeys of Bagshaw and Benzies (see Pribram and McGuinness, 1975). Mednick (1970) drew parallels with the well-documented inhibitory deficits of hippocampectomized animals and the vulnerability of the hippocampus to anoxia during birth, important in view of the higher incidence of obstetric complications during birth in the children with the psychiatric histories. Interest in birth complications as a potential contributory factor to schizophrenia breakdown (McNeil, 1978) has recently surfaced again in schizophrenia research (Murray, in press).

Limbic involvement in schizophrenia provided the theoretical background to the studies by Gruzelier and Venables (see review by Dawson, Chapter

13) of autonomic orienting and habituation in schizophrenic patients. While something of a hiatus was created by this evidence, there is now a consensus that in schizophrenia both extremes of reactivity in orienting responses may occur, with non-responding the more common feature. Normal habituation and fast habituation have also been found. However, what has not been fully assimilated by this field of research is the fact that there is nothing pathognomonic about non-responding in schizophrenia, and, in fact, both extremes of orienting activity may occur in depression (Lader and Wing, 1969), anxiety (Thornton and Gruzelier, in preparation), alcoholism, children at genetic risk for schizophrenia (Gruzelier, 1982), and in migraineurs (Gruzelier *et al.*, 1987a).

CORTICAL EVOKED POTENTIALS: THE P300

Interest in the hippocampus in schizophrenia has recently emerged from another psychophysiological domain, namely the P300 of the cortical evoked response. An absence of the P300 has been found in a percentage of schizophrenic patients, but again this is not unique to schizophrenia. The P300 is a positive-going deflection that occurs with a latency of about 300 ms and has a parioetocentral scalp derivation no matter what the modality of stimulation. The P300 provides a sensitive index of the information content of a stimulus which the subject is anticipating and searching for. It occurs to target stimuli if they are correctly detected and its amplitude varies with the confidence of detection and the improbability of the target. The complexity of the target cue is related to the latency of the P300 and to the reaction time of the behavioural response. Some form of response is essential and this may be overt or covert, though the specific nature of the response made is unimportant. Thus the P300 requires active task participation and involves a selective perceptual process for identifying particular relevant stimuli in relation to expectancy and memorized stimulus categories (Picton, Campbell, Baribeau-Braun and Proux, 1978).

Roth (1977) and Friedman (in press) have reviewed the early evidence for reductions in P300s in schizophrenia. Interesting dissociations between the cortical evoked potential and behavioural reaction time have also been observed. Sutton, Spring and Tueking (1978) found that, when a signal for a manual reaction time switches sensory modality, normal subjects show both a slowing of the manual reaction time and an increase in the P300. In contrast, schizophrenic patients, while showing a marked slowing of reaction time, failed to show the P300 augmentation. Baribeau-Braun, Picton and Gosselin (1983) also failed to find parallels between P300 amplitude and behavioural performance in schizophrenia. Unsurprisingly, the P300 deficit is not synonymous with schizophrenia, and claims have been made for an abnormal increase in P300 latency as a marker for dementia (Squires, Goodin and Starr, 1979), though this claim has been challenged (Pfefferbaum, Wenegrat, Ford, Roth and Kopell, 1984). If, as is discussed below, the medial temporal lobe is one source of the

P300 generator, then evidence of P300 abnormalities in conditions in which deficits of this brain region occur gives credence to the localization. This is in fact the case. Abnormal P300s have been found in normal elderly patients and alcoholic patients (Porjesz, Begleiter and Samuelly, 1980), dementia (Pferffer-baum *et al.*, 1984), psychotic depression (Steinhauer and Zubin, 1983), neurotic depression (Josiassen, Roemer, Shagass and Straumanis, 1986) and also in anhedonic normals (Josiassen, Shagass, Roemer and Straumanis, 1985; Simons, 1981), a condition which is associated with electrodermal non-responding (Simons, 1981).

The evidence for the source of the neural generator of the P300 is as follows. Halgren, Squires, Wilson, Rohrbaugh, Babb and Crandall (1980) recorded from bilateral electrodes implanted in the hippocampus, the hippocampal gyrus or the amygdala in order to locate epileptic foci in patients, all of whom had normal intelligence. Simultaneous scalp recordings were obtained during an oddball pitch discrimination task. Potentials were recorded from both limbic structures to infrequent and frequent tones but were found to be larger to the infrequent tones. Furthermore, if subjects were engaged in reading a book and instructed to ignore the tones, then the evoked potentials to the same tone stimuli were attenuated. These and other paradigms indicated that the potentials obeyed the criteria for a P300 being independent of stimulus modality. The amplitudes of the potentials were more than twice as high when recorded from the implanted electrodes compared with the scalp. Parallels were also found between limbic potentials and single unit recording from the same electrodes. Wood, Allison, Goff, Williamson and Spencer (1980) recorded simultaneously from the scalp and depth probes planted in frontal, central and posterior regions directed to the temporal pole. P300 amplitudes were larger in the bottom third of the probes, suggesting a subcortical rather than cortical origin. However, Johnson and Fedio (1986) cast doubt on a temporal–limbic origin of the P300 by finding in nine epileptic patients who were undergoing unilateral lobectomy that P300-like responses in seven different paradigms were obtained in all patients.

An alternative view has been proposed by Yingling and Hosobuchi (1984) who recorded from electrodes implanted in the somatosensory thalamus and periaquaductal grey in a patient with intractible pain. P300-like responses were recorded in visual and auditory paradigms, and latencies were similar in thalamus and cortex – an important feature given their observation that latencies in hippocampus in the report of Halgren *et al.* (1980) were longer than those on the scalp, casting doubt on a hippocampal generator. Yingling and Hosobuchi (1984) concluded that their single-case study provided data incompatible with the hippocampal genesis of the P300 and located the gener-ator dorsal to their recording sites. A subcortical location would be in keeping with the model of Desmedt and Debecker (1979) which implicated the reticul-othalamo-prefrontal system in the genesis of the P300. Thus, while the source of the generator is as yet unclear, the areas implicated have obvious relevance to the psychopathological conditions which show P300 abnormalities. Subcortical involvement in schizophrenia has been considered from a further perspective.

BRAIN-STEM EVOKED POTENTIALS

Auditory brain-stem functions can be examined by recording early evoked potentials to brief clicks from vertex to mastoid derivations. Six positive-going components occur within 10 ms (Jewett, Romano and Williston, 1970). Wave II is thought to reflect the earliest brain-stem activity, so that peripheral conduction time is the time elapsed from stimulus onset to wave II. Central brain-stem conduction time is the time from wave II to wave VI. Several studies of schizophrenic patients have been conducted using these techniques. Pfefferbaum, Horvath, Roth, Tinklenberg and Kopell (1980) were unable to locate any brain-stem abnormalities in 15 male, acutely ill schizophrenic patients, seven of whom were unmedicated. Szelenberger (1983) examined 15 male controls and 20 male schizophrenics who in addition completed the Eysenck EPQ questionnaire. The 'psychoticism' dimension, which has been described as reflecting aggression, eccentricity and lack of sympathy, was found associated in both groups with an inhibitory factor in the initial stages of auditory transmission. It was the later components that distinguished patients from controls and provided evidence of accelerated transmission in patients.

Syndrome relationships have been reported by Lindstrom, Klochhoff, Svedberg and Bergstrom (1987). They examined 20 schizophrenic inpatients and found a significant relationship between the presence of auditory hallucinations and abnormal brain-stem responses. This is compatible with other evidence which also associates brain-stem involvement with auditory hallucinations in schizophrenia (Gruzelier, 1985). Subgrouping of patients was also found important by Sommer (1985). He examined brain-stem auditory evoked potentials in schizophrenics on maintenance neuroleptic therapy, in drug-free alcoholics and normal subjects who were subdivided into electrodermal responders and non-responders. He found a relationship with electrodermal responding status regardless of diagnosis in response to visual but not auditory stimuli. Non-responding subjects showed longer latencies to wave V, interpreted as a sign of excessive selective filtering of stimuli in non-responders. Subcortical–cortical pathway abnormalities in schizophrenia have also been implicated in evoked potential studies designed to explore callosal transmission.

SOMATOSENSORY EVOKED POTENTIALS AND CALLOSAL TRANSMISSION

An important approach to the elucidation of disturbed inter-hemispheric relationships in schizophrenia has been the examination of bilateral somatosensory cortical evoked potentials in response to unilateral stimulation. It is assumed that the ipsilateral potential is generated by callosal fibres and that transmission across the callosum will result in an attenuation of amplitudes and a delay in latencies. Mention has been made of the methodological and theoretical difficulties encountered in the application of this technique to schizophrenia (Gruzelier, 1978b). What does emerge is clear evidence for the existence of a subgroup of schizophrenic patients who show symmetrical responses. In other words, in these patients there was no attenuation of evoked potentials recorded over somatosensory cortex on the side ipsilateral to the limb stimulated, nor were latencies delayed.

How may this effect be accounted for? One hypothesis is that an alternative route to callosal transmission has evolved through the abnormal development of ipsilateral pathways. Andrews, House Cooper and Barber (1986) have shown that it is those patients belonging to the Withdrawn syndrome (Gruzelier and Manchanda, 1982) that possess this abnormality. In a subsequent investigation (Andrews, Cooper, Barber and Raine, 1987), they replicated the syndrome relationships and also demonstrated in the Withdrawn syndrome impairments in inter-hemispheric transfer and left-sided losses of function on experimental neuropsychological tests, results which are compatible with our hemisphere-imbalance syndrome model.

CORTICAL EVOKED POTENTIALS: MIDDLE LATENCY COMPONENTS

The presence of abnormality in subcortical ipsilateral pathways is an interpretation also given to some of the irregularities revealed in auditory evoked potentials in the 100–200 ms range in schizophrenia. Connolly, Manchanda, Gruzelier and Hirsch (1985) found an absence of the contralateral dominance effect seen in N120 peak amplitudes recorded over temporal cortex in five out of ten unmedicated schizophrenic patients. Hemisphere asymmetry ratios, whether ipsilaterally or contralaterally dominant, were larger in patients than controls. It is clear that if these results are substantiated, interpretations of ear advantages in dichotic listening tasks in terms of the conventional contralateral pathway model will have to be reconsidered (Connolly, Prescott, Gruzelier and Hirsch, 1986).

In the visual modality, abnormal amplitude–intensity functions have shown topographical relationships which in one study suggested a loss of inhibitory control in the left temporal lobe to stimuli of high intensity (Connolly *et al.*, 1985). Spectral analysis of the same evoked potential waveforms has shown abnormal power–intensity relationships in schizophrenia which are compatible with abnormal cortical–subcortical interactions (Jutai, Gruzelier, Connolly, Manchanda and Hirsch, 1984). Oculomotor abnormalities in schizophrenia may also arise from abnormal subcortical–cortical interrelationships.

SMOOTH-PURSUIT EYE MOVEMENTS

Lipton, Levy, Holzman and Levin (1983) were responsible for a revival of interest in schizophrenia of disorders of the smooth ocular pursuit of a moving object such as a pendulum, a phenomenon first noticed by Diefendorf and Dodge (1908). Twin studies (Holzman, Kringlen, Levy, Proctor, Haberman and Yasillo, 1977) have shown that tracking impairments have high concordance rates in the order of 71% for monozygotic twins and 54% for dizygotic twins. However, 80% of the monozygotic twin pairs who were concordant for tracking abnormalities were, in fact, discordant for schizophrenia. Abnormal tracking has also been associated with non-psychotic and unipolar and bipolar affective disorders; apparently there is an equal prevalence in recent admissions of schizophrenia and manic depression (Lipton, Levin & Holzman, 1980; 1974). Shagass, Amadeo and Overton, 1974).

A number of different abnormalities have been documented: saccadic intrusions, where small saccades occur up to three times per second in opposite direction to one another; what is called the Type I impairment, where smooth pursuit is replaced by large-amplitude saccades; and the Type II impairment, where smooth pursuit is replaced by small-amplitude steps. Abnormal movements have also been seen during prolonged fixation of a stationary object and have been reduced during vestibulo-ocular reflex movements (Levin, Jones, Stark, Merrin and Holzman, 1982). The possibility can be excluded that smooth-pursuit impairments are an artifactual representation of brain potentials as was posited by Iacono and Lykken (1981). As yet it is unclear what the clinical or neurophysiological correlates are.

In considering cerebral involvement, one attempt has been to relate the tracking abnormalities to eye movement centres in the frontal eye fields which influence the substantia nigra (Holzman, in press; Levin, 1984a,b). A failure of the inhibitory influences of these centres via inhibitory gamma-aminobutyric acid projections has been shown after pharmacological blockade in monkeys to result in eye movement patterns such as those found in schizophrenia. However, recent evidence shows that the smooth-pursuit system involves motion detectors in the prestriate cortex which project to the medial superior temporal region and in turn to the brain stem (Newsombe, Wurtz, Dursteler and Mikami, 1985). Accordingly, unilateral temporal lobe involvement in schizophrenia should result in smooth-pursuit tracking abnormalities only in the direction towards the lesioned side.

The oculocephalic reflex, namely eye movements triggered by movement of the head, and the vestibulo-ocular reflex were found to be normal in virtually all schizophrenic patients with tracking abnormalities (Lipton *et al.* 1980). Therefore, as these reflexes require an intact brain stem and vestibular system, the tracking abnormalities must arise at a level higher than the brain stem. Another approach has been to compare full-field and partial-field optokinetic nystagmus which involve brain stem and cortical pathways, respectively. Patients with deficits in tracking exhibited partial-field but not full-field optokinetic nystagmus abnormalities, also suggesting pathophysiology at a level higher than the brain stem (Latham, Holzman, Manschrek and Tole, 1981).

It has been claimed that the saccadic system functions normally in schizophrenia (Iacono, Tuason and Johnson, 1981; Levin, Holzman, Rottenberg and Lipton, 1981; Levin *et al.*, 1982). However, full consideration has not been given to the different types of saccades, which may be classified as reflex, spontaneous and voluntary. Voluntary saccades may or may not be visually guided, as in the distinction between eye movements to real and imagined targets. The frontal eye fields are involved in voluntary saccades but not in spontaneous or reflex saccades (Fox, Fox, Raichle and Burde, 1985). Thus neurophysiological considerations suggest a number of untested hypotheses about smooth-pursuit eye movements in schizophrenia.

Before leaving schizophrenia, it can be seen that outside of lateralization theory little integration is possible across the variety of neuropsychophysiological abnormalities observed. Given the heterogeneity of schizophrenia, a syndrome approach has proven useful in the past and makes obvious sense when a brain–behaviour analysis of the condition is fully grasped. Attempts to seek markers that distinguish schizophrenic patients as a group from other diagnostic categories are unlikely to be profitable by virtue of the overlap in the symptoms of psychopathological conditions. It follows that neuropsychophysiological investigations of schizophrenia are not to be encouraged if their only interface with clinical concerns is a diagnosis of schizophrenia.

CEREBRAL LATERALITY: MOOD, SOMATIC SYMPTOMS AND THE IMMUNE SYSTEM

ANXIETY DISORDERS

Some evidence has already been reviewed showing that, under anxiety, hemispheric asymmetries in cognitive functions may be altered, such that lexical processing, for which the left hemisphere is normally superior, may be done more quickly in the right hemisphere (Gruzelier and Phelan, in press). Furthermore, high levels of anxiety in normals and patients with anxiety disorders (as defined by the *Diagnostic and Statistical Manual of Mental Disorders*, 3rd edn; DSM-III; American Psychiatric Association, 1980) may lead to a shift towards left hemispheric activational dominance (Gruzelier, 1987a; Kopp and Gruzelier, in press). Some other results are as follows.

Tucker, Antes, Stenislie and Bernhardt (1978), in an examination of anxiety measured by questionnaire in students, showed an asymmetry in favour of the right ear in loudness judgements in high trait-anxious students, an asymmetry not found in low trait-anxious students. A divided visual-field study involving processing of verbal and spatial stimuli disclosed in the same students poorer left than right hemispheric processing in the high anxious group. They inferred from these results that anxiety placed a processing load on the left hemisphere through overactivation. The processing load was seen in poorer divided visual-field processing in the left hemisphere, while overactivation was assumed from the better loudness judgements in the right ear. This inference assumes that overactivation will not impair loudness judgements which will continue to improve as anxiety increases; clearly further validation of this assumption is required.

The result of Tucker *et al.* (1978) with the divided visual-field measure was consistent with the within-subject changes observed under examination anxiety by Gruzelier and Phelan (in press). However, in our study, anxiety actually enhanced the processing abilities of the right hemisphere such that they were superior to those of the left found in the non-anxious condition. The same asymmetrical right hemispheric advantage was subsequently found in seven anxiety patients who showed left visual-field advantages for both verbal and spatial tasks (Gruzelier, 1987a).

Studies with brain imaging procedures involving positron emission tomography have also shown asymmetries in metabolism and blood flow which favour the right hemisphere in several anxiety conditions. Reivich, Gur and Alavi (1983) obtained questionnaire (Speilberger) measures of anxiety in normal subjects and undertook an examination of prefrontal regions which have connections with the limic system. They found a curvilinear relationship between local cerebral glucose metabolism and anxiety scores. Subdivision of subjects into high- and low-anxiety groups on the basis of a median split, indicated that the high-anxiety group had higher metabolic rates in the right hemisphere compared with the left, a significantly greater asymmetry than in the low-anxiety group. The same relative difference between the hemispheres has been found in studies of panic disorder (Reiman, Raichle and Butler). 1984; Reiman et al., 1986). Patients who satisfied DSM-III criteria for panic disorder were subdivided according to their vulnerability to pain induced by sodium lactate. Those patients with the vulnerability had an abnormal hemispheric asymmetry, right greater than left, in the region of the parahippocampal gyrus in measures of blood flow, blood volume and oxygen metabolism. In addition, the same group had abnormally high whole-brain oxygen metabolism.

In an earlier section of the chapter it was shown that cerebral activational dominance under anxiety may favour either hemisphere – the direction being dependent on the degree of anxiety. It is possible that the type of anxiety may reflect the direction of activational dominance, favouring the left hemisphere when there are strong cognitive components such as ruminations and obsessional thoughts, and the right hemisphere when anxiety is generalized, free floating or alexithymic (a term given to the inability to find appropriate words for feelings). In our study of anxiety in students there were some suggestions of such an association (Gruzelier, 1987a). Frustration–tension, apprehension–worrying and suspicion were associated with left hemispheric dominance in contrast to emotional instability and a lack of self-control which were associated with right hemispheric dominance.

SOMATIC SYMPTOMS

Prominent in the revival of interest in lateralization in psychopathology in the 1960s was the role of the right hemisphere in the mediation of psychogenic somatic symptoms (Galin, 1974). Conversion hysteria had last century been observed to occur more frequently on the left side of the body (Briquet, 1859). The defence mechanism of repression proposed by Galin (1974) was underpinned by functional disconnection of left hemispheric conscious verbal awareness from the unconscious ideation of the right hemisphere. Surveys were undertaken of hospital records for cases of unilateral conversion symptoms. Two surveys confirmed an association between unilateral conversion symptoms and the left side of the body (Galin, Diamond and Braff, 1977; Stern, 1977); another study showed the opposite relationship (Fallik and Sigal, 1971).

Alternative explanations for the phenomenon have been offered. The convenience theory suggests that it will be less disabling if symptoms occur on the non-dominant side. However, studies of left-handers disconfirmed this hypothesis (Stern, 1977). Another explanation was that symbolically the left side has negative associations – consider the common root of the words 'sinister' and 'sinistrality'. A third possibility was that the left side was in some way more vulnerable to genuine pathophysiology. The last possibility was examined by Axelrod, Noonan and Atanacio (1980) who carried out first a literature survey and then a survey of hospital records of 1021 consecutive admissions with unilateral complaints. Patients were classified according to whether there was organic involvement or purely psychogenic factors. No lateral bias was found in the organic cases, whereas there was a bias to the left side in the psychogenic cases. Thus the vulnerability hypothesis could be dismissed.

Another approach has been to give suggestions of sensations such as tingling, without mentioning laterality, and to examine whether the sensations were experienced on one side only (Fleminger, McClure and Dalton, 1980). Fleminger *et al.* (1980) found that in both nurses and psychiatric patients symptoms were more often expressed on the left side if they were experienced unilaterally. This lateral bias was also consistent with medical histories of psychogenic symptoms.

Pain has been suggested to occur more frequently on the left side of the body, with the exception of trigeminal neuralgia, which shows the opposite asymmetry (Merskey and Watson, 1979). Surveys of admissions to pain clinics by Hall and Clark (1982) and Hall, Hayward and Chapman (1981) have failed to confirm this and these authors have concluded that a psychogenic basis rather than an organic basis is essential to the left-sided preponderance in the survey by Merskey and Watson (1979). Nevertheless, as seen in an earlier section of this chapter, lateral imbalance and extremes of electrodermal reactivity have predicted the laterality of pain in cases of severe migraine. Furthermore, Carr, Minnitti and Pilowsky (1985) found a bimodal distribution of electrodermal orienting responses in consecutive admissions to a pain clinic. Thus central mechanisms that control the experience of pain may play an important role in the manifestation of organic symptoms, even though the psychological component is merely a state of altered mood and the physiological consequence an alteration in autonomic outflow, quite aside from any symbolic, psychological connotations. The same implication arises from the growing evidence of unilateral left-sided symptoms in patients with the hyperventilation syndrome.

HYPERVENTILATION SYNDROME

Overbreathing produces a complex of symptoms which is receiving increasing recognition and is termed the 'hyperventilation syndrome' (see also Chapter 18). It may occur in as many as 10% of general medical patients. Symptoms aside from overbreathing include palpitations, panic, fear, sweating and anxiety, and neurological symptoms may include giddiness, parasthesiae, visual disturbance, headache and non-epileptic seizures (Ames, 1955; Gowers, 1907; Lum, 1976). Remarkably, scattered reports of unilateral symptoms reveal a much higher expression on the left side of the body than would be expected by chance.

Blau, Wiles and Solomon (1983) described 12 cases whose previous diagnoses included epilepsy, migraine, multiple sclerosis, arteriovenous malformation, cerebrovascular disease and insufficiency, brachial neuritis and angina. While only one patient complained of breathlessness, these authors found that forced hyperventilation produced numbness, weakness and parasthesiae on the left side of the body in nine cases and on the right side in three cases.

Perkin and Joseph (1986) reported on 78 patients referred for neurological assessment. Bilateral symptoms of parasthesiae were observed in 21 patients and an additional seven had unilateral symptoms, all of which were manifested on the left side – in two, involving the face and in five, the left arm. Tavel (1987) described two studies, the first of which involved seven patients with unilateral symptoms such as numbness, tingling and weakness, and sometimes pain, all of which were experienced on the left side of the body. The second study involved the effects of forced hyperventilation in 90 volunteer normal subjects, 14 of whom showed an asymmetry in symptoms, which when handedness was taken into account, were in 12 subjects contralateral to the non-dominant hand.

Peripheral explanations were favoured by Tavel (1987), with hyperventilation bringing about greater vasoconstriction on the non-dominant side because of difference in vasculature linked to motor dominance. Blau *et al.* (1983) gave consideration to central factors – after all, dizziness, confusion and seizures indicate central nervous system involvement. All authors acknowledge the importance of anxiety which is an inevitable part of the hyperventilation syndrome; however, the causative role of anxiety in the syndrome is unclear, as anxiety may lead to hyperventilation which in turn may increase anxiety (Lum, 1981). As outlined above, the fact that anxiety may alter imbalances in hemispheric activation must be considered relevant. Noteworthy, too, is the fact that imbalances of hemispheric activation appear important in migraine which, in addition to the symptom of unilateral pain, includes all those somatic symptoms documented in the hyperventilation syndrome.

PSYCHONEUROIMMUNOLOGY

Lateralization may also emerge as a critical dynamic in immunological susceptibility. The immune system has until recently been regarded as an autoregulated system, but recognition is growing of the influence of psychological factors (Lloyd, 1986). As Lloyd observes, the sympathetic nervous system, the hypothalamus and the pituitary have recently been shown to play a part in immunoregulation. This evidence may now be extended to incorporate cerebral lateralization. Renoux, Biziere, Renoux, Guillaumin and Degenne (1983) have shown in the rodent that lesions to the frontoparietal cortex of the left hemisphere have a variety of influences on the immune system, including a 50% reduction in T-cell production and an improved response to antigens. An equivalent lesion to the right hemisphere gives rise to opposite effects, such as an increase in T-cells and responsiveness. Thus inter-hemispheric balance is shown to be a critical dynamic in immunoregulation.

Denenberg (1983) has delineated the importance of hemispheric balance in studies of the lateralization of emotion in the rat. Rats were assigned to a handled or non-handled regimen after birth (the effect of handling is to reduce emotionality and increase exploration in the open field). The animals were then assigned to one of four surgical treatments: no surgery, sham operation, or left or right neocortical ablation. Mouse killing was used as an index of spontaneous emotion. No differences were found between the non-handled groups. However, in the handled groups, muricide occurred more frequently in the unilateral ablation group with the left-sided lesion, whereas rats with a right-sided lesion were no different from controls. As there was no difference between the right-sided lesion and the controls, and because muricide was much more frequent after a left-sided lesion, it was inferred that the left neocortex normally acts to inhibit the right. Identical implications arose from a study of a learned fear response induced through a taste-aversion paradigm which involved pairing food with gastric upset. Evidence showed that the left hemisphere acts to inhibit the learned fear response of the right hemisphere. In studies of open-field activity, the opposite asymmetries have been observed. Thus hemisphere asymmetries of function in the rat were demonstrated for spontaneous and learned emotion, and for exploratory activity, the manifestation of which depended on the lateral imbalance in neocortical processes.

In man there is now an extensive literature on lateralization and emotion. Evidence shows that distinctions must be drawn between the perception of emotion and its expression, which as with language appears to depend on posterior and anterior functions, respectively (Davidson, 1987). In studies both of the normal and of the pathological brain, it has been commonly observed that the valence of emotion along a positive–negative dimension depends on the hemisphere functionally activated or undamaged. What is controversial is which valence is associated with which hemisphere, that is marrying a particular valence to a particular hemisphere. What is less controversial is the fact that, within studies, opposite emotions are typically associated with the two hemispheres. In schizophrenia, we have observed that Active versus Withdrawn syndromes are best unravelled with an imbalance model, such that the expression of symptoms, including whether the affect is positive or negative, depends on the hemisphere with the higher level of functional activation, which is opposite to the one revealing losses of function on neuropsychological tests. The same theoretical approach brings consistency to much of the controversy surrounding the laterality of emotion. Clearly the emotional valence associated with the functional activation of a particular hemisphere in normals would be the opposite to the one resulting from damage to the same hemisphere in patients. A majority of studies are consistent with an imbalance schema (Gainotti, 1979; Gruzelier, 1981; Sackeim *et al.*, 1983). The possibility that a damaged hemisphere may also lead to an exaggeration of that hemisphere's function must also be kept in mind, and much will depend on whether the damaged system has excitatory or inhibitory effects and on the interplay of cortical–subcortical functions (Tucker and Frederick, 1987).

Returning to the immune system, if the evidence of lateralized control of immune regulation in the rodent can be applied to man, then from the evidence that it is the lateral imbalance in frontoparietal systems that is critical, it follows that mood states may also be inextricably linked with immune competence. As a reduction in T-cells and their responsiveness occurs with a loss of left anterior functions, thereby tipping the balance towards the right, then the mood state that accompanies susceptibility will be of a depressive type. This is, in fact, one of the implications from various studies of psychological vulnerability in man.

Loneliness in university students has been inversely correlated with immune competence (Kiecolt-Glaser *et al.*, 1984), as has the need in prisoners for assertive power over others and the frustration experienced in the absence of that power (McClelland, Alexander and Marks, 1982). The stress of separation from parent or spouse, reactive depression from conjugal bereavement, and depressive psychosis are all associated with immune suppression (Bartrop, Luckhurst, Lazarus, Kiloh and Penny, 1977. Cupoli, Hallock and Barness, 1980; Schleifer, Keller, Siris, Davis and Stein, 1985).

FUTURE DIRECTIONS

THERAPEUTIC INTERVENTION

Evidence of imbalances in functional processes in functional disorders raises the possibility of therapeutic intervention with techniques addressed at altering the functional process. Awareness of neuropsychophysiological factors under-lying, for example, immune function may lead to clarification of the sometimes confusing psychodynamic formulations of the experiential concomitants of immune suppression. Conversely, a rationale is provided for the attempts, now legion, to halt or reverse immunological disorders with therapies aimed at producing positive attitudes to illness, though often initiated for curious psych-odynamic reasons.

Some progress is being made in understanding the processes involved in hypnotherapy and what constitutes the hypnotically susceptible individual.

Neuropsychophysiology and the Induction of Hypnosis

In view of the parallels between the hypnotic state and many processes associ-ated with the unconscious, attempts have been made to show that under hypnosis there is a release of right hemispheric processing and that the hypnoti-cally susceptible individual in the waking state will show right hemisphericity. The types of hypnotic phenomena associated with the right hemisphere, or a reduction in left hemispheric influences, include the dream-like quality, the use of visual imagery, the altered time-sense, amnesia for all but automatic memory processes, regression to childhood memories and to primary process thinking, disinhibition of affect, and an attitude of passive acceptance, while the use of child-like language and a singsong delivery facilitate hypnotic induction. While there has been some success in demonstrating these relationships, frequently results claimed in support of right hemispheric involvement in hypnosis on closer inspection are found to be wanting, often because while low susceptibles show the predicted effect, high susceptibles do not (Frumkin, Ripley and Cox, 1978; Graham and Pernicano, 1979; Morgan, Macdonald and Hilgard, 1974). Notwithstanding, Crawford and Allen (1983) have shown a shift in hypnotized subjects in visual memory tasks from detail-oriented processing towards holistic processing. The ability to shift between cognitive styles has also been emphasized by MacLeod-Morgan and Lack (1982) when examining left/right alpha ratios in putative left and right hemisphere tasks. Shifts in ratios in line with hemispheric cognitive specialization correlated with hypnotic susceptibility. Of particular interest is a study by McKeever, Larrabee, Sullivan, Johnson, Ferguson and Rappart (1981) in which hypnosis was undertaken with a case of partial callosectomy. Among their results was the finding that, under hypnosis, arm lowering and arm levitation occurred only with the left arm, and that tactile anomia of the left hand was reduced when coincidently speech production became anergic, suggesting a shift in hemispheric balance to the right.

Attempts to show that hypnotically susceptible individuals possess right hemisphericity have been less successful. For example, recordings of conjugate lateral eye movements in hypnotically susceptible subjects have been reported as predominantly rightward (Bakan, 1969; DeWitt and Averill, 1976; Gur and Gur, 1974), leftward (Smith, 1980) or in no consistent direction (Gur and Reyher, 1976; Joffe, 1982; Spanos, Pawlak, Mah and D'Eon, 1980; Spanos, Rivers and Gottlieb, 1979, 1980).

A somewhat different light has been cast on these issues through studies in our laboratory of bilateral skin conductance, haptic processing asymmetries and auditory cortical evoked potentials. In the first study, bilateral skin conductance was recorded in subjects undergoing hypnosis involving the presentation of a standard tone habituation paradigm about 10 min into the induction procedure. In those subjects who were hypnotically susceptible, habituation was faster than under baseline conditions and there was a reversal in lateral asymmetries in response amplitudes in the direction of a shift towards a right-greater-than-left asymmetry. Unsusceptible subjects failed to show the lateral shift and orienting responses were slower to habituate than under an awake control condition (Gruzelier and Brow, 1985). Importantly, when lateral asymmetries in orienting responses were examined in the standard tone habituation procedure, either 4 weeks earlier or later than the hypnosis session, those subjects who were hypnotically susceptible showed larger left hand responses indicative of a left hemispheric activational dominance. The same implication was obtained from two subsequent experiments with a haptic sorting task. Under hypnosis, there was a slowing in right hand processing time (sorting time minus movement time) compared with a trivial increase in left hand processing times in susceptible subjects. Prior to hypnosis, susceptible subjects showed shorter right than left hand processing times, an asymmetry not observed in unsusceptible subjects (Gruzelier, Brow, Perry, Rhonder and Thomas, 1984).

These and other experiments (Gruzelier *et al.*, 1987b) have revealed the importance of the left hemisphere in the induction of hypnosis and have led to a neuropsychophysiological model of the phenomenon (Gruzelier, 1988). Briefly, hypnosis is seen to be a multistage process, the first stage of which requires focused attention, typically achieved by visual fixation on a small object. This engages left hemispheric processes of focused attention, from which it follows that subjects with a left hemispheric activational dominance, or an ability to shift rapidly into this state, are particularly susceptible to hypnosis. The next stage involves suggestions of fatigue, eye closure and sleepiness, bringing about an inhibition of anterior brain functions, particularly of the left hemisphere, as seen in the slowing of haptic processing times of the right hand. Left-sided temporal lobe processes remain free from inhibition as the subject continues to listen to the hypnotist, as shown in recordings of middle latency cortical evoked potentials (Jutai, Golds and Gruzelier, in preparation). The third stage is the release of posterior brain functions, particularly of the right hemisphere, and hence the shift in electrodermal response asymmetries. Evidence of perceptual enhancement has also been demonstrated with a divided visual-field brightness discrimination task in which subjects with moderate degrees of susceptibility showed elevations in d' (sensory sensitivity) bilaterally compared with two awake conditions, whereas highly susceptible subjects showed increases in d' in the left visual field only. Estimates of β (criterion) remained invariant (McCormack and Gruzelier, in preparation).

It is likely that some of the basic dynamics that have emerged in the study of hypnosis will have relevance to the induction of other deep states of relaxation through medication, progressive muscle relaxation and autogenic training. The essential difference with hypnosis is that the range of applications goes far beyond those of other therapeutic procedures and encompasses hypnoanalysis and the revivification of previous experience, as well as attempts to exert control over physiological processes such as blood coagulation, the anti-inflammatory response, the autonomic nervous system, etc. To date, the neuropsychophysiological approach has provided objective evidence of altered brain function in hypnosis, preliminary evidence of markers of susceptibility, and a rationale for induction procedures and clinical application.

TOPOGRAPHICAL MAPPING WITH THE ELECTROENCEPHALOGRAM (EEG) DURING FUNCTIONAL ACTIVATION

Finally, as mentioned in the Introduction, an important advance is taking place in the application of new microcomputer-based EEG mapping systems to localization of function (Duffy, 1985; Maurer, 1988). The impetus for this approach has arisen from the clinical concern to localize the brain abnormalities, particularly those of a functional nature, which may elude or be impracticable with other forms of brain imaging such as CT, positron emission tomography, nuclear magnetic resonance scanning, etc. (Pfurtscheller and Lopes da Silva, 1988).

If limitations of scalp recording for localization of function can be overcome, then EEG topographical mapping offers many advantages. These include ethical benefits, for the EEG is non-invasive, whereas the majority of other techniques involve radioactivity. The equipment is relatively cheap, compact and portable. By virtue of these features, repeat testing is made possible. The technique is versatile in permitting multiple tests of functional activation in a single session; in the case of EEG power, only 2 min of recording is typically required to reliably characterize a particular task. The EEG is sensitive to psychological nuances, a sensitivity which has both pros and cons and requires careful experimental control to isolate the dependent variable of interest.

The initial 'if' concerns the value of distal recording sites for indexing central mechanisms, a methodological limitation in psychophysiology. The application of converging operations may minimize these limitations and provide the necessary validation. Evoked potential maps where the contribution of subcortical mechanisms to specific components recorded from the scalp is one approach. The use of neurological patients with circumscribed focal lesions is another, particularly where EEG mapping can be combined with other forms of scanning such as positron emission tomography or single photon emission tomography, measures which provide topographical maps of deep brain structures. A third approach which we have begun to explore is functional activation with neuropsychological tests which permit predictions about localization. A striking consistency between laboratories has been shown in the topography in normal subjects of unimanual sensory–motor tasks (cf. Gruzelier, Liddiard, Davis and Wilson, 1988; Pfurtscheller, 1988). In schizophrenia, double dissociation of function has been disclosed between recognition memory for words and faces, indicative of a right temporoparietal impairment, along with topographical differences between patients and controls in power spectra in the same predicted region (Gruzelier, 1988; Gruzelier and Liddiard, 1988).

If the initial promise is fulfilled, this technique of all the traditional polygraph measures offers the best index of central nervous system function. It is for this reason that the topic of EEG topographical mapping has brought the chapter to a close. The reader is offered the prediction that this application is as likely as any other to ensure a vigorous future for clinical psychophysiology and in so doing will bring central mechanisms to the forefront of research in psychophysiology.

REFERENCES

American Psychiatric Association (1980). *Diagnostic and Statistical Manual of Mental Disorders*, 3rd edn. Washington, DC: APA.

Andrews, H. B., Cooper, J. E., Barber, C., and Raine, A. (1987). Early somatosensory evoked potentials in schizophrenia: symptom pattern, clinical outcomes and inter-hemispheric functioning. In: R. Takahashi, P. Flor-Henry, J. Gruzelier and S. Niwa (Eds) *Cerebral Dynamics, Laterality and Psychopathology*, pp. 175–186. Amsterdam: Elsevier.

Andrews, H. B., House, A. O., Cooper, J. E., and Barber, C. (1986). The prediction of abnormal evoked potentials in schizophrenic patients by means of symptom pattern. *British Journal of Psychiatry* **149**, 46–50.

Axelrod, S., Noonan, M., and Atanacio, B. (1980). On the laterality of psychogenic somatic symptoms. *Journal of Nervous and Mental Disease* **168**, 517–525.

Bagshaw, M. H., and Benzies, G. (1968). Multiple measures of the orienting-reaction and their dissociation after amygdalectomy in monkeys, *Experimental Neurology* **20**, 175–187.

Bakan, P. (1969). Hypnotisability, laterality of eye movements and functional brain asymmetry. *Perceptual and Motor Skills* **28**, 927–932.

Baribeau-Braun, J., Picton, T. W., and Gosselin, J. (1983). Schizophrenia: a neurophysiological evaluation of abnormal information processing. *Science* **219**, 874–876.

Bartrop, R. W., Luckhurst, E., Lazarus, L., Kiloh, L. G., and Penny, R. (1977). Depressed lymphocyte function after bereavement. *Lancet* **1**, 843–836.

Bechtereva, N. P. (1983). Neurophysiology of intellectual and emotional processes in man. *International Journal of Psychophysiology* **1**, 7–12.

Bechtereva, N. P. (1987). Some general physiological principles of the human brain functioning. *International Journal of Psychophysiology* **5**, 235–251.

Blau, J. N., Wiles, C. M., and Solomon, F. S. (1983). Unilateral somatic symptoms due to hyperventilation. *British Medical Journal* **286**, 1108.

Boring, E. G. (1957). *A History of Experimental Psychology*. New York: Appleton-Century-Crofts.

Briquet, P. (1859). *Traite Cliniques et Therapeutique de L'Hysterie*. Paris: Baillière.

Carr, V., Minnitti, R., and Pilowsky, I. (1985). Electrodermal activity in patients with chronic pain: implications for the specificity of physiological indices in relation to psychopathology. *Psychophysiology* **22**, 208–217.

Cohen, G. (1982). Theoretical interpretations of lateral asymmetries. In: J. G. Beaumont (Ed.) *Divided Visual Field Studies of Cerebral Organisation*, pp. 87–115.

Connolly, J. F., Gruzelier, J. H., and Manchanda, R. (1983). Electrocortical and perceptual asymmetries in schizophrenia. In: P. Flor-Henry and J. Gruzelier (Eds) *Laterality and Psychopathology*, pp. 363–378. Amsterdam: Elsevier.

Connolly, J. F., Manchanda, R., Gruzelier, J. H., and Hirsch, S. R. (1985). Pathway and hemispheric differences in the event related potential (ERP) to monoral stimulation: a comparison of schizophrenic patients with normal controls. *Biological Psychiatry* **20**, 293–303.

Connolly, J. F., Prescott, J., Gruzelier, J. H., and Hirsch, S. R. (1986). The contribution of neurophysiological abnormalities to cognitive function in schizophrenia. In: C. Shagass (Ed.) *Electrical Brain Potentials and Psychopathology*, pp. 47–58. Amsterdam: Elsevier.

Cram, J. I. (1980). EMG biofeedback and the treatment of tension headaches: a systematic analysis of treatment components. *Behaviour Therapy* **11**, 699–710.

Crawford, H. J., and Allen, S. N. (1983). Enhanced visual memory during hypnosis as mediated by hypnotic responsiveness and cognitive strategies. *Journal of Experimental Psychology: General* **112**, 664–685.

Cupoli, J. M., Hallock, J. A., and Barness, L. A. (1980). Failure to thrive. *Current Problems in Paediatrics* **10**, 1–43.

Darrow, C. W., Pathman, J. and Kronenberg, G. (1946). Level of autonomic activity and the EEG. *Journal of Experimental Psychology* **36**, 355–365.

Davidson, R. J. (1987). Cerebral asymmetry and the nature of emotion: implications for the study of individual differences and psychopathology. In: R. Takahashi, P. Flor-Henry, J. Gruzelier, and S. Niwa (Eds) *Cerebral Dynamics, Laterality and Psychopathology*, pp. 71–84. Amsterdam: Elsevier.

Davison, M. A., and Koss, M. C. (1974). Brain stem loci for activation of electrodermal response in the cat. *American Journal of Physiology* **229**, 930–934.

Denenberg, V. H. (1983). Brain laterality and behavioural asymmetry in the rat. In: P. Flor-Henry and J. Gruzelier (Eds) *Laterality and Psychopathology*, pp. 29–40. Amsterdam: Elsevier.

Desmedt, J. E., and Debecker, J. (1979). Wave form and neural mechanism of the decision P350 elicited without pre-stimulus CNV or readiness potential in random sequences of near threshold auditory clicks and finger stimuli. *Electroencephalography and Clinical Neurophysiology* **77**, 648–670.

DeWitt, G. W., and Averill, J. R. (1976). Lateral eye-movements, hypnotic susceptibility and field dependence. *Perceptual and Motor Skills* **43**, 1179–1184.

Diefendorf, A. R., and Dodge, R. (1908). An experimental study of the ocular reactions of the insane from photographic records. *Brain* **31**, 451–489.

Dimond, S. J. (1979). Disconnection and psychopathy. In J. Gruzelier and P. Flor-Henry (Eds) *Hemisphere Asymmetrics of Function in Psychopathology*, pp. 35–46. Amsterdam: Elsevier.

Douglas, R. J. (1967). The hippocampus and behaviour. *Psychological Bulletin* **67**, 416–442.

Duffy, F. H. (1985). (Ed.) *Topographic Mapping of the Brain Electrical Activity*. London: Butterworths.

Elithorn, A., Piercy, M. F., and Crosskey, A. (1954). Autonomic changes after unilateral leucotomy. *Journal of Neurology, Neurosurgery and Psychiatry* **17**, 139–144.

Fallik, A., and Sigal, M. (1971). Hysteria – the choice of symptom site. *Psychotherapy and Psychosomatics* **19**, 310–318.

Fleminger, J. J., McClure, G. M., and Dalton, R. (1980). Lateral response to suggestion in relation to handedness and the side of psychogenic symptoms. *British Journal of Psychiatry* **136**, 562–566.

Flor-Henry, P. (1969). Psychoses and temporal lobe epilepsy: a controlled investigation. *Epilepsia* **10**, 363–395.

Flor-Henry, P. (1983). *Cerebral Basis of Psychopathology*. New York: Wright.

Flor-Henry, P., and Gruzelier, J. H. (Eds) (1983). *Laterality and Psychopathology*. Amsterdam: Elsevier.

Fox, P. T., Fox, J. M., Raichle, M. F., and Burde, R. M. (1985). The role of the cerebral cortex in the generation of voluntary saccades: positron emission tomographical study. *Journal of Neurophysiology* **54**, 348–369.

Friedman, D. (in press). The endogenous scalp-recorded brain potentials in schizophrenia. In: S. Steinhauer, J. Gruzelier and J. Zubin (Eds) *Handbook of Schizophrenia*, Vol. 4: *Neuropsychology, Psychophysiology and Information Processing*. Amsterdam: Elsevier.

Frumkin, L. R., Ripley, N. S., and Cox, G. B. (1978). Changes in cerebral hemisphere lateralisation with hypnosis. *Biological Psychiatry* **13**, 741–750.

Gaebel, L. W., Ulrich, G., and Frick, K. (1986). Eye movement research with schizophrenic patients and normal controls using corneal reflection–pupil centre measurement. *European Archives of Psychiatry and Neurological Sciences* **235**, 243–254.

Gainotti, G. (1979). The relationships between emotions and cerebral dominance: A review of clinical and experimental endence. In J. H. Gruzelier and P. Flor-Henry (Eds) *Hemisphere Asymmetrics of Function in Psychopathy*, pp. 21–34. Amsterdam: Elsevier.

Galin, D. (1974). Implications for psychiatry of left and right cerebral specialisation: a neurophysiological context for unconscious processes. *Archives of General Psychiatry* **31**, 572–583.

Galin, D., Diamond, R., and Braff, D. (1977). Lateralisation of conversion symptoms, more frequent on the left. *American Journal of Psychiatry* **134**, 578–580.

Geschwind, N. (1965). Disconnection syndromes in animals and men. *Brain* **88**, 237–294.

Gowers, W. R. (1907). A lecture on vaso-vagal attacks. *Lancet* **1**, 1551–1554.

Graham, K. R., and Pernicano, K. (1979). Laterality, hypnosis, and the autokinetic effect. *American Journal of Clinical Hypnosis* **22**, 79–84.

Gray, J. A. (1967). Strength of the nervous system, introversion–extroversion, condition ability and arousal. *Behaviour Research and Therapy* **5**, 151–169.

Gruzelier, J. H. (1973). Bilateral asymmetry of skin conductance orienting activity and levels in schizophrenics. *Biological Psychology* **1**, 21–41.

Gruzelier, J. H. (1982). Bimodality and lateral asymmetries in the electrodermal orienting activity of schizophrenic patients revisited. *Psychophysiology* **19**, 295–296.

Gruzelier, J. H. (1984). Hemispheric imbalances in schizophrenia. *Internation Journal of Psychophysiology* **1**, 227–240.

Gruzelier, J. H. (1985). Schizophrenia: central nervous system signs in schizophrenia. In: J. A. M. Frederick (Ed.) *Handbook of Clinical Neurology*, Vol. 2: *Neurobehavioural Disorders*, pp. 481–521. Amsterdam: Elsevier.

Gruzelier, J. H. (1986a). Lateralised CNS functions in schizophrenia. In: C. Burrows (Ed.) *Handbook of Studies on Schizophrenia*, Part 2: *Management and Research*, pp. 175–196. Amsterdam: Elsevier.

Gruzelier, J. H. (1986b). The thalamic involvement in the genesis of migraine: psych-ophysiological evidence. *Biological Psychology* **24**, 109.

Gruzelier, J. H. (1987a). Cerebral laterality and schizophrenia: a review of the inter-hemispheric disconnection hypothesis. In: A. Glass (Ed.) *Individual Differences in Hemispheric Specialisation*, pp. 357–375. London: Plenum.

Gruzelier, J. H. (1987b). Individual differences in dynamic process asymmetries in the normal and pathological brain. In: A. Glass (Ed.) *Individual Differences in Hemispheric Specialisation*, pp. 301–329. London: Plenum.

Gruzelier, J. H. (1987c). Commentary on neuropsychological and information processing deficits in psychosis and neuropsychophysiological syndrome relationships in schizophrenia. In: R. Takahashi, P. Flor-Henry, J. Gruzelier and S. Niwa (Eds) *Cerebral Dynamics, Laterality and Pathology*, pp. 23–54. Amsterdam: Elsevier.

Gruzelier, J. H. (1988). The neuropsychology of hypnosis. In: M. Heap (Ed.) *Experimental and Clinical Hypnosis: Current Clinical, Experimental and Forensic Practices*, pp. 68–76. London: Croom Helm.

Gruzelier, J. H. (in press). Lateralisation in schizophrenia after two decades of investigation. In: S. Steinhauer, J. Gruzelier and J. Zubin (Eds) *Handbook of Schizophrenia*, Vol. 4: *Neuropsychology, Psychophysiology and Information Processing*. Amsterdam: Elsevier.

Gruzelier, J. H., and Brow, T. D. (1985). Psychophysiological evidence for a state theory of hypnosis and susceptibility. *Journal of Psychosomatic Research* **29**, 287–302.

Gruzelier, J. H., and Connolly, J. F. (1980). Differential actions of a pharmacological agent on electrodermal orienting – responses as distinct from non-specific responses and electrodermal levels. In H. D. Kimmel (Ed.). *The Orienting Reflex in Humans*, pp. 701–713. New York: Erlbaum.

168 J. H. Gruzelier

Gruzelier, J. H., and Flor-Henry, P. (1979). *Hemisphere Asymmetries of Function and Psychopathology*. Amsterdam: Elsevier.

Gruzelier, J. H., and Hammond, N. V. (1976). Schizophrenia: a dominant hemisphere temporal–limbic disorder? *Research Communications in Psychology, Psychiatry and Behaviour* **1**, 33–72.

Gruzelier, J. H., and Liddiard, D. M. (1988). The neuropsychology of schizophrenia in the context of topographical mapping of electrocortical activity. In: K. Maurer (Ed.) *Topographic Brain Mapping of EEG and Evoked Potentials*. London: Springer-Verlag.

Gruzelier, J. H., and Manchanda, R. (1982). The syndrome of schizophrenia: relations between electrodermal response lateral asymmetries and clinical ratings. *British Journal of Psychiatry* **141**, 488–495.

Gruzelier, J. H., and Phelan, M. (in press). Reversal of hemisphere asymmetry in a lexical divided visual-field task under examination stress. *Neuropsychologia*.

Gruzelier, J. H., and Venables, P. H. (1973). Skin conductance responses to tones with and without attentional significance in schizophrenic and non-schizophrenic patients. *Neuropsychologia* **11**, 221–230.

Gruzelier, J. H., and Venables, P. H. (1974). Bimodality and lateral asymmetry of skin conductance orienting activity in schizophrenics: replication and evidence of lateral asymmetry in patients with depression and disorders of personality. *Biological Psychiatry* **8**, 55–73.

Gruzelier, J. H., Brow, T. D., Perry, A., Rhonder, J., and Thomas, M. (1984). Hypnotic susceptibility: a lateral predisposition and altered cerebral asymmetry under hypnosis. *International Journal of Psychophysiology* **2**, 131–139.

Gruzelier, J. H., Connolly, J. F., Eves, F. F., Hirsch, S. R., Zaki, S. A., Weller, M. F., and Yorkston, N. J. (1981a). Effect of propranolol and phenothiazines on electrodermal orienting and habituation in schizophrenia. *Psychological Medicine* **11**, 93–108.

Gruzelier, J. H., Eves, F. F., and Connolly, J. F. (1981b). Habituation and phasic reactivity in the electrodermal system: reciprocal hemispheric influences. *Physiological Psychology* **9**, 313–317.

Gruzelier, J. H., Liddiard, D. M., Davis, L., and Wilson, L. (1988). Topographical mapping of electrocortical activity in schizophrenia during directed focussed attention, recognition memory and motor programming. In: G. Pfurtscheller and F. H. Lopes da Silva (Eds) *Functional Brain Imaging*. Berlin: Springer-Verlag.

Gruzelier, J. H., Lykken, D. T., and Venables, P. H. (1972). Schizophrenia and arousal revisited: two-flash threshold and electrodermal activity in activated and non-activated conditions. *Archives of General Psychiatry* **26**, 427–432.

Gruzelier, J. H., Nikolau, T., Connolly, J. F., Peatfield, R. C., Davies, P. T. G., and Clifford-Rose, F. (1987a). Laterality of pain in migraine distinguished by interictal rates of habituation of electrodermal responses to visual and auditory stimuli. *Journal of Neurology, Neurosurgery and Psychiatry* **50**, 416–422.

Gruzelier, J. H., Sergeant, J., and Eves, F. (1988). The use of bilateral skin conductance measurement in elucidating stimulus versus response processing influence on the orienting reaction. *International Journal of Psychophysiology* **6**, 195–206.

Gruzelier, J. H., Seymour, K., Wilson, L., Jolley, T., and Hirsch, S. R. (1988) Impairments on neuropsychological tests of temporo-hippocampal and fronto-hippocampal functions and word fluency in remitting schizophrenia and affective disorders. *Archives of General Psychiatry*, **45**, 623–629.

Gruzelier, J. H., Thomas, M., Conway, A., Liddiard, D. M., Jutai, J., McCormack, K., Perry, A., Rhonder, J., and Brow, T. (1987b). Involvement of the left hemisphere in hypnotic induction: electrodermal, haptic, electrocortical and divided visual field evidence. *Advances in Biological Psychiatry*, Vol. 16: *Neurophysiological Correlates of Relaxation and Psychopathology*, pp. 6–17 Basle: Karger.

Gur, R. C., and Gur, R. E. (1974). Handedness, sex and eyedness as moderating variables in the relation between hypnotic susceptibility and functional brain asymmetry. *Journal of Abnormal Psychology 83*, 635–643.

Gur, R., and Reyher, J. (1976). The enhancement of creativity via free imagery and hypnosis. *American Journal of Clinical Hypnosis 18*, 237–249.

Halgren, E., Squires, N. K., Wilson, C. S., Rohrbaugh, J. W., Babb, T. L., and Crandall, P. H. (1980). Endogenous potentials generated in the human hippocampal formation and amygdala by infrequent events. *Science 210*, 803–805.

Hall, W., and Clark, I. M. (1982). Pain and laterality in a British pain clinic sample. *Pain 14*, 63–66.

Hall, W., Hayward, L., and Chapman, C. R. (1981). The lateralisation of pain. *Pain 10*, 337–351.

Hammond, N. V., and Gruzelier, J. H. (1978). Laterality, attention and rate effects in the auditory temporal discrimination of chronic schizophrenics: the effects of treatment with clorpromazine. *Quarterly Journal of Experimental Psychology 30*, 91–103.

Harrington, A. (1985). Nineteenth century ideas on hemisphere differences and 'duality of mind'. *Behavioural and Brain Sciences 8*, 617–669.

Harris, L. J. (1978). Sex differences in spatial ability: possible environmental, genetic, and neurological factors. In: M. Kinsbourne (Ed.) *Asymmetrical Function of the Brain*, pp. 405–522. London: Cambridge University Press.

Heilman, K. M., Schwartz, H. D., and Watson, R. T. (1978). Hypo-arousal in patients with the neglect syndrome and emotional indifference. *Neurology 28*, 229–232.

Herron, J. (1980). (Ed.) *Neuropsychology of Left-Handedness*. London: Academic Press.

Holloway, F. A., and Parsons, O. A. (1969). Unilateral brain damage and bilateral skin conductance levels in humans. *Psychophysiology 6*, 138–148.

Holzman, P. S. (in press). Eye movement dysfunctions in schizophrenia. In: S. Steinhauer, J. Gruzelier and J. Zubin (Eds) *Handbook of Schizophrenia*, Vol. 4: *Neuropsychology, Psychophysiology and Information Processing*. Amsterdam: Elsevier.

Holzman, P. S., Kringlen, E., Levy, D. L., Proctor, L. R., Haberman, S., and Yasillo, N. J. (1977). Abnormal pursuit movements in schizophrenia: evidence for a genetic marker. *Archives of General Psychiatry 34*, 802–812.

Hugdahl, K. (1984). Hemispheric asymmetry and bilateral electrodermal recordings: a review of the evidence. *Psychophysiology 21*, 371–393.

Iacono, W. G., and Lykken, D. T. (1981). Two-year retest stability of eye-tracking performance and the comparison of electro-oculographic and infra-red recording techniques: evidence of EEG and the electro-oculogram. *Psychophysiology 18*, 49–55.

Iacono, W. G., Tuason, V. B., and Johnson, R. A. (1981). Dissociation of smooth pursuit and saccadic eye tracking in remitted schizophrenics. *Archives of General Psychiatry 38*, 991–999.

Ingvar, D. H. (1976). Functional landscapes of the dominant hemisphere. *Brain Research 107*, 181–197.

Jakob, H., and Beckmann, H. (1986). Pre-natal developmental disturbances in the limbic alocortex in schizophrenics. *Journal of Neural Transmission 65*, 303–326.

Jewett, D. L., Romano, N. W., and Williston, J. F. (1970). Human auditory evoked potentials: possible brainstorm components detected on the scalp. *Science 167*, 1517–1518.

Joffe, R. (1982). Hypnotic susceptibility, cerebral asymmetry, illusion susceptibility, and a field-dependent perceptual style. Unpublished doctoral dissertation, Washington University.

Johnson, R., and Fedio, P. (1986). P300 activity in patients following unilateral temporal lobectomy: a preliminary report. In: W. C. McCallum, R. Zappoli and F. Denworth (Eds) *Cerebral Psychophysiology: Studies in Event-Related Potentials. Electroencephalography and Clinical Neurophysiology*, Suppl. 38, 552–554.

Josiassen, R. C., Roemer, R. A., Shagass, C., and Straumanis, J. J. (1986). Attention-related effects on somatosensory evoked potentials in non-psychotic dysphoric psychiatric patients. In: C. Shagass, R. C. Josiassen and R. A. Romer (Eds) *Electrical Brain Potentials and Psychopathology*, pp. 259–277. New York: Elsevier.

Josiassen, R. C., Shagass, C., Romer, R. A., and Straumanis, J. J. (1985). Attention-related effects on somatosensory evoked potentials in college students at high risk for psychopathology. *Journal of Abnormal Psychology* **94**, 507–518.

Jutai, J., Golds, J., and Gruzelier, J. H. (in preparation). An electrophysiological investigation of asymmetric hemispheric activation during hypnosis.

Jutai, J., Gruzelier, J. H., Connolly, J., Manchanda, R., and Hirsch, S. R. (1984). Schizophrenia and spectral analysis of the visual evoked potential. *British Journal of Psychiatry* **145**, 496–501.

Kiecolt-Glaser, J. K., Ricker, D., George, J., Messick, G., Speicher, C. E., Garner, W., and Glazer, R. (1984). Urinary cortisol levels, cellular immunocompetency, and loneliness in psychiatric inpatients. *Psychomatic Medicine* **46**, 15–23.

Kimble, D. P. (1968). Hippocampus and internal inhibition. *Psychological Bulletin* **79**, 285–295.

Kinsbourne, M. (1975). The mechanism of hemispheric control of the lateral gradient of attention. In: P. A. M. Rabbitt and S. Dornic (Eds) *Attention and Performance*, pp. 81–97. London: Academic Press.

Kopp, M., and Gruzelier, J. H. (in press). Electrodermally differentiated subgroups of anxiety patients and controls: II. Relationships with auditory, somatosensory and pain thresholds, agoraphobic fear, depression and cerebral laterality. *International Journal of Psychophysiology* **6**.

Krug, S. E., Scheier, I. H., and Cattell, R. B. (1976). *Handbook for the IPAT Anxiety Scale*. Champagne: Institute for Personality and Ability Testing.

Lacroix, J. N., and Comper, P. (1969). Lateralisation in the electrodermal system as a function of cognitive-hemispheric manipulation. *Psychophysiology* **16**, 116–129.

Lader, M. H., and Wing, L. (1966). *Physiological Measures, Sedative Drugs, and Morbid Anxiety*. London: Oxford University Press.

Lader, M., and Wing, L. (1969). Physiological measures in agitated and retarded depressed patients. *Journal of Psychiatric Research* **7**, 89–100.

Latham, C., Holzman, P. S., Manschrek, T., and Tole, J. (1981). Optokinetic nystagmus and pursuit eye movements in schizophrenia. *Archives of General Psychiatry* **38**, 997–1003.

Levin, S. (1984a). Frontal lobe dysfunctions in schizophrenia: I. Eye movement impairments. *Journal of Psychiatric Research* **18**, 27–42.

Levin, S. (1984b). Frontal lobe dysfunctions in schizophrenia: II. Impairments of psychological and brain functions. *Journal of Psychiatric Research* **18**, 57–71.

Levin, S., Holzman, P. S., Rothenberg, S. J., and Lipton, R. B. (1981). Saccadic eye movements in psychotic patients. *Psychiatry Research* **5**, 47–56.

Levin, S., Jones, A., Stark, L., Merrin, E. L., and Holzman, P. S. (1982). Identification of abnormal patterns in eye movements of schizophrenic patients. *Archives of General Psychiatry* **39**, 1125–1132.

Levy, J., Heller, W., Banich, N. T., and Burton, L. A. (1983). Are variations among right-handed individuals and perceptual asymmetries caused by characteristic arousal differences between the hemispheres? *Journal of Experimental Psychology: Human Perception and Performance* **9**, 329–359.

Lindstrom, L., Klochhoff, I., Svedberg, A., and Bergstrom, K. (1987). Abnormal auditory brain-stem-responses in hallucinating schizophrenic patients. *British Journal of Psychiatry* **151**, 9–14.

Lipton, R. B., Levin, S., and Holzman, P. S. (1980). Horizontal and vertical pursuit movements, the oculocephalic reflex, and the functional psychoses. *Psychiatry Research* **3**, 193–201.

Lipton, R. B., Levy, D. L., Holzman, P. S., and Levin, S. (1983). Eye movement dysfunctions in schizophrenic patients: a review. *Schizophrenia Bulletin* **9**, 13–32.

Lloyd, R. (1987). *Explorations in Psychoneuroimmunology*. London: Grune and Stratton.

Lum, L. C. (1976). The syndrome of habitual chronic hyperventilation. In: O. W. Hill (Ed.) *Modern Trends in Psychosomatic Medicine*, 3rd edn, pp. 196–230. London: Butterworths.

Lum, L. C. (1981). Hyperventilation and anxiety state. *Journal of the Royal Society of Medicine* **74**, 1–4.

Lynn, R. (1966). *Attention, Arousal, and the Orientation Reaction*. London: Pergamon.

Lykken, D. T., and Maley, M. (1968). Autonomic versus cortical arousal in schizophrenics and non-psychotics. *Journal of Psychiatric Research* **6**, 21–32.

Luria, A. R., and Homskaya, E. D. (1963). Le trouble du role regulateur du langage au cours des lesions du lobe frontal. *Neuropsychologia* **1**, 9–26.

Luria, A. R., and Homskaya, F. D. (1970). Frontal lobe and the regulation of arousal processes. In: D. Mostofsky (Ed.) *Attention: Contemporary Theory and Research*, pp. 303–330. New York: Appleton-Century-Crofts.

MacLeod-Morgan, C., and Lack, L. (1982). Hemisphere specificity: a physiological concomitant of hypnotizability. *Psychophysiology* **19**, 687–690.

Maltzman, I., Smith, N. J., and Cantor, W. (1971). Effects of stress on habituation of the orienting reflex. *Journal of Experimental Psychology* **87**, 207–217.

Maurer, K. (Ed.) (1988). *Topographic Brain Mapping of EEG and Evoked Potentials*. London: Springer-Verlag.

McClelland, D. C., Alexander, C., and Marks, F. (1982). The need for power, stress, immune function, and illness among male prisoners. *Journal of Abnormal Psychology* **91**, 61–70.

McCormack, K., and Gruzelier, J. H. (in preparation). Cerebral asymmetry and hypnosis, a signal detection analysis of divided-visual field stimulation.

McKeever, W. F., Larrabee, G. J., Sullivan, K. F., Johnson, H. J., Ferguson, S., and Rappapart, M. (1981). Unimanual tactile anomia consequent to corpuscallosotomy: reduction of anomic deficit under hypnosis. *Neuropsychologia* **19**, 179–190.

McNeil, T. F. (1978). Obstetric factors in the development of schizophrenia: complications in the births of pre-schizophrenics and in reproduction by schizophrenic parents. In: L. C. Wynne, R. L. Cromwell and S. Matthysse (Eds) *The Nature of Schizophrenia*. New York: Wiley.

Mecacci, L. (1977). Brain and history: the relationship between neurophysiology and psychology in Soviet research. New York: Brunner and Mazel.

Mednick, S. A. (1970). Breakdown in individuals at high risk of schizophrenia: possible predispositional perinatal factors. *Mental Hygiene* **54**, 50–63.

Merskey, H., and Watson, G. D. (1979). The lateralisation of pain. *Pain* **7**, 271–280.

Milner, B. (1982). Some cognitive effects of frontal-lobe lesions in man. In: D. E. Broadbent and L. Weiskrantz (Eds) *The Neuropsychology of Cognitive Function*, pp. 211–266. London: The Royal Society.

Morgan, A. H., Macdonald, H., and Hilgard, E. R. (1974). EEG alpha: lateral asymmetry related to task and hypnotizability. *Psychophysiology* **11**, 275–282.

Morrow, L., Vrtunski, P., Kim and Boller, F. (1981). Arousal responses to emotional stimuli and laterality of lesion. *Neuropsychologia* **19**, 65–71.

Moruzzi, G., and Magoun, H. W. (1949). Brain stem reticular formation and activation of EEG. *Electroencephalography and Clinical Neurophysiology* **1**, 455–473.

Moscovitch, M. (1979). Information processing and the cerebral hemispheres. In: M. S. Gazzaniga (Ed.) *Handbook of Behavioural Neurobiology*, Vol. 2: *Neuropsychology*, pp. 379–446. London: Plenum.

Murray, R. M. (in press). The neurodevelopmental origins of dementia praecox. In: P. Bebbington and P. McGuffin (Eds) *Schizophrenia: The Major Issues*. London: Heineman.

Newsombe, W. T., Wurtz, R. H., Dursteler, M. R., and Mikami, A. (1985). Deficits in visual motion processing following lesions of the middle temporal visual area of the monkey. *Journal of Neuroscience* **5**, 825–840.

Obrist, P. A. (1963). Skin resistance levels and galvanic skin response: unilateral differences. *Science* **139**, 227–228.

O'Gorman, J. G. (1977). Individual differences in habituation of human physiological responses: a review of theory, method, and findings in the study of personality correlates in non-clinical populations. *Biological Psychology* **5**, 257–318.

Overall, J. E., and Gorham, D. R. (1962). The brief psychiatric rating scale. *Psychological Reports* **10**, 799–812.

Perkin, G. D., and Joseph, R. (1986). Neurological manifestations of the hyperventilation syndrome. *Journal of the Royal Society of Medicine* **79**, 448–450.

Pfefferbaum, A., Horvath, T. B., Roth, W. T., Tinklenberg, J. R., and Kopell, B. S. (1980). Auditory brain stem and cortical evoked potentials in schizophrenia. *Biological Psychiatry* **15**, 209–223.

Pfefferbaum, A., Wenegrat, B., Ford, J. M., Roth W. T., and Kopell, B. S. (1984). Clinical application of the P3 component of event-related potentials: II. Dementia, depression and schizophrenia. *Electroencephalography and Clinical Neurophysiology* **59**, 104–124.

Pfurtscheller, G. (1988). ERD-mapping: temporal and spatial aspects. Paper read to the International Workshop on Statistics and Topography in Quantitative EEG, Rouen, March 1988.

Pfurtscheller, G., and Lopes da Silva, F. H. (Eds) (1988). *Functional Brain Imaging*. London: Springer-Verlag.

Picton, T. W., Campbell, K. B., Baribeau-Braun, J. and Proux, G. B. (1978). The neurophysiology of human attention: a tutorial review. In: J. Requin (Ed.) *Attention and Performance*, Vol. 7, pp. 122–160. Hillsdale, NJ: Erlbaum.

Porjesz, B., Begleiter, H., and Samuelly, I. (1980). Cognitive deficits in chronic alcoholics and elderly subjects assessed by evoked brain potentials. *Acta Psychiatrica Scandinavica* **62**, Suppl. 286, 15–29.

Pribram, K. H., and McGuinness, D. (1975). Arousal, activation and effort in the control of attention. *Psychological Review* **82**, 116–149.

Rabavilas, A. D., Liappas, J. A., and Stefanis, C. N. (1986). Electrodermal laterality indices in paranoid schizophrenics. In: C. N. Stefanis (Ed.) *Schizophrenia: Recent Biosocial Developments*, pp. 581–585. New York: Human Sciences Press.

Redding, F. K. (1967). Modifications of sensory cortical evoked potentials by tripocampal stimulation. *Electroencephalography and Clinical Neurophysiology* **22**, 74–83.

Reiman, E. M., Raichle, M. E., and Butler, F. K. (1984). A focal brain abnormality in panic disorder, a severe form of anxiety. *Nature* **310**, 683–685.

Reiman, E. M., Raichle, M. E., Robbins, E., Butler, F., Herscovitch, P., Fox, P., and Perlmutter, J. (1986). The application of positron emission tomography to the study of panic disorder. *American Journal of Psychiatry* **143**, 469–477.

Reivich, M., Gur, R., and Alavi, A. (1983). Positron emission tomographic studies of sensory stimuli, cognitive processes and anxiety. *Human Neurobiology* **2**, 25–33.

Renoux, G., Biziere, K., Renoux, M., Guillaumin, J.-M., and Degenne, D. (1983). A balanced brain asymmetry modulates T cell-mediated events. *Journal of Neuroimmunology* **5**, 227–238.

Roth, W. T. (1977). Late event-related potentials and psychopathology. *Schizophrenia Bulletin* **3**, 105–120.

Sackeim, H. A., Weiman, A. L., and Grega, D. M. (1984). Effects of predictors of hemispheric specialisation on individual differences in hemispheric activation. *Neuropsychologia* **22**, 55–56.

Schleifer, S. J., Keller, S. E., Siris, S. G., Davis, K. L., and Stein, M. (1985). Depression and immunity. Lymphocyte function in ambulatory depressed patients, hospitalised schizophrenic patients, and patients hospitalised for herniorrhaphy. *Archives of General Psychiatry* **42**, 129–133.

Schwartz, H. G. (1937). Effect of experimental lesions of the cortex on the 'psychogalvanic reflex' in the cat. *Archives of Neurology and Psychiatry* **38**, 308–408.

Shagass, C., Amadeo, M., and Overton, D. A. (1974). Eye-tracking performance in psychiatric patients. *Biological Psychiatry* **9**, 245–254.

Simons, R. F. (1981). Electrodermal and cardiac orienting in psychometrically defined high-risk subjects. *Psychiatry Research* **4**, 374–356.

Smith, D. E. (1980). Hypnotic susceptibility and eye movement during rest. *American Journal of Clinical Hypnosis* **22**, 147–155.

Sokolov, E. M. (1963). *Perception and the Conditioned Reflex*. New York: Macmillan.

Sommer, W. (1985). Selective attention differentially affects brainstem auditory evoked potentials of electrodermal responders and nonresponders. *Psychiatry Research* **16**, 227–230.

Sourek, K. (1965). *The Nervous Control of Skin Potentials in Man*. Praha: Nakiadateistvi Ceskoslovenska Akademie.

Spanos, N. P., Pawlak, A. E., Mah, C. D., and D'Eon, J. L. (1980). *Perceptual and Motor Skills* **50**, 287–294.

Spanos, N. P., Rivers, S. M., and Gottlieb, J. (1978). Hypnotic responsivity, meditation, and laterality of eye movements. *Journal of Abnormal Psychology* **87**, 566–569.

Speilberger, C. D. (1975). Anxiety: State-trait-process. In C. D. Speilberger and I. G. Sarason (Eds) *Stress and Anxiety Ed one*, pp. 115–143. New York: John Wiley & Sons.

Sperry, R. W. (1964). The great cerebral commissure. *Scientific American* **210**, 42–52.

Squires, A. C., Goodin, D., and Starr, A. (1979). Event related potentials in development, ageing and dementia. In: D. Lehmann and E. Calloway (Eds) *Human Evoked Potentials*, pp. 383–396. London: Plenum.

Steinhauer, S., and Zubin, J. (1983). Vulnerability to schizophrenia: information processing in the pupil and event-related potential. In: I. Hanin and E. Usdin (Eds) *Biological Markers in Psychiatry and Neurology*, pp. 371–385. Oxford: Pergamon.

Stern, D. B. (1977). Handedness and the lateral distribution of conversion reactions *Journal of Nervous and Mental Disease* **164**, 122–128.

Sutton, S., Spring, B. J., and Tueting, P. (1978). Modality shift at the cross-roads. In: L. C. Wynne, R. L. Cromwell and S. Matthysse (Eds) *The Nature of Schizophrenia*, pp. 262–270. London: Wiley.

Szelenberger, W. (1983). Brain stem auditory evoked potentials and personality. *Biological Psychiatry* **18**, 157–174.

Takahashi, R., Flor-Henry, P., Gruzelier, J. H., and Niwa, S.-I. (Eds) (1987). *Cerebral Dynamics, Laterality and Psychopathology.* Amsterdam: Elsevier.

Tavel, M. E. (1964). Hyperventilation syndrome with unilateral somatic symptoms. *Journal of the American Medical Association* **187**, 301–303.

Teuber, H. L. (1959). Some alterations in behaviour after cerebral lesions in man. In: A. D. Bass (Ed.) *Evolution of Nervous Control from Primitive Organisms to Man*, pp. 120–132. Washington: American Association for the Advancement of Science.

Thornton, S., and Gruzelier, J. H. (in preparation). Extremes of electrodermal habituation including nonresponding in anxiety disorders.

Toone, B. K., Cooke, E., and Lader, H. (1979). The effect of temporal lobe surgery on electrodermal activity: implications for an organic hypothesis in the aetiology of schizophrenia. *Psychological Medicine* **9**, 281–285.

Trimble, M. R., and Robertson, M. M. (1987). Laterality and psychopathology: recent findings in epilepsy. In: R. Takahashi, P. Flor-Henry, J. Gruzelier and S. Niwa (Eds) *Cerebral Dynamics, Laterality and Psychopathology*, pp. 359–369. Amsterdam: Elsevier.

Tucker, D. M., and Frederick, S. L. (in press). Emotion and brain lateralisation. In: H. Wager and T. Manstead (Eds) *Handbook of Psychophysiology: Social Behaviour.* London: Wiley.

Tucker, D. M., Antes, J. R., Stenslie, C. E., and Bernhardt, N. (1978). Anxiety and lateral cerebral function. *Journal of Abnormal Psychology* **87**, 380–383.

Venables, P. H. (1963a). The relationship between level of skin potential and fusion of paired light flashes in schizophrenic and normal subjects. *Journal of Psychiatric Research* **1**, 279–287.

Venables, P. H. (1967). Partial failure of cortical–subcortical integration as a factor underlying schizophrenic behaviour. In: J. Romano (Ed.) *Origins of Schizophrenia*, pp. 42–53.

Walker, E., and McGuire, S. (1982). Intra- and inter-hemispheric information processing in schizophrenia. *Psychological Bulletin* **92**, 701–725.

Wang, G. H. (1964). *The Neural Control of Sweating.* Maddison: University of Wisconsin Press.

White, C., Svali, J., and Charles, P. (1987). Psychophysiological responses, laterality, social stress and chronic schizophrenic disorder. *British Journal of Psychiatry* **150**, 365–373.

Wing, J. K., Cooper, J. E., and Sartorines, N. (1974). *The Measurement and Classification of Psychiatric Symptoms.* London: Cambridge University Press.

Wood, C. C., Allison, T., Goff, W. R., Williamson, P. D., and Spencer D. D. (1980). On the neural origin of P300 in man. In: H. H. Kornhuber and L. Deecke (Eds) *Motivation, Motor and Sensory Processes of the Brain: Electrical Potentials, Behaviour and Clinical Use*, pp. 51–55. Amsterdam: Elsevier.

Yingling, C. D., and Hosobuchi, Y. (1984). A subcortical correlate of P300 in man. *Electroecephalography and Clinical Neurophysiology* **59**, 72–76.

Chapter 6

Psychophysiological Assessment in Behaviour Therapy

Stephen N. Haynes,* Shelley Falkin† and
Kathy Sexton-Radek‡

*Department of Psychology, University of Hawaii at Manoa, 2430 Campus
Road, Honolulu, HI 96822, USA
†Department of Psychology, Illinois Institute of Technology, ITT Center,
Chicago, Il 60616, USA
‡Department of Psychology, Elmhurst College, Elmhurst, Il 60126, USA

ABSTRACT

The application of psychophysiology to behaviour therapy is reviewed. The increasing use of these techniques to investigate complex causal processes underlying behavioural and cognitive changes is emphasized. Relevant psychophysiological techniques are reviewed in relation to pre-treatment, outcome and process measures commonly obtained in behaviour therapy. The conceptual and methodological bases of these applications are critically discussed.

Handbook of Clinical Psychophysiology Edited by G. Turpin
© 1989 John Wiley & Sons Ltd

INTRODUCTION

BEHAVIOUR THERAPY

Behaviour therapy* subsumes an extensive array of underlying assumptions, interventions, and empirical methodologies. Some behavioural interventions are based on operant paradigms, while others are derived from cognitive-mediational, classical conditioning, Hullian, information-processing, stimulus–response, or broad-based social learning paradigms (Bandura, 1969; Kazdin, 1982). Intervention *procedures* are also diverse and include contingency management, systematic desensitization, cognitive restructuring, relaxation training, biofeedback, classical conditioning, modelling, imagery, behavioural rehearsal, instructions, self-monitoring, and behavioural insight training, among others (Bandura, 1959; Bellack, Hersen and Kazdin, 1982; Catania and Brigham, 1978; Kanfer and Phillips, 1971; Turner, Calhoun and Adams, 1981; Wolpe, 1982).

The commonality among these diverse intervention procedures is a strong commitment to particular *methodological principles*, rather than to particular causal assumptions or intervention strategies. These methodological principles provide a strategy for understanding the determinants of behaviour and for investigating the efficacy of intervention strategies. They include an emphasis on empiricism, operationalism, intensive longitudinal study of individuals, observable behaviour, use of controlled single-case designs, integration of assessment with therapy, and *current* determinants of behaviour (Haynes, 1978, 1984a,b; Nelson and Hayes, 1987).

A broad spectrum of socially, psychologically, and biologically based disorders are treated with behaviour therapy. These include addictive disorders, psychotic disorders, anxiety disorders, sexual dysfunctions and disorders, cardiovascular dysfunctions, aggression, sleep disorders, headaches, marital and family dysfunctions, many neurological disorders, obsessive–compulsive disorders, diabetes, affective disorders, ulcers, neuromuscular disorders, and stuttering (Barlow, 1985; Bellack *et al.*, 1982; Turner *et al.*, 1981). Behaviourally based intervention strategies are also applied in many educational, criminal justice, and community programmes (Bellack *et al.*, 1982).

The concepts, interventions, methodological foundations, and focus of behaviour therapy are particularly congruent with psychophysiological assessment. The emphases on empiricism and applications to disorders with important physiological components almost mandate psychophysiological assessment. The important role of psychophysiological assessment in behaviour therapy is

* 'Behaviour therapy' is used in the singular form throughout this chapter, but refers to multiple therapy strategies with different empirical and conceptual bases. Readers may consult the numerous behaviour therapy texts cited in this chapter for extended discussions of the definition and domain of behaviour therapy.

well documented by its prominent treatment in books on behavioural assessment (Barlow, 1985; Ciminero, Calhoun and Adams, 1986; Cone and Hawkins, 1977; Haynes, 1978; Haynes and Wilson, 1979; Nelson and Hayes, 1987).

CHAPTER FOCUS

The purpose of this chapter is to provide an overview of psychophysiological assessment in behaviour therapy. The first section will examine the degree to which psychophysiological assessment has been integrated in behaviour therapy and some of the determinants of that integration. The subsequent section will consider the utility of psychophysiological methods for pre-treatment, outcome, and process assessment in behaviour therapy. Methodological and conceptual dimensions in the use of psychophysiological assessment in behaviour therapy will be discussed in the last section.

The domain of assessment methods discussed in this chapter extends beyond those typically labelled 'psychophysiological'. Biologically based, sensitive and valid measures of physiological components of behaviour disorders, which are conceptually congruent with traditional electrophysiological methods, are included. For example, assessment methods such as the use of expired carbon monoxide and carboxyhaemoglobin as measures of smoking and substance abuse are included.

Because this chapter is only one of a series on psychophysiology in this handbook, a basic knowledge of the principles and methods of psychophysiological measurement and of the underlying physiological systems is presumed. (Readers are also referred to Andreassi, 1980; Brown, 1967; Coles, Donchin and Porges, 1986; Greenfield and Sternbach, 1972; Hassett, 1978; Stern, Ray and Davis, 1980; Venables and Martin, 1967.)

THE USE OF PSYCHOPHYSIOLOGICAL ASSESSMENT IN BEHAVIOUR THERAPY

Figure 6.1 illustrates the percentage of behaviour therapy articles that utilized psychophysiological assessment which were published in the years 1965, 1970, 1975, 1980 and 1985, in two major clinical journals: *Behavior Therapy** and the *Journal of Consulting and Clinical Psychology*. As indicated in Figure 6.1, the proportion of behaviour therapy articles that included psychophysiological assessment has demonstrated a negatively accelerating curve across the years surveyed.

Several factors may account for this trend: (a) many of the behaviour disorders targeted in behaviour therapy have physiological components, (b)

* *Behavior Therapy* was not published in 1965.

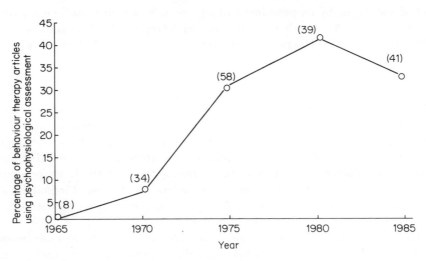

Figure 6.1. Percentage of behaviour therapy articles that used psychophysiological assessment which were published in *Behavior Therapy* and the *Journal of Consulting and Clinical Psychology*, in the years indicated. (Data for 1965 is for the *Journal of Consulting and Clinical Psychology* only.)

there is an increased recognition by behaviour therapists of the complex interactions among behavioural, cognitive, and physiological components of behaviour disorders, (c) models of behaviour disorder aetiology are including increasingly complex causal models, (d) many of the behaviour therapies have as their goal the alteration of physiological processes, and (e) the use of psychophysiological assessment is being facilitated by advances in recording and data analytical procedures.

PHYSIOLOGICAL COMPONENTS OF BEHAVIOUR DISORDERS

Many behaviour problems involve dysfunctions of physiological systems. Psychophysiological disorders such as high blood pressure, vascular and muscle-contraction headaches, insomnia, Raynaud's disease, asthma, and gastrointestinal disorders are the most obvious exemplars of disorders treated with behaviour therapy whose *primary* defining characteristics are physiological dysfunctions or subjective reports based upon assumed physiological dysfunctions such as self-reported head pain accompanying elevated cephalic muscle tension in muscle-contraction headaches (Haynes, 1981; Haynes, Cuevos and Gannon, 1982). Other disorders such as phobias and addictive disorders, although not primarily defined by physiological dysfunctions, have important physiological components (Bernstein, Borkovec and Coles, 1986).

Physiological dysfunctions in psychophysiological disorders may take several non-orthogonal forms:

(1) *Chronic dysfunction*

In some cases, such as the later stages of essential hypertension (Kaplan, 1982), a physiological system may be chronically dysfunctional.

(2) *Excessive response magnitude*

In other cases, such as the early stages of hypertension (Gross and Strasser, 1982), a physiological system may demonstrate transient but excessive response magnitude, rather than chronic dysfunction.

(3) *Conditional response*

In some disorders, such as post-traumatic stress responses (Keane, Fairbanks, Caddell, Zimering and Bender, 1985) or phobias (Bernstein *et al.*, 1986), high-magnitude responses may occur only when the person is exposed to a restricted set of stimuli.

(4) *Delayed post-stress recovery*

In some cases, a physiological disorder may be manifested by delayed recovery following the cessation of a stressor rather than an excessive response magnitude (Gannon, 1981).

(5) *Response non-occurrence*

Some disorders, such as sexual dysfunctions (Friedman, Weiler, LoPiccolo and Hogan, 1982; Leiblum, 1982) are characterized by the non-occurrence of a physiological response.

A list of disorders with important physiological components that have been treated with behaviour therapy is presented in Table 6.1.

MULTIPLE COMPONENTS OF BEHAVIOUR DISORDERS

The complex interactions among behavioural, cognitive, and physiological components of behaviour disorders are increasingly recognized by behavioural scientists (Gannon and Haynes, 1986; Grey, Sartory and Rachman, 1979; Lang, Levin, Miller and Kuzak, 1983; Vermillyea, Boice and Barlow, 1984). The degree of correlation and synchrony among them, and their importance to the aetiology of behaviour disorders varies across time, situations, and individuals. For example, one individual may exhibit primarily behavioural manifestations of anxiety, such as avoidance behaviours, while another may manifest primarily physiological indices, such as rapid heart rate. Because of probable desynchrony (low levels of correlation) among these response modalities (Gannon and Haynes, 1986), multimodal evaluation including psychophysiological assessment is necessary.

Table 6.1
Representative psychophysiological measures in behaviour therapy

Behaviour Disorder	Measure	Reference
Alcoholism	BAC Autonomic responses BA	Cannon and Baker (1981) Correa and Sutker (1986) Lindros (1982) Sobell et al. (1982)
Anger	HR	Hazaleus and Deffenbacher (1986)
Anxiety disorders	HR SC EMG	Barlow et al. (1984) Bernstein et al. (1986) Fowles (1982) Hernez and Melamed (1984)
Asthma	PEFR TRR FEV	Alexander (1981) Doleys and Bruno (1982) Miklich et al. (1977)
Convulsive disorders	SMR	Doleys and Bruno (1982)
Depression	EMG HR	Carson (1986)
Diabetes	Blood glucose	Wing et al. (1985)
Eating disorders	Calorimetry RMR Cholesterol Triglycerides	Brownell (1981) Barstuble et al. (1986) Wing et al. (1985)
Hypertension	PTT BP HR BVP	Hoelscher et al. (1986) Taylor (1982) Agras et al. (1983, 1984) McCann (1987)
Insomnia (disorders of initiating and maintaining sleep)	EEG EMG EOG HR	Youkilis and Bootzin (1981) Borkovec et al. (1979) Coates et al. (1982)
Migraine headache	Peripheral BVPA Cephalic BVPA	Sturgis et al. (1981) Gannon and Haynes (1986) Blanchard et al. (1980) Friar and Beatty (1976)
Muscle-contraction headache	Frontal EMG Neck EMG Cephalic BVPA	Blanchard et al. (1980, 1985) Haynes et al. (1982)
Post-traumatic stress disorder	HR; SC Cortisol Catecholamines	Keane and Kaloupek (1982) Davidson and Baum (1986) Malloy et al. (1983)
Raynaud's disease	Peripheral BVPA Peripheral temp.	Surwit et al. (1978)

Behaviour Disorder	Measure	Reference
Sexual dysfunctions (male)	Penile circumference Penile volume	Friedman *et al.* (1982) Heiman and Hatch (1982) Abel *et al.* (1981) Abrahanson *et al.* (1986)
Sexual dysfunctions (female)	Vaginal BVP Labial temperature Vaginal BVPA	Haynes and Wilson (1979)
Sexual disorders	Penile volume Penile circumference	McConaghy (1982) Abel *et al.* (1981) Avery-Clark and Laws (1984)
Smoking	CO SCN CH; HR	Killen *et al.*(1984) Brown *et al.* 1984) Danahar *et al.* (1976) Epstein *et al.* (1981)
Spasmodic torticollis	Site-specific EMG	Taylor (1982) Brundy *et al.* (1974) Martin (1981)
Stuttering	Masseter EMG	Lanyon and Goldsworthy (1982)
Tachycardia, premature ventricular contractions	HR and variability	Blanchard and Abel (1976) Pickering and Miller (1977) Taylor (1982)
Ulcers	EGG Gastric pH	Walker and Sandman (1981) Whitehead *et al.* (1975)

BA = blood acetaldehyde, BAC = blood alcohol concentration, BP = blood pressure, BVP = blood volume pulse, BVPA = blood volume pulse amplitude, CH = carboxyhaemoglobin, CO = carbon monoxide, EEG = electroencephalogram, EGG = electrogastrogram, EMG = electromyogram, EOG = electro-oculogram, FEV = forced expiratory volume, HR = heart rate, PEFR = peak expiratory flow rate, PTT = pulse transit time, RMR = resting metabolic rate, SC = skin conductance, SCN = serum thiocynate, SMR = sensory motor rhythm, TRR = total respiratory resistance.

COMPLEX CAUSAL PROCESSES

Complex causal models for behaviour disorders recognize that the disorders have *multiple causes*, that there are *individual differences* in their aetiology and expression, that causal factors *interact* in complex ways and that they *vary* across time or stages of a disorder (Haynes, 1988a,b). For example, migraine headaches may be a function of dietary factors, sleep patterns, oestrogen fluctuations and/or environmental stressors and may involve any of a number of cerebrovascular pathways (Bakal, 1982; Dalessio, 1980; Diamond and Dalessio, 1986). Furthermore, these can differ across individuals and across time within individuals, and can be mutually potentiating.

Because of the complexity of causal pathways and the fact that interventions are often intended to modify causal factors (Haynes, 1988a), psychophysiological assessment is necessary when identifying causal paths that might involve physiological variables.

ALTERATION OF PHYSIOLOGICAL PROCESSES IN BEHAVIOUR THERAPY

The goal of many behaviour therapies is the modification of physiological processes. For example, one goal of relaxation training (Borkovec and Sides, 1979) is to facilitate voluntary control of autonomically mediated arousal. Consistent with this function, relaxation training has been used to reduce the physiological arousal of individuals with insomnia (see review by Bornstein and Kazdin, 1985; Coates and Thoresen, 1977; Turner et al., 1981), headaches (see review by Beaty and Haynes, 1979), hypertension (see review by McCann, 1987), and anxiety disorders (McGowan, Haynes and Wilson, 1979; Michelson and Ascher, 1987).

Similarly, covert sensitization (Cautela, 1967) and classical aversion conditioning (Rimm and Masters, 1979; Wolpe, 1982) were designed to modify autonomically mediated responses to particular stimuli. For example, in a treatment programme for incarcerated sex offenders, McConaghy (1982) paired aversive stimuli with pictures and activities associated with the sexual preferences of voyeurs, paedophiliacs, and exhibitionists. The intent of the intervention was to reduce the level of sexual arousal to these stimuli by associating them with incompatible responses. Outcome was measured by the degree of penile erection to the previously sexually arousing stimuli.

The modification of physiological processes is also the goal of other behaviour therapies. For example, biofeedback (Blanchard and Epstein, 1978) provides analogue information to individuals about physiological processes for the purpose of facilitating their voluntary control. Systematic desensitization (Wolpe, 1982) pairs a relaxation response with fear-eliciting stimuli, in a hierarchical fashion, for the purpose of decreasing conditional fear responses. Flooding and implosive therapy (Stampfl and Levis, 1967) attempt to extinguish physiological arousal to conditional fear stimuli through long-duration presentation of those stimuli.

Imagery, particularly imagining a traumatic event or phobic stimulus, seems to be a particularly powerful means of eliciting physiological responses in analogous situations and is an important component of many behaviour therapies. Imagery-elicited physiological responses can be used in pre-treatment assessments and can be monitored as an index of therapy effects (e.g. Bernstein et al., 1986).

TECHNOLOGICAL ADVANCES

The utilization of any assessment procedure is partially a function of the ease or cost-effectiveness with which it can be applied. In the last ten years there have been many technological advances in psychophysiological assessment which have facilitated its application across an expanding range of populations and situations (see review by Rugh, Gable and Lemke, 1986). Examples include advances in miniaturization of recording devices, telemetric and automatic recording procedures for monitoring physiological responses in the natural environment, computer analysis, and electronic filtering capabilities. Specific examples include: (a) the monitoring of electroencephalographic patterns of insomniacs at home through portable recording devices or through the use of the home telephone as a modem for data transmission; (b) the automatic monitoring of blood pressure and heart rate throughout the day using portable recording devices (Agras, Southam and Taylor, 1983; Holden and Barlow, 1986; Keefe and Blumenthal, 1982); (c) the monitoring of peak expiratory flow rate outside the clinic through the use of relatively inexpensive portable apparatus (Alexander, 1981); and (d) the monitoring of carbon monoxide levels throughout the day of individuals on smoking programmes by having subjects exhale into polyvinyl bags (Martin and Fredericksen, 1980).

Technological advances are also reflected in a wider availability of commercial products. Many companies now manufacture user-friendly psychophysiological recording systems that provide computer-assisted graphics and data collection, reduction, integration, and analysis. These systems allow psychophysiological monitoring without extensive training in the principles of computer programming or electrophysiology.

A cautionary note is warranted. In many cases 'ease of use' is receiving considerably more attention than factors such as filtering and amplification characteristics, response sampling, and integration methods. Thus, although the operation of many psychophysiological assessment instruments does not require specialized training, the selection of quality instrumentation from the vast array of commercial products and the interpretation of the resulting data do require at least basic knowledge of physiology and medical electronics. In essence, an increase in clinical utility can, but need not, be accompanied by a decrease in validity of the derived measures.

SUMMARY

Psychophysiological assessment is well incorporated into behaviour assessment and therapy. It is congruent with the emphasis on careful assessment and quantification which characterizes behavioural construct systems and reflects the focus of behaviour therapy on disorders with significant physiological components. The importance of psychophysiological assessment in behaviour therapy is also a function of the emphasis of many of the intervention procedures on modifying physiological processes, the complex interactions among cognitive, behavioural, and physiological processes and determinants, and recent technological advances.

The next two sections will examine the clinical utility of psychophysiological assessment in pre-treatment assessment and as a method of measuring the process and outcome of intervention.

PRE-TREATMENT PSYCHOPHYSIOLOGICAL ASSESSMENT

As noted earlier in this chapter, an emphasis on systematic, empirically oriented, pre-treatment assessment is a primary characteristic of behaviour therapy (Haynes, 1984a,b; 1988a; Nelson and Hayes, 1987). This emphasis is a function of presumed individual differences in the topography and causality of behaviour problems, the operation of multiple and interacting causal factors, individual differences in response to intervention, and a mandate to measure treatment outcome. Consequently, pre-treatment assessment is a prerequisite for the identification of behaviour problems and their determinants, for the selection of appropriate intervention strategies, and for intervention evaluation.

Pre-treatment psychophysiological assessment can have a number of important functions: (a) it can help pinpoint behaviours to be targeted for intervention, (b) it can facilitate classification and diagnosis of behaviour problems, (c) it can help identify causal factors in behaviour disorders and can help identify precipitating stimuli or triggers for behaviour problems, (d) it can suggest treatment strategies, and (e) it is necessary for the prediction and monitoring of response to intervention and can help predict the probability of relapse for persons with behaviour disorders involving psychophysiological systems. These functions are considered in more detail in the following sections.

SELECTION OF TARGET BEHAVIOURS

One function of behavioural assessment is to select the targets for intervention. For example, muscle-contraction headaches may result from sustained elevated cephalic muscle tension at any of several sites (Haynes, 1981). Pre-treatment psychophysiological assessment can aid in the identification of the most involved muscle groups to be targeted through biofeedback (e.g. Philips, 1977). Similarly, the treatment of patients with low back pain may include modification of muscle tension in the lower back region through relaxation training or biofeedback, if pre-treatment assessment implicates elevated muscle tension in that region as a contributing factor (Bush, Ditto and Feuerstein, 1985; Holzman and Turk, 1986). Electromyogram (EMG) levels within normal ranges in cases of low back pain would suggest that reports of low back pain are a function of factors other than elevated muscle tension.

Pre-treatment identification of intervention targets is based on the concept of *conditional probabilities* or *discriminative associations*. That is, physiological processes are presumed to be aetiological when their level, given the occurrence of a disorder, is greater than their level in the absence of a disorder. Thus, EMG feedback from the spinalis or semispinalis muscle groups (neck region) would be indicated for muscle-contraction headache only if their measured EMG level was greater for headache than for non-headache subjects, or greater for a subject during headache than non-headache conditions (Haynes *et al.*, 1982). In many cases, these judgements are subjectively based because normative data is unavailable.

In practice, the results of pre-treatment assessment are used to indicate treatment targets only when they are consistent with an *accepted causal model* of the disorder (Haynes, 1988a). Site-specific EMG elevations in cephalic muscle groups indicate which muscle groups should be targeted for biofeedback, because the involvement of these muscle groups is consistent with commonly accepted aetiological models of muscle-contraction headache (Haynes, 1981). In contrast, elevations in the forearm extensor muscles of a subject during headache conditions would not necessarily suggest forearm biofeedback because the current causal model of muscle-contraction headache does not include elevated tension in these muscle groups as a component. Similarly, numerous studies (see review by Sturgis, Adams and Brantly, 1981) have found that frontal EMG levels are significantly higher for migraine than for non-headache control subjects. However, these EMG elevations are assumed to be a result of, rather than a cause of, migraine headache pain. Consequently, EMG feedback is not commonly used to test migraine headache.

CLASSIFICATION AND DIAGNOSIS OF BEHAVIOUR PROBLEMS

The clinical and empirical utility of a behaviour disorder classification system is related to the degree to which its categories help indicate specific causal factors or treatments (Adams and Haber, 1984; Garfield, 1984, 1986; Morey, Skinner and Blashfield, 1986). However, many currently used behaviour taxonomies (e.g. see the *Diagnostic and Statistical Manual of Mental Disorders*, 3rd edn, American Psychiatric Association, 1980) include categories in which members differ in the topography, causes and appropriate treatment of their targeted behaviour disorders, thereby limiting their utility (Kanfer, 1985).

Psychophysiological assessment can facilitate classification by aiding in the identification of homogeneous subgroups of particular categories. An example is the division of sleep-onset insomnia into 'subjective' and 'psychophysiological' subgroups (Borkovec, 1982). This classification is based on the degree of correspondence between subjectively reported and psychophysiologically measured sleep-onset latency: a low correlation between these measures is indicative of 'subjective' insomnia, while a high correlation is indicative of 'psychophysiological' insomnia. This distinction is important in that the two subgroups may require different treatments or be a function of different determinants (Borkovec, 1982).

Psychophysiological assessment has also been used to differentiate erectile dysfunctions into subgroups based on presumed psychogenic and organic aetiology (Friedman *et al.*, 1982; Haynes and Wilson, 1979; Heiman and Hatch, 1981; see also Chapter 14). For this purpose, penile erections are measured (most often by a mercury-filled strain gauge) while a subject sleeps. A normal erection response and pattern (full erections usually occur on a 90-min cycle associated with rapid eye movement sleep) in a male with erectile failure is presumed to indicate a 'psychogenic' rather than an organic aetiology. In such a case, the use of behavioural treatment programmes involving sensate focusing, stimulus control training, relaxation training, masturbatory conditioning, and/ or desensitization might be indicated (Barlow, 1985; LoPiccolo and LoPiccolo, 1978; Wincze and Lange, 1981). Organic impairment, suggested by impaired nocturnal erections, might suggest the use of prosthetic devices or hormone therapy (Tollison and Adams, 1979).

Psychophysiological assessment has also been used for diagnostic purposes with other behaviour disorders. For example, McConaghy (1982) measured penile erection responses of paedophiliacs to various slide-presented stimuli in order to identify which were most likely to elicit sexual arousal. In a similar manner, Avery-Clark and Laws (1984) attempted to differentiate dangerous from less dangerous incarcerated sex offenders by measuring their erectile responses to tape-recorded depictions of sexual activities which varied in the degree to which the partners were coerced. Offenders with a history of violent sexual behaviour demonstrated greater erectile responses to scenes depicting sexual coercion of an unwilling female than to scenes depicting sex with a willing female.

One of the most promising uses of pre-treatment psychophysiological assessment is the identification of individuals who are 'at risk' for a disorder. For example, a number of studies have noted that the degree of cardiovascular reactivity of young adults to laboratory stressors may be correlated with the probability of developing hypertension later in life (Manuck, Proietti, Rader and Polefrone, 1984). Such early identification procedures can facilitate longitudinal studies on the development of a disorder and are prerequisite to the development of prevention programmes.

Although logically appealing, the validity, utility, and cost-effectiveness of classification through psychophysiological assessment should not be presumed. For example, it has not been conclusively demonstrated that individuals with psychogenic sexual dysfunctions do not demonstrate aberrant nocturnal erection patterns, or that nocturnal erectile patterns are associated with differential responses to treatment. Also, the clinical utility of labeling sleep-onset insomniacs as 'subjective' or 'psychophysiological' has yet to be demonstrated

(Haynes *et al.*, 1982). Similarly, the past behaviour patterns of incarcerated sex offenders may be a more accurate and easily obtainable and less expensive predictor of sexual preference and behaviour than erectile responses to erotic stimuli in a laboratory situation.

IDENTIFICATION OF CAUSAL FACTORS*

In addition to identifying causal factors via classification, psychophysiological assessment may help identify causes in other ways. One particularly powerful method of identifying possible determinants of behaviour problems involves the monitoring of several psychophysiological responses while hypothesized causal (triggering) factors are systematically manipulated (Barlow and Hersen, 1984). For example, psychophysiological responses to a variety of systematically presented stimuli can be used with anxious clients to help identify specific triggers of anxiety responses (Kallman and Feuerstein, 1986). In a similar manner, Flor, Turk and Birbaumer (1985) asked patients with chronic low back pain to discuss 'personally relevant' life events to determine which topics were associated with increases in paraspinal EMG. In another example, Burns (1980) monitored inspiratory and expiratory flow rates while a variety of potentially noxious stimuli (e.g. lacquer fumes, tobacco smoke) were presented in order to identify triggers for a client's asthma attacks.

To derive valid causal indices, the stimuli must be carefully and systematically presented. However, they may be imagined, real, or analogue (e.g. slides). In all cases we infer that a particular stimulus may function as a 'triggering stimulus' when its presentation is conditionally associated with the occurrence or increased magnitude of a psychophysiological response or disorder. Confidence in this inference is a function of the degree to which methodologically sound procedures are followed (Barlow and Hersen, 1981; Sidman, 1960; and see also 'Conceptual and methodological principles of psychophysiological assessment' later in this chapter).

SELECTION OF TREATMENT STRATEGIES

As suggested in the previous sections, pre-intervention psychophysiological assessment can help indicate which intervention strategies are most appropriate

---

* The concept of 'causality' refers to the conditions associated with variance in a particular target behaviour. Causes vary in their degree of abstractness or level, and may be triggers (e.g. bright flashing lights for a seizure), environmental events (e.g. loss of reinforcement for depression), or pathophysiological processes (e.g. release of platelet-bound serotonin for a headache). In the context of this chapter, 'cause' is closely associated with the concepts of 'conditional probability' and 'functional relationship' (Haynes, 1988b). Causal factors need not be necessary, sufficient, nor infallible (James *et al.*, 1982).

for a particular client. Because behaviour problems are composed of behavioural, cognitive, and physiological components, psychophysiological assessment is necessary to estimate the causal relevance of psychophysiological variables for a particular individual. Social anxiety, for example, may or may not involve physiological arousal (Emmelkamp, 1982). Pre-intervention psychophysiological assessment (including measurement of sympathetically mediated responses such as electrodermal responses, heart waveform or peripheral vasomotor responses) of a subject with an anxiety disorder can suggest whether a treatment strategy such as systematic desensitization, relaxation training, or heart rate biofeedback, aimed at modifying these physiological responses, is warranted. In contrast, a behaviourally oriented intervention strategy, such as behaviour rehearsal, might be more appropriate in the absence of physiological components of anxiety.

PREDICTION AND MONITORING OF TREATMENT EFFECTS

Perhaps the most frequent empirical application of pre-treatment psychophysiological assessment is in the prediction of treatment outcome. For example, Barstuble, Klesges and Terbizar (1986) measured resting metabolic rate of overweight clients prior to treatment and found that it was significantly related to relapse following behavioural treatment, suggesting the need for different weight control strategies as a function of clients' pre-treatment metabolic rate. Hall, Ginsberg and Jones (1986) and Hall, Tunstall, Rugg, Jones and Benowitz (1985) used cotinine (a nicotine metabolite) levels to predict weight gain associated with smoking cessation programmes. Similarly, Suarez, Adams and McCutcheon (1976) found that the degree of pre-intervention psychophysiological reactions to fearful stimuli were associated with differential reactions to implosive therapy or systematic desensitization.

Thus, pre-intervention psychophysiological assessment may facilitate the matching of clients to particular interventions and it can suggest intervention modifications for particular clients. It can also help predict initial responses to intervention, the probability of success with a particular intervention, and the probability of relapse following intervention cessation (Haynes and Wilson, 1979). However, the identification of psychophysiological indices or 'markers' of expected intervention effects necessitates complex and carefully conducted longitudinal research programmes which take into consideration individual differences in causality of behaviour disorders and the multiple treatments available (Haynes, 1988a, b). Such research has been infrequently conducted. However, including pre-treatment assessment as an integral part of all interventions will aid in developing a body of data on predictors of treatment effects.

PSYCHOPHYSIOLOGICAL ASSESSMENT AS AN OUTCOME AND PROCESS MEASURE IN BEHAVIOUR THERAPY

An important function of behavioural assessment is the measurement of intervention effects. Consistent with this purpose, psychophysiological assessment can be used to monitor intervention outcome, intervention response generalization and maintenance, treatment side-effects, treatment mediational or independent variables, and the intervention process. These functions are discussed in the following sections.

MEASUREMENT OF INTERVENTION OUTCOME

Psychophysiological assessment is frequently used to measure changes associated with behavioural intervention. The measurement of intervention outcome is particularly important when physiological processes are targeted for intervention, as in the treatment of hypertension, headaches, Raynaud's disease, or asthma (Haynes and Gannon, 1981). Each of these disorders is characterized by a physiological dysfunction whose modification is the primary aim of intervention. Examples of physiological responses monitored during behaviour therapy are provided in Table 6.1.

Psychophysiological measurement of intervention outcome usually involves the use of *analogue stimuli and settings* – stimuli and settings that are different from, but produce responses correlated with, those occurring in the natural environment. For example, to evaluate the effects of three behaviour therapies (flooding, relaxation training, and desensitization) in the treatment of post-traumatic stress syndrome (severe anxiety reactions following transportation accidents), McCaffrey and Fairbank (1985) monitored heart rate and skin resistance of subjects in a laboratory before and after treatment while they viewed videotapes of accidents. Similarly, Karacan (1970) monitored the nocturnal erections of patients with diabetes-related erectile failure in a sleep laboratory in order to evaluate the effects of dietary intervention.

Because heightened psychophysiological reactivity to stressors is presumed to be a causal factor in many behaviour disorders (Matthews *et al.*, 1986), assessment of pre- and post-intervention stress reactivity is frequently used to evaluate intervention effects (e.g. Blanchard and Abel, 1976; McGowan *et al.*, 1979). In this assessment paradigm, clients are presented with analogue stressors (e.g. taped descriptions of feared stimuli) or naturally occurring stressors (actual exposure to feared stimuli) before and after intervention while psychophysiological responses are monitored. Without psychophysiological stress testing, inferences about intervention effects have restricted validity or clinical utility: they must be derived from self-reports or limited to effects on *resting* levels.

Post-intervention psychophysiological reactivity to unconditional or conditional stimuli may also provide information about intervention effects. For example, post-intervention penile erections to previously sexually arousing stimuli were used to evaluate the effects of a sexual reorientation programme with paedophiliacs in a study by Abel, Blanchard, Murphy, Becker and Djenderedjiam (1981). Likewise, based on the finding that the degree of cardiovascular reactivity to smoking is inversely related to an individual's recent smoking history, Epstein, Ossip, Coleman, Hughes and Weist (1981) measured cardiac reactivity to smoking in subjects who had completed a smoking-withdrawal programme.

Although infrequently measured, *post-stress recovery* rate or level may be a particularly sensitive measure of intervention effects. The latency between maximum response during a stressor and recovery following stressor termination has been shown to be a valid and useful measure of intervention outcome (Anderson, Stoyva and Vaughn, 1982; Hernez and Melamed, 1984) and may be implicated as a possible causal factor in many psychophysiological disorders (Gannon, 1981). For example, Goleman and Schwartz (1976) found that meditation training increased the degree of heart rate recovery following termination of a stressful film. Post-stressor recovery measures were also used by Keane and Kaloupek (1982) to measure the effects of flooding with a case of post-traumatic stress disorder, and by Hernez and Melamed (1984) to assess psychophysiological recovery from a stressful film in children with fears of medical procedures.

When inferences about intervention outcome are made on the basis of psychophysiological responses in analogue environments such as a laboratory, care must be exercised in presuming that the observed responses are representative of those that would occur in the natural environment. Greater confidence is possible in assuming *situational generalizability* of laboratory-based assessment if: (a) psychophysiological measures are also taken in the natural environment (e.g. Agras, Schneider and Taylor, 1984) and (b) psychophysiological assessment is only one component of a multimethod assessment programme involving other behavioural and self-report measures (Haynes, 1984b).

MEASUREMENT OF INTERVENTION GENERALIZATION AND SIDE-EFFECTS

The evaluation of intervention outcome should never be confined to the main target variable, nor should it be limited to a narrow range of situations or stimuli (Haynes, 1978; Haynes and Wilson, 1979). Narrowly focused intervention evaluations cannot provide the information necessary for a comprehensive evaluation of intervention effects. The generalization of intervention effects across situations, time, and responses, and positive and negative side-effects must also be considered.

Several published studies illustrate the importance of assessing generalized effects of behaviour therapy. For example, to examine *stimulus generalization* of classical aversive conditioning with alcoholics (e.g. Cohen and Phelan, 1972), conditioned aversion responses should be examined across a range of alcoholic and non-alcoholic beverages to ensure that conditioning has not been confined to a limited array of alcoholic beverages and has not generalized to non-alcoholic drinks. To examine *response generalization* in an intervention programme for migraineurs (Koppman, McDonald and Kunzel, 1974), the effects of biofeedback-aided modification of peripheral vasomotor responses should also be examined on temporal arteries because of their presumed involvement in the pathophysiology of migraine (Dalessio, 1980).

Intervention *side-effects* (positive or negative effects of an intervention other than those on the main target response) are also important assessment foci. They can be important indicators of intervention outcome and in some cases, can contribute more than main effects to inferences about the clinical utility of a behavioural intervention programme. For example, clinically significant tachycardia is an occasional side-effect of rapid-smoking treatment programmes (see review by Haynes and Wilson, 1979). This suggests caution in the use of this intervention with some persons, regardless of its effectiveness. In a similar vein, Ewart, Taylor, Kraemer and Agras (1984) found that marital communication training resulted in a reduction in blood pressure during a marital communication task involving 41 essential hypertension subjects. While the primary purpose of marital communication training was to modify dyadic interaction styles, the side-effect was a moderation of blood pressure elevations during communication exercises.

In summary, an adequate evaluation of the effects of behavioural intervention requires a broadly focused assessment. In some cases, the magnitude of positive or negative side-effects and response, stimulus, and setting generalization may significantly affect inferences about the clinical utility or applicability of an intervention procedure.

MEASUREMENT OF INDEPENDENT OR TREATMENT MEDIATIONAL VARIABLES

To identify which components in a behavioural intervention programme are responsible for intervention effects and to ascertain if behaviour changes can be attributed to the intervention programme rather than to extraneous events, it is necessary to demonstrate a correlation between the independent treatment variables and the target variables. For example, biofeedback treatment of muscle-contraction headache is based on the assumption that reductions in headaches result from biofeedback-aided reductions in the tension of the frontalis (forehead) muscles. However, a number of studies have monitored the frontalis muscles during biofeedback and noted non-significant correlations between EMG levels and headache reductions (Haynes et al., 1982). These findings suggest that the therapeutic effects of frontal EMG biofeedback on muscle-contraction headaches must be attributable to factors other than, or in addition to, reductions in frontalis muscle tension.

The assumption that changes in a psychophysiological variable mediate intervention effects also underlies other behaviour therapies. For example, the use of relaxation intervention with sleep-onset insomnia (Borkovec, 1982) is based upon assumptions that difficulties in initiating sleep are a function of heightened sympathetically mediated arousal and that relaxation training is effective because it can reduce arousal. Therefore, psychophysiological assessment of insomniacs throughout treatment can help determine the degree to which any positive effects can be attributed to reductions in arousal.

In summary, to differentiate active from inactive treatment components, the hypothesized independent or treatment mediational variable, as well as the primary target behaviour, must be monitored. Failure to do so will hinder our understanding of the aetiology of disorders and the derivation of more effective or efficient intervention programmes.

MONITORING THE INTERVENTION PROCESS

Ongoing intervention programmes must sometimes be modified and this can be facilitated by psychophysiological assessment during intervention. For example, failure to demonstrate conditioned aversion responses during aversive conditioning with alcoholics (Cannon and Baker, 1981), failure to demonstrate reductions in arousal during relaxation training with anxiety disorders (Barlow et al., 1984), or failure to elicit high levels of arousal during flooding with post-traumatic stress disorders (Keane and Kaloupek, 1982) suggest that the treatments are not having the intended effects and require modification.

To effectively monitor the intervention process, serial assessment, repeated measures, or time-series strategies must be used (Agras, Taylor, Kraemer, Allen and Schneider, 1980; Barlow and Hersen, 1984; Goldstein and Hersen, 1984). This allows the assessor to sensitively track intervention effects and to rapidly change intervention strategies if necessary. That is, both independent and dependent variables should be monitored frequently, both across and within therapy sessions.

Another method of evaluating the intervention process is through the use of probes. Probes are intervention-related stimuli or conditions presented systematically and intermittently during the intervention process to help monitor its effects. In psychophysiological assessment, probes may include analogue stressors. For example, difficult mental tasks may be presented to a cardiovascularly hyper-reactive client during treatment to assess its effects. Probes may also include fear stimuli (e.g. slides of fear objects presented during treatment of phobias), measures of self-control (e.g. measures of voluntary control of muscle tension during treatment of headaches), or conditional stimuli (e.g. pictures of nude adults presented during treatment of paedophilia).

Probes were used by Burns (1980) to periodically test for upper airway sensitivity to airborne stimuli during intervention with an asthmatic patient. They were also used by Blanchard (1979) to periodically test a client's ability to control peripheral temperature during biofeedback intervention of causalgia. In all cases, probes are usually presented on a variable or fixed interval time schedule that corresponds to the expected latency for behaviour change.

SUMMARY

Psychophysiological assessment plays an important role in monitoring the progress and outcome of behaviour therapy. It has numerous empirically and clinically useful functions, including the assessment of intervention outcome, treatment generalization, the side-effects of treatment, independent variables in the treatment, and the intervention process. It is most useful and valid when conducted frequently, in conjunction with a multimethod assessment programme, and when applied to a number of dependent and independent variables. As with all assessment methods, care should be exercised in presuming response, situational, and temporal generalizability of the results.

CONCEPTUAL AND METHODOLOGICAL PRINCIPLES OF PSYCHOPHYSIOLOGICAL ASSESSMENT

The clinical utility of psychophysiological assessment in behaviour therapy is constrained by the validity of inferences that can be drawn from it. These, in turn, are a function of several conceptual and methodological parameters, including the operation and interaction among physiological mechanisms, the multiple and interactive aetiology of behaviour disorders, the assessment methods used, the research designs within which the assessment occurs, methods of data reduction and analysis, and instrumentation.

PHYSIOLOGICAL PROCESSES AND THEIR INTERACTIONS

The characteristics of psychophysiological responses, their underlying physiological mechanisms, and their interactions with other response modalities affect inferences that can be drawn from psychophysiological assessment (Andreassi, 1980; Brown, 1967; Greenfield and Sternbach, 1972; Hassett, 1978; Stern, Ray and Davis, 1980; Venables and Martin, 1967). Several concepts are particularly relevant to psychophysiological assessment in behaviour therapy: (a) the characteristics of the responses measured, (b) response discordance, (c) response desynchrony, and (d) initial values.

Response Characteristics

As noted earlier in this chapter, psychophysiological assessment is frequently used to evaluate the effects of behaviour therapy on a psychophysiological response. In the psychophysiological assessment of anxiety disorders, for example, electrodermal responses must be monitored because they reflect sympathetically mediated arousal (one component of 'anxiety') in the presence of feared stimuli; the reduction of such arousal is one goal of behaviour therapy (Barlow *et al.*, 1984; Bernstein *et al.*, 1986; Emmelkamp, 1982).

To accurately interpret intervention effects in such cases, it is important to understand the *physiological basis* or determinants of the selected psychophysiological response. For example, electrodermal responses primarily reflect the tone of the sympathetic division of the autonomic nervous system. In contrast, heart rate and blood pressure changes are a function of complex interactions involving intrinsic neural stimulation, sympathetic and parasympathetic balance, metabolic demands, catecholamines, and interactions among cardiovascular events such as stroke output and peripheral resistance (Kaplan, 1982). Therefore, heart rate and blood pressure may be clinically useful *general* indices of multiple physiological mechanisms and of treatment outcome. However, it is not possible to ascribe intervention-related changes in these variables to changes in any *particular* physiological mechanism (Bernstein *et al.*, 1986).

One effect of the differing physiological determinants across psychophysiological responses is a low level of intercorrelation among them – i.e. *response fractionation* (Bernstein *et al.*, 1986; Haynes and Wilson, 1979; Holden and Barlow, 1986; Lacey, 1967). For example, biofeedback, systematic desensitization, or other cognitive imagery procedures (Wolpe, 1982) often result in physiological responses diverging from a pattern consistent with a unitary view of arousal.

Response fractionation mandates caution in the interpretation of intervention-related psychophysiological changes. In particular, *response generalization* cannot be assumed. Response fractionation also underscores the importance of establishing *convergent validity* in psychophysiological assessment (Kallman and Feuerstein, 1986) by examining the level of covariation among multiple measures of the same target. For example, convergent validity may be assessed by using at least two measures of cardiovascular activation when assessing hypertensive subjects. The degree of correlation between the measures will influence the type and level of confidence in the inferences that can be drawn.

Differing mechanisms of control among psychophysiological systems also result in differences in their *temporal latency*, *sensitivity*, or *response equilibrium*. For example, heart rate and electrodermal response are quite sensitive to discrete stimuli, and they demonstrate short response latencies. Other measures, such as urinary catecholamine levels or diastolic blood pressure (Selye, 1982), demonstrate longer response latencies and are, therefore, less 'sensitive' measures of transient arousal. However, urinary catecholamine levels and diastolic blood pressure can validly reflect responses to longer duration events or stressors. Latency to achieve maximum magnitude of response (response equilibrium), given a particular stimulus, will also vary across psychophysiological responses. As will be discussed later, these response parameters dictate appropriate sampling intervals.

The temporal sensitivity and response equilibrium of measures is particularly important when evaluating therapy outcome. The effects of smoking intervention programmes, for example, are frequently evaluated through expired carbon monoxide levels (Brown, Lichtenstein, McIntyre and Harrington-Kostur, 1984; Glasgow, Klesges, Klesges, Vasey and Gunnarson, 1986; Hall *et al.*, 1986; Killen, Maccoby and Taylor, 1984; Martin and Fredericksen, 1980; Ossip-Klein, Epstein, Winter, Stiller, Russell and Dickson, 1983; Russell, Epstein and Dickson, 1983). However, carbon monoxide levels are a valid indicator of smoking only if measured within 2 hours of smoking. On the other hand, serum thiocyanate levels can serve as a valid indicator of smoking for much longer periods (Lichtenstein and Brown, 1982). Temporal constraints on validity apply as well to blood alcohol measures and many urine tests for drugs. These measures of substance ingestion are accurate for only a few hours following ingestion (Correa and Sutker, 1986).

Other parameters of psychophysiological responses also affect their utility in behaviour therapy assessment. One important parameter is *habituation rate*: psychophysiological responses differ in the degree to which they are affected by repeated presentation of a stimulus. For example, the magnitude of penile erections can diminish with repeated presentations of an erotic stimulus (Murphy, Abel and Becker, 1980). Similarly, the frequency of electrodermal responses to novel stimuli can rapidly habituate when they are repeatedly presented (Bernstein *et al.*, 1986). Since habituation rate varies as a function of stimulus complexity, meaningfulness, and variability, stimuli used in psychophysiological research should be varied and care should be exercised to avoid attributing reductions in response magnitude to intervention effects when it might be more valid to attribute them to habituation effects.

Many psychophysiological responses also demonstrate *temporal variability* – variability in magnitude across time in the absence of stimulation. This variability may be a function of natural circadian or diurnal rhythms, interactions among physiological systems (such as the sinus arrhythmia pattern), sleep patterns (such as cyclic brain-wave patterns during sleep), or responses to regular stimuli (such as changes in caffeine-induced sympathetic arousal during the day) (Burch and Altschuler, 1975; Haynes and Gannon, 1981).

In summary, the *utility*, *validity*, and *sensitivity* of psychophysiological measures of behaviour therapy are influenced by their physiological basis, response fractionation, temporal sensitivity, habituation rate, and temporal variability. There is a complex interaction among these parameters and other aspects of an assessment programme which affect the internal validity of psychophysiological assessment in behaviour therapy. The sensitivity and validity of particular psychophysiological measures will be influenced by the particular behaviour disorder targeted, the assessment situation and procedures used, the behaviour therapy to be employed, and the physiological processes underlying the particular measures used.

These parameters suggest several important principles of psychophysiological assessment in behaviour therapy: (a) more than one psychophysiological response should be monitored, (b) psychophysiological measures should reflect the underlying physiological processes of interest, (c) the intent and timing of the assessment should be congruent with the temporal sensitivity and characteristics of the responses measured, and (d) the habituation rate of each measure should be considered if a stimulus is going to be repeatedly presented.

Response Discordance

Response concordance and discordance, as outlined by Gannon and Haynes (1986), refer to the degree of correlation between contemporaneous measures of two or more response systems assumed to measure the same construct. For example, labial temperature and subjective reports of sexual arousal in a group of women would be concordant if they were significantly correlated and discordant if they demonstrated low levels of correlation (Hensen, Rubin and Hensen, 1979).

Discordance among cognitive, physiological, behavioural, and self-report measures is commonly noted. For example, discordance has been documented in measures of anxiety (Bernstein *et al.*, 1986; Malloy, Fairbank and Keane, 1983), sexual arousal (Heiman & Hatch, 1981), sleep-onset insomnia (Borkovec, Grayson, O'Brien and Weerts, 1979), and headache (Haynes *et al.*, 1982).

Discordance among response modalities further emphasizes the complexity and idiosyncrasy of causal pathways. Cognitive, behavioural, and physiological measures of the same construct reflect different dimensions of a behaviour disorder, have different determinants, and reflect different sources of measurement error. Therefore, they should be considered as independent but interacting response channels. To illustrate, a high level of sympathetically mediated arousal cannot be *equated* with the construct of 'anxiety' and may not correlate highly with self-report or behavioural measures of anxiety. Consequently, the effects of behaviour therapy should always be evaluated through measurement of multiple response modalities.

Response Desynchrony

Response desynchrony is a special case of discordance and refers to low levels of concordance among response modalities *across time* (Hodgson and Rachman, 1974). It is most often indicated by a low correlation between *change scores* across time. Thus, intermodal (i.e. behavioural, psychophysiological) and intra-modal (i.e. *volume* and *circumference* measures of penile erections) measures will often not demonstrate parallel changes (e.g. Michelson and Mavissakalian, 1985) even if they were initially significantly correlated.

Like discordance, response desynchrony is primarily a function of variance in determinants across measures. For example, behavioural concomitants of panic may be more affected by social contingencies than are psychophysiolog-ical concomitants and would, therefore, be expected to demonstrate a greater magnitude of change with variance in that class of variables. Desynchronous responses to behaviour therapy are also a function of the differential effects of behaviour therapy across responses. Thus, desensitization would be expected to more immediately and strongly affect physiological than cognitive components of anxiety (Wolpe, 1982), while cognitive restructuring (McMullin, 1986) would be expected to more immediately affect cognitive components. It should be emphasized that the degree of response desynchrony during behav-iour therapy varies across clients and therapies, and that cases of synchronous changes across response systems commonly occur (e.g. Davidson and Baum, 1986).

Initial Values

The magnitude of psychophysiological responses to a stimulus is frequently inversely related to its pre-stimulus value. As indicated by Coles, Gratton, Kramer and Miller (1986), this 'Law of Initial Values' (LIV) renders interpret-ation of change scores (such as the degree of cardiovascular response to a cognitive stressor) difficult because they are often influenced by initial values. For this reason, analysis of covariance (Huitema, 1980; see also Chapter 3), which can partial out variance in a post-stimulus level that is attributable to the pre-stimulus level, is frequently used in statistical analyses of psychophysiol-ogical data. However, as Coles *et al.* (1986) noted, particular hypotheses may dictate that covariance not be utilized.

The LIV can complicate behaviour therapy outcome evaluation because a goal of many interventions is to effect a general reduction in arousal, and a reduction in pre-stimulus (resting) levels of a psychophysiological response may be accompanied by an increased amplitude of response to a stimulus. Thus, when evaluating intervention outcome, assessment of change in resting level may lead to different conclusions than would assessment of change in response magnitude.

The relationship between initial values and response magnitude has implications for the goals and evaluation of behaviour therapy: (a) the hypothesized inverse relationship between initial values and response magnitude suggests that, in many cases, intervention should be focused on the reduction of response magnitude as well as on the reduction of resting levels of psychophysiological responses, (b) effective intervention with resting (pre-stimulus) levels in one would not necessarily be associated with therapeutic changes in the other, and vice versa, and (c) persons and disorders vary in terms of whether resting levels or response magnitude should be targeted in therapy.

Initial values also affect interpretation of intervention effects because, in many cases, regression of elevated psychophysiological responses towards the mean would be expected in the absence of any intervention (Jacob, Kraemer and Agras, 1977). Many symptoms, as well as causal factors, demonstrate periodicity and contact with behaviour therapists is most likely during elevations in the cycle. For example, individuals are most likely to seek intervention when they are under high levels of stress and experiencing stress-related disorders such as insomnia or elevated blood pressure. Because of the transient nature of most experimental stressors, a reduction in stress, psychophysiological correlates of stress, and in stress-related psychophysiological disorders would be expected. Consequently, carefully constructed group factorial or longitudinal within-subject designs are necessary to avoid misattributing cyclic changes in these variables to treatment effects.

Summary

The characteristics and interactions among psychophysiological responses and the relationship between psychophysiological and non-psychophysiological responses have an important impact on psychophysiological assessment in behaviour therapy. Salient parameters include differences in the physiological determinants of various psychophysiological measures, the frequently low correlations among psychophysiological measures, differences in the temporal characteristics and habituation rate of psychophysiological responses, variance among measures in sensitivity to the effects of particular interventions, discordance between psychophysiological and other response modalities, desynchronous changes among measures during intervention, and the relationship between initial values and degree of change.

These are important sources of variance in psychophysiological measures and suggest that multiple psychophysiological and non-psychophysiological measures must be selected, applied, and interpreted with care. They should reflect the physiological systems of interest, be applied in a systematic manner, sampled at carefully chosen intervals, and reflect expected response latencies.

CAUSALITY OF BEHAVIOUR DISORDERS AND OF INTERVENTION EFFECTS

As indicated by Haynes (1988b), behavioural construct systems emphasize a functional analytic strategy for understanding and modifying behaviour: variables that demonstrate important functional (causal, controlling, deterministic) relationships with a target behaviour are identified and intervention programmes are then implemented to modify those variables (Baer, 1984; Ferster, 1967; Goldfried and Pomeranz, 1968). Although earlier causal models in behaviour therapy were primarily univariate and stressed the importance of response contingencies, more recent causal models acknowledge the importance of multiple, idiosyncratic, non-linear, bidirectional, and temporally unstable causes and their interactions (Haynes, 1988b).

Although complete causal models increase predictive power, they also complicate assessment. Because we frequently assess potential causal variables, the role of psychophysiological assessment will vary across disorders and across individuals manifesting the same disorder as a function of variance in the causal role of psychophysiological variables (Haynes, 1988a). For some cases of chronic back pain, for example, psychophysiological assessment may be clinically useful because it taps into possible causal pathways for the pain (Keefe, Brown, Scott and Ziesat, 1982). In other cases, however, chronic pain will be a function of behavioural, cognitive, or anatomical determinants and the utility of psychophysiological assessment will be reduced. Similarly, physiological factors may have had a role in the *original aetiology* of some disorders (such as early classical conditioning of post-traumatic stress syndrome) but be less important in the *maintenance* of the disorder.

Assessment procedures must be designed in such a way that *alternative explanations* can be evaluated and/or controlled. For example, the comparative degree of pre- and post-intervention cardiovascular reactivity to anger-arousing stimuli is sometimes used as an outcome measure in 'anger' intervention programmes (e.g. Hazaleus and Deffenbacher, 1986). However, changes in cardiovascular reactivity may also be a function of changes in diet, caffeine intake, recent exercise, aerobic fitness, habituation to assessment stimuli, assessment demand factors, client expectations, and recent life stressors (Matthews *et al.*, 1986). Similarly, evoked potentials are sometimes used to assess brain function in alcoholics (Porjesz and Begleiter, 1981) but may also be influenced by drugs, nutrition, attentional variables, pre-morbid individual differences, and instructional factors. In these cases, failure to control for alternative explanations of the obtained psychophysiological measure threatens the *internal validity* of the assessment.

Voluntary control of psychophysiological responses is another threat to the internal validity of psychophysiological assessment. Psychophysiological measures are usually assumed to *reflect* an underlying physiological process or cognitive process. Consequently, psychophysiological measures have frequently been presumed to be less susceptible than self-report measures to voluntary control or other sources of error associated with subjective report (Kallman and Feuerstein, 1986) and, therefore, may be considered more 'objective'. However, several studies have indicated that psychophysiological measures are sometimes amenable to voluntary control. The most salient example is the control, apparently through imagery and attentional processes, of penile responses to erotic stimuli (Heiman and Hatch, 1981): some males can voluntarily modify the occurrence and/or magnitude of their penile erections and appear to be sexually aroused by personally non-erotic stimuli or unaroused by personally erotic stimuli. As a result, post-treatment changes in the sexual orientation of a paedophiliac or rapist cannot be validly inferred from penile responses. Multimodal assessment can facilitate the derivation of valid inferences.

Psychophysiological measures can also be sensitive to the degree of effort or cooperation by the subject. For example, peak expiratory flow rate measures of pulmonary functioning require *forceful* expiration into the instrument (Alexander, 1981) and the resulting flow rate measure is highly sensitive to level of exertion. It should also be noted that some measures (e.g. skin conductance) can be influenced indirectly by breathing rate and amplitude (Coles *et al.*, 1986).

In summary, theories concerning the causes of behaviour disorders affect the focus and structure of psychophysiological assessment. Current complex models of causality necessitate multimethod and multimodal assessment. Additionally, alternative explanations for assessment results must be carefully considered or controlled to maximize the internal validity of the assessment.

ASSESSMENT ENVIRONMENT, PROCEDURES AND STIMULI

The validity of psychophysiological assessment is also influenced by the physical environment within which it occurs and associated procedures. Because psychophysiological measures are sensitive to variance in physical settings and interactions between subjects and assessors, these variables should be *standardized* across persons and time. Many psychophysiological measures are particularly sensitive to changes in temperature, sound, time of day, body position, length of adaptation periods, instructions and measurement sites (Coles *et al.*, 1986). These parameters must be maintained within normal limits and be appropriate for the intent of the assessment. For example, psychophysiological assessment during naps should take place during a subject's normal nap time and measures of peripheral blood volume pulse amplitude should occur within a carefully controlled temperature range.

DATA SELECTION, REDUCTION, AND ANALYSIS

For many response systems it is possible to derive a number of measures. For example, penile erections can be measured by volume or circumference, peripheral vasomotor activity can be measured by blood volume or blood volume pulse amplitude, and electrodermal measures can include skin potential responses, evoked responses, or simple resistance and conductance (Coles *et al.*, 1986). Although reflecting similar physiological processes, these measures may differ in latency, sensitivity, magnitude, habituation rate, and variability. Similarly, derived measures may reflect maximum, minimum, or average response; rate or degree of change; latency, slope, or variability. As noted in the section on 'fractionation' (see 'Response characteristics'), different measures of the same response do not always demonstrate high levels of correlation. Therefore the specific measure selected will affect the inferences that can be derived.

The selection of one measure when several are available should be based on validity and sensitivity to expected changes associated with the particular target problem and intervention. For example, vaginal blood volume pulse amplitude appears to be more highly correlated with subjective self-reports of sexual arousal in women than does vaginal blood volume (Heiman and Hatch, 1981). Also, variability in heart rate would be expected to be a more sensitive index of intervention effects of tachycardia than would mean heart rate (Natelson, 1981). When an optimal measure has not been identified, several measures may be taken and the differential validity indices of each examined. As in all research involving multiple measures, the probability of erroneously concluding that there were significant effects must be controlled.

One useful but infrequently used measure of psychophysiological dysfunction and intervention effects is *post-stress recovery* (Bernstein *et al.*, 1986; Hernez and Melamed, 1984; Pardine and Napoli, 1983). This measure is based upon the hypothesis that, for some disorders, the rate or degree of recovery from a stressor may be a more useful index of dysfunction than is the magnitude of response to a stressor. Post-stress recovery can be measured by the time required for a psychophysiological response to approximate pre-stress levels, the slope of the post-stress response–time function, or the maximum post-stress recovery within a given time period. Although it has not been sufficiently studied, it may prove to be a sensitive index of 'risk' for psychophysiological dysfunctions and of intervention effects, and may add to our understanding of the causes of psychophysiological dysfunctions.

The *rate of sampling* of psychophysiological responses can also affect the validity of derived inferences. The appropriate sampling rate depends upon the variability of the response across time (Haynes, 1978). A low sampling rate for highly variable responses is likely to result in erroneous estimates of the response parameters and excessively frequent samples, while providing more valid estimates, can be costly and inefficient. Similarly, there is an inverse relationship between sampling rate and response latency and duration: short-latency responses must be sampled at short intervals following the stimulus; short-duration responses must be sampled at high rates or for short intervals during the period of expected effects.

In order to determine the reliability of the relationships between psychophysiological and other variables and among psychophysiological variables, as well as to test the power of causal models, statistical analyses may be used (Bunge, 1959; Gottman, 1981; James, Mulaik and Brett, 1982; Ostrom, 1978). Although this topic is beyond the scope of this chapter, the clinician–researcher should be cognizant of several dimensions which affect the validity of statistically derived inferences. First, there are a large number of available methods of statistical analyses and each has a limited domain of applicability. Characteristics of the measures analysed (e.g. autocorrelation, within- versus between-subjects data acquisition, homogeneity of variance between groups, the type of scales used) affect which statistical methods can be applied and how the results of these analyses are interpreted. Second, the dependent variables are seldom linear nor normally distributed across subjects. These relationships often reflect quadratic, logarithmic, or other complex non-linear functions. Consequently, many measures must be transformed prior to most statistical analyses to render the data set congruent with the linear assumptions inherent in most statistical methods. Although such recommendations may seem unnecessary, many published studies have led to inappropriate conclusions based upon the application of unsuitable statistics.

INSTRUMENTATION

Because psychophysiological measures are usually less susceptible to the errors which influence self-report and observation measures, there is a tendency to ascribe a degree of validity to them which is often unwarranted. In addition to the many sources of variance that were reviewed in the previous sections, error variance can also be attributable to instrumentation. There are many instruments which can be used to obtain most measures and, because of unique sources of error, the measures derived from separate instruments are likely to vary. For example, measures of peak expiratory flow rate (Alexander, 1981), blood pressure (Hoelscher, Lichstein and Rosenthal, 1986), and blood sugar level (Wing, Epstein, Nowalk, Koeske and Hagg, 1985) are likely to vary as a function of which instruments are used. Measures may be affected by such instrumentation factors as sensitivity, filtering, ambient temperature, integration methods, sampling rates, calibration, and time-constants (Coles *et al.*, 1986).

All psychophysiological measures should be viewed with some scepticism and care should be exercised to avoid presuming validity for these measures.

Preferably, independent validity checks should be conducted on instruments prior to and intermittently during their use and care should be exercised in selecting instruments. Reviews of instrumentation can be found in Brown (1967), Rugh *et al.* (1986), and Venables and Martin (1967).

SUMMARY

In this section the conceptual and methodological parameters that affect the validity of psychophysiological assessment in behaviour therapy were reviewed. They include the operation and interaction among physiological systems, aetiological concepts of behaviour disorders, the methods and procedures used in assessment, the assessment environment, the research designs within which assessment occurs, methods of data reduction and analysis, and instrumentation. These parameters are important determinants of the utility, applicability, and validity of psychophysiological assessment in behaviour therapy.

SUMMARY

Psychophysiological assessment is an integral part of behaviour therapy. Its importance derives from its congruence with the empirical emphasis in behaviour therapy, the focus in behaviour therapy on disorders with important physiological components, the modification of physiological processes, and the recognition of the interactions among physiological, behavioural, and cognitive processes, and technological advances.

Psychophysiological assessment is especially useful for pre-intervention assessment and for the assessment of therapy processes and outcome. It can aid in the selection of target behaviours for intervention, the design of intervention strategies, diagnosis and classification, the detection of causal factors, the identification of triggering stimuli, and the prediction of response to intervention and recidivism. It can also aid in measuring intervention outcome, intervention response generalization, treatment side-effects, mediational or independent variables, and monitoring of the intervention process.

In all applications of psychophysiological assessment, care must be exercised in assuming the validity and generalizability of the derived measures. Psychophysiological assessment should be conducted frequently and as part of a multimethod–multimodal assessment programme.

There are numerous dimensions which affect the validity of psychophysiological assessment in behaviour therapy. These include the physiological basis of the obtained measure, response fractionation, temporal sensitivity, habituation rate, temporal variability, intervention sensitivity, discordance, response desynchrony, initial values, the causal models for behaviour disorders, voluntary control of psychophysiological responses, the assessment environment and procedures, data selection, reduction and analysis, and instrumentation. Careful attention to these dimensions is necessary for the derivation of valid inferences from psychophysiological assessment.

ACKNOWLEDGEMENTS

The authors would like to express their appreciation to Linda Gannon for her comments on an earlier version of this chapter.

REFERENCES AND FURTHER READING

Abel, G.G., Blanchard, E.B., Murphy, W.D., Becker, J.V. and Djenderedjiam, A. (1981). Two methods of measuring penile response. *Behavior Therapy* **12**, 320–328.

Abrahanson, D.J., Barlow, D.H., Sakhein, D.K., Beck, J.G. and Athanasian, R. (1986). Effects of distraction on sexual responding in functional and dysfunctional men. *Behavior Therapy* **16**, 503–515.

Adams, H.E. and Haber, J.D. (1984). The classification of abnormal behavior. In: H.E. Adams and P.B. Sutker (Eds) *Comprehensive Handbook of Psychopathology*. New York: Plenum.

Agras, W.S., Schneider, J.A. and Taylor, C.B. (1984). Relaxation training in essential hypertension: a failure of retraining in relaxation procedures. *Behavior Therapy* **15**, 191–196.

Agras, W.S., Southam, M.A. and Taylor, C.B. (1983). Long-term persistence of relaxation-induced blood pressure lowering during the working day. *Journal of Consulting and Clinical Psychology* **51**, 792–794.

Agras, W.S., Taylor, C.B., Kraemer, H.C., Allen, R.A. and Schneider, J.A. (1980). Relaxation training: twenty-four-hour blood pressure reductions. *Archives of General Psychiatry* **37**, 859–863.

Alexander, A.B. (1981). Asthma. In: S.N. Haynes and L.R. Gannon (Eds) *Psychosomatic Disorders: A Psychophysiological Approach to Etiology and Treatment*, pp. 320–358. New York: Praeger.

American Psychiatric Association (1980). *Diagnostic and Statistical Manual of Mental Disorders*, 3rd edn. Washington, DC: APA.

Anderson, C.D., Stoyva, J.M. and Vaughn, L.J. (1982). A test of delayed recovery following stressful stimulation in four psychosomatic disorders. *Journal of Psychosomatic Research* **6**, 571–580.

Andreassi, J.L. (1980). *Psychophysiology: Human Behavior and Physiological Response*. New York: Oxford University Press.

Avery-Clark, C.A. and Laws, D.R. (1984). Differential erection response patterns of sexual child abusers to stimuli describing activities with children. *Behavior Therapy* **15**, 71–83.

Baer, D.M. (1984). Future directions? Or is it useful to ask 'Where did we go wrong?' before we go? In: R.F. Dangel and R.A. Polster (Eds) *Parent Training, Foundations of Research and Practice*, pp. 547–557. New York: Guilford.

Bakal, D.A. (1982). *The Psychobiology of Chronic Headache*. New York: Springer.

Bandura, A. (1969). *Principles of Behavior Modification*. New York: Holt, Rinehart and Winston.

Bandura, A., Taylor, C.B., Williams, S.L., Mefford, I.N. and Barchas, J.D. (1985). Catecholamine secretion as a function of perceived coping self-efficacy. *Journal of Consulting and Clinical Psychology* 53, 406–414.

Barlow, D.H. (1985). *Clinical Handbook of Psychological Disorders*. New York: Guilford.

Barlow, D.H. and Hersen, M. (1984). *Single Case Experimental Designs, Strategies for Studying Behavior Change*. New York: Pergamon.

Barlow, D.H., Cohen, A.S., Waddell, M.T., Vermilegen, B.B., Klosko, J.S., Blanchard, E.B. and DiNardo, P.A. (1984). Panic and generalized anxiety disorders: nature and treatment. *Behavior Therapy* 15, 431–449.

Barstuble, J.A., Klesges, R.C. and Terbizar, D. (1986). Predictors of weight loss in a behavioral treatment program. *Behavior Therapy* 17, 288–294.

Baum, A., Gatchel, R.J. and Schaeffer, M.A. (1983). Emotional, behavioral, and physiological effects of chronic stress at Three Mile Island. *Journal of Consulting and Clinical Psychology* 51, 565–572.

Beaty, T. and Haynes, S.N. (1979). Behavioral intervention with muscle-contraction headache: a review. *Psychosomatic Medicine* 41, 165–180.

Bellack, A.S., Hersen, M. and Kazdin, A.E. (Eds) (1982) *International Handbook of Behavior Modification and Therapy*. New York: Plenum.

Bernstein, D.A., Borkovec, T.D. and Coles, M.G.H. (1986). Assessment of anxiety. In: A.R. Ciminero, K.S. Calhoun and H.E. Adams (Eds) *Handbook of Behavioral Assessment*, pp. 353–403. New York: Wiley.

Blanchard, E.B. (1979). A case study of the use of temperature biofeedback in the treatment of chronic pain due to causalgia. *Biofeedback and Self-Regulation* 4, 183–188.

Blanchard, E.B. (1981). Behavioral assessment of psychophysiologic disorders. In: Barlow (Ed.) *Behavioral Assessment in Adult Disorders*, pp. 239–269. New York: Guilford.

Blanchard, E.B. and Abel, G. (1976). An experimental case of the biofeedback treatment of rape-induced psychophysiological cardiovascular disorder. *Behavior Therapy* 7, 113–119.

Blanchard, E.B. and Epstein, L.H. (1978). *A Biofeedback Primer*. Reading, Mass.: Adison-Wesley.

Blanchard, E.B., Andrasik, F., Ahles, T.A. and Teders, S.J. (1980). Migraine and tension headache: a meta-analytic review. *Behavior Therapy* 11, 613–631.

Blanchard, E.B., Andrasik, F., Evans, D.D., Neff, D.F., Appelbaum, K.A. and Rodichok, L.D. (1985). Behavioral treatment of 250 chronic headache patients: a clinical replication series. *Behavior Therapy* 16, 308–327.

Borkovec, T.D. (1982). Insomnia. *Journal of Consulting and Clinical Psychology* 50, 607–609.

Borkovec, T.D. and Sides, J.K. (1979). Critical procedural variables related to the physiological of progressive relaxation: a review. *Behavior Research and Therapy* 17, 119–125.

Borkovec, T.D., Grayson, J.B., O'Brien, G.T. and Weerts, T.C. (1979). Relaxation treatment of pseudoinsomnia and idiopathic insomnia: an electroencephalographic evaluation. *Journal of Applied Behavior Analysis* 12, 37–54.

Bornstein, P.H. and Kazdin, A.E. (1985). *Handbook of Clinical Behavior Therapy with Children*. Illinois: Dorsey.

Brown, C.C. (1967). *Methods in Psychophysiology*. Baltimore: Williams and Wilkins.

Brown, R.A., Lichtenstein, E., McIntyre, K.O. and Harrington-Kostur, J. (1984). Effects of nicotine fading and relapse prevention on smoking cessation. *Journal of Consulting and Clinical Psychology* 52, 307–308.

Brownell, K.D. (1981). Assessment of eating disorders. In: D.H. Barlow (Ed.) *Behavioral Assessment in Adult Disorders*. New York: Guilford.

Brownell, K.D., Hayes, S.C. and Barlow, D.H. (1977). Patterns of appropriate and deviant sexual arousal: the behavioral treatment of multiple sexual deviations. *Journal of Consulting and Clinical Psychology* **45**, 1144–1155.

Brundy, J., Korein, J., Levidow, L., Grynbaum, B.B., Lieberman, A. and Friedman, L.W. (1974). Sensory feedback therapy as a modality of treatment in central nervous systems disorders of voluntary movement. *Neurology* **24**, 925–932.

Bunge, M. (1959). *Causality*. Cambridge, Mass.: Harvard University Press.

Budzynski, T.H., Styva, J.M., Adler, C.S. and Mullaney, D.J. (1973). EMG biofeedback and tension headache: a controlled outcome study. *Psychosomatic Medicine* **6**, 509–514.

Burch, N. and Altschuler, H.I. (1975). *Behavior and Brain Electrical Activity*. New York: Plenum.

Burns, K.L. (1980). Modification of an habitual upper airway constrictive response: a case study. *Behavior Therapy* **11**, 601–606.

Bush, C., Ditto, B. and Feuerstein, M. (1985). A controlled evaluation of paraspinal EMG biofeedback in the treatment of chronic low back pain. *Health Psychology* **4**, 307–321.

Cannon, D.S. and Baker, T.B. (1981). Emetic and electric shock alcohol aversion therapy: assessment of conditioning. *Journal of Consulting and Clinical Psychology* **49**, 20–33.

Carson, T.P. (1986). Assessment of depression. In: A.R. Ciminero, K.S. Calhoun and H.E. Adams (Eds) *Handbook of Behavioral Assessment*, pp. 404–445. New York: Wiley.

Catania, A.C. and Brigham, T.A. (1978). *Handbook of Applied Behavior Analysis*. New York: Wiley.

Cautela, J.R. (1967). Covert sensitization. *Psychological Record* **20**, 459–468.

Ciminero, A.R., Calhoun, K.S. and Adams, H.E. (Eds) (1986). *Handbook of Behavioral Assessment*. New York: Wiley.

Coates, T.J. and Thoresen, C.E. (1977). *How to Sleep Better: A Drug-Free Program for Overcoming Insomnia*. New Jersey: Prentice-Hall.

Coates, T.J., Killen, J.D., George, J., Marchini, E., Silverman, S. and Thoresen, C. (1982). Estimating sleep parameters: a multitrait–multimethod analysis. *Journal of Consulting and Clinical Psychology* **50**, 345–352.

Cohen, D.J. and Phelan, J.G. (1972). Differences in degree of generalization in extinction of compulsive drinking between one type and multitype beverage drinkers. *Journal of Psychology* **80**, 309–317.

Coles, M.G.H., Donchin, E. and Porges, S.W. (1986). *Psychophysiology, Systems, Processes and Applications*. New York: Guilford.

Coles, M.G.H., Gratton, G., Kramer, A.F. and Miller, G.A. (1986). Principles of signal acquisition and analysis. In: M.G.H. Coles, E. Donchin and S.W. Porges (Eds) *Psychophysiology: Systems, Processes and Applications*, pp. 183–225. New York: Guilford.

Cone, J.D. and Hawkins, R.P. (Eds) (1977). *Behavioral Assessment: New Directions in Clinical Psychology*. New York: Brunner/Mazel.

Correa, E.I. and Sutker, P.B. (1986). Assessment of alcohol and drug behaviors. In: A.R. Ciminero, K.S. Calhoun and H.E. Adams (Eds) *Handbook of Behavioral Assessment*, pp. 446–495. New York: Wiley.

Dalessio, D.J. (1980). *Wolff's Headache and Other Head Pain*. New York: Oxford University Press.

Danaher, B.G., Lichtenstein, E. and Sullivan, J.M. (1976). Comparative effects of rapid and normal smoking on heart rate and carboxyhemoglobin. *Journal of Consulting and Clinical Psychology* **44**, 556–563.

Davidson, L.M. and Baum, A. (1986). Chronic stress and posttraumatic stress disorders. *Journal of Consulting and Clinical Psychology* **54**, 303–308.

Diamond, S. and Dalessio, D.J. (Eds) (1986). *The Practicing Physician's Approach to Headache*, 4th edn. Baltimore: Williams and Wilkins.

Doleys, D.M. and Bruno, J. (1982). Treatment of childhood medical disorders. In: A.S. Bellack, M. Hersen and A.E. Kazdin (Eds) *International Handbook of Behavior Modification and Therapy*, pp. 997–1016. New York: Plenum.

Emmelkamp, P.M.G. (1982). Anxiety and fear. In: A.S. Bellack, M. Hersen and A.E. Kazdin (Eds) *International Handbook of Behavior Modification and Therapy*, pp. 349–395. New York: Plenum.

Epstein, L.H., Ossip, D.J., Coleman, D., Hughes, J. and Weist, W. (1981). Measurement of smoking topography during withdrawal or deprivation. *Behavior Therapy* **12**, 507–519.

Ewart, C.K., Taylor, C.B., Kraemer, H.C. and Agras, W.S. (1984). Reducing blood pressure reactivity during interpersonal conflict: effects of marital communication training. *Behavior Therapy* **15**, 473–484.

Faust, J. and Melamed, B.G. (1984). Influence of arousal, previous experience, and age on surgery preparation of same day of surgery and in-hospital pediatric patients. *Journal of Consulting and Clinical Psychology* **52**, 359–365.

Ferster, C.B. (1967). Classification of behavioral pathology. In: L. Krasner and P. Ullman (Eds) *Research in Behavior Modification*. New York: Holt.

Feuerstein, M. and Adams, H.E. (1977). Cephalic vasomotor feedback in the modification of migraine headache. *Biofeedback and Self-Regulation* **3**, 241–254.

Flor, H., Turk, D.C. and Birbaumer, N. (1985). Assessment of stress-related psychophysiological reactions in chronic back pain patients. *Journal of Consulting and Clinical Psychology* **53**, 354–364.

Folkow, B. (1982). Physiological aspects of primary hypertension. *Physiological Reviews* **62**, 347–504.

Fowles, D.C. (1982). Heart rate as an index of anxiety: failure of a hypothesis. In: J.T. Cacioppo and R.E. Petty (Eds) *Perspectives in Cardiovascular Psychophysiology*. New York: Guilford.

Freund, K. (1963). A laboratory method of diagnosing predominance of homo- and heteroerotic interest in the male. *Behaviour Research and Therapy* **1**, 85–93.

Friar, L.R. and Beatty, J. (1976). Migraine: management by trained control of vasoconstriction. *Journal of Consulting and Clinical Psychology* **44**, 46–53.

Friedman, J.M., Weiler, S.J., LoPiccolo, J. and Hogan, D.R. (1982). Sexual dysfunctions and their treatment. In: A.S. Bellack, M. Hersen and A.E. Kazdin (Eds), *International Handbook of Behavior Modification and Therapy*, pp. 653–716. New York: Plenum.

Gannon, L.R. (1981). The psychophysiology of psychosomatic disorders. In: S.N. Haynes and L.R. Gannon (Eds) *Psychosomatic Disorders: A Psychophysiological Approach to Etiology and Treatment*, pp. 1–31. New York: Praeger.

Gannon, L.R. and Haynes, S.N. (1986). Cognitive–physiological discordance as an etiological factor in psychophysiologic disorders. *Advances in Behavior Research and Therapy* **8**, 223–236.

Garfield, S.L. (1984). Methodological problems in clinical diagnosis. In: H.E. Adams and P.E. Sutker (Eds) *Comprehensive Handbook of Psychopathology*. New York: Plenum.

Garfield, S.L. (1986). Problems in diagnostic classification. In: T. Millon and G.L. Klerman (Eds) *Contemporary Directions in Psychopathology: Toward the DSM-IV*, pp. 99–114. New York: Guilford.

Gatchel, R.J. and Proctor, J.D. (1976). Effectiveness of voluntary heart rate control in reducing speech anxiety. *Journal of Consulting and Clinical Psychology* **44**, 381–389.

Gatchel, R.J., Hatch, J.P., Watson, P.J., Smith, D. and Gaas, E. (1977). Comparative effectiveness of voluntary heart rate control and muscular relaxation as active coping skills for reducing speech anxiety. *Journal of Consulting and Clinical Psychology* **45**, 1093–1100.

Glasgow, R.E., Klesges, R.C., Klesges, L.M., Vasey, M.W. and Gunnarson, D.F. (1986). Long-term effects of a controlled smoking program: a 2½ year follow-up. *Behavior Therapy* **16**, 303–307.

Goldberger, L. and Breznitz, S. (1982). *Handbook of Stress: Theoretical and Clinical Aspects.* New York: Macmillan.

Goldfried, M.R. and Goldfried, A.P. (1977). Importance of hierarchy content in the self-control of anxiety. *Journal of Consulting and Clinical Psychology* **45**, 124–134.

Goldfried, M.R. and Pomeranz, D.M. (1968). Role of assessment in behavior modification. *Psychological Reports* **23**, 75–87.

Goldstein, G. and Hersen, M. (1984). *Handbook of Psychological Assessment.* New York: Pergamon.

Goleman, D.J. and Schwartz, G.E. (1976). Meditation as an intervention in stress reactivity. *Journal of Consulting and Clinical Psychology* **44**, 456–466.

Gottman, J.M. (1981). *Time-Series Analysis, A Comprehensive Introduction for Social Scientists.* Cambridge: Cambridge University Press.

Gottman, J.M. and Levenson, R.W. (1985). A valid procedure for obtaining self-report of affect in marital interaction. *Journal of Consulting and Clinical Psychology* **53**, 151–160.

Greenfield, N.S. and Sternbach, R.A. (1972). *Handbook of Psychophysiology.* New York: Holt, Rinehart and Winston.

Grey, S., Sartory, G. and Rachman, S. (1979). Synchronous and desynchronous changes during fear reduction. *Behaviour Research and Therapy* **17**, 137–147.

Gross, F. and Strasser, T. (1982). *Mild Hypertension: Recent Advances.* New York: Raven.

Hall, S.M., Bass, A., Hargreaves, W.A. and Loeb, P. (1979). Contingency management and information feedback in outpatient heroin detoxification. *Behavior Therapy* **10**, 443–451.

Hall, S.M., Ginsberg, D. and Jones, R.T. (1986). Smoking cessation and weight gain. *Journal of Consulting and Clinical Psychology* **54**, 342–346.

Hall, S.M., Tunstall, C., Rugg, D., Jones, R.T. and Benowitz, N. (1985). Nicotine gum and behavioral treatment in smoking cessation. *Journal of Consulting and Clinical Psychology* **53**, 256–258.

Hassett, J. (1978). *A Primer of Psychophysiology.* San Francisco: W. H. Freeman.

Haynes, S.N. (1978). *Principles of Behavioral Assessment.* New York: Gardner.

Haynes, S.N. (1981). Muscle-contraction headache: a psychophysiological perspective of etiology and treatment. In: S.N. Haynes and L. Gannon (Eds) *Psychosomatic Disorders: A Psychophysiological Approach to Etiology and Treatment,* pp. 447–485. New York: Praeger.

Haynes, S.N. (1984a). The behavioral assessment of adult disorders. In: A. Goldstein and M. Hersen (Eds) *Handbook of Psychological Assessment.* New York: Pergamon.

Haynes, S.N. (1984b). Behavioral assessment. In: M. Hersen, A. Kazdin and A. Bellack (Eds) *The Clinical Psychology Handbook.* New York: Pergamon.

Haynes, S.N. (1988a). Causal models and the assessment–treatment relationship in behavior therapy. *Journal of Psychopathology and Behavioral Assessment,* **10**, 171–183.

Haynes, S.N. (1988b). The Gordian knot of DSM III use: integrating principles of behavior classification, complex causal models and functional analytic strategies. *Behavioral Assessment,* **10**, 95–105.

Haynes, S.N. and Gannon, L. (1981). *Psychosomatic Disorders: A Psychophysiological Approach to Etiology and Treatment.* New York: Praeger.

Haynes, S.N. and Wilson, C.C. (1979). *Behavioral Assessment: Recent Trends in Methods, Concepts and Applications*. San Francisco: Jossey Bass.

Haynes, S.N., Cueves, J. and Gannon, L.R. (1982). The psychophysiological etiology of muscle-contraction headache. *Headache* **22**, 122–132.

Hazaleus, S.L. and Deffenbacher, J.L. (1986). Relaxation and cognitive treatments of anger. *Journal of Consulting and Clinical Psychology* **54**, 222–226.

Heide, F.J. and Borkovec, T.D. (1983). Relaxation-induced anxiety: paradoxical anxiety enhancement due to relaxation training. *Journal of Consulting and Clinical Psychology* **51**, 171–182.

Heiman, J.R. and Hatch, J.P. (1981). Conceptual and therapeutic contributions of psychophysiology to sexual dysfunctions. In: S.N. Haynes and L.R. Gannon (Eds) *Psychosomatic Disorders: A Psychophysiological Approach to Etiology and Treatment*, pp. 222–268. New York: Praeger.

Hensen, C., Rubin, H.B. and Hensen, D.E. (1979). Women's sexual arousal concurrently assessed by three genital measures. *Archives of Sexual Behavior* **8**, 459–469.

Hernez, D.A. and Melamed, B.G. (1984). The assessment of emotional imagery training in fearful children. *Behavior Therapy* **15**, 156–172.

Hersen, M. and Barlow, D.H. (1976). *Single-Case Experimental Designs: Strategies for Studying Behavior Change*. New York: Pergamon.

Hodgson, R. and Rachman, S. (1974). Desynchrony in measures of fear. *Behaviour Research and Therapy* **12**, 319–326.

Hoelscher, T.J., Lichstein, K.L. and Rosenthal, T.L. (1986). Home relaxation practice in hypertension treatment: objective assessment and compliance induction. *Journal of Consulting and Clinical Psychology* **54**, 217–221.

Holden, A.E. and Barlow, D.H. (1986). Heart rate and heart rate variability recorded *in vivo* in agoraphobics and nonphobics. *Behavior Therapy* **17**, 26–42.

Holzman, A.D. and Turk, D.C. (1986). *Pain Management: A Handbook of Psychological Treatment Approaches*. New York: Pergamon.

Huitema, B.E. (1980). *The Analysis of Covariance and Alternatives*. New York: Wiley.

Jacob, R.G., Kraemer, H.C. and Agras, W.S. (1977). Relaxation therapy in the treatment of hypertension: a review. *Archives of General Psychiatry* **34**, 1417–1427.

James, L.R., Mulaik, S.A. and Brett, J.M. (1982). *Causal Analysis: Assumptions, Models and Data*. Beverly Hills: Sage.

Kallman, W.M. and Feuerstein, M.J. (1985). Psychophysiological procedures. In: A.R. Ciminero, K.S. Calhoun and H.E. Adams (Eds) *Handbook of Behavioral Assessment*, pp. 325–350. New York: Wiley.

Kaloupek, D.G. (1983). The effects of compound *in vivo* and imaginal exposure: a test of fear enhancement models. *Behavior Therapy* **14**, 345–356.

Kanfer, F.H. (1985). Target selection for clinical change programs. *Behavioral Assessment* **7**, 7–20.

Kanfer, F. and Phillips, J.S. (1971). *Learning Foundations of Behavior Therapy*. New York: Wiley.

Kaplan, N.M. (1982). *Clinical Hypertension*. Baltimore: Williams and Wilkins.

Karacan, I. (1970). Clinical value of nocturnal erection in the prognosis and diagnosis of impotence. *Medical Aspects of Human Sexuality* , April, 27–34.

Kazdin, A.E. (1982). History of behavior modification. In: A.S. Bellack, M. Hersen and A.E. Kazdin (Eds) *International Handbook of Behavior Modification and Therapy*, pp. 3–32. New York: Plenum.

Kazdin, A.E. and Wilcoxin, L.A. (1976). Systematic desensitization and nonspecific treatment effects: a methodological evaluation. *Psychological Bulletin* **83**, 729–758.

Keane, T.M. and Kaloupek, D.G. (1982). Imaginal flooding in the treatment of a posttraumatic stress disorder. *Journal of Consulting and Clinical Psychology* **50**, 138–140.

Keane, T.M., Fairbanks, J.A., Caddell, J.M., Zimering, R.T. and Bender, M.E. (1985). A behavioral approach to assessing and treating posttraumatic stress disorder in Vietnam veterans. In: C.R. Figley (Ed.) *Trauma and its Wake*, pp. 257–294.

Keane, T.M., Martin, J.E., Berler, E.S., Wooten, L.S., Fleece, E.L. and Williams, J.G. (1982). Are hypertensives less assertive? A controlled evaluation. *Journal of Consulting and Clinical Psychology* **50**, 499–508.

Keefe, F.J. and Blementhal, J.A. (Eds) (1982). *Assessment Strategies in Behavioral Medicine*. New York: Grune and Stratton.

Keefe, F.J., Brown, C., Scott, D.S. and Ziesat, H. (1982). Assessment strategies for chronic pain and illness. In: F.J. Keefe and J.A. Blumenthal (Eds) *Assessment Strategies in Behavioral Medicine*, pp. 321–351. New York: Grune and Stratton.

Kendrick, M.J., Craig, K.D., Lawson, D.M. and Davidson, P.O. (1982). Cognitive and behavioral therapy for musical-performance anxiety. *Journal of Consulting and Clinical Psychology* **50**, 353–362.

Killen, J.D., Maccoby, N. and Taylor, C.B. (1984). Nicotine gum and self-regulation training in smoking relapse prevention. *Behavior Therapy* **15**, 234–248.

Koppman, J.W., McDonald, R.D. and Kunzel, M.G. (1974). Voluntary regulation of temporal artery diameter in migraine patients. *Headache* **14**, 133–138.

Krantz, D.S. and Manuck, S.B. (1984). Acute psychophysiologic reactivity and risk of cardiovascular disease: a review and methodologic critique. *Psychological Bulletin* **96**, 435–464.

Lacey, J.I. (1967). Somatic response patterning and stress: some revisions of activation theory. In: M.H. Appley and R. Trumball (Eds) *Psychological Stress. Issues in Research*. New York: Appleton-Century-Crofts.

Lang, P.J. and Melamed, B.G. (1960). Case report: avoidance conditioning therapy of an infant with chronic ruminative vomiting. *Journal of Abnormal Psychology* **74**, 1–8.

Lang, P.J., Levin, D.N., Miller, G.A. and Kuzak, M. (1983). Fear behavior, fear imagery and the psychophysiology of emotion: the problem of affective response integration. *Journal of Abnormal Psychology* **92**, 276–306.

Lang, P.J., Melamed, B.G. and Hart, J. (1970). A psychophysiological analysis of fear modification using an automated desensitization procedure. *Journal of Abnormal Psychology* **76**, 220–234.

Lanyon, R. I. and Goldsworthy, R. J. (1982). Habit disorders. In: A. S. Bellack, M. Hersen, and A. E. Kazdin, (Eds) *International Handbook of Behavior Modification and Therapy*. New York: Plenum

Leiblum, S.R. (1982). Assessment strategies for sexual disorders. In: F.J. Keefe and J.A. Blumenthal (Eds) *Assessment Strategies in Behavioral Medicine*, pp. 373–391. New York: Grune and Stratton.

Levin, S.M., Barry, S.M., Gambaro, S., Wolfinsohn, L. and Smith, A. (1977). Variations of covert sensitization in the treatment of pedophilic behavior: a case study. *Journal of Consulting and Clinical Psychology* **45**, 896–907.

Lichtenstein, E. and Brown, R.A. (1982). Current trends in the modification of cigarette dependence. In: A.S. Bellack, M. Hersen and A.E. Kazdin (Eds) *International Handbook of Behavior Modification and Therapy*, pp. 575–611). New York: Plenum.

Lindros, K.O. (1982). Human blood acetaldehyde levels: with improved methods a clearer picture emerges. *Alcoholism: Clinical and Experimental Research* **6**, 70–74.

LoPiccolo, J. and LoPiccolo, L. (1978). *Handbook of Sex Therapy*. New York: Plenum.

Lyles, J.N., Burish, T.G., Krozely, M.G. and Oldham, R.K. (1982). Efficacy of relaxation training and guided imagery in reducing the aversiveness of cancer chemotherapy. *Journal of Consulting and Clinical Psychology* **50**, 509–524.

Malec, J. and Sipprelle, C.N. (1977). Physiological and subjective effects of Zen meditation and demand characteristics. *Journal of Consulting and Clinical Psychology* **45**, 339–340.

Malloy, P.F., Fairbank, J.A. and Keane, T.M. (1983). Validation of a multimethod assessment of posttraumatic stress disorders in Vietnam veterans. *Journal of Consulting and Clinical Psychology* **51**, 488–494.

Manuck, S.B. and Proietti, S.M. (1982). Parental hypertension and cardiovascular responses to cognitive and isometric challenge. *Psychophysiology* **19**, 481–489.

Manuck, S.B., Proietti, J.M., Rader, S.J. and Polefrone, J.M. (1984). Parental hypertension, affect and cardiovascular response to cognitive challenge. *Psychosomatic Medicine* **96**, 435–464.

Marinacci, A.A. and Horande, M. (1960). Electromyogram in neuromuscular reeducation. *Bulletin of the Los Angeles Neurological Society* **25**, 57–71.

Marshall, W.L. (1985). The effects of variable exposure in flooding therapy. *Behavior Therapy* **16**, 117–135.

Martin, J.E. and Fredericksen, L.W. (1980). Self-tracking of carbon monoxide levels by smokers. *Behavior Therapy* **11**, 577–587.

Martin, P.R. (1981). Spasmodic torticollis: investigation and treatment using EMG feedback training. *Behavior Therapy* **12**, 247–262.

Matthews, K.A., Weiss, S.M., Detre, T., Dembrowski, P.M., Faulkner, B., Manuck, S.B. and Williams, R.B. (Eds) (1986). *Handbook of Stress, Reactivity and Cardiovascular Disease*. New York: Wiley.

McCaffrey, R.J. and Fairbank, J.A. (1985). Behavioral assessment and treatment of accident-related posttraumatic stress disorder: two case studies. *Behavior Therapy* **16**, 406–416.

McCann, B.S. (1987). The behavioral management of hypertension. In: M. Hersen, R.M. Eisler and P.M. Miller (Eds) *Progress in Behavior Modification*, Vol. 21, pp. 191–229. Newbury Park: Sage.

McConaghy, N. (1967). Penile volume changes to moving pictures of male and female nudes in heterosexual and homosexual males. *Behaviour Research and Therapy* **5**, 43–48.

McConaghy, N. (1974). Measurements of change in penile dimension. *Archives of Sexual Behavior* **3**, 381–388.

McConaghy, N. (1982). Sexual deviation. In: A. S. Bellack, M. Hersen and A.E. Kazdin (Eds) *International Handbook of Behavior Modification and Therapy*, pp. 683–716. New York: Plenum.

McGowan, W.T., Haynes, S.N. and Wilson, C.C. (1979). Frontal electromyographic feedback: stress attenuation and generalization. *Biofeedback and Self-Control* **4**, 323–336.

McIntyre-Kingsolver, K., Lichtenstein, E. and Mermelstein, R.J. (1986). Spouse training in a multicomponent smoking cessation program. *Behavior Therapy* **17**, 67–74.

McMullin, R.E. (1986). *Handbook of Cognitive Therapy Techniques*. New York: Norton.

Michelson, L. and Ascher, L.M. (Eds) (1987). *Anxiety and Stress Disorders*. New York: Guilford.

Michelson, L. and Mavissakalian, L. (1985). Psychophysiological outcome of behavioral and pharmacological treatments of agoraphobia. *Journal of Consulting and Clinical Psychology* **53**, 229–236.

Miklich, D.R., Renne, C.M., Creer, T.L., Aleander, A.B., Chai, H., Davis, M.H., Hoffman, A. and Danker-Brown, P. (1977). The clinical utility of behavior therapy as an adjunctive treatment for asthma. *Journal of Allergy and Clinical Immunology* **5**, 285–294.

Miller, P.M. (1975). A behavioral intervention program for chronic public drunkenness offenders. *Archives of General Psychiatry* **32**, 915–918.

Morey, L.C., Skinner, H.A. and Blashfield, R.K. (1986). Trends in the classification of abnormal behavior. In: A.R. Ciminero, C.S. Calhoun and H.E. Adams (Eds) *Handbook of Behavioral Assessment*. New York: Wiley.

Morrison, R.L. and Bellack, A.S. (1985). Role of social competence in borderline essential hypertension. *Journal of Consulting and Clinical Psychology* **53**, 248–255.

Murphy, W.D., Abel, G.G. and Becker, J.V. (1980). Research in exhibitionism. In: D.J. Cox and R.J. Daitzman (Eds) *Exhibitionism: Description, Assessment and Treatment*. New York: Garland.

Natelson, B.H. (1981). Cardiac arrhythmias and sudden death. In: S.N. Haynes and L. Gannon (Eds) *Psychosomatic Disorders: A Psychophysiological Approach to Etiology and Treatment*, pp. 407–447. New York: Praeger.

Nelson, R. and Hayes, S.C. (1987). *Conceptual Foundations of Behavioral Assessment*. New York: Guilford.

Novaco, R.W. (1976). Treatment of chronic anger through cognitive and relaxation controls. *Journal of Consulting and Clinical Psychology* **44**, 681.

Obrist, P.A., Light, K.C., McCubbin, J.A., Hutcheson, J.S. and Hoffer, J.L. (1979). Pulse transit time: relationship to blood pressure and myocardial performance. *Psychophysiology* **16**, 292–301.

Ossip-Klein, D.J., Epstein, K.L.H., Winter, M.K., Stiller, R., Russell, P. and Dickson, B. (1983). Does switching to low tar/nicotine/carbon monoxide-yield cigarettes decrease alveolar carbon monoxide measures? A randomized controlled trial. *Journal of Consulting and Clinical Psychology* **51**, 234–241.

Ostrom, C.W., Jr (1978). Time series analysis: regression techniques. Sage University Series on Quantitative Applications in the Social Sciences, pp. 7–9. Beverley Hills: Sage.

Pardine, P. and Napoli, A. (1983). Physiological reactivity and recent life-stress experience. *Journal of Consulting and Clinical Psychology* **51**, 467–469.

Paxton, R. and Bernacca, G. (1979). Urinary nicotine concentration as a function of time since last cigarette: implications for detecting faking in smoking clinics. *Behavior Therapy* **10**, 523–528.

Philips, C. (1977). The modification of tension headache pain using EMG biofeedback. *Behaviour Research and Therapy* **15**, 119–129.

Pickering, T.G. and Miller, N.E. (1977). Learned voluntary control of heart rate and rhythm in two subjects with premature ventricular contractions. *British Heart Journal* **39**, 152–159.

Porjesz, B. and Begleiter, H. (1981). Human evoked brain potential and alcohol. *Alcoholism: Clinical and Experimental Research* **5**, 304–317.

Prue, D.M., Martin, J.E. and Hume, A.S. (1980). A critical evaluation of thiocyanate as a biochemical index of smoking exposure. *Behavior Therapy* **11**, 368–379.

Quinsey, V.L., Chaplin, T.C. and Carrigan, W.F. (1979). Sexual preferences among incestuous and nonincestuous child molesters. *Behavior Therapy* **10**, 562–565.

Rimm, D.C. and Masters, J.C. (1979). *Behavior Therapy: Techniques and Empirical Findings*. New York: Academic Press.

Rosen, G.M. (1976). Subjects' initial therapeutic expectancies and subjects' awareness of therapeutic goals in systematic desensitization: a review. *Behavior Therapy* **7**, 14–27.

Rosen, R.C. and Kopel, S.A. (1977). Penile plethysmography and biofeedback in the treatment of a transvestite-exhibitionist. *Journal of Consulting and Clinical Psychology* **45**, 908–916.

Rugh, J.D., Gable, R.S. and Lemke, R.R. (1986). Instrumentation for behavioral assessment. In: A.R. Ciminero, K.S. Calhoun and H.E. Adams (Eds) *Handbook of Behavioral Assessment*, pp. 79–108. New York: Wiley.

Russell, P.O., Epstein, L.H. and Dickson, B.E. (1983). Behavioral and physiological effects of low-nicotine cigarettes during rapid smoking. *Journal of Consulting and Clinical Psychology* **51**, 312.

Seer, P. (1979). Psychological control of hypertension: review of the literature and methodological critique. *Psychological Bulletin* **86**, 1015–1043.

Selye, Hans (1982). History and present status of stress concept. In: L. Goldberger and S. Breznitz (Eds) *Handbook of Stress: Theoretical and Clinical Aspects*, pp. 5–17. New York: Macmillan.

Shahar, A. and Marks, I. (1980). Habituation during exposure treatment of compulsive rituals. *Behavior Therapy* **11**, 397–401.

Sherry, G. and Levine, B.A. (1980). An examination of procedural variables in flooding therapy. *Behavior Therapy* **11**, 148–155.

Sidman, M. (1960). *Scientific Research: Evaluating Experimental Data in Psychology*. New York: Basic Books.

Sobell, M.B., Sobell, L.C., Ersner-Hershfield, S. and Nirenberg, T.D. (1982). Alcohol and drug problems. In: A.S. Bellack, M. Hersen and A.E. Kazdin (Eds) *International Handbook of Behavior Modification and Therapy*, pp. 501–533. New York: Plenum.

Stampfl, T.G. and Levis, D.J. (1967). Essentials of implosive therapy: a learning-theory-based psychodynamic behavioral therapy. *Journal of Abnormal Psychology* **72**, 469–503.

Steffen, J.J. (1975). Electromyographically induced relaxation in the treatment of chronic alcohol abuse. *Journal of Consulting and Clinical Psychology* **43**, 275.

Stern, R.M., Ray, W.J. and Davis, C.M. (1980). *Psychophysiological Recording*. New York: Oxford University Press.

Stickler, D., Bigelow, G., Wells, D. and Liebson, I. (1977). Effects of relaxation instructions on the electromyographic responses of abstinent alcoholics to drinking related stimuli. *Behaviour Research and Therapy* **15**, 500–502.

Sturgis, E., Adams, H.E. and Brantly, P. (1981). The parameters, etiology and treatment of migraine headache. In: S. Haynes and L. Gannon (Eds) *Psychosomatic Disorders: A Psychophysiological Approach to Etiology and Treatment*, pp. 485–516. New York: Praeger.

Suarez, Y., Adams, H.E. and McCutcheon, B.A. (1976). Implosion and systematic desensitization: efficacy in subclinical phobics as a function of arousal. *Journal of Consulting and Clinical Psychology* **44**, 337–347.

Surwit, R.S., Pilon, R.N. and Fention, C.H. (1978). Behavioral treatment of Raynaud's disease. *Journal of Behavioral Medicine* **1**, 323–336.

Taylor, C.B. (1982). Adult medical disorders. In: A.S. Bellack, M. Hersen and A.E. Kazdin (Eds) *International Handbook of Behavior Modification and Therapy*, pp. 467–499. New York: Plenum.

Tollison, C.D. and Adams, H.E. (1979). *Sexual Disorders: Treatment, Theory, and Research*. New York: Gardner.

Turner, S.M., Calhoun, K.S. and Adams, H.E. (1981). *Handbook of Clinical Behavior Therapy*. New York: Wiley.

Varni, J.W. (1981). Self-regulation techniques in the management of chronic arthritic pain in hemophilia. *Behavior Therapy* **12**, 185–194.

Venables, P.H. and Martin, I. (1967). *A Manual of Psychophysiological Methods*. New York: Wiley.

Vermillyea, J.A., Boice, R. and Barlow, D.H. (1984). Rachman and Hodgson (1974) a decade later: how do desynchronous response systems relate to the treatment of agoraphobia? *Behaviour Research and Therapy* **22**, 615–621.

Walker, B.B. and Sandman, C.A. (1981). Disregulation of the gastrointestinal system. In: A.N. Haynes and L.R. Gannon (Eds) *Psychosomatic Disorders: A Psychophysiological Approach to Etiology and Treatment*, pp. 133–178. New York: Praeger.

Watson, J.P., Gaind, R. and Marks, I.M. (1972). Physiological habituation to continuous phobic stimulation. *Behaviour Research and Therapy* **10**, 269–278.

Whitehead, W.E., Renault, P.F. and Goldiamond, I. (1975). Modification of human gastric acid secretion with operant conditioning procedures. *Journal of Applied Behavior Analysis* **8**, 147–156.

Wilder, J. (1957). The Law of Initial Values in neurology and psychiatry: facts and problems. *Journal of Nervous and Mental Disease* **125**, 73–86.

Wincze, J.P. and Lange, J.D. (1981). Assessment of sexual behavior. In: D.H. Barlow (Ed.) *Behavioral Assessment in Adult Disorders*, pp. 301–328. New York: Guilford.

Wing, R.R., Epstein, L.H., Nowalk, M.P., Koeske, R. and Hagg, S. (1985). Behavior change, weight loss, and physiological improvements in type II diabetic patients. *Journal of Consulting and Clinical Psychology* **53**, 111–122.

Wolf, S.L., Nacht, M. and Kelly, J.L. (1982). EMG feedback during dynamic movement for low back pain patients. *Behavior Therapy* **13**, 395–406.

Wolpe, J. (1982). *The Practice of Behavior Therapy*. New York: Pergamon.

Yates, E., Barbara, H.C. and Marshall, W.L. (1984). Anger and deviant sexual arousal. *Behavior Therapy* **15**, 287–294.

Youkilis, H.D. and Bootzin, R.R. (1981). A psychophysiological perspective on the etiology and treatment of insomnia. In: S.N. Haynes and L.R. Gannon (Eds) *Psychosomatic Disorders: A Psychophysiological Approach to Etiology and Treatment*, pp. 179–221. New York: Praeger.

Chapter 7

Psychophysiological Interventions in Behavioural Medicine

Andrew Steptoe

Department of Psychology,
St George's Hospital Medical School,
University of London,
Cranmer Terrace,
London SW17 0RE

ABSTRACT

Three broad classes of psychophysiological intervention are discussed in this chapter: self-regulation methods such as relaxation, biofeedback and meditation, cognitive methods, and methods based on physical exercise training. The rationales underlying the applications of these interventions in behavioural medicine are outlined, and putative mechanisms are evaluated. A number of implications for clinical practice are drawn.

Handbook of Clinical Psychophysiology Edited by G. Turpin
© 1989 John Wiley & Sons Ltd

INTRODUCTION

Behavioural medicine is a comparatively new discipline, although researchers and clinicians have been studying the relationships between psychological state and medical disorders for many decades. The first use of the term 'behavioural medicine' is generally agreed to have been made by Birk who entitled a book *'Biofeedback: Behavioral Medicine'* in 1973. Although the term was originally used to describe applications of biofeedback to clinical medical conditions, biofeedback is now only one of the many techniques employed in behavioural medicine. The field has flourished over the last decade, with the foundation of societies, journals and numerous books. The definition of behavioural medicine has also become more broad, as in this version presented by Schwartz and Weiss (1978):

> The interdisciplinary field concerned with the development and integration of behavioral and biomedical science, knowledge and techniques relevant to health and illness and to the application of this knowledge and these techniques to prevention, diagnosis, treatment and rehabilitation.

Definitions such as this are so all-embracing that they tend to fudge one of the main themes of behavioural medicine – that is the focus on medical as opposed to psychiatric disorders. Of course, such a distinction smacks of dualism, and the separation between mental and physical illness. The whole philosophy underlying behavioural medicine is that such distinctions are spurious, and that all clinical disorders are influenced in their aetiology, maintenance or management by emotion and behaviour (albeit to a variable extent). Nevertheless, in the present context a pragmatic definition of behavioural medicine will be used, restricting discussion to conditions in which physiological or systemic disturbances are central, and where psychiatric and behavioural disorders (if present) are only secondary in nature.

This chapter concerns psychophysiological interventions in behavioural medicine. Psychophysiological interventions are taken to be treatments or methods of management based on the modification of behaviour or cognition, designed to alter patterns of physiological activity. Physiological activities include striate muscular, autonomic, endocrine and immunological processes, together with electroencephalographic (EEG) phenomena. Typical psychophysiological interventions in behavioural medicine include cognitive stress management, exercise training, and what may broadly be called self-regulation methods (such as relaxation and biofeedback). They have been used in the context of general stress management, in the prevention of cardiovascular disease, and in the management of specific disorders such as hypertension, headache, chronic pain, asthma, diabetes, epilepsy and neuromuscular disorders. Several reviews of the clinical effects of these procedures have been published (e.g. Holroyd and Creer, 1986; Holzman and Turk, 1986; Lubar and Deering, 1981), and methods used in specific disorders are discussed in Section 2 of this handbook. The present chapter will therefore focus on two aspects that receive comparatively little attention, namely the rationale underlying psychophysiological intervention, and the mechanisms involved in mediating therapeutic effects.

Before these issues are discussed, it is necessary to qualify the scope of the chapter. In behavioural medicine, a variety of non-psychophysiological methods are used in which the focus of treatment is on behaviour rather than any associated physiological disturbance. Examples include operant management techniques for patients with chronic pain and asthma (Creer, 1979; Fordyce and Steger, 1979), systematic desensitization and related behaviour therapy methods for problems such as dermatitis and anticipatory nausea in patients undergoing chemotherapy (Cataldo, Varni, Russo and Estes, 1980; Morrow and Morrell, 1982), and the range of strategies designed to help people cope more adequately with chronic disease (Burish and Bradley, 1983). On the other hand, the methods described here as psychophysiological interventions are also used in areas where the primary goal is not the correction of physiological dysfunction, but some psychological change. Examples would be the use of relaxation and cognitive stress-management techniques during preparation for surgery (Mathews and Ridgeway, 1984), relaxation for the control of drug abuse (Zuroff and Schwartz, 1978), meditation as a form of psychotherapy (Smith, 1975), and cognitive methods for modifying the Type A coronary-prone behaviour pattern (Friedman and Ulmer, 1985). These applications are not discussed in the present chapter since the mechanisms are likely to be very different from those involved when psychophysiological procedures are employed primarily to produce changes in physiological function.

PSYCHOPHYSIOLOGICAL MECHANISMS IN DISEASE

Research into psychophysiological processes in the aetiology of disease is intimately related to intervention, and in particular to the rationale underlying the use of cognitive and self-regulation methods in behavioural medicine. For if it can be demonstrated that emotional or behavioural events either cause or exacerbate pathological processes, then psychological methods might be used to reverse such patterns. Extensive evidence has been collected relating organic pathology to emotion and behaviour, and this has been reviewed elsewhere (Elliott and Eisdorfer, 1982; Gentry, 1984). Relevant data are provided by animal studies, both at an individual level, assessing such parameters as life events and Type A behaviour, and psychosocial epidemiological studies of sociocultural mobility, social networks and work patterns.

The psychophysiological processes thought to be involved in this aetiological chain are based on the stress–diathesis model, and are summarized in Figure 7.1 (see Steptoe, 1984, for more details).

THE STRESS–DIATHESIS MODEL

Stage I

The first stage of the process involves some form of psychological or social stimulation. Responses are influenced not only by quantitative factors such as the duration and intensity of stimulation, but also by the pattern of inputs (novelty, predictability, etc.). However, it is recognized that responses are not simple products of external challenge, since stimuli are filtered by the psychological state and capacity of the individual. Cognitive appraisal mechanisms and underlying predispositions such as hardiness or tendencies towards hostility, all influence response patterns. The appropriate combination of psychosocial stimulation and psychosocial resources may lead to:

Stage II

The psychobiological response, involving changes at the affective, behavioural and physiological levels. Physiologically, typical responses include autonomic discharge, mobilization of the sympatho-adrenomedullary and pituitary–adren-

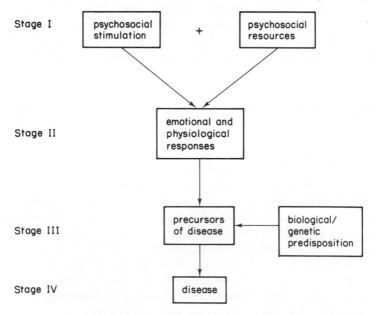

Figure 7.1. Simplified stress–diathesis model.

ocortical axes, and a variety of haemostatic and immunological changes. There is good evidence that the pattern of physiological response varies with the nature of the demands on the individual, and the coping resources that are mobilized (Steptoe, 1983).

Stage III

The diathesis or biological predisposition towards disease now comes into play to determine whether acute reactions are transformed into serious or sustained dysfunctions (*Stage IV*). At the psychophysiological level, this may be manifest in terms of individual response specificity, or the tendency of an individual to show his or her maximal reactivity in a single autonomic parameter over a variety of stimulus conditions. It has been argued that approximately one-third of healthy subjects show consistent individual response specificity, and it is possible that these people may be especially vulnerable to disease in the relevant system (Fahrenberg, 1986).

This model has been tested in animals by measuring the pathology following exposure to severe psychosocial stimulation, and irreversible lesions have been observed in the gastointestinal system, cardiovascular system and elsewhere (Weiner, 1977). Animal studies also indicate a related mechanism whereby psychophysiological responses might influence disease, not through a direct aetiological process but by exacerbating or promoting existing pathology. This is particularly apparent in the study of infection and malignancy, where the immunological disturbances caused by behavioural stimulation may permit more rapid development of disease (Anisman and Sklar, 1984).

Human studies have largely been confined to acute experiments in which the psychophysiological reactions of people with and without particular diseases are compared. However, such investigations are only weak evidence for the stress–diathesis model, since disturbed reactivity may be secondary to the disease process, rather than being primary or aetiologically relevant. Recent research has therefore focused on risk groups, notably Type A individuals and the normotensive offspring of hypertensive patients, to see whether they too show disturbed psychophysiological reactivity that is antecedent to manifest disease. Here again, results are not entirely clear-cut, since it cannot be assumed that the physiological regulatory mechanisms of such individuals are 'normal' (e.g. Doyle and Fraser, 1961).

CONCLUSION

It can be concluded that, although there is extensive evidence relating psychological factors with disease, and therefore a *prima facie* case for psychophysiological intervention, the psychophysiological pathways involved are not well understood. Psychophysiological studies in humans have tended to focus on stimulus parameters, with the consequence that the mechanisms operating at the interface between psychological and biological responses and their implications for particular medical disorders are quite unclear.

THE RATIONALES FOR PSYCHOPHYSIOLOGICAL INTERVENTION

The rationales for the various types of psychophysiological intervention are seldom expounded. Of course, it is possible to take an unashamedly empirical approach, and apply methods to a patient group with only the most general justification that mental processes influence bodily functions. But a responsible scientific attitude involves forming testable hypotheses concerning the pathways that will be affected by the treatment. In terms of the model presented in Figure 7.1, the disease process could be changed by altering the pattern of environmental stimulation or by bolstering the individual's psychosocial resources (Stage I), by modifying responsivity (Stage II), or by ameliorating the person's adverse biological disposition (Stage III). No psychophysiological interventions are presumed to alter psychosocial stimulation directly, but all the other components of the stress–diathesis process have been implicated in different therapeutic rationales. Psychophysiological interventions can, in fact, be divided into three groups, each operating primarily at a different level of the stress–diathesis model. These rationales will be briefly outlined, and their validity will be considered in the light of data concerning the mechanisms mediating treatment responses.

COGNITIVE METHODS

The rationale for cognitive methods in behavioural medicine is based on Stage I of the stress–diathesis model. By modifying the cognitive appraisal and coping processes with which the person deals with adverse environmental conditions, it may be possible to reduce or eradicate potentially damaging physiological responses. Within this framework, specific rationales can be generated for particular problems. For example, Type A individuals are thought to respond to the inevitable hassles and challenges of life in a stereotyped aggressive fashion. Training such people to perceive the environment in a more differentiated way and to respond flexibly might therefore prevent exaggerated psychophysiological activation (Roskies *et al.*, 1986).

In the case of painful conditions, the rationale for cognitive interventions is even more direct, since it is argued that cognitions and behaviours are crucial components of the experience of pain (Turk and Rudy, 1986). Laboratory studies of acute pain provide considerable evidence that cognitive strategies such as distraction and certain types of attention-focusing reduce distress and increase tolerance for nociceptive stimulation (McCaul and Malott, 1984). Clinical studies have shown associations between stressful life events, mood and pain (Feuerstein, Bortolussi, Houle and Labbe, 1983; Harrigan, Kues, Ricks and Smith, 1984). The cognitive–behavioural models that have been used to guide psychophysiological interventions in pain have been discussed by Keefe and Gil (1986).

SELF-REGULATION METHODS

It is generally postulated that self-regulation methods such as relaxation operate at Stage II of the stress–diathesis model, displacing the physiological stress responses with an incompatible relaxation response, notably reduced sympathetic nervous system activity. In addition, these techniques may improve people's ability to cope psychologically with everyday challenges, and consequently lead to modifications at Stage I. Such rationales imply that self-regulation methods are only appropriate in conditions where there is clear evidence of psychophysiological involvement in the disorder, and where the intervention is likely to produce antagonistic physiological responses. Taking this argument to its logical limits, one might then conclude that relaxation is not suitable for the management of asthma, since reductions in sympathetic activity increase rather than decrease bronchoconstriction, and that such techniques are doubtful in the treatment of tension headache, where the evidence for psychophysiological involvement of the disorder is inconsistent, to say the least (Feuerstein, Bush and Corbisiero, 1982; Haynes, Gannon, Cuevas, Heiser, Hamilton and Katranides, 1983). In conditions such as diabetes and epilepsy, the aetiological role of stress is also somewhat speculative, although there is stronger evidence for psychological factors affecting the clinical stability of patients with these problems (Lubar and Deering, 1981; Wing, Epstein, Nowalk and Lamparski, 1986). Yet in each case, treatment is carried out using self-regulation techniques, for in practice few therapists base treatment on overt evidence of excessive psychophysiological reactivity in individual patients. The inconsistency of the data hints at the possibility that self-regulation techniques may not operate through conventional psychophysiological pathways at all. It is, however, possible that selection of patients on psychophysiological principles would improve the outcome with these treatments.

EXERCISE TRAINING

Aerobic training has entered the armoury of psychophysiological interventions comparatively recently. The justification for its use derives empirically from epidemiological studies demonstrating the increased health and longevity of active as opposed to sedentary people (Kannel, Wilson and Blair, 1985). This effect appears not to be due solely to selection biases, or physical correlates such as weight loss or increased muscle strength. Rather, tonic changes in cardiovascular function take place that may be mediated by autonomic adjustments (Billman, Schwartz and Stone, 1984; Scheuer and Tipton, 1977). In terms of the stress–diathesis model, physical fitness may therefore exert an influence at Stage III, by modifying the biological predisposition to disorder. However, it has also been proposed that aerobic fitness may lead to changes in psychophysiological reactivity to behavioural challenges (Sinyor, Schwartz, Peronnet, Brisson and Seraganian, 1983). Animal studies indicate that exercise attenuates stress-induced hypertension, and the same mechanism may operate in humans (Cox, Hubbard, Lawler, Sanders and Mitchell, 1985; Mills and Ward, 1986).

MECHANISMS UNDERLYING PSYCHOPHYSIOLOGICAL INTERVENTIONS

The justification for psychophysiological interventions in behavioural medicine has been presented somewhat baldly in the last section. The reason is that the validity of rationales must be considered in the light of evidence concerning the mechanisms mobilized during treatment. When this information is evaluated, it will become clear that psychophysiological treatments may not actually operate through the pathways that are postulated, but through different processes.

AUTONOMIC AND ENDOCRINE CHANGES WITH RELAXATION

The autonomic and endocrine responses during muscle relaxation training appear well established. Borkovec and Sides (1979) reviewed the literature and found consistently greater reductions in cardiac, electrodermal and respiratory variables with relaxation than with various control treatments. Significant decreases in plasma catecholamine levels and cardiac contractility were observed by Davidson, Winchester, Taylor, Alderman and Ingels (1979) in a small group of patients relaxing during cardiac catheterization, and similar catecholamine responses have been recorded in migraine patients (Mathew, Ho, Kralik, Taylor and Claghorn, 1980). The apparent elevation in urinary adrenaline levels following relaxation reported by Wilson (1981) is difficult to interpret owing to the unstandardized collection conditions and the absence of pre-treatment assays. Surwit and Feinglos (1984) reported that Type 2 (non-insulin-dependent) diabetics showed improvements in glucose tolerance following progressive muscle relaxation, and that this effect was mediated through decreases in plasma cortisol levels. In the treatment of hypertensives using biofeedback-assisted relaxation, reductions in plasma renin and aldosterone levels have been reported, though these did not persist as long as the pressure responses (Patel, Marmot and Terry, 1981). However, it is not clear whether any of these adjustments necessarily mediate the therapeutic effects of relaxation training, since many studies have only demonstrated acute changes in autonomic and endocrine parameters. Moreover, the size of intervening physiological changes is frequently poorly correlated with treatment conditions.

RESPONSES TO MEDITATION

The study of meditation has been a confused area of research, and the physiological differences between meditation and relaxation procedures are difficult to define. In part, this is a product of inexact terminology. Many researchers have followed Benson, Beary and Carol (1974) in arguing that meditation and relaxation both lead to a common hypometabolic state called the 'relaxation response'. This has resulted in the use of the term 'relaxation response' to define a set of procedures that are in fact derived from Transcendental Meditation. Yet although systematic comparisons are not extensive, the literature suggests that meditation does not in fact produce the reductions in tonic autonomic and neuroendocrine activity found with muscle relaxation. An extensive review of controlled studies by Holmes (1984) revealed that in none of 16 experiments was heart rate lower during meditation than control treatments, while electrodermal activity was lower in only one of 13 studies. In some types of meditation, autonomic parameters actually suggest increased rather than decreased activation (Corby, Roth, Zarcone and Kopell, 1978; Travis, Kondo and Knott, 1976). Measurements of plasma catecholamines have generally shown elevated levels in meditation compared with control (Hoffman *et al.*, 1982; Lang, Dehof, Meurer and Kaufman, 1979; Morrell and Hollandsworth, 1986), although Michaels, Huber and McCann (1976) found no differences. The down-regulation of adrenergic receptor sensitivity with the 'relaxation response' postulated by Hoffman *et al.* (1982) was not confirmed by Morrell and Hollandsworth (1986). The autonomic and endocrine adjustments during meditation thus appear to differ from those induced by relaxation procedures, and are unlikely to be responsible for therapeutic effects.

PATTERNS OF MUSCULAR RELAXATION

Relaxation methods such as progressive muscle relaxation are, of course, presumed to operate in part through the generation of low levels of skeletal muscle tone, rather than through autonomic pathways. In Jacobson's (1938) technique, training was conducted over many sessions, focusing on major and minor muscle groups in turn. In the present day, most clinicians in behavioural medicine use abbreviated techniques (e.g. Bernstein and Borkovec, 1973), in which training in the relaxation of a limited set of muscle groups is carried out for a few sessions only. The assumption is that generalization of muscle relaxation will take place to other muscle groups, and to situations outside the laboratory. The presumption of generalization is even more striking in the use of electromyographic (EMG) biofeedback, where training is commonly conducted on a single set of muscles alone. Yet although a number of studies have shown EMG reductions at specifically trained sites during relaxation and biofeedback treatments, the literature suggests that generalization to the skeletal musculature in its entirety is hard to achieve.

Two problems are important in this respect. The first is that EMG recorded from the commonly used frontalis site (actually a bilateral amalgam of two muscles) is not an accurate indicator of general muscular tension (Alexander and Smith, 1979). The correlation between activity in the frontalis and other muscles is weak (Alexander, 1975; Fridlund, Fowler and Pritchard, 1980). More generally, there is little support for the notion of a general level of muscle tone related to anxiety or tension that can be indexed at any one site (Fridlund, Cottam and Fowler, 1982; Fridlund, Hatfield, Cottam and Fowler, 1986). This renders the assessment of muscle tension in clinical studies extremely laborious and practically difficult. No studies have yet shown convincingly that the therapeutic effects of relaxation or EMG biofeedback procedures are mediated through general muscular relaxation. The second problem is that many investigators have used inappropriate filtering bandwidths when assessing surface EMG (Fridland and Cacioppo, 1986). Spectral analytic studies indicate that the power of surface EMG signals is predominantly located at frequencies below 100 Hz (Van Boxtel, Goudswaard and Schomaker, 1984). In addition, the frequency distribution of the EMG varies with the strength of muscle contractions. Unfortunately, many commercial EMG amplifiers filter out wavelengths below 100 Hz in order to eliminate electrocardiographic interference. This means that many of the studies concerning patterns of muscle tension in behavioural medicine have used inadequate measures of EMG.

MECHANISMS IN BIOFEEDBACK

Biofeedback is used clinically in two different ways. First, it is employed in an attempt to produce specific control over particular physiological parameters. The parameter being monitored under these circumstances will be directly relevant to the condition being treated – for example bronchoconstriction for asthma, aberrant EEG waveforms for epilepsy, blood pressure for essential hypertension. The second and more widespread use of biofeedback is as an index of somatic activation. Heart rate, skin conductance and EMG biofeedback are employed not so much because specific control is required, but to provide an indication of general activation and relaxation. When biofeedback is used in this way, there may not be any simple association between voluntary control and symptom relief, since the feedback parameter is a correlate of the dysfunction rather than a cause. When it is recalled that biofeedback is used in the management of widely differing physiological phenomena – EEG, striate muscular and autonomic responses – it is no surprise that a single theory has not been found to account for all effects.

Early research into the instrumental control of physiological functions suggested that biofeedback might operate through direct conditioning of autonomic processes (Miller, 1969). However, the experimental basis for this hypothesis in animal research proved fragile (Miller and Dworkin, 1974), and human studies of biofeedback for parameters such as heart rate have cast doubt on the existence of direct autonomic control. It would appear that many autonomic effects may be secondary to overall changes in energy expenditure, and do not violate the normally closely integrated relationship between cardiovascular state and metabolic requirements (Moses, Clemens and Brener, 1986). Biofeedback may operate in these circumstances by enabling subjects to label existing states in their behavioural repertoire, rather than through mobilizing novel autonomic efferent responses.

The use of biofeedback in the management of conditions unrelated to the autonomic nervous system is less easy to explain within this framework. A number of systematic case studies suggest that epileptic seizure activity can be modified using biofeedback of various EEG rhythms (Lubar and Deering, 1981). The hypothesis has been put forward that these effects are mediated through the enhancement of inhibitory rhythms, but direct evidence is not available. Controlled studies have also shown enhanced motor control following biofeedback in stroke and other neurological patients (Marzuk, 1985a). Again, it is unclear whether these responses are the outcome of neuronal plasticity and reorganization, regrowth of neuro-anatomical connections or enhanced motivation and attention on the part of patients.

Biofeedback and Pain Management

Frontalis EMG biofeedback has been used extensively for tension headache, while thermal and cephalic vasomotor feedback has been employed in the treatment of migraine (Beatty, 1982; Cox and Hobbs, 1982). More recently, EMG activity from the shoulder and neck muscles has been evaluated in the treatment of chronic back pain (Bush, Ditto and Feuerstein, 1985). Although these treatments have been provided in the belief that biofeedback would promote direct control of the muscles or vasomotor responses responsible for the pain, the evidence in favour of such a rationale is slight. Thermal biofeedback has not proved to have consistent therapeutic effects, while the other treatments appear no more effective than relaxation (Holmes and Burish, 1983; Marzuk, 1985b). Few studies using EMG biofeedback even test whether patients acquire control over the muscles under study. It has been suggested that biofeedback training with one muscle might be useful in promoting control at other sites, but this has not been demonstrated in systematic studies (Alexander, White and Wallis, 1977; Carlson, Basilio and Heaukulani, 1983).

It is possible that biofeedback exerts its effect on pain not through specific muscular control nor even through mimicking the physiological responses of relaxation, but through modifications in cognitive activity. Flor, Haag, Turk and Koehler (1983) found that reductions in back pain following biofeedback were associated with decreases in negative thoughts concerning helplessness and lack of control rather than with changes in the sensory properties of the nociceptive experience. Long-term benefits in tension-headache patients were shown by Andrasik and Holroyd (1983) to be related to cognitive rather than EMG change. A direct test was carried out by Holroyd *et al.* (1984), who compared treatments with real and false EMG biofeedback in tension-headache subjects, dividing each group into high or moderate apparent-success conditions. Subjects in the two high apparent-success conditions showed greater improvements in headache than the moderate apparent-success groups, irrespective of actual EMG changes. Therapeutic effects were associated with modifications in perceived self-efficacy and self-control. Such studies may provide an indication of the mechanisms underlying not only EMG biofeedback training, but other psychophysiological interventions in behavioural medicine.

THE REGULATION OF PSYCHOPHYSIOLOGICAL REACTIONS TO STRESS

The literature presented in the last section concerned tonic physiological responses and their potential role in mediating therapeutic effects. It can be concluded that, with the exception of muscle relaxation, there is little consistent experimental evidence for sustained autonomic or endocrine change with treatment. Even in the case of relaxation, it is not certain that these modifications mediate therapeutic responses. It is possible, however, that such studies are not appropriate, since measures are carried out under benign conditions when the subject is in an undisturbed state. It may be more valuable to assess the modifications in physiological reactions to psychosocial challenge rather than resting levels, since treatments may come into their own when the patient is under stress.

A number of investigators have therefore assessed reactions to different types of psychological stimulation following training. Interpretation of these studies is sometimes hampered by the lack of suitable control groups (e.g. Shapiro and Lehrer, 1980), since reactivity to experimental tasks generally declines on repeated presentation even in the absence of any specific treatment. Another problem is that reductions in reactivity may be secondary to decreases in tonic level (Bradley and McCanne, 1981; English and Baker, 1983). Nevertheless, it would appear that autonomic reactivity to experimental tasks can be reduced with brief relaxation training (Connor, 1974; Paul, 1969). Effects have been seen both for actively challenging problem-solving tasks (Steptoe and Ross, 1982), and for passive conditions such as exposure to loud noise and anticipation of shock (Eves and Steptoe, 1986; Holmes, Frost, Bennett, Nielson and Lutz, 1981). Negative results have also been published, but mainly in studies using weak treatments, and where subjects were not explicitly prepared to cope with impending stress using the relaxation technique (e.g. Boswell and Murray, 1979).

Once again, meditation techniques produce rather different results from those demonstrated with relaxation. Kirsch and Henry (1979) showed that meditation of the type developed by Benson *et al.* (1974) had no effect on anticipatory heart rate in speech-anxious students, whereas decreases in heart rate were recorded in subjects given muscle relaxation training. Similarly, Puente and Beiman (1980) found that progressive muscle relaxation and self-relaxation led to decreases in cardiac reactions to aversive slides, while transcendental meditation did not. Other comparisons have shown similar advantages for muscle relaxation (Lehrer, Schoicket, Carrington and Woolfolk, 1980). The suggestion made by Goleman and Schwartz (1976) that the heightened stress-responsivity of meditators is in some way adaptive is unconvincing (Holmes, 1984).

BIOFEEDBACK AND REACTIVITY CONTROL

Biofeedback has also been used to train subjects to reduce their physiological reactivity to aversive stimulation (DeGood and Adams, 1976; Reeves and Shapiro, 1983). An interesting aspect of these experimental studies is that effects seem to be confined to the physiological parameter used for the feedback, and do not generalize to other measures. For example, Falkowski and Steptoe (1983) combined relaxation instructions with skin conductance biofeedback for two training sessions. Increases in skin conductance during a problem-solving task and a distressing film were reduced in the treatment group in comparison with controls, but no differences in heart rate were observed. Similarly, Gatchel, Korman, Weiss, Smith and Clarke (1978) reported that frontalis EMG feedback training led to decreases in EMG during anticipation of electric shock, but had no effect on cardiac or electrodermal responsivity. Nielson and Holmes (1980) also showed that EMG feedback reduced subsequent muscle tension stress responses, while having no effect on skin conductance. Specific cardiovascular effects were seen by Steptoe and Ross (1982) with pulse transit-time feedback.

The literature concerning generalization of biofeedback effects across physiological variables is not extensive, since most investigators have confined autonomic assessments to the feedback parameter. Nevertheless, the experimental studies described here have important implications in suggesting that biofeedback may only be an effective means of regulating stress reactivity when a specific change in the feedback parameter is required. The evidence for generalization of stress reactivity control is not convincing.

CARDIOVASCULAR REACTIVITY AND THE TREATMENT OF HYPERTENSION

An area in which the regulation of reactivity appears particularly important is the management of hypertension. A number of therapists have argued that reactivity control is a central ingredient of successful treatment. However, the evidence from laboratory tests supporting this proposition is limited. The literature has been reviewed by Johnston (1986), who concluded that only one study has convincingly demonstrated that the stress reactivity of hypertensives is reduced following training. It is notable that this particular investigation gave patients an opportunity to prepare themselves to cope by using their relaxation technique, before the onset of the aversive stimulation (Patel, 1975).

It is more typical to find that tonic rather than phasic blood pressure changes take place with psychophysiological interventions. For example, Richter-Heinrich *et al.* (1988) assessed the blood pressure responses of a group of hypertensives to laboratory stress tests before and after relaxation training. The systolic and diastolic responses to mental arithmetic were reduced by more than 30/15 mmHg following training. However, this was due primarily to a decline in tonic levels, for when responses were expressed in terms of changes from resting levels, the pre-treatment reactions averaged 28/18 mmHg, while the post-treatment mean was 22/14 mmHg. These studies in general do not indicate that cardiovascular reactivity control is central to successful psychophysiological treatment of hypertension. However, it should be added that many tests have not been appropriate for addressing this issue, and evaluations based on ambulatory recording may be more suitable.

PSYCHOPHYSIOLOGICAL REACTIVITY AND AEROBIC FITNESS

The notion that aerobic fitness is associated with reduced psychophysiological reactivity and greater effectiveness in coping with stress has received considerable attention in recent years. Table 7.1 summarizes results from a number of cross-sectional studies, comparing fit and unfit groups on a variety of tasks. It can be seen that reduced reactivity has been observed in several experiments, as has more rapid recovery and return to basal levels following termination of the stimulation. Despite this general trend, some well-conducted studies have failed to show differences, and it is worth considering the explanation for such inconsistencies.

The variable pattern of results may, of course, be a product of differences in experimental conditions and the recording of different physiological parameters. Perhaps more important are potential biases in subject selection It cannot be assumed that sedentary people and those who elect to become fit with regular exercise are the same. The biases may work in both directions. On the one hand, fit subjects may be less disturbed by the laboratory, and more capable of mastering stressful stimuli. On the other hand, certain high-fitness groups (e.g. marathon runners and other athletes) may include highly dedicated, competitive individuals, whose active striving during problem-solving mitigates any stress-reducing effects of physical training.

Our understanding of the psychophysiological consequences of aerobic training is becoming more sophisticated with the completion of studies in which volunteers are assigned at random to training and control conditions. Keller and Seraganian (1984) compared aerobic training with meditation or music appreciation, carried out over equivalent time periods. Following training, heart rate and electrodermal reactions to problem-solving tasks were unchanged, but return to basal levels following tasks was more rapid. Holmes and McGilley (1987) showed that heart rate reactions to an information-processing task were reduced following an aerobic training programme as compared with a control group, but only among subjects who were initially unfit. These effects have unfortunately not been confirmed in comparisons between aerobic conditioning, anaerobic conditioning and waiting-list control (Sinyor, Golder, Steinert and Seraganian, 1986) or between aerobic, anaerobic and cognitive stress-management programmes (Seraganian, Roskies, Hanley, Oseasohn and Collu, 1987). No differences in cardiovascular reactivity between groups trained at a high or moderate intensity and attention-placebo controls were seen by Steptoe, Moses, Edwards and Mathews (1987a).

There appears therefore to be some discrepancy between longitudinal and cross-sectional results in studies of physical activity and fitness. It should be noted that none of these longitudinal trials have involved training beyond the minimal period necessary for producing physical conditioning effects, so the differences in aerobic capacity between groups have been small in comparison with the cross-sectional studies described in Table 7.1. Seraganian *et al.* (1987) have pointed out that the time-course for physical and psychophysiological adaptation with exercise may not be the same, but that modifications of reactivity may require more prolonged training. Nor have the instructions given to subjects in the stress sessions necessarily been appropriate. It has been assumed that changes in reactivity would occur automatically, without instructing subjects to orientate themselves to coping with tasks effectively. On the other hand, it is possible that there are constitutional constraints on changes in stress reactivity with training, just as training itself produces variable effects in different individuals (Bouchard, 1986).

Research into the psychophysiological aspects of aerobic fitness is at an early stage. The effects that have been reported are suggestive but by no means conclusive. It remains to be seen whether differences between fit and unfit

Table 7.1
Psychophysiological reactions and physical fitness: cross-sectional studies

Study	Test/task	Reaction	Recovery	Comments
Sinyor *et al.* (1983)	Mental arithmetic, Stroop test, Quiz	no diff.: HR, NA, A	HR+	
Dorheim *et al.* (1984)	Video game, reaction-time task, cold pressor	no diff.: SBP, DBP, HR, NA, A, cortisol	—	Marathon runners
Hollander and Seraganian (1984)	Visual/auditory conflict overload	no diff.: HR, SCL	HR+ SCL+	Correlational design
Hull *et al.* (1984)	Film, Stroop test	DBP+ (Stroop) no diff.: SBP, HR, NA	DBP+ (film)	
	Cold pressor	no diff.	—	
Keller and Seraganian (1984; Expt 1)	Maze, Stroop test	no diff.: HR, SCL	HR+	
Holmes and Roth (1985)	Memory test	HR+	no diff.	
Lake *et al.* (1985)	Type A interview	SBP+, DBP+	—	Interactions with Type A behaviour
	Mental arithmetic	no diff.	—	
	Cold pressor	no diff.	—	
	Competitive games	DBP0	—	
Perkins *et al.* (1986)	Video game	SBP+, DBP+ no diff.: HR	—	Hypertensive subjects
	Mental arithmetic	no diff.		
Schulhan *et al.* (1986)	Easy and difficult mental arithmetic	HR+, TWA+ on difficult task	—	Phasic responses
Jamieson and Lavoie (1987)	Stroop test	HR: no diff.	no diff.	
Light *et al.* (1987)	Pseudo-shock avoidance	SBP+, HR+, PEP+	—	Self-report fitness only
	reaction time	no diff.: DBP		
	Cold pressor	no diff.	—	
Sothmann *et al.* (1987)	Stroop test	NA+ no diff.: HR, A	—	
Steptoe and Molineux (1987)	Raven's Matrices,	HR+ on difficult task no diff.: SBP, DBP	no diff.	Adolescent subjects
	Video game	no diff.	no diff.	
Steptoe *et al.* (1987a)	Raven's Matrices	HR+ no diff.: SBP, DBP	SCL+	

Study	Test/task	Reaction	Recovery	Comments
Turner *et al.*	Mental arithmetic	HR+	—	—
(1988)	Video game	HR+		

+ = unfit react more than fit, 0 = fit react more than unfit, no diff. = no difference in reaction between fit and unfit groups, — = untested, HR = heart rate, NA, A = catecholamines, noradrenaline and adrenaline, PEP = cardiac pre-ejection period, SBP and DBP = systolic and diastolic blood pressure, SCL = skin conductance level, TWA = T-wave amplitude.

people are really products of reactivity change, secondary to the tonic physiological adjustments that take place with increased fitness, or reflections of some underlying individual difference.

BEHAVIOURAL AND COGNITIVE CHANGES DURING TREATMENT

It would appear that the therapeutic effects of interventions such as relaxation, biofeedback and meditation are not fully accounted for by the traditional psychophysiological mechanisms – modification of tonic levels or responses to stimuli. It is therefore possible that cognitive and behavioural changes are responsible. The behaviours that might be relevant include alterations in habitual activities (diet, exercise, substance use) that themselves have health-promoting effects, and alterations in behaviours that prevent the elicitation of stress-related responses. After all, one of the ways in which one can eliminate the autonomic reactions associated with particular activities or social interactions is simply to avoid these situations altogether. Relaxation may also serve as a distraction in potentially stressful situations. Allied cognitive changes include the reappraisal of threatening situations as benign, the establishment of more effective coping resources, and increasing the client's perceived control over stressful situations and his or her reaction to them. Such responses are, of course, explicitly fostered during cognitive treatment. Even exercise training may have similar effects through enhancing participants' sense of mastery and achievement.

The fact that many psychophysiological interventions are used not only in behavioural medicine but in behaviour therapy for the management of anxiety-related disorders is an indication that cognition and behaviour do respond to these procedures (see Section 2). Unfortunately, there is little evidence concerning concurrent changes in these parameters during the treatment of physiological dysfunctions. Steptoe, Patel, Marmot and Hunt (1987b) found that subjects who had undergone biofeedback-assisted relaxation treatment for the modification of coronary risk reported greater improvements than controls in various aspects of their lives, including relationships at work, enjoyment of life and social relationships. However, these data were collected retrospectively, and may have been subject to social desirability biases. Johnston (1986) has suggested that relaxation training may promote an effort on the part of patients to identify and solve personal problems, and this may lead to changes in lifestyle and revision of beliefs concerning the relative value of work and leisure activities. Direct evidence is once again missing. Even in the context of overtly cognitive approaches to treatment, few investigations include measures that can be used to show that cognitions have actually changed in appropriate ways (Turk and Rudy, 1986).

The role of cognitive and behaviour change is one of the least understood aspects of psychophysiological intervention, and one that is in urgent need of development. It is crucial that future studies of interventions include thorough assessment of cognitions and behaviours, using diaries, questionnaires and direct observations, in order to understand the process of change. It may be that enthusiasm for these parameters as mediating mechanisms stems more from ignorance than fact, and that when cognitions and behaviours are properly evaluated, they too will show poor correlations with therapeutic effects. At present, however, they must be considered important candidates for the central mechanism in psychophysiological treatment.

PREDICTION OF TREATMENT RESPONSES

Studies of mechanism are important not only for understanding the treatment process, but also because they may be helpful in identifying subjects who are good candidates for psychophysiological intervention. It would clearly be a major advance to be able to conduct a battery of physiological and psychological tests which could be used to select patients for psychophysiological treatment, or even for one out of the range of possible psychophysiological treatments (e.g. cognitive versus relaxation methods). Little work of this kind has yet been published.

One of the most persistent notions is that subjects who initially show marked physiological reactivity to behavioural stress will be particularly suitable for treatment. It can be argued that a person who shows little or no increase in activity in symptom-relevant physiological parameters with a laboratory challenge is unlikely to benefit from a treatment based on stress management. Steptoe (1982) suggested on the basis of experimental studies that people with high initial cardiovascular reactions to mental stress tests produce greater improvements with relaxation and biofeedback than the less responsive, and that this effect is not simply an adaptation phenomenon.

There is a limited amount of clinical evidence in favour of these propositions. Cottier, Shapiro and Julius (1984) found that the hypertensives who responded positively to progressive muscle relaxation had higher initial sympathetic tone (indexed by heart rate, plasma noradrenaline and anxiety) than non-responders. Another study of hypertensives showed that responders were characterized by high pre-treatment levels of trait anxiety and urinary cortisol (McGrady, Utz, Woerner, Bernal and Higgins, 1986). On the other hand, low correlations have been found between pre-treatment reactions during formal mental stress testing and therapeutic responses (Goldstein, Shapiro, Thananopavarn and Sambhi, 1982; Richter-Heinrich *et al.*, 1988). In the case of tension and migraine headache, Blanchard *et al.* (1983) reported that responses to relaxation and biofeedback were associated with a variety of autonomic reactions to mental stress tests, with more labile individuals showing greater benefits. Interestingly, Blanchard *et al.* (1983) included recordings during relaxation as well as challenge in their assessment battery, and this may provide a more complete estimation of the sensitivity of patients' autonomic nervous systems to behavioural stimulation.

CONCLUSIONS

The treatment of medical disorders is an important aspect of contemporary clinical psychophysiology, and the methods that have been developed are likely to have a major impact on health care in the future. This chapter has not discussed the application or efficacy of psychophysiological interventions, since procedures used for individual disorders are discussed in later chapters of the handbook. Results for a number of conditions are promising, and some are beginning to be deployed on a large scale.

Nevertheless, the theoretical background and mechanisms of psychophysiological intervention remain poorly defined. The experimental literature concerning autonomic and endocrine responses to relaxation and other self-regulation techniques provides stronger evidence for the modification of tonic levels of activity than reductions in reactivity to stress. It cannot be assumed that all self-regulation techniques have similar effects, since muscle relaxation and meditation appear to promote different physiological adjustments in some studies. It must be said that, in clinical research, little attention has been paid to the mechanisms of change, many investigators being content to measure the target response alone and assume that the postulated autonomic and endocrine changes take place. In order to understand the process of change, it is necessary to assess mediating factors not only in the laboratory but in ambulatory settings. In addition, insufficient attention has been paid to the cognitive and behavioural responses that take place during psychophysiological treatment. These may assume a more important role in generating therapeutic effects than the psychophysiological response itself. In terms of the model presented in Figure 7.1, many treatments may operate at Stage I rather than Stage II. Such distinctions are important, since they provide an opportunity for targeting interventions more precisely on sensitive components of stress-related disease. It is to be hoped that examination of the rational basis for intervention will also assist in the prediction of response and selection of people most likely to benefit from treatment.

REFERENCES

Alexander, A.B. (1975). An experimental test of assumptions relating to the use of electromyographic biofeedback as a general relaxation technique. *Psychophysiology* **12**, 656–662.

Alexander, A.B. and Smith, D.D. (1979). Clinical applications of EMG biofeedback. In: R.J. Gatchel and K.P. Price (Eds) *Clinical Applications of Biofeedback: Appraisal and Status*. New York: Pergamon.

Alexander, A.B., White, P.D. and Wallis, H.M. (1977). Training and transfer of training effects in EMG biofeedback-assisted muscular relaxation. *Psychophysiology* **14**, 551–559.

Andrasik, F. and Holroyd, K.A. (1983). Specific and non-specific effects in the biofeedback treatment of tension headache: three-year follow-up. *Journal of Consulting and Clinical Psychology* **51**, 634–636.

Anisman, H. and Sklar, L.S. (1984). Psychological insults and pathology. Contribution of neurochemical, hormonal and immunological mechanisms. In: A. Steptoe and A. Mathews (Eds) *Health Care and Human Behaviour*. London: Academic Press.

Beatty, J. (1982). Biofeedback in the treatment of migraine: simple relaxation or specific effects? In: L. White and B. Tursky (Eds) *Clinical Biofeedback: Efficacy and Mechanisms*. New York: Guilford.

Benson, H., Beary, J.F. and Carol, M.P. (1974). The relaxation response. *Psychiatry* **37**, 37–46.

Bernstein, D.A. and Borkovec, T.D. (1973). *Progressive Relaxation Training*. Champaign, Ill.: Research Press.

Billman, G.E., Schwartz, P.J. and Stone, H.L. (1984). The effect of daily exercise on susceptibility to sudden cardiac death. *Circulation* **69**, 1182–1189.

Birk, L. (1973). *Biofeedback: Behavioral Medicine*. New York: Grune and Stratton.

Blanchard, E.B., Andrasik, F., Arena, J.G., Neff, D.F., Saunders, N.L., Jurish, S.E. and Teders, S.J. (1983). Psychophysiological responses as predictors of response to behavioral treatment of chronic headache. *Behavior Therapy* **14**, 357–374.

Borkovec, T.D. and Sides, J.K. (1979). Critical procedural variables related to the physiological effects of progressive relaxation: a review. *Behaviour Research and Therapy* **17**, 119–125.

Boswell, P.C. and Murray, E.J. (1979). Effects of meditation on psychological and physiological measures of anxiety. *Journal of Consulting and Clinical Psychology* **47**, 606–607.

Bouchard, C. (1986). Genetics of aerobic power and capacity. In: R.M. Malina and C. Bouchard (Eds) *Sport and Human Genetics*. Champaign, Ill.: Human Kinetics.

Bradley, B.W. and McCanne, T.R. (1981). Autonomic responses to stress: the effects of progressive relaxation, the relaxation response, and expectancy of relief. *Biofeedback and Self-Regulation* **6**, 235–251.

Burish, T.G. and Bradley, L.A. (1983). *Coping with Chronic Disease*. New York: Academic Press.

Bush, C., Ditto, B. and Feuerstein, M. (1985). A controlled evaluation of paraspinal EMG biofeedback in the treatment of chronic low back pain. *Health Psychology* **4**, 307–321.

Carlson, J.G., Basilio, C.A. and Heaukulani, J.D. (1983). Transfer of EMG training: another look at the general relaxation issue. *Psychophysiology* **20**, 530–536.

Cataldo, M.F., Varni, J.W., Russo, D.C. and Estes, S.A. (1980). Behavior therapy techniques in the treatment of ex-foliative dermatitis. *Archives of Dermatology* **116**, 919–922.

Connor, W.H. (1974). Effects of brief relaxation training on autonomic response to anxiety-provoking stimuli. *Psychophysiology* **11**, 591–599.

Corby, J.C., Roth, W.T., Zarcone, V.P. and Kopell, B.S. (1978). Psychophysiological correlates of the practice of Tantric yoga meditation. *Archives of General Psychiatry* **35**, 571–577.

Cottier, C., Shapiro, K. and Julius, S. (1984). Treatment of mild hypertension with progressive muscle relaxation: predictive value of indexes of sympathetic tone. *Archives of Internal Medicine* **144**, 1954–1958.

Cox, D.J. and Hobbs, W. (1982). Biofeedback as a treatment for tension headaches. In: L. White and B. Tursky (Eds) *Clinical Biofeedback: Efficacy and Mechanisms*. New York: Guilford.

Cox, R.H., Hubbard, J.W., Lawler, J.E., Sanders, B.J. and Mitchell, V.P. (1985). Exercise training attenuates stress-induced hypertension in the rat. *Hypertension* **7**, 747–751.

Creer, T.L. (1979). *Asthma Therapy: A Behavioral Health Care System for Respiratory Disorders*. New York: Springer.

Davidson, D.M., Winchester, M.A., Taylor, C.B., Alderman, E.A. and Ingels, N.B. (1979). Effects of relaxation therapy on cardiac performance and sympathetic activity in patients with organic heart disease. *Psychosomatic Medicine* **41**, 303–309.

DeGood, D.E. and Adams, A.S. (1976). Control of cardiac responses under aversive stimulation. *Biofeedback and Self-Regulation* **1**, 373–378.

Dorheim, T.A., Rüddel, H., McKinney, M.E., Tod, G.L., Mellion, N.B., Buell, J.C. and Eliot, R.S. (1984). Cardiovascular response of marathoners to mental challenge. *Journal of Cardiac Rehabilitation* **4**, 476–480.

Doyle, A.E. and Fraser, J.R.E. (1961). Essential hypertension and inheritance of vascular reactivity. *Lancet* **ii**, 509–511.

Elliott, G.R. and Eisdorfer, C. (1982). *Stress and Human Health*. New York: Springer.

English, E.H. and Baker, T.B. (1983). Relaxation training and cardiovascular response to experimental stressors. *Health Psychology* **2**, 239–259.

Eves, F. and Steptoe, A. (1986). Modification of reactivity associated with the defensive response. *Biological Psychology* **23**, 88 (Abstract).

Fahrenberg, J. (1986). Psychophysiological individuality: a pattern analytic approach to personality research and psychosomatic medicine. *Advances in Behaviour Research and Therapy* **8**, 43–100.

Falkowski, J. and Steptoe, A. (1983). Biofeedback-assisted relaxation in the control of reactions to a challenging task and anxiety-provoking film. *Behaviour Research and Therapy* **21**, 161–167.

Feuerstein, M., Bortolussi, L., Houle, M. and Labbe, E. (1983). Stress, temporal artery activity, and pain in migraine headache: a prospective analysis. *Headache* **23**, 296–304.

Feuerstein, M., Bush, C. and Corbisiero, R. (1982). Stress and chronic headache: a psychophysiological analysis of mechanisms. *Journal of Psychosomatic Research* **26**, 167–182.

Flor, H., Haag, G., Turk, D.C. and Koehler, H. (1983). Efficacy of EMG biofeedback, pseudotherapy, and conventional medical treatment for chronic rheumatic back pain. *Pain* **17**, 21–31.

Fordyce, W.E. and Steger, J.C. (1979). Chronic pain. In: O.F. Pomerleau and J.P. Brady (Eds) *Behavioral Medicine: Theory and Practice*. Baltimore: Williams and Wilkins.

Fridlund, A.J. and Cacioppo, J.T. (1986). Guidelines for human electromyographic research. *Psychophysiology* **23**, 567–589.

Fridlund, A.J., Cottam, G.L. and Fowler, S.C. (1982). In search of the general tension factor: tensional patterning during auditory stimulation. *Psychophysiology* **19**, 136–145.

Fridlund, A.J., Fowler, S.C. and Pritchard, D.A. (1980). Striate muscle tensional patterning in frontalis EMG biofeedback. *Psychophysiology* **17**, 47–55.

Fridlund, A.J., Hatfield, M.E., Cottam, G.L. and Fowler, S.C. (1986). Anxiety and striate-muscle activation: evidence from electromyographic pattern analysis. *Journal of Abnormal Psychology* **95**, 228–236.

Friedman, M. and Ulmer, D. (1986). *Treating Type A Behaviour and Your Heart*. London: Michael Joseph.

Gatchel, R., Korman, M., Weiss, C., Smith, D. and Clarke, L. (1978). A multiple-response evaluation of EMG biofeedback performance during training and stress-induction conditions. *Psychophysiology* **15**, 253–258.

Gentry, W.D. (1984). *Handbook of Behavioral Medicine*. New York: Guilford.

Goldstein, I.B., Shapiro, D., Thananopavarn, C. and Sambhi, M.P. (1982). Comparison of drug and behavioral treatments of essential hypertension. *Health Psychology* **1**, 7–26.

Goleman, D.J. and Schwartz, G.E. (1976). Meditation as an intervention in stress reactivity. *Journal of Consulting and Clinical Psychology* **44**, 456–466.

Harrigan, J.A., Kues, J.R., Ricks, D.F. and Smith, R. (1984). Moods that predict coming migraine headache. *Pain* **20**, 385–396.

Haynes, S.N., Gannon, L.R., Cuevas, J., Heiser, P., Hamilton, J. and Katranides, M. (1983). The psychophysiological assessment of muscle-contraction headache subjects during headache and non-headache conditions. *Psychophysiology* **20**, 393–399.

Hoffman, J.W., Benson, H., Arns, P.A., Stainbrook, G.L., Landsberg, L., Young, J.B. and Gill, A. (1982). Reduced sympathetic nervous system responsivity associated with the relaxation response. *Science* **215**, 190–192.

Hollander, B.J. and Seraganian, P. (1984). Aerobic fitness and psychophysiological reactivity. *Canadian Journal of Behavioral Science* **16**, 257–261.

Holmes, D.S. (1984). Meditation and somatic arousal reduction: a review of the experimental evidence. *American Psychologist* **39**, 1–10.

Holmes, D.S. and Burish, T.G. (1983). Effectiveness of biofeedback for training migraine and tension headaches: a review of the evidence. *Journal of Psychosomatic Research* **27**, 511–532.

Holmes, D.S. and McGilley, B.M. (1987). Influence of a brief aerobic training program on heart rate and subjective responses to a psychological stressor. *Psychosomatic Medicine* **49**, 366–374.

Holmes, D.S. and Roth, D.L. (1985). Association of aerobic fitness with pulse rate and subjective responses to psychological stress. *Psychophysiology* **22**, 525–529.

Holmes, D.S., Frost, R.O., Bennett, D.H., Nielson, D.H. and Lutz, D.J. (1981). Effectiveness of skin resistance biofeedback for controlling arousal in non-stressful and stressful situations: two experiments. *Journal of Psychosomatic Research* **25**, 205–211.

Holroyd, K.A. and Creer, T.L. (1986). *Self-Management of Chronic Disease*. New York: Academic Press.

Holroyd, K.A., Penzien, D.B., Hursey, K.G., Tobin, D.L., Rogers, L., Holm, J.E., Marcille, P.J., Hall, J.R. and Chila, A.G. (1984). Change mechanisms in EMG biofeedback training: cognitive changes underlying improvements in tension headache. *Journal of Consulting and Clinical Psychology* **52**, 1039–1053.

Holzman, A.D. and Turk, D.C. (1986). *Pain Management: A Handbook of Psychological Treatment Approaches*. New York: Pergamon.

Hull, E.M., Young, S.H. and Ziegler, M.G. (1984). Aerobic fitness affects cardiovascular and catecholamine responses to stressors. *Psychophysiology* **21**, 353–360.

Jacobson, E. (1938). *Progressive Relaxation*. Chicago: University of Chicago Press.

Jamieson, J.L. and Lavoie, N.F. (1987). Type A behavior, aerobic power, and cardiovascular recovery from a psychosocial stress. *Health Psychology* **6**, 361–371.

Johnston, D.W. (1986). How does relaxation training reduce blood pressure in primary hypertension? In: T.D. Dembroski, T.H. Schmidt and C. Blümchen (Eds) *Biobehavioral Factors in Coronary Heart Disease*. Basle: Karger.

Kannel, W.B., Wilson, P. and Blair, S.N. (1985). Epidemiological assessment of the role of physical activity and fitness in the development of cardiovascular disease. *American Heart Journal* **109**, 876–884.

Keefe, F.J. and Gil, K.M. (1986). Behavioral concepts in the analysis of chronic pain syndromes. *Journal of Consulting and Clinical Psychology* **54**, 776–783.

Keller, S. and Seraganian, P. (1984). Physical fitness level and autonomic reactivity to psychosocial stress. *Journal of Psychosomatic Research* **28**, 279–288.

Kirsch, I. and Henry, D. (1979). Self-desensitisation and meditation in the reduction of public speaking anxiety. *Journal of Consulting and Clinical Psychology* **47**, 536–541.

Lake, B.W., Suarez, E.C., Schneiderman, M. and Tocci, N. (1985). The Type A behavior pattern, physical fitness, and psychophysiological reactivity. *Health Psychology* **4**, 169–187.

Lang, R., Dehof, K.A., Meurer, W. and Kaufman, J. (1979). Sympathetic activity and transcendental meditation. *Journal of Neural Transmission* **44**, 117–135.

Lehrer, P.M., Schoicket, S., Carrington, P. and Woolfolk, R.L. (1980). Psychophysiological and cognitive responses to stressful stimuli in subjects practicing progressive relaxation and clinically standardised meditation. *Behaviour Research and Therapy* **13**, 293–303.

Light, K.C., Obrist, P.A., James, S.A. and Strogatz, D.S. (1987). Cardiovascular responses to stress: II. Relationships to aerobic exercise patterns. *Psychophysiology* **24**, 79–86.

Lubar, J.F. and Deering, W.M. (1981). *Behavioral Approaches to Neurology*. New York: Academic Press.

Marzuk, P.M. (1985a). Biofeedback for neuromuscular disorders. *Annals of Internal Medicine* **102**, 854–858.

Marzuk, P.M. (1985b). Biofeedback for headaches. *Annals of Internal Medicine* **102**, 128–131.

Mathew, R.J., Ho, B.T., Kralik, P., Taylor, D. and Claghorn, J.L. (1980). Catecholamines and migraine: evidence based on biofeedback-induced changes. *Headache* **20**, 247–252.

Mathews, A. and Ridgeway, V. (1984). Psychological preparation for surgery. In: A. Steptoe and A. Mathews (Eds) *Health Care and Human Behaviour*. London: Academic Press.

McCaul, K.D. and Malott, J.M. (1984). Distraction and coping with pain. *Psychological Bulletin* **95**, 516–533.

McGrady, A., Utz, S.W., Woerner, M., Bernal, G.A.A. and Higgins, J.T. (1986). Predictors of success in hypertensives treated with biofeedback-assisted relaxation. *Biofeedback and Self-Regulation* **11**, 95–103.

Michaels, R.R., Huber, M.J. and McCann, D.S. (1976). Evaluation of transcendental meditation as a method of reducing stress. *Science* **192**, 1242–1244.

Miller, N.E. (1969). Learning of visceral and glandular responses. *Science* **153**, 434–445.

Miller, N.E. and Dworkin, B.R. (1974). Visceral learning: recent difficulties with cura-
rised rats and significant problems for human research. In: P.A. Obrist, A.H. Black,
J. Brener and L.V. DiCara (Eds) *Cardiovascular Psychophysiology*. Chicago: Aldine.

Mills, D.E. and Ward, R.D. (1986). Attenuation of stress-induced hypertension by
exercise independent of training effects: an animal model. *Journal of Behavioral Medicine*
9, 599–605.

Morrell, E.M. and Hollandsworth, J.G. (1986). Norepinephrine alterations under stress
conditions following the regular practice of meditation. *Psychosomatic Medicine* **48**,
270–277.

Morrow, G.R. and Morrell, C. (1982). Behavioral treatment for the anticipatory nausea
and vomiting induced by cancer chemotherapy. *New England Journal of medicine* **307**,
1476–1480.

Moses, J., Clemens, W.J. and Brener, J. (1986). Bidirectional voluntary heart rate
control during static muscular exercise: metabolic and respiratory correlates. *Psychophysiology* **23**, 510–520.

Nielson, D.H. and Holmes, D.S. (1980). Effectiveness of EMG biofeedback training for
controlling arousal in subsequent stressful situations. *Biofeedback and Self-Regulation* **5**,
235–248.

Patel, C. (1975). Yoga and biofeedback in the management of 'stress' in hypertensive
patients. *Clinical Science and Molecular Medicine* **28** (Suppl.), 171–174.

Patel, C., Marmot, M.G. and Terry, D.J. (1981). Controlled trial of biofeedback-aided
behavioural methods in reducing mild hypertension. *British Medical Journal* **282**,
2005–2008.

Paul, G.L. (1969). Inhibition of physiological response to stressful imagery by relaxation
training and hypnotically suggested relaxation. *Behaviour Research and Therapy* **7**,
249–256.

Puente, A.E. and Beiman, I. (1980). The effects of behavior therapy, self-relaxation,
and transcendental meditation on cardiovascular stress response. *Journal of Clinical
Psychology* **36**, 291–295.

Reeves, J.L. and Shapiro, D. (1983). Heart-rate reactivity to cold pressor stress following
biofeedback training. *Biofeedback and Self-Regulation* **8**, 87–99.

Richter-Heinrich, E., Homuth, V., Heinrich, B., Knust, U., Schmidt, K.H., Wiedemann, R. and Gohlke, H.R. (1988). Behavioral therapies in essential hypertensives:
a controlled study. In: T. Elbert, W. Langosch, A. Steptoe and D. Vaitl (Eds)
Behavioural Medicine in Cardiovascular Disorders. Chichester: John Wiley & Sons.

Roskies, E., Seraganian, P., Oseasohn, R., Hanley, J.A., Collu, R., Martin, N. and
Smilga, C. (1986). The Montreal Type A Intervention Project: major findings. *Health
Psychology* **5**, 45–70.

Scheuer, J. and Tipton, C. (1977). Cardiovascular adaptations to physical training.
Annual Review of Physiology **39**, 221–251.

Schulhan, D., Scher, H. and Furedy, J.J. (1986). Phasic cardiac reactivity to psychological stress as a function of aerobic fitness level. *Psychophysiology* **23**, 562–566.

Schwartz, G.E. and Weiss, S.M. (1978). Behavioral medicine revisited: an amended
definition. *Journal of Behavioral Medicine* **1**, 249–252.

Seraganian, P., Roskies, E., Hanley, J.A., Oseasohn, R. and Collu, R. (1987). Failure
to alter psychophysiological reactivity in Type A men with physical exercise or stress
management programs. *Psychology and Health* **1**, 195–213.

Shapiro, S. and Lehrer, P.M. (1980). Psychophysiological effects of autogenic training
and progressive relaxation. *Biofeedback and Self-Regulation* **5**, 249–255.

Sinyor, D., Golden, M., Steinert, Y. and Seraganian, P. (1986). Experimental manipulation of aerobic fitness and the response to psychosocial stress: psychophysiological and self-report measures. *Psychosomatic Medicine* **48**, 324–337.

Sinyor, D., Schwartz, S.G., Peronnet, F., Brisson, G. and Seraganian, P. (1983). Aerobic fitness level and reactivity to psychosocial stress: physiological, biochemical and subjective measures. *Psychosomatic Medicine* **45**, 205–217.

Smith, J.C. (1975). Meditation as psychotherapy: a review of the literature. *Psychological Bulletin* **82**, 558–564.

Sothmann, M.S., Horn, T.S., Hart, B.A. and Gustafson, A.B. (1987). Comparison of discrete cardiovascular fitness groups on plasma catecholamines and selected behavioral responses to psychological stress. *Psychophysiology* **24**, 47–54.

Steptoe, A. (1982). Control of cardiovascular reactivity and the treatment of hypertension. In: R.S. Surwit, R.B. Williams, A. Steptoe and R. Biersner (Eds) *Behavioral Treatment of Disease*. New York: Plenum.

Steptoe, A. (1983). Stress, helplessness and control: the implications of laboratory studies. *Journal of Psychosomatic Research* **27**, 361–367.

Steptoe, A. (1984). Psychophysiological processes in disease. In: A. Steptoe and A. Mathews (Eds) *Health Care and Human Behaviour*. London: Academic Press.

Steptoe, A. and Ross, A. (1982). Voluntary control of cardiovascular reactions to demanding tasks. *Biofeedback and Self-Regulation* **7**, 149–166.

Steptoe, A. and Molineux, D. (1987). Family history of cardiovascular disease and physical fitness as determinants of cardiovascular reactions to laboratory tasks in adolescent males. *Psychophysiology* **24**, 614 (Abstract).

Steptoe, A., Moses, J., Edwards, S. and Mathews, A. (1987a). Psychophysiological reactions to challenging tasks before and after exercise training: a longitudinal approach. *Psychophysiology* **24**, 571 (Abstract).

Steptoe, A., Patel, C., Marmot, M. and Hunt, B. (1987b). Frequency of relaxation practice, blood pressure reduction and the general effects of relaxation following a controlled trial of behaviour modification for reducing coronary risk. *Stress Medicine* **3**, 101–107.

Surwit, R.S. and Feinglos, N.M. (1984). Relaxation-induced improvement in glucose tolerance is associated with decreased plasma cortisol. *Diabetes Care* **7**, 203–204.

Travis, T., Kondo, C.Y. and Knott, J.R. (1976). Heart rate, muscle tension, and alpha production of transcendental meditation and relaxation controls. *Biofeedback and Self-Regulation* **1**, 387–394.

Turk, D.C. and Rudy, T.E. (1986). Assessment of cognitive factors in chronic pain: a worthwhile enterprise? *Journal of Consulting and Clinical Psychology* **54**, 760–768.

Turner, J.R., Carroll, D., Costello, M. and Sims, J. (1988). The effects of aerobic fitness on additional heart rate during active psychological challenge. *Journal of Psychophysiology*, **2**, 91–97.

Van Boxtel, A., Goudswaard, P. and Schomaker, L.R.B. (1984). Amplitude and bandwidth of the frontalis surface EMG: effects of electrode parameters. *Psychophysiology* **21**, 699–707.

Weiner, H. (1977). *Psychobiology and Human Disease*. New York: Elsevier.

Wilson, J.F. (1981). Behavioral preparation for surgery: benefit or harm? *Journal of Behavioral Medicine* **4**, 79–102.

Wing, R.R., Epstein, L.H., Nowalk, M.P. and Lamparski, D.M. (1986). Behavioral self-regulation in the treatment of patients with diabetes mellitus. *Psychological Bulletin* **99**, 78–89.

Zuroff, D.C. and Schwartz, J.C. (1978). Effects of transcendental meditation and muscle relaxation on trait anxiety, maladjustment, locus of control and drug use. *Journal of Consulting and Clinical Psychology* **46**, 264–271.

Chapter 8

Psychophysiological and Biochemical Indices in 'Stress' Research: Applications to Psychopathology and Pathophysiology

Mats Fredrikson

Department of Medical Psychology,
Karolinska Institute,
Stockholm,
Sweden

ABSTRACT

Physiological and biochemical reactions accompanying behaviour and emotions are reviewed. Particular emphasis is placed on cardiovascular (systolic and diastolic blood pressure, and heart rate) and neuroendocrine (adrenaline, noradrenaline and cortisol) responses in anxiety states and in cardiovascular disease. Theoretical implications for the understanding of pathophysiology and psychopathology are discussed.

Handbook of Clinical Psychophysiology Edited by G. Turpin
© 1989 John Wiley & Sons Ltd

STRESS AND ITS DEFINITIONS

Stress is a popular concept and we are flooded with messages about its possible harmful effects. However, there is little agreement on how the term should be defined. Approaches fall into three broad categories. The first approach defines stress as a response and identifies patterns of physiological and psychological responses elicited by different situations. One of the pioneers of stress research, Hans Selye (1976), defined stress as the non-specific response of 'the body to any demand made upon it'. Selye in his definition emphasized that stress referred to a similarity in responses to multiple tasks. Selye (cf. 1950, 1976) also introduced a time dimension and suggested that a stressor elicited a sequale of responses, the general adaptation syndrome. This is characterized by the acute alarm phase, a more prolonged resistance phase, and finally the exhaustion phase.

A second approach to the definition of stress focuses on the stimulus, conceptualizing stress as an event. Researchers adhering to this definition have studied ecological catastrophes like fires or the accumulation of stressful events (cf. Holmes and Rahe, 1967). A third approach views stress as an interaction between the environment and an individual that induces a mismatch between the resources of the individual and the demands of the environment (cf. Frankenhaeuser, 1979; Levi, 1975). This definition of stress places particular emphasis on individual differences in how situations are experienced or appraised (cf. Lazarus and Folkman, 1984). Possibly, some of the use and misuse of the term 'stress' stems from the need to understand how we adapt and maladapt to the fast evolution of our society. The daily threats that we meet and deal with in Westernized societies by and large are psychological rather than physical. However, our physiological system has not changed markedly during the evolution occurring in the last 30–40 thousand years.

STRESS AND BODILY CHANGES

Today, symbolic rather than physical threats elicit behaviour which once served to increase the chance of survival. Regardless of whether you are about to fall off a cliff or encounter someone who insults you, the body will respond in similar ways. The metabolism increases, along with changes in heart rate (HR), blood pressure (BP), respiration rate, and muscle tension. Energy is needed, and the liver releases glucose and hormones that convert lipids into triglycerides. Blood is shunted from the skin and viscera to the muscles to facilitate action. These changes are controlled by the autonomic nervous system together with the neuroendocrine system. The hypothalamus serves to integrate the autonomic and endocrine changes, and two principal axes exist: the sympatho-adrenal system with the hormones adrenaline and noradrenaline, and the pituitary–cortical system with cortisol. Depending on whether the focus has been on the analysis of acute or of chronic effects of behavioural stress, the response has been termed the 'defence reflex' (Sokolov, 1963), the 'fight/flight response' (Cannon, 1929), or the 'alarm reaction' (Selye, 1950). Sokolov's (1963) term generally refers to short-lasting, acute changes, whereas Cannon's (1929) and Selye's (1950) concepts refer to longer lasting, chronic changes. Regardless of their designation, both short-term and long-term bodily changes may involve physiological and biochemical changes of relevance for disease. This makes it important to monitor both in order to understand the interplay of behaviour, physiology and neuroendocrinology in mental and physical disease.

Research on behavioural factors in somatic diseases has often focused on the possible deleterious effects of increased physiological or neuroendocrine reactivity associated with behaviour. For example, it has been suggested that essential hypertension (EHT) may result from or be accelerated by exaggerated cardiovascular reactivity to everyday challenges (cf. Fredrikson, 1986a, for a review). Similarly, the increased risk for cardiovascular morbidity and mortality associated with the Type A behaviour pattern (see e.g. Friedman and Rosenman, 1974) has been suggested to result from increased cardio-vascular and neuroendocrine reactions (Krantz and Manuck, 1984). Previously, the textbook notion of the sympathetic nervous system (SNS) implied simultaneous increase (or decrease) in all SNS parameters measured. However, the correlation between different SNS measures is far from perfect (cf. Fredrikson, Dimberg, Frisk-Holmberg and Ström, 1985b). In fact, there is ample evidence to suggest that differentiation of sympathetic activity is the rule rather than the exception (Wallin, 1981). One cannot identify a single 'measure of stress'; instead some research questions require monitoring of only a single parameter, whereas other questions require monitoring of several parameters. For example, in experiments on learning, skin conductance and finger pulse volume changes, by virtue of being fast and reliable to measure, may be better suited than relatively slower hormonal changes. On the other hand, if the focus is on low back pain and stress, it is evident that measures of electromyography from this part of the body may be best suited to reflect responses of interest. It is often preferable to include several measures of SNS activity in stress research, since a single measure does not adequately reflect the activity of other parameters. For several reasons it is advisable to include joint measures of biochemical and physiological activity.

First, the sympatho-adrenal system forms part of an integrated functional system, and physiological activation and endocrine activity may reflect different aspects of this process. Systems have different time-courses. For example, if the subject is under a condition of threat the electrodermal system may respond in seconds, whereas the pituitary–cortical system only responds in minutes or hours (Fredrikson, Sundin and Frankenhaeuser, 1985c). Generally, parameters of physiological activation such as skin conductance, finger pulse volume, systolic and diastolic BP, or HR are easier and cheaper to measure than biochemical ones (adrenaline, noradrenaline, cortisol, renin, sodium, calcium, etc.). The latter also generally require invasive collection methods. Venipuncture is a procedure that most people find unpleasant and therefore some biochemical measures like catecholamine levels increase due to this procedure *per se*. This then requires that subjects rest at least 30–45 min to reach resting levels of catecholamines before the experiment proper starts. This procedure is in contrast to, for example, the application of electrodes to measure skin conductance, which is a non-invasive procedure and does not cause much discomfort.

Second, catecholamine levels constitute a direct measure of SNS efferens, whereas, for example, cardiovascular activity, being an effector system, represents an indirect measure of SNS activity. The cardiovascular effects of catecholamines are determined not only by their level of output but also by the sensitivity or density of the peripheral receptors on which they act. There are also numerous factors, apart from SNS outflow, and receptor sensitivity, that may affect the response of the effector system. For example, cortisol may potentiate the vasoconstrictive effects of circulating noradrenaline (Ganong, 1983). Magnesium levels may influence the threshold for arrhythmias, and cellular levels of salt may modify the cardiac response to stress (cf. Ambrosini, Costa, Montebugnoli, Borghi and Magnani, 1981). The joint measure of plasma concentrations of noradrenaline (which has a vasoconstrictive effect through its action on beta-adrenoceptors) and BP is much more informative than any measure in isolation. A given amount of noradrenaline secretion may produce different responses at the effector organ due to different modulating factors. If the effect on the effector organ is not measured, this information will not be noticed, and, conversely, if only the biochemical measure is studied, its effect on the effector organ is only assumed.

One reason for the popularity of stress research would appear to stem from the fact that behavioural factors seem to be associated with some somatic diseases. In addition, stress-induced physiological and biochemical changes may be plausible mechanisms that may mediate the association between behaviour and disease.

STRESS AND HEALTH

Epidemiologists who study the incidence and prevalence of disease and death in humans have provided evidence to suggest that the leading causes of death have changed dramatically. During the 19th century malnutritional disease was the leading killer, whereas at the turn of the century infectious diseases such as pneumonia and tuberculosis were the main causes of morbidity and mortality. Recently, the American Academy of Science suggested that out of the ten current leading causes of death, seven are associated with behavioural factors. The three leading causes of death are coronary heart disease, cancer and accidents. This has promoted a renewed interest in behavioural factors in medical practice and in behavioural influences on disease and recovery processes.

Cardiovascular diseases, particularly EHT and coronary heart disease (CHD), have attracted special attention. There are several reasons for this. First, nervous and hormonal influences on the cardiovascular control systems are numerous (cf. Ganong, 1983). Second, emotions and behaviour exert an influence both on SNS activity and on the hormones involved in cardiovascular control. Thus, there are plausible mechanisms through which the brain could influence pathophysiological processes. This is also part of the reason that both physiological and biochemical measures, particularly in combination, are of value when trying to relate behaviour to disease. Another factor promoting interest in behavioural influences on somatic diseases is found in the Type A area. Even though exceptions exist, there are now several prospective studies showing that the Type A behaviour pattern, characterized by exaggerated competitiveness, a chronic sense of time urgency, and intense hostile feelings, is a risk factor for CHD (see Review Paniel, 1981, for a review). The prevalent hypothesis is that this behaviour pattern reflects person–environment interactions and that Type A behaviour is associated with exaggerated cardiovascular and neuroendocrine responses (cf. Krantz and Manuck, 1984). The cumulative effect of these responses may result in CHD. Research on the Type A behaviour pattern is a relatively recent development including studies both on aetiology and treatment. Traditionally, the study of behavioural factors in disease has focused on aetiology rather than on treatment or recovery. This is typified by the field of psychosomatic medicine.

PSYCHOSOMATIC MEDICINE

The classic psychosomatic disorders consist of bronchial asthma, eczema, rheumatoid arthritis, ulcerative colitis, duodenal ulcer, EHT and hyperthyroidism. They were called 'psychosomatic' because psychological influences were thought of as independent variables that had an influence on the dependent somatic manifestations. Between 1940 and 1950, the dominating theories relating psychological factors to somatic disease relied heavily on Freudian thinking. Alexander (1939), in his influential nuclear conflict theory, suggested that the presence of specific unconscious conflicts led to specific disorders. Thus, each psychosomatic symptom was viewed as the result of a central emotional conflict. For example, unconscious feelings of hostility were thought to trigger EHT, whereas unconscious feelings of dependency were held to be associated with gastrointestinal and respiratory disorders such as ulcers or asthma. Dunbar (1943) had a conceptually similar way to account for psychosomatic disorders, and argued that specific personality types were associated with specific complaints. Dunbar's theory is often called a profile theory, alluding to the fact that one particular personality profile was thought to lead to one particular disease. The validity, reliability and, ultimately, the testability of these theories have caused debate. Numerous problems with conceptualization, measurement and interpretation of these constructs exist. It has been pointed out (Steptoe, 1984) that theories relating behavioural factors to disease end-points have to satisfy two requirements. First, they must specify a plausible mechanism accounting for the relation between behaviour and the pathophysiological state. Second, they must account for individual differences. The theories of Dunbar (1943) and Alexander (1939) may satisfy the latter but not the former criteria. However, the specificity notion inherent in these theories has had a longstanding impact on research in this area (Ax, 1953; Engel and Bickford, 1961; Fredrikson, Danielsson, Engel, Frisk-Holmberg, Ström and Sundin, 1985a; Wolf, Cardon, Shepard and Wolff, 1955).

SPECIFIC AND GENERAL RESPONSE PATTERNS

Specificity theories claim that certain emotional states are associated with certain distinguishable activation patterns and, ultimately, specific disease end-points. These theories may be contrasted with the generality notion as put forward by Selye (cf. 1950). Selye pointed out that different stressors and emotions elicit both similar and different responses. The communality was termed 'stress' (Selye, 1950). The hypothesis then that 'stress' leads to disease is oversimplified and cannot account for individual differences in susceptibility (cf. Steptoe, 1981). Instead, models allowing for multiple factors and their interaction are needed. Individual differences in genetic make-up, and hence in biological predisposition and vulnerability to disease, have to be taken into account. Models that allow for such interactions are sometimes called 'mosaic' (Page, 1977) or 'stress–diathesis' models (cf. Kagan and Levi, 1974). The idea is to incorporate environmental influences and their interaction with biological and genetic factors into the model to describe physiological and endocrine responses that may be precursors of disease and eventually produce chronic disease. The physiological and endocrine responses thought to increase the risk for future disease are generally those associated with the defence reaction (see Turpin, 1983, for a discussion). There is evidence to suggest that the defence reflex (Sokolov, 1963) is elicited in fear and anxiety. Therefore, this chapter will first describe physiological and endocrine changes associated with the defence reflex and exemplify this by using fear and anxiety. The focus will be on catecholamines and cortisol, since these hormones have been implicated both in the fight/flight response, and in many theories on the role of 'stress' in disease. Since there exist many excellent reviews on the association between fear and anxiety, and catecholamines in normals (cf. Frankenhaeuser, 1979; Levi, 1975; Mason, 1975), this section will focus on clinically documented fear and anxiety only in patients. A second section will discuss the role of physiological and endocrine arousal in chronic disease and will use EHT and CHD as prime examples. The reason for this is that there exist plausible mechanisms relating behaviour to disease (i.e. increased physiological and endocrine activation), and that defined risk factors exist making it theoretically meaningful to relate risk factors to activation patterns. However, first follows a short review on basic cardiovascular and neuroendocrine functions.

BASICS OF CARDIOVASCULAR FUNCTION

The physiological basis and mechanisms involved in determining cardiac and vascular functions have been thoroughly reviewed elsewhere (cf. Schneiderman and Pickering, 1986). Generally, HR is jointly determined by the two branches of the autonomic nervous system, the sympathetic (SNS) and parasympathetic nervous system (PNS), respectively. When SNS activity increases, HR also increases, whereas when PNS activity increases, HR decreases. Conversely, HR may go up due to PNS inhibition, or down because of SNS inhibition. The pace of the neurally denervated human heart is 70–80 beats/min, indicating that there is a constant PNS inhibition, since the resting HR in humans normally is 60–70 beats/min. Thus, a change in HR to below roughly to 60–70 beats/min may result from altered SNS or PNS activity or both, whereas an increase to above 70–80 beats/min could not be accomplished without an increased SNS efferens to the heart.

Heart rate (beats/min) and stroke volume (ml) determine cardiac output (ml/min), which mainly determines systolic BP. Systolic BP is measured in millimetres of mercury (mmHg) and is a measure of the peak pressure obtained during systole (the phase where blood is pumped into the aorta). Diastolic BP is also measured in millimetres of mercury and represents the pressure during the resting phase between successive heartbeats. It is mainly determined by total systemic resistance. Systemic resistance, in turn, is essentially determined by the degree of vasoconstriction in the vascular tree, predominantly in the precapillary resistance vessels. These are innervated through the SNS only, and the release of noradrenaline causes constriction through stimulation of alpha-adrenergic receptors. The only exception to this is the coronary circulation, where increased SNS activation decreases resistance in the vessels. This has adaptive value, since the coronary circulation needs to be increased in emergency situations. Noradrenaline increases peripheral resistance in the skin and muscular beds through activation of alpha-adrenoceptors. Adrenaline causes decreased resistance in the muscular beds through activation of beta-adrenoceptors. The main reflex pathway linking short-term changes in BP to short-term changes in HR and systemic resistance is the baroreceptor reflex (Ganong, 1983). Chemoreceptors and osmotic receptors also participate in regulation of BP. The kidneys play a crucial role, particularly in long-term regulation of BP (Guyton, Coleman, Cowley, Manning, Norman and Ferguson, 1974).

Peripheral blood flow is generally determined either through venous occlusive plethysmography (cf. Fredrikson, Dimberg, Frisk-Holmberg and Ström, 1982) or digital finger pulse volume measures (Jennings, Tahmoush and Redmond, 1980). Venous occlusive plethysmography gives a calibrated volume measure of blood in the tissue in millilitres per minute. Finger pulse volume measures can only be used to determine relative constriction and the absolute change cannot be measured (for a review see Schneiderman and Pickering, 1986). Skin blood flow decreases when arteries constrict due to increased SNS activity. Circulating adrenaline stimulates the beta-2-adrenoceptors that cause dilatation in the muscle beds. A cholinergic dilatory pathway may also exist.

BASICS OF NEUROENDOCRINE FUNCTION

THE SYMPATHO-ADRENAL SYSTEM

The hypothalamus serves to integrate the autonomic and endocrine systems. Two principal axes exist: the pituitary–cortical system and the sympatho-adrenal system. Cortisol is part of the pituitary–cortical axis. Adrenaline and noradrenaline are a functional part of the sympatho-adrenal system, and are metabolized in and secreted from the adrenal medulla from tyrosine, dopa and dopamine. Secretion is controlled by preganglionic fibres of the SNS in the splanchnic area. Both adrenaline and noradrenaline may be elicited peripherally when the hypothalamus is electrically stimulated, and also when cortical regions are activated (von Euler, 1967). Adrenaline constitutes the largest proportion of the catecholamines produced and noradrenaline comprises only a small fraction. Most of the circulating noradrenaline is released from the sympathetic postganglionic nerve endings. Its half-life in blood is short, roughly 90 s. Both adrenaline and noradrenaline are thought of as emergency hormones, since their action generally prepares an organism for fight or flight. Adrenaline, for example, causes an increase in blood sugar and releases fatty acids into the bloodstream, offering substrates for short- and long-term physical action. Its cardiovascular effect is to shunt blood from the skin and intestinal tract to voluntary muscles. The firing threshold of the skeletomusculature is also reduced (Goffard and Perry, 1951). All of these changes seem to have a survival value. Noradrenaline generally has somewhat more circumscribed effects than adrenaline and is particularly important for vascular regulation, since its primary cardiovascular effect is to raise BP and increase inotropism (contractility). Noradrenaline is also involved in thermoregulation. Both adrenaline and noradrenaline levels may be measured in plasma, where arterial samples are preferred compared to venous (cf. Folkow, Di Bona, Hjemdahl, Thorén and Wallin, 1983; Hjemdahl, Freyschuss, Juhlin-Dannfelt and Linck, 1986). Adrenaline and noradrenaline and their metabolites are also excreted in urine and can be measured using fluorometric (von Euler and Lishajko, 1961) or radioenzymatic methods, or using high-performance liquid chromatography (cf. Baum, Lundberg, Grunberg, Singer and Gatchel, 1985).

THE PITUITARY–CORTICAL SYSTEM

The adrenal cortex is influenced by the adrenocorticotrophic hormone (ACTH), which activates the adrenal cortex to secrete both mineralocorticoids and glucocorticoids (cortisol in humans). Adrenocorticotrophic hormone is released from the anterior pituitary gland, given that corticotrophin releasing factor from the hypothalamus is present. Adrenocorticotrophic hormone also stimulates the release of beta-endorphins. When ACTH passes into the bloodstream, it triggers the cells of the adrenal cortex to produce cortisol, which has an inhibitory influence on the release of ACTH. Cortisol has a number of anabolic and catabolic physiological effects – some direct and some indirect. It is involved in producing glucose, primarily for delivery to the central nervous system (CNS). Cortisol also facilitates some of the lipolytic and vasoconstrictor effects of the catecholamines.

Cortisol counteracts fatigue in heart and skeletal muscles, and has facilitatory effects on the CNS, decreasing thresholds for taste and smell (DeWied, 1969). The mineralocorticoids are also involved in sodium retention. Cortisol in humans is secreted in bursts, with 20–30 min between successive bursts. Its half-life is estimated to be 60–90 min. Cortisol also induces an enzyme that will allow the adrenal medulla to synthesize adrenaline from noradrenaline. Thus, the pituitary–cortical axis may be conceived of as a functional part of the sympatho-adrenal system.

There are several practical and technical problems that need attention when collecting plasma or urine for the determination of catecholamine and cortisol levels. Generally, urinary measures are more easily collected than plasma measures and provide integrated measures over longer periods of time. Furthermore, they are non-invasive and do not cause discomfort. Venous samples of plasma catecholamines reflect local skeletal muscle sympathetic tone rather than general activation (see Steptoe, 1987, for a review). Arterial samples of catecholamines are not well correlated with venous estimations but correlate better with urinary catecholamines (Steptoe, 1987). Both arterial penetration and venipuncture cause distress, since they are uncomfortable or painful. Specimens also need to be handled with particular care to prevent oxidation of catecholamines and cortisol. Plasma samples of both catecholamines and cortisol are normally frozen immediately and urinary samples for catecholamines are acidated, whereas urinary samples for the determination of cortisol are frozen only (Baum *et al.*, 1985; von Euler, 1967). Care also needs to be taken to inform subjects who participate in studies where catecholamines are sampled to refrain from strenuous exercise and food and beverages that affect the neuroendocrine system 24 h before the experiment (Baum *et al.*, 1985).

STRESS AND PSYCHOPATHOLOGY

ANXIETY AND CATECHOLAMINES

Anxiety is an important emotion in its own right. It is the core of many psychopathological states and causes long-term suffering for many individuals. Anxiety is also an important confounding factor in studies of other psychopathological states like depression, or obsessive–compulsive neurosis, since anxiety is often present and may be considered a non-specific factor in these disorders. To understand what changes, if any, specifically relate to other emotional states and traits, it is important to disentangle the physiological and endocrinological changes that are associated with anxiety itself (Mathew, Ho, Taylor and Semchuk, 1981a).

Ever since Cannon's (1914) research, catecholamines have been the subject of study for investigations of fear and anxiety. Subsequently, catecholamines have been conceived of both as consequences and determinants of emotions. It has been suggested that anxiety is associated with a relatively greater increase in adrenaline than noradrenaline, and that anger produces a relatively greater increase in noradrenaline than adrenaline (Ax, 1953; Funkenstein, 1956). This specificity notion relating circumscribed excretion patterns to specific emotions has received some support in studies where anger and anxiety have been induced and physiological or neuroendocrine responses monitored (Ax, 1953; Funkenstein, 1956). In this context, the specificity notion may be contrasted with the general idea that catecholamines are determined not by the quality but by the intensity of emotional feelings. In particular, Frankenhaeuser (cf. 1975) has argued that emotional intensity is the prime determinant of adrenaline excretion. Similarly, Levi (1975) induced both positive and negative emotions and found that both were associated with increased catecholamine excretion, suggesting that change in catecholamine excretion is non-specific with respect to emotional quality and is determined by emotional intensity. The specificity notion has also been challenged by several studies that have used adrenaline and noradrenaline infusions to produce emotions (Mathew, Ho, Francis, Taylor and Weinman, 1982). These do not provide equivocal support for the notion that an increase in circulating adrenaline is synonymous with the experience of anxiety, nor does infusion of noradrenaline produce anger. In summary, an increase in anxiety may be a sufficient but not a necessary antecedent of increased adrenaline excretion. Conversely, an increase in adrenaline is not sufficient to produce anxiety but may be necessary.

Generally, clinical anxiety seems to be associated with increased cardio-vascular and neuroendocrine activation (Lader, 1983). For example, individuals with simple phobias react with an increase in HR when exposed to feared cues, but with an HR deceleration when exposed to neutral cues (Fredrikson, 1981). Heart rate acceleration is associaed with the defence reflex (Sokolov, 1963), whereas HR deceleration is associated with attention and the orienting response (Turpin, 1983). In addition, cephalic and finger pulse volumes decrease in phobics during exposure to feared cues (Hare, 1973). These acute changes in physiological activation could be interpreted to be examples of the defence reflex (Sokolov, 1963). Consistent with this, increases in cortisol and catecholamine excretion (Fredrikson *et al.*, 1985c; Nesse, Cameron, Buda, McCann, Curtis and Huber-Smith, 1985b), changes of a more long-term nature, are also found in phobics during fear. Catecholamine excretion seems to be increased not only in phobics but also in patients with anxiety states. For example, Dajas, Nin and Barbeite (1986) observed higher resting urinary noradrenaline excretion in patients with panic anxiety than in phobics. Levels in both patient groups were higher than in normal controls. Also Nesse *et al.* (1985a) reported higher night-time, but not daytime, plasma adrenaline and noadrenaline levels in panic-anxiety patients without mitral valve prolapse (MVP) compared to levels in controls. Panic-anxiety patients with MVP did not differ significantly from normals. Treatment with imipramine, alpha- or beta-blockers in ten patients significantly reduced anxiety levels, but a reduction in plasma catecholamines was, unfortunately, not significant.

Dental phobics compared to control patients during exposure to the phobic situation demonstrated increased plasma adrenaline but not noradrenaline levels (Edmonson, Roscoe and Vickers, 1972). Diazepam therapy lowered these levels. Wyatt, Portnoy, Kupfer, Snyder and Engelman (1971) observed higher levels of adrenaline and noradrenaline in hospitalized patients (suffering from anxiety and depression) than in a control group. There was a significant correlation between nurse-rated anxiety and plasma catecholamine concentrations. However, not all studies have been able to show a linear association between anxiety and catecholamines. This raises the questions as to what extent peripheral catecholamines determine the experience of anxiety, and to what extent they are specific in the experience of anxiety or reflect the intensity of the emotion rather than its quality.

THE EXPERIENCE OF ANXIETY AND NEUROENDOCRINE ACTIVATION

Several symptoms experienced during anxiety mimic the effects of SNS stimulation in normals. These include enhanced chronotropic (rate) and inotropic (contractility) effects on the heart, sweating, shortness of breath and tremor.

The autonomic nervous system, the endocrine system and their interaction are complex, and there are several possible ways to account for individual differences in the experience of anxiety. First, efferent sympathetic drive may be increased in highly anxious individuals and increase circulating catecholamines. For adrenaline, this seems to be the only route, since circulating adrenaline is produced by the adrenal medulla. However, there may be factors other than increased SNS activity (e.g. tumours) that lead to increased levels of adrenaline. For noradrenaline, the picture is more complex. If there is an increased sympathetic drive, this would lead to an overflow of catecholamines from the synaptic cleft into the capillaries. Noradrenaline is inactivated by catechol-*o*-methyl transferase (COMT). Theoretically, if inactivation is slower in anxious than in non-anxious individuals, noradrenaline overflow might be higher. Noradrenaline is subject to re-uptake by the presynaptic nerve ending via a noradrenaline-dependent active transport process. Thus, if re-uptake is diminished, this would also produce increased noradrenaline in the synaptic cleft and higher overflow in anxious than in non-anxious patients. There is also a feedback mechanism such that the presynaptic membrane of adrenergic fibres contains alpha-receptors. These respond to noradrenaline in the synaptic cleft and inhibit release of more noradrenaline. This mechanism may also be offset in anxious patients. Finally, adrenergic receptors may be more sensitive in anxious than in non-anxious individuals.

The assumption that peripheral physiological and endocrinological factors influence the experience of anxiety or mimic central processes operating in the brain has empirical support. Generally, an interpretation in terms of increased stimulation of the beta-adrenergic system in anxiety seems to be favoured by the data. However, the balance between sympathetic outflow, receptor sensitivity and catecholamine elimination may depend on or interact with type of anxiety.

Nesse, Cameron, Curtis, McCann and Huber-Smith (1984) observed higher resting HR, catecholamines, cortisol and growth hormone in patients with panic attacks than in controls. Patients had a decreased HR response to isoproterenol (a potent beta-adrenergic stimulator) compared to controls. These data support the notion that beta-adrenergic stimulation is increased and receptor sensitivity decreased in patients with panic attacks. Nesse *et al.* (1984) pointed out that parasympathetic activity may also be altered in patients with panic attacks, accounting for the increased HR observed. They also noted that decreased receptor sensitivity (magnitude) or receptor down-regulation (number) may result from an initially increased beta-adrenergic drive resulting from anxiety, rather than being primary to anxiety problems. Lima and Turner (1983) reached a similar conclusion based on their work on isoproterenol-stimulated cyclic adenosine monophosphate (cAMP), since in anxiety patients cAMP production was lower than in normal controls. Hormones act as an extracellular first messenger system and are secreted into the bloodstream and carried to all cells in the body. At the target organ, the hormones bind to specific receptors and produce a second intracellular messenger: cAMP. Catecholamines activate cAMP. Thus, all other things being equal, lower cAMP indicates a smaller effect at the target organ. However, this evidence of decreased receptor sensitivity possibly mediated by cAMP may be specific to patients with panic anxiety.

Fredrikson, Tuomisto, Gunnarsson, Sundin and Mörlin (1987) found that beta-blockade decreased resting HR relatively more in blood and mutilation phobics than in animal phobics. They suggested two possible explanations. Given that a similar SNS drive was present in both phobic groups, beta-adrenoceptors may have been sensitized in blood phobics. Thus, the effect of the blockade would be more pronounced due to initially sensitized receptors. However, given that receptor sensitivity is similar in the two groups, the data suggest an increased cardiac sympathetic *and* parasympathetic drive. When the beta-adrenoceptors are blocked, the initially heightened parasympathetic drive is left unbalanced, causing a greater drop in HR in this group than in animal phobics. Hence, there may be a complex interaction between, for example, receptor sensitivity and type of anxiety-related state.

With respect to inactivation factors, Mathew, Ho, Kralik, Taylor and Claghorn (1980a) found a negative correlation between COMT activity and measures of trait anxiety in anxious patients, but not in non-anxious controls. Enzyme activity did not differ between the two groups, making it unlikely that inactivation of catecholamines occurs at a slower rate in anxious patients than in normal controls. It is possible that this mechanism may operate within the anxiety disorders, since Mathew *et al* (1980a) observed a negative correlation between anxiety and COMT only in patients with anxiety problems but no correlation between COMT and anxiety in normals. However, Mathew *et al.* (1980b) were not able to replicate this finding in a subsequent study. In addition, relaxation treatment that reduced adrenaline and noradrenaline had no effect on COMT. Thus, important factors that modify COMT activity in anxiety probably exist and there is no simple relation between COMT and the experience of anxiety.

ANXIETY AND CORTISOL

Studies relating cortisol and anxiety are more sparse than those on catecholamines and anxiety, particularly if restricted to clinical studies. It can be argued that catecholamines are target responses associated with the production of symptoms such as tremor and palpitations. Cortisol, however, has mainly been considered as the index response for anxiety. Cortisol excretion is an interesting parameter in several psychopathological states, since in normal human subjects it has been related to personal control over environmental stress (cf. Frankenhaeuser, 1975) and to the experience of distress (Mason, 1975). Thus, if different psychopathological states are associated with feelings of distress and lack of control, cortisol would be expected to increase. Miyabo, Asato and Mizushima (1979) studied neurotic patients during and after a mirror drawing test and found an increase which was not present in normal controls. Further support is provided by the many studies relating depressive states and cortisol to each other (for a review see Lader, 1983).

Some studies, however, have shown increased levels of plasma cortisol during sexual arousal, which may question the specific relationship between distress and cortisol (Brown and Heninger, 1975). Sexual arousal is generally associated with pleasure, yet cortisol levels increase during this state. This indicates that cortisol excretion may be linked to emotional intensity, regardless of quality. However, several studies in both humans and animals have indicated that the cortisol response may uniquely reflect degree of control. Personal control over environmental stressors (Frankenhaeuser, 1975) or even personal control over feelings (Mason, 1975; Miyabo et al., 1979) have been found to attenuate cortisol excretion compared to feelings of no control. For example, Frankenhaeuser (1979) observed attenuation of cortisol excretion during a self-paced but not during an externally paced reaction-time task. Differences in cortisol levels mirrored differences in subjective ratings of distress. Similarly, unemployed individuals who have a sense of no control and feel helpless excrete more cortisol after being laid off than when they were employed (Arnetz et al., 1987).

It should be noted that not all studies have demonstrated an association between distress ratings and cortisol excretion. Price, Thaler and Mason (1977) found no relation between pre-operative anxiety and cortisol excretion in normal healthy volunteers. Rosenbaum et al. (1983) collected 24-h urine specimens for determination of urinary free cortisol and found no differences between highly anxious outpatients and controls. In contrast, Nesse, Curtis, Thyer, McCann, Huber-Smith and Knopf (1985b) and Fredrikson et al. (1985c) both studied patients with specific phobias and observed higher levels of cortisol excretion in phobics confronted by their phobic object when compared to resting cortisol levels (Nesse et al., 1985b) or cortisol levels in response to neutral stimulation (Fredrikson et al., 1985c). Recently, Fredrikson, Gunnarsson, Frankenhaeuser, Klein, Lindgren and Westermark (submitted, a) observed that public compared to private performance caused higher ratings of distress and also increased urinary cortisol both in anxious and non-anxious string-musicians. It appears that with increased levels of stimulation, differences between patients and controls (Miyabo et al., 1979) become more evident.

Thyer and Matthews (1986) reported a case study where prolonged phobic anxiety increased beta-endorphins. This is an interesting observation, the value of which is unclear. The authors interpret the finding as supporting the hypothesis that a possible mechanism underlying exposure therapy may exist and would involve the 'homeostatic endorphinergic response to stress'. However, stimuli that release beta-endorphins also release ACTH (Ganong, 1983).

Cortisol is increased in phobic anxiety (Fredrikson *et al.*, 1985c; Nesse *et al.*, 1985b), suggesting higher ACTH levels. Thus, the findings of Thyer and Matthews (1986) are consistent with previous reports and may suggest that the beta-endorphin effect is not independent of other catabolic hormonal effects. It is difficult, therefore, to disentangle the independent contribution of beta-endorphin from other hormonal effects, since there is a pharmacological/physiological dependency in the brain.

Most studies relating emotions to bodily changes have involved negative emotional states like anxiety, fear or apprehension and have related them to neuroendocrine and cardiovascular changes. The vast majority of studies on anxiety and peripheral neuroendocrine changes have been undertaken using normal healthy individuals. The underlying assumption has been that anxiety in patients is quantitatively but not qualitatively different from anxiety in the normal population (Lader, 1983). However, this may not be the case (cf. Boulenger and Uhde, 1982; Klein, 1980), and the monitoring of peripheral physiological and endocrinological changes in anxiety patients and phobics may help to characterize qualitative as well as quantitative differences between normal and pathological anxiety. In order to achieve this, data across different laboratories have to be compared. This necessitates the use of well-defined diagnostic criteria such as those provided by the *Diagnostic and Statistical Manual of Mental Disorders* (3rd edn; American Psychiatric Association, 1980).

TREATMENT OF ANXIETY AND NEUROENDOCRINE ACTIVATION

Mathew, Ho, Kralik, Taylor, Semchuk, Weinman and Claghorn (1980b) studied the endocrine effects of behavioural treatment in patients with generalized anxiety. They observed decreased levels of anxiety, adrenaline, noradrenaline and monoamine oxidase after 4 weeks of biofeedback-assisted relaxation and home practice with taped relaxation instructions. No differences between pre- and post-test catecholamines were observed in healthy controls. However, no correlations were found between anxiety scores and biochemical measures. The authors voice a caution in attributing the decreased catecholamine levels to decreased anxiety. Instead they state that it cannot be ruled out that the reductions may have been due to diminished reactivity to venipuncture (used to obtain the blood samples). Another possibility, not discussed by Mathew *et al.* (1981b), is that factors present in the patient group but not in the control group may have acted to reduce catecholamine excretion in patients only. First, the biochemical changes may have been due not to relaxation but to nonspecific factors related to treatment. Second, patients had higher values during pre-treatment and the regression towards the mean would have been greater in patients than in controls. Third, patients were familiarized with the hospital environment during relaxation training, whereas the controls did not visit the hospital except for pre- and post-testing. Since catecholamine levels may increase in novel situations (Mason, 1975), another possible explanation is that patients habituated to environmental cues whereas controls did not. Indeed, Jones, Hamilton and Reid (1979) found that subjects 'familiar with research routines' had lower plasma catecholamine levels than less experienced subjects. This further supports the view that non-specific factors may have influenced the decrease in catecholamines in the patient group. In short, the study by Mathew *et al.* (1981b) lacked a patient control group given placebo treatment.

This issue has been examined in a recently completed study (Gunnarsson and Fredrikson, 1987) designed to control for non-specific and familiarization factors, which included a treatment group and a placebo-control group. The two groups consisted of anxious string musicians. In the experimental group, eight musicians were given active treatment for 12 sessions (relaxation, guided imagery), whereas the placebo group were seen for discussions only. Heart rate, and adrenaline, noradrenaline and cortisol excretion during public performance in these musicians were compared before and after treatment. The experimental group showed significantly lower HR, anxiety ratings and cortisol arousal after treatment, whereas catecholamines did not differ as a function of treatment in the experimental or the control group. Admittedly, the sample was small and the failure to observe treatment effects on catecholamine excretion may reflect this. However, the data from Gunnarsson and Fredrikson (1987) may suggest that HR is a more sensitive physiological index of anxiety than are measures of catecholamines. This conclusion was also drawn by Nesse *et al.* (1985b), who found HR to be most influenced by differences in anxiety, more so than neuroendocrine variables. Moreover, Fredrikson *et al.* (submitted, a), made the same observation studying anxious and non-anxious string musicians during public and private performances. They observed a greater increase in HR during public but not private performance in anxious compared to non-anxious individuals, whereas catecholamine and cortisol levels increased similarly in the two groups from private to public performance. By and large, correlations between ratings of distress and effort on the one hand, and neuroendocrine or cardiovascular activation on the other are low. Thus, both this recent study and that of Mathew *et al.* (1981b) indicate that the relationship between anxiety and neuroendocrine activation may be non-linear. Bandura, Taylor, Williams, Mefford and Barchas (1985) recently suggested a plausible mechanism that may influence the effect of anxiety on catecholamines, namely perceived self-efficacy. They demonstrated that increased self-efficacy induced through modelling in phobics resulted in low levels of adrenaline and noradrenaline during interaction with a phobic object. Total lack of self-efficacy did not result in any increase in plasma catecholamines, whereas moderate self-efficacy resulted in substantial increases in catecholamines. These data are similar to other studies (cf. Bohlin, Eliasson, Hjemdahl, Klein, Fredrikson and Frankenhaeuser, 1986) that have shown that control gained with effort results in higher HR and BP than no control or control gained without effort. Thus, perceived self-efficacy or amount of effort devoted to a task may significantly influence the pattern of cardiovascular and neuroendocrine changes, and account for some of the non-linearity between amount of anxiety and physiological activation.

STRESS AND PATHOPHYSIOLOGY

Stress as synonymous with physiological or neuroendocrine activation has been studied in many diseases. Physiological measures of stress have ranged from global to specific and sometimes have focused on the presumed mechanisms of the illness. To give just a few examples, stress reactions have been studied in patients with peptic ulcers, asthma and headache (see Weiner, 1977, for a review). Physiological measures have included airway resistance during psychological challenge in asthmatics, and levels of muscular and vascular activity in headache sufferers (Weiner, 1977). Studies have used both epidemiological and experimental approaches. For example, Harburg, Erfurt, Hauenstein, Chape, Schull and Schork (1973) used an epidemiological approach and demonstrated that the incidence of high BP was greater in so-called 'high-stress areas', characterized by poverty and high mobility, than in more stable and richer areas. Henry and Stephens (1977) used an experimental approach and demonstrated in animals that overcrowding leads to high BP. Within epidemiological approaches, individual factors thought to buffer the effect of the environment have also been studied. Gentry, Chesney, Gary, Hall and Harburg (1982) found that the individual factor 'anger expression style' interacted with the environmental factor 'job-demand' in producing high BP. At risk of overgeneralization, it could be said that epidemiologists relate situational influences to disease end-points, whereas psychophysiologists relate situational influences to physiological response patterns. The relationship between the response patterns and disease are studied in medicine and may reveal the physiological mechanisms of the disease. Behavioural medicine encompasses all of these.

BEHAVIOURAL MEDICINE AND ESSENTIAL HYPERTENSION

The mechanism through which psychosocial stimuli may influence disease development will be exemplified by cardiovascular diseases for several reasons. First, different cardiovascular diseases are the leading cause of death in many countries. Second, there are plausible mechanisms that potentially could mediate the influence of the brain on the body and the cardiovascular system. Third, there is a relatively rich literature relating psychological and behavioural factors to physiological changes of potential importance for the development of cardiovascular disease. Fourth, it is possible to relate cardiovascular and neuroendocrine activity to established risk factors for disease.

There are several physiological and biochemical reactions associated with 'stress' that may be of relevance for the development of cardiovascular disease. For example, exaggerated HR and BP activation along with enhanced triglycerides, catecholamine and cortisol excretion, have all been suggested to initialize or accelerate the development of cardiovascular disease. Thus, it is important to focus on both physiological and biochemical measures and their relation to individual differences to understand the bodily mechanisms through which situational factors eventually translate into disease end-points. This is particularly important, since hypertension is most likely to be a multifactorial disorder and the pathophysiological mechanisms may differ according to the severity or duration of the disease (Page, 1977). High BP has been related to genetic predisposition (Ayman and Goldshine, 1938), excessive salt intake (Dahl, 1977), the autonomic nervous system (Goldstein, 1981, 1983), the renin–angiotensin–aldosterone system (Laragh, Bear, Brunner, Bühler, Sealy and Vaughn, 1976), arterial vascular smooth-muscle reactivity (Page, 1977), personality traits (Harrell, 1980; Schalling, 1985) and 'stress' (Henry and Stephens, 1977; Shapiro et al., 1979). Vascular (cf. Folkow, 1982; Sivertsson, 1970), neurogenic (Julius, 1976) and renal factors (Guyton et al., 1974) have all been ascribed primary pathophysiological importance.

BEHAVIOURAL FACTORS IN HYPERTENSION

Folkow (1982) has suggested that the repeated elicitation of the defence reaction (Hilton, 1975), and the episodes of increased cardiac output associated with it, translate into sustained hypertension by causing vascular hypertrophy in genetically 'susceptible' or 'hyper-reactive' individuals. Julius (1976) claims that sympathetic medullary activation through behavioural factors influences cardiac and vascular activity and also the renin–angiotensin–aldosterone system to increase BP (cf. Esler et al., 1977). Guyton et al. (1974) emphasize the influence of the kidneys in the long-term regulation of BP, and maintain that hypertension must be accompanied by a change in the kidney 'set point' via the blood volume and atrial receptors. Thus, even though theories emphasize different pathophysiological mechanisms, a common denominator is found in the fact that behavioural factors can influence most of the suggested mechanisms through sympathetic and adrenomedullary activation. This and similar observations have promoted a long-standing interest in behavioural and emotional influences on BP (cf. Surwit, Williams and Shapiro, 1982) and possible mechanisms associated with the development of high BP.

The epidemiology and natural history of hypertension is reviewed elsewhere in this volume (see Chapter 15). To briefly summarize, EHT increases the risk of ischaemic heart disease, myocardial infarction and stroke (Alderman, 1980;

Hypertension Detection and Follow-up Program Cooperative Group, 1979). Blood pressure is normally distributed in the population, and hence there are no naturally occurring 'set points' defining essential (or primary or sustained) hypertension (EHT) or borderline hypertension (BHT) (Pickering, 1961). The World Health Organization (WHO, 1978) defines EHT as systolic BP (SBP) >160 mmHg or diastolic BP (DBP) >95 mmHg or both, measured after 5 min of supine rest, and BHT as 140 < SBP < 160 mmHg or 90 < DBP < 95 mmHg. The US Department of Health and Human Services (1984) recently proposed a scheme in which mild hypertension is defined as 90–104 mmHg DBP, regardless of SBP. In the present chapter, the WHO definitions will be used when EHT and BHT are referred to.

HAEMODYNAMICS IN ESSENTIAL HYPERTENSION

Men before the age of 50 years generally have higher BP than women, whereas this is reversed after the age of 50. Even though exceptions exist (cf. Julius and Conway, 1968; Safar, Weiss, Levenson, London and Milliez, 1973), there seems to be a haemodynamic difference between EHT and BHT (Conway *et al.*, 1982). Essential hypertension is usually characterized by an increased systemic vascular resistance and a normal cardiac output, whereas in BHT the cardiac output is usually increased (hyperkinetic) in relation to the metabolic needs and the systemic resistance is within normal limits. This suggests circulatory dysregulation, since arterial baroreceptors (Sleight, 1980) normally tend to decrease systemic vascular resistance in response to an increased BP. Lund-Johansen (1967, 1977) followed BHT patients over a 10-year period. He observed that initially BP was maintained by an increased cardiac output, but that 10 years later the high BP was maintained by an increased vascular resistance, while the cardiac output had returned to a normal level.

Discussions on the role of behavioural factors in the development of hypertension have (cf. Shapiro *et al.*, 1979), emphasized both situational and individual influences and their interaction. Factors related to individual differences in cardiovascular and neuroendocrine reactivity to behavioural challenge have attracted particular interest (Krantz and Manuck, 1984).

SITUATIONAL AND INDIVIDUAL INFLUENCES

Situational influences that may contribute to the development of hypertension include differences between and within societies (cf. Stamler, Berkson, Lindberg, Miller, Stamler and Collette, 1967), socio-economic change (Guttman and Benson, 1971), and work-related factors such as decision latitude and job demands (Cobb and Rose, 1973; Theorell, Knox, Svensoon and Waller, 1985).

Starting with Alexander (1939) and Dunbar (1943), there is a long tradition of investigations seeking to relate enduring personality traits to the development of hypertension. By and large, the literature on personality and BP has not presented a consistent picture relating specific personality traits to the development of hypertension (for summaries see Chapter 15; Diamond, 1980; Harrel, 1980; Krantz and Manuck, 1984; Weiner, 1977), with the possible exception of introverted anger (Diamond, 1982; Dimsdale, Pierce, Schoenfeld, Brown, Zusman and Graham, 1986; Esler et al., 1977; Schalling, 1985; Schneider, Egan, Johnson, Drobuy and Julius, 1986), which is possibly linked to high renin hypertension (Perini, Rauchfleisch and Buhler, 1985; Thailer, Friedman, Harshfield and Pickering, 1985). However, introverted anger may not be a personality trait but rather an example of a coping response which interacts with situational influences (Gentry et al., 1982).

CARDIOVASCULAR REACTIVITY

Excessive SNS activity has been implicated in the development of hypertension, both in animal (Hallbäck and Folkow, 1974) and human studies. Goldstein (1981, 1983) reviewed studies on plasma catecholamines in EHT and demonstrated that noradrenaline was elevated among young BHT patients and that adrenaline was elevated in all age groups. Differences between hypertensives and normotensives were more apparent during orthostatic and exercise stress than resting conditions. Only a few studies have included measures of catecholamines during behavioural challenge and these have not been conclusive, since some studies have demonstrated hypertensive–normotensive differences, whereas others have not (Goldstein, 1981, 1983). In some studies excessive BP and HR reactivity among hypertensives have been observed in spite of no differences in neuroendocrine activation (cf. Eliasson, 1984; Fredrikson et al., 1985b). This suggests that the increased cardiovascular responsivity may not be an example of generalized SNS activation but specific to the cardiovascular system. This suggestion is further strengthened by the fact that studies which have sampled cortisol in hypertensives and normotensives often have been unable to detect differences even in circumstances where cardiovascular activation clearly was increased in hypertensives (cf. Bohlin et al., 1986; Sapira, Scheib, Moriarty and Shapiro, 1971; Sullivan et al., 1981). Similar results have been obtained when cardiovascular and electrodermal reactions have been compared between hypertensives and normotensives during 'stress'. It is possible that during the very early phase of the development of high BP, both cardiovascular and neuroendocrine responsivity is increased. Fredrikson, Tuomisto, Bergman-Losman and Frankenhaeuser (in preparation) observed increased neuroendocrine and cardiovascular responsivity to mental stress in a normotensive group with hypertensive parents compared to normotensive offspring of normotensive parents. Collins, Baer and Bourianoff (1981) have suggested that the defence reaction was more easily elicited in normotensives with a positive family history than in those with a negative family history. They studied orienting behaviour during a vigilance task and found that subjects with a positive family history showed slower skin resistance habituation and an HR increase compared to a decrease in subjects with a negative family history.

Thus, the data suggest that it is important to study both cardiovascular and neuroendocrine reactions. To the extent that differences in cardiovascular activation are genetically determined, reactions during challenge rather than resting conditions may be more relevant. In fact, Theorell, de Faire, Schalling, Adamson and Askerold (1979) showed that genetic influences on the cardiovascular system during rest are small but increase substantially during stress. This underscores the importance of cardiovascular reactivity in evaluating mechanisms and early markers for disease.

Hines and Brown (1932) observed a higher cardiovascular reactivity to the cold pressor test (the hand immersed in +4 °C water) in patients with EHT than in normotensive controls. They suggested that enhanced reactivity would predict subsequent development of hypertension and be associated with a faster rate of development of high BP. Thus, the amplitude of the cardiovascular response was thought to be of pathophysiological importance. Other authors have suggested that the recovery (return to base-level) of the cardiovascular response is of significance, in that a slow recovery may be associated with hypertension (Brod, 1971). Others again (Engel, 1983) have suggested that the patterning of several physiological responses is of pathophysiological importance and that hypertension is associated with a less flexible (more stereotyped) response pattern than normal BP.

CAUSE, CONSEQUENCE OR CORRELATE?

Prospective data relating increased cardiovascular reactivity to the development of EHT are not consistent (Harlan, Osborne and Graybiel, 1964; Wood, Sheps, Elveback and Schringer). Some data suggest that increased cardiovascular reactivity observed under laboratory conditions may predict BP levels (Steptoe, Melville and Ross, 1983) and responsivity (Matthews, Manuck and Saab, 1986) in real-life conditions. Thus, an increased reactivity to certain laboratory stressors may at least be interpreted as a sign of an increased cardiovascular load under everyday conditions. This load in turn is associated with complications from hypertension (Devereaux et al., 1983; Perloff, Sokolow and Cowan, 1983).

Lacking confirmatory or disconfirmatory prospective data, we (Fredrikson and Matthews, submitted) recently reviewed all relevant case/control studies published between 1932 and 1985 to examine whether an increased cardiovascular reactivity characterized patients with EHT. It has been pointed out that high BP may result in increased cardiovascular reactivity since secondary adaptations occur, like structural vascular changes, resetting of arterial baroreceptors and change in cardiac performance. These changes are less likely in

BHT patients than in patients with EHT, and are unlikely in normotensive offspring of hypertensives. Thus, we included these groups as well. We reviewed published studies that reported cardiovascular reactivity to behavioural, psychological or mental tasks but excluded physiological or pharmacological manipulations (dynamic and static exercise tests, orthostatic tests, infusion studies, etc). The aim was to learn how individual and situational factors interact to eventually produce increased cardiovascular reactivity in patients with EHT or BHT, and in normotensive offspring of hypertensives. This was obtained by pooling data from different studies using samples with different characteristics and a variety of stressors. The dependent measures, BP and HR, are probably compatible across different laboratories. We used meta-analytical methods to compare the published data pooled from the several independent studies.

Patients with EHT or BHT and normotensives with a positive family history were compared to controls with respect to whether cardiovascular reactivity was increased averaged over (1) all tasks, (2) tasks that required active behaviour or (3) tasks of a more passive nature. Fredrikson and Matthews (submitted) observed the following pattern: averaged across all tasks, patients with EHT or BHT and normotensive offspring of hypertensives showed an increased systolic BP reactivity when compared to controls. Parents with EHT or BHT also evidenced an increased diastolic BP reactivity. Heart rate reactivity was higher only in the BHT group.

This pattern interacted with task demands such that EHT patients showed significantly greater BP but not HR reactivity both to tasks that required behavioural activity and to tasks of a more passive nature. Borderline hypertensives and normotensive offspring to hypertensives, however, exhibited significantly greater BP and HR responses only to stressors that required an active behavioural response. In response to stressors of a more passive nature and to the cold pressor test, they did not exhibit hyper-reactivity. Since reactivity differences are more easily observed with tasks requiring an active response, this may help to explain why the cold pressor test (a passive stressor) has met with limited success in predicting subsequent development of high BP. The meta-analytic study (Fredrikson and Matthews, submitted) raises two important questions: (1) what is the pathophysiological role of a behaviourally induced cardiovascular hyper-reactivity and (2) what are its psychological and/or physiological mechanisms?

MECHANISMS OF CARDIOVASCULAR REACTIVITY

The data are compatible with the hypothesis put forward by Folkow (1982; Folkow and Hallbäck, 1977) and von Eiff (1970, 1984) that an increased cardiovascular reactivity of central origin initiates or accelerates the development of hypertension. Increased cardiovascular reactivity was observed predominantly in the borderline phase of hypertension and in response to active challenge. This suggests that increased cardiovascular reactivity is not merely an effect of secondary adaptations stemming from an already increased BP, but is primary to the disease and may have a pathophysiological role in the development of hypertension. In addition, normotensive subjects with a positive family history of hypertension, in whom secondary adaptations are unlikely, show increased cardiovascular reactivity, particularly in response to active challenge. This implies CNS involvement, since behavioural factors modify the cardiovascular response. The stressors that have been used differ on dimensions other than the active/passive one and any one of these dimensions may potentially explain the differences in reactivity. However, when a comparison was made in which care was taken that the tasks differed only in the active/passive dimension (Fredrikson, submitted), reactivity differences between patients and controls were still evident in systolic BP during active but not passive challenge. This suggests that the activity dimension is a modulator of BP reactivity *per se*, and that it interacts with disease status. Several other modulators of cardiovascular reactivity exist. For example intralymphocytic sodium content (Borghi, Costa, Boschi, Mussi and Ambrosini, 1986) affects cardiovascular reactivity. Similarly, both sodium intake and retention may play a role in modulating cardiovascular reactivity to stress. Ambrosini and co-workers (Ambrosini *et al.*, 1981; Ambrosini, Costa, Borghi, Boschi and Mussi, 1986; Borghi *et al.*, 1986) have shown that the pressor response in BHT patients and in normotensives with a positive family history of hypertension is related to lymphocytic sodium concentrations. In addition, in a group of initially borderline hypertensive subjects, only those with high intralymphocytic sodium developed EHT (Borghi *et al.*, 1986). Interestingly, Light, Koepke, Obrist and Willis (1983) demonstrated that elevated cardiovascular reactivity during a reaction-time task was associated with increased sodium retention in BHT subjects and in normotensive offspring of hypertensive patients. Anderson, Kearns and Better (1983) demonstrated in dogs that an increased sodium load was required if avoidance conditioning were to raise BP. In dogs with normal sodium levels, stress did not produce an increase in BP. Furthermore, during behavioural challenge, a greater renal vasoconstriction was observed in BHT subjects and in normotensives with a positive family history compared to normotensive controls (Brod, Fencl, Hejl and Jirka, 1959; Hollenberg, Williams and Adams, 1981). This was accompanied by abnormal responses of plasma renin activity, angiotensin II and aldosterone (Hollenberg *et al.*, 1981). Since cortisol did not change differentially, it is unlikely that the pituitary–adrenal axis was involved but rather that the abnormal renal responses were induced directly by angiotensin formation. Regardless of the mechanism, renal vasoconstriction together with aldosterone may affect sodium balance and subsequently affect cardiovascular reactivity to behavioural challenge.

In addition to an increased intralymphocytic sodium content, increased cardiovascular reactivity may be due to other factors such as increased afferent sensory input, altered central modulation, increased efferent outflow, or local factors such as differences in alpha- or beta-receptor density or sensitivity, or in vascular structure.

Central processes may influence the activity of cardiovascular regulatory centres and this has been associated with the development of experimentally produced hypertension in animals (see Brody, Haywood and Touw, 1980, for a review). One example is the theory that the defence reaction is more easily elicited in pre-hypertensives, and that this contributes to the development of EHT (von Eiff, 1970; Folkow, 1982). Another example is Julius's (1976) observation of altered central regulation of the autonomic nervous system in BHT. The question is how behavioural factors may influence these processes. Some theories have stressed the role of personality factors (Diamond, 1982), and recently Jorgensen and Houston (1986) reported that individuals unwilling to admit feelings of agression displayed increased BP reactivity compared with controls. It has also been suggested that other centrally initiated factors associated with emotions, such as anger and social (in)competence (Keane, Martin, Berler, Wooten, Fleece and Williams, 1982; Manuck, Morrison, Bellack and Polfrone, 1984), coping patterns (Hentry *et al.*, 1982; Henry and Stephens, 1977) and social position (Kaplan *et al.*, 1983) may modify cardiovascular reactivity. Some authors (Brody *et al.*, 1980; Jorgensen and Houston, 1986) have argued that the final common pathway for emotional influences is via limbic structures which exert an influence on SNS or cardiovascular regulatory structures. Others have proposed that endogenous opiate peptides exert an inhibitory influence on SNS reactivity to stress, and that this may be lacking in persons at risk of developing EHT (McCubbin, Surwit and Williams, 1985). Incidentally, the opioid system is involved in pain reduction, and if this mechanism is suboptimal in hypertension, and also if the BP increase reduces pain, it is conceivable that a BP increase may be intrinsically more reinforcing (pain reducing) in hypertensives than in normotensive persons. This was demonstrated to be the case in animals (Dworkin, Filewich, Miller, Craigwyle and Pickering, 1979).

With respect to efferent factors, Wallin, Delins and Hagbarth (1973) have concluded, on the basis of microneurography, that SNS outflow is similar in patients with EHT and in normotensive individuals. A similar conclusion was drawn by Goldstein (1981, 1983) in his reviews of plasma catecholamines in hypertension. Goldstein also claimed that a possible exception to this were young men with BHT, in whom catecholamine reactivity may be increased. In most of the studies summarized by Goldstein, venous estimates of plasma catecholamines were used. Folkow *et al.* (1983) have voiced a word of caution in interpreting catecholamine concentrations in venous samples, and argue that venous samples may not reflect arterial catecholamines properly but may underestimate sympathetic influences on the cardiovascular system. Hjemdahl *et al.* (1986) demonstrated that this was indeed the case by comparing catecholamines in venous and arterial samples. The effects of adrenaline infusions on cardiovascular responsivity and on cAMP (mediated by beta-2-adrenoceptor activation) was similar in BHT subjects and normotensives. Thus, alpha- and beta-adrenoceptor sensitivity and density do not seem to differ between hypertensives and normotensives. However, local vascular factors may be different (Zweifler and Nicholls, 1982) and it has been reported that maximal vasodilatation is less pronounced in young men with BP elevations than in young men with normal BP (Sivertsson, Sannerstedt and Lundgren, 1976). A limited vasodilatory capacity in the forearm has also been demonstrated in young men with a positive family history of hypertension. This suggests structural changes (in hypertrophy) in the resistance vessels (Takeshita, Imaizumi, Ashihara, Yamamoto, Hoka and Nakamura, 1982).

MODULATORS OF CARDIOVASCULAR REACTIVITY

The data indicate that cardiovascular reactivity is increased in patients with hypertension and in subjects with a positive family history of hypertension, although not all individual studies have always been positive. This suggests the presence of a set of important modulators which amplify or buffer the individual 'stress response'. Thus, individual modulating factors of various types may be worth studying. For example, personal control is generally believed to attenuate cardiovascular reactivity (cf. Frankenhaeuser, 1975), but recently Bohlin *et al.* (1986) demonstrated that this buffering influence is not present in BHT. Other factors known to influence cardiovascular reactivity, such as salt intake (Ambrosini *et al.*, 1981; Light *et al.*, 1983), smoking (Dembroski and MacDougall, 1986), caffeine (Lane and Williams, 1985), teine (Henry and Stephens-Larson, 1984), and the long-term effect of exercise (Svedenhag, 1985), may also be worth studying in connection with behavioural factors, and crossed with the hypertensive/normotensive distinction.

This picture is complicated, but the joint use of biochemical and cardiovascular parameters may reveal in which individuals an increased cardiovascular and/or neuroendocrine reactivity to behavioural challenge might reflect the activity of the sympatho-adrenal system, the pituitary–cortical system, the opioid system or increased efferent activity in cardiovascular pathways only.

INDIVIDUAL RESPONSE SPECIFICITY

Even though cardiovascular reactivity is modified by situational factors, the patterning of several physiological responses may be less dependent on extrinsic factors in hypertensive than in normotensive persons. This has been termed individual response specificity (Engel, 1983), response stereotopy and symptom specificity. Given that an individual has a rigid response pattern (for example he or she always reacts with an HR increase, irrespective of type of challenge), individual response specificity may translate into symptom specificity. The first demonstration of increased response specificity in patients with hypertension was provided by Engel and Bickford (1961). They subjected female EHT patients and normotensive controls to several laboratory 'stressors', and measured systolic BP, diastolic BP, HR, respiration rate, skin conductance activity, finger–toe temperature and face temperature. To enable comparisons between groups and response systems to be made, all responses were standardized. In 15 of 20 female patients with EHT, BP made the greatest response, irrespective of the task, whereas this was true only in 5 of 20 normotensives. In addition, the numerical estimate of individual response specificity – the intraclass correlation coefficient – was higher in EHT patients than in normotensives. This general finding was replicated and extended by Fredrikson et al. (1985a). We subjected male hypertensive patients and matched normotensive controls to several stressors and recorded systolic BP, diastolic BP, HR, respiration, forearm and hand blood flow, skin conductance level and fluctuations. Replicating the results of Engel and Bickford's (1961) study, male hypertensive patients were found to be more consistent than controls, as evidenced by higher intraclass correlations. Hypertensives showed their maximum responses in BP, whereas maximum responses in normotensives were variable. Individual response specificity was greater among hypertensive patients than normotensives, both during anticipation of tasks and during actual stimulation, pointing to the possibility that hypertensives both prepare for and react to behavioural demands in a less flexible manner than do normotensives.

In Engel and Bickford's (1961) study, the greater BP reactivity observed in EHT patients might have contributed to produce higher intraclass correlations in this group than in normotensives. Consequently, Fredrikson et al. (1985a) excluded BP responses in the computation of intraclass correlations. When this was done, hypertensives still showed greater individual response specificity, indicating a more consistent ordering of responses other than BP in hypertensives than in normotensives.

To further address the question of whether intraclass correlations are independent of reactivity, beta-adrenoceptor antagonists were administered to a subgroup of hypertensive patients. Beta-adrenoceptor blockade attenuated systolic BP and HR reactivity, but failed to affect individual response specificity. Thus, individual patterns of autonomic activation are less flexible and less dependent on extrinsic factors in hypertensives than in normotensives. We (Fredrikson et al., in preparation) have recently extended this finding by showing that normotensive offspring of hypertensives show increased individual response specificity compared to offspring of normotensives. This supports the notion that increased individual response specificity is primary and not secondary to hypertension.

These data are consistent with the so-called stress–diathesis theory of hypertension (cf. Kagan and Levi, 1974). The concept is as follows. An acquired or inborn tendency to emit a consistent hierarchy of responses, individual response specificity, is a predisposing factor for the development of hypertension. When a person with a specific tendency to over-respond in a certain response system is challenged, he or she will respond in this relatively rigid manner. If such rigidity is located within the cardiovascular system, it increases the risk for hypertension compared with a more flexible response style. In order to establish its clinical relevance, longitudinal studies have to determine if consistency changes when hypertension progresses, and establish if increased consistency is predictive of high BP development.

CARDIOVASCULAR REACTIVITY AND CARDIOVASCULAR RISK

High BP is one risk factor for CHD that may be influenced by behavioural factors. The other primary risk factors include plasma cholesterol levels, nicotine abuse, diabetes mellitus and obesity (Wilhelmsen, 1984). The Type A behaviour pattern characterized by an exaggerated competitiveness, a chronic sense of time urgency and intense hostile feelings has also been established as an independent risk factor for CHD (Review Panel, 1981). An increased cardiovascular and neuroendocrine reactivity to mental stress is associated with several of these, indicating that psychosocial factors may interact with the primary CHD risk factors. In hypertension, cardiovascular reactivity, especially HR, is increased among BHT patients in response to active challenge (Fredrikson and Matthews, submitted). Smoking and behavioural stress act synergistically to increase HR reactivity in healthy subjects (Dembroski and MacDougall, 1986). The type A behaviour pattern is also associated with increased cardiovascular and neuroendocrine responsivity to behavioural challenge (Williams, Lane, Kuhn, Melosh, White and Schanberg, 1982). Diabetes mellitus and obesity have not to date been associated with heightened cardiovascular reactivity, even though some evidence to suggest this has been presented (Shapiro, 1961). In two recent studies (Fredrikson and Blumenthal, in press; Fredrikson, Lundberg, Tuomisto, Melin and Frankenhaeuser, submitted) we have presented evidence that increased plasma levels of cholesterol are associated with increased cardiovascular and neuroendocrine reactivity to behavioural challenge. Thus, it may be suggested that acute cardiovascular and neuroendocrine reactions to stress may be a final common pathway initiating or accelerating the development of atherosclerosis. Case/control studies have reported that patients with CHD show larger pressor responsivity to psychological load than healthy controls (Corse, Manuck, Cantwell, Giordani and Matthews, 1982). Keys (1980) in a prospective study found that increased BP reactivity to the 'cold pressor test' predicted subsequent development of CHD over a 23-year follow-up period. Elevated HR is also an independent predictor of atherosclerotic development in man and animals (cf. Kaplan, Manuck, Clarkson, Lusso, Taub and Miller, 1983). Furthermore, experimental studies in animals have shown that psychosocial stress in monkeys housed in unstable social groups is associated with more extensive coronary artery atherosclerosis than in monkeys in stable environments (Kaplan *et al.*, 1983). This effect was potentiated in the individual animals who were most HR reactive in response to threat (Manuck, Kaplan and Clarkson, 1983). Thus, increased HR may be associated with several risk factors for CHD and may contribute to the development of atherosclerosis. This conclusion is supported by a study conducted by Beere, Glagov and Zarins (1984). They decreased HR passively in cynomolgus monkeys through surgical ablation of the sino-atrial node and compared development of atherosclerosis in these animals with sham-operated controls. Cholesterol-fed monkeys with the lowered HR had less coronary artery atherosclerosis than controls.

CARDIOVASCULAR REACTIVITY AND CARDIOVASCULAR DISEASE

Type A individuals exhibit increased cardiovascular reactivity, yet they do not develop hypertension at a higher rate than their Type B counterparts. This indicates that an increased cardiovascular reactivity may be sufficient for development of atherosclerosis but not for high BP. However, increased reactivity may be necessary for development of high BP. Differences in disease (hypertension, CHD) development could be due to situational factors and individual factors. The latter might include increased vulnerability, different physiological response patterns or coping behaviours in 'coronary prone' and 'high BP prone' individuals, or a combination of these factors. With respect to response patterning, joint use of biochemical and physiological responses to stress has indicated that the increased cardiovascular reactivity in hypertension might represent organ specificity rather than generalized SNS activation. The conclusion regarding organ specificity in EHT may be in contrast to the cardiovascular patterning in Type A subjects (Blumenthal, Lane and Williams, 1985).

In Type A subjects, but not in Type B, it has been found that a decreased vascular resistance results from behavioural stress. This may indicate that increased cardiovascular reactivity in Type A subjects is an example of generalized SNS activation rather than of localized BP and HR responses. Individuals with high BP seldom show increased neuroendocrine reactivity to behavioural challenge (Goldstein, 1981, 1983), whereas Type A individuals do. In addition, there is no evidence that patients with high BP show increased vasodilatation in response to mental stress (Brod *et al.*, 1959; Fredrikson and Engel, 1985; Fredrikson *et al.*, 1982, 1985b). However, Type A individuals do. This increased vasodilatation may help to balance the increased cardiac output observed in response to mental stress. No direct comparison of cardiovascular reactivity in patients with hypertension and Type A individuals has been published. However, differences in vasodilatory responding may be one factor that predisposes a hyper-responsive individual to CHD or hypertension.

With respect to situational factors, Steptoe (1984) has concluded that control over environmental stressors is not a critical dimension for obtaining differences in cardiovascular reactivity between Type A and Type B individuals. Bohlin *et al.* (1986) studied subjects with BHT and normotensives with and without personal control over work pace. Control over work pace reduced cardiovascular responsivity in normotensives but did not attenuate responsivity in the BHT subjects. We (Bohlin *et al.*, 1986) interpreted these data to suggest that, at least in terms of circulatory responses, individuals with BHT may profit less than normotensives from personal control over environmental demands. Thus, these data support the conclusion that the buffering effects of personal control may be lacking in those who develop EHT.

With respect to individual differences between the coronary-prone personality and individuals prone to develop high BP, one mechanism that has been implicated is individual response specificity (Steptoe, 1984). The idea is that individuals may be programmed, genetically or through their learning history, to over-respond in a certain organ system. For example, given environmental encounters that elicit cardiovascular reactivity, individuals with high individual response specificity may develop high BP, if the specificity acts to increase BP relative to any other physiological responses. Engel and Bickford (1961) and Fredrikson *et al.* (1985a) provided support for this model with their finding that patients with EHT show a greater degree of individual response specificity than do normotensive controls. Preliminary data from our laboratory also suggest that individuals with a positive family history of hypertension but not myocardial infarction show more sterotyped responding than those with a negative family history (Fredrikson *et al*, in preparation). Future comparison between coronary-prone individuals and those with BHT must be made.

Another potentially important question is to what extent cardiovascular reactivity may be conditioned. We (Fredrikson, Danielsson, Iremark and Sundin, 1987; see also Hamm and Vaitl, 1986) subjected patients with hypertension and normotensive controls to a discriminative classical conditioning paradigm and observed slower extinction of finger pulse volume responses in patients with EHT than in normotensives. This indicates that EHT patients may not only be more reactive when challenged but may also show vasoconstrictive responses when facing similar situations without being challenged. No comparison between Type A individuals and hypertensives exists with respect to the ease with which cardiovascular reactions are classically conditioned.

Theoretically, the notion that cardiovascular reactivity influences development of hypertension would be strengthened if other traditional risk factors for high BP correlated with increased cardiovascular reactivity and if protective factors correlated with decreased reactivity. For example sex, age and race are important risk factors for high BP. Before the age of 50, males are more likely than females to have high BP. Frankenhaeuser *et al.* (cf. 1979) have presented data that indicate that males are more pressor reactive whereas females are HR reactive. Thus, increased BP but not HR reactivity is correlated with sex as a risk factor. Enhanced pressor responsivity and attenuated HR is more common among the elderly (Alderman, 1980). In addition, older subjects show greater individual response specificity than younger subjects (Garwood, Engel and Capriotti, 1982). Hypertension is more common in black Americans than in white Americans. Fredrikson (1986b) and Anderson, Lane, Muranaka, Williams and Houseworth (1988) studied cardiovascular reactivity in blacks and whites using an aversive reaction-time task. The results indicated decreased cardiac responsivity in blacks compared to whites but enhanced vascular responsivity. This may suggest that cardiac reactivity is more important for the development of hypertension in whites than in blacks. However, these data may also suggest that the important 'toxic process' in the development of high BP is enhanced vascular reactivity, leading to an increased vascular resistance and vascular hypertrophy. Blacks have an increased vascular reactivity and individuals with BHT have an increased diastolic BP reactivity, which is probably correlated with increased vascular resistance. On the other hand, Type A subjects compared to their Type B counterparts show decreased vascular resistance during behavioural stress, and less of an increase during attention-provoking states (Williams *et al.*, 1982). One speculation then is that vascular responses may balance the increased cardiac reactivity and somehow protect against the development of EHT in Type A individuals.

The time is ripe for prospective studies on physiological and neuroendocrine response patterns and subsequent development of cardiovascular disease, again underscoring the necessity to monitor several physiological and biochemical parameters when exploring possible mechanisms relating behaviour to disease.

REFERENCES

Alderman, M.H. (1980). The epidemiology of hypertension: etiology, natural history and the impact of therapy. *Cardiovascular Reviews and Reports* **1**, 509–519.

Alexander, F. (1939). Emotional factors in essential hypertension. *Psychosomatic Medicine* **1**, 173–179.

Ambrosini, E., Costa, F.V., Borghi, C., Boschi, S. and Mussi, A. (1986). Cellular and humoral factors in borderline hypertension. *Journal of Cardiovascular Pharmacology* **8**, S15–S22.

Ambrosini, E., Costa, F.V., Montebugnoli, C., Borghi, C. and Magnani, B. (1981).

Intralymphocytic sodium concentration as an index of response to stress and exercise in young subjects with borderline hypertension. *Clinical Science* **61**, 25s–27s.

American Psychiatric Association (1980). *Diagnostic and Statistical Manual of Mental Disorders*, 3rd edn. Washington, DC: APA.

Anderson, D., Kearns, W. and Better, W. (1983). Progressive hypertension in dogs by avoidance conditioning and saline infusion. *Hypertension* **5**, 286–291.

Anderson, N., Lane, J.D., Muranaka, M., Williams, R.D. and Houseworth, S.J. (1988). Racial differences in the vasoconstrictive response to cold stress. *Hypertension* **50**, 57–63.

Appleby, I.L., Klein, D.F., Sachar, E.J. and Levitt, M. (1981). Biochemical indices of lactate-induced panic: a preliminary report. In: D.F. Klein and J. Rabkin (Eds) *Anxiety: New Research and Changing Concepts*. New York: Raven Press.

Arnetz, B.B., Wasserman, J., Petrini, B., Brenner. S.O., Levi, L., Eneroth, P., Salovaara, H., Hjelm, R., Salovaara, L., Theorell, T. and Petterson. I.-L. (1987). Immune function in unemployed women. *Psychosomatic Medicine* **49**, 3–12.

Ayman, D. and Goldshine, A.D. (1938). Cold as a standard stimulus of blood pressure: a study of normal and hypertensive subjects. *New England Journal of Medicine* **219**, 650–655.

Ax, A. (1953). The physiological differentiation between fear and anger in humans. *Psychosomatic Medicine* **15**, 433–442.

Bandura, A., Taylor, C.B., Williams, S.L., Mefford, I.N. and Barchas, J.D. (1985). Catecholamine secretion as a function of perceived coping self-efficacy. *Journal of Consulting and Clinical Psychology* **53**, 406–414.

Baum, A., Lundberg, U., Grunberg, N., Singer, J. and Gatchel, R. (1985). Urinary catecholamines in behavioral research in stress. In: C.R. Lake and M.G. Ziegler (Eds) *The Catecholamines in Psychiatric and Neurologic Disorders*, pp. 55–72. London: Butterworths.

Beere, P.A., Glagov, S. and Zarins, C.K. (1984). Retarding effect of lowered heart rate on coronary atherosclerosis. *Science* **226**, 180–184.

Blumenthal, J.A., Lane, J.D. and Williams, R.B. (1985). The inhibited power motive, type A behavior, and patterns of cardiovascular response during the structured interview and thematic apperception test. *Journal of Human Stress* **11**, 82–92.

Bohlin, G., Eliasson, K., Hjemdahl, P., Klein, K., Fredrikson, M. and Frankenhaeuser, M. (1986). Personal control over work pace – circulatory neuroendocrine and subjective responses in borderline hypertension. *Journal of Hypertension* **4**, 295–305.

Borghi, C., Costa, F.V., Boschi, S., Mussi, A. and Ambrosini, . (1986). Predictors of stable hypertension in young borderline subjects: a five-year follow-up study. *Journal of Cardiovascular Pharmacology* **8**, Suppl. 5, S138–S141.

Boulenger, J.P. and Uhde, T.W. (1982). Biological peripheral correlates of anxiety. *L'Encéphale* **VIII**, 119–130.

Brod, J. (1971). The influence of higher nervous processes induced by psychosocial environment on the development of essential hypertension. In: L. Levi (Ed.) *Society, Stress and Disease*, Vol. 1: *Psychosocial Environment and Psychosomatic Diseases*. London: Oxford University Press.

Brod, J., Fencl, V., Hejl, Z. and Jirka, J. (1959). Circulatory changes underlying blood pressure elevation during acute emotional stress (mental arithmetic) in normotensive and hypertensive subjects. *Clinical Science* **18**, 269–279.

Brody, M.J., Haywood, J.R. and Touw, K.B. (1980). Neural mechanisms in hypertension. *Annual Review of Physiology* **42**, 441–453.

Brown, W.A. and Heninger, G. (1975). Cortisol, growth hormone, free fatty acids, and experimentally evoked affective arousal. *American Journal of Psychiatry* **132**, 1172–1176.

Cannon, W.B. (1914). The emergency function of the adrenal medulla in pain and the major emotions. *American Journal of Physiology* **33**, 356–372.

Cannon, W.B. (1929). *Bodily Changes in Pain, Hunger, Fear and Rage.* Boston: Branford.

Cobb, S. and Rose, R.M. (1973). Hypertension, peptic ulcer and diabetes in air traffic controllers. *Journal of the American Medical Association* **224**, 489–492.

Collins, F.H., Baer, P.E. and Bourianoff, G.G. (1981). Orienting behavior of children with hypertensive fathers. *Psychophysiology* **18**, 181 (Abstract).

Conway, F.J., Lund-Johansen, P., Hansson, L., Andrén, L., Eggertsen, R., Jern, S., Sivertsson, R. and Svensson, A. (1982). Circulatory aspects of hypertension. *Acta Medica Scandinavica* **212**, 253–260.

Corse, C., Manuck, S., Cantwell, J., Giordani, B. and Matthews, K. (1982). Coronary-prone behaviour pattern and cardiovascular response in persons with and without coronary heart disease. *Psychosomatic Medicine* **44**, 449–459.

Dahl, C.K. (1977). Salt intake and hypertension. In: J. Genest, E. Koiw and O. Kuchel (Eds) *Physiopathology and Treatment.* New York: McGraw-Hill.

Dajas, F., Nin, A. and Barbeite, L. (1986). Urinary noradrenaline in panic and phobic disorders. *Journal of Neural Transmission* **65**, 75–81.

Dembroski, T.M. and MacDongall, J.M. (1986). Stress and cigarette smoking: implications for cardiovascular risk. In: T.H. Schmidt, T.M. Dembroski and G. Blumchen (Eds) *Biological and Psychological Factors in Cardiovascular Disease.* New York: Karger.

Devereaux, R.B., Pickering, T.G., Harshfield, G.A., Kleinert, H.D., Denby, L., Clark, L., Pregibon, D., Jason, M., Kleiner, B., Borer, J.S. and Laragh, J.H. (1983). Left ventricular hypertrophy in patients with hypertension: importance of blood pressure response to regularly recurring stress. *Circulation* **68**, 470–476.

DeWied, D. (1969). Effects of peptide hormones on behavior. In: L. Martini and W.F. Ganong (Eds) *Frontiers in Neuroendocrinology*, pp. 97–140. London: Oxford University Press.

Diamond, E.L. (1982). The role of anger and hostility in essential hypertension and coronary heart disease. *Psychological Bulletin* **92**, 410–433.

Dimsdale, J.E., Pierce, C., Schoenfeld, D., Brown, A., Zusman, R. and Graham, R. (1986). Suppressed anger and blood pressure. The effects of race, sex, social class, obesity and age. *Psychosomatic Medicine* **48**, 430–436.

Dunbar, H.F. (1943). *Psychosomatic Diagnosis.* New York: Hoeber.

Dworkin, B.R., Filewich, R.J., Miller, N.E., Craigwyle, N. and Pickering, T. (1979). Baroreceptor activation reduces reactivity to noxious stimulation: implications for hypertension. *Science* **205**, 1299–1301.

Edmonson, H., Roscoe, B. and Vickers, M. (1972). Biochemical evidence of anxiety in dental patients. *British Medical Journal* **iv**, 7–9.

von Eiff, A.W. (1970). The role of the autonomic nervous system in the etiology and pathogenesis of essential hypertension. *Japanese Circulation Journal* **34**, 147–153.

von Eiff, A.W. (1984). Pathophysiologie und Ätiologi der essentiellen Hypertonie. *Münchener Medizinische Wochenschrift* **126**, 165–170.

Eliasson, K. (1984). Borderline hypertension: circulatory, sympatho-adrenal and psychological reactions to stress. *Acta Medica Scandinavica*, Suppl. 692.

Engel, B.T. (1983). Assessment and alteration of physiological reactivity. In: T.D. Dembroski, T.H. Schmidt and G. Blümchen (Eds) *Biobehavioral Bases of Coronary Heart Disease.* Basle: Karger.

Engel, B.T. and Bickford, A.F. (1961). Response-specificity: stimulus-response and individual-response specificity in essential hypertensives. *Archives of General Psychiatry* **5**, 82–93.

Esler, M.O. and Nestel, P.J. (1973). Renin and sympathetic nervous system responsiveness to adrenergic stimuli in essential hypertension. *American Journal of Cardiology* **32**, 643–649.

Esler, M.D., Julius S., Zweifler, A., Randall, O., Harburg, E., Gardiner, H. and DeQuattro, V. (1977). Mild high-renin essential hypertension. Neurogenic human hypertension? *New England Journal of Medicine* **296**, 405–411.

von Euler, U.S. (1967). Adrenal medullary secretion and its neural control. In: L. Martini and W.F. Ganong (Eds) *Neuroendocrinology*, Vol. 2, pp. 283–333. New York: Academic Press.

von Euler, U.S. and Lishajko, F. (1961). Improved technique for the fluorimetric estimation of catecholamines. *Acta Physiologica* **51**, 384–355.

Folkow, B.S. (1982). Physiological aspects of primary hypertension. *Physiological Review* **62**, 347–504.

Folkow, B. and Hallbäck, M. (1977). Physiopathology of spontaneous hypertension in rats. In: J. Genest, E. Koiw and O. Kuchel (Eds) *Hypertension: Physiopathology and Treatment*. New York: McGraw-Hill.

Folkow, B., Di Bona, G.F., Hjemdahl, P., Thorén, P. and Wallin, B.G. (1983). Measurements of plasma noradrenaline concentrations in human primary hypertension. *Hypertension* **5**, 399–403.

Frankenhaeuser, M. (1975). Sympathetic–adrenomedullary activity, behaviour and the psychosocial environment. In: P.H. Venables and M.J. Christi (Eds) *Research in Psychophysiology*, pp. 71–94. London: Wiley.

Frankenhaeuser, M. (1979). Psychoneuroendocrine approaches to the study of emotion as related to stress and coping. In: H.E. Howe and R.A. Dienstbier (Eds) *Nebraska Symposium on Motivation*. Lincoln: University of Nebraska Press.

Fredrikson, M. (1981). Orienting and defensive responses to phobic and conditioned stimuli in phobics and normals. *Psychophysiology* **18**, 456–465.

Fredrikson, M. (1986a). Behavioural aspects of cardiovascular reactivity in essential hypertension. In: T.H. Schmidt, T.M. Dembroski and G. Blümchen (Eds) *Biological and Psychological Factors in Cardiovascular Disease*, pp. 325–331. Heidelberg: Springer-Verlag.

Fredrikson, M. (1986b). Racial differences in behaviorally evoked cardiovascular reactivity in essential hypertension. *Journal of Hypertension* **4**, 325–331.

Fredrikson, M. (submitted). Habituation of the electrodermal orienting reaction to signal and non-signal stimuli in mild hypertensives and normotensives.

Fredrikson, M. and Blumenthal, J.A. (in press). Lipids, catecholamines and cardiovascular responses to stress in patients recovering from myocardial infarction. *Journal of Cardiopulmonary Rehabilitation*.

Fredrikson, M. and Engel, B.T. (1985). Cardiovascular and electrodermal adjustments during a vigilance task in patients with borderline and established hypertension. *Journal of Psychosomatic Research* **20**, 235–246.

Fredrikson, M. and Matthews, K. (submitted). Cardiovascular reactivity to stress and the development of hypertension: a meta-analytic review.

Fredrikson, M., Danielsson, T., Engel, B.T., Frisk-Holmberg, M., Ström, G. and Sundin, Ö. (1985a). Autonomic nervous system function and essential hypertension: individual response specificity with and without beta-adrenergic blockade. *Psychophysiology* **22**, 167–174.

Fredrikson, M., Danielsson, T., Iremark, H. and Sundin, Ö. (1987). Autonomic nervous blockades and phobic fear responses. *Journal of Psychophysiology* **1**, 35–43.

Fredrikson, M., Dimberg, U., Frisk-Holmberg, M. and Ström, G. (1982). Haemodynamic and electrodermal correlates of psychogenic stimuli in hypertensive and normotensive subjects. *Biological Psychology* **15**, 63–73.

Fredrikson, M., Dimberg, U., Frisk-Holmberg, M. and Ström, G. (1985b). Arterial blood pressure and general sympathetic activation in essential hypertension during stimulation. *Acta Medica Scandinavica* **217**, 309–317.

Fredrikson, M., Gunnarsson, R., Frankenhaeuser, M., Klein, K., Lindgren, M. and Westermark, O. (submitted, a). Psychobiology of stage fright: the effect of public performance on neuroendocrine, cardiovascular and subjective reactions.

Fredrikson, M., Lundberg, U., Tuomisto, M., Melin, B. and Frankenhaeuser, M. (submitted, b). Do serum cholesterol levels affect cardiovascular reactivity?

Fredrikson, M., Sundin, Ö. and Frankenhaeuser, M. (1985c). Cortisol excretion in specific phobias. *Psychosomatic Medicine* **47**, 313–319.

Fredrikson, M., Tuomisto, M., Gunnarsson, M., Sundin, Ö. and Mörlin, C. (1987). Classical conditioning of vascular and electrodermal responses in mild hypertension. *Journal of Psychophysiology* **1**, 180–181.

Fredrikson, M., Tuomisto, M., Bergman-Losman, B. and Frankenhaeuser, M. (in preparation). Is neuroendocrine and cardiovascular reactivity to stress influenced by parental hypertension and myocardial infarction?

Freidman, M. and Rosenman, R.H. (1974). *Type A Behavior and Your Heart*. New York: Knopf.

Funkenstein, D. (1956). Nor-adrenaline-like and adrenaline-like substances in relation to human behavior. *Journal of Nervous and Mental Disease* **124**, 58–68.

Ganong, W.F. (1983). *Review of Medical Physiology*, 11th edn. Los Altos: Lange Medical Publications.

Garwood, M., Engel, B.T. and Capriotti, R. (1982). Autonomic nervous system function and aging: response specificity. *Psychophysiology* **19**, 378–386.

Gentry, W.D., Chesney, A.P., Gary, H., Hall, R.P. and Harburg, E. (1982). Habitual anger-coping styles: I. Effect on male/female blood pressure and hypertension status. *Psychosomatic Medicine* **44**, 195–202.

Goffard, M.I. and Perry, W.L.W. (1951). The action of adrenaline on the rate of loss of potassium ions from unfatigued striated muscle. *Journal of Physiology* **112**, 95–101.

Goldstein, D.S. (1981). Plasma norepinephrine during stress in essential hypertension. *Hypertension* **3**, 551–556.

Goldstein, D.S. (1983). Plasma catecholamines and essential hypertension. An analytical review. *Hypertension* **5**, 86–99.

Gunnarsson, R.D.R. and Fredrikson, M. (1987). Behaviour therapy in the treatment of stage-fright in musicians. Paper presented at the 8th International Conference of the Society for Test Anxiety Research, Bergen, 1987.

Guttman, M.C. and Benson, H. (1971). Interaction of environmental factors and systematic arterial blood pressure. *Medicine* **50**, 543–553.

Guyton, A., Coleman, T.G., Cowley, A.W., Jr, Manning, R.D., Jr, Norman, R.A., Jr and Ferguson, J.D. (1974). A systems analysis approach to understanding long-range arterial blood pressure control in hypertension. *Circulation Research* **35**, 159–176.

Hallbäck, M. and Folkow, B. (1974). Cardiovascular responses to acute mental stress in spontaneously hypertensive rats. *Acta Physiologica Scandinavica* **90**, 684–698.

Hamm, A. and Vaitl, D. (1986). Kardiovaskuläre und elektrodermale Reaktionsspezifität bei essentiellen Grenzwert-Hypertonikern: ein konditionierungsexperiment. *Zeitschrift für klinische Psychologie* **15**, 201–206.

Harburg, E., Erfurt, J.C., Hauenstein, L.S., Chape, D., Schull, W.J. and Schork, M.A. (1973). Socio-ecological stress, suppressed hostility, skin color, and black–white male blood pressure: Detroit. *Psychosomatic Medicine* **35**, 276–296.

Hare, R.D. (1973). Orienting and defensive responses to visual stimuli. *Psychophysiology* **10**, 453–464.

Harlan, E.R., Jr, Osborne, R.K. and Graybiel, A. (1964). Prognostic value of the cold pressor test and the basal blood pressure based on an eighteen year follow-up study. *American Journal of Cardiology* **13**, 683–687.

Harrell, J.P. (1980). Psychological factors and hypertension: a status report. *Psychological Bulletin* **87**, 482–501.

Henry, J.P. and Stephens, P.M. (1977). *Stress, Health and the Social Environment. A Sociobiological Approach to Medicine*. New York: Springer.

Henry, J.P. and Stephens-Larson, P.M. (1984). Reduction of chronic psychosocial hypertension in mice by decaffeinated tea. *Hypertension* **6**, 437–444.

Hilton, S.M. (1975). Ways of viewing the central nervous control of the circulation – old and new. *Brain Research* **87**, 213–219.

Hines, E.A. and Brown, G.E. (1932). A standard stimulus for measuring vasomotor reactions: its application in the study of hypertension. *Proceedings of Staff Meetings of the Mayo Clinic* **7**, 332–335.

Hjemdahl, P., Freyschuss, U., Juhlin-Dannfelt, A. and Linck, B. (1986). Plasma catecholamines and mental stress. In: J.N. Christiansen, O. Henriksen and N.A. Lassen (Eds) *The Sympathoadrenal System*. Copenhagen: Munksgaard.

Hoffman, J.W., Benson, H., Arns, P.C., Stainbrook, G.L., Landsberg, L., Young, J.B. and Gill, A. (1982). Reduced sympathetic nervous system responsivity associated with the relaxation response. *Science* **215**, 190–192.

Hollenberg, N.K., Williams, G.H. and Adams, D.F. (1981). Essential hypertension: abnormal renal vascular and endocrine responses to a mild psychological stimulus. *Hypertension* **3**, 11–17.

Holmes, T.H. and Rahe, R.H. (1967). The social readjustment rating scale. *Journal of Psychosomatic Research* **11**, 213–218.

Hypertension Detection and Follow-up Program Cooperative Group. (1979). Five year findings of the hypertension detection and follow-up program. *Journal of the American Medical Association*, **242**, 2562–2577.

Jennings, J.R., Tahmoush, A.J. and Redmond, D.P. (1980). Non-invasive measurement of peripheral vascular activity. In: I. Martin and P.H. Venables (Eds) *Techniques in Psychophysiology*. New York: Wiley.

Jones, D.H., Hamilton, C.A. and Reid, J.L. (1979). Choice of control groups in the appraisal of sympathetic nervous activity in essential hypertension. *Clinical Science* **57**, 339–344.

Jorgensen, R.S. and Houston, B.K. (1986). Family history of hypertension, personality patterns and cardiovascular reactivity to stress. *Psychosomatic Medicine* **48**, 102–117.

Julius, S. (1976). Neurogenic component in borderline hypertension. In: S. Julius, M.D. Esler and C.N. Ellis (Eds) *The Nervous System in Arterial Hypertension*, pp. 301–330. Springfield, Ill.: Thomas.

Julius, S. and Conway, J. (1968). Hemodynamic studies in patients with borderline blood pressure elevation. *Circulation* **38**, 282–288.

Kagan, A.R. and Levi, L. (1974). Health and environment — psychosocial stimuli: a review. *Social Science and Medicine* **8**, 225–241.

Kaplan, J.R., Manuck, S.B., Clarkson, T.B., Lusso, F.M., Taub, D.M. and Miller, E.W. (1983). Social stress and atherosclerosis in normocholesterolemic monkeys. *Science* **220**, 733–735.

Keane, T.M., Martin, J.E., Berler, E.S., Wooten, L.S., Fleece, E.L. and Williams, G. (1982). Are hypertensives less assertive? A controlled evaluation. *Journal of Consulting and Clinical Psychology* **50**, 499–508.

Keys, A. (1980). *Seven Countries. A Multivariate Analysis of Death and Coronary Disease.* Cambridge, Mass.: Harvard University Press.

Klein, D.F. (1980). Anxiety reconceptualized. *Comprehensive Psychiatry* **21**, 411–427.
Krantz, D.S. and Manuck, S.B. (1984). Measures of acute physiologic reactivity to behavioral stimuli: assessment and critique. *Psychological Bulletin* **96**, 435–464.
Lader, M. (1983). Anxiety and depression. In: A. Gale and J.A. Edwards (Eds) *Physiological Correlates of Human Behaviour. Individual Differences and Psychopathology.* London: Academic Press.
Lane, J.D. and Williams, R.B. (1985). Caffeine affects cardiovascular response to stress. *Psychophysiology* **22**, 648–656.
Laragh, J.H., Bear, L., Brunner, H.R., Bühler, F.R., Sealy, J.E. and Vaughn, E. (1976). The renin–angiotension–aldosterone system in pathogenesis and management of hypertensive vascular disease. In: J.H. Laragh (Ed.) *Hypertension Manual*, pp. 313–320. New York: New York Medical Books.
Lazarus, R.S. and Folkman, S. (1984). *Stress, Appraisal, and Coping.* New York: Springer.
Levi, L. (Ed.) (1975). *Emotions and Their Parameters and Measurements.* New York: Raven Press.
Liebowitz, M., Gorman, J., Fyer, A., Levitt, M., Dillon, D., Levy, G., Appleby, I., Anderson, S., Palij, M., Davies, S. and Klein, D.F. (1985). Lactate provocation of panic attacks. II. Biochemical and physiological findings. *Archives of General Psychiatry* **42**, 709–719.
Light, K.C., Koepke, J.P., Obrist, P.A. and Willis, P.W. (1983). Psychological stress induces sodium and fluid retention in men at high risk for hypertension. *Science* **220**, 429–431.
Lima, D.R. and Turner, P. (1983). Propranolol increases reduced beta-receptor function in severely anxious patients. *Lancet* **2**, 1505.
Lund-Johansen, P. (1967). Hemodynamics in early essential hypertension. *Acta Medica Scandinavica*, Suppl. 482, 18.
Lund-Johansen, P. (1977). Hemodynamic trends in untreated essential hypertension. Preliminary report on a 10-year follow-up study. *Acta Medica Scandinavica*, Suppl. 602, 68.
Manuck, S.B., Kaplan, J.R. and Clarkson, T.B. (1983). Behaviorally-induced heart rate reactivity and atherosclerosis in cynomalgus monkeys. *Psychosomatic Medicine* **45**, 95–108.
Manuck, S.B., Morrison, R.L., Bellack, A.S. and Polfrone, J.M. (1984). Behavioral factors in hypertension: cardiovascular responsivity, anger, and social competence. In: M. Chesney, S. Goldston and R. Rosenman (Eds) *Anger, Hostility and Behavioral Medicine.* New York: Hemisphere.
Mason, J.W. (1975). Emotion as reflected in patterns of endocrine integration. In: L. Levi (Ed.) *Emotions: Their Parameters and Measurements.* New York: Raven Press.
Mathew, R.J., Ho, B.T., Francis, D.J., Taylor, D.L. and Weinman, M.L. (1982). Catecholamines and anxiety. *Acta Psychiatrica Scandinavica* **65**, 142–147.
Mathew, R.J., Ho, B.T., Kralik, P., Taylor, D. and Claghorn, J.L. (1980a). MAO, DBH and COMT: the effect of anxiety. *Journal of Clinical Psychiatry* **41**, 25–28.
Mathew, R.J., Ho, B.T., Kralik, P., Taylor, D.L. and Claghorn, J.L. (1981b). Catecholamines and monoamine oxidase activity in anxiety. *Acta Psychiatrica Scandinavica* **63**, 245–252.
Mathew, R.J., Ho, B.T., Kralik, P., Taylor, D., Semchuk, K., Weinman, M. and Claghorn, J.L. (1980b). Catechol-*o*-methyltransferase and catecholamines in anxiety and relaxation. *Psychiatry Research* **3**, 85–91.
Mathew, R.J., Ho, B.T., Taylor, D.L. and Semchuk, K.M. (1981a). Catecholamine and dopamine-beta-hydroxylase in anxiety. *Journal of Psychosomatic Research* **25**, 499–504.
Matthews, K.A. and Rakaczky, C.J. (1986). Familial aspects of the type A behavior pattern and physiologic reactivity to stress. In: T.H. Schmidt, T.M. Dembroski

and G. Blümchen (Eds) *Biological and Psychological Factors in Cardiovascular Disease.* Heidelberg: Springer.

Matthews, K.A., Manuck, S.B. and Saab, P.G. (1986). Cardiovascular responses of adolescents during a naturally occuring stressor and their behavioral and psychophysiological predictors. *Psychophysiology* **23**, 198–209.

McCubbin, J.A., Surwit, R.S. and Williams, R.B. (1985). Endogenous opiate peptides, stress reactivity, and risk for hypertension. *Hypertension* **7**, 808–811.

Miyabo, S., Asato, T. and Mizushima, N. (1979). Psychological correlates of stress-induced cortisol and growth hormone releases in neurotic patients. *Psychosomatic Medicine* **41**, 515–523.

Nesse, R.M., Cameron, O.G., Curtis, G.C., McCann, D.S. and Huber-Smith, M.J. (1984). Adrenergic function in patients with panic anxiety. *Archives of General Psychiatry* **41**, 771–776.

Nesse, R.M., Cameron, O.G., Buda, A.J., McCann, D.S., Curtis, G.C. and Huber-Smith, M. (1985a). Urinary catecholamines and mitral valve prolapse in panic-anxiety patients. *Psychiatry Research* **14**, 67–75.

Nesse, R.M., Curtis, G.C., Thyer, B.A., McCann, D.S., Huber-Smith, M.J. and Knopf, R.F. (1985b). Endocrine and cardiovascular responses during phobic anxiety. *Psychosomatic Medicine* **47**, 320–332.

Page, I.H. (1977). Some regulatory mechanisms of renovascular and essential arterial hypertension. In: J. Genest, E. Koiw and O. Kuchel (Eds) *Hypertension: Physiopathology and Treatment*, pp. 576–587. New York: McGraw Hill.

Perini, C., Rauchfleisch, U. and Buhler, F.R. (1985). Personality characteristics and renin in essential hypertension. *Psychotherapy and Psychosomatics* **43**, 44–48.

Perloff, D., Sokolow, M. and Cowan, R. (1983). The prognostic value of ambulatory blood pressure. *Journal of the American Medical Association* **249**, 2792–2798.

Pickering, G.W. (1961). *The Nature of Essential Hypertension.* London: Churchill.

Price, D.B., Thaler, M. and Mason, J.W. (1977). Preoperative emotional states and adrenal cortical activity. *Archives of Neurology and Psychiatry* **77**, 646–656.

Review Panel on Coronary-Prone Behavior and Coronary Heart Disease (1981). Coronary-prone behavior and coronary heart disease – a critical review. *Circulation* **63**, 1199–1215.

Rosenbaum, A.H., Schatzberg, A.F., Jost III, F.A., Cross, P.D., Wells, L.A., Jiang, N.-S. and Maruta, T. (1983). Urinary free cortisol levels in anxiety. *Psychosomatics* **24**, 835–837.

Safar, M.E., Weiss, Y.A., Levenson, J.A., London, G.M. and Milliez, P.L. (1973). Hemodynamic study of 85 patients with borderline hypertension. *American Journal of Cardiology* **31**, 315–319.

Sapira, J.D., Scheib, E.T., Moriarty, R. and Shapiro, A.P. (1971). Differences in perception between hypertensive and normotensive populations. *Psychosomatic Medicine* **33**, 239–250.

Schalling, D. (1985). Personality correlates of elevated blood pressure. Anxiety, unexpressed anger and lack of assertiveness. In: C.D. Spielberger, I.G. Sarason and P.B. Deforest (Eds) *Stress and Anxiety*, Vol. 9, pp. 241–251.

Schneider, R.H., Egan, B.M., Johnson, E.H., Drobuy, H. and Julius, S. (1986). Anger and anxiety in borderline hypertension. *Psychosomatic Medicine* **48**, 242–248.

Schneiderman, N. and Pickering, T.G. (1986). Cardiovascular measures of physiologic reactivity. In: K.A. Matthews, S.M. Weiss, T. Detre, T.M. Dembroski, B. Falkner, S.B. Manuck and R.B. Williams, Jr (Eds) *Handbook of Stress, Reactivity and Cardiovascular Disease.* New York: Wiley.

Selye, H. (1950). *Stress.* Montreal: ACTA.

Selye, H. (1976). *The Stress of Life*, 2nd edn. New York: McGraw-Hill.

Sexton, M.M. (1979). Behavioral epidemiology. In: O.F. Pomerleau and J.P. Brady (Eds) *Behavioral Medicine: Theory and Practice*. Baltimore: Williams and Wilkins.

Shapiro, A.P. (1961). An experimental study of comparative responses of blood pressure to different noxious stimuli. *Journal of Chronic Disease* **13**, 293–311.

Shapiro, A.P., Benson, H., Chobanian, A.V., Herd, A.J., Julius, S., Kaplan, N., Lazarus, R.S., Ostfeld, A.M. and Syme, S.L. (1979). The role of stress in hypertension. *Journal of Human Stress* **5**, 7–26.

Sivertsson, R. (1970). The hemodynamic importance of structural vascular changes in essential hypertension. *Acta Physiologica Scandinavica*, Suppl. 343, 1–56.

Sivertsson, R., Sannerstedt, R. and Lundgren, Y. (1976). Evidence for peripheral vascular involvement in mild elevation of blood pressure in man. *Clinical Science and Molecular Medicine* **51**, 65s–68s.

Sleight, P. (Ed.) (1980). *Arterial Baroreceptors and Hypertension*. London: Oxford University Press.

Sokolov, E.N. (1963). *Perception and the Conditioned Reflex*. Oxford: Pergamon.

Stamler, J., Berkson, D.M., Lindberg, H.A., Miller, M.A., Stamler, R. and Collette, P. (1967). Socioeconomic factors in the epidemiology of hypertensive disease. In: J. Stamler, R. Stamler and T.N. Pullman (Eds) *The Epidemiology of Essential Hypertension*. New York: Grune and Stratton.

Steptoe, A. (1981). *Psychological Factors in Cardiovascular Disorders*. London: Academic Press.

Steptoe, A. (1984). Psychophysiological processes in disease. In: A. Steptoe and A. Matthew (Eds) *Health Care and Human Behaviour*. London: Academic Press.

Steptoe, A. (1987). The assessment of sympathetic nervous function in human stress research. *Journal of Psychosomatic Research* **31**, 141–152.

Steptoe, A., Melville, D.R. and Ross, A. (1983). Behavioral response demands, cardiovascular reactivity and essential hypertension. *Psychosomatic Medicine* **45**, 33–48.

Sullivan, P.A., Procci, W.R., DeQuattro, V., Schoentgen, S., Levine, D., van der Meulen, J. and Bornheimer, J.F. (1981). Anger, anxiety, guilt and increased basal and stress-induced neurogenic tone: causes or effects in primary hypertension. *Clinical Science* **61**, 380–392.

Surwit, R.S., Williams, R.B. and Shapiro, D. (1982). *Behavioral Approaches to Cardiovascular Disease*. New York: Academic Press.

Svedenhag, J. (1985). The sympatho-adrenal system in physical conditioning: significance for training-induced adaptations and dependency on the training state. *Acta Physiologica Scandinavica*, Suppl. 543.

Takeshita, A., Imaizumi, T., Ashihara, T., Yamamoto, K., Hoka, S. and Nakamura, M. (1982). Limited maximal vasodilator capacity of forearm resistance vessels in normotensive young men with a familiar predisposition to hypertension. *Circulation Research* **50**, 671–677.

Turpin, G. (1983). Unconditioned reflexes and the autonomic nervous system. In: D. Siddle (Ed.) *Orienting and Habituation: Perspectives in Human Research*. London: Wiley.

Thailer, S.A., Friedman, R., Harshfield, G.A. and Pickering, T.G. (1985). Psychologic differences between high-, normal- and low-renin hypertensives. *Psychosomatic Medicine* **47** 294–297.

Theorell, T., de Faire, U., Schalling, D., Adamson, U., and Askevold, F. (1979). Personality traits and psychophysiological reactions to a stressful interview in twins with varying degree of coronary heart disease. *Journal of Psychosomatic Research* **23**, 89–99.

Theorell, T., Knox, S., Svensson, J. and Waller, D. (1985). Blood pressure variations during working day at age 28: effects of different types of work and blood pressure at age 18. *Journal of Human Stress* **11**, 36–41.

Thyer, B.S. and Matthews, J. (1986). The effect of phobic anxiety on plasma-beta-endorphin: a single-subject experiment. *Behaviour Research and Therapy* **24**, 237–241.

US Department of Health and Human Services (1984). Report of the Joint National Committee on Detection, Evaluation and Treatment of High Blood Pressure. NIH publication no. 84–1088.

Wallin, G. (1981). Sympathetic nerve activity underlying electrodermal and cardiovascular reactions in man. *Psychophysiology* **18**, 470–476.

Wallin, B.G., Delius, W. and Hagbarth, K.-E. (1973). Comparison of sympathetic nerve activity in normotensive and hypertensive subjects. *Circulation Research* **333**, 9–21.

Weiner, H. (1977). *Psychobiology and Human Disease*. New York: Elsevier.

Weiner, H., Singer, M.T. and Reiser, M.F. (1962). Cardiovascular responses and their psychological correlates: I. A study in healthy young adults and patients with peptic ulcer and hypertension. *Psychosomatic Medicine* **24**, 477–497.

Wilhelmsen, L. (1984). Risk factors for coronary heart disease in perspective. *American Journal of Medicine* **76**, 37–40.

Williams, J., Lane, J., Kuhn, C., Melosh, A., White, S. and Schanberg, S. (1982). Type A behavior and elevated physiological and neuroendocrine responses to cognitive tasks. *Science* **218**, 483–485.

Wolf, S., Cardon, P.V., Shepard, E.M. and Wolff, H.G. (1955). *Life Stress and Essential Hypertension*. Baltimore: Williams and Wilkins.

Wood, D.L., Sheps, S.G., Elveback, L.R. and Schringer, A. (1984). Cold pressor test as a predictor of hypertension. *Hypertension* **6**, 301–306.

Wyatt, R.J., Portnoy, B., Kupfer, D.J., Snyder, F. and Engelman, K. (1971). Resting plasma catecholamine concentrations in patients with depression and anxiety. *Archives of General Psychiatry* **24**, 65–72.

Zweifler, A.J. and Nicholls, M.G. (1982). Diminished finger volume pulse in borderline hypertension: evidence for early structural vascular abnormality. *American Heart Journal* **104**, 812–815.

SECTION 2

APPLICATIONS TO SPECIFIC DISORDERS

Chapter 9

Simple Phobias

Kenneth Hugdahl

Department of Somatic Psychology,
University of Bergen,
Årstadveien 21,
N-5009 Bergen,
Norway

ABSTRACT

Simple phobias are defined and characterized, and prevalence rates, age onset, and gender differences are described. Acquisition is discussed within a 'three-systems' model. Psychophysiological measures are described, and the typical response patterns obtained in phobic reactions are outlined. Special attention is devoted to the paradoxical response seen in blood–injury phobias, and the use of beta-blockers in treatment. The chapter ends with a discussion of the role played by prepared learning in phobia acquisition and maintenance.

Handbook of Clinical Psychophysiology Edited by G. Turpin
© 1989 John Wiley & Sons Ltd

INTRODUCTION

In the present chapter I will review how psychophysiology can elucidate important aspects of phobias, and especially simple phobias. The chapter is divided into three sections. The first section is concerned with definitions and characteristics of simple phobias, focusing on recent concepts and models in research and clinical practice. The second section is devoted to a brief overview of the psychophysiology of phobias, including electrodermal and cardiovascular measures. Findings relevant to an understanding of psychophysiology of simple phobias will be presented. A third section is devoted to a discussion of the aetiology and maintenance of simple phobias, and how psychophysiology has contributed to this knowledge. This section will especially deal with the issues of prepared classical conditioning in fear behaviour.

PSYCHOPHYSIOLOGY: USE IN THE SEARCH FOR MECHANISMS VERSUS USE IN ASSESSMENT FOR TREATMENT

Before turning to a description and definition of simple phobias, it is important to distinguish between the use of psychophysiological methods in research on mechanisms in the aetiology of fear (e.g. Hugdahl, 1978; Hugdahl and Ohman, 1977; Ohman, Fredrikson, Hugdahl and Rimmo, 1976), and their use in assessment and evaluation of treatment (e.g. Haug, Brenne, Johnsen, Berntzen, Gotestam and Hugdahl, 1987; Holden and Barlow, 1986; McNally and Stekeete, 1985; Ost and Jansson, 1986; Ost, Johansson and Jerremalm, 1982).

The use of psychophysiology in research on basic mechanisms and processes has originated from the dualistic view of emotions as consisting of both a cognitive and a somatic component (e.g. James, 1884). Similarly, one of the classic benchmark papers in the history of psychophysiology was related to the differentiation of fear and anger (Ax, 1953). Thus, emotion, and especially fear, is one of the cornerstones in psychophysiology. Furthermore, the easily observed changes in physiological response to fear-relevant stimuli, like the pounding of the heart, sweaty palms, and trembling hands, make psychophysiology an obvious candidate when investigating fear behaviour. Finally, and perhaps most important, the close link between human classical conditioning and psychophysiological recordings (e.g. Ohman, 1971), and the historical conceptualization of fear and emotions in terms of conditioning (Mowrer, 1939; Watson and Raynor, 1920) make psychophysiology a suitable candidate to unravel the secrets of our emotions.

It is also important to realize that psychophysiology may not only give information about the *intensity* of fear, but in addition, may have something to tell us about the *quality* of the fear response. This is particularly interesting in the field of phobic fears where diametrically different physiological response patterns may be obtained within the same response-system to different fear-eliciting stimuli. A well-known example of this is that although heart rate increases usually accompany a phobic reaction, significant decreases are observed if the phobia under study is related to blood and injury situations (Ost, Sterner and Lindahl, 1984; Wardle and Jarvis, 1981). Thus, different physiological response patterns may be associated with different fear reactions.

The above use of psychophysiology should, however, be distinguished from the use of recordings of heart rate and electrodermal activity, in clinical practice. This latter application of psychophysiology is theoretically closely related to the conceptualization in the late 1960s and early 1970s of fear and emotions as complex response patterns involving three different components: psychophysiological, cognitive/subjective, and behavioural (Lang, 1968; Rachman, 1977; see also Hugdahl, 1981). This is further discussed later in the chapter. Thus, as argued by Ost and Jansson (1986) when discussing issues in treatment, in order to obtain as complete as possible a picture of the disorder under study, it is essential to measure not only subjective self-reports, but also psychophysiological parameters related to the fear response.

A final observation concerning the use of psychophysiology in clinical practice is the distinction between the use of psychophysiological recordings as an instrument for assessing treatment effectiveness and the use of psychophysiology directly in treatment. The best known example of the use of psychophysiology in treatment is biofeedback training where the change in a physiological parameter (e.g. heart rate) as a function of information to the subject is directly utilized in the treatment process. This will not be further discussed in the present chapter, and the reader is referred to Gatchel (1979) for a review of clinical applications of biofeedback in the treatment of fear and anxiety.

DESCRIPTION OF SIMPLE PHOBIAS

Fear is a common emotional experience found in any human population. Some people are afraid of encountering snakes and spiders, while others may be paralysed by fear upon the thought of facing an audience or when being enclosed in a small room, typically a lift.

When the fear becomes so intense that it interferes with the person's life, we speak of phobic fears or phobias. A simple phobia is thus defined as an extreme fear and avoidance of a limited set of specific situations that the individual intellectually recognizes should not be dangerous (cf. Leitenberg, 1976; Marks, 1969).

The simple phobias are defined in the *Diagnostic and Statistical Manual for Mental Disorders* (3rd edn; DSM-III; American Psychiatric Association, 1980) as 'a persistent irrational fear of, and compelling desire to avoid, an object or a situation other than being alone or in public places away from home (Agoraphobia), or of humiliation or embarrassment in certain social situations (Social phobia)' (p. 228). Since the focus in the present chapter is on simple phobias, I will not further discuss the more diffuse phobic syndromes of agoraphobia and social phobia (cf. Chapter 10).

From the above definition it follows that a phobia is irrational in the sense of being an emotional reaction out of proportion to the actual demands of the situation. In addition, phobic responses cannot be voluntarily controlled, and this is perhaps of most relevance when considering the psychophysiological reactions accompanying the response. Although phobic responses may fluctuate over time, they are usually very robust and persistent. Typically, they persist for a lifetime if no treatment is applied. Phobic reactions are not age-specific in the sense that they are tied to certain developmental stages. However, while phobias for small animals often develop before puberty (e.g. Marks and Gelder, 1966; Ost, 1985), claustrophobia usually has a later onset in the early twenties (Ost, 1985). Phobic reactions are also non-adaptive and lead to secondary social handicaps in the sense that the person is usually embarrassed by his/ her reaction which often leads to a reduction in self-confidence.

A final comment on the definition of phobias is that they seem to be learned behaviours (although with a possible biological component, see Marks, 1981; Ohman *et al.*, 1976; Seligman, 1971) that are easily acquired. However, the actual pathways to fear need not necessarily involve traumatic conditioning experiences, as fear may also be vicariously transmitted through the modelling behaviour of significant others (Ost and Hugdahl, 1981, 1985; Rachman, 1977).

CATEGORIZATION OF SIMPLE PHOBIAS

Although there are reports in the literature of unusual phobias such as fear of chocolates and fear of flowers (Rachman and Seligman, 1976), the most common phobias are about a limited set of objects or situations. Usually these fears are concerned with particular animals (especially snakes, spiders, rats, and dogs); particular situations like heights, closed spaces, and darkness; and specific fears of blood–injury, and illness.

A categorization of simple phobias into different subgroupings was made by Marks (1969) with reference to what he called phobias of external versus phobias of internal stimuli. Included in the first category were animal phobias and other miscellaneous specific fears of heights and closed spaces. The phobias of internal stimuli were blood and illness phobias and obsessive phobias (although the latter should perhaps better be categorized under obsessive–compulsive neurosis). Rosenhan and Seligman (1984) listed three main categories of specific phobias: (1) animal phobias, including snakes, spiders, dogs, cats, insects, and rats; (2) inanimate object phobias, including heights, darkness, closed spaces, and thunder; and (3) illness–injury phobias, including fear of blood–injury, and of lethal diseases.

PREVALENCE

The prevalence of a disease or of a disorder is defined as the percentage of a specified population that has the disease or the disorder. This should be distinguished from the incidence of a disease or disorder, which means the rate of newly identified cases in a given time period.

A frequently cited report of the prevalence of phobias (including also agoraphobia) is the study by Agras, Sylvester and Oliveau (1969) for a US adult population. Agras *et al.* (1969) showed that while 7.7% of the population experienced some mild form of phobia, only 0.22% had clinically relevant phobias. Furthermore, it is estimated that of all patients in psychiatric treatment, between 5 and 10% also present phobic symptoms (Marks, 1969; Rosenhan and Seligman, 1984). When looking at these figures, it should be kept in mind, however, that they include agoraphobia and social-phobia syndromes. According to Marks (1970), approximately 50–60% of all patients suffering from phobia are classified as agoraphobics.

Although agoraphobia and social phobia are more prominent within clinical populations, simple phobias such as fear of snakes and spiders may be far more common than estimated. There have to my knowledge been no large-scale epidemiological studies of specific phobias, thus nobody actually knows how common they are in the entire population. Since simple phobias probably do not lead to clinical consultation as frequently as agoraphobia, they may be more common than hitherto acknowledged. For example, Arnarson (1988) has recently reported that the prevalence of flight phobia in Iceland is 13%.

An indication of the prevalence of fear (probably not phobic, however) for animals was provided in a study by Bowd and Boylan (1984) who reported that among 78 college students, 82% reported at least one animal which they feared. These results should, however, be treated cautiously, since they only asked their subjects: 'if there are any animals you fear, please list them'. This may have initially primed subjects to come up with reports that did not actually involve fear. Second, there is no indication of the strength of fear in their study. However, an interesting aspect of the results is that fear of snakes, spiders, and dogs were the top three fears listed.

Bennett-Levy and Marteau (1984) asked 113 subjects attending a local health centre to fill out a questionnaire concerning how afraid they were of 29 different small, harmless animals and insects. Of the 29 different species, the four most-feared animals were: rats, cockroaches, spiders, and snakes in descending order. It was further shown that females rated themselves as significantly less willing to approach or pick up the ten most-feared animals than were males. This is an interesting observation considering that exposure to the situation (approach and pick up) is probably the most effective single treatment ingredient (Marks, 1981). One could thus speculate that traditional stereotyped sex-roles work against females since it is more socially accepted for them, for example, not to approach and kill an insect on the kitchen floor.

AGE OF ONSET

Phobias for specific animals are usually acquired before puberty. Ost (1985) reported a mean onset age of 6.9 years in a survey of 50 patients. Similarly, Marks and Gelder (1966) reported a mean onset age of 4.4 years in a sample of 18 subjects. Mean age of onset for blood–injury phobias has been reported as 8.8 years in a sample of 40 subjects, while the corresponding value for calustrophobia was 21.5 years (Ost, 1985). Thus, it seems that fear of animals, and of blood–injury, has a relatively early onset compared to claustrophobia.

CURRENT CONCEPTS

THE 'THREE-SYSTEMS' MODEL

According to the 'three-systems' model of fear (Hugdahl, 1981; Lang, 1968; Rachman, 1977), fear should be viewed not as a 'lump', or as an entity, but as a set of loosely coupled components: (1) psychophysiological reactivity, (2) cognitive reports, and (3) overt avoidance behaviour. The three components may further be differentially affected by various treatment methods (Rachman, 1977). It could, for instance, be argued that phobic individuals who mainly respond with physiological arousal when confronted with their phobic object should benefit more from a physiologically directed treatment method, like systematic desensitization, or relaxation. Similarly, it could be argued that a cognitive responder should benefit more from a cognitively directed treatment method, like various forms of cognitive restructuring (e.g. Meichenbaum, 1977). Since the three components do not always covary (Rachman, 1977), it seems reasonable to record from all three systems in assessment and treatment in order to get as valid as possible an evaluation of the disorder and of treatment effects. Such a multisystem approach has recently been taken by Ost and his co-workers (e.g. Ost *et al.*, 1982; Ost, Jerremalm and Jansson, 1984).

In a first study (Ost *et al.*, 1982) which employed a sample of claustrophobic patients, it was found that exposure treatment yielded better results than applied relaxation for patients categorized as mainly behavioural responders, whereas applied relaxation was superior to exposure for physiological reactors. These results would thus support the notion that greater effects are obtained when the treatment employed is consonant with the patient's most prominent pattern of responding. Similarly, Wolpe, Lande, McNally and Schotte (1985) found that clinical trainees easily learned to distinguish between classically conditioned and cognitively based phobias. The therapy students made their ratings from transcripts of excerpts from actual therapy sessions. Furthermore, Wolpe (1981) has argued that failure to carry out an analysis of the distinction between conditioned and cognitively learned phobic fears is the reason for much confusion and inconclusiveness in therapy outcome studies.

However, when the question of component expression is considered together with the origin of the phobia, i.e. the mode of acquisition, the issue becomes more complicated. In his critique of the weakness of Mowrer's (1939) traditional 'two-factor' theory of fear, Rachman (1977) discussed three different pathways to the acquisition of a phobic reaction. The first was taken to be traumatic classical conditioning. The second was concerned with vicarious experiences and modelling influences from significant others. By this Rachman (1977) meant the instigating effect which recurrent warnings and admonitions from parents could have for the acquisition of a phobic reaction in the child. The third pathway was thought of as involving fear experiences acquired through the indirect influences of the transmission of information and/or instruction, e.g. from the mass media. When describing his model of fear acquisition, Rachman (1977) also suggested that, for conditioned fears, psychophysiological and behavioural components would predominate whereas in fears acquired indirectly (vicariously or informationally), the cognitive component should be most prominent.

Ost and Hugdahl (1981, 1983, 1985; Hugdahl and Ost, 1985) asked 267 patients with phobias (including small-animal phobias, agoraphobia, claustrophobia, social phobia, and blood and dental phobia) how they recollected the origin of their phobias. A specially designed questionnaire (see Hugdahl and Ost, 1985; Ost and Hugdahl, 1981) was developed that tapped the three pathways to fear suggested by Rachman (1977). The studies by Hugdahl and Ost have consistently revealed that conditioning was by far the most prominent factor in all the subgroups of phobias studied. Second came modelling experiences, and third instruction/information.

The findings by Ost and Hugdahl (1981, 1983, 1985; Hugdahl and Ost, 1985) are in contrast to previous reports where it was maintained that conditioning plays a minimal role in the origin of phobic fears (e.g. Murray and Foote, 1979; Rimm, Janda, Lancaster, Nahl and Dittmar, 1977). However, one important difference between these studies is that while Ost and Hugdahl investigated clinical patients asking for treatment in a hospital unit, Murray and Foote (1979) used non-phobic, but fearful, undergraduate students. The findings by Hugdahl and Ost were further supported in a recent study by McNally and Stekeete (1985) where 71% of a sample of small-animal phobics attributed the origin of their fear to conditioning experiences.

However, although different pathways to phobic fear may be identified, the predicted relationship between ways of acquisition and the particular response-profile in terms of a three-systems model is more complex. In essence, the results by Ost and Hugdahl (1981, 1983, 1985, Hugdahl and Ost, 1985) have failed to identify a significant relationship between ways of acquisition and fear components.

Similarly, Ost (1985) reported in a sample of 183 patients that there was no difference in the proportion of improved patients between physiologically and cognitively based treatment methods for those patients with a background history of conditioning experiences. However, patients with indirect acquisition experiences demonstrated greater improvement when a cognitively based treatment method, like Stress-Inoculation Training (Meichenbaum, 1977), was employed.

A final comment concerning the three-systems model of fear concerns recent reports by Mathews and MacLeod (e.g. 1985, 1986; see also Foa and McNally, 1986) where the cognitive component in fear was assessed by measures of perceptual vigilance for threatening stimuli. This is an important development in research on phobic behaviour, since it has the advantage of not relying only on subjective reports when assessing the cognitive component. Specifically, Mathews and MacLeod (1985, 1986) presented colour-words that were either threatening or neutral. The subjects' task was to concentrate on naming the colour, ignoring the word. Colour-naming was found to be slowed in patients anxious about the threatening words. Furthermore, Watts, Frank, McKenna, Sharrock and Trezise (1986) used a version of the Stroop (1938) colour-naming test where spider phobics were required to colour-name spider-related words (like hairy, creepy, crawl). Subjects were given Stroop cards with either spider or control words. Results showed that spider-phobic subjects were severely retarded in colour-naming the spider words, but not the control words. Treatment with systematic desensitization reduced the interference observed with the spider words. Thus, it seems that treatment may not only change overt behaviour, but also perceptual attributes related to phobic fear. This line of research has interesting implications not only for treatment effects, but also for the elucidation of basic mechanisms in phobic reactions. In a similar vein, Foa and McNally (1986) used a dichotic listening task where fear-relevant words were presented together with an irrelevant prose passage. The fear-relevant words were detected more often than neutral words, and skin conductance responses (SCRs) were also larger in amplitude to the fear-relevant words. Interestingly, these differences between the fear-relevant and neutral words disappeared after treatment.

THE PSYCHOPHYSIOLOGY OF SIMPLE PHOBIAS

ELECTRODERMAL RECORDINGS

In a comparison between anxiety states and simple phobias, Lader (1967) showed that specific phobias revealed rapid habituation of the electrodermal orienting response, as indicated by skin conductance responses (SCRs), while skin conductance levels (SCLs) did not discriminate between groups.

Furthermore, both Geer (1966) and Wilson (1967) found larger SCRs to pictures of snakes and spiders than to control stimuli in snake and spider phobics. Control subjects did not show discriminatory responding between stimuli. Hare and Blevings (1975) compared spider phobics and controls on SCR amplitudes when they were exposed to pictures of spiders and neutral objects. As expected, the phobic group revealed larger SCRs to the spider pictures. Tonic SCLs, however, did not differentiate between groups. This has also been reported by Lader and Wing (1966). Similarly, Klorman, Weissberg, and Wiesenfeld (1977) did not find evidence for differential SCLs in phobics and controls when exposed to slides of mutilated bodies. Furthermore, Ohman, Dimberg and Ost (1985) reported larger SCR amplitudes to pictures of unknown faces in subjects high in social fear compared to those in a low-fear group. Finally, Sartory (1986) has studied orienting responses in phobic subjects using SCRs as dependent measures and has argued that phobic fears, unlike panic anxiety, are characterized by attention being directed towards external environmental cues.

Non-specific skin conductance responses (NSSCRs) have been reported as perhaps the most reliable index of heightened arousal in a fear response (see Lader and Wing, 1966, for an overview). Prigatano and Johnson (1974) found more NSSCRs in phobic subjects viewing slides of spiders, and Marks, Marsel, Boulougouris and Huson (1971) found more NSSCRs in phobic subjects imagining fear-eliciting scenes. Prigatano and Johnson (1974), however, failed to differentiate between groups when using SCR amplitude.

In summary, it seems that both frequency of NSSCRs and the amplitude of stimulus-elicited SCRs are positively related to increased fear. However, SCLs have not yielded the same consistent results. It is therefore recommended that spontaneous fluctuations (NSSCRs) and SCRs are monitored when electrodermal activity is used as an index of fear in simple phobias.

For further information, the reader is referred to Sartory and Lader (1981), and to Sartory (1983) for excellent reviews.

CARDIOVASCULAR RECORDINGS

Heart Rate Recordings

Psychophysiological cardiovascular response systems typically include measures of heart rate (HR), blood pressure, and peripheral blood flow (vasomotor activity). Since HR is influenced by both the sympathetic and the parasympathetic branches of the autonomic nervous system, it is a likely candidate for indexing phobic fear reactions.

Psychophysiologists have focused upon the second-by-second or beat-by-beat changes that occur upon repeated exposure to fear-relevant stimuli. A multiphasic response pattern is typically observed with initial deceleration compared to pre-stimulus baseline, and with a peak 2 s after stimulus onset. This is sometimes followed by an acceleration, and a second deceleration. Some authors (e.g. Bohlin and Kjellberg, 1979) have argued that the initial deceleration is related to the elicitation of an orienting response (OR) upon stimulus exposure (cf. Connor and Lang, 1969). The acceleration is similarly conceptualized as an index of a defensive reaction (DR), and seems to be related to stimulus significance and to motivational and emotional aspects of the stimulus (Coles and Duncan-Johnson, 1975). Turpin (1986) has recently reviewed the psychophysiological literature on the OR/DR distinction, and has emphasized the need for a revised scheme of OR/DR differentiation including such aspects as the response direction of the autonomic measures and the importance of the startle reflex.

Heart rate acceleration was demonstrated by Lang, Melamed and Hart (1970) who had snake phobics imagine fear-relevant scenes. Of particular interest was the fact that the amount of HR acceleration was positively correlated with the subjective experience of fear intensity. Thus, there was a linear increase in HR with increased fear ratings. In a later study by Sartory, Rachman and Grey (1977), it was shown that the linear relationship between HR acceleration and fear intensity was consistent only at relatively intense fear levels. Sartory et al. (1977) exposed fearful and volunteer subjects to phobic objects at distances which elicited fear ratings of four different intensities. The results showed that HR changes differentiated between the groups at the more intense rating levels, but not at the low levels. Thus, it seems that although HR is increased in fear states, a clear positive linear relationship is only demonstrated at more intense fear levels.

Other researchers who have reported increased HR responses to phobic stimuli include Fredrikson (1981), Hare (1973), Klorman et al. (1977), and Prigatano and Johnson (1974). Hare (1973) and Fredrikson (1981) exposed phobic and non-phobic subjects to pictures of the phobic object. Both studies demonstrated an accelerative response to fear stimuli in the phobic, but not in the non-phobic subjects, thus indicating a specific cardiovascular response in the phobic subjects. In addition, Hare and Blevings (1975) showed that it was possible to observe a conditioned HR *acceleration* in spider phobics by pairing the presentation of spider pictures with tones. Heart rate acceleration was elicited by the tones only after these had been paired with the pictures. Acceleration was also observed by Fredrikson (1981) in a sample of both spider and snake phobics, in response to slides of the phobic object. However, conditioned *deceleration* was observed in normals undergoing a conditioning procedure to pictures of snakes and spiders.

Klorman et al. (1977) presented slides of mutilation scenes to subjects fearful of these stimuli, and compared the HR response with that of non-fearful subjects. Neutral and incongruous slides were used as control stimuli. The neutral and incongruous slides elicited HR deceleration in both the fearful and non-fearful subjects. The mutilation scenes, however, elicited initial HR acceleration in the fearful subjects, while the non-fearful subjects maintained their decelerative response.

A similar response pattern was reported by May (1977) who had subjects imagining a neutral or a fearful scene. As an example, a neutral scene depicted a girl in a chair reading a magazine, while a fearful scene portrayed a girl in a chair with a snake crawling on her. The responses of the fearful subjects were differentiated between imagery scenes, with increased HR acceleration to the fear-relevant scenes. However, no such difference was found for the non-fearful group, who mainly exhibited HR deceleration.

In a recent study, Sartory (1986) compared HR responses in subjects fearful of snakes and spiders. Slides of phobic content were presented concurrently with tones. Subjects were divided into three groups (accelerators, decelerators, and medium responders) depending on their initial HR response to the first slide presentation. Interestingly, the 'accelerators' also showed a marked deceleration to the first tone, yielding an orienting-type response. This was not found in the other two groups. This is an interesting finding since it suggests that individuals with specific fears may be more prone than others to focus their attention on environmental events, since HR deceleration has frequently been employed as an index of the elicitation of an orienting response (Turpin, 1986). Sartory (1986) argues that her findings are at variance with those found in chronically anxious subjects. The latter group would appear to focus their attention on internal cues whereas simple phobics focus attention on external cues.

Johansson and Ost (1982) studied the relationship between perceived and actual changes in HR. They argued that without expensive and advanced electronic equipment, the clinician is at a disadvantage compared to the researcher in obtaining a reliable measure of physiological response. One way to achieve reliable measurement would be to administer to the patient the Autonomic Perception Questionnaire (APQ; Mandler, Mandler and Uviller, 1958), which is a self-rating scale for the perception of changes in physiological reactions. By comparing the actual change in HR with the perceived change, Johansson and Ost (1982) sought to determine the clinical significance of the APQ in a phobic sample. Previous studies (e.g. Borcovec, Stone, O'Brien and Kaloupek, 1973) had failed to find significant correlations between the APQ and HR. However, Johansson and Ost (1982) argued that most of the previous studies had used fear analogue samples, and not clinical subjects, which might explain these low correlations. If the findings by Sartory *et al.* (1977) are taken into consideration, one might expect a positive correlation between APQ and HR, at the more intense fear levels. Interestingly, Johansson and Ost (1982) found that while social phobics were quite good at estimating their actual HR change during a provocation test, this was not the case for a similar sample of claustrophobic patients. Thus, the issue of the relation of perceived changes in cardiovascular response to actual change in physiological responding may also be related to the type of phobia studied.

Peripheral Blood Flow Recordings

Hare (1973) and Hare and Blevings (1975) found that cephalic vasomotor responses differentiated between phobic and non-phobic subjects who were exposed to slides of spiders. While vasoconstriction was found in the phobic group, vasodilatation was found in the non-phobic group. In Sokolov's (1963) terminology, the former response is part of a DR, while the latter response is part of an OR. The results of these studies are consistent with the findings of HR acceleration reported in most phobic subjects.

In summary, HR is generally increased when patients with simple phobias are exposed to a phobia-relevant object. Furthermore, the HR response seems to be related to the intensity of fear experienced. Although this is the common pattern of responding, it is important to realize that it is not always the case. The best known example of an opposite HR response (i.e. deceleration) upon exposure to phobic stimuli is the paradoxical response seen in blood–injury phobia.

Cardiovascular Response in Blood–Injury Phobia

Although Agras et al. (1969) concluded that fear of blood and injury was the most common simple phobia, with a prevalence of 3.1% in a normal population, it is also the least studied among the simple phobias. Psychophysiological studies of blood–injury phobia may shed further light on the longstanding controversy in psychophysiology concerning emotional stimulus–response specificity, i.e. that different emotional stimuli produce distinct physiological response patterns. The classic example of this was the demonstration by Ax in 1953 that anger and fear yielded different cardiovascular responses in a sample of non-phobic subjects.

The uniphasic cardiovascular pattern of increased HR and blood pressure as described above in the case of simple phobias, is not observed in blood–injury phobics. Instead, the typical clinical response is feelings of dizziness, pallor, and sweating, which eventually lead to fainting, or near-fainting (Connolly, Hallam and Marks, 1976; Hugdahl and Ost, 1985). This is accompanied by clinical signs of a vasovagal phenomenon: a profound decrease in HR (bradycardia) and blood pressure are often observed (Cohn, Kron and Brady, 1976; Wardle and Jarvis, 1981). Similarly, Graham, Kabler and Lunsford (1961) have observed a biphasic cardiovascular response in blood donors, which is characterized by an initial increase in HR (tachycardia) and blood pressure, followed by a massive bradycardia and fall in blood pressure, eventually leading to fainting.

Graham *et al.* (1961) interpreted the above findings as indicating an initial sympathetic arousal response which was linked to the experience of anxiety. The increase in sympathetic activity was said to have resulted in the initial HR acceleration and increase in blood pressure. This increase in sympathetic activity was, however, said to be accompanied by an opposing increase in *parasympathetic* activity. When the anxiety suddenly cessated, the sympathetic activity would also decrease, and the parasympathetic influences were left unopposed. This second phase vasovagal syncope would then lead to bradycardia and eventually fainting.

Recently, Wardle and Jarvis (1981) reported a diphasic HR response with tachycardia preceding a massive bradycardia in a 25-year-old male afraid of blood and injury. The patient was assessed in the laboratory while having a few millilitres of blood taken. Essentially the same response pattern was also observed by Ost *et al.* (1984) in 18 clinical blood–injury phobics when exposed to a 30-min film showing details of a surgical operation. The subjects were encouraged to view the film for as long as they could, but were told that they could turn it off at any time. Heart rate, and systolic and diastolic blood pressure were monitored before, during, and after the film. The results showed an initial increase from baseline in all parameters during an instruction period when the experimenter explained the purpose and nature of the test. This was followed by a massive bradycardia (down to 30–40 beats/min) when the film started, with a peak at about 4 min after the film was turned off.

An interesting phenomenon was observed by Ost *et al.* (1984). An analysis of individual electrocardiograms (ECGs) showed periods of asystole ranging between 5 and 10 s in some patients. Thus, the average bradycardia seen in blood–injury phobia might not be caused by a reduction in stable HR, but possibly by periods of asystole, followed by periods of rapid ventricular contraction. The exact nature of this particular response pattern remains unclear.

A biphasic cardiovascular response was also observed by Curtis and Thyer (1983), who monitored HR and blood pressure in two blood–injury phobic patients undergoing exposure treatment. Their data, however, do not support the hypothesis of 'cessation of anxiety' proposed by Graham *et al.* (1961) as the cause for the vasovagal syncope, since exposure therapy eliminated both the cardiovascular *and* the subjective fear responses. On the basis of their own data, and from observations of others on the specificity of blood–injury phobias, Curtis and Thyer (1983) suggested that this kind of phobic behaviour should have a diagnostic category of its own rather than being included in the DSM-III (American Psychiatric Association, 1980) category of simple phobias.

It may be speculated that the atypical response seen in blood–injury phobias has an evolutionary background. Injury to the body with excessive bleeding is lethal to the organism. A vasovagal reflex to slow down cardiovascular effectors would thus be instrumental in preventing excessive blood loss. To exhibit a similar response when viewing *someone else* bleeding is, however, an irrational phobic response. It is as if the brain misperceives or misinterprets the source of the injury, causing the same biphasic response as that reflexively observed upon real injury to the body.

There seems, however, to be a lack of agreement amongst different explanations of this unique psychophysiological response pattern observed in blood–injury phobics. One area of interest is whether these patients show the same decrease in cardiovascular responding to *other* fear-relevant and stress-related stimuli and situations. If the responses are tied only to stimuli related to blood and injury, we may be dealing with a unique case of stimulus–response specificity which should attract interest from researchers concerned with the psychophysiology of emotions. A study by Fredrikson, Sundin and Frankenhaeuser (1985) yielded data relevant to this question. Six subjects fearful of blood and mutilation were compared with six subjects fearful of snakes and spiders. Each group was presented with slides of phobic and neutral content. Increased cortisol excretion in the urine was observed in both groups in response to the phobic stimuli compared to the neutral stimuli. There was, however, no significant difference between the groups. Thus, while blood–injury phobias display a different cardiovascular response pattern compared to other simple phobias, this is obviously not accompanied by a similarly unique neuroendocrine response pattern.

An interesting implication arises from the notion that the tachycardia/bradycardia response in blood–injury phobia is caused by a parallel increase in sympathetic nervous system (SNS) and parasympathetic nervous system (PNS) activity (with sudden SNS cessation). If the initial SNS increase could be prevented, would the subsequent PNS increase disappear? A somewhat paradoxical consequence of this suggestion is that a beta-blocker that *slows* the heart, might be effective in the treatment of blood–injury phobias, since it might prevent the occurrence of the initial increase in SNS activity.

The Effect of Beta-Blockers

The use of beta-adrenergic-blocking drugs in phobic fears may be said to have its theoretical rationale in the three-systems model of fear (Hugdahl, 1981; Lang, 1968; Rachman, 1977). If autonomic physiological arousal is one component of a phobic reaction, then pharmacologically blocking at least part of the reaction, might have a positive effect upon the subjective experience of fear, and also on any accompanying avoidance behaviour. The development of beta-blocking drugs that act directly on the frequency of the heart by blocking the synapse at the sino-atrial node of the right atrium seemed a promising tool. However, early studies that administered tolamolol to both spider and snake phobics failed to observe any significant effects on self-reported anxiety (see also Taggart, Carruthers and Sommerville, 1973). Furthermore, Tyrer and Lader (1974) found that diazepam was generally more effective in anxiety states than a beta-blocker (propranolol). However, other studies have reported significant effects of beta-blockers compared to placebo (Butollo, 1981; Erdmann and van Lindern, 1980; Kathol, Noyes, Slymen, Crowe, Clancy and Kerber, 1980), indicating that the relationship between phobic fear and beta-blockers is a complex one.

Starting from the three-systems model of fear, Fagerström, Hugdahl and Lundström (1985; see also Hallstrom, Treasaden, Guy Edwards and Lader, 1981), reasoned that beta-blockers should be most effective in those phobic subjects who could be identified as physiological responders, and especially those with marked cardiovascular reactivity. If this were true, then physiological responders should benefit more from pharmacological treatment than cognitive responders. Fagerström *et al.* (1985) compared the effects of two types of beta-blockers (propranolol and atenolol) and a placebo on fear responses in snake and spider phobics. Propranolol is a non-specific beta-blocker that easily penetrates the blood–brain barrier, whereas atenolol is a non-penetrating beta-2 selective blocker. All subjects were exposed to slide pictures of snakes or spiders depending on the particular phobia.

It was predicted that subjects with high cardiovascular reactivity would be more sensitive to beta-blocker treatment when exposed to the fear-relevant slides. The results indicated significant effects for HR and finger temperature during drug conditions compared to placebo. Diastolic blood pressure was unaffected, while systolic blood pressure differentiated between high and low reactors. Of particular interest was the effect of beta-blockers on subjective anxiety. Contrary to initial expectations, it was found that subjects high in cardiovascular reactivity showed *increased* anxiety ratings during drug conditions compared to placebo, and especially in the propanolol condition. Thus, it seems that the administration of a beta-blocker reduced subjectively experienced anxiety more in subjects characterized as low in cardiovascular reactivity.

In an attempt to explain this unexpected finding, Fagerström *et al.* (1985) suggested that high cardiovascular reactors are so conscious and skilled in assessing the ongoing status of their cardiovascular system that they become very easily aware of novel sensations. This alerts them and increases their fear. Thus, it is argued that subjects high in cardiovascular reactivity would respond with increased fear to *any* change in cardiovascular activity irrespective of the direction of the change. However, one drawback with this explanation is that several studies have shown rather low intercorrelations between scores on the APQ and actual autonomic change (e.g. Brener and Jones, 1974; Epstein and Stein, 1974).

SKELETAL MUSCLE RECORDINGS

Psychophysiological recording of skeletal muscle activity typically involves electromyography, where electrodes are placed on the skin over an active muscle, and the algebraic sum of a large number of muscle fibre depolarizations is monitored. For a review of electromyogram (EMG) recordings in psychophysiology, see Lippold (1967), Fridlund and Cacioppo (1986), and Chapter 19 in this handbook.

The most frequently used electrode sites are over the frontalis, or forearm extensor muscles. As argued by Sartory and Lader (1981), there seem to be as many studies with findings of increased EMG activity in fear and anxiety, as there are results in the opposite direction. A study by Hugdahl and Ost (1985) supports the picture of both increased and decreased skeletal muscle activity in phobias. In this study, 267 phobic patients, representing six different subgroupings, were asked to rate how intensively they experienced 11 specified physiological reactions when confronted with their phobic situation. Among the 11 items in the questionnaire, one question related to muscles becoming tense, and one question concerned muscles becoming weak. The results revealed that mixed feelings of muscles becoming both tense and weak were quite common. Thus, previous inconsistencies in the literature concerning the relation of EMG to phobic fear (see Sartory and Lader, 1981 for review) is nicely supported by the analysis of subjective feelings reported in the data by Hugdahl and Ost (1985).

ELECTROENCEPHALOGRAM RECORDINGS AND EVOKED BRAIN POTENTIALS

Traditionally, the use of electroencephalographic (EEG) measures of fear and anxiety has focused on the blocking of alpha activity in the EEG. Alpha activity refers to phasic cortical activity having a frequency range of 8–13 Hz (Hassett, 1978). The presence of alpha waves in the EEG is said to indicate a state of lowered activation and arousal, while the absence or blocking of alpha activity indicates increased activation and arousal. Anxiety and fear states would thus be indicative of reduced alpha frequencies (e.g. Lindsley, 1950). Unfortunately, the unidimensional character of activation and arousal is questionable (see Chapter 1). For example, Lacey (1967) has shown that different response systems may go in opposite directions during stressful stimulation.

By mathematically averaging short samples of EEG contingent upon repeated stimulations, it is possible to detect subtle averaged brain potentials (event-related potentials, ERPs, and contingent negative variations, CNVs) to discrete stimulation hidden in the EEG (Hassett, 1978). One of these, the CNV, is a recording of a slow negative wave which occurs between stimulus administrations in two-stimulus, or classical conditioning paradigms (Walter, Cooper, Aldridge, McCallum and Winter, 1964).

Dubrovsky, Solyom and Barbas (1978) observed larger CNVs in a sample of phobic subjects in anticipation of a phobic as compared to a neutral stimulus. Klorman and Ryan (1980), and Rizzo, Spadaro, Albani and Morocutti (1983) have reported smaller CNVs in response to visual presentations of fear-relevant stimuli. Klorman and Ryan (1980) studied subjects fearful of blood–injury when confronted with repeated presentations of mutilation slides. Smaller CNV amplitudes in response to phobia-related stimuli were also reported by Lumsden, Howard and Fenton (1986) in phobic volunteers, and in subjects reporting themselves fearful of small animals. Phobic and neutral slides were associated with two tones differing in pitch following a classical conditioning paradigm. Specifically, it was found that anticipation of the phobic slide after tone presentations yielded smaller CNVs during acquisition than did anticipation of neutral slides. However, the results were only reliable for the volunteer fearful subjects. This complicates the nature of the findings. In summary, it seems that smaller CNVs may be associated with phobic fear states, although there are conflicting data in the literature.

PSYCHOPHYSIOLOGICAL RESPONSE PATTERNS: SUMMARY

Table 9.1 summarizes the findings concerning psychophysiological response patterns reviewed in this chapter. For previous reviews, see Lader (1975) and Sartory and Lader (1981).

There is a general increase in both phasic and tonic electrodermal activity, reflecting increased SNS activity. The increase in phasic activity is related to both stimulus-elicited and non-specific responses. Non-specific activity might be a more sensitive index than stimulus-elicited responses. Increases in tonic activity seldom occur in isolation to increased phasic activity. This would indicate that changes in tonic activity are secondary to phasic responding. Moreover, habituation of the electrodermal orienting response is delayed by fear-relevant stimuli (Ohman, Eriksson, Fredrikson, Hugdahl and Olofsson, 1974), and also in clinically anxious subjects (Lader and Wing, 1966).

There is generally an increase in both HR and blood pressure in phobic reactions, accompanied by an increase in peripheral resistance (vasoconstriction). The evoked HR response typically shows an acceleratory component following presentations of fear-relevant slides in phobic subjects (Fredrikson, 1981), with a deceleratory component observed in non-phobic subjects conditioned to fear-relevant stimuli (Fredrikson and Ohman, 1979).

Skeletal muscle responses involve either increased or decreased EMGs, usually recorded from the frontalis or forearm extensor muscles. The EEG shows a reduction in alpha 8–13 Hz activity, together with reduced CNV activity, and an increase in the P300-component amplitude of the ERP to fear-

Table 9.1
Typical psychophysiological response patterns in simple phobic fears*

Electrodermal system	– Increase in skin conductance response (SCR) amplitudes. – Increase in frequency of non-specific skin conductance fluctuations (NSSCRs). – Increase in skin conductance levels (SCL), secondary to response increases. – Large initial orienting responses, with retarded habituation.
Cardiovascular system	– Increase in heart rate (HR). – Increase in systolic and diastolic blood pressure. – Peripheral vasoconstriction. – Phasic HR acceleration to repeated stimulation.
Muscles	– Both muscle tension increase and decrease (frontalis, forearm extensors).
Electrocortical system	– Reduced alpha (8–13 Hz) activity. – Reduced contingent negative variation (CNV) amplitude. – Increased P300-component amplitude of the event-related potential (ERP).

* Note exceptions for blood–injury phobia (see text).

relevant stimuli (see Donchin, Karis, Bashore, Coles and Gratton, 1986, for a review of the P300 literature).

CLASSICAL CONDITIONING AND SIMPLE PHOBIAS

The conditioning approach to the acquisition of fears and simple phobias has had a strong impact on behaviourally oriented theories and models (see Eysenck, 1979; Eysenck and Rachman, 1965). Traditionally, this has been conceptualized in terms of the two-factor theory of fear and avoidance as advocated by Mowrer (1939). Briefly, the theory assumes that fear is a conditioned response that is elicited in the presence of a conditioned stimulus. When elicited, the conditioned response energizes instrumental behaviour to avoid or escape from the situation. During the last 10–15 years, this model has been challenged by several authors (e.g. Hugdahl, 1977; Marks, 1969; Rachman, 1977; Seligman, 1971). More specifically, it has been questioned whether two-factor theory can adequately accommodate or explain the selectivity of phobias, the failure of extinction despite unreinforced presentations of the conditioned stimulus, and the one-trial acquisition observed in phobic fears.

PREPAREDNESS AND PREPARED LEARNING

In 1971, Seligman suggested that the specificity of phobic conditioning could be accounted for by what he named 'biological preparedness', or 'prepared conditioning'. Basically, Seligman (1971) proposed that the general laws of learning may not be valid for all kinds of stimuli and responses. Instead he suggested that organisms had evolved a biologically determined preparedness which led to more easily found associations between certain stimuli, or certain stimuli and reinforcers. The prototype of a prepared paradigm was the taste-aversion phenomenon (Garcia and Koelling, 1966) where rats easily developed an avoidance response to saccharin-flavoured water if this was previously paired with injections of lithium chloride (which made the animals sick), but not when paired with external shocks. A second example of prepared learning was the acquisition of phobic fears.

Using electrodermal measures, Ohman, Hugdahl and Fredrickson in Uppsala (e.g. Hugdahl and Ohman, 1977; Ohman, 1979; Ohman *et al.*, 1976) developed a psychophysiological human laboratory model of prepared fear conditioning. Electrodermal fear responses were conditioned in non-fearful subjects using different supposedly prepared stimuli (slides of snakes and spiders) that were mixed with neutral, or non-prepared stimuli. Typically, the slides signalled that an electric shock would occur 8 s later during the conditioned acquisition phase. In a second phase (extinction), the slides were presented without the shock. Subjects in the prepared group showed significantly more resistance to extinction than subjects in the neutral, or non-prepared group. Also, conditioned SCRs in the prepared group were more resistant to cognitive instructions about the non-occurrence of the shock than were responses in the neutral group (Hugdahl and Ohman, 1977). Thus, the experiments by Ohman and his colleagues showed that conditioned SCRs were selective with respect to the stimulus, that they could be acquired rapidly, and that they could not be abolished by simply instructing the subject.

In addition to the use of SCR as the dependent measure, differential responding to fear-relevant and neutral conditioned stimuli has also been observed using HR (Fredrikson and Ohman, 1979). Thus, responses to fear-relevant stimuli conditioned in the laboratory seemed to mimic the fear responses observed in clinical phobias.

However, attempts to replicate the findings by the Uppsala group have met with mixed success. McNally and Foa (1986) conditioned students high and low in fear to either fear-relevant or neutral conditioned stimuli, with shock as the unconditioned stimulus. They failed to replicate the previous finding that SCRs established to fear-relevant stimuli were more resistant to extinction than those established to neutral stimuli (see also Maltzman and Boyd, 1984; McNally, 1986). On the other hand, Cook (1983) reported significantly better resistance to extinction in a group conditioned to pictures of snakes and spiders

compared to a group conditioned to flowers and mushrooms, thus replicating
the findings by Ohman *et al.* (1976). In addition, Cook (1981) found HR
acceleration to fear-relevant stimuli, but deceleration to neutral stimuli. The
effect was also stronger in female subjects, and especially for those who reported
intense fear for snakes and spiders. However, although Cook (1983) replicated
the resistance to extinction finding, he failed to find evidence for the specificity
of resistance to instructions observed by Hugdahl and Ohman (1977), since
the interaction between instruction and stimulus content was not significant.
It should, however, be remembered that the corresponding interaction was not
significant in the study by Hugdahl and Ohman (1977) either. Because of
heterogeneous variances in the different experimental groups, Hugdahl and
Ohman (1977) compared mean differences between conditioned and unconditioned stimulus responses to the fear-relevant and neutral stimuli for the
instructed group, and found the difference to be significant. Thus, it should be
clear that the reported effect of instructed extinction to fear-relevant stimuli by
Hugdahl and Ohman (1977) did not include a significant two-way interaction
between instruction and stimulus content. (See McNally (1987) for a thorough
review of preparedness and phobias, focusing on the Ohman, Hugdahl and
Fredrickson studies.)

In summary, although the preparedness hypothesis of phobic acquisition
has an obvious theoretical appeal, the empirical psychophysiological support
for it has so far been inconsistent. This might suggest that the effect is empirically rather fragile. It may also underscore the need for the inclusion of
response measures other than psychophysiological ones, and that psychophysiological activity may not be the relevant domain to examine in relation to
prepared fear conditioning. Nevertheless, that simple phobias to a large extent
are acquired through classical conditioning seems to be a consistent finding
(Hugdahl and Ost, 1985; McNally and Stekeete, 1985; Ost and Hugdahl, 1981,
1983, 1985), at least when clinically relevant phobias are considered.

SUMMARY AND CONCLUSIONS

In the present chapter I have described the psychophysiology of simple phobias
from a three-systems conceptualization of fear and emotion (Hugdahl, 1981;
Lang, 1968; Rachman, 1977), where the phobic reaction is seen as consisting
of responses in three different systems (physiological, cognitive, and motor).

It is further argued that the use of psychophysiological indices of fear in
therapy evaluation should be separated from studies related to causal mechanisms in fear acquisition and maintenance. A general overview of simple phobias
is provided focusing on problems of definitions, age of onset, prevalence, and
mode of acquisition.

Basic psychophysiological measures are described along with a review of findings related to each response system. It is argued that recent clinical studies by Ost and Hugdahl (1981, 1983, 1985; Hugdahl and Ost, 1985; see also McNally and Stekeete, 1985; Wolpe *et al.*, 1985) have shown simple phobias in clinically relevant patients to be acquired through traumatic classical conditioning to an extent not previously acknowledged. It is further argued that psychophysiology may not only reveal the intensity of a fear reaction, but that specific psychophysiological reactions may also differentiate between various simple phobias. This is most obvious in the unique cardiovascular response seen in blood–injury phobics. The use of beta-blockers in the treatment of simple phobias, together with its psychophysiological evaluation is also reviewed. The chapter is concluded by a brief discussion of the theory of biological prepared conditioning (Seligman, 1971).

A final issue concerns the utility of psychophysiological measures for clinical research and therapy. As I have argued previously, it is important to make a distinction between the use of psychophysiological techniques in treatment evaluation, or directly in the therapy process, from its use in research on mechanisms in the aetiology of fear and of clinical processes. While the former use has been rather extensive, the latter use has not been employed to any great extent. However, it is my belief that psychophysiology may contribute also to our understanding of clinical processes and that it may play an important role in unravelling psychological aspects of disease in general. As an example, psychophysiological investigations of arousal and activation may have something to tell us of individual differences in reactivity to disease, like vulnerability to develop anticipatory nausea and vomiting after chemotherapy treatment for cancer. It may thus turn out that routine psychophysiological screening may be as relevant for clinical psychology and behavioural medicine as is current routine psychometric testing for clinical neuropsychology.

REFERENCES

Agras, W.S., Sylvester, D. and Oliveau, D. (1969). The epidemiology of common fears and phobias. *Comprehensive Psychiatry* **10**, 151–156.

American Psychiatric Association (1980). *Diagnostic and Statistical Manual of Mental Disorders*, 3rd edn (DSM-III). Washington, DC: APA.

Arnarson, E. D. (1988). Prevalence of phobias in the Icelandic population. *Paper presented at the Third Nordic Congress of Behaviour Therapy, Norway*.

Ax, A. (1953). The physiological differentiation between anger and fear in humans. *Psychosomatic Medicine* **15**, 433–442.

Bennett-Levy, J. and Marteau, T. (1984). Fear of animals: what is prepared? *British Journal of Psychology* **75**, 37–42.

Bohlin, G. and Kjellberg, A. (1979). Orienting activity in two-stimulus paradigms as reflected in heart rate. In: H.D. Kimmel, E.H. van Olst and J.F. Orlebeke (Eds) *The Orienting Reflex*. Hillsdale, NJ: Erlbaum.

Borcovec, T.-D., Stone, N.M., O'Brien, G.T. and Kaloupek, D.G. (1978). Evaluation

304 K. Hugdahl

of a clinically relevant target behavior for analog outcome research. *Behavior Therapy* **5**, 503–573.

Bowd, A.D. and Boylan, C.R. (1984). Reported fears of animals among biology and non-biology students. *Psychological Reports* **54**, 18.

Brener, J. and Jones, J.N. (1974). Interoceptive discrimination in intact humans: detection of cardiac activity. *Physiology and Behavior* **13**, 763–767.

Butollo, W. (1981). Behandling chronischer Angst mit Verhaltens-therapie und Beta-Rezeptoren-Blockern: eine empirische Untersuchung. *Psychotherapy and Medical Psychology* **31**, 53–57.

Cohn, C.K., Kron, R.E. and Brady, J.P. (1976). A case of blood–illness phobia treated behaviorally. *Journal of Mental Disorders* **162**, 65–68.

Coles, M.G.H. and Duncan-Johnson, C.C. (1975). Cardiac activity and information processing: the effects of stimulus significance, and detection and response requirements. *Journal of Experimental Psychology: Human Perception and Performance* **1**, 418–428.

Connolly, J., Hallam, R.S. and Marks, I.M. (1976). Selective association of fainting with blood–injury–illness fear. *Behavior Therapy* **7**, 8–13.

Connor, W.H. and Lang, P.J. (1969). Cortical slow-wave and cardiac rate response in stimulus orientation and reaction-time conditions. *Journal of Experimental Psychology* **82**, 310–320.

Cook, E.W. (1981). Classical conditioning, individual differences, and preparedness. Unpublished Master Thesis, Department of Psychology, University of Wisconsin-Madison.

Cook, E.W. (1983). Human classical conditioning and the preparedness hypothesis. Unpublished Doctoral Dissertation, Department of Psychology, University of Wisconsin-Madison.

Curtis, G.C. and Thyer, B. (1983). Fainting on exposure to phobic stimuli. *American Journal of Psychiatry* **140**, 771–774.

Donchin, E., Karis, D., Bashore, T.R., Coles, M.G.H. and Gratton, G. (1986). Cognitive psychophysiology and human information processing. In: M.G.H. Coles, E. Donchin and S.W. Porges (Eds) *Psychophysiology: Systems, Processes, and Applications*. Amsterdam: Elsevier.

Dubrovsky, N., Solyom, L. and Barbas, H. (1978). Characteristic of the contingent negative variation in patients suffering from specific phobias. *Biological Psychiatry* **13**, 531–540.

Epstein, L.H. and Stein, D.B. (1974). Feedback-influenced heart rate discrimination. *Journal of Abnormal Psychology* **83**, 333–338.

Erdmann, G. and van Lindern, B. (1980). The effects of beta-adrenergic stimulation and beta-adrenergic blockade on emotional reactions. *Psychophysiology* **17**, 332–338.

Eysenck, H.J. (1979). The conditioning model of neurosis. *Behavioral and Brain Sciences* **2**, 155–199.

Eysenck, H.J. and Rachman, S.J. (1965). *The Causes and Cures of Neurosis*. London: Routledge and Kegan Paul.

Fagerström, K.O., Hugdahl, K. and Lundström, N. (1985). Effect of beta-receptor blockade on anxiety with reference to the Three-Systems model of phobic behavior. *Neuropsychobiology* **13**, 187–193.

Foa, E. and McNally, R.J. (1986). Sensitivity to feared stimuli in obsessive–compulsives: a dichotic listening analysis. *Cognitive Therapy and Research* **10**, 477–485.

Fredrikson, M. (1981). Orienting and defensive reactions to phobic and conditioned fear stimuli in phobics and normals. *Psychophysiology* **18**, 456–465.

Fredrikson, M. and Ohman, A. (1979). Cardiovascular and electrodermal responses conditioned to fear-relevant stimuli. *Psychophysiology* **16**, 1–7.

Fredrikson, M., Sundin, O. and Frankenhaeuser, M. (1985). Cortisol excretion during the defense reaction in humans. *Psychosomatic Medicine* **47**, 313–319.

Fridlund, A.J. and Cacioppo, J.T. (1986). Guidelines for human electromyographic research. *Psychophysiology* **23**, 567–589.

Garcia, J. and Koelling, R.A. (1966). Relation of cue to consequence in avoidance learning. *Psychonomic Science* **4**, 123–124.

Gatchel, R.J. (1979). Biofeedback and the treatment of fear and anxiety. In: R.J. Gatchel and K.P. Price (Eds) *Clinical Applications of Biofeedback: Appraisal and Status*. New York: Pergamon.

Geer, J.H. (1966). Fear and autonomic arousal. *Journal of Abnormal Psychology* **71**, 263–255.

Graham, D.T., Kabler, J.D. and Lunsford, L. (1961). Vasovagal fainting: a diphasic response. *Psychosomatic Medicine* **23**, 319–326.

Hallstrom, C., Treasaden, I., Guy Edwards, J. and Lader, M. (1981). Diazepam, propranolol and their combination in the management of chronic anxiety. *British Journal of Psychiatry* **139**, 417–421.

Hare, R.D. (1973). Orienting and defensive responses to visual stimuli. *Psychophysiology* **10**, 453–464.

Hare, R.D. and Blevings, G. (1975). Defensive responses to phobic stimuli. *Biological Psychology* **3**, 1–13.

Hassett, J. (1978). *A Primer of Psychophysiology*. San Francisco: Freeman.

Haug, T., Brenne, L., Johnsen, B.H., Berntzen, D., Gotestam, K.G. and Hugdahl, K. (1987). A Three-Systems analysis of fear of flying: a comparison of a consonant vs. a non-consonant treatment method. *Behaviour Research and Therapy* **25**, 187–194.

Holden, A.E., Jr and Barlow, D.H. (1986). Heart rate and heart rate variability recorded *in vivo* in agoraphobics and nonphobics. *Behavior Therapy* **17**, 26–42.

Hugdahl, K. (1977). Conditioning, stimulus relevance, and cognitive factors in phobic fears. *Acta Universitas Uppsaliensis*, Abstracts from Dissertations from the Faculty of Social Sciences, University of Uppsala, no. 16.

Hugdahl, K. (1978). Electrodermal conditioning to potentially phobic stimuli: effects of instructed extinction. *Behaviour Research and Therapy* **16**, 315–321.

Hugdahl, K. (1981). The Three-Systems model of fear and emotion: a critical examination. *Behaviour Research and Therapy* **19**, 75–85.

Hugdahl, K. and Ohman, A. (1977). Effects of instruction on acquisition and extinction of electrodermal responses to fear relevant stimuli. *Journal of Experimental Psychology: Human Learning and Memory* **3**, 608–618.

Hugdahl, K. and Ost, L.G. (1985). Subjectively rated physiological and cognitive symptoms in six different clinical phobias. *Personality and Individual Differences* **6**, 175–188.

James, W. (1884). What is emotion? *Mind* **19**, 188–205.

Johansson, J. and Ost, L.G. (1982). Perception of autonomic reactions and actual heart rate in phobic patients. *Journal of Behavioral Assessment* **4**, 133–143.

Kathol, R.G., Noyes, R., Jr, Slymen, D.J., Crowe, R.R., Clancy, J. and Kerber, R.E. (1980). Propranolol in chronic anxiety disorders. *Archives of General Psychiatry* **37**, 1361–1365.

Klorman, R. and Ryan, R.M. (1980). Heart rate, contingent negative variation, and evoked potentials during anticipation of affective stimulation. *Psychophysiology* **17**, 513–523.

Klorman, R., Weissberg, R.D. and Wiesenfeld, A.R. (1977). Individual differences in fear and autonomic reactions to affective stimulation. *Psychophysiology* **14**, 45–51.

Lacey, J.I. (1967). Somatic response patterning and stress: some revisions of activation theory. In: M.H. Appley and R. Trumbull (Eds) *Psychological Stress: Issues in Research.* New York: Appleton-Century-Crofts.

Lader, M.H. (1967). Palmar skin conductance measures in anxiety and phobic states. *Journal of Psychosomatic Research* **11**, 271–281.

Lader, M.H. (1975). The psychophysiology of anxious and depressed patients. In: D.C. Fowles (Ed.) *Clinical Applications of Psychophysiology.* New York: Columbia University Press.

Lader, M.H. and Wing, L. (1966). *Physiological Measures, Sedative Drugs and Morbid Anxiety.* Maudsley Monograph no. 14. London: Oxford University Press.

Lang, P.J. (1968). Fear reduction and fear behavior: problems in treating a construct. In: J.M. Schlien (Ed.) *Research in Psychotherapy*, Vol. 3. Washington, DC: American Psychiatric Association.

Lang, P.J., Melamed, B. and Hart, J.D. (1970). A psychophysiological analysis of fear modification using an automated desensitization procedure. *Journal of Abnormal Psychology* **76**, 220–234.

Leitenberg, H. (1976). Behavioral approaches to treatment of neuroses. In: H. Leitenberg (Ed.) *Handbook of Behavior Modification and Behavior Therapy.* New York: Appleton-Century-Crofts.

Lindsley, D.B. (1950). Emotions and the electroencephalogram. In: M.L. Reymert (Ed.) *Feelings and Emotions.* New York: McGraw-Hill.

Lippold, O.C.J. (1967). Electromyography. In: P.H. Venables and I. Martin (Eds) *Manual of Psychophysiological Methods.* Amsterdam: North-Holland.

Lumsden, J., Howard, R.C. and Fenton, G.W. (1986). The contingent negative variation (CNV) to fear-related stimuli in acquisition and extinction. *International Journal of Psychophysiology* **3**, 253–261.

Maltzman, I. and Boyd, G. (1984). Stimulus significance and bilateral SCRs to potentially phobic pictures. *Journal of Abnormal Psychology* **93**, 41–46.

Mandler, G., Mandler, J.M. and Uviller, F.T. (1958). Autonomic feedback: the perception of autonomic activity. *Journal of Abnormal and Social Psychology* **56**, 367–373.

Marks, I. (1969). *Fears and Phobias.* London: Heinemann.

Marks, I.M. (1970). Epidemiology of phobic disorders. *British Journal of Social Psychiatry* **4**, 109–114.

Marks, I. (1981). *Cure and Care of Neurosis – Theory and Practice of Behavioral Therapy.* Chichester: Wiley.

Marks, I. and Gelder, M.G. (1966). Different onset ages in varieties of phobia. *American Journal of Psychiatry* **123**, 218–221.

Marks, I., Marsel, P., Boulougouris, J.D. and Huson, J. (1971). Physiological accompaniments of neutral and phobic imagery. *Psychological Medicine* **1**, 299–307.

Mathews, A. and MacLeod, C. (1985). Selective processing of threat cues in anxiety states. *Behaviour Research and Therapy* **23**, 563–569.

Mathews, A. and MacLeod, C. (1986). Discrimination of threat cues without awareness in anxiety states. *Journal of Abnormal Psychology* **95**, 131–138.

May, J.R. (1977). A psychophysiological study of self and externally regulated phobic thoughts. *Behavior Therapy* **8**, 849–861.

McNally, R.J. (1986). Pavlovian conditioning and preparedness: effects of initial fear level. *Behaviour Research and Therapy* **24**, 27–33.

McNally, R.J. (1987). Preparedness and phobias: a review. *Psychological Bulletin* **101**, 283–303.

McNally, R.J. and Foa, E.B. (1986). Preparedness and resistance to extinction to fear-relevant stimuli: a failure to replicate. *Behaviour Research and Therapy* **24**, 529–536.

McNally, R.J. and Stekeete, G.S. (1985). The etiology and maintenance of severe animal phobias. *Behaviour Research and Therapy* **23**, 431–435.

Meichenbaum, D. (1977). *Cognitive-Behavior Modification*. New York: Plenum.

Mowrer, O.H. (1939). A stimulus–response analysis of anxiety and its role as a reinforcing agent. *Psychological Review* **46**, 553–565.

Murray, E.J. and Foote, F. (1979). The origin of fear of snakes. *Behaviour Research and Therapy* **17**, 489–493.

Ohman, A. (1979). Fear relevance, autonomic conditioning, and phobias: a laboratory model. In: P.O. Sjoden, S. Bates and W.S. Dockens, III (Eds) *Trends in Behavior Therapy*. New York: Academic Press.

Ohman, A. (1971). Differentiation of conditioned and orienting response components in electrodermal conditioning. *Psychophysiology* **8**, 7–22.

Ohman, A., Dimberg, U. and Ost, L.G. (1985). Animal and social phobias: biological constraints on learned fear responses. In: S. Reiss and R.R. Bootzin (Eds) *Theoretical Issues in Behavior Therapy*. New York: Academic Press.

Ohman, A., Eriksson, A., Fredrikson, M., Hugdahl, K. and Olofsson, C. (1974). Habituation of the electrodermal orienting reaction to potentially phobic and supposedly neutral stimuli in normal human subjects. *Biological Psychology* **2**, 85–93.

Ohman, A., Fredrikson, M., Hugdahl, K. and Rimmo, P.A. (1976). The premise of equipotentiality in human classical conditioning: conditioned electrodermal responses to potentially phobic stimuli. *Journal of Experimental Psychology: General* **105**, 313–337.

Ost, L.G. (1985). Ways of acquiring phobias and outcome of behavioral treatments. *Behaviour Research and Therapy* **23**, 683–689.

Ost, L.G. and Hugdahl, K. (1981). Acquisition of phobias and anxiety response patterns in clinical patients. *Behaviour Research and Therapy* **19**, 439–447.

Ost, L.G. and Hugdahl, K. (1983). Acquisition of agoraphobia, mode of onset and anxiety response patterns. *Behaviour Research and Therapy* **21**, 623–631.

Ost, L.G. and Hugdahl, K. (1985). Acquisition of blood and dental phobia and anxiety response patterns in clinical patients. *Behaviour Research and Therapy* **23**, 27–34.

Ost, L.G. and Jansson, L. (1986). Methodological issues in cognitive–behavioral treatments of anxiety disorders. In: L. Michelson and M. Ascher (Eds) *Cognitive–Behavioral Assessment and Treatment of Anxiety Disorders*. New York: Guilford.

Ost, L.G., Jerremalm, A. and Jansson, L. (1984). Individual response patterns and the effects of different behavioral methods in the treatment of agoraphobia. *Behaviour Research and Therapy* **22**, 697–707.

Ost, L.G., Johansson, J. and Jerremalm, A. (1982). Individual response patterns and the effects of different behavioral methods in the treatment of claustrophobia. *Behaviour Research and Therapy* **20**, 445–460.

Ost, L.G., Sterner, V. and Lindahl, I.L. (1984). Physiological responses in blood phobics. *Behaviour Research and Therapy* **22**, 109–117.

Prigatano, G.P. and Johnson, H.J. (1974). Autonomic nervous system changes associated with a spider phobic reaction. *Journal of Abnormal Psychology* **83**, 169–177.

Rachman, S. (1977). The conditioning theory of fear-acquisition: a critical examination. *Behaviour Research and Therapy* **15**, 375–387.

Rachman, S. and Seligman, M.E.P. (1976). Unprepared phobias: 'be prepared'. *Behaviour Research and Therapy* **14**, 333–338.

Rimm, D.C., Janda, L.H., Lancaster, D.W., Nahl, M. and Dittmar, K. (1977). An exploratory investigation of the origin and maintenance of phobias. *Behaviour Research and Therapy* **15**, 231–238.

Rizzo, P.A., Spadaro, M., Albani, G. and Morocutti, C. (1983). Contingent negative variation in phobic disorders. *Biological Psychiatry* **9**, 73–77.

Rosenhan, D.L. and Seligman, M.E.P. (1984). *Abnormal Psychology*. New York: Norton.

Sartory, G. (1983). The orienting response and psychopathology: anxiety and phobias. In: D. Siddle (Ed.) *Orienting and Habituation: Perspectives in Human Research*. Chichester: Wiley.

Sartory, G. (1986). Effect of phobic anxiety on the orienting response. *Behaviour Research and Therapy* **24**, 251–261.

Sartory, G. and Lader, M.H. (1981). Psychophysiology and drugs in anxiety and phobias. In: M.I. Christie and P. Mellett (Eds) *Foundations of Psychosomatics*. Chichester: Wiley.

Sartory, G., Rachman, S. and Grey, S.J. (1977). An investigation of the relation between reported fear and heart rate. *Behaviour Research and Therapy* **15**, 435–438.

Seligman, M.E.P. (1971). Phobias and preparedness. *Behavior Therapy* **2**, 307–321.

Sokolov, E.N. (1963). *Perception and the Conditioned Reflex*. Oxford: Pergamon.

Stroop, J.R. (1938). Factors affecting speed in serial verbal reactions. *Psychological Monographs* **50**, 38–48.

Taggart, P., Carruthers, M. and Sommerville, W. (1973). Electrocardiogram, plasma catecholamines and lipids, and their modification by oxprenolol when speaking before an audience. *Lancet* **ii**, 341–346.

Turpin, G. (1986). Effects of stimulus intensity on autonomic responding: the problem of differentiating orienting and defense reflexes. *Psychophysiology* **23**, 1–14.

Tyrer, D.J. and Lader, M.H. (1974). Response to propranolol and diazepam in somatic anxiety. *British Medical Journal* **11**, 14–16.

Walter, W.G., Cooper, R., Aldridge, V., McCallum, W. and Winter, A. (1964). Contingent negative variation: an electrical sign of sensori-motor association and expectancy in the human brain. *Nature* **203**, 380–384.

Wardle, J. and Jarvis, M. (1981). The paradoxical fear response to blood, injury and illness – a treatment report. *Behavioral Psychotherapy* **9**, 13–24.

Watson, J.B. and Raynor, R. (1920). Conditioned emotional reactions. *Journal of Experimental Psychology* **3**, 1–14.

Watts, F.N., Frank, R., McKenna, F.P., Sharrock, R. and Trezise, L. (1986). Colour naming of phobia-related words. *British Journal of Psychology* **77**, 97–108.

Wilson, G.D. (1967). GSR responses to fear-related stimuli. *Perceptual and Motor Skills* **24**, 401–402.

Wolpe, J. (1981). The dichotomy between classically conditioned and cognitively learned anxiety. *Journal of Behavior Therapy and Experimental Psychiatry* **12**, 35–42.

Wolpe, J., Lande, S.D., McNally, R.J. and Schotte, D. (1985). Differentiation between classically conditioned and cognitively based neurotic fears: two pilot studies. *Journal of Behavior Therapy and Experimental Psychiatry* **16**, 287–293.

Chapter 10

Panic Disorder, Agoraphobia, and Social Phobia

Lars-Göran Öst

Psychiatric Research Center,
University of Uppsala,
Ulleråker Hospital,
S-750 17 Uppsala,
Sweden

ABSTRACT

Characteristic features of panic disorder, agoraphobia, and social phobia are briefly reviewed. Basic psychophysiological studies performed in the laboratory and in natural settings, and the contributions of physiological assessment to the evaluation of treatment methods are reviewed. The use of psychophysiology in the study of these disorders should be increased.

Handbook of Clinical Psychophysiology Edited by G. Turpin
© 1989 John Wiley & Sons Ltd

NATURE OF THE DISORDERS

PANIC DISORDER

The most characteristic feature of panic disorder (PD) is the occurrence of panic attacks. These are discrete periods of intense fear which occur spontaneously, 'out of the blue'. According to the *Diagnostic and Statistical Manual for Mental Disorders* (3rd edn: DSM-III; American Psychiatric Association, 1980) at least four of the following 12 symptoms must occur during an attack:

> (1) dyspnea, (2) palpitations, (3) chest pain or discomfort, (4) choking or smothering sensations, (5) dizziness, vertigo, or unsteady feelings, (6) feelings of unreality, (7) paresthesias, (8) hot and cold flashes, (9) sweating, (10) faintness, (11) trembling or shaking, (12) fear of dying, going crazy, or doing something uncontrolled during an attack.
>
> (pp. 231–232)

Furthermore, the attacks must occur outside phobic situations, and have a frequency of at least three in a 3-week period. Finally, the patient must not have developed agoraphobic avoidance, for, if this has occurred, a diagnosis of agoraphobia with panic attacks is made.

The panic attacks usually have a short onset time and generally last for 15–30 min. However, little empirical data are available on these issues. Taylor *et al.* (1986) found a mean onset time (from the first symptom to the peak) of 4 min and an average duration of increased heart rate activity of 20 min. Öst (submitted) let PD patients self-observe panic attacks and found a mean duration of 50 min.

Between panic attacks some patients are anxiety-free until the next attack, while others have varying degrees of anticipatory anxiety. Whether these patients are two subgroups distinguishable on other variables has not yet been investigated.

Panic attacks are, however, not phenomena restricted to patients with the diagnosis of PD or agoraphobia with panic attacks. A recent study by Barlow, Vermilyea, Blanchard, Vermilyea, DiNardo and Cerny (1985) showed that the following percentages of patients receiving other DSM-III diagnoses had experienced panic attacks, and fulfilled the criteria for PD, respectively: agoraphobia 98/74%, social phobia 89/50%, simple phobia 100/33%, generalized anxiety disorder 83/29%, obsessive–compulsive disorder 83%, and major depression 83%.

Furthermore, recent studies by Norton, Dorward and Cox (1986) and Norton, Harrison, Hauch and Rhodes (1985) have shown that in samples of normal college students aged 18–60 (means 28.5 and 25.5 years) panic attacks are surprisingly common. Norton *et al.* (1985) found that as many as 34.4% reported at least one panic attack during the past year, 24.1% had one attack during the last 3 weeks, and 2.1% had one attack during the last 3 weeks, and 2.1% had three panic attacks during the last 3 weeks (thus fulfilling the DSM-III frequency criterion for PD). The corresponding figures in the Norton *et al.* (1986) study were 35.9%, 22.7%, and 3.1%, respectively.

Recent epidemiological studies (Myers *et al.*, 1984; Weissman, Myers and Harding, 1978; Wittchen, 1986) found that the prevalence of PD varies between 0.4% and 1.1%, with a female : male ratio of 1.6 : 1.

Various aetiological models for PD have been suggested in the literature, e.g. biological models by Carr and Sheehan (1984) and Klein (1981), behavioural models by Barlow (1986) and Jacob and Rapport (1984), and cognitive models by Beck and Emery (1985) and Clark (1986). All of the models are formulated in such a way that specific hypotheses can be deduced and tested. Since most of the models have been formulated during the last few years, the empirical evidence is not overwhelming for any one of them.

AGORAPHOBIA

In DSM-III, agoraphobia is divided into two categories: with and without panic attacks. The differentiating criterion is whether the patient during the course of the disorder has ever experienced a panic attack. If this is the case, he/she is given the diagnosis of agoraphobia with panic attacks, even if there are no current panic attacks. Klein (1981) and others consider agoraphobia as a complication of panic disorder, which differs from 'uncomplicated' agoraphobia without panic attacks. There are today, however, few empirical studies verifying basic differences between these subgroups.

Both forms of agoraphobia are characterized by a marked fear and avoidance of 'being alone or in public places from which escape might be difficult or help not available in case of sudden incapacitation' (APA, 1980, p. 227), i.e. in most cases a panic attack or high degree of anxiety is experienced. Furthermore, this fear and avoidance leads to increasingly greater restrictions on normal activities. Many agoraphobic patients can perform a lot of activities completely without, or with only mild anxiety, if accompanied by a trusted person: husband, friend, parent, or even a child; however, on their own, almost no normal activities outside of the home are possible.

The prevalence of agoraphobia in the normal population varies between 1.2% and 3.8%, according to recent epidemiological studies (e.g. Myers *et al.*, 1984; Wittchen, 1986). The preponderance of women is marked and the sex ratio is 3 : 1.

Aetiological models for agoraphobia are, from a biological point of view, largely the same as for PD (e.g. Klein, 1981). A specific behavioural model has been put forward by Mathews, Gelder and Johnston (1981) and a cognitive view was presented by Beck and Emery (1985). As for PD, the current empirical support for the various models is rather sparse, but increasing interest in these issues can be envisaged in the future.

SOCIAL PHOBIA

The most prominent feature of social phobia is 'A persistent, irrational fear of, and compelling desire to avoid, a situation in which the individual is exposed to possible scrutiny by others and fears that he or she may act in a way that will be humiliating or embarrassing' (APA, 1980, p. 228). Examples of situations avoided by social phobics are public speaking, talking in a small group of people, eating out or going to a dinner party, performing fine motor activities while being observed, etc. The crucial fear in social phobia is the fear of being *scrutinized* by others and behaving in a humiliating way ('making a fool of oneself').

Social phobia appears to be more prevalent than was earlier thought to be the case. In a recent epidemiological study (Myers *et al.*, 1984), the figure 1.7% was reported, with a sex ratio of 2 : 1 in favour of women.

The aetiology of social phobia has not yet been a subject of interest for many researchers. However, a few attempts toward an aetiological formulation of social phobia have been published (e.g. Beck and Emery, 1985; Nichols, 1974; Öhman, Dimberg and Öst, 1985; Trower and Turland, 1984). Empirical evidence for any specific model is as yet rather meagre.

PRINCIPAL PSYCHOPHYSIOLOGICAL FINDINGS

PANIC DISORDER

Laboratory Observation

A few studies on patients experiencing a panic attack while undergoing physiological assessment for some other purpose have been reported. Lader and Mathews (1970) described three female patients who panicked spontaneously during different psychophysiological experiments. All patients displayed large increases in heart rate (HR): 90–130, 75–120, and 87–138 beats/min; as well as increases in skin conductance: 11–14, 7–12, and 7–19 $\mu\Omega$. Forearm blood flow also increased in two of the patients, and finger pulse volume decreased in the third. Spontaneous skin conductance fluctuations, and forearm electromyogram (EMG) varied in two, and increased in the third patient.

Cohen, Barlow and Blanchard (1985) reported one patient who panicked during a relaxation period as part of a pre-treatment psychophysiological assessment, and another who panicked during her third biofeedback session.

The HR of the first patient increased from 65 to 101 beats/min in 1 min and her frontalis EMG increased from 15 to 47 μV in 2 min. The second patient showed an increase of HR from 64 to 115 beats/min in 2 min and of frontalis EMG from 18 to 48 μV in 3 min.

These two studies suggest that spontaneous panic attacks are associated with large increases in HR, skin conductance and forearm blood flow over a short period of time (1–2 min), attesting to the sudden onset of panic attacks.

Ambulatory Monitoring in Natural Settings

In order to obtain physiological data during naturally occurring panic attacks, portable recorders have been used in a few studies. Taylor, Telch and Havvik (1982) studied 10 panic patients who wore a Vitalog MC-2 monitor recording HR and physical activity for 24 h. During this period 7/10 patients had a total of 8 panic attacks, and 4 of the attacks were associated with a significant increase in HR, reaching a region of 115–148 beats/min. However, in half of the panic attacks experienced, no significant HR increase was observed.

Freedman, Ianni, Ettedgui and Puthezhath (1985) compared 12 PD patients with 11 age-matched controls. The patients wore an electrocardiogram (ECG) cassette recorder for 24 h. Besides ECG, skin and ambient temperatures were monitored, and there was an event recorder for indication of panic attacks. When the average overall values for the entire recording period were compared, there were no significant differences between patients and controls on HR, skin temperature difference (between finger and ambient air), and anxiety (which was rated once every hour). However, 5/12 patients had 8 panic attacks, while the controls had none. Compared to 5 min prior to the attack, 7/8 attacks were associated with HR increases (16–38 beats/min) compared to smaller increases during high-anxiety control periods without panic (7–13 beats/min). Finger temperature increased 0.3–2.3 °C before panic attacks, and only 0–0.3 °C during control periods.

Taylor *et al.* (1986) studied 12 PD patients wearing the Vitalog MC-2 recorder for 6 days. The patients also had a diary, recording all panic attacks and periods of anticipatory anxiety. During the observation period, the patients recorded a total of 33 panic attacks and 8 periods of anticipatory anxiety. Nineteen of the 33 panic attacks (58%) were considered definitive or probable, i.e. there was an HR increase without physical activity. The mean HR for these periods was 116.8 beats/min compared to 97.4 beats/min during matched periods 24 h before or after the attack. Furthermore, the mean increase in HR from the first symptom to the peak was 38.6 beats/min. The peak occurred after an average of 4 min and the duration of HR changes was 20 min.

In summary, the results from the above studies on ambulatory monitoring show that 61% (across the three studies) of the self-observed panic attacks were associated with a significant increase in HR. This means that a fairly

314   *L.-G. Öst*

large proportion of panic attacks are not picked up physiologically, at least not by HR recording.

Panic Provocation Tests

Recently a number of studies have measured different psychophysiological parameters during the provocation of panic attacks in the laboratory. Various agents (see Table 10.1), e.g. sodium lactate, yohimbine, isoproterenol, and CO_2-inhalation have been used, as well as hyperventilation. Whether lactate infusion is a sensitive and specific way of producing panic attacks has been

Table 10.1
Results of physiological assessment in panic provocation tests

Study	HR	BP	SCL	FBF	Temp.	RR	EMG	EEG
Lactate								
Fink et al. (1970)								↗beta↙alpha
Kelly et al. (1971)	↗			↗				
Bonn et al. (1973)	↗			↗	↗neck ↙hand			
Knott et al. (1981)	↗		=				↗	↗beta↙alpha
Gorman et al. (1983)	↗	↗SBP =DBP						
Freedman et al. (1984)	↗		↗		=finger	=	=	
Lapierre et al. (1984)	↗		=				↗	↗delta
Liebowitz et al. (1985)	↗	↗SBP =DBP						
Ehlers et al. (1986)	↗	↗						
Isoproterenol								
Nesse et al. (1984)	↗	↗						
Freedman et al. (1984)	↗							
Yohimbine								
Charney et al. (1984)	↗	↗						
Caffeine								
Charney et al. (1985)	↗	↗						
CO_2-inhalation								
Ehlers et al. (1985)	↗	↗						
Hyperventilation								
Rapee (1986)	↗							

HR = heart rate, BP = blood pressure, SCL = skin conductance level, FBF = forearm blood flow, Temp. = temperature, RR = respiration rate, EMG = electromyography, EEG = electroencephalography. ↗ = significant increase, ↙ = significant decrease, = = no significant change.

questioned on methodological grounds by Margraf, Ehlers and Roth (1986), and similar criticisms can be voiced against the studies of other agents. This is, however, beyond the scope of the present chapter.

The panic provocation studies that have included some psychophysiological measure are summarized in Table 10.1. These studies contain 'panic patients', i.e. subjects with either PD or agoraphobia with panic attacks, according to DSM-III.

Heart rate has been measured in 13/15 studies, and significant increases from the baseline were obtained during the provocation phase in all studies. *Blood pressure* (BP) was assessed in 7 studies and systolic pressure increased significantly in 5/7 studies. *Skin conductance level* (SCL) was measured in 3 studies, and only one of these was a significant increase obtained. *Forearm blood flow* increased in both studies that assessed it. *Temperature* showed a more variable pattern: in one study neck temperature increased, while hand temperature decreased, and in another finger temperature was unchanged. *Respiration rate* was unchanged in both the studies that measured it. *Electromyogram level* increased in 2/3 studies. The 3 studies measuring *electroencephalogram (EEG) activity* showed similar results: decreased alpha, and increased beta and delta activity.

In summary, the results of the panic provocation tests show consistent increases in autonomic activity, while this is not the case for indicators of somatic activity and central nervous system parameters. However, the studies in general failed to demonstrate that panic episodes were physiologically different from non-panic episodes for the respective group of patients studied (e.g. Freedman *et al.*, 1984; Margraf *et al.*, 1986).

AGORAPHOBIA

Laboratory Assessment

Gelder, Bancroft, Gath, Johnston, Mathews and Shaw (1973) assessed HR and skin conductance at baseline and during neutral and phobic imagery, and found that phobic scenes led to larger physiological responses. Fisher and Wilson (1985) measured HR and SCL while patients viewed four videotaped vignettes purported to elicit anxiety. There were very small reactions overall and no difference between agoraphobic patients and control subjects was found.

In a large-scale study, Roth *et al.* (1986) compared HR and electrodermal measures for patients having agoraphobia with panic attacks and for normal controls. A standard orienting response, habituation paradigm with 19, 1-s tones (75 dB, 1000 Hz) was used, followed by an 'intensities' paradigm of 37 white-noise pips. Each paradigm was of 10-min duration. During baseline, agoraphobics had significantly higher HR and SCL than normals, and this was also the case during the habituation and intensities paradigms. During the habituation paradigm, controls displayed SCL habituation effects with steeper slopes than agoraphobics, while there was no habituation effect on HR levels. During the intensities paradigm, agoraphobics had higher SCL and habituated more slowly than the controls, as well as higher HR levels; neither group, showed HR habituation.

In-vivo Assessment

A number of studies have assessed the HR of agoraphobics during *in-vivo*, behavioural avoidance tests. Some of these are therapy outcome studies, and will be reviewed in the next section.

Mavissakalian and Michelson (1982) reported HR and subjective anxiety in 26 patients during a 0.6-km walk. In a subgroup ($N=13$) for which data were available before the walk and at follow-up, resting baseline HR was about 90 beats/min, walking baseline 111 beats/min, mean during the test 122 beats/min, and peak HR 132 beats/min. Mean HR response (difference between baseline and test) was 10.9 beats/min. In another subgroup ($N=6$) for which data were available before and during the walk, and at follow-up, the mean HR response was 13 beats/min.

Holden and Barlow (1986) compared 10 patients suffering from agoraphobia with panic attacks with 10 matched controls on HR during a 1-mile walk. The subjects took the walk seven times and the agoraphobics had a significantly higher baseline and walk mean HR on each occasion. Group means for the first walk were 124 versus 116 beats/min. However, there was no difference in HR response between patients and controls: means for the first walk were 6.7 and 8.3 beats/min, respectively. Thus, the higher HR during the walks shown by agoraphobics was due to higher resting HR, rather than anxiety-producing factors during the test.

Roth *et al.* (1986) compared 37 agoraphobics with 19 controls during a 680-m walk. Patients had significantly higher mean HR (113 vs 97 beats/min), maximum HR (121 vs 104 beats/min), and minimum HR (103 vs 84 beats/min). However, their sitting baseline before the walk was also significantly higher (92 vs 78 beats/min). This means that patients and controls had almost the same HR response: 21 versus 19 beats/min.

Finally, Woods, Charney, McPherson, Gradman and Heninger (1987) compared 18 agoraphobics with panic attacks and 13 controls in one individually chosen phobic situation, belonging to the top of each patient's hierarchy. Those patients that experienced a situational panic attack had significantly higher HR than controls (95 vs 83 beats/min) and the change (23 vs 12 beats/min) from baseline (72 vs 71 beats/min) was significantly larger. The change in systolic BP in patients (from 119 to 136 mmHg) and in controls (from 108 to 121 mmHg) did not differ significantly.

SOCIAL PHOBIA

Laboratory Assessment

In a series of studies Samuel Turner and co-workers have investigated physiological, cognitive and behavioural aspects of social anxiety. Beidel, Turner and Dancu (1985) compared 26 socially anxious and 26 non-socially anxious subjects on three behavioural tasks, while continuously monitoring HR and BP. In an unstructured interpersonal interaction with an opposite-sex confederate, the socially anxious subjects had significantly larger systolic BP response (26.9 vs 16.9 mmHg) and HR response (6.5 vs 2.3 beats/min), but not diastolic BP response. In a same-sex interaction, the reactions were smaller and non-significant on all measures. Finally, during an impromptu talk, the socially anxious group had a significantly larger systolic BP response (27.5 vs 22.1 mmHg), but not diastolic BP or HR response.

Turner and Beidel (1985) studied the same sample and assessed BP and cognitions during a 5-min impromptu speech. Using independently determined cut-off scores, 21 of the 26 socially anxious subjects fell into two categories, both having a high frequency of negative cognitions. The group with high physiological reactions ($N=12$) had a mean systolic response of 33.9 mmHg, which was significantly higher than that of the low physiological reaction group, 15.5 mmHg.

Turner, Beidel and Larkin (1986) compared the original sample of 26 socially anxious and 26 non-socially anxious subjects with a clinical sample of 17 social phobics (fulfilling DSM-III criteria). There was no difference between the socially anxious and the social phobics on the clinical rating scales, but the phobics were twice as old as the anxious subjects (40.8 vs 20.4 years). Socially anxious and phobic groups did not differ, but both had significantly higher systolic BP (144.5 and 149.2 mmHg, respectively) during the impromptu speech than during the same-sex interaction (133.3 and 134.4 mmHg). During the speech, both groups had significantly higher systolic BP than the non-socially anxious subjects (139.2 mmHg). Diastolic BP and HR did not differ significantly between the groups.

Matias and Turner (1986) studied the effect of demand characteristics on physiological variables for 40 speech-anxious subjects. The subjects given high-demand instructions showed an increase in their HR during the anticipatory phase (before starting to speak) significantly more than those in the low-demand condition. During the speech task, their mean HR (105.2 beats/min) was also significantly higher than in the low-demand group (95.4 beats/min). The groups, however, did not differ on systolic or diastolic BP.

TREATMENT EVALUATION STUDIES

PANIC DISORDER

One of the few outcome trials of PD applying physiological assessment is that of Taylor, Kenigsberg and Robinson (1982). They compared progressive relaxation, diazepam, placebo and waiting-list control. Heart rate and skin conductance were measured during a stress test and a stress interview. Only diazepam yielded a significant HR reduction ($\bar{X}$ = 6.6 beats/min) at post-test. On skin conductance no group changed significantly at post-treatment assessment.

AGORAPHOBIA

Gelder *et al.* (1973) measured HR at baseline, and during neutral and phobic imagery. The baseline mean HR decreased significantly more after desensitization ($\bar{X}$ = 7.1 beats/min) and flooding ($\bar{X}$ = 8.1 beats/min) than after the control condition ($\bar{X}$ = 1.7 beats/min).

Bonn, Readhead and Timmons (1984) measured respiration rate during a resting period. One group treated with exposure *in vivo* improved significantly after treatment (from 28.4 to 20.0 breaths/min) with a slight deterioration at the 6-month follow-up (21.6 breaths/min). However, the group treated by breathing retraining plus exposure improved continuously throughout (28.7 – 18.7 – 14.5 breaths/min), and was significantly better than the first group at follow-up. Its follow-up mean was also within the normal range.

Vermilyea, Boice and Barlow (1984) assessed HR during a 1-mile standardized walk for a group of 28 patients treated with coping self-statements and exposure *in vivo*. Overall there were only small, and non-significant changes on the different HR measures. However, a dichotomization of patients into synchronous (concordant changes in HR and subjective anxiety) and desynchronous subgroups yielded a significant HR reduction for the synchronous subjects (e.g. change in mean HR from 126 to 115 beats/min), while the change for the desynchronous patients was non-significant (from 119 to 121 beats/min).

Öst, Jerremalm and Jansson (1984) classified 40 agoraphobics into behavioural or physiological reactors on the basis of a pre-treatment behavioural test and randomized them to either exposure *in vivo* (E) or applied relaxation (AR). The behavioural reactors showed, by definition, a small HR response at pre-treatment ($\bar{X}$ = 1.58 beats/min, range −17.2–13.3 beats/min). Their improvement at post-treatmennt was fairly substantial (E = 5.3 beats/min, AR = 6.7 beats/min) but non-significant. The physiological reactors had a large pre-treatment HR response ($\bar{X}$ = 20.63, range 15.1–40.1 beats/min), and both groups improved significantly (E = 10.5 beats/min, AR = 9.9 beats/min) at post-treatment. The improvements were also sustained at a 15-month follow-up (Jansson, Jerremalm and Öst, 1986).

Telch, Agras, Taylor, Roth and Gallen (1985) treated 37 agoraphobics with either imipramine, imipramine + exposure, or placebo + exposure. Heart rate was assessed during a sitting resting baseline and a 1-km walk. Mean HR response at pre-treatment assessment was 21.6 beats/min. However, none of the groups improved significantly on this measure: both the imipramine ($\bar{X} =$ −0.3) and placebo + exposure ($\bar{X} =$ −6.0) groups in fact deteriorated, while the imipramine + exposure group showed a non-significant improvement ($\bar{X} =$ 8.5). The overall mean HR response at post-treatment was 20.6 beats/min.

In a series of excellent studies, Larry Michelson and colleagues have assessed HR in their agoraphobic patients during a sitting and a walking baseline, and during a standard walk 0.4 or 1.0 mile long.

Michelson and Mavissakalian (1985) studied 62 agoraphobics in a 2 × 2 factorial design. All patients were given instructions for self-directed exposure *in vivo* and in addition either imipramine, flooding, imipramine + flooding, or discussion (control) treatments were given. The overall pre-treatment HR means were for the walking baseline 113.6 beats/min, the standard walk 123.5 beats/min, and for HR response 10.7 beats/min. At the 1-month post-treatment assessment, flooding yielded a reduction on the walking baseline, and the imipramine + flooding group showed a deterioration on the HR response. Overall, the patients' mean for the walking baseline was 109.1 beats/min, for the walk 118.8 beats/min, and for HR response 11.1 beats/min. A comparison with a normative sample showed that at pre-treatment the patients were significantly higher on all HR measures. However, at the 1-month post-treatment assessment there were no significant differences on any measure during the walk.

Michelson, Mavissakalian and Marchione (1985) studied HR in 39 patients while on a 1-mile walk. The patients were treated with either paradoxical intention (PI), graduated exposure (GE), or relaxation training (RT). At pre-treatment assessment, the overall walking baseline was 131.8 beats/min, and the mean during the walk 138.9 beats/min. Only GE and RT groups showed significant improvements from pre- to post-assessment on both measures. At post-treatment, the PI group had actually worsened and HR was significantly higher than that of the GE and RT groups on the walking baseline. The same trend was evident in the mean during the walk. However, at the 3-month follow-up, PI subjects showed a large gain and HR was non-significantly better than in the GE and RT groups, both during baseline and during the walk.

Michelson (1986) reanalysed the data from the previous study by dichotomizing the patients into consonant and non-consonant groups. The former consisted of behavioural reactors treated with GE, physiological reactors treated with RT, and cognitive reactors treated with PI. Patients with all other combinations of response pattern and treatment were assigned to the non-consonant group. There were no significant differences between the groups at post-treatment, but at the 3-month follow-up the consonant group was significantly better than the non-consonant group on all HR measures. For example, HR during the walk had improved from 137.9 to 108.7 beats/min for the consonant group, compared to the slight deterioration in the non-consonant group HR, from 140.9 to 143.7 beats/min.

SOCIAL PHOBIA

Goldfried and Goldfried (1977) studied 42 speech-anxious adults who were treated in groups and received either (1) target-relevant self-control desensitization, (2) target-irrelevant self-control desensitization, or (3) prolonged exposure. Heart rate was measured after a 5-min anticipatory period, immediately prior to a 4-min speech. All groups displayed a significant improvement after treatment: group 1, from 98.4 to 85.3 beats/min; group 2, from 99.7 to 83.3 beats/min; and group 3, from 95.0 to 79.3 beats/min; but there was no difference between the groups.

Kanter and Goldfried (1979) investigated 68 social phobics who were divided into four groups: (1) rational restructuring, (2) self-control desensitization, (3) combination of (1) and (2), and (4) waiting list. Heart rate was measured immediately prior to a 5-min conversation between the patient and two persons (one male and one female). Only group 1's HR changed significantly after treatment (from 98.2 to 87.6 beats/min), while the other groups showed minor decreases (group 2: from 89.2 to 82.8 beats/min; group 3: from 86.5 to 83.8 beats/min) and HR for the waiting-list group increased (from 88.8 to 90.2 beats/min).

Öst, Jerremalm and Johansson (1981) divided 32 social phobics into behavioural or physiological reactors and randomized them to either social skills training (SST) or applied relaxation (AR) in a 2 × 2 design. Heart rate was measured during a rest period (after 30 min of screening interview) and continuously during a 5-min conversation with an unknown person of the opposite sex. At pre-treatment assessment, the mean HR response of the physiological reactors (23.4 beats/min) was significantly higher than that of the behavioural reactors (6.0 beats/min). Among the physiological reactors, significant HR improvements in both AR (from 103.3 to 94.1 beats/min) and SST (from 102.6 to 95.0 beats/min) groups were seen, but the difference between them was not significant. The changes for the behavioural reactors were too small to be significant.

Emmelkamp, Mersch, Vissia and van der Helm (1985) studied 34 social phobics who were treated with (1) exposure *in vivo*, (2) rational emotive therapy (RET), or (3) self-instructional training (SIT). Heart rate was measured immediately before a 5-min conversation with two persons. Only the exposure group showed an improvement in HR (from 91.3 to 85.3 beats/min), albeit not significant. The RET (from 92.4 to 94.8 beats/min) and SIT (from 86.0 to 86.4 beats/min) groups displayed some deterioration, but these changes were also non-significant.

Jerremalm, Jansson and Öst (1986) divided 38 patients into physiological or cognitive reactors, and randomized them to either AR, SIT, or a waiting-list condition. Heart rate was measured as in the Öst *et al.* (1981) study, continuously during a conversation test. At pre-treatment, the mean HR response of the physiological reactors (14.7 beats/min) was significantly higher than that of the cognitive reactors (2.8 beats/min). Among the physiological reactors, HR response in both AR (from 14.8 to 4.2 beats/min) and SIT (from 14.6 to 6.2 beats/min) groups improved significantly, while responses for the waiting-list group remained unchanged. There was no difference between AR and SIT at the post-treatment assessment. Among cognitive reactors both AR and SIT improved HR response somewhat, albeit not significantly.

In summary, 14 outcome studies have used HR, or respiration rate, in evaluating treatment. Significant improvements on the most important measure (from each study) were obtained in the only PD study, in 6/8 agoraphobia studies, and in 4/5 studies on social phobia.

DISCUSSION

ASSESSMENT

Panic Disorder

In order to compare the results from the three types of assessment situation described above, the mean HR response from baseline for each type of situation (across studies) was computed. The mean for the laboratory observation studies was 44.6 beats/min, compared to 32.8 beats/min for ambulatory monitoring, and 19.5 beats/min for the provocation studies. Furthermore, the mean time to reach the peak of the panic episode was 2, 5, and 12 min, respectively.

In a sense, the laboratory observation studies can be considered to give the most valid picture of natural panic attacks as the patients were not at all prepared for them, the purpose of the study being to measure something else. The ambulatory monitoring studies, of course, pick up panic attacks in the natural settings of the patients, but the fact that patients are carefully instructed to observe and record any panic episode whilst wearing the portable recorder may make the data somewhat less valid. Finally, the panic provocation studies can be considered the least valid as the patients usually are told the purpose of the study, and a number of persons are observing their every reaction during the provocation test (see Margraf, Ehlers and Roth, 1986, for a description of methodological problems).

Naturally, one cannot draw unequivocal conclusions from these data, but it is likely that ambulatory monitoring yields a better assessment of naturally occurring, 'unprepared' panic attacks than the provocation method.

Agoraphobia

The laboratory assessment of agoraphobic patients published so far is very meagre and needs to be increased along the lines of the Roth *et al.* (1986) study.

Somewhat more research has been done on *in-vivo* assessment of agoraphobics' physiological responses. In three of the studies a standardized walk (0.6–1.6 km) was used, and two of these had a matched control group. Both studies failed to show a higher HR response for the agoraphobic patients. However, the study by Woods *et al.* (1987) used individually chosen, top-hierarchy situations and found that the patients had a significantly higher HR response than the matched controls.

Further research in this area should compare agoraphobic patients' reactions in standardized and individualized tests, and use other physiological measures concurrently with HR, e.g. BP, skin conductance, and temperature.

Social Phobia

Some very useful laboratory assessment studies have been published comparing socially anxious and non-anxious subjects, and have demonstrated differential reactivity, both in HR and BP. However, all studies are derived from one research group, and in only one of the studies has a clinical sample of social phobics been included. Thus, there is a great need for more investigations of clinical samples both in the laboratory and in natural settings. There is no reason why the portable recorders used in PD and agoraphobia studies should not be used in studies of social phobics as well. As in agoraphobia the range of physiological parameters should be increased to include more than HR and BP, which have been used in laboratory assessment so far.

TREATMENT EVALUATION

Panic Disorder

So far physiological measures have been used to a very small extent in the evaluation of PD treatments. This is understandable, considering the nature of the disorder, which makes laboratory assessment under controlled conditions problematic. Just using a resting, non-stressful situation is not very informative, and some kind of stress or provocation test is needed. A number of these have been described in the literature, but so far none has proven sensitive enough to reliably elicit a panic attack in untreated PD patients. There is, however, continuous development in various research centres concerning this issue. Meanwhile, the use of ambulatory monitoring devices in therapy evaluation is recommended; furthermore, these probably give more valid measures than laboratory provocation tests (as described above).

Agoraphobia

Physiological assessment has been used considerably more in treatment evaluation of agoraphobia than of PD. However, considering the large number of studies in this area, the usage is still not more than about 15%. Besides one study using respiration rate (Bonn *et al.*, 1984), only HR has been used. With a few exceptions, these studies have yielded significant improvements after treatment, which do not corroborate the negative view of physiological assessment held by some authors. The recommendation that can be given is that physiological assessment should be used in evaluating agoraphobia treatments, but future research will show whether a standardized or an individualized behavioural test is the most valid.

Social Phobia

Heart rate has been used in five treatment evaluation studies, but only two of these (Jerremalm *et al.*, 1986; Öst *et al.*, 1981) actually measured HR during a behavioural test. As the majority of the studies (4/5) found significant improvements after treatment, the increased use of physiological assessments in social phobia treatment must be recommended. Naturally, the number of parameters should be increased to also include, for example, BP and skin conductance, at least in the laboratory.

TREATMENT IMPLEMENTATION

The use of physiological assessment as part of a pre-treatment analysis in order to decide on the optimal treatment for the individual patient has been used in a few studies on agoraphobia (Michelson, 1986; Öst *et al.*, 1984) and social phobia (Jerremalm *et al.*, 1986; Öst *et al.*, 1981). The general trend in these studies is that a treatment consonant with the patient's response pattern yields better treatment effects than a non-consonant treatment.

Whether PD patients can be divided into, for example, physiological and cognitive reactors has not yet been empirically tested. The ambulatory monitoring studies reviewed above, however, showed that 39% of the self-observed panic attacks were not associated with an HR increase. It is possible that these instead are characterized by a strong cognitive reaction with catastrophic thoughts, or other negative ideation. If this categorization is possible, then treatments like applied relaxation (Öst, 1988) and cognitive therapy (Clark, 1986) can be compared.

From a treatment implementation point of view, it can, thus, be concluded that psychophysiological assessment is a fruitful and necessary part of a pre-treatment evaluation that can guide the clinician in the choice of the right treatment for his/her individual patient.

ACKNOWLEDGEMENTS

The present research was supported by grant 251/83 from the Swedish Council for Research in the Humanities and Social Sciences, and grant 05452 from the Swedish Medical Research Council.

REFERENCES

American Psychiatric Association (1980). *Diagnostic and Statistical Manual for Mental Disorders*, 3rd edn. Washington, DC: APA.

Barlow, D.H. (1986). Behavioral conception and treatment of panic. *Psychopharmacology Bulletin* **22**, 802–806.

Barlow, D.H., Vermilyea, J., Blanchard, E.B., Vermilyea, B.B., DiNardo, P.A. and Cerny, J.A. (1985). The phenomenon of panic. *Journal of Abnormal Psychology* **94**, 320–328.

Beck, A.T. and Emery, G. (1985). *Anxiety Disorders and Phobias. A Cognitive Perspective*. New York: Basic Books.

Beidel, D.C., Turner, S.M. and Dancu, C.V. (1985). Physiological, cognitive and behavioral aspects of social anxiety. *Behaviour Research and Therapy* **23**, 109–117.

Bonn, J.A., Harrison, J. and Rees, L. (1973). Lactate infusion in the treatment of 'free-floating' anxiety. *Canadian Psychiatric Association Journal* **18**, 41–45.

Bonn, J.A., Readhead C.P.A. and Timmons, B.H. (1984). Enhanced adaptive behavioural response in agoraphobic patients pretreated with breathing retraining. *Lancet* **i**, 665–669.

Carr, D.B. and Sheehan, D.V. (1984). Panic anxiety: a new biological model. *Journal of Clinical Psychiatry* **45**, 323–330.

Charney, D.S., Heniger, G.R. and Breier, A. (1984). Noradrenergic function in panic anxiety. *Archives of General Psychiatry* **41**, 751–763.

Charney, D.S., Heniger, G.R. and Jatlow, P.I. (1985). Increased anxiogenic effects of caffeine in panic disorders. *Archives of General Psychiatry* **42**, 233–243.

Clark, D.M. (1986). A cognitive approach to panic. *Behaviour Research and Therapy* **24**, 461–470.

Cohen, A.S., Barlow, D.H. and Blanchard, E.B. (1985). Psychophysiology of relaxation-associated panic attacks. *Journal of Abnormal Psychology* **94**, 96–101.

Ehlers, A., Margraf, J., Roth, W.T., Taylor, C.B., Maddock, R.J. and Kopell, B.S. (1985). CO_2 as a trigger for panic in panic patients. Paper presented at the American Psychiatric Association meeting.

Ehlers, A., Margraf, J., Roth, W.T., Taylor, C.B., Maddock, R.J., Sheikh, J.; Kopell, M.L., McClenahan, K.L., Gossard, D., Blowers, G.H., Agras, W.S. and Kopell,

B.S. (1986). Lactate infusions and panic attacks: do patients and controls respond differently? *Psychiatry Research* **17**, 295–308.

Emmelkamp, P.M.G., Mersch, P.-P., Vissia, E. and van der Helm, M. (1985). Social phobia: a comparative evaluation of cognitive and behavioral interventions. *Behaviour Research and Therapy* **23**, 365–369.

Fink, M., Taylor, M.A. and Volavka, J. (1970). Anxiety precipitated by lactate. *New England Journal of Medicine* **281**, 1429.

Fisher, L.M. and Wilson, G.T. (1985). A study of the psychology of agoraphobia. *Behaviour Research and Therapy* **23**, 97–107.

Freedman, R.R., Ianni, P., Ettedgui, E., Pohl, R. and Rainey, J.M. (1984). Psychophysiological factors in panic disorder. *Psychopathology* **17**, Suppl. 1, 66–73.

Freedman, R.R., Ianni, P., Ettedgui, E. and Puthezhath, N. (1985). Ambulatory monitoring of panic disorder. *Archives of General Psychiatry* **42**, 244–248.

Gelder, M.G., Bancroft, J.H.J., Gath, D.H., Johnston, D.W., Mathews, A.M. and Shaw, P.M. (1973). Specific and non-specific factors in behaviour therapy. *British Journal of Psychiatry* **123**, 445–462.

Goldfried, M.R. and Goldfried, A.P. (1977). Importance of hierarchy content in the self-control of anxiety. *Journal of Consulting and Clinical Psychology* **45**, 124–134.

Gorman, J.M., Levy, G.F., Liebowitz, M.R., McGrath, P., Appleby, I.L., Dillon, D.J., Davies, S.O. and Klein, D.F. (1983). Effect of acute β-adrenergic blockade on lactate-induced panic. *Archives of General Psychiatry* **40**, 1079–1082.

Holden, A.E., Jr and Barlow, D.H. (1986). Heart rate and heart rate variability recorded *in vivo* in agoraphobics and nonphobics. *Behavior Therapy* **17**, 26–42.

Jacob, R.G. and Rapport, M.D. (1984). Panic disorder: medical and psychological parameters. In: S.M. Turner (Ed.) *Behavioral Theories and Treatment of Anxiety*. New York: Plenum.

Jansson, L., Jerremalm, A. and Öst, L.-G. (1986). Follow-up of agoraphobic patients treated with exposure *in vivo* or applied relaxation. *British Journal of Psychiatry* **149**, 486–490.

Jerremalm, A., Jansson, L. and Öst, L.-G. (1986). Cognitive and physiological reactivity and the effects of different behavioral methods in the treatment of social phobia. *Behaviour Research and Therapy* **24**, 171–180.

Kanter, N.J. and Goldfried, M.R. (1979). Relative effectiveness of rational restructuring and self-control desensitization in the reduction of interpersonal anxiety. *Behavior Therapy* **10**, 472–490.

Kelly, D., Mitchell-Heggs, N. and Sherman, D. (1971). Anxiety and the effects of sodium lactate assessed clinically and physiologically. *British Journal of Psychiatry* **119**, 129–141.

Klein, D.F. (1981). Anxiety reconceptualized. In: D.F. Klein and J. Rabkin (Eds) *Anxiety: New Research and Changing Concepts*. New York: Raven Press.

Knott, V., Chaudry, R. and Lapierre, Y.D. (1981). Panic induced by sodium lactate: electrophysiological correlates. *Progress in Neuro-Psychopharmacology* **5**, 511–514.

Lader, M. and Mathews, A.M. (1970). Physiological changes during spontaneous panic attacks. *Journal of Psychosomatic Research* **14**, 377–382.

Lapierre, Y.D., Knott, V.J. and Gray, R. (1984). Psychophysiological correlates of sodium lactate. *Psychopharmacology Bulletin* **20**, 50–57.

Liebowitz, M.R., Gorman, J.M., Fyer, A.J., Levitt, M., Dillon, D., Levy, G., Appleby, I.L., Anderson, S., Palij, M., Davies, S.O. and Klein, D.F. (1985). Lactate provocation of panic attacks. II. Biochemical and physiological findings. *Archives of General Psychiatry* **42**, 709–719.

Margraf, J., Ehlers, A. and Roth, W.T. (1986). Sodium lactate infusions and panic attacks: a review and critique. *Psychosomatic Medicine* **48**, 23–51.

Mathews, A.M., Gelder, M.G. and Johnston, D.W. (1981). *Agoraphobia. Nature and Treatment*. New York: Guilford.

Matias, R., Jr and Turner, S.M. (1986). Concordance and discordance in speech anxiety assessment: the effects of demand characteristics on the tripartite assessment method. *Behaviour Research and Therapy* **24**, 537–545.

Mavissakalian, M. and Michelson, L. (1982). Pattern of psychophysiological change in the treatment of agoraphobia. *Behaviour Research and Therapy* **20**, 347–356.

Michelson, L. (1986). Treatment consonance and response profiles in agoraphobia: the role of individual differences in cognitive, behavioral, and physiological treatments. *Behaviour Research and Therapy* **24**, 263–275.

Michelson, L. and Mavissakalian, M. (1985). Psychophysiological outcome of behavioral and pharmacological treatments of agoraphobia. *Journal of Consulting and Clinical Psychology* **53**, 229–236.

Michelson, L., Mavissakalian, M. and Marchione, K. (1985). Cognitive and behavioral treatments of agoraphobia: clinical, behavioral, and psychophysiological outcomes. *Journal of Consulting and Clinical Psychology* **53**, 913–925.

Myers, J.K., Weissman, M.M., Tischler, G.L., Holzer, C.E., Leaf, P.J., Orvaschel, H., Anthony, J.C., Boyd, J.H. Burke, J.D., Jr, Kramer, M. and Stoltzman, R. (1984). Six-month prevalence of psychiatric disorders in three communities. *Archives of General Psychiatry* **41**, 959–967.

Nesse, R.M., Cameron, O.G., Curtis, G.C., McCann, D.S. and Huber-Smith, M.J. (1984). Adrenergic function in patients with panic anxiety. *Archives of General Psychiatry* **41**, 771–776.

Nichols, K.A. (1974). Severe social anxiety. *British Journal of Medical Psychology* **47**, 301–306.

Norton, G.R., Dorward, J. and Cox, B.J. (1986). Factors associated with panic attacks in nonclinical subjects. *Behavior Therapy* **17**, 239–252.

Norton, G.R., Harrison, B., Hauch, J. and Rhodes, L. (1985). Characteristics of people with infrequent panic attacks. *Journal of Consulting and Clinical Psychology* **94**, 216–221.

Öhman, A., Dimberg, U. and Öst, L.-G. (1985). Animal and social phobias: biological constraints on learned fear responses. In: S. Reiss and R.R. Bootzin (Eds) *Theoretical Issues in Behavior Therapy*. Orlando: Academic Press.

Öst, L.-G. (1988). Applied relaxation vs. progressive relaxation in the treatment of panic disorder. *Behaviour Research and Therapy* **26**, 13–22.

Öst, L.-G., Jerremalm, A. and Jansson, L. (1984). Individual response patterns and the effects of different behavioral methods in the treatment of agoraphobia. *Behaviour Research and Therapy* **22**, 697–707.

Öst, L.-G., Jerremalm, A. and Johansson, J. (1981). Individual response patterns and the effects of different behavioral methods in the treatment of social phobia. *Behaviour Research and Therapy* **19**, 1–16.

Rapee, R. (1986). Differential response to hyperventilation in panic disorder and generalized anxiety disorder. *Journal of Abnormal Psychology* **95**, 24–28.

Roth, W.T., Telch, M.J., Taylor, C.B., Sachitano, J.A., Gallen, C.C., Kopell, M.L., McClenahan, K.L., Agras, W.S. and Pfefferbaum, A. (1986). Autonomic characteristics of agoraphobia with panic attacks. *Biological Psychiatry* **21**, 1133–1154.

Taylor, C.B., Kenigsberg, M.L. and Robinson, J.M. (1982). A controlled comparison of relaxation and diazepam in panic disorder. *Journal of Clinical Psychiatry* **43**, 423–425.

Taylor, C.B., Sheik, J., Agras, W.S., Roth, W.T., Margraf, J., Ehlers, A., Maddock,

R.J. and Gossard, D. (1986). Ambulatory heart rate changes in patients with panic attacks. *American Journal of Psychiatry* **143**, 478–482.

Taylor, C.B., Telch, M.J. and Havvik, D. (1982). Ambulatory heart rate changes during panic attacks. *Journal of Psychiatric Research* **17**, 261–266.

Telch, M.J., Agras, W.S., Taylor, C.B., Roth, W.T. and Gallen, C.C. (1985). Combined pharmacological and behavioral treatment for agoraphobia. *Behaviour Research and Therapy* **23**, 325–335.

Trower, P. and Turland, D. (1984). Social phobia. In: S.M. Turner (Ed.) *Behavioral Theories and Treatment of Anxiety*. New York: Plenum.

Turner, S.M. and Beidel, D.C. (1985). Empirically derived subtypes of social anxiety. *Behavior Therapy* **16**, 384–392.

Turner, S.M., Beidel, D.C. and Larkin, K.T. (1986). Situational determinants of social anxiety in clinic and nonclinic samples: physiological and cognitive correlates. *Journal of Consulting and Clinical Psychology* **54**, 523–527.

Vermilyea, J.A., Boice, R. and Barlow, D.H. (1984). Rachman and Hodgson (1974) a decade later: how do desynchronous response systems relate to the treatment of agoraphobia? *Behaviour Research and Therapy* **22**, 615–621.

Weissman, M.M., Myers, J.K. and Harding, P.S. (1978). Psychiatric disorders in a U.S. urban community. *American Journal of Psychiatry* **135**, 459–462.

Wittchen, H.-U. (1986). Epidemiology of panic attacks and panic disorders. In: I. Hand and H.-U. Wittchen (Eds) *Panic and Phobia*. Berlin: Springer.

Woods, S.W., Charney, D.S., McPherson, C.A., Gradman, A.H. and Heninger, G.R. (1987). Situational panic attacks: behavioral, physiological, and biochemical characterization. *Archives of General Psychiatry* **44**, 365–375.

Chapter 11

Obsessional–Compulsive Disorder

Gudrun Sartory

Department of Psychology,
University of Wuppertal,
Max-Horkheimer Strasse 20,
5600 – Wuppertal,
Federal Republic of Germany

ABSTRACT

Empirical work on obsessional–compulsive disorder (OCD) ranges from familial to biochemical studies. Some of the data underline the strong relationship between this disorder and depression, without, however, explaining the evident differences in symptomatology. An increased amplitude of the contingent negative variation remains the most specific psychophysiological marker of OCD. Underlying mechanisms are still obscure. Autonomic measures have also contributed to assessment and treatment outcome.

Handbook of Clinical Psychophysiology Edited by G. Turpin
© 1989 John Wiley & Sons Ltd

329

NATURE AND TREATMENT OF
OBSESSIONAL–COMPULSIVE DISORDER

Although frequently occurring together, a distinction is made between obsessions and compulsions. Obsessions are intrusive and persistent thoughts, images or impulses which are experienced as being distressing. They may be doubting thoughts such as 'Did I knock over the old lady I just passed?', distressing images of a violent or sexual nature or impulses to behave in a socially unacceptable fashion, for instance, to shout obscenities in public. These obsessions are experienced as being involuntary, and an attempt is made to suppress or ignore them.

Compulsions, on the other hand, are repetitive and stereotyped forms of behaviour, also termed rituals, which appear to serve a purpose, for instance, to prevent infections, but are too exaggerated to do so realistically. An over-powering urge to carry out these rituals is experienced despite insight regarding their senselessness in most cases. Attempts are made to resist them. Situations which give rise to rituals are experienced as distressing and the execution of the rituals frequently gives relief from tension.

The two rituals most commonly engaged in are hand-washing and checking. Hand-washing can be triggered by contact with anything that is considered contaminated with germs and, once activated, tends to be thorough and repetitive. Furthermore, decontamination rituals can extend to all items in the vicinity of the patient. Checking rituals are repetitive, stereotyped activities, such as ensuring that household appliances are switched off, windows and doors are closed, that everything is in its place, etc. Other compulsions may serve supersititious purposes. Certain objects, colours or numbers may be avoided and elaborate rituals employed to undo the harm which an encounter with the feared object might cause.

Onset of the disorder tends to be sudden in the case of 'washers', whereas it is gradual in the case of 'checkers'. The course of the disorder tends to be continuous while being exacerbated at times of stress or in the presence of additional affective disorder. A few patients may show a return to a normal lifestyle between such episodes but the majority of patients are likely to display a chronic, deteriorating course.

DEMOGRAPHIC STUDIES

Most studies are in agreement that the occurrence of obsessional–compulsive disorder (OCD) is rare among both inpatients and outpatients. Estimates vary between 0.5% and 4.0% of all patients treated in general psychiatric settings (Rasmussen and Tsuang, 1984). The variability of estimates is probably attributable to the use of different diagnostic criteria in different studies. Given the secretive nature of individuals with OCD, it is likely that a significant number remain undetected in the community, avoiding psychiatric contact. In keeping with this notion, OCD patients, rather than approaching medical institutions by themselves, are frequently encouraged by relatives to seek help. Recent community studies have indeed found a higher prevalence of OCD than would have been assumed from hospital estimates. Myers, Weissman, Tischler, Holzer, Leaf and Orvaschel (1984; cit. Rasmussen and Tsuang, 1984) found a 6-month point prevalence of 1–2% and Robins, Helzer, Weissman, Orvaschel, Grünberg and Burker (1984) a lifetime prevalence of 2–3%. Thus, it appears that only a proportion of OCD sufferers seek help.

The sex distribution tends to be equal in OCD patients. Black (1979) found a total of 651 men and 685 women amongst inpatients and outpatients when tabulating 11 studies. There is, however, a different sex ratio among checkers and washers. Six times as many men as women can be found among checkers and the opposite ratio has been found among washers (Rachman and Hodgson, 1980). Males have been more frequently (76%) represented than females when the childhood incidence of OCD is considered (Hollingsworth, Tanguay, Grossman and Pabst, 1980). This latter finding must be viewed with caution since only 17 cases were studied and continuity between childhood and adult disorder has not been sufficiently established as yet.

Celibacy rate is high (37%) among OCD patients, a level similar to that found among schizophrenics. Of those OCD patients who are married, half are judged to have a good marital relationship. This figure does not differ from that of other patients (Coryell, 1981). A high proportion of OCD patients are childless (23%) compared with the national average. Difficulties with rearing children exist in most cases.

Ordinal position of birth and parental style have sometimes been considered important determinants in the development of the disorder. It was thought that parental anxiety and lack of flexibility played an important part in giving rise to the high anxiety level and strict morality seen in OCD patients. First-born children may be reared with a less relaxed parental attitude and may therefore be disposed to develop the disorder. Yet so far, results have failed to show clearly that more first-born children are found among OCD patients than in other groups of patients. A recent study has, however, found differences in the way washers and checkers perceive their mother's parental style and her attitude towards them. A higher proportion of checkers (67%) than washers (29%) rated their mother as having high achievement expectations and as being meticulous. The prediction that washers' parents are seen to be more overprotective than those of checkers could not be substantiated (Steketee, Grayson and Foa, 1985).

GENETIC STUDIES

Little is known as yet about hereditary factors in the aetiology of OCD. Within the past 50 years there have been 32 pairs of monozygotic twins recorded as being concordant for OCD and 19 discordant pairs. This has been assumed to point to a major genetic component despite the lack of comparable data on dizygotic twins. Doubts have also been raised as to the diagnostic validity of OCD in some studies and the validity of the determination of zygosity in others. Owing to the low incidence of the disorder, many of the studies dealt with single pairs of twins. It must be assumed that cases of concordant monozygotic twins are more newsworthy and therefore publishable than discordant twins, which may explain their greater number. An investigation of the heritability of obsessional traits and symptoms in 419 pairs of normal twins (Clifford, Murray and Fulker, 1984) revealed heritability estimates of 47% for traits and 44% for symptoms. The personality traits and symptoms were highly correlated in this non-clinical population which has not been found to be the case to this extent in clinical samples (see below).

Estimates of the familial incidence of OCD have ranged between 0.5 and 37%. One of the best controlled studies of first degree relatives of OCD patients (Brown, 1942) found an OCD incidence of 8% among parents and of 7% among siblings. It can be concluded cautiously that there is a small hereditary influence on OCD but that environmental factors play a major part in the aetiology of OCD.

PERSONALITY

According to Janet and Freud, OCD patients typically show personality traits of orderliness, parsimony and obstinacy. Studies of the prevalence of pre-morbid obsessional traits in patients suffering from OCD rely heavily on self-report and must therefore be considered subject to bias. Estimates of pre-morbid personality vary between studies. One study found that about 30% of OCD patients had an obsessional pre-morbid personality, another 30% did not and the rest showed it to a moderate degree. A neurotic control group showed a similar distribution with less cases of marked pre-morbid obsessive personality traits. When not distinguishing between degree of severity, 72% of OCD patients were found to have pre-morbid obsessional traits as compared to 53% of a control group (Kringlen, 1965). A more recent study (Rasmussen and Tsuang, 1984) found that about half of 44 OCD patients met the diagnostic criteria for compulsive personality laid down by the *Diagnostic and Statistical Manual for Mental Disorders* (3rd edn; American Psychiatric Association, 1980).

Thus, the hypothesis that OCD represents a severe form of obsessive–compulsive personality traits has so far not been supported unequivocally. Personality appears to contribute to the disorder to a moderate extent only.

RELATIONSHIP WITH OTHER PSYCHIATRIC DISORDERS

Patients with OCD experience a great deal of anxiety. In the most severe cases, anxiety or tension is chronic but, in the majority, it is triggered by certain stimuli such as contaminated material or untidiness. Carrying out the ritual usually gives relief from anxiety. In some cases, however, namely in about one-third of checkers, tension increases with repeated checking. At the same time, mood also deteriorates, presumably due to the growing doubt as to whether or not the most recent check had been thorough enough.

Depression, according to some authors, is inextricably linked with OCD. Obsessional–compulsive disorder may start during an episode of depression but, in the vast majority of cases, depression appears to be the result of OCD. In most cases, OCD is aggravated during bouts of depression but sometimes ritualizing also ceases when mood deteriorates. About 30% of depressed patients have OCD features which, in their case, fail to outlast the depressive episode and would therefore not attract a diagnosis of OCD. The close relationship between depression and OCD in a proportion of OCD patients is also reflected by biochemical studies (see below).

There is now general consensus about dissimilarity between OCD and schizophrenia, although some 1–16% of OCD patients have been found to develop schizophrenia at a later date (Fenton and McGlasham, 1986). Some authors have argued, however, that some of these patients did not originally suffer from OCD. Similarly, obsessive–compulsive symptoms have been described in only 1–3.5% of schizophrenic patients. Delusions can occur among OCD sufferers, although in the absence of hallucinations. Recently, a small atypical subgroup of OCD patients has been identified, apparently showing marked psychotic features without justifying the diagnosis of schizophrenia. These patients are less anxious and depressed than typical OCD patients (Solyom, Dinicola, Phil, Sookman and Luchins, 1985), reveal no precipitants of the disorder and are characterized by 'overvalued ideation' (Foa, 1979), i.e. they believe their fears and rituals to be realistic. Neither pharmacological nor behavioural treatment has so far been effective in this group.

Finally, some researchers have considered the possibility of a link between the motor abnormalities of OCD and those of Tourette's syndrome (Montgomery, Clayton and Friedhoff, 1982). Both disorders can have an early onset and are sometimes characterized by bizarre thoughts. So far, however, evidence of a biological mechanism is scanty.

PSYCHOMETRIC DATA

Patients with OCD have been found to have a higher IQ than other neurotic patients. Their thought systems and reminiscences may require a high degree of abstract thinking and recall. Accordingly, they yield a higher digit span than other groups (Reed, 1977). Yet OCD patients have difficulties in making decisions due to doubt and lack of conviction. This may also occur when making trivial decisions. Sufferers of OCD will put off making decisions when given the chance and take less risks. In tasks requiring a trade-off between speed and accuracy, OCD sufferers will thus opt for accuracy (Gordon, 1985). When having to find communalities between items, as many categories as items may be named (Reed, 1969a, b). This could be due either to an inability to ignore irrelevant details or to an inability to make decisions. So far a hypothesis regarding abnormal allocation of attention can be supported only in relation to contents relevant to ritualizing. Foa and McNally (1986) presented neutral and fear-relevant words in the unattended channel during a dichotic listening task. Fear-relevant words were more readily detected than neutral ones. This effect disappeared following successful treatment. A similar result has been obtained for generalized anxiety (Mathews and MacLeod, 1986) and it is therefore likely to be related to the anxiety reaction aroused by relevant contents. Whether or not OCD also engenders or is engendered by abnormal information processing, such as generally heightened detection of target words in the unattended channel cannot be concluded from Foa and McNally's (1986) study, since no control group was employed. Thus the notion of overattention to irrelevant details still awaits empirical support in OCD. Difficulty in decision making, however, appears to be a major factor in this disorder.

ENDOCRINOLOGICAL FINDINGS

Since mood disturbance has been noted to be an important feature in OCD, a biochemical test considered to be a biological marker of depression has also been applied to OCD patients. The dexamethasone suppression test consists of administering dexamethasone (a synthetic glucocorticoid) at 11 p.m., followed by measurement of plasma cortisol levels the following day at 8 a.m. and 4 p.m. Plasma cortisol remains suppressed in normal individuals for 24 h following dexamethasone administration. Lack of suppression is considered indicative of a breakdown in the regulatory mechanisms of this group of hormones. Some 50% of depressives have shown a lack of suppression of plasma cortisol. Similarly, 40% of OCD patients displayed a lack of suppression (Asberg, Thorén and Bertilsson, 1982) and there is some indication that the extent of the failure to suppress is related to the severity of depression in these patients.

The similarity between depressive states in primary depressives and OCD sufferers is further underlined by their growth-hormone response to clonidine. Clonidine is a selective alpha-2-adrenergic receptor agonist which induces an increase in plasma growth hormone in humans (presumably triggered by the agonist's effect on hypothalamic alpha-2 receptors). Depressives display a blunted growth-hormone response to clonidine, which supports the notion of adrenergic receptor dysregulation in this group of patients (Siever and Uhde, 1984). The blunted growth-hormone response has been observed to persist long after clinical improvement. Insel, Mueller, Gillin, Siever and Murphy (1984) found a similarly blunted growth-hormone response in OCD patients after administration of clonidine. This response also occurred in OCD patients not suffering from secondary depression. Such data strongly support the clinical observation of a close relationship between OCD and depression, yet they fail to reveal how the particular pattern of OCD symptoms comes about.

NEUROANATOMICAL STUDIES AND PSYCHOSURGICAL TREATMENT

While no specific anatomical site has so far been implicated in OCD, similarities between OCD and the behaviour of lesioned animals point to malfunctioning of the limbic system. Thus it has been noted that hippocampectomized rats exhibit stereotyped and rigid behaviour and engage in odd rituals reminiscent of those observed in OCD patients (Devenport, Devenport and Holloway, 1981). The close relationship between mood and obsessional–compulsive behaviour also points to involvement of the limbic system in OCD, since limbic structures have traditionally been associated with emotion and motivation.

The limbic system has also been the target of surgical intervention in the treatment of OCD. Leucotomy aims at disconnecting the orbital and medial frontal cortex from the limbic system. Of 17 OCD patients treated with leucotomy, Kelly (1973) reported that 75% showed improvement. In another report, only 50% of OCD sufferers benefited from leucotomy. The intervention showed itself to be more effective in patients suffering from agitated depression and chronic anxiety (Kelly, Walter, Mitchell-Heggs and Sargant, 1972). As has been pointed out by other authors, clinical assessment of outcome was limited to the evaluation of anxiety and depression. Assessment of obsessional–compulsive behaviour may have yielded a less favourable success ratio. It is thought now that leucotomy has a general tension-reducing effect while not modifying behaviour. In any case, given the availability of other and more successful treatment modes, leucotomy cannot be the first choice of intervention. Possible long-term side-effects including poor memory, social disinhibition and epilepsy also militate against such a radical and irreversible step.

PHARMACOLOGICAL TREATMENT

Although OCD is often accompanied by severe anxiety, anxiolytic agents have failed to yield a therapeutic effect in this disorder (Ananth, 1976). While most preparations decreased physiological arousal, they were ineffective in reducing the primary symptoms of obsessions and compulsions. Thus OCD cannot be considered to be entirely determined by level of anxiety, or rather by the adrenergic system which is usually implicated in anxiolytic medication.

In exploring alternative strategies in pharmacological treatment, interest has focused on the serotonergic system. There is evidence to suggest reduced serotonergic function in depressed patients and the finding of similarly low levels of blood serotonin in OCD patients prompted Yaryura-Tobias (1977) to suggest that there are decreased functional levels of serotonin available in the synaptic cleft of OCD patients. Depletion of serotonin in animals has been shown to lead to stereotyped behaviour including excessive grooming (Shillitoe, 1970). Furthermore, the antidepressant clomipramine has been repeatedly shown to be effective in the treatment of OCD patients (Rachman *et al.*, 1979; Thorén, Asberg, Bertilsson, Mellström, Sjoqvist and Traskman, 1980). Clomipramine is thought to inhibit serotonin re-uptake, resulting in greater availability of this neurotransmitter in the synaptic cleft. The most direct evidence of its effect in OCD patients has been provided by Thorén *et al.* (1980). Examination of a serotonin metabolite in the cerebrospinal fluid failed to reveal differences between patients and control subjects but those patients with a high level of the metabolite were also the ones who improved clinically during clomipramine treatment. They also showed a significant reduction in the level of the metabolite.

It is still unclear whether clomipramine's effect is primarily antidepressant and secondarily anti-obsessional or whether it has direct anti-obsessional action. In Rachman *et al.*'s (1979) study, only depressed OCD patients benefited from medication, yet other studies have shown its effect to be independent of mood state (Mavissakalian, Turner, Michelson and Jacob, 1985). Evidence available so far suggests that OCD symptoms return after discontinuation of the drug (Thorén *et al.*, 1980). However, clomipramine's cardiac toxic effects advise against its use for permanent medication.

PSYCHOLOGICAL TREATMENT

Obsessional–compulsive disorder proved intractable and unresponsive to various forms of psychotherapy. Failure rates were generally high and the occasional clinical improvement could not be attributed to therapeutic interventions. However, a breakthrough occurred with the advent of the treatment approach of Rachman, Hodgson and Marks (1971) and Meyer, Levy and Shnurer (1974). Rachman addressed the question as to the maintenance of ritualizing. He and his co-workers showed that contact with stimuli deemed to be contaminated caused considerable discomfort to OCD patients. Subsequent cleaning or checking rituals, on the other hand, had an anxiety-reducing effect (Röper and Rachman, 1975; Röper, Rachman and Hodgson, 1973). These studies underlined the role of anxiety as giving rise to ritualizing. Furthermore, they also revealed that ritualizing had a reinforcing effect. The persistence of compulsions was therefore attributed to the contingent relief from anxiety.

A series of clinical studies followed (see Rachman and Hodgson, 1980), evaluating anxiety-reducing techniques, such as systematic desensitization, exposure *in vivo* and modelling, in the treatment of OCD. Participant modelling *in vivo* emerged as the most effective technique. In employing this technique, the therapist demonstrates 'self-contamination' with the object deemed contaminated: thus the object is touched, after which clothes, hair and skin, as well as frequently used appliances found around the room, are touched with apparent lack of concern. In the treatment of checking compulsions, objects are made to be untidy or, if indicated, the therapist may demonstrate rapid switching off and immediate walking away from appliances. As soon as possible the patient is encouraged to participate and imitate the therapist's way of dealing with the anxiety-inducing stimuli. Response prevention turned out to be a further important treatment component: following exposure, the patient is encouraged to resist carrying out the rituals usually engaged in after encountering such stimuli. The time during which the patient has to resist is normally increased over sessions. Thus response prevention aims at diminishing ritualizing and, thereby, also extending exposure.

The results of the studies attested to the efficacy of these treatment methods. A recent comparison between the two methods, exposure and response prevention, and their combined use (Foa, Steketee, Grayson, Turner and Latimer, 1984) confirmed their combination as being the more effective intervention than either component alone. Results also confirmed the specificity of the two treatment approaches. While exposure diminished anxiety to a greater extent than response prevention, the latter had a greater effect on the urge to ritualize. A controlled treatment study with a larger sample size replicated earlier results and established behavioural treatment as the most effective treatment method in OCD to date (Rachman *et al.*, 1979). Some 70% of OCD patients were either asymptomatic or much improved at the end of treatment. Follow-up data, although tainted with methodological problems, suggest the long-term effectiveness of this treatment to be better than that of any other. Given the success of behavioural treatment, it would be interesting to know whether it also brings about biochemical changes indicative of clinical improvement.

An analysis of treatment failures (Foa, Grayson, Steketee, Doppelt, Turner and Latimer, 1983) pointed to the existence of subgroups amongst OCD patients. Among those not responding to behavioural treatment were severely depressed patients whose anxiety failed to diminish over repeated exposures and a group of patients with 'overvalued ideas' who considered their fears and rituals to be realistic. It was suggested previously that these latter patients may be distinct from other OCD sufferers in that they evince psychotic features.

PSYCHOPHYSIOLOGICAL METHODS IN RESEARCH INTO OBSESSIONAL–COMPULSIVE DISORDER

A two-pronged approach with surprisingly little overlap has been used in psychophysiological research of OCD. One approach has been dedicated to the investigation of the nature and genesis of the disorder. Hypotheses regarding the underlying pathology have ranged from the possibility of neurological lesions to the likelihood of cognitive dysfunctions. Appropriately, central measures such as waking electroencephalogram (EEG), sleep EEG, event-related potentials (ERPs) and the contingent negative variation (CNV) have been employed in this line of research.

The other approach has been concerned with models of maintenance and treatment of OCD. Given that emotional mechanisms are implicated in these processes, autonomic measures such as heart rate (HR) and electrodermal activity (EDA) have been favoured.

PSYCHOPHYSIOLOGICAL MEASURES IN CLINICAL RESEARCH

Waking EEG recordings are carried out routinely in neurological assessments. Among the most noticeable EEG abnormalities are those observed in epileptic states. Synchronization of EEG activity (characteristically termed 'spikes' and 'waves'), can take place during neuronal discharges emanating from epileptic foci. Such synchronization may be a topographically isolated event, but it may also spread over the whole cortex as in *grand mal* episodes of epilepsy. Other consistently found clinical EEG results include a predominance of slow EEG rhythms in mentally retarded children.

Abnormalities of sleep EEG have more recently become a focus of research. The most consistently found sleep abnormalities in psychiatric disorders are reduced sleep time, reduced slow-wave sleep (i.e. a reduction in delta activity) and shortened latency of rapid eye movement (REM) sleep. This sleep pattern has been found in depressed patients (Gillin, Duncan, Pettigrew, Frankel and Snyder, 1979) as well as in schizophrenics (Feinberg and Hiatt, 1978).

Although not frequently employed, some ERP abnormalities have been shown in psychiatric disorders. One of them is a failure to suppress the P50 of the auditory evoked potential (AEP) in schizophrenics. Presentation of visual stimuli with short inter-stimulus intervals of half a second usually results in the suppression of the P50 of the AEP. Schizophrenics fail to show suppression and so do their first degree relatives (Siegel, Waldo, Mizner, Adler and Freedman, 1984). Early components up to 100 ms are thought to represent subcortical activity and are regarded as being highly dependent on stimulus properties, whereas late components are considered to reflect cognitive processes or 'response set' (Hillyard and Woods, 1979). Failure to suppress the

P50 component is thought to be indicative of a breakdown in filter mechanisms regulating sensory intake.

Psychiatric groups have also shown a variety of CNV abnormalities (Sartory, 1985). Among the most consistent findings are low CNV amplitude in schizophrenic and depressed patients, as well as a retarded return to baseline following the motor response (post-imperative negative variation) in both groups of patients.

Heart rate has been used in both diagnostic assessment and treatment evaluation in anxiety states (Sartory, 1981). Resting HR has been shown to be increased by 15 beats/min in patients with severe generalized anxiety compared with controls (Lader and Wing, 1966). Phobics rarely show marked elevation in resting rate, but exhibit cardiac acceleration when confronted with the phobic situation or object. Peak acceleration of the phasic cardiac response has been established to be linearly related to self-report of fear (Sartory, Rachman and Grey, 1977). Since anxiety is thought to play a major role in maintaining ritualizing, HR has also been utilized in assessing OCD states and treatment outcome.

The electrodermal response (EDR) is considered to be a component of the orienting response and is subject to rapid habituation. Some evidence has been provided that habituation is retarded during generalized anxiety states (Lader and Wing, 1966). It has also been shown that phobics display greater EDRs to phobic stimulation than non-phobics (Sartory, 1983). Number of spontaneous responses (NSRs) have also been of interest in psychiatric research. Higher NSRs have been observed in patients with generalized anxiety than in controls (Lader and Wing, 1966).

PSYCHOPHYSIOLOGICAL STUDIES IN PATIENTS WITH OBSESSIONAL–COMPULSIVE DISORDER

NEUROLOGICAL RESULTS AND SPONTANEOUS EEG IN AWAKE STATE

Given the intractability of obsessional states to psychotherapy before the advent of behaviour therapy techniques, it is perhaps not surprising that OCD was thought by some authors to be of organic aetiology. There is, in fact, some evidence to suggest that OCD is the result of neurological abnormalities. Schilder (1938) noted mild neurological symptoms including tremor, akinesia or hyperkinesia in about two-thirds of OCD patients. He thought the symptoms to be the result of a subclinical encephalitis episode. Diagnostic criteria of OCD were, however, not clearly defined until more recently. Applying more stringent criteria, some 3.4% prevalence of OCD was found among 415 patients with head injuries (Hillbom, 1960). Obsessional–compulsive disorder was more common after severe trauma but could not be related to a lesion of any particular structure.

Electroencephalogram studies in OCD patients are similarly inconclusive. Pacella, Polatin and Nagler (1940) reported that 22 of 31 OCD patients showed EEG abnormalities of a non-specific kind. The diagnosis of 'pure OCD' has to be doubted, however, since some of the patients also suffered from major motor seizures. In contrast, Rockwell and Simons (1947) found only 1 of 11 OCD patients with 'stable and well-organized personalities' to have an abnormal EEG and a similar ratio, namely 1 of 18 patients with obsessive personality traits, showed abnormalities in another study (Ingram and McAdam, 1960). Epstein and Bailine (1971) noted theta and spiking similar to that of epileptics in the awake EEG of 3 OCD patients which became more pronounced and localized during sleep. In a sample of severely impaired OCD patients, 4 out of 12 showed EEG abnormalities in the temporal region (Jenike and Brotman, 1984). However, another study which included a control group found no differences in EEG patterns between groups other than reduced left-temporal variability in OCD patients during a resting state (Flor-Henry, Yendall, Koles and Howarth, 1979).

Summarizing, no strong case can be made for the presence of cerebral abnormality on the basis of spontaneous EEG results in OCD patients. Some evidence points to temporal lobe dysfunction similar to that in epileptics but it has been found in too few patients to be implicated confidently in the aetiology of the disorder. Instead, the disorders, whenever found together, must be considered to co-exist rather than be causally related. Alternatively, the notion might be entertained of a subgroup amongst OCD sufferers whose obsessional–compulsive behaviour is related to cerebral lesions.

SLEEP EEG

Studies on the patterns of sleep EEG of OCD patients are few but results are, on the whole, more consistent than those of the awake state. The sleep patterns of OCD patients showed a number of abnormalities compared to those of controls (Gaillard, Iorio, Campajola and Kemali, 1984; Insel, Gillin, Moore, Mendelson, Loewenstein and Murphy, 1982; Insel et al., 1984). Total sleep time was reduced in Insel et al.'s (1982) study but not in that by Gaillard et al. (1984), although both groups of authors reported an increase in awake movement time in OCD patients compared with that of non-clinical control subjects. Both groups of authors were in agreement that stage 1 lasted longer in OCD patients, while stages 3 and 4, as indicated by the amount of delta activity, were markedly reduced. Patients with OCD, therefore, seem to take longer to go to sleep and have a more shallow sleep than controls. In fact, Gaillard et al. (1984) reported that 3 out of 5 OCD patients had neither stage 3 nor stage 4 sleep. Some abnormality has also been found regarding REM sleep. Insel *et al.* (1982, 1984) reported shortened REM latency in OCD patients which was not found by Gaillard *et al.* (1984), but both groups found a decreased REM efficiency index: OCD patients suffered more awake and non-REM states during what should otherwise have been REM phases.

The question arises as to how specific these sleep abnormalities are to OCD. Insel *et al.* (1982, 1984) compared OCD patients with depressed patients, whereas Gaillard *et al.* (1984) compared them with schizophrenics. Depressed patients show both a similarly increased awake movement time to OCD patients and a similarly marked reduction in slow-wave sleep. The two groups have also been found to sleep for shorter durations and have decreased REM latency (results which Gaillard *et al.* (1984) did not replicate in their OCD patients). It could be argued that the sleep pattern in OCD patients is similar to that of depressed patients because of the high incidence of secondary depression in the former group. Yet Insel *et al.* (1982) failed to find a reliable difference in sleep abnormalities between depressed and non-depressed OCD patients. Furthermore, similarities in sleep patterns between depressed patients and schizophrenics (as found by Gaillard *et al.*, 1984) would militate against the depression hypothesis. Schizophrenics show a decreased total sleep time with dramatically increased waking time compared with controls. Stage 4 sleep is also severely diminished.

It would, therefore, appear that sleep abnormalities observed in OCD patients cannot unequivocally be attributed to their specific psychopathology. It has been suggested that the regulation of slow-wave sleep involves, in part, serotonin (Jouvet, 1983), which may provide the essential link between disturbed sleep patterns in these three groups of patients.

EVOKED POTENTIAL STUDIES

In an attempt to account for the heightened tension experienced by OCD patients and their preoccupation with particular contents, such as germs, Beech and Perigault (1974) proposed that OCD was characterized by an unstable arousal system making obsessionals more vulnerable to fixed and rapid conditioning. Such a model implies altered information processing which Beech and co-workers sought to confirm by examining evoked potentials. Patients with OCD were compared with normal controls with regard to both sensory visual evoked potentials (VEPs) and cognitive evoked potentials in response to a decision-making task. No differences between groups were found regarding VEPs during flash presentation but, contrary to expectations, OCD patients exhibited a lower P130 amplitude than controls during pattern presentations. An abnormally elevated arousal should have been reflected in increased ERP amplitudes. The decision-making task had been projected either to the right or left visual field. Cognitive ERPs of obsessionals yielded a decreased N220 component compared to that of controls. In addition, this component was of shorter latency in patients during presentation to the left visual field (Ciesielski, Beech and Gordon, 1981). Results were partly replicated in a further study in which either two or three shapes had to be judged identical or not. Comparison of three shapes was deemed the more difficult task (Beech, Ciesielski and Gordon, 1983). The amplitude of the N2 component during presentation to the left visual field (right electrode position) was diminished in OCD patients during the easy task and more pronouncedly so during the difficult task. Moreover, the difficult task also engendered a lowered N2 component over the left side and a lower P3 component on both sides in OCD patients. The latency of the two components, N2 and P3, was markedly reduced in patients in both tasks and both electrode positions. While it is uncertain why the amplitude of ERP components is diminished, the shortened latency was taken as partial support of the assumption of a low level of inhibitory activity in OCD patients.

However, Shagass, Roemer, Straumanis and Josiassen (1984a,b) found no evidence of shortened ERP latencies. In their study, left and right somatosensory evoked potentials (LSEPs and RSEPs) to median nerve shocks applied to the wrist, as well as AEPs to binaural clicks and VEPs to chequerboard flashes, were recorded in OCD patients and controls. Recordings were derived from 14 scalp leads referenced to linked ears. Stimulation of the left median nerve resulted in a more pronounced N60 component contralaterally at C4 in patients than in controls. On the other hand, VEPs of OCD patients showed a lower amplitude of the N75 component and their AEPs, a smaller P50 than those of controls. Thus, somatosensory stimulation led to an increased response, whereas acoustic and visual stimuli led to a decreased one. The authors point out that an increased SEP N60 component had already been found in chronic schizophrenics, although comparison between the two groups of patients revealed a higher SEP N60 in OCD patients (Shagass *et al.*, 1984b). Some epileptics have also shown an increased SEP N60 on the side of the lesion (Williamson, Allisn, Goff and Mattson, 1977), which may point to local cortical hyperexcitability. A low amplitude VEP N75 has only been found in non-chronic schizophrenics, whereas a lowered AEP N50 had not previously been observed in a clinical group. The authors speculated that the lower amplitudes of these ERP components in OCD patients may point to a heightened degree of activation in subcortical mechanisms modulating sensory input.

The VEP results for OCD patients found by these two groups of researchers, led by Beech and Ciesielski on the one hand and by Shagass on the other, are clearly at odds. The findings of shortened latencies of VEP components by the first group was not replicated by he second. The British group also found a lower amplitude of VEP P130 in OCD patients, rather than the lower amplitude of the earlier N75 component found by Shagass *et al.* (1984a). Differences in results could be due to medication. Half of the patients studied by Beech and Ciesielski's group were on medication whereas all were drug-free in Shagass *et al.*'s (1984a,b) study. The composition of control groups may also account for differences in results. The status of controls is not certain in Shagass *et al.*'s (1984a,b) study. They may have consisted of non-patients or else of patients with 'other neuroses'. Results of reduced latencies and amplitudes of N200 and P300 in OCD patients were replicated by the British group. This time all patients had been drug-free for 48 h. In this study ERPs were also derived from P3 and P4 and elicited by a judgemental task, presumably appropriate to the pathological difficulty in decision making in OCD (although no performance data had been provided to ascertain that notion). No direct comparison can therefore be made between these results and those found in passive VEPs, and the reason for the differences between the two studies remains obscure at this stage. Yet the divergence of results underlines the importance of carrying out further ERP work in OCD patients.

SLOW-WAVE POTENTIALS

Unlike the findings in the ERP studies, those relating to the CNV in OCD patients have been consistent. McCallum and Walter (1968) were the first authors to report a higher CNV amplitude in obsessional patients than in normal controls. This finding is unique among psychiatric patients who otherwise invariably have a lower CNV amplitude compared with normals (see Sartory, 1985).

When a distracting stimulus was applied during the stimulus interval, OCD patients also showed faster CNV recovery than normals and anxious patients (McCallum and Walter, 1968). The finding of an increased CNV amplitude in OCD patients was replicated (Timsit, Konickx, Dargent, Fontaine and Dongier, 1970) and, in addition, prolonged negativity after the motor response was noted amongst OCD records. This post-imperative negative variation was, however, also observed in other groups of patients, such as schizophrenics, depressives and manics. Prolonged negativity must therefore be considered to be non-specific and may reflect dysregulation of reafferent pathways during motor responses.

The increased CNV amplitude appears specific to OCD and the question arises as to which aspect of the disorder it reflects. The above-mentioned studies had been carried out with short inter-stimulus intervals in which the 'early' and 'late' components are thought to be superimposed. In an attempt to clarify which of the two components showed an increased amplitude, a study was carried out using the traditional forewarned reaction-time paradigm, with an interval of 5 s between warning and imperative stimulus (Sartory and Master, 1984). It was assumed that the 'early' component reflected attentional processes which might be heightened in obsessional patients. Accordingly, the increased CNV amplitude found in OCD patients was predicted to be due to a heightened 'early' component. In the event, it was the second component which was increased in obsessional patients compared with controls. Concurrent HR and EDA also failed to point to heightened attention in the patient group. In any case, the assumption that the 'early' CNV component reflects orienting has turned out to be unfounded (Simons, Rockstroh, Elbert, Fiorito, Lutzenberger and Birbaumer, 1987).

The reason why OCD patients should exhibit an increased 'late' component remains unclear. No corresponding differences in reaction time between patients and controls were found and the results could not, therefore, be attributed to increased motor preparation in patients. The amplitude of the CNV had previously been found to increase with uncertainty even in tasks not demanding an immediate motor response (Simons and Lang, 1976). It is conceivable that OCD patients approached the reaction-time task with doubt as to the requirements made of them, this being reflected in the 'late' CNV component. Supportive evidence for this assumption will necessitate a paradigm with direct manipulation of doubt and uncertainty in OCD patients.

AUTONOMIC ACTIVITY

As anxiety is thought to be the driving force in maintaining obsessional ritualizing, assessment of autonomic responses is of major importance in this disorder. Most studies have been devoted to assessing whether obsessional stimuli result in greater autonomic activity than neutral ones, as is the case in phobic anxiety. A further aim has been the assessment of treatment outcome. If anxiety maintains the maladaptive behaviour, successful treatment can be expected to reduce anxiety.

In an early study, Rabavilas and Boulougouris (1974) compared HR and EDA during phases of obsessional fantasy (during which patients engaged in their idiosyncratic ruminations), during a flooding talk (during which the therapist described upsetting imagery) and during flooding practice (wherein patients rehearsed unacceptable thoughts with the imagined disastrous consequences). Reactions were compared with those during neutral fantasy and neutral thoughts. Patients had to indicate whenever imagery was present and maintain it for up to 3 min, followed by rest periods of 1 min. Patients suffering from ruminations with few or no compulsions were selected for this study. Data were analysed over 20-s periods. Heart rate was counted, as were non-specific EDRs. In addition, the maximum EDR amplitude was measured. Periods with the highest amount of activity during experimental phases were compared with those of highest activity during control phases. Heart rate proved to be higher by a mean 4.2 beats/min during obsessional fantasy than during neutral fantasy and it was also higher during flooding talk by 5 beats/min than during neutral talk, increasing by a further 2 beats/min during flooding practice. This last phase was considered to be the most disturbing one. Non-specific EDRs were more frequent during obsessional than during neutral talk, but did not differentiate among other phases. Finally, EDRs of greater amplitude were observed during experimental phases than during control ones. Both HR and EDR therefore confirmed the presence of increased autonomic activity during preoccupation with obsessional material in OCD patients.

Results of phasic second-by-second HR reactions to obsessional ruminations (Eves and Tata, in press) confirmed those found for tonic HR. Primarily, ruminating OCD patients were presented with key words representing their ruminations as well as words used to 'neutralize' danger associated with the former stimuli. Neutral contents from the same semantic class as the ruminations were also presented for comparison. Ruminative words elicited greater cardiac acceleration and also more anxiety than either of the other stimuli. Neutral stimuli were accompanied by cardiac deceleration, whereas 'neutralizing' ones showed no distinct cardiac deflections. In contrast to the previous study, EDA failed to differentiate reliably between conditions.

Other studies have been directed at the question as to whether compulsions have an anxiety-relieving effect upon obsessions. Hornsveld, Kraainmaat and Van Dam-Baggen (1979) compared OCD patients fearful of contamination (and with hand-washing rituals) with other psychiatric patients (whose complaint was not specified beyond being matched for fear and anxiety without suffering from OCD). Both groups underwent an identical procedure. To begin with they were instructed to wash their hands, after which they were given relaxation instructions. The contaminated stimulus was then placed in front of them with the instruction that they should touch it. Having done so, patients were again permitted to wash their hands. Heart rate and subjective distress were recorded throughout the procedure. Electrodermal level (EDL) and non-specific EDRs were also recorded throughout, with the exception of during the hand-washing phases. Means of autonomic data were evaluated for the 10-min relaxation phase, as well as for 15 s at the beginning and end of the hand-washing phases in the case of HR. These two periods were chosen in order to investigate whether or not hand-washing had an anxiety-relieving effect. The kind of data reduction carried out for the phases of anticipation and actual touching of the contaminated object was not described. Comparisons were carried out within groups, between active phases and relaxation. Heart rate increased during anticipation of touching the dirt stimulus but not during the actual touching. These results applied to OCD patients only. Electrodermal level and number of non-specific EDRs were raised in both groups during the two phases. Subjective distress was greater at the beginning of the second hand-washing phase (i.e. after touching the dirt stimulus) than during relaxation in the OCD group but not in the control group. Surprisingly, HR was at the highest level during hand-washing phases in both groups. Thus both groups experienced a higher degree of HR activity during the phase considered anxiety relieving.

Similar results have been found by Grayson, Nutter and Mavissakalian (1980). Patients imagined four scenes repeatedly. One consisted of the feared activity (i.e. touching contaminated material), another of the compulsive ritual without provocation (i.e. taking a shower), another the feared task together with the compulsive activity and, finally, a neutral scene. Each trial was preceded by 40-s rest, after which the scene was described for 20 s and visualized by the patients for another 30 s.

Second-by-second HR was evaluated during the first 15-s period of visualization and referred to the preceding last 5 s of rest. Imagery of obsessional content elicited cardiac acceleration compared to the brief deceleration observed during neutral imagery. Responses of compulsive washers to contaminated material therefore seem similar to those of phobics to phobic stimuli (Sartory, 1985). Surprisingly though, visualization of the compulsive activity without the provoking stimulus again produced an accelerative response. There are thus findings of HR acceleration during the actual execution of the compulsive ritual as well as during imagery of its execution. These results apparently fail to confirm the assumption that the compulsive ritual is anxiety relieving. They are also inconsistent with the lack of a cardiac response during 'neutralizing' thoughts noted by Eves and Tata (in press). The discrepancy between the results may lie in the content of imagery or activity. Studies finding cardiac acceleration during compulsions involved motor activity, real or imagined, whereas in Eves and Tata's (in press) study, compulsions involved thoughts devoid of motor activity. It is conceivable that muscular activity during the actual execution or during imagery can account for differences in results. Concurrent registration of muscular activity may have shed light on this issue.

Finally, treatment effects on physiological responses in OCD have been evaluated in three studies. Boulougouris, Rabavilas and Stefanis (1977) compared four treatment conditions: short- and long-duration fantasy as well as short and long *in-vivo* practice were administered according to a Latin square design to 12 obsessionally ruminating patients. Before and after each treatment phase, tonic HR changes, non-specific EDRs, maximum EDR and subjective ratings of discomfort were assessed to obsessional fantasy, flooding talk and flooding *in vivo*, comparing them with reactions during neutral fantasy talk. Long-duration practice yielded the greatest improvement in HR, as measured during the 'flooding *in vivo*' phase, and in EDR during this and the 'flooding talk' phase. Being generally infrequent, spontaneous EDRs were least frequent during 'flooding talk' following short practice. Subjective anxiety was again lowest following long practice in all 'active' testing phases, namely, obsessive fantasy, flooding talk and flooding *in vivo*. It thus appears that long *in-vivo* practice is more beneficial than either short practice or treatment in fantasy.

In a further study, Grayson, Foa and Steketee (1982) investigated the effect of attention-focusing and distraction on HR and subjective anxiety during exposure. The study was aimed at deciding whether directing attention to the feared object was necessary for 'functional exposure' and thereby response decrement, as was suggested by Borkovec and Grayson (1980), or, alternatively, whether the introduction of competing stimuli could facilitate reduction in discomfort (Rachman, 1976). Patients had washing compulsions. During attention-focusing, they had to touch the most feared stimulus for 90 min while being engaged by the therapist in a conversation about the contaminant and their fear of it. During the distraction condition, patients touched the contaminant while engaging in a video game with the therapist. All patients experienced both conditions on alternate days in a cross-over design. Heart rate was sampled over 20 s at the end of a 10-min rest period and at half-hour intervals throughout treatment. Subjective discomfort ratings were taken every 10 min. Both measures showed linear reduction in all treatment sessions. There was, however, a difference between treatment conditions regarding the maintenance of the clinical gain between sessions. Gains were maintained following attention-focusing, whereas the distraction condition was followed by between-session relapse. This pattern was consistent for both HR and subjective ratings of discomfort. The data thus suggest that direction of attention has an effect on maintenance of anxiety reduction between sessions. Little is known as yet about the processes underlying short- and long-term response decrement. The results support the contention that they are independent. However, it remains obscure as to why long-term response decrement should be a function of direction of attention.

Whereas the last two studies evaluated psychophysiological changes during behavioural treatment programmes, a recent study investigated those occurring during pharmacological treatment. Such an undertaking poses problems, since most psychoactive drugs can affect autonomic nervous system activity and it may be difficult to decide whether the observed autonomic changes are indeed related to clinical changes or whether they are peripheral and independent. Tricyclic antidepressants, in particular, have been shown to lead to a substantial increase in HR (Bigger, Kantor, Glassman and Perel, 1978), an effect not readily associated with concurrent reports of lowered anxiety. Zahn, Insel and Murphy (1984) nevertheless compared the effect of clomipramine (a tricyclic antidepressant thought to have a specific anti-obsessional effect) with a placebo and clorgyline (a monoamine oxidase (MAO) inhibitor), which is selective for MAO-A. This enzyme subtype preferentially metabolizes serotonin and noradrenaline. Clorgyline had been reported to be effective in primary depression. The rationale of the study was Beech and Perigault's (1974) hypothesis that OCD is characterized by abnormal fluctuations in arousal with an accompanying facilitation of fixation on certain stimuli. Were the medication clinically successful, so Zahn *et al.* (1984) argued, then fluctuations in arousal should be stabilized. Although not explicitly stated, the clorgyline condition should presumably shed light on the contribution of depression or its alleviation to clinical changes. Electrodermal activity and HR were registered during a resting phase and during habituation to tones. Such a paradigm has been shown to differentiate between states of anxiety (Lader, 1967).

Patients with OCD received clomipramine for 6 weeks followed by clorgyline, or vice versa, in a cross-over design. Prior to and between drug treatments, patients received a placebo for 4 weeks. Psychophysiological testing was carried out at the end of each period. Heart rate and bilateral EDA were recorded during a 5-min rest period, during the presentation of tones of moderate intensity and during a further period of tones of variable intensity (up to 100 dB). Finally, a two-flash threshold discrimination procedure, thought to elicit obsessional doubt, was carried out.

The clinical benefit was greater in the clomipramine condition than in either of the others. Electrodermal level and number of non-specific EDRs were markedly reduced during rest in the clomipramine condition, as was number of non-specific EDRs in the clorgyline condition compared with placebo. Both EDA indices as well as amplitude of non-specific EDRs were also reduced in the clomipramine condition during task instructions and the two-flash threshold discrimination, although performance was unchanged in this task. Clorgyline produced only a moderate decrease in EDL during the two situations. Clomipramine thus appeared to have a stabilizing effect on tonic EDA. In contrast, both drugs produced HR increases compared to the placebo, with clomipramine increasing HR by 12 beats/min and clorgyline by 6 beats/min. As to phasic responses, clomipramine reduced the amplitude of the EDR to tones of high intensity and hastened habituation of the orienting response, an effect which was most prominent during high-intensity stimulation. It may be remembered that Lader's (1967) original study of anxious patients had also been carried out with tones of 100dB. Clorgyline failed to produce any effects on habituation compared with placebo. No clear-cut results were obtained for phasic HR but the significantly different basal levels between conditions would, in any case, have presented difficulties in interpreting results. Thus clomipramine affected EDA in a stabilizing fashion similar to that of anxiety-reducing agents (Johnstone *et al.*, 1981) whereas its effect on HR was, if anything, opposite to that of an anxiolytic action. At the same time clomipramine had a greater clinical effect than clorgyline, the latter showing no improvement beyond that of the placebo. These results point to a more specific action of clomipramine than merely antidepressant and underline the contribution of the serotonergic system to OCD.

Summarizing, results of autonomic reactions parallel those of subjective ratings during the evaluation of treatment outcome. Both sets of measures point to the greater efficacy of long-term exposure among behavioural techniques and of the tricyclic antidepressant, clomipramine compared with placebo among pharmaceutical methods.

CONTRIBUTIONS OF PSYCHOPHYSIOLOGICAL METHODS TO THE UNDERSTANDING OF OBSESSIONAL–COMPULSIVE DISORDER

Practitioners are often of the opinion that psychophysiological measures add little to the knowledge obtained by other, more easily applied techniques. After all, why use complicated machinery and even more complicated data processing just to find out that HR increases to a fear-inducing stimulus, when the same information can be obtained by asking the subject how frightening he rates the object? The lack of a cardiac response after treatment will be similarly unexciting if the treatment success has already been made obvious by the more economical behavioural and self-report measures. Psychophysiological contributions to our understanding of OCD will be traced in aetiological as well as assessment and treatment research.

AETIOLOGICAL MODELS

The traditional view regards OCD as the extreme version of a personality type, the anacastic one, which is the result of a strict and inflexible upbringing. Attempts at substantiating this view suffer from the limitations that data have to be collected retrospectively and, even if differences emerge between the clinical and a non-clinical population, it cannot usually be decided unequivocally whether the differences are cause or effect of the disorder. For instance, a depressed OCD patient may well judge his upbringing to have been harsh, because the disorder causes him to select harsh memories rather than happy ones. He may also selectively perceive those qualities in his parents which he attributes to himself. Psychophysiology has made no contribution to this aetiological stance and it is difficult to see how such an aim could be achieved. The successful use of psychophysiological methods requires tight operationalization of phenomena and a degree of precision in formulating questions which this stance does not afford.

The notion that neurological disorders might underlie OCD has fared little better. Some early studies pointed to the presence of soft neurological signs but their results must be viewed with caution because diagnostic criteria of OCD have changed since the time they were carried out. Electroencephalographic recording is used routinely in the assessment of epileptic foci and a number of recent studies have found EEG abnormalities in OCD patients, sometimes similar to those of left temporal lobe epilepsy, in other cases diffuse and variable. These results have been found in too few patients to permit generalization.

Psychometric data have also not yielded evidence of psychological dysfunctions. They do, however, point to peculiarities in the way OCD patients process information and make decisions. Evoked potentials are rapidly turning into a prime instrument for the assessment of how sensory input is processed. So far, the evidence regarding abnormalities in the evoked potentials of OCD patients is inconsistent. Furthermore, given the complexity of the various potential waveforms and their sensitivity to even minute changes in the eliciting paradigm, it is as likely at this stage that OCD research will illuminate the nature of ERPs as that ERP research will shed light on the nature of OCD.

The increased CNV amplitude observed in OCD patients sets them apart from other psychiatric groups. Schizophrenia, depression, bipolar disorder, psychopathy and anxiety states are all, and presumably for different reasons, characterized by a low or altogether non-existent CNV response. The question arises as to the underlying mechanisms engendering the increased CNV amplitude in OCD. It seems unlikely that it is due to increased motor preparation; indeed, no differences were found in reaction time between OCD patients and controls (Sartory and Master, 1984). Instead, increased CNV amplitude in OCD seems to be related to uncertainty and doubt, factors which had previously been shown to yield a heightened CNV in normal subjects. This conclusion would be consonant with psychometric data in OCD, indicating that affected patients have difficulty in decision making and risk taking. Other disorders have also been shown to engender long decision-making times (Mathews and McLeod, 1985), without, however, the concurrent increased CNV amplitude. More research is clearly needed in this area: if the CNV can be shown to distinguish between groups while concurrent performance data fail to do so, then the psychophysiological measure could become a major key to the understanding of mental functioning in this disorder. It is also conceivable that mechanisms underlying these patients' peculiar CNV responses might play a major part in the aetiology of OCD, i.e. might be the reason why this particular syndrome comes about rather than any other, such as agoraphobia.

ASSESSMENT AND TREATMENT

Two major factors have been implicated in the maintenance of OCD, the first one being deterioration of mood or depression exacerbating obsessive–compulsive symptoms, and the second being anxiety or tension which is relieved by compulsive behaviour.

Obsessional–compulsive disorder and depression have been found to have common neurohormonal reactions, such as the failure to show suppression of cortisol following administration of dexamethasone and a blunted growth-hormone response to clonidine. In addition, similarities in sleep EEG patterns have also pointed to a close relationship between OCD and depression. Similar deficits have also been observed in schizophrenic patients and it is therefore likely that the disturbed sleep pattern is due to neurophysiological dysfunctions common to all three disorders.

The presence of anxiety in OCD has also been confirmed by the use of HR recording. Patients with OCD appear to react to certain stimuli similarly to the way in which phobics react. The proposed anxiety-relieving effect of compulsive activity could not however be confirmed, in that HR was further increased during both actual and imaginal execution of cleaning activity. This further HR increase seems attributable to the physical effort demanded by the cleaning activity be it *in vivo* or in imagination. Non-clinical controls exhibited HR increases similar to those of OCD patients during hand-washing.

Few treatment evaluation studies have employed psychophysiological measures. Zahn *et al.* (1984) reported stabilization of EDA similar to that produced by anxiolytic agents after administration of clomipramine. Reactions to idiosyncratic fear-inducing stimuli were assessed before and after treatment with psychological techniques in other studies. Changes in HR were shown to parallel those of subjective ratings of discomfort.

Is it of value, though, to know that HR increases in the presence of certain stimuli in OCD, when we already know from concurrent discomfort ratings that these stimuli elicit anxiety? It has been argued previously (Lang, 1979; Rachman and Hodgson, 1974) that anxiety is a multilayered reaction, consisting of experiential, physiological and behavioural components. It could be argued that each of these manifestations is equally important if shown to be abnormal, i.e. that a cardiac reaction to a stimulus when non-clinical controls have none is just as abnormal a phenomenon as an exaggerated cleaning ritual. Hence when the autonomic reaction occurs, it is as indicative of treatment-worthiness (and should therefore also be a target for treatment) as are compulsive rituals themselves. The same argument will apply to any other physiological indices once they have been firmly established. Thus if evidence of serotonin dysfunction were to be confirmed in OCD, treatment would have to provide a remedy for this dysfunction also, since it is as clinically relevant as, for example, being excessively fearful of untidiness. In consequence, psychophysiological as well as neurophysiological parameters should enter assessment procedures, first, to ascertain the presence of abnormal reactions and, secondly, to ascertain their removal by successful treatment.

BIBLIOGRAPHY

American Psychiatric Association (1980). *Diagnostic and Statistical Manual for Mental Disorders*, 3rd edn. Washington, DC: APA.

Ananth, J. (1976). Treatment of obsessive–compulsive neurosis: pharmacological approach. *Psychosomatics* **17**, 180–184.

Asberg, M., Thorén, P. and Bertilsson, L. (1982). Clomipramine treatment of obsessive disorder – biochemical and clinical aspects. *Psychopharmacological Bulletin* **18**, 13–21.

Beech, H.R. and Perigault, J. (1974). Towards a theory of obsessional disorder. In: H.R. Beech (Ed.) *Obsessional States*. London: Methuen.

Beech, K.T., Ciesielski, K.T. and Gordon, P.K. (1983). Further observations of evoked potentials in obsessional patients. *British Journal of Psychiatry* **142**, 605–609.

Bigger, J.T., Jr, Kantor, S.J., Glassman, A.H. and Perel, J.M. (1978). Cardiovascular effects of tricyclic anti-depressant drugs. In: M.A. Lipton, A.D. DiMascio and K.F. Killam (Eds) *Psychopharmacology: A Generation of Progress*. New York: Raven Press.

Black, A. (1979). The natural history of obsessional neurosis. In: H.R. Beech (Ed.) *Obsessional States*. London: Methuen.

Borkovec, T.D. and Grayson, J.B. (1980). Consequences of increasing the functional impact of internal emotional stimuli. In: K. Blankstein, P. Pliner and J. Policy (Eds) *Advances in the Study of Communication and Affect: Assessment and Modification of Emotional Behavior*, Vol. 6. New York: Plenum.

Boulougouris, J.C., Rabavilas, A.D. and Stefanis, C. (1977). Psychophysiological responses in obsessional–compulsive patients. *Behaviour Research and Therapy* **15**, 221–230.

Brown, F.W. (1942). Heredity in the psychoneuroses. *Proceedings of the Royal Society of Medicine* **35**, 785–790.

Ciesielski, K.T., Beech, H.R. and Gordon, P.K. (1981). Some electrophysiological observations in obsessional states. *British Journal of Psychiatry* **138**, 479–484.

Clifford, C.A., Murray, R.M. and Fulker, D.W. (1984). Genetic and environmental influences on obsessional traits and symptoms. *Psychological Medicine* **14**, 791–800.

Coryell, W. (1981). Obsessive–compulsive disorder and primary unipolar depression: comparisons of background, family history, course, and mortality. *Journal of Nervous and Mental Disease* **169**, 220–224.

Devenport, C.D., Devenport, J.A. and Holloway, F.A. (1981). Reward induced stereotype: modulation by the hippocampus. *Science* **212**, 1288–1289.

Epstein, A.W. and Bailine, S.H. (1971). Sleep and dream studies in obsessional neurosis with particular reference to epileptic states. *Biological Psychiatry* **3**, 149–158.

Eves, F. and Tata, P. (in press). Phasic cardiac and electrodermal reactions to idiographic stimuli in obsessional subjects. *Behavioural Psychotherapy*.

Feinberg, D.F. and Hiatt, J.F. (1978). Sleep patterns in schizophrenia: a selective review. In: R.C. Williams and I. Karacan (Eds) *Sleep Disorders: Diagnosis and Treatment*. New York: Wiley.

Fenton, W.S. and McGlasham, T.H. (1986). The prognostic significance of obsessive–compulsive symptoms in schizophrenia. *American Journal of Psychiatry* **143**, 437–441.

Flor-Henry, P., Yendall, L.T., Koles, Z.J. and Howarth, B.G. (1979). Neuropsychological and power spectral EEG investigations of the obsessive–compulsive syndrome. *Biological Psychiatry* **14**, 119–130.

Foa, E.B. (1979). Failure in treating obsessive–compulsives. *Behaviour Research and Therapy* **17**, 169–176.

Foa, E.B. and McNally, R.J. (1986). Sensitivity to feared stimuli in obsessive–compulsives: a dichotic listening analysis. *Cognitive Therapy and Research* **10**, 477–485.

Foa, E.B., Grayson, J.B., Steketee, G., Doppelt, H.G., Turner, R.M. and Latimer, P.L. (1983). Success and failure in the behavioral treatment of obsessive–compulsives. *Journal of Consulting and Clinical Psychology* **15**, 287–297.

Foa, E.B., Steketee, G., Grayson, J.B., Turner, R.M. and Latimer, P.R. (1984). Deliberate exposure and blocking of obsessive–compulsive rituals: immediate and long-term effects. *Behaviour Therapy* **15**, 450–472.

Gaillard, J.M., Iorio, G., Campajola, P. and Kemali, D. (1984). Temporal organization of sleep in schizophrenics and patients with obsessive–compulsive disorder. *Advances in Biological Psychiatry* **15**, 76–83.

Gillin, J.C., Duncan, W., Pettigrew, K., Frankel, B.L. and Snyder, F. (1979). Successful separation of depressed, normal, and insomniac subjects by EEG sleep data. *Archives of General Psychiatry* **33**, 85–90.

Gordon, P.K. (1985). Allocation of attention in obsessional disorder. *British Journal of Clinical Psychology* **24**, 101–107.

Grayson, J.B., Foa, E.B. and Steketee, G. (1982). Habituation during exposure treatment: distraction vs. attention-focussing. *Behaviour Research and Therapy* **20**, 323–328.

Grayson, J.B., Nutter, D. and Mavissakalian, M. (1980). Psychophysiological assessment of imagery in obsessive–compulsives: a pilot study. *Behaviour Research and Therapy* **18**, 590–593.

Hillbom, E. (1960). After-effects of brain injuries. *Acta Psychiatrica Neurologica Scandinavica*, Suppl. 142, **35**, 105–145.

Hillyard, S. and Woods, D. (1979). Electrophysiological analysis of human brain function. In: R.E. Gazzaniga (Ed.) *Handbook of Behavioural Neurobiology*, Vol. 2., pp. 345–378. New York: Plenum.

Hollingsworth, C.E., Tanguay, P.E., Grossman, L. and Pabst, P. (1980). Long-term outcome of obsessive–compulsive disorder in childhood. *Journal of the American Academy of Child Psychiatry* **19**, 134–144.

Hornsveld, R.H.J., Kraainmaat, F.W. and Van Dam-Baggen, R.M.J. (1979). Anxiety/discomfort and handwashing in obsessive–compulsive and psychiatric control patients. *Behaviour Research and Therapy* **17**, 223–228.

Ingram, I.M. and McAdam, W.A. (1960). The electroencephalogram, obsessional illness and obsessional personality. *Journal of Mental Science* **106**, 686–691.

Insel, T.R., Gillin, J.C., Moore, A., Mendelson, W.B., Loewenstein, R.J. and Murphy, D.L. (1982). The sleep of patients with obsessive–compulsive disorder. *Archives of General Psychiatry* **39**, 1372–1377.

Insel, T.R., Mueller, E.A., III, Gillin, C., Siever, L.J. and Murphy, D.L. (1984). Biological markers in obsessive–compulsive and affective disorders. *Journal of Psychiatric Research* **18**, 407–423.

Jenike, M.A. and Brotman, A.W. (1984). The EEG in obsessive–compulsive disorder. *Journal of Clinical Psychiatry* **45**, 122–124.

Johnstone, E.C., Bourne, R.C., Frith, C.D., Gamble, S., Lofthouse, R., Owen, F., Owens, D.G.C., Robinson, J. and Stevens, M. (1981). The relationship between clinical response, psychophysiological variables and plasma levels of amitriptyline and diazepam in neurotic outpatients. *Psychopharmacology* **72**, 233–240.

Jouvet, M. (1983). Hypnogenic indolamine-dependent factors and paradoxical sleep rebound. In: W.P. Koella (Ed.) *Sleep 1981*, Proceedings of the 6th European Congress of Sleep Research, 1982, pp. 2–18. Basle: Karger.

Kelly, D. (1973). Therapeutic outcome in limbic leucotomy in psychiatric patients. *Psychiatria, Neurologia, Neurochirurgia* **76**, 353–363.

Kelly, D., Walter, C.J.S., Mitchell-Heggs, N. and Sargant, W. (1972). Modified leucotomy assessed clinically, physiologically and psychologically at six weeks and eighteen months. *British Journal of Psychiatry* **120**, 19–29.

Kringlen, E. (1965). Obsessional neurotics: a long term follow-up. *British Journal of Psychiatry* **111**, 709–722.

Lader, M.H. (1967). Palmar skin conductance measures in anxiety and phobic states. *Journal of Psychosomatic Research* **11**, 271–281.

Lader, M.H. and Wing, L. (1966). Physiological measures. Sedative drugs and morbid anxiety. *Maudsley Monograph*, no. 14. London: Oxford University Press.

Lang, P.J. (1979). A bio-informational theory of emotional imagery. *Psychophysiology* **17**, 179–192.

Mathews, A. and MacLeod, C. (1985). Selective processing of threat cues in anxiety states. *Behaviour Research and Therapy* **23**, 563–569.

Mathews, A. and MacLeod, C. (1986). Discrimination of threat cues without awareness in anxiety states. *Journal of Abnormal Psychology* **95**, 131–138.

Mavissakalian, M., Turner, S.M., Michelson, L. and Jacob, R. (1985). Tricyclic antidepressants in obsessive–compulsive disorder: antiobsessional or antidepressant agents? II. *American Journal of Psychiatry* **142**, 572–576.

McCallum, W.C. and Walter, G.W. (1968). The effects of attention and distraction on the contingent negative variation in normal and neurotic subjects. *Electroencephalography and Clinical Neurophysiology* **25**, 319–329.

Meyer, V., Levy, R. and Schnurer, A. (1974). The behavioral treatment of obsessional–compulsive disorder. In: H.R. Beech (Ed.) *Obsessional States*. London: Methuen.

Montgomery, M.A., Clayton, P.J. and Friedhoff, A.J. (1982). Psychiatric illness in Tourette Syndrome patients and first degree relatives. In: A.J. Friedhoff and T.N. Chase (Eds) *Gilles de la Tourette Syndrome*, pp. 335–339. New York: Raven Press.

Pacella, B.L., Polatin, P. and Nagler, S.H. (1940). Clinical and EEG studies in obsessive–compulsive states. *American Journal of Psychiatry* **100**, 830–838.

Rabavilas, A.D. and Boulougouris, J.C. (1974). Physiological accompaniments of ruminations, flooding and thought-stopping in obsessive patients. *Behaviour Research and Therapy* **12**, 239–243.

Rachman, S. (1976). The modification of obsessions, a new formulation. *Behaviour Research and Therapy* **14**, 437–443.

Rachman, S. and Hodgson, R. (1974). Synchrony and desynchrony in fear and avoidance. *Behaviour Research and Therapy* **12**, 311–318.

Rachman, S. and Hodgson, R.T. (1980). *Obsessions and Compulsions*. Englewood Cliffs, NJ: Prentice-Hall.

Rachman, S., Cobb, J., Grey, S., McDonald, B., Mawson, D., Sartory, G. and Stern, R. (1979). The behavioral treatment of obsessional–compulsive disorders with and without clomipramine. *Behaviour Research and Therapy* **17**, 467–478.

Rachman, S., Hodgson, R. and Marks, I. (1971). The treatment of chronic obsessional neurosis. *Behaviour Research and Therapy* **9**, 237–247.

Rasmussen, S.A. and Tsuang, M.T. (1984). The epidemiology of obsessive compulsive disorders. *Journal of Clinical Psychiatry* **45**, 450–457.

Reed, G.F. (1969a). 'Under-inclusion' – a characteristic of obsessional personality disorder I. *British Journal of Psychiatry* **115**, 781–785.

Reed, G.F. (1969b). 'Under-inclusion' – a characteristic of obsessional personality disorder II. *British Journal of Psychiatry* **115**, 787–790.

Reed, G.F. (1977). Obsessional personality disorder and remembering. *British Journal of Psychiatry* **130**, 177–183.

Robins, L.N., Helzer, J.I., Weissman, M.M., Orvaschel, H., Grünberg, E. and Burker, J. (1984). Lifetime prevalence of specific psychiatric disorders in three sites. *Archives of General Psychiatry* **41**, 949–958.

Rockwell, F.V. and Simons, D.J. (1947). The electroencephalogram and personality organization in the obsessive–compulsive reactions. *Archives of Neurological Psychiatry* **57**, 71–77.

Rohrbaugh, J.W., Syndulko, K. and Lindsley, D.B. (1976). Brain wave components of the contingent negative variation in humans. *Science* **191**, 1055–1057.

Röper, G. and Rachman, S. (1975). Obsessional–compulsive checking: experimental replication and development. *Behaviour Research and Therapy* **14**, 25–32.

Röper, G., Rachman, S. and Hodgson, R. (1973). An experiment on obsessional checking. *Behaviour Research and Therapy* **11**, 271–277.

Sartory, G. (1977). The fearless avoiders: comparisons of various strains of rats in an active avoidance task. *Behaviour Research and Therapy* **15**, 149–157.

Sartory, G. (1981). Some psychophysiological issues in behavioural psychotherapy. *Behavioural Psychotherapy* **9**, 215–230.

Sartory, G. (1983). The orienting response and psychopathology: anxiety and phobias. In: D. Siddle (Ed.) *Orienting and Habituation: Perspectives in Human Research.* New York: Wiley.

Sartory, G. (1985). The CNV in psychiatric states. In: D. Papakostopulos, S. Butler and I. Martin (Eds) *Clinical and Experimental Neuropsychophysiology.* London: Croom Helm.

Sartory, G. and Master, D. (1984). Contingent negative variation in obsessional–compulsive patients. *Biological Psychology* **18**, 253–267.

Sartory, G., Rachman, S. and Grey, S.J. (1977). An investigation of the relation between reported fear and heart rate. *Behaviour Research and Therapy* **15**, 435–438.

Schilder, P. (1938). The organic background of obsessions and compulsions. *American Journal of Psychiatry* **94**, 1397–1416.

Shagass, C., Roemer, R.A., Straumanis, J.J. and Josiassen, R.C. (1984a). Evoked potentials in obsessive–compulsive disorder. *Advances in Biological Psychiatry* **15**, 69–75.

Shagass, C., Roemer, R.A., Straumanis, J.J. and Josiassen, R.C. (1984b). Distinctive somatosensory evoked potentials feature in obsessive–compulsive disorder. *Biological Psychiatry* **19**, 1507–1524.

Shillitoe, E.E. (1970). The effect of parachlorphenylalanine on social interaction of male rats. *British Journal of Pharmacology* **38**, 305–315.

Siegel, S., Waldo, H., Mizner, G., Adler, L. and Freedman, R. (1984). Deficits in sensory gating in schizophrenic patients and their relatives. *Archives of General Psychiatry* **41**, 607–612.

Siever, L.J. and Uhde, T.W. (1984). New studies and perspectives on the noradrenergic receptor system in depression: effects of the α_2-adrenergic agonist clonidine. *Biological Psychiatry* **19**, 131–156.

Simons, R.F. and Lang, P.J. (1976). Psychophysical Judgement: electrocortical and heart-rate correlates of accuracy and uncertainty. *Biological Psychology* **4**, 51–64.

Simons, R.F., Rockstroh, B., Elbert, T., Fiorito, E., Lutzenberger, W. and Birbaumer, N. (1987). Evocation and habituation of autonomic and event-related potential responses in a nonsignal environment. *Journal of Psychophysiology* **1**, 45–59.

Solyom, L., Dinicola, V.F., Phil, M., Sookman, D. and Luchins, D. (1985). Is there an obsessive psychosis? Aetiological and prognostic factors of an atypical form of obsessive–compulsive neurosis. *Canadian Journal of Psychiatry* **30**, 372–380.

Steketee, G.S., Grayson, J.B. and Foa, E.B. (1985). Obsessive–compulsive disorder: differences between washers and checkers. *Behaviour Research and Therapy* **23**, 197–201.

Thorén, P., Asberg, M., Bertilsson, L., Mellström, B., Sjoqvist, F. and Traskman, L. (1980). Clomipramine treatment of obsessive–compulsive disorders: II. Biochemical aspects. *Archives of General Psychiatry* **37**, 1289–1294.

Timsit, M., Koninckx, N., Dargent, J., Fontaine, O. and Dongier, M. (1970). Variations contingentes négatives en psychiatrie. *Electroencephalography and Clinical Neurophysiology* **28**, 41–47.

Williamson, P.D., Allison, T., Goff, W.R. and Mattson, R.H. (1977). Evoked potential abnormalities in epilepsy: the E-wave. *Electroencephalography and Clinical Neurophysiology* **42**, 729–730.

Yaryura-Tobias, J.A. (1977). Obsessive–compulsive disorders: a serotonin hypothesis. *Journal of Orthomolecular Psychiatry* **6**, 317–326.
Zahn, T.P., Insel, T.R. and Murphy, D.L. (1984). Psychophysiological treatment of patients with obsessive–compulsive disorder. *British Journal of Psychology* **145**, 39–44.

Chapter 12

Affective Disorders

Jeffrey B. Henriques and Richard J. Davidson

Department of Psychology,
University of Wisconsin-Madison,
USA

ABSTRACT

The authors review studies of depression and mania that have used at least one of
the following psychophysiological indicators: cardiac activity, electrodermal activity,
regional cerebral blood flow, glucose metabolism, electroencephalogram, or evoked
potentials. Measures of autonomic activity reveal that depressives have higher heart
rates, lower skin conductance levels, and smaller skin conductance responses than do
non-depressed subjects. Studies of central activation are much less consistent, but
there is a trend toward decreased left anterior activation and decreased right posterior
activation.

INTRODUCTION

At any one time, 10% of the population is suffering from an affective disorder
(Tomb, 1981). The central feature of an affective disorder is depression (Zahn,

Handbook of Clinical Psychophysiology Edited by G. Turpin
© 1989 John Wiley & Sons Ltd

1986). It may appear by itself (unipolar depression), or alternate with periods of mania (bipolar I, commonly known as manic depression) or hypomania (bipolar II) (Spitzer, Endicott and Robbins, 1978).

By most accounts, depression is a heterogeneous disorder (cf. Akiskal and McKinney, 1973; Kupfer, Pickar, Himmelhoch and Detre, 1975; Willner, 1985; Winokur, 1979). There have been many attempts to categorize depression throughout the history of psychology. Kraepelin classified severe mood disorders as manic–depressive psychosis and considered these to be biological in origin, while less extreme forms were believed to be psychogenic in origin and were referred to as neurotic. Kraepelin's two subtypes evolved into the endogenous/reactive dichotomy. Although endogenous and reactive depressions were presumed to be different illnesses, research suggested that these subtypes were different points along a continuum (Kendell, 1968). Garmany (1958) reported that 'stress factors' were found in 95% of reactive depressions and in 79% of endogenous depressions. Garmany (1958) also observed that the 'constitutional loading' that was supposed to distinguish endogenous depressions was present in 55% of the reactive depressives he examined. Kendell (1968), in a 14-year investigation, studied 1080 depressed patients and found that many patients had diagnostic scores indicative of neurotic depression on one admission and scores in the endogenous range on the next admission, or vice versa, suggesting that these subtypes were not different illnesses. In recent years, the distinction has been between endogenous and non-endogenous depression (e.g. Feinberg and Carroll, 1982; Zimmerman, Coryell, Pfhol and Stangl, 1986). This distinction is believed to reflect biological differences in the two types of depression as evidenced by differential performance on the dexamethasone suppression test (DST) (Feinberg and Carroll, 1982). More work needs to be done to demonstrate that these are indeed different illnesses and not just differences in severity. Akiskal and McKinney (1973) have suggested that, although a depressive episode may have different causes (biological, behavioural, or life events), there is a common final pathway that results in the syndrome of depression. This suggests that we would find similarities on some physiological measures among these different types of depression.

One of the more accepted classifications of affective disorders is the bipolar/ unipolar dichotomy (cf. *Diagnostic and Statistical Manual of Mental Disorders*, 3rd edn; DSM-III; American Psychiatric Association, 1980; Perris, 1966). However, even this categorization has its critics (e.g. Smeraldi, Negri and Melica, 1977; Taylor, Abrams and Hayman, 1980). Bipolar depression, as the name suggests, conceives of mania and depression as polar opposites. We might expect that during the manic phase of the illness scores on psychophysiological measures would be at one extreme, while the swing to depression would be associated with extreme scores in the opposite direction. This polarity view has been challenged by some researchers who hold that unipolar and bipolar illnesses are different points on the continuum of affective disorders (Gershon, Baron and Leckman, 1975; Smeraldi *et al.*, 1977). This view holds that bipolar disorder is the more severe form of disturbance, and implies that psychophysiological investigations would find that the scores of bipolars would be more deviant than those of unipolars. The issue of the validity of diagnostic subtypes is one that psychophysiologists are just beginning to explore (e.g. Nyström, Matousek and Hällström, 1986) and one that holds great promise.

PSYCHOPHYSIOLOGICAL APPROACHES TO THE STUDY OF AFFECTIVE DISORDERS: CONCEPTUAL ISSUES

A variety of conceptual strategies have been adopted in the psychophysiological study of affective disorders. Most studies compare one or more clinical groups with a control group on one or more psychophysiological measures. The measures can be obtained during the resting state and/or in response to stimulation. The clinical status of the psychiatric groups has varied among studies. Some investigators have studied patients during the acute stage of the illness, while others have studied patients in the normothymic state. To at least some extent, these variations among studies are a function of the conceptual approach adopted by the investigator. The purpose of this section is to make explicit the different conceptual approaches that have been used in research in this area and to underscore the methodological consequences of each (see also Chapters 1 and 2).

CLINICAL STATUS OF SUBJECTS

Some studies are explicitly designed to examine differences between controls and previously depressed or manic patients now in a normothymic state (e.g. Iacono, Lykken, Haroian, Peloquin, Valentine and Tuason, 1984). These studies make the assumption that at least some physiological measures will reflect state-independent differences between clinical and normal groups. In such studies, both groups are in a normothymic state at the time of testing. An implicit assumption in these studies is that the physiological measure itself will show stability within subjects over time. If the chosen measure does not possess this characteristic, it would be inappropriate to expect that the measure would be a state-independent marker. It is also imperative in studies of this kind to confirm that subjects in both groups are indeed in the same 'state'. To establish that depressed subjects are no longer depressed on the basis of an interview or a rating scale does not necessarily mean that both groups are in the same state. For example, the formerly depressed subjects might display more anxiety in the testing session compared with controls, and physiological differences found between groups might reflect this state anxiety rather than any trait-like differences. Thus, studies which purport to identify state-independent markers of affective disorders must take unusual precautions in ascertaining the state of the subjects at the time of testing. This should include measures of a variety of different constructs which might potentially differ between formerly depressed or manic subjects and controls.

RESTING VERSUS TASK-ELICITED DIFFERENCES

According to certain models, subjects with affective disorders are assumed to differ from normal controls on certain psychophysiological measures *at rest*. Such models assume that the resting physiology of subjects with affective disorders is different from that of controls since the former group has a different trait compared with the latter group. To the extent that the groups differ in subjective state at rest, the physiological differences cannot be assumed to reflect more than this state difference. Empirically, most studies which have compared depressed subjects and controls on resting measures of physiology, and which also have included a measure of state at the time of testing, have found the groups to differ in subjective state (e.g. Schaffer, Davidson and Saron, 1983).

A number of studies have also recorded physiological responses to a variety of different stimulus classes (see Zahn, 1986, for a review). Such studies make the assumption that subjects with affective disorders will react to stimuli in a different manner compared with controls. The nature of the eliciting stimuli has varied widely among studies. Most of the studies on autonomic differences between groups have used simple sensory stimuli presented successively in a habituation paradigm. Unfortunately, very few studies have used more complex cognitive and/or affective stimuli (see Davidson, Chapman and Chapman, 1987; Henriques, Davidson, Straus, Senulis and Saron, 1987, for examples). It is more likely that patients with affective disorders will differ from controls in response to more complex tasks of this nature and it would appear fruitful to examine physiology in response to such challenges. Such a strategy has been very productive in recent studies on schizophrenia, where it has been found that cognitive challenges such as the Wisconsin Card Sort reveal dramatic differences in regional cerebral blood flow which differentiate between schizophrenics and controls (e.g. Weinberger, Berman and Zec, 1986).

CORRELATES OR CONCOMITANTS?

Physiological activity which differentiates between tasks or groups can be conceptualized in one of two basic ways – either as a *correlate* or as a *concomitant* of the behaviour or group of interest. Correlation implies that the particular physiological change is not an integral part of the behaviour or process of interest. For example, it would be reasonable to suggest that an electrodermal response is a correlate of orienting. It is not a concomitant in the sense that peripherally blocking the electrodermal change would not prevent the orienting response from occurring; there would still be physiological and behavioural signs which mark the occurrence of orienting. Concomitance implies that the measured physiological change is a part of the biobehavioural process itself. If a physiological change which is a concomitant of a process or trait is peripherally altered, it would in turn transform the behaviour in question. For example, according to Lacey and Lacey (1978), the heart rate deceleration which accompanies orienting is a concomitant of the process. Therefore modification of the cardiac response should alter the orienting process itself. In the domain of affective disorders, it is reasonable to propose that some of the physiological findings which have been reported should be conceptualized as concomitants, while others should be conceived of as correlates. Unfortunately, few investigators make explicit the objective of their study with respect to this issue. However, different types of research programmes have different goals which would lead the investigator to focus more on one type of physiological association compared with another. When the goal is understanding the biological substrates of a particular disorder, it would be most prudent to focus one's efforts on the identification of concomitants, since such physiological findings would represent an integral part of the disease process. Research efforts which have as their principal goal the specification of markers of a disorder for identification in high-risk samples could use either a correlate or a concomitant, as long as it was specifically associated with the target disorder.

This chapter will selectively review the psychophysiological research on affective disorders. We hope to integrate the results from different areas of psychophysiology and discuss the implications of these findings. We plan to offer suggestions on questions that have not yet been answered and problems that now need to be addressed.

STUDIES OF CARDIOVASCULAR ACTIVITY

Although autonomic nervous system function has played an important role in studies of emotion since the beginnings of scientific psychology, much less attention has been paid to autonomic indices in research on affective disorders. As the review below suggests, studies of electrodermal function in depression constitute the bulk of the research on autonomic activity in this disorder. Probably the ease of measurement of electrodermal activity (EDA) is at least partially responsible for this state of affairs.

Comparatively less work has been done on cardiac activity in depression and most of it has examined relatively gross measures of cardiac function. For example, some investigators, although finding no overall difference between depressives and controls, have observed, not surprisingly, that agitated depressives had higher pulse rates than non-agitated depressives (e.g. Lader and Wing, 1969; Kelly and Walter, 1968). Using digital pulse volume as a measure of the sympathetically mediated vasoconstrictory response, Lapierre and Butter (1980) also found differences between agitated and retarded subtypes of depression. The deviant group on this measure was the retarded depressives who showed a less pronounced vasoconstrictory response compared with both agitated depressives and normal controls, who did not differ from one another.

Strian, Klicpera and Caspar (1977) studied changes in cardiac activity which occur over the course of electroconvulsive therapy (ECT) in depressives. These investigators found that the measure which showed the most pronounced change over the course of treatment was heart rate variance. As patients progressed through a course of ECT, there was an increase in heart period variance. Consistent with these data are the recent findings of Imaoka, Inoue, Inoue, Hazama, Tanaka and Yamane (1985), who found that depressed patients had less heart period variability compared with controls during a resting baseline.

In an important study on the diagnostic utility of a number of autonomic measures, Dawson, Schell, Braaten and Catania (1985) found a number of cardiovascular indices which were effective in discriminating depressed patients from controls. The two cardiovascular measures which were most effective were tonic heart rate level at rest and heart rate response to task-related stimuli. The subjects were 20 inpatients with major depressive disorder who were about to undergo a course of ECT. Nineteen of the 20 patients were medicated with tricyclics at the time of testing. The results indicated that the depressed subjects had higher resting heart rates and less of a heart rate orienting response as compared with non-depressed subjects. The sensitivity and specificity of the tonic heart rate group difference (using a *post-hoc* cut-off point which maximized group separation) were 85% and 95%. For the heart rate orienting response measure, the comparable statistics were 100% and 65%. Dawson *et al.* (1985) presented data on the pre-medication heart rates of their depressed patients and found that they were virtually equivalent to the heart rates post-medication. On the basis of these data, they reasoned that the medication of the patients played a relatively small role in the cardiac differences that were found to differentiate the groups. These authors also reviewed prior evidence which suggests that at least some of these autonomic differences exhibit trait-like properties and change very little after a series of clinically effective ECTs. In other work, these investigators (Dawson, Schell and Catania, 1977) explored the relation between heart rate and specific subtypes of depression and found that tonic heart rate was related to agitation/retardation symptoms. This pattern was previously observed by Lader and Wing (1969), who found that heart rate in response to loud tones was elevated in agitated depressives, but not in retarded depressives.

Other workers have found a pattern of heart rate activity in depressed subjects similar to that described above. For example, Lahmeyer and Bellur (1987) found that patients with endogenous major depressive disorder had a higher resting heart rate than a group of matched controls. This heart rate difference was preserved during sleep. While heart rate was found to increase during movements in sleep in all subjects, the magnitude of this increase was attenuated in depressed subjects. The authors suggested that the pattern of cardiac differences observed in their depressed patients reflected decreased cholinergic or increased adrenergic activity, or a loss of autonomic control of heart rate.

In a study of the relation between changes in subjective anxiety in response to neutral and affective imagery and changes in psychophysiological measures in depressed patients and controls, Rabavilas, Stefanis, Liappas, Perissaki and Rinieris (1982) found an interesting pattern which they interpreted as reflecting more desynchrony among the depressives. The subjects were 12 drug-free involutional depressives and age- and sex-matched controls. The diagnostic criteria for the depressives were not described. Rabavilas *et al.* (1982) found that in response to imagery of loss, depressed subjects show a small increase in subjective anxiety relative to a neutral imagery period. However, heart rate and skin conductance showed large and significant rises during this condition. During scenes of imagined hostility and guilt, the subjective anxiety of the depressives rose while the rise in heart rate and skin conductance was considerably less pronounced. Unfortunately, these effects are based upon a comparison of mean differences across conditions in psychophysiological measures and measures of anxiety. It would have been more appropriate to examine correlations between anxiety and the psychophysiological measures for the patients and controls. Nevertheless, the report of increased desynchrony between self-report and physiological measures among the depressives is similar to the desynchrony reported by Brown, Schwartz and Sweeney (1978) between behavioural and self-report measures of emotion in depressed inpatients.

Bruno, Myers and Glassman (1983) performed what is probably the most comprehensive assessment of cardiovascular functioning in unipolar depressives. They studied the relation between several cardiovascular measures and severity of depression (total Hamilton score) in 22 drug-free major unipolar depressives. Forearm blood flow (FBF), digital blood flow (DBF) and pre-ejection period (PEP) were measured under several different conditions including: baseline, mental arithmetic, cold pressor pain, and tilt. The FBF response to mental arithmetic was included because of evidence that the increase in FBF elicited by this stressor results from sympathetic cholinergic vasodilator fibre stimulation of the forearm muscle vessels (Blair, Glover, Greenfield and Roddie, 1959). The marked digital vasoconstriction which is normally seen contralaterally in response to cold pressor stimulation results from sympathetic alpha-adrenergic stimulation of skin vessels (Downey and

Darling, 1971). Pre-ejection period measures were obtained in the light of evidence suggesting that PEP is a measure of the speed of the myocardial response following stimulation by atrioventricular node depolarization – a function which is primarily controlled by sympathetic beta-adrenergic mechanisms (Newlin and Levenson, 1979). The results indicated that both FBF and DBF were inversely correlated with severity of depression. This pattern was present during both the baseline condition and in response to the cold pressor challenge for the DBF and in response to mental arithmetic for the FBF. The direction of these relations indicates that increased vasoconstriction is associated with increased severity of depression. In response to the tilt procedure, decreased FBF and increased forearm resistance {[(pulse pressure/3) + diastolic blood pressure]/FBF} were correlated with severity of depression. Pre-ejection period, both raw and corrected for heart rate, was positively correlated with severity of depression. From this pattern of data, the authors concluded that, as severity of depression increases, cholinergic sympathetic activity decreases and sympathetic adrenergic activity increases. These findings suggest a specific autonomic profile which varies with depressive severity. Unfortunately, these investigators were examining only depressed patients. A control group was not included. Thus, while relations with severity of depression were demonstrated, we have no information on where normal subjects would fall on these measures.

The data reviewed above on cardiovascular concomitants of depressive disorders indicate that some cardiac indices have reliably differentiated between depressed subjects and controls. Heart rate has been found to be elevated among depressives, particularly those of the agitated and endogenous subtypes. Some investigators have found this to be a state-independent effect which does not recover with symptomatic improvement. Other cardiac differences between depressives and controls, such as heart period variance (Strian *et al.*, 1977), have been found to be state-dependent. From these studies, it cannot be determined to what extent these observed cardiac differences are peripheral in origin or are manifestations of central activity. What is needed are studies that combine the measurement of autonomic and central nervous system activity so that relations between these systems can be examined.

ELECTRODERMAL STUDIES

As we noted earlier, the majority of the studies that examined autonomic activity in affective disorders have looked at EDA. The recording of EDA in affective disorders was first done by Richter in 1928, but it is only in the last 25 years that interest in EDA and depression has increased (e.g. Bagg and Crookes, 1966; Byrne, 1975; Gruzelier and Venables, 1973, 1974; Iacono and Tuason, 1983; Kamenskaya and Mikhailova, 1985; Lader and Wing, 1969;

Noble and Lader, 1971, 1972; Storrie, Doerr and Johnson, 1981). Unfortunately, many of the studies should be viewed with some caution due to the use of inadequate recording methods, such as improper electrolyte (i.e. Lapierre and Butter, 1980; Mirkin and Coppen, 1980) or non-standard electrode placement (i.e. Donat and McCullough, 1983; Noble and Lader, 1971, 1972; Toone, Cooke and Lader, 1981). For recommndations on proper techniques for recording EDA, the reader is referred to Fowles, Christie, Edelberg, Grings, Lykken and Venables (1981). Other problems facing many studies of EDA in depressives are the lack of formal diagnostic criteria (e.g. Byrne, 1975; Donat and McCullough, 1983; Myslobodsky and Horesh, 1978; Rabavilas *et al.*, 1982) or the lack of a normal control group (e.g. Breyer-Pfaff, Gaertner and Giedke, 1982; Gruzelier and Venables, 1973; Noble and Lader, 1971). Fortunately, the results of the studies which have used less than ideal methodology have for the most part been in agreement with those investigations that utilize proper recording methods (e.g. Gruzelier and Venables, 1973; Iacono and Tuason, 1983; Lenhart, 1985; Storrie *et al.*, 1981; Ward and Doerr, 1986).

There are ten reports in the literature investigating EDA and affective disorders that have used the recording techniques suggested by the Fowles *et al.* (1981) committee report (Gruzelier and Venables, 1973, 1974; Iacono and Tuason, 1983; Iacono *et al.*, 1984; Iacono, Lykken, Peloquin, Lumry, Valentine and Tuason, 1983; Lenhart, 1985; Lenhart and Katkin, 1986; Storrie *et al.*, 1981; Ward and Doerr, 1986; Ward, Doerr and Storrie, 1983). Of these, only two (Ward and Doerr, 1986; Ward *et al.*, 1983) report on a group of currently depressed subjects and a comparable control group that have been diagnosed with formal diagnostic criteria. These two studies found that depressed subjects had significantly lower skin conductance levels (SCL) than did non-depressed control subjects. Storrie *et al.* (1981), in a preliminary report, also included the skin conductance responses (SCRs) of a portion of the depressed subjects examined by Ward *et al.* (1983). They found that depressed subjects had lower SCRs, in response to blowing in a pressure gauge, then did the non-depressed subjects. Other investigators have also found that depressives have lower resting SCLs than non-depressed subjects (Donat and McCullough, 1983; Lapierre and Butter, 1980; Noble and Lader, 1971; Rabavilas *et al.* 1982) and that the SCRs of depressed subjects are smaller (Kamenskaya and Mikhailova, 1985). Only Toone *et al.* (1981) failed to find differences between depressed and control subjects on EDA variables.

The lowered SCLs and SCRs of these depressed subjects did not increase upon recovery (Storrie *et al.*, 1981), suggesting that the lowered EDA of depressed subjects may be a trait marker for depression. Dawson *et al.* (1977) found similar results: treatment with ECT did not alter the observed lower SCLs in unipolar depressives diagnosed using Research Diagnostic Criteria (RDC). Other studies (Breyer-Pfaff *et al.*, 1982; Noble and Lader, 1971) have also shown that recovery did not produce changes in EDA measures. Iacono *et al.* (1983) examined bipolar and unipolar subjects in remission and found that these subjects had lower SCLs and lower SCRs, in response to tones and familiar sounds, than did a group of normal controls. Retesting a year later (Iacono *et al.*, 1984) revealed that the significant differences between the groups were still present. Other evidence supporting the idea that lowered EDA is a trait rather than a state marker of affective disorders comes from Lenhart's work (Lenhart, 1985; Lenhart and Katkin, 1986). Screening students with the GBI (Depue, Slater, Wolfstetter-Kausch, Klein, Goplerud and Farr, 1981), Lenhart found that high-risk subjects had significantly smaller SCRs in response to a series of tone stimuli than did a group of matched controls. These high-risk subjects also exhibited non-significantly lower SCLs.

Several investigations have attempted to use EDA measures to discriminate between subtypes of depression. Lader and Wing (1969) reported that retarded depressives had lower SCLs than did controls, while the values of agitated depressives were higher than controls. Lapierre and Butter (1980), however, were unable to find differences between these two subgroups. Two studies (Mirkin and Coppen, 1980; Noble and Lader, 1972) found differences between endogenous and reactive depressives. These results should be regarded as suggestive, however, because other variables may account for the group differences. For instance, it has been shown that females have lower SCL values than males (Ward and Doerr, 1986) and neither of these studies reported the breakdown of males and females in their diagnostic subgroups. It should also be noted that Ward and Doerr (1986) have been unable to distinguish diagnostic subgroups on the basis of SCL.

To date, only one study has examined bipolar subjects in either a depressed or manic state (Toone *et al.*, 1981, tested only four manic subjects and did not report extensively on their results). Kamenskaya and Mikhailova (1985) examined 50 subjects suffering from manic–depressive psychosis in the depressive phase. They found that in response to neutral stimuli depressives had lower amplitude electrodermal responses. In response to stress (the threat of shock), no group differences were observed. They did not report on the presence or absence of baseline differences. Unfortunately, these authors provided no information about their recording techniques or on which EDA measure they were recording. It is also not clear whether Soviet and Western diagnostic systems are comparable. Therefore these results would best be viewed as preliminary. However, taken together with the findings of Iacono *et al.* (1983), it would appear that bipolar subjects exhibit a pattern of EDA similar to that seen in unipolar depressives, i.e. lower SCL and decreased SCRs.

Several investigators have examined bilateral EDA in an attempt to find evidence of a lateralized dysfunction in affectively disordered subjects. Gruzelier and Venables (1974) reported finding that depressed subjects had higher left-hand SCLs during periods of both high and low arousal. The depressed subjects had lower SCLs on both hands in comparison to both schizophrenic and personality-disorder subjects, but the greater relative left-hand SCL observed in the depressed subjects was a function of the decrease in right-hand SCL. They also found that during the low-arousal period, a tone habituation task, depressed subjects had a greater relative left-hand SCR (Gruzelier and Venables, 1974). This difference was a result of diminished right-hand response amplitudes. Myslobodsky and Horesh (1978) found that endogenous depressives had greater left-hand SCRs in response to both neutral and emotional verbal and visual stimuli, but they were unable to find any consistent pattern in a group of reactive depressives. The greater left-hand SCR that Myslobodsky and Horesh (1978) observed in their depressed subjects was a function of greater left-hand responses in reaction to the auditory stimuli and diminished right-hand responses to the neutral visual stimuli. Greater left-handed SCRs in response to tones have also been found in a group of subjects at risk for bipolar depression (Lenhart and Katkin, 1986), although this investigation did not reveal any lateral differences at rest. This difference was the result of smaller right-hand responses in the high-risk subjects. Other investigators have been unable to find any lateral differences in EDA, either in resting SCL or SCR (Iacono and Tuason, 1983; Storrie *et al.*, 1981; Toone *et al.*, 1981).

The interpretation of the asymmetry findings is problematic. In a review of the bilateral EDA literature, Hugdahl (1984) concluded that observed asymmetries are indicative of hemispheric asymmetries in activation, although which hemisphere was responsible for the observed asymmetry was a question that could not be answered. Both Gruzelier and Venables (1974) and Lenhart and Katkin (1986) have interpreted their results as indicative of a right hemisphere dysfunction. Gruzelier and Venables (1974) concluded that a right hemisphere dysfunction was producing the decreased right-hand responses that they observed, while Lenhart and Katkin (1986) concluded that abnormal right hemisphere arousal produced the greater left-hand responses that they observed in their subjects. It is obvious that more research is needed to determine if, in fact, there are reliable lateral differences, and studies that examine neural activity concurrent with EDA are needed to illuminate what sort of central dysfunction is responsible for the observed differences.

With all the work done so far documenting differences between depressed and non-depressed subjects, few attempts have been made to explain the cause of these group differences. Noble and Lader (1972) noted that decreased EDA was correlated with weight loss and they suggested that both disturbances may reflect a disturbance in hypothalamic control. Donat and McCullough (1983), however, found group differences on SCL even though both depressed and non-depressed subjects were normal weight. Some authors (Dawson *et al.*, 1977; Donat and McCullough, 1983; Lenhart and Katkin, 1986) have argued that the observed differences in EDA are reflective of the depressives' preoccupation with internal events and withdrawal from the environment. Ward and Doerr

(1986) pointed out that sweat gland activity is influenced by sympathetic cholinergic and beta-adrenergic activity. They also pointed out that vasoconstriction, which is mediated by alpha-adrenergic activity, can indirectly inhibit EDA. It is their view that decreases in cholinergic and beta-adrenergic activity and increases in alpha-adrenergic activity could all produce the lowered EDA seen in depressed subjects (Ward and Doerr, 1986). This interpretation is consistent with the conclusions reached by Bruno *et al.* (1983) on the basis of their cardiac data.

REGIONAL CEREBRAL BLOOD FLOW AND POSITRON EMISSION TOMOGRAPHY SCAN STUDIES

Both regional cerebral blood flow (rCBF) and cerebral glucose metabolism have been used to index regional cerebral activation. It is only within this decade that these measures have been used to explore differences in the patterns of cerebral activation in subjects suffering from affective illness.

Regional cerebral blood flow, in its present form, is a relatively non-invasive technique that involves the inhalation of an inert gas, most often ^{133}Xe, and the use of scintillation detectors to measure the uptake and clearance of the gas. A two-compartment model is utilized to provide an estimate of cerebral blood flow. The first component is a measure of fast clearing cortical grey matter flow, expressed as f_g or f_1, and the second component is a composite of white matter flow and of extracerebral tissue. Only the first component is used in the analysis, because the second component is contaminated by saturation in the extracerebral tissues. The initial slope index (ISI) is highly correlated with f_g and often used in its place (Stump and Williams, 1980).

Cerebral glucose metabolism is measured via positron emission tomography (PET). This procedure involves the intravenous injection of [^{18}F]2-fluoro-2-deoxy-D-glucose (FDG). Approximately 40 min after FDG injection, the subject is scanned and a series of slices are imaged.

In reviewing studies of cerebral function in affective disorders, it is important to consider not only factors such as age, sex, and handedness but also factors such as sensory state and P_{CO_2}. Women have been shown to have higher levels of cerebral blood flow than men (Gur *et al.*, 1984) and increasing age has been associated with decreases in blood flow (Warren, Butler, Katholi, McFarland, Crews and Halsey, 1984). Mazziotta, Phelps, Carson and Kuhl (1982) demonstrated that a subject's level of sensory deprivation has effects on both the global level of glucose metabolism and on the pattern of metabolic symmetry. They showed that subjects scanned in either eyes-closed or ears-closed conditions had symmetrical patterns of left/right metabolism. When subjects were scanned in the both-closed condition, a left greater than right asymmetry emerged. Systemic P_{CO_2} can produce changes in rCBF that are not the result of changes in cerebral function (Phelps, Mazziotta and Huang, 1982). These changes in blood flow are global, and thus relative regional differences in blood flow reflect real differences. It is in comparing absolute levels of rCBF that differences in P_{CO_2} can obscure or confound results.

Because these studies are invasive and involve the use of radioactive ligands, it can be difficult to recruit large numbers of subjects. Therefore many reports in the literature involve reanalyses of data from the same subjects or data from extended studies (e.g. Buchsbaum *et al.*, 1984a,b, 1986; Mathew, Meyer, Francis, Semchuk, Mortel and Claghorn, 1980a; Mathew, Meyer, Semchuk, Francis, Mortel and Claghorn, 1980b,c). In the interest of reducing confusion we will attempt to limit ourselves by referring to only one published work from each project.

Most studies have looked at global levels of cerebral activation and the majority report no differences between affectively disordered subjects and normal controls (e.g. Gur *et al.*, 1984; Kling, Metter, Riege and Kuhl, 1986; Kuhl, Metter and Riege, 1985; Risberg, 1980). In unipolar depressed subjects, Gur *et al.* (1984) found that the ISI at rest did not differ from that of non-depressed control subjects. Kuhl *et al.* (1985) examined seven unipolar subjects using PET and found that global cerebral metabolic rates for glucose did not distinguish between depressed and control subjects. Baxter *et al.* (1985) also used FDG injection and found that the whole brain metabolic rates of unipolar depressed subjects did not differ from those of control subjects.

Other investigators, using more broadly defined subject groups, have for the most part found similar results (Chabrol, Barrere, Guell, Bes and Moron, 1986; Guenther, Moser, Mueller-Spahn, von Oefele, Buelle and Hippius, 1986; Johanson, Risberg, Silfverskiöld and Gustafson, 1979). There have been some exceptions to these findings (Hoyer, Oesterreich and Wagner, 1984; Mathew *et al.*, 1989c; Warren *et al.*, 1984). Mathew *et al.* (1980c) found reduced grey matter flow in both hemispheres of RDC major depressives, but the flow values obtained from their control subjects have been criticized as being abnormally high (Gustafson, Risberg and Silfverskiöld, 1981a). Although Gustafson, Risberg and Silfverskiöld (1981b) found that the mean flow values of depressed subjects were lower than those of controls, they believe that differences in age and P_{CO_2} were responsible for the observed differences. Warren *et al.* (1984) tested a mixed group of DSM-III diagnosed depressives and dysthymics and compared them to a group of age-, sex-, and handedness-matched control subjects. They found that depressed subjects had lower resting grey matter flow values than did controls. It should be noted that these investigators covaried P_{CO_2}, blood pressure, age, and education in their analyses. Only age was related to grey matter flow.

Though the majority of evidence suggests that unipolar depressed subjects do not differ from controls in measures of global activation, there is some evidence which indicates that unipolar subjects do differ from controls in the pattern of regional activation. Chabrol *et al.* (1986) found that depressed subjects had a loss of the hyperfrontal pattern of activation that is seen in normal control subjects. This diminished anterior/posterior (AP) ratio was most evident in subjects diagnosed as unipolar depressed, and it reverted to normal during antidepressant treatment. It is unclear, however, whether the AP normalization was accompanied by an improvement in mood. It is also not possible to determine from their report whether the diminished AP ratio is the result of decreased frontal activation, increased posterior activation, or some combination of both. Contradictory results have been found by Buchsbaum *et al.* (1986), who reported that depressed subjects have higher AP ratios than controls. The authors cautioned that their report was based on only four unipolar subjects. Buchsbaum *et al.* (1986) also use a different testing paradigm. Somatosensory stimulation (shock) is administered to the subjects' right forearm during the period of FDG uptake, so as to ensure that both groups are in the same psychological state. Normal subjects show a contralateral increase in glucose metabolism in the scan that includes the somatosensory strip, while unipolar subjects fail to show any asymmetry (Buchsbaum *et al.*, 1986). Guenther *et al.* (1986) examined changes in rCBF during an activation task. They had subjects squeeze a handle once a second during the 4-min examination period. They used a measure based on algorithms that included grey and white matter flow and found, in their group of unipolar and bipolar depressed subjects, that less severely depressed subjects showed bilateral increases in activation, while the more severely depressed subjects exhibited a lack of activation (increases 2% from baseline values) in the contralateral motor area, suggestive of a left hemisphere dysfunction.

Other investigators have looked for lateral differences at rest. Their results are mixed. Gur *et al.* (1984), although not specifying exactly where their detectors were placed, reported that right-hand unipolar depressed subjects had increased left hemisphere flow in the most anterior probe and an increased right hemisphere flow in the first posterior probe. Using relative values so as to avoid the effects of variations in age, subjective state, and Pco_2, Uytdenhoef, Portelange, Jacquy, Charles, Linkowski and Mendlewicz (1983) also found increases in left frontal activation, but decreases in right posterior activation. These investigators do not report the handedness of their subjects, and further examination revealed that these effects were only seen in DST suppressors. Non-suppressors were similar to controls and did not exhibit any asymmetry (Charles, Uytdenhoef, Portelange, Wilmotte, Mendlewicz and Jacquy, 1983). Different findings were observed by Kuhl *et al.* (1985). They found that the pattern of glucose metabolism in unipolar subjects differed from controls in only one region: depressed subjects had decreased metabolism in the left posterior-inferior frontal cortex. However, they noted that this may be a function of the larger left than right Sylvian fissure observed in the computerized tomography scans of depressed subjects (Kuhl *et al.*, 1985). Decreases in left frontal activation have also been observed in a subgroup (3/11) of the unipolar subjects tested by Baxter *et al.* (1985), but these investigators have been unable to determine which variables differentiate this subgroup from the other unipolar subjects.

It is not clear why these investigators have obtained such divergent results. The observed differences may be a function of the differences among the depressed subjects tested by these examiners. No two of these studies examined the same subject population. The subjects have been similar on some measures and not on others. For instance, both Gur *et al.* (1984) and Baxter *et al.* (1985) studied younger depressives, but the subjects in Gur *et al.*'s (1984) study were on a variety of medications, while the subjects in Baxter *et al.*'s (1985) study were drug-free at the time of testing. Kuhl *et al.* (1985) tested only male subjects and Uytdenhoef *et al.* (1983) examined predominantly female subjects. Two of the studies tested only right-handed subjects (Gur *et al.*, 1984; Kuhl *et al.*, 1985) while others provide no handedness information (e.g. Baxter *et al.*, 1985; Uytdenhoef *et al.*, 1983). These differences may have added enough variance to produce these divergent results. It is also clear that additional study is required before any final conclusions can be drawn.

In studies that have been done on bipolar subjects, it appears that the results obtained depend on the state of the bipolar subject at testing. Baxter *et al.* (1985) found that bipolar subjects in a manic state had whole brain metabolic rates that did not differ from controls; however, bipolar depressed subjects had global metabolic rates that were significantly lower. They also tested a small group of bipolar mixed subjects and found that these subjects had metabolic rates similar to the bipolar depressed subjects. Bipolar subjects in a normo-thymic state exhibit decreased global cerebral blood flow as compared to controls and unipolar depressives (Gustafson *et al.*, 1981b). The authors attri-bute these differences to medication, although medication was not tested as a covariate in any of the analyses. Buchsbaum *et al.* (1986) found that bipolar depressed subjects, in response to stimulation, had increased metabolic activity in each PET scan slice as compared to controls. These subjects did, however, exhibit diminished AP ratios, which was a result of a decrease in relative frontal activation (Buchsbaum *et al.*, 1986).

The results of these studies of blood flow and glucose metabolism are far from conclusive. There are a number of considerations that need to be addressed if future research is to shed new light on rCBF and glucose metabolism in affective disorders. Gur *et al.* (1984) noted that women had higher rCBF levels than men. Studies that compare female depressives with male control subjects may be obscuring real group differences in cerebral activation (e.g. Baxter *et al.*, 1985; Buchsbaum *et al.*, 1986; Uytdenhoef *et al.*, 1983). A number of the studies reported here examined laterality differences between affectively disordered subjects and controls. Many of these studies either used both right- and left-handed subjects (Buchsbaum *et al.*, 1986; Mathew *et al.*, 1980c; Warren *et al.*, 1984) or do not provide any information on handedness (i.e. Baxter *et al.*, 1985; Gustafson *et al.*, 1981; Johanson *et al.*, 1979; Kling *et al.*, 1986; Utydenhoef *et al.*, 1983). It is possible that left/right regional differences are being obscured because of these mixed subject groups. We would strongly urge that all future studies separate right-handed from non-right-handed subjects.

We have noted earlier in this chapter the need for clearly specified homogeneous patient groups in all research efforts. Many of the studies that utilize either rCBF or PET methodology either do not clearly diagnose their subjects with regard to the bipolar/unipolar dichotomy (i.e. Mathew *et al.*, 1980c; Uytdenhoef *et al.*, 1983) or group subjects with mixed diagnoses into one 'depressed' group (i.e. Chabrol *et al.*, 1983; Guenther *et al.*, 1986; Warren *et al.*, 1984).

It has been pointed out that variations in subjective state may be responsible for observed group differences (Buchsbaum *et al.*, 1986). The solution proposed by Buchsbaum and his associates has been to use somatosensory stimulation to ensure that all subjects are in a similar state. This approach has two problems. First, although both groups are subjected to the same stimulation condition, this alone does not ensure comparable states across subject groups. Data are available which suggest that depressed subjects have a higher pain threshold than do non-depressed subjects (Davis, Buchsbaum and Bunney, 1979). A second problem with this solution is that the pattern of brain activation in response to painful stimuli may be similar across subject groups and thus obscure any differences that do exist between groups. One possible solution to this potential problem would be to assess subjective state via a self-report checklist. This would enable the researcher to see if indeed there are any differences between subject groups and to examine the proportion of variance in the dependent measure of interest accounted for by subjective state versus group membership.

It has been suggested that group differences in P_{CO_2} may be producing illusory differences in rCBF (Gustafson *et al.*, 1981b). Some authors (Guenther *et al.*, 1986; Gur *et al.*, 1984) correct rCBF values for each millimitre of mercury change in P_{CO_2}. A more powerful solution to this potential problem would be to use analysis of covariance and covary P_{CO_2} levels (see e.g. Warren *et al.*, 1984).

Although both rCBF and PET are potentially very powerful technologies for inferring regional cerebral activation, relatively few consistent findings have emerged from studies of affective disorders. The inconsistencies in the literature may be largely a function of differences across studies in diagnostic criteria and in the conditions during which the scans are obtained. It is hoped that eliminating this variance in future studies will produce more consistent results. It will also be fruitful to explore behavioural differences among subtypes defined on the basis of patterns of regional cerebral activation. The currently available categories provided by descriptive psychiatry may map very imperfectly onto the subtypes that emerge from studies of regional brain activation.

ELECTROENCEPHALOGRAM STUDIES

Pauline Davis was one of the first investigators to use the electroencephalogram (EEG) in the study of affective disorders. She found that visual inspection of the EEG revealed very few differences between the manic and depressed states of manic-depressive psychotics (Davis, 1941). During the depressed phase there was a tendency towards a lower peak alpha frequency and during the manic phase the peak alpha frequency increased. Hes (1960) examined a patient with rapid cycles and found that during the depressed phase there were no signs of paroxysmal activity, while periods of mania were associated with short bursts of symmetrical high-voltage slow-wave activity in the frontal regions.

Many investigators (e.g. Abrams and Taylor, 1979; Cook, Shukla and Hoff, 1986; Crighel and Solomonovici, 1968; Nyström *et al.*, 1986) have found higher than expected percentages of abnormal records among subjects with affective disorders. Among bipolar subjects, abnormalities in EEG records have been found to be negatively correlated with a family history of affective disorder (Cook *et al.*, 1986; Dalén, 1965; Kadrmas and Winokur, 1979). The observed abnormalities vary in type and location. Abrams and Taylor (1979) found that the abnormalities were predominantly in the right parieto-occipital region, while other investigators (Crighel and Solomonovici, 1968; Cook *et al.*, 1986) have found that disturbances, when unilateral, were most often left-sided.

It is only in recent years that there has been widespread use of computers to analyse patterns of brain electrical activity. Most of the studies that have compared depressed and non-depressed subjects on patterns of brain electrical activity have been performed on resting EEG. It is to this literature that we will turn first. Some of the earliest work was done by d'Elia and Perris (1973, 1974). They examined the mean integrated amplitude (MIA) and the within-patient variability (WPV) of the integrated amplitude in depressed subjects, as recorded from bipolar centro-occipital leads. They found that, although the MIA did not differ between the two hemispheres, the WPV in the dominant left hemisphere was significantly lower in depression and this variability in the left hemisphere increased upon recovery. They interpreted this finding as suggestive of greater left hemisphere involvement in depression (d'Elia and Perris, 1973, 1974; Perris, 1975). Greater relative right hemisphere variability has also been found in neurotic depressives (Rochford, Swartzburg, Chowdhrey and Goldstein, 1976), in a mixed group of adolescents displaying depressed affect (Rochford, Weinapple and Goldstein, 1981), and in both depressed and manic subjects (Flor-Henry, 1979). It should be noted that Rochford *et al.*

(1976, 1981) recorded from over the temporal and occipital regions and selected for each subject the pair of homologous leads that showed the greatest lateral difference in variation. von Knorring (1983), recording from the central region, found that depressed subjects had significantly more polymodal distributions of the MIA in the right hemisphere. This study found that depressives with polymodal distributions in the right hemisphere were more anxious, while patients with polymodal distributions in the left hemisphere were more depressed (von Knorring, 1983). Goldstein (1981) recorded from the temporal region and computed the number of modes in frequency histograms of the cumulated amplitude. He found that depressed subjects had a greater number of modes in the right hemisphere as compared to the left hemisphere, which again suggests greater variability in right hemisphere activation. A major problem with studies of variability is the lack of a clear consensus as to what differences in variability mean. Until we know more about what variability reflects, the functional significance of the group differences that have been reported using this measure will remain obscure.

More recently, investigators have begun to examine group differences in power in different frequency bands. Although many studies have examined activity in more than one frequency band (e.g. Brenner *et al.*, 1986; Matousek, Capone and Okawa, 1981; Perris, von Knorring, Cumberbatch and Marciano, 1981), all examined activity in the alpha band (8–13 Hz). Activity in the alpha band is inversely correlated with relative brain activation, with a *decrease* in alpha power indicative of an *increase* in brain activation. Kemali, Vacca, Nolfe, Iorio and De Carlo (1980) recorded from the frontal, parietal, and occipital regions and found no differences in asymmetry between neurotic reactive depressives and controls, although both groups had less right than left parietal alpha. These investigators did not, however, look at the magnitude of the observed asymmetries to see if the groups differed. A second study by the same group (Kemali, Vacca, Marciano, Nolfe and Iorio, 1981) found that a mixed group of neurotic reactive and endogenous depressives also exhibited less right than left alpha, but controls no longer had this pattern. The one region where control and depressed subjects differed was in the right occipital region. Depressed subjects had less right occipital alpha compared to controls, although neither depressives nor controls had a significant asymmetry in this region. These studies should be regarded with some caution, however, because the authors did not use a hamming window when computing the Fast Fourier Transform. A hamming window is a cosine wave shaped multiplier that is used to attenuate the spurious frequency sidelobes at the beginning and end of each epoch.

Examination of temporal and parietal activation by Flor-Henry, Koles, Howarth and Burton (1979) revealed that both depressed and manic subjects had greater right parietal activation than controls during an eyes-open baseline. A more recent study (Flor-Henry and Koles, 1984) found that this effect was no longer significant. It should be noted that Flor-Henry's group do not eliminate epochs that are contaminated by muscle artifact in the belief that muscle artifact is symmetrical. This seems to be a mistaken assumption. Volavka, Abrams, Taylor and Reker (1981) looked at asymmetry in the 24–51 Hz band, and found that failure to remove artifact resulted in a reversal of the pattern of temporal asymmetry seen in schizophrenics and depressives. Although muscle artifact is most noticeable in the higher frequency bands, muscle activity can intrude into the alpha band, and this may be a confound in the work by Flor-Henry's team. Matousek *et al.* (1981) used only artifact-free data, but they did not use a hamming window. They compared the data from 63 records collected from 27 endogenous depressives with 26 records from 26 normal controls. They found that depressed subjects had more relative left-sided alpha activity in the frontal region than controls, though this difference was not significant (Matousek *et al.*, 1981).

Schaffer *et al.* (1983) did find significant group differences in the frontal region. They tested subclinically depressed college students and measured alpha activity at rest in the frontal and parietal regions. They found the pattern of activation in the parietal regions did not differ between depressed and control subjects, although the direction of the means indicated that controls showed greater relative right parietal activation. The groups did differ significantly in frontal asymmetry. Depressed subjects had significantly greater right than left activation, while controls showed the opposite pattern. This was a result of depressed subjects having decreased activity in the left frontal region. We have recently replicated this study with a larger number of subjects (Davidson *et al.*, 1987) and found once again that depressed subjects exhibit greater right frontal activation. This study also revealed significant differences in parietal activation in the same direction as we found in the previous study: depressed subjects showed left parietal activation while non-depressed subjects had right activation (Davidson *et al.*, 1987). A study examining induced mood (Tucker, Stenslie, Roth and Shearer, 1981) also points to a relation between depressed mood and relative left frontal inactivation. This study recorded activity over the frontal, central, parietal and occipital regions while both depressed and euphoric moods were induced. The only significant change in asymmetry was in the frontal regions, with the depressed mood associated with an increase in left-sided alpha and a decrease in right-sided alpha (Tucker *et al.*, 1981).

A study by Perris *et al.* (1981) examined frontal, central, and parietal activation, and found that a mixed group of depressed subjects had more left hemisphere activation in the central region while non-depressed subjects had a pattern of right-sided activation. Another study that found relative left activation in posterior regions (Nyström *et al.*, 1986) examined subtypes and symptoms of major depressive disorder and looked for correlations with a multitude of EEG variables. It does not appear that these investigators attempted to control for family-wise error, so it is unclear if the observed correlations would have occurred by chance. The strongest correlation observed was between relative left hemisphere activation in the parieto-occipital leads and anxiety ($r=0.60$) (Nyström *et al.*, 1986).

We have recently found that the pattern of asymmetry during a resting baseline condition reliably discriminates between non-depressed subjects with and without a past history of depression (Henriques and Davidson, 1988). Non-depressed subjects who have had a past depression were found to have greater relative right mid-frontal activation and greater relative left-sided activation in the posterior temporal, central, and parietal regions as compared to control subjects with no past history of depression. Using a computer-averaged ears reference the group difference in asymmetry was highly significant in the mid-frontal region, with previously depressed subjects showing less frontal activation (i.e. more alpha) than controls. A discriminant function was computed from asymmetry scores and revealed a sensitivity of 87.5% and a specificity of 100% (Henriques and Davidson, 1988).

There are a number of studies that have reported EEG measures of cerebral activation in depressed subjects, but have not compared these subjects to a normal control group. As a result, we can only speculate on whether the observed patterns of activation differ from that seen in controls. Abrams, Taylor and Volavka (1983) examined temporal activation in a combined group of depressed and manic patients. They found that these subjects had more power in the left temporal region for all frequency bands and this effect was strongest for the delta and theta bands and marginally significant for the alpha band (Abrams *et al.*, 1983). Perris, Monakhov, von Knorring, Botskarev and Nikiforov (1978) examined activation in the frontal, parietal, and occipital regions in search of 'bioelectrical structures'. Although these investigators were not looking or testing for asymmetries in activation, their figures reveal that depressed patients had more left than right alpha power in all regions. Ulrich, Renfordt, Zeller and Frick (1984) examined changes in occipital activation as a result of drug therapy, but they did not use artifact rejection or a hamming window. They found that drug responders had a decrease in both left and right occipital leads, although this effect was only significant on the left side. The authors also report that, though it was not significant, a left lateralization of alpha power seemed related to clinical response while a right lateralization seemed related to non-response (Ulrich *et al.*, 1984). In other words, subjects who had an increase in relative right occipital activation (increased relative left alpha) in response to medication improved, while those who had an increase in relative left occipital activation did not improve.

There are two studies that have failed to find any differences in asymmetry in elderly depressed and control subjects (Brenner *et al.*, 1986; Visser, Van Tilburg, Hooijer, Jonker and De Rijke, 1985). Visser *et al.* (1985) compared normal controls to a group of psychiatric patients, consisting mainly of depressives, and found no significant within-group differences in hemispheric activation between homologous leads. They did not, however, compare the two groups on the pattern of asymmetry, so it is possible that there might have been a significant effect. Brenner *et al.* (1986) deleted epochs in which there was excessive temporal artifact. However, they did not delete the concurrent data from the parasagittal derivations, which ignores the possibility that other leads could have picked up this muscle artifact.

Among all the observed effects that we have reported, there are two effects in the baseline EEG data that are somewhat consistent. We hesitate to call them consistent because there are so few studies that are methodologically sound, but they are worth noting. There seems to be a left frontal and a right posterior inactivation in depression. These effects can occur separately (Nyström *et al.*, 1986; Perris *et al.*, 1981; Schaffer *et al.*, 1983; Tucker *et al.*, 1981; Ulrich *et al.*, 1984) or together (Davidson *et al.*, 1987; Henriques and Davidson, in preparation).

Several studies have examined activation asymmetries in response to cognitive or emotional stimuli. Flor-Henry and Koles (1984) examined asymmetry in the temporal and parietal regions during a verbal and a spatial task drawn from the Wechsler Adult Intelligence Scale. Depressed and manic subjects did not differ from controls in alpha power during these tasks. Performance level data were not reported. Davidson *et al.* (1987) used verbal and spatial tasks matched on item difficulty as well as mean difficulty, variance, and internal reliability. The behavioural data revealed that depressed subjects performed more poorly than the controls on the spatial task, while the groups did not differ on the verbal task. The EEG data paralleled the behavioural data in that, for the controls, the expected task-dependent shifts in alpha asymmetry were observed in the central and parietal regions, with more relative left-sided activation observed during the verbal task compared to the spatial task. The depressed subjects actually showed task differences in the reverse direction.

In examining the pattern of asymmetry in response to emotion-eliciting film clips, we have found that non-depressed subjects have a positive correlation between change in self-reported happiness and change in relative left-sided activation, in the mid-frontal and anterior temporal regions, across happy and disgust-provoking films ($r=0.47$ frontal, $r=0.45$ temporal). In other words, for the controls, shifts toward greater relative left-sided anterior activation are accompanied by more intense reports of felt happiness. Depressed subjects show little relation between changes in anterior asymmetry and self-reports of happiness ($r=-0.15$ frontal, $r=-0.02$ temporal). These differences are the result of depressed subjects showing left-sided activation to the disgust-provoking films, while the non-depressed subjects had a pattern of right-sided activation (Henriques *et al.*, 1987).

Although there is a paucity of studies that have examined differences between bipolar and unipolar depressed subjects, there have been studies that looked for differences between manic and depressed subjects. Unfortunately, these studies do not specify if the depressed subjects are unipolar or bipolar depressives, so it is unclear if the observed differences are differences between different phases of the same disorder or differences between different disorders. Shagass, Roemer and Straumanis (1982) found that manics had more posterior activation, as indicated by lower mean amplitudes, compared with depressives. The same pattern of results was found by Flor-Henry and Koles (1984). Flor-Henry *et al.*'s (1979) study looked for differences in parietal and temporal asymmetry between manic and depressed subjects and found that these groups did not differ in EEG asymmetry. Another study (Abrams *et al.*, 1983) combined depressed and manic subjects into one group, leading us to speculate that both groups showed the same pattern of asymmetry. There is also a case report by Harding, Lolas-Stepke and Jenner (1976) of a bipolar patient with rapid cycles. They recorded alpha activity from the occipital region over a period of 4 months, and found that periods of mania and depression were both characterized by left occipital activation. Treatment with lithium produced a stabilization of mood and a pattern of relative right occipital activation.

Another study by Flor-Henry's group (Flor-Henry, Koles and Tucker, 1982) found that manic subjects had greater cerebral activation in both temporal and parietal regions, as compared to control subjects. This may be a state-independent difference, because Knott, Waters, Lapierre and Gray (1985) found this same difference between euthymic bipolars and their discordant siblings. Although lithium has been shown to produce changes in EEG (Fetzer, Kader and Danahy, 1981; Ghadirian and Lehmann, 1980; Heninger, 1978; Ulrich, Frick, Stieglitz and Müller-Oerlinghausen, 1987), most subjects were not receiving medication at the time of testing, and lithium, while lowering the peak alpha frequency (Heninger, 1978; Ulrich *et al.*, 1987), has not been shown to decrease alpha activity, but rather to increase it (Ulrich *et al.*, 1987).

Unfortunately, no strong conclusion can be drawn from the studies that we have reviewed. A number of studies have found different patterns of hemispheric activation when comparing depressed and non-depressed subjects. Many of the studies that we have cited have used different recording and analytical procedures, which probably accounts for a substantial proportion of the variability among studies. Moreover, several studies have not included measures of frontal EEG, which we have found to be most strongly and consistently related to emotion (see review by Davidson, 1984; Davidson, 1988). We would urge that interested investigators review the suggestions of Etevenon, Samson-Dulfus, Kemali and Perris (1982). These authors discuss a number of important methodological issues, such as anti-aliasing filters, and argue for a set of standards in EEG research on psychopathology that will allow meaningful across-laboratory comparisons. It is clear that until some accepted recording and analysis standards are adopted, inconsistencies among studies will resist resolution.

EVOKED POTENTIAL STUDIES

The study of event-related potentials (ERPs) in affective disorders has had a long history. The relative ease of obtaining these measures in conjunction with the possibility that they may provide useful information on neural substrates of the disorder has in large measure been responsible for the growth of research in this area. It is not our purpose in this section to provide a comprehensive overview of this literature. The interested reader is referred to Zahn (1986) for a recent review. Rather, this section will illustrate what we consider to be the more promising approaches using ERPs to study affective disorders. One of the unique advantages of this methodology is the capacity to study the timing of the neural operations that presumably underlie mental operations. A growing body of literature is examining the timing of information-processing stages, in an attempt to better understand the nature of the psychomotor retardation that so frequently accompanies depression. It is this literature which we will emphasize in our discussion.

A number of investigators have studied aspects of P300 latency and amplitude in depressed subjects. The logic of studying the P300 component of the ERP is that extensive previous research has shown that the latency of this component is associated with stimulus evaluation time (see Donchin, 1979, for a review). A promising approach is the examination of both reaction time and P300 latency in order to determine whether the delayed responding often observed in depressed patients (e.g. Miller, 1975) is a function of delays in stimulus evaluation time and/or response-related processes. For example, Giedke, Thier and Bolz (1981) examined reaction time and P300 amplitude and latency in response to infrequently presented tone stimuli in an oddball paradigm. The subjects were 13 primary depressives diagnosed according to the Feighner criteria (Feighner, Robins, Guze, Woodruff, Winokur and Munoz, 1972) and 13 age- and sex-matched controls. The depressed subjects were drug-free for a minimum of 6 days. On the reaction-time measure, the depressed subjects were significantly slower than the controls. There were no significant main effects for group on measures of either P300 amplitude or latency, suggesting that the delayed reaction time in the depressives is a function of impairments in the activation of motor processes, rather than in stimulus evaluation.

The lack of any P300 amplitude or latency difference in depressed subjects found by Giedke *et al.* (1981) has not been consistently observed. Pfefferbaum, Wenegrat, Ford, Roth and Kopel (1984), using a much larger sample of depressed patients, have reported both longer latency and smaller amplitude P300s in depressed patients compared with age-matched controls. These effects were significant only for unmedicated depressed patients and occurred in response to both auditory and visual stimuli. The reason for the discrepancy between these findings and those of Giedke *et al.* (1981) is not entirely clear.

Pfefferbaum *et al.* (1984) used the RDC diagnostic criteria while Giedke *et al.* (1981) used the Feighner criteria. Differences in sample size may also be a factor.

In a recent study of 10 major depressives and 10 matched controls, Diner, Holcomb and Dykman (1985) reported that depressed subjects had smaller P300 amplitudes in response to visual stimuli than non-depressed subjects. In addition, among the depressed subjects, P300 amplitude was inversely correlated with severity of depressive symptomatology as indexed by the Hamilton scale ($r=-0.41$). As in the Giedke *et al.* (1981) study, no differences were found between groups on P300 latency. In addition, and again consistent with the finding of Giedke *et al.* (1981), Diner *et al.* (1985) found significant differences between the groups in reaction time, with depressed subjects exhibiting longer reaction times than non-depressed subjects. The authors interpreted the diminished P300 amplitude as reflecting the anhedonic component of depression (see e.g. Miller, Simons and Lang, 1984; Simons, 1982).

In a recent study, Thier, Axmann and Giedke (1986) reasoned that if the P300 component does indeed index stimulus evaluation and since the majority of studies have found little or no difference between depressed and non-depressed subjects on this measure, the study of psychomotor retardation in depression must focus on processes occurring after stimulus evaluation, i.e. processes involved in selection, activation, and/or execution of the motor response. They therefore designed an experiment that would provide information on these response-related processes. The experiment consisted of a choice reaction-time paradigm in which each new trial was initiated by the subject closing a microswitch. One and a half seconds following switch closure, one of two different pitch tones was presented. The tone type specified whether or not the subject was to respond. As expected, depressed patients had a longer reaction time than controls. The *Bereitschaftspotential* (Kornhuber and Deecke, 1965) which developed prior to the production of the spontaneous voluntary response required for trial initiation, did not differentiate between the two groups. The major difference between the groups was a markedly more negative post-imperative negative variation (PINV), which follows the go/no-go signal, in the depressives when compared with the controls. The authors suggested that since the PINV starts with the presentation of the imperative stimulus, prior to response execution, it may interfere with a quick motor response. Unfortunately, correlations between reaction time and PINV amplitude were not significant within either group, casting some doubt on the authors' interpretation. It should be noted that the sample sizes in this study were small so that the lack of significant correlations could be a function of insufficient power.

Knott and Lapierre (1987) performed a recent study which attempted to decompose response-related processing into several discrete substages in order to specify with increased precision where the deficits in depressed subjects appear. Twenty-one females meeting DSM-III and Feighner criteria for major depressive disorder and having a Hamilton rating of 18 or more after a drug-washout period of 3–7 days were tested. Age- and sex-matched hospital staff with no psychiatric history served as controls. Subjects were tested in a fixed foreperiod, two-choice visual reaction-time task. The warning signal (S1) was an auditory stimulus that was followed by one of two visual (green or red light) imperative stimuli (S2). The task required that subjects respond as quickly as possible with their dominant index finger to random presentations of the two coloured stimuli by releasing a 'home key' and depressing the correct 'response key', which terminated S2. Subjects were instructed not to release the home key until they had definitely decided which response key was to be selected. By utilizing such a paradigm, the authors were able to derive several different reaction-time measures: decision time (DT) was the time to release the home key from the onset of S2; movement time (MT) was the time from release of the home key to depression of the response key; and total time (TT) was DT + MT. Both EEG and forearm electromyogram (EMG) were measured, which allowed for the measurement of the timing of a number of hypothetical processing stages. Input processing time (IPT) was defined as the latency from stimulus onset to the N1 peak of the ERP elicited by S2. Central processing time (CPT) was taken as the time from the N1 peak to the EMG onset time, and motor execution time (MET) was defined as the time from EMG onset to the behavioural DT.

The results indicated that on all of the behavioural measures of response latency the depressed subjects exhibited longer latencies than controls. The electrophysiological data helped to specify at which stage the delayed processing occurs. The IPT measure did not differentiate between the two groups. The depressed patients were found to have significantly longer CPT components compared with controls. The groups did not differ on the MET component. Within the depressed group, no significant correlations were found between any of these measures and ratings of depressive severity. The authors argue that the pattern of both CPT and MT delay in the depressed patients provides evidence for a deficiency in both central processing as well as some relative impairment in peripheral psychomotor speed. The fact that IPT was found to be equivalent in the two groups suggests that the delays among the depressed subjects are not a function of any delays at early stages of perceptual processing or selective attention.

While the studies reviewed above all took advantage of information provided by the ERP on the timing of neural operations, a large number of studies have been performed comparing depressed and non-depressed subjects on basic features of sensory evoked potentials. This experimental strategy is an explicitly empirical one. It begins with the identification of well-defined peaks in the sensory evoked response and compares clinical groups with controls on these measures. Since this literature has been recently reviewed (Zahn, 1986), only brief highlights will be noted here. Shagass, Roemer, Straumanis and Amadeo (1980) have reported that the P90, N130, and P290 peaks of the somatosensory evoked potential show more posterior maxima in depressed than in control subjects, while P185 is maximal more anteriorly in depressives. Unfortunately, unipolar and bipolar depressives were combined in this study.

Ågren and his associates (Ågren, Österberg and Franzén, 1983a; Ågren, Österberg, Niklasson and Franzén, 1983b) have studied relations between somatosensory evoked potentials and cerebrospinal fluid monoamine and purine metabolites in 32 major depressives. They found a number of complex relationships between different evoked potential indices and the neurochemical indices which they measured. Unfortunately, the authors report a total of 120 correlations and the number that reached significance did not exceed that expected by chance.

A number of older studies in the literature have examined differences between depressed and non-depressed subjects in evoked potential measures of augmentation/reduction. Many of these findings are equivocal in the light of the numerous methodological problems that have been noted in evoked response studies of augmentation/reduction (see e.g. Iacono, Gabbay and Lykken, 1982). The interested reader is urged to consult Zahn (1986).

The study of ERPs in depression and other affective disorders has generated a large literature. The findings that seem particularly noteworthy are those that have used methods to decompose the specific stages of information processing which are deficient in depression. Most of these studies have only recorded ERPs from a few midline locations. Information about the scalp topography of these potentials would be potentially valuable in specifying the neural systems which may underlie the information-processing deficits. The single most important feature that is currently lacking in ERP studies of affective disorders is the lack of any guiding theory. Event-related potentials are ideally suited to test specific hypotheses derived from theoretical conceptions of laterality and emotion. Such potentials could be elicited in response to affectively significant stimuli. We anticipate the adoption of this strategy in future studies in this area.

CONCLUSION

In concluding this review of psychophysiological investigations of affective disorders, it is obvious that results of studies of peripheral autonomic activity are much more consistent than those obtained from examinations of central activation. Most of these observed effects seem to reflect trait differences between depressed and non-depressed subjects. The most reliably observed pattern of autonomic activity in the depressive is increased heart rate, lowered SCL, and diminished SCR compared with controls. This pattern is consistent with the suggestion of Bruno *et al.* (1983), who argue that depressives show decreased cholinergic and increased adrenergic sympathetic activity. The diminished heart period variance that has been observed in depressed subjects seems to be the only consistently observed state effect.

The most consistent evoked potential data have not focused on the identification of any particular abnormal biological parameter *per se*. Rather, the studies in this area have used this methodology to examine the timing of information processing in depressives. The data suggest that the typical delay in motor responding characteristic of the depressive is not a function of delays in input processing. The delay appears to be most pronounced in measures of central processing. It would be valuable for future studies in this area to attend more to scalp topography. Most of the studies which used evoked potentials to examine information-processing differences in patients with affective disorders have recorded from midline sites only. Additional information concerning the localization of these processing differences might be provided by examining the scalp topography of these evoked potentials.

Studies that have examined patterns of cerebral activation have found a number of different results. As we have noted earlier, there are a number of reasons that may possibly account for these observed differences. Among these are differences in recording and analytical methodologies, and differences in subject type. Despite the considerable problems with the literature, there do seem to be some trends in the data. These are a decrease in left anterior activation and a decrease in right posterior activation. Visual inspection of EEG records has shown that affectively disordered subjects have a predominance of abnormalities in either the left fronto-temporal region (Cook *et al.*, 1986; Crighel and Solomonovici, 1968) or in the right parieto-occipital region (Abrams and Taylor, 1979). Blood flow and metabolism studies have also found differences in these regions. Kuhl *et al.* (1985) found decreased glucose metabolism in the left posterior-inferior frontal cortex, and Baxter *et al.* (1985) found similar results for a subset of their subjects. It has also been shown that motor activity failed to produce increases in the left motor area (Guenther *et al.*, 1986). Charles *et al.* (1983) found that DST suppressors had decreased right posterior blood flow. Diminished right posterior activation has also been seen in EEG studies (Davidson *et al.*, 1987; Henriques and Davidson, 1988; Nyström *et al.*, 1986; Perris *et al.*, 1981), and increases in right posterior activation have been associated with clinical improvement (Ulrich *et al.*, 1984). We have also observed decreases in left frontal activation (Davidson *et al.*, 1987; Schaffer *et al.*, 1983). All of these data are congruent with the lesion data of Robinson, Kubos, Starr, Rao and Price (1984), who have found that the severity of a post-stroke depression is positively correlated with the lesion's proximity to the frontal pole in the left hemisphere or with its proximity to the posterior pole in the right hemisphere.

However, not all of the data fit with this model (i.e. Gur *et al.*, 1984; Kemali *et al.*, 1981) and just cannot be dismissed as resulting from methodological shortcomings. Clearly more work needs to be done to examine patterns of cerebral asymmetry in depression. One of the most important questions for which we currently do not have an answer is whether the patterns of resting regional hemispheric activation that have been reported by many investigators are stable over time within subjects. If these patterns of neural activity are to be viewed as a trait-like attribute of subjects, it is imperative to establish their stability.

Another critical issue in need of study is the degree to which the subgroups formed on the basis of measures of regional brain activation are phenotypically meaningful. We suspect that the current diagnostic categories may not capture the true biological heterogeneity of affective disorders. One strategy for future research is to select subjects on the basis of deviance on a biological characteristic theoretically assumed to be related to some aspect of affective disorder and then to study such subjects longitudinally. Ideally, this work could be conducted in young children who are likely to be pre-symptomatic. They could then be followed to determine what specific patterns of behaviour are related to the underlying biological characteristic. A related approach would be to examine the relation between clinical subtype and the pattern of cerebral activation. This could be investigated by looking at specific subtypes of depression to determine if patterns of physiology distinguish among them. Investigators could also look at differences in physiology and try to discover if groups defined on the basis of their physiology differ in the types of clinical symptoms that they manifest. For instance, are there differences between subjects who display a decrease in left frontal activation and subjects who have a decrease in right posterior activation? Another line of investigation would be to look at changes in physiology over the course of an illness. There have been studies of autonomic functioning before and after treatment (i.e. Strian *et al.*, 1977), but relatively little has been done with central measures of activation. Such an approach would help to differentiate between state-dependent and state-independent physiological differences.

With increased attention to theory-based research in this area, along with a growing appreciation of the methodological constraints of different psychophysiological measures, we expect that this research area will enjoy increased attention and recognition. It is principally psychophysiological research which is committed to the difficult task of understanding the relation between biological processes, on the one hand, and behavioural and subjective state on the other. This enterprise will be critical for the understanding of how biological abnormalities result in disturbances in affect.

ACKNOWLEDGEMENTS

Preparation of this chapter was supported by NIMH grant MH 40747 to R.J. Davidson.

REFERENCES

Abrams, R. and Taylor, M.A. (1979). Differential EEG patterns in affective disorder and schizophrenia. *Archives of General Psychiatry* **36**, 1355–1358.

Abrams, R., Taylor, M.A. and Volavka, J. (1983). Interhemispheric power ratios in schizophrenia and affective disorder. In: P. Flor-Henry and J. Gruzelier (Eds) *Laterality and Psychopathology*, pp. 219–223. New York: Elsevier.

Ågren, H., Österberg, B. and Franzén, O. (1983a). Depression and somatosensory evoked potentials: II. Correlations between SEP and depressive phenomenology. *Biological Psychiatry* **18**, 651–659.

Ågren, H., Österberg, B., Niklasson, F. and Franzén, O. (1983b). Depression and somatosensory evoked potentials: I. Correlations between SEP and monoamine and purine metabolites in CSF. *Biological Psychiatry* **18**, 635–649.

Akiskal, H.S. and McKinney, W.T. (1973). Depressive disorders: toward a unified hypothesis. *Science* **182**, 20–28.

American Psychiatric Association (1980). *Diagnostic and Statistical Manual of Mental Disorders*, 3rd edn. Washington, DC: APA.

Bagg, C.E. and Crookes, T.G. (1966). Palmar digital sweating in women suffering from depression. *British Journal of Psychiatry* **112**, 1251–1255.

Baxter, L.R., Phelps, M.E., Mazziotta, J.C., Schwartz, J.M., Gerner, R.H., Selin, C.E. and Sumida, R.M. (1985). Cerebral metabolic rates for glucose in mood disorders. *Archives of General Psychiatry* **42**, 441–447.

Blair, D.A., Glover, W.E., Greenfield, A.D.M. and Roddie, I.C. (1959). Excitation of cholinergic vasodilator nerves to human skeletal muscles during emotional stress. *Journal of Physiology (London)* **148**, 633–637.

Brenner, R.P., Ulrich, R.F., Spiker, D.G., Sclabassi, R.J., Reynolds, C.F., Marin, R.S. and Boller, F. (1986). Computerized EEG spectral analysis in elderly normal, demented and depressed subjects. *Electroencephalography and Clinical Neurophysiology* **64**, 483–492.

Breyer-Pfaff, U., Gaertner, H.J. and Giedke, H. (1982). Plasma levels, psychophysiological variables, and clinical response to amitriptyline. *Psychiatric Research* **6**, 223–234.

Brown, S.-L., Schwartz, G.E. and Sweeney, D.R. (1978). Dissociation of self-reported and observed pleasure in depression. *Psychosomatic Medicine* **40**, 536–548.

Bruno, R.L., Myers, S.J. and Glassman, A.H. (1983). A correlational study of cardiovascular autonomic functioning and unipolar depression. *Biological Psychiatry* **18**, 227–235.

Buchsbaum, M.S., Cappelletti, J., Ball, R., Hazlett, E., King, A.C., Johnson, J., Wu, J. and DeLisi, L.E. (1984a). Positron emission tomographic image measurement in schizophrenia and affective disorders. *Annals of Neurology* **15** (Suppl.), S157–S165.

Buchsbaum, M.S., DeLisi, L.E., Holcomb, H.H., Cappelletti, J., King, A.C., Johnson, J., Hazlett, E., Dowling-Simmerman, S., Post, R.M., Morihisa, J., Carpenter, W., Cohen, R., Pickar, D., Weinberger, D.R., Margolin, R. and Kessler, R.M. (1984b). Anteroposterior gradients in cerebral glucose: use in schizophrenia and affective disorders. *Archives of General Psychiatry* **41**, 1159–1166.

Buchsbaum, M.S., Wu, J., DeLisi, L.E., Holcomb, H., Kessler, R., Johnson, J., King, A.C., Hazlet, E., Langston, K. and Post, R.M. (1986). Frontal cortex and basal ganglia metabolic rates assessed by positron emission tomography with [^{18}F]2-deoxyglucose in affective illness. *Journal of Affective Disorders* **10**, 137–152.

Byrne, D.G. (1975). A psychophysiological distinction between types of depressive states. *Australian and New Zealand Journal of Psychiatry* **9**, 181–185.

Chabrol, H., Barrere, M., Guell, A., Bes, A. and Moron, P. (1986). Hyperfrontality of cerebral blood flow in depressed adolescents. *American Journal of Psychiatry* **143**, 263–264 (Letter to the editor).

Charles, G., Uytdenhoef, P., Portelange, P., Wilmotte, J., Mendlewicz, J. and Jacquy, J. (1983). The dexamethasone suppression test and cerebral blood flow in primary major depression. *Biological Psychiatry* **18**, 1336–1338 (Letter to the editor).

Cook, B.L., Shukla, S. and Hoff, S.L. (1986). EEG abnormalities in bipolar affective disorder. *Journal of Affective Disorders* **11**, 147–149.

Crighel, E. and Solononovici, A. (1968). Electroclinical correlations in neurosis with anxiety and depression. *Psychiatrica Clinica* **1**, 143–151.

Dalén, P. (1965). Family history, the electroencephalogram and perinatal factors in manic conditions. *Acta Psychiatrica Scandinavica* **41**, 527–563.

Davidson, R.J. (1984). Affect, cognition and hemispheric specialization. In: C.E. Izard, J. Kagan and R. Zajonc (Eds) *Emotion, Cognition and Behavior*, pp. 320–365. New York: Cambridge University Press.

Davidson, R.J. (1988). Cerebral asymmetry, affective style and psychopathology. In: M. Kinsbourne (Ed.) *Hemisphere Function in Depression*. Washington, DC: American Psychiatric Association Press.

Davidson, R.J., Chapman, J.P. and Chapman, L.J. (1987). Task-dependent EEG asymmetry discriminates between depressed and non-depressed subjects. *Psychophysiology* **24**, 585.

Davis, G.C., Buchsbaum, M.S. and Bunney, W.E. (1979). Analgesia to painful stimuli in affective illness. *American Journal of Psychiatry* **136**, 1148–1151.

Davis, P.A. (1941). Electroencephalograms of manic–depressive patients. *American Journal of Psychiatry* **98**, 430–433.

Dawson, M.E., Schell, A.M., Braaten, J.R. and Catania, J.J. (1985). Diagnostic utility of autonomic measures for major depressive disorders. *Psychiatry Research* **15**, 261–270.

Dawson, M.E., Schell, A.M. and Catania, J.J. (1977). Autonomic correlates of depression and clinical improvement following electroconvulsive shock therapy. *Psychophysiology* **14**, 569–578.

Depue, R.A., Slater, J.F., Wolfstetter-Kausch, H., Klein, D., Goplerud, E. and Farr, D. (1981). A behavioral paradigm for identifying persons at risk for bipolar depressive disorder: a conceptual framework and five validation studies. *Journal of Abnormal Psychology* **90**, 381–437.

Diner, B.C., Holcomb, P.J. and Dykman, R.A. (1985). P$_{300}$ in major depressive disorder. *Psychiatry Research* **15**, 175–184.

Donat, D.C. and McCullough, J.P. (1983). Psychophysiological discriminants of depression at rest and in response to stress. *Journal of Clinical Psychology* **39**, 315–320.

Donchin, E. (1979). Event-related brain potentials: a tool in the study of human information processing. In: H. Begleiter (Ed.) *Evoked Brain Potentials and Behavior*, pp. 13–106. New York: Plenum.

Downey, J.A. and Darling, R.C. (1971). *Physiological Basis of Rehabilitation Medicine*. Philadelphia: Saunders.

d'Elia, G. and Perris, C. (1973). Cerebral functional dominance and depression. *Acta Psychiatrica Scandinavica* **49**, 191–197.

d'Elia, G. and Perris, C. (1974). Cerebral functional dominance and memory functions. *Acta Psychiatrica Scandinavica* **255** (Suppl.), 143–157.

Etevenon, P., Samson-Dulfus, D., Kemali, D. and Perris, C. (1982). In quest of the best spectral EEG parameters towards a multicentric consensus for measuring normality, psychopathology and psychotropic drug effects. *Advances in Biological Psychiatry* **9**, 28–38.

Feighner, J., Robins, E., Guze, S., Woodruff, R., Winokur, G. and Munoz, R. (1972). Diagnostic criteria for use in psychiatric research. *Archives of General Psychiatry* **26**, 201–214.

Feinberg, M. and Carroll, B.J. (1982). Separation of subtypes of depression using discriminant analysis: I. Separation of unipolar endogenous depression from non-endogenous depression. *British Journal of Psychiatry* **140**, 384–391.

Fetzer, J., Kader, G. and Danahy, S. (1981). Lithium encephalopathy: a clinical, psychiatric, and EEG evaluation. *American Journal of Psychiatry* **138**, 1622–1623.

Flor-Henry, P. (1979). Laterality, shifts of cerebral dominance, sinistrality and psychosis. In: J. Gruzelier and P. Flor-Henry (Eds) *Hemisphere Asymmetries of Function in Psychopathology*, pp. 3–19. New York: Elsevier/North-Holland.

Flor-Henry, P. and Koles, Z.J. (1984). Statistical quantitative EEG studies of depression, mania, schizophrenia and normals. *Biological Psychology* **19**, 257–279.

Flor-Henry, P., Koles, Z.J., Howarth, B.G. and Burton, L. (1979). Neurophysiological studies of schizophrenia, mania and depression. In: J. Gruzelier and P. Flor-Henry (Eds) *Hemisphere Asymmetries of Function in Psychopathology*, pp. 189–222. New York: Elsevier/North-Holland.

Flor-Henry, P., Koles, Z.J. and Tucker, D.M. (1982). Studies in EEG power and coherence (8–13 Hz) in depression mania and schizophrenia compared to controls. *Advances in Biological Psychiatry* **9**, 1–7.

Fowles, D.C., Christie, M.J., Edelberg, R., Grings, W.W., Lykken, D.T. and Venables, P.H. (1981). Publication recommendations for electrodermal measurements. *Psychophysiology* **18**, 232–239.

Garmany, G. (1958). Depressive states; their aetiology and treatment. *British Medical Journal* **2**, 341–344.

Gershon, E.S., Baron, M. and Leckman, J.F. (1975). Genetic models of the transmission of affective disorders. *Journal of Psychiatric Research* **12**, 301–317.

Ghadirian, A.M. and Lehman, H.E. (1980). Neurological side effects of lithium: organic brain syndrome, seizures, extrapyramidal side effects, and EEG changes. *Comprehensive Psychiatry* **21**, 327–335.

Giedke, H., Thier, P. and Bolz, J. (1981). The relationship between P_3-latency and reaction time in depression. *Biological Psychology* **13**, 31–49.

Goldstein, L. (1981). Statistical organizational features of the computerized EEG under various behavioral states. *Advances in Biological Psychiatry* **6**, 12–16.

Gruzelier, J.H. and Venables, P.H. (1973). Skin conductance responses to tones with and without attentional significance in schizophrenic and nonschizophrenic psychiatric patients. *Neuropsychologia* **11**, 221–230.

Gruzelier, J.H. and Venables, P.H. (1974). Bimodality and lateral asymmetry of skin conductance orienting activity in schizophrenics: replication and evidence of lateral asymmetry in patients with depression and disorders of personality. *Biological Psychiatry* **8**, 55–73.

Guenther, W., Moser, E., Mueller-Spahn, F., von Oefele, K., Buelle, U. and Hippius, H. (1986). Pathological cerebral blood flow during motor function in schizophrenic and endogenous depressed patients. *Biological Psychiatry* **21**, 889–899.

Gur, R.E., Skolnick, B.E., Gur, R.C., Caroff, S., Rieger, W., Obrist, W.D., Younkin,

D. and Reivich, M. (1984). Brain function in psychiatric disorders. II. Regional cerebral blood flow in medicated unipolar depressives. *Archives of General Psychiatry* **41**, 695–699.

Gustafson, L., Risberg, J. and Silfverskiöld, P. (1981a). Cerebral blood flow in dementia and depression. *Lancet* **i**, 275 (Letter to the editor).

Gustafson, L., Risberg, J. and Silfverskiöld, P. (1981b). Regional cerebral blood flow in organic dementia and affective disorders. *Advances in Biological Psychiatry* **6**, 109–116.

Harding, G.F.A., Lolas-Stepke, F. and Jenner, F.A. (1976). Alpha rhythm, laterality, lithium, and mood. *Lancet* **ii**, 1248 (Letter to the editor).

Heninger, G.R. (1978). Lithium carbonate and brain function. Cerebral-evoked potentials, EEG, and symptom changes during lithium treatment. *Archives of General Psychiatry* **35**, 228–233.

Henriques, J.B. and Davidson, R.J. (1988 EEG). activation asymmetries discriminate between normothymic depressives and normal controls *Psychophysiology* **25**, 453–454.

Henriques, J.B., Davidson, R.J., Straus, A., Senulis, J.A. and Saron, C. (1987). Emotion-elicited EEG asymmetries differ in depressed and control subjects. *Psychophysiology* **24**, 591.

Hes, J.P. (1960). Manic depressive psychosis. A case report. *Electroencephalography and Clinical Neurophysiology* **12**, 193–195.

Hoyer, S., Oesterreich, K. and Wagner, O. (1984). Depression in old age and its relation to primary dementia: variations in brain blood flow and oxidative metabolism. *Monographs of Neural Science* **11**, 187–192.

Hugdahl, K. (1984). Hemispheric asymmetry and bilateral electrodermal recordings: a review of the evidence. *Psychophysiology* **21**, 371–393.

Iacono, W.G. and Tuason, V.B. (1983). Bilateral electrodermal asymmetry in euthymic patients with unipolar and bipolar affective disorders. *Biological Psychiatry* **18**, 303–315.

Iacono, W.G., Gabbay, F.H. and Lykken, D.T. (1982). Measuring the average evoked response to light flashes: the contribution of eye-blink artifact to augmenting–reducing. *Biological Psychiatry* **17**, 897–911.

Iacono, W.G., Lykken, D.T., Haroian, K.P., Peloquin, L.J., Valentine, R.H. and Tuason, V.B. (1984). Electrodermal activity in euthymic patients with affective disorders: one-year retest stability and the effects of stimulus intensity and significance. *Journal of Abnormal Psychology* **93**, 304–311.

Iacono, W.G., Lykken, D.T., Peloquin, L.J., Lumry, A.E., Valentine, R.H. and Tuason, V.B. (1983). Electrodermal activity in euthymic unipolar and bipolar affective disorders: a possible marker for depression. *Archives of General Psychiatry* **40**, 557–565.

Imaoka, K., Inoue, H., Inoue, Y., Hazama, H., Tanaka, T. and Yamane, N. (1985). R–R intervals of ECG in depression. *Folia Psychiatrica et Neurologica Japonica* **39**, 485–488.

Johanson, M., Risberg, J., Silfverskiöld, P. and Gustafson, L. (1979). Regional cerebral blood flow related to acute memory disturbance following electroconvulsive therapy in depression. *Acta Neurologica Scandinavica* **60** (Suppl. 72), 534–535.

Kadrmas, A. and Winokur, G. (1979). Manic depressive illness and EEG abnormalities. *Journal of Clinical Psychiatry* **40**, 306–307.

Kamenskaya, V.M. and Mikhailova, E.S. (1985). Ratios of electroencephalographic and autonomic indexes in a stress situation in patients with different types of depression. *Neuroscience and Behavioral Physiology* **15**, 483–487.

Kelly, D.H.W. and Walter, C.J.S. (1968). The relationship between clinical diagnosis and anxiety, assessed by forearm blood flow and other measurements. *British Journal of Psychiatry* **114**, 611.

Kemali, D., Vacca, L., Marciano, F., Nolfe, G. and Iorio, G. (1981). CEEG findings in schizophrenics, depressives, obsessives, heroin addicts and normals. *Advances in Biological Psychiatry* **6**, 17–28.

Kemali, D., Vacca, L., Nolfe, G., Iorio, G. and De Carlo, R. (1980). Hemispheric EEG quantitative asymmetries in schizophrenics and depressed patients. *Advances in Biological Psychiatry* **4**, 14–20.

Kendell, R.E. (1968). The classification of depressive illnesses. *Maudsley Monograph*, No. 18. London: Oxford University Press.

Kling, A.S., Metter, E.J., Riege, W.H. and Kuhl, D.E. (1986). Comparison of PET measurement of local brain glucose metabolism and CAT measurement of brain atrophy in chronic schizophrenia and depression. *American Journal of Psychiatry* **143**, 175–180.

von Knorring, L. (1983). Interhemispheric EEG differences in affective disorders. In: P. Flor-Henry and J. Gruzelier (Eds) *Laterality and Psychopathology*, pp. 315–326. New York: Elsevier.

Knott, V.J. and Lapierre, Y.D. (1987). Electrophysiological and behavioral correlates of psychomotor responsivity in depression. *Biological Psychiatry* **22**, 313–324.

Knott, V., Waters, B., Lapierre, Y. and Gray, R. (1985). Neurophysiological correlates of sibling pairs discordant for bipolar affective disorder. *American Journal of Psychiatry* **142**, 248–250.

Kornhuber, H. and Deecke, L. (1965). Hirnpotentialänderungen bei Willkürbewegungen und passiven Bewegungen des Menschen: Bereitschaftspotential und reafferentes Potential. *Pflügers Archiv. European Journal of Physiology* **284**, 1–17.

Kuhl, D.E., Metter, E.J. and Riege, W.H. (1985). Patterns of cerebral glucose utilization in depression, multiple infarct dementia, and Alzheimer's disease. In: L. Sokoloff (Ed.) *Brain Imaging and Brain Function*, pp. 211–226. New York: Raven Press.

Kupfer, D.J., Pickar, D., Himmelhoch, J.M. and Detre, T.P. (1975). Are there two types of unipolar depression? *Archives of General Psychiatry* **32**, 866–871.

Lacey, B.C. and Lacey, J.I. (1978). Two-way communication between the heart and the brain: significance of time within the cardiac cycle. *American Psychologist* **33**, 99–113.

Lader, M.H. and Wing, L. (1969). Physiological measures in agitated and retarded depressed patients. *Journal of Psychiatric Research* **7**, 89–100.

Lahmeyer, H.W. and Bellur, S.N. (1987). Cardiac regulation and depression. *Journal of Psychiatric Research* **21**, 1–6.

Lapierre, Y.D. and Butter, H.J. (1980). Agitated and retarded depression: a clinical psychophysiological evaluation. *Neuropsychobiology* **6**, 217–223.

Lenhart, R.E. (1985). Lowered skin conductance in a subsyndromal high-risk depressive sample: response amplitudes versus tonic levels. *Journal of Abnormal Psychology* **94**, 649–652.

Lenhart, R.E. and Katkin, E.S. (1986). Psychophysiological evidence for cerebral laterality effects in a high-risk sample of students with subsyndromal bipolar depressive disorder. *American Journal of Psychiatry* **143**, 602–607.

Mathew, R.J., Meyer, J.S., Francis, D.J., Semchuk, K.M., Mortel, K. and Claghorn, J.L. (1980a). Cerebral blood flow in depression. *American Journal of Psychiatry* **137**, 1449–1450.

Mathew, R.J., Meyer, J.S., Semchuk, K.M., Francis, D., Mortel, K. and Claghorn, J.L. (1980b). Regional cerebral blood flow in depression: a preliminary report. *Journal of Clinical Psychiatry* **41**, 71–72.

Mathew, R.J., Meyer, J.S., Semchuk, K.M., Francis, D., Mortel, K. and Claghorn, J.L. (1980c). Cerebral blood flow in depression. *Lancet* **i**, 1308 (Letter to the editor).

Matousek, M., Capone, C. and Okawa, M. (1981). Measurement of the inter-hemispheral differences as a diagnostic tool in psychiatry. *Advances in Biological Psychiatry* **6**, 76–80.

Mazziotta, J.C., Phelps, M.E., Carson, R.E. and Kuhl, D.E. (1982). Tomographic mapping of human cerebral metabolism: sensory deprivation. *Annals of Neurology* **12**, 435–444.

Miller, G.A., Simons, R.F. and Lang, P.J. (1984). Electrocortical measures of information processing deficits in anhedonia. *Annals of the New York Academy of Sciences* **425**, 598.

Miller, W. (1975). Psychological deficit in depression. *Psychological Bulletin* **32**, 238–260.

Mirkin, A.M. and Coppen, A. (1980). Electrodermal activity in depression: clinical and biochemical correlates. *British Journal of Psychiatry* **137**, 93–97.

Myslobodsky, M.S. and Horesh, N. (1978). Bilateral electrodermal activity in depressive patients. *Biological Psychiatry* **6**, 111–120.

Newlin, D.B. and Levenson, R.W. (1979). Pre-ejection period: measuring beta-adrenergic influences upon the heart. *Psychophysiology* **16**, 546–553.

Noble, P. and Lader, M. (1971). The symptomatic correlates of the skin conductance changes in depression. *Journal of Psychiatric Research* **9**, 61–69.

Noble, P. and Lader, M. (1972). A physiological comparison of 'endogenous' and 'reactive' depression. *British Journal of Psychiatry* **120**, 541–542.

Nyström, C., Matousek, M. and Hällström, T. (1986). Relationships between EEG and clinical characteristics in major depressive disorder. *Acta Psychiatrica Scandinavica* **73**, 390–394.

Perris, C. (1966). A study of bipolar (manic–depressive) and unipolar recurrent depressive psychoses. *Acta Psychiatrica Scandinavica* **42** (Suppl. 194), 7–189.

Perris, C. (1975). EEG techniques in the measurement of the severity of depressive syndromes. *Neuropsychobiology* **1**, 16–25.

Perris, C., Monakhov, K., von Knorring, L., Botskarev, V. and Nikiforov, A. (1978). Systemic structural analysis of the electroencephalogram of depressed patients. General principles and preliminary results of an international collaborative study. *Neuropsychobiology* **4**, 207–228.

Perris, C., von Knorring, L., Cumberbatch, J. and Marciano, F. (1981). Further studies of depressed patients by means of computerized EEG. *Advances in Biological Psychiatry* **6**, 41–49.

Pfefferbaum, A., Wenegrat, B.G., Ford, J.M., Roth, W.T. and Kopel, B.S. (1984). Clinical application of the P3 component of event-related potentials. II. Dementia, depression and schizophrenia. *Electroencephalography and Clinical Neurophysiology* **59**, 104–124.

Phelps, M.E., Mazziotta, J.C. and Huang, S.-C. (1982). Study of cerebral function with positron computed tomography. *Journal of Cerebral Blood Flow and Metabolism* **2**, 113–162.

Rabavilas, A.D., Stefanis, C.N., Liappas, J., Perissaki, C. and Rinieris, P. (1982). Synchrony of subjective and psychophysiological responses in involutional depression. *Neuropsychobiology* **8**, 156–161.

Richter, C.P. (1928). The electrical skin resistance. *Archives of Neurology and Psychiatry* **19**, 488–508.

Risberg, J. (1980). Regional cerebral blood flow measurements by ^{133}Xe-inhalation: methodology and applications in neuropsychology and psychiatry. *Brian and Language* **9**, 9–34.

Robinson, R.G., Kubos, K.L., Starr, L.B., Rao, K. and Price, T.R. (1984). Mood disorders in stroke patients. *Brian* **107**, 81–93.

Rochford, J.M., Swartzburg, M., Chowdhrey, S.M. and Goldstein, L. (1976). Some quantitative EEG correlates of psychopathology. *Research Communications in Psychology Psychiatry and Behavior* **1**, 211–226.

Rochford, J.M., Weinapple, M. and Goldstein, L. (1981). The quantitative hemispheric EEG in adolescent psychiatric patients with depressive or paranoid symptomatology. *Biological Psychiatry* **16**, 47–54.

Schaffer, C.E., Davidson, R.J. and Saron, C. (1983). Frontal and parietal electroencephalogram asymmetry in depressed and nondepressed subjects. *Biological Psychiatry* **18**, 753–762.

Shagass, C., Roemer, R.A. and Straumanis, J.J. (1982). Relationships between psychiatric diagnosis and some quantitative EEG variables. *Archives of General Psychiatry* **39**, 1423–1435.

Shagass, C., Roemer, R.A., Straumanis, J.J. and Amadeo, M. (1980). Topography of sensory evoked potentials in depressive disorders. *Biological Psychiatry* **15**, 183–207.

Simons, R. (1982). Physical anhedonia and future psychopathology: an electrocortical continuity? *Psychophysiology* **19**, 433–441.

Smeraldi, E., Negri, F. and Melica, A.M. (1977). A genetic study of affective disorders. *Acta Psychiatrica Scandinavica* **56**, 382–398.

Spitzer, R.L., Endicott, J. and Robins, E. (1978). Research diagnostic criteria: rationale and reliability. *Archives of General Psychiatry* **35**, 773–782.

Storrie, M.C., Doerr, H.O. and Johnson, M.H. (1981). Skin conductance characteristics of depressed subjects before and after therapeutic intervention. *Journal of Nervous and Mental Disease* **69**, 176–179.

Strian, F., Klicpera, C. and Caspar, F. (1977). Autonomic activation and endogenous depression. *Archives of Psychiatry and Neurological Sciences* **223**, 203–218.

Stump, D.A. and Williams, R. (1980). The noninvasive measurement of regional cerebral circulation. *Brain and Language* **9**, 35–46.

Taylor, M.A., Abrams, R. and Hayman, M.A. (1980). The classification of affective disorders – a reassessment of the bipolar–unipolar dichotomy: a clinical, laboratory, and family study. *Journal of Affective Disorders* **2**, 95–109.

Thier, P., Axmann, D. and Giedke, H. (1986). Slow brain potentials and psychomotor retardation in depression. *Electroencephalography and Clinical Neurophysiology* **63**, 570–581.

Tomb, D.A. (1981). *Psychiatry for the House Officer*. Baltimore: Williams and Wilkins.

Toone, B.K., Cooke, E. and Lader, M.H. (1981). Electrodermal activity in the affective disorders and schizophrenia. *Psychological Medicine* **11**, 497–508.

Tucker, D.M., Stenslie, C.E., Roth, R.S. and Shearer, S.L. (1981). Right frontal lobe activation and right hemisphere performance. *Archives of General Psychiatry* **38**, 169–174.

Ulrich, G., Frick, K., Stieglitz, R.-D. and Müller-Oerlinghausen, B. (1987). Interindividual variability of lithium-induced EEG changes in healthy volunteers. *Psychiatry Research* **20**, 117–127.

Ulrich, G., Renfordt, E., Zeller, G. and Frick, K. (1984). Interrelation between changes in the EEG and psychopathology under pharmacotherapy for endogenous depression: a contribution to the predictor question. *Pharmacopsychiatry* **17**, 178–183.

Uytdenhoef, P., Portelange, P., Jacquy, J., Charles, G., Linkowski, P. and Mendlewicz, J. (1983). Regional cerebral blood flow and lateralized hemispheric dysfunction in depression. *British Journal of Psychiatry* **143**, 128–132.

Visser, S.L., Van Tilburg, W., Hooijer, C., Jonker, C. and De Rijke, W. (1985). Visual evoked potentials (VEP's) in senile dementia (Alzheimer type) and in non-organic behavioral disorders in the elderly: comparisons with EEG parameters. *Electroencephalography and Clinical Neurophysiology* **60**, 115–121.

Volavka, J., Abrams, R., Taylor, M.A. and Reker, D. (1981). Hemispheric lateralization of fast EEG activity in schizophrenia and endogenous depression. *Advances in Biological Psychiatry* **6**, 72–75.

Ward, N.G. and Doerr, H.O. (1986). Skin conductance: a potentially sensitive and specific marker for depression. *Journal of Nervous and Mental Disease* **174**, 553–559.

Ward, N.G., Doerr, H.O. and Storrie, M.C. (1983). Skin conductance: a potentially sensitive test for depression. *Psychiatry Research* **10**, 295–302.

Warren, L.R., Butler, R.W., Katholi, C.R., McFarland, C.E., Crews, E.L. and Halsey, J.H. (1984). Focal changes in cerebral blood flow produced by monetary incentive during a mental mathematics task in normal and depressed subjects. *Brain and Cognition* **3**, 71–85.

Weinberger, D.R., Berman, K.F. and Zec, R.F. (1986). Physiologic dysfunction of dorsolateral prefrontal cortex in schizophrenia. I. Regional cerebral blood flow evidence. *Archives of General Psychiatry* **43**, 114–124.

Willner, P. (1985). *Depression: A Psychobiological Synthesis*. New York: Wiley.

Winokur, G. (1979). Unipolar depression: is it divisible into autonomous subtypes? *Archives of General Psychiatry* **36**, 47–52.

Zahn, T.P. (1986). Psychophysiological approaches to psychopathology. In: M.G.H. Coles, E. Donchin and S.W. Porge (Eds) *Psychophysiology: Systems, Processes, and Applications*, pp. 508–610. New York: Guilford.

Zimmerman, M., Coryell, W., Pfohl, B. and Stangl, D. (1986). The validity of four definitions of endogenous depression: II. Clinical, demographic, familial, and psychosocial correlates. *Archives of General Psychiatry* **43**, 234–244.

Chapter 13

Schizophrenic Disorders

Michael E. Dawson*, Keith H. Nuechterlein* and
Robert M. Adams
Department of Psychology,
University of Southern California and
*Department of Psychiatry and Biobehavioral Sciences,
University of California,
Los Angeles,
USA

ABSTRACT

This chapter examines the relationship between the schizophrenic disorders and three psychophysiological measures: electrodermal responses, the P300 component of brain event-related potentials, and smooth-pursuit eye movements. The principal anomalies found to be associated with the schizophrenias are reviewed for each measure, and implications of these findings are discussed.

Handbook of Clinical Psychophysiology Edited by G. Turpin
© 1989 John Wiley & Sons Ltd

INTRODUCTION

In this chapter, we examine several psychophysiological measures which have been widely studied in relation to the schizophrenias. Although a large number of psychophysiological variables have been studied in this regard (for a thorough review, see Zahn, 1986), we have chosen to focus on the three most extensively investigated measures: electrodermal responses, the P300 component of brain event-related potentials, and smooth-pursuit eye movements. First, we provide an overview of the nature of schizophrenic disorders. Next, we review each of the three measures in turn and discuss the major findings and unresolved issues associated with each. Finally, implications of these findings and directions for further research are discussed.

THE NATURE OF SCHIZOPHRENIC DISORDERS

The mental disorders that are alternatively termed schizophrenic disorders, the schizophrenias, or simply schizophrenia are the most prominent forms of 'madness'. The diversity of the manifestations of schizophrenic disorders was clearly noted by Emil Kraepelin (1919), who brought together this group of disorders under the earlier name 'dementia praecox':

> The complexity of the conditions which we observe in the domain of dementia praecox is very great, so that their inner connection is at first recognizable only by their occurring one after the other in the course of the same disease. In any case certain fundamental disturbances, even though they cannot for the most part be regarded as characteristic, yet return frequently in the same form, but in the most diverse combinations.
>
> (p. 5, 1971 edn)

The diversity of the manifestations of 'schizophrenia' is sufficient to have caused Eugene Bleuler (1911) to emphasize the existence of a group of schizophrenias and for the third edition of the *Diagnostic and Statistical Manual for Mental Disorders* (DSM-III) of the American Psychiatric Association (1980) to use the plural 'schizophrenic disorders' rather than a singular term. As might be expected in this situation, the most useful clinical boundaries for these disorders have been difficult to determine precisely. The movement in recent years to operational criteria for psychiatric disorders has nowhere been more evident than in attempts to define schizophrenic disorders, so that at the present time several sets of operational criteria for schizophrenia are available, including DSM-III, Research Diagnostic Criteria, Schneider's first-rank signs, CATEGO, Feighner's (Washington University) criteria, and Taylor and Abrams' criteria (see Brockington, Kendell and Leff, 1978; Endicott, Nee, Fleiss, Cohen, Williams and Simon, 1982; Wing, Cooper and Sartorius, 1974).

These major sets of operational criteria appear to be of essentially equal reliability, but differ considerably in the breadth of the concept of schizophrenia employed and in their handling of cases in which prominent affective symptoms accompany psychotic symptoms (Brockington *et al.*, 1978; Endicott *et al.*, 1982). Thus, the researcher should choose carefully the diagnostic system that is most appropriate for a given application and should strongly consider cross-classifying cases by other major systems to determine whether the diagnostic system employed affects the principal results.

The core symptoms of schizophrenic disorders common to all these systems are delusions, hallucinations, and formal thought disorder that cannot be accounted for by known neurological disease or toxic conditions, although other associated features are often also required for a diagnoses of schizophrenia. In DSM-III, the widely used official nomenclature of the American Psychiatric Association (1980), at least one clear symptom from this core group is required. If this symptom is formal thought disorder, it must be accompanied by either blunted or inappropriate affect, delusions or hallucinations, or catatonic or other grossly disorganized behaviour. In addition, for a diagnosis of schizo-phrenia, DSM-III requires functional impairment, continuous signs of the illness for at least 6 months (including prodromal or residual phases), onset before age 45 years, and either absence of a full depressive or manic syndrome or the presence of such an affective syndrome only after the psychotic symptoms or for a brief duration relative to the psychotic symptoms. In DSM-III, a disorder that lasts between 2 weeks and 6 months, but which meets the remaining criteria for a schizophrenic disorder, is termed a schizophreniform disorder. The diagnosis of schizophrenia by the Research Diagnostic Criteria (Spitzer, Endicott and Robins, 1978) incorporates most cases that would be classified as either schizophrenic or schizophreniform disorder in DSM-III. Earlier studies that employed DSM-II criteria (American Psychiatric Association, 1968) for schizophrenia are likely to have included a broader range of cases than those included by DSM-III, Research Diagnostic Criteria, and other current major sets of operational criteria.

The subcategorization of schizophrenia into positive and negative symptoms or syndromes has been a focus of much recent interest (e.g. Andreasen, 1985; Crow, 1985). The most prominent positive symptoms of schizophrenic disorders involve aspects of excess functioning such as hallucinations and delusions. On the other hand, negative symptoms of schizophrenia involve aspects of dimin-ished functioning. The optimal breadth of the concept of negative symptoms is currently being debated, with Crow (1985) favouring a narrow conception that involves flattening of affect and poverty of speech, while Andreasen (1985) favours a broad conception that adds avolition and apathy, anhedonia and asociality, and attentional impairment. Negative symptoms appear to be associ-ated with poorer outcome, cognitive impairments, and poorer response to neuroleptic medication (Andreasen, 1985; Crow, 1985). Crow (1980, 1985) has hypothesized that positive and negative syndromes involve different dimensions of pathological processes within schizophrenia.

Although the aetiology of schizophrenic disorders remains unknown, evidence for genetic factors in vulnerability to schizophrenia is strong (Gottesman and Shields, 1982). The most prominent theoretical framework for the aetiology of schizophrenic disorders is a diathesis/stress or vulnerability/stress model, in which genetically influenced vulnerability factors interact with environmental stressors to precipitate schizophrenic breakdown (Gottesman and Shields, 1982; Nuechterlein and Dawson, 1984a; Rosenthal, 1970). Thus, in addition to studies of schizophrenic patients, we will also review in this chapter studies that have sought to isolate relevant vulnerability factors in groups at heightened risk for schizophrenic disorder (Garmezy and Streitman, 1974). Children of a schizophrenic parent, who have a 10–15% chance of developing schizophrenia as compared to the general population rate of less than 1% (Gottesman and Shields, 1982), have been the most popular focus of this research. Whenever possible, we will also address the related question of whether psychophysiological anomalies found in schizophrenic patients are enduring, trait-like qualities or transient, state-related phenomena.

ELECTRODERMAL ACTIVITY

ASSESSMENT PROCEDURES

The relative ease with which electrodermal activity may be recorded, combined with its sensitivity to psychological processes, has led to it becoming the most widely employed measure in the psychophysiological study of the schizophrenias. Although a number of aspects of this activity are available for study, the electrodermal measure which has stimulated the most research in this area has been the rate of habituation of specific skin conductance responses (SCRs). A specific SCR is a phasic increase in skin conductance elicited by an identifiable stimulus and occurs as a component of the orienting response (OR) to novel or significant stimuli, or, alternatively, as a component of the defensive response to aversive stimuli. These responses are generally considered to reflect the degree of attention and information processing allocated to the eliciting stimulus (Öhman, 1979; Sokolov, 1963; Spinks and Siddle, 1983), and thus may help to shed some light on important attentional dysfunctions associated with the schizophrenias.

In the typical SCR-OR paradigm, a simple innocuous stimulus, usually a tone of moderate intensity and controlled rise-time (in order to avoid startle), is presented at variable intervals ranging from 20 to 50 s. The elicitation and subsequent habituation of SCRs are then measured and quantified. Although definitions of SCR habituation have varied widely (Siddle, Stephenson and

Spinks, 1983), the most common index used in the study of schizophrenic disorders has been the number of stimulus repetitions required before three consecutive presentations fail to elicit an SCR-OR. Generally, this habituation criterion is reached after 2–8 repetitions of an innocuous stimulus in normal subjects.

Other important electrodermal measures include non-specific SCRs (NS-SCRs) and skin conductance level (SCL). Non-specific SCRs, also referred to as 'spontaneous' SCRs, are phasic increases in skin conductance which occur despite the absence of a discrete, identifiable stimulus. A typical normal subject will exhibit between 1 and 3 NS-SCRs per minute while at rest, with the number tending to increase during heightened autonomic arousal. Skin conductance level refers to the tonic level of skin conductivity and can vary widely between subjects. As with NS-SCR activity, this measure generally increases as a function of overall autonomic arousal.

PRINCIPAL FINDINGS

A reliable finding obtained with the simple SCR-OR paradigm is that a sizeable subgroup of schizophrenic patients, typically 40–50%, fails to exhibit any SCR-ORs to innocuous stimuli, compared to a 5–10% rate of non-responsiveness in the normal population. The reliability of this phenomenon has been noted in several recent reviews of the literature (Dawson and Nuechterlein, 1984; Öhman, 1981; Spohn and Patterson, 1979; Zahn, 1986), and has been confirmed in an analysis of independently collected SCR-OR data (Bernstein *et al.*, 1982). Although the reported size of this non-responder subgroup varies between studies, the phenomenon has been observed among both acute and chronic patient populations, irrespective of medication status. Apparently, this lack of electrodermal responsiveness is not merely the result of a peripheral effector problem, as most schizophrenic non-responders are capable of responding if the stimulus intensity is increased (e.g. Bernstein, Taylor, Starkey, Juni, Lubowsky and Paley, 1981) or if the stimuli are made task-significant (Gruzelier and Venables, 1973). The degree of this increased responsiveness has been found to vary between studies, however. Whereas Gruzelier and Venables (1973) found schizophrenics to display approximately normal electrodermal responsiveness to task-significant stimuli, Zahn, Carpenter and McGlashan (1981a) found that responsiveness remained significantly lower in schizophrenics than in normal controls. Variables such as the type of task employed and patient characteristics may serve to explain these disparate findings.

There is considerably less agreement in the literature regarding SCR-OR activity among the remaining subgroup of schizophrenics: those who do exhibit SCR-ORs to innocuous stimuli. The majority finding is that this responder subgroup exhibits either abnormally fast habituation of the SCR-OR (Bernstein *et al.*, 1982) or an approximately normal rate of habituation (Öhman, 1981). However, a consistent minority finding, particularly from Gruzelier and his colleagues, is that the responder subgroup shows abnormally slow habituation (e.g. Gruzelier, Eves, Connolly and Hirsch, 1981).

Levinson, Edelberg and Bridger (1984) have proposed a rather simple resolution of this long-standing controversy. They noted that previous studies which reported a high incidence of slow habituation used a long response-latency scoring window (usually 1–5 s following stimulus onset), while studies reporting fast-to-normal habituation used a short scoring window (usually 1–3 s). After noting this relationship, Levinson *et al.* (1984) collected SCR-OR data from 36 chronic schizophrenic patients and 11 normal controls and scored the data using both short and long scoring windows. The authors found clusters of non-habituators with the long scoring window which virtually disappeared with the short scoring window, leading them to conclude that the apparent lack of habituation observed among subgroups of subjects when utilizing a long scoring window was due to the mis-scoring of some non-specific SCRs as SCR-ORs. Despite this promising suggestion, it remains to be seen whether use of different scoring windows can fully account for the different results reported in the literature, and particularly whether use of a long scoring window can account for the differentially higher rate of slow habituation among the patients and controls.

In any event, the general responder/non-responder distinction is reliable across studies and appears to be theoretically and clinically useful. It is theoretically relevant that the responder subgroup generally exhibits autonomic hyperarousal compared to normal controls, as indicated by a higher frequency of NS-SCRs and higher SCLs (e.g. Gruzelier and Venables, 1972; Gruzelier *et al.*, 1981), as well as higher heart rate levels, skin temperature, and systolic blood pressure (Gruzelier and Venables, 1975). As Öhman (1981) has suggested, when these tonic levels are taken into account, the two subgroups of schizophrenic patients appear to be best described as phasic hyporeactives (non-responders) versus tonic hyperactives (responders).

Aside from purely physiological differences, the schizophrenic responder and non-responder subgroups have been found to differ in their performance on cognitive and attentional tasks. For example, Straube (1979) found that non-responders tend to make more errors, particularly errors of omission, on a dichotic listening and verbal shadowing task than responders, suggesting that the non-responder subgroup possesses impaired selective attention capabilities. Non-responders have also been found to exhibit poorer perceptual resolution than responders as measured by the two-flash threshold (Gruzelier and Venables, 1974). On a signal-detection vigilance task, schizophrenics classified as either non-responders or non-habituators both performed more poorly than fast habituators (Patterson and Venables, 1980). It has been proposed that this latter finding may be explained in terms of an inverted-U relationship between arousal and performance, a hypothesis which receives support from studies demonstrating that phenothiazine medication tends to improve signal-detection performance among the responder subgroup, while tending to impair the performance of non-responders (Zahn, 1986).

The responder/non-responder distinction also seems to be related to important clinical phenomena. Gruzelier (1976) found that slow-habituation responders were rated by nurses as more manic, anxious, assaultive, belligerent, and attention-demanding than non-responders, while both Straube (1979), with acute patients, and Bernstein *et al.* (1981), with chronic patients, observed that non-responders were rated higher than responders on conceptual disorganization and emotional withdrawal and lower on excitement. These results suggest that the SCR-OR responder/non-responder distinction may be related to a dimension of positive versus negative symptomatology.

Electrodermal measures may also be related to another important clinical consideration: prediction of short-term outcome. Frith, Stevens, Johnstone and Crow (1979) found that a group of schizophrenic patients who failed to exhibit SCR-OR habituation showed significantly less subsequent clinical improvement than the subgroup of patients who did habituate. The non-habituators also exhibited higher SCLs and more frequent NS-SCRs than the habituators. Results consistent with these findings have also been obtained by Zahn, Carpenter and McGlashan (1981b). Thus, slow SCR-OR habituation, accompanied by high tonic electrodermal arousal, appears to be related to, and predictive of, poor short-term outcome. It is important to note that the subgroups of patients studied by Frith *et al.* (1979) and by Zahn *et al.* (1981b) did not differ symptomatically at the time of testing, and hence the autonomic dysfunctions appear to be predictive of short-term outcome independent of symptomatic severity.

The question naturally arises as to whether the electrodermal anomalies noted among schizophrenic patients are secondary effects of symptomatic states. In this regard, Iacono (1982) measured SCR-ORs to a series of mild innocuous tones in a group of remitted schizophrenic outpatients and found that 46% were non-responsive to the tones, while the remainder tended to display the same abnormally high SCLs and NS-SCR frequencies characteristic of responder schizophrenics. Although further research is needed, these results lend support to the notion that these electrodermal patterns are not merely a reaction to symptomatology, but rather represent enduring physiological traits.

Related to the above issue, electrodermal responses have been studied in populations at increased risk for schizophrenia in order to determine whether autonomic abnormalities develop long before the onset of symptomatology (see reviews by Dawson and Nuechterlein, 1984; Öhman, 1981; Zahn, 1986). Studies utilizing a genetic relationship to a schizophrenic patient to select a population at increased risk have yielded rather mixed results. Early studies indicated that the offspring of schizophrenic patients were electrodermally hyperaroused and hyper-reactive, particularly to aversive loud noises (Mednick and Schulsinger, 1968; Prentky, Salzman and Klein, 1981; Van Dyke, Rosenthal and Rasmussen, 1974). However, more recent studies have found either no electrodermal abnormalities or trends suggestive of hyporeactivity (Erlenmeyer-Kimling, Friedman, Cornblatt and Jacobsen, 1985; Kugelmass, Marcus and Schmueli, 1985).

Personality traits considered indicative of risk for future schizophrenia have also been studied in relation to electrodermal activity; again, the results have been mixed. Simons (1981) found that 67% of college students reporting physical anhedonia, a putative risk factor for schizophrenia (Chapman and Chapman, 1978), were SCR-OR non-responders, compared to 14% of the non-anhedonic controls. In contrast, Nielsen and Petersen (1976) developed a Schizophrenism Scale which emphasizes social withdrawal and attentional dysfunction, and found it to be related to high electrodermal arousal and high SCR-OR responsivity. It is interesting, and a little perplexing, that none of the studies of at-risk samples have reported obtaining the distinctive responder/ non-responder subgroups commonly found among symptomatic patients.

The findings discussed thus far have been concerned primarily with SCR-ORs elicited by simple laboratory stimuli. An interesting recent line of research has measured the frequency of NS-SCRs of schizophrenics in the presence of relatives who had been rated as high or low in 'expressed emotion' (EE) (see reviews of this line of research by Dawson, Liberman and Mintz, in press; Turpin, Tarrier and Sturgeon, in press). In a study conducted by Tarrier, Vaughn, Lader and Leff (1979), electrodermal activity of remitted schizophrenic outpatients was recorded in the patient's home. It was found that, while all of the patients exhibited higher than normal rates of NS-SCRs when tested with only the experimenter present, those whose relatives had been rated as low EE showed a gradual decline in arousal when in the presence of their relatives. In contrast, those patients whose relatives had been rated as high EE continued to exhibit heightened electrodermal arousal when in the presence of their relatives. Related results have been obtained by Sturgeon, Turpin, Kuipers, Berkowitz and Leff (1984) with acutely ill schizophrenic inpatients. Utilizing procedures very similar to those used in the Tarrier *et al.* (1979) study, these investigators found that those patients who had high-EE relatives exhibited much greater tonic arousal throughout the entire test period than the patients with low-EE relatives, regardless of whether the relative was present in the test situation. Although the different results obtained from acutely ill as opposed to remitted patients is puzzling, both studies indicate that the degree of sympathetic arousal in schizophrenic patients bears a relationship to the EE levels of relatives, and may help to explain the higher rates of relapse observed among patients with high-EE relatives (Brown, Birley and Wing, 1972; Vaughn and Leff, 1976; Vaughn, Snyder, Freeman, Jones, Falloon and Liberman, 1982).

P300 AND OTHER ENDOGENOUS COMPONENTS OF THE EVENT-RELATED POTENTIAL

ASSESSMENT PROCEDURES

While electrodermal measurements reflect the activity of the autonomic nervous system, measurements of brain event-related potentials (ERPs) yield direct information about central nervous system activity. The ERP waveform is recorded from the scalp in the same manner as the electroencephalogram (EEG) and consists of a transient series of voltage oscillations that are time-locked to an external stimulus. Due to the relatively small amplitude of ERPs in comparison to the background EEG, the signal is usually averaged across multiple trials in order to distinguish ERPs from the background EEG signals.

The ERP waveform comprises a number of components which may be divided into two general categories: 'exogenous' and 'endogenous' (Donchin, Ritter and McCallum, 1978). Exogenous ERP components form the initial post-stimulus portion of the ERP waveform and represent activity that is for the most part determined solely by the physical characteristics of the eliciting stimulus. In contrast, the later endogenous components are generally insensitive to specific physical properties of stimuli, but are highly sensitive to psychological factors such as task complexity, motivation, stimulus significance, etc. As the endogenous ERP components would appear to reflect higher level aspects of stimulus processing, rather than initial stimulus registration, their measurement has been increasingly employed by researchers investigating the schizophrenias.

Although several endogenous ERP components have been widely studied, including the contingent negative variation (CNV), N100, and the slow wave (SW), the component that has received the most attention, and with which we shall be primarily concerned here, is termed P300. The P300 component is a wave of positive polarity which reaches its peak approximately 300 ms following the onset of an eliciting stimulus (thus the term 'P300'), and occurs in response to novel, surprising, and/or task-relevant stimuli. In this regard, the P300 component appears similar to the autonomic OR (Donchin *et al.*, 1984; Roth and Tinklenberg, 1982). Thus, variations in the P300 waveform, particularly amplitude, may yield important information concerning abnormalities in attentional functioning that are associated with the schizophrenias.

As the P300 tends to occur most reliably in response to rare and/or task-significant stimuli, most studies investigating this phenomenon have utilized versions of the so-called 'oddball' paradigm. In this paradigm, a subject is exposed to infrequent target stimuli intermixed within a series of much more frequent non-target stimuli. The stimuli can be either auditory, visual, or somatosensory in nature. It has been demonstrated that, utilizing this paradigm, P300 amplitude is inversely proportional to the *a-priori* probability of target stimuli presentation (Duncan-Johnson and Donchin, 1977).

Before examining the principal findings regarding P300 and schizophrenia, it should be noted that many studies include a second endogenous component which is closely allied with P300, the SW. Taken together, these two components comprise what is known as the late positive complex (LPC). Although the inclusion of the SW may lead to somewhat different results under certain conditions, studies examining the LPC have yielded essentially the same results as those dealing only with P300, and thus no attempt is made here to evaluate them separately. The reader interested in the complexities associated with the family of components which make up the LPC should consult Sutton and Ruchkin (1984).

PRINCIPAL FINDINGS

Regardless of the specific paradigm used, studies have consistently found that the P300 amplitude is significantly attenuated in schizophrenic patients as compared to normal subjects (for reviews see Mirsky and Duncan, 1986; Pritchard, 1986; Roth, 1977; Zahn, 1986), with the amount of this reduction ranging from approximately 26 to 53% for studies that utilize a version of the oddball paradigm which requires an active response to target stimuli (Pritchard, 1986, p. 53). Other studies have also found attenuated P300s in schizophrenics in response to infrequently occurring, task-irrelevant stimuli (Roth and Cannon, 1972; Shagass, Straumanis, Roemer and Amadeo, 1977), although this effect is less pronounced than when the stimuli are task-relevant. This attenuation does not appear to simply reflect medication effects, as it has been found to an equal degree in unmedicated patients (Brecher and Begleiter, 1983; Roth, Pfefferbaum, Horvath, Berger and Kopell, 1980b).

As the attenuated P300s of schizophrenic patients are often paralleled by poor task performance (Cohen, Sommer and Hermanutz, 1981; Pass, Klorman, Salzman, Klein and Kaskey, 1980), one might wonder whether the attenuated P300 merely reflects a lack of motivation and task involvement. This question has been indirectly answered by the results of a study conducted by Duncan-Johnson, Roth and Kopell (1984), who sought to determine whether schizophrenic subjects formulate trial-to-trial expectancies for events in a random series in the same manner as normal controls. As the P300 is a sensitive index of the degree to which an eliciting stimulus is expected, P300s were evaluated as a function of the preceding sequences of stimuli. If schizophrenic subjects are sensitive to these manipulations in the same manner as controls, their varying levels of expectancy, as reflected by P300 amplitude, should parallel those of the controls. Indeed, this was precisely what these researchers found. Although the schizophrenics displayed an overall attenuated P300 amplitude as compared to the control subjects, the fact that they displayed equal sensitivity to the stimulus different sequences suggests that they were engaged in the task to a similar degree as the controls.

Attempts to find a relationship between P300 characteristics and degree of symptomatology in schizophrenia have produced rather mixed results. Brecher and Begleiter (1983) failed to find any correlation between P300 amplitude and symptomatology as measured by the Brief Psychiatric Rating Scale (BPRS). On the other hand, two other studies (Roth, Horvath, Pfefferbaum and Kopell, 1980a; Roth, Horvath, Pfefferbaum, Tinklenberg, Mezzich and Kopell, 1979) reported a significant inverse correlation between BPRS thought-disorder scores and P300 amplitude, although the Roth *et al.* (1980a) study found this relationship in only one of three paradigms used. More research in this area is clearly needed before any firm conclusions may be drawn.

Another issue with interesting but equivocal results concerns the possibility that P300 attenuation represents an underlying trait marker for vulnerability to schizophrenia. Barrett, McCallum and Pocock (1986), for example, found attenuated P300s in a subgroup of symptom-free schizophrenic outpatients who previously displayed positive schizophrenic symptoms. These results are consistent with the possibility that the P300 abnormality is an enduring trait-like characteristic. However, Duncan, Perlstein and Morihisa (in press) obtained preliminary evidence from a subgroup of schizophrenic patients tested while on and off medication indicating that neuroleptics tend to normalize P300 amplitude among patients who respond well clinically. Although the lack of a normal control group prevents making conclusions about the degree of this normalization, the Duncan *et al.* (in press) results support the possibility that P300 attenuation is a temporary state-like characteristic. It should be noted that both sets of findings may prove to be correct in that P300 amplitude may tend to normalize with neuroleptic-induced remission (Duncan *et al.*, in press) but does not completely normalize during remission (Barrett *et al.*, 1986).

Another line of research which addresses the state versus trait issue has attempted to determine whether ERP abnormalities exist among populations statistically at-risk for schizophrenia. Friedman, Vaughn and Erlenmeyer-Kimling (1982) reported reduced P300 amplitudes in the offspring of schizo-phrenic patients relative to the offspring of normal controls. However, after rediagnosing the parents of their high-risk population using more stringent Research Diagnostic Criteria and DSM-III criteria, and including the offspring of non-schizophrenic psychiatric patients as a second control group, these researchers obtained negative results (Friedman, Erlenmeyer-Kimling and Vaughn, 1985). By contrast, another study which utilized the siblings of schizo-phrenics, as opposed to their offspring, found significant P300 attenuation in these subjects relative to controls (Saitoh, Niwa, Hiramatsu, Kameyama, Rymar and Itoh, 1984). Pritchard (1986) has argued that a possible expla-nation for these divergent findings lies in the type of task utilized in each study. While Friedman *et al.* (1985) used a fairly easy auditory oddball task, Saitoh *et al.* (1984) required subjects to perform a more difficult syllable discrimination task. As current evidence indicates that the attentional performance of genetically defined high-risk subjects is poorer than controls only for rather demanding tasks (Nuechterlein and Dawson, 1984b), the paradigm utilized by Saitoh *et al.* (1984) may have been a more sensitive test of whether P300 attenuation can be demonstrated in genetic high-risk populations.

A study that selected subjects on hypothesized personality correlates of risk for schizophrenia also reported attenuated P300s in its target subjects. Simons (1982) examined the LPC in college students and found that subjects who scored high on the Revised Physical Anhedonia scale (Chapman, Chapman and Raulin, 1976) exhibited significantly smaller P300s than controls to warning tones preceding erotic stimuli, but showed normal P300 amplitude to non-signal tones. These interesting results must be interpreted with some caution, as the presence of anhedonia blurs the distinction between trait and state. Nevertheless, these findings demonstrate that attenuated P300s in response to stimuli normally of high interest can be found among subjects at hypothesized risk for schizophrenia who are not currently psychotic.

SMOOTH-PURSUIT EYE MOVEMENT

ASSESSMENT PROCEDURES

The prominence of smooth-pursuit eye movement (SPEM) procedures in recent schizophrenia research followed the reports by Holzman, Proctor and Hughes (1973) and Holzman, Proctor, Levy, Yasillo, Meltzer and Hurt (1974) demonstrating that 50–85% of schizophrenic patients and about 45% of their first-degree relatives show abnormalities in such movements. Smooth-pursuit eye movements involve those eye movements that are employed in following a continuously moving object, as differentiated from the high-velocity saccadic shifts of the eyes that function to fixate the image of an object onto the fovea. Although a number of variations have been used across studies, the most common procedure in schizophrenia research has involved having subjects track a small target moving horizontally in a sinusoidal fashion over 20° of visual arc at a frequency of 0.4 Hz. Electro-oculographic (EOG) or infra-red techniques have been employed to record the eye movements, with the former being most common and much more convenient but the latter being less vulnerable to bioelectrical artifacts and more accurate when very small eye movements need to be registered (Iacono and Lykken, 1983; Lindsey, Holzman, Haberman and Yasillo, 1978).

Scoring has usually involved making a qualitative judgement of the smoothness of the tracking record as displayed on a polygraph and, in addition, using one or more quantitative measures. The qualitative measure typically assesses the overall adequacy of the tracking on a five-point scale (Shagass, Amadeo and Overton, 1974), with emphasis on the extent to which saccadic intrusions disrupt smooth pursuit, and is often used to dichotomize subjects into 'good' and 'bad' trackers (e.g. Holzman, Solomon, Levin and Waternaux, 1984; Levin, Lipton and Holzman, 1981). In the initial studies, the quantitative measure involved obtaining the first derivative of the direct SPEM signal and counting the 'velocity arrests' per pendulum cycle (e.g. Holzman *et al.*, 1974). Velocity arrests are occasions when the eye movement velocity required for smooth tracking of the target stimulus is momentarily interrupted and becomes close to zero.

Improvements in quantitative scoring have been made which have led to replacement of the velocity arrest count. Lindsey *et al.* (1978) suggested that the count of velocity arrests be replaced by computation of the natural logarithm signal : noise ratio ($\ln (S/N)$) for the 0.4-Hz signal frequency relative to higher frequencies, because the latter yields more reliable scores across EOG and infra-red recording techniques. Alternatively, Iacono and Lykken (1979a,b) have successfully employed a root-mean-square error deviation to quantify overall tracking performance. Lykken, Iacono and Lykken (1981) and Iacono and Lykken (1983) have noted that the root-mean-square measure is closely related mathematically to the signal : noise ratio if all non-signal frequencies are included as noise in the latter, although the relationship is not linear. Phase lag, the extent to which the eye movements lag behind the location of the target, can be computed if the placement of the target stimulus is recorded simultaneously with the eye movement signal and has proven to be a very interesting additional SPEM measure (Iacono and Koenig, 1983). Measures of more specific components of abnormal eye movements have also been explored in an attempt to classify the types of abnormalities found in schizophrenic patients (Levin, Jones, Stark, Merrin and Holzman, 1982), but these measures have not been widely used.

PRINCIPAL FINDINGS

The basic finding of a substantially heightened frequency of abnormal smooth-pursuit eye tracking in schizophrenic patients has been a very reliable one across studies and laboratories, with 50–85% of schizophrenic patients showing abnormal tracking as compared to about 8% of normal comparison subjects (Holzman *et al.*, 1973, 1974; Mialet and Pichot, 1981; Pivik, 1979; Shagass *et al.*, 1974). The SPEM abnormalities do not appear to be caused by gross inattention or lack of cooperation (Holzman, Levy and Proctor, 1976, 1978b; Lipton, Frost and Holzman, 1980a) or neuroleptic medication (David, 1980; Holzman, Levy, Uhlenhuth, Proctor and Freedman, 1975). Shagass, Roemer and Amadeo (1976) introduced a secondary task – silently reading arabic numbers attached to the pendulum that was to be tracked – to recruit more voluntary attention to the tracking task. They found that this manipulation led to significant improvement but not complete normalization of the SPEM performance of schizophrenic patients, a finding that was replicated by Holzman *et al.* (1976, 1978b). Because schizophrenic patients continued to show impaired SPEM even during the number-reading task, Holzman *et al.* (1978b) concluded that the SPEM dysfunction in schizophrenia is not due to voluntary attentional systems. Furthermore, differentiating between two types of SPEM dysfunctions, they suggested that the number-reading procedure does not affect type-II dysfunctions (intrusion of small-amplitude rapid movements into smooth tracking) as markedly as type I (almost complete replacement of smooth pursuit by large saccadic shifts). The intrusion of multiple discrete, very small saccades into the SPEMs of some schizophrenic patients was later shown more dramatically by Levin *et al.* (1982), using an infra-red methodology that allowed a finer-grained analysis of the nature of SPEM abnormalities in a small group of schizophrenic patients.

The most appropriate theoretical constructs with which to describe SPEM abnormalities in cognitive processing terms remain open to speculation. The intrusion of rapid, small-amplitude saccadic movements into smooth pursuit (type-II dysfunctions) has been viewed as reflecting a deficit in involuntary attention that is connected to 'a failure of some inhibiting, modulating or integrating control centers' (Holzman *et al.*, 1978b, p. 108). Although initial theorizing focused on possible brain-stem mediation, Levin (1984a,b) has more recently suggested that these smooth-pursuit dysfunctions are related to a cortical regulatory system for saccades, which may involve the frontal lobe.

The SPEM task appears to be very sensitive to performance deficits in first-degree biological relatives of schizophrenics, as mentioned earlier, with about 35–45% of such relatives showing impaired tracking (Holzman *et al.*, 1973, 1974, 1984). Additional data from monozygotic and dizygotic twin pairs in which at least one member is schizophrenic have added further evidence that is consistent with the postulation that eye-tracking performance may be a genetic marker for a schizophrenia-prone genotype (Holzman, Kringlen, Levy and Haberman, 1980; Holzman, Kringlen, Levy, Proctor and Haberman, 1978a).

The presence of SPEM abnormalities in non-schizophrenic first-degree relatives of schizophrenic patients indicates that such anomalies can exist in the absence of psychotic symptomatology. This conclusion is also supported by evidence from relatively remitted schizophrenic patients. Although Pivik (1979) did not find significantly increased velocity arrests among schizophrenic outpatients in an early study, Iacono, Tuason and Johnson (1981) demonstrated in a well-documented study that relatively remitted schizophrenic patients showed significantly less accurate smooth pursuit than normal subjects. Furthermore, in a study of patients in relative remission an average of 5 years after their last hospitalization for major psychiatric disorder, Salzman, Klein and Strauss (1978) found that SPEM disorders were significantly correlated with degree of psychosis during the last hospitalization. However, SPEM dysfunction was not correlated with narrowly defined schizophrenia *per se* nor with current psychosis or mental health ratings. Thus, these cross-sectional studies suggest that SPEM dysfunctions may be an enduring index of vulnerability to psychosis which is relatively independent of current clinical state, although direct longitudinal evidence would demonstrate this independence from clinical state more convincingly.

Relatively little longitudinal evidence is available regarding whether variations in degree of SPEM dysfunction occur in relationship to changes in clinical state within schizophrenic patients. Most of the studies that have measured SPEM performance across time in schizophrenic patients have involved examination of the effect of medication. Holzman *et al.* (1974) noted that 10 chronic schizophrenic patients who were removed from medication for 10 days showed no change in their SPEM. Holzman *et al.* (1975), in a more systematic study of drug effects on SPEM, found that normal subjects did not show a significant disruption of SPEM when administered single doses of chlorpormazine (0.667 and 1.334 mg/kg) or diazepam (0.071, 0.142, and 0.284 mg/kg). Sccobarbital (100 mg) did increase the number of velocity arrests and in some subjects also produced qualitative disruption. Levy, Lipton, Holzman and Davis (1983) found that, although only 2 of 8 schizophrenic subjects showed impaired SPEM at the end of a drug-free washout baseline period, the SPEM performance of all 8 patients remained stable at four subsequent weekly intervals while antipsychotic medication was reintroduced. In non-clinical subjects, Iacono and Lykken (1981) have found a high level of SPEM stability over 2 years, suggesting that such stability is also a possibility in schizophrenic patients. Although the evidence thus far favours stability across clinical states in schizophrenic patients, the conclusion of Lipton, Levy, Holzman and Levin (1983) regarding longitudinal stability of the SPEM abnormalities continues to be noteworthy: 'it remains unclear whether smooth pursuit impairment is a trait variable or whether in certain instances it reflects state-related variability in functioning, such as severity of psychosis' (p. 20). Additional data involving repeated testing across psychotic and remission periods within schizophrenic and affective disorder patients would be very useful.

Because the SPEM deviations have been viewed as a possible genetic marker specifically for schizophrenic disorder (Holzman *et al.*, 1974, 1984), considerable attention has focused on the extent to which these abnormalities appear in other psychiatric disorders. Holzman *et al.* (1974) found originally, using DSM-II criteria (American Psychiatric Association, 1968), that 52% of recently hospitalized (less than 6 months) schizophrenic patients and 86% of chronic (more than 5 years of total hospitalization time) schizophrenic patients showed SPEM tracking that was judged qualitatively deviant, compared to 22% of manic–depressive patients, 21% of non-psychotic patients, and 8% of the normal group. Shagass *et al.* (1974) reported weaker specificity of deviant SPEM to schizophrenia, finding such deviations to a similar degree in affective psychoses as well, but not in non-psychotic psychiatric patients. In a study that employed the Washington University diagnostic criteria (Feighner, Robins, Guze, Woodruff, Winokur and Munoz, 1972) to yield groups with greater clinical homogeneity, Lipton, Levin and Holzman (1980b) found that about half of the patients with schizophrenia and with manic–depression illness showed smooth-pursuit dysfunction. Impaired tracking in a significant portion of acute affective psychoses was also apparent in a study of consecutive admissions classified by the Research Diagnostic Criteria (Lipton, Moulthrop, Holzman and Schwab, as discussed in Lipton *et al.*, 1983). Although a somewhat elevated frequency of impaired smooth-pursuit performance may characterize functional psychoses in general (Lipton *et al.*, 1983), some aspects of these eye movement dysfunctions, such as phase lag (Iacono and Koenig, 1983), seem to differentiate the performance of schizophrenic and affective disorder patients. Furthermore, recent evidence suggests that SPEM abnormalities in bipolar patients may frequently be a by-product of lithium therapy (Iacono, Peloquin, Lumry, Valentine and Tuason, 1982; Levy *et al.*, 1985). Finally, familial evidence for specificity has recently been reported (Holzman *et al.*, 1984), with 34% (13 of 38) of the parents of schizophrenic patients compared to 10% (2 of 21) of parents of manic–depressive patients showing SPEM dysfunctions.

In summary, SPEM abnormalities are found in a disproportionate number of schizophrenic patients. Evidence regarding SPEM changes over repeated testing suggest that these movements are not significantly affected by neuroleptics in schizophrenic or normal individuals and that they tend to be highly stable in at least normal subjects. Available data on the heightened frequency (35–45%) of SPEM disorders in the first-degree relatives of schizophrenic patients imply that these dysfunctions are not only part of the schizophrenic psychotic period, but may index vulnerability to schizophrenia. Furthermore, data from twins discordant for schizophrenia are consistent with genetic transmission of impaired SPEM tracking. The significant correlation of SPEM performance in remitted patients with severity of psychosis during the last hospitalization also supports the hypothesis that SPEM disorders are an enduring index of vulnerability to psychosis.

IMPLICATIONS AND DIRECTIONS FOR FURTHER RESEARCH

Several psychophysiological abnormalities that are reliably associated with the schizophrenias have been reviewed in the present chapter. First, whereas an abnormally large subgroup of schizophrenic patients exhibits SCR-OR non-responsiveness to innocuous stimuli, the remaining subgroup of SCR-OR responders usually displays autonomic hyperarousal. Second, an attenuated P300 component of the ERP waveform, elicited by rare and/or task-significant stimuli, has consistently been found in schizophrenic patients. Third, abnormalities in SPEMs have been found in a disproportionate number of schizophrenic patients and in their first-degree relatives. These findings, although intriguing, raise several important overlapping issues which must be dealt with before their true significance can be ascertained.

The first issue concerns the degree to which these psychophysiological anomalies are specific to the schizophrenias. Abnormally high rates of SCR-OR non-responsiveness have also been found among patients with endogenous depression (Mirkin and Coppen, 1980), while abnormally high electrodermal arousal has been found among anxiety neurotics (Lader and Wing, 1966). Likewise, both unipolar depressive and dementia patients have been found to exhibit attenuated P300s (Pfefferbaum, Wenegrat, Ford, Roth and Kopell, 1984), and some studies have found increased rates of deviant SPEM in major affective disorders as well as in schizophrenia (Lipton *et al.*, 1980b; Shagass *et al.*, 1974). However, as noted earlier, the impaired SPEM in bipolar patients now appears to be associated with lithium therapy (Iacono *et al.*, 1982; Levy *et al.*, 1985). Furthermore, the parents of manic–depressive patients do not show the increased rate of deviant SPEM that is found among parents of schizophrenic patients (Holzman *et al.*, 1984).

It would appear that the SPEM abnormalities are more specifically associated with schizophrenia (after psychopharmacological effects are eliminated), whereas the electrodermal and P300 abnormalities discussed in this chapter may not be unique to the schizophrenias. However, further evidence suggests that any conclusion regarding the non-specificity of electrodermal and P300 abnormalities may be somewhat premature. For example, Bernstein *et al.* (1986) found high rates of SCR-OR non-responding to innocuous tones in both schizophrenics and depressives, but only the schizophrenics were non-responsive with a finger pulse volume measure of orienting. Moreover, when the tones were made task-significant, the SCR-ORs of schizophrenics tended to normalize whereas those of the depressives did not normalize. Thus, although both schizophrenics and depressives exhibited SCR-OR non-responding to innocuous tones, the two patient groups could be distinguished by consideration of the patterns of non-responding across different stimulus situations and response systems.

A second issue concerns the delineation of meaningful diagnostic subgroups subsumed under the general heading of schizophrenia. As discussed in the section on electrodermal activity, schizophrenic patients may be reliably divided into two fairly distinct subgroups based upon SCR-OR responsiveness: non-responders and responders. Although this distinction probably represents a continuum rather than a dichotomy, the fact that it might be related to positive versus negative symptom dimensions (Zahn, 1986), as well as factors such as the apparent role of genetic components in schizophrenia (Alm, Lindström, Öst and Öhman, 1984) and medication effects (Zahn, 1986), provides converging evidence for the possible existence of two symptom complexes within schizophrenia. These lines of evidence suggest the possibility that there may be different vulnerability factors for the development of positive versus negative symptoms of schizophrenia and that psychophysiological variables may be differentially related to these vulnerabilities (Nuechterlein, 1987).

Neither P300 nor SPEM measures appear to be related to the responder/ non-responder SCR-OR distinction. These measures seem quite likely to reflect different, more universal, aspects of schizophrenia. Thus, these measures may tap more central biological and/or cognitive 'schizophrenic' dysfunctions which both the responder and non-responder subgroups have in common.

A third issue concerns the role of psychophysiological abnormalities in the developmental course of schizophrenia. Specifically, do these abnormalities reflect enduring trait-like characteristics related to vulnerability factors for schizophrenia, temporary state-like characteristics related to symptomatic status, or both? Although further research is clearly needed, preliminary evidence indicates that each of the abnormalities discussed in this chapter is at least partly a function of trait-like factors. For example, relatively remitted schizophrenic patients have been reported to exhibit psychophysiological abnormalities similar to those found in symptomatic patients for electrodermal measures (Iacono, 1982), for P300s (Barrett et al., 1986), and for SPEMs (Salzman et al., 1978). Simons' (1981, 1982) finding that anhedonic college students possess high rates of SCR-OR non-responsiveness and attenuated P300s is also possibly relevant to this issue, as anhedonia has been suggested as a vulnerability indicator for schizophrenia (Chapman, Chapman and Raulin, 1976). Perhaps most impressive is the finding of increased rates of SPEM dysfunction among the first-degree relatives of schizophrenic patients (Holzman et al., 1974, 1984). This finding suggests that deviant SPEM may not only be a vulnerability indicator for schizophrenia, but that it may also serve as a genetic marker for vulnerability among relatives of schizophrenic patients.

Dawson and Nuechterlein (1984, 1987) and Nuechterlein and Dawson (1984a) have suggested that certain psychophysiological abnormalities may exhibit characteristics of both enduring trait-like vulnerability indicators and of fluctuating state-like symptom indicators. That is, these abnormalities may exist in an attenuated form while patients are symptom-free, and then become more deviant as subclinical symptoms begin to emerge. Because changes in these measures may index processes which mediate the development of psychotic symptoms, these variables have been referred to as possible 'mediating vulnerability factors'. For example, as noted earlier, an individual may exhibit an attenuated P300 amplitude as part of the vulnerability to schizophrenia but also may exhibit variability in the degree of this attentuation as symptoms begin to exacerbate or remit. Given the possibility that the psychophysiological measures may change before the overt behavioural symptoms, it would be desirable to frequently monitor psychophysiological measures in schizophrenic outpatients in order to detect changes which could cue the initiation of more aggressive treatment interventions designed to head off an impending relapse.

Another important issue concerns the need to better understand which psychological and physiological constructs can be related to the psychophysiological abnormalities. Although knowledge of these abnormalities is of limited utility when viewed in isolation, their usefulness should increase as more explicit theoretical networks are developed. Thus far, most of the psychophysiological research dealing with schizophrenia has been guided and organized by the general concepts of 'arousal' and 'attention', but more specific and integrative theoretical constructs are now needed. As a step in this direction, SCR-ORs and P300s have been related to the initiation of information processing in a limited-capacity central processor (Bernstein *et al.*, 1981; Dawson, Schell, Beers and Kelly, 1982; Donchin, Kramer and Wickens, 1986; Jennings, 1986; Öhman, 1979; Posner, 1978; Roth and Tinklenberg, 1982). The view that SCR-ORs and P300s index the allocation of limited attentional resources, or the 'call' for such processing, is potentially testable and may serve to bridge experimental psychophysiology with the study of psychopathology in general, and the schizophrenias in particular. This framework may also help to relate psychophysiological abnormalities to the cognitive and attentional deficits frequently observed to be associated with the schizophrenias. The theoretical constructs concerning SPEM dysfunctions are similarly in need of further development. Current suggestions that the SPEM dysfunctions represent problems of involuntary attention and failures of central integrating functions have been helpful, but improved linkage of the SPEM dysfunctions to current models of human information processing seems warranted.

In order to understand better the nature and meaning of these abnormalities, two areas urgently need to be pursued further in future research. First, longitudinal research is needed in which psychophysiological measures are obtained from the same patients while symptomatic and while remitted. Such research will permit a better understanding of the specific relationship between psychophysiological measures and symptomatology. Second, the development of more explicit conceptual models is necessary in order to integrate psychophysiological findings with psychological and physiological factors, thereby permitting investigators to select more rationally the experimental paradigms and psychophysiological measures through which to explore the nature of the schizophrenias.

REFERENCES

Alm, T., Lindström, L., Öst, L.G. and Öhman, A. (1984). Electrodermal non-responding in schizophrenia: relationships to attentional, clinical, biochemical, computed tomographical and genetic factors. *International Journal of Psychophysiology* 1, 195–208.

American Psychiatric Association (1968). *Diagnostic and Statistical Manual of Mental Disorders*, 2nd edn. Washington, DC: APA.

American Psychiatric Association (1980). *Diagnostic and Statistical Manual of Mental Disorders*, 3rd edn. Washington, DC: APA.

Andreasen, N.C. (1985). Positive vs. negative schizophrenia: a critical evaluation. *Schizophrenia Bulletin* 11, 380–389.

Barrett, K., McCallum, W.V. and Pocock, P.V. (1986). Brain indicators of altered attention and information processing in schizophrenic patients. *British Journal of Psychiatry* 148, 414–420.

Bernstein, A.S., Frith, C.D., Gruzelier, J.H., Patterson, T., Straube, E., Venables, P.H. and Zahn, T.P. (1982). An analysis of the skin conductance orienting response in samples of American, British and German schizophrenics. *Biological Psychology* 14, 155–211.

Bernstein, A.S., Riedel, J.A., Graae, F., Seidman, D., Steele, H., Connolly, J. and Lubowsky, J. (1988 orienting response). Schizophrenia is associated with altered orienting response; depression with electrodermal (cholinergic?) deficit and normal orienting response. *Journal of Abnormal Psychology* 97, 3–12.

Bernstein, A.S., Taylor, K.W., Starkey, P., Juni, S., Lubowsky, J. and Paley, H. (1981). Bilateral skin conductance, finger pulse volume, and EEG orienting response to tones of differing intensities in chronic schizophrenics and controls. *Journal of Nervous and Mental Disease* 169, 513–528.

Bleuler, E. (1911). *Dementia Praecox or the Group of Schizophrenias*. 1950 edn; J. Zinkin (trans.). New York: International Universities Press.

Brecher, M. and Begleiter, H. (1983). Event-related brain potentials to high incentive stimuli in unmedicated schizophrenics. *Biological Psychiatry* 18, 661–674.

Brockington, I.F., Kendell, R.E. and Leff, J.P. (1978). Definitions of schizophrenia: concordance and prediction of outcome. *Psychological Medicine* 8, 387–398.

Brown, G., Birley, J.L.T. and Wing, J.K. (1972). Influence of family life on the course of schizophrenia. *British Journal of Psychiatry* 121, 241–248.

Chapman, L.J. and Chapman, J.P. (1978). *Revised Physical Anhedonia Scale*. Unpublished test.

Chapman, L.J., Chapman, J.P. and Raulin, M.L. (1976). Scales for physical and social anhedonia. *Journal of Abnormal Psychology* 85, 374–382.

Cohen, R., Sommer, W. and Hermanutz, M. (1981). Auditory event-related potentials in chronic schizophrenics: effects of electrodermal response type and demands on selective attention. In: C. Perris, D. Kemali and L. Vacca (Eds) *Advances in Biological Psychiatry*, Vol. 6: *Electroneurophysiology and Psychopathology*, pp. 180–194. Basle: Karger.

Crow, T.J. (1980). Molecular pathology of schizophrenia: more than one dimension of pathology? *British Medical Journal* 280, 66–68.

Crow, T.J. (1985). The two-syndrome concept: origins and current status. *Schizophrenia Bulletin* 11, 471–486.

David, I. (1980). Disorders of smooth pursuit eye movements in schizophrenics and the effect of neuroleptics in therapeutic doses. *Activitas Nervosa Superior* 22, 155–156.

Dawson, M.E. and Nuechterlein, K.H. (1984). Psychophysiological dysfunctions in the developmental course of schizophrenic disorders. *Schizophrenia Bulletin* 10, 204–232.

Dawson, M.E. and Nuechterlein, K.H. (1987). The role of autonomic dysfunctions within a vulnerability/stress model of schizophrenic disorders. In: D. Magnusson and A. Ohman (Eds) *Psychopathology: An Interactional Perspective*, pp. 41–57. New York: Academic Press.

Dawson, M.E., Liberman, R.P. and Mintz, L.I. (in press). Sociophysiology of expressed emotion in the course of schizophrenia. In: P.R. Barchas (Ed.) *Sociophysiology of Social Relationships*. New York: Oxford University Press.

Dawson, M.E., Schell, A.M., Beers, J.R. and Kelly, A. (1982). Allocation of cognitive processing capacity during human autonomic conditioning. *Journal of Experimental Psychology: General* **111**, 273–295.

Donchin, E., Heffley, E., Hillyard, S.A., Loveless, N., Maltzman, I., Öhman, A., Rösler, F., Ruchkin, D. and Siddle, D. (1984). Cognition and event-related potentials: II. The orienting reflex and P300. In: R. Karrer, J. Cohen and P. Tueting (Eds) *Brain and Information: Event-Related Brain Potentials*, pp. 39–57. New York: New York Academy of Sciences.

Donchin, E., Kramer, A.F. and Wickens, C. (1986). Applications of brain event-related potentials to problems in engineering psychology. In: M.G.H. Coles, E. Donchin and S.W. Porges (Eds) *Psychophysiology: Systems, Processes, and Applications*, pp. 702–778. New York: Guilford.

Donchin, E., Ritter, W. and McCallum, W.C. (1978). Cognitive psychophysiology: the endogenous components of the ERP. In: E. Callaway, P. Tueting and S. Koslow (Eds) *Event-Related Brain Potentials in Man*, pp. 349–442. New York: Academic Press.

Duncan, C.C., Perlstein, W.M. and Morihisa, J.M. (in press). The P300 metric in schizophrenia: effects of probability and modality. *Electroencephalography and Clinical Neurophysiology*.

Duncan-Johnson, C.C. and Donchin, E. (1977). On quantifying surprise: the variation in event-related potentials with subjective probability. *Psychophysiology* **14**, 456–467.

Duncan-Johnson, C.C., Roth, W.T. and Kopell, B.S. (1984). Effects of stimulus sequence on P300 and reaction time in schizophrenics: a preliminary report. In: R. Karrer, J. Cohen and P. Tueting (Eds) *Brain and Information: Event-Related Potentials*, pp. 570–577. New York: New York Academy of Sciences.

Endicott, J., Nee, J., Fleiss, J., Cohen, J., Williams, J.B.W. and Simon, R. (1982). Diagnostic criteria for schizophrenia: reliabilities and agreement between systems. *Archives of General psychiatry* **39**, 884–889.

Erlenmeyer-Kimling, L., Friedman, D., Cornblatt, B. and Jacobsen, R. (1985). Electro-dermal recovery data on children of schizophrenic parents. *Psychiatry Research* **14**, 148–161.

Feighner, J.P., Robins, E., Guze, S.B., Woodruff, R.A., Winokur, G. and Munoz, R. (1972). Diagnostic criteria for use in psychiatric research. *Archives of General Psychiatry* **21**, 57–62.

Friedman, D., Erlenmeyer-Kimling, L. and Vaughan, H. (1985). Auditory event-related potentials in children at risk for schizophrenia revisited: re-diagnosis of the patient parents and inclusion of the psychiatric control group. *Psychophysiology* **22**, 590.

Friedman, D., Vaughan, H.G. and Erlenmeyer-Kimling, L. (1982). Cognitive brain potentials in children at risk for schizophrenia: preliminary findings. *Schizophrenia Bulletin* **8**, 514–531.

Frith, C.D., Stevens, M., Johnstone, E.C. and Crow, T.J. (1979). Skin conductance responsivity during acute episodes of schizophrenia as a predictor of symptomatic improvement. *Psychological Medicine* **9**, 101–106.

Garmezy, N. and Streitman, S. (1974). Children at risk: the search for the antecedents of schizophrenia. Part I. Conceptual models and research methods. *Schizophrenia Bulletin* **1**, 14–90.

Gottesman, I.I. and Shields, J. (1982). *Schizophrenia: The Epigenetic Puzzle.* Cambridge: Cambridge University Press.

Gruzelier, J.H. (1976). Clinical attributes of schizophrenic skin conductance responders and nonresponders. *Psychological Medicine* **6**, 245–249.

Gruzelier, J.H. and Venables, P.H. (1972). Skin conductance orienting activity in a heterogeneous sample of schizophrenics: possible evidence of limbic dysfunction. *Journal of Nervous and Mental Disease* **155**, 277–287.

Gruzelier, J.H. and Venables, P.H. (1973). Skin conductance responses to tones with and without attentional significance in schizophrenic and nonschizophrenic psychiatric patients. *Neuropsychologia* **11**, 221–230.

Gruzelier, J.H. and Venables, P.H. (1974). Two-flash threshold, sensitivity, and β in normal subjects and schizophrenics. *Quarterly Journal of Experimental Psychology* **26**, 594–604.

Gruzelier, J.H. and Venables, P.H. (1975). Evidence of high and low levels of physiological arousal in schizophrenics. *Psychophysiology* **12**, 55–73.

Gruzelier, J., Eves, F., Connolly, J. and Hirsch, S. (1981). Orienting, habituation, sensitization, and dishabituation in the electrodermal system of consecutive, drug free, admissions for schizophrenia. *Biological Psychology* **12**, 187–209.

Holzman, P.S., Kringlen, E., Levy, D.L. and Haberman, S.J. (1980). Deviant eye tracking in twins discordant for psychosis: a replication. *Archives of General Psychiatry* **37**, 627–631.

Holzman, P.S., Kringlen, E., Levy, D.L., Proctor, L.R. and Haberman, S. (1978a). Smooth pursuit eye movements in twins discordant for schizophrenia. In: L.C. Wynne, R.L. Cromwell and S. Matthysse (Eds) *The Nature of Schizophrenia: New Approaches to Research and Treatment,* pp. 376–386. New York: Wiley.

Holzman, P.S., Levy, D.L. and Proctor, L.R. (1976). Smooth pursuit eye movements, attention, and schizophrenia. *Archives of General Psychiatry* **33**, 1415–1420.

Holzman, P.S., Levy, D.L. and Proctor, L.R. (1978b). The several qualities of attention in schizophrenia. *Journal of Psychiatric Research* **14**, 99–110.

Holzman, P.S., Levy, D.L., Uhlenhuth, E.H., Proctor, L.R. and Freedman, D.X. (1975). Smooth pursuit eye movements, and diazepam, CPZ, and secobarbitol. *Psychopharmacologia* **44**, 111–115.

Holzman, P.S., Proctor, L.R. and Hughes, D.W. (1973). Eye-tracking patterns in schizophrenia. *Science* **181**, 179–181.

Holzman, P.S., Proctor, L.R., Levy, D.L., Yasillo, N.J., Meltzer, H.Y. and Hurt, S.W. (1974). Eye-tracking dysfunctions in schizophrenic patients and their relatives. *Archives of General Psychiatry* **31**, 143–151.

Holzman, P.S., Solomon, C.M., Levin, S. and Waternaux, C.S. (1984). Pursuit eye movement dysfunctions in schizophrenia: family evidence for specificity. *Archives of General Psychiatry* **41**, 136–139.

Iacono, W.G. (1982). Bilateral electrodermal habituation–dishabituation and resting EEG in remitted schizophrenics. *Journal of Nervous and Mental Disease* **170**, 91–101.

Iacono, W.G. and Koenig, W.G.R. (1983). Features that distinguish the smooth-pursuit eye-tracking performance of schizophrenic, affective-disorder and normal individuals. *Journal of Abnormal Psychology* **92**, 29–41.

Iacono, W.G. and Lykken, D.T. (1979a). Electro-oculographic recording and scoring of smooth pursuit and saccadic eye tracking: a parametric study using monozygotic twins. *Psychophysiology* **16**, 94–107.

Iacono, W.G. and Lykken, D.T. (1979b). Eye tracking and psychopathology: new procedure applied to a sample of normal monozygotic twins. *Archives of General Psychiatry* **36**, 1361–1369.

Iacono, W.G. and Lykken, D.T. (1981). Two-year retest stability of eye tracking performance and a comparison of electro-oculographic and infra-red recording techniques: evidence of EEG in the electro-oculogram. *Psychophysiology* **18**, 49–55.

Iacono, W.G. and Lykken, D.T. (1983). The assessment of smooth tracking dysfunction. *Schizophrenia Bulletin* **9**, 44–50.

Iacono, W.G., Peloquin, L.J., Lumry, A.E., Valentine, R.H. and Tuason, V.B. (1982). Eye tracking in patients with unipolar and bipolar affective disorders in remission. *Journal of Abnormal Psychology* **91**, 35–44.

Iacono, W.G., Tuason, V.B. and Johnson, R.A. (1981). Dissociation of smooth-pursuit and saccadic eye tracking in remitted schizophrenics. *Archives of General Psychiatry* **38**, 991–996.

Jennings, J.R. (1986). Bodily changes during attending. In: M.G.H. Coles, E. Donchin and S.W. Porges (Eds) *Psychophysiology: Systems, Processes, and Applications*, pp. 268–289. New York: Guilford.

Kraepelin, E. (1919). *Dementia Praecox and Paraphrenia*. 1971 edn; R.B. Barclay (trans.). Huntington, NY: Krieger.

Kugelmass, S., Marcus, J. and Schmueli, J. (1985). Psychophysiological reactivity in high-risk children. *Schizophrenia Bulletin* **11**, 66–73.

Lader, M.H. and Wing, L. (1966). *Physiological Measures, Sedative Drugs, and Morbid Anxiety*. London: Oxford University Press.

Levin, S. (1984a). Frontal lobe dysfunctions in schizophrenia. I. Eye movement impairments. *Journal of Psychiatric Research* **18**, 27–55.

Levin, S. (1984b). Frontal lobe dysfunctions in schizophrenia. II. Impairments of psychological and brain functions. *Journal of Psychiatric Research* **18**, 57–72.

Levin, S., Jones, A., Stark, L., Merrin, E.L. and Holzman, P.S. (1982). Identification of abnormal patterns in eye movements of schizophrenic patients. *Archives of General Psychiatry* **39**, 1125–1130.

Levin, S., Lipton, R.B. and Holzman, P.S. (1981). Pursuit eye movements in psychopathology: effects of target characteristics. *Biological Psychiatry* **16**, 255–267.

Levinson, D.F., Edelberg, R. and Bridger, W.H. (1984). The orienting response in schizophrenia: proposed resolution of a controversy. *Biological Psychiatry* **19**, 489–507.

Levy, D.L., Dorus, E., Shaughnessy, R., Yasillo, N.J., Pandey, G.N., Janicak, P.G., Gibbons, R.D., Gaviria, M. and Davis, J.M. (1985). Pharmacologic evidence for specificity of pursuit dysfunction to schizophrenia: lithium carbonate associated with abnormal pursuit. *Archives of General Psychiatry* **42**, 335–341.

Levy, D.L., Lipton, R.B., Holzman, P.S. and Davis, J.M. (1983). Eye tracking dysfunction unrelated to clinical state and treatment with haloperidol. *Biological Psychiatry* **18**, 813–819.

Lindsey, D.T., Holzman, P.S., Haberman, S. and Yasillo, N.J. (1978). Smooth pursuit eye movements: a comparison of two measurement techniques for studying schizophrenia. *Journal of Abnormal Psychology* **87**, 491–496.

Lipton, R.B., Frost, L.A. and Holzman, P.S. (1980a). Smooth pursuit eye movements, schizophrenia, and distraction. *Perceptual and Motor Skills* **50**, 159–167.

Lipton, R.B., Levin, S. and Holzman, P.S. (1980b). Horizontal and vertical eye movements, the oculocephalic reflex, and the functional psychoses. *Psychiatry Research* **3**, 193–203.

Lipton, R., Levy, D.L., Holzman, P.S. and Levin, S. (1983). Eye movement dysfunctions in psychiatric patients: a review. *Schizophrenia Bulletin* **9**, 13–32.

Lykken, D.T., Iacono, W.G. and Lykken, J.D. (1981). Measuring deviant eye tracking. *Schizophrenia Bulletin* **7**, 204–205.

Mednick, S.A. and Schulsinger, F. (1968). Some premorbid characteristics related to breakdown in children with schizophrenic mothers. In: D. Rosenthal and S.S. Kety (Eds) *Transmission of Schizophrenia*, pp. 267–291. New York: Pergamon.

Mialet, J.P. and Pichot, P. (1981). Eye-tracking patterns in schizophrenia: an analysis based on incidence of saccades. *Archives of General Psychiatry* **38**, 183–186.

Mirkin, A.M. and Coppen, A. (1980). Electrodermal activity in depression: clinical and biochemical correlates. *British Journal of Psychiatry* **137**, 93–97.

Mirsky, A.F. and Duncan, C.C. (1986). Etiology and expression of schizophrenia: neurobiological and psychosocial factors. *Annual Review of Psychology* **37**, 291–319.

Nielsen, T.C. and Petersen, K.E. (1976). Electrodermal correlates of extraversion, trait anxiety and schizophrenia. *Scandinavian Journal of Psychology* **17**, 73–80.

Nuechterlein, K.H. (1987). Vulnerability models for schizophrenia: state of the art. In: H. Hafner, W.F. Gattaz and W. Janzarik (Eds) *Search for the Causes of Schizophrenia*, pp. 297–316. New York: Springer.

Nuechterlein, K.H. and Dawson, M.E. (1984a). A heuristic vulnerability/stress model of schizophrenic episodes. *Schizophrenia Bulletin* **10**, 300–312.

Nuechterlein, K.H. and Dawson, M.E. (1984b). Information processing and attentional functioning in the developmental course of schizophrenic disorders. *Schizophrenic Bulletin* **10**, 160–203.

Öhman, A. (1979). The orienting response, attention and learning: an information processing perspective. In: H.D. Kimmel, E.H. Van Olst and J.F. Orlebeke (Eds) *The Orienting Reflex in Humans*, pp. 443–471. Hillsdale, NJ: Lawrence Erlbaum.

Öhman, A. (1981). Electrodermal activity in schizophrenia: a review. *Biological Psychology* **12**, 87–145.

Pass, H.L., Klorman, R., Salzman, L.F., Klein, R.H. and Kaskey, G.B. (1980). The late positive component of the evoked response in acute schizophrenics during a test of sustained attention. *Biological Psychiatry* **15**, 9–20.

Patterson, T. and Venables, P.H. (1980). Auditory vigilance: normals compared to chronic schizophrenic subgroups defined by skin conductance variables. *Psychiatry Research* **2**, 107–112.

Pfefferbaum, A., Wenegrat, B.G., Ford, J.M., Roth, W.T. and Kopell, B.S. (1984). Clinical applications of the P3 component of event-related potentials: II. Dementia, depression, and schizophrenia. *Electroencephalography and Clinical Neurophysiology* **59**, 104–124.

Pivik, R.T. (1979). Smooth pursuit eye movements and attention in psychiatric patients. *Biological Psychiatry* **14**, 859–879.

Posner, M.I. (1978). *Chronometric Explorations of Mind.* Hillsdale, NJ: Lawrence Erlbaum.

Prentky, R.A., Salzman, L.F. and Klein, R.H. (1981). Habituation and conditioning of skin conductance responses in children at risk. *Schizophrenia Bulletin* **7**, 281–291.

Pritchard, W.S. (1986). Cognitive event-related potential correlates of schizophrenia. *Psychological Bulletin* **100**, 43–66.

Rosenthal, D. (1970). *Genetic Theory and Abnormal Behavior.* New York: McGraw-Hill.

Roth, W.T. (1977). Late event-related potentials and psychopathology. *Schizophrenia Bulletin* **3**, 105–120.

Roth, W.T. and Cannon, E.H. (1972). Some features of the auditory evoked response in schizophrenics. *Archives of General Psychiatry* **27**, 466–471.

Roth, W.T. and Tinklenberg, J.R. (1982). A convergence of findings in the psychophysiology of schizophrenia. *Psychopharmacology Bulletin* **18**, 78–83.

Roth, W.T., Horvath, T.B., Pfefferbaum, A. and Kopell, B.S. (1980a). Event-related potentials in schizophrenics. *Electroencephalography and Clinical Neurophysiology* **48**, 127–139.

Roth, W.T., Horvath, T.B., Pfefferbaum, A., Tinklenberg, J.R., Mezzich, J. and Kopell, B.S. (1979). Late event-related potentials and schizophrenia. In: H. Begleiter (Ed.) *Evoked Brain Potentials and Behavior*, pp. 499–515. New York: Plenum.

Roth, W.T., Pfefferbaum, A., Horvath, T.B., Berger, P.A. and Kopell, B.S. (1980b). P3 reduction in auditory evoked potentials of schizophrenics. *Electroencephalography and Clinical Neurophysiology* **49**, 497–505.

Saitoh, O., Niwa, S., Hiramatsu, K., Kameyama, T., Rymar, K. and Itoh, K. (1984). Abnormalities in late positive components of event-related potentials may reflect a genetic predisposition to schizophrenia. *Biological Psychiatry* **19**, 293–303.

Salzman, L.F., Klein, R.H. and Strauss, J.S. (1978). Pendulum eye tracking in remitted psychiatric patients. *Journal of Psychiatric Research* **14**, 121–126.

Shagass, C., Amadeo, M. and Overton, D.A. (1974). Eye-tracking performance in psychiatric patients. *Biological Psychiatry* **9**, 245–260.

Shagass, C., Roemer, R.A. and Amadeo, M. (1976). Eye-tracking performance and engagement of attention. *Archives of General Psychiatry* **33**, 121–125.

Shagass, C., Straumanis, J.J., Roemer, R.A. and Amadeo, M. (1977). Evoked potentials of schizophrenics in several sensory modalities. *Biological Psychiatry* **12**, 221–235.

Siddle, D., Stephenson, D. and Spinks, J.A. (1983). Elicitation and habituation of the orienting response. In: D. Siddle (Ed.) *Orienting and Habituation: Perspectives in Human Research*, pp. 109–182. New York: Wiley.

Simons, R.F. (1981). Electrodermal and cardiac orienting in psychometrically defined high-risk subjects. *Psychiatry Research* **4**, 347–356.

Simons, R.F. (1982). Physical anhedonia and future psychopathology: an electrocortical continuity? *Psychophysiology* **19**, 433–441.

Sokolov, E.N. (1963). *Perception and the Conditioned Reflex*. New York: Macmillan.

Spinks, J.A. and Siddle, D. (1983). The functional significance of the orienting response. In: D. Siddle (Ed.) *Orienting and Habituation: Perspectives in Human Research*, pp. 237–314. New York: Wiley.

Spitzer, R.L., Endicott, J. and Robins, E. (1978). Research Diagnostic Criteria: rationale and reliability. *Archives of General Psychiatry* **35**, 773–782.

Spohn, H.E. and Patterson, T. (1979). Recent studies of psychophysiology in schizophrenia. *Schizophrenia Bulletin* **5**, 581–611.

Straube, E.R. (1979). On the meaning of electrodermal nonresponding in schizophrenia. *Journal of Nervous and Mental Disease* **167**, 601–611.

Sturgeon, D., Turpin, G., Kuipers, L., Berkowitz, R. and Leff, J. (1984). Psychophysiological responses of schizophrenic patients to high and low expressed emotion relatives: a follow-up study. *British Journal of Psychiatry* **145**, 62–69.

Sutton, S. and Ruchkin, D.S. (1984). The late positive complex: advances and new problems. In: R. Karrer, J. Cohen and P. Tueting (Eds) *Brain and Information: Event-Related Potentials*, pp. 1–23. New York: New York Academy of Sciences.

Tarrier, N., Vaughn, C., Lader, M.H. and Leff, J.P. (1979). Bodily reactions to people and events in schizophrenics. *Archives of General Psychiatry* **36**, 311–315.

Turpin, G., Tarrier, N. and Sturgeon, D. (1988). Social psychophysiology and the study of biopsychosocial models of schizophrenia. In: H. Wagner (Ed.) *Social Psychophysiology and Emotion: Theory and Clinical Applications*, pp 251–272. Chichester: Wiley.

Van Dyke, J.L., Rosenthal, D. and Rasmuussen, P.V. (1974). Electrodermal functioning in adopted-away offspring of schizophrenics. *Journal of Psychiatric Research* **10**, 199–215.

Vaughn, C. and Leff, J.P. (1976). The influence of family and social factors on the course of psychiatric illness. *British Journal of Psychiatry* **129**, 125–137.

Vaughn, C., Snyder, K.S., Freeman, W., Jones, S., Falloon, I.R.H. and Liberman, R.P. (1982). Family factors in schizophrenic relapse: a replication. *Schizophrenia Bulletin* **8**, 425–426.

Wing, J.K., Cooper, J.E. and Sartorius, N. (1974). *The Measurement and Classification of Psychiatric Symptoms: An Instruction Manual for the PSE and CATEGO Programs*. London: Cambridge University Press.

Zahn, T.P. (1986). Psychophysiological approaches to psychopathology. In: M.G.H. Coles, E. Donchin and S.W. Porges (Eds) *Psychophysiology: Systems, Processes, and Applications*, pp. 508–610. New York: Guilford.

Zahn, T.P., Carpenter, W.T. and McGlashan, T.H. (1981a). Autonomic nervous system activity in acute schizophrenia. I. Method and comparison with normal controls. *Archives of General Psychiatry* **38**, 251–258.

Zahn, T.P., Carpenter, W.T. and McGlashan, T.H. (1981b). Autonomic nervous system activity in acute schizophrenia. II. Relationships to short-term prognosis and clinical state. *Archives of General Psychiatry* **38**, 260–266.

Chapter 14

Sexual Disorders

James H. Geer and Cathy Orman Castille

Department of Psychology,
Louisiana State University,
Baton Rouge,
Louisiana,
USA

ABSTRACT

The contributions of psychophysiology to the study of human sexuality, sexual disorders, and sexual dysfunctions are examined. Psychophysiological techniques of genital measurement employed in the evaluation and treatment of sexual disorders are discussed. Specific methods of genital measurement, including vaginal photometry and penile tumescence measurement techniques are described and evaluated. Problems encountered in genital measurement are described.

Handbook of Clinical Psychophysiology Edited by G. Turpin
© 1989 John Wiley & Sons Ltd

THE NATURE OF SEXUAL DISORDERS

'Sexual disorder' is a term which encompasses many different, often seemingly unrelated, behaviours. These disorders represent a broad spectrum of problems reflected in such common labels as 'impotence' or 'frigidity'. The simplicity of such terms is misleading, as the disorders themselves are quite complex. Unresolved issues in aetiology, gender differences, classification, assessment, and treatment of sexual disorders underscore the complexity of the problems. It is not the intention of this paper to address these broad issues, but rather to focus on how psychophysiology has been and may be relevant to understanding sexual disorders. We wish to note that the contribution of psychophysiology to our understanding of sexual disorders is, as yet, rather limited in scope.

Cultural and social concerns strongly influence the examination of human sexuality. These become accentuated when sexual disorders are considered. Ethical and moral considerations limit researchers in the type of data that can be gathered, and restrict the populations that can be studied. Longitudinal data are difficult to assess because of rapid changes in cultural attitudes and definitions, making it difficult to establish the incidence and prevalence of sexual disorders. Given these limitations, and the nature of the available data, it is clear that sexual disorders represent a significant problem in society today which cannot be ignored. On the other hand, advances in research methodology in sexuality have occurred, albeit at a slow pace, and the sex therapy literature has progressed from case studies to treatment comparisons using untreated controls.

Before addressing the topic of sexual disorders, it is helpful to gain a historical perspective. Attitudes towards sexuality and the interpretation of sexual events have changed through time, and definitions of normal and abnormal sexuality are not easily agreed upon. Societal attitudes towards sexuality at any given time greatly influence perceptions of sexual normality and abnormality. For instance, prior to the age of 'sexual enlightenment', a woman who complained of inorgasmia, or any other sexual dysfunction, would have been reassured that she was normal, virtuous, and decent (LoPiccolo and Heiman, 1978). During the early twentieth century, sexual normalcy was narrowly defined according to three major themes: intercourse was the only acceptable sexual activity; women had no sex drive; and pleasure during sex was to be kept at a minimum, lest dangerous forces undo civilization. Thus, suppression of sexual activity was the main method of prevention of sexual problems (LoPiccolo and Heiman, 1978). Kinsey's (Kinsey, Pomeroy and Martin, 1948; Kinsey, Pomeroy, Martin and Gebhard, 1953) work forced the recognition that non-coital sexual activities were widely practised (in spite of religious, legal, and cultural restrictions) and challenged the belief that intercourse was the only natural form of sexuality. Similarly, more recent cultural influences have affected the study of sexuality, by establishing a more accepting context. This has permitted the beginnings of the empirical study of sexuality.

We will now turn our attention to the problems that make up the sexual disorders. Because of the complexity of sexual disorders, aetiological references are not generally tied to the major classification systems, but, rather, the focus is upon the behaviour *per se*. The term 'psychosexual disorder', used in the third edition of the *Diagnostic and Statistical Manual of Mental Disorders* (DSM-III; American Psychiatric Association, 1980), assumes that the cause of the disorder is at least in part psychological. There is some consensus on the current and maintaining factors involved in sexual disorders, but very little is understood about the causes.

Kaplan (1979) points out that conceptualizations of the human sexual response have evolved over the years. Until recently, the sexual response was considered a single event, passing from desire to orgasm. All sexual problems were defined relatively simply by the terms 'impotence' or 'frigidity', depending on whether they appeared in men or women. Impotence included premature ejaculation, inability to achieve an erection, and inability to ejaculate; while frigidity included the lack of desire and inorgasmia (Qualls, 1978). It followed quite naturally from the unitary event model that treatment was also undifferentiated. This monistic view was challenged in the 1950s. Today, the sexual response is viewed as a multicomponent cycle with a range of treatments; however, the details of the components, as well as their treatments, are still under scrutiny and discussion.

Although several models have been proposed to describe the course of sexual arousal (Geer, Heiman and Leightenberg, 1984), the most widely used system is derived from the work of Masters and Johnson (1966). They proposed that the sexual response cycle is divided into four sequential phases: (1) excitement, (2) plateau, (3) orgasmic, and (4) resolution. Kaplan (1974) modified the Masters and Johnson (1966) model and suggested that the sexual response cycle could be conceptualized by only three phases: desire, excitement, and orgasm. Kaplan's (1974) tripartite system of classification was influential in formulating the eight different sexual dysfunctions presented in DSM-III (APA, 1980). It is assumed that sexual dysfunctions can arise at any point or points in the cycle, and they are described as such in the DSM-III (APA, 1980). Temporal and situational dimensions are also considered. Hence, the temporal dimension refers to whether the dysfunction is lifelong or acquired. An acquired dysfunction is one in which a period of normal functioning is followed by a period of dysfunction. Dysfunctions may also be situational or generalized, and partial or total. Situational dysfunctions are those limited to particular circumstances or partners, while generalized dysfunctions are exhibited across situations or partners. The partial/total dichotomy refers to the degree or frequency of the disturbance (APA, 1980). Sexual deviations are categorized in the DSM-III according to the broad headings of gender identity disorders, paraphilias, and other psychosexual disorders, which include ego-dystonic homosexuality. The next version of the DSM will certainly be changed, and one should not be lulled into assuming that current views are the 'correct' ones.

Aetiological theories of sexual disorders can be divided into several broad classifications. At the most global level, disorders are often divided into those caused by organic factors, such as illness or physiological malfunction, and those caused by psychological factors. Clearly, this organic/psychological dichotomy is too simplistic, because sexual behaviour, like other forms of behaviour, is the result of an interaction between the organism and the environment. The aetiology of sexual disorders, as perhaps with all behavioural events, involves complicated interrelationships among the individual's biological make-up, his/her environment, and his/her experiences.

Several different aetiological schema have been suggested. Malatesta and Adams (1984) classify aetiology temporally by discussing predisposing, precipitating, and maintaining factors. Kaplan (1974), on the other hand, describes aetiology according to psychoanalytic theory, learning theory, and dyadic theory. These classification schemes are not necessarily exclusive of one another, and in many ways compliment each other. It could be suggested that psychoanalytic theory primarily deals with predisposing factors, while learning theory and dyadic theory deal more with the precipitating and maintaining factors of sexual dysfunction.

What is needed is a workable and parsimonious method of conceptualizing sexual disorders. One way of approaching this goal is to think of all sexual disorders as deficits or excesses present within the sexual response cycle. A workable method of organizing these excesses and deficits is in terms of the stimulus–organism–response (S–O–R) model that has been successfully used in describing behavioural phenomena. Disorders in any one or more of these conceptual units will disrupt healthy, normal, highly integrated sexual functioning. This scheme makes explicit the interactional nature of sexuality, and forces recognition that influences on one component will affect the others.

An immediate issue faced by the proposed classification model is how to deal with cognitive factors. While cognitive processes are events within the organism, they are perhaps poorly represented as 'organismic factors' since they are influenced by environmental, physiological, and experiential events. There is ample evidence of the role of cognitive factors in sexuality (Geer and Fuhr, 1976; Heiman and Hatch, 1982). Additionally, cognitive factors have been proposed as being implicated in many sexual dysfunctions (Barlow, 1986). We view the S–O–R formulation as being in concert with a recognition of the role of cognitive factors in sexuality. Cognitive conceptualizations of emotion, such as those proposed by Lang (1984), provide a potentially useful tool for understanding the interactions among the components of sexuality. We believe that the clarification and understanding of cognitive events are crucial to understanding sexuality. Although the S–O–R formulation we propose to use in classifying disorders is, perhaps, too simplistic, it is strengthened by reference to cognitive events.

Using the S–O–R formulation to categorize sexual disorders, we suggest that those falling within the 'stimulus' category would include the paraphilias, in which arousal occurs to a sexual object or situation that is not normative. In paraphilias, sexual excitement is dependent upon the presence of stimuli which could be considered to be bizarre or unusual. The arousing stimuli can be either real or imagined. The DSM-III states that these acts or images generally involve preference for a non-human object for sexual arousal, repetitive sexual activity with humans involving real or imagined suffering or humiliation, or repetitive sexual activity with non-consenting partners. The idea of an excess must be applied here, since certain paraphilic stimuli would also be sexually arousing to a normal individual. The differentiating factor is that in the paraphilic individual, the stimulus *must* be present for arousal to occur.

Disorders involving the 'organismic' variable would include any anomalies occurring in the physiological component of the sexual response cycle. Until recently, organic factors in sexual dysfunction were believed to be extremely rare. This conclusion was due partly to the psychoanalytic heritage of sexuality, and partly to technological limitations. As a consequence, organismic factors were often overlooked in favour of experiential factors. This bias towards psychological explanations continues to influence assessment and, in doing so, limits the recognition of organicity. Nevertheless, the possible existence and influence of organic factors must be carefully examined in order to properly treat sexual disorders. Known organic factors that influence sexual functioning include genetic abnormalities, neurological disorders, surgical procedures, illness, endocrine disorders, vascular disorders, aging, and both recreational and medicinal drug usage.

Disorders of the 'response' component would include most of the psychosexual dysfunctions which are not primarily attributable to organic factors, and which do not fall into the classification of a paraphilia. Masters and Johnson (1970) coined the term 'sexual dysfunction' to describe sexual behaviours whose response qualities are considered to be deficient. The disorders contained in this category include problems of sexual desire or excitement, inhibition of orgasm, premature ejaculation, functional dyspareunia, and functional vaginismus. Sexual dysfunctions are described in terms of both qualitative and quantitative dimensions of the response, such as duration, latency, frequency, intensity, and elicitation threshold. Psychophysiology, which focuses upon responding, is a field well suited to the study of these parameters. We now turn to the description of specific psychophysiological techniques employed in the study of sexuality and sexual disorders.

PSYCHOPHYSIOLOGICAL TECHNIQUES EMPLOYED IN THE EVALUATION AND TREATMENT OF SEXUAL DISORDERS

Masters and Johnson's (1966) model of the sexual response cycle has served as a foundation for psychophysiological research. This work, which described both genital and non-genital changes in sexual arousal, gave initial direction to much subsequent psychophysiological research. Psychophysiological measures of the sexual response cycle have, at times, included both genital and extra-genital measurements. Extra-genital measures for the most part have not, however, been very helpful in uniquely defining the sexual response, or in differentiating sexual from non-sexual responses. The non-specific nature of measures such as heart rate, electrodermal activity (galvanic skin response), skin temperature, etc., make their use as independent indices of sexual arousal questionable (Hoon, 1979; Zuckerman, 1971). Masters and Johnson (1966) have described the non-genital physiological sexual response system in detail. Few studies have included both genital and extra-genital measures (see Rosen and Beck, in press). To date, direct genital measures appear to be much more appropriate to the examination of sexuality than non-genital measures. Nevertheless, extra-genital measures have been of value in painting the complete picture of sexual responding, and their importance should not be minimized. Multiple measures always strengthen research designs when their collection does not interfere with outcome. We ought to note, parenthetically, that measures of central nervous system activity hold promise (Rosen and Beck, in press) for the development of complete understanding of sexual responding.

Masters and Johnson (1966) described the two most widespread physiological responses in sexual arousal as being myotonia and vasocongestion. Although vasocongestion occurs in vascular response sites located throughout the body, the response is more specific to sexual arousal in the genitals. This is most obvious in the occurrence of erections in males and vaginal lubrication in females. The latter is believed to be a by-product of vasocongestion (Masters and Johnson, 1966). More research has been conducted utilizing genital measurement in males than in females, probably because of the wider awareness of the sexual response in the male, the relative ease of obtaining measures of the response, and cultural restraints on studying feminine sexuality. We will first discuss genital measurement in males, and then turn our attention to female genital measurement.

GENITAL MEASUREMENT IN MALES

Most studies of male sexual response have concentrated on the measurement of penile tumescence. Penile tumescence is the result of a complex interaction betwen the arterial and venous systems, the central, autonomic, and somatic nervous systems, and the hypothalamic–pituitary–gonadal axis (Rivard, 1982). In spite of the complexity of the mechanism of penile erection, rather straightforward approaches have been developed to quantify changes in penile tumescence. The two most commonly used techniques utilize either volumetric or circumferential measurements. Both types of measures have been shown to be sensitive to penile changes, and therefore represent an important index of sexual arousal. To date, volumetric and circumferential measures are commonly believed to be the most reliable methods of distinguishing sexual arousal from other types of arousal in the male. Temperature and photometric measures have also been recently developed to study penile changes but with, as yet, limited success.

The first major category of penile measurement device, allowing volumetric measurement, includes two main types: air and water plethysmographs. These operate by enclosing the penis in an air- or water-tight chamber. Changes in the volume of the penis result in fluid or air displacement, which is transduced and then recorded in a manner that can be calibrated in units of volume change. Freund (1963) and McConaghy (1967) have developed variations of the air-filled plethysmograph. We illustrate the device used by Freund (1963) in Figure 14.1. The water-filled plethysmograph developed by Fisher, Gross and Zuch (1965) was found to be excessively bulky and therefore has been used only infrequently (Rosen and Keefe, 1978). The air-filled device has

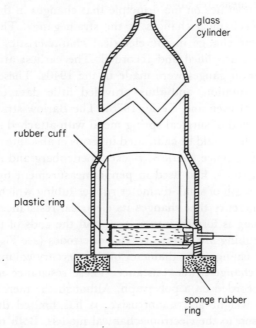

Figure 14.1. Freund's volumetric penile plethysmograph.

been utilized more frequently. However, the obtrusiveness of both varieties of volumetric instruments has limited their use. In addition to the sheer bulkiness of these plethysmographs, other problems exist, including confounds such as stimulation from the devices themselves and vulnerability to movement artifacts (Zuckerman, 1971).

Despite the drawbacks of volumetric plethysmographic devices, they have proven to be reliable, and more sensitive to volume changes than any other physiological method of penile measurement (Zuckerman, 1971). The relationship between circumferential change and volumetric change is not necessarily linear. Three-dimensional or volumetric changes describe the erection response more completely than any two-dimensional (circumferential) measurement (McConaghy, 1974). For example, Freund and Blanchard (1981) report that, in some subjects, tumescence begins with a decrease in circumference accompanied by penile elongation. They conclude that circumferential methods may not be sensitive to changes in the penis that occur early in the sexual response sequence.

The second major category of penile measurement device, allowing penile circumference measurement, typically involves some type of strain gauge placed around the penis. Strain gauges, as the name suggests, respond in a known manner to strain or stress placed upon them. Most circumference methods are either electromechanical or resistance strain gauges. The electromechanical type of strain gauge operates on the principle that changes in the diameter of the penis produce mechanical changes in the strain gauge. The mechanical changes yield a linear change in the electrical characteristics of the strain gauge which are then amplified and recorded. The earliest attempts to use electromechanical strain gauges were made in the 1940s. These gauges only recorded binary information, and thus provided little data on relative or absolute tumescence (Rosen and Keefe, 1978). The Barlow strain gauge (see Figure 14.2), constructed of surgical spring metal with attached strain gauges, produced recordings that could be calibrated in terms of absolute circumference and changes in circumference (Barlow, Becker, Leitenberg and Agras, 1970).

Resistance strain gauges, first used in penile measurement by Fisher *et al.* (1965), consist of a length of small-diameter rubber tubing which is filled with a material such as mercury that changes its electrical resistance proportional to its form. The tubing is formed into a loop, and the ends of the column of mercury within the tubing are pierced by two electrodes (see Figure 14.3). As penile circumference changes, the diameter of the mercury column in the loop changes, yielding a change in its resistance. These resistance measurements are amplified and recorded on a polygraph. Although the mercury-in-rubber strain gauge is lightweight and unobtrusive, it has limited durability and shelf-life in comparison to the electromechanical models. Both resistance and electromechanical gauges accurately detect and measure small changes in

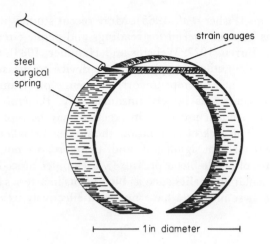

Figure 14.2. A schematic view of the Barlow strain gauge.

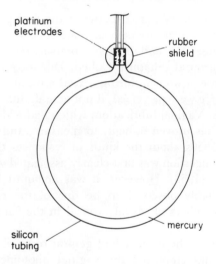

Figure 14.3. A schematic view of a mercury strain gauge.

penile circumference and can be readily calibrated to yield absolute measures of circumference.

Since one important factor in the mechanism of penile erection is a change in circulatory patterns, attempts to develop measures which reflect changes in the vascular system of the penis have been made. These have included the use of temperature and photometric measures of penile responding. Temperature-related measurements of tumescence are typically made by attaching a small thermistor to the dorsal surface of the penis. Initial attempts to utilize temperature as an indication of penile responding were less than satisfactory, due to methodological problems (Fisher *et al.*, 1965). More recent studies have shown fairly high correlations between thermistor readings and penile circumference measures (Solnick and Birren, 1977; Webster and Hammer, 1983).

Bancroft and Bell (1985) utilized a photometric device to measure penile arterial pulse amplitude. Their attempt to correlate penile pulse amplitude to circumference measurements was largely unsatisfactory. Bancroft and Bell (1985) suggest that independent processes in erection may be represented in the different measures. The lack of correlation should not be taken to mean that these measurements are not significant, and, therefore, are not worthy of further study. Measures of penile blood pressure via Doppler procedures have been used to assess vascular anomalies such as blood clots in arteries branching into the penis. As yet these measures have not been effectively used to index sexual arousal.

GENITAL MEASUREMENT IN FEMALES

Nearly one-quarter of a century passed between the first published report of an attempt at the objective measurement of male sexual arousal (Ohlmeyer, Brilmayer and Hullstrung, 1944) and the first promising reports of the measurement of female sexual arousal (Shapiro, Cohen, Dibianco and Rosen, 1968). Since the genital response of women during sexual arousal was not as obvious as the male erection, there were perceived, if not actual, difficulties in studying female genital responses. Vaginal lubrication, which had widely been observed during sexual arousal, has proven difficult to measure, and little was known during the 1940s and 1950s about the kinds of responses that needed to be assessed. Vaginal vasocongestion was first clearly associated with female sexual arousal by Kinsey *et al.* (1953). However, it was not until 1966 that vaginal vasocongestion was reliably observed to be one of the earliest and most consistent physiological indices of sexual arousal in the female (Masters and Johnson, 1966).

The most widely used of the measures of genital responding during sexual arousal in the female has employed the vaginal photometer. This device, developed by Sintchak and Geer (1975), measures changes in vaginal vascular response and consists of a clear plastic cylinder about the size and shape of a tampon, which contains a light source and a photoelectric transducer (see Figure 14.4). When placed in the vagina, the light source shines onto the vaginal lumen, and the transducer measures the amount of reflected light. The light reflected by the tissues is affected by changes in the vascular bed in the vaginal wall.

Both vaginal blood volume and pulse amplitude can be measured with the vaginal photometer. Vaginal blood volume is thought to represent blood pooling in the vagina, and is reflected in the direct current component of the photometer's output. Vaginal pulse amplitude, reflected in the alternating

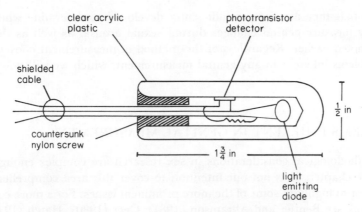

Figure 14.4. A schematic representation of a vaginal photometer.

current component of the output, represents the arrival of the pulse wave with each heartbeat. Both of these measures have been investigated as correlates of sexual arousal. There is evidence to suggest that vaginal pulse amplitude is the more sensitive of the two measures (Hatch, 1979).

While the vaginal photometer is currently the most popular of the female genital measurement devices, research into other methods continues. Cohen and Shapiro (1971) reported using a thermistor mounted on a cervical diaphragm to measure heat dissipation into vaginal tissues in order to index blood flow. Unfortunately, the device has not proven to be practical, because of its delicate nature and the fact that it requires individual fitting. A similar technique has been developed to measure vaginal temperature (Fugl-Meyer, Sjogren and Johannson, 1984). Of particular interest was the inclusion of a transmitting system in the circuitry of this device which allowed continuous measurement of temperature changes even during intercourse. Careful evaluation of this device is clearly warranted. Wagner and Levin (1978) have also attempted to measure vaginal blood flow by measuring the transcutaneous movement of oxygen through the vaginal surface. While very sophisticated, the device is expensive and intrusive. With design improvements, this methodology holds great promise because of its relationship to important physiological phenomena that occur during genital responding.

Other attempts have been made to develop physiological measures that can assess similar genital activity in both males and females. Bohlen and Held (1979) have developed a probe which is capable of measuring either vaginal or anal muscular activity during sexual arousal. Perhaps anal measures are similar between sexes. Thus far, this device has not been widely used. Another approach has been the use of thermography, which allows direct comparisons of surface temperature changes between the sexes (Seeley, Abramson, Perry, Rothblatt and Seeley, 1980). The problem with techniques that look at both sexes is that they are not yet sufficiently developed to determine whether or not they measure genital changes during sexual arousal as well as the techniques noted earlier. Regardless of the method of measurement chosen, there are problems inherent in any genital measurement, which we will now briefly address.

PROBLEMS INHERENT IN GENITAL MEASUREMENT

The methodological considerations in sex research are complex enough for a complete chapter. It is not our intention to cover this area comprehensively, but rather to highlight some of the more prominent issues. For a more complete discussion, see Bentler and Abramson (1981), Geer (1980), Hatch (1979) and Hoon (1979).

The interpretation of some measurements obtained from genital measuring devices is difficult. Many devices do not have an absolute scale that reflects physiological events. This means that difficult quantification decisions must be made. It is often necessary to use an arbitrary scale, such as estimating percentage of a full erection or millimetres of pen deflection when measuring vaginal pulse amplitude. Without calibration to known physiological events, obvious problems occur when attempts are made to compare data across subject groups or conditions. The issue is further complicated when attempts are made to compare male and female responses. For example, why should what appears to be a common measure like pen change be similar when considering penile and vaginal responses? Scaling methodologies must carefully address these problems.

Another major problem with genital measurement devices is that the device itself may result in stimulation either directly or 'psychologically', which could result in modified responses. This situation could quite obviously confound any conclusions drawn. In a similar vein, the demand characteristics of participation in any type of sex research should be seriously considered. Volunteer bias, while not invalidating findings, must be considered in evaluating outcomes (Wolchik, Spencer and Lisi, 1983). Problems of bias and reactivity to the conditions of measurement underscore the necessity for a continuing search for less invasive methods.

The study of sexual behaviour carries with it specific ethical responsibilities, over and above that involved in most research utilizing human subjects. The current concern over acquired immune-deficiency syndrome and other sexually transmitted diseases requires that instrumentation devices be sterilized to prevent the iatrogenic transmission of such diseases (Geer, 1978). Societal and cultural attitudes towards sexuality require that research be done in an especially safe and confidential manner. Researchers must be particularly sensitive to the emotional concerns of participants in sex research. The sex researcher must recognize that societal concerns and values strongly influence what questions can be addressed and the methodologies that can be used.

PSYCHOPHYSIOLOGICAL RESEARCH IN HUMAN SEXUALITY

The following section provides only a very brief outline of psychophysiological research in human sexuality. Most research has dealt with aspects of both basic research and clinical application, and has been comprehensively reviewed elsewhere (Geer, O'Donohue and Schorman, 1986). Heiman and Hatch (1982) note, however, that there have been relatively few attempts to integrate psychophysiology with studies of sex therapy. Two exceptions to this generalization are studies using biofeedback and the assessment or diagnosis of sexual disorders. Because of conflicting results (Bancroft, 1980), biofeedback has received little support as a useful treatment modality in sexual dysfunctions.

The use of psychophysiology in assessment of sexual functioning has shown promise but is still in the investigative stages. One clinical application which has found fairly widespread usage is in the psychophysiological assessment of penile function during sleep, in the attempt to rule out or confirm organicity in erectile disorders. Although controversial, another application that is said to have considerable promise is in the assessment of sex offenders. In this situation, the offender might be considered cured if he/she no longer experiences genital changes when exposed to stimuli associated with the offending situation.

We will now discuss more fully the use of psychophysiological techniques in the study of sexual disorders. It is important to emphasize again that the S–O–R formulation that we employ is merely a way of conceptualizing disorders of the sexual cycle, and that interactions among the components necessarily occur. A disruption in one component will affect the other components. It is also important to point out that even when a disorder neatly fits into the stimulus or organismic category, psychophysiological techniques are limited to measurement of responses. We may be able to make the inference that a disorder fits into the stimulus category by measurement of the response to different stimuli, or similarly, the organismic category by noting that an organismic variable contributes heavily to the response variance. We must take care that when considering a sexual disorder typically manifested symptomatically in the response component, that the stimulus and organismic features are not overlooked.

STIMULUS CATEGORY

Psychophysiological techniques have been utilized in the study of atypical sexual interests. Such techniques have been helpful in determining which stimuli an individual finds arousing. Some of the first work utilizing sexual psychophysiology with regard to clinical issues was intended to differentiate homosexual males from heterosexual males. Early studies showed that when males were shown erotic pictures of same-sex and opposite-sex individuals, their penile responses reflected their sexual preference (Freund, 1963; McConaghy, 1967). Similar designs have been used in the identification of paedophiles (Freund, 1967). In related research, a rape index scale was developed using penile tumescence. This scale reportedly differentiated sexually aggressive from non-aggressive males (Abel, Becker, Blanchard and Djenderedjian, 1978). Recently, however, the use of penile tumescence to identify and/or classify sex offenders has been brought into question. A study by Murphy, Krisak, Stalgaitis and Anderson (1984), found that penile tumescence measures did not differentiate between incarcerated rapists and incarcerated non-rapists. In attempting to explain the equivocal results of different studies, Freund and Blanchard (1981) conclude that penile tumescence is not a reliable tool for diagnosing erotic preferences, particularly when these preferences are those which an individual does not want to admit. Regardless, one of the most widespread uses of psychophysiology has been, and will likely continue to be, the assessment of stimulus factors in sexual disorders.

ORGANISMIC CATEGORY

There has been considerable attention focused on the differentiation between organic and psychological causes of sexual dysfunctions. These studies make up most of what we include in the organismic category. This is most clearly seen in the studies of nocturnal penile tumescence (NPT) in the aetiological differentiation of psychogenic and biological erectile failure (e.g. Fisher, Schiavi, Lear, Edwards, Davis and Witkin, 1975). It has been established that periods of rapid eye movement sleep are frequently accompanied by penile tumescence (Aserinsky and Kleitman, 1955). In the study of NPT, the individual's penile tumescence is monitored during sleep on one or more nights. If the male with erectile problems has nocturnal erections, it is then assumed that there is no physiological basis for the problem. Since the mechanism of erection works, it is then assumed that the problem is psychological, not physiological. Differential diagnosis in erectile failure is important to ensure that unnecessary surgery or inappropriate sex therapy is avoided. However, to complicate the issue, some researchers (i.e. Maddock, 1980) claim that there is no such thing as a totally organic cause of a sexual disturbance, while others question the value of NPT as a diagnostic tool (Wasserman, Pollak, Spielman and Weitzman, 1980), since NPT can occur in the presence of certain physiological conditions.

Investigations have begun to establish whether there are vaginal arousal patterns exhibited in sleeping women (Cohen and Shapiro, 1970; Fisher *et al.*,

1983). The nocturnal evaluation of vaginal circulatory patterns offers potential in identifying cases of sexual dysfunction in women in which organic factors are important (Rogers, Van de Castle, Evans and Critelli, 1985). At this time, however, there is no evidence that this search will prove fruitful.

Vaginal vasocongestive responses have been studied in relationship to the stages of the menstrual cycle. It has been suggested that the phase of the menstrual cycle is related to sexual responsiveness, with the highest rate of intercourse occurring at the time of ovulation (Udry and Morris, 1968). In one study, it was found that subjective–genital response correlations were higher in the luteal phase of the menstrual cycle (Schreiner-Engel, Schiavi and Smith, 1981). Anorgasmia and arousal dysfunctions in women have been studied utilizing the vaginal probe in an attempt to locate a physiological marker of female sexual dysfunction (Hoon, Coleman, Amberson and Ling, 1981). Hoon *et al.* (1981) have suggested that women with anorgasmia may not reach the levels of vaginal vasocongestion required for orgasm to occur. Although preliminary in scope, this research shows promise. Findings such as these, if replicated and expanded, may have implications for disorders of sexual desire. The influence of hormonal factors neatly fits the organismic category and is an area of study only barely touched upon.

RESPONSE CATEGORY

The issue of which topics should be discussed in the response category is somewhat arbitrary. Psychophysiological research uses response measures as the data of primary interest; however, these measures are often used to evaluate cognitive and behavioural phenomena. Sexual arousal, obviously a complicated phenomenon, has both physiological and cognitive components. The relationship between these two components and the behavioural aspects of sexuality is a complex and intriguing area of research that has implications for the sexual disorders.

Genital responding as it relates to the subjective (cognitive) experience of sexual arousal has been suggested to play a role in sexual dysfunction (Kaplan, 1974). Speiss, Geer and O'Donohue (1984) studied the relationship between subjective and genital responding in males diagnosed as premature ejaculators. Contrary to Kaplan's (1974) theoretical expectations, clinical and control subjects did not differ in the correlation between subjective and genital responding. There have been conflicting results concerning the correlation between subjective reports of sexual arousal and physiological arousal in non-clinical populations. Geer, Morokoff and Greenwood (1974) found no correlation, while others (Heiman, 1977; Henson, Rubin, Henson and Williams, 1977; Korff and Geer, 1983) have found significant correlations.

The effects of erotic stimuli on sexually functional and dysfunctional women have been studied with the use of vaginal photometry. In one representative study, differences were found between functional and dysfunctional women who were exposed to an erotic film, an erotic audiotape, and self-generated fantasy (Morokoff and Heiman, 1980). These differences were reflected in a non-significant correlation between physiological and subjective measures of arousal in the dysfunctional group prior to treatment, while a significant positive correlation was present in the functional group. The dysfunctional group exhibited a significant positive physiological/subjective correlation following formal sex therapy (Morokoff and Heiman, 1980).

It has been suggested that a wide range of variables affect the subjective/ physiological correlation, including methodological and subject variables. While as yet only briefly examined, this area of study may be important in understanding sexual disorders.

A different approach to this problem is the use of the habituation paradigm. In one study, it was found that the decrement in genital responding to repeated presentations of erotic stimuli was influenced by the same variables that affect habituation in other psychophysiological response systems (O'Donohue and Geer, 1985). Habituation to an erotic stimulus has been suggested as a model for explaining the sexual disorder commonly referred to as inhibited sexual desire. At this point in time, psychophysiology has more promise than reality in contributing to our understanding of response factors in sexual disorders.

There have been several studies evaluating the role of distraction in genital responding (Beck, Barlow, Sakheim and Abrahamson, in press; Geer, 1984). The findings indicate that distraction powerfully affects genital responding, and it has therefore been suggested as playing a role in sexual disorders. The implication is that the reduction in sexual response that is characteristic of erectile failure may stem from distractions produced by intrusive non-erotic thoughts. The research on this topic illustrates the potential that response measurement has for helping clarify issues that relate to sexual disorders, although at present, we must speak of promise rather than direct pay-off.

THE CONTRIBUTION OF PSYCHOPHYSIOLOGY TO THE STUDY OF HUMAN SEXUALITY

Human sexual functioning is difficult to study under the best of circumstances. Although animal studies have enriched the amount of knowledge available, animal models are insufficient to describe human sexuality. The complexity of human sexual functioning would appear to be heavily dependent upon cognitive processes that are missing in the animal model. To further complicate matters, the study of human sexuality is fraught with complications that are largely specific to this area. Psychophysiologists must contend with these limitations and constraints, and as a result, psychophysiology at present has contributed primarily to the assessment of sexual functioning and to addressing limited theoretical concerns. Only secondarily has there been a contribution to the outcome of sexual therapy.

Since direct physiological research in human sexuality encounters a host of problems, we must often rely on the more indirect methods of study. The rationale for conducting psychophysiological research is that it allows inferences to be made concerning the physiological workings of the phenomena under study. Although the methodology is available for the psychophysiological measurement of a variety of important sexual behaviours (e.g. self-stimulatory behaviours, fantasy, and responding to erotica), to date, there is no widely accepted method of measuring genital responding during sexual intercourse. Thus, a major limitation on the behaviour that can be studied must be acknowledged. Preliminary attempts have been made to develop such techniques in women (Fugl-Meyer *et al.*, 1984), but without major methodological advances, the study of genital responses during coitus remains an elusive goal. This means that a central behavioural event is not available to the psychophysiologist for study.

Another major area of concern is whether we are measuring the appropriate response. The relative emphasis on measures of sexual arousal should not discount the importance of other aspects of the sexual cycle. For example, in females does lubrication, temperature change, or vasodilation more accurately reflect the sexual response cycle? Perhaps some combination is the most appropriate measure. Likewise, in males, is penile buckling pressure (Karacan, Salis and Williams, 1978) a more behaviourally relevant parameter to measure than tumescence, or is there another, as yet unidentified measure that should be assessed? These issues are not easily addressed, and only with continued research will the answers to these questions become clearer.

There is more research utilizing psychophysiology in male sexual disorders than in female sexual disorders. There are multiple reasons for this, including societal influences, a relative lack of information on the female sexual response, and difficulties in genital assessment in females. This subject bias contributes to our limited understanding of the psychophysiology of sexual disorders.

The assessment of genital responses provides a unique opportunity in psychophysiology. Historically, psychophysiology was developed as a strategy in the study of emotion. The responses that were obtained were in general, only indirectly related in most instances to the behavioural aspects of emotion. In sexuality, however, genital responses are very often central to the behavioural phenomenon. This fact provides the opportunity for psychophysiology to contribute directly to sexuality. Elsewhere we (Geer *et al.*, 1986) have argued that this close relationship may allow sexuality to provide a setting in which basic questions concerning emotion and emotion theory may be fruitfully studied. The examination of this relationship has begun, and holds the real promise of providing insights into emotion (Steinberg, 1986).

FUTURE DEVELOPMENTS

There are many unanswered questions concerning sexuality that may be usefully studied using psychophysiological methodology. Variables such as sexual experience and practice, hormonal variations, detailed examination of menstrual cycle effects, and the effects of disease and treatment must be addressed. In addition, further study of the sexual response in both sexes, particularly at higher levels of arousal, is necessary.

In order to make dramatic progress, there is a crucial need for the development of less intrusive psychophysiological measures. For example, if thermography could be developed so that temperature could be measured while the subject is clothed, investigations with dramatically reduced intrusiveness could be undertaken. The development of more behaviourally relevant measures are also needed. For example, the availability of an adequate measure of vaginal lubrication would be useful. As noted, a start has been made toward measuring 'buckling strength' of the penis (Karacan *et al.*, 1978). This latter measure could be the genital measure of direct behavioural importance.

Researchers should increase efforts to combine genital measures with additional psychophysiological measures. In addition to concurrent subjective and behavioural measures, there is a need to assess activity in other aspects of the autonomic nervous system in order to gather the most information possible. The start made using electroencephalographic measures (e.g. Rosen and Beck, in press) warrants further study. Research on individual differences in sexual responding is an area which is in need of examination. Knowledge of individual differences within both normal and clinical populations is crucial to understanding sexuality. The variables that influence physiological/subjective agreement need further study. Patterns of physiological/subjective correlation may be dependent upon a wide range of variables such as the level of sexual arousal, and/or individual differences. The central role that cognitions play in sexuality makes it clear that this relationship merits further study. In conclusion, well-planned research using psychophysiological methodologies will contribute to our understanding of sexual disorders, and we are forced to report that this is a promise, not a reality.

REFERENCES

Abel, G.G., Becker, J.V., Blanchard, E.B. and Djenderedjian, A. (1978). Differentiating sexual aggressives with penile measures. *Criminal Justice and Behavior* **5**, 315–332.

American Psychiatric Association (1980). *Diagnostic and Statistical Manual of Mental Disorders*, 3rd edn. Washington, DC: APA.

Aserinsky, E. and Kleitman, N. (1955). Two types of ocular motility occurring in sleep. *Journal of Applied Psychology* **8**, 1–10.

Bancroft, J. (1980). Psychophysiology of sexual dysfunction. In: M. Lader (Ed.) *Hand-*

book of Biological Psychiatry: Brain Mechanisms and Abnormal Behaviour–Psychophysiology, pp. 359–392. New York: Marcel Decker.

Bancroft, J.H. and Bell, C. (1985). Simultaneous recording of penis diameter and penile arterial pulse during laboratory-based erotic stimulation in normal subjects. *Journal of Psychosomatic Research* **29**, 303–313.

Barlow, D.H. (1986). Causes of sexual dysfunction: the role of anxiety and cognitive interference. *Journal of Consulting and Clinical Psychology* **54**, 140–148.

Barlow, D.H., Becker, R., Leitenberg, H. and Agras, W.S. (1970). A mechanical strain gauge for recording penile circumference change. *Journal of Applied Behavior Analysis* **3**, 73–76.

Beck, J.G., Barlow, D.H., Sakheim, D.K. and Abrahamson, D.J. (in press). Shock threat and sexual arousal: the role of selective attention, thought content, and affective states. *Psychophysiology*.

Bentler, P.M. and Abramson, P.R. (1981). The science of sex research: some methodological considerations. *Archives of Sexual Behavior* **10**, 225–251.

Bohlen, J. and Held, J.P. (1979). An anal probe for monitoring vascular and muscular events during sexual response. *Psychophysiology* **16**, 318–323.

Cohen, H. and Shapiro, A. (1970). Vaginal blood flow during sleep. *Psychophysiology* **7**, 338 (Abstract).

Cohen, H. and Shapiro, A. (1971). A method for measuring sexual arousal in the female. *Psychophysiology* **8**, 251.

Fisher, C., Cohen, H., Schiavi, R., Davis, D., Furman, B., Ward, K., Edwards, A. and Cunningham, J. (1983). Patterns of female sexual arousal during sleep and waking: vaginal thermoconductance studies. *Archives of Sexual Behavior* **12**, 97–122.

Fisher, C., Gross, J. and Zuch, J. (1965). Cycle of penile erection synchronous with dreaming (REM) sleep. *Archives of General Psychiatry* **12**, 29–45.

Fisher, C., Schiavi, R., Lear, H., Edwards, A., Davis, D. and Witkin, A. (1975). The assessment of nocturnal REM erection in the differential diagnosis of sexual impotence. *Journal of Sex and Marital Therapy* **1**, 277–289.

Freund, K. (1963). A laboratory method for diagnosing predominance of homo- or hetero-erotic interest in the male. *Behavior Research and Therapy* **1**, 85–93.

Freund, K. (1967). Erotic preference in pedophilia. *Behavior Research and Therapy* **5**, 339–348.

Freund, K. and Blanchard, R. (1981). Assessment of sexual dysfunction and deviation. In: M. Hersen and A.S. Bellack (Eds) *Behavioral Assessment: A Practical Handbook*, pp. 427–455. New York: Pergamon.

Fugl-Meyer, A.R., Sjogren, K. and Johannson, K. (1984). A vaginal temperature registration system. *Archives of Sexual Behavior* **13**, 247–260.

Geer, J.H. (1978). Sterilization of genital devices. *Psychophysiology* **15**, 385.

Geer, J.H. (1980). Measurement of genital arousal in human males and females. In: I. Martin and P.H. Venables (Eds) *Techniques in Psychophysiology*, pp. 431–458. New York: Wiley.

Geer, J.H. (1984). Distraction effects on female sexual arousal: repeated exposure and possible recovery. Paper presented at the Meeting of the American Psychological Association, Toronto, Canada, August 1984.

Geer, J.H. and Fuhr, R. (1976). Cognitive factors in sexual arousal: the role of distraction. *Journal of Consulting and Clinical Psychology* **44**, 238–243.

Geer, J.H., Heiman, J.R. and Leightenberg, H. (1984). *Human Sexuality*. Englewood Cliffs, NJ: Prentice-Hall.

Geer, J.H., Morokoff, P. and Greenwood, P. (1974). Sexual arousal in women: the development of a measurement device for vaginal blood volume. *Archives of Sexual Behavior* **3**, 559–564.

Geer, J.H., O'Donohue, W.T. and Schorman, R.H. (1986). Sexuality. In: M.G.H. Coles, E. Donchin and S.W. Porges (Eds) *Psychophysiology: Systems, Processes and Applications*, pp. 407–427. New York: Guilford.

Hatch, J.P. (1979). Vaginal photoplethysmography: methodological considerations. *Archives of Sexual Behavior* **8**, 357–374.

Heiman, J. (1977). A psychophysiological exploration of sexual arousal patterns in females and males. *Psychophysiology* **14**, 266–274.

Heiman, J.R. and Hatch, J.P. (1982). Conceptual and therapeutic contributions of psychophysiology to sexual dysfunction. In: S.N. Haynes and L. Gannon (Eds) *Psychosomatic Disorders*, pp. 222–268. New York: Praeger.

Henson, D., Rubin, H., Henson, C. and Williams, J. (1977). Temperature change of the labia minora as an objective measure of human female eroticism. *Journal of Behavior Therapy and Experimental Psychiatry* **8**, 401–410.

Hoon, P.W. (1979). The assessment of sexual arousal in women. In: P. Hersen, R. Eisler and P. Miller (Eds) *Progress in Behavior Modification*, Vol. 7, pp. 1–61. New York: Academic Press.

Hoon, P.W., Coleman, E., Amberson, J. and Ling, F. (1981). A possible physiological marker of female sexual dysfunction. *Biological Psychiatry* **16**, 1101–1106.

Kaplan, H.S. (1974). *The New Sex Therapy*. New York: Bruner/Mazel.

Kaplan, H.S. (1979). *Disorders of Sexual Desire*. New York: Simon and Schuster.

Karacan, I., Salis, P.J. and Williams, R.L. (1978). The role of the sleep laboratory in diagnosis and treatment of impotence. In: R.L. Williams and I. Karacan (Eds) *Sleep Disorders: Diagnosis and Treatment*. New York: Wiley.

Kinsey, A., Pomeroy, W. and Martin, C. (1948). *Sexual Behavior in the Human Male*. Philadelphia: Saunders.

Kinsey, A., Pomeroy, W., Martin, C. and Gebhard, P. (1953). *Sexual Behavior in the Human Female*. Philadelphia: Saunders.

Korff, J. and Geer, J.H. (1983). The relationship between sexual arousal experience and genital response. *Psychophysiology* **20**, 121–127.

Lang, P.J. (1984). Cognition in emotion: concept and action. In: C. Izard, J. Kagan and R. Zajonc (Eds) *Emotion, Cognition, and Behavior*. New York: Cambridge University Press.

LoPiccolo, J. and Heiman, J. (1978). The role of cultural values in the prevention and treatment of sexual problems. In: C.B. Qualls, J.P. Wincze and D.H. Barlow (Eds) *The Prevention of Sexual Disorders: Issues and Approaches*, pp. 43–74. New York: Plenum.

Maddock, J.W. (1980). Assessment and evaluation protocol for surgical treatment of impotence. *Sexuality and Disability* **3**, 39–49.

Malatesta, V. and Adams, H. (1984). The sexual dysfunctions. In: H.E. Adams and P. Sutker (Eds) *Comprehensive Handbook of Psychopathology*, pp. 725–775. New York: Plenum.

Masters, W.H. and Johnson, V.E. (1966). *Human Sexual Response*. Boston: Little, Brown.

Masters, W.H. and Johnson, V.E. (1970). *Human Sexual Inadequacy*. Boston: Little, Brown.

McConaghy, N. (1967). Penile volume changes to moving pictures of male and female nudes in heterosexual and homosexual males. *Behavior Research and Therapy* **5**, 43–48.

McConaghy, N. (1974). Measurements of change in penile dimensions. *Archives of Sexual Behavior* **4**, 381–388.

Morokoff, P. and Heiman, J. (1980). Effects of erotic stimuli on sexually functional and dysfunctional women: multiple measures before and after sex therapy. *Behavior Research and Therapy* **18**, 127–137.

Murphy, W.D., Drisak, J., Stalgaitis, S. and Anderson, K. (1984). The use of penile tumescence measures with incarcerated rapists: further validity issues. *Archives of Sexual Behavior* **13**, 545–554.

O'Donohue, W.T. and Geer, J.H. (1985). The habituation of sexual arousal. *Archives of Sexual Behavior* **14**, 233–246.

Ohlmeyer, P., Brilmayer, H. and Hullstrung, H. (1944). Periodische Vorgange im Schlaf. *Pfluegers Archives Gesamte Physiologische* **248**, 559–560.

Qualls, C.B. (1978). The prevention of sexual disorders: an overview. In: C.B. Qualls, J.P. Wincze and D.H. Barlow (Eds) *The Prevention of Sexual Disorders: Issues and Approaches*, pp. 1–42. New York: Plenum.

Rivard, D. (1982). Anatomy, physiology, and neurophysiology of male sexual function. In: A. Bennett (Ed.) *Management of Male Impotence*, pp. 1–25. Baltimore: Williams and Wilkins.

Rogers, G.S., Van de Castle, R.L., Evans, W.S. and Critelli, J.W. (1985). Vaginal pulse amplitude response patterns during erotic conditions and sleep. *Archives of Sexual Behavior* **14**, 327–342.

Rosen, R.C. and Beck, J.G. (1988). *Sexual Psychophysiology: Concepts and Methods in Laboratory Sex Research*. New York: Guilford.

Rosen, R.C. and Keefe, F.J. (1978). The measurement of human penile tumescence. *Psychophysiology* **15**, 366–376.

Schreiner-Engel, P., Schiavi, R. and Smith, H. (1981). Female sexual arousal: relation between cognitive and genital assessments. *Journal of Sex and Marital Therapy* **7**, 256–267.

Seeley, T.T., Abramson, P.R., Perry, L.B., Rothblatt, A.B. and Seeley, D.M. (1980). Thermographic measurement of sexual arousal: a methodological note. *Archives of Sexual Arousal* **9**, 77–85.

Shapiro, A., Cohen, A., Dibianco, P. and Rosen, G. (1968). Vaginal blood flow changes during sleep and sexual arousal. *Psychophysiology* **4**, 394 (Abstract).

Sintchak, G. and Geer, J.H. (1975). A vaginal plethysmograph system. *Psychophysiology* **12**, 113–115.

Solnick, R.L. and Birren, J.E. (1977). Age and male erectile responsiveness. *Archives of Sexual Behavior* **6**, 1–9.

Speiss, W., Geer, J.H. and O'Donohue, W. (1984). Premature ejaculation: a psychophysiological and psychophysical investigation of ejaculatory latency. *Journal of Abnormal Psychology* **94**, 242–245.

Steinberg, J.L. (1986). The psychology of sexual arousal: an information processing analysis. Unpublished doctoral dissertation, State University of New York, Stony Brook.

Udry, J.R. and Morris, N.M. (1968). Distribution of coitus in the menstrual cycle. *Nature* **220**, 593–596.

Wagner, G. and Levin, R. (1978). Oxygen tension of the vaginal surface during sexual stimulation in the human. *Fertility and Sterility* **30**, 50–53.

Wasserman, M., Pollak, C., Spielman, A. and Weitzman, E. (1980). Theoretical and technical problems in the measurement of nocturnal penile tumescence for the differential diagnosis of impotence. *Psychosomatic Medicine* **42**, 575–585.

Webster, J.S. and Hammer, D. (1983). Thermistor measurement of male sexual arousal. *Psychophysiology* **20**, 111–115.

Wolchik, S.A., Spencer, S.L. and Lisi, I.S. (1983). Volunteer bias in research employing vaginal measures of sexual arousal. *Archives of Sexual Behavior* **12**, 399–408.

Zuckerman, M. (1971). Physiological measures of sexual arousal in the human. *Psychological Bulletin* **75**, 297–329.

Chapter 15

Hypertension

Iris B. Goldstein

Department of Psychiatry,
University of California,
Los Angeles,
California 90024,
USA

ABSTRACT

Methods and problems in recording blood pressure are discussed. Contributions of psychophysiology to the understanding of hypertension are reviewed in terms of the following: studies of anger and Type A behaviour; stress response of hypertensives and individuals with a family history of hypertension; and effects of behavioural treatment on blood pressure control.

Handbook of Clinical Psychophysiology Edited by G. Turpin
© 1989 John Wiley & Sons Ltd

INTRODUCTION

Hypertension is a major life-threatening disorder which affects between 10 and 20% of the adult population (Swales, 1984). It has been defined as chronically elevated blood pressure in excess of 160/95 mmHg (World Health Organization, 1978). For some patients hypertension can be traced to clearly definable causes such as certain drugs and chemicals, diseases of pregnancy, and organic diseases such as kidney dysfunction, coarctation of the aorta, and adrenal disorders. In 96–99% of cases the causes cannot be clearly identified, and the disorder is referred to as essential or primary hypertension (Gross, Pisa, Strasser and Zanchetti, 1984). In spite of the fact that the precise causes of hypertension have not been identified, it is known that multiple psychological, physiological, behavioural, dietary, and other factors contribute to its aetiology. Both aetiology and the related issue of epidemiology have been discussed in a number of reviews (Epstein, 1983; Paul, 1975; Rose, 1985; Swales, 1984).

Consideration of hypertension as a major health problem stems not only from its prevalence but also from the risk it carries towards cardiovascular and cerebrovascular diseases. It is one of three major risk factors for heart attack and stroke (the others are raised cholesterol levels and cigarette smoking) and is an accurate predictor of the later development of these conditions (Beevers, 1983). It has been estimated that hypertensives have more than twice the likelihood of developing peripheral artery disease, 3 times the incidence of coronary disease, 5 times as much congestive failure, and 8 times as much cerebrovascular disease. Not only can hypertension directly lead to death, but it also causes approximately one-third of deaths from coronary attacks and strokes (Kannel, 1977). In general, the risk of developing either fatal or non-fatal complications is directly related to level of blood pressure (Freis, 1974). For each increment of blood pressure above 100/60 mmHg, there is a corresponding increase in death risk from a variety of disorders (Eyer, 1975).

In discussing hypertension, this chapter will highlight some of the problems frequently encountered in the recording of blood pressure, as well as describe some commonly used methods for assessing blood pressure. There will also be a review of hypertension research in terms of three major areas, all of which underscore the important contributions of psychophysiology. The first of these involves personality studies in the areas of anger and Type A behaviour. A second area of research centres around the response of hypertensives and individuals with a family history of hypertension to various laboratory stressors. Finally, there will be a discussion of studies concerning the effects of various behavioural treatments on the control of blood pressure in hypertensives.

PSYCHOPHYSIOLOGICAL ASSESSMENT OF BLOOD PRESSURE

PROBLEMS IN ASSESSMENT

In studies of hypertensives in the psychophysiological literature, several different types of measurement techniques are frequently utilized. These can range from estimates of catecholamines and sodium levels, to measures of sympathetic functions such as the electrodermal response. Although a number of measures of cardiovascular functioning (see Larsen, Schneiderman and Pasin, 1986; Tursky and Jamner, 1982) are relevant to this chapter, emphasis will be placed on the recording of the blood pressure response itself.

When one records blood pressure, there are a number of sources of variance that can occur to distort the readings. To the extent that many of these sources are under the control of the clinician or the experimenter, efforts should be made to reduce them as much as possible. One method of increasing the reliability of blood pressure measurement is to follow the suggested guidelines for recording blood pressure, including recommendations for position and state of the subject, cuff size, rate of deflation of cuff, etc. (for details see Gross *et al.*, 1984; North, 1981; Petrie, O'Brien, Littler and De Swiet, 1986). It is also possible to reduce the variability in blood pressure measurement by controlling physical activity, smoking, caffeine, alcohol intake, and the effects of eating (see Shapiro, Mainardi and Surwit, 1977). Blood pressure swings in response to daily (Weber, Drayer, Nakamura and Wyle, 1984) and seasonal variations (Brennan, Greenberg, Miall and Thompson, 1982) should be accounted for. When recording blood pressure in women, one should be aware of variations in blood pressure which are related to different phases of the menstrual cycle (Kelleher, 1986). Many errors, both random and systematic, can be reduced by the replication of measurements (Rose, 1980).

METHODOLOGY

Standard Techniques

Standard blood pressure measurement is based on the occluding cuff technique and involves apparatus consisting of a manometer, cuff, inflation–deflation device, and a stethoscope (Kirkendall, Burton, Epstein and Freis, 1967). This technique is accurate and reliable for use in most settings. Either a mercury or an aneroid manometer may be used, although it is essential that the aneroid meter is periodically recalibrated (Petrie *et al.*, 1986). In spite of widespread usage, the limitations of having to rely on a few measurements have prompted investigators to utilize a number of other blood pressure devices.

Random-Zero Recorders

The Hawksley Random Zero and the London School of Medicine sphygmo-manometers both provide 'blind' readings, thereby avoiding observer bias (Rose, 1980). The Hawksley, a simple modification of the conventional mercury instrument, is used more often, because it is less cumbersome and easier to move around than the London machine. While the Hawksley machine compares well with the mercury column device (Labarthe, Hawkins and Remington, 1973), a source of error sometimes occurs due to the overinflation needed to compensate for the unknown zero level (Barker, Hediger, Katz and Bowers, 1984).

Ambulatory Measurement

The primary advantage of ambulatory recorders over the standard cuff device is their capability for providing repeated blood pressure readings over long time periods while an individual is engaged in normal activities. Such recordings are not only more representative than those yielded by the standard clinical method but also more accurately reflect the degree of concomitant target organ damage and are predictive of cardiovascular morbidity secondary to hypertension (Mancia, 1983; Rion, Waeber, Graf, Jaussi, Porchet and Brunner, 1985).

Ambulatory devices can either be direct (intra-arterial) or indirect (non-invasive) and usually record blood pressure and heart rate. Direct methods record blood pressure continuously with each heartbeat and provide a degree of precision that exceeds that of any other technique for the assessment of blood pressure. Because of its invasive nature, however, the direct recording of blood pressure has limited use and has generally been confined to research settings in Great Britain (Horan, 1985). While not as accurate as direct methods, non-invasive ambulatory devices are safer, more comfortable, and sufficiently accurate to provide clinically valid readings. The following should be noted, however: none of these recorders works with every patient; they must be calibrated against conventional sphygmomanometers for a given patient; and inaccurate readings can result from movement artifact (Pickering, Harsh-field, Devereux and Laragh, 1985).

Home Blood Pressure Monitors

A recent trend is for patients to purchase blood pressure monitors and record their blood pressures at home. Home recordings provide more information on blood pressure patterns, give patients active participation in their own treatment, help in drug compliance, and can be an important part of behavioural treatment (Carnahan and Nugent, 1975). Home monitors vary from mercury and aneroid devices used in conjunction with a standard stethoscope to newer electronic machines. While the stethoscope methods are the most accurate, they are dependent upon a patient's skill and are subject to observer bias. The easier usage and relative low cost of electronic monitors have led to a surge in their sales in the last few years. However, because of their sensitivity, electronic machines are likely to become inaccurate over time, a situation which can be aided by periodic calibrations (Grissom, Gust and Olson, 1986). Because of added features, such as digital output, a printer, and good agreement with a random-zero sphygmomanometer, some electronic machines, such as the Copal UA-251, have been recommended (Steptoe and Molineux, 1986).

Other Measures of Blood Pressure

Indirect tracking methods monitor blood pressure on a continuous basis but utilize surface techniques rather than intra-arterial recording. Among these tracking methods (see Tursky and Jamner, 1982), the constant-cuff (Shapiro, Tursky, Gershon and Stern, 1969) and the tracking-cuff (Shapiro, Greenstadt, Lane and Rubinstein, 1981) systems are probably the most frequently utilized in psychophysiological research and have both been validated against intra-arterial recordings. While the tracking-cuff can assess changing blood pressure trends over a series of beats, there is considerable lag with large blood pressure changes.

Pulse wave velocity and pulse transit time have been suggested as measures of blood pressure change but seem to be related more to sympathetic tone than to actual blood pressure (Larsen *et al.*, 1986). Some investigators have recommended specific automatic devices such as the Arteriosonde recorder, which operates on the Doppler principle from an ultrasound signal (Rose, 1980), and the Dinamap monitor, which measures oscillations in cuff pressure (Baker, 1986). However, when these machines were tested against the mercury column and random-zero machines, there were problems with accuracy, and neither of the methods could be accepted unequivocally. Furthermore, it has been strongly recommended that neither the Dinamap, Arteriosonde, nor any other blood pressure device be used interchangeably with one another (see Barker *et al.*, 1984; Labarthe *et al.*, 1973; Rubin, McLean and Reid, 1980).

PSYCHOPHYSIOLOGICAL RESEARCH RELEVANT TO HYPERTENSION

In the hypertension literature there are three basic areas of potential interest to the clinician which have been investigated by psychophysiologists and which will be discussed. One area, that of personality theory, has been particularly fruitful in generating research on concepts of anger and hostility and Type A behaviour as related to hypertension. A second area has been concerned with the response to stress by hypertensives and individuals with a family history of hypertension. Finally, of particular relevance to the clinician are studies aimed at the control of blood pressure by means of such behavioural treatments as biofeedback and relaxation.

PERSONALITY THEORY

Anger and Hostility

In spite of the fact that attempts to associate hypertension with personality have not always been successful (see Goldstein, 1981; Harrell, 1980), hostility and anger (terms that will be used interchangeably here) have emerged as important factors in the psychological literature (Diamond, 1982). For almost 50 years, since Alexander (1939) first described hypertensives as being incapable of overtly expressing anger, investigators have pursued this topic and sometimes reported negative evidence for this hypothesis (Mann, 1977; McDonough, 1964; Ostfeld and Lebovits, 1959; Pilowsky, Spalding, Shaw and Korner, 1973). Early psychophysiological studies added fuel to this controversy by describing distinctive physiological patterns accompanying different emotional states (Ax, 1953; Funkenstein, King and Drolette, 1954). Hokanson and Burgess (1962) reported that the suppression of anger during a frustrating task led to sustained systolic blood pressure and an elevation in heart rate, but once the aggression was expressed there was a return to pre-frustration levels. Using emotive images, Schwartz, Weinberger and Davidson (1981) found that there was a specific physiological pattern of anger that was associated with an increase in diastolic blood pressure, high peripheral resistance, and increased baroreceptor firing.

Investigating urban blacks, Naditch (1974) suggested that there was some underlying hostility associated with chronic frustration among hypertensive males. In a carefully executed study of blacks and whites in four areas of Detroit, a strong relationship was found to exist between suppressed hostility and high blood pressure, both of which were prevalent among black males in high stress areas (Harburg, Erfurt, Hauenstein, Chape, Schull and Schork, 1973).

The relationship between suppressed anger and blood pressure appears to be related to a number of variables. For example, mild hypertensives with high renin levels were found to have a high level of unexpressed anger when compared with normal-renin mild hypertensives and normotensive controls (Esler *et al.*, 1977). Cottington, Matthews, Talbott and Kuller (1986) reported that the prevalence of hypertension in a random sample of factory workers was highest among men who suppressed anger and reported high job stress but low among men who suppressed anger and reported low levels of job stress. Furthermore, in a recent study of 507 hypertensive and normotensive subjects, systolic (but not diastolic) blood pressure was related to suppressed anger (Dimsdale, Pierce, Schoenfeld, Brown, Zusman and Graham, 1986). Gerardi, Blanchard, Andrasik and McCoy (1985) found that a group of hypertensives whose blood pressure was consistently elevated both at home and in the physician's office had higher scores on measures of anger and hostility than office responders or a group whose blood pressure was only high at home. Confirmatory results were obtained by Schneider, Egan, Johnson, Drobny and Julius (1986), who indicated that borderline hypertensives whose blood pressure remains high at home are more likely to report more angry feelings in response to time pressure and to suppress anger more than a comparable group whose home blood pressure returns to normal.

Confirming the early findings of Schachter (1957), it was reported that patients with essential hypertension had more anger, anxiety, and guilt than patients with secondary hypertension or normotensive controls. Following mental arithmetic and isometric handgrip, subjects with high levels of anxiety and anger responded with increased norepinephrine and systolic blood pressure (Sullivan *et al.*, 1981a). An exaggerated pressor response to laboratory stressors was associated with more anger, regardless of whether subjects were mild or transient hypertensives or normotensives (Steptoe, Melville and Ross, 1984). Compared to borderline hypertensives without suppressed aggression and normotensives with or without suppressed aggression, borderline hypertensives who suppressed aggression had higher heart rates and diastolic blood pressure during rest and mental stress and higher norepinephrine responses to stress (Perini, Müller, Rauchfleisch, Battegay and Bühler, 1986).

Type A Research

Because elevated blood pressure is a major determinant of coronary heart disease, the research of Friedman and Rosenman (1959) on an overt behaviour pattern associated with a high prevalance of coronary heart disease (Type A) is relevant to the study of hypertension. Furthermore, Type A behaviour bears a relationship to hostility, in that hostility is an important component of the Type A scale. Although recent studies have indicated that the relationship between Type A behaviour and resting blood pressure is weak and inconsistent, Type A individuals generally respond to stressful situations with marked increases in heart rate and blood pressure, particularly when confronted with complex psychomotor or verbal tasks (see review by Surwit, Williams and Shapiro, 1982).

If cardiovascular reactivity to challenging situations is a risk factor for hypertension as well as a characteristic of Type A individuals, then Type A behaviour itself may play some role in predicting whether or not an individual will develop hypertension. Although studies on this topic are limited, Type A scores for female, but not male, college students were associated with a family history of hypertension (Waldron *et al.*, 1980). Some relationship between Type A behaviour and hypertension has been reported in a few studies of women (Rosenman and Friedman, 1961; Shekelle, Schoenberger and Stamler, 1976). In other studies on hypertensives (Steptoe *et al.*, 1984) and individuals with a family history of hypertension (Hastrup, Kraemer, Hotchkiss and Johnson, 1986; Hastrup, Light and Obrist, 1982), blood pressure reactivity to laboratory stressors was found to be unrelated to Type A scores.

Overview

Although there are conflicting results, the preponderance of evidence supports a relationship between hypertension and hostility, particularly with regard to the concept of suppressed anger. Some clarity to this issue may come from not viewing all hypertensives as the same and in perceiving anger in terms of different patterns and expressions. Manuck, Morrison, Bellack and Polefrone (1985a) reported that during role playing a group of hypertensives judged to be more assertive displayed cardiac output and systolic pressor responses that were greater than normotensives and a less assertive group of hypertensives. Lesser assertion in hypertensives was associated with more of a diastolic blood pressure response, brought about by changes in peripheral resistance. With regard to Type A behaviour, there is no strong evidence that most hypertensives display such behaviour. Since Type A individuals do not seem to be particularly likely to develop hypertension, Steptoe *et al.* (1984) have hypothesized that coronary-prone behaviour and cardiac pathology are linked through catecholamines or regional vasomotor activity rather than through blood pressure reactivity.

STUDIES OF REACTIVITY

Hypertensives

A substantial portion of the literature has been concerned with the response of hypertensives to stress and the extent to which these reactions to various stimuli may differ from those of normotensives. The basic assumption of these investigations has been that patients with elevated blood pressure are also hyper-reactive in response to a variety of stimuli. Although not always well controlled, studies utilizing interview techniques have shown that, while most individuals respond to topics of conflict with rises in blood pressure, hypertensives exhibit much greater increases, with a slower return to baseline (Wolf, Cardon, Shepard and Wolff, 1955). Blood pressure elevations were particularly prevalent during strong personal involvement (Hardyck, Singer and Harris, 1962; Williams, Kimball and Williard, 1972), such as in discussions involving self-references (Innes, Miller and Valentine, 1959) or topics like personal failure or loss of status (Adler, Hermann, Schäfer, Schmidt, Schonecke and Vexküll, 1977).

Hines and Brown (1933) were among the first to demonstrate the blood pressure response to a cold pressor stimulus, which was more prolonged in patients with essential hypertension. A fairly common mental stressor, performance of arithmetic under duress, led to increases in blood pressure that persisted longer in hypertensives than among normotensives (Brod, Fencl, Hejl and Jurka, 1959) and showed a protracted fall at the end of the task (Baumann, Ziprian, Gödicke, Hartrodt, Naumann and Läuter, 1973). The exaggerated blood pressure response of hypertensives has also been demonstrated during exercise (Groen *et al.*, 1977), to a set of complex visual puzzles (Nestel, 1969), and to a variety of stimuli in sequence (Shapiro, 1961). Engel and Bickford (1961) found that hypertensives reacted to any stressor with a maximal blood pressure response, regardless of the stimulus.

In spite of evidence showing that hypertensives exhibit elevated responses to stressful stimuli, failure to clearly differentiate hypertensives and normals was found with a cold pressor stimulus (Voudoukis, 1978) and with handgrip, mental arithmetic, and the Stroop test (colour/word interference) (Fredrikson, Dimberg, Frisk-Holmberg and Ström, 1982; Sullivan *et al.*, 1981b). Other investigators have found that the results vary with the particular stimulus, as well as with the degree of severity of the hypertension. Steptoe *et al.* (1984) reported that mild hypertensives had greater systolic and diastolic reactions than normotensives to conditions demanding active behavioural coping (the Stroop test and a video game) as compared with a passive condition (a distressing movie). Transient hypertensives with an initial high reading exhibited exaggerated diastolic and heart rate responses during active stimulus conditions. Increased diastolic blood pressure readings were also found in borderline hypertensives during mental arithmetic (Jern, 1982) and the Stroop test, but during orthostatic stress and cold pressor testing, borderline and stable hypertensives and normotensives exhibited similar blood pressures (Eliasson, Hjemdahl and Kahan, 1983).

The response to orthostatic stress implies that altered baroreceptor sensitivity may be a mechanism in the development of hypertension. McCrory, Klein and Rosenthal (1982) noted that increases in both norepinephrine and blood pressure were blunted in young adults (aged 7–20 years) with sustained and borderline hypertension upon change to upright posture. Similar abnormalities among borderline hypertensives have been noted by others (Hull, Wolthuis, Cortese, Longo and Triebwasser, 1977; Safar, Weiss, Levenson, London and Milliez, 1973).

There is evidence that individuals, such as borderline hypertensives, who exhibit symptoms of early hypertension may differ physiologically from hypertensives with established hypertension. Fredrikson and Engel (1985) demonstrated that although patients with established and borderline hypertension had higher blood pressure responses to a signalled reaction-time task than normals, the borderline patients showed skin conductance levels which exceeded the levels of the other two groups. Schulte, Rüddel, Jacobs and von Eiff (1986) found not only stronger systolic and diastolic reactions to mental stress in borderline hypertensives, but greater increases in heart rate and cardiac output, as well as decreases in total peripheral resistance. These findings are consistent with the concept of increased sympathetic arousal to stress among mild and borderline hypertensives. Fredrikson and Engel's (1985) data suggest that there is an exaggerated response among hypertensives and borderlines that is specific to the cardiovascular system but not exhibited consistently in the electrodermal response. While there are indications of greater cardiovascular responsivity to stressors among some borderline hypertensives, these results are not unequivocal (see Falkner, 1986; Frohlich, 1986; Lund-Johansen, 1986).

Normotensives with a Family History of Hypertension

According to the Report of the Task Force on Blood Pressure Control in Children (1977), parental hypertension is one of the primary risk factors for hypertension. Falkner, Onesti, Angelakos, Fernandes and Langman (1979) reported that in response to a stressful mental arithmetic task, the adolescent offspring of adults with hypertension manifested greater systolic, diastolic, and heart rate responses and higher plasma catecholamine levels than did offspring of normotensive parents. Lawler and Allen (1981) found that children (11–12 years old) of hypertensive parents had higher levels of systolic blood pressure and resting heart rate, and a tendency to greater diastolic reactivity. Ninth and tenth graders with familial risk of hypertension were best typified by diminished pulse pressure due to lower systolic blood pressure, higher diastolic blood pressure, and reduced systolic response to mental stress (Ewart, Harris, Zeger and Russell, 1986). Hastrup et al. (1986), in looking at the children and grandchildren of hypertensive individuals, found that only the middle-aged first generation offspring exhibited hyper-responsivity of heart rate during stressful reaction-time and spelling tasks. The second generation children (aged 7–10 years), perhaps because they were younger than children in other studies, did not exhibit the same responsiveness to stressors as their parents.

Light and Obrist (1980) reported that the incidence of parental hypertension was highest among normotensive college students who demonstrated high heart rate reactivity to a shock avoidance task and occasional systolic levels of 135 mmHg or greater. When compared with sons of normotensive parents, sons of hypertensive parents had elevated systolic blood pressure during frustrating cognitive tasks but no differences in heart rate and diastolic blood pressure (Manuck, Giordani, McQuaid and Garrity, 1981; Manuck and Proietti, 1982). In a more recent study, Manuck, Proietti, Rader and Polefrone (1985b) found that heart rate and diastolic (but not systolic) blood pressure rose during mental arithmetic in the sons of hypertensive parents.

Researchers have theorized that stressors that encourage active coping lead to greater heart rate and blood pressure increases than other kinds of stressors (Light, 1981). In line with this concept, Ditto (1986) reported that systolic differences between young men with and without a family history of hypertension are present during mental arithmetic and the Stroop test but not in response to handgrip. Furthermore, only those individuals with a parental history of hypertension who performed well on the Stroop test exhibited greater heart rate responses to the task than similar high-performance men without such a history. Although men with a positive family history of hypertension had higher systolic blood pressure and heart rate than men with a negative family history during baseline and two different stressors (cold pressor and reaction time), the responses of the groups were most divergent during the reaction-time task (Hastrup *et al.*, 1982). Gintner, Hollandsworth and Intrieri (1986) demonstrated that heart rate and both systolic and diastolic blood pressure were greater in men with parental hypertension during a reaction-time task than in men with normotensive parents.

Studies of children (Remington, Lambarth, Moser and Hoobler, 1960) and young adult males (Weipert, Shapiro and Suter, 1987) have indicated an aberrant blood pressure and heart rate response during orthostatic stress in offspring of hypertensive parents, which could be the result of an alteration of baroreceptor sensitivity or some other abnormal vascular properties (Brown, 1981). Further indication of a possible abnormality comes from a study by Light, Koepke, Obrist and Willis (1983), which showed that, during competitive tasks, sodium excretion decreased in hypertensive offspring who had high heart rates. The control group (negative family history) exhibited increased sodium excretion. After 14 days of oral salt loading, Falkner, Onesti and Angelakos (1981b) reported that there was little effect on the offspring of normotensives, whereas hypertensive offspring exhibited higher baseline blood pressure, greater blood pressure elevation, and decreased heart rate in response to mental arithmetic. The failure of the kidneys to maintain blood pressure within normal limits by excreting sodium and water may be an important factor in the establishment of hypertension (Guyton, Coleman, Crowley, Schell, Manning and Norman, 1972).

Overview

Apparently, the critical factor in distinguishing hypertensives from normotensives is not just the level of response but the prolonged reaction that hypertensives have to stressful stimuli (Goldstein, 1981). Furthermore, although various stressors elicit blood pressure increases, they do so by different haemodynamic mechanisms. For example, Andrén and Hansson (1981) found that, whereas the cold pressor task increased total peripheral resistance, mental arithmetic led to elevation in heart rate and cardiac output. The results of studies of borderline hypertensives are similar to family history research, in that both kinds of investigations point to increases, not only in blood pressure, but in heart rate reactivity, as well. In spite of this, inconsistency exists in the literature (see reviews by Falkner, 1986; Krantz and Manuck, 1985) with regard to the particular physiological variable (systolic blood pressure, diastolic blood pressure, or heart rate) or stressor that differentiates between groups of subjects who might later develop hypertension. The ability to evoke active coping (Light, 1981) and sufficient emotional stress (Neus, Gödderz, Otten, Rüddel and von Eiff, 1985) are important stimulus variables in obtaining greater responsivity among borderline hypertensives and normotensives with a family history of hypertension. Finally, it is important to note that in groups of individuals who are at risk for hypertension, a substantial number will remain disease-free throughout their lives (Weder and Julius, 1985).

BEHAVIOURAL METHODS OF TREATMENT

Biofeedback

The development of behavioural methodology for reducing blood pressure has stemmed from research in psychophysiological laboratories. Much of the basic human research on the voluntary control of blood pressure by means of biofeedback techniques follows the procedures first described by Shapiro *et al.* (1969). Early adaptation of this procedure to hypertensives resulted in fairly sizeable blood pressure reductions (Benson, Shapiro, Tursky and Schwartz, 1971; Kristt and Engel, 1975), although the lack of control groups and the small numbers of subjects in these studies makes it difficult to establish that the lowering of blood pressure resulted strictly from biofeedback. Reeves and Shapiro (1978), in a review of the early studies, concluded that biofeedback does reduce blood pressure in patients with essential hypertension. Seer (1979) has questioned whether the decreases in pressure, although statistically significant, were large enough to be clinically meaningful and could persist over time.

Many forms of feedback are based upon the supposition that the more relaxed an individual is, the lower his or her blood pressure will be. In order to achieve maximal relaxation, Moeller (1973) trained hypertensive patients in progressive relaxation combined with autogenic phrases, and also provided electromyogram (EMG) feedback from the frontalis muscle. The results suggested that feedback combined with relaxation might be an effective means of reducing blood pressure in hypertensives. More recently, Goldstein, Shapiro and Thananopavarn (1984) found that combining a modified form of progressive relaxation with EMG feedback was effective, but no more so than the relaxation procedure itself. In contrast, Glasgow, Gaarder and Engel (1982) reported that relaxation and blood pressure biofeedback were more effective than either treatment alone. However, the administration of the treatments in sequence, rather than simultaneously, may have influenced the potency of the treatment.

Patel (1973) combined feedback from a galvanic skin response (GSR) device with a set of yoga exercises involving passive relaxation training and meditation. Presumably, skin resistance increases would reflect sympathetic nervous system decreases, which would be expected during relaxation. Not only did blood pressures drop, but drug requirements were reduced (Patel, 1975). Another group of hypertensives taught relaxation with yoga exercises and then given GSR and EMG feedback showed very large blood pressure reductions (26/15 mmHg) (Patel and North, 1975). Although such blood pressure decreases are much larger than those generally reported, it is impossible to determine how much the biofeedback contributed to the lowering of pressures, because relaxation and biofeedback have always been combined in Patel's studies.

Relaxation

Although for years various techniques have existed for the purpose of altering states of consciousness, in recent times relaxation procedures have been associated with treatment for a variety of stress-related disorders. Most of the methods have developed from procedures such as progressive relaxation (Jacobson, 1939), autogenic training (Schultz and Luthe, 1969), and various forms of meditation (Wallace and Benson, 1972). Reviews of some of the early studies (Frumkin, Nathan, Prout and Cohen, 1978; Jacob, Kraemer and Agras, 1977; Tarler-Benlolo, 1978) have confirmed the general success of relaxation methods in the reduction of blood pressure. Seer (1979) reported across-session reduction in relaxation studies ranging from 7 to 17 mmHg for systolic blood pressure and 4 to 10 mmHg for diastolic blood pressure, which have frequently been maintained for several months. Taylor, Farquhar, Nelson and Agras (1977) indicated that the effects of a relaxation exercise (adapted from progressive relaxation) on blood pressure were greater than the effects attributed either to medical treatment alone, or to a non-specific treatment introduced with apparent enthusiasm.

Crowther (1983) looked at relaxation imagery, relaxation imagery plus stress management training, and blood pressure checks. The two treatment conditions did not differ from one another but were more effective in lowering blood pressure than the control condition during treatment and during 6 months of follow-up in the clinic as well as at home. In contrast, Cottier, Shapiro and Julius (1984) found that progressive muscle relaxation, when compared to an attention control, led to small differences in home blood pressures with no clinic differences.

The fact that relaxation does not always lead to blood pressure reductions which are greater than control conditions was demonstrated by Jacob, Fortmann, Kraemer, Farquhar and Agras (1985). They found no differences between a group of hypertensives trained to relax at home with instructions about salt intake and weight reduction and a group that visited the clinic for weekly blood pressure monitoring. Similarly, Wadden (1984) reported no differences between the following three groups: relaxation alone, relaxation training with a significant other, and cognitive therapy. In both studies, all conditions were equally effective in reducing blood pressure, a result which may be partially attributable to the subjects' feelings of having maintained some degree of control over their blood pressure and the expectancy of positive outcome.

A Comparison of Different Behavioural Methods

In early studies comparing a variety of behavioural techniques, relaxation methods either had greater effects in reducing blood pressure than biofeedback or there were only small differences between treatments. Among the few well-controlled studies demonstrating positive biofeedback effects as compared with relaxation are those of Blanchard and his associates. In a comparison of blood pressure biofeedback, EMG feedback, and simple relaxation instructions, patients in the blood pressure feedback group exhibited significant systolic decreases, although diastolic blood pressure remained unchanged (Blanchard, Miller, Abel, Haynes and Wicker, 1979). A study still in progress (McCaffrey and Blanchard, 1985) indicates that a thermal biofeedback (hand-warming) group shows larger blood pressure reductions and more successful drug withdrawal than a group of hypertensives given training in progressive relaxation. Goldstein, Shapiro, Thananopavarn and Sambhi (1982) found that while the blood pressure in self-monitoring and meditation groups increased, blood pressure feedback led to a decrease in diastolic blood pressure.

Some research has suggested that rather than either one of the two techniques (biofeedback or relaxation) being superior, a combination of strategies may result in more effective blood pressure control (Fey and Lindholm, 1978). Glasgow *et al.* (1982) found that while relaxation and systolic feedback were equally effective in lowering systolic blood pressure, relaxation had a greater effect on diastolic blood pressure. Furthermore, a combination of relaxation and biofeedback (with biofeedback treatment occurring before relaxation and each treatment being presented sequentially) produced better results than either treatment alone. Contrary to these results, Frankel, Patel, Horwitz, Friedewald and Gaarder (1978) found that a combination of blood pressure feedback, EMG feedback, and verbal relaxation (autogenic training and progressive relaxation) was no more effective than sham feedback. Goldstein *et al.* (1984) also found relaxation and relaxation combined with EMG biofeedback to be equally effective in reducing blood pressure.

While the superiority of one behavioural technique over another, or even a combination of techniques, has not been clearly established, it may be that the effectiveness of a given technique is related to individual differences. Glasgow *et al.* (1982) have proposed that reductions in blood pressure resulting from relaxation and biofeedback are achieved through different mechanisms, with blood pressure feedback affecting peripheral resistance and relaxation affecting cardiac output. Depending on the underlying mechanisms of a given hypertensive disorder, one behavioural treatment may be more effective than another in lowering blood pressure.

Overview

There are a number of critical issues in the area of behavioural treatment. To begin with, investigators have often noted that the amount of blood pressure decrease in a given individual is dependent upon that person's initial blood pressure (Jacob *et al.*, 1977). Also, no-treatment control conditions are often as effective as behavioural treatments in reducing the blood pressure of hypertensives. Blood pressure sometimes decreases because patients are suddenly given increased attention by a team of psychologists and physicians, and they gain more information about their disorder. If patients are asked to record home blood pressures, daily blood pressure logs provide them with a form of feedback, possibly telling them what activities lead to corresponding increases and decreases in blood pressure. Agras, Horne and Taylor (1982) suggested that expectancy of blood pressure changes may have an important effect upon whether or not blood pressure is reduced as a result of a behavioural treatment. In addition, involving patients in a treatment programme will probably have an effect on drug compliance (Haynes *et al.*, 1976).

In spite of problems with drugs, there is little question that they can lower blood pressure more dramatically than any of the behavioural treatments. In comparisons of pharmacological and behavioural treatments, drugs almost always produced larger blood pressure reductions (Goldstein *et al.*, 1982; Luborsky *et al.*, 1982). At present, until more research is done, behavioural techniques can be effective as methods of blood pressure control; and, while they cannot always replace antihypertensive medication, they can serve as useful adjuncts to pharmacological treatment. Because relaxation is at least as effective as biofeedback in controlling blood pressure, the relative low cost and ease in learning relaxation techniques makes them a preferable alternative to biofeedback (Goldstein, 1982).

CRITIQUE: EVALUATION OF CONTRIBUTIONS OF PSYCHOPHYSIOLOGY

THEORIES OF AETIOLOGY AND MAINTENANCE

Although little is known about the precise causes of hypertension, psychophysiology has contributed significantly to hypotheses about aetiology. Results of research imply that the recurrence of cardiovascular and endocrine responses to stressful situations eventually lead to essential hypertension in individuals who are at risk for hypertension (see also Chapter 8). Investigations of laboratory stressors have expanded our understanding of the chronic disease process by indicating that certain stimuli bring about large changes in the sympathetic nervous system in hypertensives and their offspring. It is also possible that the response of anger (particularly if suppressed) may further contribute to elevating cardiovascular responses. Response levels during stress have been found to predict hypertension more effectively than casual blood pressures (McKinney *et al.*, 1985). If one assumes that laboratory stressors reflect physiological levels achieved during actual life situations, then laboratory conditions can simulate processes by which blood pressure becomes elevated.

Some investigators have speculated that pressor effects of acute and repeated stress could be implicated in the alteration of blood vessel morphology. According to Obrist's (1981) hypothesis, the increased cardiac output found in pre-hypertensives can over time lead to elevated resistance in the peripheral vasculature. It has also been suggested that cardiovascular reactivity can contribute to hypertension by a disruption in the regulation of blood volume and the kidney's control of blood pressure. This is supported by the finding that stressors that induce active coping lead to decreased sodium and fluid excretion in either borderline hypertensives or in those individuals with a familial predisposition to hypertension (Light *et al.*, 1983).

ASSESSMENT

Psychophysiological studies of reactivity have not only contributed to theories of aetiology but have also emphasized the importance of measuring the response to stress in addition to standard resting measures. This can be accomplished in the natural environment by making greater use of 24-h ambulatory monitoring devices and, at considerably less expense, by training patients to use home blood pressure machines. Such home measures provide accurate indices of morbidity and mortality (Ibrahim, Tarazi, Dustan and Gifford, 1977) and can play a crucial role in pharmacological as well as behavioural treatment (Glasgow *et al.*, 1982). Furthermore, since blood pressure during laboratory-induced stress is more highly correlated with average blood pressure measured during ambulatory monitoring than casual blood pressure measurement

(McKinney *et al.*, 1985), the use of laboratory stressors could be an important tool for determining the risk of developing stress-induced hypertension.

The constant-cuff and tracking-cuff systems, which assess continuous blood pressure responses without invasive techniques, have been developed for psychophysiological research (Shapiro *et al.*, 1981; Tursky, Shapiro and Schwartz, 1972), but could provide valuable information in a clinical setting. Glasgow *et al.* (1982) utilized a modification of the constant-cuff technique to provide blood pressure biofeedback for patients at home. The recording of blood pressure on a beat-to-beat basis in a clinical setting could allow one to observe the constant variation that occurs at each beat both at rest and in response to different stimuli. This is particularly important when one is studying situations such as postural change or the Valsalva response, where the blood pressure changes are extremely rapid. To assume that these response patterns can be represented by one or two blood pressure measurements can be a gross oversimplification.

TREATMENT

The development of blood pressure biofeedback stemmed directly from psychophysiological experimentation as an offshoot of the constant-cuff method (Shapiro *et al.*, 1969). Since the first report on the use of biofeedback training in hypertensives (Benson *et al.*, 1971), a number of investigators have followed this strategy. It demonstrated the possibilities of reducing blood pressure by non-pharmacological methods. Biofeedback is an attractive treatment strategy, because it can be oriented to control specific physiological response systems relevant to a given patient's hypertension and can also be used to modify a pattern of simultaneous changes in several physiological functions. These studies have led to research on other behavioural methods, which now play a vital role in the treatment of hypertension. As such they can be adjunctive to standard medical approaches to treatment and can be used to enhance the effectiveness of antihypertensive drugs, to reinforce compliance with drug regimes, to reduce drug dosage in some cases, or to substitute for drug treatment that is not effective or results in intolerable side-effects (Shapiro and Goldstein, 1982). Research in behavioural techniques has also clarified the importance of non-specific effects by helping to explain how such events as repeated measurement and positive expectancy can lead to reductions in blood pressure (Chesney and Black, 1986).

FUTURE RESEARCH AND DEVELOPMENT

Our level of understanding of hypertension and the mechanisms involved would be expanded if we considered it more as a heterogeneous disorder and less as being unidimensional. For example, even though a number of factors, such as genetics, diet, stress, etc., contribute to aetiology, there is probably no single factor that applies to all individuals. In the personality literature there is evidence that more than one pattern of behaviour may be linked to hypertension (Baer, Collins, Bourianoff and Ketchel, 1979). In addition, Esler *et al.* (1977) reported that high-renin essential hypertensives differ both behaviourally and physiologically from normal-renin hypertensives. Looking at different response dimensions may help clarify discrepancies in the literature.

Focusing on heterogeneity among hypertensives should change the direction of treatment research towards looking more at individual differences. Anyone involved in this area knows that some patients exhibit large blood pressure declines after treatment, whereas others show no change at all. Thus far, investigators have been unable to isolate those patients who would derive the most benefit from treatment. Another variable that needs to be studied is why individuals differ so much in their commitment to treatment. More attention must be given to factors that get people to join programmes and comply with requirements. A proper assessment of motivation, involvement, and cooperation is needed to understand factors that reinforce a patient's commitment to his or her own treatment. Investigators should develop programmes that meet the needs of specific individuals. The patient who benefits from blood pressure biofeedback may not be the same one who shows blood pressure reductions during progressive relaxation or EMG biofeedback. Cottier *et al.* (1984) found that in a sample of borderline hypertensives, those who responded to progressive relaxation had faster heart rates, higher norepinephrine levels, and higher anxiety scores. Other characteristics such as obesity may necessitate the inclusion of dietary modification in a treatment programme.

Since the blood pressure reaction to stress is exaggerated in most hypertensives, treatment programmes should emphasize reducing the pressor response in addition to baseline blood pressure. This approach was demonstrated by Patel (1975), who showed that a combination of behavioural methods resulted in lower blood pressure during rest and in response to both exercise and cold pressor stimulation. Similarly, by means of heart rate biofeedback, Victor, Mainardi and Shapiro (1978) found it possible to alter the heart rate response of normotensives to the cold pressor test. This is clearly an area where more research with hypertensives is needed. If it can be demonstrated that hypertensives can be trained to control their pressor response to laboratory stimuli, further attempts should be made to generalize these reactions to relevant situations in everyday life.

The importance of being able to generalize the results of laboratory studies to the clinic and to the natural environment cannot be overemphasized. A therapy has no value if the desired outcome occurs only in the laboratory. Moreover, the results of reactivity to laboratory stressors among hypertensives and those at risk for hypertension should be applied to a natural environment. It is necessary for blood pressure measurements to be taken at various times of the day both during routine activities and perhaps even during sleep. The use of 24-h ambulatory monitoring devices can convey information regarding tonic as well as phasic changes in blood pressure. The generalizability of behavioural treatments to work settings (Southam, Agras, Taylor and Kraemer, 1982) and during sleep (Agras, Taylor, Kraemer, Allen and Schneider, 1980) has been demonstrated by the use of ambulatory recorders. Patients can also be trained in the use of home self-monitoring devices to assess blood pressure outside of standardized laboratory conditions.

Finally, the testing of many of the hypotheses advanced in this area requires the use of follow-up or longitudinal research. Long-term studies will help to determine the effectiveness of behavioural treatment over extended periods and will tell us whether or not prolonged periods of stress or unexpressed anger will lead to essential hypertension. They could also provide clues as to why some normotensives at risk for hypertension develop the disorder, while others do not. A possible model for such long-term studies is a 41-month follow-up study by Falkner, Kushner, Onesti and Angelakos (1981a) in which adolescents with borderline blood pressures, a strong family history of hypertension, high resting heart rates, and an exaggerated cardiovascular response to stress developed fixed hypertension. In the treatment area, Patel, Marmot, Terry, Carruthers, Hunt and Patel (1985) demonstrated that a group of hypertensives initially taught to lower blood pressure by behavioural methods maintained reduced pressures relative to a control group for up to 4 years. Clearly there is a need for more longitudinal studies of this nature.

REFERENCES

Adler, R., Hermann, J.M., Schäfer, N., Schmidt, T., Schonecke, O.W. and Vexküll, T.V. (1976/77). A context study of psychological conditions prior to shifts in blood pressure. *Psychotherapy and Psychosomatics* **27** 198–204.

Agras, W.S., Horne, M. and Taylor, C.B. (1982). Expectation and the blood-pressure-lowering effects of relaxation. *Psychosomatic Medicine* **44**, 389–395.

Agras, W.S., Taylor, C.B., Kraemer, H.C., Allen, R.A. and Schneider, J.A. (1980). Relaxation training: 24-hour blood pressure reductions. *Archives of General Psychiatry* **37**, 859–865.

Alexander, F. (1939). Emotional factors in essential hypertension. *Psychosomatic Medicine* **1**, 173–179.

Andrén, L. and Hansson, L. (1981). Circulatory effects of stress in essential hypertension. *Acta Medica Scandinavica* **646**, 69–72.

Ax, A.F. (1953). The physiological differentiation between fear and anger in humans. *Psychosomatic Medicine* **5**, 433–442.

Baer, P.E., Collins, F.H., Bourianoff, G.G. and Ketchel, M.F. (1979). Assessing personality factors in essential hypertension with a brief self-report instrument. *Psychosomatic Medicine* **41**, 321–330.

Baker, L.K. (1986). Dinamap Monitor versus direct blood pressure measurements. *Dimensions of Critical Care Nursing* **5**, 228–235.

Barker, W.F., Hediger, M.L., Katz, S.H. and Bowers, E.J. (1984). Concurrent validity studies of blood pressure instrumentation: the Philadelphia Blood Pressure Project. *Hypertension* **6**, 85–91.

Baumann, R., Ziprian, H., Gödicke, W., Hartrodt, W., Naumann, E. and Läuter, J. (1973). The influence of acute psychic stress situations on biochemical and vegetative parameters of essential hypertensives at the early stage of the disease. *Psychotherapy and Psychosomatics* **22**, 131–140.

Beevers, D.G. (1983). Risks of hypertension and benefits of treatment. In: J.I.S. Robertson (Ed.) *Handbook of Hypertension*, Vol. 1: *Clinical Aspects of Essential Hypertension.* Amsterdam: Elsevier.

Benson, H., Shapiro, D., Tursky, B. and Schwartz, G.E. (1971). Decreased systolic blood pressure through operant conditioning techniques in patients with essential hypertension. *Science* **173**, 740–742.

Blanchard, E.B., Miller, S.T., Abel, G.G., Haynes, M.R. and Wicker, R. (1979). Evaluation of biofeedback in the treatment of borderline essential hypertension. *Journal of Applied Behavior Analysis* **121**, 99–109.

Brennan, P.J., Greenberg, G., Miall, W.E. and Thompson, S.G. (1982). Seasonal variation in arterial blood pressure. *British Medical Journal* **285**, 919–923.

Brod, J., Fencl, V., Hejl, Z. and Jurka, J. (1959). Circulatory changes underlying blood pressure elevation during acute emotional stress (mental arithmetic) in normotensive and hypertensive subjects. *Clinical Science* **18**, 269–279.

Brown, M. (1981). What the baroreceptors tell the brain in hypertension. In: J.P. Buckley and C.M. Ferrario (Eds) *Central Nervous Mechanisms in Hypertension.* New York: Raven Press.

Carnahan, J.E. and Nugent, C.A. (1975). The effects of self-monitoring by patients on the control of hypertension. *American Journal of Medical Science* **269**, 69–73.

Chesney, M.A. and Black, G.W. (1986). Behavioral treatment of borderline hypertension: an overview of results. *Journal of Cardiovascular Pharmacology* **8** (Suppl. 5), s57–s63.

Cottier, C., Shapiro, A. and Julius, S. (1984). Treatment of mild hypertension with progressive muscle relaxation: predictive value of indexes of sympathetic tone. *Archives of Internal Medicine* **144**, 1954–1958.

Cottington, E.M., Matthews, K.A., Talbott, E. and Kuller, L.H. (1986). Occupational stress, suppressed anger, and hypertension. *Psychosomatic Medicine* **48**, 249–260.

Crowther, J.H. (1983). Stress management training and relaxation imagery in the treatment of essential hypertension. *Journal of Behavioral Medicine* **6**, 169–187.

Diamond, E.L. (1982). The role of anger and hostility in essential hypertension and coronary heart disease. *Psychological Bulletin* **92**, 410–433.

Dimsdale, J.E., Pierce, C., Schoenfeld, D., Brown, A., Zusman, R. and Graham, R. (1986). Suppressed anger and blood pressure: the effects of race, sex, social class, obesity, and age. *Psychosomatic Medicine* **48**, 430–436.

Ditto, B. (1986). Parental history of essential hypertension, active coping, and cardiovascular reactivity. *Psychophysiology* **23**, 62–70.

Eliasson, K., Hjemdahl, P. and Kahan, T. (1983). Circulatory and sympatho-adrenal responses to stress in borderline and established hypertension. *Journal of Hypertension* **1**, 131–139.

Engel, B.T. and Bickford, A.F. (1961). Response specificity: stimulus–response and individual-response specificity in essential hypertensives. *Archives of General Psychiatry* **5**, 478–489.

Epstein, F.H. (1983). The epidemiology of essential hypertension. In: J.I.S. Robertson (Ed.) *Handbook of Hypertension*, Vol. 1: *Clinical Aspects of Essential Hypertension.* Amsterdam: Elsevier.

Esler, M., Julius, S., Zweifler, A., Randall, O., Harburg, E., Gardiner, H. and De Quattro, V. (1977). Mild high-renin essential hypertension: neurogenic-human hypertension. *New England Journal of Medicine* **296**, 405–411.

Ewart, C.K., Harris, W.L., Zeger, S. and Russell, G.A. (1986). Diminished pulse pressure under mental stress characterizes normotensive adolescents with parental high blood pressure. *Psychosomatic Medicine* **48**, 489–501.

Eyer, J. (1975). Hypertension as a disease of modern society. *International Journal of Health Services* **5**, 539–558.

Falkner, B. (1986). Cardiovascular characteristics of the young with borderline hypertension. *Journal of Cardiovascular Pharmacology* **8** (Suppl. 5), s44–s47.

Falkner, B., Kushner, H., Onesti, G. and Angelakos, E.T. (1981a). Cardiovascular characteristics in adolescents who develop essential hypertension. *Hypertension* **3**, 521–527.

Falkner, B., Onesti, G. and Angelakos, E.T. (1981b). The effect of salt loading on the cardiovascular response to stress in adolescents. *Hypertension* **3** (Suppl. II), II195–II199.

Falkner, B., Onesti, G., Angelakos, E.T., Fernandes, M. and Langman, C. (1979). Cardiovascular response to mental stress in normal adolescents with hypertensive parents: hemodynamics and mental stress in adolescents. *Hypertension* **1**, 23–30.

Fey, S.G. and Lindholm, E. (1978). Biofeedback and progressive relaxation: effects on systolic and diastolic blood pressure and heart rate. *Psychophysiology* **15**, 239–247.

Frankel, B.L., Patel, D.J., Horwitz, D., Friedewald, W.T. and Gaarder, K.R. (1978). Treatment of hypertension with biofeedback and relaxation techniques. *Psychosomatic Medicine* **40**, 276–293.

Fredrikson, M. and Engel, B.T. (1985). Cardiovascular and electrodermal adjustments during a vigilance task in patients with borderline and established hypertension. *Journal of Psychosomatic Research* **29**, 235–246.

Fredrikson, M., Dimberg, U., Frisk-Holmberg, M. and Ström, G. (1982). Haemodynamic and electrodermal correlates of psychogenic stimuli in hypertensive and normotensive subjects. *Biological Psychology* **15**, 63–73.

Freis, E.D. (1974). The clinical spectrum of essential hypertension. *Archives of Internal Medicine* **133**, 982–987.

Freidman, M. and Rosenman, R.H. (1959). Association of specific overt behavior pattern with blood and cardiovascular findings. *Journal of American Medical Association* **169**, 1286–1296.

Frohlich, E.D. (1986). Clinical assessment of the patient with borderline hypertension. *Journal of Cardiovascular Pharmacology* **8**, (Suppl. 5), s98–s102.

Frumkin, K., Nathan, R.J., Prout, M.F. and Cohen, M.C. (1978). Nonpharmacologic control of essential hypertension in man: a critical review of the experimental literature. *Psychosomatic Medicine* **40**, 294–320.

Funkenstein, D.H., King, S.H. and Drolette, M.E. (1954). The direction of anger during a laboratory stress-inducing situation. *Psychosomatic Medicine* **16**, 404–413.

Gerardi, R.J., Blanchard, E.B., Andrasik, F. and McCoy, G.C. (1985). Psychological dimensions of 'office hypertension'. *Behavior Research and Therapy* **23**, 609–612.

Gintner, G.G., Hollandsworth, J.G. and Intrieri, R.C. (1986). Age differences in cardiovascular reactivity under active coping conditions. *Psychophysiology* **23**, 113–120.

Glasgow, M.S., Gaarder, K.R. and Engel, B.T. (1982). Behavioral treatment of high blood pressure. II. Acute and sustained effects of relaxation and systolic blood pressure biofeedback. *Psychosomatic Medicine* **44**, 155–170.

Goldstein, I.B. (1981). Assessment of hypertension. In: L.A. Bradley and C.K. Prokop (Eds) *Medical Psychology: A New Perspective*. New York: Academic Press.

462 *I. B. Goldstein*

Goldstein, I.B. (1982). Biofeedback in the treatment of hypertension. In: L. White and B. Tursky (Eds) *Clinical Biofeedback: Efficacy and Mechanisms.* New York: Guilford.

Goldstein, I.B., Shapiro, D. and Thananopavarn, C. (1984). Home relaxation techniques for essential hypertension. *Psychosomatic Medicine* **46**, 398–414.

Goldstein, I.B., Shapiro, D., Thananopavarn, C. and Sambhi, M.P. (1982). Comparison of drug and behavioral treatments of essential hypertension. *Health Psychology* **1**, 7–26.

Grissom, R.L., Gust, W.F. and Olson, R. (1986). Home blood pressure monitoring. *Nebraska Medical Journal* **71**, 327–329.

Groen, J.J., Hansen, B., Hermann, J.M., Schäfer, N., Schmidt, T.H., Selbmann, K.H., Vexküll, T.V. and Weckmann, P. (1977). Haemodynamic responses during experimental emotional stress and physical exercise in hypertensive and normotensive patients. *Progress in Brain Research* **47**, 301–308.

Gross, F., Pisa, Z., Strasser, T. and Zanchetti, A. (1984). *Management of Arterial Hypertension. A Practical Guide for the Physician and Allied Health Workers.* Geneva: World Health Organization.

Guyton, A.H., Coleman, T.G., Crowley, A.W., Schell, K.W., Manning, R.D. and Norman, R.A. (1972). Arterial pressure regulation. *American Journal of Medicine* **52**, 584–594.

Harburg, E., Erfurt, J.C., Hauenstein, L.S., Chape, C., Schull, W.J. and Schork, M.A. (1973). Socio-ecological stress, suppressed hostility, skin color, and black–white male blood pressure: Detroit. *Psychosomatic Medicine* **35**, 276–295.

Hardyck, C., Singer, M.T. and Harris, R.E. (1962). Transient changes in affect and blood pressure. *Archives of General Psychiatry* **7**, 15–20.

Harrell, J.P. (1980). Psychological factors and hypertension: a status report. *Psychological Bulletin* **87**, 482–501.

Hastrup, J.L., Kraemer, D.L., Hotchkiss, A.P. and Johnson, C.A. (1986). Cardiovascular responsivity to stress: family patterns and the effects of instructions. *Journal of Psychosomatic Research* **30**, 233–241.

Hastrup, J.L., Light, K.C. and Obrist, P.A. (1982). Parental hypertension and cardiovascular response to stress in healthy young adults. *Psychophysiology* **99**, 615–622.

Haynes, R.B., Gibson, E.S., Hackett, B.C., Sackett, D.L., Taylor, D.W., Roberts, R.S. and Johnson, A.L. (1976). Improvement of medication compliance in uncontrolled hypertension. *Lancet* **i**, 1265–1268.

Hines, E.A. and Brown, G.E. (1933). A standard test for measuring the variability of blood pressure: its significance as an index of the prehypertensive state. *Annals of Internal Medicine* **7**, 209–217.

Hokanson, J.E. and Burgess, M. (1962). The effects of status, type of frustration, and aggression on vascular processes. *Journal of Abnormal and Social Psychology* **65**, 232–237.

Horan, M.J. (1985). Role of ambulatory blood pressure recording in the diagnosis, prognosis, and management of hypertension. *Clinical and Experimental Hypertension [A]* **2**, 205–216.

Hull, D.H., Wolthuis, R.A., Cortese, T., Longo, M.R. and Triebwasser, J.H. (1977). Borderline hypertension versus normotension: differential response to orthostatic stress. *American Heart Journal* **94**, 414–420.

Ibrahim, M.M., Tarazi, R.C., Dustan, H.P. and Gifford, R.W. (1977). Electrocardiogram in evaluation of resistance to antihypertensive therapy. *Archives of Internal Medicine* **137**, 1125–1129.

Innes, G., Miller, W.M. and Valentine, M. (1959). Emotion and blood pressure. *Journal of Medical Science* **105**, 840–851.

Jacob, R.G., Fortmann, S.P., Kraemer, H.C., Farquhar, J.W. and Agras, W.S. (1985).

Combining behavioral treatments to reduce blood pressure: a controlled outcome study. *Behavioral Medicine* **9**, 32–53.

Jacob, R.G., Kraemer, H.C. and Agras, S. (1977). Relaxation therapy in the treatment of hypertension. *Archives of General Psychiatry* **34**, 1417–1427.

Jacobson, E. (1939). Variation of blood pressure with skeletal muscle tension and relaxation. *Annals of Internal Medicine* **12**, 1194–1212.

Jern, S. (1982). Psychological and hemodynamic factors in borderline hypertension. *Acta Medica Scandinavica* **662** (Suppl.), 1–55.

Kannel, W.B. (1977). Importance of hypertension as a major risk factor in cardiovascular disease. In: J. Genest, E. Koiw and O. Kuchel (Eds) *Hypertension*. New York: McGraw-Hill.

Kelleher, C. (1986). Blood pressure alters during the normal menstrual cycle. *British Journal of Obstetrics and Gynaecology* **93**, 523–526.

Kirkendall, W.M., Burton, A.C., Epstein, F.H. and Freis, E.D. (1967). Report of a subcommittee of the Postgraduate Education Committee, American Heart Association: recommendations for human blood pressure determination by sphygmomanometers. *Circulation* **36**, 980–988.

Krantz, D.S. and Manuck, S.B. (1985). Measures of acute physiologic reactivity to behavioral stimuli: assessment and critique. In: A.M. Ostfeld and E.D. Eaker (Eds) *Measuring Psychosocial Variables in Epidemiologic Studies of Cardiovascular Disease*. Bethesda: National Institutes of Health.

Kristt, D.A. and Engel, B.T. (1975). Learned control of blood pressure in patients with high blood pressure. *Circulation* **51**, 370–378.

Labarthe, D.R., Hawkins, C.M. and Remington, R.D. (1973). Evaluation of performance of selected devices for measuring blood pressure. *American Journal of Cardiology* **32**, 546–553.

Larsen, P.B., Schneiderman, N. and Pasin, R.D. (1986). Physiological basis of cardiovascular psychophysiology. In: M.G.H. Coles, E. Donchin and S.W. Porges (Eds) *Psychophysiology: Systems, Processes, and Applications*. New York: Guilford.

Lawler, K.A. and Allen, M.T. (1981). Risk factors for hypertension in children: their relationship to psychophysiological responses. *Journal of Psychosomatic Research* **23**, 199–204.

Light, K. (1981). Cardiovascular responses to effortful active coping: implications for the role of stress in hypertension development. *Psychophysiology* **18**, 216–225.

Light, K.C. and Obrist, P.A. (1980). Cardiovascular reactivity to behavioral stress in young males with and without marginally elevated casual systolic pressures: comparison of clinic, home and laboratory measures. *Hypertension* **2**, 802–808.

Light, K.C., Koepke, J.P., Obrist, P.A. and Willis, P.W. (1983). Psychological stress induces sodium and fluid retention in mean risk for hypertension. *Science* **220**, 429–431.

Luborsky, L., Crits-Cristoph, P., Brady, J.P., Kron, R.E., Weiss, T., Cohen, M. and Levy, L. (1982). Behavioral versus pharmacological treatments for essential hypertension – a needed comparison. *Psychosomatic Medicine* **44**, 203–213.

Lund-Johansen, P. (1986). Hemodynamic patterns in the natural history of borderline hypertension. *Journal of Cardiovascular Pharmacology* **8** (Suppl. 5), s8–s14.

Mancia, G. (1983). Methods for assessing blood pressure values in humans. *Hypertension* **5** (Supp. III), III-5–III-13.

Mann, A.H. (1977). Psychiatric morbidity and hostility in hypertension. *Psychological Medicine* **7**, 653–659.

Manuck, S. and Proietti, J.M. (1982). Parental hypertension and cardiovascular response to cognitive and isometric challenge. *Psychophysiology* **19**, 481–489.

Manuck, S.B., Giordani, B., McQuaid, K.J. and Garrity, S.J. (1981). Behaviorally-induced cardiovascular reactivity among sons of reported hypertensive parents. *Journal of Psychosomatic Research* **25**, 261–269.

Manuck, S.B., Morrison, R.L., Bellack, A.S. and Polefrone, J.M. (1985a). Behavioral factors in hypertension: cardiovascular responsivity, anger, and social competence. In: M.A. Chesney and R.H. Rosenman (Eds) *Anger and Hostility in Cardiovascular Disorders*. New York: Hemisphere.

Manuck, S.B., Proietti, J.M., Rader, S.J. and Polefrone, J.M. (1985b). Parental hypertension, affect, and cardiovascular response to cognitive challenge. *Psychosomatic Medicine* **47**, 189–200.

McCaffrey, R.J. and Blanchard, E.B. (1985). Stress management approaches to the treatment of essential hypertension. *Annals of Behavioral Medicine* **7**, 5–12.

McCrory, W.W., Klein, A.A. and Rosenthal, R.A. (1982). Blood pressure, heart rate, and plasma catecholamines in normal and hypertensive children and their siblings at rest and after standing. *Hypertension* **4**, 510–513.

McDonough, L.B. (1964). Inhibited aggression in essential hypertension. *Journal of Clinical Psychology* **20**, 447.

McKinney, M.E., Miner, M.H., Rüddel, H., McIlvain, H.E., Witte, H., Buell, J.C., Eliot, R.S. and Grant, L.B. (1985). The standardized mental stress test protocol: test–retest reliability and comparison with ambulatory blood pressure monitoring. *Psychophysiology* **22**, 453–463.

Moeller, T.A. (1973). Reduction of arterial blood pressure through relaxation training and correlates of personality in hypertensives. Unpublished doctoral dissertation, Nova University, Fort Lauderdale, Florida.

Naditch, M.P. (1974). Locus of control, relative discontent and hypertension. *Social Psychiatry* **9**, 111–117.

Nestel, P.J. (1969). Blood pressure and catecholamine excretion after mental stress in labile hypertension. *Lancet* **i**, 692–694.

Neus, H., Gödderz, W., Otten, H., Rüddel, H. and von Eiff, A. (1985). Family history of hypertension and cardiovascular reactivity of mental stress: effects of stimulus intensity and environment. *Journal of Hypertension* **3**, 31–37.

North, L.W. (1981). Blood pressure measurement: techniques and tips for accurate readings. *Journal of Practical Nursing* **31**, 23–24, 38.

Obrist, P.A. (1981). *Cardiovascular Psychophysiology*. New York: Plenum.

Ostfeld, A.M. and Lebovits, B.Z. (1959). Personality factors and pressor mechanisms in renal and essential hypertension. *Archives of Internal Medicine* **104**, 43–52.

Patel, C.H. (1973). Yoga and biofeedback in the management of hypertension. *Lancet* **ii**, 1053–1055.

Patel, C. (1975). 12 month follow-up of yoga and biofeedback in the management of hypertension. *Lancet* **i**, 62–64.

Patel, C.H. and North, W.R.S. (1975). Randomized controlled trial of yoga and biofeedback in management of hypertension. *Lancet* **ii**, 93–95.

Patel, C., Marmot, M.G., Terry, D.J., Carruthers, M., Hunt, B. and Patel, M. (1985). Trial of relaxation in reducing coronary risk: four year follow up. *British Medical Journal* **290**, 1103–1106.

Paul, O. (Ed.) (1975). *Epidemiology and Control of Hypertension*. New York: Grune and Stratton.

Perini, C., Müller, F.B., Rauchfleisch, U., Battegay, R. and Bühler, F.R. (1986). Hyperadrenergic borderline hypertension is characterized by suppressed aggression. *Journal of Cardiovascular Pharmacology* **8** (Suppl. 5), s53–s56.

Petrie, J.C., O'Brien, E.T., Littler, W.A. and De Swiet, M. (1986). Recommendations on blood pressure measurement. *British Medical Journal* **293**, 611–615.

Pickering, T.G., Harshfield, G.A., Devereux, R.B. and Laragh, J.H. (1985). What is the role of ambulatory blood pressure monitoring in the management of hypertensive patients? *Hypertension* **7**, 171–177.

Pilowsky, I., Spalding, D., Shaw, J. and Korner, P.I. (1973). Hypertension and personality. *Psychosomatic Medicine* **35**, 50–56.

Reeves, J.L. and Shapiro, D. (1978). Biofeedback and relaxation in essential hypertension. *International Review of Applied Psychology* **27**, 121–135.

Remington, R.D., Lambarth, B., Moser, M. and Hoobler, S.W. (1960). Circulatory reactions of normotensive and hypertensive subjects and the children of normal and hypertensive parents. *American Heart Journal* **59**, 58–70.

Report of the Task Force on Blood Pressure Control in Children (1977). *Pediatrics* **59**, 797–820.

Rion, R., Waeber, B., Graf, H.J., Jaussi, A., Porchet, M. and Brunner, H.R. (1985). Blood pressure response to antihypertensive therapy: ambulatory versus office blood pressure readings. *Journal of Hypertension* **3**, 139–143.

Rose, G. (1980). The measurement of blood pressure. In: A.J. Marshall and D.W. Barritt (Eds) *The Hypertensive Patient*. Kent: Pitman.

Rose, G. (1985). Hypertension in the community. In: C.J. Bulpitt (Ed.) *Handbook of Hypertension*, Vol. 6: *Epidemiology of Hypertension*. Amsterdam: Elsevier.

Rosenman, R.H. and Friedman, M. (1961). Association of specific behavior pattern in women with blood and cardiovascular findings. *Circulation* **24**, 1173–1184.

Rubin, P., McLean, K. and Reid, J. (1980). A comparative study of automated blood pressure recorders. *Postgraduate Medical Journal* **56**, 815–817.

Safar, M.E., Weiss, J.A., Levenson, J.A., London, G.M. and Milliez, P.L. (1973). Hemodynamic study of 85 patients with borderline hypertension. *American Journal of Cardiology* **31**, 315–319.

Schachter, J. (1957). Pain, fear, and anger in hypertensives and normotensives. *Psychosomatic Medicine* **19**, 17–29.

Schneider, R.H., Egan, B.M., Johnson, E.H., Drobny, H. and Julius, S. (1986). Anger and anxiety in borderline hypertension. *Psychosomatic Medicine* **48**, 242–248.

Schulte, W., Rüddel, H., Jacobs, U. and von Eiff, A.W. (1986). Hemodynamic abnormalities in borderline hypertension during mental stress. *Journal of Cardiovascular Pharmacology* **8** (Suppl. 5), s128–s130.

Schultz, J.H. and Luthe, W. (1969). *Autogenic Therapy: Autogenic Methods*, Vol. 1. New York: Grune and Stratton.

Schwartz, G.E., Weinberger, D.A. and Davidson, R.A. (1981). Cardiovascular differentiation of happiness, sorrow, anger, and fear following imagery and exercise. *Psychosomatic Medicine* **43**, 343–367.

Seer, P. (1979). Psychological control of essential hypertension: review of the literature and methodological critique. *Psychological Bulletin* **86**, 1015–1043.

Shapiro, A.P. (1961). An experimental study of comparative responses of blood pressure to different noxious stimuli. *Journal of Chronic Diseases* **13**, 293–311.

Shapiro, D. and Goldstein, I.B. (1982). Biobehavioral perspective on hypertension. *Journal of Consulting and Clinical Psychology* **50**, 841–858.

Shapiro, D., Greenstadt, L., Lane, J.D. and Rubinstein, E. (1981). Tracking cuff system for beat-to-beat recordings of blood pressure. *Psychophysiology* **18**, 129–136.

Shapiro, D., Mainardi, J.A. and Surwit, R.S. (1977). Biofeedback and self-regulation in essential hypertension. In: G.E. Schwartz and J. Beatty (Eds) *Biofeedback: Theory and Research*. New York: Academic Press.

Shapiro, D., Tursky, B., Gershon, E. and Stern, M. (1969). Effects of feedback and reinforcement on the control of systolic blood pressure. *Science* **163**, 588–590.

Shekelle, R.B., Schoenberger, J.A. and Stamler, J. (1976). Correlates of the JAS type A behavior pattern score. *Journal of Chronic Diseases* **29**, 381–394.

Southam, M.A., Agras, W.S., Taylor, C.B. and Kraemer, H.C. (1982). Relaxation training: blood pressure lowering during the working day. *Archives of General Psychiatry* **39**, 715–717.

Steptoe, A. and Molineux, D. (1986). Evaluation of an electronic sphygmomanometer suitable for the self-monitoring of blood pressure. *Behavior Research and Therapy* **24**, 223–226.

Steptoe, A., Melville, D. and Ross, A. (1984). Behavioral response demands, cardio-vascular reactivity, and essential hypertension. *Psychosomatic Medicine* **46**, 33–48.

Sullivan, P.A., Procci, W.R., De Quattro, V., Schoentgen, S., Levine, D., Van Der Meulen, J. and Bornheimer, J.F. (1981a). Anger, anxiety, guilt and increased basal and stress-induced neurogenic tone: causes or effects in primary hypertension? *Clinical Science* **61**, 389s–392s.

Sullivan, P., Schoentgen, S., De Quattro, V., Procci, W., Levine, D., Van Der Meulen, J. and Bornheimer, J. (1981b). Anxiety, anger and neurogenic tone at rest and in stress in patients with primary hypertension. *Hypertension* **3** (Suppl. II), II119–II123.

Surwit, R.S., Williams, R.B. and Shapiro, D. (1982). *Behavioral Approaches to Cardio-vascular Disorders*. New York: Academic Press.

Swales, J.D. (1984). Aetiology of hypertension. *British Journal of Anaesthesiology* **56**, 677–688.

Tarler-Benlolo, L. (1978). The role of relaxation in biofeedback training: a critical review of the literature. *Psychological Bulletin* **85**, 727–755.

Taylor, C.B., Farquhar, J.W., Nelson, E. and Agras, S. (1977). Relaxation therapy and high blood pressure. *Archives of General Psychiatry* **34**, 339–342.

Tursky, B. and Jamner, L.D. (1982). Measurement of cardiovascular functioning. In: J.T. Cacioppo and R.E. Petty (Eds) *Perspectives in Cardiovascular Psychophysiology*. New York: Guilford.

Tursky, B., Shapiro, D. and Schwartz, G.E. (1972). Automated constant-cuff pressure sysyem to measure average systolic and diastolic blood pressure in man. *IEEE Transactions on Biomedical Engineering* **19**, 271–276.

Victor, R., Mainardi, J.A. and Shapiro, D. (1978). Effect of biofeedback and voluntary control procedures on heart rate and the perception of pain during the cold pressor test. *Psychosomatic Medicine* **40**, 216–225.

Voudoukis, I.J. (1978). Cold pressor test and hypertension. *Angiology* **29**, 429–439.

Wadden, T.A. (1984). Relaxation therapy for essential hypertension: specific or nonspecific effects? *Journal of Psychosomatic Research* **28**, 53–61.

Waldron, I., Hickey, A., McPherson, C., Butensky, A., Gruss, L., Overall, K., Schmader, A. and Wohlmuth, D. (1980). Type A behavior pattern: relationship to variation in blood pressure, parental characteristics, and academic and social activities of students. *Journal of Human Stress* **6**, 16–27.

Wallace, R.K. and Benson, H. (1972). The physiology of meditation. *Scientific American* **226**, 85–90.

Weber, M.A., Drayer, J.I., Nakamura, D.K. and Wyle, F.A. (1984). The circadian blood pressure pattern in ambulatory normal subjects. *American Journal of Cardiology* **54**, 115–119.

Weder, A.B. and Julius, S. (1985). Behavior, blood pressure variability, and hypertension. *Psychosomatic Medicine* **47**, 406–414.

Weipert, D., Shapiro, D. and Suter, T. (1987). Family history of hypertension and cardiovascular responses to orthostatic stress. *Psychophysiology* **24**, 251–257.

Williams, R.B., Kimball, C.P. and Williard, II.N. (1972). The influence of interpersonal interaction on diastolic blood pressure. *Psychosomatic Medicine* **34**, 194–198.

Wolf, S., Cardon, P.V., Shepard, E.M. and Wolff, H.G. (1955). *Life Stress and Essential Hypertension*. Baltimore: Williams and Wilkins.

World Health Organization (1978). *Arterial Hypertension: Report of WHO Expert Committee*. Technical Report Series, No. 628. Geneva: WHO.

Chapter 16

Raynaud's Disease

Robert R. Freedman

Behavioural Medicine Laboratory,
Lafayette Clinic,
Departments of Psychiatry and Psychology,
Wayne State University,
Detroit, Michigan,
USA

ABSTRACT

The symptoms and physiological phenomena associated with Raynaud's disease are described. Various aetiological mechanisms are reviewed, together with evidence that emotional stress may provoke Raynaud's disease attacks. Methods of measuring finger blood flow are also reviewed. In particular, the use of these techniques to evaluate behavioural treatments of Raynaud's disease are discussed. Finally, the contribution of psychophysiology to understanding these phenomena is assessed.

Handbook of Clinical Psychophysiology Edited by G. Turpin
© 1989 John Wiley & Sons Ltd

469

SYMPTOMS

Raynaud's disease is a disorder of the peripheral circulation characterized by episodic vasospasms and associated colour changes in the fingers and, sometimes, the toes. The attacks are precipitated by cold exposure and/or emotional stress (Freedman and Ianni, 1983a), and generally begin in the tips of one or more fingers, but may eventually affect all the phalanges. The typical colour progression is from pallor to cyanosis to rubor, but not all patients manifest all three phases. Although the initial pallor is thought to be due to digital artery vasospasms, their exact location has not been proven. The cyanosis is presumably caused by slow blood flow in dilated capillaries and venules (McGrath and Penny, 1974). Patients typically complain of cold or numb fingers during these phases. The attacks, which can last from a few minutes to several hours, often terminate with reactive hyperaemia, characterized by redness and painful, throbbing or burning sensations.

The term 'Raynaud's disease' refers to the primary form of the disorder, in which the attacks cannot be explained by connective tissue diseases (such as scleroderma, rheumatoid arthritis, or lupus erythematosus), vibration trauma, occlusive arterial disease, thoracic outlet syndrome, or other disorders. It is five times more common in women than in men (Spitell, 1980), with the age of onset generally in the second or third decades of life (Blain, Coller and Carver, 1951). Presently, the diagnosis of Raynaud's disease is based on the following criteria (Allen and Brown, 1932): (1) episodes of bilateral colour changes precipitated by cold or emotion, (2) absence of severe gangrene, (3) absence of any systemic disease that might account for the attacks, and (4) duration of symptoms for at least 2 years. Using these criteria, a study in Denmark found a prevalence of 22% among women aged 21–50 years based on responses to a questionnaire (Olsen and Nielsen, 1978). The frequency and severity of the attacks generally increase during cold weather, and although the extremities are usually otherwise normal, sclerodactyly (tense and atrophic skin, deformed nails) occurs in approximately 10% of the patients (Gifford and Hines, 1957).

PHYSIOLOGICAL CONTROL OF DIGITAL BLOOD FLOW

Research on the pathophysiology of Raynaud's disease is most easily understood in the context of the mechanisms controlling normal finger blood flow. The digital vasculature is almost entirely cutaneous and plays a fundamental role in the regulation of body temperature. The palmar surface and tip of the finger are rich in arteriovenous anastomoses (or shunts) which function in parallel with the capillary bed. These shunts have the capacity to rapidly vary their lumen size and rate of blood flow in response to changes in external temperature. This is accomplished mainly through sympathetic adrenergic vasoconstrictor nerves (Figure 16.1). Body cooling causes reflex finger vasoconstriction through increased neural activity and, conversely, body heating produces vasodilation through withdrawal of this activity. Finger capillary blood flow is somewhat affected by sympathetic nervous system (SNS) activity,

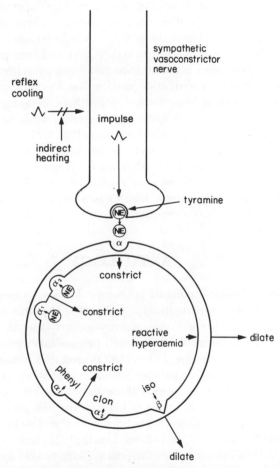

Figure 16.1. Control of digital blood flow. Reflexive cooling causes digital vasoconstriction through the liberation of norepinephrine (NE) from sympathetic nerve endings, which can be reduced by indirect heating. Injection of tyramine causes vasoconstriction by displacing NE from the nerves. Vasoconstriction can also be caused by the interaction of circulating NE or synthetic agonists such as phenylephrine (PHENYL) or clonidine (CLON) with alpha-1- and alpha-2-adrenergic receptors. Synthetic beta-adrenergic agonists such as isoproterenol (ISO) cause vasodilation through interaction with beta-receptors. Reactive hyperaemia produces vasodilation through the accumulation of unknown compounds during ischaemia.

though to a lesser extent than arteriovenous shunt flow (Coffman, 1972). There are no known vasodilating nerves in the human finger, although such nerves do exist in the skin of the forearm (Shepherd, 1963).

Finger blood flow is also controlled through the interactions of circulating vasoactive substances with alpha- and beta-adrenergic receptors to produce vasoconstriction and vasodilation. Circulating catecholamines, released from the adrenal medulla and from other nerve endings 'upstream', act at alpha-adrenergic receptors to produce vasoconstriction. These alpha receptors are probably closer to the lumen than those which respond to norepinephrine released from sympathetic nerve endings. Alpha and beta receptors have been divided into two subtypes based on their relative sensitivities to different agonists. A beta-adrenergic vasodilating mechanism has recently been discovered in the finger by injecting isoproterenol, a synthetic beta-adrenergic agonist, in the brachial artery and then blocking this effect with propranolol, a beta-adrenergic antagonist (Cohen and Coffman, 1981). However, an endogenous ligand which acts at these beta receptors has not yet been found.

The sensitivities of vascular adrenergic receptors change according to temperature and represent one means of local control of blood flow. Other local influences include changes in blood gases and metabolism, myogenic tone, and the axon reflex (Vanhoutte, 1980).

AETIOLOGY

The aetiology of Raynaud's disease remains unknown, although several theories have been put forth to explain it. Raynaud (1888) hypothesized an SNS overactivity leading to an increased vasoconstrictor response to cold, while Lewis (1929) postulated a 'local fault' in which precapillary resistance vessels were hypersensitive to local cooling. Lewis (1929) produced ischaemic attacks in the fingers of Raynaud's disease patients using local cooling, and also found local structural changes, such as intimal thickening and thrombosis. He was later criticized on the grounds that most of his patients had very advanced forms of the disease and that their vascular changes were therefore of a secondary nature (Halperin and Coffman, 1979). Indeed, Lewis (1938) later reported three cases of mild Raynaud's disease where the precapillary vessels appeared normal.

Evidence regarding Lewis's cold hypersensitivity hypothesis is mixed. Downey and Frewin (1973) measured the response of hand blood flow to a cold stimulus and recovery times after removal of the stimulus; they found no differences between patients with Raynaud's disease and normals. Miller and Walder (1972) measured finger blood flow and temperature before and after local cooling in normal subjects and patients with Raynaud's disease and also found no differences. However, Lottenbach (1971) found reduced heat elimination (i.e. lower blood flow) at 19 °C in fingers of patients with Raynaud's disease when compared to normal controls. Chucker, Fowler, Motomuja, Singh and Hurley (1971), using thermography, found prolonged rewarming time after ice-water immersion of the hands in Raynaud's disease patients as compared to normals. Another study found that local cooling of the hand enhanced reflexive sympathetic vasoconstriction following ice application to the neck in patients with Raynaud's disease or scleroderma but not in normal subjects (Jamieson, Ludbrook and Wilson, 1971). Using measurements in controlled laboratory conditions and in the natural environment, Freedman and Ianni (1983a) showed that patients with Raynaud's disease had significantly lower finger temperatures than normal persons or those with scleroderma during local cold stress and in normal thermal conditions. Coffman and Cohen (1971) also found that Raynaud's disease patients had lower finger blood flows than normals in cold and warm environments. In addition, by using sophisticated measurement techniques, these investigators were able to distinguish specific components of finger blood flow and demonstrated that, in a cold environment, capillary blood flow was severely reduced in Raynaud's disease patients but not in normals.

In support of the theory of excessive sympathetic activity as the cause of Raynaud's disease, average hand blood flow in a group of patients with this disorder was found to be abnormally low when compared to normals (Peacock, 1959a). After sympathetic release produced by body warming, hand blood flow in patients with mild forms of the disease rose to normal levels. Peacock (1959a) argued that this normal vasodilatation was evidence against structural arterial disease. Willerson, Thompson and Hookman (1970) found low superficial digital blood flows in patients with Raynaud's disease as compared to normals and also suggested the hypothesis of increased sympathetic activity. However, the failure of Downey and Frewin (1973) to find increased reflex sympathetic vasoconstriction to a cold stimulus in affected patients argues against this theory. In addition, more recent research (Fagius and Blumberg, 1985) has failed to find differences between Raynaud's disease patients and normals using microneurographic recordings of sympathetic nerve activity during cold stimulation.

Peacock (1959b) also found an increased level of catecholamines in wrist venous blood in Raynaud's disease patients, which he took as evidence for continuous sympathetic vasoconstrictor hyperactivity. However, these results were not replicated in several other studies of patients with Raynaud's disease, or in patients with Raynaud's phenomenon secondary to scleroderma (Kontos and Wasserman, 1969; Mendlowitz and Naftchi, 1959; Sapira, Rodnan, Scheib, Klaniecki and Rizk, 1972; Surwit, Allen, Gilgor, Schanberg, Kuhn and Duvic, 1983). Mendlowitz and Naftchi (1959) also studied digital blood pressure and flow in 20 Raynaud's disease patients before and after vasodilatation and identified two groups. In one group, the intrinsic vascular calibre after vasodilatation was normal, but vasomotor tone was high; in the second group,

vascular calibre was decreased, but vasomotor tone was normal. It was hypothesized that the first group had heightened vasomotor tone but no organic
obstructive disease, and that the second group had vascular obstruction,
although it was not known whether this was a cause or an effect of the disease.
As the researchers could not show increased epinephrine or norepinephrine
levels in venous blood from the hands, or hypersensitivity to infused norepinephrine, the increased vasomotor tone of patients in the first group was
attributed to heightened activity of sympathetic innervation.

Other research has examined physical properties of the blood in Raynaud's
disease. Pringle, Walder and Weaver (1965) found blood hyperviscosity associated with hyperfibrinogenaemia and increased erythrocyte aggregation,
although these findings were not confirmed by later work (Johnsen, Neilsen
and Skovborg, 1977; McGrath, Peek and Penny, 1978). Two other studies
failed to find increased plasma fibrinogen levels in patients with Raynaud's
disease (Charles and Carmick, 1970; Jamieson *et al.*, 1971).

In summary, a satisfactory explanation of the cause(s) of Raynaud's disease
has not yet been found. Theories of increased sympathetic activity, catecholamine blood levels, blood viscosity, sensitivity to local cooling and vessel
obstruction have not been proven. Altered sensitivities and/or densities of a
variety of pharmacological receptors have been implicated in the pathophysiology of many disease states (Lefkowitz, Caron and Stiles, 1984): decreased
alpha- and/or decreased beta-adrenergic receptor density and/or sensitivity
could contribute to the vasospastic attacks of Raynaud's disease. This hypothesis is particularly attractive since local cooling enhances the vasoconstrictive
response to norepinephrine in certain blood vessels (Flavahan and Vanhoutte,
1986).

We recently compared finger blood flow responses of Raynaud's disease
patients and normal subjects to dose-ranging brachial artery infusions of phenylephrine, an alpha-1 agonist; clonidine, an alpha-2 agonist; isoproterenol, a
beta agonist; and tyramine, which causes vasoconstriction by releasing norepinephrine from sympathetic nerve endings (Freedman, Sabharwal, Wenig and
Mayes, 1989). Twenty-eight patients with idiopathic Raynaud's disease, 24
women and 4 men aged 22–69 years, were screened to meet the Allen and
Brown (1932) criteria, have negative antinuclear antibody tests, normal nailfold
capillaries, and normal finger blood flow responses to a maximum vasodilation
test. In the latter procedure, subjects were subjected to total body heating and
peripheral reactive hyperaemia, to verify the patency of finger blood vessels.
They were matched by age and baseline finger blood flow level with 24 normal
women and 5 normal men, aged 22–66 years. Subjects were supine in a 23 °C
room while finger blood flow was measured with venous occlusion plethysmography and the above four compounds were given by pump, in successively
doubling doses, through a brachial artery catheter. The doses employed did
not change blood pressure or heart rate. Analysis of variance showed that

phenylephrine caused dose-related vasoconstriction ($P < 0.005$) which was greater in the patients than the normals ($P < 0.002$). Similarly, dose-related vasoconstriction produced by clonidine ($P < 0.02$) was greater in patients than in normals ($P < 0.05$). There were no significant differences in responses to isoproterenol or tyramine. Thus, equal levels of circulating catecholamines acting at alpha-adrenergic receptors would cause a greater degree of peripheral vasoconstriction in Raynaud's disease patients than in matched controls.

EMOTIONAL STRESS AND RAYNAUD'S DISEASE

It has generally been thought that Raynaud's disease attacks are precipitated wholly or in part by emotional stress (Abramson, 1974; Halperin and Coffman, 1979; Spitell, 1980). This is not surprising, since the attacks are clearly vaso-constrictive in nature and since digital vasoconstriction has been reliably prod-uced in normal persons using various laboratory stressors (Bloom and Trautt, 1977; Cook, 1974). Until recently, however, evidence of the effects of stress in Raynaud's disease has been largely anecdotal. Mittelmann and Wolff (1939) presented data from one patient showing that a combination of low environ-mental temperature and emotional stress (induced by an interview) was necessary to provoke an attack. In a study of 10 Raynaud's patients, Freedman, Lynn and Ianni (1982) found that 22.4% of 838 attacks were reported to be caused by stress. These patients also had significantly higher ratings of state anxiety and subjective emotional stress immediately prior to attacks than during asymptomatic periods.

A controlled study of stress in Raynaud's disease (Halperin, Cohen and Coffman, 1983) found digital vasodilation rather than vasoconstriction in response to mental arithmetic, a 'standard' stressor which produces finger vasoconstriction in normals. The explanation for this paradoxical finding is not known. In our laboratory, we constructed emotional stressors having thematic relevance to Raynaud's disease patients and which could be repeatedly admin-istered in a controlled manner (Freedman and Ianni, 1985). Thirty-two Raynaud's disease patients and 22 normal subjects listened to three brief tape-recorded scripts in the laboratory: a general stress script (social embarrass-ment), a stress script specifically relevant to Raynaud's disease (lost gloves in a snowstorm), and a neutral script (beach scene). Analysis of variance showed that the two groups differed significantly ($P < 0.05$) only in their pattern of finger temperature responses to the specific stress script: Raynaud's patients vasoconstricted while normals did not. Both groups vasoconstricted in response to the general stress script and showed no temperature response to the neutral script.

We were also interested in the role of stress in actual vasospastic attacks, which are not readily provoked in the laboratory. We therefore employed ambulatory monitoring techniques to obtain temperature, electrocardiogram (ECG), and stress rating data from 32 patients with Raynaud's disease, 24 with Raynaud's phenomenon and scleroderma, and 22 normal subjects (Freedman and Ianni, 1983a). Fifty-six attacks were recorded in 12 Raynaud's disease patients. Increased stress ratings occurred in 39% of these attacks and tachycardia occurred in 37%. Declines in ambient temperature were not detected during 34% of the Raynaud's disease attacks, but almost always accompanied attacks in scleroderma patients. Thus, about one-third of the Raynaud's disease attacks in this study appeared to be precipitated by stress. Interestingly, attacks which occurred above the average stress rating were accompanied by significantly higher finger temperatures than those occurring below it. Thus, the addition of an emotionally stressful stimulus may cause an attack at a level of blood flow which is insufficient to produce an attack in the absence of stress.

MEASUREMENT OF FINGER BLOOD FLOW

In intact human extremities, blood flow can be measured only by indirect methods. Behavioural studies have most often used the temperature of the skin as an index of peripheral blood flow. Measurement may be made on the surface of the skin (thermometry) or at a distance (thermography). Visual observation of portions of the peripheral circulation can be accomplished by capillary microscopy or angiography. Plethysmographic techniques measure changes in the volume of extremities and include pneumatic, girth, photoelectric, and ultrasonic methods. Although the psychophysiologist will not have direct access to all of these procedures, it is likely that some of them will be employed by collaborators from other areas (e.g. vascular surgery). The most commonly used methods will therefore be described, along with examples of their use in the assessment of Raynaud's disease.

THERMAL METHODS

Thermometry

The temperature of the surface of the skin may be easily measured to an accuracy of 0.1 °C using an electronic thermometer. The procedure involves attaching to the skin a thermistor, whose electrical resistance changes with temperature, or a thermocouple, which generates a voltage proportional to its temperature. The appropriate electrical factor is then measured with an electronic meter or saved on a recording instrument.

We (Freedman and Ianni, 1983a) recorded finger temperatures of patients with Raynaud's disease, Raynaud's phenomenon secondary to scleroderma, and normal subjects during 24-h ambulatory monitoring and in the laboratory. Raynaud's disease patients had significantly lower temperatures than the other two groups under all conditions; laboratory and ambulatory finger temperatures were significantly correlated ($P < 0.01$).

The use of skin temperature or other thermal methods as indices of peripheral blood flow carries the risk of several sources of error. Skin temperature depends upon both the rate of heat supply to the skin and the rate of heat removal, i.e. upon the temperature and flow rate of the blood, and the insulation and temperature difference between the skin and the environment (Fetcher, Hall and Schaub, 1949). Environmental factors, such as ambient temperature, air currents, and clothing must be well controlled. Even if this is done, physiological problems remain (Burton, 1948). The temperature of inflowing arterial blood may be affected by that of venous blood in adjacent vessels. Muscle blood flow in the forearm tends to vary inversely with cutaneous flow and may affect finger circulation 'downstream'. The thermal capacity of tissues between the blood vessels and the skin surface varies with the size of the digit and the skin temperature. During conditions of constant temperature, thermal capacity remains relatively constant. However, if blood flow changes rapidly, changes in skin temperature may lag by several seconds or even minutes. Lastly, skin temperature may fall due to evaporation of perspiration, irrespective of changes in blood flow. The advantages of skin temperature measurement are mainly practical ones. High-quality instruments are relatively inexpensive, easy to apply, and do not require frequent recalibration. The units of measurement (°C or °F) are easily used in statistical analysis, although their relationship to actual blood flow is not always clear. Since the method is relatively insensitive to movement artifacts, it may be used in ambulatory monitoring, as opposed to other measures, such as plethysmography.

Thermography

The human skin emits radiation primarily as a function of its temperature. Thermography is an electro-optical means of translating variations of surface temperature into visual images. Thermography was used to examine total digital rewarming time in 24 Raynaud's disease patients and 51 controls (Chucker *et al.*, 1971). After immersion of both hands in ice-water for 1 min, only 2 patients achieved complete rewarming after 45 min, as opposed to 49 controls.

Like other thermal methods, thermography is an indirect measure of blood flow and, as such, is subject to the same sources of error. In addition, the required equipment is quite expensive. Its advantages lie in its fast response time (16 measurements/second), the capability of simultaneously measuring large surfaces, and the absence of physical contact with the object being measured.

VISUAL METHODS

Capillary Microscopy

Since vasospastic attacks occur at zero or near-zero levels of blood flow, the observation of the movement of red blood cells permits the determination of the complete standstill of capillary circulation (Maricq, Downey and LeRoy, 1976) as well as the measurement of cell velocities (Bollinger, Mahler and Meier, 1977; Mahler, Meier, Frey, Bollinger and Anliker, 1977). If the nailfold is moistened with immersion oil and observed under magnifications of approximately ×50 to ×300, the capillaries and red blood cells can be seen. Using this technique in a 16 °C room, Maricq *et al.* (1976) found that complete or intermittent standstill of capillary blood flow occurred in all 15 patients with Raynaud's phenomenon secondary to scleroderma, and in 5 of 6 patients with Raynaud's disease, but in none of the normal controls. By filming or videotaping the blood cells through the microscope and measuring the distance travelled over time, their velocity may be calculated. Under normal resting conditions the red blood cell velocities of Raynaud's disease patients were not different from those of controls (Bollinger *et al.*, 1977), but with finger cooling by −10 °C air, the cell velocities were significantly slower. Complete flow stoppages also occurred significantly more frequently in the patients than in the controls during the cold stressor.

Since patients with Raynaud's disease may have very low levels of capillary blood flow, capillary microscopy may be a useful evaluation procedure (Maricq *et al.*, 1976). Observation, however, is limited to a relatively small field of capillaries in the nailfold, and the thermal environment may be altered by the use of immersion oil. The calculation of cell velocities from films or videotapes is time consuming, although automated techniques are being developed to facilitate the computations (Bollinger *et al.*, 1977).

Angiography

This is a radiographic technique in which arteries are X-rayed using injected radioactive contrast agents. Results of this procedure were compared in 34 mixed Raynaud's phenomenon patients and 5 normal controls (Rosch, Porter and Grolino, 1977). Raynaud's symptoms were classified as mild (occasional attacks with minimal functional impairment), moderate (daily attacks in cool weather with moderate functional impairment), or severe (frequent attacks with significant progression and ulcerations). Symptoms were related to vasospasms seen in the angiograms, graded on a five-point scale. Under resting baseline conditions, the patients had more severe vasospasms than the normals, but the degree of spasm did not significantly correlate with the severity of clinical symptoms. After hand immersion in cold water, the patients' degree of vasospasm was significantly greater than that of the controls. After treatment with intra-arterial reserpine, the patients showed a significant decrease in cold-exposure vasospasm but not in baseline vasospasm. At 1-year follow-up, the difference in cold-spasm decrease between patients who rated their therapeutic results as excellent and those who rated them as poor was statistically significant.

Although angiography permits the visualization of arterial obstructions and vasospasm over a large area, it is an invasive procedure which involves risk to the patient. Objective quantification of the data is difficult.

PLETHYSMOGRAPHIC METHODS

Pneumoplethysmography

In this technique, a limb or digit is enclosed in a rigid container so that changes in volume in the enclosed part cause displacements of the substance (air or water) in the container. These pulsations are detected by a pressure transducer and output is displayed on a chart recorder. If the limb is maintained at the level of the heart, the amplitude of the pulsations is closely related to total blood flow (Burton, 1939). A similar method involves the measurement of changes in limb girth by encircling it with a strain gauge whose electrical resistance varies with changes in circumference. These procedures are most often employed in venous occlusion plethysmography, which determines blood flow from the increase in volume of the limb after venous outflow is occluded by a sphygmomanometer cuff.

Using this technique, patients showed significantly lower hand blood flows than normals when the temperature of the water in the plethysmograph was maintained at 32, 27, and 20 °C (McGrath et al., 1978). The percentage decrease in flow with cooling was also greater in Raynaud's patients; similar changes were found in the contralateral, uncooled hands. Also using venous occlusion plethysmography, Jamieson et al. (1971) found similar results in Raynaud's disease and scleroderma patients using ice applied to the neck as the cold stimulus.

Venous occlusion plethysmography is relatively well accepted because it permits the calculation of blood flow in absolute units. However, continuous measurement is not possible since blood flow must be permitted to return to resting values between occlusions.

Photoelectric Plethysmography

Pulse waves may also be detected using an infra-red light source to transmit through, or reflect light from, a segment of tissue and converting the light to electricity with a photodetector. Since infra-red light is scattered by blood, the output of the photodetector is related to the volume of blood within the tissue (Jennings, Tahmoush and Redmond, 1980). However, since a suitable method of calibration for this technique has not yet been developed, it provides only a relative measure of blood flow.

Pulse amplitude recovery time was measured with this method in 12 Raynaud's patients and 11 controls after immersion of both hands in ice-water for 1 min (Chucker, Fowler and Hurley, 1973). Recovery times (time required for amplitude to reach pre-stress baseline) were longer for patients than controls (significance not tested), and agreed in each case with measurements obtained with thermography. The digital pulse wave disappeared completely in Raynaud's disease patients (number not specified) but not in controls when room temperature was lowered to 18 °C (Mishima, 1978). An electronic integrator was used to analyse the pulse volumes of 3 Raynaud's disease patients during temperature biofeedback training (Freedman, Sattler and Ianni, 1979b). The average correlation between integrated pulse volume and adjacent finger temperature was 0.67.

As noted, photoplethysmography provides only a relative measure of blood flow. In addition, it is subject to error, due to changes in physical characteristics of the blood (e.g. haematocrit and orientation of red blood cells) which do not affect other plethysmographic methods. The advantages of photoplethysmography lie in the ease of transducer application and in the fact that it detects primarily cutaneous, rather than total, blood flow.

Doppler Ultrasound

In this procedure, high-frequency sound waves transmitted towards and reflected by the red blood cells moving within a vessel are detected by an electronic receiver. The red cells shift the transmitted frequency by an amount proportional to their velocity (the Doppler effect). This frequency shift can provide an audible signal as well as a visual record of pulse waves on a chart recorder (Wells, 1977).

In the diagnosis of Raynaud's disease, Doppler ultrasound has been used mainly to detect the presence or absence of vessel occlusions, and thereby differentiate between Raynaud's disease and Raynaud's phenomenon. Of 27 patients presenting with symptoms of these disorders, 10 were found to have occlusion of the digital artery by the ultrasound method, all later confirmed by arteriograms (Yao, Gourmas, Papathanasion and Irvine, 1972).

The output waveform of the Doppler flow meter is only proportional to relative blood velocity. Determination of true velocity requires knowledge of the angle between the ultrasonic beam and the flowing blood, which is impossible to delineate in practice. Doppler ultrasound is particularly useful in the detection of deep venous thromboses, which are inaccessible to most non-invasive procedures (Wells, 1977).

OTHER METHODS

Isotope Clearance

The rate of disappearance of a radioisotope from the skin is proportional to the rate of blood flow within it. Finger blood flow rates obtained by this method have been found to correlate significantly ($r = 0.95$) with those determined by venous occlusion plethysmography when ^{133}Xe was used as the isotope (Chumoskey, 1972).

Coffman and Cohen (1971) postulated that isotope clearance rate represented capillary flow, that values obtained by venous occlusion plethysmography measured total finger flow, and that the difference between these values represented arteriovenous shunt flow. Using $Na^{131}I$ as the isotope, they found that patients with Raynaud's phenomenon or primary Raynaud's disease had significantly smaller total and capillary fingertip blood flows than normals, and that arteriovenous shunt flow was only smaller in a 20 °C room.

This is the first investigation to differentiate abnormalities in specific components of finger blood flow in Raynaud's disease. The validity of this method rests on the assumption that the isotope is injected only into the capillary circulation and is not cleared through shunts. Also, it requires at least 2–3 min to perform a measurement and therefore cannot be used to assess the effects of brief stimuli.

Digital Blood Pressure

Finger systolic pressure (FSP), defined as the highest cuff pressure where pulses can be detected during cuff deflation (Brown, 1972), may be recorded using a small occluding cuff on the proximal phalanx attached to a pressure gauge and a distal strain-gauge plethysmograph to detect pulses. Since the pallor of a Raynaud's attack may be due to digital artery closure, FSP should fall to zero during this period. Finger systolic pressure was measured in 18 Raynaud's disease patients and 22 normals while cooling the finger with a small water-filled cuff on the mid-phalanx (Nielsen, 1978). Sixty-one per cent of the patients showed digital artery closure between 20 °C and 10 °C, as opposed to none of the controls. By adding body cooling with a water-filled blanket, closure was provoked in all but one of the remaining patients, as opposed to none of the controls.

Given the excellent differentiation of Raynaud's patients from normals, it is possible that the FSP technique will be useful in evaluating treatment outcome in Raynaud's disease. This study illustrates that a combination of local and environmental cold is probably necessary to reliably produce vasospastic symptoms. However, Nielsen (1978) does not report the appearance of actual attacks in his study. The FSP technique cannot be used to obtain continuous measurements as cuff occlusion is necessary. It would be desirable to use this technique to simultaneously measure several digits.

AMBULATORY MONITORING

For reasons which are not known, it has been notoriously difficult to produce Raynaud's attacks in the laboratory using a variety of thermal and emotional stressors. Therefore, ambulatory monitoring has been useful in obtaining psychophysiological measurements during attacks experienced in the natural environment (Freedman and Ianni, 1983a). It has also been valuable in testing the generalization of behavioural procedures outside the laboratory in normal persons (Freedman and Ianni, 1983b) and in Raynaud's patients (Freedman, Ianni and Wenig, 1983).

The basic method employs a four-channel 'Medilog' (Oxford Medical Instruments) cassette recorder to continuously measure finger and ambient temperatures, ECG, and time and event signals for 24-h periods. Finger temperature is recorded with a Yellow Springs no. 731 thermistor taped to one finger-pad and ambient temperature is measured with another no. 731 thermistor attached 4 cm away from the dorsal side of the wrist of the same hand and shielded from body heat by a Plexiglas holder (Figure 16.2). The ECG is obtained with disposable stick-on electrodes in a Lead II configuration. An hourly time code is internally generated on one channel in addition to patient-event signals produced by a push-button mounted on the side of the recorder. Patients are typically instructed to press the button each time an attack occurs, in addition to entering stress ratings and descriptive information of the events surrounding the attack on diary cards. The physiological data are replayed at 60 times real time on a separate playback unit and high-speed recorder. Accuracy of temperature measurement with this system is 0.1 °C.

BEHAVIOURAL TREATMENT OF RAYNAUD'S DISEASE

Medical treatments for Raynaud's disease have been generally unsuccessful. Surgical sympathectomies have been employed to abolish sympathetic nerve activity and reduce peripheral vasomotor responses to cold and stress. However, vascular tone generally recovers within a few weeks and the clinical benefits subsequently deteriorate (Robertson and Smithwick, 1951). Pharmacological treatments are problematic since they can rarely be directed towards the extremities alone. Since the vasodilator drugs dilate most of the blood vessels in the body and the digits are at the distal ends of the vascular tree, these compounds may actually reduce blood flow in the extremities (Coffman, 1979). Severe side-effects also occur with some compounds.

RELAXATION PROCEDURES

Behavioural treatments for Raynaud's disease do not suffer from the above problems. Since finger blood flow is controlled, for the most part, by the SNS through vasoconstricting nerves and circulating catecholamines, a general reduction in SNS activity should increase digital circulation. This is the rationale for the use of relaxation procedures, such as autogenic training and progressive relaxation, in the treatment of Raynaud's disease.

In the first controlled study of behavioural treatments for Raynaud's disease (Surwit, Pilon and Fenton, 1978), 30 patients were randomly assigned to receive either autogenic training alone or in combination with temperature feedback. Half the subjects in each group received 12 45-min laboratory training sessions, while half received home training and three instructional group meetings. In addition, for a 1-month period, half the subjects served as a waiting-list control group for the other half and then received treatment. All subjects were instructed in a response-generalization technique in which they practised hand-warming many times each day using visual aids as reminders. Since the investigators hypothesized that reduced SNS activity would produce increased finger blood flow, their major endpoint was finger temperature during whole-body cold stress – which produces digital vasoconstriction through increased SNS activity. Subjects as a whole showed significant improvement in response to this test and reported fewer attacks after treatment. However, the decline in symptom frequency reported by treated subjects (32%) did not differ significantly from that reported by the waiting-list controls (10%). There were no significant differences between subjects who received autogenic training alone and those who also received biofeedback, or between subjects trained at home and those trained in the laboratory. Also, subjects' heart rates were significantly higher during the post-treatment cold stress test than during the pre-treatment test. One year later, the cold stress responses of 19 follow-up subjects returned to pre-treatment levels, although reported symptom frequency remained improved (Keefe, Surwit and Pilon, 1979). In a subsequent study (Keefe, Surwit and Pilon, 1980) of 21 patients, no outcome differences were found among those receiving progressive relaxation, autogenic training, or a combination of autogenic training and temperature feedback; patients as a whole showed significant improvements in response to the cold stress test and in reported symptom frequency. All patients were treated at home in that study.

Jacobson, Manschreck and Silverberg (1979) treated 12 Raynaud's disease patients with 12 brief sessions of progressive relaxation alone or in combination with temperature feedback. Patients generally showed temperature elevations during training and rated themselves as improved; however, there were no outcome differences between the two groups.

TEMPERATURE BIOFEEDBACK

The first controlled group studies of temperature biofeedback in normal subjects were performed by Keefe (1975, 1978) and Keefe and Gardner (1979), who showed that various combinations of brief temperature feedback training and thermal suggestions produced significant increases in finger temperature ranging from 0.8 to 1.3 °C. Subjects generally acquired the response early in training and the magnitude of the response was not increased by additional training sessions. One study (Keefe, 1978) showed that the training effect was maintained at 1- and 2-week follow-up sessions.

Two studies conducted by Freedman and Ianni (1983b) were designed to assess the ability to increase finger temperature without feedback, as well as outside the laboratory, and to determine if physiological relaxation is necessary for feedback-induced vasodilation. In the first experiment, 32 subjects were randomly assigned to receive six sessions of either finger temperature feedback, frontalis EMG feedback, autogenic training or simple instructions to increase finger temperature. Each session consisted of a 16-min baseline period, a 24-min training or instruction period, and a final 16-min baseline. The ability to voluntarily increase temperature without feedback was tested before training, after training, and outside the laboratory during ambulatory monitoring. In addition to finger temperature, heart rate, respiration rate, frontalis EMG, and skin conductance level were continuously recorded during each session.

In the pre-training voluntary control session, subjects declined in finger temperature, demonstrating that voluntary vasodilation was not possible prior to training. During training, subjects receiving temperature feedback showed significant increases in finger temperature during the first 12 min of the first session only, an effect not shown by the other subjects. During the subsequent five training sessions, significant elevations were not shown by any group. Subjects as a whole showed within-session declines in heart rate, respiration rate, and frontalis EMG level. During the post-training test of voluntary control in the laboratory, only the temperature-feedback group produced a significant elevation in digital temperature. In the final voluntary control test, conducted outside the laboratory with ambulatory monitoring, no temperature increases were found.

It was hypothesized that finger temperature elevations produced during temperature feedback might be time-limited or that excessive session length might impede training. Kluger and Tursky (1982) also found that feedback-induced temperature increases peaked early in the session and subsequently declined. We therefore performed a second experiment in which the training periods were shortened from 24 to 16 min and the final baseline period eliminated. Sixteen subjects were randomly assigned to receive either finger temperature feedback or simple instructions to increase finger temperature. Half the subjects in each group received 6 training sessions and half received 10. As in the previous study, subjects were unable to raise their finger temperature when requested to do so prior to training. However, during training, temperature-feedback subjects consistently increased their finger temperature (+ 0.42 °C, $P < 0.05$) while those receiving instructions only did not. Increasing the number of training sessions from 6 to 10 had no effect. Subjects in the instructions-only group showed significant declines in heart rate and muscle tension during training, while temperature-feedback subjects did not. During the first post-training voluntary control test, temperature-feedback subjects were the only ones who demonstrated significant increases in digital temperature (+ 0.56 °C). There were no group differences on other physiological measures. During a similar test performed outside the laboratory with ambulatory monitoring, these subjects were again the only ones to show significant finger temperature elevations. These increases were of substantially larger magnitude (2.41 °C) than those produced during prior sessions. Thus, shortening the session length resulted in a robust laboratory training effect and also enhanced generalization of the response to an extra-laboratory setting. Subjects as a whole showed significant heart rate declines during this session.

Given the vasoconstrictive nature of the symptoms of Raynaud's disease and the ability of normal subjects to learn to increase peripheral blood flow using temperature feedback, it was logical to employ this procedure in the treatment of this disorder. In one investigation (Freedman, Lynn, Ianni and Hale, 1981), 6 patients with Raynaud's disease and 4 with secondary Raynaud's phenomenon received 12 56-min training sessions of finger temperature biofeedback. Patients showed significant reductions in reported symptom frequency which were maintained for a 1-year follow-up period. Small but significant elevations in finger temperature were found during training and were not accompanied by physiological relaxation. Increased finger temperature was, in fact, significantly correlated with increased respiration rate, skin conductance level, and frontalis EMG activity.

In a review of the literature on transfer of training in biofeedback, Lynn and Freedman (1979) concluded that 'Transfer will tend to be minimal when the training stimulus is nonrepresentative of the population of stimuli to which the response is to be transferred.' Since the Raynaud's disease patient must be able to control finger blood flow in cold conditions as well as in the comfortable laboratory environment, a study was performed in which a local cold stimulus was introduced during temperature-feedback training (Freedman, Ianni, Hale and Lynn, 1979a). Six Raynaud's disease and 2 Raynaud's phenomenon patients first received six temperature feedback training sessions as described above. During six subsequent sessions, a thermal cooling device was applied to the finger which was being monitored for feedback. The temperature of this device was decreased from 30 to 20 °C at a rate of 1 °C/min and then held at 20 °C for 10 min. The addition of this device, of course, greatly increased the difficulty of finger temperature elevation during feedback. However, patients again showed significant reductions in attack frequency, which were maintained throughout the following year.

In a subsequent investigation (Freedman *et al.*, 1983), the relative efficacy of standard temperature feedback and temperature feedback under cold stress was tested in a controlled manner. Thirty-two Raynaud's disease patients were randomly assigned to receive ten 32-min training sessions in either one of these procedures, autogenic training, or frontalis EMG feedback. The last procedure was chosen to control for the effects of receiving feedback of any physiological information and to assess the role of relaxation in treatment. In addition, since emotional stress is a factor in some Raynaud's attacks (Freedman and Ianni, 1983a), cognitive stress management was employed with half the patients in each group. Patients were tested for the ability to increase temperature without feedback prior to treatment, after treatment, and 1 year later. This was done both with and without cold stress. All vasospastic attacks were recorded for 1 month before and 1 year following treatment. In addition, patients received ambulatory monitoring of finger temperature, ambient temperature, and ECG for 24 h prior to treatment and at the 1-year follow-up evaluation.

During training, subjects receiving temperature feedback (TEMP) or temperature feedback under cold stress (TEMPCS) showed significant increases (0.60 °C) in finger temperature, whereas those receiving autogenic instructions or EMG feedback did not. Autogenic and EMG subjects showed significant declines in muscle tension and reported stress, and non-significant declines in heart rate, while the other groups did not. During post-training cold stress and voluntary control tests, the temperature elevations of the TEMP subjects were superior to those of the other three groups. One year later, however, the TEMPCS group showed the best performance (+ 0.5 °C) on the voluntary control test. The change shown by the TEMP group (+ 0.3 °C) was still significant, but smaller than that shown previously. Final temperatures during the follow-up test were significantly related to the number of reported attacks. Decrements in reported symptoms were greatest for the TEMPCS group (92.5%), next greatest for the TEMP group (66.8%), followed by the autogenic group (32.6%) and the EMG group (17.0%). During 1-year follow-up Medilog recordings, greater finger-ambient temperature differences were needed to produce attacks in TEMP and TEMPCS subjects compared to EMG and autogenic subjects. The addition of cognitive stress management had no significant effects on any procedure. Data recently obtained from the TEMP and TEMPCS subjects show that their symptom reductions were retained 3 years after treatment, although the ability to voluntarily increase finger temperature in the lab was lost at the 2-year follow-up point (Freedman, Ianni and Wenig, 1985).

MECHANISMS OF BEHAVIOURAL TREATMENT

We have shown in normal persons (Freedman and Ianni, 1983b) and in Raynaud's disease patients that the effects of temperature feedback are physiologically different from those of autogenic training, frontalis EMG feedback, or simple instructions to increase finger temperature. Temperature feedback produces digital vasodilation without bradycardia or decreased muscle tension, whereas the other techniques do produce bradycardia and lower EMG levels but not increased finger temperature. Recent research has uncovered a physiological mechanism which may explain increased digital blood flow in the absence of decreased generalized physiological arousal. It was previously thought that vascular control of digital blood flow resulted solely from sympathetically mediated alpha-adrenergic vasoconstriction. However, recently an active beta-adrenergic vasodilating mechanism has been identified in the human finger (Cohen and Coffman, 1981). We have shown that this mechanism is operative during temperature feedback in both normal persons and patients with Raynaud's disease by local beta-blockade of the vasodilation with intra-arterial infusions of propranolol (Freedman, Sabharwal, Ianni, Desai, Wenig and Mayes, 1988).

We first randomly assigned 18 patients with idiopathic Raynaud's disease and 16 normal subjects to receive ten sessions of temperature feedback or autogenic training using the methods of the previous study (Freedman, Ianni and Wenig, 1983). Following training, in a separate session, a catheter was placed in the right brachial artery using a local anaesthetic and connected to two Harvard infusion pumps, one containing 0.9% saline solution, the other containing propranolol, a beta-adrenergic antagonist. Saline was infused at a rate of 2 ml/min throughout the experiment except when indicated below. The pumps were housed in a sound-proofed box and controlled remotely by the experimenter from the polygraph in a separate room. Finger blood flow was measured in both hands with venous occlusion plethysmography, and capillary blood flow was recorded by injecting 2 μCi of $Na^{131}I$ subcutaneously in one finger-pad on the right hand and measuring its disappearance with a scintillation counter.

After a 20-min adaptation period and 16 min of baseline recordings, the temperature-feedback signals or autogenic tape were activated. After 6 min the infusion was switched from saline to propranolol (0.5 mg/min) for 2 min, then saline for 4 min, propranolol (same dose) for 2 min, and saline for 4 min. These changes occurred without the subject's knowledge. Significant bilateral vasodilation occurred in the temperature-feedback subjects and was significantly reduced by propranolol in the infused but not the control hand. The magnitudes of these effects were not significantly different in the Raynaud's disease and normal subjects. However, capillary blood flow increased significantly during feedback in the patients but not the normal subjects. There were no significant blood flow changes at all in the patients or normals who received autogenic training. There were no significant heart rate or blood pressure changes in the temperature-feedback group; the autogenic group showed a significant decline in heart rate during the autogenic instructions. Thus, a beta-adrenergic mechanism is involved in feedback-induced vasodilation.

The only known efferent vasomotor nerves in human fingers are adrenergic; neurogenic vasoconstriction is caused by the interaction of released norepinephrine with post-junctional alpha-adrenergic receptors. Our finding of a beta-adrenergic mechanism in temperature biofeedback thus raised the question of whether feedback-induced vasodilation is neurally mediated. Since it is possible to block the digital nerves by local injection of an anaesthetic, a method was available to test this hypothesis. Since digital nerve blockade raises finger blood flow to near ceiling levels, we reduced it to mid-range by infusing norepinephrine (NE) (0.25 μg/min), in the right brachial artery. To control for all of the manipulations, we measured blood flow in 3 fingers: right, nerve-blocked + NE; right, no block + NE; left, no block, no NE. We then repeated the propranolol infusion of the previous study. In two separate studies of normal subjects ($N = 8$, $N = 9$) and a subsequent study with Raynaud's disease patients ($N = 10$), we found that vasodilation produced by temperature feedback was not attenuated by nerve-blockade or norepinephrine, but was reduced by propranolol. This also occurred for capillary blood flow in the patients, but not the normal subjects. Thus, the beta-adrenergic vasodilating mechanism of temperature feedback does not appear to be mediated through the digital nerves.

CONTRIBUTION OF PSYCHOPHYSIOLOGICAL METHODS TO RESEARCH ON RAYNAUD'S DISEASE

No physiological method, invasive or non-invasive, has been developed to diagnose idiopathic Raynaud's disease. Although the attacks are visually distinct, they are difficult to provoke in the laboratory, even with intense cooling. Therefore, the classification of a patient as having primary Raynaud's disease rests largely on his/her self-report of these symptoms after the exclusion of all other likely diseases.

Most studies have found that Raynaud's disease patients have, on average, lower levels of finger temperature (Freedman and Ianni, 1983b), total finger blood flow (Coffman and Cohen, 1971), and finger capillary blood flow (Coffman and Cohen, 1971) compared to normal persons under a variety of thermal conditions. However, these studies have found substantial overlap of temperature and blood flow measurements from normal and patient populations, reducing their value as diagnostic tools. One study (Nielsen, 1978) reported a fall to zero of finger systolic pressure during combined finger and body cooling in 6 of 7 patients reported to have primary Raynaud's disease. However, other patient groups were not investigated and the study has not been replicated.

Surface measurements of finger temperature in the laboratory and during ambulatory monitoring have been somewhat more useful in assessing the role of stress in Raynaud's disease. In the laboratory, an emotionally stressful script having thematic relevance to Raynaud's disease reduced finger temperature, on the average, in patients but not controls (Freedman and Ianni, 1985). During ambulatory monitoring, finger temperature declined and heart rate and stress ratings increased in about one-third of the Raynaud's attacks (Freedman and Ianni, 1983b), which were interpreted as being stress-related. This is in reasonable agreement with patient diary data (Freedman *et al.*, 1982) from a previous study. It is important to note that ambulatory finger temperatures were sufficiently sensitive to detect some but not all vasospastic attacks; patient-event signals were also needed for this purpose.

Since finger temperature is a non-linear, slowly changing correlate of blood flow, it cannot be used where quantitative measurements are needed. In studying blood flow responses to infused adrenergic drugs, venous occlusion plethysmography was therefore employed (Freedman, Sabharwal, Ianni, Desai, Wenig and Mayes, 1988; Freedman *et al.*, 1989). Since this measure responds more rapidly than temperature, it also reflects ongoing SNS activity in addition to the pharmacological effects. It is possible to control for this activity mathematically, by measuring finger blood flow in the non-infused hand and subtracting it from measurements in the infused hand.

Measurements of SNS activity have, with one exception, not been elucidative in the study of Raynaud's disease. At least four studies, cited earlier, have measured venous catecholamine levels in Raynaud's patients and normals and produced inconsistent results. A more direct method employed microelectrode recordings of sympathetic nerve activity in Raynaud's patients and normal volunteers (Fagius and Blumberg, 1985). Although it is difficult to quantify the actual number of nerve impulses with this technique, it is possible to analyse intra-individual data using percentage change scores.

Traditional psychophysiological measurements have been most commonly employed in studies of behavioural treatments for Raynaud's disease and similar investigations of biofeedback and relaxation procedures in normal subjects. Measurements of heart and respiration rates, and EMG and skin conductance levels have shown that physiological relaxation is not necessary for vasodilation during finger temperature biofeedback (Freedman and Ianni, 1983a; Freedman *et al.*, 1983). Finger temperature has been almost exclusively employed as the mode of feedback for peripheral vasodilation. Recognizing the fact that finger temperature is a slowly changing measure of blood flow, Kluger, Jamner and Tursky (1985) compared the effects of blood flow feedback by photoplethysmograph with those of standard finger temperature feedback.

Since no differences were found between the two methods, the amount of information conveyed to the subject by finger temperature appears to be sufficient for vasodilation to occur.

Since laboratory provocation of Raynaud's attacks is unreliable and no standard cold stress test has been developed, the patient's reported attack frequency has been most frequently used as the major outcome measure in clinical studies. Patients given finger temperature feedback reported significantly fewer attacks at follow-up than those given relaxation-based procedures, were superior in their ability to voluntarily increase finger temperature, and required significantly colder temperatures to produce attacks during ambulatory monitoring (Freedman *et al.*, 1983). Thus, although not precisely correlated, there was some concordance among physiological and self-report measures. However, at 2- and 3-year follow-up points, patients' reported symptoms remained improved but the ability to voluntarily increase finger temperature was lost (Freedman *et al.*, 1985).

The dissociation between physiological and self-report measures was found in a previous follow-up study of behavioural treatments for Raynaud's disease (Keefe *et al.*, 1980) and is an important area for further research. Since finger capillary blood flow is most severely reduced in Raynaud's disease, but represents only a small portion of total finger blood flow, it is possible that patients retain the ability to increase it at long-term follow-up but that this is not reflected by finger temperature measurements. New research in our laboratory has shown that Raynaud's disease patients given temperature feedback can voluntarily increase finger capillary blood flow, measured by radioisotope clearance, and retain this ability at 1-year follow-up. Work is currently in progress to determine if this effect persists for longer periods of time.

A laser Doppler flow meter has recently been developed and was claimed to represent a non-invasive measure of capillary blood flow. However, this method operates on essentially the same principle as photoelectric plethysmography and more recent research has shown that it responds to changes in both shunt and capillary blood flow (Kristensen, Englehart and Nielsen, 1983). Thus, the additional expense of this instrument ($10,000) is not justified. Recent developments in digital vascular imaging currently permit accurate, high-quality images of coronary arteries and may eventually be enhanced to allow imaging of smaller digital blood vessels. Such a device might help specify the vascular fault in idiopathic Raynaud's disease.

The use of pharmacological probes, in conjunction with quantitative measures of finger blood flow, has enabled the identification of alpha-adrenergic hyper-responsiveness in idiopathic Raynaud's disease. However, the aetiology of this receptor difference is not known, nor is its precise involvement in the production of vasospastic attacks. Pharmacological probes have also identified a non-neural beta-adrenergic vasodilating mechanism in temperature biofeedback. However, the endogenous vasodilating substance which mediates this effect is not known. Although psychophysiologists have not typically employed manipulations of this nature, these findings will hopefully encourage their use in attempts to solve these and other problems of Raynaud's disease and its treatment.

ACKNOWLEDGEMENTS

Research conducted by the author was supported by research grants HL-23828 and HL-30604 from the National Heart, Lung, and Blood Institute.

REFERENCES

Abramson, D. (1974). *Vascular Disorders of the Extremities*. New York: Harper and Row.

Allen, E. and Brown, G. (1932). Raynaud's disease: a critical review of minimal requisites for diagnosis. *American Journal of Medical Science* **183**, 187–195.

Blain, A., Coller, F. and Carver, G. (1951). Raynaud's disease: a study of criteria for prognosis. *Surgery* **29**, 387–397.

Bloom, L. and Trautt, G. (1977). Finger pulse volume as a measure of anxiety: further evaluation. *Psychophysiology* **14**, 541–544.

Bollinger, A., Mahler, F. and Meier, B. (1977). Velocity patterns in nailfold capillaries of normal subjects and patients with Raynaud's disease and acrocyanosis. *Bibliotheca Anatomica* **16**, 142–145.

Brown, C. (1972). Instruments in psychophysiology. In: N. Greenfield and R. Sternbach (Eds) *Handbook of Psychophysiology*. New York: Holt, Rinehart, and Winston.

Burton, A. (1939). The range and variability of the blood flow in the human fingers. *American Journal of Physiology* **127**, 437–453.

Burton, A. (1948). Temperature of skin: measurement and use as index of peripheral blood flow. In: V. Potter (Ed.) *Methods in Medical Research*. Chicago: Yearbook.

Charles, R. and Carmick, E. (1970). Skin temperature changes after griseofulvin. *Archives of Dermatology* **101**, 331–336.

Chucker, F., Fowler, R. and Hurley, G. (1973). Photoplethysmometry and thermography in Raynaud's disorders. *Angiology* **24**, 612–618.

Chucker, F., Fowler, R., Motomuja, T., Singh, B. and Hurley, W. (1971). Induced temperature transients in Raynaud's disease measured by thermography. *Angiology* **22**, 580–593.

Chumoskey, J. (1972). Skin blood flow by ^{133}Xe disappearance validated by venous occlusion plethysmography. *Journal of Applied Physiology* **32**, 432–435.

Coffman, J.D. (1972). Total and nutritional blood flow in the finger. *Clinical Science* **42**, 243–250.

Coffman, J.D. (1979). Vasodilator drugs in peripheral vascular disease. *New England Journal of Medicine* **300**, 713–717.

Coffman, J. and Cohen, A. (1971). Total and capillary fingertip blood flow in Raynaud's phenomenon. *New England Journal of Medicine* **285**, 259–263.

Cohen, R. and Coffman, J. (1981). Beta-adrenergic vasodilator mechanism in the finger. *Circulation Research* **49**, 1196–1201.

Cook, M. (1974). Psychophysiology of peripheral vascular changes. In: P. Obrist, A. Black, J. Brener and L. DiCara (Eds) *Cardiovascular Psychophysiology*. Chicago: Aldine.

Downey, J. and Frewin, D. (1973). The effect of cold on blood flow in the hands of patients with Raynaud's phenomenon. *Clinical Science* **44**, 279–287.

Fagius, J. and Blumberg, H. (1985). Sympathetic outflow to the hand in patients with Raynaud's phenomenon. *Cardiovascular Research* **19**, 249–253.

Fetcher, E., Hall, J. and Shaub, H. (1949). The skin temperature of an extremity as a measure of its blood flow. *Science* **110**, 422–432.

Flavahan, N. and Vanhoutte, P. (1986). The effect of cooling on alpha₁ and alpha₂ adrenergic responses in canine saphenous and femoral veins. *Journal of Pharmacology and Experimental Therapeutics* **238**, 139–147.

Freedman, R. and Ianni, P. (1983a). Role of cold and emotional stress in Raynaud's disease and scleroderma. *British Medical Journal* **287**, 1499–1502.

Freedman, R. and Ianni, P. (1983b). Self-control of digital temperature: physiological factors and transfer effects. *Psychophysiology* **20**, 682–688.

Freedman, R. and Ianni, P. (1985). Effects of general and thematically relevant stressors in Raynaud's disease. *Journal of Psychosomatic Research* **29**, 275–280.

Freedman, R., Ianni, P., Hale, P. and Lynn, S. (1979a). Treatment of Raynaud's phenomenon with biofeedback and cold desensitization. *Psychophysiology* **16**, 182 (Abstract).

Freedman, R., Ianni, P. and Wenig, P. (1983). Behavioural treatment of Raynaud's disease. *Journal of Consulting and Clinical Psychology* **51**, 539–549.

Freedman, R., Ianni, P. and Wenig, P. (1985). Behavioural treatment of Raynaud's disease: long-term followup. *Journal of Consulting and Clinical Psychology* **53**, 136.

Freedman, R., Lynn, S. and Ianni, P. (1982). Behavioural assessment of Raynaud's disease. In: F. Keefe and J. Blumenthal (Eds) *Assessment Strategies in Behavioral Medicine*, pp. 99–130. New York: Grune and Stratton.

Freedman, R., Lynn, S., Ianni, P. and Hale, P. (1981). Biofeedback treatment of Raynaud's disease and phenomenon. *Biofeedback and Self-Regulation* **6**, 355–365.

Freedman, R., Sabharwal, S., Ianni, P., Desai, N., Wenig, P. and Mayes, M. (1988). Non-neural beta-adrenergic vasodilating mechanism in temperature biofeedback. *Psychosomatic Medicine* **50**, 394–401.

Freedman, R., Sabharwal, S., Ianni, P. and Wenig, P. (1984). Beta-adrenergic vasodilating mechanism in temperature feedback. *Psychophysiology* **21**, 577–578.

Freedman, R., Sabharwal, S., Wenig, P. and Mayes, M. (1989). Increased alpha-adrenergic responsiveness in Raynaud's disease. *Arthritis and Rheumatism*, **33**, 61–65.

Freedman, R., Sattler, H. and Ianni, P. (1979b). Analysis of photoplethysmographic data. *Psychophysiology* **16**, 182.

Gifford, R. and Hines, E. (1957). Raynaud's disease among women and girls. *Circulation* **16**, 1012–1025.

Halperin, J. and Coffman, J. (1979). Pathophysiology of Raynaud's disease. *Archives of Internal Medicine* **139**, 89–92.

Halperin, J., Cohen, R. and Coffman, J. (1983). Vasodilation during mental stress in Raynaud's disease. *Cardiovascular Research* **17**, 671–677.

Jacobson, A., Manschreck, T. and Silverberg, E. (1979). Behavioural treatment for Raynaud's disease: a comparative study with long-term follow-up. *American Journal of Psychiatry* **136**, 844–846.

Jamieson, G., Ludbrook, J. and Wilson, A. (1971). Cold hypersensitivity in Raynaud's phenomenon. *Circulation* **44**, 254–264.

Jennings, J.R., Tahmoush, A.J. and Redmond, D.P. (1980). Non-invasive measurement of peripheral vascular activity. In: I. Martin and P.H. Venables (Eds) *Techniques in Psychophysiology*. New York: Wiley.

Johnsen, T., Nielsen, S. and Skovborg, F. (1977). Blood viscosity and local response to cold in primary Raynaud's phenomenon. *Lancet* **ii**, 1001–1002.

Keefe, F. (1975). Conditioning changes in differential skin temperature. *Perceptual and Motor Skills* **40**, 283–288.

Keefe, F. (1978). Biofeedback vs. instructional control of skin temperature. *Journal of Behavioral Medicine* **1**, 323–335.

Keefe, F. and Gardner, E. (1979). Learned control of skin temperature: effects of short and long-term biofeedback training. *Behavior Therapy* **10**, 202–210.

Keefe, F., Surwit, R. and Pilon, R. (1979). A 1-year follow-up of Raynaud's patients treated with behavioural therapy techniques. *Journal of Behavioral Medicine* **2**, 385–391.

Keefe, F., Surwit, R. and Pilon, R. (1980). Biofeedback, autogenic training, and progressive relaxation in the treatment of Raynaud's disease: a comparative study. *Journal of Applied Behavior Analysis* **13**, 3–11.

Kluger, M.A., Jamner, L.D. and Tursky, B. (1985). Comparison of the effectiveness of biofeedback and relaxation training on hand warming. *Psychophysiology* **22**, 162–166.

Kluger, M. and Tursky, B. (1982). A strategy for improving finger temperature biofeedback training. *Psychophysiology* **19**, 329 (Abstract).

Kontos, H.A. and Wasserman, A.J. (1969). Effect of reserpine in Raynaud's phenomenon. *Circulation* **39**, 259–266.

Kristensen, J.K., Engelhart, M. and Neilsen, T. (1983). Laser-Doppler measurement of digital blood flow regulation in normals and in patients with Raynaud's phenomenon. *Acta Dermatovener (Stockholm)* **63**, 43–47.

Lefkowitz, R., Caron, M. and Stiles, G. (1984). Mechanisms of membrane receptor regulation. *New England Journal of Medicine* **310**, 1570–1579.

Lewis, T. (1929). Experiments relating to the peripheral mechanism involved in spasmodic arrest of circulation in the fingers, a variety of Raynaud's disease. *Heart* **15**, 7–101.

Lewis, T. (1938). The pathological changes in the arteries supplying the fingers in warm handed people and cases of so-called Raynaud's disease. *Clinical Science* **3**, 287–300.

Lottenbach, K. (1971). Vasomotor tone and vascular responses to local cold in primary Raynaud's disease. *Angiology* **22**, 4–8.

Lynn, S. and Freedman, R. (1979). Transfer and evaluation of biofeedback treatment. In: A. Goldstein and F. Kanfer (Eds) *Maximizing Treatment Gains – Transfer Enhancement in Psychotherapy.* New York: Academic Press.

Mahler, F., Meier, B., Frey, R., Bollinger, A. and Anliker, M. (1977). Reaction of red blood cell velocity in nailfold capillaries to local cold in patients with vasospastic disease. *Bibliotheca Anatomica* **16**, 155–158.

Maricq, H., Downey, J. and LeRoy, E. (1976). Standstill of nailfold capillary blood flow during cooling in scleroderma and Raynaud's syndrome. *Blood Vessels* **13**, 338–349.

McGrath, M., Peek, R. and Penny, R. (1978). Raynaud's disease: reduced hand blood flows with normal blood viscosity. *Australian and New Zealand Journal of Medicine* **8**, 126–131.

McGrath, M. and Penny, R. (1974). The mechanisms of Raynaud's phenomenon, Part 1. *Medical Journal of Australia* **2**, 328–333.

Mendlowitz, M. and Naftchi, N. (1959). The digital circulation in Raynaud's disease. *American Journal of Cardiology* **4**, 480–484.

Miller, I. and Walder, D. (1972). Raynaud's disease and cooling of the fingers. *British Journal of Surgery* **59**, 313.

Mishima, Y. (1978). Pathophysiology of Raynaud's phenomenon. *Journal of Cardiovascular Surgery* **19**, 521–526.

Mittelmann, B. and Wolff, H. (1939). Affective states and skin temperature: experimental study of subjects with 'cold hands' and Raynaud's syndrome. *Psychosomatic Medicine* **1**, 271–292.

Nielsen, S. (1978). Raynaud's phenomenon and finger systolic pressure during cooling. *Scandinavian Journal of Clinical Laboratory Investigation* **38**, 765–770.

Olsen, N. and Nielsen, S. (1978). Prevalence of primary Raynaud's phenomenon in young females. *Scandinavian Journal of Clinical Laboratory Investigation* **38**, 761–765.

Peacock, J. (1959a). A comparative study of the digital cutaneous temperatures and hand blood flows in the normal hand, primary Raynaud's disease, and primary acrocyanosis. *Clinical Science* **8**, 25–33.

Peacock, J. (1959b). Peripheral venous blood concentration of epinephrine and norepinephrine in primary Raynaud's disease. *Circulation Research* **7**, 831–837.

Pringle, R., Walder, D. and Weaver, J. (1965). Blood viscosity and Raynaud's disease. *Lancet* **iii**, 1085–1088.

Raynaud, M. (1888). *New Research on the Nature and Treatment of Local Asphyxia of the Extremities*, T. Barlow (trans.). London: The New Sydenham Society.

Robertson, C. and Smithwick, R. (1951). The recurrence of vasoconstrictor activity after limb sympathectomy in Raynaud's disease and allied vasomotor states. *New England Journal of Medicine* **245**, 317–320.

Rosch, J., Porter, J. and Grolino, B. (1977). Cryodynamic hand angiography in the diagnosis and management of Raynaud's syndrome. *Radiology* **55**, 807–814.

Sapira, J., Rodnan, G., Scheib, E., Klaniecki, T. and Rizk, M. (1972). Studies of endogenous catecholamines in patients with Raynaud's phenomenon secondary to progressive systemic sclerosis. *American Journal of Medicine* **52**, 330–337.

Shepherd, J.T. (1963). *Physiology of the Circulation in Human Limbs in Health and Disease.* Philadelphia: Saunders.

Spitell, J.A., Jr (1980). Raynaud's phenomenon and allied vasospastic disorders. In: J.L. Juergens, J.A. Spitell, Jr and J.F. Fairbairn (Eds) *Peripheral Vascular Diseases.* Philadelphia: Saunders.

Surwit, R.S., Allen, L.M., III, Gilgor, R.S., Schanberg, S., Kuhn, C. and Duvic, M. (1983). Neuroendocrine response to cold in Raynaud's syndrome. *Life Sciences* **32**, 995–1000.

Surwit, R., Pilon, R. and Fenton, C. (1978). Behavioural treatment of Raynaud's disease. *Journal of Behavioral Medicine* **1**, 323–335.

Vanhoutte, P.M. (1980). Physical factors of regulation. In: D. Bohr, A. Somylo and H. Sparks (Eds) *Handbook of Physiology*, Vol. II. Baltimore: American Physiological Society.

Wells, P.N.T. (1977). *Biomedical Ultrasonics.* New York: Academic Press.

Willerson, J., Thompson, R. and Hookman, P. (1979). Reserpine in Raynaud's disease and phenomenon. *Annals of Internal Medicine* **72**, 17–27.

Yao, S., Gourmas, C., Papathanasion, K. and Irvine, W. (1972). A method for assessing ischemia of the hand and fingers. *Surgery, Gynecology and Obstetrics* **135**, 373–378.

Chapter 17

Gastrointestinal Disorders

Rupert Hölzl

Psychophysiological Research Unit,
Max Planck Institute of Psychiatry,
Kraepelinstrasse 9,
D-8000 Munich 40,
Federal Republic of Germany

ABSTRACT

Historically, experimental and clinical research on the psychophysiology of the gastrointestinal system originated from early physiological (Beaumont, Pavlov, Cannon) and psychosomatic work (Wolff and others). Controlled human laboratory studies on psychophysiological determinants of gastrointestinal function remained scarce until about 1978, mainly because reliable noninvasive recording methods were lacking. Since then major methodological advances and behavioural medicine research on functional gastrointestinal disorders, particularly in the field of the irritable bowel syndrome and fecal incontinence, have converged in the rapidly developing field of clinical psychophysiology of the gastrointestinal system. It is characterized by a more detailed discussion of some of its basic issues.

Basic technical and methodological requirements of psychophysiological studies in the gastrointestinal system and their clinical applications are described with particular

Handbook of Clinical Psychophysiology Edited by G. Turpin

emphasis on noninvasive recording techniques of relevant functional parameters and representative psychophysiological test paradigms. In particular, techniques for the measurement of secretion, motility, emptying and transit, as well as the assessment of sphincter function, visceral perception, and visceral pain are considered.

The main part of the chapter deals with the application of psychophysiological methods to analysis, diagnosis, and treatment of functional gastrointestinal disorders. The concepts of functional disorder and of psychopathophysiological mechanisms as categories of analysis and diagnostic criteria are elaborated. This is followed by a selective review of disorders in the light of these categories: oesophageal disorders, peptic ulcer disease and nonulcerative dyspepsia, inflammatory bowel diseases, irritable bowel syndrome, fecal incontinence.

The final part of the chapter is devoted to research perspectives such as central-autonomic and psychoendocrinological links of the gastrointestinal peptide system and applied interoception research.

HISTORICAL INTRODUCTION

It may be considered a trivial statement to say, that motor and secretory functions of the *gastrointestinal tract (GIT)* are influenced by psychological variables, and that, vice versa, gastrointestinal afferents exert significant control over central processes and overt behaviour. But astonishingly, until recently little firm information on the particulars of these interactions in health and disease has been published, despite the enormous growth of knowledge in gastrointestinal physiology.

Clinical knowledge of these relationships is as old as medicine, and their existence has been common knowledge to laymen psychologists and medical practitioners alike. The conviction, that gastrointestinal disorders such as peptic ulcers are of 'nervous' origin, that is, psychogenic, dates back far beyond the advent of psychoanalytic formulations of '*psychosomatics*' (Alexander, 1950). The idea found early scientific support in the well-known work of Beaumont (1833) and Cannon (1909, 1929), and more recently in that by Wolf and Wolff (1943). The early evidence on gastrointestinal correlates of emotions was supplemented by Pavlov's (1927) demonstration of conditionability or respondent learning of the GIT.

Compared with this long tradition the history of gastrointestinal psychophysiology is short. Around 1977 there were some texts on neuronal control of gastric motor and secretory functions (e.g. Brooks and Evers, 1977) and the results of animal research on experimental ulcers and GIT effects of 'experimental neuroses' had been published (Brady, Porter, Conrad and Mason, 1958; Bykov and Kurzin, 1966; Weiss, 1977). The abundant and contradictory 'psychosomatic' literature on personality characteristics of peptic ulcer patients was based on clinical correlative studies if empirical at all (Weiner, 1977).

Explicit analyses of the functional connections between psychological and physiological regulatory systems which could mediate those assumed correlations were not available. Experimental laboratory work within the classical field of human psychophysiology was scarce, mostly limited to problematic surface recordings of gastric motility, and of a comparatively low methodological standard (Russell and Stern, 1967; Walker and Sandman, 1977; see review by Hölzl, 1983). At that time, however, several lines of methodological experimental, and clinical research on functional GIT disorders converged with *'behavioural medicine'* approaches to produce a sudden increase of interest in *gastrointestinal psychophysiology* (Hölzl and Whitehead, 1983).

Since then, increasing numbers of original articles, chapters, and books have appeared. They deal with *recording methods* suitable for human psychophysiology (Stern and Koch, 1985) and general psychophysiology of the GIT, and with laboratory studies of human *gastrointestinal responses* to different *'stress'* conditions (Hölzl, 1989). Psychological and physiological mechanisms of *functional GIT disorders*, with particular emphasis on the 'irritable bowel syndrome' (IBS), have been studied (Area Review, 1987; Dotevall, 1985; Whitehead and Schuster, 1985). Applications of psychophysiological tools to *diagnostic analysis* and *biofeedback therapy* of specific dysfunctions of somatic origin like faecal incontinence have emerged (Wald and Handen, 1987; Whitehead and Schuster, 1985, Ch. 11). Stimulated by results on the mechanism of continence and by findings on altered visceral pain perceptions in IBS, emphasis has shifted from assessment of GIT responses to psychophysiological functions of *afferent visceral processes*. Meanwhile, these clinical analyses have converged with recent physiological evidence on autonomic regulatory systems in which gastrointestinal afferents take part and on the mechanisms of visceral nociception (cf. Jänig, 1986; Jänig and Morrison, 1986).

MEASUREMENT TECHNIQUES

Experimental and clinical analyses of psychophysiological GIT mechanisms require (*1*) highly specific sets of reliable and practically acceptable *methods of recording* physiologically and pathophysiologically relevant aspects of gastrointestinal function in the intact human being; and (*2*) *controlled stimulation* procedures related to the kind of pathophysiological or psycho-pathophysiological mechanism under investigation. Progress has been made during the last decade to meet the first requirement. The developmental state of standard stimulation procedures for psychophysiological assessment is less satisfactory. The set of required recording methods may be derived from pathophysiological mechanisms assumed to be involved in functional or 'psychosomatic' GIT disorders. Only functions for which suitable psychophysiological measurement techniques have been devised are dealt with in the following paragraphs under the basic recording categories of *secretion, motility, emptying and transit, sphincter function*, and *interoception*. Test procedures are described in sections on those GIT disorders to which they have been applied.

An obvious reason for the slow development of gastrointestinal psychophysiology lies in the difficulties of assessing relevant parameters of gastrointestinal functions under the conditions of human psychophysiological studies. Conventional gastroenterological techniques are mostly invasive and use intraluminal probes or X-raying. They cause discomfort to the subject, alter the function under investigation, or involve radiation hazard. Clinical methods like aspiration of gastric juices, usually provide only discrete samples over longer intervals. With such measures functional changes elicited by transient psychological stimulation are difficult to evaluate. To overcome these limitations quite early efforts were made to develop *non-invasive methods* and utilize them for psychophysiological investigation. The use of surface gastrograms or 'electrogastrograms' (EGGs) to indicate electromotor activity of the stomach marked the first attempts of this kind (Russell and Stern, 1967). Other important GIT functions cannot be assessed without introducing some kind of intraluminal probe and/ or substance. Fortunately, probes and methods have been developed which are well suited to dealing with the specialized questions raised by psychophysiology.

SECRETION

Usually, only *gastric acid secretion* has been recorded in psychophysiological studies. It can be recorded almost continuously by a combination of intragastric pH measurement and titration consisting of discrete or continuous neutralization of hydrochloric acid by hydrocarbonate solution *per os*. Acid concentration is measured through intragastric pH-sensors fastened to a nasopharyngeal probe or a telemetric capsule (for practical version, see Stacher, 1983a). For long-term recording (up to 24 h) nasopharyngeal pH-probes have been described, which are connected to portable digital recorders. This technique is now widely used in gastroenterology to measure hypersecretion and circadian secretory patterns in ulcer patients, etc. Direct psychophysiological applications are still rare, although the method has been shown to be well tolerated by patients. It should be noted that recording of intragastric pH indicates only the concentration of unbuffered acid. This is not a valid measure of the amount of acid actually secreted per time unit. Acid concentration in the stomach depends also on the rate of gastric emptying and on the production of mucus, which dilutes and buffers the acid component.

MOTILITY

The term 'motility' usually refers to contractions of smooth muscles of a specified segment of the GIT. But it is also often used as a global term, which includes the electrical events at smooth muscle membranes correlated with mechanical activity. Both aspects of the complex electromotor activity of the GIT require different approaches to measurement. They should not be confused, as did commonly occur in the earlier psychophysiological literature. The relations between contractile and electrical activity of gastrointestinal muscles are by no means simple, nor are their psychophysiological connections.

Measurement of contractile activity generally requires the use of direct methods with some kind of intraluminal probe such as manometric catheters, balloons, or telemetric capsules by which contraction correlated pressure changes in the lumen of a GIT segment are picked up. Because the transduction of wall movements to pressure changes is not as simple as often implied, some caveats are appropriate. Special considerations are necessary for large or multicompart-mented structures like the stomach and colon. Despite these limitations, *manometric methods* using perfused catheters with extracorporal pressure transducers have become the standard methods of assessing motility of practically all GIT segments. As to psychophysiological applications, the same limitations apply as for intragastric pH-probes. But flexible manometric probes are available which produce little discomfort when applied through the nose (for gastroduodenal recording) or the anus (for rectal and colonic measurement) (see Hölzl and Whitehead, 1983).

Apart from these accepted methods there exist a few interesting but debatable non-invasive techniques producing indirect indices of mechanical activity, which despite their variable validity, have proved to be of some value in addressing the specialized questions of psychophysiology. The oldest of these techniques is the use of the so-called '*magnetogastrogram*' *(MGG)*, which goes back to Wenger, Henderson and Dinning (1957). Magnetogastrography consists of recording magnetic field changes over the epigastric region which are induced by the movements of a little magnet or iron rod swallowed by the subject. The method is too unreliable to record even relative contraction amplitude. Frequency of gastric rhythms may be evaluated (see review and critique by Hölzl, 1983, 1989). One variant called '*conjoint gastrography*' *(CSG)* uses the MGG only in combination with the EGG to increase signal-to-noise ratios of surface recordings (Müller, Hölzl and Brüchle, 1983).

Currently, *impedance gastrographies* are being developed out of epigastric impedance recordings originally designed to measure gastric emptying. They may also provide non-invasive measures of stomach wall movements by extracting their phasic information content (see 'Emptying and Transit'). These methods are very promising because they provide direct information on wall movements instead of indirect indices.

Non-invasive recordings of contractile activity from other segments of the GIT, e.g. the small bowel, are not possible. In this case pressure-sensitive telemetric capsules are the only way to avoid nasopharyngeal catheters and the like. Various suitable devices have been described early in the literature (e.g. Fink and Stacher, 1972).

In general, *direct recording of electrical activity* of the GIT is seldom feasible in psychophysiological studies, but suitable probes have been constructed for the distal colon and the rectum, which are easy to apply and present no detectable discomfort to the subject. Some of them combine ring and needle electrodes with ports for manometric recording of contractions. They were constructed for the study of motility changes in irritable bowel patients under conditions of minimal strain, and have been shown to be well suited for psychophysiological assessment of various kinds (e.g. Erasmus, 1989; Lederer, 1985).

Non-invasive recording of electrical activity of the GIT requires the detection of smooth muscle potentials from the abdominal surface. This is not difficult for the stomach, because of the large and well-structured summation potentials, which can be detected over the epigastric region by electrogastrography. Recording from other parts requires direct methods. Surface recordings from the colon have been attmpted, but were not successful (Duthie, 1974). Practical applications of the EGG to problems of clinical psychophysiology have been presented by various laboratories.

Since the first attempt to record an *EGG* from the abdominal surface by Alvarez (1922), a number of improvements on the basic method have appeared (Hölzl, 1983; Stern and Koch, 1985). But only recently have reliable methods of recording and signal analysis, as well as convincing demonstrations of the physiological significance of EGG parameters, become available (e.g. Hölzl, Löffler, and Müller, 1985; Smout, 1980). Recording techniques are similar in these variants. Preferably, bipolar epigastric recordings from a hexagonal multi-electrode configuration should be used to ensure independence from anatomical variations and variable electrical vector orientation. Gastric slow rhythms at about 1 and 3 cycles/min correlated with gastric pacemaker and/or contractile rhythms may be extracted reliably, provided that adequate methods of analysis like Fourier decomposition of records of sufficient length are used. These are the only EGG components which have been successfully validated so far. Interpretation of single waveforms is doubtful. For older parameters like direct current shifts, etc. (Russell and Stern, 1967) no gastric correlates have been identified. Some of the problems of classical EGG are substantially reduced by CSG (Hölzl, 1989; Hölzl *et al.*, 1985; Müller *et al.*, 1983). The method basically consists of combined recording and conjoint Fourier analysis of multichannel EGGs from a hexagonal epigastric electrode field and three-axes MGG over the same area. Cross-spectral analysis is used to identify common periodic components in this two-fold array of surface gastrograms. Because MGGs reflect mechanical events, only those EGG rhythms associated with contractile activity are extracted.

EMPTYING AND TRANSIT

Transport of substance through the GIT and emptying of specified compartments such as the stomach are functions of motility but not simply related to it. Therefore, motility recordings and transit measures are no substitutes for each other. The study of gastric emptying and small and large bowel transit requires ingestion of test substances by the subject, which can be detected in direct or indirect ways. At present, radionuclides are preferred as marker substances for diagnostic measurement of emptying. Absolute and selective measurements in specified GIT compartments may be made by appropriate scanning devices. Double marking by technetium and indium isotopes allows separate study of emptying of liquid and solid substances (Minami and McCallum, 1984). Despite these obvious advantages *radioisotope methods* have not been used in psychophysiology, mainly because of radiation hazards, and other non-invasive techniques have been looked for.

There are three candidates for non-invasive transit measurement which may become more important for psychophysiological assessments. The first of these employs an inert *ferromagnetic marker* substance (magnesium ferrite), which is traced by sensitive magnetometric methods (Benmair, 1975; Frei, Benmair, Yerushalmi and Dreyfuss, 1970). Unfortunately, although initial trials seemed very promising, this method has never been fully developed. The second method makes use of bacterial decomposition of non-absorbable carbohydrates such as lactulose in the large bowel (Armbrecht, Jensen, Eden and Stockbrügger, 1986). This produces hydrogen, which diffuses into the bloodstream and is exhaled through the lungs. Detecting the corresponding rise of hydrogen concentration in expired air allows relatively precise definition of the time when the test substance enters the caecum. The *hydrogen exhalation method* has been used to measure mouth–caecum transit time in several studies on the effects of psychological stress on gastrointestinal transit. Variants have been described, which use naturally occurring carbohydrates, e.g. laevulose in beans instead of artificial test substances (Cann *et al.*, 1983b). The third non-invasive method to be mentioned here is the use of *impedance gastrography* (IGG) to measure gastric emptying. It is still in the developmental stage, but operational versions have been presented (e.g. Gilbey and Watkins, 1987). The method is based on epigastric impedance changes associated with changing filling states of the stomach. There is no doubt that this method will become the method of choice for psychophysiological studies in the near future. Apart from the slow drift due to changes in gastric filling, epigastric impedance signals also contain phasic components correlated with changes in stomach contour during contractions. Thus, IGG offers the possibility of recording motility and emptying of the stomach simultaneously.

SPHINCTER FUNCTION, INTEROCEPTION, AND VISCERAL PAIN

Practical methods of sphincter assessment have been described for oesophageal and anal sphincters. Measuring upper and lower *oesophageal sphincter responses* involves intraluminal pressure probes (Schuster, 1983; Stacher, 1983b) or radionuclides for assessment of *gastro-oesophageal reflux*. Only a few psychophysiological applications have been published. Contrary to oesophageal sphincter functions, *anal sphincter mechanisms* have found considerable interest in clinical psychophysiology (Engel, 1978; Whitehead and Schuster, 1983). Elaborate, but still straightforward, manometric methods of assessing contractile sphincter responses are available, which use Schuster's (1968) three-balloon probe or similar devices.

These methods involve assessment of rectal perception as an essential part of sphincter mechanisms. They may be classified equally well under *interoceptive methods*, together with other methods of evaluation of gastrointestinal afferent processes and their psychophysiological relations. This requires intraluminal balloon probes through which controlled distension stimuli may be presented, and phasic and tonic contractile response can be recorded. New probes and stimulation devices have been reported, which allow reliable near-threshold measurements and provide for the requirements of psychophysical analysis of interoception in the distal colon and rectum (Erasmus, 1989; Erasmus, Hermsdörfer, Püll and Hölzl, 1987). Similar techniques are applied to the analysis of *visceral pain perception* in clinical syndromes like IBS (Kratzmair, Erasmus, Hölzl and Hartl, 1987). Estimation of pain thresholds has improved. By use of new psychophysical methods separation of peripheral and central factors in pain perception has become possible (see 'Irritable Bowel Syndrome' later in this Chapter).

FUNCTIONAL GASTROINTESTINAL DISORDERS

THE CONCEPT OF FUNCTIONAL DISORDERS

Clinical psychophysiology of the GIT primarily deals with (*1*) *physiological dysfunctions or disorders* in which psychological determinants or psychophysiological mechanisms play a role in primary or secondary aetiology, and (*2*) *disorders of primarily somatic origin* which may be influenced substantially by psychological variables and/or psychological treatment. For the first category the term 'psychophysiological disorders' has been coined. There is some overlap with other terms like 'functional disorder' and 'psychosomatic disease', which need clarification.

According to Whitehead and Schuster (1985, p. 2), the term *'psychophysiological disorder'* refers to disorders in which 'there is a demonstrable interaction between physiological events on the one hand and environmental events that have psychological significance on the other hand . . . a symptom for which there is no physiological basis (a hypochondriacal complaint) is not considered a psychophysiological disorder . . . simple exclusion of organic disease is not . . .' sufficient; and positive psychological criteria should be included (presence of psychopathology, indications for psychological factors in pathogenesis, covariation of subjective distress with symptoms, symptom relief in response to psychological interention). 'Psychophysiological disorders' in this sense comprise both *'functional disorders'* and *'psychosomatic diseases'*. In the latter tissue damage (e.g. peptic lesions) is implied, which is believed to be caused or exacerbated by psychological factors. 'Functional disorder', in contrast, refers to a disorder or syndrome for which no physical symptom cause in morphological or histological pathology has been found. The criterion of tissue damage is artificial, because psychosomatic lesions presumably result from abnormal physiological activity which is not different in principle from pathophysiological events seen in 'functional disorders'.

These distinctions are helpful, but the attempt to define a class of psychophysiological disorders as disease unities is problematic from both a nosological and a practical diagnostic point of view. Adding positive psychological diagnostic criteria to somatic symptoms for which no morphological basis can be identified does not by itself create a specified class of disorders, as long as we are unable to identify an underlying mechanism which connects pathophysiological and psychological events. The existence of a unique *psycho-pathophysiological mechanism* is an empirical question, which at present must be left open for most of these disorders. For classificatory purposes, a more cautious concept of *'functional GIT disorder'* is used here (Hölzl, 1987a). It refers to a syndrome rather than a disease. Its aetiological basis is to be found in the relation to observable physiological dysfunctions, which eventually may or may not lead to tissue damage. This relation is hierarchical (Figure 17.1): the somatic end-product is governed by *'peripheral pathogenetic mechanisms'* which are not considered to constitute a unique disorder by themselves. Several aetiological routes may lead to the same result (e.g. gastric lesions or 'functional' symptoms like obstipation). These routes may contain purely somatic as well as 'psychosomatic' aetiologies, they may be mixed within a syndromatic group, or appear combined in a single patient. In classifying patients we have to rely on co-occurrence of subjective complaints, somatic symptoms, and certain gross dysfunctions of the GIT, which are sometimes attributable to more specific functional changes. This constitutes a functional GIT syndrome or disorder. Boundaries between somatic and psychophysiological disorders become

---

LEVEL 3:
PSYCHOLOGICAL AND BEHAVIOURAL PROCESSES

Examples of Subsystems: Arousal and Attention, Body Perception, Pain Perception, Emotional Control, Maintenance Behaviour, Attribution

---

LEVEL 2:
INTERMEDIARY PSYCHOPHYSIOLOGICAL PROCESSES

Examples of Subsystems: Direct Psychoautonomic Effects, Indirect Autonomic Effects by Catecholamines, Psychoendocrinological Effects by Corticosteroids

---

LEVEL 1:
PERIPHERAL PATHOPHYSIOLOGICAL MECHANISMS

Examples of Subsystems: Gastric Secretory, Motor, and Humoural Variables in Ulcer Formation, Patterns of Motor Dysfunction in Proximal and Distal Colon, Impairment of Continence Organ and its Control System

---

Figure 17.1. The functional schema of hierarchical pathogenesis in psychosomatics and the concept of psycho-pathophysiological mechanism.

At least three levels of subsystems may be distinguished on the basis of their internal connectivity and relative functional autonomy: (1) *Peripheral pathogenetic mechanisms*: local system of pathophysiological variables; example: secretory, motility, and humoural processes producing mucosal lesions. (2) *Intermediary psychophysiological mechanisms*: processes which connect level 1 mechanisms to higher brain functions and psychological processes through peripheral and central autonomic nervous and neuroendocrinological control systems; example: short-term and long-term responses to specific 'stressors', specified by patterns of autonomic innervation of the gastrointestinal tract (GIT) and adrenal medulla, and by hypothalamic–hypophyseal stimulation of steroid secretion by the adrenal cortex. (3) *Psychological and behavioural mechanisms*: mechanisms which can (or must be) specified in purely psychological or behavioural terms, such as respondent conditioning, operant contingencies, 'sensitivity' and 'bias' of visceral perception, predictability and controllability, etc. The schema is no 'model'. It arranges categories of measurable variables and processes in hierarchical order which allows distinction of classes of pathogenetic mechanisms. A genuine psycho-pathophysiological mechanism is characterized by an identifiable subsystem of variables on both levels 1 and 2 leading to identifiable dysfunctions; it is not sufficiently specified by level 1 variables alone which specify pathophysiological mechanisms and their correlations with level 3 variables.

blurred, because clinically relevant effects of psychological variables on GIT dysfunctions are not limited to the latter (if they exist). This is demonstrated by psychophysiological studies on GIT pathologies associated with somatic disorders like diabetes mellitus (Strian, Hölzl and Haslbeck, 1987). 'Functional GIT disorder' in this sense is the broader category, which may contain hypothetical nosological unities such as 'psychophysiological disorders' and 'psychosomatic diseases' besides 'purely' physiological dysfunctions. *Clinical psychophysiology of the GIT* has to deal with all of them. It has (*1*) to provide tools to *analyse psycho-pathophysiological processes* in GIT disorders regardless of etiology; (*2*) to make use of this analysis in *differential diagnostic assessment* of peripheral versus central variables in gastrointestinal dysfunctions; and (*3*) to develop *specific treatments* based on (1) and (2).

OESOPHAGEAL DISORDERS

Three motor dysfunctions are often considered as functional oesophageal disorders: *globus sensation* ('lump in the throat'), *diffuse oesophageal spasms (DES)*, and *gastro-oesophageal reflux (GEF)*. Psychophysiological mechanisms have been discussed for *globus* sensation and DES (Malcomson, 1966; Schuster, 1983). Although there is no evidence of psychological factors in GEF, Schuster's group has shown instrumental learning of pressure responses in the lower oesophageal sphincter (LES). Incompetence of the LES is related to GEF. Various clinical and other observations point to psychological influences on oesophageal functions, but research into mechanisms is scarce.

There is no doubt about the psychophysiological nature of the *rumination syndrome*, which occurs mainly in infants and mentally handicapped people. The syndrome refers to excessive regurgitation of food and chewing it anew, after which it is reswallowed or spat out. This is a well-controlled voluntary act (DeMeester, Johnson, Guy, Toscano, Hall and Skinner, 1976). It is initiated by stimulation of the palate by the finger or tongue. Descent of the diaphragm and LES relaxation may also be involved. Finally, food is forced up by contraction of the abdominal muscles.

Several mechanisms are supposed to underly the genesis and maintenance of pathological rumination. None of them could be called psycho-pathophysiological, but may be described in purely behavioural terms. This is despite the fact that voluntary and reflexive physiological events are involved at various points in the sequence. The only direct psychophysiological approach to rumination seems to have been that of Shay, Rosenthal and Johnson (1983). They taught normally intelligent, adult ruminators with oesophageal reflux to avoid abdominal muscle contractions accompanying regurgitation by biofeedback of the electromyogram of the rectus abdomini muscles. This resulted in rapid reduction of reflux and rumination.

Psychophysiological mechanisms are also involved in certain kinds of *vomiting.* It is problematic to try to isolate distinct categories of vomiting disorders like 'psychogenic vomiting'. However, there are disorders like anorexia and bulimia nervosa where self-induced vomiting can become a major component of the syndrome. It may be analysed mainly at the behavioural level as in the case of rumination. Nevertheless, there is a background of functional GIT problems in a fraction of these patients (Dubois, Gross and Ebert, 1984; Lautenbacher, Galfe, Hölzl and Pirke, in press).

A distinct psychophysiological mechanism exists for *anticipatory nausea and vomiting* in patients undergoing cancer chemotherapy (Redd and Andrykowski, 1982). A strong case has been made that these symptoms are classically conditioned to environmental stimuli associated with the adverse effects of cytostatica much like taste aversions to radiation or sickness-inducing drugs (Bernstein and Webster, 1980; Garcia and Rusiniak, 1977).

PEPTIC ULCER DISEASE AND NON-ULCERATIVE DYSPEPSIA

Peptic ulcer disease (PUD) refers to chronically recurrent lesions in the wall of the stomach or duodenum. They can be distinguished from acute lesions developed under severe stress by histology and predominant localization (e.g. Oi, Toriumi, Miho and Kijima, 1971). Gastric and duodenal ulcers themselves must be considered as distinct disorders, too, but they are pathophysiologically related (Bonnevie, 1975).

Peptic ulcer disease has multiple causes, including hereditary factors. Ulcer episodes are the final common result of an imbalance of aggressive and defensive factors at the level of the mucosal walls, due to varying combinations of pathophysiological changes. These include hypersecretion, changes in gastric emptying and pyloric function, reduction of mucosal resistance, and impaired buffering of acid by gastric and pancreatic juices. Accordingly, no single pathopsychophysiological mechanism for PUD can be identified. Earlier animal models of experimental ulcers induced under psychological stress (Weiss, 1977) turned out to be pathophysiologically different from chronic primary ulcers in humans and to be more like acute stress lesions. However, the contribution of psychological stress to the aetiology and exacerbation of PUD in predisposed individuals is well supported.

Several possible psychophysiological links between psychological factors and peripheral pathogenesis can be identified for subjects at risk (e.g. Hölzl, 1979). Transient hyposecretion followed by prolonged hypersecretion may be elicited by stressful events and emotional states (e.g. Polish, Brady, Mason, Thach and Neimeck, 1962). Depending on the pattern of changes in antral motility and pyloric tone which they induce, gastric emptying may be either accelerated or retarded by stressful stimulation (cf. Malagelada, 1981). The first effect would increases acid contact with the duodenal walls, thus increasing the risk for a duodenal ulcer, while retarded emptying tends to lead to gastric lesions. Filling state is also important.

Unfortunately, psychophysiological studies on stress responses in the stomach have usually included only one parameter such as acid secretion or antral motility, in isolation. Integrated temporal patterns of functional changes in the gastroduodenal regulation system under controlled psychological stimulation have not been considered. Studies on intermediary psychophysiological mechanisms at the level of the autonomic nervous system are lacking. Practically all human laboratory studies rely on the notion that the antagonism of sympathetic and parasympathetic commands to the GIT is reflected in a simple antagonism of effects on GIT functions such as secretion and antral motility. This is not supported by contemporary physiology (cf. Dotevall, 1985, pp. 6–10). Complex effects of autonomic innervation patterns have been shown which arise from interactions with intrinsic autoregulatory systems of the GIT, the enteric nervous system and the system of regulatory peptides. It is for such reasons that previous studies on gastrographic responses in ulcer patients etc. have not improved our knowledge on psycho-pathophysiological processes (see Hölzl, 1989).

Finally, mention should be made of a neglected pathway which produces 'psychosomatic correlations' but is not directly related to psychophysiological processes *per se*: certain types of overt intake behaviour such as alcohol consumption are related to occupational stress and emotional disturbances and, at the same time, strongly increase the probability of ulcer episodes (Hölzl, 1979). Weiner (1977) called this mechanism *'mediated causation'* of a psychosomatic disease, indicating that a third variable (overt risk behaviour) causes correlations between psychological conditions and somatic disorders without direct involvement of psycho-pathophysiological mechanisms. It may be questioned whether such a disease should be called 'psychosomatic' at all.

Some authors have defined a syndrome of upper GIT symptoms called *non-ulcerative dyspepsia (NUD)*, which is very similar to complaints found in PUD patients (except nightly pain), but has no morphological basis. It is debatable, whether it is a separate disorder or whether it only represents upper GIT symptoms frequently accompanying IBS but forming no stable syndrome itself (Dotevall, 1985). Originally, NUD was considered as an early functional form of PUD. But neither data on PUD risk in NUD patients nor studies on pathophysiology have supported this notion. No relation to hypersecretion could be found. Present pathophysiological hypotheses relate NUD symptoms to non-secretory mechanisms similar to those shown for IBS. They imply reduced compliance to gastric distension, unspecific gastroduodenal hypersensitivity to intraluminal and central stimuli (Soll and Isenberg, 1983), and disturbed gastroduodenal motility (Fielding and Doyle, 1982).

INFLAMMATORY BOWEL DISEASES

Crohn's disease (*Morbus Crohn*) and *colitis ulcerosa* are small and large bowel diseases which involve inflammation of gastrointestinal walls. They have been subsumed under the common term of 'inflammatory bowel disease' (IBD) (Kirsner and Shorter, 1982). But there are some characteristic differences, too. In ulcerative colitis only the mucosa of the colon is inflamed and ulcerates, while Crohn's disease starts with submucosal inflammation and oedema, which extend through all layers of the bowel and eventually may lead to bowel obstruction and fistulas. The main symptoms differ according to these distinctions, but diarrhoea, abdominal pain and anorexia with weight loss are common to both.

Traditionally, IBDs have been considered to be classical psychosomatic diseases. But although there is evidence for psychosomatic contributions, the hypothesis of psychosomatic genesis by Engel and (e.g. 1954) others is no longer supported (Whitehead and Schuster, 1985, pp. 137 f.). Earlier results based on Engel's intensive case study approach were impossible to reproduce with more controlled methods. However, there is some evidence on positive outcomes of psychotherapy studies.

As has been pointed out earlier, neither symptom exacerbation under stress nor beneficial effects of psychological treatments are proof of psychosomatic genesis. There are good empirical arguments for an immune deficiency or autoimmune process in IBD. In this case *psychoimmunological mechanisms* may influence the time course of the disease and the severity of symptoms by direct interaction, although they need not be part of the initial pathogenetic chain. There are more indirect causal ways, too. One of them involves psycho-pathophysiological mechanisms, another does not. Gastrointestinal responses to stress and emotional disturbances may cause dramatic changes in GIT functions, especially in small bowel transit (Cann *et al.*, 1983b). These changes need not be related to the primary inflammatory process, but could suffice to explain aggravation as well as amelioration of symptoms in IBD patients. The second way by which psychological factors may influence IBD symptoms and therapy relates to Weiner's (1977) mechanism of 'mediated causation' which was discussed earlier in relation to PUD.

IRRITABLE BOWEL SYNDROME

The irritable bowel syndrome (IBS) has become a major focus of clinical psychophysiological research for a number of reasons. One is its enormous practical importance. Prevalence in the general population and in the population of patients seeking help from gastroenterologists is very high (8–17% and 22–50%, respectively; see Whitehead and Schuster, 1985, p. 155). This is contrasted by the absence of specific treatments with enduring effects. Other reasons relate to the relative ease by which essential pathophysiological variables can be measured since the advent of sufficiently reliable recording techniques. Important reasons for the fast growth of IBS research derive from the nature of the disorder itself; that is: (*1*) its demonstrated *functional nature* and syndromatic coherence, despite unsolved problems of classification; (*2*) overwhelming evidence for the *psychological determination* of pathogenesis, maintenance of symptoms and therapy; and (*3*) the existence of *specific patho-psychophysiological mechanisms* for certain aspects of the disorder, such as increased sensitivity to intraluminal mechanical stimuli.

According to Whitehead and Schuster (1985), 'IBS is considered a syndrome . . . rather than a disease because there is no general agreement on the pathophysiological mechanism for the symptoms' (p. 155). It is characterized by abnormal bowel habits (diarrhoea, constipation, or both) in combination with abdominal pain, and positive exclusion of underlying somatic disease. Some authors have included painless diarrhoea and constipation in the syndrome, but there is disagreement on this point. The same is true for other characteristics like relief of pain by bowel movement (Manning, Thompson, Heaton and Morris, 1978). At present, Whitehead and Schuster's (1985, p. 164) attempt to formulate diagnostic research criteria for IBS is most promising. They emphasize exclusion of lactose malabsorption, because it cannot be distinguished from IBS by clinical criteria. The inclusion of positive psychological criteria such as covariation of symptoms with anxiety or depression scores is problematic (see critique above). In addition to Whitehead and Schuster's (1985) criteria, Kruis' diagnostic index of IBS should be considered (Kruis, Thieme, Weinzierl, Schüssler, Holl and Paulus, 1984).

Several pathophysiological explanations of IBS have been put forward. As they are intimately related to central factors, the physiological and psychophysiological processes involved are discussed together. No attempt is made at completeness (see Whitehead and Schuster, 1985, pp. 179 ff. for a well-balanced discussion). The following *patho-psychophysiological mechanisms* have been related to IBS symptoms:

(*1*) *Increased colon motility* in response to psychological stimuli, stress episodes, or emotional disturbance, either (a) due to increased central stimulation related to psychopathology (Almy, 1951; Latimer, 1983), or (b) from nonspecific hyper-reactivity of smooth bowel muscles to various stimuli including intraluminal distension, meals, and psychological events (Whitehead, Engel, Schuster, 1980).

(*2*) *Acceleration or retardation of small bowel transit* by psychological factors (Cann, Read, Brown, Hobson and Holdsworth, 1983a).

(*3*) *Altered interoception* of intraluminal distension including general or localized hyperalgia of the colon (Ritchie, 1973, Swarbrick, Hegarty, Bat, Williams and Dawson, 1980).

(4) *Instrumental learning* and maintenance *of pathological bowel activity* through differential social reinforcement of associated complaints (Whitehead, Winget, Fedoravicius, Wooley and Blackwell, 1982).

(5) *Discriminative instrumental learning of heightened wall tonus* with subsequent lowering of pain thresholds (Hölzl, 1987b).

These mechanisms will now be considered more fully:

(*1*) *and* (*2*): Abnormal motility such as increased total, single spastic, or 'paradoxical' activity of the colon has been assumed to underly altered bowel habits as well as pain symptoms in IBS patients. Attempts to find stable physiological markers based on motility under resting conditions alone produced inconsistent results. Methodological problems are also involved, but have been largely overcome (cf. Löffler, 1988). Functional changes in smooth muscle activity depend on stimulus conditions, including psychological ones. This explains why findings on hyper-reactivity of the bowel to various stimuli show more consistency than basal recordings. Stepwise distension tests of the distal colon and stimulation by meals and/or cholecystokinin (CCK) were developed to assess hypersensitivity of visceral reflexes. Over-responding to test meals or CCK is correlated with post-prandial pain in a subgroup of IBS patients. Similarly, procedures to assess stress-dependent changes in small bowel transit have been designed (Cann *et al.*, 1983a,b), because the adverse consequences on colon function seem to be associated with symptoms in some subjects. Psychological stimulation procedures to be used in this connection are not yet agreed on. Several unsolved problems have prevented use of these 'tests' in actual diagnostic applications. 'Abnormal colonic response to stress' has no simple interpretation. It may result from abnormal colon responses elicited by normal psychological stress responses or normal colon responses to abnormal psychological stress responses; and it may indicate a more generalized tendency to psychoautonomic over-responding. Furthermore, the physiological tests mentioned are not psychologically neutral and may have differential effects on psychologically disturbed persons like many IBS patients. Response differences in comparison to non-anxious subjects may result from this interaction and lead to wrong conclusions.

(*3*): Interoceptive afferent processes associated with intraluminal stimuli in the colon may be changed at various levels of the gut–brain axis, and these changes may assume several functional roles in mediating IBS symptoms. Increased visceral reflex activity may be caused by altered transduction of wall distension instead of hypersensitivity in the efferent branch of the reflex arc. The same mechanism leads to lowered pain thresholds as smaller volumes suffice to cause suprathreshold discharge of stretch receptors. This was shown to be a very probable explanation of colonic hyperalgia in specified subsyndromes of IBS (Kratzmair, Erasmus, Hölzl and Hartl, 1987). Increased sensitivity to intraluminal stimuli and lowered pain thresholds may also be localized in the afferent transmission chain (cf. Jänig and Morrison, 1986). Finally, there is good evidence for altered visceral pain perception of IBS patients at the psychological level. Changes may be found at the perceptual level or be due to non-perceptual factors such as operant pain behaviour. Differentiation of these levels requires systematic use of psychophysical tools as they have been developed in similar approaches to somatosensory pain (Bromm, 1984). Distinguishing between altered sensitivity and response criteria is a major problem.

(4) and (5): Findings on instrumental maintenance of overt illness behaviour of IBS patients led to the hypothesis that abnormal bowel motility might have been learned instrumentally through social reinforcement of associated complaints. Based on this argument behavioural treatments were constructed ('contingency management'; Whitehead and Schuster, 1985, p. 218). A rational indication for this promising approach would require the positive proof that this mechanism really works in particular individuals. Instrumental factors could also work more indirectly via inadequate health behaviour, e.g. laxative abuse and diet. A similar argument holds for the attempt to link colonic hyperalgia to instrumental learning processes (Hölzl, 1987b). According to this hypothesis, hypersensitive visceroception might also be developed through discriminative learning of increased smooth muscle tonus, which lowers pain thresholds; cf. (3). Again, operation of instrumental factors on this specific mechanism has yet to be shown.

Utilization of these pathogenetic considerations in designing specific and efficient treatments for IBS is not satisfactory. Although there is a placebo response to any novel treatment, improvements do not persist. This is proof of nonspecificity of treatment effects: heterogeneous in the population and compository in single patients. Powerful tactics of differential functional assessment of pathophysiological networks are needed which allow differential assignment of treatment components. The tools used in the research on mechanisms just described can be transferred to the task of differential diagnosis. Psychophysiological treatments can also be constructed. But so far large-scale diagnostic studies are lacking, and so are controlled outcome studies making use of their results in the differential indication of specific treatments for symptomatic subgroups. At present, only more or less hypothetical assignments of special treatment elements to single functional pathologies can be derived. For instance, supportive psychotherapy, relaxation, and stress management have been recommended to reduce stress-related abnormal motility. More specifically, biofeedback-assisted relaxation of striated abdominal muscles has been used to reduce abnormal bowel motility on the basis of somatovisceral spinal reflexes (Hölzl and Kröger, 1988). Biofeedback training of spontaneous colon motility and intraluminal pressure responses to stepwise distension were employed to reduce pathological contraction patterns or to increase colonic compliance (e.g. Hölzl and Kröger, 1988; Whitehead, 1985).

FAECAL INCONTINENCE

Faecal incontinence (FI) refers to inappropriate loss of stool from the anus. It is usually distinguished from encopresis in which there is no organic cause for soiling. This distinction is in part artificial. It could be shown that behavioural mechanisms presumed to cause encopresis are operating in FI with organic reasons as well. Conversely, cryptic alterations in afferent and efferent systems which normally guarantee continence cannot always be excluded in encopretic cases. Psycho-pathophysiological mechanisms are relevant for certain forms of FI and their treatment by biofeedback. Only these will be discussed. It should be noted, however, that therapies for encopresis also make use of psychophysiological relations such as conditioned rectal and colonic responses to facilitate control of bowel movements.

Faecal incontinence involves disturbance of at least one component of the continence system. This consists of coordinated reflexes of internal and external anal sphincters, as well as overlearned automatic instrumental responses of the latter to afferent signals from rectal stretch receptors. Accordingly, two basic forms of FI may be distinguished, which are caused by disturbances in the efferent or the afferent branch of this system. They require different treatment.

Disturbance of efferent parts consists of a weakness in rectal sphincter function, usually a result of impairment of the external sphincter or its innervation. When faeces enter the rectum, the internal sphincter (smooth muscle) relaxes reflectorily. Continence is preserved by timely contraction of the external sphincter (striate muscle). There is convincing evidence that this response is no reflex but an automated discriminative operant. If its response strength is too weak because of efferent factors, treatment is directed towards restrengthening. This can take the form of simple muscle exercises or biofeedback training.

The second type of FI is due to *defective afferent signals* necessary for discriminative control of external sphincter contractions by rectal distension. Sphincter function itself is basically normal in this case. Consequently, therapy is directed towards re-establishing discriminative control of the externus contractions by the weakened sensations from the rectum. This can be achieved by appropriate perception training in which rectal sensations are assisted by biofeedback displays of manometric records of sphincter activity to the subject under controlled distension of the rectum by a balloon.

Relative contributions of the two aspects of FI to the symptoms of a patient are evaluated diagnostically by the same analytical tools which were developed for research on FI mechanisms. Separation of dysfunctions in efferent parts of the continence organs from loss of rectal sensation by neuropathic deafferentation, etc. is achieved with Whitehead and Schuster's (1983) test procedure or similar routines. The rectal probe which has been mentioned earlier (see 'Measurement Techniques') is used for this purpose. Apart from distinguishing afferent from efferent impairment, further distinctions of clinical relevance are to be made on the basis of degrees of sensory loss. If rectal thresholds have been raised over critical values of around 30–50 ml, re-establishing discriminative control of sphincter responses by standard biofeedback must be supplemented by perception training. There are several other kinds of FI and more than one mechanism involved in a single category of the disorder. Severe simplifications were necessary for our purpose. The reader is referred to Whitehead and Schuster (1985, pp. 229 ff.), and Wald and Handen (1987), for a more detailed account of diagnostic categories and pathophysiological mechanisms.

Biofeedback therapies for FI have become most widely known, because of their established efficacy. They are also worth noting for their unique property of making use of the very same techniques by which the mechanisms of FI were analysed scientifically and by which patients are differentially diagnosed. The basic operation consists simply of supplying the patient with augmented exteroceptive feedback of his/her rectal pressure recordings and corresponding sphincter responses together with appropriate instructions. To be maximally effective in practice, however, therapy has to follow a more complex plan constructed according to established behavioural principles. This has been overlooked in some critical accounts of outcome studies in the medical literature. Details of elaborated therapy protocols and discussions of available outcome data are to be found in the basic sources cited above.

FUTURE PERSPECTIVES

The early development of gastrointestinal psychophysiology was largely determined by the pace of methodological progress. Although further improvement of recording tools is still important, the technological state reached has allowed a dramatic expansion of basic and clinical research on psychophysiological GIT mechanisms since about 1980. Recent methodological advances in visceral perception research brought the study of afferent GIT mechanisms and their disorders within reach of human psychophysiology and psychophysics. Despite this progress, a large part of the physiological knowledge on gastrointestinal regulatory mechanisms and gut–brain interactions has not been connected with the tactics of psychophysiological investigations. This is particularly true for gastrointestinal peptides and the enteric nervous system.

Interoception research like the psychophysiological analysis of FI and its therapeutic applications pioneered an important *change in paradigm*: it marked a turn to *mechanism-oriented* rather than correlative or 'index'-oriented *strategies* in general and clinical psychophysiology. Research into IBS is following this trend. It is probably not by accident that the earliest and most successful applications of this approach were demonstrated in the field of gastrointestinal psychophysiology. The strong orientation towards basic physiology and the necessity of constructing advanced techniques of measurements were certainly helpful. However, the *unique gut–brain relationships* involved and their psychophysiological counterparts seem to have been most stimulating. They strongly involve afferent mechanisms which gave rise to intensive research on interoceptive processes. It appears that this is spreading to other areas like cardiovascular psychophysiology and the psychology of subjective reports of bodily symptoms in general (Pennebaker, 1982).

REFERENCES

Alexander, F. (1950). *Psychosomatic Medicine: Its Principles and Applications*. New York: Norton.

Almy, T.P. (1951). Experimental studies on the irritable colon. *American Journal of Medicine* **9**, 60–67.

Alvarez, W.C. (1922). The electrogastrogram and what it shows. *Journal of the American Medical Association* **79**, 1116–1119.

Area Review (1987). Gastrointestinal disorders. *Annals of Behavioral Medicine* **9**, complete issue no. 3.

Armbrecht, U., Jensen, J., Eden, S. and Stockbrügger, R. (1986). Assessment of orocecal transit time by means of a hydrogen breath test as compared to radiological control method. *Gastroenterology* **21**, 670–677.

Beaumont, W. (1833). *Experiments and Observations of the Gastric Juices and Physiology of Digestion*. Plattsburg: Allen.

Benmair, Y. (1975). *Use of ferromagnetic tracer for measurement of gastric emptying and some other medical physic purposes*. PhD thesis, Weizman Institute, Rehovot.

Bernstein, I.L. and Webster, M.M. (1980). Learned taste aversions in humans. *Physiology and Behavior* **25**, 363–366.

Bonnevie, O. (1975). The incidence in Copenhagen County of gastric and duodenal ulcers in the same patients. *Scandinavian Journal of Gastroenterology* **10**, 529–536.

Brady, J.V., Porter, R.W., Conrad, D.G. and Mason, J.W. (1958). Avoidance behavior and the development of gastroduodenal ulcers. *Journal of the Experimental Analysis of Behavior* **1**, 69–73.

Bromm, B. (Ed.) (1984). *Pain Measurement in Man. Neurophysiological Correlates of Pain*. Amsterdam: Elsevier.

Brooks, F.P. and Evers, P.H. (1977). *Nerves and the Gut*. Thorofare: Slack.

Bykov, K.M. and Kurzin, I.T. (1966). *Kortiko–viszerale Pathologie*. Berlin: Volk und Gesundheit.

Cann, P.A., Read, N.W., Brown, C., Hobson, N. and Holdsworth, C.D. (1983a). Irritable bowel syndrome: relationship of disorders in the transit of a single solid meal to symptom patterns. *Gut* **24**, 405–411.

Cann, P.A., Read, N.W., Cammack, I., Childs, H., Holden, S., Kashman, R., Longmore, I., Nix, S., Simms, K., Swallow, K. and Weller, J. (1983b). Physiological stress and the passage of a standard meal through the stomach and the small intestine in man. *Gut* **24**, 236.

Cannon, W.B. (1909). The influence of emotional states on the functions of the alimentary canal. *American Journal of Medical Science* **137**, 480–487.

Cannon, W.B. (1929). *Bodily Changes in Pain, Hunger, Fear and Rage*. New York: Appleton-Century-Crofts.

DeMeester, T.R., Johnson, L.F., Guy, J.J., Toscano, J.S., Hall, A.W. and Skinner, D.B. (1976). Patterns of gastroesophageal reflux in health and disease. *Annals of Surgery* **184**, 459–470.

Dotevall, G. (1985). *Stress and Common Gastrointestinal Disorders: A Comprehensive Approach.* New York: Praeger.

Dubois, A., Gross, H.A. and Ebert, M.H. (1984). Gastric function in primary anorexia nervosa. In: K.M. Pirke and D. Ploog (Eds) *The Psychobiology of Anorexia Nervosa.* Berlin: Springer.

Duthie, H.L. (1974). Electrical activity of gastrointestinal smooth muscle. *Gut* **15**, 669–681.

Engel, B.T. (1978). The treatment of fecal incontinence by operant conditioning. *Automedica* **2**, 101–108.

Engel, G.L. (1954). Studies of ulcerative colitis. II. The nature of the somatic processes and the adequacy of psychosomatic hypothesis. *American Journal of Medicine* **16**, 416–433.

Erasmus, L.-P. (1989). *Psychophysikalische Untersuchungen zur gastrointestinalen Interozeption: Apparatur, Methodik, Ergebnisse.* Frankfurt: Lang Verlag.

Erasmus, L.-P., Hermsdörfer, J., Püll, O. and Hölzl, R. (1987). Method and apparatus for gastrointestinal interoception research. *Psychophysiology* **24**, 587–588.

Fielding, J.F. and Doyle, G. (1982). The prevalence and significance of gastritis in patients with lower irritable bowel (irritable colon) syndrome. *Journal of Clinical Gastroenterology* **4**, 507.

Fink, G. and Stacher, G. (1972). Eine neue Endoradiosonde zur Messung intraluminaler Drucke im Magendarmtrakt. *Acta Chirurgica Australica* **4**, 1–6.

Frei, E.H., Benmair, Y., Yerushalmi, S. and Dreyfuss, F. (1970). Measurements of the stomach with a magnetic tracer material. *IEEE Transactions on Magnetics* **6**, 348–349.

Garcia, J. and Rusiniak, K.W. (1977). Visceral feedback and the taste signal. In: J. Beatty and H. Legewie (Eds) *Biofeedback and Behavior.* New York: Plenum.

Gilbey, S.G. and Watkins, P.J. (1987). Measurement by epigastric impedance of gasgric emptying in diabetic autonomic neuropathy. *Diabetic Medicine* **4**, 122–126.

Hölzl, R. (1979). Noninvasive measurement in gastrointestinal motility in experimental psychosomatics. In: W.H.G. Wolters and G. Sinnema (Eds) *Psychosomatics and Biofeedback.* Utrecht: Nijhoff.

Hölzl, R. (1983). Surface gastrograms as measures of gastric motility. In: R. Hölzl and W.E. Whitehead (Eds) *Psychophysiology of the Gastroinestinal Tract: Experimental and Clinical Applications.* New York: Plenum.

Hölzl, R. (1987a). Funktionelle Diagnostik und Kriterien verhaltensmedizinischer Intervention. In: F. Strian, R. Hölzl and M. Haslbeck (Eds) *Verhaltensmedizin und Diabetes Mellitus.* Berlin: Springer.

Hölzl, R. (1987b). Discriminative functions and centrifugal control of afferent signals from the gastrointestinal tract. *Psychophysiology* **24**, 575.

Hölzl, R. (1989). *Psychophysiologische Untersuchungen im Gastrointestinalsystem.* Frankfurt: Lang Verlag.

Hölzl, R. and Kröger, C. (1988). Verhaltensmedizinische Aspekte funktioneller Verdauungsstörungen. In: H.-U. Wittchen and I. Hand (Eds) *Verhaltenstherapie und Medizin.* Berlin: Springer.

Hölzl, R. and Whitehead, W.E. (Eds) (1983). *Psychophysiology of the Gastrointestinal Tract: Experimental and Clinical Applications.* New York: Plenum.

Hölzl, R., Löffler, K. and Müller, G. (1985). On conjoint gastrography or what the surface gastrograms show. In: R.M. Stern and K.L. Koch (Eds) *Electrogastrography. Methodology, Validation, and Applications.* New York: Praeger.

Jänig, W. (1986). Spinal cord integration of visceral sensory systems and sympathetic nervous system reflexes. In: F. Cervero and J.F.B. Morrison (Eds) *Progress in Brain Research, Vol. 67: Visceral Sensation.* Amsterdam: Elsevier.

Jänig, W. and Morrison, J.F.B. (1986). Functional properties of spinal visceral afferents supplying abdominal and pelvic organs, with special emphasis on visceral nociception. In: F. Cervero and J.F.B. Morrison (Eds) *Progress in Brain Research, Vol. 67: Visceral Sensation.* Amsterdam: Elsevier.

Kirsner, J.B. and Shorter, R.G. (1982). Recent developments in 'nonspecific' inflammatory bowel disease. *New England Journal of Medicine* **306**, 775–785.

Kratzmair, M., Erasmus, L.-P., Hölzl, R. and Hartl, L. (1987). Influence of predistension, stimulus duration, and rise time on the perception of colonic distension. *Journal of Psychophysiology* **1**, 302–303.

Kruis, W., Thieme, C., Weinzierl, M., Schüssler, P., Holl, J. and Paulus, W. (1984). A diagnostic score for the irritable bowel syndrome: its value in the exclusion of organic disease. *Gastroenterology* **87**, 1–7.

Latimer, P.R. (1983). *Functional Gastrointestinal Disorders: A Behavioral Approach.* New York: Springer.

Lautenbacher, S., Galfe, G., Hölzl, R. and Pirke, R.M. (in press). Gastrointestinal transit is delayed in patients with bulimia. *International Journal of Eating Disorders* **7**.

Lederer, P.C.H. (1985). *Rechnergestützte Auswertung gastrointestinaler Motilitätsparameter: Ösophagus, Magen, Kolon.* Postdoctoral thesis, Faculty of Medicine, University of Erlangen-Nürnberg, Erlangen.

Löffler, K.G. (1988). *Signalanalytische und biometrische Untersuchungen psychophysiologischer Magen-Darm-Reaktionen bei Gesunden und Kranken Patienten mit funktionellen Darmstörungen.* Frankfurt: Lang Verlag.

Malagelada, J.-R. (1986). Gastric, pancreatic, and biliary responses to a meal. In: L.R. Johnson (Ed.) *Physiology of the Gastrointestinal Tract.* New York: Raven.

Malcomson, K.G. (1966). Radiological findings in *globus hystericus. British Journal of Radiology* **39**, 583–586.

Manning, A.P., Thompson, W.G., Heaton, K.W. and Morris, A.F. (1978). Towards positive diagnosis of the irritable bowel. *British Medical Journal* **2**, 653–654.

Minami, H. and McCallum, R.W. (1984). The physiology and pathophysiology of gastric emptying in humans. *Gastroenterology* **86**, 1592–1610.

Müller, G.M., Hölzl, R. and Brüchle, H.A. (1983). Conjoint gastrography: principles and techniques. In: R. Hölzl and W.E. Whitehead (Eds) *Psychophysiology of the Gastrointestinal Tract: Experimental and Clinical Applications.* New York: Plenum.

Oi, M., Toriumi, T., Miho, O. and Kijima, M. (1971). Location of experimental ulcers as compared with that of human peptic ulcer. In: C.J. Pfeiffer (Ed.) *Peptic Ulcer.* Copenhagen: Munksgaard.

Pavlov, I.P. (1927). *Conditioned Reflexes. An Investigation of the Physiological Activity of the Cerebral Cortex.* London: Oxford University Press.

Pennebaker, J.W. (1982). *The Psychology of Physical Symptoms.* New York: Springer.

Polish, E., Brady, J.V., Mason, J.W., Thach, J.S. and Niemeck, W.M. (1962). Gastric contents and the occurence of duodenal lesions in the rhesus monkey during avoidance behavior. *Gastroenterology* **43**, 193–201.

Redd, W.E. and Andrykowski, M.A. (1982). Behavioral intervention in cancer treatment: controlling aversion reactions to chemotherapy. *Journal of Consulting and Clinical Psychology* **50**, 1018–1029.

Ritchie, J. (1973). Pain from distension of the pelvic colon by inflating a balloon in the irritable bowel syndrome. *Gut* **14**, 125–132.

Russell, R.W. and Stern, R.M. (1967). Gastric motility: the electrogastrogram. In: P.H.

Venables and I. Martin (Eds) *A Manual of Psychophysiological Methods*. Amsterdam: North-Holland.

Schuster, M.M. (1968). Motor action of rectal and anal sphincter in continence and defecation. *Handbook of Physiology: Section 6. Alimentary Canal, Vol. IV: Motility*. Washington, D.C.: American Physiological Society.

Schuster, M.M. (1983). Disorders of the esophagus: applications of psychophysiological methods to treatment. In: R. Hölzl and W.E. Whitehead (Eds) *Psychophysiology of the Gastrointestinal Tract: Experimental and Clinical Applications*. New York: Plenum.

Shay, S.S., Rosenthal, R. and Johnson, L.F. (1983). *Biofeedback therapy of patients with chronic dyspepsia and gastroesophageal reflux*. Paper presented at the Fourth Annual Meeting of the Society for Behavioral Medicine. Baltimore, Md.

Soll, A.H. and Isenberg, J.I. (1983). Duodenal ulcer disease. In: M.H. Sleisenger and J.S. Fordtran (Eds) *Gastrointestinal Disease: Pathophysiology, Diagnosis, Management*. Philadelphia, Pa.: Saunders.

Smout, A.J.P. (1980). *Myoelectric Activity of the Stomach (Gastroelectromyography and Electrogastrography)*. Delft: University Press.

Stacher, G. (1983a). Telemetric and isotope methods of measuring gastric acid secretion, motility and emptying. In: R. Hölzl and W.E. Whitehead (Eds) *Psychophysiology of the Gastrointestinal Tract: Experimental and Clinical Applications*. New York: Plenum.

Stacher, G. (1983b). The responsiveness of the esophagus to environmental stimuli. In: R. Hölzl and W.E. Whitehead (Eds) *Psychophysiology of the Gastrointestinal Tract: Experimental and Clinical Applications*. New York: Plenum.

Stern, R.M. and Koch, K.L. (Eds) (1985). *Electrogastrography. Methodology, Validation, and Applications*. New York: Praeger.

Strian, F., Hölzl, R. and Haslbeck, M. (Eds) (1987). *Verhaltensmedizin und Diabetes mellitus*. Berlin: Springer.

Swarbrick, E.T., Hegarty, J.E., Bat, I., Williams, C.B. and Dawson, A.M. (1980). Site of pain from the irritable bowel. *Lancet* ii, 443–446.

Wald, A. and Handen, B.L. (1987). Behavioral aspects of disorders of defecation and fecal incontinence. *Annals of Behavioral Medicine* 9, 19–23.

Walker, B.B. and Sandman, C.A. (1977). Physiological response patterns in ulcer patients: phasic and tonic components of electrogastrogram. *Psychophysiology* 14, 393–400.

Weiner, H.D. (1977). *Psychobiology and Human Disease*. New York: Elsevier.

Weiss, J.M. (1977). Psychological and behavioral influences on gastrointestinal lessions in animal models. In: J.D. Maser and M.E.P. Seligman (Eds) *Psychopathology: Experimental Models*. San Francisco: Freeman.

Wenger, M.A., Henderson, E.B. and Dinning, J.S. (1957). Magnetometer method for recording gastric motility. *Science* 125, 990–991.

Whitehead, W.E. (1985). Psychotherapy and biofeedback in the treatment of irritable bowel syndrome. In: N.W. Read (Ed.) *Irritable Bowel Syndrome*. London: Grune and Stratton.

Whitehead, W.E. and Schuster, M.M. (1983). Manometric and electromyographic techniques for assessment of the anorectal mechanism for continence and defecation. In: R. Hölzl and W.E. Whitehead (Eds) *Psychophysiology of the Gastrointestinal Tract: Experimental and Clinical Applications*. New York: Plenum.

Whitehead, W.E. and Schuster, M.M. (1985). *Gastrointestinal Disorders: Behavioral and Physiological Basis of Treatment*. Orlando: Academic Press.

Whitehead, W.E., Engel, B.T. and Schuster, M.M. (1980). Irritable bowel syndrome: physiological and psychological differences between diarrhea-predominant and constipation-predominant patients. *Digestive Diseases and Sciences* 25, 404–413.

Whitehead, W.E., Winget, C., Fedoravicius, A.S., Wooley, S. and Blackwell, B. (1982). Learned illness behavior in patients with irritable bowel syndrome and peptic ulcer. *Digestive Disease and Sciences* **27**, 202–208.

Wolf, S. and Wolff, H.G. (1943). *Human Gastric Function.* New York: Oxford University Press.

Chapter 18

Respiratory Disorders: Asthma and Hyperventilation Syndrome

Paul Grossman* and Cornelis J. E. Wientjes†

*Forschungsgruppe Psychophysiologie,
University of Freiburg,
Belfortstrasse 20, and
D-7800 Freiburg,
Federal Republic of Germany,
†TNO Institute for Perception,
Kampweg 5,
3769 ZG Soesterberg,
The Netherlands

ABSTRACT

The application of psychophysiology to understanding two respiratory disorders, asthma and hyperventilation syndrome, is reviewed. The physiological mechanisms underlying each disorder are detailed, together with aspects of psychophysiological measurement. The role of psychophysiology in identifying factors associated with the clinical presentation, aetiology, maintenance and treatment of these disorders is discussed.

Handbook of Clinical Psychophysiology Edited by G. Turpin

INTRODUCTION

This chapter will focus upon two important respiration-related disorders that may benefit from a psychophysiological perspective: hyperventilation syndrome (HVS) and bronchial asthma. The basic aim of our presentation is to provide a review of the current state of knowledge concerning the psychophysiology of these disorders. Unfortunately, much of the abundant psychosomatic literature regarding these syndromes suffers from rather severe methodological problems. Consequently, we have chosen not to cover comprehensively all the relevant literature, but to focus upon what, in our opinion, are the best and most recent scientific publications.

BRONCHIAL ASTHMA

Modern conceptions concerning the contribution of psychological factors to the aetiology and maintenance of bronchial asthma date back to at least 100 years ago, when MacKenzie (1886) putatively observed an asthmatic who, allergic to flowers, succumbed to an asthmatic attack upon exposure to an artificial rose. Several generations of psychosomatic investigators subsequently formed various theories concerning the origins of a psychogenic type of asthma in which personality characteristics and classical conditioning often played major roles. Although the role of conditioning factors appears to have withstood the test of time (i.e. not being proven but also not being disproven, cf. Weiner, 1977), the aetiological contribution of dispositional traits, such as neuroticism and dependency, have fared less well (e.g. Neuhaus, 1958; Rosenthal, Aitken and Zealley, 1973).

More current psychophysiological approaches to asthma focus upon psychological factors that may be involved in triggering discrete asthmatic attacks, as well as the manner in which psychological elements may interact with management and the course of the disorder. In the following sections we will begin by discussing physiological and medical aspects of the disorder and then proceed to consider psychophysiological factors.

PHYSIOLOGICAL CHARACTERISTICS AND MEASUREMENT TECHNIQUES

Bronchial asthma is defined in terms of increased reactivity of the trachea and bronchi to various agents and is manifested by widespread constriction of the airways. Such narrowing of the air passages, furthermore, must be largely reversible, either spontaneously or as a result of therapy (American Thoracic Society, 1962). The range of severity of disorder is great, extending from individuals with asthmatic episodes less than once a year who otherwise have perfectly normal pulmonary functioning to those chronic perennial sufferers who endure multiple, severe attacks each week and for whom lung function values between attacks are clearly abnormal.

Typical symptoms of the disorder include wheezing, breathlessness and sometimes coughing and sputum production. The proximal physiological mechanism responsible for symptoms is usually bronchospasm (i.e. airway constriction due to sudden contraction of the smooth muscles), although airway inflammatory responses and mucus secretion may also be involved (Boushey, Holteman, Sheller and Nadel, 1980). The bronchial tree is composed of larger air passages that branch out into increasingly smaller bronchioles. There is considerable evidence of differential involvement of larger and smaller airways in the asthmatic reactions of different individuals, and this may be of special interest in understanding the psychophysiological mechanisms to be discussed later (e.g. Lehrer, Hochron, McCann, Swartzman and Reba, 1986).

Young children are at increased risk for asthma and this appears likely to be partially due to such physical factors as the presence of more mucus glands, smaller airways that obstruct more easily and less smooth muscle in the small airways as compared to adults (Siegel and Rachelefsky, 1985).

A cursory examination of the natural history of asthmatics suggests that the onset of asthma can be very abrupt, reports indicating that foreign environmental agents are sometimes able to bring about dramatic asthmatic reactions within minutes of exposure to individuals with no pre-existing histories of bronchial hyper-reactivity or respiratory complaints. Furthermore, these individuals are transformed into rather typical asthmatics who may suffer frequent attacks for years to come (Brooks, Weiss and Bernstein, 1985). On the other hand, spontaneous remission, as well as relapse, appears to be very common among asthmatics of many different age groups (Bronniman and Burrows, 1986). Consequently, one may characterize asthma as frequently unstable in its natural course. How behavioural factors may influence the progress of the disorder remains unclear.

Types of Asthma

Generally, there are four major types of asthma that are distinguished. They are extrinsic (or allergic) asthma, intrinsic asthma, exercise-induced asthma and occupational asthma. The first three varieties largely reflect different primary mechanisms that are capable of triggering attacks; nevertheless, it is likely that a particular individual may be susceptible to more than one form of asthma, since hyper-reactivity of the airways to a variety of agents is common in the vast majority of asthmatics (e.g. Boushey *et al.*, 1980).

Extrinsic asthma is characterized by an immunologically mediated allergic response which affects the airways. Antigen–antibody reactions in allergic asthmatics lead to the formation of immunoglobulin E (IgE) antibodies which circulate through the blood to protect against specific antigens. These antigen–antibody interactions stimulate the bronchial mast cells (pervasive cells of the connective tissue) to release humoural mediators such as histamine. The mediators, in turn, induce contraction of the smooth muscle cells which results in bronchial constriction, as well as enhancement of mucus secretion and stimulation of vagal afferent fibres. Allergy mediated by IgE plays an important role in asthma, since different studies have found allergic responses in the majority of asthmatic patients (66–84%; see DeShazo and Salvaggio, 1985). Although allergic asthmatics have been reported to have three times the number of mast cells to that of non-allergic individuals, there is also evidence of neural factors contributing to extrinsic asthma (DeShazo and Salvaggio, 1985; Mathews, 1982), since sympathetic beta-2-adrenergic systems are blunted, whereas parasympathetic responses are heightened. This is consistent with the fact that increased levels of parasympathetic activity are known to produce bronchoconstriction whereas elevated beta-adrenergic activity enhances airway dilatation. Thus immunological and autonomic influences appear jointly related to extrinsic asthma, although the details of this inter-relationship remain a mystery.

Intrinsic asthma, on the other hand, is apparently unrelated to immunological responses. Intrinsic asthmatics may respond with their airways to bacterial or viral infection and a host of other vaguely specified environmental agents but show no sign of elevated IgE serum levels. Intrinsic asthma is often a diagnosis of exclusion, and allergic asthmatics for whom an unsuspected allergen has not been identified may sometimes slip into this category (Pepys and Hutchcroft, 1975). However, the validity of intrinsic asthma as a discrete form does gain support from recent research indicating that intrinsic asthmatics manifest particularly exaggerated levels of parasympathetic activity as compared to normals, atopic non-asthmatics and atopic asthmatics (Sturani, Sturani and Tosi, 1985). Presumably then, increased cholinergic tone and direct non-immunological effects of environmental irritants and/or infection jointly conspire to elicit bronchospasm in intrinsic asthma.

Seventy to 80 per cent of all intrinsic and extrinsic asthmatics additionally suffer from exercise-induced asthma, which is defined as an increase in airway resistance occurring after several minutes of strenuous exercise (Anderson, 1985). Occasionally, exercise is the only stimulus condition that provokes asthma for certain individuals (McFadden, 1980). Exercise-induced asthma presents a significant problem, especially for children and young adults who may particularly feel forced to limit their levels of physical activity. The physiological mechanisms underlying exercise-induced asthma are fairly well understood: loss of water vapour in the airway lumen and sometimes cooling of the airways occurring with exercise stimulate production of bronchoactive substances in the mast and epithelial cells, and the effects upon the airways are potentiated by simultaneously occurring increases in vagal efferent activity

(Anderson, 1985). Additional evidence also points to reduced beta-adreno-ceptor responsiveness in exercise-induced asthma (Martinsson, Larsson and Hjemdahl, 1985).

The last major category of asthma is occupational asthma, defined as variable airway constriction causally related to exposure to certain substances (e.g. dusts or vapours) in the working environment (Chan-Yeung and Lam, 1986). Occupational asthma may result from allergic and non-allergic responses, and in many cases the precise mechanisms remain unknown. Work involved with platinum salts, grain dust, flour, laboratory animals or insects, to mention just a few causes, is associated with a high prevalence of asthma. For example, 20% of all professional bakers apparently suffer from this disorder, and the prevalence rates run even higher for other types of work. Perhaps more distressing is the fact that many studies have found that after removal of susceptible individuals from exposure to provoking factors, the majority of patients remain symptomatic for periods of many years (Chan-Yeung and Lam, 1986).

In summary, it is obvious that asthma is a disorder with several different subtypes that vary in eliciting causes and underlying physiological mechanisms. All these variations in type, age-related factors, chronicity and severity of asthma pose problems for a single psychophysiological approach to the study of the disorder. For example, it would seem unlikely that psychological factors are equally related to the different varieties of asthma, either in terms of psychological contributions to eliciting an asthmatic attack or to the long-term course and medical outcome of the disorder. Unfortunately, however, there are very few psychophysiological studies of asthma that have paid great attention to these distinctions.

Diagnostic Procedure

Diagnosis of asthma requires special procedures to elicit bronchial hyper-reactivity, since spontaneous asthma infrequently occurs in the clinician's office and airway function of asthmatics during non-symptomatic periods may be normal. Furthermore, diagnosis based on anamnesis of symptoms, such as wheezing and breathlessness, is simply insufficient for differential recognition of the disorder. Consequently, bronchial challenge tests have been developed in order to assess the level of airway reactivity to specific inhaled substances. Inasmuch as the bronchi of asthmatics are usually hyper-responsive to a great many substances, two bronchoconstrictive agents are frequently used in these challenge procedures: methacholine and histamine (Pepys and Hutchcroft, 1975). Methacholine is a synthetic acetylcholine-like substance, and histamine is an agent produced by the mast cells. Both are potent bronchoconstrictors for asthmatics. A 15–20% increase in airway resistance is generally considered the minimum criterion for positive diagnosis. Like most diagnostic procedures, this one also has its shortcomings: non-asthmatic individuals suffering from chronic cough, hay fever, rhinitis and cold infections have also been shown to manifest heightened levels of bronchial reactivity to such provocation tests (Boushey *et al.*, 1980; Hargreave, O'Byre and Ramsdale, 1985).

Aspects of Measurement

One of the major problem areas in studying asthmatic and normal changes in airway resistance revolves around difficulties of measurement, and this may be an especially crucial issue for psychophysiological investigation of asthma. The most commonly used indices of airway resistance in medical practice and in the scientific literature are spirometric or air-flow measures such as forced vital capacity (FVC; the maximal amount of air expired after a full inspiration), forced expiratory volume after 1 s (FEV₁), peak expiratory flow rate (PEFR) and maximal mid-expiratory flow (MMEF). Perhaps most important for psychological investigations, these measures are to a significant degree effort-dependent and thus rely upon the motivation and cooperation of the subject, as well as upon the instructions and enthusiasm of the tester (Harm, Marion, Creer and Kotses, 1985a). However, although these measures have often been spurned by psychophysiological investigators, they remain frequently employed in physiological studies. These measures are typically derived from individual breaths into a spirometer or a peak flow meter, and only indirectly reflect the calibre of the airways, influenced as they are by such additional factors as airway collapsibility and pleural pressure changes (van de Woestijne and Clement, 1972). Furthermore, the deep inspiration required to accompany these manoeuvres can itself influence bronchial tone in variable ways in normals and asthmatics (Orehek, Nicoli, Delpierre and Beaupre, 1981). However, these measures are relatively easily and inexpensively obtained, and may often be quite useful, provided adequate care is given to maximizing motivational factors and standardizing the demand characteristics of the test situation. Cheap and portable peak flow meters also remain the only available possibility for approximating ambulatory monitoring of airway resistance, whereas MMEF is probably the only easily obtainable index of peripheral airway constriction (Bouhuys and van de Woestijne, 1970). Furthermore, several of these measures (i.e. FEV₁, PEFR and MMEF) appear sensitive enough to detect clinically significant changes in airway resistance (e.g. Spector, Luparello, Kopetzky, Souhrada and Kinsman, 1976). Hence, until there is clear evidence to the contrary, cautious employment of spirometric measures in asthma research seems warranted.

The best instrument for directly estimating airway calibre, however, is the body plethysmograph, a small enclosed cabin which permits monitoring of both airway and cabin volume and pressure. Whole-body plethysmography makes possible continuous measurement of thoracic gas volume (T_{gv}: the amount of gas in the lungs and other airways at the end of expiration), airway resistance (R_{aw}: airway pressure/airway flow), airway conductance (G_{aw}: $1/R_{aw}$), and specific airway conductance (SG_{aw}: G_{aw}/T_{gv}). Inasmuch as increases and decreases in lung volume influence airway resistance by altering the elastic force upon the lungs (Dubois, Brody, Lewis and Burgess, 1956), measurement of R_{aw} or G_{aw} alone provides an inaccurate reflection of the specific bronchial and upper airway resistance when T_{gv} shifts. SG_{aw} is used as an attempt to correct for alterations in lung volume and thus is generally considered the most sensitive measure of specific airway calibre.

Although the body plethysmograph accurately measures respiratory parameters, the instrument itself is expensive, and the enclosure of the subject in such a confined space may sometimes induce anxiety responses which alter respiratory function. Two other methods of continuously measuring respiratory resistance which largely circumvent these problems are the forced-oscillation technique and the shutter, or interrupter, method (Goldman, Knudson, Mead, Peterson, Schwaber and Wohl, 1970; Klein, Urbanek, Kohler and Matthys, 1983; Shaw, Chiang, Wsieh and Milic-Emili, 1983). Neither procedure yields results as accurate as the body plethysmograph; none the less, resistance values derived from both techniques are highly correlated with plethysmographic measures (e.g. Shaw *et al.*, 1983; Vachon and Rich, 1976). Both measurement techniques employ different methods of disturbing the airstream (i.e. imposed oscillations vs brief interruption) so that airway pressure–flow relations may be analysed and total respiratory resistance (R_t) can be determined. Since R_t varies with thoracic gas volume, due to elastic changes of the lungs (as previously explained), T_{gv} must be kept relatively constant in order to accurately reflect the airway resistance of interest.

In summary, there are several different direct and indirect procedures for estimating the calibre of the airways, each of them having their advantages and disadvantages. Additionally, there are other important measures of functioning, and these include records of medicine usage, diaries of respiratory function and symptoms, and physician's ratings, medical charts, hospitalization data and school or work absenteeism. Since many of these measures tend not to be strongly correlated with each other or with more objective measures of respiratory function (e.g. Chai, Purcell, Brady and Falliers, 1968; Dirks, Brown and Robinson, 1982a; Dirks, Ruback, Feiguine and Covina, 1982b; Heim, Blaser and Waidelich, 1972; Kinsman, Dahlem, Spector and Staudenmayer, 1977), these dimensions are likely to reflect the results of specific patterns of coping and adaptation to asthma. Hence, their concurrent use with objective respiratory measures is of great value in unravelling the complex interactions between physical dysfunction and psychological factors which may determine not only the specific pattern of coping with the disorder but perhaps also how the disorder itself progresses (e.g. Steiner, Higgs, Fritz, Laszlo and Harvey, 1987).

PSYCHOPHYSIOLOGICAL ASPECTS OF ASTHMA

Interactions with Psychological Traits and Situational Behavioural Responses

The often long-term nature of the syndrome predisposes asthmatics to the same sort of psychological consequences and coping strategies as those of other sufferers of chronic diseases. Thus, the psychological characteristics of asthmatics that early psychosomatic researchers took to be aetiological in origin, such as insecurity and emotional dependency, have turned out to be typical responses to prolonged debilitating disease (e.g. Benjamin, 1977; Neuhaus, 1958). None the less, there is much recent evidence that indicates the importance of individual differences in psychological traits and situational behavioural responses of asthma sufferers for issues related to the management and treatment of their disorder. Some of these psychological factors may even have bearing, among severe asthmatics, upon the probability of survival. Thus, one study found that only when psychological factors (e.g. emotional disturbance, family conflict and disregard of symptoms) were included along with physiological risk characteristics was it possible to distinguish accurately between severe asthmatic children who died from their disorder and those who did not (Strunk, Mrazek, Fuhrman and LaBrecque, 1985).

Other findings relating the course of the disorder to variations in behavioural dimensions have been reported by Dirks and colleagues (e.g. Dirks, 1982; Dirks *et al.*, 1982a,b). For example, ratings on both personality and situational behavioural dimensions associated with a tendency towards panic and fear have been found to be predictive of length of hospitalization, rehospitalization rates and intensity of prescribed medicine regimes among severe asthmatics, and these relations were independent of physiological factors (Dirks, Jones and Kinsman, 1977; Kinsman *et al.*, 1977; Kinsman, Spector, Shucard and Luparello, 1974; Staudenmayer, Kinsman, Dirks, Spector and Wangaard, 1979). Obviously such findings point to complex interactions between physiological manifestations of asthma and individual-specific behavioural styles.

Psychological Precipitants of Asthma

There is abundant evidence that psychological elements are specifically implicated in the precipitation of episodes of airway bronchoconstriction and pulmonary symptoms among certain asthma sufferers. Several laboratory investigations have provided rather convincing evidence that asthmatics differ from normal individuals in their airway and respiratory responses to psychological stimuli (e.g. Florin, Freudenberg and Hollaender, 1985; Hollaender and Florin, 1983; Levenson, 1979; Mathé and Knapp, 1971; Smith, Colebatch and Clarke, 1979; Tal and Miklich, 1976). Suggestion of asthma and of emotionally laden situations, as well as actual laboratory stressors of diverse varieties, produce tonic elevations of airway resistance among some asthmatics, but no responses or even a decrease in resistance in normals. However, in most studies, the mean level of stress-related increase in airway resistance among asthmatics has been small and not clinically significant.

Possibly the most fascinating and best replicated findings concerning psychological precipitants of asthmatic responses come from studies that have incorporated suggestion of bronchoconstriction and bronchodilatation into typical airway-challenge test procedures (Horton, Suda, Kinsman, Souhrada and Spector, 1978; Lewis, Lewis and Tattersfield, 1984; Luparello, Leist, Lourie and Smeet, 1970; Luparello, Lyons, Bleecker and McFadden, 1968; McFadden, Luparello, Lyons and Bleecker, 1969; Nield and Cameron, 1985; Philip, Wilde and Day, 1972; Spector *et al.*, 1976; Strupp, Levenson, Manuck, Snell, Hinrichsen and Boyd, 1974). Although a number of these investigations suffer from various methodological weaknesses, there is a great consistency of findings across studies. In these experiments, asthmatic subjects were presented with aerosol inhalant agents that were suggested to be either bronchoconstrictive or bronchodilatory substances. In reality, depending upon the experimental condition, either inert saline solution or actual constrictive or dilatational agents were administered, after which airway conductance was directly or indirectly assessed. In this manner, it became possible to tease apart the separate effects of suggestion and the specific agents.

To summarize the results, suggestion of constriction or dilatation while inhaling an inert substance was usually found to produce actual corresponding changes in airway calibre, and these effects were consistently statistically significant. Furthermore, suggestions that ran opposite to the true effects of the inhaled agent generally produced attenuated bronchial responses to those which were normally seen, whereas suggestions which accurately reflected the effects of the substance generally seemed to potentiate pulmonary reactions. Additionally, there was also evidence that asthmatic reactivity to suggestion was reproducible over time (McFadden *et al.*, 1969), an important point when considering the vagaries of asthmatic responsivity (Tal and Miklich, 1976).

These investigations provide the clearest evidence that rather subtle psychological factors, such as suggestion, can play a role in the pulmonary responsiveness of asthmatic patients. However, only about one-quarter to two-thirds of asthmatics in these studies appeared to be highly susceptible to such psychological influences. Unfortunately, with the exception of one methodologically flawed study (Philip *et al.*, 1972), all investigations have used criteria for subject selection that cut across diagnostic subcategories of asthma; hence it is unclear whether certain types of asthmatics are more susceptible to suggestion than others. Nevertheless, it may be derived from these many studies that suggestion exerts its effects over a wide range of severity of the disorder.

Individual differences among asthma patients in airway responses to emotional stimuli are, of course, of fundamental concern for a psychophysiological approach to this disorder. Identification of asthmatics who regularly manifest potent airway reactions to emotional triggers may have obvious implications for issues related to treatment and management of the disorder. This is clearly illustrated by a well-controlled study which found that juvenile asthmatics with a history of asthma triggered by family-related conflicts improved when they were experimentally separated from their family (Purcell, Brody, Muser, Molk, Gordon and Means, 1969a).

Other evidence also suggests that asthmatic children who physiologically respond beneficially to separation from their families differ from non-responsive asthmatics in terms of both their own and their parent's psychological profiles. Thus such children appear to be more neurotic and anxious, whereas their parents are often more controlling, hostile, intolerant and authoritarian (Purcell and Metz, 1962; Purcell, Bernstein and Bukantz, 1961; Purcell, Muser, Micklich and Dietikor, 1969b). This research points to the possibility that emotional conflicts, typically revolving around family disputes, may often be important factors in the precipitation of bronchospastic episodes and may influence the particular course that asthma may take in some individuals. Although interview-based studies suggest that four major categories of affect (i.e. anger, fear, excitement and depression) may often precede and stimulate episodes of bronchoconstriction among many asthmatics (see Wiener, 1977), future work is needed to verify these and other classes of emotional stimuli as potent triggers of asthma. Furthermore, much more research is needed to investigate just how prominent a role emotional factors actually play in the precipitation of asthma attacks, as well as whether specific types of asthma are differentially related to emotional triggers.

Mechanisms of Psychogenic Contributions to Bronchospastic Episodes

Most of the psychophysiological stress literature clearly points to specific neural and visceral adaptations occurring to psychological or physical demands and stressors. Although the particular patterns of physiological responses to stressors appear to depend upon both individual differences and the particular nature of the stressor, the general pattern of reaction is that of autonomic activation, often including increased production and/or release of catecholamines and corticosteroids. Nevertheless, the relationship between psychological precipitants and asthma is difficult to understand within the normal psychophysiological framework of stress responses. In asthmatics, airway diameter increases upon enhanced sympathetic and adrenocortical stimulation and decreases upon vagal stimulation. Indeed, sympathetic agonists, parasympathetic antagonists and corticosteroids have long been used therapeutically in the management of asthma. One might expect, therefore, that emotional stressors, known to produce just this pattern of sympathetic and vagal responses, would provide relief to asthmatic individuals. In reality, emotional stimuli have been shown to induce episodic bronchospasm in patients (e.g. Levenson, 1979).

A clear explanation for this apparent paradox is presently lacking. However, several clues point to the involvement of aberrant autonomic function playing a central role in asthma in general, and in behaviourally related asthmatic episodes in particular. First, regarding sympathetic activity, there are several studies which indicate a selective damping of the beta-adrenergic system among many asthmatics. Asthmatics show both a blunted release of adrenaline to behavioural stress (Mathé and Knapp, 1971) and an often attenuated cardio-vascular response to pharmacological and behavioural beta-2-agonists (Barnes, 1986). However, there are almost no sympathetic nerve fibres in the smooth muscle of the airways and there is no evidence of direct adrenergic innervation. Furthermore, neither beta-adrenergic blockade or surgical removal of the adrenal glands transforms normals into asthmatics (Barnes, 1986), making it unlikely that a sympathetic defect is primary in asthma, or is important for psychologically associated mechanisms.

Current evidence suggests that, whereas sympathetic and specifically adre-naline-related factors may secondarily modulate primary asthmatic responses, the parasympathetic system may be more centrally involved, and could be of special importance for psychologically induced bronchoconstrictive episodes (Barnes, 1986). Hence, asthmatics have been repeatedly shown to exhibit exaggerated parasympathetic cardiac and pupillary reactions which, in turn, have been related to both clinical severity and degree of bronchial hyper-reactivity (e.g. Kallenbach *et al.*, 1985; Sturani *et al.*, 1985). Specifically regarding psychological factors, pharmacological blockade of the vagus or of cholinergic airway receptors has been shown to eliminate bronchial responses to suggestion (McFadden *et al.*, 1969; Nield and Cameron, 1985). Similarly, bronchial responses to suggestion have been found to be positively related to presumably vagally mediated reactivity to histamine and methacholine chal-lenges (Horton *et al.*, 1978). Furthermore, recent studies indicate that bronchial effects of suggestion occur primarily in the larger airways (Ewer and Stewart, 1986; Lehrer *et al.*, 1986), just where vagal fibres and receptors are most prolific and where parasympathetically active drugs are known to have their effects (Ewer and Stewart, 1986; O'Cain, Hensley, McFadden and Ingram, 1979). Behavioural acts such as laughing and crying, which directly irritate the airway epithelium in asthmatics, are also thought to produce constrictive responses via the vagus (Boushey *et al.*, 1980; Weinstein, 1984).

Although most findings seem to point to vagal mediation of behavioural effects upon asthma, the fact remains that psychological stressors, known to induce bronchospasm in asthmatics, should be more likely to reduce, rather than enhance, general levels of vagal activity. Thus the puzzle of stress-related asthmatic reactions would still appear to be unresolved. Nevertheless, several investigations point to a plausible hypothesis that involves hyperventilatory responses to psychological stressors. On the one hand, hyperventilation is a physiological response which may often occur to psychological stress and has been particularly implicated in the reactions of asthmatics to hypnotic suggestion of the same negative emotional states and bronchoconstrictive episodes also known to produce actual bronchospastic reactions in patients (Clarke and Gibson, 1980; Smith *et al.*, 1970). On the other hand, hyperventilation exerts bronchoconstrictive influences via two mechanisms, at least one of which is mediated by the vagus.

Thus hypocapnia and overbreathing-induced airway cooling independently bring about bronchoconstrictive responses (Clarke, 1971; O'Cain *et al.*, 1979; Sterling, 1968; Wilson, Barnes, Vickers and Silverman, 1982), and at least the large airway reactions seem to be mediated by the vagus, since vagal blockers eliminate these responses. Additional evidence is provided by a study which has shown no effects of suggestion upon asthmatic bronchial tone once airway cooling is controlled (Lewis *et al.*, 1984), also indicating the possible mediating effects of hyperventilation. Unfortunately, simultaneous monitoring of airway tone, ventilation and blood-gas responses to suggestion and other psychological stimuli has not yet been reported in the literature, and the hyperventilation hypothesis, although a plausible explanation for apparently paradoxical stress reactions of asthmatics, awaits an adequate empirical test.

Psychophysiological Approaches to Treatment of Asthma

Behavioural Therapy Approaches

Various behavioural treatments have been applied to asthma, including relaxation therapy, systematic desensitization, assertiveness training, hypnosis, respiratory and muscular biofeedback, and both operant and classical conditioning procedures. An extensive review of the experimental literature concerning these treatments is beyond the scope of this chapter, and there are several reviews already available (Cluss, 1986; Erskine-Millis and Schonell, 1981; Knapp and Wells, 1978; Richter and Dahme, 1982; Steptoe, 1983). Hence, we shall only summarize and supplement the existing reviews.

The results of evaluation studies of most type of behavioural procedures provide an unclear picture regarding the promise of such therapies for primary or adjunctive treatments for asthma. On the one hand, there are many investigations that report significant improvements in pulmonary responses, frequency of medication use and other medical interventions, and subjective measures of wellbeing. However, the real evidence for objective and clinically significant benefits in pulmonary function is, indeed, quite slender, once distinctions are made between statistical and clinical significance and between methodologically sound and unsound investigations (e.g. see Richter and Dahme, 1982). Regarding the latter point, only about half of the existing treatment studies included an adequate control group with which to compare their experimental therapy group, another half did not control for severity of the disorder, and only 10% of the studies actually followed up subjects for a period of longer than 6 months in order to determine long-term effects of treatment (Cluss, 1986). Furthermore, most therapy-evaluation experiments have employed spirometric measures as dependent indices of pulmonary function which, besides being effort-dependent, also reflect airway elasticity as well as resistance. These measures are particularly ill-suited for investigating effects of behavioural interventions since motivational factors and experimental demand characteristics may differentially affect the effort expended among experimental and control subjects; this in turn could largely account for experimental group improvements in spirometric measures, especially when spirometric flow improvement is modest. Alexander, Cropp and Chai (1979), for example, reported relaxation therapy to enhance flow measures slightly (and statistically significantly) among asthmatic children; however, more objective plethysmographic measures of resistance remained unaltered.

To the best of our knowledge, there have only been eight behavioural treatment studies that have employed more objective plethysmographic or forced-oscillation estimates of airway resistance as dependent measures (Alexander *et al.*, 1979; Ben-Zvi, Young and Kattan, 1982; Ewer and Stewart, 1986; Feldman, 1976; Janson-Bjerklie and Clark, 1982; Steptoe, Philips and Harburg, 1981; Vachon and Rich, 1976; Wilson, Honsberger, Chiu and Novey, 1975). The behavioural treatments used include hypnosis (Ben-Zvi *et al.*, 1982; Ewer and Stewart, 1986), relaxation (Alexander *et al.*, 1979), meditation (Wilson *et al.*, 1975) and biofeedback of total respiratory resistance. Clear statistically significant improvements were reported for behavioural treatments in only half the studies, and in some of these there were also suggestions of clinical significance. However, none of these investigations has assessed long-term benefits. An additionally important point is that the majority of these (and other) studies have evaluated treatment effects under basal conditions. Since asthma is intermittent and airway functioning often approximates normal values among asthmatics between attacks, the clinical significance of these behavioural techniques remains in question. Under bronchial provocation challenges (i.e. exercise), behavioural treatments have been found to provide either no improvement in resistance measures or the same level as placebo-control procedures, and behavioural interventions fare significantly worse than medication regimens (Ben-Zvi *et al.*, 1982; Ewer and Stewart, 1986).

In summary, then, the progress made in the last few years regarding behavioural treatment of asthma has been modest. The literature is marred by methodological and measurement problems which limit our drawing any clear conclusions concerning the potential effectiveness of behavioural procedures. Much research therefore is still needed.

Management Approaches

Whereas the effectiveness of behavioural therapies for the improvement of objective airway functioning in asthma remains unclear, much of the psychophysiological literature on the disorder seems to suggest the usefulness of integrating biobehavioural aspects into programmes of management and self-management of asthma. The frequency and severity of diverse effects of asthma can be reduced for many individuals by the conscious learning and avoidance of known precipitants (whether environmental or psychological), by the proper timing and administration of appropriate medication and by the acquisition of new coping strategies to deal with the acute and chronic aspects of the disorder. There have been several nation-wide management programmes in the US which have attempted such a comprehensive approach to childhood asthma (see Creer and Winder, 1986), although there is a scarcity of refereed research reports in this area. The aims of these programmes have been to educate participants and their families concerning physiological and medical aspects of asthma, as well as to teach problem-solving and decision-making skills (Creer and Winder, 1986). The latter elements include ways to control possible triggers of asthma, manage attacks and face problems that result from the asthma, such as those relating to school and sporting activities.

Underlying these global skills are more detailed learning processes that investigators have begun to systematically examine. The use of the peak flow meter has figured importantly in studies aimed at improving the typically poor ability of asthmatics accurately to perceive objective changes in pulmonary functioning (see Steiner *et al.*, 1987). Thus in a recent controlled experiment, multiple daily self-monitoring of peak flow over 4 weeks enhanced the veridicality of perceived airway obstruction (Higgs, Richardson, Lea, Lewis and Laszlo, 1986). Other studies have shown that patients' abilities to predict future attacks can be greatly improved by utilizing daily peak flow values and base-rate data concerning attacks in conditional probability procedures (Harm, Marion, Creer and Kotses, 1985b; Talpin and Creer, 1978).

Still other approaches to skill acquisition have focused upon the application of behavioural methods to the reduction of undesirable behaviour patterns, such as unnecessary hospitalizations, non-compliance with medical regimes and improper use of inhalators (see Creer and Winder, 1986). Despite the fact that these procedures have encompassed a wide range of learning techniques, the reported results are consistently positive and lend promise to future developments in behavioural management of asthma.

CONCLUSIONS AND FUTURE DIRECTIONS

Asthma is a respiratory disorder characterized by airway hyper-responsiveness that may be due to a number of separate mechanisms. Although there is little evidence of psychogenic factors playing any role in producing the disorder, psychological elements certainly seem to contribute to discrete asthmatic attacks and may figure significantly in the natural course and professional management of the illness. Although the autonomic–behavioural interactions in asthma appear paradoxical, it seems that the parasympathetic pathway mediates the behavioural effects upon airway calibre. Emotional hyperventilatory responses have also been suggested to elicit bronchoconstrictive episodes among certain asthmatics. Indeed, a recent report points toward a possible link between hyperventilation syndrome and asthma (Demeter and Cordasco, 1986). Future studies should explore the effects of behaviourally mediated variations in both parasympathetic tone and hyperventilatory breathing in order to assess the validity of these proposed relationships.

HYPERVENTILATION SYNDROME

INTRODUCTION

Hyperventilation syndrome (HVS) is a disorder characterized by a range of somatic and psychological symptoms, which are not secondary to any organic disease state, but are considered to result from episodes of hyperventilation, or from more or less chronic levels of hypocapnia (arterial carbon dioxide levels below normal). Individuals suffering from HVS typically report respiratory, cardiac, central neural and/or gastrointestinal complaints usually coupled importantly to anxiety and fear responses (see e.g. Grossman and de Swart, 1984). Although investigators of the disorder frequently provide evidence suggesting that the incidence of HVS in the general medical population is high (Brashear, 1983; Magarian, 1982; Pfeffer, 1978; Weimann, 1968), basic scientific research aimed at validation of the syndrome as a distinct disorder, inexorably tied to the consequences of aberrant ventilatory patterns, has not been rapidly forthcoming. When the sparse strands of validation research are braided together, it becomes apparent that a simple model in which all symptoms of HVS are regarded directly or indirectly as consequences of hyperventilation or hypocapnia provides a naive and inadequate approach to the disorder. Whereas the already available evidence indicates a real, if somewhat modest, relationship between HVS and ventilatory activity, previously overlooked interactions between physiological functioning and psychological processes associated with enhanced tendencies to report somatic complaints and to focus upon bodily sensations, contribute to a far more credible analysis of the aetiology of the syndrome than that generally offered. Such an approach has diverse implications for issues related to diagnosis, treatment and even the proper name for the disorder.

PHYSIOLOGICAL BACKGROUND AND MEASUREMENT ISSUES

Respiration

In this section, respiratory physiology is briefly described. (For more detailed accounts of respiratory processes, see, for example, Comroe, 1965; Guyton, 1966.) The main function of respiration is the transport of oxygen from the atmosphere to the tissues and of carbon dioxide (a metabolic waste product) from the tissues back to the atmosphere. Respiration can be described and quantified on different levels. In the first place, one can measure the volume of air that moves in and out of the lungs. This is expressed in the minute respiratory volume, which is the product of the tidal volume (the volume of air that flows in and out of the lungs with each normal breath) and respiratory rate. A second level of description and quantification concerns the exchange of gases in the alveoli of the lungs. The rate of gas exchange is determined by the force the gases exert on the alveolar membrane in attempting to diffuse through it. This force is, in turn, dependent upon the partial pressures of the gases that are involved. As a consequence of the pressure gradients of oxygen and carbon dioxide, oxygen diffuses from the alveoli into the arterial blood and carbon dioxide, conversely, from the blood into the alveoli. Most of the oxygen is transported to the tissues in chemical combination with the haemoglobin in the red blood cells. The transport of carbon dioxide from the tissues to the lungs is accomplished in four different chemical forms: as dissolved carbon dioxide, in chemical combination with haemoglobin, and in combination with water as carbonic acid, which, in turn, dissociates to a large extent into hydrogen and bicarbonate ions. The acid–base balance of blood is, therefore, directly affected by the carbon dioxide partial pressure (P_{CO_2}): a lower P_{CO_2} in the arterial blood typically results in a lower concentration of hydrogen ions (higher pH, i.e. alkalosis), whereas a relatively high P_{CO_2} usually leads to more hydrogen ions and lower pH (acidosis). Therefore, respiration plays a very significant role in the maintenance of the acid–base equilibrium.

Neural Control of Respiration

Respiratory processes are partially controlled by a number of closely interacting neural pools in the brain stem that together are often referred to as 'the respiratory centre'. The main purpose of this respiratory centre is to adjust the rate of alveolar ventilation to the ever-changing metabolic demands of the body. The activity of this centre is sensitive to both humoural and neural factors. Among the most important humoural influences are the concentrations of carbon dioxide and hydrogen ions in the tissue fluids of the respiratory centre. In addition, special receptors located in the carotid and aortic bodies (called chemoreceptors) are responsive to changes in carbon dioxide, hydrogen ions and oxygen.

Respiration is also jointly under the control of cortical and mid-brain mechanisms (Bass and Gardner, 1985a; Hugelin, 1986). The feedback mechanisms involved in the automatic, brain-stem control of ventilation are often overridden by influences from these higher brain areas upon the respiratory centre and respiratory muscles. Such influences include the sleep/wake cycle, arousal, cognitive functioning and emotional states.

Hyperventilation and Hypocapnia

Hyperventilation is physiologically defined in a very precise way. It occurs whenever alveolar ventilation increases beyond metabolic requirements. Elimination of carbon dioxide thus occurs at a faster rate than production of it in the tissues. Hyperventilation may be accomplished voluntarily, by overriding the normal regulation of ventilation, or it may occur involuntarily in emotional states, at high altitude, in certain disease states, and in response to certain drugs or toxins. The immediate consequence of hyperventilation is a drop in the arterial carbon dioxide partial pressure below normal levels of 36–45 mmHg (i.e. hypocapnia), and a rapid shift in the blood acid–base balance towards alkalosis. During moderate or severe hyperventilation, an *acute* hypocapnic state is achieved within minutes, which is characterized by a low P_{CO_2}, and an elevated pH. When, however, the hypocapnia is sustained for longer periods of time, renal compensatory mechanisms come into action, and after 36–72 h of hypocapnia, a *chronic* hypocapnic state is established with a low P_{CO_2} and pH values around normal.

The effects of hypocapnia upon other body functions are numerous and complicated. Among the most important consequences are hypophosphataemia (Magarian, 1982), increase in lactic acid production (Balke, Ellis and Wells, 1958) and reductions in cerebral and coronary perfusion (Magarian, 1982). Even relatively small reductions in P_{CO_2} are sufficient to decrease cerebral blood flow considerably (Kenneally, McLennan, Loudon and McLaurin, 1980). Acute, pronounced hypocapnia can also dramatically decrease myocardial blood flow and oxygen delivery to the musculature of the heart (Rowe, Castillo and Crumpton, 1962). There is clear evidence that hyperventilation may compromise the myocardial oxygen supply of individuals suffering from cardiac insufficiency (see Grossman and Wientjes, 1985) and may produce life-threatening coronary occlusion in a substantial proportion (25%) of certain heart-disease patients (Rasmussen, Jull, Bagger and Henningsen, 1987). Therefore, hyperventilation seems to be of special significance for coronary artery disease. In addition, a number of electrocardiogram abnormalities may be observed during hypocapnia, including T-wave flattening or inversion, and S–T depression (see Grossman and Wientjes, 1985). The autonomic effects of hyperventilation seem to be an increase of sympathetic activity and withdrawal of cardiac vagal tone (see Grossman and Wientjes, 1985).

Physiological Measurements

Because hyperventilation is defined as an excessive removal of carbon dioxide from the blood, hyperventilation is operationalized in terms of a reduction in arterial P_{CO_2}. The direct measurement of arterial P_{CO_2}, however, is invasive, and it is therefore often substituted by measurement of the alveolar carbon dioxide partial pressure (alveolar P_{CO_2}), which is generally considered to be an accurate estimate of arterial P_{CO_2} (Gardner, Meah and Bass, 1986). For practical purposes, alveolar P_{CO_2} can be estimated by measuring the P_{CO_2} of the expired air at the *end* of a normal expiration (end-tidal P_{CO_2}), as measured by means of an infra-red gas analyser. When respiration is very shallow, however, the expired air will consist mainly of gases that have not been in contact with the alveolar membrane and, therefore, the end-tidal P_{CO_2} will, in this case, not be representative of the true alveolar P_{CO_2}. During the measurement of end-tidal P_{CO_2}, breaths with a low percentage of alveolar air can easily be recognizd by the fact that the CO_2 waveform does not reach a horizontal pleateau but, rather, increases steeply and then breaks off suddenly. Such breaths should not be included in analyses.

Recently, a new technique has become available, employing transcutaneous measurement of carbon dioxide concentration by means of an electrochemical sensor (Hibbert, 1986). However, its reliability of measurement has not yet been sufficiently established.

It should be noted that hyperventilation cannot be assessed merely by measuring ventilation. However, respiratory parameters, including time and volume components are essential for research purposes. There are a number of techniques available for the measurement of respiration, such as relatively intrusive spirometry and pneumotachography (which involve a mouthpiece and noseclip, or face mask), or indirect measurement of respiratory parameters by means of (calibrated) bands or strain gauges across the chest and abdomen (see Morel, Forster and Suter, 1983). The major advantage of the indirect measurement techniques is that they do not interfere with spontaneous breathing.

Questionnaires

The use of self-reports has become common both in HVS research and in clinical practice. The reasons for this are obvious: the most important signs and symptoms of HVS and related disturbances manifest themselves primarily in terms of subjective reports and experiences, rather than in terms of objectively measurable phenomena. Typically, however, the use of self-report techniques poses a number of methodological problems, including such aspects as differences in response tendencies, labelling processes, social desirability, and experimental demand characteristics (Lazarus, 1966). One should always be aware of these problems, and a number of techniques have been developed that attempt to deal with them. The use of standardized symptom checklists and questionnaires may help to minimize the effects of linguistic confusion, whereas the inclusion of 'dummy items' (i.e. items that are clearly unrelated to the symptomatology of HVS) may serve to assess response tendencies. Although a number of standardized questionnaires have been developed for specific use among HVS patients (e.g. van Dixhoorn and van Duivenbode, 1985; Grossman and de Swart, 1984), much remains to be accomplished with regard to standardization and scoring methods.

CLINICAL MANIFESTATIONS OF HVS

The typical episodic, physical symptoms of HVS patients encompass a variety of functional complaints that appear to be related to different physiological systems (see Table 18.1). The constellation of symptoms, furthermore, varies both in type, number and severity between patients and often mimics organic disease states (Grossman and de Swart, 1984). Such a diffuse symptomatology of potentially serious somatic symptoms provides a double-edged threat for mistaken diagnosis: on the one hand, patients inappropriately diagnosed as having HVS may actually suffer from serious, sometimes life-threatening, physical conditions unrelated to hyperventilation or in which hyperventilation is a purely secondary physiological response to organic disease. Thus, common organic causes of hyperventilation include central nervous system abnormalities (e.g. stroke and infection), pulmonary emboli, salicyclate poisoning, acidaemia, hypoxaemia and fever (Gennari and Kassirer, 1982), whereas chest and respiratory symptoms representing cardiac conditions or diabetes, may be erroneously attributed to HVS (e.g. Magarian and Hickam, 1986; Treasure, Fowler, Millington and Wise, 1987). On the other hand, where HVS is instead mistaken for organic disease, patients may be referred from specialist to specialist or receive long-term medical treatments that are ineffective and have detrimental side-effects, while their actual problem remains untreated. For these reasons, it is obviously necessary for patients suspected of having HVS to be subjected initially to a thorough medical examination to exclude organic disease. Conversely, physicians should consider the possibility of HVS when organic disorders have been convincingly excluded.

In addition to the major presenting symptoms of a somatic nature, an important feature of HVS patients seems to be their great psychological vulnerability (Brashear, 1983; Lum, 1976; Garssen, 1980; Magarian, 1982). On standardized psychological inventories, these individuals manifest low levels of self-esteem and high levels of neuroticism and anxiety (Grossman, de Swart and Defares, 1985). Combined clinical interviews and tests have also revealed that one-half of a group of HVS patients were afflicted to a serious degree by psychiatric disorder (Bass and Gardner, 1985b). In addition, other reports suggest a frequent association between HVS and both agoraphobia and panic

Table 18.1
Frequency of positive responses to chronic complaint items among 200 HVS and 200
non-HVS subjects diagnosed on the basis of the provocation test (see 'Diagnosis';
from Grossman and de Swart, 1984)

Item	Percentage of positive responses		Significance level
	HVS	non-HVS	
Fits of crying	14.5	6.5	0.01
Unable to breathe deeply enough	44.5	33.5	0.03
Suffocating feeling	54.5	41.0	0.009
Rapid heartbeat	41.5	27.0	0.003
Feeling of unrest, panic	54.5	38.5	0.002
Tingling in feet	20.0	17.0	
Nausea	38.0	31.5	
Confused or dream-like feeling	35.0	27.5	
Feeling of heat	42.0	34.0	
Pounding heart	50.0	27.0	0.0000
Stomach cramps	19.0	18.0	
Toe or leg cramps	10.5	12.5	
Shivering	25.5	16.5	
Irregular heartbeat	18.5	11.5	0.07
Tingling in legs	16.0	11.5	
Feeling anxious	30.0	21.0	0.05
Chest pain around heart region	40.0	37.5	
Stiffness in fingers or arms	18.5	13.0	
Cold hands or feet	20.5	20.5	
Feeling of head warmth	29.0	20.0	0.05
Stiffness about mouth	6.5	4.5	
Stomach feels blown up	21.5	18.0	
Pressure or knot in throat	23.0	13.5	0.02
Tingling in arms	20.5	14.0	
Faster or deeper breathing than normal	42.5	18.5	0.0000
Hands tremble	38.5	25.0	0.005
Dizziness	69.0	50.5	0.0002
Stiffness in legs	7.5	5.0	
Blacking out	45.5	35.5	0.05
Tingling in body	5.0	4.0	
Tenseness	51.5	36.5	0.003
Need for air	27.5	16.0	0.008
Fainting	15.0	15.5	
Tingling in fingers	26.5	17.5	0.04
Tiredness	64.0	55.5	0.10
Headaches	47.0	51.0	
Tingling in face	10.0	4.0	0.03

disorder (Bass and Gardner, 1985a; Garssen, van Veenendaal and Bloemink,
1983).

Often, greater psychological vulnerability seems to be combined with higher levels of real or perceived psychoenvironmental stressors. Attacks of HVS, correspondingly, are frequently reported to be triggered by stressful experiences, such as sexual problems, relational conflicts, occupational or financial difficulties or by anxiety reactions to situations such as crowded shops, stations, small enclosed places or travelling by public transport (Garssen, 1980). Furthermore, at the time of the first attack, serious life-events are frequently indicated to have occurred, such as loss of a relative, or physical trauma (Garssen, 1980). Patients with HVS typically report experiencing symptom attacks as profoundly stressful, characterizing themselves during attacks as very fearful, anxious, tense and confused (Grossman and de Swart, 1984). They also perceive themselves as severely incapacitated by their disorder (Gardner *et al.*, 1986).

Types of HVS

Several investigators have proposed a distinction between two types of HVS (Gardner *et al.*, 1986; Magarian, 1982). One form, termed acute HVS, is characterized by sudden attacks of symptoms triggered by episodic hyperventilation. Between attacks, however, patterns of breathing and levels of CO_2 are within normal range. The other type of HVS, called chronic HVS, is marked by a persistent pronounced hypocapnia in the absence of any organic disease. Whereas recent investigations provide support for the existence of the two forms (Freeman, Conway and Nixon, 1986; Gardner *et al.*, 1986), there is no data yet available bearing upon differences among these forms with respect to symptom constellation, aetiological factors or incidence rates.

Incidence of HVS

Evaluation of incidence rates of HVS is hampered by the loose assessment techniques generally used to diagnose the disorder (see next section); hence the available estimates should be taken as merely suggestive of the disorder. Nevertheless, among various medical specialities, estimates have run between 5% and 11% of all patients (Brashear, 1983; Magarian, 1982; Pfeffer, 1978; Weimann, 1968). Furthermore, most investigators report that HVS occurs at least twice as frequently among women then men (e.g. Doelle, 1964; Pincus, 1978; Weimann, 1968). Regarding age, it appears that those between 20 and 40 years of age are most likely to be at risk (Doelle, 1964; Pincus, 1978; Weimann, 1968). The disorder also seems to occur among children and adolescents, although incidence rates have not been established (e.g. Herman, Stickler and Lucas, 1981; Joorabchi, 1977).

DIAGNOSIS OF HVS

Although several diagnostic procedures are in current use, correct identification of HVS patients presents significant problems. First of all, HVS as a discrete clinical disorder is predicated upon the assumption that hyperventilation is the proximal trigger of symptom attacks. In order to verify this with an individual patient, it is necessary to monitor his/her P_{CO_2} during a symptomatic episode. However, these attacks are generally rather brief in duration, and they are unlikely to occur during occasional contacts with doctors or psychologists. Since ventilation may be normal during non-symptomatic periods, and other clear and objective physiological criteria are frequently lacking, ventilatory or other physiological assessment often cannot serve as the decisive diagnostic criterion. Secondly, a major problem revolves around the fact that subjective perceptions and reports of somatic and psychological complaints play such a large role in the definition of the syndrome. It is well established that various parameters of symptom reporting may be heavily influenced by psychological factors of a situational, historical and personality nature, and that symptom reports are often more powerfully correlated with psychological characteristics than with actual variations in physiological activity (see Pennebaker, 1982). In the same vein, we have shown that seemingly typical HVS symptoms often occur in the absence of hyperventilation, and that an increased tendency to report such symptoms in everyday life is associated with a propensity to report the same symptoms under stressful conditions in which no hyperventilation occurs (Svebak and Grossman, 1985; Wientjes, Grossman, Gaillard and Defares, 1985a,b). Thus tacit acceptance of reported symptoms as both as veridical and evidence of HVS would seem naive in the light of current evidence.

With rare exceptions (Bass and Gardner, 1985b; Gardner et al., 1986), research investigations, as well as clinical practice, have chosen to ignore these considerations. Hence presenting symptoms that are, in the absence of disease, likely to be related to hyperventilation are often assumed to provide sufficient evidence for a positive diagnosis. A seemingly more sophisticated diagnostic procedure utilizes, along with symptom reports, a ventilatory challenge, known as the hyperventilation provocation test (HVPT). After obtaining information concerning presenting complaints, patients are required to hyperventilate voluntarily during a 3 min period so that a substantial level of sustained hypocapnia ensues (see Grossman and de Swart, 1984; Magarian, 1982). After termination of the hyperventilation, the patient is asked to identify those symptoms that were experienced during the hyperventilation. A correspondence between these acute HVPT symptoms and the major presenting symptoms is assumed to indicate a positive diagnosis. However, careful consideration reveals this procedure also to be a flawed procedure: (1) Although it is generally assumed that the HVPT symptoms result specifically from the induced hypocapnic state, we have shown that other types of challenges, not involving hyperventilation, may produce comparable numbers and types of symptoms (Svebak and Grossman, 1985; Wientjes *et al.*, 1986a,b). Therefore, the assumption of symptom specificity of the HVPT may often be unsubstantiated, and symptom reporting during the HVPT appears (at least partially) to be under control of factors other than hyperventilation (e.g. factors of a psychological nature). (2) Even if certain HVPT-produced symptoms, indeed, specifically result from the hypocapnia, generalization of this finding to the causal mechanisms that are involved in symptom production in daily life may, in some cases, be unwarranted. Hence the HVPT is not a diagnostic tool capable of distinguishing between symptom complexes resulting specifically from hyperventilation-associated factors and those unrelated to hyperventilation.

Some workers in the area have attempted to append a more objective physiological criterion to the HVPT. Noting the sizeable amount of individual differences in the rate of recovery of end-tidal CO_2 immediately after termination of hyperventilation, Hardonk and Beumer (1979) suggested that HVS patients, in contrast to healthy controls, manifested a delayed post-hyperventilation recovery of CO_2. However, later investigations have found it to be an ineffective diagnostic technique for identifying HVS patients (e.g. Gardner *et al.*, 1986; Wientjes, Grossman and Defares, 1984).

One group of investigators has employed, perhaps, safer diagnostic criteria which include a characteristic symptom picture and pronounced hypocapnia during spontaneous breathing (Pco_2 less than 30 mmHg) (Bass and Gardner, 1985b; Gardner *et al.*, 1986). This diagnostic approach has the obvious advantage of providing clear evidence of aberrant ventilation among patients but is likely to miss individuals who typically maintain normal levels of ventilation and only hyperventilate to specific situational stimuli.

Another experimental assessment approach of potential promise evaluates the ventilatory responses of potential HVS patients to hypnotically induced suggestions of personally relevant experiences previously reported to have been associated with symptom attacks (Freeman *et al.*, 1986). Suspected HVS sufferers in this study typically showed much more pronounced hyperventilation to such suggestions, compared to a healthy control group presented with suggestions of emotionally aversive experiences. This procedure has the advantage of taking into account the individually specific nature of circumstances likely to produce an episode of complaints; however, individual differences in suggestibility present a problem for this procedure. Furthermore, these results need to be replicated and extended before the technique can be clinically applied.

Finally, another potential diagnostic tool may involve the use of ambulatory monitoring of transcutaneous Pco_2 (Hibbert, 1986), provided this method should prove to yield reliable data. Ambulatory CO_2 monitoring could make it possible to study whether patients actually hyperventilate during symptom attacks, as well as to assess the incidence of hyperventilation episodes in daily life, and their relation to symptom experience and triggering stimuli.

In summary, many of the commonly applied diagnostic procedures have inherent inadequacies, but there appear to be promising future avenues for diagnostic assessment of HVS. A significant issue with which to conclude our discussion of diagnostic issues relates to whether or not it is critical to distinguish accurately between non-organic symptom complexes that are specifically related to hyperventilation (i.e. HVS) and those that are perhaps a consequence of factors unrelated to hyperventilation (e.g. other physiological reactions or psychological responses). Such a distinction may be more academic than practically useful in terms of furthering our understanding of aetiology, prevention and treatment. At the present state of knowledge only future research can resolve this issue.

AETIOLOGY OF HVS

The previous description of various aspects of HVS has pointed toward an interwoven fabric of physiological and psychological factors being involved in the aetiology of the disorder. A more detailed consideration of potential psychophysiological mechanisms should make it apparent that respiratory stress responses seem to interact with both situational and dispositional psychological characteristics to determine the development of the syndrome.

Dispositional and Situational Variations in Ventilation

Many different studies indicate that baseline levels of arterial or end-tidal CO_2 are somewhat depressed among HVS patients and among those with symptom complexes similar to HVS, in contrast to controls (e.g. Folgering and Colla, 1978; Gardner et al., 1986; Liebowitz et al., 1985; Rapee, 1986; Wientjes et al., 1984, 1985a,b). Even where upper and lower quartiles of symptom complainers and non-complainers were distinguished among a sample of normals, the high-complaint group showed significantly (but modestly) reduced CO_2 levels that were still maintained 1 year later (Wientjes et al., 1986a,b). Likewise, baseline minute ventilation volume was also elevated in this and another study (Huey and West, 1983) among high-complaint normals in comparison with low-complaint controls. Other recent investigations also report greater irregularity of respiratory parameters during rest among HVS patients than controls (Hormbrey, Patil, Jacobi and Saunders, 1986).

A point of caution is, however, in order concerning interpretation of these findings: it is important to acknowledge that the baseline ventilatory differences between HVS patients and controls which have been found may reflect a variant of situational responding rather than any general biological disposition. Gardner *et al.* (1986), in this regard, have found that the awake state, *per se*, is associated with depressed CO_2 levels in certain patients and that CO_2 becomes normalized during sleep. Since cortical and mid-brain influences upon respiration are absent during non-REM (rapid eye movement) sleep (when medullary metabolic control of ventilation prevails; Phillipson and Bowes, 1986), the results of this study suggest that higher brain controls of respiration are affected in HVS and may manifest themselves as metabolically exaggerated ventilatory responses across a wide range of normal situations. This hypothesis is also supported by a lack of evidence that HVS individuals differ from normal controls in a measure of lower brain (medullary) ventilatory control (Gardner *et al.*, 1986; Pearson, Peattie, Auadiri and Finn, 1986).

The likely involvement of higher brain mechanisms in the baseline ventilatory deviations of HVS patients, in turn, suggests that psychological factors may be prepotent in the development of HVS. This possibility is further supported by findings that increased respiratory function and hypocapnia are characteristic of clinical populations suffering from depression, anxiety neurosis and phobias, all psychological dimensions frequently associated with HVS (see Grossman, 1983, for a review). It thus seems plausible that the elevated emotional arousal characteristic of these affective states also overactivates the higher brain impulses to respiration among HVS patients.

Variations between HVS subjects and healthy controls in ventilatory reactivity to psychological stressors tend to give additional substance to this psychogenic hypothesis. Whereas mild-to-moderate hyperventilation is characteristic of normal respiratory responses to threat, pain and passive coping (Allen, Sherwood and Obrist, 1986; Dudley, Holmes, Martin and Ripley, 1964; Garssen, 1980; Motta, Fagiani, Dolcetti, Bellone and Borello, 1971; Suess, Alexander, Smith, Sweeney and Marion, 1980), several studies have found that hyperventilatory reactions of HVS patients or similar individuals exceed those of normal controls when subjects are confronted with emotionally evocative, threatening or aversive stimuli (Freeman *et al.*, 1986; Liebowitz *et al.*, 1985). Exaggerated hyperventilation among HVS patients during emotionally stressful, naturally occurring situations has also been verified in a few case studies (Hibbert, 1986; Salkovskis, Warwick, Clark and Wessels, 1986). On the other hand, no differences in ventilatory reactions between HVS patients and normal controls were manifested in another study utilizing an active coping stressor involving demanding mental tasks, although substantial task-related respiratory changes were seen for both groups (Wientjes *et al.*, 1986a,b). These opposing results suggest that the excessive ventilation of HVS patients may often be related specifically to emotionally aversive situations, possibly of a passive nature.

Somatic Symptom Formation

There is ample evidence that hyperventilation, hypocapnia and their physiological concomitants can elicit numerous somatic and psychological symptoms
among normals that seem very similar to the typical symptom complexes of
HVS sufferers (Clark and Helmsley, 1982; Huey and West, 1983; Svebak and
Grossman, 1985; Wientjes *et al.*, 1984). However, that does not imply that
hyperventilation should be considered a necessary and/or sufficient stimulus
for the triggering of symptom attacks. On the contrary, there are indications
that HVS patients and other individuals with a similar symptom picture
experience and report a greater number and intensity of complaints than
normal controls in response to laboratory behavioural stressors that evoke
equivalent levels of physiological activation in all groups but little or no hyperventilation (Svebak and Grossman, 1985; Wientjes *et al.*, 1986a,b). These
findings point to the involvement of psychological mechanisms in the formation
and reporting of symptoms. Several investigations of symptom responses to
laboratory stressors (including hyperventilation) have, in fact, found systematic
relationships between the degree of symptom reporting and variations in several
dispositional psychological traits (Clark and Helmsley, 1982; Heim *et al.*, 1972;
Pennebaker, 1982; Wientjes *et al.*, 1984). Furthermore, other research indicates
that highly neurotic and/or anxious individuals generally tend, in the absence
of organic disease states, to report more somatic symptoms than others (Costa
and McCrae, 1985; Kellner and Sheffield, 1973; Morrell and Wale, 1976). To
explain these findings, it has been proposed that certain individuals, as a result
of specific personality factors and developmental experiences, are more likely
to direct their attention to internal, rather than to external, events. Consequently, such individuals seem to focus more closely upon bodily sensations
than other people, and this form of heightened somatic self-perception tends
to result in negative evaluations and anxiety-provoking thoughts (Mechanic,
1972; Pennebaker, 1982). Since ventilatory responses are insufficient to explain
all the symptom reports of HVS patients and since HVS is characterized by
high levels of anxiety and neurosis (Grossman *et al.*, 1985), the evidence points
toward an important contribution of altered perceptual mechanisms in the
experience of symptoms among HVS patients. Unfortunately, little research
has been done in this area regarding HVS.

**Psychophysiological Implications for a Causal Model of HVS: Over-
reactivity of Soma or Psyche?**

The previous analysis provides evidence that HVS is characterized by tendencies toward ventilatory hyper-reactivity and an enhanced perception and/or
reporting of somatic and psychological symptoms. However, it becomes clear
that it is unnecessary that both characteristics are mutually present for the

experience of symptoms to take place: as already indicated, most normal people experience a range of symptoms during hyperventilation without possessing any unusual propensity to focus upon internal sensations; on the other hand, HVS patients may often be hyper-responsive with regard to stress-related symptom reporting without presenting evidence of greater-than-normal physiological reactions. This potential dissociation of physiological responses and somatic perception must be addressed in any adequate aetiological model of HVS.

Unfortunately, there is little direct knowledge concerning the development or maintenance of HVS. Nevertheless, a few aetiological possibilities appear plausible based upon the existing empirical literature. First, the ventilatory and somatic–perceptual over-reactivity typically found among HVS patients may bear no direct association to each other, but their co-occurrence in the disorder may be solely due to the underlying relationship that each shares with certain psychological dimensions, especially anxiety and neurosis. An alternative explanation involves a more direct relationship between hyperventilation and symptoms at least in the early stages of the disorder: it is conceivable that more frequent and profound episodes of stress-related physiological reactions occur among particular anxious, neurotic individuals than among other people, and this may sensitize them at an early stage to bodily sensations. In addition, tendencies toward enhanced negative appraisals of external events may generalize to negative evaluations of internal somatic perceptions. This could gradually result in conditioned responses of heightened somatic awareness and symptom complaints to aversive situational stimuli, even in the absence of exaggerated physiological reactivity. Other more extreme stimuli, producing actual bouts of hyperventilation (whether frequent or occasional), would serve to reinforce this response.

It should be mentioned that both proposed models differ from the frequently proposed 'vicious spiral' model of the syndrome, in which threatening stimuli, hyperventilation and disturbing bodily sensations form a loop of progressive exacerbation, finally culminating in a full-blown attack of symptoms (e.g. Clark, Salkovskis and Chalkley, 1985). The latter hypothesis suggests that all three precipitating elements are always essential for attacks to occur and that the absence of any one would interrupt the loop, thus preventing the appearance of an symptomatic episode.

In both our aetiological models proposed above, it is assumed that psychogenic factors may be prepotent in the development and maintenance of the syndrome. One implication of this assumption is that HVS patients may *not* be characterized by a specific over-responsivity of the respiratory system which distinguishes them in a qualitative fashion from non-HVS populations, as suggested by Garssen (1980). On the contrary, we propose that HVS may be conceived as one extreme end of a continuum of susceptibility to ventilatory and somatic–perceptual over-reactivity in response to psychoenvironmental stressors that can be seen in a normal population. This view is supported by several studies among normals revealing a continuum of responses concerning symptom severity during daily-life and laboratory stress. Furthermore, these symptom responses have been found to be significantly correlated with individual differences in ventilation and psychological characteristics, including neuroticism and anxiety (Clark and Helmsley, 1982; Huey and West, 1983; Wientjes *et al.*, 1984, 1986a,b).

One possible qualitative distinction that can be made between HVS patients and non-HVS populations relates to the fact that some individuals actively seek professional help for their complaints whereas others do not. Hence, it may be useful for HVS researchers in the future to explore issues related to individual differences in such characteristics as complaint threshold, attributional factors in symptom formation, previous experiences with illness, and social and developmental factors (Bass and Gardner, 1985b; Ingham and Miller, 1983).

Treatment of HVS

Several types of behavioural therapies have been proposed as treatments for HVS. However, there have been very few well-controlled studies investigating the effectiveness of the different procedures. Central to all the assessed treatment techniques are attempts to alter the breathing pattern of HVS patients. Thus, one approach has been to use repeated voluntary hyperventilation initially to elicit symptom attacks. This is followed by an explanation to the patient by the therapist concerning the causal relationship between symptom occurrence and hyperventilation, with an emphasis placed upon the patient learning to reattribute the cause of the disturbing somatic sensations to the hyperventilation, as opposed to inferring some threatening physical disease state. Lastly, some form of slow breathing exercises are taught which are incompatible with hyperventilation (Clark *et al.*, 1985; Compernolle, Hoogduin and Joele, 1979). Although quantitative evaluation of this procedure remains inadequate, there are indications that either specific or non-specific components of this therapeutic programme may provide substantial long-term reduction of attack frequency among HVS sufferers (Clark *et al.*, 1985).

The other major approach to treatment has focused exclusively upon alteration of the resting breathing pattern via respiratory biofeedback (Grossman *et al.*, 1985) or by means of breathing exercises (Bonn *et al.*, 1984). Both techniques seem to achieve marked symptomatic improvement. Furthermore, in one study comparing the effects of biofeedback-assisted changes in breathing pattern versus a placebo-treatment control (Grossman *et al.*, 1985), only the real-therapy group showed improvements in both state and dispositional psychological characteristics. Additionally, differentially greater benefits were found for this group, in contrast to the placebo subjects, with respect to respiratory variables.

Although these positive findings concerning the effects of breathing therapy upon HVS would appear to suggest that alterations in ventilatory parameters are central to symptom formation and alleviation (see Grossman *et al.*, 1985), an alternative explanation is possible: the types of changes in breathing pattern utilized by these therapies are typically associated with relaxation (Grossman, 1983). Therefore, it may well be that breathing therapies provide the opportunity for patients to learn to attribute positive, relaxing qualities to bodily processes that have previously been perceived as extremely threatening. Furthermore, the new ability to gain control over a physiological system in such a manner as to produce pleasant, calming, physical and mental sensations would seem to counteract the frightening loss of control over somatic functioning that occurs with an episode of disturbing symptoms. Thus both physiological and psychological elements may synergistically combine to produce their beneficial effects. This hypothesis would appear worth empirical examination.

Another more purely psychological approach has been proposed for patients with serious somatic symptoms in the absence of organic disease (but not yet adopted specifically to HVS; Mechanic, 1980). Assuming that these kinds of individuals have a greatly increased tendency to focus upon internal states and bodily sensations, a counselling therapy is offered that is aimed at (1) a redirection of the patient's attention towards the external environment and away from internal sensations, (2) the formation of more adequate coping techniques, and (3) modifying aspects of the psychological appraisal process. Given that somatic perceptual and appraisal processes are significantly involved in HVS, this form of therapy should be tested with HVS patients.

REFERENCES

Alexander, A.B., Cropp, G. and Chai, H. (1979). Effects of relaxation training on pulmonary mechanics in children with asthma. *Journal of Applied Behavior Analysis* **12**, 27–35.

Allen, M.T., Sherwood, A. and Obrist, P.A. (1986). Interactions of respiratory and cardiovascular adjustments to behavioral stressors. *Psychophysiology* **23**, 532–541.

American Thoracic Society Committee on Diagnostic Standards for Nontuberculosis Respiratory Disease (1962). *American Review of Respiratory Diseases* **875**, 761.

Anderson, S.D. (1985). Issues in exercise-induced asthma. *Journal of Allergy and Clinical Immunology* **76**, 763–772.

Balke, B., Ellis, J.P. and Wells, J.G. (1958). Adaptive responses to hyperventilation. *Journal of Applied Physiology* **12**, 269–277.

Barnes, P.J. (1986). Endogenous catecholamines and asthma. *Journal of Allergy and Clinical Immunology* **77**, 791–793.

Bass, C. and Gardner, W. (1985a). Emotional influences on breathing and breathlessness. *Journal of Psychosomatic Research* **29**, 592–609.

Bass, C. and Gardner, W.N. (1985b). Respiratory and psychiatric abnormalities in chronic symptomatic hyperventilation. *British Medical Journal* **290**, 1387–1390.

Bass, C., Wade, C. and Gardner, W.N. (1983). Unexplained breathlessness and psychiatric morbidity in patients with normal and abnormal coronary arteries. *Lancet* **i**, 605–609.

Benjamin, S. (1977). Is asthma a psychosomatic illness? I: A retrospective study of mental illness and social adjustment. *Journal of Psychosomatic Research* **21**, 463–470.

Ben-Zvi, Z., Young, S.H. and Kattan, M. (1982). Hypnosis for exercise-induced asthma. *American Review of Respiratory Disease* **125**, 392–395.

Bonn, J.A., Readhead, C.P.A. and Timmons, B.H. (1984). Enhanced adaptive behavioural response in agoraphobics pretreated with breathing retraining. *Lancet* **ii**, 665–669.

Bouhuys, A. and van de Woestijne, K.P. (1970). Respiratory mechanics and dust exposure in byssinosis. *Journal of Clinical Investigation* **49**, 106–112.

Boushey, H.A., Holteman, M.J., Sheller, J.R. and Nadel, J.A. (1980). Bronchial hyperreactivity. *American Review of Respiratory Disease* **12**, 389–413.

Brashear, R.E. (1983). Hyperventilation syndrome. *Lung* **161**, 257–273.

Bronniman, S. and Burrows, B. (1986). A perspective study of the natural history of asthma: remission and relapse rates. *Chest* **90**, 480–484.

Brooks, S.M., Weiss, M.A. and Bernstein, I.L. (1985). Reactive airways dysfunction syndrome: persistent asthma syndrome after high level irritant exposures. *Chest* **88**, 376–384.

Chai, H., Purcell, K., Brady, K. and Falliers, C.J. (1968). Therapeutic and investigational evaluation of asthmatic children. *Journal of Allergy* **41**, 23–46.

Chan-Yeung, M. and Lam, S. (1986). State of art: occupational asthma. *American Review of Respiratory Disease* **133**, 686–703.

Clark, D.M. (1986). A cognitive approach to panic. *Behavior Research and Therapy* **24**, 461–470.

Clark, D.M. and Helmsley, D.R. (1982). The effects of hyperventilation: individual variability and its relation to personality. *Journal of Behavior Therapy and Experimental Psychiatry* **13**, 41–47.

Clark, D.M., Salkovskis, P.M. and Chalkley, A.J. (1985). Respiratory control as a treatment for panic attacks. *Journal of Behavior Therapy and Experimental Psychiatry* **16**, 23–30.

Clarke, P.S. (1971). Effect of disodium cromoglycate on exacerbations of asthma produced by hyperventilation. *British Medical Journal* **1**, 317–319.

Clarke, P.S. and Gibson, J.R. (1980). Asthma hyperventilation and emotion. *Australian Family Physician* **9**, 715–719.

Cluss, P.A. (1986). Behavioral interventions as adjunctive treatments for chronic asthma. In: M. Hersen, R.M. Eisler and P.M. Miller (Eds) *Progress in Behavior Modification*, Vol. 20. Orlando: Academic Press.

Compernolle, T., Hoogduin, K. and Joele, L. (1979). Diagnosis and treatment of the hyperventilation syndrome. *Psychosomatics* **19**, 612–625.

Comroe, J.H. (1965). *Physiology of Respiration*. Chicago: Year Book Medical.

Costa, P.T. and McCrae, R.R. (1985). Hypochondriasis, neuroticism, and aging: when are somatic complaints unfounded? *American Psychologist* **40**, 19–28.

Creer, T.L. and Winder, J.A. (1986). Asthma. In: K.A. Holroyd and T.L. Creer (Eds) *Self-Management of Chronic Disease*. New York: Academic Press.

Demeter, S. and Cordasco, E.M. (1986). Hyperventilation syndrome and asthma. *American Journal of Medicine* **81**, 989–994.

deShazo, R.D. and Salvaggio, J.E. (1985). Allergy and immunology. *Journal of the American Medical Association* **254**, 2257–2259.

Dirks, J.F. (1982). The battery of asthma illness behavior. I: Independence from age of asthma onset. *Journal of Asthma* **19**, 75–78.

Dirks, J.F., Brown, E.L. and Robinson, S.K. (1982a). The battery of asthma illness behavior. II: Independence from airways hyperreactivity. *Journal of Asthma* **19**, 79–83.

Dirks, J.F., Jones, N.F. and Kinsman, R.A. (1977). Panic-fear: a personality dimension related to intractability of asthma. *Psychosomatic Medicine* **39**, 120–126.

Dirks, J.F., Ruback, L.A., Feiguine, R.J. and Covina, N.A. (1982b). The battery of asthma illness behavior. III: Independence from longitudinal pulmonary functions. *Journal of Asthma* **19**, 85–89.

van Dixhoorn, J. and van Duivenbode, H.J. (1985). Efficacy of Nijmegen Questionnaire in recognition of the hyperventilation syndrome. *Journal of Psychosomatic Research* **29**, 199–206.

Doelle, W. (1964). Hyperventilation und Hyperventilationssyndrom. *Medische Klinik* **59**, 695–699.

Dubois, A.B., Brody, A.W., Lewis, D.H. and Burgess, B.F. (1956). Oscillation mechanics of lungs and chest in man. *Journal of Applied Physiology* **8**, 587–594.

Dudley, D.L., Holmes, T.H., Martin, C.J. and Ripley, H.S. (1964). Changes in respiration associated with hypnotically induced emotion, pain and exercise. *Psychosomatic Medicine* **26**, 46–57.

Enzer, N.B. and Walker, P.A. (1967). Hyperventilation syndrome in childhood. *Pediatrics* **70**, 521–532.

Erskine-Millis, J. and Schonell, M. (1981). Relaxation therapy in asthma: a critical review. *Psychosomatic Medicine* **43**, 365–372.

Ewer, T.C. and Stewart, D.E. (1986). Improvement in bronchial hyperresponsiveness in patients with moderate asthma after treatment with a hypnotic technique: a randomized controlled trial. *British Medical Journal* **293**, 1129–1132.

Feldman, G.M. (1976). The effect of biofeedback on respiratory resistance of asthmatic children. *Psychosomatic Medicine* **38**, 27–34.

Florin, I., Freudenberg, G. and Hollaender, J. (1985). Facial expressions of emotion and psychologic reactions in children with bronchial asthma. *Psychosomatic Medicine* **47**, 382–393.

Folgering, H. and Colla, P. (1978). Some anomalies in the control of $PACO_2$ in patients with a hyperventilation syndrome. *Bulletin European Physiopathologie Respiratoire* **14**, 503–512.

Freeman, L.J., Conway, A. and Nixon, P.G.F. (1986). Physiological responses to psychological challenge under hypnosis in patients considered to have the hyperventilation syndrome: implications for diagnosis and therapy. *Journal of the Royal Society of Medicine* **79**, 76–83.

Gardner, W.N., Meah, M.S. and Bass, C. (1986). Controlled study of respiratory responses during prolonged measurements in patients with chronic hyperventilation. *Lancet* **i**, 826–830.

Garssen, B. (1980). Role of stress in the development of the hyperventilation syndrome. *Psychotherapy and Psychosomatics* **33**, 214–225.

Garssen, B., van Veenendaal, W. and Bloemink, R. (1983). Agoraphobia and the hyperventilation syndrome. *Behavior Research and Therapy* **21**, 643–649.

Gennari, F.J. and Kassirer, J.P. (1982). Respiratory alkalosis. In: J.J. Cohen and J.P. Kassirer (Eds) *Acid/Base*. Boston: Little, Brown.

Goldman, M., Knudson, R.J., Mead, J., Peterson, W., Schwaber, J.R. and Wohl, M.E.

(1970). A simplified measurement of respiratory resistance by forced oscillation. *Journal of Applied Physiology* **28**, 113–120.

Grossman, P. (1983). Respiration, stress and cardiovascular function. *Psychophysiology* **20**, 284–300.

Grossman, P. and de Swart, J.C.G. (1984). Diagnosis of hyperventilation syndrome on the basis of reported complaints. *Journal of Psychosomatic Research* **28**, 97–104.

Grossman, P. and Wientjes, C.J.E. (1985). Respiratory–cardiac coordination as an index of cardiac functioning. In: J.F. Orlebeke, G. Mulder and L.J.P. van Doornen (Eds) *Psychophysiology of Cardiovascular Control*. New York: Plenum.

Grossman, P., de Swart, J.C.G. and Defares, P.B. (1985). A controlled study of breathing therapy for treatment of hyperventilation syndrome. *Journal of Psychosomatic Research* **29**, 49–58.

Guyton, A.C. (1966). *Textbook of Medical Physiology*. London: Saunders.

Hardonk, H.J. and Beumer, H.M. (1979). Hyperventilation syndrome. In: P.J. Vinken and G.W. Bruyn (Eds) *Handbook of Clinical Neurology*, Vol. 38. Amsterdam: North Holland.

Hargreave, F.E., O'Byre, P.M. and Ramsdale, E.H. (1985). Mediators, airways responsiveness and asthma. *Journal of Allergy and Clinical Immunology* **76**, 272–276.

Harm, D.L., Marion, R.J., Creer, T.L. and Kotses, H. (1985a). Effects of instructions upon pulmonary function tests. *Journal of Asthma* **22**, 289–294.

Harm, D.L., Marion, R.J., Creer, T.L. and Kotses, H. (1985b). Improving the ability of peak expiratory flow rates to predict asthma. *Journal of Allergy and Clinical Immunology* **76**, 688–694.

Heim, E., Blaser, A. and Waidelich, E. (1972). Dyspnea: psychophysiologic relationships. *Psychosomatic Medicine* **34**, 405–423.

Herman, S.P., Stickler, G.B. and Lucas, A.R. (1981). Hyperventilation syndrome in children and adolescents: long-term follow-up. *Pediatrics* **67**, 183–187.

Hibbert, G.A. (1986). Ambulatory monitoring of transcutaneous pCO_2. In: L. Lacey and D. Sturgeon (Eds) *Proceedings of the 15th European Conference on Psychosomatic Research*. London: Libby.

Higgs, C.M., Richardson, R.B., Lea, D.A., Lewis, G.T. and Laszlo, G. (1986). Influence of knowledge of peak flow on self assessment of asthma: studies with a coded peak flow meter. *Thorax* **41**, 671–675.

Hollaender, J. and Florin, I. (1983). Expressed emotion and airway conductance in children with bronchial asthma. *Journal of Psychosomatic Research* **27**, 307–311.

Hormbrey, J.M., Patil, C.P., Jacobi, M.S. and Saunders, K.B. (1986). Hyperventilation syndrome – analysis of irregularity of breathing. *Bulletin European Physiopathologie Respiratoire* **22**, 518.

Horton, D.J., Suda, W.L., Kinsman, R.A., Souhrada, J. and Spector, S.L. (1978). Bronchoconstrictive suggestion in asthma: a role for airways hyperreactivity and emotions. *American Review of Respiratory Disease* **117**, 1029–1038.

Huey, S.R. and West, S.G. (1983). Hyperventilation: its relation to symptom experience and to anxiety. *Journal of Abnormal Psychology* **92**, 422–432.

Hugelin, A. (1986). Forebrain and midbrain influences on respiration. *Handbook of Physiology: The Respiratory System*, Vol. 2. Bethesda, Md: American Physiological Society.

Ingham, J.G. and Miller, P.McC. (1983). Self-referral: social and demographic determinants of consulting behavior. *Journal of Psychosomatic Research* **27**, 233–242.

Janson-Bjerklie, S. and Clark, E. (1982). The effects of biofeedback training on bronchial diameter in asthma. *Heart and Lung* **11**, 200–207.

Joorabchi, B. (1977). Expression of the hyperventilation syndrome in childhood. *Clinical Pediatrics* **16**, 1110–1115.

Kallenbach, J.M., Webster, T., Dowdeswell, R., Reinach, S.G., Millar, R.N., Scott, N. and Zwi, S. (1985). Reflex heart rate control in asthma. *Chest* **87**, 644–648.

Kellner, R. and Sheffield, B.F. (1973). The one-week prevalence of symptoms in neurotic patients and normals. *American Journal of Psychiatry* **130**, 102–105.

Kenneally, J.A., McLennan, J.E., Loudon, R.G. and McLaurin, R.L. (1980). Hyperventilation-induced cerebral hypoxia. *American Review of Respiratory Disease* **122**, 407–412.

Kinsman, R.A., Dahlem, N.W., Spector, S. and Staudenmayer, H. (1977). Observations on subjective symptomatology, coping behavior and medical decisions in asthma. *Psychosomatic Medicine* **39**, 102–119.

Kinsman, R.A., Spector, S.L., Shucard, D.W. and Luparello, T.J. (1974). Observations on patterns of subjective symptomatology of acute asthma. *Psychosomatic Medicine* **36**, 129–146.

Klein, G., Urbanek, R., Kohler, D. and Matthys, H. (1983). Inhalative bronchiale Provocationstests bei Kindern: Vergleichende Messungen der Oszillations-, Verschluss- Druck- und Plethysmographischen Resistance. *Clinical Pediatrics* **195**, 33–37.

Knapp, T.J. and Wells, L.A. (1978). Behavior therapy for asthma: a review. *Behavior Research and Therapy* **16**, 103–115.

Lazarus, R.S. (1966). *Psychological Stress and the Coping Process.* New York: McGraw-Hill.

Lehrer, P., Hochron, S., McCann, B., Swartzman, L. and Reba, P. (1986). Relaxation decreases large-airway but not small-airway asthma. *Journal of Psychosomatic Research* **30**, 13–25.

Levenson, R.W. (1979). Effects of thematically relevant and general stressors on specificity of responding in asthmatic and nonasthmatic subjects. *Psychosomatic Medicine* **41**, 28–39.

Lewis, R.A., Lewis, M.N. and Tattersfield, A.E. (1984). Asthma induced by suggestion: is it due to airway cooling? *American Review of Respiratory Disease* **129**, 691–695.

Liebowitz, M.R., Gorman, J.M., Fyer, A.J., Levitt, M., Dillon, D., Levy, G., Appleby, I.L., Anderson, S., Palij, M., Davies, S.O. and Klein, D.F. (1985). Lactate provocation of panic attacks. II. Biochemical and physiological findings. *Archives of General Psychiatry* **42**, 709–719.

Lum, L.C. (1976). The syndrome of habitual hyperventilation. In: O.W. Hill (Ed.) *Modern Trends in Psychosomatic Medicine.* London: Butterworths.

Luparello, T.J., Leist, N., Lourie, C.H. and Smeet, P. (1970). The interaction of psychologic stimuli and pharmacologic agents on airway reactivity in asthmatic subjects. *Psychosomatic Medicine* **32**, 509–513.

Luparello, T., Lyons, H.A., Bleecker, E.R. and McFadden, E.R. (1968). Influences of suggestion on airways reactivity in asthmatic subjects. *Psychosomatic Medicine* **30**, 819–825.

MacKenzie, J.N. (1886). The production of rose asthma by an artifical rose. *American Journal of Medical Science* **91**, 45–57.

Magarian, G.J. (1982). Hyperventilation syndromes: infrequently recognized common expressions of anxiety and stress. *Medicine* **61**, 219–236.

Magarian, G.J. and Hickam, D.H. (1986). Noncardiac causes of angina-like chest pain. *Cardiovascular Disease* **29**, 65–80.

Martinsson, A., Larsson, K. and Hjemdahl, P. (1985). Reduced β_2-adrenoceptor responsiveness in exercise-induced asthma. *Chest* **87**, 594–598.

Mathé, A.A. and Knapp, P.H. (1971). Emotional and adrenal reactions to stress in bronchial asthma. *Psychosomatic Medicine* **33**, 323–340.

Mathews, K.P. (1982). Respiratory atopic diseases. *Journal of the American Medical Association* **248**, 2587–2610.

McFadden, E.R. (1980). Exercise-induced asthma. *American Journal of Medicine* **68**, 471–472.

McFadden, E.R., Luparello, T., Lyons, H.A. and Bleecker, E. (1969). The mechanism of suggestion in the induction of acute asthma attacks. *Psychosomatic Medicine* **31**, 134–143.

Mechanic, D. (1972). Social psychologic factors affecting the presentation of bodily complaints. *New England Journal of Medicine* **286**, 1132–1139.

Mechanic, D. (1980). The experience and reporting of common physical symptoms. *Journal of Health and Social Behavior* **21**, 146–155.

Morel, D.R., Forster, A. and Suter, P.M. (1983). Noninvasive ventilatory monitoring with bellows pneumographs in supine subjects. *Journal of Applied Physiology* **55**, 598–606.

Morrell, D.C. and Wale, C.J. (1976). Symptoms perceived and recorded by patients. *Journal of the Royal College of General Practitioners* **26**, 308–403.

Motta, P.E., Fagiani, M.B., Dolcetti, A., Bellone, E. and Borello, G. (1971). Modificazioni dei Gas nel Sangue nello Stato Ansioso di media gravita. *Archivio per le Scienze Mediche* **128**, 111–119.

Neuhaus, E.C. (1958). A personality study of asthmatic and cardiac children. *Psychosomatic Medicine* **20**, 181–190.

Nield, J.E. and Cameron, I.R. (1985). Bronchoconstriction in response to suggestion: its prevention by an inhaled anti-cholinergic agent. *British Medical Journal* **290**, 674.

O'Cain, C.F., Hensley, M.J., McFadden, E.R. and Ingram, R.H. (1979). Pattern and mechanism of airway response to hypocapnia in normal subjects. *Journal of Applied Physiology* **47**, 8–12.

Orehek, J., Nicoli, M., Delpierre, S. and Beaupre, A. (1981). Influence of the previous deep inspiration on the spirometric measurement of provoked bronchoconstriction in asthma. *American Review of Respiratory Disease* **123**, 269–272.

Pearson, M.G., Peattie, B., Auadiri, M.R. and Finn, R. (1986). Abnormalities of respiratory centre function and potassium homeostasis in the chronic hyperventilation syndrome. *Biological Psychology* **22**, 190.

Pennebaker, J.W. (1982). *The Psychology of Physical Symptoms.* New York: Springer Verlag.

Pepys, J. and Hutchcroft (1975). Bronchial provocation tests in etiological diagnosis of asthma. *American Review of Respiratory Disease* **112**, 829–859.

Pfeffer, J.M. (1978). The aetiology of the hyperventilation syndrome: a review of the literature. *Psychotherapy and Psychosomatics* **30**, 47–55.

Philip, R.L., Wilde, G.J. and Day, J.H. (1972). Suggestion and relaxation in asthmatics. *Journal of Psychosomatic Research* **16**, 193–204.

Phillipson, E.A. and Bowes, G. (1986). Control of breathing during sleep. *Handbook of Physiology: The Respiratory System.* Bethesda, Md: American Physiological Society.

Purcell, K. and Metz, J.R. (1962). Distinctions between subgroups of asthmatic children: some parent attitude variables related to age of onset of asthma. *Journal of Psychosomatic Research* **6**, 251–259.

Purcell, K., Bernstein, L. and Bukantz, S.C. (1961). A preliminary comparison of rapidly remitting and persistently steroid-dependent asthmatic children. *Psychosomatic Medicine* **23**, 305–313.

Purcell, K., Brody, K., Muser, J., Molk, L., Gordon, N. and Means, J. (1969a). The effect of asthma in children of experimental separation from the family. *Psychosomatic Medicine* **31**, 144–152.

Purcell, K., Muser, J., Micklich, D. and Dietikor, K.E. (1969b). A comparison of psychological findings in variety defined asthmatic subgroups. *Journal of Psychosomatic Research* **13**, 67–75.

Rapee, R. (1986). Differential response to hyperventilation in panic disorder and generalized anxiety disorder. *Journal of Abnormal Psychology* **95**, 24–28.

Rasmussen, K., Jull, S., Bagger, J.P. and Henningsen, P. (1987). Usefulness of ST deviation induced by prolonged hyperventilation as a predictor of cardiac death in angina pectoris. *American Journal of Cardiology* **59**, 763–768.

Richter, R. and Dahme, B. (1982). Bronchial asthma in adults: there is little evidence for the effectiveness of behavioral therapy and relaxation. *Journal of Psychosomatic Research* **26**, 533–540.

Rosenthal, S.V., Aitken, R.C. and Zealley, A.K. (1973). The Cattell 16PF Personality Profile of asthmatics. *Journal of Psychosomatic Research* **17**, 9–14.

Rowe, G.G., Castillo, C.A. and Crumpton, C.W. (1962). Effects of hyperventilation on systemic and coronary hemodynamics. *American Heart Journal* **63**, 67–77.

Salkovskis, P.M., Warwick, H.M.C., Clark, D.M. and Wessels, D.J. (1986). A demonstration of hyperventilation during naturally occurring panic attacks. *Behavior Research and Therapy* **24**, 91–94.

Shaw, C.F., Chiang, S.T., Wsieh, X.C. and Milic-Emili, J. (1983). A new method for measurement of respiratory resistance. *Journal of Applied Physiology* **54**, 594–597.

Siegel, S.C. and Rachelefsky, G.S. (1985). Asthma in infants and children. *Journal of Allergy and Clinical Immunology* **76**, 1–14.

Smith, M.M., Colebatch, H.J. and Clarke, P.S. (1970). Increase and decrease in pulmonary resistance with hypnotic-suggestion in asthma. *American Review of Respiratory Disease* **102**, 236–242.

Spector, S., Luparello, T.J., Kopetzky, M.T., Souhrada, I. and Kinsman, R.A. (1976). Response of asthmatics to metacholine and suggestion. *American Review of Respiratory Disease* **113**, 43–50.

Staudenmayer, H., Kinsman, R.A., Dirks, J.F., Spector, S.L. and Wangaard, C. (1979). Medical outcome in asthmatic patients: effects of airways hyperreactivity and symptom focused anxiety. *Psychosomatic Medicine* **41**, 109–118.

Steiner, W., Higgs, C.M.B., Fritz, G.K., Laszlo, G. and Harvey, J.E. (1987). Defense style and the perception of asthma. *Psychosomatic Medicine* **49**, 35–44.

Steptoe, A. (1983). Psychological aspects of bronchial asthma. In: S. Rachman (Ed.) *Contributions to Medical Psychology*. London: Pergamon.

Steptoe, A., Philips, J. and Harburg, J. (1981). Biofeedback and instructions in the modification of total respiratory resistance: an experimental study of asthmatic and nonasthmatic volunteers. *Journal of Psychosomatic Research* **25**, 541–552.

Sterling, G.M. (1968). The mechanism of bronchoconstriction due to hypocapnia in man. *Clinical Science* **34**, 277–285.

Strunk, R.C., Mrazek, D.A., Fuhrman, G.S. and LaBrecque, J.F. (1985). Physiologic and psychological characteristics associated with death due to asthma in childhood: a case-controlled study. *Journal of the American Medical Association* **254**, 1193–1198.

Strupp, H.H., Levenson, R.W., Manuck, S.B., Snell, J.D., Hinrichsen, J.J. and Boyd, S. (1974). Effects of suggestion on total respiratory resistance in mild asthmatics. *Journal of Psychosomatic Research* **18**, 337–346.

Sturani, C., Sturani, A. and Tosi, I. (1985). Parasympathetic activity assessed by diving reflex and by airway response to metacholine in bronchial asthma. *Respiration* **48**, 321–328.

Suess, W.M., Alexander, A.B., Smith, D.D., Sweeney, H.W. and Marion, R.J. (1980). The effects of psychological stress on respiration: a preliminary study of anxiety and respiration. *Psychophysiology* **17**, 535–540.

Svebak, S. and Grossman, P. (1985). The experience of psychosomatic symptoms in the hyperventilation provocation test and in non-hyperventilation tasks. *Scandinavian Journal of Psychology* **26**, 327–335.

Tal, A. and Miklich, D.R. (1976). Emotionally induced decreases in pulmonary flow rates in asthmatic children. *Psychosomatic Medicine* **38**, 190–200.

Talpin, P.S. and Creer, T.L. (1978). A procedure for using peak expiratory flow rate data to increase the pedictability of asthma episodes. *Journal of Asthma Research* **16**, 15–19.

Treasure, R.A., Fowler, P.B., Millington, W.T. and Wise, P.H. (1987). Misdiagnosis of diabetic ketoacidosis as hyperventilation syndrome. *British Medical Journal* **294**, 630.

Vachon, L. and Rich, E.S. (1976). Visceral learning in asthma. *Psychosomatic Medicine* **38**, 122–130.

Weimann, G. (1968). *Das Hyperventilationssyndrom*. Munich: Urban and Schwarzenberg.

Weiner, H. (1977). *Psychobiology and Human Disease*. New York: Elsevier.

Weinstein, A.G. (1984). Cry-induced bronchospasm in childhood asthma. *Journal of Asthma* **21**, 161–165.

Wientjes, C.J.E., Grossman, P. and Defares, P.B. (1984). Psychosomatic symptoms, anxiety and hyperventilation in normal subjects. *Bulletin European Physiopathologie Respiratoire* **20**, 90–91.

Wientjes, C.J.E., Grossman, P., Gaillard, A.W.K. and Defares, P.B. (1986a). *Breathing and Stress*. (Dutch.) Soesterberg, The Netherlands: TNO/Institute for Perception.

Wientjes, C.J.E., Grossman, P., Gaillard, A.W.K. and Defares, P.B. (1986b). Individual differences in respiration and stress. In: R. Hockey, A.W.K. Gaillard and M. Coles (Eds) *Energetics and Human Information Processing*. Dordrecht: Nijhoff.

Wilson, A.F., Honsberger, R., Chiu, J.T. and Novey, H.S. (1975). Transcendental meditation and asthma. *Respiration* **32**, 74–80.

Wilson, N.M., Barnes, P.J., Vickers, H. and Silverman, M. (1982). Hyperventilation-induced asthma: evidence for two mechanisms. *Thorax* **37**, 657–662.

van de Woestijne, K.P. and Clement, J. (1972). Functional assessment of airway calibre. *Bulletin Physiopathologie Respiratoire* **8**, 555–563.

Chapter 19

Motor Disorders

Marjan Jahanshahi and C. David Marsden

MRC Human Movement and Balance Unit,
Department of Clinical Neurology,
Institute of Neurology,
The National Hospital,
Queen Square,
London WC1N 3BG

ABSTRACT

A number of applications of psychophysiology to the assessment and treatment of motor disorders are considered, with a major emphasis on electromyographic biofeedback treatment of three groups of motor disorders: the focal dystonias, paralysis and spasticity secondary to stroke, and cerebral palsy. Methodological shortcomings of the existing biofeedback literature are highlighted.

INTRODUCTION

Within the field of motor disorders, clinical electromyography (EMG), nerve conduction and evoked potential investigations are performed for diagnosis or

Handbook of Clinical Psychophysiology Edited by G. Turpin

research. Detailed discussion of these uses of physiological recording in motor
disorders is outside the scope of this chapter, because of limitations of space,
and because, in terms of the techniques and paradigms used, these types of
recording fall within the boundaries of neurophysiology rather than psychophysiology. The major emphasis will be on the application of psychophysiology in
the treatment of motor disorders. More specifically, an overview of EMG and
other types of biofeedback (BF) that have been employed to treat a range of
motor disorders will be provided, following a brief presentation of the common
assessment procedures.

MEASUREMENT AND ASSESSMENT

ELECTROMYOGRAPHY AND OTHER MEASUREMENT TECHNIQUES

Recording of electrical activity of muscles (EMG) is the most widely employed
physiological measure in motor disorders. Electromyographic recording
requires suitable equipment including amplifiers, integrators, filters, chart and
magnetic-tape recorders, analogue to digital convertors, and laboratory
computers. Other considerations involve the choice of the type (surface, needle)
and size of electrodes, type of recording (monopolar, bipolar), selection and
preparation of the site of electrode placement, adequate grounding, removal of
artifacts, and testing of resistance at the subject/electrode interface, as well as
filtering, rectification, integration, data sampling and analysis. An excellent
and comprehensive recent review by Fridlund and Cacioppo (1986) sets out
the guidelines of human EMG research for psychophysiologists.

While the laboratory has been the traditional place for EMG recording,
telemetric (Barto, Supinski and Skinner, 1984) and ambulatory (Rugh and
Solberg, 1974) devices allow EMG measurement in the patient's natural
environment. In telemetry, physiological responses are transmitted from a
subject outside the laboratory to a recorder in the laboratory. Ambulatory
monitoring employs portable devices which measure physiological responses
and are worn or carried by the patient (see Chapter 1). These allow assessment
of the effect of stressors operative in the patient's natural environment on the
physiological responses, and can be valuable for determining whether therapeutic change achieved in the clinic has generalized to the natural environment.
A major problem with ambulatory equipment, however, is the presence of
movement artifact.

Besides EMG recording, many other physiological parameters are measured
in motor disorders. For example, accelometers are used in the measurement of
tremor (Hughes and McLellan, 1985). Force of voluntary muscular contractions is assessed with hand-held dynamometers or specially built chairs (Wiles

and Karni, 1983). Because of the nature of the symptoms and resulting disability, adoption of a three-systems (subjective, behavioural, physiological) approach in the assessment of movement disorders is appropriate. Behavioural measures such as reaction time, time to walk a set distance, tapping speed, performance on the peg-board test, and assessment of the range of motion in the affected body part can provide useful information. In addition, numerous scales have been developed which allow clinical rating of the severity and progression of different motor disorders and the evaluation of disability in activities of daily living. Videotapes provide a permanent record which can later be used for more objective assessment, for example, by using multiple and 'blind' observers/raters. A more detailed outline of the techniques used in the assessment of extrapyramidal disorders is provided by Marsden and Schachter (1981).

BIOFEEDBACK EQUIPMENT

For learning of the desired response, the feedback provided to the patient has to be accurate and immediate. To meet these requirements, BF equipment must meet certain specifications, which have been covered by Gaarder and Montgomery (1979). In practical terms, BF equipment should provide sufficient amplification of the EMG signal and filter out artifacts. High resolution and coverage of a wide range of EMG values are other considerations in the choice of appropriate EMG BF equipment (Fischer-Williams, Nigl and Sovine, 1986).

A variety of types of feedback can be provided both in terms of the feedback modality (visual or auditory) and the relation of the feedback signal to the physiological response being monitored. In analogue feedback, the signal is continuously present and directly proportional to changes in the physiological response. In the case of binary feedback, a threshold level of response is determined and the feedback signal is turned on or off only when it is above or below the threshold.

The type of feedback provided also varies in informational content and attentional demands. For example, simultaneous visual feedback from antagonist muscles has been provided by some in training of muscle coordination (Davis and Lee, 1980). Simpler forms of feedback can be easily attended to by the patient, and may be less likely to interfere with the state of passive volition often considered necessary for success with BF. More complex feedback, on the other hand, may be interesting and helpful in maintaining motivation; however, it should not be so complex as to result in informational overload.

Studies have not revealed a clear-cut superiority for any one modality (Yates, 1980). A main consideration in choosing the feedback modality is the characteristics of the disorder being dealt with. For example, problems may arise using visual feedback in a patient with blepharospasm, who starts treatment unable to see as a result of spasms in the eyelids. A second consideration is the preferences of the patient. Some find feedback tones irritating and prefer visual feedback; others prefer their eyes closed during relaxation and so choose auditory feedback.

Biofeedback equipment has been classified into three types by Girdano (1976): research equipment, clinical trainers and home trainers, in decreasing order of cost and technical sophistication. Equipment in each category has its specific use. Home trainers can be valuable in ensuring generalization of the change obtained in the clinic to the patient's natural environment. More recently, functions such as the processing of the physiological response, control of the feedback signal, and data storage and display have all been performed by a laboratory computer (Kolotkin, Billingham and Feldman, 1981; Montgomery, Howland, Cleeland, Mueller and Dearing, 1984). A list of American suppliers of BF equipment is provided by Rugh and Schwitzgebel (1975).

Besides EMG BF equipment, a number of other feedback devices have been used to treat motor disorders. Since the 1970s, various head-position trainers have been developed for patients with cerebral palsy. The most widely used of these devices is the Head Position Trainer developed at the Ontario Crippled Children's Center (Wooldridge and Russell, 1976). Other positional feedback devices have also been used for treating torticollis (Harrison, Garrett, Henderson and Adams, 1985) and scoliosis (Dworkin et al., 1985). These positional feedback machines essentially consist of mercury switches or potentiometers that are sensitive to changes in the position of the body/limb/head in one or more of the three bodily axes. Any deviations from pre-set positions are detected and activate the feedback signal. Feedback goniometers have also been used to increase active range of motion (Brown, DeBacher and Basmajian, 1979), for kinaesthetic feedback training (Greenberg and Fowler, 1980), or for gait training (Flodmark, 1986). The limb-load monitor, consisting of a load-sensitive insole inserted in the shoe, is another feedback device used in gait training (Seeger, Caudrey and Scholes, 1981).

PROCEDURAL CONSIDERATIONS

Attendance at a psychophysiological laboratory can be stressful for the patient. In the interests of reliability and validity, such effects should be minimized through provision of simple information about the equipment and procedures, use of pre-experimental 'adaptation' periods, and multiple baseline EMG recording to determine intra- and inter-subject variability (see Chapter 1). Furthermore, a treatment rationale providing the patient with information regarding the relationship between his symptoms, the training tasks and the feedback signal can help promote appreciation of the contingencies that operate during the BF sessions.

Another source of variability is that the EMG alters with even slight variations in electrode placement (van Boxtel, Goudswaard and Schomaker, 1984). When repeated recordings from the same site are made (as in EMG BF), the electrode sites can be marked with indelible ink or, more practically, exactly calculated in relation to anatomical landmarks (for example nasion, inion, mastoid process) on each occasion. Major sites of electrode placement for EMG BF are given in Basmajian and Blumenstein's (1980) book, and by Davis (1952), and Lippold (1967).

In EMG BF treatment of motor disorders, initial baseline EMG levels are likely to vary across patients, so some form of mathematical correction (Kinsman and Staudenmayer, 1978) may be appropriate, although some have questioned the usefulness of *pro-forma* covariance analysis, baseline corrections, and range corrections of EMG signals (Fridlund and Cacioppo, 1986). Baseline recording as part of various single-case designs for BF has been covered by Barlow, Blanchard, Hayes and Epstein (1977). In BF, pre- and post-sessional baseline recording, in addition to the initial pre-treatment baseline sessions, will allows examination of within-sessional and cross-sessional effects. Inclusion of self-control or instructional baselines (during which the patient is simply instructed to change the physiological response in the target direction but is provided with no feedback) can also be of value in interpreting the treatment result. Such self-control trials introduced before and after feedback trials (for example, Lang, Troyer, Twentyman and Gatchel, 1975) serve a dual purpose: they make it possible to ascertain whether the effect of feedback provision is over and above instruction for self-control alone, and whether there is generalization of learning from feedback trials to no-feedback instruction trials within and across sessions.

As the majority of motor disorders are susceptible to the effects of stress, a 'stress profile' analysis undertaken following baseline assessment and prior to BF training can be informative. Such an analysis identifies how a range of 'stimuli' quantitatively or qualitatively affect EMG from the target muscle(s) and other physiological responses. Relevant 'stimuli' may be stressful (mental arithmetic, stressful imagery, cold-pressor task, noise exposure, threat of shock), involve postural changes (standing, walking) or be movement related. This approach can yield a hierarchy of body or limb postures that can be used as graded tasks during BF. Also, a hierarchy of stressful situations from the patient's everyday life may be constructed, which can be used as imaginal stimuli in a systematic desensitization procedure during BF training.

In some disorders, identification of the target muscle may require a neurological examination or multiple-site EMG recording. For instance, torticollis takes many forms depending on the involved muscles, which can be the sternocleidomastoid, splenium or trapezius muscles (or deeper cervical muscles) contralateral or ipsilateral to the direction of abnormal head deviation. The specificity–generality issue renders the use of the appropriate muscle as the target of EMG BF training pertinent. Evidence exists that EMG BF produces change that is specific to the trained muscle, and which does not generalize to untrained muscles (Alexander, 1975; Shedivy and Kleinman, 1977).

As most physiological measures are state dependent, the effect of factors such as time of day, fatigue, menstrual cycle and length of recording session, as well as the level of noise and lighting in the laboratory, should be minimized or kept constant within and across subjects. Mulder and Hulstijn (1984) reported that, while fatigue led to decreased efficiency of one of the ankle dorsiflexors, there was a concomitant rapid and significant paradoxical increase in EMG. This inverse relationship between efficient muscle activity and EMG output necessitates BF trials of short duration (e.g. 20–30 s) and rest periods in between to prevent muscular fatigue.

A frequent confounding variable in BF is the effect of medication that most patients with motor disorders may be concurrently taking. For example, the benzodiazepines and anticholinergics currently in vogue in treating focal dystonias affect attention and learning (Dunne and Hartley, 1985; Ghoneim and Mewaldt, 1977). Electromyographic BF is essentially a learning therapy requiring patients' selective attention to their physiological response and the feedback signal, and such medication may hamper therapeutic gains. Furthermore, to be able to attribute change to the BF treatment, patients should ideally not be on any medication. If this is not practical, the amount of medication should be kept constant throughout BF training. Also, patients who are on medication should be seen at the same time of day on every occasion, to control for variations in the time since medication was last taken.

BIOFEEDBACK IN THE TREATMENT OF MOTOR DISORDERS

Application of BF to motor disorders has three major distinctions. First, the use of EMG BF in the treatment of motor disorders has the longest history, and can be traced back to the early studies of Marinacci and Horande (1960) and Mims (1956). Second, it is an area in which conclusions of efficacy have been somewhat over-optimistic (for example Fernando and Basmajian, 1978; Fotopoulos and Sunderland, 1978). Third, BF for motor disorders has been at the forefront of the expansion that has been occurring in the field. It is being applied to an increasing range of motor disorders such as scoliosis (Dworkin et al., 1985).

The major therapeutic aims in BF for motor disorders fall into four categories:

(1) Training of recruitment of activity in non-functional or weak muscles, for example in hemiplegia.

(2) Training of inhibition of undesired excessive muscle activity, for example in spasticity.

(3) Training of coordinated muscle activity (which may necessitate initial training as in (1) and (2) above), as, for example, in spasmodic torticollis, where the two antagonist sternocleidomastoid muscles need to be trained to achieve muscular balance, coordinated movement and a midline posture of the head.

(4) Training of appropriate postural control, for example head-position training in cerebral palsy.

Application of BF to three groups of motor disorders will be reviewed: the focal dystonias, cerebral palsy, and paralysis and spasticity. These have been the major focus of clinical and research effort in this area.

THE FOCAL DYSTONIAS

Dystonia is a syndrome of sustained muscle contractions, frequently causing twisting and repetitive movements, or abnormal postures (*Ad Hoc* Committee of the Dystonia Medical Research Foundation, 1984). A distinction is made between focal, segmental and generalized dystonia, when, respectively, one part, two or more contiguous regions, or multiple parts of the body including the legs are affected by muscle spasms (Marsden, Harrison and Bundey, 1976). The site of the spasm in a focal dystonia may be the neck muscles (spasmodic torticollis), the orbicularis oculi muscles around the eyes (blepharospasm), the hand and forearm muscles during writing (writer's cramp), the muscles of the jaw, mouth and tongue (oromandibular dystonia), the laryngeal muscles involved in speech production (spasmodic dysphonia), or the pharyngeal muscles, resulting in difficulty with swallowing (spasmodic dysphagia). The exact prevalence and incidence of focal dystonias are unknown, although they are not uncommon disorders. The aetiology of dystonia is uncertain. The idiopathic dystonias are considered to be due to a functional biochemical abnormality in the basal ganglia, although the precise site or nature of this are at present unknown.

Three features have been noted as characteristic of the electrophysiology of dystonias. Although none are specific to dystonia, cumulatively they may underlie the abnormal muscular contractions. These are: (1) co-contraction of antagonist muscles, which suggests an abnormality of reciprocal inhibition in dystonia; (2) overflow of contraction to remote muscles not engaged in the production of the voluntary movement; and (3) paradoxic contraction of passively shortened muscles, the so-called 'Westphal phenomenon'.

The pathophysiology of dystonia has been studied by Rothwell, Obeso, Day and Marsden (1983) in 35 patients, 15 of whom had focal dystonia. At rest, involuntary muscle contractions were absent or greatly reduced in those with focal or segmental dystonia, but persisted in the patients with generalized dystonia. Somatosensory evoked potentials were normal, and no time-locked electroencephalographic (EEG) event preceded the spasms. An additional finding was the abnormality of the time-course of reciprocal inhibition from forearm extensor to flexor muscles. The fact that all movements were not equally affected suggested that, in dystonia, the fault cannot lie solely in the common motor outflow pathways and that there must also be a problem in the production of the motor command.

Spasmodic Torticollis

In spasmodic torticollis (ST), involuntary contractions of the neck muscles result in abnormal head posture and/or involuntary head movement. The abnormal posture can be rotation (torticollis) or tilt (laterocollis) to the left or right, forward flexion (antecollis) or backward extension (retrocollis) of the head, or a combination. The muscles most frequently involved are the sterno-cleidomastoids, the trapezius and the splenius (Podivinsky, 1968). The ratio of male to female sufferers is roughly equal (Patterson and Little, 1943). Onset which is usually gradual, predominantly occurs in the third to fifth decades of life (Patterson and Little, 1943). The severity of the abnormal posture and of the involuntary movements of the head is affected by body position, often being worse when walking and relieved in the supine position. Patients use 'trick' movements (*geste antagoniste*) to keep the head in the midline.

The treatment of ST with EMG BF was first reported by Brudny, Grynbaum and Korein (1973) and Cleeland (1973). Cleeland (1973) compared EMG BF alone with EMG BF plus shock to the finger contingent on neck spasm in the treatment of 10 cases of ST. Nine patients showed marked to moderate improvement, and greater reduction of spasm with BF plus shock was noted in 8 cases. At follow-up, 1–40 months after treatment, moderate or marked improvement was maintained by 60% of the patients. Better treatment outcome was noted in younger and less chronic patients. The number of patients treated with EMG BF and shock was subsequently increased to 52. Of these, 44 (84.6%) showed marked to moderate improvement at the end of treatment and 26 (50%) maintained this at follow-up (Cleeland, 1983). Besides the obvious lack of any control groups and the limitations of the outcome criteria, it is not possible to isolate the effects of EMG BF from those of the shock. From the procedural details provided by Cleeland (1983), it appears that the results of the BF treatment are further confounded by simultaneous provision of physical therapy and mirror exercises.

Brudny and his colleagues have treated the largest number of ST patients with EMG BF. Results of BF treatment of 9 (Brudny, Grynbaum and Korein, 1973, 1974a), 13 (Brudny, Korein, Levidow, Grynbaum, Lieberman and Fried-mann, 1974b), 48 (Brudny et al., 1976; Korein, Brudny, Grynbaum, Sachs-

Frankel, Weisinger and Levidow, 1976) and 69 (Korein and Brudny, 1976) patients with ST have been reported. The outstanding characteristics of BF treatment by this team include its procedural sophistication (simultaneous feedback from agonist and antagonist neck muscles), the large number of treatment sessions (60 or more), the long follow-ups (up to 4 years) and the very positive outcomes achieved. In Korein and Brudny's (1976) report, 37 of the 69 ST patients (56.3%) were considered treatment successes, with 30 patients (43.4%) maintaining their gains at follow-up. However, there have been no controls of any kind, no quantitative data are provided, and clinical gradings are the major outcome criterion. These positive and negative features of the design, when considered jointly, necessitate caution in interpreting the findings of this team.

Fernando (see Fernando and Basmajian, 1978) has had a success rate of 20–30% in treating a series of 25 ST patients with a combination of EMG BF, muscular relaxation training and psychological counselling. The efficacy of BF for torticollis has also been reported in a number of single-case investigations, which vary in their design sophistication. These have used EMG BF from the sternocleidomastoid muscle (Jankel, 1978; Jones, Massong and Buckley, 1983), frontalis muscle (Roxanas, Thomas and Rapp, 1978), frontalis and sternocleidomastoid muscles combined with cutaneous shock (Russ, 1975) or from the frontalis and trapezius muscles plus kinaesthetic reconditioning (Counts, Gutsch and Hutton, 1978), or have employed heart rate feedback (Williams, 1975). Although the successful use of heart rate feedback and EMG BF from the frontalis have been reported, a better outcome may be achieved with disorder-specific procedures providing feedback from the involved neck muscle, instead of feedback aiming at a general relaxation effect.

Martin's (1981) series of 6 single-case studies constitutes the most methodologically sound study. An A–B–BC–C–BC design (A = baseline, B = EMG BF, C = home management, involving neck exercises and relaxing in front of a mirror) was employed. Each phase consisted of three sessions, and patients were followed up for 3 months. The procedures were standardized across patients. The outcome measures included cervical EMG, range of movement of the head, hourly torticollis severity ratings, length of time that the patient could maintain the head in the body midline, and patient and spouse ratings of change. From comparison of EMG levels across the different phases, the author concluded that EMG BF was associated with lower muscular activity at the trained site, although the effects of feedback were weak. None of the 6 patients were asymptomatic, but they had all benefited to some extent.

Successful reduction of muscular activity in the trained muscles with EMG BF is not always tantamount to the patient being clinically asymptomatic, as shown by Martin's (1981) results. Also, in some cases where EMG BF has been considered a success, EMG recording with needle electrodes has revealed abnormal muscular activity in the target muscle (Korein and Brudny, 1976).

Therefore, as noted by Yates (1980), the degree to which voluntary control of head posture and movement in successfully treated cases can be attributed to learning of voluntary control of the target muscles is in doubt.

The only study aiming at head position rather than muscular training has been reported by Harrison, Garrett, Henderson and Adams (1985). A multiple baseline design and feedback of forward and lateral head flexion were used to treat a female torticollis sufferer. The treatment was successful, and the patient's head tilt was reduced from a mean baseline level of 11.5° to 0°. As forward and lateral flexion of the head are not totally independent, use of a multiple baseline design across these head positions is not appropriate. It remains debatable whether training in control of head position or training in the more elementary task of controlling the activity of involved neck muscles is more fruitful.

Physiological responses were recorded as outcome measures in some behaviour therapy studies of ST (Agras and Marshall, 1965) or to test specific hypotheses (Meares, 1973; Meares and Lader, 1971). Several 'subtypes' of ST (for example, simple vs complex) have been distinguished through analysis of EMG records from neck muscles (Podivinsky, 1968; Rondot, Jedynak and Ferrey, 1981). The effects of proprioceptive and tactile cutaneous stimulation, the *geste antagoniste* ('trick' movements), and mental arithmetic on EMG recordings from the neck muscles have been examined by a number of investigators (Matthews, Beasley, Parry-Jones and Garland, 1978; Meares and Lader, 1971; Podivinsky, 1968; Rondot *et al.*, 1981), although the results are inconclusive.

Blepharospasm

In blepharospasm, the orbicularis oculi muscles are the site of involuntary spasms, which result in contractions of the eyelids and eye closure. The spasms may occur so frequently that the patient is virtually 'blind'. They can be triggered by bright sunlight, wind, dust, reading, watching television, driving, fatigue and stress. 'Trick' manoeuvres such as yawning, jaw opening, neck extension or manual eye opening may be developed by patients to open their eyes. Blepharospasm often presents in adult life usually in the sixth decade, and women are more frequently affected than men (Marsden, 1976). Besides occurring as a focal dystonia, blepharospasm is in many cases coupled with oromandibular dystonia as part of Meige's disease (Marsden, 1976).

The pathophysiology of belpharospasm has been investigated by Beradelli, Rothwell, Day and Marsden (1985), who studied 16 patients with blepharospasm (12 of whom also had oromandibular dystonia) and 10 normals. Dystonic spasms in the periocular and jaw muscles had EMG characteristics similar to that previously noted in other dystonic muscles (Rothwell *et al.*, 1983, discussed above). The latency of the R1 and R2 components of the blink and corneal reflexes were normal, whereas the amplitude and duration of R1 and R2 and duration of the corneal reflex were increased. The excitability cycle of recovery of the R2 component of the blink reflex was enhanced in the patients. Blepharospasm was not preceded by any EEG potential, but voluntary blinks were preceded by a *Bereitschaftspotential* beginning about 500 ms before. In 40–50% of the patients, exteroceptive suppression in the contracting orbicularis oculi or masseter muscles was absent. The authors concluded that in belpharospasm and oromandibular dystonia, the neuronal arcs of the facial muscles are normal, but there is an abnormal excitatory drive, possibly from the basal ganglia, to the facial motor neurones and interneurones mediating the facial reflexes.

Compared to surgery and botulinum toxin injections (Sanders, Massey and Buckley, 1985), BF is a less invasive therapeutic approach to blepharospasm and has therefore been used increasingly. Reports of its application, however, are restricted to single-case studies. These vary in sophistication, and use a variety of procedures and diverse outcome measures. A combination of avoidance training and feedback from the electro-oculograph eye-blink potentials (Ballard, Doerr and Varni, 1972), and a combination of relaxation training and EMG BF from the frontalis and forearm muscles (Stephenson, 1976), have been reported successful in belpharospasm, with patients being symptom-free at 9- and 6-month follow-up, respectively. Three other single-case reports have used frontalis EMG BF in conjunction with other techniques, including relaxation and assertiveness training (Norton, 1976), relaxation exercises and finger temperature BF (Rowan and Sedlacek, 1981), and ophthalmological treatment, hypnosis and concurrent EMG BF from the orbicularis oculi (Murphy and Fuller, 1984). Besides methodological shortcomings, two issues are relevant to evaluation of the results of these reports. First, none of these single-case reports have evaluated the effect of BF *per se*, but have reported the cumulative effects of the joint application of a number of therapeutic techniques. Second, although there is evidence that eye closure in blepharospasm involves the agonist orbicularis oculi and its antagonist frontalis muscle (Beradelli *et al.*, 1985), EMG BF from the former muscle may be a more direct and specific method of training.

Three single-case reports are noteworthy for using EMG BF alone and providing quantitative pre- and post-treatment EMG data. Peck's (1977) 17 sessions of EMG BF from orbicularis oculi and frontalis reduced mean EMG levels from 25 to 7 μV after seven sessions, and spasm frequency per 20-min from 1600 prior to treatment to 15 during the last three treatment sessions. Increased control of spasm at home and maintenance of improvement at 4-month follow-up were reported. Roxanas *et al.* (1978) employed feedback from the frontalis muscle in treating a case of blepharospasm and torticollis. At the end of treatment, mean frontalis EMG was reduced from 329 to 9.4 μV, and average distance between the eyelids improved by 30%. Improvement in affect and daily activities, and maintenance of gains at 6-month follow-up were also noted. An A–B–A–C–A design was used by Brantley, Carnrike, Faulstich and Barkemeyer (1985). Five days of baseline assessment were followed by the sequence of 5.5 weeks of taking the drug trihexyphenidyl (Artane), a 3-week washout period and 5 days of baseline assessment, 23 sessions of auditory frontalis EMG BF, and follow-up assessment at 1, 2, 4, 8, 24 and 42 weeks. Electromyographic levels during the two baseline and the drug-treatment phases were equivalent, although there was a reduction in eyeblink frequency during the drug phase. Substantial decreases in EMG level and eyeblink frequency occurred during the feedback and follow-up phases, and social functioning improved.

Writer's Cramp

Sheehy and Marsden (1982) have suggested a distinction between simple and dystonic writer's cramp. In the former, involuntary spasms of the hand and forearm muscles occur only when writing, other acts with the hand being performed normally. In dystonic writer's cramp, muscle spasms in the hand occur not only when writing but also during other manual acts such as handling a knife and fork, mechanical tools, etc. Simple writer's cramp can progress into the dystonic type. Abnormal posture of the fingers, hands or wrists are evident when the patient attempts to write, and tremor is a frequent accompanying feature. The resulting script is usually of poor quality. The onset of writer's cramp is often between the ages of 20 and 50 years, and is most prevalent amongst those who make their living through writing or use of their hand (for example, playing musical instruments). Patients often teach themselves to write with the other hand (Sheehy and Marsden, 1982).

Hughes and McLellan (1985) compared the performance of 11 patients with writer's cramp with that of 11 sex- and age-matched normal controls on a series of writing and non-writing tasks. The patients showed significantly higher EMG in all arm muscles, especially in the triceps, which was overactive in all but one of the tasks. The writing task was the best discriminator between groups, with the patients showing significantly higher EMG levels in all arm muscles, thus indicating increased co-activation. Five patients showed postural tremor with a mean frequncy of 6 Hz in the right and 6.7 Hz in the left hand.

Biofeedback is the latest in a long line of behavioural treatments for writer's cramp, and has been reviewed by Ince, Leon and Christidis (1986). The aim is to teach relaxation of muscles involved in the production of spasm or cramp during writing. As in BF treatment of the other dystonias, single-case studies prevail, and controlled outcome studies are absent. Electromyographic BF combined with relaxation guided by feedback of electrodermal activity and writing retraining (Reavley, 1975), or as part of a package including progressive relaxation or autogenic training and systematic desensitization (Uchiyama, Lutterjohann and Shah, 1977), or in conjunction with self-monitoring, relaxation training, graduated *in-vivo* practice and home practice (Furlong, 1980), has been reported to be successful in treating writer's cramp. Successful application of finger temperature BF and home exercise to a case of musician's cramp (LeVine, 1983), and tactile feedback provided by a piece of tape over the thumb to treat writer's cramp (Grassick, 1979), have also been reported.

The results of EMG BF in treating multiple cases of writer's cramp have been less encouraging. Bindman and Tibbetts (1977) treated 6 of 10 cases of writer's cramp with EMG BF. One patient was symptom-free, 3 improved (but two of these continued to be disabled at work), and 2 patients were unchanged after 3–7 weeks of treatment. At follow-up, 3–12 months later, one patient had relapsed, one had improved further and 4 were unchanged. The poor outcome may have resulted from the inappropriate placement of electrodes over the tendons of the finger flexors instead of over the muscles themselves. In another multiple-case study, Cottraux, Juenet and Collet (1983) treated 4 of 15 patients with writer's cramp with EMG BF from the forearm extensor, and the remaining 9 with a multimodal treatment consisting of BF, autogenic training, systematic desensitization, and assertiveness training. Only 9 patients completed the treatment; all were improved on the basis of clinical evaluation of handwriting, although only one had normal handwriting at follow-up. It is difficult to arrive at any conclusions regarding the efficacy of BF for writer's cramp, as it has virtually always been used in combination with other behavioural techniques. Available evidence from multiple-case studies, however, suggest that consistently positive effects are not obtained in all cases.

CEREBRAL PALSY

Cerebral palsy (CP) involves non-progressive brain damage incurred before, during or shortly after birth, resulting in impaired control of movement (Kurland, 1957). While prematurity is the commonest aetiological factor, a large proportion of cases of CP have no known perinatal, natal or postnatal complications (O'Reilly and Walentynowicz, 1981). Cerebral palsy is one of the most common of childhood handicaps, with an incidence of 1.5–5 per 1000 births and a prevalence of 400,000 in the United States (Lord, 1984).

Cerebral palsy is classified into a number of clinical types, the major distinction being between spastic, athetoid, ataxic, and mixed types (Minear, 1956). Persistence of primitive reflexes, failure of mature postural mechanisms to emerge and delayed motor development are often the first clinical signs. Head control, maintenance of an upright posture, and walking may be delayed or never become fully developed. One or more of the extremities may be involved. Intellectual retardation in about 50–70% of cases, ocular abnormalities and hearing deficits, seizures, scoliosis, hip dislocation and other musculoskeletal problems are often associated features (Lord, 1984).

Management of CP has included a variety of surgical procedures, medication, physiotherapy, and use of adaptive seating with special chairs, ambulatory aids, braces and devices for postural correction. Two major types of BF have been used in the treatment of CP: EMG BF and head-position training. Harris' (1971) model suggesting that CP may involve a faulty servomechanical feedback control system can be considered as providing a rationale for the BF studies.

Finley and his colleagues have carried out a series of multiple-case studies of EMG BF in the treatment of CP. In one study (Finley, Niman, Standley and Ender, 1976), 12 sessions of frontalis EMG BF were given to reduce muscle tone in 6 athetoid CP patients. Comparison of pre- and post-treatment measures showed a significant reduction of frontalis EMG (from a mean of 28.9 μV to a mean of 13 μV) for all but one subject, significant improvements in gross and fine motor function for all subjects, and improvement of speech in 4 patients.

An A–B–A–B design was used in their second study (Finley, Niman, Standley and Wansley, 1977) of 4 spastic CP children. During the first baseline phase of two to four sessions, frontalis and forearm flexor EMG was recorded, and speech, fine and gross motor functions were evaluated. This was followed by 12 sessions of frontalis EMG BF (B1), 6 weeks of no training (A2) and 4 weeks of frontalis EMG BF (B2). At the end of each phase, 'blind' speech and motor evaluations were repeated. Within all sessions, a 5-min baseline was taken before and after the feedback training. Besides the more sophisticated design, an interesting feature of this study was the use of a 'Universal Feeder' which dispensed a toy, candy or token if the child's cumulative integrated frontalis EMG was below a criterion threshold at the end of each 60-s epoch. During the first 12 BF sessions there was a decrease in frontalis EMG, and improvements in speech and motor function were noted. Deterioration was evident on all measures following the 6 weeks of return to baseline, which was rectified by reinstitution of BF.

The attention given to motivational factors in BF treatment of children, by developing the Universal Feeder, is an important feature of Findley et al.'s work. However, both studies have shortcomings. With regards to the issue of specificity versus generality of relaxation effects, the training from the frontalis cannot be assumed to result in a generalized reduction of muscle tone (Alexander, 1975). The fact that a deterioration was evident on all measures during the return to baseline phase (A2) in the second study demonstrates that the benefits obtained with 12 sessions of BF (B1) were short-lived, making the need for long-term follow-up obvious. No follow-up data was reported in either study. As the number of patients treated in each study was very small, caution must be exercised in interpreting the results.

Successful use of feedback has been reported in the treatment of spasticity using an aversive conditioning paradigm (Sachs and Mayhall, 1971), of involuntary muscle activity in 4 adults with mixed CP (Neilson and McCaughey,

1982), and of foot-dragging in a case of athetoid CP using a portable feedback device (Spearing and Poppen, 1974). The last study, the only one to include a follow-up, noted relapse 3 months later. Three single-case studies of BF treatment of choreoathetoid CP patients by Cataldo, Bird and Cunningham (1978) demonstrate the pitfalls of relying on either reversal or multiple baseline single-case designs. In case 1 reversal did not occur, and in case 3 using a multiple baseline design, generalization to untrained muscles occurred. Both these effects, which are positive from a therapeutic perspective, limit the conclusions that can be drawn regarding the mechanisms of change.

Biofeedback has mainly been used to treat dysfunctional muscles (e.g. increased tone) or abnormal gross motor behaviour (e.g. spastic head movement). Some applications of BF in CP, however, have been directed at finer motor control. Harrison and Connolly (1971) reported that, although spastic patients took longer to achieve fine control of the forearm flexor muscle compared to normals, they were not different in the control finally achieved. In a similar study, but using wire electrodes, Robertson, Lee and Jacobs (1984) noted that 3 patients with CP and 3 normals were similar in their ability to produce a discrete whole muscle contraction, to isolate and maintain firing of a single motor unit (SMU), and to turn an SMU on with visual feedback from an oscilloscope. In contrast to the normals, the CP patients were not consistently able to inhibit SMUs or whole muscle activity, if the SMU or muscle had been active for some time.

Other uses of BF with CP patients have been directed towards teaching head control or gait training. In a number of small case studies with CP patients, successful training of head control using head-position training devices has been reported by Ball, McCrady and Hart (1975); Catanese and Sandford (1984); Harris, Spelman and Hymer (1974); Leiper, Miller, Lang and Herman (1981); Walmsley, Crichton and Droog (1981); Wooldridge and Russell (1976). However, some CP patients failed to achieve head control with such training (Walmsley *et al.*, 1981; Wooldridge and Russell, 1976). Furthermore, those who tested transfer of learned head control to other situations found a lack of generalization beyond the training sessions (Catanese and Sandford, 1984; Leiper *et al.*, 1981). Symmetrical gait training using auditory feedback from a limb-load monitor was achieved in 4 children with CP (Seeger *et al.*, 1981), although the improvements were not maintained at follow-up 18–24 months later (Seeger and Caudrey, 1983). Gait training with a joint-position feedback device was not consistently successful across all CP patients (Flodmark, 1986).

Recording of physiological responses in CP has been used as an investigative tool in conjunction with other procedures. Nwaobi, Brubaker, Cusick and Sussman (1983) examined whether different seating positions on a Mulholland chair had any effect on the tonic EMG activity of the low-back extensors in 11 children with CP. Electromyographic activity was least with a seat surface elevation of 0° and a backrest inclination of 75°. An extension of this study (Nwaobi, 1986) examined the effects of body position (upright vs reclined) on EMG recorded from three muscles. It was concluded that although a reclined seat may give the impression of a more relaxed individual, it may not necessarily be so. Given the widespread use of adaptive seating in cerebral palsy, investigations of this kind are important in evaluating the appropriate use of such seating devices.

Barto et al. (1984) used dynamic telemetric EMG to identify deforming muscles prior to surgery for foot deformities in spastic CP. Electromyographic records were obtained through wire electrodes from eight muscles. Information about various aspects of gait was provided by compression-closing foot switches taped to the bottom of the foot. On the basis of the EMG findings, suggestions for surgical procedures were made. In 13 of the 15 patients who had undergone surgery, the surgeon performed the procedure recommended by dynamic EMG. Traditional clinical examination cannot determine the timing of muscle contractions during gait, and dynamic EMG can refine the diagnostic process.

PARALYSIS AND SPASTICITY SECONDARY TO STROKE

By far the largest number of studies using EMG BF have been concerned with its application to the rehabilitation of patients following cerebrovascular accident (CVA). In North America, the reported incidence of stroke varies between 1.8 and 2.73 per 1000, with 2 in 3 patients surviving (Licht, 1975). Of the half a million or so survivors, a large majority have permanent or temporary loss of motor function in the upper or lower extremities. Some spontaneous recovery of function may occur within at least the first 6 months after a CVA.

A CVA can cause paralysis (denoted by the suffix 'plegia'), or weakness (denoted by the suffix 'paresis'), or spasticity. Depending on the site and extent of the dysfunction, various prefixes are employed: for example, monoplegia (paralysis of one limb), hemiplegia (paralysis of one arm and leg on the same side of the body), paraplegia (paralysis of the lower limbs), tetraplegia or quadriplegia (paralysis of all four limbs). Footdrop, shoulder subluxation and hand function have been the three major symptoms used as targets of BF treatment of stroke patients (Basmajian, Regenos and Baker, 1977). Analysis and treatment of impaired gait patterns have also been among the objectives of BF training (Takebe and Basmajian, 1976).

The rationale behind EMG BF treatment of paralysis is that some residual muscular activity remains which may be insufficient to produce movement but is sufficient for EMG measurement. The existence of residual motor activity in apparently paralysed muscles has been shown by SMU studies (Basmajian, 1974). The first aim of BF in such cases is to demonstrate the existence of residual muscular activity to the patient. When both spasticity and paralysis are present, training initially focuses on the reduction of spasticity. Increasing the strength of flaccid muscles is then followed by development of coordinated movement through simultaneous monitoring of agonist and antagonist muscles. Spasticity and lower limb dysfunction are often the initial target of BF treatment (Wolf, Baker and Kelly, 1979). Detailed coverage of the strategies and procedures commonly employed in BF training of stroke patients is provided by several sources (Binder-Macleod, 1983; DeBacher, 1983; Kelly, Baker and Wolf, 1979).

Electromyographic BF studies in this area consist mainly of single-case, multiple-case or single-group studies. An excellent critical review has been made recently by Wolf (1983). Therefore, only the control group studies and their major findings will be discussed below. Biofeedback studies in this area can be distinguished on the basis of whether the upper or lower extremities are the target of therapeutic efforts. This is a rather artificial distinction, as some studies have involved the treatment of both. Nevertheless, this dichotomy will be used since, as discussed later, there is evidence for prognostic differences between the two (Wolf *et al.*, 1979, 1980).

Lower Extremity

One of the first studies which included a control group was reported by Basmajian, Kukulka, Narayan and Takebe (1975), who compared groups of 10 patients assigned to conventional physical therapy or conventional physical therapy plus EMG BF. Although both groups of patients improved, combined BF and physical therapy was more effective. The conclusions of this study are, however, subject to several criticisms. Fish, Mayer and Herman (1976) have noted that the two groups were not equated for time since occurrence of the CVA (the combined treatment group being more acute); post-treatment evaluations were performed at variable times after the cessation of treatment in the two groups; and statistical analysis of the results showed in significant differences between the two groups only in one of the outcome measures. Treatment outcome in the Basmajian *et al.* (1975) study was also assessed by peroneal nerve conduction velocity measurement, the results of which were reported in a subsequent publication (Takebe, Kukulka, Narayan and Basmajian, 1976). The latter study found no change in nerve conduction velocity following either of the treatments.

A number of subsequent studies (Binder, Moll and Wolf, 1981; Burnside, Tobias and Bursill, 1982; Shahani, Connors and Mohr, 1977) have included control groups, in a design similar to that of Basmajian *et al.* (1975), comparing BF plus physical therapy to physical therapy alone. This does not constitute a true control design which would enable isolation of BF-specific effects, but compares the additive effects of BF and physical therapy with those of the latter treatment alone. Biofeedback plus physical therapy has been consistently reported superior to physical therapy in these studies.

Wolf and Binder-Macleod (1983a) have reported the only treatment study of lower extremity (LE) dysfunction that had more than one control group. Post-CVA LE dysfunction in a group given LE EMG BF ($N=7$, 'experimental' group) was compared with an EMG BF for upper extremity (UE) group ($N=16$), a general relaxation training through EMG BF group ($N=8$), and a no-treatment group ($N=6$). Of the 18 t-tests reported, comparing the experimental group with each of the control groups, only seven were statistically significant. The LE BF group showed improvement in active range of movement at the knee and the ankle (compared to the relaxation and no-treatment groups only). Of the 12 comparisons of change of EMG, only two were significant. Therefore, the group who received LE BF showed more change, but their results were not consistently superior to all three groups or across all measures.

The conclusions that can be drawn from the results of this study are limited by a flaw in its design. Three of the patients in the experimental group were also included in each one of the three other groups. In effect, the true size of the experimental group was 4. Furthermore, patients in the EMG BF groups received 60 sessions of treatment, while the relaxation training group had only 20 sessions of treatment.

Upper Extremity

Brudny and his colleagues have been mainly concerned with the BF training of upper limb function in hemiparetics. As with torticollis, their various publications mainly constitute uncontrolled reports of multiple cases treated over the years. Their contribution has been in terms of the procedural sophistication of the EMG BF treatment, including simultaneous monitoring of agonist and antagonist muscles, and reports of long-term follow-up. Their results are impressive. They describe functional gains for 61% of 70 hemiparetics treated with EMG BF in their 1979 report (Brudny, Korein, Grynbaum, Belandres and Gianutsos, 1979). However, these results need to be interpreted cautiously as no experimental control is attempted and although integrated EMG is recorded, its pre- versus post-treatment values are not reported and the main outcome measure is based on clinical judgement.

As characteristic of outcome evaluations for many other disorders, reports of treatment failure or limitation are rare events. Nevertheless, several investigators (Honer, Mohr and Roth, 1982; Lee, Hill, Johnston and Smiehorowski, 1976; Mroczek, Halpern and McHugh, 1978; Turczynski, Hartje and Sturm, 1984) have reported that BF was of limited value in the treatment of UE dysfunction.

More recently, several control-group studies of BF treatment of UE dysfunction have appeared, comparing EMG BF plus physical therapy with physical therapy alone (Basmajian, Gowland, Brandstater, Swanson and Trotter, 1982; Inglis, Donald, Monga, Sproule and Young, 1984), or kinaesthetic feedback with occupational therapy (Greenberg and Fowler, 1980). Although improvement was noted with treatment, in none of these studies were the differences in outcome between BF and the control groups significant.

In the only study to include a no-treatment control group, Wolf and Binder-Macleod (1983b) compared 22 chronic stroke patients with UE dysfunction who received 60 sessions of EMG BF with a no-treatment control group of 9 patients, on a very large number of measures including various EMG recordings. The BF group showed significant changes from pre- to post-treatment on neuromuscular but not on functional measures, and differed from the control group mainly with regard to change in neuromuscular measures. Only 5 of the 22 patients in the BF group initially had or developed better hand function with the treatment.

Until recently, UE and LE dysfunctions have been jointly evaluated in terms of degree of post-CVA recovery. In a review of 229 patients, Gowland (1982) reported that only 5% regained functional use of their hand and arm following physical therapy. Wolf *et al.* (1979), in a review of the BF treatment of 48 UEs and 44 LEs of 52 stroke patients concluded that LEs responded more favourably to treatment. Reports on the limited value of BF seem more numerous in the case of UE dysfunction.

In some of the more recent studies, a number of patient characteristics such as time since stroke and initial motor function in the UE (Basmajian *et al.*, 1982), site of lesion (Shahani *et al.*, 1977), greater active range of movement in the UEs and less hyperactivity in spastic muscles (Wolf and Binder-Macleod, 1983b) have emerged as related to outcome. The association of patient characteristics with the outcome of EMG BF for stroke patients has been the subject of a report by Wolf *et al.* (1979), and a 1-year follow-up report by the same authors (Wolf *et al.*, 1980). Age, sex, side of hemiparesis, time since stroke, previous rehabilitation, and number of BF sessions were not associated with outcome in the BF treatment of 48 UEs and 44 LEs in 52 stroke patients. Proprioceptive impairment and presence of aphasia were associated with poorer outcome (Wolf *et al.*, 1979). One year follow-up data obtained from 34 (65.4%) of the original sample revealed that improvements achieved with BF were maintained, and again none of the variables previously considered were associated with outcome at follow-up (Wolf *et al.*, 1980). The number of BF sessions was not associated with outcome in either report, which raises questions with regard to the cost–efficacy and value of the large number of treatment sessions employed by some studies (for example, Brudny *et al.*, 1979; Wolf and Binder-Macleod, 1983a).

METHODOLOGICAL CONSIDERATIONS AND DIRECTIONS FOR FUTURE RESEARCH

Other disorders of movement such as tics (Moldofsky, 1971; Obeso, Rothwell and Marsden, 1981), Parkinson's disease (Hallett, Shahani and Young, 1977; Shumaker, 1980), tremor (Le Boeuf, 1976), Huntington's chorea (MacPherson, 1967), and other focal dystonias (Haynes, 1976; Henschen and Burton, 1978) have also been the subject of physiological investigation or BF treatment. Physiological recording is therefore an indispensable part of the assessment and treatment of a wide range of motor disorders.

The diverse uses of physiological recording are well illustrated by studies of the focal dystonias. Electromyographic recording has allowed classification of ST into various 'types' on the basis of the muscles involved. The effect of a number of factors including stress, tactile and proprioceptive stimulation on the neck EMG has been examined. Electromyographic recording has been used as an outcome measure in some behavioural treatments of ST, or to test various hypotheses. Most significantly, in the absence of pathological studies, pathophysiological studies such as those of Beradelli *et al.* (1985) and Rothwell *et al.* (1983) promote an understanding of the underlying physiological deficits in dystonias and generate hypotheses regarding the possible loci of dysfunction in these disorders. Electromyographic recording has also been employed to confirm denervation following botulinum toxin (Sanders *et al.*, 1985), or surgical denervation of muscles. Biofeedback has constituted an alternative and less invasive treatment in these disorders. The other varied uses of EMG recording have included determination of the best applications of prosthetic devices and the identification of involved muscles prior to surgery in CP, and the assessment of the levels of muscle activity required by different physical therapy exercises (Soderberg and Cook, 1983).

Like pathophysiological studies, investigations using BF have the potential of clarifying the nature of deficits in neuromuscular disorders. This use of BF was stated over 20 years ago in Smith and Henry's (1967) review. As noted by Yates (1980), with a few exceptions, this potential has remained largely unexplored, as most investigators have been concerned with the therapeutic application of BF. The potential of BF can be partly realized through studies of normal processes of motor function and control, such as those of Kukulka and Basmajian (1975) and Middaugh (1978). Studies such as these can provide information about how BF operates and also pre-test BF procedures and measures before application to clinical populations.

Biofeedback, being a treatment fundamentally based on physiological recording, does not challenge the organic models of motor disorders, which might appear to be the case with other behavioural treatments. For this reason, BF has credibility for the patient. This, combined with the sophisticated equipment employed, necessity of active participation of the patient, and the often large number of treatment sessions, make it an ideal candidate for the label 'ultimate placebo' (Stroebel and Glueck, 1973). It is therefore surprising and disappointing that during the last 20 years so few controlled outcome studies have been carried out. Single-case reports and single-group studies dominate, based on the assumption (often false) of symptom stability in these chronic disorders. Recovery of function especially in the first 6 months after a CVA is well recognized, spontaneous remissions do occur in some dystonic disorders (Jayne, Lees and Stern, 1984), and medication, surgery and physiotherapy are effective for a proportion of treated patients. The use of control groups, therefore, is essential in any assessment of BF in these conditions. The handful of controlled studies that have been performed have mainly compared BF in conjunction with physical therapy, with physical therapy alone; they do not allow evaluation of BF effects in isolation. Studies which have compared BF alone with physical therapy have not consistently found a significant superiority for BF. Also, the majority of control-group studies have suffered from limitations of design which restrict the generality of their findings.

Most studies have various methodological shortcomings. In a large number of reports, procedural details as well as EMG data are lacking, the patients do not form a homogeneous group, treatments are not standardized across patients, patients concurrently receive several treatments including medication, outcome measures are limited to clinical gradings, and differences in pretreatment levels are not taken into account. All these deficits limit interpretation of the results. The length of feedback trials are quite variable, ranging from a few seconds to a few minutes. Despite evidence showing specificity rather than generality of change obtained with EMG BF, relaxation training from the frontalis continues, and identification and treatment of the muscle most implicated in the individual's motor dysfunction are rarely undertaken.

As distinct from statistical significance, the issue of clinical significance of treatment outcome is intimately bound with those of multidimensionality (physiological, behavioural and subjective), generalization and maintenance of gains. The changes in muscular activity achieved with EMG BF are clinically significant only in so far as they result in functionally valuable behavioural changes that are appreciated by the patient, and which are manifest in the patient's natural environment and persist over time. Most studies have failed to examine the associations between EMG, functional improvement (range of movement, length of time correct posture is maintained, gait analysis, etc.), behavioural improvement in activities of daily living and self-reported change. The patterns of synchrony and desynchrony that may occur between these various aspects of changed functioning have implications for the obtained results and future refinement of therapeutic techniques. The fact that generalization of change to the natural environment and long-term maintenance of effects cannot be assumed but need to be assessed is rendered evident by the results of studies that have reported absence of such effects when they were assessed (Catanese and Sandford, 1984; Leiper *et al.*, 1981; Seeger and Caudrey, 1983).

Considerable variability exists in the number of sessions of BF given, varying from as low as two (Middaugh and Miller, 1980) to 60 (Brudny *et al.*, 1979). The issue of cost–efficacy, often raised with regard to the expensive equipment required for BF, is also pertinent to the demands on therapist and patient time when large numbers of treatment sessions are given. Also related to the issue of cost–efficacy has been the indiscriminate use of BF for all patients. Recent attempts to identify patient characteristics that are related to outcome (Wolf *et al.*, 1979, 1980) are moves in the right direction. As the mechanisms of change in BF are largely unknown, assessment of factors such as kinaesthesia, position sense, ability to discriminate muscle tension, locus of control, and perceived self-efficacy may at least reveal some aspects of this process of change.

The shortcomings of existing studies, and the paucity of controlled studies, render over-optimistic Fernando and Basmajian's (1978) comment in the task force report of the Biofeedback Society of America (BSA) that BF for neuro-muscular disorders is past the experimental mode. In another BSA task force report, Fotopoulos and Sunderland (1978) concluded that there appears to be enough evidence to support the claim that EMG BF is highly effective in reducing torticollis symptoms, a conclusion that we cannot support. It is evident that BF alone or in combination with a variety of other techniques may turn out to be successful in improving various motor dysfunctions. What remains to be demonstrated, however, is that such gains are specific to the feedback component of the treatment package, as opposed to alternative features of such treatment. More cautious views have been expressed by Wolf (1983), Yates (1980) and Keefe and Surwit (1977), and by the report of the Health and Public Policy Committee (1985). From the available evidence, including the results of the more recent studies employing control groups, we conclude that BF will remain an 'unfulfilled promise' unless it is supported by solid evidence soon.

REFERENCES

Ad Hoc Committee (1984). *Ad Hoc* Committee of the Dystonia Medical Research Foundation. See Fahn, S., Marsden, C.D. and Calne, D.B. (1987). Classification and investigation of dystonia. In: C.D. Marsden and S. Fahn (Eds) *Movement Disorders*, vol. 2. London: Butterworths.

Agras, S. and Marshall, C. (1965). The application of negative practice to spasmodic torticollis. *American Journal of Psychiatry* **122**, 579–582.

Alexander, A.B. (1975). An experimental test of assumptions relating to the use of electromyographic biofeedback as a general relaxation technique. *Psychophysiology* **12**, 656–662.

Ball, T.S., McCrady, R.E. and Hart, A.D. (1975). Automated reinforcement of head posture in two cerebral palsied retarded children. *Perceptual and Motor Skills* **40**, 619–622.

Ballard, P., Doerr, H. and Varni, J. (1972). Arrest of a disabling eye disorder using biofeedback. *Psychophysiology* **9**, 271 (Abstract).

Barlow, D.H., Blanchard, E.B., Hayes, S.C. and Epstein, L.H. (1977). Single-case designs and clinical biofeedback experimentation. *Biofeedback and Self-Regulation* **2**, 221–239.

Barto, P.S., Supinski, R.S. and Skinner, S.R. (1984). Dynamic EMG findings in varus hindfoot deformity and spastic cerebral palsy. *Developmental Medicine and Child Neurology* **26**, 88–93.

Basmajian, J.V. (1974). *Muscles Alive: Their Functions Revealed by Electromyography*. 3rd ed. Baltimore: Williams and Wilkins.

Basmajian, J.V. and Blumenstein, R. (1980). *Electrode Placement in EMG Biofeedback*. Baltimore: Williams and Wilkins.

Basmajian, J.V., Gowland, C., Brandstater, M.E., Swanson, L. and Trotter, J. (1982). EMG feedback treatment of upper limb in hemiplegic stroke patients: a pilot study. *Archives of Physical Medicine and Rehabilitation* **63**, 613–616.

Basmajian, J.V., Kukulka, C.G., Narayan, M.G. and Takebe, K. (1975). Biofeedback treatment of foot-drop after stroke compared to standard rehabilitation technique: effects on voluntary control and strength. *Archives of Physical Medicine and Rehabilitation* **56**, 231–236.

Basmajian, J.V., Regenos, E.M. and Baker, M.P. (1977). Rehabilitating stroke patients with biofeedback. *Geriatrics* **32**, 85–88.

Beradelli, A., Rothwell, J.C., Day, B.L. and Marsden, C.D. (1985). Pathophysiology of blepharospasm and oromandibular dystonia. *Brain* **108**, 593–608.

Binder, S.A., Moll, C.B. and Wolf, S.L. (1981). Evaluation of electromyographic biofeedback as an adjunct to therapeutic exercise in treating the lower extremities of hemiplegic patients. *Physical Therapy* **61**, 886–893.

Binder-Macleod, S.A. (1983). Biofeedback in stroke rehabilitation. In: J.V. Basmajian (Ed.) *Biofeedback: Principles and Practice for Clinicians*, 2nd edn. Baltimore: Williams and Wilkins.

Bindman, E. and Tibbetts, R.W. (1977). Writer's cramp – a rational approach to treatment? *British Journal of Psychiatry* **131**, 143–148.

van Boxtel, A., Goudswaard, P. and Schomaker, L.R.B. (1984). Amplitude and bandwidth of the frontalis surface EMG: effects of electrode parameters. *Psychophysiology* **21**, 699–707.

Brantley, P.J., Carnrike, C.L.M., Jr, Faulstich, M.E. and Barkemeyer, C.A. (1985). Blepharospasm: a case study comparison of trihexyphenidyl (Artane) versus EMG biofeedback. *Biofeedback and Self-Regulation* **10**, 173–180.

Brown, D.M., DeBacher, G.A. and Basmajian, J.V. (1979). Feedback goniometers for hand rehabilitation. *American Journal of Occupational Therapy* **33**, 458–463.

Brudny, J., Grynbaum, B.B. and Korein, J. (1973). New therapeutic modality for treatment of spasmodic torticollis. *Archives of Physical Medicine and Rehabilitation* **54**, 575 (Abstract).

Brudny, J., Grynbaum, B.B. and Korein, J. (1974a). Spasmodic torticollis: treatment by feedback display of the EMG. *Archives of Physical Medicine and Rehabilitation* **55**, 403–408.

Brudny, J., Korein, J., Grynbaum, B.B., Belandres, P.V. and Gianutsos, J.G. (1979). Helping hemiparetics to help themselves. *Journal of American Medical Association* **241**, 814–818.

Brudny, J., Korein, J., Grynbaum, B.B., Friedmann, L.W., Weinstein, S., Sachs-

Frankel, G. and Belandres, P.V. (1976). EMG feedback therapy: review of treatment of 114 patients. *Archives of Physical Medicine and Rehabilitation* **57**, 55–61.

Brudny, J., Korein, J., Levidow, L., Grynbaum, B.B., Lieberman, A. and Friedmann, L.W. (1974b). Sensory feedback therapy as a modality of treatment in central nervous system disorders of voluntary movement. *Neurology* **24**, 925–932.

Burnside, I.G., Tobias, H.S. and Bursill, D. (1982). Electromyographic feedback in the remobilization of stroke patients: a controlled trial. *Archives of Physical Medicine and Rehabilitation* **63**, 217–222.

Cataldo, M.F., Bird, B.L. and Cunningham, C.E. (1978). Experimental analysis of EMG feedback in treating cerebral palsy. *Journal of Behavioral Medicine* **1**, 311–322.

Catanese, A.A. and Sandford, D.A. (1984). Head-position training through biofeedback: prosthetic or cure? *Developmental Medicine and Child Neurology* **26**, 369–374.

Cleeland, C.S. (1973). Behavioral technics in the modification of spasmodic torticollis. *Neurology* **23**, 1241–1247.

Cleeland, C.S. (1983). Biofeedback and other behavioral techniques in the treatment of disorders of voluntary movement. In: J.V. Basmajian (Ed.) *Biofeedback: Principles and Practice for Clinicians*, 2nd edn. Baltimore: Williams and Wilkins.

Cottraux, J.A., Juenet, C. and Collet, L. (1983). The treatment of writer's cramp with multimodal behaviour therapy and biofeedback: a study of 15 cases. *British Journal of Psychiatry* **142**, 180–183.

Counts, D.K., Gutsch, K.U. and Hutton, B.O. (1978). Spasmodic torticollis treatment through biofeedback training. *Psychotherapy: Theory, Research and Practice* **15**, 13–15.

Davis, A.E. and Lee, R.G. (1980). EMG biofeedback in patients with motor disorders: an aid for co-ordinating activity in antagonistic muscle groups. *Le Journal Canadien Des Sciences Neurologiques* **7**, 199–206.

Davis, J.F. (1952). *Manual of Surface Electromyography*. Montreal: Laboratory for Psychological Studies, Allan Memorial Institute of Psychiatry.

DeBacher, G. (1983). Biofeedback in spasticity control. In: J.V. Basmajian (Ed.) *Biofeedback: Principles and Practice for Clinicians*, 2nd edn. Baltimore: Williams and Wilkins.

Dunne, M.P. and Hartley, L.R. (1985). The effects of scopolamine upon verbal memory: evidence for an attentional hypothesis. *Acta Psychologica* **58**, 205–217.

Dworkin, B., Miller, N.E., Dworkin, S., Birbaumer, N., Brines, M.L., Jonas, S., Schwentker, E.P. and Graham, J.J. (1985). Behavioural method for the treatment of idiopathic scoliosis. *Proceedings of the National Academy of Sciences of the USA* **82**, 2493–2497.

Fernando, C.K. and Basmajian, J.V. (1978). Biofeedback in physical medicine and rehabilitation. Task Force Report of the Biofeedback Society of America. *Biofeedback and Self-Regulation* **3**, 435–455.

Finley, W.W., Niman, C., Standley, J. and Ender, P. (1976). Frontal EMG-biofeedback training of athetoid cerebral palsy patients. *Biofeedback and Self-Regulation* **1**, 169–182.

Finley, W.W., Niman, C.A., Standley, J. and Wansley, R.A. (1977). Electrophysiologic behavior modification of frontal EMG in cerebral-palsied children. *Biofeedback and Self-Regulation* **2**, 59–79.

Fischer-Williams, M., Nigl, A.J. and Sovine, D.L. (1986). *A Textbook of Biological Feedback*. New York: Human Sciences.

Fish, D., Mayer, N. and Herman, R. (1976). Biofeedback. *Archives of Physical Medicine and Rehabilitation* **57**, 152.

Flodmark, A. (1986). Augmented auditory feedback as an aid in gait training of the cerebral-palsied child. *Developmental Medicine and Child Neurology* **28**, 147–155.

Fotopoulos, S.S. and Sunderland, W.P. (1978). Biofeedback in the treatment of psychophysiologic disorders. Task Force Report of Biofeedback Society of America. *Biofeedback and Self-Regulation* **3**, 331–361.

Fridlund, A.J. and Cacioppo, J.T. (1986). Guidelines for human electromyographic research. *Psychophysiology* **23**, 567–589.

Furlong, F.W. (1980). Behavioural and biofeedback treatment of writer's cramp. *Canadian Journal of Psychiatry* **25**, 44–48.

Gaarder, K.R. and Montgomery, P.J. (1979). *Clinical Biofeedback: A Procedural Manual for Behavioral Medicine*, 2nd edn. Baltimore: Williams and Wilkins.

Ghoneim, M.M. and Mewaldt, S.P. (1977). Studies on human memory: the interactions of diazepam, scopolamine, and physostigmine. *Psychopharmacology* **52**, 1–6.

Girdano, D. (1976). Buying biofeedback. In: Barber, T.X., DiCara, L.V., Kamiya, J., Miller, N.E., Shapiro, D. and Stoyva, J. (Eds) *Biofeedback and Self-Control*. Chicago: Aldine.

Gowland, C. (1982). Recovery of motor function following stroke: profile and predictors. *Physiotherapy* **34**, 77–84.

Grassick, G.P. (1979). The rapid treatment of a case of writer's cramp using band-aid biofeedback. *Journal of Behaviour Therapy and Experimental Psychiatry* **10**, 87–88.

Greenberg, S. and Fowler, R.S., Jr (1980). Kinesthetic biofeedback: a treatment modality for elbow range of motion in hemiplegia. *American Journal of Occupational Therapy* **34**, 738–743.

Hallett, M., Shahani, B.T. and Young, R.R. (1977). Analysis of stereotyped voluntary movements at the elbow with Parkinsons' disease. *Journal of Neurology, Neurosurgery, and Psychiatry* **40**, 1129–1135.

Harris, F.A. (1971). Inapproprioception: a possible sensory basis for athetoid movements. *Physical Therapy* **51**, 761–770.

Harris, F.A., Spelman, F.A. and Hymer, J.W. (1974). Electronic sensory aids as treatment for cerebral palsied children. *Physical Therapy* **54**, 354–365.

Harrison, A. and Connolly, K. (1971). The conscious control of fine levels of neuromuscular firing in spastic and normal subjects. *Developmental Medicine and Child Neurology* **13**, 762–771.

Harrison, D.W., Garrett, J.C., Henderson, D. and Adams, H.E. (1985). Visual and auditory feedback for head tilt and torsion in a spasmodic torticollis patient. *Behaviour Research and Therapy* **23**, 87–88.

Haynes, S.N. (1976). Electromyographic biofeedback treatment of a woman with chronic dysphagia. *Biofeedback and Self-Regulation* **1**, 121–126.

Health and Public Policy Committee, American College of Physicians (1985). Biofeedback for neuromuscular disorders. *Annals of Internal Medicine* **102**, 854–858.

Henschen, T.L. and Burton, N.G. (1978). Treatment of spastic dysphonia by EMG biofeedback. *Biofeedback and Self-Regulation* **3**, 91–97.

Honer, J., Mohr, T. and Roth, R. (1982). Electromyographic biofeedback to dissociate an upper synergy pattern. *Physical Therapy* **62**, 299–303.

Hughes, M. and McLellan, D.L. (1985). Increased co-activation of the upper limb muscles in writer's cramp. *Journal of Neurology, Neurosurgery, and Psychiatry* **48**, 782–787.

Ince, L.P., Leon, M.S. and Christidis, D. (1986). EMG biofeedback for handwriting disabilities: a critical examination of the literature. *Journal of Behaviour Therapy and Experimental Psychiatry* **17**, 95–100.

Inglis, J., Donald, M.W., Monga, T.N., Sproule, M. and Young, M.J. (1984). Electromyographic biofeedback and physical therapy of the hemiplegic upper limb. *Archives of Physical Medicine and Rehabilitation* **65**, 755–759.

Jankel, W.R. (1978). Electromyographic feedback in spasmodic torticollis. *American Journal of Clinical Biofeedback* **1**, 28–29.

Jayne, D., Lees, A.J. and Stern, G.M. (1984). Remission in spasmodic torticollis. *Journal of Neurology, Neurosurgery, and Psychiatry* **47**, 1236–1237.

Jones, G.E., Massong, S.R. and Buckley, M.F. (1983). Treatment of spasmodic torticollis through spasm control and muscle re-education: a case study. *Behavior Therapy* **14**, 178–184.

Keefe, F.J. and Surwit, R.S. (1978). Electromyographic biofeedback: behavioral treatment of neuromuscular disorders. *Journal of Behavioral Medicine* **1**, 13–24.

Kelly, J.L., Baker, M.P. and Wolf, S.L. (1979). Procedures for EMG biofeedback training in involved upper extremities of hemiplegic patients. *Physical Therapy* **59**, 1500–1507.

Kinsman, R.A. and Staudenmayer, H. (1978). Baseline levels in muscle relaxation training. *Biofeedback and Self-Regulation* **3**, 97–104.

Kolotkin, R.L., Billingham, K.A. and Feldman, H.S. (1981). Computers in biofeedback research and therapy. *Behavior Research Methods and Instrumentation* **13**, 532–542.

Korein, J. and Brudny, J. (1976). Integrated EMG feedback in the management of spasmodic torticollis and focal dystonia: a prospective study of 80 patients. In: M.D. Yahr (Ed.) *The Basal Ganglia*. New York: Raven Press.

Korein, J., Brudny, J., Grynbaum, B.B., Sachs-Frankel, G., Weisinger, M. and Levidow, L. (1976). Sensory feedback therapy of spasmodic torticollis and dystonia: results in treatment of 55 patients. In: R. Eldridge and S. Fahn (Eds) *Advances in Neurology*, Vol. 14. New York: Raven Press.

Kukulka, C.G. and Basmajian, J.V. (1975). Assessment of an audio-visual feedback device used in motor training. *American Journal of Physical Medicine* **54**, 194–209.

Kurland, L.T. (1957). Definitions of cerebral palsy and their role in epidemiologic research. *Neurology (Minneapolis)* **7**, 641–654.

Lang, P.J., Troyer, W.G., Twentyman, C.T. and Gatchel, R.J. (1975). Differential effects of heart rate modification training on college students, older males and patients with ischemic heart disease. *Psychosomatic Medicine* **37**, 429–446.

Le Boeuf, A. (1976). The treatment of a severe tremor by electromyogram biofeedback. *Journal of Behaviour Therapy and Experimental Psychiatry* **7**, 59–61.

Lee, K.-H., Hill, E., Johnston, R. and Smiehorowski, T. (1976). Myofeedback for muscle retraining in hemiplegic patients. *Archives of Physical Medicine and Rehabilitation* **57**, 588–591.

Leiper, C.I., Miller, A., Lang, J. and Herman, R. (1981). Sensory feedback for head control in cerebral palsy. *Physical Therapy* **61**, 512–518.

LeVine, W.R. (1983). Behavioral and biofeedback therapy for a functionally impaired musician: a case report. *Biofeedback and Self-Regulation* **8**, 101–107.

Licht, S. (Ed.) (1975). *Stroke and its Rehabilitation*. Physical Medicine Library Series, vol. 12. Baltimore: Williams and Wilkins.

Lippold, O.C.J. (1967). Electromyography. In: P.H. Venables and I. Martin (Eds) *Manual of Psychophysiological Methods*. Amsterdam: North-Holland.

Lord, J. (1984). Cerebral palsy: a clinical approach. *Archives of Physical Medicine and Rehabilitation* **65**, 542–548.

MacPherson, E.L.R. (1967). Control of involuntary movement. *Behaviour Research and Therapy* **5**, 143–145.

Marinacci, A.A. and Horande, M. (1960). Electromyogram in neuromuscular re-education. *Bulletin of the Los Angeles Neurological Society* **25**, 57–71.

Marsden, C.D. (1976). Blepharospasm–oromandibular dystonia syndrome (Brueghel's syndrome) A variant of adult-onset torsion dystonia? *Journal of Neurology, Neurosurgery, and Psychiatry* **39**, 1204–1209.

Marsden, C.D. and Schachter, M. (1981). Assessment of extrapyramidal disorders. *British Journal of Clinical Pharmacology* **11**, 129–151.

Marsden, C.D., Harrison, M.J.G. and Bundey, S. (1976). Natural history of idiopathic torsion dystonia. In: R. Eldridge and S. Fahn (Eds) *Advances in Neurology*, Vol. 14. New York: Raven Press.

Martin, P.R. (1981). Spasmodic torticollis: investigation and treatment using EMG feedback training. *Behavior Therapy* **12**, 247–262.

Matthews, W.B., Beasley, P., Parry-Jones, W. and Garland, G. (1978). Spasmodic torticollis: a combined clinical study. *Journal of Neurology, Neurosurgery, and Psychiatry* **41**, 485–492.

Meares, R. (1973). Behaviour therapy and spasmodic torticollis. *Archives of General Psychiatry* **28**, 104–107.

Meares, R. and Lader, M. (1971). Electromyographic studies in patients with spasmodic torticollis. *Journal of Psychosomatic Research* **15**, 13–18.

Middaugh, S. (1978). EMG feedback as a muscle re-education technique: a controlled study. *Physical Therapy* **58**, 15–22.

Middaugh, S.J. and Miller, M.C. (1980). Electromyographic feedback: effect of voluntary muscle contractions in paretic subjects. *Archives of Physical Medicine and Rehabilitation* **61**, 24–29.

Mims, W.H. (1956). Electromyography in clinical practice. *Southern Medical Journal* **49**, 804–806.

Minear, W.L. (1956). A classification of cerebral palsy. *Pediatrics* **18**, 841–852.

Moldofsky, H. (1971). A psychophysiological study of multiple tics. *Archives of General Psychiatry* **25**, 79–87.

Montgomery, G.K., Howland, E.W., Cleeland, C.S., Mueller, W.C. and Dearing, M.P. (1984). Versatility in computer automation of biofeedback: the Behavioral Assessment and Rehabilitative Training System (BARTS). *Biofeedback and Self-Regulation* **9**, 325–337.

Mroczek, M., Halpern, D. and McHugh, R. (1978). Electromyographic feedback and physical therapy for neuromuscular retraining in hemiplegia. *Archives of Physical Medicine and Rehabilitation* **59**, 258–267.

Mulder, T. and Hulstijn, W. (1984). The effects of fatigue and task repetition on the surface electromyographic signal. *Psychophysiology* **21**, 528–534.

Murphy, J.K. and Fuller, A.K. (1984). Hypnosis and biofeedback as adjunctive therapy in belpharospasm: a case report. *American Journal of Clinical Hypnosis* **27**, 31–37.

Neilson, P.D. and McCaughey, J. (1982). Self-regulation of spasm and spasticity in cerebral palsy. *Journal of Neurology, Neurosurgery, and Psychiatry* **45**, 320–330.

Norton, G.R. (1976). Biofeedback treatment of long-standing eye closure reactions. *Journal of Behaviour Therapy and Experimental Psychiatry* **7**, 278–280.

Nwaobi, O.N. (1986). Effects of body orientation in space on tonic muscle activity of patients with cerebral palsy. *Developmental Medicine and Child Neurology* **28**, 41–44.

Nwaobi, O.M., Brubaker, C.E., Cusick, B. and Sussman, M.D. (1983). Electromyographic investigation of extensor activity in cerebral-palsied children in different seating positions. *Developmental Medicine and Child Neurology* **25**, 175–183.

Obeso, J.A., Rothwell, J.C. and Marsden, C.D. (1981). Simple tics in Gilles de la Tourette's syndrome are not prefaced by a normal premovement EEG potential. *Journal of Neurology, Neurosurgery, and Psychiatry* **44**, 735–738.

O'Reilly, D.E. and Walentynowicz, J.E. (1981). Etiological factors in cerebral palsy: an historical review. *Developmental Medicine and Child Neurology* **23**, 633–642.

Patterson, R.M. and Little, S.C. (1943). Spasmodic torticollis. *Journal of Nervous and Mental Disease* **98**, 571–599.

Peck, D.F. (1977). The use of EMG feedback in the treatment of a severe case of blepharospasm. *Biofeedback and Self-Regulation* **2**, 273–277.

Podivinsky, F. (1968). Torticollis. In: Vinken, P.K. and Bruyn, G.W. (Eds) *Handbook of Clinical Neurology*, Vol. 6. Amsterdam: North-Holland.

Reavley, W. (1975). The use of biofeedback in the treatment of writer's cramp. *Journal of Behaviour Therapy and Experimental Psychiatry* **6**, 335–338.

Robertson, D.W., Lee, W.A. and Jacobs, M. (1984). Single motor-unit control by normal and cerebral-palsied males. *Developmental Medicine and Child Neurology* **26**, 323–327.

Rondot, P., Jedynak, C.-P. and Ferrey, G. (1981). *Le Torticolis Spasmodique.* Paris: Masson.

Rothwell, J.C., Obeso, J.A., Day, B.L. and Marsden, C.D. (1983) Pathophysiology of dystonias. In: J. Desmedt (Ed.) *Motor Control in Health and Disease.* New York: Raven Press.

Rowan, G.E. and Sedlacek, K. (1981). Biofeedback in the treatment of blepharospasm: a case study. *American Journal of Psychiatry* **138**, 1487–1489.

Roxanas, M.R., Thomas, M.R. and Rapp, M.S. (1978). Biofeedback treatment of blepharospasm with spasmodic torticollis. *Canadian Medical Association Journal* **119**, 48–49.

Rugh, J.D. and Schwitzgebel, R.L. (1975). Biofeedback apparatus: list of suppliers. *Behavior Therapy* **6**, 238–240.

Rugh, J.D. and Solberg, W.K. (1974). The identification of stressful stimuli in natural environments using a portable biofeedback unit. Paper presented at a meeting of the Biofeedback Research Society, Colorado Springs.

Russ, K.L. (1975). EMG biofeedback of spasmodic torticollis: a case study. *Annual Proceedings of the Biofeedback Research Society.*

Sachs, D.A. and Mayhall, B. (1971). Behavioral control of spasms using aversive conditioning with a cerebral palsied adult. *Journal of Nervous and Mental Disease* **152**, 362–363.

Sanders, D.B., Massey, E.W. and Buckley, E.C. (1985). EMG monitoring of botulinum toxin in blepharospasm. *Neurology* **35** (Suppl.), 272.

Seeger, B.R. and Caudrey, D.J. (1983). Biofeedback therapy to achieve symmetrical gait in children with hemiplegic cerebral palsy: long-term efficacy. *Archives of Physical Medicine and Rehabilitation* **64**, 160–162.

Seeger, B.R., Caudrey, D.J. and Scholes, J.R. (1981). Biofeedback therapy to achieve symmetrical gait in hemiplegic cerebral palsied children. *Archives of Physical Medicine and Rehabilitation* **62**, 364–368.

Shahani, B.T., Connors, L. and Mohr, J.P. (1977). Electromyographic audiovisual feedback training effect on the motor performance in patients with lesions of the central nervous system. *Archives of Physical Medicine and Rehabilitation* **58**, 519 (Abstract).

Shedivy, D.I. and Kleinman, K.M. (1977). Lack of correlation between frontalis EMG and either neck EMG or verbal ratings of tension. *Psychophysiology* **14**, 182–186.

Sheehy, M.P. and Marsden, C.D. (1982). Writer's cramp – a focal dystonia. *Brain* **105**, 461–480.

Shumaker, R.G. (1980). The response of manual motor functioning in Parkinsonians to frontal EMG biofeedback and progressive relaxation. *Biofeedback and Self-Regulation* **5**, 229–234.

Smith, K.U. and Henry, J.P. (1967). Cybernetic foundations for rehabilitation. *American Journal of Physical Medicine* **46**, 379–467.

Soderberg, G.L. and Cook, T.M. (1983). An electromyographic analysis of qiadriceps femoris muscle setting and straight leg raising. *Physical Therapy* **63**, 1434–1438.

Spearing, D.L. and Poppen, R. (1974). The use of feedback in the reduction of foot-dragging in a cerebral palsied client. *Journal of Nervous and Mental Disease* **159**, 148–151.

Stephenson, N. (1976). Successful treatment of blepharospasm with relaxation training and biofeedback. *Biofeedback and Self-Regulation* **1**, 331 (Abstract).

Stroebel, C.F. and Glueck, B.C. (1973). Biofeedback treatment in medicine and psychiatry: an ultimate placebo? *Seminars in Psychiatry* **5**, 379–393.

Takebe, K. and Basmajian, J.V. (1976). Gait analysis in stroke patients to assess treatments of foot-drop. *Archives of Physical Medicine and Rehabilitation* **57**, 305–310.

Takebe, K., Kukulka, C.G., Narayan, M.G. and Basmajian, J.V. (1976). Biofedback treatment of foot drop after stroke compared with standard rehabilitation technique (Part 2): affect on nerve conduction velocity and spasticity. *Archives of Physical Medicine and Rehabilitation* **57**, 9–11.

Turczynski, B.E., Hartje, W. and Sturm, W. (1984). Electromyographic feedback treatment of chronic hemiparesis: an attempt to quantify treatment effects. *Archives of Physical Medicine and Rehabilitation* **65**, 526–528.

Uchiyama, K., Lutterjohann, M. and Shah, M.D. (1977). Biofeedback-assisted desensitization treatment of writer's cramp. *Journal of Behaviour Therapy and Experimental Psychiatry* **8**, 169–171.

Walmsley, R.P., Crichton, L. and Droog, B. (1981). Music as a feedback mechanism for teaching head control to severely handicapped children: a pilot study. *Developmental Medicine and Child Neurology* **23**, 739–746.

Liles, C.M. and Karni, Y. (1983). The measurement of muscle strength in patients with peripheral neuromuscular disorders. *Journal of Neurology, Neurosurgery, and Psychiatry* **46**, 1006–1013.

Williams, R.B. (1975). HR feedback in the treatment of torticollis: a case report. *Psychophysiology* **12**, 237 (Abstract).

Wolf, S.L. (1983). Electromyographic biofeedback applications to stroke patients: a critical review. *Physical Therapy* **63**, 1448–1459.

Wolf, S.L. and Binder-Macleod, S.A. (1983a). Electromyographic biofeedback applications to the hemiplegic patient: changes in lower extremity neuromuscular and functional status. *Physical Therapy* **63**, 1404–1413.

Wolf, S.L. and Binder-Macleod, S.A. (1983b). Electromyographic biofeedback applications to the hemiplegic patient: changes in upper extremity neuromuscular and functional status. *Physical Therapy* **63**, 1393–1402.

Wolf, S.L., Baker, P. and Kelly, J.L. (1979). EMG biofeedback in stroke: effect of patient charactristics. *Archives of Physical Medicine and Rehabilitation* **60**, 96–102.

Wolf, S.L., Baker, P. and Kelly, J.L. (1980). EMG biofeedback in stroke: a 1-year follow-up on the effect of patient characteristics. *Archives of Physical Medicine and Rehabilitation* **61**, 351–355.

Wooldridge, C.P. and Russell, G. (1976). Head position training with the cerebral palsied child: an application of biofeedback techniques. *Archives of Physical Medicine and Rehabilitation* **57**, 407–414.

Yates, A.J. (1980). *Biofeedback and the Modification of Behavior*. New York: Plenum.

Author Index

Abel, G.G. 181, 189–90, 195, 204–5, 212, 432, 436, 454, 460
Abrahamson, D.J. 181, 204, 434, 437
Abrams, R. 358, 375–6, 378, 383, 385, 391, 392
Abramson, D. 475, 491
Abramson, P.R. 429, 430, 437, 439
Ackles, P.A. 25, 38, 74, 102
Adams, A.S. 227, 235
Adams, D.F. 263, 275
Adams, H. 422, 438
Adams, H.E. 176–7, 185–6, 188, 196, 204, 206–7, 213, 558, 564, 579
Adams, N.E. 22, 33
Adamson, U. 261, 278
Ad hoc Committee of the Dystocia Medical Research Foundation 561, 576
Adler, C.S. 206
Adler, L. 338, 355
Adler, L.E. 66, 69
Adler, R. 449, 459
Agras, S. 466, 564, 576
Agras, W.S. 29, 39, 180, 183, 190–2, 198, 204, 207, 209, 287, 294, 303, 319, 324, 326, 327, 426, 437, 453–5, 459, 462–3, 466
Agren, H. 382, 385

Ahles, T.A. 205
Aitken, R.C. 520, 553
Akiskal, H.P. 56, 59, 66
Akiskal, H.S. 358, 385
Alavi, A. 156, 173
Albani, G. 299, 308
Alderman, E.A. 222, 235
Alderman, M.H. 258, 270
Aldridge, V. 299, 308
Aldrige, V.J. 356
Alexander, A.A. 86, 103
Alexander, A.B. 180, 183, 200, 202, 204, 211, 224, 226, 234, 245, 246, 531, 543, 547, 553, 560, 568, 576
Alexander, C. 161, 171
Alexander, F. 259, 270, 456, 459, 494, 514
Allen, C.R. 66
Allen, E. 470, 474, 491
Allen, L.M. 473, 494
Allen, M.T. 450, 463, 543, 547
Allen, R.A. 192, 204, 459
Allen, S.N. 161, 165
Allison, T. 151, 174, 342, 356
Alm, T. 410, 412
Almy, T.P. 509, 514
Alterman, I.S. 61, 69
Altschuler, H.I. 195, 206
Alvarez, W.C. 500, 514

Amadeo, M. 154, 173, 382, 391, 402, 405, 417
Amaducci, L. 70
Amberson, J. 433, 438
Ambrosini, E. 244, 263, 265, 270, 271
American Psychiatric Association 56, 66, 120, 122–4, 131, 155, 164, 185, 204, 255, 271, 310–12, 324, 332, 351, 358, 385, 394, 395, 407, 412, 421, 436
American Thoracic Society Committee on Diagnostic Standards for Nontuberculosis Respiratory Disease 520, 547
Aminoff, M.J. 7, 33
Ananth, J. 335, 351
Anastasiades, P. 5, 34
Ancoli, S. 86, 100
Anderer, P. 53, 69
Anderson, A.B. 87, 98
Anderson, C.D. 190, 204
Anderson, D. 263, 271
Anderson, J.R. 108, 110, 131
Anderson, K. 432, 439
Anderson, M.A. 67
Anderson, N. 270–1
Anderson, S. 276, 325
Anderson, S.D. 522–3, 547, 551
Andrasik, F. 11, 23, 24, 31, 33, 88, 98, 205, 226, 234, 447, 461
Andreasen, N.C. 395, 412
Andreassi, J.L. 23, 33, 53, 66, 177, 193, 204
Andrén, L. 272, 451, 459
Andresen, B. 91, 98
Andrew, R.J. 8, 33
Andrews, H.B. 153, 165
Andrykowski, M.A. 506, 516
Angelakos, E.T. 450, 451, 459, 461
Anisman, H. 219, 234
Anliker, M. 493
Antes, J.R. 155, 174
Anthony, E.J. 15, 43
Anthony, J.C. 326
Appelbaum, K.A. 205
Appleby, I.L. 271, 276, 325, 551
Arena, J.G. 6, 11, 24, 29–31, 33, 42, 88, 98, 234
Armbrecht, U. 501, 514
Arnetz, B.B. 254, 271
Arns, P.A. 236
Arns, P.C. 275

Asato, T. 254, 277
Asberg, M. 334, 336, 351, 356
Ascher, L.M. 182, 211
Aserinsky, E. 432, 436
Ashihara, T. 265, 278
Askevold, F. 261, 278
Atanacio, B. 157, 165
Athanasian, R. 204
Auadiri, M.R. 543, 552
Averill, J.R. 74, 99, 162, 166
Avery, D. 48, 66
Avery-Clark, C.A. 181, 186, 204
Ax, A.F. 9, 33, 246, 250, 271, 284, 294, 303, 446, 459
Axmann, D. 380, 391
Axelrod, S. 157, 165
Ayman, D. 258, 271

Babb, T.L. 151, 169
Bächer, P. 88, 100
Baer, D.M. 199, 204
Baer, P.E. 260, 272, 458, 459
Bagg, C.E. 364, 385
Bagger, J.P. 535, 553
Bagshaw, M.H. 165
Bailine, S.H. 340, 352
Bakal, D.A. 181, 204
Bakan, P. 162, 165
Baker, L.K. 445, 459
Baker, M.P. 570–1, 577, 580
Baker, S. 30, 36, 84, 100
Baker, T.B. 180, 192, 206, 226, 235
Balke, B. 535, 547
Ball, R. 385
Ball, T.S. 569, 577
Ballard, P. 565, 577
Baltes, P.B. 77, 102
Bancroft, J. 428, 431, 436, 437
Bancroft, J.H.J. 315, 325
Bandeira, M. 26, 32, 33
Bandura, A. 22, 33, 176, 204–5, 256, 271
Banich, N.T. 146, 170
Barbara, H.C. 214
Barbeite, L. 251, 272
Barber, C. 153, 165
Barchas, J.D. 205, 256, 271
Bardach, E. 118, 119, 131
Baribeau-Braun, J. 150, 165, 172
Barkemeyer, C.A. 566, 577
Barker, W.F. 444, 445, 460
Barlow, D.H. 22, 26, 29, 32–3, 37, 121, 127, 132, 176–7, 179–80, 183,

186–7, 192, 194, 204–5, 209, 213, 284, 305, 310–12, 316, 318, 324–5, 327, 422, 426, 434, 437, 559, 577
Barnes, P.J. 530, 547, 554
Barness, L.A. 161, 165
Baron, M. 49, 66, 359, 387
Barrere, M. 369, 386
Barrett, C.L. 27, 42
Barrett, K. 403, 410, 412
Barron, K.D. 11, 33
Barrowclough, C. 27, 42
Barry, S.M. 210
Barstuble, J.A. 180, 188, 205
Barto, P.S. 556, 570, 577
Bartrop, R.W. 161, 165
Basajian, J.V. 558–60, 563, 570–1, 573–4, 576–78, 583
Bashore, T.R. 10, 35, 300, 304
Basilio, C.A. 226, 235
Basilvesky, A. 87, 98
Bass, A. 208
Bass, C. 535–8, 540–1, 546–9
Bat, I. 509, 517
Battegay, R. 447, 464
Battig, K. 70
Bauer, R.M. 130, 131
Baum, A. 180, 197, 205–6, 249–50, 271
Baumann, R. 449, 460
Baxter, L.R. 369, 371–2, 383, 385
Bear, L. 258, 276
Beary, J.F. 223, 234
Beasley, P. 564, 581
Beaty, T. 182, 205
Beatty, J. 180, 207, 225, 234
Beaumont, W. 495, 514
Beaupre, A. 524, 552
Bechtereva, N.P. 136, 165
Beck, A.T. 125, 131, 311–12, 324
Beck, J.G. 204, 422, 434, 436, 437, 439
Becker, J.V. 190, 195, 204, 212, 432, 436
Becker, R. 426, 437
Beckmann, H. 148, 169
Beech, H.R. 342, 347, 351–2
Beech, K.T. 341, 352
Beere, P.A. 268, 271
Beers, J.R. 411, 413
Beevers, D.G. 442, 460
Begleiter, H. 51, 66, 151, 172, 199, 212, 402–3, 412
Beidel, D.C. 127, 134, 317, 324, 327
Beiman, I. 227, 238
Belandres, P.V. 572, 577–8

Bell, B. 70
Bell, C. 428, 437
Bellack, A.S. 176, 205, 212, 264, 276, 448, 464
Bellone, E. 543, 552
Bellur, S.N. 363, 389
Belmaker, R.H. 66
Bender, M.E. 179, 210
Benjamin, S. 526, 548
Benmair, Y. 501, 514, 515
Bennett, D.H. 227, 236
Bennett-Levy, J. 287, 303
Benowitz, N. 188, 208
Ben-Shakhar, G. 83, 99
Benson, H. 23, 33, 223, 227, 234, 236, 259, 274–5, 278, 452–3, 457, 460, 466
Benson, K.L. 48, 70
Bentler, P.M. 430, 437
Benzier, G. 165
Ben-Zvi, Z. 531, 548
Beradelli, A. 564–5, 574, 577
Berdzen, D. 284, 305
Berg, W.K. 32, 38, 86, 101
Berger, P.A. 48, 70, 402, 417
Bergman-Losman, B. 260, 274
Bergstrom, K. 171
Berkowitz, R. 15, 42, 400, 417
Berkson, D.M. 259, 278
Berler, E.S. 210, 264, 275
Berman, K.F. 360, 392
Bernacca, G. 212
Bernal, G.A.A. 223, 237
Bernard, B.A. 31, 43
Bernhardt, N. 155, 174
Bernstein, A.S. 10, 13–15, 34, 43, 397, 399, 409, 411–12
Bernstein, D.A. 22, 34, 178–80, 182, 194–6, 201, 205, 223, 234
Bernstein, I.L. 506, 514, 521, 548
Bernstein, L. 528, 552
Bergstrom, K. 152
Bertilsson, L. 334, 336, 351, 356
Bes, A. 369, 386
Better, W. 263, 271
Betts, G.H. 117, 131
Beumer, H.M. 541, 550
Bickford, A.F. 246, 266, 269, 272, 449, 460
Biersner, R. 6, 42
Bigelow, G. 213
Bigger, J.T. 52, 67, 347, 352

Bihari, B. 66
Billingham, K.A. 558, 580
Billman, G.E. 222, 234
Binder-MacLeod, S.A. 571–3, 577, 583
Bindman, E. 567, 577
Birbaumer, N. 187, 207, 344, 356, 578
Bird, B.L. 569, 578
Birk, L. 215, 234
Birley, J.L.T. 400, 412
Birren, J.E. 428, 439
Biziere, K. 159, 173
Black, A. 331, 352
Black, G. W. 457, 460
Blackburn, I.M. 27, 34
Blackwell, B. 510, 518
Blain, A. 470, 491
Blair, D.A. 363, 385
Blair, S.N. 221, 237
Blanchard, E.B. 6, 11, 21–4, 26, 31–4, 88,
    98, 121, 132, 180–2, 189–90, 193,
    204–5, 233–4, 310, 312, 324, 426,
    432, 436–7, 447, 454, 460–1, 464,
    559, 577
Blank, S. 99
Blaser, A. 525, 550
Blashfield, R.K. 12, 14, 34, 39, 185, 211
Blau, J.N. 158, 159, 165
Bleecker, E.R. 527, 551, 552
Bleuler, E. 394, 412
Blevings, G. 291, 292, 294, 305
Bloch, D.L. 22, 34
Bloemink, R. 538, 549
Bloom, L. 475, 491
Blouin, D.C. 31, 35, 43
Blowers, G.H. 324
Blumberg, H. 473, 489, 492
Blumenstein, R. 559, 577
Blumenthal, J.A. 183, 210, 267–8, 271,
    273
Blythe, S.T. 80, 103
Bock, R.D. 81, 99
Bohlen, J. 429, 437
Bohlin, G. 256, 260, 265, 269, 271, 292,
    303
Boice, R. 179, 213, 318, 327
Boller, F. 139, 172, 385
Bollinger, A. 478, 491, 493
Bolz, J. 379, 387
Bonham, K.G. 27, 34
Bonilla, E. 67
Bonn, J.A. 314, 318, 323–4, 546, 548
Bonnevie, O. 506, 514

Boomsa, D.I. 54, 66
Bootzin, R.R. 180, 214
Borcovec, T.D. 291, 302
Borden, R.J. 119, 132
Borello, G. 543, 552
Borer, J.S. 272
Borghi, C. 244, 263, 270, 271
Boring, E.G. 136, 165
Borkovec, T.D. 22, 28, 30, 34, 178, 180,
    182, 185–6, 192, 196, 205, 209,
    222–3, 234, 347, 352
Bornheimer, J.F. 278
Bornstein, P.H. 182, 205
Bortolussi, L. 221, 235
Boschi, S. 263, 270, 271
Boswell, P.C. 227, 234
Botskarev, V. 376, 390
Bouchard, C. 229, 234
Bouchard, M.A. 26, 32, 33
Bouhuys, A. 524, 548
Boulenger, J.P. 255, 271
Boulougouris, J.C. 115, 131, 293, 308,
    344, 346, 352, 354
Bourianoff, G.G. 260, 272, 458, 459
Bourne, R.C. 353
Boushey, H.A. 521, 524, 529, 548
Boven, K.H. 15, 42
Bowd, A.D. 287, 304
Bower, G.H. 108, 112, 113, 131
Bowers, E.J. 444, 460
Bowes, G. 543, 552
Boyd, G. 301, 306
Boyd, J.H. 352
Boyd, S. 5
Boylan, C.R. 7, 37, 287, 304
Braaten, J.R. 362, 386
Bradley, B.W. 226, 234
Bradley, L.A. 217, 234
Bradley, M.M. 109, 115, 132
Brady, J.P. 294, 304, 463
Brady, J.V. 496, 506, 514, 516
Braff, D. 157, 167
Brandstater, M.E. 573, 577
Brandt, D. 76, 103
Brantley, P.J. 566, 577
Brantly, P. 185, 213
Brashear, R.E. 533, 537, 539, 548
Brecher, M. 402, 403, 412
Breier, A. 324
Bremer, J. 225, 238
Brennan, P.J. 443, 460
Brener, J. 297, 304

Brenne, L. 284, 305
Brenner, R.P. 374, 376–7, 385
Brenner, S.-O. 271
Brett, J.M. 202, 209
Breyer-Pfaff, U. 365, 385
Brezniz, S. 208
Brickner, R.M. 352
Bridger, W.H. 398, 415
Brigham, T.A. 176, 206
Brilmayer, H. 428, 439
Brines, D.M. 528
Briquet, P. 157, 165
Brisson, G. 222, 239
Brockington, I.F. 394, 395, 412
Brod, J. 261, 263, 269, 271, 449, 460
Brody, A.W. 525, 549
Brody, K. 525, 528, 548, 552
Brody, M. 264, 271
Bromm, B. 511, 514
Bronniman, S. 521, 548
Brooks, F.P. 498, 514
Brooks, S.M. 523, 548
Brotman, A.W. 340, 353
Brow, T.D. 162, 167, 168
Brown, A. 260, 272, 447, 460
Brown, C. 492, 509, 514
Brown, C.C. 177, 203, 205, 210
Brown, D.M. 558, 577
Brown, E.L. 525, 549
Brown, F.W. 332, 352
Brown, G. 400, 412, 470, 474, 481, 491
Brown, G.E. 261, 275, 449, 462
Brown, M. 451, 460
Brown, R.A. 181, 193, 195, 199, 205, 210
Brown, S.-L. 363, 385
Brown, W.A. 254, 271
Brownell, K.D. 180, 205
Brubaker, C.E. 569, 581
Brüchle, H.A. 499, 516
Brundy, J. 181, 206, 562–3, 572–3, 576–8, 580
Bruni, A. 70
Brunner, H.R. 258, 276, 444, 465
Bruno, J. 180, 207
Bruno, R.L. 363, 368, 383, 385
Buchanan, D.C. 22, 39
Buchsbaum, M.S. 16, 37, 51, 55–6, 59, 61, 66–7, 69–70, 369–72, 386
Buckley, E.C. 565, 582
Buckley, M.F. 563, 580
Buda, A.J. 251, 277
Budzynski, T.H. 206

Buell, J.C. 39, 235, 464
Buelle, U. 369, 287
Bühler, F.R. 258, 260, 275–7, 447, 464
Bukantz, S.C. 528, 552
Bundey, S. 561, 581
Bunge, M. 202, 206
Bunney, W.E. 372, 386
Burch, N. 195, 206
Burde, R.M. 155, 166
Burgess, B.F. 525, 549
Burgess, M. 446, 462
Burish, T.G. 210, 217, 225, 234, 236
Burke, J.D. 326
Burker, J. 331, 355
Burns, K.L. 187, 193, 206
Burnside, Z.G. 571, 578
Burr, W. 89, 103
Burrows, B. 521, 548
Burshill, D. 571, 578
Burton, A. 477, 479, 491
Burton, A.C. 443, 463
Burton, L. 374, 387
Burton, L.A. 146, 170
Burton, N.G. 574, 579
Bush, C. 184, 206, 221, 225, 234, 235
Butensky, A. 466
Butler, F.K. 156, 172, 173
Butler, R.W. 368, 392
Butollo, W. 297, 304
Butter, H.J. 362, 365, 366, 389
Buzzi, R. 70
Bykov, K.M. 496, 514
Byrne, D.G. 364–5, 386

Cacioppo, J.T. 18, 23, 29–30, 34, 86, 97, 99–100, 224, 236, 298, 305, 556, 559, 579
Caddell, J.M. 179, 210
Calhoun, K.S. 176, 177, 206, 213
Callaway, E. 35
Cameron, I.R. 527, 529, 552
Cameron, O.G. 251, 252, 277, 326
Cammack, I. 514
Campajola, P. 340, 353
Campbell, D.T. 84, 99
Campbell, K.B. 150, 172
Campbell, M.E. 79, 99
Candrey, D.J. 558, 569, 576, 582
Cann, P.A. 501, 508–10, 514
Cannon, D.S. 180, 192, 206
Cannon, E.H. 402, 416
Cannon, W.B. 243, 250, 272, 497–8, 514

Cantor, W. 143, 171
Cantwell, J. 267, 272
Capone, C. 374, 389
Cappelletti, J. 385
Capriotti, R. 270, 274
Cardon, P.V. 246, 279, 448, 467
Carlson, J.G. 226, 235
Carmick, E. 474, 491
Carnahan, J.E. 444, 460
Carnrike, C.L.M. 566, 577
Caroff, S. 387
Carol, M.P. 223, 234
Caron, M. 474, 493
Carpenter, W. 385
Carpenter, W.T. 15, 44, 397, 399, 418
Carr, D.B. 311, 324
Carr, V. 158, 165
Carrigan, W.F. 212
Carrington, P. 227, 237
Carroll, B.J. 56, 66, 358, 387
Carroll, D. 5, 6, 23, 34, 239
Carruthers, M. 297, 308, 459, 464
Carson, R.E. 368, 390
Carson, T.P. 180, 206
Carver, G. 470, 491
Caspar, F. 362, 391
Castillo, C.A. 535, 553
Cataldo, M.F. 217, 235, 569, 578
Catanese, A.A. 569, 576, 578
Catania, A.C. 176, 206
Catania, J.J. 362, 386
Cattell, R.B. 142, 170
Cautela, J.R. 182, 206
Cerny, J.A. 310, 324
Cervero, F. 516
Chabrol, H. 369, 370, 372, 386
Chai, H. 211, 525, 531, 547, 548
Chalkeley, A.J. 545, 548
Chan-Yeung, M. 523, 548
Chape, C. 446, 462
Chape, D. 257, 274
Chaplin, T.C. 212
Chapman, C.R. 158, 169
Chapman, J.P. 62, 66, 360, 386, 400, 404,
    410, 412
Chapman, L.J. 62, 66, 360, 386, 400, 404,
    410, 412
Charles, G. 370, 383, 386, 391
Charles, P. 145, 174
Charles, R. 474, 491
Charney, D.S. 314, 316, 324, 327
Chase, W.G. 352

Chaudry, R. 325
Chernik, D. 48, 67
Chesney, A.P. 257, 274
Chesney, M.A. 457, 460
Cheung, M.N. 87, 99
Chiang, S.T. 525, 553
Chila, A.G. 236
Childs, H. 514
Chiu, J.T. 531, 554
Chobanian, A.V. 278
Chomsky, N. 109, 131
Chowdhrey, S.M. 373, 390
Christidis, D. 566, 579
Christie, M.J. 32, 36, 86, 100, 365, 387
Chucker, F. 473, 477, 480, 491
Chumoskey, J. 481, 491
Ciesielski, K.T. 342, 352
Ciminero, A.R. 6, 35, 177, 206
Claghorn, J.L. 222, 237, 253, 255, 276,
    369, 389
Claiborn, J.M. 21, 40, 128, 134
Clancy, J. 297, 305
Claridge, G. 8, 9, 34
Clark, D.M. 311, 324, 543–6, 548, 553
Clark, E. 531, 550
Clark, I.M. 158, 169
Clark, L. 272
Clark, L.A. 87, 99
Clark, M.S. 113, 131
Clarke, L. 227, 236
Clarke, P.S. 526, 530, 548, 553
Clarkson, T.B. 268, 275, 276
Clayton, P.J. 333, 354
Cleary, P.J. 79, 90, 99
Cleeland, C.S. 558, 562, 581
Clemens, W.J. 225, 238
Clement, D.L. 89, 103
Clement, J. 524, 554
Clement, R.A. 7, 37
Clements, K. 25, 34
Clifford, C.A. 332, 352
Clifford-Rose, F. 143, 168
Clifton, R.K. 353
Cluss, P.A. 530–1, 548
Coates, T.J. 180, 182, 206
Cobb, J. 354
Cobb, S. 259, 272
Coffman, J.D. 472, 481, 482, 487, 488,
    491, 492–3
Cohen, A. 428, 439, 491
Cohen, A.S. 312, 324
Cohen, B.H. 80, 103

Cohen, D.J. 191, 205, 206
Cohen, G. 137, 165
Cohen, H. 429, 432, 437
Cohen, J. 394, 413
Cohen, M. 463
Cohen, M.C. 453, 461
Cohen, R. 385, 402, 412, 472, 482, 491
Cohn, C.K. 294, 304
Cole, H.W. 74, 102
Cole, J.D. 52, 70
Colebatch, H.J. 526, 553
Coleman, D. 190, 207
Coleman, E. 433, 438
Coleman, T.G. 248, 274, 451, 462
Coles, M.G.H. 5, 10, 17, 22–3, 26, 31–2, 34–5, 53, 67, 177–8, 197, 200–2, 205–6, 292, 300, 304
Colla, P. 542, 549
Coller, F. 472–3, 475, 481, 487, 489, 491
Collet, L. 567, 578
Collette, P. 259, 278
Collins, F.H. 260, 272, 458, 459
Collu, R. 229, 238
Comper, P. 140, 170
Compernolle, T. 546, 548
Comroe, J.H. 534, 548
Conally, P.M. 67
Cone, J.D. 9, 20, 34, 177, 206
Conneally, D.M. 70
Connolly, J. 294, 304, 398, 412, 414
Connolly, J.F. 140, 143, 146, 153, 165, 167–8, 170
Connolly, K. 569, 579
Connor, W.H. 227, 235, 292, 304
Conors, L. 571, 582
Conrad, D.G. 496, 514
Conway, A. 168, 539, 549
Conway, F.J. 259, 272, 275
Cook, B.L. 373, 383, 386
Cook, E.W. 107–8, 117, 119, 132, 133, 301–2, 304
Cook, M. 470, 491
Cook, T.M. 574, 583
Cooke, E. 139, 174, 365, 391
Cooper, J.E. 11, 44, 144, 153, 165, 174, 394, 418
Cooper, L.A. 110, 134
Cooper, R. 35, 297, 306, 356
Coppen, A. 365–6, 390, 409, 416
Corah, N. 52, 68
Corbisiero, R. 221, 235
Corby, J.C. 223, 235

Cordasco, E.M. 533, 548
Corder-Bolz, C.R. 81, 99
Cornblatt, B. 61, 66, 400, 413
Correa, E.I. 180, 195, 206
Corse, C. 267, 272
Cortese, T. 449, 462
Corvell, W. 331, 352, 358, 392
Costa, F.V. 244, 263, 270, 271
Costa, P.T. 544, 548
Costello, M. 239
Cotch, P.A. 31, 33, 88, 98
Cottam, G.L. 224, 236
Cottier, C. 232, 235, 453, 458, 460
Cottington, E.M. 446, 460
Cottraux, J.A. 567, 578
Counts, D.K. 563, 578
Coursey, R.D. 56, 61, 66, 69
Covina, N.A. 525, 549
Cowan, R. 261, 277
Cowley, A.W. Jr 248, 274
Cox, B.J. 310, 326
Cox, D.J. 225, 235
Cox, G.B. 161, 166
Cox, R.H. 222, 235
Cox, T. 9, 34
Coyne, L. 70
Craig, K.D. 210
Craigwyle, N. 264, 272
Cram, J.L. 144, 165
Crandall, P.H. 151, 169
Craske, M. 127, 132
Crawford, H.J. 161, 165
Creer, T.L. 211, 216–17, 235, 236, 524, 532, 548, 550, 554
Crews, E.L. 368, 392
Crichton, L. 569, 583
Crider, A.B. 14, 34
Crighel, E. 373, 383, 386
Critelli, J.W. 433, 439
Crits-Christoph, P. 6, 35, 463
Cronbach, L.J. 78, 89–90, 97, 99
Crookes, T.G. 364, 385
Cropp, G. 531, 547
Cross, P.D. 277
Crosskey, A. 139, 166
Crow, T.J. 15, 36, 395, 399, 412–13
Crowe, R.R. 297, 305
Crowley, A.W. 451, 462
Crowther, J.H. 453, 460
Crumpton, C.W. 535, 553
Cueves, J. 178, 209, 221, 236
Cullen, T.D. 88, 103

Cumberbatch, J. 374, 390
Cunningham, C.E. 569, 578
Cunningham, J. 437
Cupoli, J.M. 161, 165
Cusich, B. 571, 581
Curtis, G.C. 251–2, 254, 277, 295, 304, 326
Cuthbert, B.N. 107, 109, 115, 132

Dahl, C.K. 258, 272
Dahlem, N.W. 525, 551
Dahlén, P. 373, 386
Dahme, B. 530, 553
Dajas, F. 251, 272
Dalais, J.C. 70
Dalessio, D.J. 181, 191, 206, 207
Dalton, R. 157, 166
Danahar, B.G. 181, 206
Danahy, S. 378, 387
Dancu, C.V. 317, 324
Danielsson, T. 246, 269, 273
Danker-Brown, P. 211
Dargent, J. 343, 356
Darling, R.C. 364, 386
Darrow, C.W. 149, 166
Davey, G. 10, 35
David, I. 405, 412
Davidson, D.M. 222, 235
Davidson, L.M. 180, 197, 206
Davidson, P.O. 210
Davidson, R.A. 446, 465
Davidson, R.J. 97, 99, 160, 166, 360, 375–8, 383, 386, 388, 391
Davies, P.T.G. 143, 168
Davies, S. 276
Davies, S.O. 325, 553
Davis, A.E. 557, 578
Davis, C.M. 23, 42, 213
Davis, D. 432, 437
Davis, G.C. 372, 386
Davis, J.F. 559, 578
Davis, J.M. 68, 407, 415
Davis, K.L. 161, 173
Davis, L. 164, 168
Davis, M.H. 177, 193, 211
Davis, P.A. 373, 386
Davison, M.A. 139, 166
Dawson, A.M. 509, 517
Dawson, M.E. 10–11, 16, 23, 35, 37, 40, 362, 365, 367, 386, 396–7, 399–400, 404, 410–11, 413, 416
Day, B.L. 561, 564, 577, 582

Day, J.H. 527, 552
Dearing, M.P. 558, 581
DeBacher, G. 558, 571, 577, 578
Debecker, J. 151, 166
De Carlo, R. 374, 389
Dedon, M.F. 86, 100
Deecke, L. 354, 380, 389
Deering, W.M. 217, 221, 225, 237
Defares, P.B. 537, 540, 541, 550, 554
Deffenbacher, J.L. 180, 199, 209
Degenne, D. 159, 173
DeGood, D.E. 227, 235
Dehof, K.A. 223, 237
de Jong, J.B. 21, 40, 128, 134
Dekker, J. 128, 132
D'Elia, G. 373, 386, 387
DeLisi, L.E. 385, 386
Delius, W. 264, 279
Delpierre, S. 524, 552
Dembroski, T.M. 265, 267, 272
Dembrowski, P.M. 211
DeMeester, T.R. 505, 515
Demeter, S. 533, 548
Denby, L. 99, 272
Denenberg, V.H. 159, 166
D'Eon, J.L. 162, 173
Depue, R.A. 13, 35, 60, 66, 366, 386
DeQuattro, V. 278, 461, 466
De Rijke, W. 376, 391
Desai, N. 475, 492
DeShazo, R.D. 522, 549
Desmedt, J.E. 35, 151
De Swart, J.C.G. 533, 537–40, 550
De Swiet, M. 443, 465
Detre, T.P. 211, 358, 389
Devenport, C.D. 335, 352
Devenport, J.A. 335, 352
Devereaux, R.B. 261, 272, 444, 465
DeWied, D. 249, 272
DeWitt, G.W. 162, 166
Diamond, E.L. 260, 264, 272, 446, 460
Diamond, R. 167
Diamond, S. 181, 207
Dibianco, P. 428, 439
Di Bona, G.F. 248, 273
Dickson, B. 195, 212
Diefendorf, A.R. 154, 166
Dietikor, K.E. 528, 552
Dillon, D.J. 276, 325, 551
Dillon, O. 325
Dimberg, U. 243, 248, 273, 291, 307, 312, 326, 449, 461

Dimond, S.J. 138, 157, 166
Dimsdale, J.E. 89, 99, 260, 272, 447, 460
DiNardo, P.A. 121, 132, 205, 310, 324
Diner, B.C. 380, 386
Dinicola, V.F. 333, 356
Dinning, J.S. 499, 517
Dirks, J.F. 525, 526, 549, 553
Dittmar, K. 287, 305
Ditto, B. 184, 206, 225, 234, 451, 460
Dixhoorn, J. van 537, 549
Djenderedjiam, A. 190, 204, 432, 436
Dodge, R. 154, 166
Doelle, W. 541, 551
Doerr, H.O. 12, 43, 365–6, 368, 391, 392, 565, 577
Dolchetti, A. 543, 552
Doleys, D.M. 6, 35, 180, 207
Donald, M.W. 573, 579
Donat, D.C. 365, 367, 386
Donchin, E. 10, 17, 32, 34–5, 53, 67, 177, 206, 300, 304, 379, 386, 401–2, 411, 413
Dongier, M. 343, 356
Doppelt, H.G. 337, 352
Dorheim, T.A. 230, 235
Dorus, E. 68, 415
Dorward, J. 310, 326
Dotevall, G. 497, 507, 515
Douglas, R.J. 149, 166
Dowdeswell, R. 553
Dowling-Simmerman, S. 385
Downey, J.A. 363, 386, 489, 492, 493
Doyle, A.E. 219, 235
Doyle, G. 507, 515
Drachman, D. 70
Dranon, M. 56, 66
Drayer, J.I.M. 89, 103, 443, 466
Drayna, D. 49, 66
Dreyfuss, F. 501, 515
Drisak, J. 432, 439
Drobuy, H. 260, 277, 447, 465
Drolette, M.E. 446, 461
Droog, B. 571, 583
Drumer, D. 66
Dubois, A. 506, 515
Dubois, A.B. 525, 549
Duchmann, E.G. 31, 35
Dudley, A.B. 543, 549
Duffy, E. 8, 35, 97, 99
Duffy, F.H. 163, 166
Duivenbode, H.J. van 537, 549
Dunbar, H.F. 245–6, 259, 272

Duncan, C.C. 402–3, 413, 416
Duncan, W. 338, 353
Duncan-Johnson, C.C. 292, 304, 402, 413
Dunne, M.P. 560, 578
Durac, J. 33, 38
Dursteler, M.R. 154, 172
Duston, H.P. 456, 462
Duthie, H.L. 500, 515
Duvic, M. 472, 473, 478, 494
Dworkin, B.R. 225, 238, 264, 272, 558, 560, 578
Dworkin, S. 578
Dykman, R.A. 380, 386

Ebert, M.H. 506, 515
Edelberg, R. 32, 36, 64, 66, 86, 100, 365, 387, 398, 415
Eden, S. 501, 514
Edmonson, H. 251, 272
Edwards, A. 432, 437
Edwards, J.A. 8, 27, 32, 36, 74, 100, 229
Edwards, S. 239
Efron, B. 86, 99
Egan, B.M. 260, 277, 447, 465
Egeland, J.A. 50, 66
Eggertsen, R. 272
Ehlers, A. 29, 39, 314, 315, 221, 324, 326
Eisdorfer, C. 217, 235
Ekman, P. 18, 35
Elbert, T. 344, 356
Eliasson, K. 256, 260, 271, 272, 449, 460
Eliot, R.S. 39, 235, 464
Elithorn, A. 139, 166
Elliott, G.R. 217, 235
Ellis, J.P. 535, 547
Elveback, L.R. 261, 279
Emery, G. 311, 312, 324
Emmelkamp, P.M.G. 188, 194, 207, 320, 325
Ender, P. 568, 578
Endicott, J. 358, 391, 394–5, 413, 417
Eneroth, P. 271
Engel, B.T. 5–6, 9, 17, 32, 35, 261, 266, 269, 270, 272–4, 449–50, 452, 460–1, 463, 502, 509, 515, 517
Engel, G.L. 6, 18, 35, 245, 246, 508, 515
Engelhart, M. 490, 493
Engelman, K. 251, 279
English, E.H. 226, 235
Enzer, N.B. 549
Epstein, A.W. 340, 352
Epstein, F.H. 442, 443, 460, 463

Epstein, L.H. 6, 22–4, 26, 32–4, 88, 99,
    181–2, 190, 195, 202, 205, 207, 212,
    214, 221, 239, 297, 304, 559, 577
Epstein, S. 125, 132
Erasmus, L.-P. 500, 502, 510, 515, 516
Erbaugh, J. 125, 131
Erdmann, G. 84, 99, 297, 304
Erfurt, J.C. 257, 274, 446, 462
Eriksson, A. 299, 307
Erlenmeyer-Kimling, L. 61, 66, 67, 400,
    403, 413
Erskine-Millis, J. 22, 35, 530, 549
Ersner-Hershfield, S. 213
Esler, M. 446, 458, 461
Esler, M.O. 260, 272, 273
Estes, S.A. 217, 235
Etevenon, P. 378, 387
Ettedgui, E. 313, 325
Evans, C.R. 354
Evans, D.D. 205
Evans, I.M. 20, 35
Evans, W.S. 433, 439
Everaerd, W. 128, 132
Evers, P.H. 496, 514
Eves, F.F. 140, 168, 227, 235, 345, 346,
    352, 398, 414
Ewart, C.K. 191, 207, 450, 461
Ewer, T.C. 529, 531, 549
Eyer, J. 442, 461
Eysenck, H.J. 8, 35, 300, 304

Fagerström, K.O. 297, 304
Fagiani, M.B. 543, 552
Fagius, J. 473, 489, 492
Fahrenberg, J. 9, 35, 74, 82, 84, 88–90,
    94–5, 99–100, 219, 235
Fair, P.L. 128, 134
Fairbank, J.A. 179, 189, 196, 211
Faire, U. de 261, 278
Falkner, B. 450, 451, 452, 459, 461
Falkowski, J. 227, 235
Falliers, C.J. 528, 548
Fallik, A. 157, 166
Falloon, I.R.H. 400, 418
Farquhar, J.W. 453, 454, 462, 466
Farr, D. 60, 66, 366, 386
Faulkner, B. 211
Faulstich, M.E. 31, 35, 43, 566, 577
Faust, J. 207
Fedio, P. 151, 170
Fedoravicius, A.S. 510, 518
Feighner, J.P. 59, 66, 379, 387, 408, 413

Feiguine, R.J. 525, 549
Feinberg, D.F. 338, 352
Feinberg, M. 56, 66, 358, 387
Feinglos, N.M. 222, 239
Feldman, G.M. 531, 549
Feldman, H.S. 558, 580
Feldman, R.G. 70
Fencl, V. 263, 271, 449, 460
Fention, C.H. 213
Fenton, C. 483, 494
Fenton, G.W. 299, 306
Fenton, W.S. 333, 352
Fenz, W.D. 125, 132
Ferguson, J.D. 248, 274
Ferguson, S. 162, 171
Fernandes, M. 450, 461
Fernando, C.K. 560, 563, 576, 578
Ferrcy, G. 564, 582
Ferster, C.B. 199, 207
Fetcher, E. 477, 492
Fetzer, J. 378, 385
Feuerstein, M. 6, 24, 33, 35, 38, 184, 187,
    194, 200, 206–7, 209, 221, 225,
    234–5
Fey, S.G. 454, 461
Fielding, J.F. 507, 515
Filewich, R.J. 264, 272
Fink, G. 502, 515
Fink, M. 314, 325
Finley, W.W. 568, 578
Finn, R. 545, 552
Fiorito, E. 344, 356
Fischer-Williams, M. 557, 578
Fish, D. 571, 578
Fisher, A.E. 353
Fisher, C. 425–6, 432, 437
Fisher, J.G. 23, 37
Fisher, L.M. 315, 325
Flavahan, N. 474, 492
Fleece, E.L. 210, 264, 275
Fleiss, J. 394, 413
Fleminger, J.J. 157, 166
Fletcher, R.P. 70
Flodmark, A. 558, 569, 578
Flor, H. 187, 207, 226, 235
Flor-Henry, P. 137–8, 144, 166, 168, 174,
    340, 352, 373–5, 377–8, 387
Florin, I. 526, 549, 550
Foa, E.B. 115, 129, 132, 290, 304, 331,
    333–4, 337, 346, 352–3, 356
Foerster, F. 9, 35, 79–84, 88, 90–1, 95,
    100, 102

Foerster, K. 15, 42
Folgering, H. 542, 549
Folkman, S. 242, 276
Folkow, B. 207, 248, 258, 260, 262, 264, 273–4
Foncin, J-F. 70
Fontaine, O. 343, 356
Foote, F. 287, 305
Ford, J.M. 150, 172, 379, 390, 409, 416
Fordtran, J.S. 517
Fordyce, W.E. 217, 236
Forgue, D.F. 21, 40, 128, 134
Forster, A. 536, 552
Fortmann, S.P. 454, 462
Fotopoulos, S.S. 560, 576, 578
Fowler, P.B. 537, 554
Fowler, R. 473, 480, 491
Fowler, R.S. Jr 558, 573, 579
Fowler, S.C. 97, 100, 224, 236
Fowles, D.C. 6, 8–9, 13, 18, 32, 35–6, 86, 100, 180, 207, 338, 353, 365, 387
Fox, J.M. 155, 166
Fox, P. 173
Fox, P.T. 155, 166
Francis, D. 369, 389
Francis, D.J. 250, 276
Frank, R. 288, 306
Frankel, B.L. 338, 353, 54, 461
Frankenhaeuser, M. 242–3, 246, 250, 253–4, 256, 260, 265, 267, 270–1, 273–4, 299, 305
Franzén, O. 382, 385
Fraser, J.R.E. 219, 235
Frederick, S.L. 160, 174
Fredericksen, L.W. 183, 195, 211
Fredrikson, M. 243, 246, 248, 251, 253–6, 260–3, 266–7, 269–71, 273–4, 282, 290, 294, 297, 299–300, 302–3, 305, 449–50, 461
Freedman, D.X. 405, 414
Freedman, R. 52, 66, 69, 333, 355
Freedman, R.R. 313–15, 325, 469–70, 473–6, 480, 482, 484, 485–90, 492–4
Freeman, L.J. 539, 541, 543, 549
Freeman, W. 400, 418
Freeman, W.J. 111, 112, 130, 132
Frei, E.H. 501, 515
Freidman, M. 274
Freis, E.D. 442, 443, 461, 463
Freixa i Baqué, E. 88, 100
Freudenberg, G. 526, 549
Freund, K. 107, 425–6, 432, 437

Frewin, D. 472, 473, 492
Frey, R. 478, 493
Freyschuss, U. 249, 275
Friar, L.R. 180, 207
Frick, K. 146, 166, 376, 378, 391
Fridlund, A.J. 10, 18, 36, 86, 97, 100, 224, 236, 296, 303, 556, 559, 579
Friedewald, W.T. 454, 461
Friedhoff, A.J. 333, 354
Friedman, D. 61, 66, 69, 150, 166, 400, 403, 413
Friedman, J.M. 179, 186, 207
Friedman, L.W. 181, 206, 562, 578
Friedman, M. 217, 236, 447, 448, 461, 465
Friedman, R. 260, 278
Friersen, W.V. 18
Frisk-Holmberg, M. 243, 246, 248, 273, 449, 461
Frith, C.D. 15, 36, 353, 399, 412–13
Fritz, G.K. 525, 553
Frohlich, E.D. 450, 461
Frommelt, P. 70
Frost, L.A. 405, 415
Frost, R.O. 227, 236
Frumkin, K. 453, 461
Frumkin, L.R. 161, 166
Fugl-Meyer, A.R. 429, 435, 437
Fuhr, R. 422, 437
Fuhrman, G.S. 526, 553
Fulker, D.W. 332, 352
Fuller, A.K. 565, 581
Funkenstein, D.H. 250, 274, 446, 461
Furby, L. 78, 99
Furedy, J.J. 21, 36, 79, 103, 238
Furlong, F.W. 567, 579
Furman, B. 437
Fyer, A.J. 276, 325, 551

Gaarder, K.R. 452, 454, 461, 557, 579
Gaas, E. 207
Gabbay, F.H. 382, 388
Gable, R.S. 24, 41, 183, 212
Gabrielli, W.F. Jr 51, 54, 66, 67
Gaebel, L.W. 146, 166
Gaertner, H.J. 365, 385
Gaillard, A.W.K. 540, 554
Gaillard, J.M. 340–1, 353
Gaind, R. 214
Gainotti, G. 160, 166
Gale, A. 8, 27, 30, 32, 36, 74, 84, 100
Galfe, G. 506, 516

Galin, D. 138, 157, 167
Gallant, D. 61
Gallen, C.C. 326, 327
Gambaro, S. 210
Gamble, S. 353
Gannon, L.R. 6, 37, 178–80, 189–90,
  195–6, 207–9, 236
Ganong, W.F. 244, 247, 254, 274
Garcia, J. 301, 305, 506, 515
Gardiner, H. 273, 461
Gardner, E. 484, 493
Gardner, W.N. 535–43, 546–9
Garfield, S.L. 185, 207
Garland, F.N. 88, 101
Garland, G. 564, 581
Garmany, G. 358, 387
Garmezy, N. 396, 414
Garner, W. 170
Garrett, J.C. 558, 564, 579
Garrity, S.J. 450, 464
Garssen, B. 537–9, 543, 545, 549
Garwood, M. 270, 274
Gary, H. 257, 274
Gasser, T. 53, 67, 86, 88, 100
Gatchel, R.J. 6, 23, 36, 205, 207, 227,
  236, 249, 271, 285, 305, 559, 580
Gath, D.H. 315, 325
Gavira, M. 68, 415
Gebhard, P. 420, 438
Geer, J.H. 291, 305, 21–2, 428, 430–1,
  433–5, 437–9
Gelder, M.G. 119, 132, 286, 288, 304,
  311, 315, 318, 325, 326
Gellhorn, E. 106, 132
Gennari, F.J. 537, 549
Gentry, W.D. 6, 36, 217, 236, 257, 274
George, J. 170, 206
Gerardi, R.J. 21, 34, 447, 461
Gerhard, D.S. 66
Gerner, R.H. 385
Gershon, E.S. 51, 57, 63, 67, 69, 359, 387,
  466
Geschwind, N. 138, 167
Gevins, A.S. 86, 100
Ghadirian, A.M. 378, 387
Ghanshym, N.P. 68
Ghoneim, M.M. 560, 569
Gianutsos, J.G. 572, 577
Gibbons, R.D. 68, 415
Gibson, E.L. 10, 36
Gibson, E.S. 462
Gibson, J.R. 530, 548

Giedke, H. 365, 379, 380, 385, 387, 391
Gifford, R. 470, 493
Gifford, R.W. 456, 462
Gil, K.M. 221, 237
Gilbey, S.G. 501, 515
Gilgor, R.S. 473, 494
Gill, A. 275
Gillin, C. 335, 353
Gillin, J.C. 338, 340, 353
Ginsberg, D. 188, 208
Gintner, C.G. 52, 67
Gintner, G.G. 451, 461
Giordani, B. 267, 272, 450, 464
Girdane, D. 558, 579
Glagov, S. 268, 271
Glasgow, M.S. 452, 455, 456, 457, 454,
  461
Glasgow, R.E. 195, 208
Glassman, A.H. 52, 67, 347, 352, 363,
  385
Glazer, R. 170
Gleser, G.C. 89, 97, 99
Glover, W.E. 363, 385
Glueck, B.C. 575, 583
Gödderz, W. 452, 464
Gödicke, W. 449, 460
Goff, W.R. 35, 151, 174, 342, 356
Goffard, M.I. 248, 274
Gohlke 238
Goldband, S. 23, 41
Goldberg, T.E. 53, 68
Goldberger, L. 208
Golden, M. 229, 238
Golden, R.R. 58, 69
Goldfried, A.P. 208, 320, 325
Goldfried, M.R. 20, 36, 199, 208, 320,
  325
Goldiamond, I. 214
Goldman, M. 527, 549
Golds, J. 163, 170
Goldshine, A.D. 258, 271
Goldstein, D.S. 258, 260, 264, 268, 274
Goldstein, G. 192, 208
Goldstein, H. 77, 78, 79, 100
Goldstein, I.B. 233, 236, 446, 451, 452,
  454, 455, 457, 461, 462, 465
Goldstein, L. 373–4, 387, 390, 391
Goldstein, R. 53, 70
Goldsworthy 181
Goleman, D.J. 190, 208, 227, 236
Gollob, H.F. 90, 101
Gong, G. 86, 99

Goodin, D. 150, 173
Goodwin, D.W. 60, 69
Goperlund, E. 60, 66
Goperud, E. 366, 386
Gordon, N. 530, 554
Gordon, P.K. 334, 342, 352, 353
Gorham, D.R. 146, 172
Gorman, J.M. 276, 314, 325, 551
Gossard, D. 324, 327
Gosselin, J. 150, 165
Götestam, C.G. 284, 305
Gottesman, I.I. 47, 49, 55–6, 60, 62–3, 65, 67, 69, 396, 414
Gottlieb, J. 162, 173
Gottman, J.M. 18, 28, 39, 87, 101, 202, 208
Goudswaard, P. 224, 239, 559, 577
Gourmas, C. 480, 494
Gowers, W.R. 158, 167
Gowland, C. 573, 577, 579
Graae, F. 412
Gradman, A.H. 316, 327
Graf, H.J. 444, 465
Graham, D.T. 129, 132, 294–5, 305, 326
Graham, F.K. 5, 36, 129, 132, 352, 353
Graham, J.J. 578
Graham, K.R. 161, 167
Graham, R. 260, 272, 447, 460
Gramling, S. 6, 24, 42
Granger, L. 26, 32–3
Grant, L.B. 39, 464
Grassick, G.P. 567, 579
Gratton, G. 10, 35, 53, 67, 197, 206, 300, 304
Gray, J.A. 8, 36, 39, 149, 167
Gray, R. 325, 378, 389
Graybiel, A. 261, 274
Grayson, J.B. 196, 205, 311, 373, 345–7, 352–3, 356
Greenberg, G. 443, 460
Greenberg, L.S. 10, 36, 52, 67
Greenfield, A.D.M. 363, 385
Greenfield, N.S. 23, 32, 36, 86, 103, 177, 193, 208
Greenspoon, L. 14, 34
Greenstadt, L. 445, 465
Greenwood, P. 433, 437
Grega, D.M. 146, 173
Grey, J.A. 292–3, 308
Grey, S. 179, 208
Grey, S.J. 15, 22, 36, 338, 354, 355
Grice, G.R. 90, 101

Griegberg, S. 558, 573, 579
Griffin, R. 67
Grimm, L.G. 23, 36
Grings, W.W. 23, 32, 36–7, 86, 100, 365, 387
Grissom, R.L. 445, 462
Groen, J.J. 449, 462
Grolino, B. 478, 494
Gross, F. 179, 208, 442, 443, 462
Gross, H.A. 506, 515
Gross, J. 425, 437
Grossman, L. 331, 353
Grossman, P. 533, 535, 537–41, 543–4, 546–7, 554
Growden, J. 70
Grünberg, E. 331, 355
Grunberg, N. 249, 271
Gruss, L. 466
Gruzelier, J.H. 11, 13–15, 37, 137–8, 140–50, 152–3, 155–7, 160, 152–71, 174, 364–7, 387, 397–9, 412, 414
Grynbaum, B.B. 206, 562, 572, 577, 578, 580
Guell, A. 369, 386
Guenther, W. 369–72, 384, 387
Guillaumin, J.-M. 159, 173
Gunnarson, D.F. 195, 208
Gunnarsson, M. 253, 254, 274
Gunnarsson, R.D.R. 256, 274
Gur, R.C. 156, 162, 169, 173, 387
Gur, R.E. 162, 169, 368–72, 384, 387
Gusella, J. 50, 67, 68, 70
Gust, W.F. 445, 462
Gustafson, A.B. 239
Gustafson, L. 369, 371–2, 388
Gutsch, K.V. 563, 578
Guttman, M.C. 259, 274
Guy, J.J. 505, 515
Guy Edvards, J. 297, 305
Guyton, A. 248, 258, 274
Guyton, A.C. 534, 550
Guyton, A.H. 451, 462
Guze, S.B. 6, 37, 59, 66, 379, 387, 408, 413

Haag, G. 226, 235
Haber, J.D. 185, 204
Haberman, S. 154, 169, 404, 406, 414–15
Hackett, B.C. 462
Hagbarth, K.-E. 264, 279
Hagg, S. 202, 214
Haier, R.J. 16, 37, 59, 66, 69

Haines, J.L. 70
Hale, P. 485, 492
Halgren, E. 151, 169
Hall, A.W. 505, 515
Hall, J. 477, 492
Hall, J.R. 236
Hall, R.A. 52, 67
Hall, R.P. 257, 274
Hall, S.M. 188, 195, 208
Hall, W. 158, 169
Hallam, R.S. 294, 304
Hallbäck, M. 260, 262, 273, 274
Hallett, M. 574, 579
Halliday, A.M. 7, 37
Hallock, J.A. 161, 165
Hallstrom, C. 297, 305
Hällström, T. 359, 390
Halperin, J. 472, 475, 492
Halpern, D. 572, 581
Halsey, J.H. 368, 392
Hamann, M.S. 127, 133
Hamburger, R. 66
Hamilton, C.A. 256, 275
Hamilton, J. 221, 236
Hamm, A. 269, 274
Hammer, D. 428, 439
Hammond, N.V. 138, 144, 145, 168, 169
Hand, I. 515
Handen, B.L. 497, 513, 517
Hanin, I. 12, 43
Hanley, J.A. 103, 229, 238
Hansen, B. 462
Hanson, D.R. 56, 67
Hansson, L. 272, 451, 459
Harburg, E. 257, 273–4, 446, 461, 462
Harburg, J. 531, 553
Harding, G.F.A. 7, 37, 378, 388
Harding, P.S. 311 327
Hardonk, H.J. 541, 550
Hardy, A.B. 22, 33
Hardyck, C. 448, 462
Hare, R.D. 251, 274, 291–2, 294, 305
Hargreave, F.E. 524, 550
Hargreaves, W.A. 208
Harlan, E.R. Jr 261, 274
Harm, D.L. 524, 532, 550
Harmony, T. 7, 37
Haroian, K.P. 46, 68, 359, 388
Harrell, J.P. 258, 260, 275, 446, 462
Harrigan, J.A. 221, 236
Harrington, A. 137, 169
Harrington-Kostur, J. 195, 205

Harris, F.A. 568, 569, 579
Harris, L.J. 142, 169
Harris, R.E. 448, 462
Harris, R.J. 90, 97, 101
Harris, W.L. 450, 461
Harrison, A. 569, 579
Harrison, B. 310, 326
Harrison, D.W. 558, 564, 579
Harrison, J. 324
Harrison, M.J.G. 561, 581
Harshfield, G.A. 99, 260, 272, 278, 444, 465
Hart, A.A. 569, 577
Hart, B.A. 239
Hart, J.D. 108, 133, 210, 292, 306
Hartje, W. 572, 583

Hartl, L. 502, 510, 516
Hartley, L.R. 560, 578
Hartmann, E. 14, 17, 37
Hartrodt, W. 449, 460
Harvey, J.E. 525, 553
Haslbeck, M. 505, 515, 517
Hassett, J. 177, 193, 208, 298, 305
Hastrup, J.L. 30, 37, 52, 67, 448, 450–1, 462
Hatch, J.P. 23, 37, 181, 186, 200–1, 207, 209, 422, 429–31, 438
Hatfield, M.E. 224, 236
Hauch, J. 310, 326
Hauenstein, L.S. 257, 274, 446, 462
Haug, T. 284, 305
Hauri, P. 48, 67
Hause, A.O. 153, 165
Havvik, D. 313, 327
Hawkins, C.M. 444, 463
Hawkins, D. 48, 67
Hawkins, M.F. 24, 44
Hawkins, R.P. 9, 34, 177, 206
Hayes, S.C. 20, 26, 32–3, 39, 176–7, 184, 205, 212, 559, 577
Hayman, M.A. 358, 391
Haynes, M.R. 454, 460
Haynes, R.B. 455, 462
Haynes, S.N. 6, 24, 28, 37, 176–82, 184–92, 194–6, 199, 201, 205, 207–11, 221, 236, 574, 579
Hayward, L. 158, 169
Haywood, J.R. 264, 271
Hazaleus, S.L. 180, 199, 209
Hazama, H. 362, 388
Hazlett, E. 385, 386

Health and Public Policy Committee 576, 579
Heath, H.A. 80, 101
Heaton, K.W. 509, 516
Heaukulani, J.D. 226, 235
Hebb, D.O. 111, 126, 132
Hediger, M.L. 444, 460
Heffley, E. 413
Hegarty, J.E. 511, 519
Heide, F.J. 209
Heilman, K.M. 139, 169
Heim, E. 525, 544, 550
Heiman, J.R. 181, 186, 200–1, 209, 420–2, 431, 433–4, 437–8
Heinrich, B. 238
Heiser, P. 221, 236
Heijl, Z. 263, 271, 449, 460
Held, J.P. 429, 437
Heller, W. 146, 170
Helmsley, D.R. 27, 37, 544, 546, 548
Helzer, J.I. 331, 355
Henderson, D. 558, 564, 579
Henderson, E.B. 499, 517
Heninger, G. 254, 271
Heninger, G.R. 316, 324, 327, 378, 388
Henningsen, P. 535, 553
Henriques, J.B. 360, 376–7, 383, 388
Henry, D. 227, 237
Henry, J.P. 257–8, 264–5, 275
Henry, J.R. 574, 582
Henschen, T.L. 574, 579
Hensen, C. 196, 209
Hensen, D.E. 196, 209
Hensley, M.J. 531, 552
Henson, C. 433, 438
Henson, D. 433, 438
Herd, A.J. 278
Herman, J. 61, 67
Herman, R. 569, 571, 578, 580
Herman, S.P. 539, 550
Hermann, J.M. 449, 459, 462
Hermanutz, M. 402, 412
Hermsdörfer, J. 502, 515
Hernez, D.A. 180, 190, 201, 209
Herron, J. 142, 169
Herscovitch, P. 173
Hersen, M. 26, 32–3, 176, 187, 192, 205, 208–9
Hes, J.P. 373, 388
Heslegrave, R.J. 79, 103
Heston, L. 55–6, 67, 69
Hiatt, J.F. 338, 352

Hibbert, G.A. 536, 541, 543, 550
Hickam, D.H. 537, 551
Hickey, A. 466
Higgins, J.T. 233, 237
Higgs, C.M.B. 525, 532, 550, 553
Hilgard, E.R. 161, 172
Hill, D. 84, 101
Hill, E. 574, 581
Hillbom, E. 338, 353
Hillyard, S. 338, 353
Hillyard, S.A. 35, 413
Hilton, S.M. 258, 275
Himmelhoch, J.M. 358, 389
Hines, E.A. 261, 275, 449, 462, 470, 492
Hinrichsen, J.J. 527, 553
Hippius, H. 369, 387
Hiramatsu, K. 69, 403, 417
Hirsch, S.R. 147, 153, 165, 168, 170, 398, 414
Hjelm, R. 271
Hjemdahl, P. 248–9, 256, 265, 271, 273, 275, 449, 460, 523, 551
Ho, B.T. 222, 237, 250, 253, 255, 276
Hobbs, W.J. 70, 225, 235
Hobson, N. 509, 514
Hochron, S. 521, 551
Hodgson, R. 12, 20–2, 37, 40, 197, 209, 331, 336–7, 351, 354–5
Hoelscher, T.J. 180, 202, 209
Hoff, S.L. 373, 386
Hoffer, J.L. 212
Hoffman, A. 211, 223
Hoffman, J.W. 236, 275
Hogan, D.R. 179, 207
Hoka, S. 265, 278
Hokanson, J.E. 446, 462
Holcomb, H.H. 380, 385–6
Holcomb, P.J. 386
Holden, A.E. 22, 29, 37, 183, 194, 209, 282, 303, 316, 325
Holden, S. 514
Holdsworth, C.D. 509, 514
Holl, J. 509, 516
Hollaender, J. 526, 549–50
Hollander, B.J. 103, 230
Hollandsworth, J.G. 20–22, 24, 37, 67, 223, 238, 451, 461
Hollenberg, N.K. 263, 275
Hollingsworth, C.E. 331, 353
Holloway, F.A. 140, 141, 169, 335, 352
Holm, J.E. 236

Holmes, D.S. 223, 225, 227, 229–30, 236, 238
Holmes, T.H. 242, 275, 543, 549
Holroyd, K.A. 216, 226, 234, 236
Holteman, M.J. 521, 548
Holzer, C.E. 326
Holzer, E.C. 331, 354
Hölzl, R. 497, 499–500, 502–3, 505–7, 510–11, 515–17
Holzman, A.D. 184, 209, 216, 237
Holzman, P.S. 51, 57, 68–70, 154–5, 169–71, 404–9, 414–15
Homskaya, E.D. 139, 171
Homuth, V. 238
Honer, J. 572, 579
Honsberger, R. 531, 554
Hoobler, S.W. 451, 465
Hoogduin, K. 546, 548
Hooijer, C. 376, 391
Hookman, P. 473, 494
Hoon, P.W. 424, 430, 433, 438
Hopkins, H.K. 67
Horan, M.J. 444, 462
Horande, M. 211, 560, 583
Horesh, N. 365, 367, 390
Hormbrey, J.M. 542, 550
Horn, T.S. 239
Horne, M. 455, 459
Hornsveld, R.H.J. 345, 353
Horton, D.J. 527, 529, 550
Horvath, T.B. 14, 37, 152, 172, 402–3, 416–17
Horwitz, D. 454, 461
Hosobuchi, Y. 151, 174
Hostetter, A.M. 66
Hotchkiss, A.P. 448, 462
Houle, M. 221, 235
Houseworth, S.J. 270–1
Housman, D. 50, 66, 68
Houston, B.K. 264, 275
Howard, R.C. 299, 306
Howarth, B.G. 340, 352, 374, 387
Howells, G.N. 22, 33
Howland, E.W. 558, 581
Hoyer, S. 369, 388
Huang, S.-C. 369, 390
Hubbard, J.W. 222, 235
Huber, M.J. 223, 237
Huber-Smith, M.J. 251, 252, 254, 277, 326
Huey, S.R. 542, 544, 546, 550
Hugdahl, K. 20, 37, 140, 169, 282–4,

286–8, 294, 296–303, 305, 307, 367, 388
Hugelin, A. 535, 550
Hughes, D.W. 404, 414
Hughes, J. 190, 207
Hughes, M. 556, 566, 579
Huitema, B.E. 78, 80, 101, 197, 209
Hull, D.H. 449, 462
Hull, E.M. 230, 237
Hullstrung, H. 428, 439
Hulstijn, W. 560, 581
Hum, D.J. 87, 98
Hume, J.S. 212
Hunt, B. 231, 239, 459, 464
Hurley, G. 473, 480, 491
Hursey, K.G. 236
Hurt, S.W. 68, 404, 414
Huson, J. 291, 306
Hutchcroft, 522, 523, 552
Hutcheson, J.S. 32, 38, 86, 101, 212
Hutchinson, K.M. 31, 35
Hutton, B.O. 563, 578
Hymer, J.W. 569, 579

Iacono, W.G. 16, 27, 37–8, 46, 51–3, 55, 61–2, 64–5, 68–9, 88, 101, 154–5, 169, 359, 364–7, 382, 388, 399, 404–10, 414–16
Ianni, P. 325, 470, 473, 475–6, 480, 482, 484, 485–89, 492–3
Ibrahim, M.M. 456, 462
Imaizumi, T. 265, 278
Imaoka, K. 362, 388
Ince, L.P. 566, 579
Ingels, N.B. 222, 235
Ingham, J.G. 546, 550
Inglis, J. 573, 579
Ingram, I.M. 340, 353
Ingram, R.H. 529, 552
Ingvar, D.H. 141, 169
Innes, G. 448, 462
Inoue, H. 362, 388
Inoue, Y. 362, 388
Insel, T.R. 335, 340–1, 347, 353, 356
Intrieri, R.C. 67, 451, 461
Iorio, G. 340, 353, 374, 388, 389
Iremark, H. 269, 273
Irvine, W. 480, 494
Isenberg, J.I. 507, 517
Itil, T.M. 51–2, 67–70
Itoh, K. 69, 403, 417
Izard, C.E. 18, 36

Jacob, R. 336, 354
Jacob, R.G. 198, 209, 311, 325, 453–5, 462–3
Jacobi, M.S. 542, 550
Jacobs, M. 573, 582
Jacobs, U. 450, 465
Jacobsen, E. 223, 237
Jacobsen, R. 400, 413
Jacobson, A. 484, 492
Jacobson, E. 453, 463
Jacquy, J. 370, 386, 391
Jakob, H. 148, 169
James, L.R. 187, 202, 209
James, S.A. 237
James, W. 284, 305
Jamieson, G. 473–4, 479, 492
Jamieson, J.L. 230, 237
Jamner, L.D. 443, 445, 466, 489, 493
Janda, L.H. 289, 307
Janes, C.L. 17, 42
Janicak, P.G. 68, 415
Jänig, W. 499, 513, 518
Janke, W. 84, 99
Jankel, W.R. 563, 579
Janson-Bjerklie, S. 531, 550
Jansson, L. 22, 38, 284–5, 290, 307, 318–19, 321, 325–6
Jarris, M. 285, 294–5, 308
Jason, M. 272
Jatlow, P.I. 324
Jaussi, A. 444, 465
Jayne, D. 577, 580
Jedynak, C.P. 564, 582
Jenike, M.A. 340, 353
Jenner, F.A. 378, 388
Jennings, J.R. 5, 25, 31, 32, 34, 38, 86, 101, 248, 275, 411, 415, 480, 493
Jensen, J. 501, 514
Jern, S. 272, 449, 463
Jerremalm, A. 22, 38, 284, 288, 307, 318–21, 323, 325, 326
Jewett, D.L. 152, 169
Jiang, N.-S. 277
Jirka, J. 263, 271
Joele, L. 546, 548
Joffe, R. 162, 169
Johanson, M. 369, 372, 388
Johansson, J. 293, 307, 320, 326
Johansson, K. 429, 437
Johnsen, B.H. 284, 305
Johnsen, T. 474, 493
Johnson, A.L. 462

Johnson, C.A. 448, 462
Johnson, E.H. 260, 277, 447, 465
Johnson, H.J. 162, 171, 291–2, 307
Johnson, J. 66, 385, 386
Johnson, L. 52, 68
Johnson, L.F. 505, 515, 517
Johnson, M.C. 22, 34
Johnson, M.H. 365, 391
Johnson, R.A. 151, 155, 169, 170, 406, 415
Johnson, V.E. 421, 423–4, 428, 438
Johnston, D.W. 228, 231, 237, 311, 315, 325–6
Johnston, R. 374, 580
Johnstone, E.C. 15, 36, 348, 353, 399, 413
Jolley, T. 147, 168
Jonas, S. 578
Jones, A. 154, 170, 405, 415
Jones, D.H. 256, 275
Jones, G.E. 563, 580
Jones, J.N. 297, 304
Joncs, N.F. 526, 549
Jones, R.T. 188, 208
Jones, S. 400, 418
Jonker, C. 376, 391
Joorabchi, B. 539, 551
Jorgensen, R.S. 264, 275
Joseph, R. 158, 172
Josiassen, R.C. 151, 170, 342, 355
Jost III, F.A. 277
Jouvet, M. 341, 353
Juenet, C. 567, 578
Juhlin-Dannfelt, A. 249, 275
Julius, S. 232, 235, 258–60, 264, 273, 275, 277–8, 447, 452–3, 460–1, 465–6
Jull, S. 536, 553
Jung, C.G. 19
Juni, S. 397, 412
Jurish, S.E. 234
Jurka, J. 449, 460
Jutai, J. 153, 163, 168, 170

Kabler, J.D. 129, 132, 294–5, 305
Kader, G. 378, 387
Kadrmas, A. 373, 388
Kagan, A.R. 246, 267, 275
Kahan, T. 449, 460
Kallenbach, J.M. 529, 551
Kallman, W.M. 24, 38, 187, 194, 200, 209
Kallus, W. 84, 99

Kaloupek, D.G. 20, 38, 180, 190, 192, 209–10, 293, 304
Kamenskaya, V.M. 364–5, 388
Kameyama, T. 69, 403, 417
Kanfer, F.H. 176, 185, 209
Kannel, W.B. 221, 237, 442, 463
Kanter, N.J. 320, 325
Kantor, S.J. 347, 352
Kaplan, B.J. 30, 41, 43, 88, 102
Kaplan, H.S. 421–2, 433, 438
Kaplan, J.R. 264, 268, 275, 276
Kaplan, N. 278
Kaplan, N.M. 179, 194, 209
Karacan, I. 189, 209, 435–6, 438
Karis, D. 10, 35, 300, 304
Karni, Y. 557, 583
Karson, C.N. 53, 68
Kartsounis, L.D. 28, 38
Kashman, R. 514
Kaskey, G.B. 402, 416
Kassirer, J.P. 537, 549
Kathol, R.G. 297, 305
Katholi, C.R. 368, 392
Katkin, E.S. 23, 41, 353, 365–7, 389
Katranides, M. 221, 236
Kattan, M. 531, 548
Katz, S.H. 444, 460
Kaufman, J. 223, 237
Kazdin, A.E. 27, 38, 176, 182, 205, 209
Kazrin, A. 33, 38
Keane, T.M. 179–80, 190, 192, 196, 211, 264, 275
Kearns, W. 263, 271
Keefe, F.J. 183, 199, 210, 221, 237, 425–6, 439, 484, 490, 492, 576, 580
Kelleher, C. 443, 463
Keller, S. 229–30, 237
Keller, S.E. 161, 173
Kellner, R. 544, 551
Kelly, A. 411, 413
Kelly, D. 314, 325, 335, 354
Kelly, D.H.W. 362, 388
Kelly, J.L. 214, 571, 580, 583
Kelotkin, R.L. 558, 580
Kemali, D. 340, 353, 374, 378, 384, 387–9
Kendall, M.G. 78, 79, 101
Kendell, R.E. 358, 389, 394, 412
Kendrick, M.J. 210
Kenigsberg, M.L. 318, 326
Kenneally, J.A. 535, 551
Kerber, R.E. 297, 305
Kessler, R.M. 385, 386

Ketchel, M.F. 458, 459
Keys, A. 267, 275
Kidd, K.K. 66
Kiecolt-Glaser, J.K. 161, 170
Kijima, M. 506, 516
Killen, J.D. 181, 195, 206, 210
Kiloh, L.G. 161, 165
Kim, 139, 172
Kimball, C.P. 448, 467
Kimble, D.P. 149, 170
Kimmel, H.D. 31, 40, 90, 102
King, A.C. 385, 386
King, D. 56, 66
King, S.H. 446, 461
Kinsbourne, M. 137, 146, 170
Kinsey, A. 420, 428, 438
Kinsman, R.A. 524–7, 549–51, 553
Kirk, R.E. 87, 91, 95, 101
Kirkendall, W.M. 443, 463
Kirsch, I. 227, 237
Kirsner, J.B. 508, 516
Kissin, B. 66
Kjellberg, A. 292, 303
Klaniecki, T. 473, 494
Klein, A.A. 449, 464
Klein, D. 60, 66, 366, 386
Klein, D.F. 254–6, 271, 275–6, 311, 325, 551
Klein, G. 525, 551
Klein, K. 271, 274
Klein, R.H. 400, 402, 406, 416–17
Kleiner, B. 272
Kleinert, H.D. 272
Kleinman, K.M. 560, 582
Kleitman, N. 432, 436
Klerman, G.L. 128, 134
Klesges, L.M. 195, 208
Klesges, R.C. 188, 195, 205, 208
Klett, C.J. 97, 102
Klicpera, C. 362, 391
Kling, A.S. 369, 372, 389
Klochhoff, I. 152, 171
Klorman, R. 402, 416
Klosko, J.S. 205
Kluger, M.A. 484, 489, 493
Knapp, T.J. 529, 551
Knapp, P.H. 526, 530, 551
Knight, M.L. 119, 132
Knop, J. 60, 69
Knopf, R.F. 254, 277
Knorring, L. von 374, 376, 389, 390
Knott, J.R. 223, 239

Knott, V.J. 52, 68, 314, 325, 378, 380, 389
Knox, S. 259, 278
Knudson, R.J. 525, 549
Knust, U. 238
Koch, K.L. 497, 500, 515, 517
Koehler, H. 226, 235
Koelling, R.A. 301, 305
Koenig, W.G.R. 405, 408, 414
Koepke, J.P. 263, 276, 451, 463
Koeske, R. 202, 214
Kohler, D. 525, 551
Kolb, L.C. 21, 34
Koles, Z.J. 340, 352, 374, 377–8, 387
Kondo, C.Y. 223, 239
Konickx, N. 343, 356
Kontos, H.A. 473, 493
Kopel, S.A. 212
Kopell, B.S. 150, 152, 172, 223, 235, 324–5, 379, 390, 402–3, 409, 413, 416–17
Kopell, M.L. 324, 326
Kopetzky, M.T. 524, 553
Kopp, M. 142, 143, 155, 170
Koppman, J.W. 191, 210
Korein, J. 206, 562–3, 572, 577–8, 580
Korff, J. 433, 438
Korman, M. 227, 236
Korner, P.I. 446, 465
Kornhuber, H.H. 354, 380, 389
Koss, M.C. 139, 166
Kosslyn, S.M. 110, 132
Kotsch, W.E. 97, 102
Kotses, H. 524, 532, 550
Kozak, M.J. 27, 38, 107, 115–17, 129, 132–3
Kraainmaat, F.W. 345, 353
Kraemer, D.L. 448, 462
Kraemer, H.C. 191–2, 198, 204, 207, 209, 453–4, 459, 461–3, 466
Kraepelin, E. 394, 415
Kralik, P. 222, 237, 253, 255, 276
Kramer, A.F. 197, 206, 411, 413
Kramer, M. 326
Krantz 259, 260
Krantz, D. 89, 101
Krantz, D.S. 210, 243, 245, 276, 452, 463
Kratochwill, T.R. 26, 32, 38
Kratzmair, M. 502, 510, 516
Krautze, D.S. 276
Kringlen, E. 154, 169, 332, 354, 406, 414
Kristensen, J.K. 490, 493

Kristt, D.A. 452, 463
Kröger, C. 511, 515
Kron, R.E. 294, 304, 463
Kronenberg, G. 149, 166
Krozely, M.G. 210
Krug, S.E. 142, 170
Kruis, W. 516
Kubos, K.L. 383, 390
Kuczmierczyk, A.R. 6, 35
Kues, J.R. 221, 236
Kugelmass, S. 400, 415
Kuhl, D.E. 268–71, 383, 389, 390
Kuhn, C. 267, 279, 473, 495
Kuipers, L. 15, 42, 400, 417
Kukulka, C.G. 571, 574, 577, 580
Kuller, L.H. 446, 460
Kunzel, M.G. 191, 210
Kupfer, D.J. 48, 68, 251, 279, 358, 389
Kurland, L.T. 567, 580
Kurzin, I.T. 496, 514
Kushner, H. 461
Kushner, S. 66
Kuzak, M. 179, 210

Labarthe, D.R. 444, 445, 463
Labbe, E.E. 6, 35, 221, 235
LaBreque, J.F. 526, 553
Lacey, B.C. 5, 38, 88, 101, 361, 389
Lacey, J.I. 5–6, 9, 19–20, 38, 74, 80, 88, 97, 101, 194, 210, 298, 306, 361, 389
Lack, L. 162, 171
Lacoursieve, R.B. 70
Lacroix, J.N. 140, 170
Lader, H. 139, 174
Lader, M. 82, 101, 251, 254–5, 276, 312, 325, 564, 581
Lader, M.H. 6, 8–9, 12–14, 16, 18–19, 24, 29, 38, 40, 42–3, 119, 132, 143, 150, 170, 290–1, 297–9, 306, 308, 338, 348, 354, 362, 364–7, 389–91, 400, 409, 415, 417
Lahmeyer, H.W. 363, 389
Lake, B.W. 230, 237
Lam, S. 523, 548
Lambarth, B. 451, 465
Lamparski, D.M. 221, 239
Lancaster, D.W. 289, 307
Land, R. 237
Landsberg, L. 275
Lane, J.D. 52, 68, 265, 267–8, 270–1, 276, 279, 445, 465
Lang, J. 571, 580

Lang, P.J. 6, 10, 12, 19–20, 24, 38–9, 106–9, 113–20, 122, 126–7, 131–4, 179, 210, 285, 288, 292, 296, 302, 306, 344, 351, 354, 356, 380, 390, 422, 438, 559, 580
Lange, J.D. 186, 214
Lange, K. 57, 69
Langman, C. 450, 461
Langston, K. 386
Lanyon 181
Lanzetta, J.T. 90, 102
Lapidus, L.B. 13, 41
Lapierre, Y.D. 314, 325, 362, 365–6, 378, 380, 389
Laragh, J.H. 99, 258, 272, 276, 444, 465
Larkin, K.T. 317, 327
Larrabee, G.J. 162, 171
Larsen, P.B. 443, 445, 463
Larsson, K. 523, 551
Laszlo, G. 525, 532, 550, 553
Latham, C. 155, 170
Latimer, P.L. 352
Latimer, P.R. 337, 352, 509, 516
Lautenbacher, S. 506, 516
Lauter, J. 449, 460
Lavoie, N.F. 230, 237
Lawler, J.E. 222, 235
Lawler, K.A. 450, 463
Laws, D.R. 181, 186, 204
Lawson, D.M. 210
Lazarus, L. 161, 165
Lazarus, R.S. 9, 10, 39, 242, 276, 536, 551
Lazovik, A.D. 115, 133
Lea, D.A. 532, 550
Leaf, P.J. 326, 331, 354
Lear, H. 432, 437
LeBoeuf, A. 514, 580
Lebovits, B.Z. 446, 464
Leckman, J.F. 359, 387
Lederer, P.C.H. 500, 516
Lee, K.H. 572, 580
Lee, R.G. 557, 578
Lee, W.A. 569, 582
Lees, A.J. 575, 580
Leff, J.P. 15, 29, 42, 394, 400, 412, 417
Lefkowitz, R. 474, 493
Lehman, H.E. 378, 387
Lehrer, P. 521, 529, 551
Lehrer, P.M. 226–7, 237–8
Leiblum, S.R. 179, 210
Leigh, H. 6, 39

Leightenberg, H. 421
Leist, N. 527, 551
Leitenberg, H. 285, 306, 426, 437
Lemke, R.R. 24, 41, 183, 212
Lenhart, R.E. 365–7, 389
Leon, M.S. 566, 579
LeRoy, E. 478, 493
Lesezi, J.P. 53, 68
Levenson, J.A. 259, 277, 449, 465
Levenson, R. 18, 19, 28, 39
Levenson, R.W. 208, 364, 390, 526–7, 529, 551, 553
Levey, A.B. 31, 39, 82, 101
Levi, L. 242, 246, 250, 267, 271, 275–6
Levidow, L. 206, 562–3, 578, 580
Levin, D.N. 108, 116–19, 133, 210
Levin, R. 429, 439
Levin, S. 154, 155, 170, 171, 405–8, 414–15
Levin, S.M. 179, 210
Levine, B.A. 213
Levine, D. 278, 466
Levine, W.R. 567, 580
Levinson, D.F. 398, 415
Levis, D.J. 20, 38, 182, 213
Levitt, M. 271, 276, 325, 551
Levy, D.L. 53, 68, 154, 169, 171, 404–9, 414–15
Levy, G. 278, 551
Levy, G.F. 325
Levy, J. 146, 170
Levy, L. 463
Levy, R. 336, 354
Lewis, D.H. 525, 549
Lewis, G.T. 532, 550
Lewis, M.N. 527, 551
Lewis, R.A. 527, 530, 551
Lewis, T. 472, 493
Liappas, J.A. 145, 172, 363, 390
Liberman, R.P. 400, 413, 418
Licht, S. 570, 580
Lichstein, K.L. 84, 101, 202, 209
Lichtenstein, E. 195, 205–6, 210–11
Lidberg, L. 82, 101
Liddiard, D.M. 164, 168
Lieberman, A. 206, A. 562, 578
Liebowitz, M.R. 276, 314, 325, 542–3, 551
Liebson, I. 213
Light, K. 463
Light, K.C. 52, 67, 212, 230, 237, 263,

265, 276, 448, 450, 451, 452, 456, 462, 463
Lima, D.R. 252, 276
Linck, B. 249, 275
Lindberg, H.A. 259, 278
Linden, W. 30, 39
Lindgren, M. 254, 274
Lindholm, E. 454, 461
Lindros, K.O. 180, 210
Lindsey, D.T. 404–5, 415
Lindsley, D.B. 298, 306, 355
Lindstrom, L. 40, 152, 171
Lindström, L. 410, 412
Ling, F. 433, 438
Linkowski, P. 370, 391
Lippold, O.C.J. 298, 306, 559, 580
Lipton, R.B. 154, 155, 170, 171
Lishayko, F. 249, 273
Little, B.C. 52, 68
Little, S.C. 562, 581
Littler, W.A. 443, 465
Lipton, R.B. 405, 407–9, 415
Lisi, I.S. 430, 439
Lloyd, R. 159, 171
Lobowsky, J. 397, 412
Loeb, P. 208
Loewenstein, R.J. 340, 353
Löffler, K.G. 500, 510, 515–16
Lofthouse, R. 353
Lolas-Stepke, F. 378, 388
London, G.M. 259, 277, 449, 465
Long, J.M. 29, 39
Longmore, I. 514
Longo, M.R. 449, 462
Loofbourrow, G.N. 106, 132
Look 122–4
Lopes da Silva, F.H. 137, 164, 172
LoPiccolo, J. 179, 186, 207, 210, 420, 438
LoPiccolo, L. 186, 210
Lord, J. 567, 580
Losito, B.D. 61, 70
Lottenbach, K. 472, 493
Loudon, R.G. 535, 551
Lourie, C.H. 527, 551

Loveless, N. 413
Lubar, J.F. 216, 221, 225, 237
Luborsky, L. 455, 463
Lucas, A.R. 539, 550
Luchins, D. 333, 356
Luckhurst, E. 161, 165
Ludbrook, J. 473, 492

Lum, L.C. 158–9, 171, 537, 551
Lumry, A.E. 16, 38, 62, 68, 365, 388, 408, 415
Lumsden, J. 299, 306
Lundberg, U. 249, 267, 271, 274
Lundgren, Y. 265, 278
Lund-Johansen, P. 259, 272, 276, 450, 463
Lundström, N. 297, 305
Lunsford, L. 294–5, 305
Luparello, T.J. 524, 526–7, 551–3
Luper, C.I. 571, 576, 580
Luria, A.R. 139, 171
Lusso, F.M. 268, 275
Luthe, W. 453, 465
Lutterjohann, M. 566, 583
Lutz, D.J. 227, 236
Lutzenberger, W. 344, 356
Lykken, D.T. 13, 27, 32, 36–7, 46, 55, 58, 62, 68, 81–2, 86, 88, 100–1, 149, 154, 168–9, 171, 359, 365, 382, 387–8, 404–5, 407, 414–16
Lykken, J.D. 416
Lyles, J.N. 210
Lynch, J.P. 29, 39
Lynn, R. 144, 171
Lynn, S. 475, 485, 492–4
Lyons, H.A. 527, 551, 552

Mabel, P. 291, 306
McAdam, W.A. 340, 353
McCaffrey, R.J. 189, 211, 454, 464
McCallum, R.W. 501, 516
McCallum, W. 299, 308
McCallum, W.C. 343, 354, 356, 401, 413
McCallum, W.V. 403, 412
McCann, B. 521, 551
McCann, B.S. 127, 134, 180, 182, 211
McCann, D.S. 223, 237, 251, 252, 254, 277, 326
McCanne, T.R. 226, 234
McCaul, K.D. 221
Maccoby, N. 195, 210
McClelland, D.C. 161, 171
McClelland, J.L. 110, 133
McClenahan, K.L. 324, 326
McClure, G.M. 157, 166
McConaghy, N. 181–2, 186, 211, 425–6, 432, 438
McCormack, K. 163, 168, 171
McCouchghey, J. 568, 581
McCoy, G.C. 447, 461

McCrady, R.E. 569, 577
McCrae, R.R. 544, 548
McCrory, W.W. 449, 464
McCubbin, J.A. 212, 264, 277
McCubbin, R.J. 353
McCullough, J.P. 365, 367, 386
McCutcheon, B.A. 188, 213
McDonald, B. 354
Macdonald, H. 161, 172
McDonald, R.D. 191, 210
McDonough, L.B. 446, 464
MacDougall, J.M. 265, 267, 272
McEachern, H.M. 30, 39
McFadden, E.R. 522, 527, 529, 551, 552
McFarland, C.E. 368, 392
McGilley, B.M. 229, 236
McGlashan, T.H. 15, 44, 333, 352, 397, 399, 418
McGowan, W.T. 182, 189, 211
McGrady, A. 233, 237
McGrath, M. 470, 474, 479, 493
McGrath, P. 325
McGuinness, D. 9, 40, 149, 172
McGuire, S. 138, 174
McHugh, R. 572, 581
McHugo, G.J. 90, 102
McIlvain, H.E. 39, 464
McIntyre, K.O. 195, 205
McIntyre-Kingsolver, K. 211
McKeever, W.F. 162, 171
McKenna, F.P. 129, 134, 290, 308
MacKenzie, J.N. 520, 551
McKenzie, S.J. 31, 35
McKinney, M.E. 30, 39, 235, 456, 457, 464
McKinney, W.T. 358, 385
McKoon, G. 112, 133
McKusick, V.A. 49, 69
McLaurin, R.L. 535, 551
McLean, A. Jr 118, 133
McLean, K. 445, 465
McLellan, D.L. 556, 566, 579
McLennan, J.E. 535, 551
MacLeod, C. 116–17, 129–30, 133, 288, 304, 334, 350, 354
MacLeod-Morgan, C. 162, 171
MacMillan, F.W. 61, 70
McMullin, R.E. 197, 211
McNally, R.J. 284, 287, 289–304, 306, 334, 352
McNeil, D.W. 107, 132
McNeil, T.F. 149, 171

McPherson, C.A. 316, 327, 466
MacPherson, E.L.R. 574, 580
McQuaid, K.J. 450, 464
Maddock, J.W. 432, 438
Maddock, R.J. 324, 326–7
Magarian, G.J. 533, 535, 537, 539–40, 551
Magnani, B. 244, 270
Magoun, H.W. 149, 172
Mah, C.D. 162, 173
Maher, B.A. 14, 34
Mahler, F. 478, 491, 493
Mainardi, J.A. 443, 458, 465, 466
Malagelada, J.-R. 506, 516
Malatesta, V. 422, 438
Malcomson, K.G. 505, 516
Malec, J. 210
Maley, M. 149, 171
Malinow, K.L. 29, 39
Malloy, P.F. 180, 196, 211
Malott, J.M. 221, 237
Maltzman, I. 143, 171, 301, 306, 413
Manchanda, R. 144, 146, 153, 165, 168, 170
Mancia, G. 444, 463
Mandel, B. 66
Mandel, M.R. 128, 134
Mandell, 143
Mandler, G. 293, 306
Mann, A.H. 446, 463
Manning, A.P. 509, 516
Manning, R.D. 248, 274, 451, 462
Manschrek, T. 155, 170, 484, 493
Manuck, S.B. 88–9, 101, 186, 210–11, 243, 245, 259–61, 264, 267–8, 272, 275–7, 448, 450, 452, 463–4, 527, 553
Marchini, E. 206
Marchione, K. 22, 39, 319, 326
Marciano, F. 374, 388, 390
Marcille, P.J. 236
Marcus, J. 400, 415
Margolin, R. 385
Margraf, J. 29, 39, 315, 321, 324, 326
Maricq, H. 478, 493
Marin, P.R. 563, 581
Marin, R.S. 385
Marinacci, A.A. 211, 560, 580
Marion, R.J. 524, 532, 543, 550, 553
Marks, F. 161, 171
Marks, I. 213–14, 326, 355
Marks, I.M. 115, 119, 131–3, 285–8, 291, 294, 300, 306

Marmot, M.G. 223, 231, 238–9, 459, 464
Marsden, C.D. 557, 561, 564, 566, 574, 577, 580–2
Marset, P. 115, 131
Marshall, C. 564, 576
Marshall, W.L. 211, 214
Marshall-Goodell, B. 23–4, 34
Marteau, T. 287, 303
Martin, B. 19, 20, 39
Martin, C. 420, 438
Martin, C.J. 543, 549
Martin, D. 238
Martin, I. 23, 25, 30–2, 39, 177, 193, 203, 213, 517
Martin, J.B. 67
Martin, J.E. 183, 195, 211–12, 264, 275
Martin, N.D. 103
Martin, P.R. 181, 211
Martinsson, A. 523, 551
Maruta, T. 277
Maser, J.D. 517
Mason, J.W. 246, 253–4, 256, 276–7, 496, 506, 514, 516
Massey, E.W. 565, 582
Massong, S.R. 563, 580
Master, D. 343, 350, 355
Masters, J.C. 182, 212
Masters, W.H. 421, 423–4, 428, 438
Mathé, A.A. 526, 529, 551
Mathew, R.J. 222, 237, 250, 253, 255–6, 276, 369, 372, 389
Mathews, A. 129, 130, 133, 217, 229, 237, 239, 290, 306, 334, 350, 354
Mathews, A.M. 311–12, 315, 325–6
Mathews, K.P. 522, 552
Matias, R. Jr 317, 326
Matousek, M. 359, 374–5, 389–90
Matthews, J. 279
Matthews, K. 254–5, 261–2, 267, 272–3, 276–7
Matthews, K.A. 189, 199, 211, 446, 460
Matthews, W.B. 564, 581
Matthys, H. 525, 551
Matthysse, S. 57, 64, 69
Mattson, R.H. 342, 356
Maudler, J.M. 293, 306
Maurer, K. 137, 163, 171
Mavissakalian, L. 197, 211
Mavissakalian, M. 22, 30, 39, 127, 133, 316, 319, 326, 336, 345, 353, 354
Mawson, D. 354
May, J.R. 293, 306

Mayer, N. 571, 582
Mayes, M. 474, 489, 492
Mayhall, B. 568, 582
Mazziotta, J.C. 368–9, 385, 390
Mead, J. 525, 549
Meah, M.S. 538, 549
Means, J. 528, 552
Meares, R. 14, 37, 564, 581
Mecacci, L. 136, 171
Mechanic, D. 544, 547, 552
Mednick, S.A. 52, 60, 67, 69–70, 149, 171, 400, 416
Meehl, P.E. 58, 69
Mefferd, R.B. 84, 104
Mefford, I.N. 205, 256, 271
Meichenbaum, D. 288, 290, 307
Meier, B. 478, 491, 493
Melamed, B.G. 107–8, 132–3, 180, 190, 201, 207, 209–10, 292, 306
Melica, A.M. 358, 391
Melin, B. 267, 274
Mellion, N.B. 235
Mellström, B. 336, 356
Melosh, A. 267, 279
Meltzer, H.Y. 68, 404, 414
Melville, D.R. 261, 278, 447, 466
Mendels, J. 48, 67
Mendelsohn, M. 125, 131
Mendelson, W.B. 340, 353
Mendlewicz, J. 370, 386, 391
Mendlowitz, M. 473, 493
Meredith, R.L. 35
Mermelstein, R.J. 211
Merrens, M.R. 22, 44
Merrin, E.L. 154, 170, 405, 415
Mersch, P.-P. 320, 325
Merskey, H. 157, 158, 171
Messick, G. 170
Messick, S. 78, 80, 102
Metter, E.J. 369, 389
Metz, J.R. 528, 552
Meulen, J. van der 278
Meurer, W. 223, 237
Mewaldt, S.P. 560, 579
Meyer, J.S. 369, 389
Meyer, V. 336, 354
Mezzich, J.E. 127, 134, 403, 417
Mialet, J.P. 405, 416
Miall, W.E. 443, 460
Michaels, R.R. 223, 237
Michelson, L. 22, 30, 39, 182, 197, 211, 316, 319, 323, 326, 336, 354

Micklich, D. 528, 552
Middaugh, S.J. 574, 576, 581
Miho, O. 506, 516
Mikami, A. 154, 172
Mikhailova, E.S. 364–6, 388
Mikkelsen, U. 60, 69
Miklich, D.R. 180, 211, 526–7, 554
Milberg, S. 113, 131
Milic-Emili, J. 525, 553
Millar, R.N. 551
Miller, A. 569, 580
Miller, E.W. 268, 275
Miller, G.A. 16, 27, 38–9, 107, 116–17,
  120, 132–3, 179, 197, 206, 210, 380,
  390
Miller, I. 472, 493
Miller, M.A. 259, 278
Miller, M.C. 576, 581
Miller, N.E. 23, 39, 181, 212, 225, 237–8,
  264, 272, 578
Miller, P.M. 211
Miller, P. McC. 546, 550
Miller, S.T. 454, 460
Miller, W. 379, 390
Miller, W.M. 448, 462
Milliez, P.L. 259, 477, 449, 465
Millington, W.T. 537, 554
Milner, B. 147, 171
Mills, D.E. 222, 238
Mims, W.H. 560, 581
Minami, H. 591, 516
Minear, W.L. 567, 581
Miner, M.H. 39, 464
Minnitti, R. 158, 165
Mintz, L.I. 400, 413
Mirkin, A.M. 365–6, 390, 409, 416
Mirsky, A. 61, 67
Mirsky, A.F. 402, 416
Mishima, Y. 480, 493
Mitchell, V.P. 222, 235
Mitchell-Heggs, N. 325, 335, 354
Mittelmann, B. 475, 494
Miyabo, S. 254, 277
Mizner, G. 69, 338, 355
Mizushima, N. 254, 277
Möck, J. 86, 100
Mock, J. 125, 131
Mocks, J. 53, 67
Moeller, T.A. 452, 464
Mohr, J.P. 573, 582
Mohr, T. 574, 579
Moldofsy, H. 574, 581

Molineaux, D. 445, 466
Molineux, D. 230, 239
Molk, L. 528, 552
Moll, C.B. 571, 577
Monakhov, K. 376, 390
Monga, T.N. 573, 579
Montebugnoli, C. 244, 270
Montgomery, G.K. 558, 581
Montgomery, M.A. 333, 354
Montgomery, P.J. 557, 579
Moore, A. 340, 353
Morel, D.R. 536, 552
Morey, L.C. 12, 39, 185, 211
Morgan, A.H. 161, 172
Moriarty, R. 260, 277
Morihisa, J.M. 385, 403, 413
Morimoto, T. 52, 69
Mörlin, C. 253, 274
Morokoff, P. 433–4, 437, 438
Moron, P. 369, 386
Morozutti, C. 299, 308
Morrell, C. 217, 238
Morrell, D.C. 544, 552
Morrell, E.M. 223, 238
Morris, A.F. 509, 516
Morris, N.M. 433, 439
Morrison, D.F. 90–1, 97, 102
Morrison, J.F.B. 497, 511, 516
Morrison, R.L. 212, 264, 276, 448, 464
Morrow, G.R. 217, 238
Morrow, L. 139, 172
Mortel, K. 369, 389
Moruzzi, G. 149, 172
Moscovitch, M. 137, 172
Moser, E. 369, 387
Moser, M. 451, 465
Moses, J. 225, 229, 238–9
Motomuja, T. 473, 491
Motta, P.E. 543, 552
Moulthrop 408
Mowrer, O.H. 284, 289, 300, 307
Mrazek, D.A. 526, 553
Mroczele, M. 572, 581
Mueller, E.A. 335, 353
Mueller, W.C. 558, 581
Mueller-Spahn, F. 369, 387
Mulaik, S.A. 202, 209
Mulder, T. 560, 581
Mulholland, T. 354
Mullaney, D.J. 206
Müller, F.B. 447, 464
Müller, G.M. 499–509, 515–16

Müller, W. 82, 84, 88, 95, 100
Müller-Oerlinghausen, B. 378, 391
Munoz, R. 59, 66, 379, 387, 408, 413
Munro, R. 352
Muranaka, M. 270, 271
Murphy, D.L. 16, 37, 56, 61, 66, 69, 335, 340, 347, 353, 356
Murphy, J.K. 565, 581
Murphy, W.D. 190, 195, 204, 212, 432, 439
Murray, E.J. 227, 234, 289, 307
Murray, R.M. 149, 172, 332, 352
Muser, J. 528, 552
Mussi, A. 263, 270–1
Myers, J.K. 311–12, 326–7, 331, 354
Myers, P.E. 31, 33, 88, 98
Myers, R.H. 70
Myers, S.J. 363, 385
Myrtek, M. 79–82, 84, 88, 95, 100, 102
Myslobodsky, M.S. 365, 367, 390

Nacht, M. 214
Nadel, J.A. 521, 548
Naditch, M.P. 446, 464
Naftchi, N. 473, 493
Nagler, S.H. 340, 354
Nahl, M. 287, 305
Nakamura, D.K. 443, 466
Nakamura, M. 265, 278
Nanda, H. 89, 99
Napoli, A. 201, 212
Narayan, M.G. 571, 577, 583
Natelson, B.H. 201, 212
Nathan, R.J. 453, 461
Naumann, E. 449, 460
Nay, W.R. 28, 39
Naylor, S.L. 67
Neale, J.M. 12, 39
Nebylitsyn, V.D. 8, 39
Nee, J. 394, 413
Nee, L. 70
Neff, D.F. 205
Negri, F. 358, 391
Neilsen, T. 474, 493
Nelson, E. 453, 466
Nelson, R. 176–7, 184, 212
Nelson, R.O. 20, 39
Nesse, R.M. 251–2, 254–6, 277, 314, 326
Nesselroade, J.R. 77–8, 102
Neste, P.J. 272
Nestel, P.J. 449, 464
Neuhaus, E.C. 520, 526, 552

Neus, H. 84, 102, 452, 464
Newlin, D.B. 364, 390
Newman, J.B. 10, 36
Newman, M. 66
Newsombe, W.T. 154, 172
Nicassio, P.M. 22, 39
Nicholls, M.G. 265, 279
Nichols, K.A. 312, 326
Nicoli, M. 524, 552
Nield, J.E. 527, 529, 552
Nielsen, S. 470, 481, 489, 491, 493, 494
Nielsen, T.C. 400, 416
Nielson, D.H. 227, 236, 238
Niemeck, W.M. 506, 516
Nigl, A.J. 557, 578
Nikiforov, A. 376, 390
Niklasson, F. 382, 385
Nikolau, T. 143, 168
Nil, R. 70
Niman, C. 468, 578
Nin, A. 251, 272
Nirenberg, T.D. 213
Niwa, S.-I. 69, 137, 174, 403, 417
Nix, S. 514
Nixon, P.G.F. 539, 549
Noble, P. 365–7, 390
Noble, P.J. 13–14, 40
Nolfe, G. 374, 388–9
Noonberg, A.R. 6, 23, 40
Noonan, M. 157, 165
Norman, R.A. Jr 248, 274, 451, 462
North, L.W. 443, 464
North, W.R.S. 453, 464
Norton, G.R. 310, 326, 574, 582
Novaco, R.W. 212
Novey, H.S. 531, 554
Nowalk, M.P. 202, 214, 221, 239
Noyes, R. 297, 305
Nuechterlein, K.H. 11, 16, 40, 396–7, 399, 404, 410, 413, 416
Nugent, C.A. 444, 460
Nulson, P.D. 568, 581
Nunnally, J. 97, 102
Nutter, D. 345, 353
Nutz, B. 84, 99
Nwaobloi, O.N. 569–70, 581
Nyström, C. 359, 373, 375–7, 383, 390

Obeso, J.A. 561, 574, 581
O'Brien, E.T. 443, 465
O'Brien, G.T. 121, 132, 196, 205, 293, 304

Obrist, P.A. 5, 11, 24, 32, 38, 40, 83, 85–6, 93, 101–2, 114, 116, 133, 141, 172, 212, 263, 276, 448, 450–1, 456, 462–4, 543, 547
Obrist, W.D. 387
O'Byre, P.M. 524, 550
O'Cain, C.F. 529, 530, 552
O'Donohue, W.T. 431, 433–4, 438, 439
Oesterreich, K. 369, 388
O'Gorman, J.G. 8, 40, 143, 172
Ohlmeyer, P. 428, 439
Ohlund, L. 15, 40
Ohman, A. 6, 10, 13, 15, 17–18, 28, 40, 52, 69, 127, 134, 284, 286, 291, 299, 301–2, 305, 307, 312, 326, 396–9, 410–13, 416
Oi, M. 506, 516
Okawa, M. 374, 389
Oken, D. 80, 101
Oldham, R.K. 210
Olivieu, D. 291, 294, 303
Olofsson, G. 299, 307
Olsen, N. 470, 494
Olson, R. 445
Oltmanns, T.F. 12, 39
Olton, D.S. 6, 23, 40
Onesti, G. 450, 451, 459, 461
Opton, E.M. 74, 99
Orehek, J. 524, 552
O'Reilly, D.E. 567, 581
Orr, S.P. 128, 134
Orvaschel, H. 326, 331, 354, 355
Osborne, R.K. 261, 274
Oseasohn, R. 229, 238
Osgood, C. 114, 134
Ossip, D.J. 190, 207
Ossip-Klein, D.J. 195, 212
Ost, L.-G. 22, 38, 40, 282–4, 286–9, 293–5, 298, 305, 307, 310, 318–21, 323–6, 410, 412
Österberg, B. 382, 385
Ostfeld, A.M. 278, 446, 464
Ostrom, C.W. Jr 202, 212
O'Toole, D.M. 53, 69
Otten, H. 452, 464
Ottina, K. 67
Overall, J.E. 146, 172
Overall, J.F. 77, 97, 102
Overall, K. 466
Overton, D.A. 154, 173, 405, 417
Owen, F. 353
Owens, D.G.C. 353

Pabst, P. 331, 353
Pacella, B.L. 340, 354
Page, I.H. 246, 258, 277
Paivio, A. 112, 134
Paley, H. 397, 412
Palij, M. 276, 325, 553
Pallmeyer, T.P. 21, 34
Pandey, G.N. 415
Panksepp, J. 106, 134
Papathansion, K. 480, 494
Pardine, P. 201, 212
Parry-Jones, W. 564, 581
Parsons, O.A. 140, 141, 169
Pasin, R.D. 443, 463
Paskewitz, D.A. 29, 39
Pass, H.L. 402, 416
Patel, C.H. 453, 458, 459, 464
Patel, D.J. 454, 461
Patel, G.L. 223, 228, 231, 238, 239
Patel, M. 459, 464
Pathman, J. 149, 166
Patil, C.P. 542, 550
Patterson, R.M. 562, 581
Patterson, T. 397–8, 412, 416–17
Paul, G.L. 227, 238
Paul, O. 442, 464
Paul, R. 7, 37
Pauls, D.L. 66
Paulus, W. 509, 516
Pavlov, I.P. 8, 40, 495–6, 516
Pawlak, A.E. 162, 173
Paxton, R. 212
Peacock, J. 473, 494
Pearson, M.G. 543, 552
Peatfield, R.C. 143, 168
Peattie, B. 543, 552
Peck, D.F. 565, 582
Peek, R. 474, 493
Peloquin, L.J. 16, 38, 46, 62, 68, 359, 365, 388, 408, 415
Pennebaker, J.W. 514, 516, 540, 544, 552
Penny, R. 161, 165, 470, 474, 493
Penzien, D.B. 236
Pepys, J. 523, 552
Perel, J.M. 347, 352
Perigault, J. 341, 347, 351
Perini, C. 260, 277, 447, 464
Perissaki, C. 363, 390
Perkin, G.D. 158, 172
Perkins 230
Perlmutter, J. 173
Perloff, D. 261, 277

Perlstein, W.M. 403, 413
Pernicano, K. 161
Peronnet, F. 222, 239
Perris, C. 358, 373–8, 383, 386–7, 390, 412
Perry, A. 162, 168
Perry, L.B. 429, 439
Perry, W.L.W. 248, 274
Petrini, B. 271
Petersen, K.E. 400, 416
Peterson, L. 20, 40
Peterson, W. 525, 549
Petrie, J.C. 443, 465
Petterson, I-L. 271
Pettigrew, K. 338, 353
Petty, R.E. 18, 23, 29, 34, 97, 99
Pfeffer, J.M. 533, 539, 552
Pfefferbaum 150–2, 172, 326, 379–80, 390, 402–3, 409, 416–17
Pfeiffer, C.J. 516
Pfohl, B. 358, 392
Pfurtscheller, G. 137, 164, 172
Phelan, J.G. 191, 206
Phelan, M. 143, 146, 155, 156, 168
Phelps, M.E. 368–9, 385, 390
Phil, M. 333, 356
Philip, R.L. 527, 552
Philips, C. 184, 212
Philips, C.H. 21, 27, 28, 37, 40
Philips, J. 531, 557
Phillips, J.S. 176, 209
Phillipson, E.A. 543, 552
Piacentini, S. 70
Pichot, P. 405, 416
Pickar, D. 358, 385, 389
Pickering, G.W. 259, 277
Pickering, T.G. 99, 181, 212, 247–8, 260, 264, 272, 277–8, 444, 465
Picton, T.W. 150, 165, 172
Pierce, C. 260, 272, 447, 460
Piercy, M.F. 139, 166
Pilbram, K.H. 172
Pilon, R.N. 213, 483, 493, 494
Pilowsky, I. 158, 165, 446, 465
Pincus, 539
Pinker, S. 110, 132
Pirke, K.M. 506, 515
Pirke, R.M. 516
Pisa, Z. 442, 462
Pitman, R.K. 21, 40, 128, 134
Pivik, R.T. 405–6, 416
Plapp, J.M. 6, 42

Plewis, I. 76, 102
Ploog, D. 515
Pocock, P.V. 403, 412
Podivinsky, F. 562, 564, 582
Pohl, R. 325
Polatin, P. 340, 354
Polefrone, J.M. 89, 101, 186, 211, 264, 276, 448, 450, 464
Polinsky, R.J. 70
Polish, E. 506, 516
Pollack, C. 432, 439
Pollen, D. 70
Pollock, V.E. 67
Pomeranz, D.M. 199, 208
Pomeroy, W. 420, 438
Pope, A.T. 24, 40
Poppen, R. 571, 583
Porchet, M. 444, 465
Porges, S.W. 17, 34, 74, 86, 101, 102, 177, 206
Porjesz, B. 66, 151, 172, 199, 212
Portelange, P. 370, 386, 391
Porter, J. 478, 494
Porter, R.W. 498, 514
Portnoy, B. 251, 279
Posner, M.I. 411, 416
Post, R.M. 385, 386
Powell, G.E. 27, 43
Pregibon, D. 99, 272
Prentky, R.A. 400, 416
Prescott, J. 153, 165
Presslich, O. 53, 69
Priabram, K.H. 9, 40, 149, 172
Price, D.B. 254, 277
Price, K.P. 6, 23, 36
Price, T.R. 383, 390
Prigatano, G.P. 291–2, 307
Pringle, R. 474, 494
Pritchard, D.A. 224, 236
Pritchard, W.S. 402–3, 416
Procci, W.R. 278, 466
Proctor, J.D. 207
Proctor, L.R. 68, 154, 169, 404–6, 414
Proietti, J.M. 450, 463, 464
Proietti, S.M. 186, 211
Prout, M.F. 453, 461
Proux, G.B. 150, 172
Prue, D.M. 212
Puente, A.E. 227, 238
Püll, O. 504, 515
Purcell, K. 525, 528, 538, 552
Puthezhath, N. 313, 325

Puzantin, V.R. 56, 66
Pylyshyn, Z.W. 108–10, 134

Qualls, C.B. 421, 439
Quillian, M.R. 108, 134
Quinsey, V.L. 212

Rabavilas, A.D. 145, 172, 344, 346, 352,
    354, 363, 365, 390
Rachelefsky, G.S. 521, 553
Rachman, S. 10, 12, 15, 20–2, 28, 34,
    36–7, 40, 108, 115, 134, 179, 197,
    208–9, 285, 288–9, 292–30, 296, 300,
    302, 307–8, 331, 336–8, 347, 351,
    354–5
Raczyuski, J.M. 6, 24, 41, 74, 102
Rader, S.J. 186, 211, 450, 464
Rafaelsen, O.J. 6, 43, 48, 66
Raftery, E.B. 89, 103
Rahe, R.H. 242, 275
Raichle, M.F. 155–6, 166, 172–3
Raine, A. 153, 165
Rainey, J.M. 325
Rajaratnam, N. 89, 99
Rakaczky, C.J. 276
Raman, A.C. 70
Ramsdale, E.H. 524, 550
Randall, O. 273, 461
Rao, K. 383, 390
Rapaport, J. 355
Rapee, R. 314, 326, 542, 553
Rapp, N.S. 563, 582
Rappapart, M. 67, 162, 171
Rapport, M.D. 311, 325
Rasmussen, K. 535, 553
Rasmussen, P.V. 400, 417
Rasmussen, S.A. 330–2, 355
Ratcliff, R. 112, 133
Rauchfleisch, U. 260, 277, 447, 464
Raulin, M.L. 62, 66, 404, 410, 412
Ray, R.L. 31, 90, 102
Ray, W.J. 6, 23–4, 40–2, 74, 102, 177,
    193, 213
Raynaud, M. 469, 470, 472–91, 494
Raynor, R. 284, 307
Read, N.W. 509, 514, 517
Readhead, C.P.A. 318, 324, 550
Reavky, W. 566, 582
Reba, P. 521, 551
Redd, W.E. 508, 516
Redding, F.K. 149, 172
Redmond, D.P. 248, 275, 480, 492

Reed, G.F. 334, 355
Reed, S.D. 23, 24, 41
Rees, L. 324
Reeves, J.L. 227, 238, 452, 465
Regenes, E.M. 570, 577
Reich, W. 19, 41
Reid, J. 445, 465
Reid, J.L. 256, 275
Reiman, E.M. 156, 172, 173
Reinach, S.G. 551
Reiser, M.F. 279
Reivich, M. 156, 173, 388
Reker, D. 375, 392
Remington, R.D. 444, 451, 463, 465
Renault, P.F. 214
Renfordt, E. 376, 391
Renne, C.M. 211
Renoux, G. 159, 173
Renoux, M. 159
Report of the Task Force on Blood
    Pressure Control in Children 450,
    465
Reyher, J. 162, 169
Reynolds, C.F. 385
Rhodes, L. 310, 326
Rhonder, J. 162, 168
Rice, D.G. 86, 103
Rich, E.S. 525, 554
Richardson, R.B. 532, 550
Richter, C.P. 364, 390
Richter, R. 530, 553
Richter-Heinrich, E. 228, 233, 238
Ricks, D.F. 221, 236
Ricks, N. 61, 67
Ridgeway, V. 217, 237
Riedel, J.A. 412
Rieder, R.O. 57
Riege, W.H. 369, 389
Rieger, W. 387
Rimm, D.C. 182, 212, 289, 307
Rimmo, P.A. 284, 301, 302, 307
Rinieris, P. 363, 390
Rion, R. 444, 465
Ripley, H.S. 543, 549
Ripley, N.S. 166
Risberg, J. 369, 388, 390
Risch, N. 66
Risk, M. 494
Ritchie, J. 509, 516
Ritter, W. 401, 413
Rivard, D. 425, 439
Rivers, S.M. 162, 173

Rizzo, P.A. 299, 308
Robbins, E. 173
Roberts, R. 118, 134
Roberts, R.S. 462
Robertson, C. 482, 494
Robertson, D.W. 569, 582
Robertson, M.M. 138, 174
Robins, E. 59, 66, 358, 379, 387, 391, 395, 408, 413, 417
Robins, L.N. 331, 355
Robinson, J. 353
Robinson, J.W. 30, 32, 41, 43, 88, 102, 318, 326
Robinson, R.G. 383, 390
Robinson, S.K. 525, 549
Robinson, T.E. 9, 43
Rochford, J.M. 373, 390–1
Rockstroh, B. 344, 356
Rockwell, F.V. 340, 355
Roddie, I.C. 363, 385
Rodichok, L.D. 205
Rodman, G. 473, 494
Roemer, R.A. 151, 170, 342, 355, 378, 382, 391, 402, 405, 417
Rogers, G.S. 433, 439
Rogers, L. 236
Rogosa, D.R. 76, 78, 81, 103
Rohrbaugh, J.W. 151, 169, 355
Rolf, J.E. 15, 43
Romano, N.W. 152, 169
Rondot, P. 564, 582
Röper, G. 336, 355
Rosch, J. 478, 494
Roscoe, B. 251, 272
Rose, G. 442–5, 465
Rose, R.M. 259, 272
Rose, S.C. 61, 70
Rosen, A.A. 352
Rosen, G. 428, 439
Rosen, G.M. 212
Rosen, R.C. 212, 424–6, 436, 439
Rosenbaum, A.H. 254, 277
Rosenhan, D.L. 286–7, 307
Rosenman, R.H. 243, 274, 447, 448, 461, 465
Rosenthal, D. 18, 41, 396, 416–17
Rosenthal, R. 505, 517
Rosenthal, R.A. 449, 464
Rosenthal, S.V. 520, 553
Rosenthal, T. 56, 66
Rosenthal, T.L. 202, 209
Roskies, E. 103, 220, 229, 238

Rösler, F. 74, 102–3, 413
Ross, A. 239, 261, 278, 447, 466
Ross, J. 113, 131, 227
Roth, D.L. 230, 236
Roth, R. 572, 579
Roth, R.S. 375, 391
Roth, W.T. 29, 39, 150, 152, 172–3, 223, 315–16, 319, 321–2, 324, 326–7, 379, 390, 401–3, 409, 411, 413, 416–17
Rothblatt, A.B. 429, 439
Rothenberg, S.J. 155, 170
Rothwell, J.C. 561, 565, 574, 577, 581, 582
Routtenberg, A. 9, 41
Rowan, G.E. 565, 582
Rowe, G.G. 535, 553
Roxans, N.R. 563, 565, 582
Ruback, L.A. 525, 549
Rubens, R.L. 13, 41
Rubin, H. 433, 438
Rubin, H.B. 196, 209
Rubin, P. 445, 465
Rubinstein, E. 445, 465
Ruchkin, D.S. 402, 417
Rüddel, H. 39, 235, 450, 452, 464, 465
Ruddle, F.H. 49, 69
Rudy, T.E. 220, 232, 239
Rugg, D. 188, 208
Rugh, J.D. 23, 24, 37, 41, 183, 203, 212, 556, 558, 582
Rumelhart, D.E. 110, 133
Rusiniak, K.W. 506, 515
Russ, K.L. 563, 582
Russel, R.W. 497, 498, 516
Russell, G. 558, 569, 583
Russell, G.A. 450, 461
Russell, P. 212
Russell, P.O. 195, 212
Russo, D.C. 217, 235
Ryan, P. 21, 34
Ryan, R.M. 299, 305
Rymar, K. 69, 403, 417

Saab, P.G. 261, 277
Sabharwal, S. 474, 487, 489, 492
Sachar, E.J. 6, 43, 271
Sachitano, J.A. 326
Sachs, D.A. 568, 582
Sachs-Frankel, G. 562, 578, 580
Sackeim, H.A. 146, 160, 173
Sackett, D.L. 462

Safar, M.E. 259, 277, 449, 465
Safian, P. 88, 100
Safran, J.D. 10, 36
St George-Hyslop, P.H. 50, 70
Saitoh, O. 51, 69, 403–4, 417
Sakaguchi, A.Y. 67
Sakheim, D.K. 204, 434, 437
Saletu, B. 52, 69
Saletu, M. 69
Salis, P.J. 435, 438
Salkovskis, P.M. 543, 545, 548, 553
Sallis, J.F. 84, 101
Salmon, D. 70
Salovaara, L. 271
Salt, P. 128, 134
Salvaggio, J.E. 522, 549
Salzman, L.F. 400, 402, 406, 410, 416–17
Sambhi, M.P. 233, 236, 454, 462
Samson-Dulfus, D. 378, 387
Samuelly, I. 151, 172
Sanders, B.J. 222, 235
Sanders, D.B. 565, 582
Sanderson, W.C. 127, 132
Sandford, D.A. 569, 576, 578
Sandman, C.A. 181, 213, 497, 517
Sannerstedt, R. 265, 278
Sapira, J.D. 260, 277, 473
Sarbin, T.R. 126, 134
Sargant, W. 335, 354
Saron, C. 360, 388, 391
Sartorius, N. 11, 44, 144, 174, 394, 418
Sartory, G. 10, 15, 24, 26, 41, 179, 208,
    291–3, 398–9, 308, 338, 343, 346,
    350, 354–6
Sattler, H. 480, 492
Saunders, K.B. 542, 550
Saunders, N.L. 11, 33
Savignano-Bowman, J. 70
Schachter, J. 447, 465
Schachter, S. 9, 41
Schaeffer, M.A. 205
Schäfer, N. 449, 459, 462
Schaffer, C.E. 360, 375, 377, 383, 391
Schales, J.R. 558, 582
Schalling, D. 258, 260, 261, 277, 278
Schanberg, S. 267, 279, 473, 494
Schater, M. 557, 581
Schatzberg, A.F. 277
Scheib, E.T. 260, 277, 473, 494
Scheier, I.H. 142, 170
Schell, A.M. 10, 35, 362, 286, 411, 413
Schell, K.W. 451, 462

Scher, H. 79, 103, 238
Scheuer, J. 222, 238
Schiavi, R. 432–3, 437, 439
Schilder, P. 338, 355
Schleifer, S.J. 161, 173
Schlömer, P. 84, 99
Schmader, A. 466
Schmid, H. 15, 42
Schmidt, K.H. 238
Schmidt, T.H. 449, 459, 462
Schmueli, J. 400, 415
Schneider, H.J. 82–4, 88, 95, 100
Schneider, J.A. 190, 192, 204, 459
Schneider, R.H. 260, 277, 447, 465
Schneider, W. 111, 130, 132
Schneiderman, N. 237, 247, 248, 277,
    443, 463
Schnurer, A. 336, 354
Schoenberger, J.A. 448, 466
Schoenecke, O.W. 449, 459
Schocnfeld, D. 260, 272, 447, 460
Schoentgen, S. 278, 466
Schoicket, S. 227, 237
Schomaker, L.R.B. 224, 239, 559, 577
Schonell, M. 22, 35, 530, 549
Schork, M.A. 257, 274, 446, 462
Schorman, R.H. 431, 438
Schotte, D. 288, 303, 308
Schreiner-Engel, P. 433, 439
Schringer, A. 261, 279
Schulhan, D. 230, 238
Schull, W.J. 257, 274, 446, 462
Schulsinger, F. 51, 60, 67, 69–70, 400,
    416
Schulte, W. 450, 465
Schulz, J.H. 453, 465
Schüssler, P. 511, 516
Schuster, M.M. 497, 502, 503, 505,
    508–13, 517
Schuster, P. 53, 69
Schwab 408
Schwaber, J.R. 525, 549
Schwartz, G.E. 6, 10, 18, 20, 24, 33, 35,
    41, 97, 100, 103, 110, 128, 134, 190,
    208, 216, 227, 236, 238, 363, 385,
    446, 452, 457, 460, 465–6
Schwartz, H.D. 139, 140, 169, 173
Schwartz, J.C. 217, 239
Schwartz, J.M. 385
Schwartz, P.J. 222, 234
Schwartz, S.G. 222, 239
Schwentler, E.P. 578

Schwitzgebel, R.L. 558, 582
Sclabassi, R.J. 385
Scott, D.S. 199, 210
Scott, N. 551
Scott, P.O. 21, 40
Sealy, J.E. 258, 276
Sedlacek, K. 565, 582
Seeger, B.R. 558, 569, 576, 582
Seeley, D.M. 429, 439
Seeley, T.T. 429, 439
Seer, P. 213, 452–3, 465
Seidman, D. 412
Selbmann, K.H. 462
Seligman, M.E.P. 10, 41, 286–7, 300–1,
    303, 307–8, 517
Selin, C.E. 385
Selye, H. 195, 213, 242–3, 246, 277–8
Semchuk, K.M. 250, 255, 276, 369, 389
Semlitsch, H.W. 53, 69
Senulis, J.A. 360, 388
Seraganian, P. 88, 103, 222, 229, 230,
    236–9
Sergeant, J. 140, 168
Sexton, M.M. 278
Seymour, K. 147, 168
Shafii, M. 27, 42
Shagass, C. 7, 41, 151, 154, 170, 173,
    42–3, 355, 378, 382, 291, 402, 405,
    408–9, 417
Shah, M.D. 566, 583
Shahani, B.T. 571, 573–4, 579, 582
Shahar, A. 213
Shapiro, A. 428–9, 432, 437, 439, 449,
    453, 465–7
Shapiro, A.P. 258–9, 267, 277–8
Shapiro, D. 227, 233, 236, 260, 278, 443,
    445, 447, 451–2, 545, 457–8, 460,
    462, 465–6
Shapiro, K. 232, 235, 453, 460
Shapiro, S. 226, 238
Sharpe, J.A. 53, 69
Sharrock, R. 129, 134, 290, 308
Shaub, H. 492
Shaughnessy, R. 68, 415
Shaw, C.F. 525, 553
Shaw, J. 446, 465
Shaw, P.M. 315, 325
Shaw, W.A. 109, 134
Shay, S.S. 505, 517
Shearer, S.L. 375, 391
Shedivy, D.I. 560, 582
Sheehan, D.V. 324

Sheehan, P.W. 117, 121, 134
Sheehy, M.P. 566, 582
Sheffield, B.F. 544, 551
Sheikh, J. 311, 324, 326
Shekelle, R.B. 448, 466
Sheller, J.R. 521, 548
Shepard, E.M. 246, 279, 448, 467
Shepard, R.N. 110, 134
Shepherd, J.T. 472, 494
Sheps, S.G. 261, 279
Sherman, D. 325
Sherry, G. 213
Sherwood, A. 543, 547
Shields, J. 47, 49, 55, 60, 62–3, 65, 67,
    69, 396, 414
Shillitoe, E.E. 336, 355
Shorter, R.G. 508, 516
Shoulson, I. 67
Shucard, D.W. 526, 551
Shukla, S. 373, 386
Shumaker, R.G. 574, 582
Shwartz, S.P. 132
Siddle, D.A.T. 10, 17, 25, 41, 356, 396,
    413, 417
Sides, J.K. 182, 205, 222, 234
Sidman, M. 187, 213
Siegal, C. 51, 69
Siegel, S. 338, 355
Siegel, S.C. 521, 553
Siever, L.J. 61, 69, 335, 353, 355
Sigal, M. 157, 166
Silfverskiöld, P. 369, 388
Silverberg, E. 483, 492
Silverman, M. 530, 554
Silverman, S. 206
Simms, K. 514
Simon, R. 394, 413
Simons, D.J. 340, 355
Simons, R. 380, 391
Simons, R.F. 16, 41, 61–2, 70, 151, 173,
    344, 356, 380, 390, 400, 404, 410,
    417
Sims, J. 239
Singer, J. 249, 271
Singer, M.T. 279, 448, 462
Singer, S. 9, 41
Singh, B. 473, 491
Sinnema, G. 515
Sintchak, G. 428, 439
Sinyor, D. 229–31, 238, 239
Sipprelle, C.N. 210
Siris, S.G. 161, 173

Sivertsson, R. 258, 265, 272, 278
Sjogren, K. 429, 437
Sjoqvist, F. 336, 356
Skinner, B.F. 107, 134
Skinner, D.B. 505, 515
Skinner, H.A. 12, 39, 97, 103, 185, 211
Skinner, S.R. 556, 577
Sklar, L.S. 219, 234
Skolnick, B.E. 387
Skovborg, F. 474, 493
Slade, P. 23, 41
Slater, J.F. 60, 66, 366, 386
Sleight, P. 259, 278
Sleisinger, M.H. 517
Slymen, D.J. 297, 305
Smeet, P. 527, 551
Smeraldi, E. 358-9, 391
Smichorowski, T. 572, 580
Smilga, C. 103, 238
Smith, A. 210
Smith, D. 207, 227, 236
Smith, D.D. 224, 234, 543, 553
Smith, D.E. 162, 173
Smith, G.E. 110, 132
Smith, H. 433, 439
Smith, J.C. 217, 239
Smith, K.V. 574, 582
Smith, M.M. 528, 530, 553
Smith, N.J. 143, 171
Smith, R. 221, 236
Smithwick, R. 482, 494
Smout, A.J.P. 500, 517
Snell, J.D. 527, 553
Snyder, F. 251, 279, 338, 353
Snyder, K.S. 400, 418
Sobell, L.C. 180, 213
Sobell, M.B. 213
Soderberg, B.L. 574, 583
Sokolov, E.M. 144, 173
Sokolov, E.N. 243, 246, 278, 396, 417
Sokolov, Y.N. 356
Sokolow, M. 251, 261, 277
Solberg, W.K. 556, 582
Soll, A.H. 507, 517
Solnick, R.L. 428, 439
Solomon, C.M. 405, 414
Solomon, F.S. 158, 165
Solononovici, A. 373, 383, 386
Solyom, L. 333, 356
Sommer, W. 152, 173, 402, 412
Sommerville, W. 297, 308
Sookman, D. 333, 356

Sorbi, S. 70
Sostek, A.J. 69
Sothmann, M.S. 230, 239
Souhrada, I. 524, 553
Souhrada, J. 527, 550
Sourek, K. 139, 173
Southam, M.A. 183, 204, 459, 466
Sovine, D.L. 557, 578
Spadaro, M. 299, 308
Spalding, D. 446, 465
Spanos, N.P. 162, 173
Spector, S.L. 524-7, 550-1, 553
Speicher, C.E. 170
Speilberger, C.D. 173
Speiss, W. 433, 439
Spelman, F.A. 569, 579
Spencer, D.D. 151, 174
Spencer, S.L. 430, 439
Spering, D.L. 569, 583
Sperry, R.W. 111, 134, 138, 173
Spielman, A. 432, 439
Spiker, D.G. 385
Spinks, J.A. 396-7, 417
Spitell, J.A. Jr 470, 475, 494
Spitzer, R.L. 358, 391, 395, 417
Spohn, H.E. 52, 70, 397, 417
Sprafkin, J.N. 20, 36
Spring, B.J. 18, 44, 150, 173
Sproule, M. 573, 579
Squires, A.C. 150-1, 173
Squires, N.K. 169
Sroka, L. 53, 67, 86, 100
Stacher, G. 498, 500, 502, 515, 517
Stainbrook, G.L. 275
Stalgaitis, S. 432, 439
Stamler, J. 259, 278, 448, 466
Stamler, R. 259, 278
Stampfl, T.G. 182, 213
Standley, J. 568, 578
Stangl, D. 358, 392
Stanley, J.C. 84, 99
Stark, L. 154, 170, 405, 415
Starkey, P. 397, 412
Starr, A. 150, 173
Starr, L.B. 383, 390
Staudenmayer, H. 525-6, 551, 553
Steele, H. 412
Stefan, H. 89, 103
Stefanis, C.N. 145, 172, 346, 352, 363, 390
Steffen, J.J. 213
Steger, J.C. 217, 236

Stein, D.B. 297, 304
Stein, M. 161, 173
Steinberg, H. 88, 100
Steinberg, J.L. 128, 134, 435, 439
Steiner, W. 525, 532, 553
Steinert, Y. 229, 238
Steinhauer, S. 48, 70, 151, 173
Steketee, G.S. 284, 289, 302–3, 307, 331,
  337, 346, 352–3, 356
Stemmler, G. 82, 84, 91, 97, 98, 103
Stenislie, C.E. 155, 174
Stenslie, C.E. 375, 391
Stephens, P.M. 257, 258, 264, 275
Stephens-Larson, P.M. 265, 275
Stephenson, D. 396, 417
Stephenson, N. 565, 583
Steptoe, A. 6, 9, 11, 18, 28, 42, 218–19,
  227, 229–32, 235, 239, 246, 249,
  261, 269, 278, 445, 447–9, 466,
  530–1, 553
Sterling, G.M. 530, 553
Stern, D.B. 157, 173
Stern, G.M. 577, 580
Stern, J.A. 4–6, 17, 19, 34, 42, 43, 53, 70
Stern, M. 466
Stern, R. 354
Stern, R.M. 23, 42, 177, 193, 213, 497–8,
  500, 515, 517
Sternbach, R.A. 4, 23, 32, 36, 42, 86, 103,
  177, 193, 208
Sterner, U. 285, 307
Stevens, J.R. 53, 70
Stevens, M. 15, 36, 353, 399, 413
Stewart, D.E. 529, 531, 549
Stewart, G.D. 70
Stickler, D. 213
Stickler, G.B. 539, 550
Stieglitz, R.-D. 378, 391
Stigler, S.M. 77, 102
Stiles, G. 474, 493
Stiller, R. 195, 212
Stockbrücker, R. 501, 514
Stoker, P.B. 195
Stoltzman, R. 326
Stone, H.L. 222, 234
Stone, N.M. 293, 304
Storrie, M.C. 365, 367, 391–2
Stott, F.D. 89, 103
Strasser, T. 179, 208, 442, 462
Straube, E.R. 15, 42, 398–9, 412, 417
Straumanis, J.J. 151, 170, 342, 355, 378,
  382, 291, 402, 417

Straus, A. 360, 388
Strauss, J.S. 407, 417
Streitman, S. 396, 414
Strian, F. 362, 364, 384, 391, 505, 515–16,
  517
Strogatz, D.S. 237
Ström, G. 243, 246, 248, 273, 449, 461
Struebel, C.F. 577, 583
Strunk, R.C. 526, 553
Strupp, H.H. 527, 553
Stuart, A. 78–9, 101
Stump, D.A. 368, 391
Sturani, A. 522, 553
Sturani, C. 522, 529, 553
Sturgeon, D. 11, 42–3, 400, 417
Sturgis, E. 6, 24, 29, 30, 42, 180, 185, 213
Sturn, W. 572, 583
Stoyva, J.M. 190, 204
Styva, J.M. 190, 204, 206
Suarez, E.C. 237
Suarez, Y. 188, 213
Suci, G. 114, 134
Suda, W.L. 527, 550
Suess, W.M. 543, 553
Sullivan, J.M. 206
Sullivan, K.F. 162, 171
Sullivan, P. 447, 449, 466
Sullivan, P.A. 260, 278
Sumida, R.M. 385
Sunderland, W.P. 560, 576, 578
Sundin, Ö. 243, 246, 253, 269, 273–4, 303
Supinski, R.S. 556, 577
Surwillo, W.W. 27, 42
Surwit, R.S. 6, 42, 180, 213, 222, 239,
  258, 264, 277–8, 443, 447, 465–6,
  473, 483, 493, 494, 576, 580
Sussex, J.N. 66
Sussman, M.D. 569, 581
Sutarman, M. 25, 42
Suter, P.M. 536, 552
Suter, T. 451, 467
Sutton, S. 35, 150, 173, 402, 417
Svali, J. 145, 174
Svebak, S. 540–1, 544, 554
Svedberg, A. 152, 171
Svedenhag, J. 265, 278
Svensson, A. 259, 272
Svensson, J. 259, 278
Swales, J.D. 442, 466
Swallow, K. 514
Swanson, L. 573, 577
Swarbrick, E.T. 509, 517

Swartzburg, M. 373, 390
Swartzman, L. 521, 551
Sweeney, D.R. 363, 385
Sweeney, H.W. 543, 553
Sylvester, D. 287, 294, 303
Sylvester, T.O. 53, 69
Syme, S.L. 278
Syndulko, K. 355
Szelenberger, W. 152, 173

Taggart, P. 295, 306
Tahmoush, A.J. 248, 275, 480, 492
Takahashi, R. 137, 174
Takebe, K. 570, 571, 577, 583
Takeshita, A. 265, 278
Tal, A. 526–7, 554
Talbott, E. 446, 460
Talpin, P.S. 532, 554
Tanaka, J.S. 80, 103
Tanaka, T. 362, 388
Tanguay, P.E. 331, 353
Tannenbaum, P. 114, 134
Tanzi, R.E. 67, 70
Tarazi, R.C. 456, 462
Tarler-Benlolo, L. 453, 466
Tarrier, N. 6, 11, 18, 27, 29, 30, 42–3,
    400, 417
Tata, P. 130, 133, 345–6, 352
Tattersfield, A.E. 527, 551
Taub, D.M. 268, 275
Tavel, M.E. 158, 159, 174
Taylor, C.B. 29, 39, 180–1, 183, 190–2,
    195, 204–5, 207, 210, 213, 222, 235,
    256, 271, 310, 313, 318–19, 326–7,
    453, 455, 459, 466
Taylor, D. 222, 237
Taylor, D.L. 250, 255, 276
Taylor, D.W. 462
Taylor, K.W. 397, 412
Taylor, M.A. 325, 358, 373, 375–6, 383,
    385, 391–2
Teasdale, T.W. 60, 69
Teders, S.J. 205, 234
Teece, J.J. 52, 70
Telch, M.J. 313, 319, 326–7
Terbizar, D. 188, 205
Terry, D.J. 223, 238, 459, 464
Teuber, H.L. 148, 174
Thailer, S.A. 260, 278
Thaler, M. 254, 277
Thach, J.S. 506, 516

Thananopavarn, C. 233, 236, 452, 454,
    462
Thayer, J.F. 31, 43, 80, 90, 103
Theorell, T. 259, 261, 271, 278
Thieme, C. 516
Thier, P. 379–80, 387, 391
Thomas, M. 162, 168
Thomas, N.R. 563, 582
Thomas, S.A. 29, 39
Thompson, K. 70
Thompson, R. 473, 494
Thompson, S.G. 443, 460
Thompson, W.G. 509, 516
Thomson, M.L. 25, 42
Thorell, L.H. 15, 42
Thorén, P. 248, 273, 334, 336, 351, 356
Thoresen, C.E. 182, 206
Thornton, S. 150, 174
Thyer, B. 295, 304
Thyer, B.A. 254–5, 277
Thyer, B.S. 279
Tibbetts, R.W. 567, 577
Timm, N.H. 90, 97, 103
Timmons, B.H. 318, 324, 548
Timsit, M. 343, 356
Tinklenberg, J.R. 152, 172, 401, 403, 411,
    416–17
Tischler, G.L. 326, 331, 354
Tobias, H.S. 571, 578
Tobin, D.L. 236
Tocci, N. 237

Tod, G.L. 235
Tole, J. 155, 170
Tollison, C.D. 186, 213
Tomb, D.A. 357, 391
Toone, B.K. 139, 174, 365–7, 391
Toriumi, T. 506, 516
Toscano, J.S. 505, 515
Tosi, I. 524, 553
Touw, K.B. 264, 271
Tranel, D.T. 353
Traskman, L. 336, 356
Trautt, G. 475, 491
Travis, T. 223, 239
Treasure, R.A. 537, 554
Treise, L. 290, 308
Treasaden, I. 297, 305
Trezise, L. 129, 134
Triebwasser, J.H. 449, 462
Trimble, M.R. 138, 174
Trotter, J. 573, 577

Author Index 619

Trower, P. 312, 327
Troyer, W.G. 559, 580
Truax, S.R. 74, 102
Tsuang, M.T. 330–2, 355
Tuason, V.B. 16, 38, 46, 62, 68, 155, 169, 359, 364–5, 367, 388, 406, 408, 415
Tucker, D.M. 155, 156, 160, 174, 375, 377–8, 387, 391
Tueting, P. 150, 173
Tukey, J.W. 86, 103
Tunstall, C. 188, 208
Tuomisto, M. 253, 260, 267, 274
Turczynski, B.E. 572, 583
Turk, D.C. 184, 187, 207, 209, 216, 220, 226, 232, 235, 237, 239
Turland, D. 312, 327
Turner, J.R. 239
Turner, P. 252, 276
Turner, R.M. 337, 352
Turner, S.M. 127–8, 134, 176, 182, 213, 231, 317, 324, 326–7, 336, 354
Turpin, G. 7, 9–11, 15–16, 18, 23–30, 32, 34, 38, 41–3, 86, 101, 246, 251, 278, 292–3, 308, 356, 400, 417
Tursky, B. 443, 445, 452, 457, 460, 466, 484, 489, 493
Twentyman, C.T. 559, 580

Uchiyama, K. 566, 583
Udry, J.R. 433, 439
Uhde, T.W. 255, 271, 335, 355
Uhlenhuth, E.H. 405, 414
Ulett, J.A. 52, 70
Ulmer, D. 217, 236
Ulrich, G. 146, 166, 374, 377–8, 383, 391
Ulrich, R.F. 385
Urbanek, R. 525, 551
Usdin, E. 12, 43
Utz, S.W. 233, 237
Uviller, F.T. 293, 306
Uytdenhoef, P. 370–2, 386, 391

Vacca, L. 374, 388–9
Vachon, L. 525, 531, 554
Vaitl, D. 269, 274
Valentine, M. 448, 462
Valentine, R.H. 16, 38, 46, 62, 68, 359, 365, 388, 408, 415
Van Boxtel, A. 224, 239, 559, 577
Van Dam-Baggen, R.M.J. 345, 353
Van de Castle, R.L. 433, 439
van de Woestijne, K.P. 524, 548, 554

van der Helm, M. 320, 325
Van Der Meulen, J. 466
Vanderwolf, C.H. 9, 43
Van Dyke, J.L. 400, 417
Van Egeren, L.F. 90, 103
Vanhoutte, P.M. 472, 474, 492, 494
Van Lindern, B. 297, 304
Van Praag, H.M. 6, 18, 24, 43
Van Tilburg, W. 376, 391
van Veenendaal, W. 538, 549
Varni, J. 565, 577
Varni, J.W. 213, 217, 235
Vasey, M.W. 31, 43, 90, 103, 195, 208
Vaughan, H. 61, 66–7
Vaughan, H.G. 413
Vaughn, C. 400, 403, 417–18
Vaughn, C.E. 29, 42
Vaughn, E. 258, 276
Vaughn, L.J. 190, 204
Venables, P.H. 8–10, 13–16, 23, 25, 30–2, 36–7, 39, 43, 51–2, 61, 68, 70, 86, 100, 138, 141, 144, 149, 168, 174, 177, 193, 203, 213, 364–7, 387, 397–8, 412, 414, 416, 517
Vermilegen, B.B. 205
Vermilyea, B.B. 310, 324
Vermilyea, J.A. 179, 213, 310, 318, 324, 327
Vexküll, T.V. 449, 459
Vickers, H. 530, 554
Vickers, M. 251, 272
Victor, R. 458, 466
Visser, S.L. 376, 391
Vissia, E. 320, 325
Volavka, J. 67, 325, 375–6, 385, 392
von Eiff, A.W. 84, 102, 262, 264, 272, 450, 452, 464–5
Von Euler, U.S. 248–9, 273
von Oefele, K. 369, 387
Voudoukis, I.J. 449, 466
Vrana, S.R. 109, 115, 132
Vrtunski, P. 139, 172

Waddell, M.T. 121, 132, 205
Wadden, T.A. 454, 466
Wade, C. 548
Waeber, B. 444, 465
Wagner, G. 429, 439
Wagner, O. 369, 388
Wagner, W. 15, 42
Waidelich, E. 525, 550
Wainer, H. 86, 103

Wald, A. 497, 513, 517
Walder, D. 472, 474, 493
Waldo, H. 338, 355
Waldo, M. 66, 69
Waldron, I. 448, 466
Wale, C.J. 544, 552
Walentynowicz, J.E. 567, 581
Walker, B.B. 181, 213, 497, 517
Walker, E. 138, 174
Walker, P. 56, 66
Walker, P.A. 549
Wallace, M.R. 67
Wallace, R.K. 466
Waller, D. 259, 278
Wallin, B.G. 82, 101, 243, 249, 264, 273, 279
Wallis, H.M. 226, 234
Walmsley, R.P. 569, 583
Walrath, L.C. 19, 43, 53, 70
Walschburger, P. 82, 83, 100
Walter, C.J.S. 335, 354, 362, 388
Walter, G.W. 343, 354, 356
Walter, W.G. 299, 308
Wang, G.H. 140, 174
Wangaard, C. 526, 553
Wansley, R.A. 568, 578
Ward, C.H. 125, 131
Ward, K. 437
Ward, N.G. 12, 43, 365–6, 368, 392
Ward, R.D. 222, 238
Wardle, J. 285, 294–5, 308
Warren, L.R. 369, 372, 392
Warwick, H.M.C. 543, 553
Wasserman, A.J. 473, 493
Wasserman, M. 432, 439
Waternaux, C.S. 405, 414
Waters, B. 378, 389
Waters, W.F. 24, 31, 32, 43, 44
Watkins, D.C. 67
Watkins, P.C. 70
Watkins, P.J. 501, 515
Watson, G.D. 157, 158, 171
Watson, J.B. 284, 308
Watson, J.P. 214
Watson, P.J. 207
Watson, R.T. 139, 169
Watt, N.F. 15, 16, 43
Watts, F.N. 115, 129, 130, 134, 288, 306
Weaver, J. 474, 494
Weber, M.A. 80, 89, 103, 443, 466
Webster, J.S. 88, 99, 428, 439
Webster, M.M. 506, 514

Webster, T. 551
Weckmann, P. 462
Weder, A.B. 452, 466
Weerts, T.C. 118–19, 131, 134, 196, 205
Weiler, S.J. 179, 207
Weiman, A.L. 146, 173
Weimann, G. 533, 539, 554
Weinapple, M. 373, 391
Weinberger, D.A. 446, 465
Weinberger, D.R. 360, 385, 392
Weiner, H. 6, 18, 43, 219, 239, 257, 260, 279, 520, 528, 554
Weiner, H.D. 497, 507–8, 517
Weinman, M.L. 250, 255, 276
Weinstein, A.G. 529, 554
Weinstein, S. 578
Weinzierl, M. 509, 516
Weipert, D. 451, 467
Weisberg, H.I. 78, 103
Weisinger, M. 563, 580
Weiss, C. 216, 227, 236
Weiss, J.A. 449, 465
Weiss, J.M. 496, 506, 517
Weiss, M.A. 521, 548
Weiss, S.M. 211, 238
Weiss, T. 463
Weiss, Y.A. 259, 277
Weissborg, R.D. 291–2, 306
Weissman, M.M. 311, 326–7, 331, 354, 355
Weist, W. 190, 207
Weitzman, E. 432, 439
Weller, J. 514
Weller, M.F. 168
Wells, D. 213
Wells, J.G. 535, 547
Wells, L.A. 277, 530, 551
Wells, P.N.T. 480, 494
Wenegrat, B.G. 150, 172, 379, 390, 409, 416
Wenger, M.A. 19, 43, 88, 103, 499, 517
Wenig, P. 474, 482, 486–89, 492
Wessels, D.J. 543, 553
West, S.G. 542, 544, 546, 550
Westermark, O. 254, 274
Westervelt, W.W. 25, 38
Wexler, N.S. 67
Weyer, G. 103
White, C. 145, 174
White, P.D. 226, 234
White, R. 49, 66
White, S. 267, 279

Whitehead, W.E. 181, 214, 497, 499, 502–3, 508–13, 515–18
Whitsett, S.F. 30, 41, 43, 88, 102
Wickens, C. 411, 413
Wicker, R. 454, 460
Wiedemann, R. 238
Wieland, B.A. 84, 104
Wientjes, C.J.E. 535, 540–4, 546, 550, 554
Wieselgren, I. 40
Wiesenfeld, A.R. 291–2, 306
Wiggins, J.S. 74, 104
Wilcoxin, L.A. 209
Wilde, G.J. 527, 552
Wilder, J. 79–80, 104, 214
Wildschiodtz, G. 48, 66
Wiles, C.M. 158, 165, 556, 583
Wilhelmsen, L. 267, 279
Willerson, J. 473, 494
Willett, J.B. 81, 103
Williard, H.N. 448, 467
Williams, C.B. 509, 517
Williams, G. 264, 275
Williams, G.H. 263, 275
Williams, J. 210, 267, 270, 279, 433, 438
Williams, J.B.W. 394, 413
Williams, R. 368, 391
Williams, R.B. 6, 42, 52, 68, 258, 265, 268, 276–8, 447–8, 466–7, 563, 583
Williams, R.D. 270–1
Williams, R.H. 81, 104
Williams, R.L. 435, 438
Williams, S.L. 205, 256, 271
Williamson, D.A. 24, 31, 35, 43–4
Williamson, P.D. 151, 174, 342, 356
Willis, G. 264, 275
Willis, P.W. 276, 451, 463
Williston, J.F. 152, 169
Willner, P. 358, 392
Wilmotte, J. 370, 386
Wilson, A. 473, 492
Wilson, A.F. 531, 554
Wilson, C.C. 6, 24, 28, 37, 151, 177, 181–2, 186, 188, 190–1, 194, 209–11
Wilson, C.S. 169
Wilson, G.D. 291, 308
Wilson, G.T. 315, 325
Wilson, J.F. 239
Wilson, L. 147, 164, 168
Wilson, N.M. 530, 554
Wilson, P. 221, 222, 237
Winchester, M.A. 222, 235

Wincze, J.P. 186, 214
Winder, J.A. 532, 548
Wing, J.K. 11, 14, 43, 44, 144, 150, 174, 394, 400, 412, 418Wing, L. 13, 38, 143, 170, 297, 304, 338, 354, 362, 364, 366, 389, 409, 415
Wing, R.R. 180, 202, 214, 221, 239
Winget, C. 510, 518
Winokur, G. 59, 66, 358, 373, 379, 387–8, 392, 408, 413
Winter, A. 299, 308
Winter, A.L. 356
Winter, M.K. 195, 212
Wise, P.H. 537, 554
Witkin, A. 432, 437
Wittchen, H.-U. 311, 327, 515
Witte, H. 39, 464
Wittkower, E.D. 5, 44
Wittmann, W.W. 90, 104
Woerner, M. 233, 237
Wohl, M.E. 525, 549
Wohlmuth, D. 466
Wolchik, S.A. 430, 439
Wolf, S. 246, 279, 448, 467, 518
Wolf, S.L. 214, 571, 572, 573, 576, 577, 580, 583
Wolff, H. 475, 494
Wolff, H.G. 246, 279, 448, 467, 495–6, 518
Wolff, W.T. 22, 44
Wolfinsohn, L. 210
Wolfstetter-Kausch, H. 60, 66, 366, 386
Wolpe, J. 176, 182, 194, 197, 214, 288–9, 303, 308
Wolters, W.H.G. 515
Wolthuis, R.A. 449, 462
Wood, C.C. 31, 38, 151, 174
Wood, D.L. 261, 279
Wooldridge, C.P. 558, 569, 583
Woodruff, R. 379, 387
Woodruff, R.A. 59, 66, 408, 413
Woods, D. 338, 353
Woods, S.W. 316 322, 327
Woodson, P.P. 52, 70
Wooley, S. 510, 518
Woolfolk, R.L. 237
Wooten, L.S. 210, 264, 275
Woodward, J.A. 77, 102
World Health Organization 442, 467
Wright, S.L. 89, 103
Wsieh, X.C. 525, 553

Wu, J. 385, 386
Wurtz, R.H. 154, 172
Wyatt, R.J. 251, 279
Wyle, F.A. 443, 466
Wynne, L.C. 15, 43

Yamane, N. 362, 388
Yamamoto, K. 265, 278
Yao, S. 480, 494
Yaryura-Tobias, J.A. 336, 356
Yasillo, N.J. 68, 154, 169, 404,
    414–15
Yates, A.J. 557, 564, 574, 576, 583
Yates, E. 214
Yeager, C.L. 86, 100
Yellin, A.M. 52, 67
Yendall, L.T. 340, 352
Yerushalmi, S. 501, 515
Yingling, C.D. 151, 174
Yorkston, N.J. 168
Youkilis, H.D. 180, 214
Younkin, D. 387–8
Young, A.B. 67
Young, J.B. 275
Young, M.C. 84, 101
Young, M.J. 573, 579
Young, R.R. 574, 579
Young, S.H. 237, 531, 548

Zahn, T.P. 6, 10–13, 15, 17, 44, 46, 52,
    68, 70, 347, 351, 356–7, 360, 379,
    381–2, 392, 394, 397, 399, 402, 410,
    418
Zajonc, R.B. 9, 10, 44
Zaki, S.A. 168
Zanchetti, A. 442, 462
Zarcone, V. 48, 70, 223, 235
Zarins, C.K. 268, 271
Zealley, A.K. 520, 553
Zec, R.F. 360, 392
Zeger, S. 450, 461
Zeitlin, G.M. 86, 100
Zeller, G. 376, 391
Ziegler, M.G. 237
Ziesat, H. 199, 210
Zimering, R.T. 179, 210
Zimmerman, M. 358, 392
Zimmermann, D.W. 81, 104
Zimowski, M. 76, 103
Ziprian, H. 449, 460
Zubin, J. 18, 44, 48, 70, 151, 173
Zuch, J. 425, 437
Zuckerman, M. 424, 426, 440
Zuroff, D.C. 239
Zusman, R. 260, 272, 447, 460
Zweifler, A. 265, 273, 279, 461
Zwi, S. 551

Subject Index

Acid secretion, 488
Activation, *see also* Arousal
  dimensions of, 98
  intensity and pattern, 97–98
  multicomponent model, 74, 90
Adrenocorticotrophic hormone (ACTH),
  249
Aetiological heterogeneity, 46, 56, 63
Affective disorders, 357–392, *see also*
  Depression
  classification, 358–359
  nature, 358–359
  psychophysiological studies, 359–385
Affective processing, 105 –134
Agoraphobia, 309–327
  information processing, 113–114,
    119–120, 123–128
  nature, 311–312
  psychophysiological studies, 315–317
  treatment studies, 318–324
Airways resistance, 524–525
alarm reaction (Selye's), 244
Alcohol problems, 51, 180
Alpha-adrenergic receptors and blood
  flow, 471–475, 487–490
Ambulatory monitoring, 29, *see also*
  Telemetry
  agoraphobia, 316

blood pressure, 444
  heart rate, 313–314, 316
  hypertension, 444
  panic disorder, 313–314
  'pH' measurement, 498
  transcutaneous pCO_2, 541
Analysis, *see* Statistical analysis
Anal spincter, 512, *see also* Faecal
  incontinence
  rectum retraining, 513
Anger, 180, *see also* Hostility
  hypertension, 446–447
Animal phobias, *see* Phobia
Angiography, 476, 478, 479
Anhedonia, 404, *see also* Psychosis
  proneness scales
Anorexia nervosa, 506
Anxiety disorders, 105–134, 180,
  283–308, 309–327, *see also*
  Agoraphobia, Panic disorder,
  Phobia, Social phobia
  cerebral laterality, 155–157
  enodocrine function, 250–257
  information processing, 105–134
  memory organization, 125–128
Arousal, 8, *see also* Activation
Artifacts in physiological data, 86–87

Assessment, *see* Psychophysiological
assessment
Asthma, 180, 520–533
assessment, 525–526
management, 532–533
mechanisms, 528–530
nature, 521, 525
personality factors, 526
precipitants for attacks, 526
psychophysiological studies, 526–533
treatment, 530–533
Attention, 10, 17, 411, *see also* Orienting
responses
Autogenic training, 483, 484, 486–488
Autoimmune processes, 508, *see also*
Psychoimmunology
Autonomic lability score, 82, 83
Autonomic nervous system, 25, 346–350

Baselines, 30, 84–86
Base rates, 55–57
Behavioural medicine, 11, 23–24,
215–239, 257–258, 497, *see also*
Behaviour therapy
definition, 215
disease mechanisms, 217–220
psychophysiological interventions,
217–226
stress–diathesis models, 218–220
Behaviour therapy, 18–23, 175–214, *see
also* Behavioural medicine
anxiety disorders, 105–134, 255–257,
283–308, 309–327
asthma, 530–533
definition, 175–176
gastrointestinal disorders, 502–518
hypertension, 217–226, 452–455
hyperventilation 'syndrome', 546, 547
motor disorders, 555, 576
obsessional–compulsive disorders,
336–337
psychophysiological assessment,
175–214
Raynaud's disease, 483–491
sexual disorders, 431–436
Beta-adrenergic receptors
blood flow, 471–474, 487–491
Beta-blockers
phobia, 296–297
Raynaud's disease, 472, 487, 488
Beta-endorphins and anxiety, 254–255

Biochemical indices, 241–279, *see also*
Endocrine measures
Biochemical markers
limitations of, 58
Biofeedback, 23, *see also* EMG
biofeedback
EMG, 556–576
equipment requirements, 557–558
gastro-intestinal disorders, 505, 511,
513
hypertension, 452–453
mechanisms, 224–228
methodological considerations,
558–560
motor disorders, 556–576
procedural considerations, 558–560
Raynaud's disease, 483–487
Bio-informational theory, 108–110, 130
Bipolar disorders, 357–392, *see also*
Affective disorders
linkage markers, 49, 50
Blepharospasm
clinical features, 564
pathophysiology, 564
biofeedback treatment, 565, 566
Blink rate
factors affecting, 52, *see also* EOG
Blood flow, *see also* Plethysmography
effects of cooling, 471–474, 478–481,
485, 488
measurement, 476–482
phobia, 294
Raynaud's disease, 469–470, 472–474,
476, 481, 483, 486
Blood pressure (diastolic and systolic
BP), *see also* Cardiovascular
variables
cuff-occlusion, 443–444
factors affecting, 52
home measurement, 444–445
measurement, 443–445
mechanisms, 247–248
pulse transit time, 445
Body plethysmography, 524
Bulimia nervosa, 506

Capillary blood flow, 471–478, 488–490,
see also Blood flow
Cardiac output, 247
Cardiovascular disease, *see* Blood
pressure, Coronary heart disease,
Hypertension

Cardiovascular function, *see also* Blood
     flow, Blood pressure, Cardiac output,
     Heart rate, Stroke volume
  affective disorders, 361–364
  parasympathetic influences, 247–248
  sympathetic influences, 247–248
Cardiovascular reactivity, 227–231,
     260–265, 448–450
Catecholamines, 243–250
  anxiety, 250–257
  Raynaud's disease, 472–475, 482
Catechol-*o*-methyl transferase (COMT)
  anxiety, 252
Central Nervous System (CNS), *see*
     Electroencephalogram (EEG) and
     Event-related potentials (ERPs)
Cerebral laterality, 137–174
  affective disorders
     electrodermal measures, 366–368
     EEG, 373–378
  anxiety disorders, 157–158
  hyperventilation 'syndrome', 158–159
  migraine, 143–144
  schizophrenic disorders, 144–148
  somatic symptoms, 157–158
Cerebral mechanisms, 136
Cerebral palsy, 558, 570
  clinical features, 567
  management, 569, 570
  biofeedback treatment, 567–570
Change, measurement of, 76–84
Chromosomal linkage markers, 49, 50
Classical conditioning, 10
  phobia, 284, 289, 301, 302, 303
Clinical assessment, *see*
     Psychophysiological assessment
Clinical psychophysiology, *see also*
     Psychophysiology
  assessment, 18–23
  definition, 5–7
  principles and rationales, 11–17
  treatment
     outcome measures, 12, 189–190,
        318–321
     process measures 22, 23, 191–193
Clonidine, 471, 474, 475
Cognitive appraisal, 10
Cognitive treatments,
  behavioural medicine, 270
Cold pressor test, 228, 261, 479
Colitis ulcerosa, *see* Inflammatory Bowel
     Disease (IBD)

Colon, 500
Compliance of bowel wall, 510, 511
Computed tomography (CT),
  affective disorders, 368–373
  schizophrenia, 148–150
Conjoint gastrography (CSG), 499
  cross-spectral analysis, 500
  relation to contractile activity, 500
Continence system, 512
Contingency management
  gastro-intestinal disorders, 511
Contingent Negative Variation (CNV),
     see Event-related potentials (ERPs)
Contractile activity, 499
Convulsive disorders, 180
Coronary heart disease (CHD), 215–239,
     257–279, 441–467
  risk factors, 267–268, 450–451
Correlation
  between
     conditions, 93
     subjects, 91–92
  pre- and post-stimulus scores, 77
  pre-stimulus and change scores, 79
  residual, 93–94
  within
     conditions, 94
     subjects, 94
  Cortical measures, *see*
     Electroencephalogram (EEG) and
     Event-related potentials (ERPs)
Cortisol, 249
  anxiety, 253–257
Crohn's disease, *see* Inflammatory Bowel
     Disease (IBD)
Cyclic adenosine monophosphate
     (cAMP),
  anxiety, 252–253

Deafferentation, autonomic, neuropathic,
     512
Defence responses (reflexes, DRs), 10,
     243
Depression, 180, 357–392, *see also*
     Affective disorders
Desynchrony, 20, 197
Diabetes, 180
Diagnosis, 11–17, 185–187, *see also*
     Markers
  clinical subtypes, 15
  diagnostic markers, 13
  imprecision, 56–59

Diagnosis—*continued*
  sensitivity, 12, 56
  specificity, 12, 56
  subgroup classification, 14
  vulnerability markers, 15
Diathesis-stress models, *see* Stress-
  diathesis, Vulnerability models
Digital blood flow, *see* Blood flow,
  Plethysmography
Difference scores
  as a response measure, 83
  assignment to groups, 78
  individual treatment effects, 77
  interpretation of, 80
  normalized, 83
  reliability, 31, 76, 77
Diffuse oesophageal spasm, 505
Discordance, 20
Discriminant function, 96
  analysis, 97
Discrimination, 11–17
Discriminative learning
  gastro-intestinal symptoms, 511
  hyperalgia, 511
DNA markers, 50
Doppler ultrasound,
  blood flow, 480
Duodenal ulcers, *see* peptic ulcers

Eating disorders, 180, 502, 518
Electrical safety, 24
Electrodermal activity (EDA), 141–148
  affective disorders, 51, 364–468
  anxiety disorders, 121–125
  bilateral, 138–148
  factors affecting, 52
  habituation, 141–148
  index of psychiatric risk, 51, 61–62, 64
  individual differences, 141–148
  non-responding, 397
  obsessional-compulsive disorders,
    344–348
  phobia, 290, 291
  publication guidelines, 32
  relation to clinical state and outcome,
    399
  schizophrenia, 51, 138–141, 396–400
Electroencephalogram (EEG), *see also*
  Event-related potentials (ERPs)
  affective disorders, 51, 373–378
  factors affecting, 52
  obsessional–compulsive, 339–341

  phobia, 298
  topographical mapping, 163
Electrogastrogram, 498, 499
  hexagonal leads, 500
  physiological significance, 500
  signal analysis, 500
Electromyography, 556, 576, (EMG), *see*
  also Biofeedback
  biofeedback, 484–486, 556, 560, 576
  motor disorders, 556, 576
  phobia, 298
Electromotor activity, *see* motility
Electro-oculography (EOG), 53, *see also*
  Blink rate, Eye movements, SPEM
Emotion, 9, 106, *see also* Affective
  processing
Emotional imagery, 10
Emptying, 501
  ferromagnetic methods, 501
  impedance method, 501
  radioisotope methods, 501
Encopresis, 512
Endocrine measures, 241–279, *see also*
  Neuroendocrine factors
Endophenotype, 49
Enteric nervous system, 517
Epilepsy, *see* Convulsive disorders
Equipment, *see* Psychophysiological
  methodology and techniques
Essential hypertension (EHT), *see*
  Hypertension 257–279
Event-related potentials (ERPs), 341,
  401–402
  brainstem-evoked potentials, 152
  contingent negative variation (CNV)
  affective disorders, 380–382
  factors affecting, 52
  obsessional–compulsive disorder,
    343–344
  phobia, 299
  schizophrenic disorders, 401–404
  factors affecting, 52
  middle latency and schizophrenia,
    153–154
  N2 and obsessional compulsive
    disorders, 342
  P50 as an index of psychiatric risk, 51
  P3/P300
    affective disorders, 379–382
    index of psychiatric risk, 51, 61
    obsessional–compulsive disorder,
      342–343

phobia, 299–30
schizophrenic disorders, 150–152,
    401–404
ocular artifacts, 53
sexual disorders, 424
slow wave potentials and
    obsessional–compulsive
    disorders, 343–344
somatosensory, 138–141
visual evoked potential, 51
Exercise training, 221
Experimental design, 26–29, 45–70
groups x conditions, 96
repeated measures, 31, 96
Expressed emotion, 29, 400
Eye blinks, *see* Blink
Eye movements, *see* Electro-oculography
    (EOG) and Smooth Pursuit Eye
    Movements (SPEM)

Faecal incontinence, 512
and encopresis, 512
behavioural mechanisms, 512
biofeedback, 512
differential diagnosis, 512
pathophysiology, 512
rectal perception training, 512
Family studies, 55, 57
Fear, 284–285
Feedback, *see* Biofeedback
Finger blood flow, *see* Blood flow,
    Plethysmography
Focal dystonias, 563, 569, 576, 572, *see
    also* Motor disorders
biofeedback, 562, 567
pathophysiology, 561, 562, 564, 566
Forced oscillation technique, 525
Functional disorders, 502
concept, 502, 505
hierarchical mechanisms, 503, 504
of oesophagus, 505
of stomach, 506
of colon, 508
of rectum, 512
relation to eating disorders, 506
schema, 504

Galvanic skin response (GSR), *see*
    Electrodermal activity
Gastric
secretion, 498
motility, 499

rhythm, 499, 500
emptying, 499, 501
compliance and NUD, 507
Gastric ulcers, *see* Peptic ulcers
Gastrointestinal
afferents, 496
disorders, 495
    autoimmune processes, 508
    psychoimmunological mechanisms
emptying, 501
motility, 496, 499
peptides, 513
psychophysiology, 495, 497
recording methods, 497–498
rhythms, 499
secretion, 496
stress responses, 497
transit, 501
Gastro-oesophageal reflux, 502, 505
Generalizability, 73, 89
Genetic predisposition, 47, 49
Genetics of psychophysiology variables, 54
Genital measurement
males, 424–428
females, 428–431
Globus sensation, 505
Growth models, 80, 82
Gut–brain relationships, 514

Habituation, *see* Electrodermal acitivity,
    Orienting response
Haemodynamics, *see also* Cardiovascular
    function
hypertension, 259
Headache, 11, *see also* Migraine
migraine, 143, 144, 180
muscle-contraction, 180
Heart rate (HR), 247–248, *see also*
    Cardiovascular function
agoraphobia, 315, 316, 318–320
affective disorders, 361–364
anxiety disorders, 120–125
factors affecting, 52
measurement, 24
obsessional–compulsive disorder,
    345–348
panic disorder, 312–315, 318
phobia, 291, 292, 293
social phobia, 317, 320, 321
High risk studies, 60–62
advantages of, 60
genetic markers in, 60–62

High risk studies—*continued*
  limitations, 60
Hormonal indices, 241–279, *see also*
  Neuroendocrine factors
Hostility, *see* Anger
Hydrogen exhalation method, 501
Hyperalgia, visceral/colonic, 509
Hypertension, 180, 257–279, *see also*
  Coronary heart disease
  aetiology, 456–457
  assessment, 443–445
  behavioural medicine, 228–231
  personality factors, 260, 446–448
  psychophysiological studies, 445–459
  reactivity, 448–450
  risk, 450–451
  treatment, 452–455
Hyperventilation 'syndrome', 158–159,
  533–554
  aetiology, 542–546
  nature, 539–542
  psychophysiological studies, 534–537
  treatment, 546–547
Hypnosis, 161
Hypocapnia, 533–547, *see also*
  Hyperventilation 'syndrome'
Hypomania, 357–392

Identical twins, studies of, 55, 56–57, 58
Illness behaviour, 511
Imagery, 105–134
Impedance gastrography, 499, 501
Incontinence, *see* Faecal incontinence
Individual differences, 73, 83
  components of, 96
  electrodermal measures, 141–143
Individual response specificity (IRS), 32,
  74–75, 96
  cardiovascular reactivity, 265–267
Inflammatory bowel disease (IBD), 508
  autoimmune process, 508
  psychological stress, 508
  psychoimmunological mechanisms,
    508
  psychosomatic genesis, 508
  psychotherapy effects, 508
Information processing, 10, 11, 17, 105,
  111, 130
  schizophrenic disorders, 411
Insomnia, 180
Instrumentation, *see* Psychophysiological
  methodology and techniques

Intermediary psychophysiological
  processes, 504
Interoception, 502, 513
Irritable Bowel Syndrome (IBS), 497,
  500, 502, 508, 513
  colon motility, 509
  definition, 509
  hyperalgia, colonic, 509
  hypersensitivity, visceral, 509
  pain symptoms, 497, 508, 509, 511
  prevalence, 508
  psycho-pathophysiological
    mechanisms, 509
  treatment, 511
  visceral pain mechanism, 510

Laboratory, *see also* Psychophysiological
  methodology and techniques
  field comparisons, 94
  settings, 27, 29
Laterality, *see* Cerebral laterality
Law of Initial Values (LIV), 79, 81, 197
  'Anti-LIV', 79, 80
  as a growth model, 80
  consequences, 80
  correction, 80
  empirical findings, 79
  individual activation differences, 80
  questions to ask before correction, 81
  statistical definition, 79
Laxative abuse, 511
Lower oesophageal sphincter, 505
Lung function measures, 524–525

Magnetogastrogram, 499, 500
  in conjoint gastrography, 500
Mania, 357–392, *see also* Affective
  disorders
Manic depression, 357–392, *see also*
  Affective disorders
Manometry, 499
Markers, 11–17, 59–65, *see also* Diagnosis,
  Stress-diathesis models,
  Vulnerability models
  applications
    delimiting high risk groups, 60–62
    identifying mode of inheritance,
      62–63
    illuminating nature of pathogenesis,
      63–65
    predicting outcome, 15, 62
    refining diagnosis, 14, 15, 59

correlations between, 63
defining cutoff value, 57
definition of, 47
episode, 15–17, 48, 51, 53
genetic, 48–49
  altering expression of, 49
  aetiology, 49
  criteria for identification, 54–57
  distinction from linkage markers, 50
  distinction from vulnerability
    markers, 48, 54
  examples, 51
heritability of, 55
identification and validation, 15–17,
  50–57
  studies of normal subjects, 54–56
  studies of patients, 54, 56, 57
sensitivity of, 12, 56
specificity of, 12, 56
stability of, 55
standardized measurement of, 58
vulnerability, 15–17, 48
  distinction from genetic markers, 48,
    54
  examples, 51
  identification, 53, 64, 65
Measurement, *see also*
  Psychophysiological methodology
  and responses models, 78, 81–84
Mechanical activity, *see* Contractile
  activity
'Mediated causation', 507
Meditation
  behavioural medicine, 223
Memory organization, 125–128
Migraine headache, 11, 143–144, 180
Missing data, 86–87
Motility of gastrointestinal tract, 499
  biofeedback, 511
Motor disorders, 555–576
  biofeedback treatment, 560–576
  blepharospasm, 557, 561, 564–566
  central palsy, 558, 561, 567–570
  focal dystonias, 561–567, 574, 575
  measurement and assessment, 556–557
  paralysis and spasticity, 561, 570–573
  torticollis, 561–564, 574, 576
  writers' cramp, 561, 566–567
Muscle-contraction headache, 11, 180

N2 etc., *see* Event-related potentials

Nausea, anticipatory, in cancer
  chemotherapy, 506
Neuroendocrine measures, 248–250
  anxiety, 250–257
  stress research, 241–279
Neurology, 7
Neuropsychology, 136
Nocturnal penile tumescence (NPT), 186,
  432
Noninvasive methods, 498–501
Non-ulcerative dyspepsia (NUD), 507
  and PUD, 507
  and IBS, 507
Nuisance variables in psychophysiology,
  29, 30, 52–53, 63–64, 84–85

Obsessional–compulsive disorder,
  329–356
  aetiology, 349–351
  demographic characteristics, 330–331
  endocrine studies, 334–335
  genetic studies, 332
  nature, 330
  neuroanatomical studies, 335
  personality, 332
  pharmacological treatment, 335–336
  psychological treatment, 336–337
  psychometric studies, 333–334
  psychophysiological studies, 338–351
Oesophagus, 502, 505
Orienting response (OR), 10, 396, *see also*
  Attention, Defence response
Outliers in physiological data, 86–87

P300 etc., *see* Event-related potentials
Pain, *see* Visceral pain
Panic disorder, 252, 309–327
  nature, 310, 311
  psychophysiological studies, 312, 315
  treatment studies 318
Paralysis and spasticity
  secondary to stroke, 561, 570–573
Partioning of variance and co-variance,
  90–96, *see also* Correlation,
    Statistical analysis
  definitions, 91
  example, 94–96
Pathophysiology, 7
Penile plethysmography, 21, 181, 186,
  424–428
Peptic ulcer 180, 506–507
  and emptying, 506

Peptic ulcer—*continued*
  autoregulation, 507
  autonomic innervation, 507
  hereditary factors, 506
  hypersecretion, 506
  mediated causation, 507
  personality factors, 506
  relation to NUD, 507
Perception, *see* Interoception, Visceral
  pain
Peripheral pathogenic/pathophysiological
  mechanism, 503
Personality
  asthma, 526
  hypertension, 260, 446–448
  obsessional–compulsive disorder, 332
  peptic ulcer, 506
  theories, 8
'pH' measurement, 498
  intragastric, 498
  portable digital recorders, 498
  telemetric, 498
Phobia, 105–134, 180, 283–308, 309–327,
  see also Anxiety disorders,
  Agoraphobia, Panic disorder, Social
  phobia
  beta-blockers, 296–297
  blood injury, 294–295
  classical conditioning, 284, 289, 301,
    302, 303
  nature, 285–288
  prepared learning, 301, 302
  psychophysiological studies, 300–303
  simple phobia, 113–114, 116–117,
    119–120, 122, 124–128, 283–308
  social phobia, 113, 116–117, 119–120,
    124–128, 309–327
  three systems model, 288–300
Physiological parameter
  meaning of, 72
Pituitary–cortical system, 243–250
Plethysmography, *see also* Blood flow
  digital blood flow, 474, 477, 479, 481,
    488–491
  penile, 21, 181, 186, 424–428
Positron emission tomography (PET), *see
  also* Computed tomography
  affective disorders, 368–373
Post-traumatic stress disorder (PTSD),
  21, 180
Prepared learning, *see* Phobia

Profile, psychophysiological, 93–94,
  97–98
  analysis, 97–98
  condition profiles, 93–94
  elevation, 93, 97–98
  scatter, 93, 97–98
  shape, 93, 97–98
  similarity, 97
  variable, 97
Propositional structure of images,
  109–111, 116
Psychoimmunology, 159–161, 508
Psychometrics in psychophysiology,
  84–89
Psychophysics, 502, 512
Psychopathology, *see also*
  Psychophysiological applications
  limitations of traditional studies, 46–47
  nuisance variables, 11–15, 46–51
Psychophysiology, 3–44, *see also* Clinical
  psychophysiology,
  Psychophysiological applications,
  assessment and methodology
  definition, 4
  principles and rationales, 11–17, 73
  theories, 8–11
Psychophysiological
  applications to
    affective disorders, 357–392
    agoraphobia, 309–327
    alcohol problems, 51, 180
    anxiety disorders, 105–134, 180,
      283–308, 309–327
    asthma, 520–533
    convulsive disorders, 180
    coronary heart disease, 215–239,
      257–279, 441–467
    diabetes, 180
    encopresis, 512
    epilepsy, 180
    faecal incontinence, 512
    gastro-intestinal disorders, 495
    hyperventilation 'syndrome',
      158–159, 533–554
    hypomania, 357–392
    insomnia, 180
    mania, 357–392
    manic depression, 357–392
    migraine headache, 11, 143–144, 180
    motor disorders, 555–576
    muscle-contraction headaches, 11,
      180

obsessional–compulsive disorder, 329–356
panic disorder, 252, 309–327
phobia, 105–134, 180, 283–308, 309–327
Raynaud's disease, 180, 469–491
sexual disorders, 21, 181, 419–440
social phobia, 309–327
Tourette's syndrome, 27
ulcers, 180, 506–507
assessment, 18–23, 71–104, 175–214
classification and diagnosis, 185
desynchrony amongst measures, 20, 197
discordance amongst measures, 20, 196
identification of causal factors, 187
mediational variables, 191
monitoring treatment, 188
multicomponent model, 75
selection of target behaviours, 184
selection of treatments, 187
treatment outcome, 21, 189, 190
treatment process, 22, 192
deviations, interpretation of, 49, 63–65
disorders, 503
markers, 47, 58–59, *see also* Markers
methodology and techniques, 3–44
artifacts, 86–87
biofeedback equipment, 557–558
data reduction and analysis, 30, 71–104, 201–204, *see also* Statistical analysis
designs and paradigms, 26
electrical safety, 24
instrumentation, 202
interpretation, 31
nuisance variables, 29, 30, 52–53, 63–64, 84–85
reliability, 31, 76, 81, 195
response fractionation, 74, 194
response habituation, 195
selection of measures, 24
sensitivity, 195
situational factors, 29, 200
types of measure, 24
responses, 25, *see also* Response
blink, 52
blood flow, 476–482
blood pressure, 443–445
defence, 10, 243

electrodermal, 32, 52, 141–148, 396–400
electroencephalogram, 52, 373–378, 339–341
electrogastrogram, 498, 499
electromyography, 556–576
electro-oculography, 53
event-related potentials, 52, 341, 401–402
heart rate, 24, 247–248
hormonal, 241–279
lung function, 524–525
magnetogastrogram, 499, 500
orienting, 10, 396
penile plethysmography, 21, 181, 186, 424–428
respiratory, 534–537
thermography, 473–476, 477, 480
vaginal photometers, 428–430
Psychosis proneness scales, 61–62, *see also* Anhedonia
Psychosomatic
disease, 503
medicine, 245–246
Pulse wave velocity and transit time, 445, *see also* Blood pressure

Questionnaire on Mental Imagery (QMI), 117, 121, 123, 124, 126

Rapid eye movement (REM) sleep latency, 48
Raynaud's disease, 180, 469–491
aetiology, 472, 491
emotional stress, 469, 470, 475, 486
nature, 470
psychophysiological studies, 488–491
treatment, 483–491
Rectal
probe (three balloon), 512
sensation (loss of), 512
Rectum, 500
Regression towards the mean, 77–79
'AHA' estimate, 80
Kendall and Stuart's cases, 78
Relaxation treatments, 23, 220
anxiety, 255–256
behavioural medicine, 220
hypertension, 453–454
Raynaud's disease, 482–483, 486, 490
Reliability, 31, 76, 81, 87, 195

Research questions
  designs and paradigms, 26–29
  nomothetic versus individual
    differences, 83
Respiration, *see also* Asthma,
    Hyperventilation 'syndrome'
  measurement, 534–537
  neural control, 534–535
  disorders of, 519–554
Response
  fractionation, 74
  measures, 81–84, *see also* Autonomic
    liability score, Difference score,
    Psychophysiological responses,
    Statistical analysis
    and experimental design, 83
    and growth models, 83
    and individual differences, 83
    choice among, 83–84
    indicand–indicator relationships, 82
    normalized difference scores, 83
    normalized scores, 83
    percentage scores, 83
    range-corrected, 83
    raw scores, 83, 89
    sample dependencies, 83
    transformations, 83
Risk behaviours
  coronary heart disease, 267–268,
    450–451
  peptic ulcer, 507
Rumination syndrome, 505

Schizophrenic disorders, 393–418
  central nervous system signs, 148–155
  cerebral laterality, 138–174
  nature, 394–396
  psychophysiological studies, 13–17, 51,
    138–155, 396–418
  relapse, 21–22
  relation to arousal and attention, 411
  social factors, 29, 400
Scleroderma, 470, 473, 476, 478, 479
Secretion, *see* Gastric secretion
Self-efficacy
  anxiety, 256
Self-regulation treatments
  behavioural medicine, 221
Sexual disorders, 21, 181, 419–440, *see also*
    Penile plethysmography, Vaginal
    photometry
  genital measurement, 424–431

nature, 420–421
non-genital 'arousal', 424
psychophysiological studies, 431–436
Simple phobias, *see* Phobia
Single-case methodology, 26
Skin conductance, potential and
    resistance (SCR, SRR and SPR), *see*
    Electrodermal activity
Sleep, 17
  EEG and obsessional–compulsive
    disorders, 340–341
Slow wave potentials, *see* Event-related
    potential
Small bowel, 500
Smoking, 181
Smooth pursuit eye movements (SPEM),
    404
  factors affecting, 52
  genetic transmission, 64
  prediction of clinical outcome, 62
  psychiatric disorders, 51, 61
  schizophrenia, 51, 154–155, 404–408
Social phobia, 309–327
  nature, 312
  psychophysiological studies, 317
  treatment, 320–324
Social reinforcement, 511
Somatic symptoms, 505
Somatosensory event-related potentials,
    see Event-related potentials
Somatovisceral reflexes, 511
Spasmodic torticollis, 180
Specificity of physiological responses
  individual-situation-specific, 75, 92, 93,
    94
  individual-specific, 75, 96
  situation-specific, 74, 92, 93, 96
Speech anxiety, 317, *see also* Social phobia
Sphincter, 502
State-dependent learning, 112–113, 115
Stability
  empirical findings, 87–89
  measurement of change, 77
  retest interval, 88
Statistical analysis, 30, 71–104, 201–204,
    see also Research questions,
    Responses, Single-case methodology
  change, measurement of, 76–84
  correlation, 77–79, 91–94
  difference scores, 77–83
  discriminant analysis, 96–97
  experimental design, 26–29, 45–70, 96

generalizability, 73, 89
growth models, 80, 82
'Law of Initial Values', 79, 81, 197
measurement models, 78, 81–84
missing data, 86–87
multivariate, 90–98
outliers, 86–87
partitioning of variance and
    covariance, 90–96
profile analysis, 93–94, 97–98
psychometrics, 84–89
regression towards mean, 77–80
reliability, 31, 76, 81, 87, 195
repeated measures, 31, 96
response fractionation, 74–84
specificity of responses, 75–96
stability, 77–89
transfer/function, 82, 83
trends, 84–86
true-score ANCOVA, 78
validity, 72–74
Strain gauges, 424–428
Stress, 9, 242–245
bodily changes, 242–244
definitions, 242
relation to health, 244–245
Stress–diathesis models, 47, 63, 65,
    218–220, 246, *see also* Markers,
    Vulnerability models
Stroke volume, 247
Stroop test, 129–130
Subjective symptoms, 503, 514
Surface gastrograms, 498–499
Sympatho–adrenal system, 243–250

Tachycardia
premature ventricular contractions,
    180
Taste aversion, conditioned, 506
Telemetry, 498, 499, *see also* Ambulatory
    monitoring
Temperature biofeedback, 480,
    484–491

Thermistors, 476, 482
Thermography, 473, 476, 477, 480
Three systems model, 107, 131, 288–300,
    see also Desynchrony, Discordance
Torticollis, 561–564, 574, 576
biofeedback, 562–564, 576
clinical features, 562
Tourette's syndrome, 27
Transfer function
person-specific, 83
variable-specific, 82
Transit, gut, *see also* Emptying
effect of stress, 501
hydrogen method, 501
Trends in physiological data, 84–86
permutation of tasks, 85
reference to initial rest period, 85
reference to multiple baselines, 85
steady state, 85
True-score ANCOVA, 78
Type A/B behaviour, 268–270, 447–448

Ulcers, 180, *see also* Peptic ulcer
experimental, 496

Vaginal photometers, 428–430
Validity, 72–74
construct, 72
external, 73
Visceral pain, 497, 502
Visceroception, *see* Interoception,
    Visceral pain
Visual evoked potential, *see* Event-related
    potentials
Vomiting, 506
Vulnerability models, 15–18, 393–418, *see*
    also Markers, Stress–diathesis
    models

Writers' cramp, 561, 566–567
biofeedback, 566–567
clinical features, 566
pathophysiology, 561–562, 566